Dictionary *of* Aeronautical Terms

Dictionary *of* Aeronautical Terms FIFTH EDITION

Over 11,000 Entries

Dale Crane

Aviation Supplies & Academics, Inc.
Newcastle, Washington

Dictionary of Aeronautical Terms, Fifth Edition
Based on all previous editions by Dale Crane, and continually revised and edited by ASA
Editorial Staff.

Aviation Supplies & Academics, Inc.
7005 132nd Place SE
Newcastle, Washington 98059-3153
Email: asa@asa2fly.com
Website: www.asa2fly.com

Visit **www.asa2fly.com/reader/dat** for the "Reader Resources" page for additional
information as new terms and definitions are collected.

Printed in the United States of America
2016   2015   2014   2013   2012   9   8   7   6   5   4   3   2   1

ASA-DAT-5
ISBN   1-56027-864-1
         978-1-56027-864-1

Library of Congress Cataloging-in-Publication Data
Crane, Dale
        Dictionary of aeronautical terms / compiled and edited by Dale Crane.— 3rd ed.
            p.   cm.
        New ed. of: Capstan's dictionary of aeronautical terms.
            1. Aeronautics—Dictionaries. I. Crane, Dale. Capstan's dictionary
        of aeronautical terms. II. Title.
        TL509.C73 1997
        629.13'003—dc21   97-29690
                                                  CIP

02

Contents

Preface ....*vii*

Definitions *1*

Appendices

Appendix 1   **Acronyms and Abbreviations** *729*

Appendix 2   **Periodic Table of Chemical Elements** *769*

Appendix 3   **Trigonometric Functions** *771*

Appendix 4   **International Phonetic Alphabet
and Morse Code** *773*

Preface to the Fifth Edition

There is no aspect of modern technology that encompasses so many disciplines as aviation: physics, chemistry, aerodynamics, thermodynamics, structural and fluid mechanics, electronics, acoustics, reciprocating and turbine engine technology, meteorology, and navigation. In addition, aviation is governed by an extremely complex set of federal regulations.

Each discipline and regulation has its own unique vocabulary, and it is difficult to find a single reference source that includes terms specific to the aviation application of these fields. To this end, ASA's editors have searched aviation periodicals, aviation-related textbooks, service manuals, manufacturers' literature, engineering reports, military training manuals, and especially all of the publications produced by the FAA for applicable terms.

This fifth edition of ASA's *Dictionary of Aeronautical Terms* is more than a lexicon; it explains as well as defines over 11,000 accurate, aviation-specific terms and includes nearly 500 illustrations and four appendices.

The officially recognized definitions for many of the aviation terms are included in 14 CFR Part 1 *Definitions and Abbreviations*. In all instances where a definition in this dictionary is taken directly from this document, it is identified by the prefix *14 CFR Part 1:*, and the definition is in quotation marks.

The information contained here is as accurate and up-to-date as it has been possible to make it, but because of the speed with which changes are taking place in aviation, some of the terms are taking on new meanings, and their relative importance is changing. Because of this, and because of ASA's dedication to working together for excellence, we will appreciate any criticism, or suggestion you have that will make subsequent revisions of this work more useful for you.

Editor's Note: If you do not find a word or acronym you were looking for in the *Dictionary of Aeronautical Terms*, please email ASA at **feedback@asa2fly.com** and we will try to find the definition for you. Also, be sure to visit the "Reader Resource" webpage for this book (www.asa2fly.com/reader/dat) to check for updates as new terms and definitions are collected in between book printings.

Alfa

AAM (air-to-air missile). A missile carried on an aircraft for use against other aircraft. The missile is guided to its target by radar or infrared sensors.

AAR (airport acceptance rate) (air traffic control). A dynamic input parameter specifying the number of arriving aircraft which an airport or airspace can accept from the ARTCC per hour. The AAR is used to calculate the desired interval between successive arrival aircraft.

A & B hydraulic brake system. A form of backup brake system used in some large aircraft multiple-disk power brake installations. Wheels using the A & B system have several small actuating cylinders built into the brake housing. Half of the cylinders are actuated by fluid from the A-hydraulic system and the others by fluid from the B-system. The brakes operate normally with either system.

A & P mechanic. A person who holds an aircraft mechanic certificate with both the airframe and powerplant ratings. This certification is issued by the Federal Aviation Administration under the provisions of 14 CFR Part 65.

Mechanic certification with an A&P rating is now referred to as Aviation Maintenance Technician (AMT) certification.

AAS (airport advisory service). A service provided by FAA Flight Service Stations located at airports not served by a control tower.

AAS provides information to arriving and departing aircraft concerning wind direction and speed, favored runway, altimeter setting, pertinent known traffic, pertinent known field conditions, airport taxi routes, traffic patterns, and authorized instrument approach procedures. AAS information is advisory in nature and does not constitute an ATC clearance.

abampere. A basic unit of electrical current in the electromagnetic-centimeter-gram-second system. One abampere is equal to 10 amperes in the absolute meter-kilogram-second-ampere system. The abbreviation for abampere is aA.

A-battery. A dry-cell battery used in vacuum tube radios to supply power to the heaters, or filaments, of the tubes.

A-batteries usually have a voltage ranging between 1.5 to 6.0 volts and are capable of supplying a reasonable amount of current.

abbreviated briefing. In meteorology, this is a shortened weather briefing to supplement the widely-disseminated aviation weather data.

abbreviated IFR flight plan (air traffic control). An authorization by ATC requiring pilots to submit only that information needed for the purpose of separation and control. An abbreviated flight plan includes only a small portion of the usual IFR flight plan information which may be only aircraft identification, location, and pilot request.

Abbreviated flight plans are frequently used by aircraft which are airborne and desire an instrument approach, or by aircraft which are on the ground and desire a climb to VFR-On-Top.

abcoulomb. A basic unit of electrical charge in the electromagnetic-centimeter-gram-second system. One abcoulomb is equal to 10 coulombs in the absolute meter-kilogram-second-ampere system. The abbreviation for abcoulomb is aC.

abeam. A relative location approximately at right angles to the longitudinal axis of an aircraft. When an object is beside the aircraft, it is said to be abeam of it.

abeam fix. A fix, NAVAID, point, or object positioned approximately 90 degrees to the right or left of the aircraft track along a route of flight. Abeam indicates a general position rather than a precise point.

abfarad. A basic unit of electrical capacitance in the electromagnetic-centimeter-gram-second system. One abfarad is equal to 10^9 farads in the absolute meter-kilogram-second-ampere system. The abbreviation for abfarad is aF.

abhenry. A basic unit of electrical inductance in the electromagnetic-centimeter-gram-second system. One abhenry is equal to 10^{-9} henries in the absolute meter-kilogram-second-ampere system. The abbreviation for abhenry is aH.

abmho. A basic unit of electrical conductance in the electromagnetic-centimeter-gram-second system. One abmho is equal to 10^9 mhos in the absolute meter-kilogram-second-ampere system. The abbreviation for abmho is $(a\Omega)^{-1}$. An abmho is also known as an absiemens, aS.

abort. To terminate an operation prematurely when it is seen that the desired results will not be obtained.

aborted start (gas turbine engine operation). Termination of the start procedures in a gas turbine engine when it is seen that normal combustion has not taken place within the prescribed time limits.

aborted takeoff. A takeoff terminated prematurely when it is determined that some condition exists which makes takeoff or further flight dangerous.

abradable seal (gas turbine engine component). A general term for a knife-edge seal inside a gas turbine engine that wears away (abrades) slightly to produce an extremely close fit between a rotating and a stationary part of the engine.

abradable shroud (gas turbine engine component). A special shroud ring built into the outer turbine case of a gas turbine engine. The shroud fits tightly around the outside of the turbine wheel, which is equipped with special knife edges around its periphery.

If the turbine blades creep (grow in length because of heat and high centrifugal loads), the knife edges will wear away the abradable shroud and do no damage.

abradable strip (gas turbine engine component). A strip of material in the compressor housing of some axial-flow gas turbine engines. The tip of the compressor blade touches the abradable strip and actually wears, or abrades, a groove in it. This groove ensures that the blade operates with the minimum amount of tip clearance.

abradable tip (compressor blade tip). The tip of some axial-flow compressor blades made in such a way that it will abrade, or wear away, when it contacts the compressor housing. The abradable tip wears away to allow the engine to have a minimum amount of tip clearance between the blade and the housing.

abrade. To wear away a surface or a part by mechanical or chemical action. A rough surface may be made smooth by mechanically abrading it with sandpaper. Extremely smooth surfaces may be roughened enough for paint to adhere by rubbing the surface with abrasive paper or by chemically abrading it with an etching solution.

abrasion. A form of damage to a surface made by roughening or wearing it away with scratches or gouges. Abrasion is often caused by foreign matter trapped between two surfaces having relative motion between them.

abrasion resistant. The ability of a material to resist damage by abrasion.

abrasive. A material containing minute particles of a hard substance used to wear away a softer surface. Aluminum oxide, silicon carbide, and glass beads are abrasives commonly used in aircraft maintenance.

abrasive blasting. A method of removing carbon and other contaminants from machine parts. In abrasive blasting, the parts are sprayed with a high-velocity blast of air containing fine particles of abrasive material such as sand, aluminum oxide, or glass beads.

abrasive tip (turbine blade). A turbine blade with a hardened insert at the tip that is able to cut into the turbine shroud ring. *See* abradable shroud.

abscissa. A coordinate representing the distance from the Y-, or vertical, axis in a plane Cartesian coordinate system.

The abscissa is measured along the X-, or horizontal, axis and the ordinate along the Y-, or vertical, axis.

abscissa

absolute accuracy. The ability to determine present position in space independently, most often used by pilots.

absolute altimeter. An electronic altimeter used to indicate the exact height of an aircraft above the terrain. *See* radio altimeter.

absolute altitude. The actual distance between an aircraft and the terrain over which it is flying. Absolute altitude is measured with an electronic altimeter.

absolute ceiling. The maximum height above sea level at which an aircraft can maintain level flight under standard atmospheric conditions.

absolute humidity. The actual amount of water vapor present in a specific volume of air. If one cubic meter of air contains 100 grams of water, the absolute humidity of the air is 100 grams per cubic meter.

absolute instability (meteorology). The state of a layer of air within the atmosphere in which the vertical distribution of temperature is such that a parcel of air, if given an upward or downward push, will move away from its initial level without further outside force being applied.

absolute pressure. Pressure measured relative to zero pressure, or a vacuum. Absolute pressure is measured with a barometer, and in aviation usage is often expressed in inches of mercury. Manifold pressure in a reciprocating engine is an example of an absolute pressure.

absolute pressure controller (reciprocating engine control). A type of turbocharger controller which limits the maximum discharge pressure the turbocharger compressor can produce while the aircraft is flying below its critical altitude.

absolute pressure gage. A pressure measuring instrument that measures pressure referenced from a vacuum. An aneroid barometer is one of the more accurate types of absolute pressure gages. It measures the changes in the dimensions of an evacuated bellows as it is affected by the pressure of the ambient air.

absolute pressure regulator (pneumatic system component). A regulator valve at the compressor inlet in an aircraft high-pressure pneumatic system. Regulating the inlet air pressure prevents excessive speed variation and/or compressor overspeeding.

absolute temperature. Temperature referenced from absolute zero, the temperature at which all molecular movement has ceased.

There are two absolute temperature scales, Kelvin and Rankine. The Kelvin scale uses the same size increments as the Celsius scale, and the Rankine scale uses the same size increments as the Fahrenheit scale. *See* temperature.

absolute value. The numerical value of a number without considering whether its sign is plus or minus. For example, positive eight (+8) has the same absolute value as negative eight (–8).

absolute vorticity (meteorology). The swirling motion, or vorticity, imparted to the atmosphere by the combination of the rotation of the earth and the circulation of the air relative to the earth.

absolute zero. The temperature at which all molecular movement inside a material stops. Absolute zero is 0° Kelvin, 0° Rankine, –273° Celsius, and –460° Fahrenheit.

absorptance (electromagnetic radiation). The ratio of the total unabsorbed radiation to the total amount of radiation falling on the object whose absorptance is being measured.

abstractions. Words that are general rather than specific. Aircraft is an abstraction; airplane is less abstract; jet is more specific; and jet airliner is still more specific.

abvolt. A basic unit of electromotive force in the electromagnetic-centimeter-gram-second system. One abvolt is equal to 10^{-8} volts in the absolute meter-kilogram-second-ampere system. The abbreviation for abvolt is aV.

AC (Advisory Circular). Information published by the FAA explaining the Federal Aviation Regulations and describing methods of performing certain maintenance and inspection procedures. Compliance with ACs is not mandatory, and the information in the ACs is not necessarily approved data.

AC (alternating current). Electrical current in which the electrons continually change their rate of flow and periodically reverse their direction.

ACARS (aircraft communication addressing and reporting system). A two-way communication link between an airliner in flight and the airline's main ground facilities.

Data is collected in the aircraft by digital sensors and transmitted to the ground facilities. Replies from the ground may be printed out so the appropriate flight crewmember can have a hard copy of the response.

ACC (active clearance control). A system for controlling the clearance between tips of the compressor or turbine blades and the case of high-performance turbofan engines.

When the engine is operating at maximum power, the blade tip clearance should be minimum, and the ACC system sprays cool fan-discharge air over the outside of the engine case. This cool air causes the case to shrink enough to decrease the tip clearance. For flight conditions not requiring such close clearance, the cooling air is turned off, and the case expands to its normal dimensions. Control of the ACC system is done by the FADEC, or Full-Authority Digital Electronic Control.

accelerate. To increase the speed of an object, or make it move faster.

accelerated-life test. A form of operational test of a system or component in which unusual conditions are used to cause a premature failure. An accelerated-life test is used to locate weak points and predict the service life the system or component will likely have under normal operating conditions. The test conditions used in an accelerated-life test are much more severe than will ever be encountered in normal operation.

accelerate-go distance. For multi-engine flying, the distance required to accelerate to V_1 with all engines at takeoff power, experience an engine failure at V_1, and continue the takeoff on the remaining engine(s). The required runway length includes the distance required to climb to 35 feet by which time V_2 speed must be attained.

accelerate-stop distance (aircraft performance). The length of runway needed for an aircraft to accelerate to a specified speed, and then, in case of engine failure, be able to stop on the runway.

accelerating agent. A component or substance used to hasten a chemical action or change.

accelerating pump (carburetor component). A small pump in a carburetor used to produce a momentarily rich fuel-air mixture to the engine when the throttle is suddenly opened.

The fuel supplied by the accelerating pump prevents the hesitation that would otherwise occur between the time the engine stops operating on the idle metering system and the time there is enough air flowing through the carburetor for it to supply fuel through the main metering system.

acceleration. The amount the velocity of an object, measured in feet per second, is increased by a force during each second it is acted upon by that force. Acceleration is normally expressed in terms of feet per second, per second (fps^2).

acceleration caused by gravity. The acceleration of a freely falling body caused by the pull of gravity. Acceleration caused by gravity is expressed as the rate of increase of velocity over a given unit of time. This rate, in a vacuum, near sea level at a location of 40° north latitude is 32.2 feet, or 9.8 meters, per second, per second. This acceleration decreases with an increase in altitude until it becomes zero outside of the earth's gravitational field.

acceleration check (gas turbine engine maintenance check). A maintenance check of a gas turbine engine in which the time required for the engine to accelerate from idle RPM to its rated-power RPM is compared with the time specified for this acceleration by the engine manufacturer.

acceleration control unit. *See* ACU.

acceleration error (magnetic compass error). An error in the indication of a magnetic compass that shows up when the aircraft accelerates or decelerates while flying on an easterly or westerly heading.

The float in an aircraft magnetic compass is unbalanced to compensate for the downward pull of the vertical component of the earth's magnetic field (dip error), and the inertia caused by a change in speed acts on this unbalanced condition.

When the aircraft accelerates on an easterly or westerly heading, the compass indicates that the aircraft is turning to the north, and when it decelerates on either of these headings, the compass indicates that the aircraft is turning to the south.

acceleration switch. A switch in a piece of airborne electronic equipment actuated by an abnormal acceleration. Emergency Locator Transmitters (ELTs) have an acceleration switch that causes them to begin transmitting if the aircraft crashes and subjects the ELT to an abnormally high longitudinal acceleration. Acceleration switches are also called inertia switches.

acceleration well (carburetor component). An enlarged annulus around the discharge nozzle of some float-type carburetors. The acceleration well fills with fuel when the engine is idling, and when the throttle is suddenly opened, this additional fuel discharges into the engine through the main discharge nozzle.

accelerator (plastic resin component). A substance added to a catalyzed resin to shorten the time needed for the resin to cure.

accelerator system (carburetor system). A system in an aircraft carburetor used to supply additional fuel to the engine when the throttle is suddenly opened. If an acceleration system were not used, the engine would get a momentarily lean mixture until enough air is pulled through the carburetor to meter the correct amount of fuel into the cylinders.

accelerator winding (voltage regulator component). A series winding on the voltage regulator coil in a vibrator-type generator control unit.

Current flowing through the accelerator winding produces a magnetic field which helps hold the points tightly closed against the force of a spring. As soon as the points begin to open, this field collapses, and the spring snaps the points open quickly.

accelerometer. A sensitive instrument that measures the amount of force exerted on an object because of its acceleration. Accelerometers are calibrated in G-units (Gravity units). One G-unit is a force equal to the weight of the object.

acceptable data. Data found in such aviation maintenance documents as manufacturer's maintenance manuals, service bulletins and letters, and AC 43.13-1 and 43.13-2. Acceptable data may be submitted to the FAA for a particular repair or alteration, and it may or may not be approved, depending upon its applicability to the specific job.

acceptable risk (risk assessment, aeronautical decision making). A result of risk assessment, when a pilot determines that a certain level of risk or hazard is manageable and acceptable for a certain flight. As the first task of system safety, all possible hazards or risks are identified within practical limitations; then those risks are assessed as to their manageability in flight, or whether they can be reduced through some other prior action. The resultant level of risk is then subject to a decision as to whether or not to expose oneself to that level of risk; this decision is the pilot's responsibility and affects the "go or no-go" of each flight. *See also* unacceptable risk, residual risk.

acceptance test. A test made by a person who buys equipment to be sure the equipment is exactly as specified in the purchase contract. All large and expensive aircraft are given extensive acceptance tests before the customer accepts them.

acceptor atom (solid state electronics). An atom of a chemical element alloyed with silicon or germanium to give the material a deficiency of electrons, making the material into a P-type material. *See* acceptor impurity.

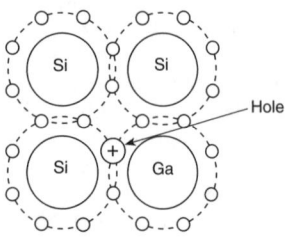

acceptor atom

acceptor impurity (solid state electronics). A trivalent chemical element alloyed with a semiconductor material to produce atoms that accept free electrons to complete their covalent bond.

Boron, aluminum, gallium, and indium are elements commonly used as acceptor impurities.

access door. A door which provides access to the inside of an aircraft structure.

accessories (engine components). Devices used with an aircraft engine that are not parts of the engine itself. Magnetos, carburetors, generators, and fuel pumps are commonly installed engine accessories.

accessory drive gearbox. A portion of an aircraft engine containing the drive gears to operate such accessories as fuel pumps, air pumps, and generators. These accessories mount on pads on the accessory-drive gearbox.

accessory drive shaft. A shaft used in some gas turbine engines to drive the accessory gearbox. The accessory drive shaft is driven by bevel gears from the compressor shaft.

accessory end. The end of a reciprocating engine away from the propeller on which many of the accessories are mounted. The accessory end is also called the antipropeller end.

accessory gear train. A group of gears that drive an accessory from the crankshaft of a reciprocating engine or from the compressor drive shaft of a gas turbine engine.

accessory section (reciprocating engine). The portion of an aircraft engine crankcase on which such accessories as magnetos, carburetors, generators, fuel pumps, and hydraulic pumps are mounted.

access panel. An easily removable panel that allows access to some portion of an aircraft structure for inspection and maintenance.

accident. An event that happens by chance or from some unknown cause. An accident is usually thought to be an unfortunate situation or event.

accumulated error. The sum of all the errors occurring in the operation of a system or in the manufacture of a part. If the errors are in opposite directions, they cancel, but if they are in the same direction, the accumulated error is greater than any of the individual errors.

accumulator (British terminology). An electrical storage battery.

accumulator (electronic computer). A device in a digital computer that stores a number and, upon the receipt of a second number, adds the two and stores the sum.

accumulator (hydraulic system component). A component in a hydraulic system that allows a noncompressible fluid, such as oil, to be stored under pressure. An accumulator has two compartments separated by a flexible or movable partition such as a diaphragm, bladder, or piston. One compartment contains compressed air or nitrogen, and the other is connected into the source of hydraulic pressure.

When oil is pumped into the accumulator, the partition moves over and increases the pressure of the air. This air pushing against the partition holds pressure on the oil.

An accumulator in an aircraft hydraulic system acts as a shock absorber and provides a source of additional hydraulic power when heavy demands are placed on the system.

accumulator air preload (precharge). The charge of compressed air or nitrogen in one side of an accumulator. The air preload is normally about one third of the system hydraulic pressure. When fluid is pumped into the oil side of the accumulator, the air is further compressed, and the air pressure and the fluid pressure become the same.

If the air preload pressure is too low, there will be almost no time between the regulator reaching its kick-in and kick-out pressures, and the system will cycle far more frequently than it should.

If there is no air pressure gage on the accumulator, the amount of air preload may be found by watching the hydraulic system pressure gage as the pressure is slowly bled off the system. The pressure will drop slowly, until a point is reached at which it drops suddenly. This point is the air preload pressure.

accuracy. A measure of the amount of error, or difference between an actual value and its indicated value. Accuracy is usually expressed in terms of percentage of the full range of measurement.

For example, if voltage is measured on a voltmeter having a full-scale range of ten volts, and the meter has an accuracy of plus or minus two percent of its full-scale reading, the voltage indication will be accurate to within 2% of ten volts, or it will be accurate within plus or minus 0.2 volt.

accurate. Free from error, or conforming exactly to a standard or pattern.

AC/DC (type of electrical component). Electrical components that can operate equally well on alternating current or direct current.

ACDO (air carrier district office). An FAA field office staffed with Flight Standards personnel. ACDOs serve the aviation industry and general public on matters related to the certification and operation of scheduled air carriers and other large aircraft operations.

ace. A term used in warfare to identify a pilot who has downed five or more enemy aircraft. This term was first used during World War I.

acetone. A flammable liquid ketone used as a solvent and as an ingredient in many types of aircraft finishes.

acetylene gas. A colorless, nontoxic flammable gas (C_2H_2)generated when calcium carbide is dissolved in water. Acetylene gas is used as a fuel gas for welding.

acetylene regulator. A single- or two-stage pressure regulator that is used to decrease the pressure of acetylene gas to a value that is appropriate for the torch being used. Most regulators have two pressure gages, one to indicate the pressure of the gas in the cylinder and the other to indicate the pressure being delivered to the torch.

AC flared tube fittings. A series of flare-type fittings used in some of the older aircraft hydraulic systems. AC fittings have a 35° flare cone, and they may be distinguished from a similar appearing AN fitting by the threads on an AC fitting extending all the way to the flare cone, while there is a slight shoulder between the cone and the first thread of an AN fitting.

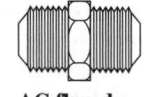

AC flared tube fitting

AC 43.13-1. An advisory circular in book form issued by the Federal Aviation Administration, giving examples of acceptable methods, techniques, and practices for aircraft inspection and repair. The procedures described in this advisory circular are considered by the FAA to be acceptable data and can be submitted to them for approval for specific repairs.

AC 43.13-2. An advisory circular issued by the Federal Aviation Administration, giving examples of acceptable methods, techniques, and practices for aircraft alterations.

A-check. *See* maintenance checks.

acid. A chemical substance that contains hydrogen, has a characteristically sour taste, and is prone to react with a base, or alkali, to form a salt and to accept electrons from the alkali.

acid diluent (finishing system component). A component in a wash primer used to mildly etch the surface of a metal being primed. The etched surface provides a good bond between the finishing system and the metal.

acid-resistant paint. A paint used on the portion of an aircraft structure near the battery box. Some acid-resistant paints have a rubber or tar base, but polyurethane enamel is the most generally used modern acid-resistant paint.

"Acknowledge" (air traffic control). A request meaning "Let me know that you have received my message."

ACLT (actual calculated landing time) (air traffic control). The frozen calculated landing time of a flight. ACLT is an actual time determined at freeze calculated landing time (FCLT) or meter list display interval (MLDI) for the adapted vertex for each arrival aircraft, based on runway configuration, airport acceptance rate, airport arrival delay period, and other metered arrival aircraft.

ACLT is either the vertex time of arrival (VTA) of the aircraft, the tentative calculated landing time, or the actual calculated landing time (TCLT/ACLT) of the previous aircraft plus the arrival aircraft interval (AAI), whichever is later. ACLT will not be updated in response to the aircraft's progress.

acorn nut. A nut with a domed top. The threaded hole does not go completely through the nut, but the end of the threads is covered by the dome. Acorn nuts, also called cap nuts, are used on the bolts to produce a finished, smooth appearance.

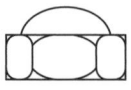

acorn nut

acoustical liners (turbine engine component). Sound absorbing liners used in an engine nacelle or around the tail pipe to reduce the amount of noise produced by the engine.

acoustics. The science of the production, transmission, reception, and effects of sound.

AC plate resistance (electron tube characteristic). The ratio of a small change in the plate voltage to the small change in the plate current it causes. The AC plate resistance, measured in ohms, is actually the internal resistance of the tube to the flow of alternating current.

acrobatic category airplane. An airplane certificated under 14 CFR Part 23 for flight without restrictions other than those shown to be necessary as the result of a required flight test. An acrobatic category airplane is stressed for a limit maneuvering load factor of +6.0, and −3.0.

acrobatic flight. An intentional maneuver involving an abrupt change in an aircraft's attitude, an abnormal attitude, or abnormal acceleration not necessary for normal flight. Loops, spins, and rolls are normally considered to be acrobatic flight.

acrylic lacquer. An aircraft finishing material consisting of an acrylic resin vehicle and certain volatile solvents.

acrylic resin. A transparent, thermoplastic material used for aircraft windshields and side windows. Lucite®, Plexiglas®, and Perspex® are registered trade names for materials made from acrylic resin.

actinium. A radioactive chemical element found in uranium ores. Actinium's symbol is Ac, and its atomic number is 89. Actinium is used as a source of alpha rays.

activated charcoal. Powdered or granulated charcoal. Because activated charcoal is full of tiny pores, it has an extremely large surface area for its volume. Activated charcoal is used as a filter for liquids and as a medium to absorb gases.

active clearance control. *See* ACC.

active component (electrical component). An electrical component that can control current or voltage for switching or amplification. Vacuum tubes, transistors, and magnetic amplifiers are active components.

active current. The current in an AC circuit in phase with the voltage. It is active current that produces true power in an AC circuit.

active detection systems. Radar, radio, and sonar systems that require the transmission of energy. Active systems are distinguished from passive systems that receive but do not transmit energy.

active infrared detection. The method of detection in which a beam of infrared rays is transmitted toward a suspected target. Reflected rays from the target are used to detect and identify it.

active runway (air traffic control). Any runway or runways currently being used for takeoff or landing. When multiple runways are used, they are all considered to be active runways.

active waypoint. The waypoint used by the FMS/RNAV as the reference navigation point for course guidance.

Actual Navigation Performance (ANP). A measure of the current estimated navigational performance Also referred to as Estimated Position Error (EPE).

actuating cylinder (fluid power system component). A cylinder and piston arrangement used to convert hydraulic or pneumatic fluid pressure into work. Fluid under pressure moves the piston that does the work.

actuating horns. Levers attached to aircraft control surfaces to which control cables are connected to move the surfaces.

actuator (fluid power system component). A device which transforms fluid pressure into mechanical force. Actuators may be linear, rotary, or oscillating, and they may be actuated by either hydraulic or pneumatic pressure.

ACU (acceleration control unit) (turbine engine fuel control). The section in a turbine engine fuel control that schedules the rate of increase of the fuel to the nozzles when the engine controls call for acceleration. The ACU prevents the engine from stalling during acceleration.

acute angle. An angle of less than 90°. An acute angle is also called a closed angle.

AD (airworthiness directive). A regulatory notice sent out by the FAA to the registered owner of an aircraft informing him or her of the discovery of a condition that prevents the aircraft from continuing to meet its conditions for airworthiness.

Airworthiness directives, called AD notes, are covered by Title 14 of the Code of Federal Regulations Part 39 (*Airworthiness Directives*). They must be complied with within the specified time limit, and the fact of compliance, the date of compliance, and the method of compliance must be recorded in the aircraft maintenance records.

ADAHRS. *See* air data attitude and heading reference system.

adapter. An apparatus that modifies a device so some component can be attached to it. Adapters, for example, are used on the ends of air hoses to attach them to air drills and rivet guns.

ADC. *See* air data computer.

Adcock antenna (radio antenna). A type of directional radio transmitting antenna made of two vertical conductors from which electromagnetic energy radiates. These conductors are connected in such a way that the signals radiated from them are opposite in phase. An Adcock antenna radiates its signal in a field shaped much like a figure eight.

adder (electronic computer). An arrangement of logic gates in a computer that adds two bits (binary digits) and produces a sum and a carry bit.

addition (mathematics). The process of computing with sets of numbers to find their sum.

additive (lubricating oil component). A chemical added to an engine lubricating oil to alter its basic characteristics. Additives are used to prevent foaming, improve viscosity index, and increase corrosion inhibiting properties.

additive primary colors. Primary colors which can be mixed to produce other colors, but which cannot be formed by the mixing of colors. The additive primary colors used to produce color television images are red, green, and blue.

address (electronic computer). A binary numerical word used to designate a specific location in a computer memory where data is located.

Adel clamp. The registered trade name for a cushioned clamp used to attach fluid lines and wire bundles to an aircraft structure.

ADF (automatic direction finder). A piece of electronic navigation equipment which operates in the low- and medium-frequency bands. ADF uses a directional loop antenna and a nondirectional sense antenna to find the direction to a radio station. This direction is shown on an instrument that looks much like the dial of a compass, with zero degrees representing the nose of the aircraft, rather than north. The needle on the ADF indicator shows the pilot the number of degrees clockwise from the nose of the aircraft to the radio station being received.

adherend. The surface to which an adhesive adheres.

adhesion. The tendency caused by intermolecular forces for matter to cling together.

adhesive. A material used to provide a bond between two surfaces by chemical means. The adhesive wets the surfaces, and as it dries, it pulls the surfaces tightly together.

adiabat. The plotted line on a thermodynamic chart that relates the pressure and temperature of a substance (such as air) that is undergoing a transformation in which no heat is exchanged with its environment.

adiabatic change. A physical change taking place within a material in which heat energy is neither added to the material nor taken from it. For example, if a container of gas is compressed, with no heat energy added to it and none taken from it, the gas will become hotter—its temperature will rise. This is an adiabatic change.

adiabatic cooling. The process of cooling the air through expansion. For example, as air moves up a slope it expands with the reduction of atmospheric pressure and cools as it expands.

adiabatic heating. The process of heating dry air through compression. For example, as air moves down a slope it is compressed, which results in an increase in temperature.

adiabatic lapse rate (meteorology). The rate at which air cools as it is forced upward or warms as it sinks, if no heat energy is added to it and none is taken from it. Under standard conditions, the adiabatic lapse rate of dry air is 3°C (5.4°F) per thousand feet.

adiabatic process (meteorology). The process by which fixed relationships are maintained during changes in temperature, volume, and pressure in a body of air when heat is neither added to nor removed from it.

ADI fluid (antidetonation injection fluid). A mixture of water and methanol, which is injected into the carburetor of an aircraft reciprocating engine to prevent detonation when the engine is producing its maximum power. The methanol is used primarily to prevent the water freezing at high altitude, and a small amount of water-soluble oil is added for corrosion prevention.

ADI system (antidetonation injection system). A system used with some of the large reciprocating engines in which a mixture of water and alcohol (methanol) is sprayed into the engine with the fuel when operating at extremely high power. The fuel-air mixture is automatically leaned to allow the engine to develop its maximum power, and the ADI fluid absorbs the excessive heat when it vaporizes.

ADI does not increase the engine power, but, by absorbing some of the heat released during full-power operation, the engine is able to develop more power without detonating.

ADIZ (air defense identification zone). Airspace over land or water, extending upward from the surface, within which the ready identification, the location, and the control of aircraft are required in the interest of national security. Domestic ADIZs are within the United States along the international boundaries. Coastal ADIZs are over the coastal waters of the United States.

adjacent side (mathematics). The two sides of a triangle that have a common angle. In the study of trigonometry, the adjacent side of one of the acute angles of a right triangle is the side of the triangle other than the hypotenuse that forms the angle.

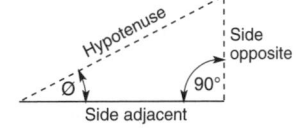

adjacent side of a right triangle

adjust. To change a condition to make it more satisfactory or to make it operate better. We adjust the hands of a clock so they show the correct time, and we adjust the fuel-air mixture on the carburetor of a reciprocating engine to get the proper mixture ratio for the best operation of the engine.

adjustable-pitch propeller. An aircraft propeller which has provisions for adjusting the pitch of the blades on the ground when the engine is not running.

adjustable split die. A tool used for cutting external threads on round stock. The circular die has a split from the threaded hole in its center to its edge. An adjusting screw can spread this split to adjust the depth of the threads being cut.

adjustable stabilizer (airplane flight control). A horizontal stabilizer that can be adjusted in flight to trim the airplane, so it will fly hands-off at any given airspeed.

ADM. *See* aeronautical decision making.

Administrator (FAA). The politically appointed head of the Federal Aviation Administration. *14 CFR Part 1:* "The Federal Aviation Administrator or any person to whom he has delegated his authority in the matter concerned."

admittance (electrical characteristic). The ease with which alternating current can flow in a circuit. Admittance (Y) is the reciprocal of impedance ($Y = 1/Z$) and is expressed in siemens. It was formerly expressed in mhos (ohm spelled backward).

AD oil (ashless dispersant oil). A mineral-base lubricating oil used in reciprocating engines. This oil does not contain any metallic ash-forming additives, but has additives that disperse the contaminants so they remain suspended in the oil, preventing their clumping together and forming sludge. The contaminants remain in the oil until they are removed by the filters.

ADS-B. *See* automatic dependent surveillance–broadcast.

ADS-B In. An appropriately equipped aircraft's ability to receive and display another aircraft's ADS-B Out information as well as the ADS-B In services provided by ground systems. *See* automatic dependent surveillance–broadcast (ADS-B), *and* ADS-B Out.

ADS-B Out. A function of an aircraft's onboard avionics that periodically broadcasts the aircraft's state vector (3-dimensional position and 3-dimensional velocity) and other required information. It is the capability necessary to transmit ADS-B messages. *See* automatic dependent surveillance–broadcast (ADS-B), *and* ADS-B In.

advance. To move forward.

advanced composites. High-strength structural materials made by encapsulating a fibrous material in a resin matrix. Advanced composites have superior strength and stiffness and are lightweight. Kevlar and graphite fibers encapsulated in an epoxy matrix are widely used in modern aircraft construction.

Advanced Surface Movement Guidance and Control System (A-SMGCS) (ICAO). A system providing routing, guidance, and surveillance for the control of aircraft and vehicles, in order to maintain the declared surface movement rate under all weather conditions within the aerodrome visibility operational level (AVOL) while maintaining the required level of safety.

advanced timing (reciprocating engine ignition timing). Timing of the ignition of the fuel-air mixture in the cylinders of a reciprocating engine, so the mixture is completely burned by the time the piston reaches the top of its stroke. Advanced timing allows the maximum pressure to be produced in the cylinder as the piston starts downward.

advancing blade (helicopter rotor blade). The blade in a helicopter rotor system moving in the same direction the helicopter is traveling.

advection. A method of heat transfer by horizontal movement of a fluid. Advection is different from convection in that convection transfers heat by vertical, rather than horizontal, movement of the fluid.

advection currents (meteorology). Currents of air moving horizontally over a surface.

advection fog (meteorology). Fog that forms when moist air moves horizontally across a surface cold enough to cool the air to a temperature below its dew point. Moisture condenses and remains suspended in the air to obstruct visibility.

adverse loaded CG check. A weight and balance check to determine that no condition of legal loading of an aircraft can move the center of gravity (CG) outside of its allowable limits.

adverse yaw (flight operation). A flight condition at the beginning of a turn in which the nose of an airplane starts to move in the direction opposite the direction the turn is being made. Adverse yaw is caused by the induced drag produced by the downward-deflected aileron holding back the wing as it begins to rise.

"Advise intentions" (air traffic control). A request meaning "Tell me what you plan to do."

Advisory Circular. *See* AC.

Advisory Service. Advice and information provided by an FAA facility to assist pilots in the safe conduct of flight and aircraft movement.

aeration. The process of mixing air in a liquid. When lubricating oil passes through an engine, it picks up a good deal of air and is said to be aerated. This air must be removed by a process called deaeration.

aerial (aeronautical). A term having to do with the air or with aircraft. It is used in such terms as aerial photography, aerial mapping, or aerial refueling.

aerial (radio communications). A term used for a radio antenna.

aerial photography. The business of taking pictures from aircraft in flight. There are two basic types of aerial photography: oblique and vertical.

Vertical photography is used for mapping. In this process, the aircraft is flown at a high altitude, and special cameras take pictures of the terrain directly below the aircraft.

Oblique photography, in which handheld cameras are used to take pictures of objects on the ground, is used for news photography and advertising. Doors or windows are usually removed from the aircraft used for oblique aerial photography.

aerial refueling. A method used to extend the range of military aircraft by refueling them in the air. Flying tankers rendezvous (meet) with the aircraft to be refueled, and large amounts of fuel are transferred in flight.

Aerodrome. The name given by Dr. Samuel P. Langley to the flying machines built under his supervision between the years of 1891 and 1903.

aerodrome. A defined area on land or water intended to be used either wholly or in part for the arrival, departure, and movement of aircraft. The term also includes any buildings, installations, and equipment in this area.

aerodrome beacon (ICAO). An aeronautical beacon used to aid in locating an aerodrome from the air.

aerodrome control service (ICAO). Air traffic control service for aerodrome traffic.

aerodrome control tower (ICAO). A unit established to provide air traffic control service to aerodrome traffic.

aerodrome elevation (ICAO). The elevation of the highest point of the landing area.

aerodrome traffic circuit (ICAO). The specified path to be flown by aircraft operating in the vicinity of an aerodrome.

aerodynamic balance (aircraft flight control component). The portion of a control surface on an airplane extending ahead of the hinge line. Air striking this portion of the control surface produces an aerodynamic force that aids the movement of the control.

aerodynamic blockage thrust reverser. A form of thrust reverser used on turbojet or turbofan engines. Thin airfoils or obstructions are placed in the engine's exhaust stream to duct the high-velocity exhaust gases forward. These forward-flowing gases create a large amount of aerodynamic drag to decrease the landing roll of the airplane.

aerodynamic braking. The use of reverse thrust from a propeller or a gas turbine engine to produce a great deal of aerodynamic drag. This drag is used to slow the aircraft on its landing roll, before the brakes are applied, or to allow the aircraft to descend at a steep angle without building up excessive airspeed.

aerodynamic ceiling. The point (altitude) at which, as the indicated airspeed decreases with altitude, it progressively merges with the low-speed buffet boundary where pre-stall buffet occurs for the airplane at a load factor of 1.0 G.

aerodynamic center. The point along the chord of an airfoil where all changes in lift effectively take place. The aerodynamic center is not affected by the camber, the thickness of the airfoil, nor the angle of attack. For a subsonic airfoil, the aerodynamic center is located between 23% and 27% of the chord length back from the leading edge, and for a supersonic airfoil it is located 50% of the chord length back from the leading edge.

aerodynamic coefficients. *14 CFR Part 1:* "Nondimensional coefficients for aerodynamic forces and moments."

aerodynamic drag. The total resistance to the movement of an object through the air. Aerodynamic drag is composed of both induced and parasite drag. *See* induced drag and parasite drag.

aerodynamic forces. The basic forces acting on an aircraft in flight that are caused by the movement of air over the surfaces.

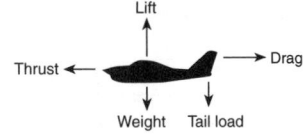
aerodynamic forces

    Thrust acts forward, drag acts rearward, and lift acts vertically upward. The weight of the aircraft produces a force that acts vertically downward. A downward-acting aerodynamic force produced by the horizontal tail surfaces balances the weight force about the center of gravity to provide longitudinal stability.

aerodynamic heating. The temperature rise caused by the friction of high-speed air flowing over a surface.

aerodynamic lift. A force produced by air moving over a specially shaped surface called an airfoil. Lift acts in a direction perpendicular to the direction the air is moving. Airplane wings and helicopter rotors produce vertical lift, and propellers produce aerodynamic lift (thrust) in a horizontal plane.

The amount of aerodynamic lift is determined by the density of the air, the speed of the air, and the direction the air is flowing as it approaches the airfoil.

$$L = \frac{C_L \, \sigma \, V^2 \, S}{295}$$

L	=	Lift (pounds)
CL	=	Coefficient of lift (dimensionless)
σ	=	Air density ratio (dimensionless)
V^2	=	Square of airstream velocity (knots)
S	=	Airfoil planform area (square feet)
295	=	A constant used when velocity is given in knots

aerodynamics. The branch of science that deals with the forces produced by air flowing over specially shaped surfaces called airfoils. Wings and helicopter rotors produce a vertical aerodynamic force, and propellers produce a horizontal force. Aerodynamic forces inside a turbojet engine produce pressure and velocity changes in the air as it passes through the compressor and turbine.

aerodynamic shape. The shape of an object with reference to the airflow over it. Certain shapes cause an air pressure difference across the surface which produces lift. Other shapes are designed in such a way that they produce the minimum amount of drag.

aerodynamic twisting force. *See* ATF.

aerodynamic twisting moment. The tendency of a propeller or rotor blade to twist toward high pitch. Centrifugal twisting moment opposes aerodynamic twisting moment.

aeroelastic tailoring. The design of an aerodynamic surface whose strength and stiffness are matched to the aerodynamic loads imposed upon it.

Aerofiche. The registered trade name for a form of microfiche used in the aircraft industry. Two hundred and eighty-eight frames of information can be placed on a single four-by-six card of film called a fiche.

Aeromatic propeller. A patented propeller that has counterweights around the blade shanks and the blades angled back from the hub to increase the effects of aerodynamic and centrifugal twisting forces. This propeller automatically maintains a relatively constant RPM for any throttle setting.

aeronaut. A person who operates or travels in a balloon or airship.

aeronautical beacon. A visual navigational aid displaying flashes of white and/or colored light. These flashes indicate the location of an airport, a heliport, a landmark, a certain point of a Federal airway in mountainous terrain, or an obstruction.

The colors and meaning of the more commonly used beacons are:

Color	Meaning
white and green	lighted land airport
green	lighted land airport
white	unlighted land airport
white and yellow	lighted water airport
yellow	lighted water airport
green, yellow and white	lighted heliport
white (dual peaked) and green	military airport
white and red	landmark or navigation point

aeronautical chart. A map used in air navigation containing all or part of the following: topographic features, hazards and obstructions, navigation aids, navigation routes, designated airspace, and airports.

aeronautical decision making (ADM). A systematic approach to the mental processes used by pilots to consistently determine the best course of action in response to a given set of circumstances. The direct and best result of this type of decision-making is the action a pilot intends to take based on the latest information he or she has and processes correctly.

Aeronautical Information Manual. *See* AIM.

aeronautics. The branch of science that deals with flight and with the operation of all types of aircraft. Aerodynamics and aerostatics are both branches of aeronautics.

AeroNav (Aeronautical Navigation Products). Previously the National Aeronautical Charting Office (NACO), now "AeroNav," or AeroNav Products. This FAA office (AJV-372) supports pilots, air traffic controllers, and aviation planners with products and services to promote safe aeronautical navigation. AeroNav develops and maintains the FAA's instrument flight procedures, performance-based navigation procedures to support NextGen, and is responsible for the creation and publication of aeronautical charts and maintaining their distribution to the aviation industry.

aerosol. A liquid or solid that is divided into extremely fine particles and dispersed into the air. Smoke is an aerosol of carbon and ash, and a cloud in the sky is an aerosol of water droplets.

Modern aerosol products such as paint, hair spray, and insecticides are usually liquids broken into tiny drops and sprayed into the air by the use of a gaseous propellant such as carbon dioxide, nitrogen, or Freon.

aerospace. The branch of science and technology that deals with travel in the space above the surface of the earth. Aerospace includes travel in the atmosphere, as well as in the vast regions outside of the earth's atmosphere.

aerospace vehicle. A flight vehicle capable of flight in both the atmosphere surrounding the earth and in the space beyond the atmosphere. The space shuttle is an aerospace vehicle.

aerostat. A device supported in the air by displacing more than its weight of air. Balloons and dirigibles are examples of aerostats.

aerostatics. The branch of science that deals with the flight of lighter-than-air vehicles, such as balloons, dirigibles, or blimps. These vehicles are filled with hot air or with a gas lighter than the air surrounding it. This gas enables the balloon to rise in the air by displacing more than its own weight of air.

Aerostatic lift, which is produced by displacing a mass of air, is different from aerodynamic lift in that it does not require relative motion between the lifting body and the air.

aero-thermodynamic duct. *See* athodyd.

AFCS (automatic flight control system). The full system of automatic flight control which includes the autopilot, flight director, horizontal situation indicator, air data sensors, and other avionics inputs. An aircraft with an AFCS can be flown in a completely automatic mode.

A/FD. *See* Airport/Facility Directory.

affective domain. A grouping of learning levels associated with a person's attitudes, personal beliefs, and values that range from receiving (at the most basic level) to responding, valuing, organization, and characterization.

AFM. *See* airplane flight manual.

"Affirmative" (air traffic control). The term used by ATC for "yes."

aft. The direction toward the rear of an aircraft.

afterbody (aircraft structure). The rearward portion of an engine nacelle or pod. The portion of the structure that surrounds the tail pipe.

afterbody length. Length from the step, to the stern of a float, or hull of a flying boat.

after bottom center (reciprocating engine piston position). The position of the piston in the cylinder of a reciprocating engine after the crankshaft, turning in its normal direction of rotation, has caused the piston to pass the bottom of its stroke and start back up.

afterburner (gas turbine engine component). A device in the exhaust system of a turbojet or turbofan engine, used to increase the thrust for takeoff and for special flight conditions.

Since much of the air passing through a gas turbine engine is used only for cooling, it still contains a great deal of oxygen. Fuel is sprayed into the hot, oxygen-rich exhaust in the afterburner, where it burns and produces additional thrust.

Afterburners, called reheaters in the United Kingdom, use a large amount of fuel, but the extra thrust they produce makes them efficient for high-performance aircraft.

afterfiring (turbine engine). Fire that continues in the combustor after the engine is shut down. Afterfiring is normally caused by a malfunctioning manifold drain valve.

afterfiring (reciprocating engines). A condition that can exist in a reciprocating engine when an excessive amount of fuel is taken into the cylinders. Some of this fuel is still burning when it is forced out of the cylinders, and it continues to burn in the exhaust system. Afterfiring is sometimes called torching.

afterglow (cathode-ray tube). The light, or glow, remaining on the phosphorescent screen of a cathode-ray tube after the electron beam passes.

after top center (reciprocating engine piston position). The position of the piston in the cylinder of a reciprocating engine after the crankshaft, turning in its normal direction of rotation, has caused the piston to pass the top of its stroke and start back down.

aft-fan engine. A turbofan engine with the fan constructed as an extension of some of the turbine blades, rather than as an extension of the compressor blades. This fan pulls large volumes of air around the outside of the gas generator portion of the engine.

aft flap. The rearmost section of a triple-slotted, segmented wing flap. *See* triple-slotted flap.

age hardening (aluminum alloy heat treatment). The process of increasing the strength and hardness of aluminum alloy after it has been solution heat-treated. Age hardening occurs at room temperature and continues for a period of several days until the metal reaches its full-hard state.

aging. A change in the characteristics of a material that takes place over a period of time under specified environmental conditions. Aging may cause the physical condition of the material either to improve or to deteriorate. Certain aluminum alloys do not have their full strength when they are first removed from the quench bath after they have been heat-treated, but they gain this strength after a few days by the natural process of aging.

agitate. To stir something or to shake it up to mix its components. Agitating a mixture of ice and water causes the water to become uniformly cooled.

AGL altitude. Altitude, expressed in feet measured above ground level.

agonic line. An irregular imaginary line across the surface of the earth along which the magnetic and geographic poles are in alignment and along which there is no variation error. The term agonic comes from the two Greek words "a," meaning no, and "gonic," meaning angle.

agricultural aircraft. Aircraft especially designed and built for use in agriculture. The main use of agricultural aircraft is that of applying chemicals to crops for insect and weed control, and for seeding and fertilizing large areas in a minimum of time.

Agricultural aircraft are ruggedly built, can carry large loads, can operate from unimproved landing strips, are highly maneuverable, and are built to protect the pilot in the event of a crash.

agronautics. The branch of the aviation industry dealing with agriculture.

AHRS. *See* attitude heading reference system.

aileron (airplane flight control). A primary flight control surface mounted on the trailing edge of an airplane wing, near the tip. Ailerons operate by lateral movement of the control wheel or stick, and their displacement causes the airplane to rotate about its longitudinal axis.

aileron angle. The angle of deflection of an aileron from its neutral, or trailing, position. Aileron angle is positive when the trailing edge of the aileron is below its neutral position and negative when it is above neutral.

aileron spar. A short partial spar in the wing of an airplane that serves as a point of attachment for the aileron hinges. An aileron spar is sometimes called a false spar.

aileron station. Reference locations along the span of an aileron. Aileron stations are measured from the inboard end outward.

AIM (Aeronautical Information Manual). A primary FAA publication whose purpose is to instruct airmen about operating in the National Airspace System of the U.S. The AIM provides basic flight information, ATC procedures, and general instructional information concerning health, medical facts, factors affecting flight safety, accident and hazard reporting, and types of aeronautical charts and their use.

air. A physical mixture of gases that make up the atmosphere of the earth. Pure dry air contains approximately 78% nitrogen and 21% oxygen by volume, with the remainder made up of small parts of carbon dioxide, argon, neon, xenon, and helium. Dry air weighs 0.07651 pound per cubic foot under standard sea-level conditions.

air adapter (gas turbine engine component). A component in a centrifugal-compressor gas turbine engine. The air adapter is located between the diffuser and the combustor and is used to direct the airflow into the combustor at the proper angle.

air bleed (carburetor component). A small hole in the fuel passage between the float bowl and the discharge nozzle of a float carburetor. Air drawn into the liquid fuel through the air bleed breaks the fuel up into an emulsion, making it easy to atomize and thus to vaporize.

airborne. The condition of an aircraft when it is off the ground and supported in the air by aerodynamic or aerostatic forces.

airborne delay (air traffic control). The amount of delay to be encountered in airborne holding.

airborne intercept radar. A short-range airborne radar system carried in fighter and attack aircraft to locate and track their targets.

airborne moving target indicator (radar system). A type of airborne radar that filters out stationary objects and displays only moving targets.

airborne navigation equipment. A phrase embracing many systems and instruments. These systems include VHF omnirange (VOR), instrument landing systems (ILS), distance measuring equipment (DME), automatic direction finders (ADF), Doppler systems, and inertial navigation systems (INS).

air brake (aerodynamic component). A device that can be extended from the structure of an airplane to produce a large amount of parasite drag. Air brakes allow an airplane to increase its descent angle without building up an excessive amount of speed. Also called dive brakes, air brakes differ from flaps in that they produce no useful lift.

air-breathing engine (heat engine). An engine that requires an intake of air to supply the oxygen it needs to operate. Reciprocating and turbine engines are both air-breathing engines, but most rockets carry an oxidizing agent with their fuel. The oxidizing agent furnishes the needed oxygen.

air capacitor (electrical component). A capacitor that uses air as the dielectric. A variable tuning capacitor in a radio is an example of an air capacitor.

air carrier. An organization or person involved in the business of transporting people or cargo by air for compensation or hire.

14 CFR Part 1: "A person who undertakes directly by lease, or other arrangement, to engage in air transportation."

Air Carrier District Office. *See* ACDO.

air commerce. The portion of the transportation industry that deals with the carriage of people or cargo by air for compensation or hire. *14 CFR Part 1:* "Interstate, overseas, or foreign air commerce or the transportation of mail by aircraft or any operation or navigation of aircraft within the limits of any Federal airway or any operation or navigation of aircraft which directly affects, or which may endanger safety in, interstate, overseas, or foreign air commerce."

air conditioning. The process of treating the air in a building or compartment to control its temperature, humidity, cleanliness, and velocity of its movement. Air conditioning in an aircraft also includes the pressurization of the air inside the cabin.

air conditioning system. An environmental control system whose function is to maintain a comfortable air temperature within the aircraft fuselage. It is designed to perform any or all of the following functions: (1) Supply ventilation air, (2) supply heated air, and (3) supply cooling air.

air-cooled engine. A reciprocating engine whose excess heat is removed by transferring it directly into the air flowing over the engine. The cylinders of an air-cooled engine are fitted with fins to increase the surface area exposed to the air.

air-cooled oil cooler. An oil-to-air heat exchanger in the lubrication system of an aircraft engine. Heat is removed from the oil and transferred into the air flowing through the cooler.

air-cooled turbine blades. Hollow blades on the turbine wheel of certain high-power gas turbine engines. These blades are cooled by compressor bleed air flowing through them.

air cooling. The removal of unwanted heat by transferring it directly into the air that flows over the component.

air-core transformer (electrical transformer). A transformer containing two or more coils wound on a core of paper or other nonmagnetic material. Air-core transformers are normally used for radio-frequency alternating current.

air-core
transformer

aircraft. Any weight-carrying device designed to be supported by the air. Airplanes, helicopters, gliders, and balloons are all types of aircraft.

14 CFR Part 1: "A device that is used or intended to be used for flight in the air."

aircraft accident. Any damage or injury that occurs when an aircraft is moving with the intention of flight, and in which any person suffers death or serious injury, or in which the aircraft receives substantial damage.

aircraft alteration. The modification of an aircraft, its structure, or its components which changes the physical or flight characteristics of the aircraft. The Federal Aviation Administration classifies all alterations as either major alterations or minor alterations. *See* major alterations, minor alterations.

aircraft approach category. A grouping of aircraft based on a speed of 1.3 times their stall speed in the landing configuration at maximum gross landing weight.

Category A...Speed less than 91 knots
Category B...Speed between 91 and 121 knots
Category C...Speed between 121 and 141 knots
Category D...Speed between 141 and 166 knots
Category E...Speed of 166 knots or more

aircraft basic operating weight. The basic weight of an aircraft, including the crew, ready for flight but without payload and fuel. This term is used only for transport aircraft.

aircraft battery. A source of electrical energy for an aircraft that may be used for starting the engine and as auxiliary electrical power when the engine-driven generator is not operating.

aircraft checkouts. An instructional program designed to familiarize and qualify a pilot to act as pilot in command of a particular aircraft type.

aircraft classes (wake turbulence separation). For the purpose of wake turbulence separation minimums, ATC has classified aircraft as heavy, large, and small:

Heavy. Aircraft capable of takeoff weights of more than 255,000 pounds whether or not they operate at this weight during a particular phase of flight.

Large. Aircraft of more than 41,000 pounds, maximum certificated takeoff weight, up to 255,000 pounds.

Small. Aircraft of 41,000 pounds or less maximum certificated takeoff weight.

aircraft classification (by certification weight). Classification of aircraft according to their maximum certificated gross weight:

Small aircraft. Aircraft weighing up to 12,500 pounds certificated takeoff weight.

Large aircraft. Aircraft of more than 12,500 pounds maximum certificated takeoff weight.

aircraft conflict (air traffic control). Predicted conflict, within URET (user request evaluation tool), of two aircraft, or between aircraft and airspace. A Red alert is used for conflicts when the predicted minimum separation is 5 nautical miles or less. A Yellow alert is used when the predicted minimum separation is between 5 and approximately 12 nautical miles. A Blue alert is used for conflicts between an aircraft and predefined airspace.

aircraft control cable. Stranded steel cable used to actuate the controls of an aircraft. Aircraft control cable is made of either stainless steel or galvanized carbon steel. There are three types of aircraft control cable: nonflexible, flexible, and extra-flexible cable. Nonflexible cable is made of seven (1 x 7) or 19 (1 x 19)

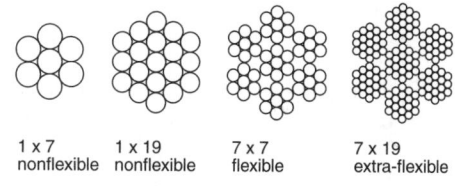

| 1 x 7 | 1 x 19 | 7 x 7 | 7 x 19 |
| nonflexible | nonflexible | flexible | extra-flexible |

aircraft control cable

strands of steel wire. Flexible cable is made of seven strands of wire, with each strand having seven separate wires. This is called 7 x 7 cable.

Extra-flexible cable, the one most generally used, is made of seven strands of wire, with each strand made of 19 small wires. Extra-flexible cable is called 7 x 19 cable and is used in locations where the cable must pass over a pulley.

aircraft engine. *14 CFR Part 1:* "An engine that is used or intended to be used for propelling aircraft. It includes turbosuperchargers, appurtenances, and accessories necessary for its functioning, but does not include propellers."

aircraft incident. An occurrence other than an accident, associated with the operation of an aircraft, that affects or could affect the safety of operations.

aircraft inspection. A systematic check of an aircraft and its components. The purpose of an aircraft inspection is to detect any defects or malfunctions before they become serious. Preflight, 100-hour, annual, and progressive inspections are the most commonly used types of aircraft inspections.

aircraft lighting system. A system for providing light to both the interior and exterior of an aircraft, including the lighting of instruments, cabins, cockpits as well as landing and position lights.

Aircraft Listings. Information sheets, published by the Federal Aviation Administration, that contain pertinent specifications for certificated aircraft of which there are fewer than fifty of that model still registered.

aircraft logs. Aircraft records containing the operational or maintenance history of the aircraft.

aircraft maintenance manual (AMM). A manual provided by the aircraft manufacturer that contains maintenance instructions for all systems installed in the aircraft.

aircraft operating instructions. A document developed by aircraft manufacturers and accepted by the Federal Aviation Administration (FAA). It is specific to a particular make and model powered parachute by serial number and contains operating procedures and limitations.

aircraft plumbing. The hoses, tubing, fittings, and connections used for carrying fluids through an aircraft.

aircraft quality. A term used to indicate that a particular piece of equipment or material meets the rigid standards established by the military services or by an aircraft manufacturer for use in an aircraft.

aircraft records. Documentation of the flight time and the maintenance that has been performed on an aircraft, its engines, or its components.

aircraft repair. Restoration of an aircraft and/or its components to a condition of airworthiness after a failure or the occurrence of damage or wear.

aircraft rigging. The final adjustment and alignment of the various component parts of an aircraft to give it the proper aerodynamic characteristics.

aircraft situation display. *See* ASD.

Aircraft Specifications. Documentation that includes the pertinent specifications for aircraft certificated under the Civil Air Regulations (CARs). Specifications are also available for Engines and Propellers. The information in Aircraft Specifications that is pertinent to aircraft certificated under Federal Aviation Regulations (14 CFR) is contained in the Type Certificate Data Sheets.

air-cycle cooling system. A system for cooling the air in the cabin of a turbine-powered aircraft. Compressor bleed air passes through a primary heat exchanger and gives up some of its heat. It then passes through a centrifugal compressor driven by an expansion turbine. The compressor uses energy from the turbine to raise the temperature and pressure of the partially cooled bleed air. This additional heat is removed as the air flows through a secondary heat exchanger. The air then flows through the expansion turbine where it gives up still more of its energy as the turbine drives the compressor.

When the air, with much of its energy removed, leaves the turbine, it expands and its pressure and temperature drop further, providing cold air for cooling the cabin.

air-cycle machine. The component in an air-cycle cooling system that includes the expansion turbine and the compressor.

air data attitude and heading reference system (ADAHRS). An integrated flight instrument system that combines the functions of an air data computer (the "AD" is short for ADC) and an attitude heading reference system (AHRS) into one unit.

air data computer (ADC). An electronic computer in an aircraft that senses pitot pressure, static pressure, and total air temperature. The air from the static ports and pitot tube is vented to the ADC instead of the flight instruments themselves. The ADC then converts the air data into electronic information that is displayed on the primary flight display. The ADC produces an indication of altitude, indicated airspeed, true airspeed, and Mach number, and its output is usable by any of the engine or flight control computers.

air defense emergency (air traffic control). A military emergency condition declared by a designated authority. This condition exists when an attack upon the continental U.S., Alaska, Canada, or U.S. installations in Greenland by hostile aircraft or missiles is considered probable, is imminent, or is taking place.

Air Defense Identification Zone. *See* ADIZ.

air density. The mass of air in a given volume. In the English system of measurements, air density is measured in slugs per cubic foot. Air at standard sea level conditions has a density of 0.002378 slug per cubic foot.

air-dry. To remove moisture from a material by exposing it to the air.

airfield. Any area in which aircraft may land, take off, and park. An airfield may also be called an airport, airstrip, or aerodrome. The term airfield includes the buildings, equipment, and maintenance facilities used to store or service aircraft.

air filter (induction system component). A filter through which air entering the induction system of a reciprocating engine must pass. Filters remove sand and dust, preventing them from entering the engine.

Because of the possibility of the filter being obstructed by ice, provisions are made to bypass it and allow the engine to take in warm, unfiltered air from the engine compartment.

air filter system (engine inlet air). A filter element, a door, and an electrically operated actuator in the inlet air passage of a turboprop engine installed in a helicopter. When the filter system is operating, air is drawn through a louvered access panel that does not face directly into the airstream. With this entrance location, considerable dust is removed as the air is forced to turn and enter the duct.

airfoil. Any surface designed to obtain a useful reaction, or lift, from air passing over it. Airplane wings, propeller blades, and helicopter rotors are examples of airfoils.

airfoil characteristic curves. A set of curves for an airfoil section plotted from wind tunnel data that shows the effect of angle of attack on the coefficient of lift, coefficient of drag, lift over drag ratio, and the movement of the center of pressure.

airfoil profile. The outline of an airfoil section.

airfoil section. The cross-sectional shape of an airfoil, viewed as if it were cut through in a fore-and-aft plane.

airframe. *14 CFR Part 1:* "The fuselage, booms, nacelles, cowlings, fairings, airfoil surfaces (including rotors but excluding propellers and rotating airfoils of engines), and landing gear of an aircraft and their accessories and controls."

airframe mechanic (technician). A person holding a certificate issued by the Federal Aviation Administration that authorizes him or her to perform maintenance and inspections on the airframe of FAA-certificated aircraft.

air-fuel mixture ratio. The ratio of the weight of the air to that of the fuel in the mixture being fed into the cylinders of a reciprocating engine.

air gap (electromagnet). A nonmagnetic separation in the magnetic path between an electromagnet and a plunger (workpiece). Air gaps can be actual air separation or separation by a nonmagnetic material. Air gaps exponentially reduce the holding value.

air impingement (aircraft finish defect). A fault resembling haze in an enamel or lacquer finish of an aircraft. Air impingement is caused by microscopic-sized bubbles in the finish that form when the finishing material is applied using too high an atomizing air pressure.

air impingement starter (gas turbine engine starter). A type of starter used on some gas turbine engines in which a stream of high-pressure compressed air is directed onto the blades of the compressor or turbine to rotate the engine for starting.

air inlet duct (turbine engine component). The portion of the aircraft ahead of the engine compressor that takes the air into the aircraft and directs it into the engine at the correct speed and direction.

airline. A company or organization that operates aircraft for the transportation of persons or cargo for compensation or hire.

airliner. A large transport-type aircraft used in air commerce for the transportation of passengers and/or cargo.

Airloc fastener. A patented form of cowling fastener in which the actual locking is done by rotating a steel cross-pin in a spring-steel receptacle.

air lock (fluid system malfunction). A pocket of air trapped in a line which carries a liquid. The air blocks the flow of the liquid.

airman. A person involved in flying, maintaining, or operating aircraft.

airman certificate. The certificate issued by the Federal Aviation Administration authorizing a person to perform certain aviation-related duties. Airman certificates are issued to pilots, mechanics, and parachute riggers.

airmanship. Consists of a satisfactory understanding of the principles of flight, the ability to operate an airplane with competence and precision both on the ground and in the air, and the exercise of sound judgment that results in optimal operational safety and efficiency.

airmanship skills. The skills of coordination, timing, control touch, and speed sense in addition to the motor skills required to fly an aircraft.

air mass (meteorology). An extensive body of air within which the conditions of temperature and moisture in a horizontal plane are essentially uniform.

air mass classification (meteorology). A system used to identify and characterize the different air masses according to a basic scheme. The system most commonly used classifies air masses primarily according to the thermal properties of their source regions: tropical (T); polar (P); and Arctic or Antarctic (A). They are further classified according to moisture characteristics as continental (c) or maritime (m).

AIRMET. An inflight weather advisory message issued only to amend an area forecast concerning weather phenomena of operational interest to all aircraft and potentially hazardous to aircraft having limited capability because of lack of equipment, instrumentation, or pilot qualifications.

  AIRMETs cover moderate icing, moderate turbulence, sustained winds of 30 knots or more at the surface, widespread areas of ceiling less than 1,000 feet and/or visibility less than three miles, and extensive mountain obscurement.

air metering force (fuel metering system). The force used in pressure carburetors and certain fuel injection systems to determine the amount of fuel to be metered into the engine. The air metering force is a balance between ram air pressure picked up by impact tubes and a low pressure produced in a venturi.

air navigation facility. Any facility used, available for use, or designated for use as an aid in air navigation. This includes landing areas, lights, and any apparatus or equipment for disseminating weather information. It also includes radio and other electrical communications equipment used for signaling, for radio-directional finding, and for guiding or controlling the takeoff and landing of aircraft and for flight in the air.

air-oil cooler. A heat exchanger that uses a flow of ambient air to remove heat from engine lubricating oil.

air-oil separator (gas turbine engine lubrication system component). A component in a turbine engine lubrication system that removes the air from the scavenged oil before the oil is returned to the tank.

airplane. *14 CFR Part 1:* "An engine-driven, fixed-wing aircraft heavier than air, that is supported in flight by the dynamic reaction of the air against its wings."

airplane flight manual (AFM). A document developed by the airplane manufacturer and approved by the Federal Aviation Administration (FAA). It is specific to a particular make and model airplane by serial number and contains operating procedures and limitations. (Sometimes referred to as "aircraft flight manual")

airplane owner/information manual. A document developed by the airplane manufacturer containing general information about the make and model of an airplane. The airplane owner's manual is not FAA-approved and is not specific to a particular serial numbered airplane. This manual is not kept current, and therefore cannot be substituted for the AFM or POH.

airport. *14 CFR Part 1:* "An area of land or water that is used, or intended to be used for the landing and takeoff of aircraft, and includes its buildings and facilities, if any."

airport acceptance rate (AAR) (air traffic control). An established hourly rate of aircraft arrivals that a given airport can manage, accounting for staffing and equipment considerations.

airport advisory area. The area within ten miles of an airport without a control tower or where the tower is not in operation and on which a Flight Service Station is located.

airport advisory service. *See* AAS.

airport diagram. A full-page depiction of an airport that includes the same features as the airport sketch plus additional details such as taxiway identifiers, airport latitude and longitude, and building identification. Airport diagrams are located in the U.S. Terminal Procedures booklet following the instrument approach charts for a particular airport.

airport elevation. The highest point of an airport's usable runways measured in feet above mean sea level.

Airport/Facility Directory (A/FD). A publication of the Federal Aviation Administration containing information on all airports, seaplane bases, and heliports open to the public. The A/F Directory contains communications data, navigational facilities, and certain special notices and procedures.

airport information desk. An unmanned facility at an airport designed for pilot self-service briefing, flight planning, and filing of flight plans.

airport lighting. The various lighting aids installed on an airport. These include:
Approach Light Systems (ALS)—
   ALSF-1. Approach light system with sequenced flashing lights in ILS category-I configuration
   ALSF-II. Approach light system with sequenced flashing lights in ILS category-II configuration
   SSALF. Simplified short approach light system with sequenced flashing lights
   SSALR. Simplified short approach light system with runway alignment indicator lights
   MALSF. Medium intensity approach light system with sequenced flashing lights
   MALSR. Medium intensity approach light system with runway alignment indicator lights
   RLLS. Runway lead-in light system
   RAIL. Runway alignment indicator lights
   ODALS. Omnidirectional approach lighting system
Runway lights/Runway edge lights
Touchdown zone lighting
Runway center line lighting

Continued

airport lighting. *Continued*
 Threshold lights—
  REIL. Runway End Identifier Lights
  VASI. Visual Approach Slope Indicator lights
  PAPI. Precision Approach Path Indicator
 Boundary lights

airport marking aids. Markings used on runway and taxiway surfaces to identify a specific runway, a runway threshold, a center line, a hold line, etc. A runway should be marked in accordance with its present usage, such as visual, nonprecision instrument, and precision instrument.

airport reservation office. The office responsible for monitoring the operation of the high-density air traffic. This office receives and processes requests for IFR operations at high-density-traffic airports.

airport rotating beacon. A visual aid to navigation located at lighted airports. The color of the beacon flashes indicates the type of airport. The colors and meaning of the more commonly used rotating beacons are:

Color	Meaning
white and green	lighted land airport
green	lighted land airport
white	unlighted land airport
white and yellow	lighted water airport
yellow	lighted water airport
green, yellow and white	lighted heliport
white (dual peaked) and green	military airport

airport sketch. Depicts the airport's runways and their length, width, and slope; the touchdown zone elevation; the lighting system installed on the end of the runway; and the taxiways. Airport sketches are located on the lower left or right portion of instrument approach charts.

airport surface detection equipment (ASDE). Radar equipment specifically designed to detect all principal features on the surface of an airport, including aircraft and vehicular traffic, and to present the entire image on a radar indicator console in the control tower. ASDE is used to augment visual observation by tower personnel of aircraft and/ or vehicular movements on runways and taxiways; it enables air traffic controllers to detect potential runway conflicts by providing detailed coverage of such movement. There are three ASDE systems deployed in the NAS:
 a. ASDE–3—this is a Surface Movement Radar.
 b. ASDE–X—a system that uses an X-band Surface Movement Radar and multilateration. Data from these two sources are fused and presented on a digital display. By collecting data from a variety of sources, ASDE-X has the combined ability to track vehicle and aircraft movement and obtain identification information from aircraft transponders.
 c. ASDE–3X—this is an ASDE–X system that uses the ASDE–3 Surface Movement Radar.

airport surveillance radar. *See* ASR.

airport surveillance radar approach. An instrument approach in which ATC issues instructions for pilot compliance based on aircraft position in relation to the final approach course and distance from the end of the runway as displayed on the controller's radar scope.

airport taxi charts. Aeronautical charts designed to expedite safe and efficient flow of ground traffic at an airport.

airport traffic area. Normally, the airspace within a horizontal radius of five statute miles from the geographical center of any airport having an operating control tower. An airport traffic area extends upward from the surface to, but not including, an altitude of 3,000 feet above the elevation of the airport.

air route surveillance radar. *See* ARSR.

air route traffic control center. *See* ARTCC.

air scoop. A hooded opening used to direct outside air into an aircraft structure in flight. The ram effect caused by movement of the aircraft through the air increases the amount of air taken into the structure.

airscrew. The British term for an aircraft propeller.

air seal. A seal around a rotating shaft, used to keep air from passing out of the housing holding the shaft. Air seals are often made of thin alternate fixed and rotating blades which act as air dams to prevent air flowing past the seal.

airship. *14 CFR Part 1:* "An engine-driven lighter-than-air aircraft that can be steered."

airspace. The space above a certain geographical area.

airspeed. The rate at which an aircraft is moving through the air.

airspeed indicator. A differential air pressure gage which measures the difference between ram, or impact, air pressure and the local static air pressure. The dial of an airspeed indicator is calibrated to convert this differential air pressure into units of knots, miles per hour, or kilometers per hour.

air start (aircraft engine operation). The process of starting an aircraft engine in flight with the engine rotated by aerodynamic forces acting on the propeller or compressor blades.

air taxi (helicopter operation). Movement of a helicopter above the surface but at an altitude of less than 100 feet above ground level.

air temperature control (carburetor operations). A means of preventing or eliminating ice accumulation in an induction system by preheating the air before it enters the carburetor. The heat is obtained from a muff around an exhaust component or from a warm area within the engine cowling.

air traffic. *14 CFR Part 1:* "Aircraft operating in the air or on an airport surface, exclusive of loading ramps and parking areas."

air traffic clearance. *14 CFR Part 1:* "An authorization by air traffic control, for the purpose of preventing collision between known aircraft, for an aircraft to proceed under specified traffic conditions within controlled airspace."

air traffic control. The control of aircraft traffic from the ground. Air traffic control is done from control towers whose personnel direct air traffic in the vicinity of an airport and air route traffic control centers whose personnel direct air traffic along the airways between airports.

Effective air traffic control is possible because of efficient two-way radio communications and radar that allow controllers to keep track of all the aircraft they are controlling.

14 CFR Part 1: "A service operated by appropriate authority to promote the safe, orderly and expeditious flow of air traffic."

air traffic control radar beacon system (ATCRBS). Sometimes called secondary surveillance radar (SSR), an ATCRBS is a radar system that requires a complementary transponder in the aircraft. The ground equipment consists of an interrogating unit in which the beacon antenna is mounted so it rotates with the surveillance antenna. The interrogating unit transmits a coded pulse sequence that actuates the aircraft transponder. The transponder answers the coded sequence by transmitting a preselected coded sequence back to the ground equipment, providing a strong return signal and positive aircraft identification, as well as other data.

air traffic control specialist. A person authorized by the FAA to provide air traffic control service.

air traffic control system command center. *See* ATCSCC.

Air Traffic Security Coordinator (ATSC). Working in the System Operations Security section of the FAA's Air Traffic Organization (ATO), an ATSC is an air traffic control specialist who has been provided with additional training and responsibilities in the area of air security and air defense.

air traffic service. A generic term meaning flight information service, alerting service, air traffic advisory service, and air traffic control service, including area control service, approach control service, and airport control service.

air traffic service (ATS) route. A specified route designated for channeling the flow of traffic as necessary for the provision of air traffic services. The term "ATS route" refers to a variety of airways, including jet routes, area navigation (RNAV) routes, and arrival and departure routes. An ATS route is defined by route specifications, which may include: (1) an ATS route designator; (2) the path to or from significant points; (3) the distance between significant points; (4) reporting requirements; and (5) the lowest safe altitude determined by the appropriate authority.

Air Transport Association (ATA) Specification 100. *See* ATA 100.

air transportation. The business of moving people, mail, or cargo by air.

14 CFR Part 1: "Interstate, overseas, or foreign air transportation or the transportation of mail by aircraft."

air turbine starter (gas turbine engine starter). An air-driven turbine used to spin the engine compressor through a system of reduction gears. A large volume of compressed air from an auxiliary power unit or bleed air from an operating engine is directed into the air-turbine starter. This air spins the turbine inside the starter, and the starter, which is geared to the main engine compressor, spins the engine fast enough for it to start.

airway. An airway is based on a centerline that extends between one navigation aid or intersection to (or through) another navigation aid or intersection. Airways are used to establish a known route for enroute procedures between terminal areas.

airway beacon. A light beacon used to mark certain segments of airways in remote mountainous areas. These beacons flash Morse code to identify their location.

Airworthiness Alert. A notice sent by the FAA to certain interested maintenance personnel, identifying problems with aircraft that have been gathered from Malfunction and Defect Reports. These are problems being studied at the time the Airworthiness Alert is issued yet not fully evaluated at the time the material goes to press.

Airworthiness Certificate. A certificate issued by the Federal Aviation Administration to aircraft which meet the minimum standards for airworthiness as specified in the appropriate part of the Federal Aviation Regulations.

Airworthiness Directive. *See* AD.

airworthy. A condition in which the aircraft or component meets the conditions of its type design and is in a condition for safe operation.

AJW-3 (FAA department). The principal government entity within the Technical Operations Services (AJW-0) that is directly responsible for the in-flight inspection of air navigation facilities, obstacle clearance verification, final approval of substitute routes, and for the development and maintenance of instrument flight procedures throughout the United States and its territories. Also, various branches of AJW-3 are responsible for the production and distribution of aeronautical charts and related publications and products.

albedo (meteorology). The ratio of the amount of electromagnetic radiation reflected by a body to the amount falling on it. Albedo, which is normally expressed as a percentage, is used in reference to solar radiation. For example, the albedo of wet sand is 9, meaning that about 9% of the electromagnetic radiation from the sun falling on the sand is reflected.

Albedo ranges upward to 80–85 for fresh snow cover. The average albedo for the earth and its atmosphere has been calculated to range from 35 to 43.

Alclad. The trade name registered by the Aluminum Company of America for clad structural aluminum alloy. Aluminum alloy corrodes easily, but pure aluminum does not. Alclad sheets are made of high-strength aluminum alloy sandwiched between thin layers of pure aluminum. The coatings of pure aluminum, which are rolled onto the alloy sheet in the rolling mill, make up about five percent of the thickness of the sheet. Alclad sheets resist corrosion as long as the cladding is not scratched through or worn off.

alcohol. A colorless, volatile, flammable liquid produced by the fermentation of certain types of grain, fruit, or wood pulp. Alcohol is used as a cleaning fluid, as a solvent in many of aircraft finishes, and as a fuel for certain types of specialized engines.

Ethyl alcohol (the alcohol used in liquor) is distilled from fruit or grain, and methyl alcohol, which is poisonous, is distilled from wood pulp.

alcohol anti-icing system. A system installed on some aircraft to prevent ice from forming on the windshield, carburetors, and propellers. Isopropyl alcohol is sprayed over the surface being protected to lower the freezing point of any water on these surfaces and prevent the formation of ice.

ALERFA (alert phase) (ICAO). A situation in which there is apprehension as to the safety of an aircraft and its occupants.

alert area (air traffic control). An area in which there is a high volume of pilot training or an unusual type of aeronautical activity.

alerting service. A service provided by the FAA to notify appropriate organizations regarding aircraft in need of search and rescue aid and to assist such organizations as required.

algebra. The branch of mathematics that uses letters or symbols to represent numbers in formulas and equations.

algebraic expression. A quantity made up of letters, numbers, and other symbols. The parts of the expression separated by a plus or a minus sign are called the terms of the expression.

An algebraic expression having only one term is called a monomial, and one with two or more terms is called a polynomial. The algebraic expressions AB, 2Y, and $6X^2$ are monomials. The expression $AB + 2Y - 6X^2$ is a polynomial. It is actually a trinomial, because it has three terms.

algorithm. A systematic set of rules or processes by which a problem can be solved in a specific number of individual steps.

alignment (electronic). The adjustment of the components in an electronic circuit so they will be resonant at the required frequency.

alignment. The arrangement, or position, of parts of an object or system in correct relationship to each other.

alignment pin. A pin installed in a helicopter rotor blade to serve as an index when aligning the blades of a semirigid rotor system.

alignment tool (electronic tool). A nonmetallic screwdriver or socket wrench used to adjust trimmer and padder capacitors to align the circuits in a piece of electronic equipment.

aliphatic naphtha. A petroleum product similar to gasoline and kerosine. Aliphatic naphtha is used as a cleaning agent to remove grease from a surface prior to painting.

alkali. A chemical substance, usually the hydroxide of a metal. An alkali has a characteristically bitter taste and is prone to react with an acid, furnishing the electrons to form a salt.

alkaline. Having the property of reacting with an acid to form a salt by giving up electrons to the acidic material.

alkaline cell. A type of primary electrochemical cell that uses powdered zinc as the anode, powdered graphite and manganese dioxide as the cathode, and potassium hydroxide as the electrolyte. An alkaline cell has an open-circuit voltage of 1.5 volts, and it has from 50% to 100% more capacity than a carbon-zinc cell of comparable size.

alkyd resin. A type of synthetic resin used as the base for certain enamels and primers.

all-cargo operation. Any operation for compensation or hire that is other than a passenger-carrying operation or, if passengers are carried, they are only those specified in 14 CFR §121.583(a) or §135.85.

Allen screw. A screw with a hexagonal hole, or socket, in its head.

Allen wrench. A hexagonal rod used to turn an Allen screw. The most common Allen wrenches are bent with a 90° angle so they have a short and a long leg.

alligator clip. A spring-type clip used on the end of an electrical wire to make temporary connections in an electrical circuit. An alligator clip has long, narrow, spring-loaded jaws with meshing teeth.

allowable. Permissible.

allowance. The difference between the nominal dimension of a part and its upper or lower limit.

alloy. A physical mixture of chemical elements combined with a metal to change its characteristics.

alloying agent. A chemical element mixed with a base metal to form an alloy. The alloying agents change the characteristics of the base metal.

alloy steel. Steel into which certain chemical elements have been mixed. Alloy steel has different characteristics from those of simple carbon steel.

all-weather spark plug. A type of shielded spark plug for use in an aircraft reciprocating engine for high-altitude operation. The ceramic insulator is recessed into the shell to allow a resilient grommet on the ignition harness lead to provide a watertight seal. All-weather spark plugs, also called high-altitude spark plugs, are identified by their 3/4-20 shielding threads.

almanac data. Information the global positioning system (GPS) receiver obtains from one satellite describing the approximate orbital positioning of all satellites in the constellation. This information is necessary for the GPS receiver to know what satellites to look for in the sky at a given time.

Alnico. The registered trade name for an alloy of iron, aluminum, nickel, and cobalt. Alnico, which has an extremely high permeability and excellent retentivity, is used in the manufacture of permanent magnets.

ALNOT (Alert Notice). A message sent by a Flight Service Station or Air Route Traffic Control Center that requests an extensive communications search for an overdue, unreported, or missing aircraft.

Alodine. The registered trade name for a conversion-coating chemical which forms a hard, unbroken oxide film on a piece of aluminum alloy. The oxide film produced by Alodine serves the same function as the film produced by anodizing, but does not require an electrolytic bath. Alodine conforms to specifications MIL-C-5541B.

Alodizing. A method of corrosion protection by the formation of a hard, airtight oxide coating on the surface of aluminum alloy parts by chemical means. The name is taken from the registered trade name of the chemical Alodine.

along-track distance (ATD) (air traffic control). The distance measured from a point in space, by ATC systems that use area navigation reference capabilities and that are not subject to slant-range errors.

alpha (transistor operation). A measure of emitter-to-collector current gain of a transistor in a common-base amplifier circuit. Alpha of a junction transistor is never greater than one. Its output is always less than its input.

alpha cutoff frequency (transistor characteristic). The frequency at which the current gain (alpha) of a common-base transistor stage drops off to 0.707 of its low-frequency value.

alpha hinge (helicopter rotor). The hinge at the root of a helicopter rotor blade that allows the tip of the blade to move back and forth in its plane of rotation. The axis of the alpha hinge is perpendicular to the plane of rotor rotation. An alpha hinge is also called a lead-lag hinge.

alpha iron. The arrangement of the molecules in iron when its temperature is below 911°C.

alpha mode of operation (turboprop operation). The operation of a turboprop engine that includes all flight operations from takeoff to landing. Alpha operation is typically between 95 percent to 100 percent of the engine operating speed. Also called "alpha control range."

alphanumeric symbols. Symbols made up of all of the letters in our alphabet, numerals, punctuation marks, and certain other special symbols.

alpha particle. A positively charged nuclear particle having the same mass as the nucleus of a helium atom. Alpha particles consist of two protons and two neutrons and are emitted at a high speed in certain types of radioactivity.

alpha ray (electromagnetic radiation). A stream of alpha particles which ionize the gas through which they pass. These particles cause a fluorescent screen to glow. An alpha ray is made up of the lowest-frequency radio emission.

alpha wave (brain waves). Electrical signals produced in the brain that have a pulse frequency of eight to 13 hertz. Alpha waves are produced by a normal human brain when in its relaxed state.

alpha wave detector. A sensitive electronic device used to detect and display alpha waves from the human brain.

ALS. *See* approach lighting system.

alteration. A change to a certificated aircraft, aircraft engine, propeller, or appliance.

alternate aerodrome (ICAO). An aerodrome to which an aircraft may proceed when it becomes either impossible or inadvisable to proceed to or to land at the aerodrome of intended landing.

alternate airport. *14 CFR Part 1:* "An airport at which an aircraft may land if a landing at the intended airport becomes inadvisable."

alternate air valve (reciprocating engine induction system). A valve in the induction system of a reciprocating engine that directs air either from the air filter or from a point inside the engine nacelle into the carburetor or the fuel injection system. The alternate air valve on an engine equipped with a carburetor is called a carburetor heat valve.

alternate static air valve (aircraft instrument system). A valve in the static air system that supplies reference air pressure to the altimeter, airspeed indicator, and vertical speed indicator.

Normally these instruments pick up their reference air pressure from a static vent on the outside of the aircraft. If this vent ever becomes clogged with ice, the alternate static air valve can be opened, and the instruments will be supplied with static air from some unpressurized area inside the aircraft.

alternating current (AC). Electricity in which the flow of electrons periodically reverses its direction and continually changes its amplitude.

alternation (alternating current electricity). One half of a cycle of alternating current or voltage. There are two alternations in one cycle: the positive alternation and the negative alternation. *See* illustration for sine wave.

alternator (electrical machine). A rotating electric generator that produces alternating current. While all rotating generators produce AC, a DC generator uses some type of rectifier to change the AC into DC before it leaves the generator.

Alternators used on light airplanes are three-phase AC generators with built-in three-phase, solid-state rectifiers to change the AC into DC before it leaves the alternator.

alternator control unit. The solid-state control for an alternator that contains the voltage and current sensors and controls the alternator field current to maintain the correct voltage and current within the alternator rating.

altimeter. An aneroid barometer whose dial is calibrated in feet or meters above a reference pressure level. An altimeter measures the difference between the pressure of the air surrounding it and a reference pressure which is set on the barometric pressure dial on the face of the instrument. This pressure difference is expressed in feet or meters.

altimeter setting. Station pressure (the barometric pressure at the location the reading is taken) which has been corrected for the height of the station above sea level. When the altimeter setting is entered into the barometric pressure window of an altimeter, the instrument will indicate its height above mean, or average, sea level. This is called indicated altitude.

altimeter setting indicator. A precision aneroid barometer at a weather observation station, calibrated to indicate directly the altimeter setting.

altitude. The height of an object expressed in units of distance above a reference plane, usually above mean sea level (MSL) or above ground (AGL). *See* corrected altitude, density altitude, indicated altitude, pressure altitude, radar altitude, and true altitude.

altitude (geometric figure). The greatest perpendicular distance from any side of the figure to its opposite side.

altitude alerting system. The system that provides the pilot with a visual and/or auditory alert when the airplane approaches or deviates from a preselected altitude.

altitude capture. An autopilot function that enables the autopilot to automatically level the airplane at a selected altitude.

altitude chamber. A device that simulates high-altitude conditions by reducing the interior pressure. The occupants will suffer from the same physiological conditions as they would during flight at altitude in an unpressurized aircraft.

altitude engine. An aircraft reciprocating engine equipped with a supercharger that allows it to maintain its rated sea-level horsepower to a specified higher altitude.

14 CFR Part 1: "A reciprocating aircraft engine having a rated takeoff power that is producible from sea level to an established higher altitude."

altitude function. An autopilot function that maintains the present altitude of the airplane.

altitude readout (radar display). The altitude of an aircraft transmitted via the Mode C transponder feature that is visually displayed in 100-foot increments on a radarscope having altitude readout capability.

altitude reservation (air traffic control). Airspace utilization under prescribed conditions normally employed for the mass movement of aircraft or other special user requirements which cannot otherwise be accomplished. ALTRVs are approved by the appropriate FAA facility.

altitude restriction. An altitude or altitudes stated in the order flown, which are to be maintained until reaching a specific point or time. Altitude restrictions may be issued by ATC (air traffic control) because of traffic, terrain, or other considerations.

"Altitude restrictions are canceled" (air traffic control directive). A statement meaning that adherence to previously imposed altitude restriction is no longer required during a climb or descent.

altitude sensing unit (turbine engine fuel control). *See* ASU.

altocumulus (meteorology). White or gray layers or patches of cloud often having a wavy appearance. Cloud elements appear as rounded masses or rolls and are composed mostly of liquid water droplets which may be supercooled. Altocumulus clouds may contain ice crystals at subfreezing temperatures.

altocumulus castellanus (meteorology). A species of middle cloud of which at least a fraction of its upper part has evidence of vertical development. Vertical development shows up as billowing tops, some of which are taller than they are wide. This gives the top of the cloud layer a crenelated or turreted appearance, especially when viewed from the side. These clouds usually have a common base arranged in lines; they indicate instability and turbulence at the altitude of the cloud.

ALTRV (altitude reservation). Airspace utilization under prescribed conditions. ALTRV is normally employed for the mass movement of aircraft or other special user requirements which cannot otherwise be accomplished.

alumel. An alloy of nickel, aluminum, manganese, and silicon that is the negative element in a thermocouple used to measure exhaust gas temperature.

alumina. Natural aluminum oxide (Al_2O_3). Alumina occurs in nature in the form of corundum, a hard mineral crystal, or in the form of bauxite, a clay.

aluminium. The British term for aluminum.

aluminizing. A form of corrosion protection for steel parts. Molten aluminum is sprayed onto the steel by a high-velocity jet of air. The aluminum coating protects the steel from corrosion by preventing air or moisture reaching the surface of the steel.

aluminum. A bluish-silvery, metallic chemical element whose atomic number is 13, atomic weight is 26.9815, and symbol is Al. Aluminum is produced from the clay bauxite, a form of aluminum oxide. Aluminum is lightweight, malleable, ductile, a good conductor of heat and electricity, and a good reflector of heat and light. Pure aluminum is highly resistant to corrosion.

In its natural state, aluminum is soft and weak, but it can be alloyed with such metals as copper, magnesium, manganese, and zinc to give it strength.

aluminum alloy. Aluminum to which has been added one or more other chemical elements. These alloying elements increase the hardness, toughness, durability, or resistance to fatigue of the aluminum.

Aluminum alloys are the primary metals used in the construction of aircraft and other structures which require high strength and light weight.

aluminum electrolytic capacitor (electronic component). An electrolytic capacitor which uses strips of aluminum as the plates. An oxide film formed on the surface of the aluminum acts as the dielectric. The aluminum plates are separated by layers of absorbent paper saturated with a liquid electrolyte.

aluminum oxide. A compound of aluminum and oxygen whose chemical formula is Al_2O_3. Aluminum oxide is extremely hard and is used as an abrasive.

aluminum paste (aircraft finishing material). Extremely fine flakes of aluminum suspended in a vehicle such as an oil. Aluminum paste is mixed with clear dope to make aluminum-pigmented dope.

aluminum-pigmented dope (aircraft finishing material). Clear aircraft dope in which tiny flakes of aluminum are suspended. When aluminum-pigmented dope is sprayed over the clear dope used on aircraft fabric, the tiny flakes of aluminum spread out and form an opaque coating that prevents ultraviolet rays from the sun damaging the clear dope and the fabric.

aluminum wool. Shavings of aluminum formed into a pad. Aluminum wool can be used to remove corrosion products from aluminum alloy parts and also to smooth out minor scratches on the surface of aluminum sheets or tubing.

AM (amplitude modulation). A system of changing the voltage of a radio-frequency carrier to allow it to carry information.

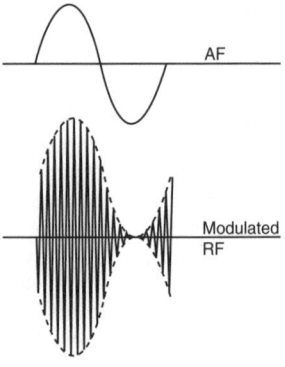

AM

The amplitude of the carrier is changed (modulated) by superimposing an information-carrying audio-frequency signal on it. The amplitude of the modulated carrier varies in the same way as the amplitude of the audio-frequency information wave.

amalgam. A mixture of different elements or ingredients that have been merged into a single body as a physical mixture, rather than a chemical compound. Concrete is an example of an amalgam of sand, portland cement, and gravel.

amalgamate. To combine or join ingredients to form a single body.

amateur-built aircraft. Aircraft built by individuals as a hobby rather than by factories as commercial products. Amateur-built, or homebuilt, aircraft are not required to meet the stringent requirements imposed on FAA-certificated commercially built aircraft.

amateur rocket. An unmanned rocket that: (1) is propelled by a motor or motors having a combined total impulse of 889,600 newton-seconds (200,000 pound-seconds) or less; and (2) cannot reach an altitude greater than 150 kilometers (93.2 statute miles) above the earth's surface.

amber. A hard, yellowish, translucent, fossilized tree resin that is currently used to make small ornaments. Centuries ago it was discovered that when a piece of amber was rubbed with wool, it attracted small bits of straw and was thus one of the materials used in early studies of electricity.

ambient. Surrounding.

ambient air. Air that surrounds an object.

ambient air pressure. The pressure of the air that surrounds an object.

ambient air temperature. The temperature of the air surrounding an object.

ambient light. The visible light that falls on a surface.

ambiguity. Not having a clear meaning. In radio navigation, 180° ambiguity is an error inherent in some of the simpler types of direction finding equipment. Because of this error, the equipment does not show whether the station being received is directly ahead of or directly behind the aircraft.

AMC (automatic mixture control). The device in a fuel metering system such as a carburetor or fuel injection system that keeps the fuel-air mixture ratio constant as the density of the air changes with altitude.

AME. *See* aviation medical examiner.

amendment status. The circulation date and revision number of an instrument approach procedure, printed above the procedure identification.

American Standards. Dimensional standards for fasteners issued by the American Standards Association (ASA).

American Wire Gage. *See* AWG.

americium. A chemical element in the actinide series. The symbol for americium is Am, its atomic number is 95, and the mass number of its isotope having the longest half life is 243.

ammeter. An instrument installed in series with an electrical load to measure the amount of current flowing through the load. Ammeters which measure very small rates of flow are called milliammeters (thousandths of an ampere) and microammeters (millionths of an ampere).

ammeter shunt. A low-resistance precision resistor installed in parallel with an ammeter between a source of electrical energy and an electrical load to allow the meter to read a flow of current which exceeds the limit of the instrument.

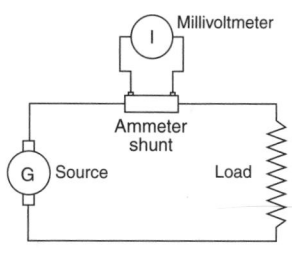

Most of the current in the circuit flows through the shunt and produces a voltage drop. The ammeter, acting as a millivoltmeter, measures the voltage drop across the shunt and indicates, on a special scale, the amount of current flowing through the circuit.

ammeter shunt

ammonia. A pungent, invisible gas made up of one atom of nitrogen and three atoms of hydrogen (NH_3). Ammonia becomes a liquid at $-28°F$ and freezes at $-107.6°F$.

Ammonia is used to case harden steel by the nitriding process. In this process, the ammonia combines with aluminum, which has been alloyed with the steel, to form aluminum nitride. Aluminum nitride gives the steel a very hard surface.

amorphous. Without shape ("a" means without, and "morphous" means shape) or without a definite character or nature. Clay is a form of amorphous soil, but sand, which is made of crystals, is not amorphous. The crystals have a definite shape.

ampere (A). A measure of electron (current) flow. One ampere is equal to a flow of one coulomb (6.28 billion billion electrons) past a point in one second. One ampere is also the amount of current that can be forced through one ohm of resistance by a pressure of one volt. *See* coulomb.

ampere-hour. The quantity of electricity that passes through a circuit when one ampere flows for one hour.

ampere-hour capacity. A rating that indicates the amount of electrical energy a battery can supply. The ampere-hour rating is the product of the current flow in amperes, multiplied by the length of time, in hours, the battery can supply this current. A 35-ampere-hour battery can supply seven amperes of current for five hours, or one ampere for 35 hours.

ampere-hour meter. An electrical meter that measures the amount of current per unit of time used in a circuit.

ampere-turn. A measure of magnetomotive force (mmf) of an electromagnet. One ampere turn is the amount of mmf produced when one ampere of current flows through one turn of wire in a coil. One ampere turn is equal to 1.26 gilberts.

amphibian aircraft. An aircraft with a landing gear that allows it to operate from either water or land surfaces.

amphibious floats. Floats which may be attached to an aircraft to allow it to operate from either land or water. Retractable wheels mounted inside the floats can be extended for operation on land.

amplification (electrical characteristic). The increase in either voltage or current that takes place in a device or an electrical circuit. Amplification is normally measured as a ratio of the output quantity to the input quantity.

amplification factor. The ratio of the amplitude of the output of an electrical or electronic circuit, to the amplitude of its input.

amplifier. An electronic circuit in which a small change in voltage or current at its input controls a much larger change in voltage or current at its output.

amplitude. The amount a value changes from its at-rest, or normal, condition to its maximum condition.

amplitude modulation. *See* AM.

AMS (Aeronautical Materials Specifications). Materials and process specifications for aircraft components which conform to established engineering and metallurgical practices in the aircraft industries.

AMT. *See* aviation maintenance technician.

anabatic wind. A wind that blows up the slope of a hill or mountain due to increased heating along the valley walls.

anaerobic resin. A single-component polyester resin that hardens when all air is excluded from it.

AN aeronautical standard drawings. Dimensional standards for aircraft fasteners developed by the Aeronautical Standards Group. Part numbers for the fasteners described in these drawings carry the prefix AN.

analog. A physical variable that keeps a fixed relationship with another variable as it changes. For example, the position of the hands of a clock keeps a fixed relationship with time. It is because of this relationship that we can tell the time of day by knowing the positions of the clock hands. The position of the clock hands is an analog of time.

analog computer. An electronic computer which operates by converting different levels of voltage or current into numerical values in the decimal number system. One level of voltage (or current) represents the number one, another level represents two, and so on. Adding or subtracting the voltages (or currents) which are analogs of the numbers produces a voltage (or current) which is the electrical equivalent of the sum or the difference of the numbers. There are also mechanical analog computers that combine mechanical analogs of numbers to solve mathematical problems.

analog data. Data or information represented by a continuously varying voltage or current. Analog data differs from digital data in that digital data has only two conditions: high and low, on and off, or one and zero.

analog electronics. Electronics in which values change in a linear fashion. Output values vary in direct relationship to changes of input values.

analog indicator. An indicator that shows the value of the parameter being measured by the amount a pointer moves across a numerical scale.

analog-to-digital conversion. The conversion that changes analog information into a digital form. Analog-to-digital conversion is done with an analog-to-digital (A-to-D) converter, which changes the varying values of an analog signal into combinations of conditions that are either on or off. The digital values can be processed in a digital computer.

anchor. A heavy hook connected to a seaplane by a line or cable, intended to dig into the bottom of the lake or riverbed and keep the seaplane from drifting. Anchoring, or using an anchor to hold the plane in place, is considered the easiest way to secure a seaplane on the water surface.

anchor light. A white light shown at night on a seaplane, ship, or boat when the vessel is anchored.

anchor nut (aircraft hardware). A nut riveted or welded to a structure in such a way that a screw or bolt can be screwed into it. An anchor nut does not need to be held with a wrench to keep it from turning.

AND gate. A logic device in which the logic condition (zero or one) of its single output is one only when the conditions of all of its inputs are logic one.

AND gate

anechoic room (radar test facility). A special room whose walls are covered with radar absorbing materials. Anechoic rooms are used for testing radar components in an environment in which there are no echoes.

anemometer. An instrument used to measure the velocity of moving air. A cup-type anemometer uses a series of hemispherical metal cups mounted on arms on a shaft. The air blows the cups and rotates the shaft. A counter measures the number of revolutions the shaft makes in a given period of time and converts this into wind speed.

A fan-type anemometer uses a small, multibladed propeller, turned by the air moving through it. The faster the air flows, the faster the fan turns.

The dial on the anemometer may be marked in feet per second, meters per second, kilometers per hour, miles per hour, or knots.

aneroid. The sensitive component in an altimeter or barometer that measures the absolute pressure of the air. An aneroid is a sealed, flat capsule made of thin disks of corrugated metal soldered together and evacuated by pumping all of the air out of it.

Evacuating the aneroid allows it to expand or collapse as the air pressure on the outside changes. The pressure of the air can be found by measuring the amount the aneroid expands or collapses.

aneroid barometer. An instrument that measures the absolute pressure of the atmosphere by balancing the weight of the air above it against the spring action of a specially shaped evacuated metal bellows.

AN flared tube fittings. A series of flare-type fittings for fluid lines installed in an aircraft. AN fittings have a 37° flare angle and a short shoulder between the ends of the flare cone and the first thread.

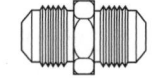

AN flared tube fitting

angel (radar meteorology). An echo caused by a physical phenomenon that is not necessarily discernible to the eye. Angels may be observed when abnormally strong temperature and/or moisture gradients exist, and they are sometimes attributed to insects or birds flying in the radar beam.

angle. The plane figure formed when two lines extend from the same point. A right angle has 90° between the lines.

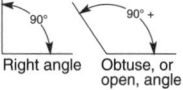

Acute, or closed, angle   Right angle   Obtuse, or open, angle

angle

angle drill. A type of drilling tool in which a twist drill is held in a chuck mounted at an angle to the spindle of the drill motor. Angle drills are often used in aircraft sheet metal work to drill holes in locations where a normal drill cannot be used.

angle of arrival (radio propagation). The angle, measured at the receiving antenna, between the line of propagation of a radio wave and the surface of the earth.

angle of attack (α). The acute angle formed between the chord line of an airfoil and the direction of the air that strikes the airfoil.

Wing chord line
Angle of attack α
Relative wind

angle of attack

angle of attack (gas turbine engine compressor). The acute angle formed between the chord line of the compressor blades and the direction the air strikes the blades. This angle of attack is affected by both the velocity of the air flowing through the compressor and the RPM of the compressor.

If the RPM of the compressor is too high for the velocity of the air flowing through the engine, the angle of attack will be excessively high, and the compressor blades can stall.

angle of attack (propeller). The acute angle between the chord line of a propeller blade and the relative wind. The angle of attack is affected by both the engine RPM and the forward speed of the aircraft.

angle of attack indicator (aircraft flight instrument). An instrument that measures the angle between the local airflow around the direction detector and the fuselage reference plane.

angle of azimuth. An angle, measured in a horizontal plane, clockwise from north.

angle of bank. The angle formed by the lateral axis of an aircraft and a horizontal plane.

angle of departure (radio propagation). The angle, measured at the transmitting antenna, between the angle of propagation of a radio wave and a horizontal plane.

angle of incidence (airplane specification). The acute angle formed between the chord line of an airfoil and the longitudinal axis of the aircraft on which it is mounted.

angle of incidence (electromagnetic energy). The angle between a beam of electromagnetic radiation and a line perpendicular to the surface the beam strikes.

angle of refraction (light). The angle between a beam of light as it passes through a medium and a line perpendicular to the surface of the medium.

angle of yaw. The acute horizontal angle formed between the plane of symmetry of an aircraft and the direction from which the wind is striking the aircraft.

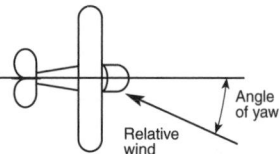

angle of yaw

angstrom. A convenient unit used to measure the wavelength of light. One angstrom, or A, is one ten-millionth of a micron. This is 0.000 000 01 (10^{-8}) centimeters. The wavelength of visible light extends from about 4,000 to 8,000 angstroms.

angular acceleration. The rate at which a rotating object increases its rotational speed.

angular measurement. Units of measurement used to specify the difference in direction of two lines that radiate from a common point. Three units of angular measurements are commonly used: The degree, the radian, and the grad:

One degree is the amount of separation between two lines that is equal to $^1/_{360}$ of a circle.

One radian is the amount of separation between two lines that is equal to $360° \div 2\pi$, or 57.3°.

One grad is the amount of separation between two lines that is equal to $^1/_{400}$ of a circle, or $^1/_{100}$ of a right angle.

angular momentum. The momentum possessed by a body because of its rotation.

angular velocity. The rate of change of angle as a shaft rotates. Angular velocity is measured in degrees per second, or in radians per second.

AN hardware. Standard hardware items such as bolts, nuts, screws, and rivets made according to standards established by the Air Force and Navy. AN hardware is approved for use in both military and civilian aircraft.

anhedral. A downward slant from root to tip of an aircraft's wing or horizontal tail surface. This is also called cathedral, or negative dihedral.

anhydrous. A material that contains no water.

anion. A negative ion that moves toward the anode (the positive electrode) in the process of electrolysis.

anisotropic. The property of being directionally dependent. In composite construction an anisotropic material has the fibers oriented in such a way that they provide the greatest strength for the particular application.

anneal. To soften a plastic or metal by means of heat treatment.

annealed wire. Wire that has been softened by heat after its diameter has been decreased by drawing it through dies. Annealed copper wire is used as electrical hookup wire.

annealing (metal heat treatment). A method of heat treatment in which a metal is softened so it loses some of its hardness and brittleness. Steel is annealed by heating it to a specified temperature and allowing it to cool very slowly, in an oven. Copper is annealed by heating it red-hot and quenching it in water.

annual inspection (aircraft inspection). A complete inspection of the airframe and powerplant required for FAA-certificated aircraft operating under 14 CFR Part 91 *(General Operating and Flight Rules)* that are not on one of the authorized special inspection programs.

An annual inspection must be conducted every 12 calendar months by an Aviation Maintenance Technician who holds an Aircraft rating with an Inspection Authorization. The scope of an annual inspection is the same as that of a 100-hour inspection.

annual rings. The rings that appear in the end of a log cut from a tree. The number of annual rings per inch gives an indication of the strength of the wood. The more rings there are and the closer they are together, the stronger the wood.

The alternate light and dark rings are caused by the difference in the growth rate of the tree. A tree grows fast in the spring and summer, producing the light-colored, less dense rings. The slower growth during the fall and winter produces the dark-colored, denser rings.

annular combustor (gas turbine engine component). A single-piece combustor for a gas turbine engine made in the shape of a ring or a cylinder. Fuel is sprayed from nozzles mounted around a fuel manifold into the inner liner of the combustor. There, it is mixed with air from the compressor and burned.

Annular combustors make the most effective use of the space they occupy, and they are the most efficient type of combustor used in both large and small gas turbine engines.

annular duct. A duct, or passage, that surrounds an object. An annular fan-discharge duct surrounds the gas generator of a turbofan engine.

annular orifice. A ring-shaped orifice, normally one that surrounds another orifice.

annulus. A ring or groove cut around the outside of a circular body or shaft. An annulus gets its name from its resemblance to the circular shape of the annual rings (the growth rings) which form in the trunk of a tree.

annunciator panel. A panel of warning lights in plain view of the pilot of an airplane or the operator of other types of equipment. The lights are identified by the name of the system they represent and are usually covered with a colored lens to show the meaning of the condition they announce. Red lights are used to indicate a dangerous condition, amber lights show that some system is armed, or active, and green lights show that a condition is safe.

By having all the lights together in an annunciator panel, the pilot or operator can determine the overall operating condition of the equipment at a glance.

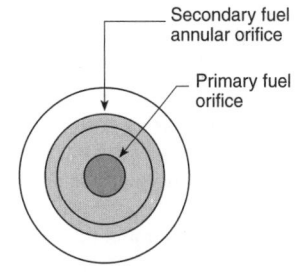

Secondary fuel
annular orifice

Primary fuel
orifice

annular orifice

anode. The electrode in a vacuum tube or semiconductor diode to which the electrons travel after they leave the cathode. The anode in a vacuum tube is called the plate.

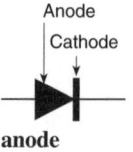

The anode of a semiconductor diode is the end made of P-type material. It is not marked—the cathode has the mark. In the diode symbol, the anode is shown by the arrowhead.

anode current. Current that flows in the anode of an electrical device. In an electron tube, anode current is commonly called plate current.

anode of a chemical cell. The area in a chemical cell from which electrons have migrated. When electrons leave an area, it becomes less negative, or takes on a positive charge. Electrons then try to move from an area having an excess of electrons, the cathode of the cell, to this anodic area.

anodic area. An area inside a piece of metal that has lost some of its electrons. This leaves a net positive charge which attracts negative ions from the electrolyte. Positive metallic ions and negative ions from the electrolyte unite to form the salts of corrosion.

anodizing. A method of preventing corrosion of aluminum alloy parts. A hard oxide film is formed on the surface of the metal by an electrolytic process. This film prevents oxygen reaching the surface of the metal. The aluminum alloy is the anode of the electrolytic cell, and chromic acid is used as the electrolyte.

anomalous propagation (radar meteorology). The greater-than-normal bending of a radar beam which causes echoes to be received from ground targets at greater distances than normal ground clutter.

anoxia. A severe case of hypoxia, or the serious effect on the human body caused by a lack of oxygen.

A-N radio range (radio navigation aid). The low-frequency radio range which was one of the first practical radio navigational aids.

Two antennas, arranged so they are at approximately right angles to each other, radiate low-frequency signals in the form of two figure eights. One antenna transmits the Morse code letter A (. –), and the other transmits the letter N (– .).

A pilot flying an airplane in the area where the two signals overlap hears a solid tone. As the airplane moves to one side or the other, the letter A or N predominates, and this indicates to the pilot the side to which he has moved. The area of overlapping signals, usually about three degrees wide, is called the "beam."

antenna. A conductor used with a radio transmitter or receiver to radiate or receive electromagnetic energy.

antenna coupler (radio equipment). A special transformer used to connect an antenna to a radio receiver or transmitter. The antenna coupler allows the maximum amount of energy to be transferred between the antenna and the receiver and between the transmitter and the antenna.

antenna current. The amount of radio-frequency current flowing in a radio antenna.

antenna duplexer. A device that allows two transmitters to use a single antenna without either transmitter interfering with the other.

antenna lens (microwave antenna component). A device installed near a microwave antenna that focuses the radiated energy in much the same way a glass lens focuses light waves.

antenna matching (radio installation). The process of matching the impedance of a radio antenna with the impedance of the transmission line carrying the signal from the transmitter to the antenna.

For the maximum amount of energy to be transferred, the impedance of the transmission line must be the same as the impedance of the antenna. Antenna matching is done by the selection of proper components in the antenna system.

antenna wire (aircraft radio antenna). A type of wire having a low electrical resistance and a high tensile strength. Copperweld, a form of copper-plated steel wire, is often used for antennas.

antiblush thinner (aircraft finishing material). A slow-drying thinner used with certain types of lacquer or dope to slow the evaporation of the solvents. When the solvents evaporate too rapidly, the evaporation drops the temperature of the surrounding air enough to cause moisture to condense out of the air. This moisture causes the dope or lacquer to blush.

anticathode (X-ray tube component). The electrode, or target, in an X-ray tube which, when struck by the stream of electrons from the cathode, emits X-rays.

anticollision light. A flashing light on the vertical fin or belly of an aircraft. Anticollision lights increase the visibility of the aircraft, especially at night and under conditions of poor visibility.

anticollision radar. A radar system installed in an aircraft to warn the pilot of the presence of any targets that could be on a collision course with the aircraft.

anticyclone (meteorology). An area of high atmospheric pressure in which the air has a closed circulation. In the northern hemisphere, the circulation of air out of a high-pressure area is clockwise (anticyclonic). In the southern hemisphere, the circulation out of a high is counterclockwise (cyclonic). At the equator, the circulation is indefinite; it can go either way.

antidetonation injection system. *See* ADI system.

antidrag wire. A diagonal, load-bearing member of a Pratt truss wing. Antidrag wires run from the rear spar inboard, to the front spar outboard, and are crossed by the drag wires. Antidrag wires oppose the aerodynamic loads on the wing that try to move the tip of the wing forward. *See* Pratt truss.

antifreeze. A chemical added to a liquid to lower its freezing point. Ethylene glycol, a form of alcohol, is an antifreeze agent that is normally used as the coolant in liquid-cooled reciprocating engines.

antifriction bearing. Any bearing that supports a rotating shaft with a rolling contact, rather than a sliding contact. Ball bearings, roller bearings, and needle bearings are all antifriction bearings. Plain bearings and bushings which support rotating shafts with a sliding contact between the bearing and the shaft are called friction-type bearings.

antiglare paint. A black or dark paint that dries to a dull or, nonspecular, finish. Antiglare paint is applied to a surface, such as the deck in front of the windshield of an aircraft, to prevent glare interfering with the flight crew's visibility.

anti-icing. The prevention of the formation of ice on a surface. Ice may be prevented by the use of heat or by covering the surface with a chemical which prevents water adhering to the surface. Anti-icing should not be confused with deicing, which is the removal of ice after it has formed on the surface.

anti-icing additive (turbine engine fuel). A chemical added to turbine-engine fuel used in some aircraft. This additive mixes with water that condenses from the fuel and lowers its freezing temperature so it will not freeze and block the fuel filters. It also acts as a biocidal agent and prevents the formation of microbial contamination in the tanks.

anti-icing fluid. A fluid, usually made of some form of alcohol and glycerine, that is sprayed on an aircraft to keep ice from forming on the surfaces. Anti-icing fluid is also carried in the aircraft and is sprayed over the windshield, along the propeller blades, and into the carburetor throat in flight.

anti-icing system (airframe system). A system that prevents the formation of ice on an aircraft structure.

anti-icing system (gas turbine engine system). A system in a gas turbine engine in which hot compressor bleed air is routed through the engine air inlet system to warm it so ice will not form on it.

antiknock rating (antidetonation characteristics). The rating of a reciprocating engine fuel that refers to the ability of the fuel to resist detonation. The antiknock rating is generally called the octane rating of the fuel because iso-octane is used as the reference fuel for the rating.

antileak check valve (reciprocating engine lubrication system component). A check valve used in the oil tank of some aircraft reciprocating engines equipped with dry-sump lubrication systems.

Antileak check valves hold the oil in the tank against the pull of gravity, but as soon as the oil pump puts a low pressure on the check valve, it opens and allows oil to flow from the tank into the engine.

antilogarithm. The number from which a logarithm is derived. The symbol for antilogrithm is $\log^{-1}$.

antimissile missile. A missile launched from the surface or from an aircraft to locate and destroy another missile.

antimony. A hard, brittle, lustrous, silvery-white metallic chemical element. Antimony's symbol is Sb, its atomic number is 51, and its atomic weight is 121.75. Antimony expands as it changes from its molten state into a solid state, and because of this, it is an important alloying element with lead for type metal and for making lead-acid storage batteries.

antipropeller end (aircraft engine). The end of an aircraft engine opposite the end to which the propeller is attached. Front or back is not always a good way to identify the ends of an aircraft engine, because the engine may be used with the propeller either in front or in back. To identify the ends of an engine correctly, the terms propeller end and antipropeller end are used. The antipropeller end is often called the accessory end.

antiseize compound. A lubricant used on threads to prevent their locking together. Anti-seize compound is specially needed on spark plugs in reciprocating engines and on threaded fasteners in the hot section of gas turbine engines.

antiservo tab. A tab installed on the trailing edge of a stabilator. The tab automatically moves in the same direction as the stabilator to produce a stabilizing aerodynamic force that tries to bring the surface back to a streamline position. An antiservo tab is also called an antibalance tab.

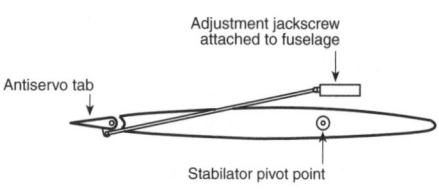

antiservo tab

antiskid brake system. An electrohydraulic control in an airplane's power brake system that prevents the wheels skidding on wet or icy runways.

A wheel-speed sensor monitors the deceleration rate of every main landing gear wheel. If any wheel decelerates too rapidly, indicating an impending skid, pressure to that brake is released and the wheel stops decelerating. Pressure is then reapplied at a slightly lower value.

antitear strips. Strips of aircraft fabric laid under the reinforcing tape before the fabric is stitched to an aircraft wing.

antitorque pedals (helicopter controls). Foot pedals used by the pilot to control the pitch of the antitorque rotor on the tail of a single-rotor helicopter. Controlling the pitch of the antitorque rotor allows the pilot to rotate the helicopter about its vertical axis.

antitorque rotor. *See* tail rotor.

anvil. A hard-faced block used as a surface on which parts may be hammered or shaped.

anvil cloud (meteorology). The popular term given to the top portion of a cumulonimbus cloud because of its anvil shape.

anxiety. Mental discomfort that arises from the fear of anything, real or imagined. Anxiety can have a potent effect on actions and the ability to learn from perceptions.

aperiodic compass. A form of aircraft magnetic compass that has damping vanes on the float. These vanes keep the compass from oscillating when flying in rough air or when the aircraft is turned to a new heading.

aperiodic damping. Damping which prevents an object overswinging, or moving past its at-rest position. If a pendulum does not have aperiodic damping, when it is disturbed from its at-rest position, it will move back toward this position but will overshoot and oscillate back and forth, with each oscillation smaller than the swing before it.

An aperiodically damped pendulum will not swing back and forth, but will stop just as it reaches its at-rest position. Aperiodic damping is also called dead-beat damping.

aperture antenna. An antenna whose beam width is controlled by the size of the reflector, horn, or lens used.

apex line. A line attached to the top of most balloons to assist in inflation or deflation. Also called crown line or top handling line.

API scale. A scale developed by the American Petroleum Institute to measure the specific gravity of a liquid.

apogee. The point at which an orbiting vehicle is the greatest distance from the center of the object it is circling.

apparent power (electrical power). The power in an alternating-current circuit which is the product of the total current and the source voltage. Apparent power, measured in volt-amps, must be multiplied by the power factor to get true power in watts.

apparent weight. The weight of an object when it is immersed in a liquid. It is the weight of the object, less the weight of the liquid it displaces, and is the difference between the force of gravity acting downward on the object and the buoyant force produced by the liquid acting upward.

appliance. Any device used in the operation of an aircraft that is not a part of the airframe, engine, or propeller. Pumps, actuators, generators, instruments, and radio receivers and transmitters are all examples of appliances.

14 CFR Part 1: "Any instrument, mechanism, equipment, part, apparatus, appurtenance, or accessory, including communications equipment that is used or intended to be used in operating or controlling an aircraft in flight, is installed in or attached to the aircraft, and is not part of an airframe, engine, or propeller."

application (in learning process). A basic level of learning at which the student puts something to use that has been learned and understood. Application is the third step of the teaching process, where the student performs the procedure or demonstrates the knowledge acquired in the lesson. In the telling-and-doing technique of flight instruction, this step consists of the student doing the procedure while explaining it.

approach. The part of an aircraft flight in which the aircraft is positioned in such a way that it can touch down at the correct part of the runway on landing.

approach arm mode. *See* terminal mode.

approach clearance. Authorization by Air Traffic Control for a pilot to conduct an instrument approach.

approach control facility. A terminal Air Traffic Control facility that provides approach control service in a terminal area.

approach control service (air traffic control). Air traffic control provided by an approach control facility for arriving and departing VFR/IFR aircraft and, on occasion, en route aircraft. At some airports not served by an approach control facility, the ARTCC provides limited approach control service.

approach end of runway (AER). The first portion of the runway available for landing. If the runway threshold is displaced, use the displaced threshold latitude/longitude as the AER.

approach fix. From a database coding standpoint, an approach fix is considered to be an identifiable point in space from the intermediate fix (IF) inbound. A fix located between the initial approach fix (IAF) and the IF is considered to be associated with the approach transition or feeder route.

approach gate. A point on the final approach course which is one mile from the final approach fix on the side away from the airport or five miles from the landing threshold, whichever is farther from the landing threshold.

approach lighting system (ALS). Provides lights that will penetrate the atmosphere far enough from touchdown to give directional, distance, and glidepath information for safe transition from instrument to visual flight.

approach lights. High-intensity lights located along the approach path at the end of an instrument runway. Approach lights aid the pilot in transitioning from instrument flight conditions to visual conditions at the end of an instrument approach.

approach mode/function. An autopilot function or mode of the FMS/GPS RNAV unit that allows the pilot to capture and track any VOR radial or localizer with a higher degree of accuracy, which activates upon reaching a point 2 NM prior to the final approach waypoint.

approach sequence (air traffic control). The order in which aircraft are positioned while on approach or awaiting approach clearance.

approach speed. The recommended airspeed listed in the aircraft manual to be used by pilots when making an approach for landing.

approach with vertical guidance (APV). An instrument approach that uses WAAS to add vertical guidance to GPS. Considered a "semi-precision" approach, an APV provides the pilot with an electronic glideslope, but the accuracy is not high enough to be considered full precision. APVs include LNAV/VNAV and LPVs. The lowest altitude on these approaches, like on an ILS, are called decision altitudes (DAs).

appropriate ATS authority (ICAO). The relevant authority designated by the state responsible for providing air traffic services in a particular airspace. In the United States the "appropriate ATS authority" is the Program Director for Air Traffic Operations, ATO-1.

approved. *14 CFR Part 1:* Unless used with reference to another person, this means approved by the FAA or any person to whom the FAA has delegated its authority in the matter concerned, or approved under the provisions of a bilateral agreement between the United States and a foreign country or jurisdiction.

approved data. Data which may be used as authorization for the techniques or procedures employed when making an alteration or repair to an FAA-certificated aircraft. Approved data consist of such documents as Type Certificate Data Sheets, Airworthiness Directives, Supplemental Type Certificates, and special repair instructions issued by the engineering department of the aircraft manufacturer and approved by the FAA.

approved inspection system. A program approved by the Federal Aviation Administration for the inspection and maintenance of an aircraft that will maintain the aircraft in an airworthy condition.

approved repair station. A facility approved and certificated by the Federal Aviation Administration under 14 CFR Part 145 *Repair Stations* to perform certain types of repairs to certificated aircraft.

Approved Type Certificate. *See* ATC.

approximate. Something that is nearly, but not exactly, correct. Approximate also means close to, but not exactly at the same location.

apron (aircraft service area). The paved area in front of an aircraft hangar where aircraft can be parked and tied down. Aprons are sometimes called ramps or tarmacs.

APU (auxiliary power unit). A small self-contained turbine- or reciprocating-engine-powered generator, hydraulic pump, and air pump.

APUs are installed in an aircraft and are used to supply electrical power, air, and hydraulic pressure for ground operation and for starting the main engines.

Aquadag. The registered trade name for a lubricant made of graphite suspended in water. Aquadag is used as a lubricant for components in an oxygen system. Oil or other petroleum products cannot be used with oxygen system components, because the oxygen can react with the petroleum to cause it to spontaneously ignite and burn.

Arabic numerals. The numerals 0, 1, 2, 3, 4, 5, 6, 7, 8, and 9.

aramid fibers. Fibers made from an organic compound of carbon, hydrogen, oxygen, and nitrogen. They have high strength and low density and are flexible under load. They have the ability to withstand impact, shock, and vibration. Kevlar® is a well-known aramid fiber.

arbor press. A press with either a mechanically or hydraulically operated ram used in a maintenance shop for a variety of pressing functions.

arc (geometric figure). The portion of the circumference of a circle between any two points on the circumference.

arc (trigonometric function). A prefix used with trigonometric functions. Arc means the inverse, or the opposite, of a function, or the angle whose function is the number given.

arc cosine. The trigonometric function that means "the angle whose cosine is." For example, arc cos 0.866 = 30°, means that the angle whose cosine is 0.866 is 30°. Arc cosine is usually written $\cos^{-1}$. *See* cosine.

arch (structure). A form of structure with curving sides and a wedge-shaped keystone at the top. An arch supports weight by transmitting the force caused by its weight through its curving sides into the structure supporting it. The forces supported by the arch are transmitted into the sides through the keystone.

Archimedes' principle. The principle of buoyancy, propounded by the Greek mathematician Archimedes. Archimedes' principle states that an object immersed in a fluid loses as much of its own weight as the weight of the fluid it displaces. The sciences of hydrostatics and aerostatics are based on Archimedes' principle.

arcing. Sparking between a commutator and brush or between switch contacts when the flow of current is interrupted. Arcing occurs when induction tries to keep the current flowing across the broken contact.

arc lamp. A source of light produced by an electric arc which is an intense and continuous spark. The arc is produced when electrons flow through ionized gases between two electrodes.

arc sine. The trigonometric function that means "the angle whose sine is." For example, arc sin 0.707 = 45°, means that the angle whose sine is 0.707 is 45°. Arc sine is usually written $\sin^{-1}$. *See* sine.

arc tangent. A value used in trigonometry that is the inverse, or opposite, of the tangent. This is the same as one divided by the tangent. The tangent of an angle is the ratio of the length of the side opposite the angle, to the length of the side adjacent, or next to, the angle.

If the sides of a triangle that form a right angle are two inches and three inches, the tangent of one of the angles is 2/3, or 0.667. The arc tangent is the angle whose tangent is 0.667, and this is 33.7°. This is normally written as Tan^{-1} 0.667. *See* tangent.

arctic air. The air in a mass formed over an arctic area of ice and snow. The air has the characteristics of this type of area.

arctic front (meteorology). The surface discontinuity between very cold (arctic) air flowing directly from the arctic region and another less cold and, consequently, less dense air mass.

arc welding. A form of electric welding in which the intense heat needed to melt the metal is produced by an electric arc.

area. A measurement of the amount of surface of an object. Area is usually expressed in such units as square inches or square centimeters for small surfaces or in square feet or square meters for larger surfaces.

area chart. A chart, part of the low-altitude enroute chart series, that furnishes terminal data at a larger scale for congested areas.

area control center (ICAO). An ICAO term for an air traffic control facility primarily responsible for ATC services being provided IFR aircraft during the en route phase of flight. The U.S. equivalent is an air route traffic control center (ARTCC).

area forecast (FA). This forecast type gives a picture of clouds, general weather conditions, and visual meteorological conditions (VMC) expected over a large area encompassing several states, providing vital information to enroute operations as well as forecast information for smaller airports that do not have terminal forecasts.

area navigation (RNAV) (electronic navigation). A method of aircraft electronic navigation that permits aircraft operations on any desired flight path within the coverage of station-referenced navigation signals, or within the limits of a self-contained system's capability. These station-referenced navigation signals are referred to as "way-points"; the RNAV flight path goes from one waypoint to the next.

area navigation (RNAV) route. *14 CFR Part 1.* "An air traffic service (ATS) route based on RNAV that can be used by suitably equipped aircraft."

area of operation. A phase of the practical test within the Practical Test Standards (PTS).

area-rule fuselage. The fuselage of a supersonic airplane built so the combined frontal area of the fuselage and the wing form a smooth curve from nose to tail. An airplane with an area-rule fuselage has the minimum transonic drag.

argon. A colorless, odorless, inert, gaseous chemical element. Argon has an atomic number of 18 and an atomic weight of 39.998. The symbol for argon is Ar. Argon is commonly used to fill electric light bulbs and the envelopes of electron tubes. The argon takes the place of air, which contains oxygen, and by keeping oxygen away from the hot filaments in the bulbs and tubes, the filaments will not burn out, or oxidize.

ARINC (Aeronautical Radio Incorporated). A corporation whose principal stockholders are the airlines. Its function is to operate certain communication links between airliners in flight and the airline ground facilities. ARINC also sets standards for communication equipment used by the airlines.

arithmetic. The basic foundation of all the systems of mathematics. Operations in arithmetic are: addition, subtraction, multiplication, and division of both whole numbers and fractions. Arithmetic deals only with real numbers. *See* real number.

arithmetic sum. The arithmetic sum of two or more numbers is the value obtained when the absolute values of the quantities are added. *See* absolute value.

arm (lever). The distance on a lever between the fulcrum and the point of application of the force or the weight.

arm (weight and balance). The horizontal distance in inches between a reference datum line and the center of gravity of an object. If the object is behind the datum, the arm is positive, and if it is ahead of the datum, the arm is negative.

armature. The rotating element in an electric motor or generator.

armature core (electrical machine). The assembly of soft iron laminations on which the coils of an armature are wound.

armature gap (electrical machine). The space between the armature core and the field poles of an electric motor or generator.

armature reaction. The distortion of the magnetic flux between the field poles in an electric generator or motor caused by the magnetic field produced by current flowing in the winding of the armature.

armed. A condition in which a device is made ready for actuation.

Armed Forces. *14 CFR Part 1:* "The Army, Navy, Air Force, Marine Corps, and Coast Guard, including their regular and reserve components and members serving without component status."

Army Aviation Flight Information Bulletin. A bulletin that provides air operation data covering Army, National Guard, and Army Reserve aviation activities.

aromatic compound. A chemical compound such as toluene, xylene, and benzene that is blended with gasoline to improve its antidetonation characteristics. Aromatic compounds have the bad feature of softening rubber hoses, diaphragms, and seals used in fuel metering system components.

aromatic gasoline. Aviation gasoline that has had its antidetonation characteristics improved by blending in some of the aromatic additives, such as benzene, toluene, or xylene.

aromatic naphtha. A coal tar derivative used as an additive in certain reciprocating engine fuels. Aromatic naphtha should not be used for cleaning aircraft parts.

AROW. The mnemonic aid to remember the certificates and documents required to be onboard an aircraft to determine airworthiness: Airworthiness certificate, Registration certificate, Operating limitations, Weight and balance data.

ARP (airport reference point). The approximate geometric center of all usable runway surfaces.

arresting system. A safety system installed on some airports to prevent aircraft from overrunning runways when the aircraft cannot be stopped after landing or during an aborted takeoff. These systems consist of two major components: engaging, or catching, devices and energy absorption devices. Arresting systems are called by such names as arresting gear, hook devices, and wire barrier cables.

arrival aircraft interval (AAI) (air traffic control). The desired optimum interval between successive arrival aircraft over the vertex. The AAI is internally generated by the ATC or ARTCC computer via an algorithm, calculated in hundredths of minutes based upon the airport acceptance rate (AAR).

arrival center (air traffic control). The ARTCC having jurisdiction for the impacted airport.

arrival delay (air traffic control). A parameter which specifies a period of time in which no aircraft will be metered for arrival at the specified airport.

arrival sector (air traffic control). An operational control sector that contains one or more meter fixes.

arrival sector advisory list (air traffic control). A list of data on arrivals displayed at the plan-view display (PVD) of the sector which controls the meter fix.

arrival sequencing program (air traffic control). The automated program designated to assist in sequencing aircraft destined for the same airport.

arrival time. The time an aircraft touches down on arrival.

arsenic. A highly poisonous metallic chemical element. Arsenic's symbol is As, its atomic number is 33, and its atomic weight is 74.9216. Arsenic, which has five valence electrons, is used as a pentavalent impurity in the manufacture of N-type semiconductor devices.

ARSR (air route surveillance radar). Air route traffic control center radar used primarily to detect and display an aircraft's position while en route between terminal areas. The ARSR enables controllers to provide radar air traffic control service when aircraft are within the ARSR coverage.

ARTCC (air route traffic control center). A facility established to provide air traffic control service to aircraft operating on IFR flight plans within controlled airspace and principally during the en route phase of flight. When equipment capabilities and controller workload permit, certain advisory/assistance services may also be provided to VFR aircraft.

articulated connecting rod (reciprocating engine component). A link rod which connects the pistons in a radial engine to the master rod. There is one less articulated rod than there are cylinders in each row of cylinders in a radial engine.

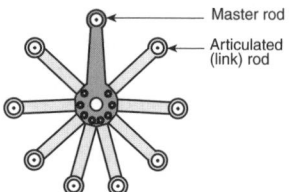

articulated rod

articulated rotor (helicopter rotor). A helicopter rotor in which each blade is connected to the rotor hub in such a way that it is free to move up and down (flap), move back and forth in its plane of rotation (drag), and change its pitch angle (feather).

artificial aging. A method of aluminum alloy heat treatment in which the part is heated and quenched (solution heat-treated) and then held at a specified elevated temperature for a period of time. The metal gains additional strength by this process. Artificial aging is also called precipitation heat treatment.

artificial antenna (radio antenna). A device attached to the output of a radio transmitter to use when adjusting its output. The artificial antenna, also called a dummy load, has the same impedance as the antenna, but the radio signal put into the artificial antenna is not radiated.

artificial feel (aircraft control system). A type of force feedback used in the automatic flight control systems of some aircraft. Artificial feel produces an opposition to the pilot's movement of the controls that is proportional to the aerodynamic loads acting on the control surfaces.

artificial horizon. A flight instrument that provides the pilot with a visual reference when the natural horizon is not visible. A bar or display, held in a constant relationship with the earth's horizon by a gyro, serves as the reference.

ARTS (automated radar terminal systems). A term used to define several automated air traffic control systems:

ARTS II. An automated, nontracking radar system with capability for air traffic control at terminals with low to medium activity.

ARTS III. A beacon-tracking automated radar system used in medium- to high-activity terminals. ARTS III detects, tracks, and predicts secondary radar-derived aircraft targets.

ARTS IIIA. A radar-tracking and beacon-tracking automated radar system that tracks and predicts primary as well as secondary radar-derived aircraft targets.

asbestos. A fiber of magnesium silicate that is highly resistant to fire and has good insulating qualities.

A-scan (radarscope). A type of radar display in which the time base (distance or range) is displayed on a horizontal line and the target appears as a vertical displacement along the time base.

ASD (aircraft situation display) (air traffic control). A computer system that receives radar track data from all 20 Continental U.S. air route traffic control centers, organizes this data into a mosaic display, and presents it on a computer screen.

The ASD provides the traffic management coordinator with multiple methods of selection and highlighting of individual aircraft or groups of aircraft. The user has the option of superimposing these aircraft positions over any number of background displays, which include ARTCC boundaries, any stratum of en route sector boundaries, fixes, airways, military and other special-use airspace, airports, and geopolitical boundaries.

By using the ASD, a coordinator can monitor any number of traffic situations or the entire systemwide traffic flow.

ash. The solid residue left after certain materials have burned.

ashless dispersant oil. *See* AD oil.

ASM (air-to-surface missile). A missile carried on an aircraft and used against a surface target. The missile is guided to its target by an internal guidance system or by signals from the launch aircraft.

ASOS. *See* Automated Surface Observing System.

aspect ratio. The ratio of the length, or span, of an airfoil to its width, or chord. For a nonrectangular airfoil, the aspect ratio is found by dividing the square of the span by the area.

$$\text{Aspect Ratio} \quad = \quad \frac{\text{Span}^2}{\text{Area}}$$

asphalt. A heavy, brownish-black mineral found in crude oil. Asphalt is used as a base for some acid-resisting paints.

aspheric (optics). The characteristics of an optical element that contains one or more surfaces that are not spherical.

ASR (airport surveillance radar). Approach control radar used to detect and display an aircraft's position in the terminal area. ASR provides range and azimuth information but does not provide elevation data. Coverage of the ASR can extend up to 60 miles.

assembly. The process of fitting together all the parts to form a complete structure or unit.

assembly break. A joint in the structure of an aircraft formed when two subassemblies are removed from their jigs and joined together to form a single unit.

assembly drawing. An aircraft drawing which shows a group of parts laid out in the relationship they will have when they are assembled.

assembly line (aircraft manufacturing). An arrangement of work stations in an aircraft factory that allows a certain function to be performed on all aircraft at a particular physical location. Special tools and specially trained personnel stay in one location, and each aircraft is moved to this location for the function to be performed.

assigned frequency (radio communications). The frequency of the carrier signal produced by a radio transmitter. This carrier frequency is assigned by the Federal Communications Commission (FCC) for the particular transmitter or the particular type of transmission.

astable. Not stable; "a" means not. An astable electronic device has two conditions of temporary stability, but no condition of permanent stability.

astable multivibrator. An electronic oscillator that has no stable condition. Astable multivibrators, also called free-running multivibrators, contain two devices such as transistors to control the flow of electrons. When one transistor is conducting, the other is not conducting. The two transistors alternate between conditions of conducting and not conducting.

astatine. A highly unstable radioactive chemical element. Astatine's symbol is At, and its atomic number is 85. Astatine is the heaviest of the halogen elements.

astern. A location or direction measured from an aircraft. Astern means to the rear of, or behind. This term comes from "stern," which is the aft, or rear part, of a ship.

ASTM (American Society for Testing Materials). An organization which sets various standards, called ASTM standards, used in the aircraft industry.

astrocompass. A navigational instrument that determines direction relative to the stars. Astrocompasses are not affected by the errors inherent in magnetic compasses and gyrocompasses.

astrodome. A transparent hemispherical dome in the upper skin of an aircraft, over or near the navigator's station. The navigator uses the astrodome to make observations of the sun or stars when navigating by celestial navigation.

astronaut. A person who travels beyond the earth's atmosphere.

astronautics. The branch of science that deals with space flight. Astronautics includes the design, construction, and operation of space vehicles and their related support equipment and activities.

astronomical twilight. The period of time before sunrise and after sunset when the sun is not more than 18° below the horizon.

astronomical unit. A unit for measuring distance in astronomy. One astronomical unit is the average distance between the earth and the sun. This is approximately 93 million miles.

astrophysics. The branch of science which deals with the physical characteristics of the heavenly bodies. These characteristics include their mass, density, temperature, size, luminosity, and origin.

ASU (altitude sensing unit—turbine engine fuel control). A subsystem in a turbine engine fuel control that regulates the fuel scheduling as a function of altitude changes.

asymmetrical. A condition of a body in which its shape is not the same on both sides of its center line.

asymmetrical airfoil. An airfoil section that is not the same on both sides of the chord line. Asymmetrical airfoils are the most commonly used type for fixed-wing aircraft, but because the location of the center of pressure changes as the angle of attack changes, they are seldom used for rotary-wing aircraft.

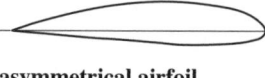

asymmetrical airfoil

asymmetrical lift (helicopter flight). A condition of uneven lift produced by the rotor system of a helicopter when it is in forward flight. When a helicopter is hovering in still air, the lift is uniform across its rotor disk. But when it is moving in flight, the blade traveling in the same direction as the helicopter, the advancing blade, has a speed equal to its own speed plus the speed of the helicopter. The blade on the other side, the retreating blade, has a speed equal to its own speed minus the speed of the helicopter. Since the amount of aerodynamic lift is determined by airspeed, the difference between the airspeed over the rotor blades on the two sides of the helicopter causes the lift on the side of the advancing blade to be greater than the lift produced by the retreating blade.

asymmetrical loading (propeller thrust). The loading of a propeller disk in such a way that one side produces more thrust than the other side.

asymmetrical thrust. The left-turning tendency of an airplane at high angles of attack and high power settings. The descending propeller blade on the right produces more thrust than the ascending blade on the left, causing the aircraft to yaw to the left. This occurs when the aircraft's longitudinal axis is in a climbing attitude in relation to the relative wind.

asymptote (mathematics). A curve that comes nearer and nearer to a given line without ever touching it.

asynchronous (electronic circuit operation). Operations at a speed determined by circuit functions and not by any timing device.

ATA 100 (Air Transport Association Specification No. 100). The standardized format for aircraft maintenance manuals developed by the Airline Transport Association. This classification of aircraft systems and components allows standardization of maintenance information. This spec has been updated and is now referred to as ATA-2200.

ATC (air traffic control). *See* air traffic control.

ATC (Approved Type Certificate). A certificate of approval issued by the Federal Aviation Administration for the design of an airplane, engine, or propeller. An ATC certifies that the product meets at least the minimum design standards.

"ATC advises" (air traffic control). A phrase used to prefix a message of noncontrol information when it is relayed to an aircraft by other than an air traffic controller.

ATC assigned airspace. Airspace defined by vertical and lateral limits assigned by ATC for the purpose of providing air traffic segregation between specified activities being conducted within the assigned airspace.

ATCCC (air traffic control command center). An air traffic service facility that consists of four operational units:

Central flow control function (CFCF). Responsible for coordination and approval of all major intercenter flow control restrictions.

Central altitude reservation function (CARF). Responsible for coordinating, planning, and approving special user requirements under the altitude reservation concept.

Airport reservation office (ARO). Responsible for approving IFR flights at designated high-density traffic airports.

ATC contingency command post. A facility which enables the FAA to manage the ATC system when significant portions of the system's capabilities have been lost or threatened.

"ATC clears" (air traffic control). A phrase used to prefix an ATC clearance when it is relayed to an aircraft by other than an air traffic controller.

ATC instructions (air traffic control). Directives issued by air traffic control for the purpose of requiring a pilot to take specific actions. Typical instructions are "turn left heading two five zero," "go around," and "clear the runway."

ATC preferred route notification (air traffic control). A notification within the user request evaluation tool (URET) at the controller's station, regarding a destination airport that is a preferred route. An ATC preferred route notification is applied to a specific location or airport; it subsequently applies to any aircraft or flight headed to that destination airport. Upon seeing the alert within URET, the controller acts on the notification by applying the preferred routing to that flight.

ATCRBS. *See* air traffic control radar beacon system.

"ATC requests" (air traffic control). A phrase used to prefix an ATC request when it is relayed to an aircraft by other than an air traffic controller.

ATCSCC (air traffic control system command center). *See* ATCCC.

ATC security services. Communications and security tracking provided by an ATC facility in support of the Department of Homeland Security (DHS), the Department of Defense (DOD), or other federal security elements in the interest of national security. Such security services are only applicable within designated areas. ATC security services do not include ATC basic radar services or flight following.

ATC security services position. The position responsible for providing ATC security services as defined. This position does not provide ATC, IFR separation, or VFR flight following services, but is responsible for providing security services in an area comprising airspace assigned to one or more ATC operating sectors. This position may be combined with control positions.

ATC security tracking. The continuous tracking of aircraft movement by an ATC facility in support of the Department of Homeland Security (DHS), the Department of Defense (DOD), or other security elements for national security using radar tracking or other means (e.g., manual tracking) without providing basic radar services (including traffic advisories).

ATF (aerodynamic twisting force). The aerodynamic force that acts on a rotating propeller blade to increase its blade angle.

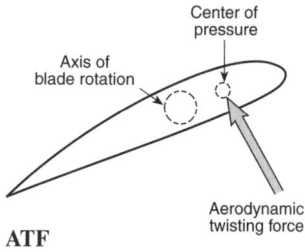

ATF

The axis of rotation of a blade is near the center of its chord line, and the center of pressure is between the axis and the leading edge. Aerodynamic lift acting through the center of pressure tries to rotate the blade to a higher pitch angle.

athodyd. A ram-jet engine. An athodyd (Aero-THermO-DYnamic-Duct) is an open tube whose inside is specially shaped to produce thrust when fuel is burned in it.

When the athodyd moves through the air at a high speed, the air in its front end is compressed. Fuel is added to this compressed air and burned, and the burning fuel heats the air and expands it. This expansion accelerates the air to the rear and produces thrust.

athwartships. A direction across, or at right angles to, the longitudinal axis of an aircraft.

ATIS (automatic terminal information service). Recorded noncontrol information continuously broadcast in selected terminal areas. ATIS information contains appropriate weather observations, altimeter setting, instrument approaches in use, and airport information needed by pilots approaching the airport.

The use of ATIS frees the controller of having to repeat this basic information on the initial call-up from each pilot.

atmosphere. The layer of gases surrounding the earth, from the surface upward to a height of about 22 miles. The atmosphere consists of a mixture of nitrogen, oxygen, and small quantities of a number of other gases. The lowest level of the atmosphere, called the troposphere, extends upward to about 36,000 feet. This is the area in which clouds form. Above the troposphere is the stratosphere, where there is no water vapor; therefore clouds cannot form.

The atmosphere presses down on the surface of the earth with a pressure of 29.92 inches (760 millimeters) of mercury. Its standard weight at sea level is 0.07651 pound per cubic foot, and it becomes lighter, or less dense, as its height above the earth increases.

The temperature of the atmosphere drops as its altitude increases, to about 36,000 feet. Here, the temperature stabilizes at −67°F (−55°C), and it remains at this temperature until it reaches an altitude of about 82,000 feet.

atmospheric electricity. Static electricity that exists between clouds and between clouds and the surface of the earth.

atmospheric noise (radio reception). Noise produced in radio equipment by electricity in the atmosphere.

atmospheric pressure. The pressure exerted by the atmosphere because of the attraction of gravity exerted on the air directly above the measuring instrument.

Under standard conditions, at sea level, the atmospheric pressure is 14.69 pounds per square inch, 29.92 inches of mercury, 1013.2 millibars and 1.01325 newtons per square meter. This is called one atmosphere of pressure (one atm). Atmospheric pressure is also called barometric pressure.

atmospheric propagation delay. A bending of the electromagnetic (EM) wave from the satellite that creates an error in the GPS system.

atmospherics (radio reception). A form of static in radio reception caused by atmospheric electrical phenomena such as electrical storms.

atmospheric sounding. A measure of atmospheric variables aloft, usually pressure, temperature, humidity, and wind.

atmospheric stability. Describes a state in which an air parcel will resist vertical displacement, or once displaced (for example, by flowing over a hill) will tend to return to its original level.

atom. The smallest particle of a chemical element that can exist, either alone or in combination with other atoms.

An atom is made up of a nucleus, which contains protons and neutrons and electrons, which spin around the nucleus. In a balanced atom, there are as many electrons spinning around the nucleus as there are protons in the nucleus.

atomic fission. The reaction that causes the nucleus of a heavy atom such as uranium to split and form the nucleus of a lighter atom. When the nucleus splits, a tremendous amount of energy, usually in the form of heat and light, is released.

atomic fusion. The reaction that causes two light atomic nuclei to combine to form a heavier nucleus. When the nuclei combine, a tremendous amount of energy, usually in the form of heat and light, is released.

atomic number. The number of protons in the nucleus of an atom of the element. The atomic number of an element determines the position of the element in the periodic table of elements.

atomic weight. The weight of an atom of a chemical element. It is approximately equal to the number of protons and neutrons in the nucleus of the atom.

atomization. The process of breaking a liquid into tiny droplets or a fine spray. Atomized liquids vaporize easily.

atomize. To break up a liquid into a very fine spray of tiny droplets. A paint spray gun atomizes the liquid finishing material and then blows the atomized liquid onto the surface being painted.

atomizer. A device that breaks a liquid into a fine spray to aid in its vaporization.

ATR racking system. A system of standardized mounting racks for electronic equipment installed in an aircraft.

ATS route (ICAO). A specified route designed for channeling the flow of traffic as necessary for the provision of air traffic services.

attenuate. To weaken, or lessen the intensity, of an action. The volume control of a radio attenuates the sound allowed to come from the speaker. The amount of attenuation can be expressed as a ratio of the strength of the output signal to the strength of the input signal.

attenuation (radar meteorology). Any process which reduces power density in radar signals. Precipitation attenuation reduces the power density because of absorption or reflection of energy by precipitation. Range attenuation is the reduction in radar power density because of distance from the antenna. Range attenuation occurs in the outgoing beam at a rate that is proportional to $1/range^2$. The return signal is also attenuated at the same rate.

attenuator (electrical equipment). A network of resistors used to decrease the amplitude of an electrical signal without causing any phase shift or frequency distortion.

attitude. A personal motivational predisposition to respond to persons, situations, or events in a given manner that can, nevertheless, be changed or modified through training as a sort of mental shortcut to decision-making.

attitude (aircraft flight condition). The relationship between the axes of an aircraft and a fixed reference. The earth's horizon is often used as this reference.

attitude and heading reference system (AHRS). A 3-axis sensor that provides aircraft heading, attitude, and yaw information. Recent advances have allowed AHRS to replace mechanical gyros and bring costs down. AHRS are integrated into electronic flight instrument systems (EFIS).

attitude director indicator (ADI). An aircraft attitude indicator that incorporates flight command bars to provide pitch and roll commands.

attitude indicator (aircraft flight instrument). A gyroscopic flight instrument that gives the pilot an indication of the attitude of the aircraft relative to its pitch and roll axes. The attitude indicator in an autopilot is in the sensing system that detects deviation from a level-flight attitude.

attitude instrument flying. Controlling the aircraft by referencing the instruments rather than outside visual cues.

attitude management. The ability to recognize hazardous attitudes in oneself and the willingness to modify them as necessary through the application of appropriate antidote thoughts.

attraction. A force which acts between particles of matter to try to draw them together.

audio-frequency amplifier (electronic component). An electronic amplifier capable of amplifying alternating current whose frequency is in the range that can be heard by the human ear.

audio-frequency oscillator (electronic component). An electronic circuit that produces an alternating current whose frequency is in the audio-frequency range.

audio-frequency vibrations. Vibrations at a frequency which produce sound that can be heard by the normal human ear. Audio frequencies range from about 16 hertz to 16,000 hertz.

audiovisual system (communications system). A system of communications that produces signals that can be both seen and heard. Television is a form of audiovisual communications system.

augend (mathematics). The number in an addition problem to which another number, the addend, is added.

augmentor. Another name for afterburner. *See* afterburner.

augmentor tube. A long, specially shaped, stainless steel tube mounted around the exhaust tail pipe of an aircraft reciprocating engine. As the exhaust gases flow through the augmentor tube, they produce a low pressure in the engine compartment which draws cooling air into the compartment through the fins on the cylinders. Heat may be taken from the augmentor tubes and directed through the leading edges of the wings for thermal anti-icing.

aural radio range (aerial navigation system). The first radio aid to navigation; it is no longer in use. Referred to as the "L/MF range," the four-course, low-frequency range directed the pilot with an audible signal. The pilot would fly down the center of the course line by positioning the aircraft so that a solid tone was heard. If the aircraft drifted to one side of the course line, the letter N in Morse code (–.) was heard. If it drifted to the other side, the letter A (.–) was heard.

aural warning device. A warning device that signals the presence of a problem by emitting a signal that can be heard.

aurora (meteorology). A luminous, radiant emission over middle and high latitudes confined to the thin air of high altitudes and centered over the earth's magnetic poles. These interesting sights are called "aurora borealis" (northern lights) in the northern hemisphere and "aurora australis" (southern lights) in the southern hemisphere.

austenite. A form of iron in which a supersaturated solution of carbon is dissolved in the iron. Austenite exists in the iron only when the iron is at a high temperature.

austenite steel. Gamma iron into which carbon can dissolve. Below its critical temperature, iron carbides are scattered throughout the iron matrix in a physical mixture. At its critical temperature, the carbon dissolves into the matrix and becomes a solid solution rather than a physical mixture.

authentic assessment. An assessment in which the student is asked to perform real-world tasks and demonstrate a meaningful application of skills and competencies.

authorized. Having a legal right to act in a certain way or to perform certain duties.

autoclave. A pressure vessel in which the air inside can be heated to a high temperature and the pressure raised to a high value. Autoclaves are used in the composite manufacturing industry to apply heat and pressure to plastic resins. Heat and pressure decrease the amount of time needed to cure plastic resins and improve the quality of the curing process.

autoclave molding. A method of molding laminated reinforced plastic components. The reinforced resin is laid up over a form having the required shape and is covered with a vacuum bag. Air is pumped out of the bag, and the entire assembly is placed in an autoclave where the temperature is raised and the air pressure is increased. The pressure inside the autoclave forces the plastic resin into the reinforcing material and forces out any air left in the resin.

autofeather. The portion of a propeller control system which causes the propeller to feather automatically if the engine on which it is mounted is shut down in flight.

autogiro. A heavier-than-air rotor-wing aircraft that is sustained in the air by rotors turned by aerodynamic forces rather than by engine power. When the name Autogiro is spelled with a capital A, it refers to a specific series of machines built by Juan de la Cierva or his followers.

autoignition system. A system on a turbine engine that automatically energizes the igniters to provide a relight if the engine should flame out.

autokinesis. A visual illusion caused by staring at a single point of light against a dark background for more than a few seconds, after which the light appears to move on its own.

autoland approach (air traffic control). A precision instrument approach to touchdown and, in some cases, through the landing rollout. An autoland approach is performed by the aircraft autopilot which is receiving position information and/or steering commands from onboard navigation equipment.

auto lean (reciprocating engine fuel-air mixture). A fuel-air mixture whose ratio is kept constant in the lean range by an automatic mixture control in the carburetor or fuel injection system.

automated flight service station (AFSS). An FAA air traffic facility that provides pilot briefings, enroute radio communications, and VFR search-and-rescue services.

automated information transfer (AIT) (air traffic control). A pre-coordinated process, specifically defined in facility directives, during which altitude control and/or radar identification is transferred using information communicated in a full data block, without verbal coordination between controllers.

automated mutual-assistance vessel rescue system (air traffic control). A facility which can deliver, in a matter of minutes, a surface picture (SURPIC) of vessels in the area of a potential or actual search and rescue incident, including their predicted positions and their characteristics.

automated problem detection (APD) (air traffic control). An automation processing capability that compares aircraft trajectories in order to predict conflicts within that ATC facility's boundaries, and which is part of the user request evaluation tool (URET).

automated problem detection boundary (APB) (air traffic control). The adapted distance beyond a facility's boundary defining the airspace within which the user request evaluation tool (URET) performs conflict detection.

automated problem detection inhibited area (APDIA) (air traffic control). Airspace surrounding a terminal area within which automated problem detection (APD) is inhibited for all flights within that airspace, acting as a filter to reduce the amount of conflict detection that occurs in some areas around a terminal that do not need to be evaluated by URET.

automated radar terminal systems. *See* ARTS.

Automated Surface Observing System (ASOS). A U.S. weather reporting system that provides surface observations every minute via digitized voice broadcasts and printed reports. ASOS is operated jointly by the NWS, FAA, and Department of Defense.

automated UNICOM. A completely automated system providing weather, radio check capability, and airport advisory information via UNICOM. These systems offer a variety of features, typically selectable by microphone clicks, on the UNICOM frequency. Availability will be published in the *Airport/Facility Directory* and approach charts.

Automated Weather Observing System (AWOS). A U.S. automated weather reporting system consisting of various sensors, a processor, a computer-generated voice subsystem, and a transmitter to broadcast weather data. AWOS is operated jointly by the NWS, FAA, and Department of Defense.

Automated Weather Sensor System (AWSS). The AWSS is part of the Aviation Surface Weather Observation Network suite of programs and provides pilots and other users with weather information through the Automated Surface Observing System. The AWSS sensor suite automatically collects, measures, processes, and broadcasts surface weather data.

automated weather system. Any of the automated weather sensor platforms that collect weather data at airports and disseminate the weather information via radio and/or landline. The systems currently consist of the Automated Surface Observing System (ASOS), Automated Weather Sensor System (AWSS) and Automated Weather Observing System (AWOS).

automatic. An operation with the ability to perform by itself. An automatic operation has all the necessary signals built into it so that it performs its function without any external decisions having to be made.

automatic adjuster (aircraft brake component). A subsystem in an aircraft disk brake that compensates for disk or lining wear. Each time the brakes are applied, the automatic adjuster is reset for zero clearance, and when the brakes are released, the clearance between the disks or the disk and lining is returned to a preset value.

automatic altitude reporting. A function of a radar beacon transponder that responds to Mode C interrogations by transmitting the aircraft's altitude in 100-foot increments.

automatic carrier landing system. U.S. Navy final approach equipment consisting of precision tracking radar coupled to a computer data link to provide continuous information to the aircraft, monitoring capability to the pilot, and a backup approach system.

automatic dependent surveillance (ADS). A surveillance method that, rather than relying on radar coverage, relies instead on data-link reports from an aircraft's avionics and position-fixing systems, which occur automatically whenever specific events occur, or specific time intervals are reached. ADS is "dependent" on the aircraft's data-link reports and does not require an independent surveillance source (such as a radar antenna) to operate; therefore it can provide accurate surveillance reports in remote and oceanic areas that for many reasons would never be inside radar coverage. The ADS reports, including aircraft identification, four dimensional position, and additional data as appropriate, are converted by data-link equipped ground stations into an ADS track. This is then presented on the controller's display to provide enhanced situational awareness and the potential for reduced separation standards. There are two current implementations of ADS; *see* automatic dependent surveillance-broadcast (ADS-B) *and* automatic dependent surveillance-contract (ADS-C).

automatic dependent surveillance–broadcast (ADS-B). An ADS implementation method that operates in a broadcast mode, in which an aircraft periodically broadcasts its GPS-derived positional (and other, such as velocity) information on a regular basis into the ether via data-link, which is received by a ground-based transmitter/receiver (transceiver) for processing and display at an ATC facility to identify aircraft location. The ADS-B transmitter in the aircraft broadcasts the position of the airplane to any appropriately-equipped station, including other aircraft and ground stations. The ADS-B system can also accept broadcasts with information on other traffic locations and weather. The reporting rate for ADS-B is significantly higher than ADS-C; therefore the FAA plans to use ADS-B to eventually eliminate traditional rotating radar. *See also* automatic dependent surveillance-contract (ADS-C), *and* ADS-B In, ADS-B Out.

automatic dependent surveillance–contract (ADS-C). An ADS implementation method established by the ground station via data-link, following a log-on with an aircraft that establishes "contracts" with the aircraft's avionics. Once established, these contracts automatically provide reports whenever specific events occur, or specific time intervals are reached, to the ground-based transmitter/receiver that transmits them for processing and display at an ATC facility.

Its main difference from ADS-B is that ADS-C relies on contracts, or prior agreements that were established between the ground system and the aircraft's avionics. Reports from the aircraft are generated in accordance with the contract agreement set up prior to the provision of ADS-C services. The contract specifies under what conditions ADS-C reports would be initiated, and what data is requested for the reports; the aircraft then automatically complies to supply the data requested when it is technically possible to do so. ADS-C reporting is controlled by the ground station in all situations other than emergency contracts.

automatic direction finder. *See* ADF.

automatic flight control system. *See* AFCS.

automatic flight information service (AFIS) (Alaska FSS's only). The continuous broadcast of recorded non-control information at airports in Alaska where a flight service station (FSS) provides a local airport advisory service. The AFIS broadcast automates the repetitive transmission of essential but routine information such as weather, wind, altimeter, favored runway, breaking action, airport NOTAMs, and other applicable information. The information is continuously broadcast over a discrete VHF radio frequency (usually the ASOS/AWSS/AWOS frequency.)

automatic frequency control (electrical power circuit). A circuit within an aircraft electrical power system that maintains the frequency of the alternating current within specified limits.

automatic frequency control (radio receiver circuit). A circuit in a radio receiver that keeps the receiver tuned to a desired frequency within specific limits.

automatic gain control (electronic circuit). An electronic circuit within a radio receiver that keeps the output volume relatively constant, even though the strength of the signal picked up by the receiver changes.

automatic intake valve (reciprocating engine component). An intake valve that is opened by the low pressure created inside the cylinder as the piston moves down. There is no mechanical means of opening it.

automatic mixture control (aircraft fuel metering system component). *See* AMC.

automatic pilot. An automatic flight control device that controls an aircraft about one or more of its three axes. The primary purpose of an autopilot is to relieve the pilot of the control of the aircraft during long periods of flight. Automatic pilots may be directed by the human pilot, or they may be coupled to a radio navigation signal.

automatic pilot controller. The component in an automatic pilot system that allows the human pilot to direct the aircraft to hold a specified heading and/or altitude or to couple to one or more of the navigation radios for cruise flight or for a landing approach. Other controls allow the pilot to command a turn, and to trim the aircraft about any of its three axes.

automatic-reset circuit breaker. A thermally actuated electrical circuit protection device installed in some electric motors that opens the power circuit when the motor overheats and automatically closes to restore the circuit when the motor cools down. Automatic-reset circuit breakers are not approved for use in aircraft electrical systems.

automatic terminal information service. *See* ATIS.

automatic volume control (radio receiver circuit). A circuit in a radio receiver that keeps the volume relatively constant as the input signal strength varies.

automation (manufacturing process). A process in which various manufacturing steps are programmed so they can be performed automatically, without requiring any input from a human operator.

automaton. A robot that can be programmed to automatically follow a predetermined set of instructions.

autopilot. *See* automatic pilot.

auto rich (reciprocating engine fuel air mixture). A fuel-air mixture whose ratio is kept constant in the rich range by an automatic mixture control in the carburetor or fuel injection system.

autorotation (aircraft flight condition). The rotation of an aircraft about any of its three axes caused by an aerodynamic force. An aircraft in a spin rotates because of an autorotative force.

autorotation (helicopter operation). Descent of a helicopter without engine power applied to its rotor. An aerodynamic force causes the rotors to spin.

If the engine in a helicopter fails, the freewheeling unit between the engine and the rotor allows the rotor to free-wheel, or turn without engine power, and an aerodynamic force, called an autorotative force, turns the rotor.

A landing made in a helicopter without the use of engine power is called an autorotative landing.

14 CFR Part 1: "A rotorcraft flight condition in which the lifting rotor is driven entirely by action of the air when the rotorcraft is in motion."

autorotation region (helicopter rotor). The portion of the rotor disk of a helicopter which produces an autorotative force. *See* autorotative force.

autorotative force. An aerodynamic force which causes an autogiro or helicopter rotor to turn when no power is supplied to it. It is an autorotative force that causes a spinning airplane to rotate about its spin axis.

Autosyn system. The registered trade name of a remote indicating instrument system. The rotors in an Autosyn system are two-pole electromagnets, and the stators are delta-connected, three-phase, distributed-pole windings in the stator housings.

The rotors in the transmitter and indicator are connected in parallel and are excited with 26-volt, 400-hertz AC. The rotor in the indicator follows the movement of the rotor in the transmitter.

autotransformer. A single-winding electrical transformer that uses a carbon brush riding on a bare portion of the winding to select the number of turns used as the secondary.

Autotransformers produce a secondary voltage that can be varied from almost zero to a value higher than the primary voltage. Autotransformers do not isolate the secondary voltage from the primary voltage.

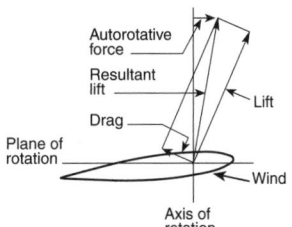

autorotative force

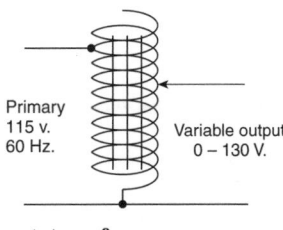

autotransformer

auxiliary. Anything supplemental to, or additional to, a main device or value.

auxiliary flight control. Lift-modifying devices on an aircraft. Flaps, slats, and slots are examples of auxiliary flight controls.

auxiliary fuel pump. An electrically operated fuel pump used to supply fuel to the engine for starting or in the case of failure of the engine-driven pump.

auxiliary hydraulic pump. A pump used as an alternate source of hydraulic pressure for an emergency or to produce hydraulic pressure when the aircraft engines are not operating.

auxiliary power unit. *See* APU.

auxiliary rotor (helicopter component). A small rotor on the tail of a single-main-rotor helicopter which produces a force to counteract the torque of the main rotor. The pitch of the blades of an auxiliary rotor may be controlled by the pilot to rotate the helicopter about its vertical axis.

14 CFR Part 1: "A rotor that serves either to counteract the effect of the main rotor torque on a rotorcraft or to maneuver the rotorcraft about one or more of its three principal axes."

auxiliary view (aircraft drawing). A view used on some aircraft drawings made at an angle to one of the three views of the main drawing. Auxiliary views show details that cannot be shown in the regular views used in the drawing.

available landing distance (ALD). The portion of a runway available for landing and roll-out for aircraft cleared for landing and hold short operations (LAHSO). This distance is measured from the landing threshold to the hold-short point.

avalanche diode (electrical component). Another name for a zener diode.

average value of sine wave alternating current. 0.637 times the peak value of the sine wave alternating current.

AVGAS. Aviation gasoline.

aviation. The branch of science, business, or technology that deals with any part of the operation of machines that fly through the air.

aviation maintenance technician (AMT). A person who holds an aircraft mechanic certificate with both the airframe and powerplant ratings. Also called A&P certificate. This certification is issued by the FAA under the provisions of 14 CFR Part 65, and it indicates the holder is authorized to perform certain maintenance and inspection tasks on airframes and powerplants in the United States.

aviation medical examiner (AME). A physician with training in aviation medicine designated by the Civil Aerospace Medical Institute (CAMI).

aviation medicine. A special field of medicine that establishes standards of physical fitness for airmen.

aviation routine weather report. *See* METAR.

aviation snips. Compound-action hand shears used for cutting sheet metal. Aviation snips come in sets of three. One pair cuts to the left, one pair cuts to the right, and the third pair cuts straight.

aviation weather. Specific characteristics of weather which pertain to flight or to the operation of aircraft.

aviation weather service. *See* AWS.

aviators breathing oxygen. Oxygen that has had all of the water and water vapor removed from it.

avionics. The branch of technology that deals with the design, production, installation, use, and servicing of electronic equipment mounted in aircraft.

Avogadro's principle. A principle of physics which states that under equal pressure and temperature, equal volumes of all gases contain equal numbers of molecules.

avoirdupois weight. The system used in most English-speaking countries for measuring the weight of most substances except drugs and precious metals. In avoirdupois weight, one pound is equal to 453.6 grams. One ounce is equal to $\frac{1}{16}$ pound, and one dram is equal to $\frac{1}{16}$ ounce.

AWG (American Wire Gage). The standard used for measuring the diameter of round wires and the thickness of certain nonferrous metal sheets. The American Wire Gage is also known as the Brown and Sharpe Gage.

awl. A smooth, sharp-pointed tool used to make holes in soft materials such as leather, plastic, or wood.

AWOS. *See* Automated Weather Observing System.

AWS (aviation weather service). A service provided by the National Weather Service (NWS) and FAA which collects and disseminates pertinent weather information for pilots, aircraft operators, and ATC. Available aviation weather reports and forecasts are displayed at each NWS office and FAA FSS.

axes of an aircraft. Three mutually perpendicular imaginary lines about which an aircraft is free to rotate. The longitudinal axis passes through the center of gravity of the aircraft from front to rear. The lateral axis passes through the center of gravity from wing tip to wing tip, and the vertical axis passes through the center of gravity from top to bottom.

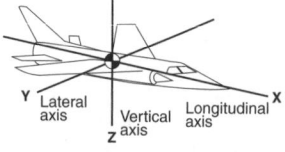

axes of an airplane

axial-centrifugal compressor (gas turbine engine component). A combination axial and centrifugal compressor used in a gas turbine engine. The axial-flow portion of the compressor serves as the low-pressure stage, and the centrifugal portion serves as the high-pressure stage.

axial-flow compressor (gas turbine engine component). A type of compressor used in gas turbine engines in which the air passes through the compressor in essentially a straight line, parallel to the axis of the compressor. The compressor is made of a number of stages of rotating compressor blades between stages of stationary stator vanes. The compression ratio is determined by the number of stages of compression.

axial-lead resistor (electrical component). A discrete electrical component which provides a given amount of resistance to a circuit. The wire leads of an axial-lead resistor extend from the ends in a direction parallel to the axis of the resistor. The resistance value and tolerance is indicated by a series of colored bands *See* illustration for resistor color code.

axial load (bearing load). The load on a bearing parallel to the shaft on which the bearing is mounted. Axial loads are usually carried by ball bearings or tapered roller bearings. The thrust load produced by a propeller is an axial load, and it is carried into the engine crankcase through the thrust bearing.

axial loading (gas turbine engine compressor force). An aerodynamic force that tries to move the compressor forward in its case. Axial loading is supported in a gas turbine engine in ball bearings.

axial turbine (gas turbine engine component). A turbine turned by a fluid flowing through it in a direction approximately parallel to the shaft on which the turbine wheel is mounted.

axis. A straight line about which a body can rotate.

axis of rotation (helicopter rotor). The line through the rotor head of a helicopter at right angles to the plane of rotation. The blades rotate around this axis.

axis of rotation (propeller). The center line about which a propeller rotates.

axis of symmetry. An imaginary center line about which a body or object is symmetrical, or has the same shape on either side.

axle. The shaft on which a wheel is mounted and about which the wheel is free to rotate.

axonometric projection (aircraft drawings). A projection used in mechanical drawing that shows a solid, rectangular object inclined in such a way that three of its faces are visible. An isometric projection is a form of axonometric projection.

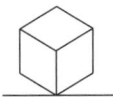

axonometric projection

azimuth. Angular measurement made in a horizontal plane and in a clockwise direction from a fixed reference direction to an object.

azimuth card. A card that may be set, gyroscopically controlled, or driven by a remote compass.

babbitt. A soft, silvery alloy of tin, lead, copper, and antimony used for main bearing inserts in some aircraft reciprocating engines. Babbitt has a very low coefficient of friction, and its dimensions change very little with changes in its temperature.

back (propeller nomenclature). The curved surface of a propeller blade. The back of a propeller blade corresponds to the upper surface of an airplane wing.

back course (BC) (instrument flight). The reciprocal of the localizer course for an ILS (Instrument Landing System). When flying a back-course approach, an aircraft approaches the instrument runway from the end on which the localizer antennas are installed.

back current (semiconductor device). Current that flows in a semiconductor when the junction is reverse-biased. Back current is also called reverse current.

backfire (reciprocating engine). A loud noise, or explosive sound, made by a reciprocating engine when the fuel-air mixture in the induction system is ignited by gases which are still burning inside the cylinder when the intake valve opens.

A lean fuel-air mixture burns more slowly than a rich mixture, and it can still be burning during the time of valve overlap (the time when both the intake and the exhaust valves are open). This causes a backfire.

backfire (welding). A condition in which the flame burns back inside the tip of an oxy-gas torch. If a backfire occurs, the gases must be shut off at the regulator to stop the fire inside the torch.

background noise (electronic equipment). Any noise heard or seen in a piece of electronic equipment when no signal is present. Background noise in a radio receiver is normally heard as a steady hiss.

backhand welding. A method of welding in which the flame is directed back over the finished weld, rather than ahead of the weld.

backing (meteorology). Shifting of the wind in a counterclockwise direction with respect to either space or time. Backing is the opposite of veering and is commonly used by meteorologists to refer to a cyclonic shift (counterclockwise in the Northern Hemisphere and clockwise in the Southern Hemisphere).

backing plate (sheet metal repair). A reinforcing plate used when making a sheet metal repair. Backing plates are often called doublers.

backlash. The play, or relative movement, between the teeth of mating gears caused by improper preload adjustment or worn teeth.

backlash check (gear measurement). A check for the proper mesh between gears. This is done by measuring the amount of clearance between the teeth of the two gears. One of the gears is held rigid and the amount the other gear can move is measured to determine the amount of backlash.

backplate (brake component). A floating plate on which the wheel cylinder and the brake shoes are attached on an energizing-type brake.

back pressure (reciprocating engine). The pressure inside the exhaust system of a reciprocating engine that prevents complete scavenging of the burned gases from the cylinders. Back pressure is caused by mufflers and such power-recovery devices as turbochargers and power-recovery turbines (PRT). *See* turbocharger and PRT.

backsaw (woodcutting saw). A fine-toothed hand saw which has a stiff spine along its upper edge. Backsaws are used to make straight or angled cuts across a board and are often used with a miter box to cut an accurate angle.

backscatter (radar meteorology). Radar energy that has been reflected or scattered by a target. Backscatter is also called an echo.

back side of the power curve. A flight condition in which flight at a higher airspeed requires a lower power setting and flight at a lower airspeed requires a higher power setting in order to maintain altitude.

back-suction mixture control. A type of mixture control used in some float carburetors that regulates the fuel-air mixture ratio by varying the pressure of the air above the fuel in the float bowl.

back taxi (air traffic control). A term used by air traffic controllers to taxi an aircraft on the runway opposite to the traffic flow. The aircraft may be instructed to back-taxi to the beginning of the runway or at some point before reaching the runway end for the purpose of departure or to exit the runway.

backup ring. A flat leather or Teflon ring installed in the groove in which an O-ring or T-seal is placed. The backup ring is on the side of the seal away from the pressure, and it prevents the pressure extruding the seal between the piston and the cylinder wall.

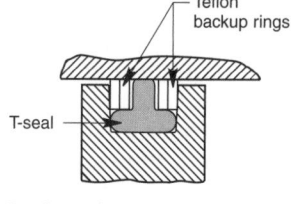

backup ring

backup system. A reserve, or substitute, system that can be put into effect if the main or primary system should fail.

back voltage (counter-electromotive force). Voltage induced in a conductor when it is carrying a changing current. As the magnetic field produced by the changing current builds up and decays, it cuts across the conductor and induces a voltage in it.

The polarity of this induced voltage is opposite that of the voltage which caused the original current to flow.

bacteria. Microscopic plant life that lives in water entrapped inside aircraft fuel tanks. The growth of bacteria in jet aircraft fuel tanks forms a film of scum which holds water against the aluminum alloy surfaces and causes corrosion to form.

bactericide. A material used to destroy bacteria.

baffle. A part of a structure used to impede, regulate, or alter the rate or direction of flow of a fluid, light, or sound.

baffle (air-cooled engine component). A sheet metal shield used to direct the flow of air between and around the cylinders of an air-cooled reciprocating engine. Forcing this air to flow through the fins on the cylinders removes the maximum amount of heat from the engine.

baffle system (fuel tanks). A series of baffles, or partitions, inside an aircraft fuel tank. These baffles have holes in them that allow the fuel to feed to the tank outlet, but prevent the fuel from surging enough to uncover the outlet. Aircraft fuel tanks carry such large quantities of fuel that the sloshing (surging back and forth) of the fuel in a partially full tank could cause severe control problems.

bagging (composites). Preparation of a composite lay-up by applying a layer of impermeable film over an uncured part and sealing the edges. This allows a vacuum to be drawn to assist in the curing.

bag molding. A method of applying pressure to a piece of laminated plastic material so all the layers are held in tight contact with each other. The reinforcing material is impregnated with liquid resin and laid up over a rigid mold in as many layers as are needed.

A sheet of flexible, airtight plastic material is placed over the mold, and the edges are sealed to form a bag over the part. The entire assembly is then placed in an autoclave, and the air pressure is increased to force the layers of material tightly together. If an autoclave is not used, a vacuum pump can be attached to the inside of the bag and the air pumped out. The atmospheric pressure pressing on the outside of the bag supplies the needed force.

bag side (composites). The side of a composite lay-up that is cured against the vacuum bag.

bail out. To jump from an aircraft in flight and use a parachute for descent.

bail-out bottle (oxygen supply). A small high-pressure oxygen bottle attached to a parachute harness. The bail-out bottle supplies the oxygen used during a parachute descent.

Bakelite. The registered trade name for a phenol resin often used as an electrical insulation.

baking soda. The common term for bicarbonate of soda ($NaHCO_3$). A solution of baking soda and water can be used to neutralize electrolyte spilled from a lead-acid battery.

balance. A condition of equilibrium, or rest. A lever is in balance when all the forces acting on one side of the fulcrum, or pivot point, are exactly equal to all the forces acting on the opposite side.

balance cable (airplane control system component). The cable in an airplane control system that ties the upside of both ailerons together. When the control wheel is rotated, a cable from the cockpit pulls one aileron down and relaxes the cable going to the other aileron. The balance cable pulls the other aileron up.

balance chamber (gas turbine engine component). An air chamber inside a gas turbine engine that is used to absorb some of the thrust load produced by the rotating compressor.

balance checks. Checks performed on rotating components after they have been repaired or overhauled to determine their condition of static and dynamic balance.

balance panel (airplane control system component). A flat panel hinged to the leading edge of some ailerons that produces a force which assists the pilot in holding them deflected.

The balance panel divides a chamber ahead of the aileron in such a way that when the aileron is deflected downward, for example, air flowing over its top surface produces a low pressure that acts on the balance panel and causes it to apply an upward force to the leading edge as long as it is deflected.

balance point. The point within an object about which all the forces trying to rotate it are balanced. These forces are equal in amount, but they act on the opposite sides of the balance point.

balance tab (airplane control). A small adjustable tab on a primary control surface of an airplane. The tab is automatically actuated in such a way it moves in the direction opposite to the direction the control surface on which it is mounted moves. Air flowing over the balance tab produces a force on the control surface that reduces the amount of force needed by the pilot to move the surface.

balance to unbalance transformer. *See* balun.

balanced actuator (fluid-power actuator). A linear actuator in a fluid-power system that produces the same amount of force in either direction of piston movement. The two sides of the piston in a balanced actuator have the same area for the fluid to push against.

balanced amplifier (electronic circuit). An electronic amplifier with two output circuits. The output signals from these two circuits are equal in amplitude but opposite in phase. A balanced amplifier is also called a push-pull amplifier.

balanced bridge (electrical measuring circuit). An electrical measuring circuit that uses three known resistances (R_1, R_2, and R_3) and one unknown resistance (R_4). The bridge is balanced ($R_1 : R_2 = R_3 : R_4$) when no current flows through the indicator.

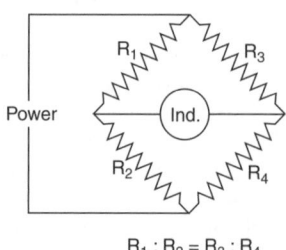

$$R_1 : R_2 = R_3 : R_4$$

balanced bridge

balanced control surface (airplane control). A movable primary control surface on an airplane designed in such a way that aerodynamic forces help the pilot move the surface.

A portion of the surface, called the balance area, extends ahead of the hinge line, and the force of the air pushing on this balance area aids the pilot in moving the surface.

balanced design (composites). A method of orienting the filaments in filament-wound reinforced plastics. The winding pattern is designed in such a way that the stresses in all filaments are equal.

balanced field length. The runway length in which the takeoff distance is the same as the number of feet required to accelerate an airplane to a go/no-go speed, decide to abort the takeoff, and come to a complete stop.

balanced laminate (composites). A composite laminate in which all of the plies are oriented, in pairs, at angles other than 0°. These plies are not necessarily adjacent.

balanced laterally (flight condition). A flight condition in which the aircraft is balanced in such a way that the wings tend to remain level.

balanced pressure torch (welding torch). A welding torch in which the oxygen and fuel gas are supplied at the same pressure. Each gas has its own valve to control the amount delivered to the tip.

balanced transmission line (radio-frequency electrical energy transmission). A transmission line having equal impedance between each conductor and ground, and between each conductor and any other electronic circuit to which it is connected.

balked landing. A go-around, or landing that has been discontinued.

ball bearing. A popular form of antifriction bearing used in many types of machinery. The outer race, consisting of a grooved hardened steel ring, is mounted in the stationary housing. And an inner race with a matching groove is mounted on the rotating shaft. Polished hardened steel balls ride in the grooves and support the shaft. Special deep-groove ball bearings are used in aircraft engines to transmit thrust from the propeller into the engine nose section.

ball bearing assembly. An antifriction bearing assembly that consists of grooved inner and outer races and one or more sets of balls. In bearings designed for disassembly, a removable sheet metal retainer holds the balls in place.

ball check valve (fluid power system component). A type of flow control valve used in a fluid power system to allow fluid to flow in one direction but not in the other.

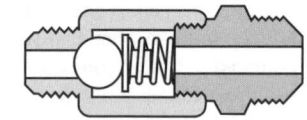

ball check valve

A ball check valve contains a spring-loaded ball that seats in one side of the valve. The ball is forced tightly against its seat by fluid entering the valve from the end containing the spring, and the fluid cannot flow through the valve. Pressure on the side of the valve containing the ball forces the ball off its seat and fluid flows through the valve. Fluid flowing through the valve is opposed only by the force of the spring.

ball joint (exhaust system). A flexible expansion joint used in an aircraft engine exhaust system to allow relative movement between the parts as heat causes them to expand and contract.

ball peen hammer. A hammer with one side of its head shaped like a ball. The ball is used to peen, or flatten, the heads of rivets driven in commercial sheet metal.

ballast (aircraft balance). A weight permanently installed in an aircraft to move the center of gravity to a location within its allowable limits.

ballast lamp (electrical equipment). An incandescent lamp installed in series with an electrical load to maintain a constant current. If the current increases, the filament gets hotter and its resistance increases. This brings the current back to its original value.

ballistic missile. A self-propelled missile which is guided as it goes upward. However, as it comes down, it follows a ballistic trajectory, its natural curved path.

balloon (aerostatic device). A lighter-than-air (LTA) aircraft that is not engine-driven, and that sustains flight through the use of either gas buoyancy or an airborne heater.

Balloon Federation of America (BFA). A national association for balloon pilots and enthusiasts in the United States, and affiliated with the National Aeronautic Association. Information about the BFA can be found at www.bfa.net.

balloon flight manual. A manual containing operating instructions, limitations, weight, and performance information that must be available in the balloon during flight. Portions of the flight manual are FAA approved.

ballooning (flight condition). A momentary climb during landing roundout caused by the misjudgment of the rate of sink during landing. The pilot tends to increase the pitch attitude and angle of attack too rapidly, causing the descent to stop and the plane to start climbing.

balsa wood. A soft, strong, lightweight wood from the tropical American balsa tree. Balsa wood is used in aircraft structure as the core for sandwich-type material. Planks of balsa are cut across the grain and are bonded (glued) between sheets of thin aluminum alloy. The balsa sandwich is strong, lightweight, and rigid.

balun. A type of balanced-to-unbalanced radio frequency transformer used in aircraft radio installation. A balun is used to connect a balanced two-conductor antenna to an unbalanced transmission line.

bamboo. A tropical plant whose stalk (stem) is made up of strong, lightweight, hollow sections with a tubular shape. The stalks were used as a structural material for some of the very first airplanes.

banana oil. Nitrocellulose dissolved in amyl acetate. Banana oil, so called because of its banana-like smell, was used as a dope on the fabric covering of some of the early airplanes.

banana plug (electrical component). A device used to make a temporary connection to an electrical circuit. The contacts of a banana plug are springs having the general shape of a banana. These springs press out against the walls of the banana jack to make a low-resistance contact. Banana plugs are installed on the leads of test instruments such as volt-ohm-milliammeters (VOMs).

band (electrical frequencies). A range of frequencies acceptable to a piece of electronic equipment.

bandpass filter (electronic circuit). An electronic filter that passes a band of frequencies with little attenuation (loss in power), while attenuating, or blocking, all frequencies above or below the band it passes.

band-reject filter (electronic circuit). An electronic filter that rejects, or attenuates, a band of frequencies, while passing with little loss all frequencies on either side of this band.

band saw (power tool). A form of power saw used to cut wood, plastics, or metal. The band saw blade is a narrow strip of steel with teeth along one edge. The ends of the blade are welded together to form a continuous loop, and the loop passes over two large wheels, one above and the other below the saw table.

One of the wheels is driven by an electric motor, and its speed is controllable to allow the operator to match the speed of the blade to the type and thickness of material being cut. For cutting the inside of a hole, many band saws have an attachment that allows the saw blade to be cut in two and an end put through a hole in the work. The ends are then welded back together and the weld ground smooth.

bandwidth (electrical circuit characteristic). The difference between the highest and the lowest frequencies in a band of frequencies.

bank (airplane flight maneuver). To rotate an airplane about its longitudinal axis, or tilt its wings, by using the ailerons. An airplane is turned by banking it.

The lift produced by the wings of an airplane always acts perpendicular to the lateral axis of the airplane. When the airplane is banked, the lift tilts, and its horizontal component pulls the nose of the airplane around in a curved flight path. The rudder of an airplane is used only to start the nose moving in the correct direction as the airplane begins to turn.

bank attitude. The angle of the lateral axis relative to the horizon.

bank indicator (aircraft flight instrument). A flight instrument used to show the pilot whether or not the bank angle being used is correct for the rate of turn being made; it is a curved glass tube partially filled with a clear liquid and containing a black glass ball. The ball rolls back and forth inside the tube to show the relationship between the centrifugal force, caused by the rate of turn, and the force of gravity, determined by the angle of bank. The position of the ball in the tube shows the pilot whether or not the angle of bank is proper for the rate of turn.

When the bank angle is correct for the rate of turn, the force of gravity acting on the ball exactly balances the centrifugal force, and the ball stays in the center of the tube. If the angle of bank is too steep for the rate of turn, the ball rolls to the inside of the turn, and if the angle of bank is not steep enough, the ball rolls to the outside of the turn.

A bank indicator is built into the face of a turn and slip indicator. *See* turn and slip indicator.

banking. The act of rotating an aircraft about its longitudinal axis.

banner cloud (meteorology). A banner-like cloud streaming downwind from a mountain peak.

bar (unit of pressure). A unit of absolute pressure equal to one million dynes per square centimeter. The millibar, one thousandth of a bar, is a unit of absolute pressure used in meteorology. The standard absolute pressure of the atmosphere at sea level is 1013.2 millibars.

bar folder. A type of sheet-metal forming tool used to make bends or folds along the edge of thin sheets of metal.

bar graph. A form of graph used to show relationships existing between different values. In a bar graph, each value is represented by a bar of appropriate length. By comparing the lengths of the bars, we can easily visualize the comparison between the different values. The bars on a bar graph can be either horizontal or vertical.

bare conductor (electrical wiring). An electrical conductor not covered by any type of insulation. Bare conductors can be used only where there is no possibility of anything touching them. These conditions may be found inside the cabinets of certain types of electrical or electronic equipment.

barium. A soft, silvery-white, alkaline-earth, metallic chemical element. Barium's symbol is Ba, its atomic number is 56, and its atomic weight is 137.34.

barnstormers. Aviation pioneers who traveled around the country carrying passengers from unimproved fields. Many of the major airports in the United States were started by barnstormers who leased or bought some farmer's field and built it into an airport. Most of the barnstorming was done between the end of World War I and 1926, at which time the federal government began to require licenses for airplanes and pilots.

baro-aiding. A method of augmenting the GPS integrity solution by using a nonsatellite input source. To ensure that baro-aiding is available, the current altimeter setting must be entered as described in the operating manual.

barograph (meteorological instrument). An absolute-pressure measuring instrument (a type of barometer) that produces a permanent record of the time and the pressure it is measuring. Barographs are often sealed and are carried aloft to make a permanent record of the altitude that has been reached by the aircraft.

barometer (pressure measuring instrument). An instrument used to measure the absolute pressure of the atmosphere. A mercury barometer measures the atmospheric pressure by the height of a column of mercury held up in a tube by the pressure of the atmosphere. An aneroid (no liquid) barometer measures the pressure by the amount an evacuated bellows is collapsed by the atmospheric pressure.

barometric altimeter. A pneumatic altimeter. *See* pneumatic altimeter.

barometric pressure. The pressure produced on the surface of the earth by the weight of the surrounding air. Barometric pressure is normally measured in inches of mercury, absolute.

barometric scale. A scale on the dial of a sensitive pneumatic altimeter to which the pilot sets the barometric pressure level from which the altitude shown on the altimeter is measured. When the scale is set to the standard sea level pressure of 29.92 inches of mercury, the altimeter indicates pressure altitude. When it is set to the existing altimeter setting, the altimeter reads indicated altitude.

barometric tendency (meteorology). The change of barometric pressure within a specified period of time. For aviation weather observations, the time period is normally three hours.

barrage balloon. A tethered, gas-filled balloon used during wartime to protect an area from low-flying airplanes. An airplane is prevented from making a strafing run in an area protected by barrage balloons by the danger of flying into the tethering cables.

barrel roll (airplane flight maneuver). A flight maneuver of an airplane in which the airplane rolls around its longitudinal axis. The term barrel roll has been replaced in modern usage; the maneuver is now called an aileron roll, or slow roll.

barrier voltage (semiconductor parameter). The voltage across a forward-biased PN junction in a semiconductor diode or transistor. When the mobile charges are drawn away from the junction, ionic charges are left. These ionic charges cause a voltage, or potential difference, to exist across the junction. The positive barrier voltage is in the N-material, and the negative barrier voltage is in the P-material. The barrier voltage across the junction in a silicon diode is about 0.7 volt, and approximately 0.3 volt in a germanium diode.

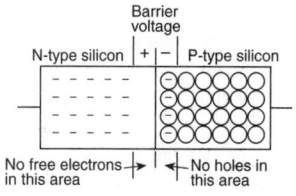

barrier voltage

base (mathematics). The number in an exponential expression that is multiplied by itself the number of times shown by the exponent.

base (transistor electrode). The electrode of a bipolar transistor between the emitter and the collector. Controlling a small flow of electrons moving into or out of the base controls a much larger flow of electrons between the emitter and the collector. The base of a transistor compares with the grid of a vacuum tube.

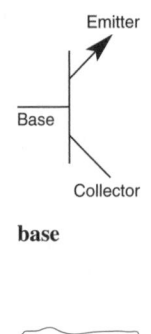

base

baseball stitch. A type of hand stitch used to join two pieces of fabric that butt together, but do not overlap. Baseball stitches are used to sew together the edges of a tear in the fabric used to cover an aircraft structure. It gets its name from this type of stitch being used to sew the cover on a baseball.

baseball stitch

base leg. A flight path at right angles to the landing runway off its approach end, and extending from the downwind leg to the intersection of the extended runway centerline.

base line. A line used as a datum, or reference line, for measuring.

base metal (metallurgy). Metal to which alloying agents are added.

base metal (welding). The metal to be welded, soldered, or brazed.

BASIC (computer language). A commonly used high-level language for digital computers. The commands used in BASIC are similar to commands used in the English language. The acronym BASIC comes from Beginners All-purpose Symbolic Instruction Code.

basic empty weight (GAMA). (1) Standard empty weight plus optional equipment. (2) The weight of the standard rotorcraft, operational equipment, unusable fuel, and full operating fluids, including full engine oil.

basic flight maneuvers. The four fundamental basic flight maneuvers upon which all flying tasks are based: straight-and-level flight, turns, climbs, and descents. All controlled flight consists of one, or a combination or more than one of these basic maneuvers.

basic ground instructor certificate. An FAA-issued certificate that authorizes the holder to provide the following training: (1) Ground training in the aeronautical knowledge areas required for the issuance of a sport pilot certificate, recreational pilot certificate, private pilot certificate, or associated ratings; (2) Ground training required for a sport pilot, recreational pilot, and private pilot flight review; and (3) A recommendation for a knowledge test required for the issuance of a sport pilot certificate, recreational pilot certificate, or private pilot certificate.

basic need. A perception factor that describes a person's ability to maintain and enhance the organized self.

basic operating index (weight and balance). The moment (weight times arm) of the airplane at its basic operating weight divided by the appropriate reduction factor.

basic operating weight. *See* BOW.

basic radar service. The services provided for VFR aircraft by all commissioned terminal radar facilities. Basic radar service includes safety alerts, traffic advisories, limited radar vectoring when requested by the pilot, and sequencing at locations where procedures have been established for this purpose and/or when covered by a letter of agreement.

basket. That portion of a hot air balloon that carries the pilot, passengers, cargo, fuel, and instruments.

basket weave (composites). A weave in which two or more warp yarns are interlaced under two or more fill yarns. The result is a fabric that is not as stable as the plain weave, but is more pliable and has the ability to conform to simple contours.

bastard file. A double-cut, metalworking file with the next to the coarsest teeth. There are five grades of double-cut files based on their teeth. From the coarsest to the finest, these are: coarse-cut, bastard-cut, second-cut, smooth-cut, and dead-smooth-cut.

batch. In general, a quantity of material formed during the same process or in one continuous process and having identical characteristics throughout. Also called a lot.

bathtub capacitor (electrical component). A type of capacitor sealed in a metal container. The bathtub capacitor takes its name from its shape, which is similar to that of a bathtub.

battery (electrical component). An electrochemical device, normally made of a number of individual cells. Electrical energy is stored in a battery by changing it into chemical energy.

battery symbol

Chemical energy in the battery causes a potential difference between the negative and the positive terminals, and when a conductor joins the two terminals, electrons flow from the negative terminal to the positive terminal.

battery analyzer. A special transformer-rectifier unit used to charge nickel-cadmium batteries. In addition to a source of direct current, the analyzer has a built-in load bank, timers, indicators, and controls for deep-cycling and recharging these batteries.

battery bus. A tie point in an aircraft electrical system to which the battery is connected. Electrical loads connected to the battery bus get their power from the bus.

battery charger. A transformer-rectifier unit that changes alternating current into direct current of the proper voltage to charge storage batteries. The battery charger is connected to the battery with the positive terminal of the charger connected to the positive terminal of the battery, and the battery is charged until its voltage is the same as that of the charger.

battery ignition system. An ignition system similar to that used in most automobiles. The source of energy is a battery or generator rather than a magneto. A cam, driven by the engine, opens a set of breaker points to interrupt the flow of current in the primary winding of the ignition coil. The resulting collapsing magnetic field induces a high voltage in the secondary winding of the ignition coil, which is directed to the proper spark plug by a distributor.

baud (computer operation). A unit of speed for binary data transmission equal to one bit per second.

bauxite. A type of clay or rock, the source of aluminum. To extract the aluminum, the bauxite is changed into alumina (aluminum oxide). Then, the alumina is reduced to metallic aluminum by an electrolytic process.

bay (structural component). A compartment in the structure of an aircraft. A bay is the portion of the structure between adjacent bulkheads, frames, or struts.

bayonet exhaust stack (aircraft reciprocating engine component). The elongated and flattened end of the exhaust stack used on an aircraft reciprocating engine. The gases leave the stack through a slot parallel to its length. Bayonet stacks decrease both exhaust back pressure and noise and prevent cold air from flowing into the exhaust stack during such maneuvers as slips. This cold air could cause the valves to warp.

bayonet fueling nozzle. A type of nozzle used to fuel aircraft with a pressure, or single-point, fueling system. The nozzle is connected to the fueling receptacle in the aircraft, and the handles are turned a portion of a turn to lock it in place.

bayonet gage. A term for a dip stick, such as that used to measure the quantity of a liquid in a tank or a reservoir.

bayonet thermocouple probe. A thermocouple pickup used to measure cylinder head temperature on an air-cooled aircraft engine. The bayonet probe fits into an adapter screwed into the cylinder head and a spring holds the end of the probe tightly against the cylinder head.

B-battery. A source of high-voltage direct current needed for vacuum tubes. Vacuum tubes must have a high positive DC voltage on their plates and screen grids to pull electrons across the vacuum from the cathode. This high voltage is called B plus (B+) voltage.

BBC. *See* before bottom center.

BC. *See* back course

BCD (binary coded decimal). A system used for changing decimal numbers into binary numbers. Each digit from 0 through 9 is represented with four binary digits:

Decimal	Binary		Decimal	Binary
0	= 0000		5	= 0101
1	= 0001		6	= 0110
2	= 0010		7	= 0111
3	= 0011		8	= 1000
4	= 0100		9	= 1001

The decimal number 126 for example, expressed in BCD, is: 0001 0010 0110.

B-check. *See* maintenance checks.

BDC. *See* bottom dead center.

beaching. Pulling a seaplane up onto a suitable shore so that its weight is supported by relatively dry ground rather than water.

beacon (navigational aid). A fixed radio transmitter that broadcasts distinctive signals as a navigational aid.

bead (tire component). The high-strength carbon-steel wire bundles that give an aircraft tire its strength and stiffness where it mounts on the wheel.

bead (tubing). A rounded ridge formed near the end of a piece of rigid tubing used for carrying fluids in an aircraft. A hose is slipped over the end of the tube, and a hose clamp is installed between the end of the hose and the bead. The bead keeps the tube from being pulled out of the hose.

bead (welding). The ridge of filler metal that sticks up above the surface of metal that has been welded. The appearance of the bead usually indicates the condition of the weld. The bead of a good weld is uniform in height, has a smooth, uniform ripple on its surface, and blends evenly into the base metal.

bead heel (tire component). The outer edge of the tire bead that fits against the wheel flange.

bead seat area of a wheel. The flat surface of an aircraft wheel on which the bead of the tire seats. The bead seat area of wheels that have tubeless tires installed on them must be very smooth and free of damage. Only then can the tire form an airtight seal with the wheel.

bead thermistor (fire detection system component). A component in a fire detection system that signals the presence of a fire or overheat condition. Beads of a thermistor material (a material, such as germanium, whose resistance changes with its temperature) support a wire that forms part of the fire detection circuit. The bead-supported wire is enclosed in a metal tube routed through the area to be protected.

If the tube is heated by a fire, the thermistor material changes from an insulator into a conductor

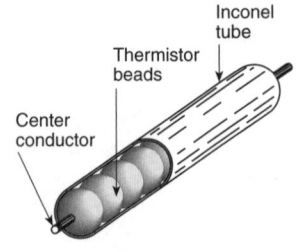

bead thermistor

and completes an electrical circuit between the central wire and the tube. This completed circuit initiates the fire-warning procedure by turning on the fire-warning light and sounding the fire-warning bell.

bead toe (tire component). The inner edge of the tire bead closest to the tire centerline.

bead welds (electric arc welding). A type of weld made by holding a short arc and welding in a straight line at a constant speed, with the electrode inclined 5° to 15° in the direction of welding. The proper arc can be recognized by a sharp cracking sound heard all during the time the electrode is being moved to and above the surface of the metal.

Some characteristics of good bead welds are (1) very little spatter on the surface of the metal, and (2) the arc crater (or depression) in the bead when the arc has been broken is approximately $1/16$ inch deep.

beaded coaxial cable (radio frequency transmission line). A form of coaxial transmission line in which the inner conductor is centered in the outer conductor by a series of beads made of insulating material.

beam (radio navigation). The beam is a descriptive term which refers to an invisible path produced by radio signals. An aircraft can follow the beam when going to or from a navigational fix. The term beam became popular with the four-course, low-frequency radio range that projected four clearly defined beams, or courses, from each of the transmitting stations. When a pilot was flying an aircraft along one of these courses, he was said to be "on the beam."

beam (structural member). A long, heavy, metal or wood member in any type of structure used to support both bending and shear loads.

beam antenna (radio antenna). A radio transmitting antenna that concentrates its radiation into a narrow beam. This beam can be oriented in any direction needed.

beam-power tube (electron tube). A form of tetrode (four-element) electron tube that uses two beam-forming electrodes, or plates, to shape the flow of electrons so they travel from the cathode to the plate in definite beams. The screen grid is wound in such a way that its wires are in the shadow cast by the control grid, and keeping the screen grid out of the path of the electrons helps minimize screen current. Beam power tubes are power amplifier tubes, rather than voltage amplifiers.

beam resolution (radar technology). The ability of radar to distinguish between targets at approximately the same range but along different azimuths.

bearing (mechanical equipment). A device fitted into a hole to reduce the friction present when a shaft rotates in the hole. Plain bearings are liners for the hole made of a material such as bronze or babbitt metal which have a low coefficient of friction. Antifriction bearings consist of a pair of hardened and polished steel races, with either hardened steel rollers or balls rolling between them.

bearing (navigation). The horizontal direction to one object from another. True bearing is the direction measured in degrees clockwise from true north. Relative bearing between two objects is the direction measured in degrees clockwise from a reference point on the first object, such as the nose of an aircraft, to the second object.

bearing burnishing (engine overhaul). The process which creates a highly polished surface on new bearings and bushings that have been installed during engine overhaul. The burnishing is usually accomplished during the first periods of engine run-in at comparatively slow engine speeds.

bearing cage (antifriction bearing component). A thin sheet metal separator that keeps the rollers or balls in an antifriction bearing evenly spaced around the races. The bearing cage should never touch either of the bearing races.

bearing cone (antifriction bearings). The tapered bearing races used with some roller bearings. For wheel bearings, the inner cone is slipped over the axle, and the outer cone fits into a recess inside the wheel. Hardened steel rollers ride between the two cones.

bearing cup (wheel bearing). The hardened-steel outer race of a tapered roller bearing installed in an airplane wheel. The complete bearing consist of the cup, which is a shrink-fit in the bearing cavity of the wheel, a bearing cone (the inner race), and rollers. Grease seals and retainers keep dirt out of the bearing.

bearing failure (riveted structural failure). A type of failure of a riveted joint in a sheet metal structure. A joint fails in bearing when the metal tears at the rivet holes before the rivets shear.

bearing friction. Friction that is caused by bearings.

bearing race. The hardened steel surface upon which the balls or rollers of an antifriction bearing ride.

bearing rollers. Hardened steel rollers that support a rotating shaft. The rollers ride between two hardened steel races and are usually spaced evenly around the races by a thin sheet metal separator.

bearing strength (sheet metal specification). The amount of pull needed to cause a piece of sheet metal to tear at the points it is held together with rivets. The bearing strength of a material is affected by both its thickness and the diameter of the rivet.

bearing stress (composites). The applied load divided by the bearing area. Maximum bearing stress is the maximum load in pounds, sustained by a specimen during the test, divided by the original bearing area.

bearing support (gas turbine engine component). The portion of the case of a gas turbine engine in which the main bearings are mounted.

bearing surface. A surface which supports a moving load. Bearing surfaces are normally treated in some way to decrease the friction between the surface and the load being moved.

beat (vibration). A low-frequency sound, or vibration, produced when two sources of vibration having almost, but not exactly, the same frequency, act on an object at the same time.

For example, in a multi-engine airplane, if one engine is turning at 1,850 RPM and the other is turning at 1,880 RPM, the airframe vibrations caused by these engines will produce a very noticeable beat of 30 cycles per minute. This beat is caused by the difference in the frequency of the two vibrations.

beat frequency. The frequency of vibration produced when two sources of vibration act on a common body. The beat frequency is the difference between the frequencies of the two original vibrations.

Beaufort scale. A number rating from zero to 12, used by the weather bureau to describe wind speed.

Beaufort Force	Velocity (knots)	Indication
0	less than 1	smoke rises vertically
1	1 – 3	wind blows smoke
2	2 – 7	wind felt on face
3	8 – 12	leaves in motion
4	13 – 18	raises dust and loose paper
5	19 – 24	sways small trees
6	25 – 31	moves large branches of trees
7	32 – 38	whole trees in motion
8	39 – 46	breaks twigs off of trees
9	47 – 54	slight structural damage
10	55 – 63	uproots trees
11	64 – 72	widespread damage
12	73 – 136	devastation

beef up. To strengthen.

beehive spring (riveting gun component). A hard steel, coil-spring retainer used to hold a rivet set in a pneumatic rivet gun. A beehive spring, which gets its name from its shape, screws onto the end of the rivet gun and allows the rivet set to move back and forth, but prevents it being driven out of the gun.

beep button (helicopter control). A switch on the collective control of a turbine engine-powered helicopter. The beep button is used to adjust the steady-state RPM of the engine.

beeswax. A natural wax applied to rib lacing cord used to attach the fabric to a fabric-covered aircraft. Beeswax protects the cord from moisture and keeps knots in the cord from slipping.

before bottom center (reciprocating engine piston position). The position of the piston in the cylinder of a reciprocating engine as the piston is moving downward, toward the bottom of its stroke, with the crankshaft turning in the direction of normal rotation. The position is normally expressed in degrees BBC, which is the number of degrees the crankshaft must rotate before the piston reaches its bottom dead center position.

before top center (reciprocating engine piston position). The position of the piston in the cylinder of a reciprocating engine as the piston is moving upward, toward the top of its stroke, with the crankshaft turning in the direction of normal rotation. The position is normally expressed in degrees BTC, which is the number of degrees the crankshaft must rotate before the piston reaches its top dead center position.

behaviorism. Theory of learning that stresses the importance of having a particular form of behavior reinforced by someone other than the student to shape or control what is learned.

bel. A dimensionless number used to express the ratio of two powers or intensities. The number of bels is the logarithm of the ratio of the two values. A decibel (dB), one tenth of a bel, is more commonly used than the bel.

bellcrank. A double lever in an aircraft control system used to change the direction of motion. Bellcranks are often used in the aileron system of an airplane to change spanwise movement of a push-pull rod into fore-and-aft movement of the control rod that raises or lowers the aileron.

bell gear. The large gear in a planetary gear system. The bell gear may be either stationary or driven, and it surrounds, and meshes with, the planetary gears as they rotate around the sun gear.

bell jar. A heavy glass jar with a dome-shaped top and an open bottom. Bell jars are used as vacuum chambers in science laboratories. The bottom of the bell jar is ground perfectly flat, so it forms an airtight seal with a flat surface plate, and a vacuum pump connected to the inside of the bell jar pumps all the air out of it.

bell mouth. The shape of a smooth convergent duct. The bell-mouth shape allows the maximum amount of air to be drawn into the duct with a minimum of loss.

bell-mouth inlet duct (gas turbine engine component). A form of convergent inlet air duct used to direct air into the inlet of a gas turbine engine. The area of a convergent duct gets smaller as the air flows into the engine. A bell-mouth inlet duct is extremely efficient, and is used where there is little ram pressure available to force the air into the engine. Bell-mouth ducts are used in engine test cells and on engines installed in helicopters.

bellows (pressure measuring device). Circular corrugated metal capsules that are either evacuated or filled with an inert gas under a specific pressure. Bellows are used to measure pressure. As the pressure acting on the outside of the bellows changes, the bellows expand or contract. The change in the thickness of the bellows is measured, and this change relates to the change in pressure acting on the bellows.

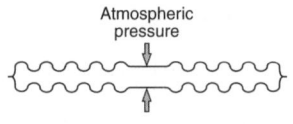

bellows

Bellville washer. A cupped, spring steel washer used to produce a large amount of compressive force, but with a limited amount of movement.

below minimums (air traffic control). Weather conditions below the minimums prescribed by regulations for the particular action involved. These are conditions such as landing minimums, takeoff minimums.

belt frame (aircraft structural component). A frame that goes around the inside of the fuselage of an aircraft. Belt frames are normally made in the form of a channel or hat section.

bench check. A functional test of a piece of equipment in which the equipment is set up on a test bench and operated to find out whether or not it functions as it should. A bench check can tell whether or not a piece of equipment is working satisfactorily by itself, but it tells little about the way it will perform when it is interconnected with other equipment.

bench plate. A flat cast-iron plate built into a bench used for working sheet metal. Holes in the bench plate support stakes used to form sheet metal.

bench timing (magneto timing). A method of setting the internal timing of a magneto. It involves timing the breaker points to open when the rotating magnet is in the position that produces the maximum flux, the E-gap position. The finger of the distributor rotor is set to point to the high tension terminal for the correct spark plug to fire.

bend allowance (sheet metal layout). The amount of material actually needed to make a bend in a piece of sheet metal. When a flat layout of a piece of sheet metal is being made, an allowance must be made for the bend. The amount of material in the bend is determined by both the radius of the bend and the number of degrees the metal is bent. The amount of material in the bend is usually found by using a bend allowance chart.

bending strength. The resistance a piece of material offers to bending stresses.

bending stress. The type of stress that tries to pull up or push down on one end of a beam while the other end is held stationary. When a beam is bent down, the top is under a tensile stress, and the bottom is under a compressive stress.

Bendix fuel injection system (Precision Airmotive system). A continuous-flow fuel injection system that uses airflow forces to measure engine air consumption. Fuel is metered to a flow divider and discharged at each intake valve on the basis of the air flowing into the engine.

bend radius (sheet metal layout). The radius of the inside of a bend in a piece of sheet metal, tubing, or wire bundle.

bend tangent line (sheet metal layout). A line made in a sheet metal layout that indicates the point at which the bend is started. The material on one side of the bend tangent line is the flat surface, and the material on the other side is the bend allowance.

benzene. A colorless, volatile, flammable, aromatic hydrocarbon liquid which has the chemical formula C_6H_6. Benzene, sometimes called benzoil, is used as a solvent, as a cleaning fluid, and as a fuel for some special types of reciprocating engines.

berkelium. A synthetic, radioactive chemical element in the actinide series. Berkelium's properties resemble those of cerium. Berkelium's symbol is Bk, and its atomic number is 97.

Bernoulli's principle. A fundamental principle of physics that explains the relation between kinetic and potential energy in a fluid in motion.

When the total energy in a column of moving fluid remains constant, any increase in the kinetic energy of the fluid (its velocity) results in a corresponding decrease in its potential energy (its pressure).

beryllium. A high-melting-point, lightweight, corrosion-resistant, steel-gray metallic chemical element. Beryllium's symbol is Be, its atomic number is 4, and its atomic weight is 9.0122. Beryllium's main importance is in its use as an alloying agent for copper.

beryllium bronze. An alloy of copper combined with about three percent beryllium. Beryllium bronze is used for making springs, bellows, and diaphragms for pressure-measuring instruments.

best angle-of-climb airspeed (V_X). The airspeed at which an aircraft will gain the greatest amount of altitude in a given distance.

best-economy mixture (reciprocating engine fuel-air mixture ratio). The fuel-air mixture ratio used in a reciprocating engine that gives the aircraft its greatest range of flight. The best-economy fuel-air mixture ratio, which is in the range of 0.055 to 0.065 (18:1 to 15:1 air-fuel ratio). This mixture ratio does not provide any additional fuel for cooling, so it can be used only when the engine is operating with reduced power.

best glide speed (best L/D speed). The airspeed that results in the least amount of altitude loss over a given distance. The aircraft's manufacturer publishes the best glide (L/D) airspeed for specified weights and the resulting glide ratio. For example, a glide ratio of 36:1 means that the glider will lose 1 foot of altitude for every 36 feet of forward movement in still air at this airspeed.

best-power mixture (reciprocating engine fuel-air mixture ratio). The fuel-air mixture ratio used in a reciprocating engine that allows the engine to develop its greatest amount of power. The best-power fuel-air mixture ratio, which is in the range of 0.074 to 0.087 (13.5:1 to 11.5:1 air-fuel ratio), is richer than the ratio used for the best economy. The additional fuel in this mixture is used to remove some of the heat from the cylinders when the engine is producing its best power.

best rate-of-climb airspeed (V_Y). The airspeed at which an aircraft will gain the greatest amount of altitude in a given unit of time.

beta (electronic measurement). The current gain of a transistor connected as a grounded-emitter (common emitter) amplifier. Beta is the ratio of the change in collector current to the change in base current when the collector voltage is held constant.

beta control range (turboprop engine operation). The range of operation of a turboprop powerplant normally used for inflight approach and ground handling of the engine and aircraft. Typically the beta mode includes operations from 65% to 95% of the engine's rated RPM.

beta particle (nuclear particle). A particle emitted from the nucleus of an atom during radioactive decay. A negative beta particle is the same as an electron, and a positive beta particle (called a positron) has the same mass as an electron, but has a positive charge.

beta tube (turboprop control). A tube in a Garrett TPE331 turboprop engine that extends into the propeller pitch control to act as a follow-up device. It provides proportional movement of the propeller blades with movement of the power lever.

bevel. The angle formed by one surface with another surface when the angle is not a right angle.

bevel gears. A pair of toothed wheels with the teeth cut on a surface at an angle other than 90° to the axis of the shaft on which the wheels are mounted. Bevel gears allow one shaft to drive another shaft that is not parallel to it.

bezel. The rim which holds the glass cover in the case of an aircraft instrument.

BFO (beat-frequency oscillator). A variable radio-frequency electronic oscillator used with communications receivers when receiving unmodulated CW (continuous wave) signals. The unmodulated CW has a frequency that is too high to hear, so it is mixed with the output of the BFO. When the BFO is adjusted so its frequency is nearly the same as that of the CW signal being received, the two signals beat together and produce an audio-frequency signal that can be heard. The frequency of this AF is the difference between the frequency of the unmodulated CW and that produced by the BFO.

B-H curve (magnetic specifications). A curve showing the relationship between the flux density (B) in a piece of magnetized material and the magnetizing force (H) needed to produce the flux density. Each type of ferromagnetic material, material that contains iron and is magnetizable, has a different B-H curve.

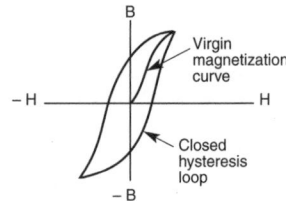

B-H curve

Each B-H curve consists of the virgin magnetization curve, the curve of B and H, when the material is first magnetized, and the closed hysteresis loop that shows the effect of hysteresis, the magnetism that remains in the material.

BHP (brake horsepower). The horsepower actually delivered to the output shaft of a rotating machine. Brake horsepower gets its name from the fact that this power was originally measured with a prony brake. Today, brake horsepower is measured with a dynamometer. BHP is actually the usable horsepower.

biannual. Occurring twice each year. Biannual must not be confused with biennial, which means occurring every two years.

bias (composites). The orientation of the warp and fill fibers in a fabric that are at an angle to the length of the material.

bias current (transistor operation). Current flowing in the emitter-base circuit of a transistor. The amount of bias current can be adjusted by the choice of components to set the operating conditions of the transistor.

bias-cut surface tape (aircraft covering material). A fabric tape in which the threads run at an angle, usually 45°, to the length of the tape. Bias-cut tape is often used as a surface tape when covering an aircraft, because it can be stretched around a compound curve without wrinkling.

bias voltage (vacuum tube operation). The DC voltage placed on the grid of an electron tube which sets the operating point about which an AC input signal is applied. The proper bias voltage allows the tube to amplify the signal applied to its grid without distortion.

bicarbonate of soda. Common baking soda ($NaHCO_3$).

bicycle landing gear. *See* bogie landing gear.

bidirectional antenna (radio antenna). A radio antenna that produces a maximum signal strength in two directions.

bidirectional data transfer. A method of data transfer in which signals can travel in either direction.

bidirectional fibers. Fibers in a piece of composite material oriented in such a way that they can sustain loads in two directions.

bidirectional laminate. A reinforced plastic laminate with the fibers oriented in two directions in the plane of the laminate; a cross-laminate.

bifilar vibration absorber (helicopter rotor system). A system designed to reduce rotor vibration at the rotor head. The absorber, consisting of a four-arm plate with attached weights, is mounted on top of the hub.

bifiliar resistor (electrical component). A special type of wire-wound resistor used in electrical circuits. A bifiliar resistor is wound of wire that is doubled back on itself to decrease the inductance in the resistor.

bifiliar transformer (electrical component). A type of electrical transformer in which the two windings, the primary and the secondary, are wound side-by-side. Bifiliar winding increases the coefficient of coupling between the windings.

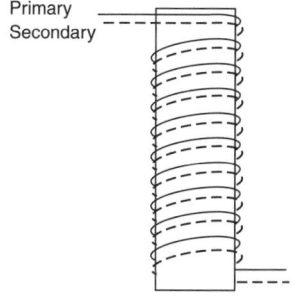

bifiliar transformer

bifurcated exhaust duct. A split duct exhaust system used on most turbofan engines.

bilge area. The lowest part of an aircraft structure in which water and contaminants collect, and corrosion is likely to form. The area under the cabin floor is normally called the bilge.

bilge pump. A pump used to extract water that has leaked into the bilge of a float or flying boat.

bill of materials (aircraft drawing). A list of all of the materials used in the component or assembly shown in an aircraft drawing.

billet (metal manufacturing). A bar of semifinished steel. A billet is rolled from an ingot, and it generally has a square cross section.

billow cloud. A cloud consisting of broad parallel bands oriented perpendicular to the wind. It is created from instability associated with airflows having marked vertical shear and weak thermal stratification.

bimetallic circuit breaker (electrical component). A circuit breaker in which one of the current-carrying contacts is mounted on a bimetallic strip. If more than the rated current flows through a bimetallic circuit breaker, the bimetallic strip will heat up and warp. When it warps, it snaps the contacts apart and opens the circuit.

bimetallic hairspring. A flat, spiral-wound spring made of two strips of metal laid side-by-side and welded together. The two metals have different coefficient of expansion, and as the temperature changes, the spiral either tightens or loosens. The pointer of an analog thermocouple-type temperature indicator is mounted on a bimetallic hairspring to compensate its indication for changes in temperature of the reference junction.

bimetallic strip. A strip made of two different types of metal fastened together, side-by-side. When heated, these two metals expand differently, causing the strip to warp, or bend. Bimetallic strips are used in some types of thermometers and circuit breakers.

binary coded decimal. *See* BCD.

binary number system. The number system whose base is two. It uses only two values, zero and one.

Each position represents a value twice that of the position to its right. For example:

64	32	16	8	4	2	1		
0	0	0	0	0	0	1	=	1
0	0	0	0	0	1	0	=	2
0	0	0	0	1	0	0	=	4
0	0	0	1	0	0	0	=	8
0	0	1	0	0	0	0	=	16
0	1	0	0	0	0	0	=	32
1	0	0	0	0	0	0	=	64

Continued

binary number system. *Continued*

The binary number system is useful when working with digital electronics, because the two basic conditions of electricity, on and off, can be used to represent the two bits of the binary number system. When the system is on, the bit one is represented, and when it is off, zero is represented.

binding post (electrical equipment). A connector used to fasten a conductor to an electrical test panel. Most binding posts have an insulated nut that can be turned with the fingers to grip the wire. Some binding posts have, in addition to the nut, holes for a banana plug.

binoculars. A form of handheld optical instrument used to observe distant objects. Binoculars have a set of magnifying lenses for each eye, and prisms are used to get a high degree of magnification in a short physical length.

binomial. An algebraic expression that contains two terms. $4X + 2Y$ is a binomial expression.

bioastronautics. The branch of science dealing with the medical and biological aspects of astronautics.

biochemistry. The branch of chemistry dealing with chemical compounds and processes involved with living organisms.

biocidal action. The action of certain chemicals that kill bacteria. Biocidal agents are used in turbine engine fuel to kill the bacteria and microbes living in water that condenses inside aircraft fuel tanks. If these microscopic organisms are not killed, they will multiply and form a scum that holds water against the aircraft skin and promotes corrosion. Biocidal additives are also put in aircraft dope used on cotton or linen fabric to kill bacteria that can destroy either of these organic fabrics.

biocidal agent. A chemical compound that is destructive to certain types of living organisms.

biodegradable. A condition of a material that allows it to be broken down into simple products by the action of certain types of microorganisms. Paper and wood are normally biodegradable. If they are buried, they will, in time, change into simpler chemical compounds. Some man-made materials are not biodegradable, and they will not change. Disposing of large volumes of nonbiodegradable materials can be an environmental problem.

biological warfare. Warfare using disease-producing microorganisms or toxic biological products to cause death or injury to humans, animals, or plants.

biophysics. The branch of physics dealing with the application of physical laws to biological problems.

biplane. An airplane having two main supporting aerodynamic surfaces (wings). The wings of a biplane are normally mounted so that one is approximately above the other.

bipolar transistor. A solid-state component in which the flow of current between its emitter and collector is controlled by a much smaller flow of current into or out of its base. Bipolar transistors may be of either the NPN or PNP type.

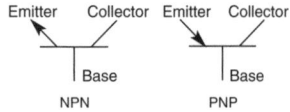

bipolar transistors

bipropellant rocket. A rocket using two separate propellants which are kept separate until they are mixed in the combustion chamber.

bisector of a line. A point on the line that divides it into two segments of equal length.

bisector of an angle. A line that divides an angle into two equal angles.

bismaleimide (BMI). A type of thermoset polyimide that cures by an additional reaction, thus avoiding formation of volatiles. It exhibits temperature capabilities between those of epoxy and polyimide.

bismuth. A heavy metallic, pentavalent chemical element. Bismuth is brittle, grayish-white, crystalline, and highly diamagnetic. Bismuth's symbol is Bi, its atomic number is 83, and its atomic weight is 208.980.

Bismuth is often used to dope silicon or germanium to make P-type semiconductor material and is also used as an alloying agent for changing the characteristic of certain metals.

bistable. A condition of a mechanical or electrical device in which either of two conditions may exist as a steady state.

bistable circuit (electronic circuit). A circuit having two stable conditions. Either condition may be chosen, and the circuit will operate in that condition until it is purposely changed. The circuit will not change its condition by itself.

bistable multivibrator (electronic circuit). A type of oscillator using two transistors. Only one transistor conducts at a time, and it will continue to conduct until an external pulse causes it to stop conducting. When the first transistor stops conducting, the second transistor automatically begins to conduct. A bistable multivibrator is called a flip-flop, and it is often used in digital electronics.

bistatic radar. A radar system in which the transmitter and receiver use separate antennas and are usually located some distance from each other.

bit. A binary digit (the word bit comes from the words **bi**nary dig**it**). A bit, either a zero or a one, is the smallest particle of information in a binary digital system, and all digital information is made up of bits. Bits are usually written as 1 for yes, true, or high, and 0 for no, false, or low.

BITE (built-in test equipment). A troubleshooting system installed in many modern jet aircraft. BITE monitors the engine and airframe systems and when a fault is found, isolates it and provides the maintenance personnel with a code that identifies the LRU, or line replaceable unit, that contains the fault.

bitumen. A general name given to tar-like hydrocarbon materials. Bitumens are the last of the products left in the fractional distillation of crude oil. Asphalt and tar are two common bitumens.

bituminous paint. A heavy, thick, tar-base paint used as a water and acid-resistant covering. Bituminous paint is used around battery compartments for lead-acid batteries and in some compartments of flying boat hulls and seaplane floats.

black blizzard (meteorology). Another name for a dust storm.

black body (radiated energy). An ideal body which absorbs all the light that falls on it. It appears perfectly black at all wavelengths because it does not reflect any wavelength of light.

black box (electronic system). A term used for any portion of an electrical or electronic system that can be removed as a unit. In troubleshooting a system using flow charts, only the information entering and leaving the black box is given. In order to understand the device or system, it is necessary to know the input and output signals and the function of the black box, but it is not necessary to know its internal circuits. A black box does not have to be a physical box.

black ice. *See* clear ice (meteorology).

black light. Ultraviolet light, or electromagnetic radiation whose wavelengths are just shorter than those visible to the human eye. Black light is used to excite certain fluorescent materials, such as some forms of oil and some rocks. When black light strikes a fluorescent material, it causes the material to fluoresce, or give off visible light.

bladder-type fuel cell. A plastic-impregnated fabric bag supported in a portion of an aircraft structure so that it forms a cell in which fuel is carried.

blade (helicopter rotor component). A rotating airfoil driven by a helicopter engine to produce vertical lift.

blade (propeller component). A rotating airfoil driven by an aircraft engine to produce a thrust force approximately in line with the longitudinal axis of the aircraft.

blade (turbine engine compressor component). A rotating airfoil which is part of an axial-flow compressor in a gas turbine engine. The compressor blades, driven by the turbine, accelerate the air as it flows through the engine.

blade alignment (helicopter rotor maintenance). Adjustment of the drag braces or latch pins of a helicopter rotor blade to align the blades about their lead-lag axis. Blade alignment is sometimes called chordwise balance.

blade angle (propeller blade). The angle formed between the face of a propeller blade and its plane of rotation. Blade angle is normally specified at a particular blade station.

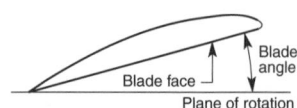

blade angle

blade antenna (radio antenna). A wide-band, quarter-wavelength antenna used on aircraft for communications or navigation in the UHF or VHF bands.

blade area (helicopter rotor). The total area of all of the rotor blades of a helicopter. Blade area is a constant for each helicopter.

blade back (propeller blade). The curved portion of a propeller blade. The back of a propeller blade is the same part of the airfoil as the upper surface of an aircraft wing.

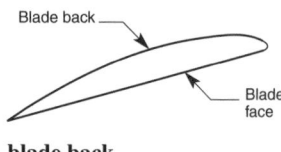

blade back

blade beam (propeller tool). *See* blade wrench.

blade blending (propeller repair). Removing shallow scratches from blades using sanding techniques to restore the blended surface finish to that of the original surface finish.

blade butt (propeller blade). The root end of a propeller blade. The blade butt fits into the hub of the propeller.

blade chord (propeller blade). A straight line through a propeller blade between its leading edge and its trailing edge.

blade coning (helicopter rotor). An upward sweep of rotor blades as a result of lift and centrifugal force.

blade coning angle (helicopter rotor blade). The angle formed between the spanwise axis of a helicopter rotor blade, when the rotor system is producing lift, and a plane at right angles to the rotor mast. The coning angle is caused by the relationship between the centrifugal force acting on the rotor blade and the lift produced by the blades.

blade cuff (propeller blade component). A metal, wood, or plastic cuff installed around the shank of a propeller blade to carry the airfoil shape of the blade all the way to the propeller hub. The airfoil shape of the cuff pulls cooling air into the engine.

blade damper (helicopter rotor blade component). A shock absorbing mechanism installed between a helicopter rotor blade and the hub to dampen lead- and lag-vibrations of the blade.

blade droop (helicopter rotor). The angle formed between the spanwise axis of the rotor blades, when the blades are not rotating, and the plane of rotation of the blades perpendicular to the rotor shaft. The only force acting on the blade to cause droop is gravity.

blade face (propeller blade). The flat surface of a propeller blade. The face of a propeller blade compares with the flat bottom portion of a wing airfoil section. *See* illustration for blade back.

blade feather or feathering (helicopter rotor). The rotation of the blade around its spanwise (pitch change) axis.

blade flap (helicopter rotor). The ability of the rotor blade tip to move in a vertical direction. Blades may flap independently or in unison.

blade flapping (helicopter rotor blades). Movement of a helicopter rotor blade in which the blades rise and descend as they rotate. Blade flapping compensates for asymmetrical lift. The advancing blade flaps up, decreasing its angle of attack and the amount of lift it produces. At the same time, the retreating blade flaps downward, increasing its angle of attack and the amount of lift it produces.

blade grips (helicopter rotor blade component). The portion of a helicopter rotor hub into which the blades fit. Blade grips are sometimes called blade forks. The rotor blade is attached to the blade grip with a lead-lag hinge pin.

blade inspection method (BIM) (helicopter rotor). A system for detecting rotor blade cracking. Each rotor blade has a hollow spar containing pressurized nitrogen gas; the pressure is monitored by a gage wired to a warning light. If a spar cracks, the gas leaks, and the BIM gage warns the pilot that the rotor may fail.

blade lead or lag (helicopter rotor). The fore and aft movement of the blade tip in the plane of rotation; sometimes called hunting or dragging.

blade loading (helicopter rotor blades). The amount of weight each square foot of a helicopter rotor blade supports. Blade loading is found by dividing the total weight of the helicopter by the area of the rotor blades.

    Blade loading is not to be confused with disk loading, which is the total weight of the helicopter divided by the area of the disk swept by the rotor blades.

blade root (propeller blade). The portion of a propeller blade that fits into the hub. The blade root is also called the blade butt.

blade section (propeller blade). A cross section of a propeller blade perpendicular to the span of the blade.

blade shank (propeller blade). The thick, rounded portion of a propeller blade near the hub.

blade span (helicopter rotor blade). The length of a helicopter rotor blade from its tip to its root.

blade stall (helicopter rotor flight condition). A condition of flight of a helicopter when the retreating blade is operating at an angle of attack higher than will allow the air to flow over its upper surface without turbulence. Blade stall occurs when the helicopter is in high-speed forward flight or when it is settling with power.

blade station (propeller blade). The distance, measured in inches, between the center line of the propeller shaft and a location along the blade of a propeller. Blade station measurements are used to identify locations along the blade of a propeller.

blade sweeping (helicopter rotor). The adjustment of chordwise balance of a helicopter rotor by moving the tip of one of the blades backward or forward in its plane of rotation by changing the length of the drag brace.

blade tabs (helicopter rotor component). Fixed tabs mounted on the trailing edge of a helicopter rotor blade. Blade tabs are adjusted to cause the rotor blades to track properly.

blade tip (propeller blade). The part of a propeller blade the greatest distance from the hub.

blade track (helicopter rotor). The condition of a helicopter rotor in which each blade follows in exactly the same path as the blade ahead of it.

blade tracking (helicopter rotor). The maintenance procedure in which the blades of a helicopter rotor are adjusted so the tip of each blade follows the same path as the tip of the blade ahead of it. Blade tracking minimizes vibration by causing the blades to travel in the same plane.

blade twist (helicopter rotor). The progressive change in the angle of incidence of a helicopter rotor blade from root to tip. Blade twist is normally built into the blade when it is manufactured, but some degree of twist can also be caused by aerodynamic forces.

blade twist (propeller blade). The decrease in the pitch angle of a propeller blade as the distance from the hub increases.

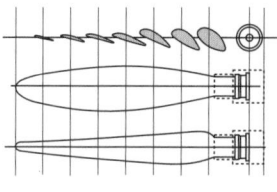

blade twist

The amount of thrust produced by a propeller blade is determined by the pitch angle of the blade and the speed at which the blade is moving through the air. The speed of the blade increases as the distance from the hub increases, so, to maintain a constant thrust along the blade, the blade angle must be decreased—the blade is twisted.

blade wrench (propeller maintenance tool). A paddle-like tool with an airfoil-shaped cutout that is slipped over the propeller blade. A handle on the blade wrench is used to apply a twisting force to the blade. Blade wrenches are also called blade beams.

blank blade (helicopter rotor). A reference point on one blade of a helicopter rotor during electronic balancing. The other blade is referred to as the target blade.

blanket method of aircraft covering. The method of installing fabric on an aircraft structure in which the fabric is applied in the form of a sheet, or blanket, wrapped around the structure and fastened by sewing or cementing it in place.

The other method of installing fabric is the envelope method, in which the fabric is sewed into the form of an envelope and slipped over the structure. The ends are then secured by sewing or cementing.

blanking (sheet metal fabrication). Cutting a large sheet of stock into smaller pieces suitable for the next operation in stamping, such as drawing and forming.

blast fence. A barrier installed on an airport to divert or dissipate jet or propeller blast.

blast pad. A surface adjacent to the ends of a runway provided to reduce the erosive effect of jet blast and propeller wash.

blast valve (hot air balloon). The valve on a propane burner that controls the flow of propane burned to produce heat.

bleed (composite forming). (1) An escape passage at the parting line of a mold, similar to a vent but deeper. It allows material to escape or bleed out. (2) The evacuation of air or gases.

bleed air. Compressed air taken from one or more stages of the compressor of a gas turbine engine. Bleed air is used for anti-icing, deicing, cabin pressurization, and cabin heating or cooling.

bleed orifice. A calibrated orifice, or hole, used in some fluid power systems to allow a controlled flow of fluid while the system is in operation. When the system is shut down, all of the pressure bleeds off through the bleed orifice.

bleed valve (gas turbine engine). A valve in the compressor case of an axial-flow gas turbine engine that allows some of the air to bleed off. By bleeding off some of the pressure, the airflow through the engine is improved, and there is less danger of compressor stall or surge.

bleeder (composite structure component). A material such as glass cloth or mat placed over a composite layup to absorb the excess resin that is forced out of the ply fibers when pressure is applied.

bleeder current. A steady current that flows from the output of a power supply through a bleeder resistor to ground. Bleeder current improves the voltage regulation of a power supply.

bleeder resistor (electrical circuit component). A high-resistance resistor placed between the output of an electrical power supply and ground. The function of a bleeder resistor is to draw a fixed current for improved regulation, or stabilization, and to bleed off high-voltage charges from the capacitors when the equipment is shut off.

bleeding (hydraulic system maintenance). Purging air out of a hydraulic system cylinder and lines.

bleeding brakes (maintenance procedure). A maintenance procedure in which air is removed from the hydraulic fluid in an aircraft brake system. Air in the fluid will compress when the brakes are applied, and the brakes will feel spongy and will not be effective. To bleed the brakes, a bleeder hose is installed in the brake cylinder, and fluid is pumped through the system until no trace of bubbles appears in the fluid.

bleeding dope. Aircraft finishing materials containing certain types of pigments that bleed through any finish applied over them. Bleeding dopes can sometimes be successfully covered with a coat of aluminum-pigmented dope applied before the final topcoats.

bleedout (composites). The excess liquid resin that appears on the surface, primarily during filament winding.

blemish. A visible imperfection that damages an object or destroys its value.

blending (turbine engine maintenance). A method of repairing damaged compressor and turbine blades. The damage is removed and the area is cleaned out with a fine file to form a shallow depression with generous radii. The file marks are then removed with a fine abrasive stone so the surface of the repaired area will match the surface of the rest of the blade.

blimp. The name given to a cigar-shaped, nonrigid airship. Nonrigid airships were originally called limp airships.

blind flight. A term used in the early days of aviation to refer to flight by reference to instruments when the natural horizon is not visible. The term blind flight has been replaced by the more accurate term instrument flight.

blind rivet. A special rivet used in a sheet metal structure that can be installed when there is access to only one side of the metal. The most widely used type of blind rivet has the end of its hollow shank upset by pulling a tapered plug up into the shank.

blind speed (air traffic control). The rate of departure or closing of a target relative to the radar antenna at which the cancellation of the primary radar target by moving target indicator (MTI) circuits in the radar equipment causes a reduction or complete loss of signal.

blind spot (radio operation). An area from which radio transmissions and/or radar echoes cannot be received.

blind spot (visual operation). An area on an airport not visible from the control tower.

blind transmission (radio transmission). A transmission from one station to another in circumstances where two-way communication cannot be established but where it is believed that the called station is able to receive the transmission.

blind velocity (ICAO). The radial velocity of a moving target, such that the target is not seen on primary radars fitted with certain forms of fixed echo suppression.

blinker. An oxygen flow indicator used with a demand oxygen regulator. The indicator appears to blink each time the user inhales.

blink Zyglo. A form of nondestructive inspection of parts subject to vibration. In this method of inspection, the part is cleaned and soaked with a fluorescent penetrant for an appropriate length of time. Then the part is rinsed, and all the penetrant is cleaned from its surface. The part is vibrated while it is being examined under a black light. If the vibration opens up a crack that has accepted some of the penetrant, the crack will show up as a blinking light.

blip (radar indication). A spot of light on a radar scope caused by a received signal, or a return from a reflecting object. Blips are also called echoes.

blisk (turbine engine component). A turbine stage machined from a single slab of steel. The disk and blades are an integral unit.

blister (evidence of corrosion). A raised spot on a piece of metal that contains the salts of corrosion. Corrosion forms under the surface of the metal, and since its salts have so much more volume than the metal they displace, the surface layer of metal is pushed out to form the blister.

blizzard (meteorology). Severe weather conditions characterized by low temperatures and strong winds bearing a great amount of snow, either falling or picked up from the ground.

block altitude. A block of altitudes assigned by ATC to allow altitude deviations; for example, "Maintain block altitude 9 to 11 thousand."

block diagram. A functional diagram of a system in which the units are represented by blocks that describe the functions of the unit and show its relationship to the other units of the system. Arrows between the blocks show the direction of flow of energy or information within the system. Block diagrams do not show any of the actual components.

"Blocked" (air traffic control communications). The phrase used to indicate that a radio transmission has been distorted or interrupted due to multiple simultaneous radio transmissions.

block heater (sheet metalworking tool). An electrical heater embedded in the die used for hot dimpling sheet metal.

blocking capacitor (electronic circuit component). A capacitor having a high impedance to DC and low-frequency AC, but a low impedance, or a small opposition, to the AC signal being passed through the circuit.

block plane. A small handheld woodcutting tool used for cutting across the grain of wood and for planing the ends of a board to make them smooth.

block test (aircraft engine test). An operational test of an aircraft engine installed in a test cell. Block tests are used to determine the condition of the engine.

block-to-block time (aircraft records). The amount of elapsed time between an aircraft leaving the departure ramp for the purpose of flight and its reaching the arrival ramp at the end of the flight.

bloom (metal processing). A semifinished mass of steel formed from an ingot in the process of being rolled into a billet.

blowback (helicopter operation). The tendency of the rotor disc to tilt aft in forward flight as a result of flapping.

blow-by (reciprocating engine malfunction). The loss of pressure in the engine cylinder caused by leakage past the piston rings.

blow-down turbine (reciprocating engine component). A power-recovery device used in the exhaust system of a reciprocating engine.

blower. A mechanical device, such as a fan, used to move a volume of air.

blower (reciprocating engine component). An internal gear-driven supercharger in an aircraft reciprocating engine. Blowers increase the pressure of the air after it passes through the carburetor and improve the uniformity of the distribution of the fuel-air mixture to all the cylinders.

blower section (reciprocating engine crankcase section). The section of an aircraft reciprocating engine crankcase that houses the internal, gear-driven supercharger.

blow-in doors. Spring-loaded doors in the inlet duct of some turbojet or turbofan engine installations that are opened by an air pressure differential when the inlet air pressure becomes a certain amount lower than that of the ambient air. Air flowing through the doors adds to the normal inlet air passing through the engine and helps prevent compressor stall.

blowing dust (meteorology). Dust particles picked up locally from the surface and blown about in clouds or sheets.

blowing sand (meteorology). Sand picked up locally from the surface and blown about in clouds or sheets.

blowing snow (meteorology). Snow picked up locally from the surface by the wind and carried to a height of six feet or more.

blowing spray (meteorology). Water particles picked up by the wind from the surface of a large body of water.

blow molding. A form of plastic molding in which a hollow tube of thermoplastic material is heated inside a mold. Air pressure is applied to the inside of the tube, and the soft plastic material is forced out against the walls of the mold. The outside of the part takes the form of the inside of the mold. The mold is then opened and the molded part removed. A blow-down turbine is a velocity-type turbine driven by the exhaust gases from the engine and coupled through a fluid coupling to the engine crankshaft. Blow-down turbines are also called power-recovery turbines, or PRTs.

blown boundary layer control (aerodynamics). A method of decreasing aerodynamic drag on the surface of an airplane wing. The boundary layer is the layer of air which flows in a random fashion directly over the surface of the wing.

Blown boundary layer control uses high-velocity air blown through ducts or jets to energize, or add energy to, the boundary layer. Energizing this air speeds it up and causes it to flow straight across the wing.

blowout plug. A safety plug on the outside skin of an aircraft fuselage near the installation of high-pressure oxygen or fire extinguisher agent. If, for any reason, the pressure of the gas in the cylinders rises to a dangerous level, the blowout plug will blow out and relieve the pressure. Colored disks in the blowout plugs identify the system that has been relieved in this manner.

blowtorch. A handheld torch that uses liquid gasoline as a fuel. Air is pumped into the fuel tank, and the liquid fuel sprays out into the burner where it becomes a vapor. The air compressed in the tank blows through the flame and intensifies it.

Gasoline blowtorches have been replaced, to a great extent, by torches using propane or other liquified petroleum products as their fuel.

bluckets (turbofan engine component). The portions of aft-fan blades that are in the exhaust of the core engine. Bluckets drive the fan by energy received from the hot gases leaving the core engine.

blue line (instrument marking). A blue radial line is used on an aircraft instrument to indicate a special operating condition. A blue line on the airspeed indicator of a mul-tiengine airplane indicates the best single-engine rate of climb speed. On a helicopter airspeed indicator, it indicates the maximum safe autorotation speed.

blueprint. A type of engineering drawing used in the design and manufacture of aircraft, aircraft engines, and various components. Lines in the drawing appear white on a dark blue background.

The original drawing is made with black ink on translucent drawing paper or cloth. This drawing is then used as a negative, and sensitized paper is exposed through the drawing by exposing it to a high-intensity light. After the exposure, the print is developed by washing it in water.

Blueprints have been replaced in many engineering departments by prints made by the Ozalid process, in which the exposed sensitized paper is developed by exposing it to ammonia fumes.

blush (aircraft finishing system defect). A defect in a lacquer or dope finish caused by moisture condensing on the surface before the finish dries. If the humidity of the air is high, the evaporation of the solvents cools the air enough to cause the moisture to condense. The water condensed from the air mixes with the lacquer or dope and forms a dull, porous, chalky-looking finish. This is called blush. A blushed finish is neither attractive nor protective.

BMEP (brake mean effective pressure). The average pressure inside the cylinder of a reciprocating engine during the power stroke. BMEP, measured in pounds per square inch, relates to the torque produced by the engine, and can be calculated when the brake horsepower and RPM of the engine are known.

B-nut. A type of tubing nut used to attach a piece of flared tubing to a threaded fitting. B-nuts are used with a sleeve slipped over the tubing before the tubing is flared. The B-nut forces the sleeve tight against the flare, which seals against the flare cone of the male fitting.

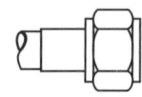

B-nut

board-foot. A unit of measurement commonly used for lumber. One board-foot is the amount of lumber in a piece of wood one foot long, one foot wide, and one inch thick. A board-foot is also used for the dimensions of any piece of board whose volume is equal to 144 cubic inches.

bob weight (aircraft control system component). A mechanical weight in the elevator control system of some airplanes. The bob weight is used to apply a nose-down force on the elevator control system. This force is counteracted by an aerodynamic force caused by the elevator trim tab. If the aircraft slows down enough that the aerodynamic force on the trim tab is lost, the bob weight forces the nose down, and the airplane picks up speed.

bogie landing gear (aircraft landing gear). The landing gear of an aircraft that uses tandem wheels mounted along the center line of the aircraft fuselage. Some aircraft having bogie landing gear are supported while parked by outrigger wheels mounted far out on the wing.

bogus parts. Parts not approved for use in aircraft maintenance. Bogus parts are normally made to look like legitimate parts. They carry the same part number as the legitimate part, and are often packaged in boxes that look like the box in which the original part was sold. When bogus parts are installed in an aircraft, safety is often compromised.

boiling point. The temperature at which a liquid begins to change into a gas. The boiling point of a liquid varies with the pressure of the air above it. The boiling point of water, under standard sea level conditions, is 212°F, or 100°C.

bolt. A threaded fastener which has an enlarged head on one end and threads on the other. Bolts used in aircraft normally have hexagonal heads, but some high-strength bolts have a round head with a hexagonal-shaped hole. These special bolts are turned with an Allen wrench. Bolts fasten pieces of material together by clamping them between the bolt head and a nut screwed onto the bolt threads.

bolt boss. The raised section of a casting where the bolt is passed through.

bomb tester (spark plug tester). A shop tool used to test spark plugs after they have been cleaned and gapped. After a spark plug has been serviced, it is screwed into the bomb tester, and about 200-psi air pressure is applied to the firing end. High voltage is directed into the terminal cavity of the spark plug, and the electrodes are observed to see the type and amount of spark being produced. If a spark plug operates properly in a bomb tester, it will almost always work properly when it is installed in an aircraft engine.

bomber. A military aircraft designed to carry a bomb load over enemy territory and release it in such a way that it will do the maximum amount of damage.

bond (chemical force). The strong attractive force that holds the atoms together in a molecule.

bonded structure. Aircraft structure joined together by chemical methods, rather than mechanical fasteners. Components made of laminated fiberglass, honeycomb material, and the advanced composite materials are examples of aircraft bonded structure.

Bonderizing. The registered trade name for a patented process of coating steel parts with a phosphate film. Bonderizing protects the parts from corrosion.

bonding (electrical). The process of electrically connecting all isolated components to the aircraft structure. Bonding provides a path for return current from the components and provides a low-impedance path to ground to minimize radio interference from static electrical charges collected on the component. Shock-mounted instrument panels have bonding braids connected across the shock mounts, so that return current from the instruments can flow into the main structure and thus return to the alternator or battery.

bonding (structural). A method of joining parts by using chemical adhesives, rather than any form of mechanical fastener.

bonding agent (structural). An adhesive used to bond together materials used in aircraft construction.

bonding braid (electrical bonding). A flat copper braid used to electrically connect isolated components to the aircraft structure to drain off any static electrical charges that could otherwise build up high enough to cause a spark, or interfere with electronic equipment.

bonding jumper (electrical systems). A low-resistance wire or metal strap used to connect a structural component or an electrical component to the basic structure of an aircraft. Bonding jumpers carry the return current from an electrical component back to the battery. Small bonding jumpers connect flight control surfaces to the main structure to carry static electrical charges that build up when air flows over the surface into the main structure. Bonding prevents sparks that could cause radio interference.

bond ply (composites). The ply of fabric that comes in contact with the honeycomb core in a repair.

bond strength. The stress required to rupture a bond formed by an adhesive between two objects.

bonnet assembly (fire extinguisher). The connector between a high-rate discharge (HRD) bottle of fire extinguishing agent and the line that carries the agent to the discharge point. An electrically ignited powder charge blows a cutter through a frangible disk that seals the bottle and allows the instantaneous discharge of the agent.

Boolean algebra (mathematics). A system of mathematical logic used to permit computations to be performed by binary electrical circuits. Gates such as AND, OR, NAND, NOR, and EXCLUSIVE OR are used to make electrical models of the Boolean algebraic functions.

boost (manifold pressure). A term for manifold pressure which has been increased above atmospheric pressure by a supercharger.

boost charge (batteries). A constant-voltage charge given to a partially discharged storage battery for a short period of time.

boost pump (aircraft fuel system component). An electrically driven centrifugal pump mounted in the bottom of the fuel tanks in large aircraft.

Boost pumps are used to provide a positive flow of fuel under pressure to the engine for starting and to serve as an emergency backup in the event the engine-driven pump should fail. They are also used to transfer fuel from one tank to another and to pump fuel overboard when it is being dumped.

Continued

boost pump (aircraft fuel system component). *Continued*
Boost pumps maintain pressure on the fuel in the line to the engine-driven pump to prevent a vapor lock forming in these lines. Centrifugal boost pumps have a small agitator propeller on top of the pump impeller. This agitator causes the vapors in the fuel to be released before the fuel leaves the tank.

boost system (flight controls). A hydraulic system that assists in the movement of flight controls.

boost venturi. A small, auxiliary venturi whose discharge is located in the throat of a larger venturi. Boost venturis increase the pressure drop produced by the main venturi. They are installed in such devices as carburetors and in the large venturi tubes used to provide the low pressure for some vacuum-operated flight instruments.

boosted brake (aircraft hydraulic brake). A form of power brake which uses hydraulic system pressure to help the pilot apply force to the brake master cylinder. When the brake pedal is depressed, hydraulic system pressure acts on the piston in the brake master cylinder to apply the brakes. Boosted brakes and power brakes are not the same. Power brake systems use hydraulic system pressure in the brake wheel cylinders themselves.

boosted control system (aircraft flight controls). Flight controls of large, high-performance aircraft actuated by hydraulic cylinders. Hydraulic fluid under pressure is directed into the cylinders by valves actuated by the cockpit flight controls.

booster coil (ignition system component). An induction coil excited by pulsating DC supplied by the aircraft battery and a vibrator. Booster coils produce a high voltage, which is directed to an auxiliary trailing finger on the rotor of the magneto distributor. When this high voltage jumps to ground across the electrodes of the spark plug, it produces a hot and late spark for starting the engine.

booster magneto. A small, auxiliary, hand-cranked magneto used with some of the older aircraft engines to provide a hot, retarded spark for starting the engine.

bootstrapping. A self-initiating or self-sustaining action. In a turbocharger system, bootstrapping describes a transient increase in engine power that causes the turbocharger to speed up, which in turn causes the engine to produce more power. The word bootstrap comes from the figure of speech "a person lifts himself by his own bootstraps."

bore (dimension). The diameter of a round hole. The distance across the hole at its widest point.

bore (engine dimension). The diameter of the inside of the cylinder of a reciprocating engine.

borescope (inspection instrument). An instrument used to examine the inside of a structure through a very small hole. The inside of a turbine engine and the inside of the cylinder of a reciprocating engine, for example, can be examined by inserting the probe of the borescope through a small inspection hole or through a spark plug hole.
A borescope furnishes its own light, and some borescopes have different ranges of magnification. Some borescopes are fitted to a camera to photograph the inside of the structure. A modern trend in borescopes is to place a video pickup on the borescope tube and display the results on a small television screen.

boric acid. A white crystal (H_3BO_3) that can be dissolved in water to make a weak acid solution. A boric acid solution can be used to neutralize spilled electrolyte from nickel-cadmium batteries.

boring (machining operation). A method of increasing the size of a hole in a piece of material by cutting it with a rotary cutting tool.

boron. A soft, brown, nonmetallic, trivalent chemical element. Boron's symbol is B, its atomic number is 5, and its atomic weight is 10.811. Boron is used to add stiffness and strength to some of the modern composite structural materials, and to dope silicon or germanium to make a P-type semiconductor material.

boron fiber (composites). A fiber, usually of a tungsten-filament core, with elemental boron vapor deposited on it to impart strength and stiffness properties.

boss. An enlarged area in a casting or machined part. A boss provides additional material to strengthen the part where holes are drilled for mounting or attaching parts.

bottle bar. A special bucking bar with a recessed hole to hold a rivet set.

bottled gas. Any gas stored in heavy steel containers, with the gas kept under pressure. Acetylene, propane, oxygen, and nitrogen are commonly used bottled gases.

bottom. *See* cone bottoming.

bottom dead center (reciprocating engine piston position). The position of the piston in a reciprocating engine cylinder when the piston is at the bottom of its stroke and the wrist pin, crankpin, and center of the crankshaft are all in line.

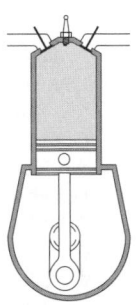

bottoming reamer (metalworking tool). A reamer used to smooth and enlarge blind holes. The blades of a bottoming reamer are parallel; they have no taper.

bottoming tap (metalworking tool). A tool used to cut threads all the way to the bottom of a hole. A bottoming tap has a flat end and no taper. It is used after the hole has been partially tapped with a plug tap.

bottom-of-descent point. The end point of the descent, as calculated by the FMS/RNAV.

bottom dead center

boundary layer (aerodynamics). The layer of air that flows next to an aerodynamic surface. Because of the design of the surface and local surface roughness, the boundary layer often has a random flow pattern, sometimes even flowing in a direction opposite to the direction of flight. A turbulent boundary layer causes a great deal of aerodynamic drag.

boundary-layer control. A method of decreasing aerodynamic drag caused by the turbulent flow of the boundary layer. Boundary-layer control can use either a high-velocity blast of air to blow the random-flowing air off the surface, or it can use a low pressure inside the structure to suck the boundary layer air off the surface through tiny holes or slots.

boundary lights. Lights defining the perimeter of an airport or landing area. *See* airport lighting.

Bourdon tube. The measuring element used in certain types of pressure-measuring instruments. A thin-walled metal tube, having an elliptical cross section, is formed into a curve. One end of the tube is sealed and is connected to an arm that moves a pointer. The other end of the tube is open and is secured to the instrument case. The pressure to be measured is connected to the open end of the tube, and this pressure causes the elliptical cross section to try to become round and thus begin to straighten the tube. The amount the tube straightens is proportional to the pressure inside the tube, and as it straightens, it moves a pointer across the calibrated instrument dial.

bow. Front end of floats or the hull of a flying boat.

BOW (basic operating weight). The weight of an aircraft, including the crew, ready for flight but without payload and fuel. This term applies only to transport category aircraft.

Bowden cable (aircraft control system). A form of control system which uses a spring steel wire, enclosed inside a helically wound wire casing. A Bowden cable transmits both pushing and pulling motion to the device being actuated. Bowden cable systems are often used for moving such aircraft engine controls as the throttle and the mixture control.

bowline knot. A handy knot used for such aeronautical purposes as securing an aircraft to prevent wind damage. A properly tied bowline knot will not slip, and it is easy to untie.

bow wave (supersonic aircraft flight). A shock wave which forms when an aircraft is flying at a speed faster than the speed of sound, a speed greater than Mach one. A bow wave either forms immediately ahead of the aircraft or is attached to the nose of the aircraft.

box beam (aircraft structural member). The main spanwise structural member of a wing made in the form of a box. Tensile and compressive stresses are carried in the top and the bottom of the box beam, and the sides act as webs to give the beam rigidity. The top and bottom of the box beam oppose the greatest loads and are the strongest parts of the beam. A box beam is also called a box spar.

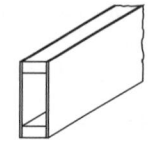

box beam

box brake (metal-forming shop tool). A metal-forming machine similar to a leaf, or cornice, brake. It is used to make straight bends across a piece of sheet metal. The holding jaws of a box brake are made in the form of fingers. All four sides of a box can be formed on a box brake by allowing the sides that have been bent to fit between the fingers of the clamp while the last bends are being made. A box brake is also called a finger brake.

boxing of paint. A mixing procedure in which the pigment in a can of paint is thoroughly mixed with the vehicle. The paint is poured back and forth between two containers until the pigment and the vehicle are completely and uniformly mixed.

box spar. *See* box beam.

box wrench (mechanic's hand tool). A wrench with an enclosed end shaped with six, eight, or twelve points to fit a square- or hexagonal-head bolt or nut. Box wrenches can be used in close spaces, and they can be used to apply a greater force than can be applied with an open-end wrench.

Boyle's law. One of the basic gas laws, which states that the product found by multiplying the pressure of a gas by its volume is always constant. If the volume of a container of gas is decreased without changing the absolute temperature of the gas, the pressure of the gas will increase.

brace. A part of a structure that supports or strengthens the main load-carrying portion of the structure.

bracing wires. High strength steel wires with threaded ends used to align and stabilize some flight surfaces and floats.

bracketing (flight procedure). A series of minor corrections left or right as required, to maintain or regain the desired course.

brad. A thin wire nail with a small-diameter, barrel-shaped head.

brad-point drill. A special drill used for drilling cured Kevlar-reinforced composite materials. The tendency of Kevlar fibers to pull and stretch when they are cut with a drill is minimized by using a brad-point drill.

brad-point drill

braid (electrical shielding and bonding component). A woven metal tube used to encase a wire carrying alternating current. This braid, called shielding, intercepts the electromagnetic field produced by the AC and prevents the field causing radio interference. Braid can also be flattened and used as a bonding strap, to conduct static electricity away from a component insulated by shock mounts. Bonding helps reduce static electricity that causes radio interference.

braided shield (electrostatic shielding). A cable shield that is applied by braiding bunches of copper strands, called picks, around an insulated, center conductor.

brake (aircraft landing gear component). A mechanism inside an aircraft wheel used to apply friction to the wheel to slow or stop its rotation.

brake (sheet metalworking tool). A metalworking shop tool used to make straight bends across sheets of metal. Brakes can be adjusted to make bends with the proper bend radius and bends having the correct number of degrees. *See* box brake, cornice brake, finger brake, and press brake.

brake back plate (aircraft landing gear component). A floating plate in an energizing-type brake to which the wheel cylinder and the brake shoes attach.

brake caliper (disk brake component). A hydraulically operated clamp that holds the brake linings on either side of a brake disk. When the brakes are applied, the calipers squeeze the linings tight against the disk to produce the required friction.

brake horsepower. *See* BHP. *14 CFR Part 1:* "The power delivered to the propeller shaft (main drive or main output) of an aircraft engine."

brake line. *See* sight line.

brake lining (aircraft landing gear component). A material with a high coefficient of friction and the ability to maintain its friction and strength when it is hot. Brake linings were at one time made with asbestos, but modern brake linings contain no asbestos.

brake mean effective pressure. *See* BMEP.

brake puck. Small, easily replaceable pads of brake lining material used in disk brakes. One or more pucks are on each side of the disk, and when the brakes are applied the pucks are forced tightly against the disk to supply the required friction. *See* brake lining (aircraft landing gear component).

brake specific fuel consumption. *See* BSFC.

braking action advisories. A condition noted in an ATIS broadcast when the tower has received a runway braking action report of "poor" or "nil." When a braking action advisory is in effect, ATC will issue the latest braking action report for the runway in use to all arriving and departing pilots.

braking action report. A report of conditions on the airport movement area providing a pilot with a degree/quality of braking that he might expect. Braking action is reported in terms of good, fair, poor, or nil.

branching. A programming technique that allows users of interactive video, multimedia courseware, or online training to choose from several courses of action in moving from one sequence to another.

brashness (wood condition). A condition of wood which causes it to have low shock resistance so that it fails abruptly when it is bent.

brass. An alloy of copper and zinc made up of approximately 67% copper and 33% zinc. Brass is malleable and ductile and is used for certain types of aircraft hardware and locking wire (safety wire) where corrosion resistance is important.

Brayton thermodynamic cycle. The constant-pressure cycle of energy release used to describe the action of a gas turbine engine. Fuel is added to the air passing through the engine and is burned. Heat from the burning fuel-air mixture expands the air, and since this air is not confined, it accelerates as it moves through the engine.

The Brayton cycle, a constant-pressure cycle, is an open cycle because all the events, compression, combustion, expansion, and exhaust take place at the same time, but in different locations within the engine.

The Brayton cycle differs from the Otto cycle used in reciprocating engines because the Otto cycle is a constant-volume cycle. *See* Otto thermodynamic cycle.

braze welding. A method of joining pieces of metal by wetting their surfaces with a molten brass alloy. The brass rod used for braze welding melts at a temperature above 800°F, but below the melting temperature of the metals being joined. Braze welding differs from brazing in that it does not use capillary action to pull the molten alloy between the pieces of metal being joined.

brazier-head rivet. A thin protruding-head rivet that was at one time popular for aircraft sheet metal construction. Brazier-head rivets have been superseded and may be replaced by MS20470 (AN 470) universal-head rivets.

brazing. A method of joining metals by allowing capillary action to pull molten, nonferrous filler metal between close-fitting parts. When the filler metal solidifies, it holds the parts together. Brazing differs from soldering in the melting temperature of the filler metals used. Soldering uses filler metals that melt at temperatures below 800°F, and brazing metals melt at temperatures above 800°F.

breadboard (electrical circuit). A device for building experimental electrical circuits that allows the components to be temporarily connected into the circuit, making it easy to exchange components. After a circuit functions as it should on the breadboard, and all the correct components are chosen, the circuit is redesigned into its final configuration.

   Many modern circuits are first built on solderless breadboards that allow the substitution of parts without their having to be soldered into the circuit.

break-before-make switch (type of electrical switch). A form of double-throw switch that breaks one circuit before it makes contact with the other circuit.

break line (aircraft drawings). A wavy line or a line containing a series of zig-zags, used to show that a part of the component has been left off the drawing.

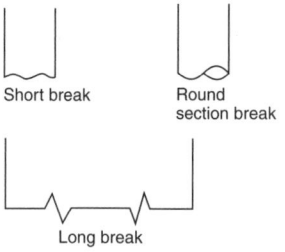

Short break

Round section break

Long break

break lines

breakdown voltage (electrical component rating). The voltage that must be placed across the dielectric in an electrical or electronic component to cause the dielectric to break down and conduct current.

breaker-point bounce. A condition in which the breaker points in an aircraft magneto bounce open, rather than remaining closed when the cam follower moves off of the cam lobe. Breaker-point bounce is caused by a weak breaker-point spring.

breaker points (magneto component). Electrical contacts in the primary circuit of an aircraft magneto that are opened by a cam turned by the engine. The breaker points are timed to open at the instant the ignition spark should occur. When the points open, the primary current stops flowing, and its magnetic field collapses.

   The lines of flux from the collapsing primary magnetic field cut across the many turns of the secondary winding and induce a high voltage in the secondary circuit. It is this high secondary voltage that causes a spark to jump across the gap in the spark plug.

breakers (tire component). Layers of reinforcing fabric (cords) in an aircraft tire between the casing plies and the tread rubber. Breakers protect the casing plies and strengthen the tire.

breakout (air traffic control). A technique used to direct aircraft out of the approach stream. In the context of close parallel operations, a breakout is used to direct threatened aircraft away from a deviating aircraft.

breast drill. A handheld drill motor used to drill relatively large holes in wood or metal. The handle of the drill motor is fitted with a curved plate that allows the user to apply a pushing force with his upper body as the drill cuts the hole.

breather (engine lubricating system). A vent line in an aircraft engine that allows the air pressure inside the engine crankcase to be the same as the pressure of the surrounding air. An effective breather system prevents pressure building up inside the engine and forcing oil out of the crankcase.

breather-pressurizing valve (turbine engine lubrication system component). An aneroid-operated valve in the overboard vent line of the lubrication system of some turbine engines. The breather-pressurizing valve is open at sea level, but closes with increasing altitude to maintain sea level pressure inside the vent system as the aircraft goes up in altitude.

breech chamber (cartridge-pneumatic starter). A locking chamber in a cartridge starter that holds a pyrotechnic cartridge (a powder charge). The cartridge is placed in the breech, the breech is closed and locked, and the cartridge is fired. The expanding gases produced by the burning powder spin the turbine in the starter.

breeder reactor (nuclear energy). A reactor that produces fissionable material as well as consuming it.

bridge circuit (electrical circuit). An electrical circuit containing four impedances connected in such a way that their schematic diagram forms a square. One pair of diagonally opposite corners is connected to an input device, and the other two corners are connected to the output device. *See* illustration for balanced bridge.

bridge-type rectifier. An electrical rectifier circuit using four diodes to change alternating current into full-wave rectified direct current.

bridging (composites). The condition in which fibers do not move into or conform to radii and corners during molding. This results in voids and dimensional control problems.

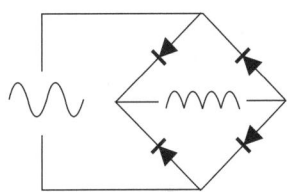

bridge-type rectifier

briefing. An oral presentation where the speaker presents a concise array of facts without inclusion of extensive supporting material.

bright band (radar meteorology). A narrow, intense echo on the range-height indicator scope resulting from water-covered ice particles of high reflectivity at the melting level.

brine (heat treatment of metal). A solution of salt (sodium chloride) and water, used as a quenching medium in the heat treatment of metal. Steel parts quenched in brine are harder than parts quenched in either water or oil.

Brinell hardness test. A method of measuring the hardness of metal. A hardened steel sphere is pressed into the surface of the metal by a specific force and is held for a specified period of time. The force is removed and the diameter of the indentation caused by the ball is measured with a special microscope. The larger the diameter of the dent, the softer the metal.

brinelling (bearing damage). A form of damage to the hardened surface of a bearing roller or race caused by excessive radial loads on the bearings. When a bearing is overloaded, the rollers are forced into the race, and they leave small dips (indentations) in the race or flat spots on the surface of the roller. Bearings that have been brinelled must be replaced.

British thermal unit. *See* Btu.

brittleness. A physical characteristic of a material that causes it to break, or fracture, without bending or distorting in any appreciable amount. Brittleness is the opposite of malleability.

broaching (metalworking procedure). The process of removing excess metal by pushing or pulling a cutting tool through a hole or the inside of a cylinder. The points inside a socket wrench are cut by broaching.

broad-band antenna (radio antenna). A radio antenna capable of receiving or transmitting a broad band of frequencies.

broadcast. The transmission of information not addressed to a specific station or person, and for which no acknowledgment is expected.

broadcast (ICAO). A transmission of information relating to air navigation that is not addressed to a specific station or stations.

broadcast weather service. A weather service that prepares weather products and transmits them to participating aircraft, also known as a data link weather service.

broken-line graph. A type of graph used to show the way values change. The horizontal axis of the graph represents time, and the vertical axis represents the changing value. Straight lines are used to connect points that show the values at each plotted time.

bromine. A heavy, volatile, corrosive, reddish-brown, nonmetallic, liquid chemical element. Bromine's symbol is Br, its atomic number is 35, and its atomic weight is 79.904. Bromine is used as an antiknock additive for gasoline and as a component in dyes.

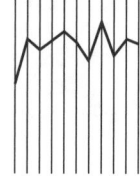

broken-line graph

bronze. A copper alloy containing tin and sometimes small amounts of zinc and phosphorus. Bronze's low coefficient of friction makes it useful for bearings and bushings.

brush (electrical component). The component in an electric motor or generator through which current flows into and out of the armature. Brushes used in generators are made of a carbon compound, and they slide over the surface of the copper commutator bars. Current induced into the armature windings is brought out of the windings through the brushes. Starter motor bushes which must carry large amounts of current are often made of a copper alloy.

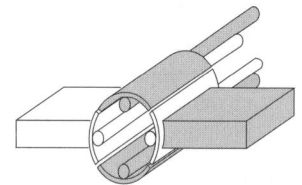

brush and commutator

brush (paintbrush). A device used to apply paint to a surface. A paintbrush is made by attaching a bundle of bristles to a wood or plastic handle. The bristles are made of animal hair or synthetic fibers. The bristles are dipped into the paint and then moved over the surface to be painted. Good quality brushes allow the paint to flow out smoothly over the surface.

brush guard (helicopter tail rotor protector). A protective frame at the tail of a single-rotor helicopter used to protect the tail rotor from damage during ground operation.

BSFC (brake specific fuel consumption). A measure of the amount of fuel used for a given amount of power developed by a heat engine. BSFC is expressed in pounds of fuel burned per hour for each brake horsepower the engine is developing.

BTC. *See* before top center.

Btu (British thermal unit). A unit of heat measurement. The amount of heat energy needed to raise the temperature of 1 pound of pure water from 60° to 61°F.

bubble. A small volume of gas entrapped in a liquid.

bubble memory (computer memory). A method of digital data storage in which individual bits (0s and 1s) are stored in the form of extremely small localized magnetic fields in a thin film of magnetic crystalline material. Bits of stored data can be moved about by the use of an external magnetic field.

bubble octant (navigation instrument). A type of celestial navigation instrument. A bubble level in the octant provides an artificial horizon which allows the navigator to find the angle between a line tangent to the earth's surface (the horizon) and a line to the stars being used for navigation.

bucket. Colloquial, or informal, term for a turbine blade.

bucket wheel. A turbine wheel in a turbosupercharger or in a gas turbine engine.

bucking (rivet bucking). The process in which a shop head is formed on a solid aircraft rivet. The rivet is inserted into holes drilled through the metal sheets being joined. The manufactured head of the rivet is hammered with a pneumatic hammer through a rivet set that fits the shape of the head.

A hardened-steel bucking bar is held against the shank of the rivet, and the hammering causes the end of the shank to expand and become shorter, forming the shop head that clamps the metal pieces together.

bucking bar (sheet metalworking tool). A heavy steel block or bar with smooth, hardened surfaces, or faces. A bucking bar is held flat against the end of the shank of a solid rivet when the head is driven with a rivet gun. Driving the rivet flattens the end of the shank against the bucking bar and forms the bucked, or shop, head.

bucking voltage. A voltage used to oppose another voltage. When one voltage is bucked by another which has the same value but opposite polarity, the result is zero voltage.

buckle (sheet metal damage). A wrinkle or kink in the surface of a sheet metal aircraft structure caused by an excessive bending or compressive load on the structure.

buckling (composites). A failure mode usually caused by compressive action and characterized by fiber deflection rather than breaking.

buffer (digital electronic component). A digital electronic component that has one input and one output, with the output having the same condition as the input. A buffer is used to isolate an input or strengthen a signal.

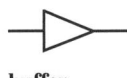

buffer

buffer amplifier (electronic circuit). An amplifier used to isolate one circuit from another circuit. Buffer amplifiers prevent one circuit from loading the other and causing it to operate improperly.

buffet (aerodynamic force). Turbulent movement of the air over an aerodynamic surface. Buffeting can cause flight control problems ranging from a vibration, or buzzing, felt in the controls, to a complete loss of control.

bug (instrument marker). A movable marker on a flight instrument that may be set to reference a particular indication of the instrument. A bug on the airspeed indicator can be set to reference a particular airspeed for the pilot or the airspeed-hold function of an autopilot to hold. A bug on the horizontal situation indicator can be used to direct the automatic pilot to turn to and hold the heading on which the bug is set.

bug (malfunction). A commonly used term for anything that prevents a system or component functioning as it should. This term has gained much use in the field of computer programs in which some small error can keep the program from working. Most newly written programs must be debugged before they work as they should.

bug light (aircraft maintenance tool). A handy tool for rough troubleshooting an aircraft electrical system. A bug light has a flashlight bulb and batteries to check for continuity in the aircraft wiring, and a bulb of the proper voltage to check for the presence of voltage in the part of the system being examined.

building block concept. A concept of learning that maintains that new knowledge and skills are best based on a solid foundation of previous experience and/or old learning. As knowledge and skills increase, the base expands, supporting further learning.

build-up and vent valve (liquid oxygen system). A manually operated valve on a liquid-oxygen converter used to control the amount of pressure inside the converter. When the valve is in the build-up position, pressure inside the converter is allowed to build up to a preset value. When the valve is moved to the vent position, gaseous oxygen is vented into the atmosphere without building up pressure.

bulb angle (aircraft structural material). An L-shaped metal extrusion having an enlarged, rounded edge that resembles a bulb on one of its legs. A bulb angle is used to provide stiffness to a structure, while keeping the weight to a minimum.

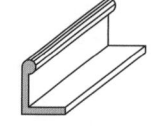

bulb angle

bulb root (turbine blade attachment method). A rounded end on a turbine blade that mates with a rounded hole in the periphery of the turbine disk, or wheel. Bulb-root blades are loose when the wheel is cold to allow for different rates of expansion between the blades and the wheel, while holding the blade against the centrifugal loads. Other types of blade roots are the dovetail and the fir-tree.

bulk cargo. Cargo capable of being stacked on the floor of the aircraft carrying it.

bulkhead. A structural partition that divides the fuselage of an aircraft into compartments or bays. A bulkhead strengthens the structure and acts as a wall.

bumping (sheet metal forming method). A method of shrinking or stretching sheet metal into compound curves by hand-hammering it into a sandbag or into or around wood or metal forming blocks.

bundled cable. An electrical cable made up of individually insulated wires. A bundled cable is tied together with lacing cord or with special plastic wire-wrapping straps.

bungee cord. An elastic cord made of a series of small strips of rubber or rubber bands. These strips or bands are encased in a braided cloth cover that holds and protects the rubber, yet allows the rubber to stretch. Bungee cords are used in some of the simpler aircraft landing gears to absorb shock, and the energy in a stretched bungee cord may be used to crank a large aircraft reciprocating engine.

buntover (gyroplane operation). The tendency of a gyroplane to pitch forward when rotor force is removed.

buoyancy. The uplifting force produced on an object when it is placed in a fluid. If a block of wood is placed in a container of water, the wood will displace some of the water, and the water on the outside of the block will push against it. The buoyancy, or the force with which the water pushes on the block, is the same as the weight of the water displaced by the block. When the block floats, it displaces, or takes the place of, its own weight of water.

burble (aerodynamic turbulence). Turbulence which forms on an airfoil surface when the angle of attack becomes so great that the air no longer flows smoothly over the surface but breaks away.

burble point (aerodynamic turbulence). The angle of attack at which air flowing over an aerodynamic surface no longer flows smoothly, but breaks away and forms a turbulent flow (it burbles).

burn (balloon operations). A common term meaning to activate the main blast valve and produce a full flame for the purpose of heating the air in the envelope.

burn-down coat (aircraft finishing system). A coat of lacquer or dope in which some of the thinner is replaced with an equal amount of retarder. When this mixture is sprayed over a blushed surface, the thinner softens and restores the blushed material. The retarder slows the drying so the new film will not blush.

burner. *See* combustor.

burner cans (gas turbine engine component). Individual combustion chambers of a gas turbine engine.

burner compartment. The portion of an engine pod or nacelle of a turbojet-powered aircraft that houses the burner section of the engine.

burner pressure (gas turbine engine parameter). The static pressure inside the combustors, or burners, of a gas turbine engine. Burner pressure, whose symbol is Pb, is one of the parameters used to compute the mass airflow through the engine.

burning. The process in which a material is consumed by fire. The material, called the fuel, is consumed when it reacts with the oxygen in the air to form new compounds. These compounds usually include carbon dioxide and water. In the process of burning, a large amount of heat and light are usually produced.

burning in (electronic components). A process in the manufacture of sensitive electronic equipment in which the equipment is operated for a specified period of time. The burning-in period shows up weak or faulty components, and stabilizes the operating characteristics of the components.

burning point (petroleum specification). The lowest temperature at which a petroleum product in an open container will continue to burn when it is ignited by an open flame held near its surface.

burnish (*verb*). To smooth the surface of metal that has been damaged by a deep scratch or gouge. The metal that has piled up at the edge of the damage is pushed back into the damage with a smooth, hard steel burnishing tool.

burr (type of metal damage). A sharp, rough edge of a piece of metal left when the metal is sheared, punched, or drilled.

burst RPM (gas turbine engine parameter). The compressor speed of an engine at which the centrifugal loads are so high the compressor will fly apart. The engine actually explodes.

bus (electrical system). A point within an electrical system from which the individual circuits get their power.

bus bar (aircraft electrical system component). A power distribution point in an aircraft electrical system. Bus bars are usually strips of metal to which generator or battery power is connected and from which circuit breakers pick up this power and carry it to the appropriate circuits within the aircraft.

bus tie breaker. A circuit breaker used to connect two electrical bus bars.

bushing. A type of friction bearing consisting of a removable cylinder made of some material, such as bronze, that has a low coefficient of friction. The bushing is pressed into a hole, and it is reamed to a size that fits the shaft with the correct amount of clearance for lubrication. Some bushings are made of Oilite, a porous bronze material that is impregnated with oil and requires no additional lubrication.

butt fusion. A method of joining two pieces of thermoplastic material. Butt fusion is done by heating the ends of the two pieces until they are in a molten state and forcing them together before they cool and harden.

butt joint (welded joint). A type of welded joint in which the pieces of metal to be joined are placed so their edges touch, but do not overlap. The edges of both pieces of metal are melted, and filler rod is added to form a bead between the two pieces.

butt rib (wing rib). The rib at the inboard end of a wing panel.

butterfly tail (airplane control surfaces). A type of tail configuration used on some models of the Beech Bonanza. A butterfly, or V-tail, has two fixed surfaces and two movable surfaces, which produce aerodynamic forces to rotate the aircraft about its vertical and lateral axes in the same way as the three fixed and three movable surfaces used in the conventional inverted T-tail.

butterfly valve. A flat, disk-shaped valve used to control the flow of fluid in a round pipe or tube. When the butterfly valve is across the tube, the flow is shut off, and when it is turned parallel with the tube, the obstruction caused by the valve is minimum, and the flow is the greatest. Butterfly-type throttle valves are used to control the airflow through a reciprocating engine fuel metering system.

buttock line (aircraft lofting term). A line used to locate a position to the right or left of the center line of an aircraft structure. Buttock lines, or butt lines, are identified by their distance in inches to the right or left of buttock line zero, which is the center line of the structure. Buttock line 12R is 12 inches to the right (facing forward) of the center line.

Butyl. The trade name for a synthetic rubber product made by the polymerization of isobutylene. Butyl withstands such potent chemicals as phosphate-ester-base (Skydrol) hydraulic fluids.

butyrate dope. An aircraft finishing product having a film base of cellulose fibers dissolved in a mixture of acetic and butric acids. Butyrate dope, also called CAB (cellulose-acetate, butyrate) dope, contains, in addition to the film base, the necessary solvents, thinners, and plasticizers to make it bond to the fabric and shrink it. Butyrate dope has, to a great extent, replaced nitrate dope because it is less flammable than nitrate.

Buys Ballot's law (meteorology). A law of meteorology that helps understand the circulation of the wind. Buys Ballot's law states that if, in the northern hemisphere, we stand with the wind striking us at our back, the center of the low-pressure area, around which the wind is blowing, is ahead of us and to our left.

bypass air. The part of a turbofan's induction air that bypasses the engine core.

bypass capacitor (electrical circuit component). A capacitor that provides a low-impedance path for alternating current to flow around, or bypass, a circuit component which is being used to produce a DC voltage drop.

bypass duct (turbofan engine). An annular passage that allows some of a turbofan's airflow to bypass the engine core, or gas generator.

bypass engine (type of gas turbine engine). A gas turbine engine in which a portion of the air moved by the first stages of the compressor bypasses the combustion chambers of the engine and mixes with the hot gases in the tail pipe. A turbofan engine is a bypass engine.

bypass ratio (turbofan engine specification). The ratio of the mass airflow, in pounds per second, through the fan section of a turbofan engine to the mass airflow that passes through the gas generator portion of the engine.

bypass valve (fluid power system). A valve used to maintain a specific pressure in a fluid power system by bypassing some of the fluid back to the inlet of the system-pressure pump. Engine oil pressure in most aircraft engines is maintained at the correct value by the use of a bypass valve.

byte (digital computer term). A group of binary digits (bits) operated on as a unit. A byte normally consists of eight bits.

cabane (airplane structure). An arrangement of struts or other supporting structure that holds the wing of an airplane above the fuselage. A high-wing monoplane whose wing is held above the fuselage with a cabane is called a parasol monoplane.

cabin (aircraft structure). The portion of an aircraft structure in which the passengers ride.

cabin altitude. The equivalent altitude at which the cabin pressure of a pressurized aircraft is maintained. If the aircraft is flying at an altitude of 20,000 feet, the cabin can be pressurized so its pressure is the same as that which exists at 10,000 feet.

cabin differential pressure. The difference in the pressure inside the cabin of a pressurized aircraft and the pressure of the air outside of the cabin. The maximum cabin differential pressure that can be maintained is determined by the strength of the aircraft structure.

cabinet file (cutting tool). A coarse file with one flat face and one convex, or rounded, face. A cabinet file, also called a half-round file, is used for both metalworking and woodworking.

cabin pressure regulator (pressurization system component). The regulator in an aircraft pressurization system that controls the position of the outflow valve to maintain the air in the cabin at the desired pressure.

cabin pressurization safety valve. A combination pressure relief, vacuum relief, and dump valve that prevents cabin pressure from exceeding a predetermined pressure above the ambient pressure.

cabin supercharger. An air compressor which supplies compressed air to pressurize the cabin of an aircraft. Pressurization is needed when aircraft fly at high altitudes. If the cabin is not pressurized, the occupants must use supplemental oxygen.

cable (electrical). A piece of stranded wire or a number of individually insulated wires enclosed in single bundle or group.

cable drum (control system component). A drum in a trim tab control system on which the control cable is wound. Rotation of the drum by the trim tab control wheel moves the cable to deflect the trim tab.

cable guard (aircraft control cable component). A pin in a control-cable pulley bracket that prevents the cable moving out of the pulley groove when cable tension is loosened.

cable rigging tension chart (aircraft control cable). A chart, normally included in an aircraft maintenance manual, that shows the proper control cable tension for any given ambient air temperature.

CAD. *See* computer-aided design.

CADD. *See* computer-aided design drafting.

cadmium. A silvery-white, malleable, ductile, metallic chemical element. Cadmium's symbol is Cd, its atomic number is 48, and its atomic weight is 112.40. Cadmium is used for plating steel aircraft hardware to protect it from corrosion.

cadmium cell (electrical standard cell). A type of electrical standard cell which produces an accurate reference voltage for use when making precision electrical measurements. The voltage produced by a cadmium cell at 20°C is 1.0186 volts.

cadmium plating. A form of corrosion protection for steel parts. A thin coating of cadmium is electroplated onto the surface of the steel part to be protected. The cadmium is more chemically active than the steel part it protects, and in the process of corrosion, the cadmium acts as the anode and is changed into cadmium oxide. This method of corrosion protection is called sacrificial corrosion.

CAE. *See* computer-aided engineering.

cage (*verb*) (gyroscopic instrument). The procedure of locking the gimbals of a gyroscopic instrument so it will not be damaged by abrupt flight maneuvers or rough handling.

cage (turn coordinator component). The vertical black lines on the ball indicator in a turn coordinator or turn and slip indicator. When the ball is within the two black lines, the bank angle is correct for the existing rate of turn.

caging system (gyroscopic instrument). A mechanism inside a gyroscopic instrument that locks the gimbals in a rigid position and holds the gyro so it cannot tumble if the aircraft maneuvers exceed the tumble limits of the gyro. The caging system also restores a tumbled gyro to its operating position.

calcium. A silvery, moderately hard, metallic chemical element. Calcium's symbol is Ca, its atomic number is 20, and its atomic weight is 40.08. Calcium is used as an alloying element for other metals and as a component in plaster and portland cement.

calcium carbide. A compound of calcium and carbon which decomposes, or breaks down, in water to produce acetylene gas.

calculated landing time (air traffic control). A term that may be used in place of tentative or actual calculated landing time, whichever applies.

calendar month. A period of time used by the FAA for inspection and certification purposes. One calendar month from a given day extends from that day until midnight of the last day of that month. A calendar month beginning on June 6 ends at midnight of June 30.

calender (fabric treatment). To pass fabric through a series of heated rollers to give it a smooth and shiny surface.

calibrated airspeed. *See* CAS.

calibrated orifice. An orifice, or hole, having a specific diameter, length, and approach and departure angles. A calibrated orifice is used to control the amount of fluid that can flow under a specific pressure. Carburetor metering jets are calibrated orifices.

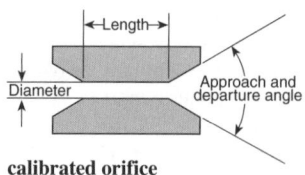

calibrated orifice

calibration (instrument accuracy check). The procedure in which the indication of an instrument is compared with a standard value. Calibration is done to determine the accuracy of an instrument. A pressure gage, for example, can be calibrated by comparing its readings with the known pressure produced by a dead-weight tester.

calibration card (instrument accuracy). A card usually mounted near an instrument to show the amount of error in the instrument. Correct information can be obtained by reading the instrument and applying the correction shown on the calibration card.

calibration curve (instrument accuracy). A curve plotted to show the instrument errors at different points on the scale. The error at each point is plotted on a graph, and these points are joined by a smooth curve. By using the calibration curve, it is possible to interpolate the error at points between those which have been plotted.

californium. A radioactive, synthetic chemical element produced by bombarding curium with helium isotopes. Californium's symbol is Cf, and its atomic number is 98.

C

call for release (ATC term). Used when the overlying ARTCC requires a terminal facility to initiate verbal coordination to secure ARTCC approval for release of a departure into the enroute environment.

call-outs (aircraft drawings). Numbers and names used to identify components or parts in an aircraft drawing. Call-outs are normally placed near the part being identified and are connected to the part by a thin leader line.

call sign (radio communications). Any combination of letters or numbers that identifies a communications facility.

call-up (radio communications procedure). The initial voice contact between a facility and an aircraft. The call-up should include the identification of the facility being called and the facility initiating the call.

calm (meteorology). The absence of wind or apparent motion of the air.

calorie. The unit of heat energy in the centimeter-gram-second system of measurements.
  A large calorie (Calorie) is the amount of heat energy needed to raise the temperature of one kilogram of water one degree Celsius. A small calorie (calorie) is the amount of heat energy needed to raise the temperature of one gram of pure water from 14.5° to 15.5°C. One calorie is equal to 4.1868 joules of energy.

calorimeter. An instrument used to measure quantities of heat released or absorbed during chemical reactions or physical changes of state.

cam. An eccentric, or lobe, on a rotating shaft that changes rotary motion into linear motion. A cam, or lobe, on the cam shaft of a reciprocating engine opens the intake and exhaust valves at the proper time relative to the position of the piston in the cylinder.

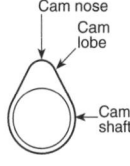

cam

CAM. *See* computer-aided manufacturing.

camber (aerodynamic shape). The amount of curve of an airfoil section. The curve on the top of the airfoil is called the upper camber, and the curve on the bottom is called the lower camber. The mean camber is a line drawn through a series of points, each of which is located midway between the upper and the lower camber.

camber (wheel alignment). The amount the wheels of an aircraft are inclined, or tilted, from the vertical. If the top of the wheel tilts outward, the camber is positive, and if it tilts inward, the camber is negative.

cambric. A closely woven, firm fabric with a slightly glossy surface.

cam dwell. The number of degrees a cam rotates during the time the object controlled by the cam does not move. The breaker points in the ignition system of a reciprocating engine are opened by a cam. The cam dwell, or cam dwell angle, is the number of degrees the cam rotates between the time the breaker points close and the time they open.

cam engine (reciprocating engine). A reciprocating engine with axial cylinders arranged around a central shaft. Rollers in the open end of the pistons press against a sinusoidal cam mounted on the shaft to rotate the shaft.

cam-ground piston (reciprocating engine component). A specially shaped piston used in an aircraft reciprocating engine. The piston is not round, but is ground in such a way that its diameter parallel to the wrist pin is slightly smaller than its diameter perpendicular to the pin. The mass of metal used in the wrist pin boss, the enlarged area around the wrist pin hole, expands when it is heated, and when the piston is at its operating temperature, it has expanded until it is perfectly round.

cam lobe. An eccentric used to change rotary motion into linear motion. The valve operating cams used in a reciprocating engine are eccentrics made onto the cam shaft. These eccentrics are enlarged portions of the cam shaft that rotate about a center different from the shaft's center. The cam followers that operate the valves ride on the cam lobes, and as the cam shaft rotates, the cam lobes move the cam followers up and down in a direction perpendicular to the axis of the cam shaft.

cam nose. The peak, or highest point, on a cam. The cam nose is the part of the cam that pushes up on the cam follower.

cam pawl. A device that allows a wheel to turn in one direction, but prevents its turning in the opposite direction. The cam pawl, an eccentric that rides over the surface of a wheel, allows the wheel to turn in one direction, but when it tries to turn in the opposite direction, the cam wedges against the wheel and prevents its turning.

cam ring (radial engine component). A ring or plate with lobes ground around its periphery. Cam rings are used in radial aircraft engines to push against cam followers and push rods to open the intake and exhaust valves.

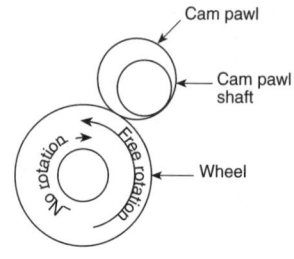

cam pawl

camshaft (reciprocating engine component). A straight, gear-driven shaft that contains lobes used to operate the intake and the exhaust valves. The camshaft is geared to the crankshaft in such a way that the valves open and close at the proper time relative to the position of the piston in the cylinders.

Canadian minimum navigation performance specification airspace. That portion of Canadian domestic airspace within which MNPS separation may be applied.

can-annular combustor (gas turbine engine component). A type of combustor used in some of the large turbojet and turbofan engines. It consists of individual cans into which the fuel is sprayed and ignited. These cans all mount on an annular duct through which the hot gases from the individual cans are collected and directed uniformly into the turbine.

canard (type of airplane). A type of airplane in which the horizontal auxiliary control is mounted ahead of the main lifting plane.

canard (aircraft component). A horizontal control surface mounted ahead of the main wing to provide longitudinal stability and control.

> *14 CFR Part 1:* "The forward wing of a canard configuration and may be a fixed, movable, or variable geometry surface, with or without control surfaces."

canard configuration. *14 CFR Part 1:* "A configuration in which the span of the forward wing is substantially less than that of the main wing."

candela. A measurement of luminous intensity in the International System of measurements. The candela is also known as the new candle, or the international candle.

candlepower. A measure of light intensity. One candlepower is the amount of light intensity produced by one international candle or one candela.

cannibalize. To take serviceable components from one unit and use them on another. Military and industrial surplus equipment is often used as a source of components that can be obtained by cannibalizing the equipment.

canopy (aircraft structure). The transparent enclosure that covers an aircraft cockpit. Most modern canopies are formed in the shape of a bubble from a single piece of transparent plastic material.

canopy (parachute). The fabric body of a parachute.

can tap valve. A valve attached to a sealed can of liquid refrigerant that controls the flow of refrigerant into an aircraft vapor-cycle cooling system. When the valve is securely attached, a seal on the can is pierced, allowing the refrigerant to flow.

canted bulkhead. The wall of a compartment in an aircraft that, because of structural reasons, is not straight up and down. A canted bulkhead angles upward from the deck.

canted rate gyro. A rate gyro whose gimbal axis is tilted so it can sense rotation of the aircraft about its roll axis as well as its yaw axis.

cantilever beam. A beam with all of its support inside the beam itself. It uses no external struts, braces, or wires. A diving board is an example of a cantilever beam.

cantilever wing. A wing with no external bracing—all of the strength of the wing is inside its structure. The wing spars are built in such a way that they carry all the bending and torsional loads.

can-type combustor (gas turbine engine component). A combustor, or burner section of a gas turbine engine made up of several individual burner cans. These cans are long cylinders of thin sheet metal consisting of an outer housing and an inner liner, arranged axially around the power shaft of the engine, more or less parallel to it.

Discharge air from the compressor flows through the cans where fuel is sprayed into it and burned to add energy. Cooling air flows between the housing and inner liner, and through holes in the inner liner to keep the temperature of the cans low enough that they will not be damaged. Can-type combustors were used on some of the early turbojet engines, but most modern engines use the more efficient annular, or can-annular combustors.

canvas. A heavy, tightly woven cloth made of cotton.

capacitance (electrical quantity). The amount of electrical charge that can be stored in a capacitor under a given amount of electrical pressure (voltage). The formula for capacitance is $C = Q \div E$, in which C is the capacitance in farads, Q is the quantity (amount) of charge in coulombs, and E is the electrical pressure, in volts. Capacitance is measured in farads, microfarads, or picofarads.

capacitance afterfiring (reciprocating engines). The continuation of the spark across the gap in a shielded spark plug after the fuel-air mixture in the cylinder is ignited. Capacitance afterfiring is caused by the return of electrical energy stored in the capacitance of the shielded ignition leads. Capacitance afterfiring is eliminated by installing a resistor inside the spark plug.

capacitance box. A piece of electrical test equipment made up of a number of capacitors and selector switches. Any amount of capacitance needed in a circuit can be selected on the switches and the capacitance box inserted into the circuit where the capacitance is needed.

capacitance bridge. A piece of precision electrical test equipment used to measure capacitance. The bridge measures the capacitance of an unknown capacitor by comparing its capacitive reactance with that produced by a known value of capacitance.

capacitance-type fuel quantity indicating system. A type of fuel quantity indicating system that shows the amount of fuel in the tanks of an aircraft. The sending units (probes) inside the fuel tank are cylindrical capacitors made of two concentric metal tubes. These probes, connected in parallel, reach across the tank from top to bottom. When the tank is full of fuel, the fuel acts as the dielectric, but when the tank is empty, air is the dielectric.

The capacitance of a capacitor is directly proportional to the dielectric constant (k) of the material between its plates. Air has a k of one, and the fuel has a k of approximately two, depending upon its temperature and thus its density.

Continued

capacitance-type fuel quantity indicating system. *Continued*
The system contains an automatic balancing capacitance bridge and an indicator. The bridge measures the capacitance of the tank probes, which varies directly with the amount of fuel in the tanks. The capacitance is converted into terms of pounds of fuel in the tanks, and this is shown on the indicator.

capacitive coupling (electronic circuit). A method of joining stages of electronic circuits with capacitors. Capacitors isolate the stages with regard to DC, but allow them to operate at the same AC potential.

capacitive feedback (electronic circuit). A process in which part of the energy in the output of an electronic circuit is fed back to the input through a capacitor.

capacitive load (electrical circuit). An electrical load that produces more capacitive reactance than inductive reactance in the circuit. Current leads the voltage in a capacitive load.

capacitive reactance. Opposition to the flow of alternating current caused by capacitance in the circuit. Capacitive reactance, whose symbol is X_C, is measured in ohms and is determined by the capacitance in the circuit and the frequency of the AC.
The formula for capacitive reactance is:

$$X_C = \frac{1}{2\pi f C}$$

X_C = Capacitive reactance in ohms
2π = A constant, 6.28
f = Frequency of the AC in hertz
C = Capacitance in farads

capacitive time constant. The amount of time, measured in seconds, needed for the voltage across a capacitor to rise to 63.2% of the source voltage. The time constant is determined by the resistance and the capacitance of the circuit.
The formula for capacitive time constant is:

TC = R · C
TC = Time constant in seconds
R = Resistance in ohms
C = Capacitance in farads

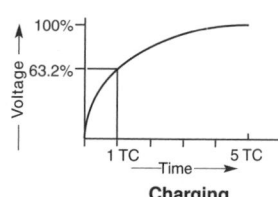

Charging

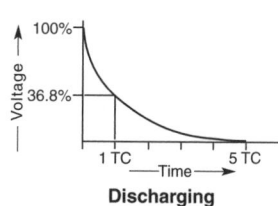

Discharging

capacitive time constant

capacitor. An electrical component made of two conductors separated by an insulator, or dielectric. A capacitor can store an electrical charge in an electrostatic field. The capacitance of a capacitor is measured in farads, microfarads (10^{-6} farad), or picofarads (10^{-12} farad).
The capacitance of a capacitor is determined by three things: the area of the plates, the amount of separation between the plates, and the kind of insulating material, or dielectric, between the plates. Capacitors were at one time called condensers.

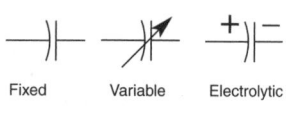

Fixed   Variable   Electrolytic

capacitors

capacitor-discharge ignition system (gas turbine engine ignition system). A type of high-energy ignition system that produces a hot spark for starting a gas turbine engine. In a capacitor-discharge ignition system, electrons are stored under high voltage in capacitors. When these electrons are released, they cause a high-intensity spark to jump across the gap in the igniters.

capacitor-input filter (electronic filter). A type of electrical filter used to smooth the pulsations in the output of an electronic power supply. A capacitor is installed in parallel with the rectifier output, and an inductor is in series.

capacitor-start induction motor. An AC motor whose rotor is excited by voltage induced into it from the stator windings. A capacitor-start motor has two stator windings: a start winding and a run winding. The start winding is in series with a capacitor that shifts the phase of the current flowing through it, so it is out of phase with the current flowing through the run winding.

    The magnetic field produced by the start winding and the field produced by the run winding work together to produce a magnetic field that rotates within the motor housing. The rotor follows this rotating field. When the rotor has accelerated to a specified speed, a centrifugal switch opens the start winding circuit, and the motor continues to operate on the run winding alone. Capacitor-start motors have a good starting torque.

capacity (battery specification). The total amount of current available in a battery or electrical cell. Capacity is normally measured in ampere-hours.

cap cloud (meteorology). A standing, or stationary, cap-like cloud that forms on mountain or ridge tops caused by cooling of moist air rising on the upwind side, followed by warming and drying by downdrafts on the lee side. Also called a foehn cloud. *See also* foehn.

cape chisel. A narrow-blade cold chisel with either a single or double bevel. Cape chisels are used to knock the head off a rivet after it has been drilled through, and to cut narrow grooves and keyways in metal components.

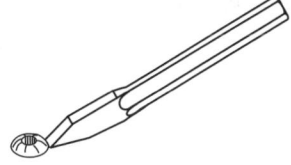

cape chisel

capillary action. The action that causes a liquid to climb the walls of a container or to be drawn up into extremely tiny tubes or between close-fitting parts.

    The force of adhesion between the liquid and the solid wall of the container is greater than the force of cohesion between the molecules of the liquid. The stronger force of adhesion causes the liquid to try to spread out and wet the walls. Capillary action causes a piece of blotting paper to pick up a liquid, and the lack of capillary action causes a drop of water to form into a ball on a waxed surface.

capillary tube. A metal or glass tube with such a small inside diameter that capillary action causes liquid to move in the tube. A soft copper capillary tube is used with a vapor-pressure thermometer connecting the temperature-sensing bulb to the Bourdon tube. The tube is protected from physical damage by enclosing it in a braided metal wire jacket.

capping (meteorology). A statically stable layer at the top of the atmospheric boundary layer. This term is used more loosely for any stable layer (potential temperature increasing with height) at the top of the boundary layer.

capsize. To overturn.

cap screw. A threaded fastener whose shank passes through a clear hole in one piece of material and screws into threads cut into the second piece. The head of the cap screw, which is turned with a wrench, clamps the two pieces of material together.

capstan (aircraft controls). A device in the control system of an aircraft that allows the automatic pilot to move the control surfaces.

The capstan is a grooved drum-like wheel mounted on the automatic pilot servo motor. A bridle of control cable is wound around the capstan, and the ends of the bridle are attached to the aileron, elevator, or rudder control cable. When the servo motor turns, it winds the bridle around the capstan, and the bridle moves the main control cable.

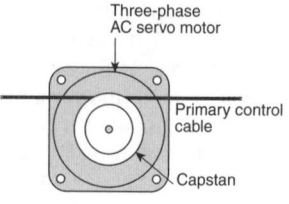

capstan

capstan screw. A form of machine screw whose head has several radial holes, holes that go across the head, through it. A bar can be passed through these holes and used to turn the screw.

cap strip. The main top and bottom members of a wing rib. The cap strips give the rib its aerodynamic shape.

capsule (aircraft instrument component). A flat container made of thin disks of corrugated metal soldered together and used to sense changing pressure. When the pressure inside the capsule changes, the capsule expands or contracts, and the change in its physical dimensions is proportional to the change in the pressure.

captive balloon. A lighter-than-air device anchored to the ground with a steel cable. Captive balloons were used in the American Civil War as aerial observation platforms. In both World War I and World War II, captive balloons were used as obstructions to keep low-flying airplanes from bombing and strafing vital ground installations.

captive screw. A screw that has a section of the threads on its shank next to its head cut away. A captive screw is free to turn in the body in which it is mounted, but it will not drop out when it is unscrewed from the part it is holding.

carbide. A chemical compound of carbon and a metallic element. Carbides are normally very hard materials.

carbide tool (machine tool). A metal-cutting machine tool whose cutting faces are surfaced with tungsten carbide, tantalum carbide, or titanium carbide. These carbides keep their hardness and cutting ability even when they are extremely hot.

Carboloy. The registered trade name for certain cutting tools and dies that have tungsten carbide bonded to their cutting or wearing surfaces.

carbon. An abundant, nonmetallic chemical element that occurs in all organic compounds and in many inorganic compounds. Carbon's symbol is C, its atomic number is 6, and its atomic weight is 12.01115. Among carbon's many important uses is that of acting as an electrical resistance element.

carbon arc. An electric arc produced when current flows through ionized air from the tip of one carbon rod to the tip of another. The intense heat produced by the passage of the current causes the tips of the carbon rods to vaporize and glow with a brilliant white light.

carbon black. A form of soft and fluffy carbon. Carbon black is produced by burning certain types of gas with a flame that contains insufficient oxygen for complete combustion. Carbon black is used in the manufacture of aircraft tires and as a pigment for some types of paint.

carbon brake (aircraft brake). A special multiple-disk brake using pure carbon for both rotating and stationary disks. Carbon brakes are used on some high-performance aircraft because of their ability to dissipate much more energy than a metal-disk brake of similar weight.

carbon deposits (engine operation). A deposit of hard carbon that forms on engine parts when lubricating oil is trapped in a hot location, allowing it to decompose into hard carbon, or coke. *See* coking (lubrication system problem).

carbon dioxide (CO_2). A colorless, odorless, and tasteless gas that is about 1.5 times as heavy as air. Carbon dioxide, composed of one atom of carbon and two atoms of oxygen, makes up about five hundredths of one percent of the air we breathe. Green plants take in carbon dioxide and combine it with water to make sugar. Humans and animals give off carbon dioxide in their exhaled breath.

Even though carbon dioxide makes up only an extremely small part of the air we breathe, it is necessary, because it helps control our rate of breathing. Carbon dioxide is important commercially because of its use as a fire extinguishing agent.

carbon dioxide fire extinguisher. A fire extinguisher that holds carbon dioxide gas under a pressure of about 800 to 900 pounds per square inch. When carbon dioxide, CO_2, is sprayed on a fire, it comes out of the extinguisher in the form of a snow and blankets the fire. The snow changes into CO_2 gas and pushes away all the oxygen. When there is no more oxygen to combine with the fuel, the fire goes out.

carbon fiber (composites). A reinforcing fiber known for its light weight, high strength, and stiffness. It is produced from an organic fiber by breaking down complex molecules into simpler molecules by heat in an inert atmosphere at temperatures above 1,800°F.

carbon-film resistor (electrical component). An electrical resistor made by vacuum-depositing a thin film of carbon on a ceramic cylinder. Wires attached to each end of the carbon film allow the resistor to be connected into an electrical circuit.

carbon fouling (spark plug condition). A spark plug condition, identified by dull black, sooty deposits in the electrode end of the plug. Common causes of carbon fouling are excessive ground idling with a rich idle mixture, and the use of a spark plug with too cold a heat range.

carbon knock (reciprocating engines). The knocking sound made in a reciprocating engine by detonation that follows preignition. Preignition occurs when incandescent (red-hot) carbon particles inside the cylinder ignite the fuel-air mixture before the engine is ready for ignition to occur. Early ignition allows the cylinder pressure and temperature to build up high enough to cause the fuel to detonate, or explode, rather than burn smoothly as it should. It is this explosion that causes the sound we hear.

carbon microphone. A type of microphone used in a telephone and with some types of radio transmitters. The sensitive element in a carbon microphone is a tube of carbon granules, or grains of carbon. A flexible diaphragm acted on by sound waves presses against the carbon inside the tube. When the diaphragm pushes the carbon granules together (compresses them), the resistance of the carbon becomes less than when the diaphragm allows the granules to relax. The looseness or tightness of the granules in the tube determines the resistance of the carbon, and this resistance changes in the same way the air pressure caused by the sound waves changes.

carbon monoxide (CO). A colorless, odorless gas that forms from incomplete combustion of an organic fuel. Carbon monoxide is poisonous to human and animal life.

carbon monoxide detector. A packet of chemical crystals mounted in the aircraft cockpit or cabin where they are easily visible. The crystals change their color from yellow to green when they are exposed to carbon monoxide.

carbon pile (electrical component). A type of variable resistor used in some electrical equipment. A carbon pile is made of a stack of thin, pure carbon disks whose resistance is changed by varying the pressure on the stack. Carbon piles are used as the control element in some types of voltage regulators. They are also used for dissipating (using up) large amounts of electrical power in certain types of electrical load banks and test equipment.

carbon pile voltage regulator. A voltage regulator used with some high-output DC generators in which a stack of pure carbon disks acts as the resistance element in the field circuit. When the generator output voltage is low, a spring compresses the carbon pile and reduces its resistance, allowing a large amount of field current to flow.

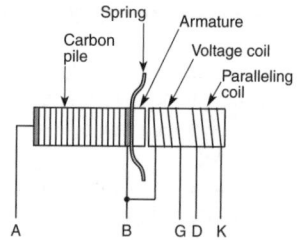

**carbon pile
voltage regulator**

When the generator output is high, the electromagnetic field produced by a voltage-sensing coil overcomes the spring force and loosens the carbon pile, increasing its resistance and decreasing the field current.

carbon resistor (electrical component). A component used to insert a controlled amount of resistance into an electrical circuit.

Carbon resistors are made of a mixture of carbon and an insulating material formed into a small cylinder and baked. Its resistance is then measured and its value marked in the form of colored bands around one end.

carbon seal (gas turbine engine component). A rubbing seal in a gas turbine engine between a rotating shaft and a fixed housing. The seal, made of carbon, rides on a highly polished steel surface, and the close fit between the carbon and the steel keeps oil from flowing into the gas path of the engine.

carbon steel. Steel in which carbon is the chief, or principal, alloying agent. Low-carbon steel which, containing less than 0.20% carbon, is relatively soft and weak, but high-carbon steel containing up to about 0.95% carbon can be hardened until it is very strong, but also very brittle.

carbon tetrachloride. A colorless, dense, liquid halogenated hydrocarbon that has, in the past, been used as a fire extinguishing agent and as a cleaning fluid for clothing. Carbon tetrachloride is no longer used for either of these purposes because it is harmful to the human body. When carbon tetrachloride is sprayed on a fire, it changes into the poisonous gas, phosgene.

carbon tracking (magneto distributor malfunction). An ignition system malfunction caused by a fine track of carbon deposited inside the distributor of an aircraft magneto. The resistance of the air inside the distributor at high altitude is so low that it is possible for a spark to jump between the distributor terminals. As this spark moves across the surface of the distributor block, it leaves a thin track of carbon. The resistance of this carbon track is so much lower than that of the material of which the distributor block is made that high voltage leaks through it during normal engine operation. This high-voltage leakage can cause misfiring, loss of engine power, and possible engine damage.

carbon-zinc cell (electrical cell). An electrochemical cell that changes chemical energy into electrical energy. The cell is made of a zinc can filled with a paste of ammonium chloride. A carbon rod is supported by the ammonium chloride in such a way that it cannot touch the zinc can.

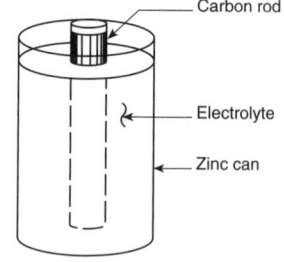

carbon-zinc cell

Electrical energy is produced as electrons leave the zinc can and travel through an external circuit to the carbon rod. A carbon-zinc cell has an open-circuit voltage of approximately 1.5 volts.

C

Carborundum. The registered trade name for several types of man-made abrasives. Carborundum is similar to emery (a natural abrasive), and it is used to make grinding wheels. Fine particles of Carborundum are bonded to paper and cloth to make sheets and strips of abrasive materials.

carburetor (reciprocating engine component). A type of fuel metering system used on some reciprocating engines. When air flows into the engine, it passes through a venturi in the carburetor. The venturi produces a pressure drop proportional to the volume of air flowing into the engine cylinders.

The low pressure caused by the venturi pulls the correct amount of fuel through a metering jet, and this fuel is mixed with the air before it enters the cylinders.

carburetor air heater. A sheet metal jacket surrounding part of the engine exhaust system. Air from inside the engine nacelle or compartment flows between this jacket and the exhaust system component and picks up heat. The heated air is carried through a carburetor heater valve, and when carburetor air temperature is low, can be directed into the carburetor; otherwise it is dumped overboard. Air that flows through the carburetor air heater is not filtered.

carburetor air temperature. The temperature of the air as it enters the carburetor. It is important that the temperature of the fuel-air mixture be kept above the freezing point of water to prevent the formation of carburetor ice, but it is difficult to measure the temperature of this mixture. By measuring and controlling the temperature of the air as it enters the carburetor, it is possible to keep the mixture temperature high enough to prevent water condensing out of the air and freezing, and at the same time to keep the temperature of the air entering the engine low enough to prevent detonation.

carburetor air temperature gage. An instrument that indicates the temperature of the air in the ram air intake duct before it enters the carburetor. Keeping this air temperature sufficiently above the freezing point of water prevents ice forming in the throat of the carburetor.

carburetor ice. Ice that forms inside the throat of a carburetor installed on an aircraft reciprocating engine. When air flows through the carburetor venturi, it speeds up, and both its pressure and temperature drop. When liquid fuel is discharged into the throat of the venturi, it vaporizes, and this change of state drops its temperature.

When the temperature of the air is low enough, moisture in the air condenses out and freezes. It is possible for carburetor ice to build up inside the venturi and restrict the air flowing into the engine enough to cause the engine to stop. Carburetor ice is normally prevented by heating the air before it enters the carburetor.

carburizing (steel heat treatment). A form of heat treatment of steel in which the surface absorbs extra carbon and becomes hard and brittle, while the center of the steel remains relatively soft and tough.

The part to be carburized is packed in a material containing a large amount of carbon (finely ground bone is often used) and is heated in a furnace until the correct amount of carbon is absorbed into the surface of the steel.

carburizing flame (oxy-acetylene welding). A flame produced by an oxy-acetylene torch when there is too much acetylene gas for the amount of oxygen being metered by the torch. A carburizing flame, identified by a definite feather around the inner cone, is not normally used, because it adds carbon to the molten metal and makes the weld weaker than the metal being welded.

carcass (tire component). The layers of rubberized fabric that make up the body of an aircraft tire.

cardinal altitudes. Odd or even thousand-foot altitudes or flight levels.

cardinal heading (aircraft navigation). The heading of an aircraft along any of the four cardinal directions shown on a compass. The cardinal directions are North, East, South, and West.

cardioid microphone. A microphone that is directional in its ability to pick up sounds, picking up sounds in front of it while rejecting sounds behind it. A cardioid microphone gets its name from the Greek word *kardia*, which means heart. The sound pickup pattern of a cardioid microphone is roughly in the shape of a heart.

caret (mathematics). A small inverted V (^) used to show the new location of the decimal in multiplication and division problems using decimal fractions.

cargo. Material transported in an airplane, ship, truck, or train.

Carnot cycle (energy release cycle). An ideal reversible, but unattainable, cycle of energy transformation that explains the operation of a perfect heat engine. The four events that occur in a Carnot cycle are:

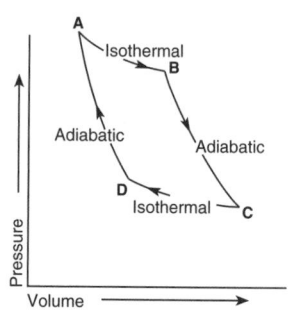

Carnot cycle

1. An isothermal expansion of the working fluid from A to B. Heat energy is neither added to nor taken from the air. The temperature remains constant at T_1.
2. An adiabatic expansion from B to C with the temperature changing from T_1 to T_2.
3. An isothermal compression from C to D at temperature T_2.
4. An adiabatic compression of the gas from D to A, returning it to its original conditions.

carriage bolt. A round-headed bolt with a square section of the shank just below the head. A carriage bolt is used to hold pieces of wood together. The square section of the shank embeds itself in the wood and keeps the bolt from turning when the nut is tightened on the threads.

carrier frequency (radio transmission). The frequency of the alternating current carrier that produces the electromagnetic waves which radiate from a radio transmitting antenna. The audio-frequency signal from the microphone modulates (changes the amplitude or the frequency) of the carrier.

cart. The engine and seats, attached by a structure to wheels; sometimes referred to as the fuselage, cockpit, chaise, or airframe.

cartridge fuse (electrical component). A type of fuse used to protect an electrical circuit from an excess of current. The fusible link, the part of the fuse that melts when too much current flows through it, is held between metal ferrules, or caps, that screw onto each end of an insulating tube. The ferrules are held in special fuse clips inside the fuse box.

cartridge-pneumatic starter (gas turbine engine starter). A pneumatic starter for a gas turbine engine that uses gas pressure produced when powder in a cartridge burns in the breech of the starter. The high-pressure gas produced by the burning powder spins a turbine geared to the engine compressor.

cartridge starter (reciprocating engine starter). A type of starter used on some large aircraft reciprocating engines. A cartridge, looking much like a shotgun cartridge, is fired in the breech of the starter. The gas produced by the burning powder pushes down on a piston inside a cylinder. The piston is attached to a helical spline, a spline cut in the shape of a spiral, in such a way that as the piston moves down, the spline twists. The twisting spline turns a gear that meshes with a gear on the engine crankshaft. When the cartridge is fired and the piston is pushed down, the helical spline turns the gear and cranks the engine fast enough for it to start.

cartridge-type fluid filter (fuel and oil filter). A disposable filter element used in an aircraft fuel or lubrication system. These filters are of the depth type and are made of cellulose fibers that trap and hold most of the contaminants in the fuel or oil that passes through them.

CAS (calibrated airspeed). A measure of the speed at which an aircraft is moving through the air. Calibrated airspeed is found by correcting the airspeed shown on the airspeed indicator, the indicated airspeed (IAS), for any errors in the instrument or those caused by its installation (installation, or position errors). *See* position error.

14 CFR Part 1: "The indicated airspeed of an aircraft, corrected for position and instrument error. Calibrated airspeed is equal to true airspeed in standard atmosphere at sea level."

cascade (electrical circuits). A method of connecting multiple stages of electrical circuits so the output of one stage feeds the input of the next stage.

cascade effect. The cumulative effect that occurs when the output of one series of components serves as the input to the next series.

cascade reverser (thrust reverser). A thrust reverser normally used on turbofan engines. A blocker door and a series of cascade vanes redirect exhaust gases in a forward direction.

cascade transformer (electrical equipment). A device that can be used in an electrical circuit to get a high voltage. The secondary winding of a step-up transformer is connected to the primary winding of another step-up transformer. As many transformers as are needed to get the required output voltage can be cascaded in this manner.

cascade vanes (thrust reverser component). Vanes in an aerodynamic blockage-type thrust reverser used to turn the stream of exhaust gases to produce a reverse thrust.

case hardening (steel heat treatment). A method of heat treatment of steel in which the surface of the metal is hardened while its inside stays strong and tough. Case hardening may be done by causing the steel on the surface to absorb extra carbon or by changing the surface into a very hard chemical compound called aluminum nitride.

Case hardening is used on such steel parts as engine crankshafts. Only the surfaces where the bearings ride are made very hard and brittle. The inside of the crankshaft remains tough and strong.

casein glue. A form of powdered glue made from milk. Casein glue powder is mixed with cold water to form a creamy paste. Casein glue was formerly used for joining wood parts of aircraft, but it is no longer used because better types of glue are now available.

case pressure (fluid pump pressure). A relatively low pressure maintained inside the bearing cavities of an engine-driven hydraulic pump. If the shaft or the bearings (bushings) of the pump should become damaged, case pressure will force hydraulic fluid out of the pump, rather than allowing air to be pulled in.

casing (aircraft tire component). The rubber and fabric body of a pneumatic tire. The casing is the same as the carcass of the tire.

casing nail. A form of wire nail made of smaller gage wire than that used for a common nail of the same length.

castellated nut. A form of hexagonal nut (a six-sided nut) that has slots cut across its end. A cotter pin is passed through the slots and through a hole in the shank of the bolt to lock the nut to the bolt. Castellated nuts are often called castle nuts.

casting. A method of forming an object by pouring molten metal or liquid plastic resin into a mold. The material is allowed to harden inside the mold and, when hard, it is removed. Castings are less expensive than forgings, but they usually have much less strength. Reciprocating engine crankcases are normally castings.

cast iron. Iron that contains carbon and silicon. Cast iron is heavy, brittle, and hard, and cannot be formed by forging. It is used for making objects that do not require a great deal of strength and can be made by pouring the molten iron into molds. The main use of cast iron in aircraft technology is in the manufacture of piston rings for reciprocating engines.

cast off (seaplane operation). To release or untie a seaplane from its mooring.

CAT (clear air turbulence). Extreme turbulence found at high altitude. Clear air turbulence is created when a difference in the temperature causes a violent movement of the air. CAT cannot be seen, because there is no moisture at the altitude at which it occurs. In the lower altitudes, where there is moisture, turbulence in the air causes recognizable cloud patterns.

catalyst. A substance used to change the speed or rate of a chemical action without being chemically changed itself. Water functions as a catalyst in the process of iron turning into rust (iron oxide). Dry iron does not rust nearly as fast as iron with water on its surface. The water itself is not affected, but the iron unites with oxygen from the air to become iron oxide, or rust.

catalytic cracking (petroleum refining). A method of refining petroleum products. In catalytic cracking, a catalyst is used to change high-boiling-point hydrocarbons into low-boiling-point hydrocarbons.

catalyzed resin (composites). A resin mixture that is in a workable state after it has been mixed with catalyst or hardener.

catapult. A mechanism used to hurl, or launch, an object at a high rate of speed. Catapults are used to launch heavily loaded aircraft from the decks of aircraft carriers.

catch point (navigation). A fix/waypoint that serves as a transition point from the high altitude waypoint navigation structure to an arrival procedure (STAR) or the low altitude ground-based navigation structure.

category (aircraft classification). *14 CFR Part 1:*
"(1) As used with respect to the certification, ratings, privileges, and limitations of airmen, means a broad classification of aircraft. Examples include: airplane; rotorcraft; glider; and lighter-than-air; and
(2) As used with respect to the certification of aircraft, means a grouping of aircraft based upon intended use or operating limitations. Examples include: transport, normal, utility, acrobatic, limited, restricted, and provisional."

Category A. *14 CFR Part 1:* "With respect to transport category rotorcraft, means multiengine rotorcraft designed with engine and system isolation features specified in Part 29 and utilizing scheduled takeoff and landing operations under a critical engine failure concept which assures adequate designated surface area and adequate performance capability for continued safe flight in the event of engine failure."

Category B. *14 CFR Part 1:* "With respect to transport category rotorcraft, means single-engine or multiengine rotorcraft which do not fully meet all Category A standards. Category B rotorcraft have no guaranteed stay-up ability in the event of engine failure and unscheduled landing is assumed."

Category II operations. *14 CFR Part 1:* "With respect to the operation of aircraft, means a straight-in ILS approach to the runway of an airport under a Category II ILS instrument approach procedure issued by the Administrator or other appropriate authority."

Category III operations. *14 CFR Part 1:* "With respect to the operation of aircraft, means an ILS approach to and landing on, the runway of an airport using a Category III ILS approach procedure issued by the Administrator or other appropriate authority."

catenary curve. A curve formed by a flexible cable suspended between two points at the same level.

cathedral (aerodynamics). Negative dihedral. The wings of an airplane, as they are viewed from the front, are not usually straight; they normally angle upward from the center. This upward angling is called positive dihedral, and it improves the stability of the airplane. However, when maneuverability is more important than stability, as it is on some military fighters and acrobatic airplanes, the wings are set with negative dihedral (cathedral). The wings angle downward from the center. Cathedral decreases the stability of an airplane and makes it more maneuverable.

cathode of an electrochemical cell. The active element in an electrochemical cell that is reduced, or loses oxygen in the chemical action which causes electrons to flow.

cathode of a semiconductor diode. The end of a semiconductor diode made of N-type material. When the diode is forward biased with the negative terminal of the power source connected to the cathode of the diode, electrons flow through the diode. The cathode of a semiconductor diode is identified by the bar in the diode symbol.

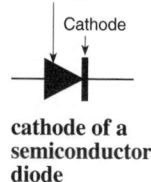

Anode

Cathode

cathode of a semiconductor diode

cathode rays. Streams of electrons emitted by the cathode in a special form of electron tube called a cathode-ray tube (CRT). These electrons are accelerated by the attraction of a positive voltage on special grids called accelerator grids. The cathode rays strike a phosphorescent material that covers the inside of the face of the tube, and when they strike it, the material glows. Cathode-ray tubes are used as the display in computers and oscilloscopes.

cathode-ray tube. *See* CRT.

cathodic area. An area within a piece of metal to which electrons from the anodic area have migrated.

cathodic protection. Another name for sacrificial corrosion. A material that is more anodic than the material being protected is attached to or plated on the material. This becomes the anode and is corroded, while the part being protected is the cathode and it is not damaged.

cation. A positive ion that moves toward the cathode in the process of electrolysis.

catwalk. A narrow walkway inside a structure that allows a person to move through an area that is otherwise inaccessible.

caul plates (composites). Smooth metal plates free of surface defects with the same size and shape as a composite lay-up. Caul plates contact the lay-up during curing to transmit pressure and heat to the finished laminate, producing a smooth surface.

caustic material. Any material that can eat away another material by chemical action. Both strong acids and strong aklalis are caustic materials.

caustic soda. A common name for sodium hydroxide, NaOH. Caustic soda is often called lye.

cavitation. A condition that exists in a fluid pump when there is not enough pressure in the reservoir to force fluid to the inlet of the pump. The pump picks up air instead of fluid.

cavity. An empty (unfilled) space. A cavity is the same as a hole.

C-battery (radio battery). A small, low-voltage battery used in some of the older, battery-powered, tube-type radios to provide a grid bias voltage for some of the vacuum tubes. C-batteries have generally been replaced by a method of biasing the tubes with the voltage drop across a resistor.

CBI. *See* computer-based instruction.

CBT. *See* computer-based training.

C-check. *See* maintenance checks.

CCL (convective condensation level). The lowest level at which condensation will occur as a result of convection due to surface heating. When condensation occurs at this level, the layer between the surface and the CCL will be thoroughly mixed, the temperature lapse rate will be dry adiabatic (3°C per 1,000 feet), and the mixing ratio will be constant.

C-clamp. A screw-type clamp made in the shape of the letter C. One jaw is fixed, and the other is mounted on a screw.

CD. *See* compact disk.

CD duct. *See* convergent-divergent duct.

CDI (course deviation indicator). An indicator used with VOR, LORAN, or GPS navigation systems to indicate the direction and relative amount of deviation from the desired course. CDIs are often called Left-Right indicators.

CDU (control display unit). A component in a flight management computer system that contains a cathode-ray tube and a keyboard with alphanumeric keys and mode-select and line-select keys. The CDU allows the flight crew to access the data to be displayed.

Ceconite. The registered trade name for an inorganic aircraft fabric woven of polyester fibers. Ceconite is installed on the structure and then shrunk with heat.

ceiling (meteorological condition). *14 CFR Part 1:* "The height above the earth's surface of the lowest layer of clouds or obscuring phenomena reported as 'broken,' 'overcast,' or 'obscuration,' and not classified as 'thin' or 'partial.'"

ceiling balloon (meteorology). A small, black, helium-filled balloon used to find the height of a base of clouds. The balloon is released by a weather observer, and the time needed for it to disappear into the clouds is measured. Since both the rate of rise of the balloon and the time it took to disappear into the clouds are known, the height of the base of the clouds can be determined.

ceiling light (meteorology). A light used by weather observers to measure the height of the bottom of a layer of clouds at night. A beam of light, shone vertically upward, makes a spot of light on the bottom of the cloud.

A theodolite (an instrument used to measure angles), located a known distance away from the light, is used to measure the angle up to the spot of light on the cloud base. By knowing the distance between the theodolite and the ceiling light and the angle measured by the theodolite, the height of the cloud base can be determined.

ceilometer (meteorology). A cloud-height measuring system. A ceilometer projects a beam of light on the cloud base, detects the reflection by a photoelectric cell, and determines the cloud-base height by triangulation.

celestial navigation. A form of navigation used by airplanes and ships. Location fixes are found by observing the angle between the observer and one of the navigational stars, and noting the exact time the observation is made. The exact location of the navigational star at the time of the observation is found by referring to a nautical almanac.

The location on the earth's surface of the star at the time of observation and the angle between the star and the observer are plotted on a navigational chart. Celestial navigation has been almost entirely replaced by various forms of electronic navigation, which are more accurate and easier to use.

cell (electrochemical). An electrochemical device consisting of two electrodes surrounded by an electrolyte. A potential difference exists between the electrodes that causes electrons to flow.

Celluloid. The registered trade name for one of the early thermoplastic materials. Celluloid is made from cellulose nitrate and camphor.

cellulose. A material obtained from natural fibrous plants such as cotton and kapok. Cellulose is treated with certain acids to make the base for some plastic materials.

C

cellulose acetate butyrate dope (aircraft finishing material). A form of finishing material for fabric-covered aircraft made of a cellulose fiber dissolved in a mixture of acetic and butyric acids. Plasticizers, solvents, and thinners are mixed with the film base to give it the proper working qualities. Cellulose acetate butyrate dope, also called CAB dope or, more simply, butyrate dope, has become more popular than the older cellulose nitrate dope because it is far less flammable than nitrate dope.

cellulose nitrate. A compound made by treating cellulose with a mixture of nitric and sulfuric acids. Cellulose nitrate is used as the base for certain plastics, and as a component in the manufacture of explosives. Cellulose nitrate is also known as nitrocellulose and guncotton.

cellulose nitrate dope (aircraft finishing material). A form of finishing material for fabric-covered aircraft made of a cellulose fiber dissolved in nitric and sulfuric acids. Plasticizers, solvents, and thinners are mixed with the film base to give it the proper working qualities.

Cellulose nitrate dope (generally called nitrate dope) is an excellent adhesive, but it is being replaced to a great extent by butyrate dope. Butyrate dope is not as good an adhesive, but it is much less flammable.

Celsius temperature. Temperature measured on a scale that sets the freezing point of water at 0° and its boiling point at 100°. There are 100 equal graduations called degrees between these two points. Absolute zero is −273°C. Celsius temperature was formerly called centigrade temperature.

CEMF (counterelectromotive force). A voltage produced in the armature of an electric motor as the armature windings cut across the fixed magnetic field. The polarity of the CEMF is opposite the polarity of the voltage applied to the motor, and it opposes the applied voltage.

CENRAP-plus. A computer program developed to provide a back-up system for airport surveillance radar in the event of a terminal secondary radar system failure. The program uses a combination of Air Route Traffic Control Center Radar and terminal airport surveillance radar primary targets displayed simultaneously for the processing and presentation of data on the ARTS IIA or IIIA displays.

center. A point within an object that is the same distance from all points on the surface of the object.

center drill. A cutting tool which combines a twist drill and a 60° countersink. A center drill is used to drill the center hole in a piece of metal so it can be mounted between the centers in a lathe.

centering (glider operations). In thermal soaring flight (called "thermalling"), centering the thermal is used to determine where the best lift is and move the glider into it for a most consistent climb. After entering a thermal, the pilot adjusts circling turns in order to achieve the greatest average climb. *See also* thermalling.

centering cam (landing gear component). A cam on the shock strut of a retractable nose gear that aligns the wheel when there is no weight on the landing gear, so it will fit into the nose wheel well.

centering cones (propeller component). Cones installed on a splined propeller shaft to hold the propeller hub centered. The rear cone is a single-piece split bronze cone, and the front cone is a two-piece chrome-plated steel cone.

center line (aircraft drawings). A thin line consisting of alternate long and short dashes used in an aircraft drawing to show the center of a part.

center line

center-line thrust airplane. A twin-engine airplane with both engines mounted in the fuselage. One is installed as a tractor in the front of the cabin, and the other as a pusher behind the cabin. The empennage is mounted on booms.

center of buoyancy. The average point of buoyancy in floating objects. Weight added above this point will cause the floating object to sit deeper in the water in a level attitude.

center of gravity. *See* CG.

center of gravity envelope (aircraft weight and balance). An envelope drawn on a graph included in aircraft Type Certificate Data Sheets and aircraft flight operations manuals showing the center of gravity limits for all weights up to the maximum allowable gross weight of the aircraft.

Any combination of weight and center of gravity location that falls within the envelope is an approved loading condition for the aircraft.

center of gravity limits (aircraft weight and balance). The specified forward and aft points beyond which the CG must not be located during flight. These limits are indicated in the Type Certificate Data Sheets (TCDS) for the aircraft.

center of gravity moment envelope. An enclosed area on a graph of the airplane's loaded weight and loaded moment. If lines drawn from the weight and loaded moment cross within the CG envelope, the airplane is properly loaded. *See* center of gravity envelope (aircraft weight and balance).

center of gravity range (aircraft weight and balance). The distance in inches between the forward allowable center of gravity and the rearward allowable center of gravity.

The allowable center of gravity range changes with the gross weight of the aircraft, and the gross weight must be specified for the center of gravity range to be meaningful. In most modern aircraft, this center of gravity range is shown in the aircraft Type Certificate Data Sheets in the form of a center of gravity envelope.

center of lift (aerodynamic parameter). The location along the chord line of an airfoil at which all the lift forces produced by the airfoil are considered to be concentrated.

center of mass. The location within a body at which its entire mass is considered to be balanced.

center of pressure (aerodynamics). The point on the chord line of an airfoil (a line through the airfoil that joins the leading edge and the trailing edge) where all the aerodynamic forces are considered to be concentrated.

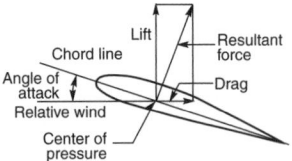

center of pressure

center of pressure coefficient (airfoil data). The distance between the leading edge of an airfoil and the location of the center of pressure expressed as a ratio of this distance to the length of the airfoil chord line.

If the center of pressure coefficient, which is expressed as "cp" on a set of airfoil characteristic curves, is 0.3, the center of pressure is located 30% of the chord line length behind the leading edge of the airfoil.

center of thrust. A line through an aircraft along which the thrust from an engine acts.

center punch. A small, metalworking punch used to make an impression in a piece of metal to hold the point of a twist drill so it can start cutting without walking over the surface of the metal. The point of a center punch forms an angle of approximately 60°. This angle allows the drill to start cutting easily.

center radar ARTS presentation/processing (CENRAP) (air traffic control). A computer program developed to provide a backup system for airport surveillance radar in the event of a failure or malfunction. The program uses ARTCC radar for the processing and presentation of data on the ARTS IIA or IIIA displays.

Additionally, "CENRAP-Plus" (or, center radar ARTS presentation/processing-plus) is a backup system in the event of a terminal secondary radar system failure, using a combination of ARTCC radar and terminal airport surveillance radar primary targets displayed simultaneously.

center's area (air traffic control). Specified airspace within which an air traffic control center (ARTCC) provides air traffic control and advisory service.

center-tapped winding (electrical transformer winding). A winding on an electrical transformer that has a tap, or connection, located in its electrical center. A center tap is used to divide the winding into two halves which have opposite polarities. A center-tapped secondary winding of a power transformer is needed for a two-diode, full-wave rectifier.

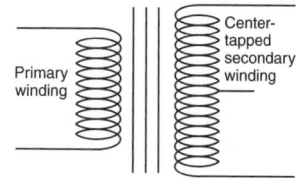

center-tapped winding

center TRACON automation system (CTAS). A computerized set of programs designed to aid Air Route Traffic Control Centers and TRACONs in the management and control of air traffic.

center weather advisory (meteorology). An unscheduled weather advisory issued by center weather service unit meteorologists for ATC use to alert pilots of existing or anticipated adverse weather conditions within the next two hours.

centigrade temperature. The name formerly used for Celsius temperature. The name centigrade means 100 graduations. *See* Celsius temperature.

centimeter-gram-second system. The system of metric measurement in which the centimeter is the basic unit of linear measurement, the gram is the basic unit of mass, and the second is the basic unit of time. This is known as the cgs system.

central east pacific. An organized route system between the U.S. West Coast and Hawaii.

central processing unit (digital computer). *See* CPU.

central refueling system (aircraft fuel system). A type of fuel system used in large aircraft that allows all the fuel tanks to be fueled from a single point, usually under the wing. A central refueling system is also called a single-point fueling system, or a pressure fueling system.

centrifugal brake. A friction brake used on a hoist drum. A centrifugal brake automatically applies friction to stop the hoist if the drum ever turns at a speed faster than is allowed.

centrifugal clutch. A form of friction clutch that engages when the drive wheel reaches a certain speed. The clutch is engaged by centrifugal force acting on a flyweight mechanism.

centrifugal compressor (gas turbine engine component). A compressor in a gas turbine engine that uses a scroll-type impeller. Air is taken into the center, or eye, of the impeller and slung outward by centrifugal force into the diffuser where its velocity is decreased and its pressure increased.

Centrifugal compressors were used on the first gas turbine aircraft engines, and are used on some modern engines as a high-pressure stage that receives its input air from a low-pressure axial-flow stage.

centrifugal filter. A filter that separates contaminants from a fluid by centrifugal action. The contaminants are thrown by rotary motion into traps that hold them until they can be removed.

centrifugal force. A force that acts outwardly on any body moving in a curved path. Centrifugal force tries to move a body away from the center of its rotation, and this force is opposed by centripetal force.

centrifugal moment. A force which tries to cause rotation. A centrifugal moment is the product of the amount of centrifugal force acting on an object, multiplied by the distance between the object and the center of its rotation.

centrifugal pump (fluid pump). A variable displacement pump which moves fluid by taking it into the center of a scroll-type impeller and slinging it outward by centrifugal action. Aircraft fuel boost pumps installed inside the fuel tanks are almost always centrifugal pumps.

centrifugal switch. An electrical switch actuated by centrifugal force and mounted inside of a piece of rotating machinery. Centrifugal switches are used in capacitor-start induction motors to disconnect the start winding when the rotor reaches a specified speed.

centrifugal tachometer. A type of mechanical tachometer used to measure the speed of rotation of a shaft or wheel. Two or three flyweights are mounted on a collar around a rotating shaft in such a way that, as they spin, centrifugal force pulls them away from the shaft. As they move away from the shaft, the collar moves up the shaft. As the collar moves up, it causes a pointer to move over a dial to indicate the speed being measured.

centrifugal twisting force. *See* CTF.

centrifugal twisting moment. *See* CTM.

centrifuge (physical separator). A device used to separate a liquid mixture or suspension into its various components which have different specific gravities. A container of the liquid mixture is spun at a high speed, and the components having the higher specific gravities are slung to the outside where they are drawn off.

centrifuge (space travel simulator). A large machine having a long motor-driven arm which moves a vehicle in a circular path at various rotational speeds. Humans and animals are carried in the vehicle to study the effect of prolonged acceleration, such as they would find while traveling in a spacecraft or rocket.

centrifuging. A method of separating liquids which have different densities by spinning them in a centrifuge.

centripetal force. The force within a body that opposes centrifugal force as the body rotates or spins. Centripetal force acts inside a piece of rotating machinery and tries to pull the rotating object in toward the center of its rotation.

centroid. The center of mass of a body. It is the point about which all the mass can be considered to be concentrated.

ceramic. Any of several hard, brittle, heat-resistant, noncorrosive materials made by shaping and then firing a mineral, such as clay, at a high temperature. Ceramic electrical insulators are stronger than glass, and they withstand high temperatures better than glass.

ceramic magnet. A permanent magnet made by pressing together a mixture of ceramic material and sintered magnetic particles. Ceramic magnetic material is called ferromagnetic ceramic.

CERAP (combined center-rapcon). An air traffic control facility which combines the function of an air route traffic control center (ARTCC) and a radar approach control facility.

cerium. A lustrous, iron-gray, malleable, metallic, rare-earth chemical element. Cerium's symbol is Ce, its atomic number is 58, and its atomic weight is 140.12. Cerium is used as a getter in the manufacture of electron tubes and as a constituent in friction-lighter flints.

cermet. Any of a group of strong, heat-resistant materials made by sintering metals with ceramic. Sintering is a process of pressing powdered materials together under enough heat that they are almost, but not, quite melted. Cermet, also known as ceramet, or metal ceramic, is used to make turbine blades for gas turbine engines.

certificated aircraft. An aircraft whose design specifications meet at least the minimum requirements specified by the Federal Aviation Administration for the particular type of aircraft. An approved type certificate (ATC) is issued for the aircraft design, and when an aircraft is built according to these specifications and maintained in such a way that it continues to meet these specifications, it is considered to be legally airworthy.

certificate holder. A person who holds or is required to hold an air carrier certificate or operating certificate issued under 14 CFR Part 119.

certificate-holding district office. The flight standards district office that has responsibility for administering the certificate and is charged with the overall inspection of the certificate holder's operations.

Certificate of Airworthiness. *See* Airworthiness Certificate.

certified flight instructor. A flight instructor authorized by the FAA to provide flight instruction in designated category of aircraft.

certified tower radar display (CTRD). An FAA radar display certified for use in the NAS.

cesium. A soft, silvery-white, ductile, metallic chemical element. Cesium's symbol is Cs, its atomic number is 55, and its atomic weight is 132.905. Cesium is an important element used in the manufacture of photoelectric cells.

CFI. *See* certified flight instructor.

CFR. *See* Code of Federal Regulations.

CFR engine. A special test engine used by the Cooperative Fuel Research to determine the octane rating of a hydrocarbon fuel. A CFR engine has a variable compression ratio, and it can be adjusted to cause any fuel being tested to detonate, or explode, rather than burn evenly. The fuel being tested is run in the CFR engine and the compression ratio is adjusted until the fuel detonates.

With the engine adjusted to cause detonation, the fuel under test is shut off, and a reference fuel, which is a mixture of iso-octane and normal heptane, is directed into the engine. The ratio of the iso-octane to heptane is changed until the reference fuel detonates the same as the fuel being tested.

The percentage of iso-octane in the reference fuel having the same detonation characteristics in the CFR engine as the fuel being tested is the octane number given the fuel.

CFRP (carbon fiber reinforced plastic). A high-strength, high-stiffness composite material made of carbon fibers encased in a resin matrix.

CG (center of gravity). The point in an object at which all of the weight is considered to be concentrated. The algebraic sum of the moments about the center of gravity is zero. The center of gravity may be expressed in inches from the datum or in percent of the mean aerodynamic chord.

Center of gravity may also be thought of as the point within an object about which all the moments trying to rotate the object are balanced.

cgs system. *See* centimeter-gram-second system.

chafe. To wear something away by a rubbing action.

chafer (aircraft tire component). Layers of rubberized fabric that wrap around the edges of the carcass plies and enclose the bead area of the tire. Chafers provide good chafe resistance between the tire bead and the wheel.

chaff (radar countermeasure). A material used to confuse enemy radar. Chaff is made of thin strips of metal foil packaged in such a way that it can be ejected from an airplane. When the chaff is ejected, it spreads out in the air and makes a large radar return.

chafing tape. A fabric tape used to cover edges of metal sheets, screw and rivet heads, and any surface discontinuity on an aircraft structure that is to be covered by aircraft fabric. Covering these parts with chafing tape prevents their rubbing holes in the fabric.

chain gear. A form of toothed wheel, or sprocket, used to transmit motion from one shaft to another. Sprockets on both shafts are joined by a roller chain, and when one shaft is turned, the roller chain pulls the other shaft around. The rear wheel of a bicycle is driven by a roller chain passing over two chain gears.

chain hoist. A form of tackle used in a shop to lift heavy weights. A chain hoist uses an endless loop of chain to rotate the drive gear in a planetary gear system. The chain that supports and lifts the load is pulled up by the driven gear in the planetary system. A chain hoist is sometimes called a chain block or a chain fall.

chain reaction. A self-sustaining action in which one event causes other events of the same kind to happen. It is a chain reaction in nuclear fission that releases so much energy that a neutron is knocked out of the nucleus of an atom. This neutron knocks other neutrons out, and each of them knocks out still other neutrons.

chamfer. A bevel cut on the edge of a piece of metal or plastic. Chamfered edges are more attractive than sharp edges, and they are less likely to cut a person who contacts the edge.

chamfer (*verb*). The act of cutting a bevel on the edge of a piece of metal or plastic.

chamfered edge. A beveled edge.

chamfered point (threaded fastener). The point of a threaded fastener, such as a bolt or a screw, that is formed in the shape of a cone with its top cut off (a truncated cone). The distance across the flat point of the cone is usually slightly less than the minor diameter of the threads, the diameter of the bolt or screw, measured at the bottom of the threads.

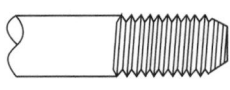

chamfered point

Chamfered points are used when easy entry into the hole for starting is important.

chamfered tooth (timing device). A tooth of a gear that has had one of the edges of its point chamfered, or beveled. The chamfered edge identifies the tooth that must be meshed with marked teeth on the mating gear to properly time the mechanism driven by the gears.

Magneto distributor gears and the gears that drive the valve mechanism in a reciprocating engine often use chamfered teeth to aid in timing.

chamois skin. A piece of soft, pliable leather, from the skin of a chamois, a goat-like antelope. Chamois skin is used to filter gasoline. Gasoline will pass through a chamois skin, but water will not. Gasoline that has been filtered through a chamois skin can be considered to be free from water.

chandelle (airplane maneuver). A maximum performance flight maneuver used in pilot training to develop skill in control and coordination. The airplane is put into a maximum-rate climb and turned in such a way that its heading changes 180° by the time the airspeed drops off to a given value.

change of state (meteorology). The transformation of water from one form into another. Five changes of state are designated by these terms:
• Condensation is the change of water vapor into liquid water.
• Evaporation is the change of liquid water into water vapor.
• Freezing is the change of liquid water into solid water (ice).
• Melting is the change of ice into liquid water.
• Sublimation is the change of ice into water vapor or water vapor into ice.

changeover points (COPs). A point along the route or airway segment between two adjacent navigation facilities or waypoints where a changeover in navigation guidance should occur.

Channel-Chrome cylinders. The registered trade name for reciprocating engine cylinders whose walls are plated with hard chromium by a patented process. The surface of this chrome plating forms a spider web of tiny stress cracks. After the plating is completed, deplating current is used to enlarge the cracks and form channels that hold lubricating oil on the cylinder wall.

channel iron. A form of extruded steel whose cross section is in the shape of the letter U. Extruded steel is formed by forcing it through a specially shaped die.

channel section (structural material). A structural material having the cross-sectional shape of a channel, or the letter U. A channel section can be formed (bent) from a flat sheet of metal, or it can be extruded (squeezed through a specially shaped die).

channel wing (aeronautics). A special type of airplane wing made in the form of half of a cylinder. The upper camber of the airfoil section of the channel wing is on the inside of the cylinder, and it forms one half of a venturi. The propeller is installed in such a way that it pulls air through the channel, across the top of the airfoil, and produces lift even when the aircraft has almost no forward speed. Channel wing aircraft have flown, but technical difficulties have prevented them from becoming popular.

chapter. Associated group of electronic "pages" of information from databases found in FMS and GPS RNAV units similar in contents, such as airports, VORs, software/unit settings, and feature selections.

charcoal. A form of black, porous carbon. Charcoal is made by charring, or partially burning, wood in a kiln (a special type of oven) in which there is not enough air for the wood to burn completely.

charge (electrical condition). A condition in which there is an excess or deficiency of electrons on a body. If there is an excess of electrons, the charge is negative. A deficiency of electrons results in a positive charge.

charging a battery. The process of restoring the active material on the plates of a battery to a condition that allows it to convert chemical energy into electrical energy. When a battery is discharged, the active material on the plates changes its chemical composition, and when the battery is charged, this material is restored to its original condition.

Charging a lead-acid battery is done by passing direct current of the correct voltage and polarity through the battery. When the electricity flows through the battery, the lead sulfate on the positive plate changes into lead peroxide, and the lead sulfate on the negative plate changes into pure lead. The electrolyte takes on a heavier concentration of sulfuric acid, its specific gravity increases.

charging current (battery charging). The direct current forced through the secondary cells of a battery to charge them. Charging current restores the active material on the plates to a condition that allows them to change chemical energy into electrical energy.

charging stand (air conditioning service equipment). A compact arrangement of air conditioning servicing equipment. A charging stand contains a vacuum pump, a manifold gage set, and a method of measuring and dispensing the refrigerant.

Charles's law. The basic gas law that describes the relationship between the temperature and the volume of a gas. Charles's law states that if the pressure of the gas is held constant and its absolute temperature is increased, the volume of the gas will also increase.

chart (engineering data). A graphic presentation that shows the way the value of one variable changes with variations in other variables. A chart allows a person to visualize the way a change in one action affects other actions.

chart (navigation). A special map used for aerial navigation that gives the location and all information necessary about the aids to navigation. A chart also shows the grids of latitude and longitude and provides a surface for plotting courses and locating fixes.

charted VFR flyways (air traffic control). Flight paths recommended for use to bypass areas heavily traversed by large turbine-powered aircraft. Pilot compliance with recommended flyways and associated altitudes is strictly voluntary. VFR Flyway Planning Charts are published on the back of existing VFR Terminal Area Charts.

charted visual flight procedure (CVFP). A CVFP may be established at some towered airports for environmental or noise considerations, as well as when necessary for the safety and efficiency of air traffic operations. Designed primarily for turbojet aircraft, CVFPs depict prominent landmarks, courses, and recommended altitudes to specific runways.

charted visual flight procedure approach (air traffic control). An approach conducted while operating on an instrument rules (IFR) flight plan which authorizes the pilot of an aircraft to proceed visually and clear of clouds to the airport via visual landmarks and other information depicted on a charted visual flight procedure. This approach must be authorized and under the control of the appropriate air traffic control facility. The weather minimums required are depicted on the approach chart.

chase aircraft. An aircraft flown in proximity to another aircraft normally to observe its performance during flight testing.

chasing threads. The process of restoring damaged threads on a bolt or shaft. A die is screwed over the threads to remove any of the damage.

chassis (electronic equipment). The sheet metal frame inside a piece of electronic equipment on which components are mounted.

chassis ground. An electrical reference point in a piece of equipment that is not connected to the earth ground. A chassis ground is also called a floating ground.

chatter (hydraulic system malfunction). A type of rapid vibration of a hydraulic pump caused by the pump taking in some air along with the hydraulic fluid.

chassis ground

chattering (brake malfunction). A malfunctioning condition of aircraft brakes that produces heavy vibrations. Chattering is caused by a glazed surface on the disk that alternately produces friction and then allows the lining to slip over the disk. High-frequency chattering is called brake squeal.

CHDO. An FAA Flight Standards certificate holding district office.

check (wood defect). Longitudinal cracks in a piece of wood, generally extending across the annual rings.

check flight (aircraft maintenance procedure). A test flight of an aircraft conducted to find out if all the systems are functioning as they should. Check flights are normally conducted after an aircraft has been inspected or repaired.

checklist. A systematic and sequential list of all operations that must be performed to properly accomplish a complex task. Checklists are used in preflight inspections as well as 100-hour and annual inspections of aircraft, to ensure that no required operation is overlooked.

check nut. A thin nut that can be jammed down tightly against a plain nut on a bolt. The check nut keeps the plain nut from vibrating loose.

checkpoint (navigation). A location that can be positively identified either visually or electronically. When an aircraft flies over a checkpoint, the pilot knows his exactly location.

checkride. The test a pilot takes in the airplane to earn a certificate or rating. Also known as the Practical Test.

check valve (fluid power system component). A valve that allows fluid to flow through it in one direction, but prevents it flowing through in the opposite direction. *See* the illustration of ball check valve.

cheek (reciprocating engine crankshaft). The offset portion of a crankshaft that forms the crankpin to which the connecting rod big end is attached.

cheesecloth. A lightweight cotton gauze which has no sizing in it. Sizing is a substance, such as starch, used to make a cloth stiff. Cheesecloth is used as a straining element to remove lumps and contaminants from liquids.

chemical bond (composites). The physical phenomenon in which chemical substances are held together by attraction of atoms to each other through sharing, as well as exchanging, of electrons or electrostatic forces.

chemical compound. A combination of two or more atoms of chemical elements which have joined together to form molecules. A compound is different from a mixture in that the elements in a compound unite in specific amounts to form a substance different from any of the original elements. In a mixture, the elements keep their identity.

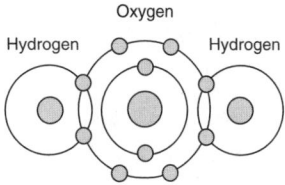

chemical compound

When two atoms of hydrogen join one atom of oxygen by sharing some of their electrons, the chemical compound water (H_2O) is formed.

chemical element. One of the fundamental building blocks of which all matter is made. There are just a few more than 100 different chemical elements. Some elements exist in nature by themselves, and others exist only in chemical compounds. Oxygen, carbon, gold, silver, and hydrogen are examples of chemical elements.

chemical energy. Energy that exists in a chemical element or in a chemical compound. This energy may be released when the element or compound joins (reacts with) other chemicals to produce new compounds.

For example, when gasoline (C_8H_{18}) burns, it reacts with oxygen (O_2) in the air and forms carbon dioxide (CO_2) and water (H_2O). It also releases a large amount of energy in the form of light and heat.

chemical etching (metal processing). A process in which a chemical is used to microscopically roughen the surface of a metal. Chemical etching is used to prepare a metal so primer will form a tight bond to its surface.

chemical fire extinguisher. Any of three types of fire extinguishers: vaporizing liquid, carbon dioxide, or dry powder. All three types of fire extinguishers expel the extinguishing agent and blanket the fire with an inert gas to keep oxygen away from it. When a fire can no longer get oxygen, it will go out.

chemical milling. A method of machining large sheets of metal by chemically etching away part of the surface. The inside of the skins of some high-performance aircraft are etched to remove metal not needed for strength. Removing this metal by chemical milling reduces the weight of the aircraft. Chemical milling produces a lightweight skin with all the needed strength and rigidity far more economically than can be done with conventional machining or by building up a skin with riveted-on stiffeners.

chemical oxygen candle system. An oxygen system used for emergency or backup use. Solid blocks of a material that releases oxygen when burned are carried in special fireproof fixtures. When oxygen is needed, the candles are ignited with a built in igniter, and oxygen flows into the tubing leading to the masks.

chemical reaction. A change in the chemical nature (the chemical characteristics) of elements when they unite to form a chemical compound. Hydrogen is a lighter-than-air gas, and oxygen is also a gas. But when two atoms of hydrogen unite with one atom of oxygen, one molecule of water (H_2O), a liquid, is formed. The compound water has different chemical characteristics from those of either of the elements oxygen or hydrogen. When hydrogen and oxygen combine to form water, a chemical reaction takes place.

chemical salt. A product that forms when an acid combines with a metal. For example, when hydrochloric acid reacts with zinc, zinc chloride, a salt, forms. Most chemical salts are porous and powdery and have no strength.

chemistry. The branch of science that deals with the composition, properties, and structure of matter. Chemistry is primarily concerned with the materials of which matter is made, and with the energy absorbed or released during changes in the characteristics of these materials.

Cherrylock® rivet. A special type of Cherry rivet in which a locking collar is swaged into a groove between the stem and the rivet head to prevent the stem from coming out of the installed rivet. Cherrylock rivets can normally be used to replace solid rivets on a size-for-size basis. *See* Cherry rivet.

cherry picker (maintenance equipment). A long, hydraulically operated boom with a man-carrying bucket on its end. A person can be lifted in the bucket of the cherry picker so he can work at a high location. They are used in aircraft maintenance for working on large airplanes. Cherry pickers are usually mounted on a truck so that they can be moved from place to place where they are needed.

Cherry rivet. A patented blind rivet manufactured by the Cherry Rivet Division of Townsend, Inc. The shank of the rivet is inserted through a hole in the metals to be joined and is upset by pulling a tapered stem through the hollow shank. After the shank is upset, further pulling on the stem breaks it off.

chevron seal. A form of one-way seal used on the piston in some fluid-power actuators. Chevron seals are made of a resilient material in the shape of the letter V, a chevron. The pressure being sealed with a chevron seal must be applied to the open side of the V.

chilled iron. A form of cast iron which has been cast in a steel mold. The steel mold cools the surface of the casting quickly so that it retains most of the carbon and is quite hard.

chin (aircraft structure). A part of an aircraft structure that sticks out from the bottom of the forward part of the fuselage. Some multiengine military aircraft have chin turrets. These are turrets in which guns are mounted below the nose of the aircraft.

chine. A longitudinal member of a seaplane hull or float that forms the joint between the bottom and the side of the structure.

chine tire. An aircraft nose wheel tire that has a special deflector, or chine, molded into its sidewall. Chine tires are mounted on the nose wheel of jet aircraft whose engines are mounted on the rear of the fuselage. When the aircraft lands on a wet or icy runway, the chine throws water and slush out to the side so that none of it gets into the engines.

chinook (meteorology). A warm, dry wind that blows down the eastern slopes of the Rocky Mountains in the United States. The air in a chinook lost most of its moisture as it blew up the western slopes of the mountains, and it is dry and warm as it blows down the eastern slopes.

chip detector (lubrication system component). A component in a lubrication system that attracts and holds ferrous metal chips that may be circulating with the engine oil. Some chip detectors are part of an electrical circuit. When a metal particle shorts across the two contacts in the detector, the circuit is completed, and a warning light is turned on to inform the flight crew that metal particles are loose in the lubrication system.

chisel. A hardened steel cutting tool with a narrow cutting edge. Chisels used to cut wood normally have a wooden handle which is hit with a mallet to drive the chisel blade into the wood. Chisels used to cut metal are called cold chisels.

chlorate candle (oxygen supply). A block of solid sodium chlorate that is burned in a special housing to release breathing oxygen. Oxygen systems using chlorate candles are commonly called solid, or chemical, oxygen systems. They are used as backup oxygen supplies in some large aircraft, and as a portable oxygen supply carried in small aircraft when oxygen is rarely needed.

chlorine. A highly irritating, greenish-yellow, gaseous, halogen chemical element. Chlorine's symbol is Cl, its atomic number is 17, and its atomic weight is 35.543. Chlorine is used as a disinfectant and as an agent to purify water.

chlorobromomethane (fire extinguishing agent). A liquefied gas, Halon 1011, with a UL toxicity rating of 3. It is commonly referred to as "CB." It is more toxic than CO_2, is corrosive to aluminum, magnesium, steel and brass, and is not recommended for aircraft use.

chock. A triangular block of metal or wood used to wedge in front of and behind the tires of an aircraft to keep the aircraft from rolling.

choke (electrical component). An inductor used to impede, or oppose, the changes of pulsating direct current. The opposition caused by a choke is inductive reactance, which produces a back voltage opposing the changing voltage in the pulsations. Chokes are used with capacitors to make filter circuits to smooth out the voltage variations and change pulsating DC into smooth DC.

choke coil (electrical component). An inductor used in an electrical circuit to suppress or limit the flow of alternating current without affecting the flow of direct current.

choked flow (gas turbine engine condition). The condition in which a gas or fluid under pressure travels through a restriction into a lower-pressure environment; the mass flow rate is directly proportional to the area of the restriction for a wide range of conditions.

choked nozzle (gas turbine exhaust system). A nozzle in a gas turbine engine that limits the speed of the gases flowing through it. The gases speed up until they reach the speed of sound. At this point, a normal shock wave forms that prevents further acceleration.

choke-ground cylinder (reciprocating engine cylinder). A cylinder of a reciprocating engine ground in such a way that its diameter at the top of the barrel is slightly smaller than the diameter in the center of the barrel.

The large mass of metal in the cylinder head absorbs enough heat to cause the top end of the barrel to expand enough more than the remainder of the barrel that, at the normal operating temperature, the diameter of choke-ground cylinders becomes uniform throughout.

choke-input filter (electronic filter). A form of filter used with an electronic power supply to change pulsating direct current into smooth DC. A choke, or inductor, is the first element in the filter, and one or more capacitors are installed in parallel with the output of the power supply following the choke.

choke of a cylinder. The difference between the bore diameter of a reciprocating engine cylinder in the area of the head and in the center of the barrel.

choo-choo (gas turbine engine operating condition). A mild compressor surge caused by an obstruction of the airflow through the compressor. The name comes from the sound made by the engine.

chop (sea condition). A roughened condition of the sea surface caused by local winds. It is characterized by irregularity, short distance between crests, and whitecaps.

chopper (electrical component). An electronic or electromagnetic device used to interrupt DC or low-frequency AC at regular intervals to produce a pulsating voltage whose frequency is high enough that it can be amplified by an AC amplifier.

chord. The straight-line distance across an airfoil from leading edge to trailing edge.

chord line. An imaginary straight line drawn from the leading edge of an airfoil to the trailing edge.

chord of a circle. A straight line across a circle that touches the circumference at two points. The chord passing through the center of a circle is called the diameter.

chord of an airfoil. An imaginary line drawn through an airfoil from its leading edge to its trailing edge. The chord, or chord line, is used as a reference, or datum, for laying out the curve of the airfoil.

chordwise. The direction from the leading edge to trailing edge of an airfoil.

chordwise axis. A term used in reference to semirigid rotors describing the flapping or teetering axis of the rotor.

chromel. An alloy of nickel and chromium. Chromel is highly resistant to oxidation and has a high electrical resistance. It is one of the metals used in a thermocouple to measure the exhaust gas temperature in both reciprocating and gas turbine engines.

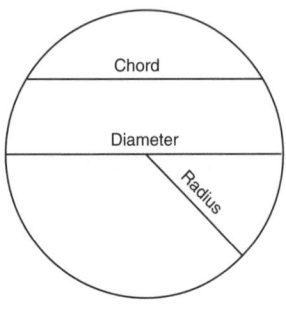

chord of a circle

chord of an airfoil

chromel-alumel thermocouple. A thermocouple used to measure the temperature of the exhaust gas in either reciprocating or gas turbine engines. It can be used for measuring temperatures up to 1,000°C.

Chromel is the positive lead, and it is normally enclosed in a white insulation for color coding. Alumel is the negative lead, and it is normally enclosed in a green insulation. The alumel lead can also be distinguished from the chromel lead because alumel is magnetic.

chrome molybdenum steel. A high-strength alloy steel in which chromium and molybdenum are the chief alloying agents. It is easy to machine and weld, and has high strength for its weight. Most welded tubular steel aircraft structure is made of chrome molybdenum tubing. Chrome molybdenum steels are the SAE 41xx series.

chrome nickel steel. An alloy of steel used for making many of the fittings and fasteners used in aircraft structure. Chrome nickel steels are the SAE 3xxx series.

chrome pickling. A method of forming a hard oxide film on the surface of a piece of magnesium to protect it from corrosion. To form this film, the magnesium is soaked in a solution of potassium dichromate. Chrome pickling is also called dichromate conversion. The surface of the metal is converted into a dense oxide film.

chrome plating. An electroplating process in which a thin film of chromium is plated on the surface of a steel part. There are two types of chrome plating: hard chrome and decorative chrome. Hard chrome is used to plate the inside walls of an engine cylinder to form a wear-resistant surface. Decorative chrome is used on such components as automobile bumpers to provide a durable, weather-resistant, and attractive surface.

chrome vanadium steel. A very tough alloy of steel with chromium and vanadium. Chrome vanadium steel is used for making wrenches and other tools that require high strength and good impact resistance.

chromic acid. An acid used for etching aluminum alloys to prepare them for painting. Chromic acid reacts with the aluminum to form a durable film on the surface that keeps oxygen away from the metal and inhibits the formation of corrosion.

chromium. A lustrous, hard, steel-gray, metallic chemical element. Chromium's symbol is Cr, its atomic number is 24, and its atomic weight is 51.996. Chromium is used to harden alloy steels and as an alloying agent to make corrosion-resistant steels.

chronometric tachometer. An instrument used to measure the speed in revolutions per minute of the crankshaft of an aircraft reciprocating engine. A chronometric tachometer repeatedly counts the number of revolutions in a given period of time and displays the average speed on its dial.

chuck (machine tool component). The device on a lathe or drill press used to hold either the material being worked or the machine tool used to work on the material. Chucks have three or more jaws to clamp and hold the material or the tool.

chugging (gas turbine engine operating condition). A noise heard in a gas turbine engine caused by unstable airflow in the engine. The chugging noise is produced by a mild compressor stall.

chute. A sloping channel used to allow objects or materials to slide from one level to a lower level.

cigarette (ignition system component). A ceramic or synthetic rubber insulator used on the end of an ignition lead that attaches to a shielded spark plug. A steel coil spring on the end of the cigarette conducts the high voltage from the lead wire to the center electrode of the spark plug.

circle. A closed plane figure with every point an equal distance from the center. A circle has the greatest area for its circumference of any enclosed shape.

circle graph. A visual presentation of data in which the entire quantity is shown as a circle. Each portion of the data is shown as a segment of the circle. Circle graphs are also called pie charts, because all the data resembles a complete pie, and each individual portion resembles a slice of the pie.

circle-to-land maneuver. A maneuver initiated by the pilot to align the aircraft with a runway for landing when a straight-in landing from an instrument approach is not possible or is not desirable.

"Circle to runway (runway number)" (air traffic control). A phrase used by ATC to inform the pilot that he must circle to land because the runway in use is other than the runway aligned with the instrument approach procedure. When the direction of the circling maneuver in relation to the airport/runway is required, the controller will state the direction and specify a left or right downwind or base leg as appropriate.

circling approach (or maneuver). *See* circle-to-land maneuver.

circling minima. *See* landing minimums.

circuit (electrical). The complete path followed by electrons from the negative terminal of the source of electrical energy, through the electrical load, back to the positive terminal of the source. All electrical circuits must have at least three components: the source of electrical energy, the electrical load, and conductors to connect the source and the load.

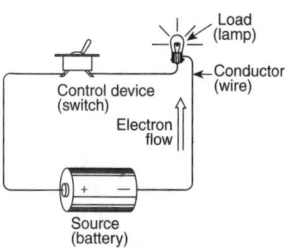

circuit (electrical)

circuit breaker (electrical circuit component). A device which opens an electrical circuit when an excess of current flows. A circuit breaker may be reset to restore the circuit after the fault causing the excessive current has been corrected. Circuit breakers may operate either by heat or a magnetic field, and some have an exposed control so they may be used as a switch as well as a circuit protector.

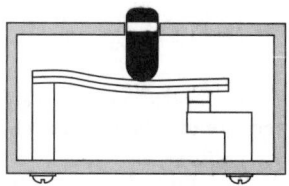

circuit breaker

circuit diagram. A drawing which uses conventional symbols to show the way the components in an electrical system or fluid power system are connected. Circuit diagrams do not show the physical relationship of the components, but the flow of electrons or fluid can be traced by following the circuit diagram.

circuit protection (electrical circuit). Provision in an electrical circuit to prevent the flow of an excessive amount of current. Circuit breakers, fuses, and current limiters open the circuit when excessive current flows.

circular inch. A measurement of area of circular objects. One circular inch is the area of a circle whose diameter is one inch. One circular inch is equal to 0.7854 square inch.

circular magnetization. A method of magnetizing a part for magnetic particle inspection. Current is passed through the part, and the lines of magnetic flux surround it. Circular magnetization makes it possible to detect faults that extend lengthwise through the part.

circular mil. A measurement of area used for round electrical conductors. A circular mil is the area of a circle whose diameter is one mil, or 0.001 inch. One circular mil is equal to 0.7854 square mil.

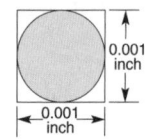

circular motion. Motion of an object along a curved path in which the object stays a constant distance from a given point, called the center of motion.

circular mil

circular saw. A powered saw that uses a thin, circular blade driven by an electric motor. In a table saw, the blade is mounted on an arbor, and only a portion of the blade sticks up above the surface of the table. In a radial-arm saw, the blade is mounted on the shaft of an electric motor which is suspended on an arm above the work. The saw is pulled across the work. A circular saw blade may also be mounted on a handheld electric motor and used as a hand saw.

circular slide rule. A slide rule with its scales arranged in rings on the surface of a disk. Transparent cursors, attached at the center of the disk, may be moved over the scale to add or subtract portions of the scales to perform the various mathematical operations.

circumference of a circle. The total linear distance around the outside of a circle. The length of the circumference of a circle is always 3.1416, or pi (π), times the length of the diameter of the circle (the distance across the circle at its center).

circumferential coil spring. A coil spring that is formed into a ring. This type of spring, also called a garter spring, is used to hold ring-type carbon seals tightly against a rotating shaft.

circumferential frame (aircraft structural component). A frame that gives an aircraft fuselage or engine nacelle its shape. A circumferential frame is also called a belt frame, or a transverse frame.

circumscribed circle. A circle drawn around the outside of a regular polygon in such a way that all the points of the polygon touch the circumference of the circle.

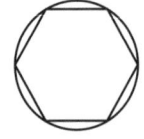

cirriform (meteorology). All species and varieties of cirrus, cirrocumulus, and cirrostratus clouds. Cirriform clouds are composed mostly or entirely of small ice crystals, usually transparent and white. Cirriform clouds often produce a halo around the sun or moon that is not observed with other cloud forms. The average height of cirriform clouds range upward from 20,000 feet in the middle latitudes.

circumscribed circle

cirrocumulus (meteorology). A cirriform cloud that appears as a thin sheet of small white puffs resembling flakes or patches of cotton without shadows. Cirrocumulus clouds are sometimes confused with altocumulus.

C

cirrostratus (meteorology). A cirriform cloud that appears as a whitish veil, usually fibrous, but sometimes smooth. Cirrostratus may totally cover the sky, and often forms a halo around the sun or moon.

cirrus (meteorology). A cirriform cloud in the form of thin, white featherlike patches or narrow bands. Cirrus clouds have a fibrous and/or silky sheen. Large ice crystals often trail downward for a considerable vertical distance in fibrous, slanted, or irregularly curved wisps called mare's tails.

cistern. A reservoir used to store a liquid. The container for the mercury in a mercury barometer is called a cistern.

civil aircraft. *14 CFR Part 1:* "Aircraft other than public aircraft."

civil twilight. The period of time before sunrise and after sunset when the sun is not more than six degrees below the horizon.

clad aluminum. A sheet of aluminum alloy which has a coating of pure aluminum rolled on one or both of its sides. Aluminum alloys corrode easily, but pure aluminum does not. By rolling a thin coating of pure aluminum onto the surface of an alloy sheet, the high strength of the alloy and the corrosion resistance of pure aluminum may be combined. Because the pure aluminum coating is weaker than the alloy sheet, cladding slightly reduces the strength of the material.

cladding. A method of protecting aluminum alloys from corrosion by rolling a coating of pure aluminum onto the surface of the alloy. Cladding is done in the rolling mill.

clamp-on ammeter (electrical measuring instrument). A handheld ammeter for measuring the amount of alternating current flowing in a circuit without opening the circuit. The jaws of the ammeter are opened and slipped over the current-carrying wire and then clamped shut. The magnetic field caused by the current flowing through the wire induces a voltage in the ammeter jaws, proportional to the amount of current flowing in the circuit.

clamp-on ski. Skis that attach to the aircraft wheel and benefit from the additional shock absorbing qualities of the tires.

clamshell device. A mechanism having two doors which open on opposite sides of the device in the same way the shell of a clam opens. *See* clamshell thrust reverser.

clamshell thrust reverser (turbojet engine component). A thrust reverser that fits in the exhaust system of a turbojet engine. In normal operation, the clamshell doors form a part of the tail pipe, but when the reverser is deployed, the doors move into position to block the normal tail pipe and duct the exhaust gases around so they flow forward to oppose the forward movement of the aircraft.

claret red. A dark or grayish purplish red to dark purplish pink.

class (aircraft classification). *14 CFR Part 1:*
"(1) As used with respect to the certification, ratings, privileges, and limitations of airmen, means a classification of aircraft within a category having similar operating characteristics. Examples include: single engine; multiengine; land; water; gyroplane; helicopter; airship; and free balloon; and
(2) As used with respect to the certification of aircraft, means a broad grouping of aircraft having similar characteristics of propulsion, flight, or landing. Examples include: airplane; rotorcraft; glider; balloon; landplane; and seaplane."

Class A airspace. Generally, that airspace from 18,000 feet MSL up to and including FL 600, including the airspace overlying the waters within 12 nautical miles of the coast of the 48 contiguous States and Alaska; and designated international airspace beyond 12 nautical miles of the coast of the 48 contiguous States and Alaska within areas of domestic radio navigational signal or ATC radar coverage, and within which domestic procedures are applied.

class-A amplifier (electronic amplifier). An electronic amplifier whose output current flows at all times. The output of a class-A amplifier has the same waveform as the input, but the amplitude of the output is greater.

Class A fire. A fire involving solid combustible materials such as wood, paper, and cloth as its fuel.

Class B airspace. Generally, that airspace from the surface to 10,000 feet MSL surrounding the nation's busiest airports in terms of IFR operations or passenger enplanements. The configuration of each Class B airspace is individually tailored and consists of a surface area and two or more layers (some Class B airspace areas resemble upside down wedding cakes), and is designed to contain all published instrument procedures once an aircraft enters the airspace. An ATC clearance is required for all aircraft to operate in the area, and all aircraft so cleared receive separation services within the airspace. The cloud clearance requirement for VFR operations is "clear of clouds."

class-B amplifier (electronic amplifier). An electronic amplifier whose output current flows only during one half of the input cycle. Two class-B amplifiers can be connected in such a way that each amplifies one half of the input signal. Both amplifiers are connected to a single output device. Class-B amplifiers are called push-pull amplifiers.

Class B fire. A fire that has combustible liquids as its fuel.

Class C airspace. Generally, that airspace from the surface to 4,000 feet above the airport elevation (charted in MSL) surrounding those airports that have an operational control tower, are serviced by radar approach control, and that have a certain number of IFR operations or passenger enplanements. Although the configuration of each Class C airspace area is individually tailored, the airspace usually consists of a 5 NM radius core surface area that extends from the surface up to 4,000 feet above the airport elevation, and a 10 NM radius shelf area that extends from 1,200 feet to 4,000 feet above the airport elevation.

class-C amplifier (electronic amplifier). An electronic amplifier whose output current flows only during a small portion of one half of the input cycle. Class-C amplifiers are used to sustain radio-frequency oscillators by supplying pulses of energy to replace the energy lost in the resistance in the circuit.

Class C fire. A fire which involves energized electrical equipment.

Class D airspace. Generally, that airspace from the surface to 2,500 feet above the airport elevation (charted in MSL) surrounding those airports that have an operational control tower. The configuration of each Class D airspace area is individually tailored, and when instrument procedures are published, the airspace will normally be designed to contain the procedures.

Class D fire. A fire in which a metal such as magnesium burns.

Class E airspace. Generally, if the airspace is not Class A, Class B, Class C, or Class D, and it is controlled airspace, it is Class E airspace.

Class G airspace. Generally that airspace that is uncontrolled, and has not been designated as Class A, Class B, Class C, Class D, or Class E airspace.

class of thread (threaded fastener condition). A method of classifying the fit of threads used in bolts and nuts. A class-1 fit is a loose fit, a class-2 fit is a free fit, a class-3 fit is a medium fit, a class-4 fit is a close fit, and a class-5 fit is a wrench fit. Most fasteners used in aircraft structure have a class-3 fit.

claw hammer. A hammer used for driving and removing nails from wood. The claws which are used to remove nails may be either straight or curved.

clean configuration. An aircraft in a clean configuration is one in which all flight control surfaces have been placed so as to create minimum drag; in most aircraft this means flaps and gear retracted.

clean room. A special room used for manufacturing and servicing precision equipment. The air in a clean room is filtered, and special precautions are taken to prevent dust, dirt, or other contamination entering the room. The workers wear special clothing to prevent contamination from their street clothes or from their hair.

clear air turbulence. *See* CAT.

clearance (physical clearance). The distance or space between moving parts that allows free movement.

clearance delivery. Control tower position responsible for transmitting departure clearances to IFR flights.

clearance fit. *See* free fit.

clearance limit (air traffic control). The fix, point, or location to which an aircraft is cleared when issued an air traffic clearance.

clearance on request. An IFR clearance not yet received after filing a flight plan.

"Clearance void if not off by (time)" (air traffic control). A phrase used by ATC to advise an aircraft that the departure clearance is automatically canceled if takeoff is not made prior to a specific time. The pilot must obtain a new clearance or cancel his IFR flight plan if not off by the specified time.

clearance void time (ICAO). A time specified by an air traffic control unit at which a clearance ceases to be valid unless the aircraft concerned has already taken action to comply therewith.

clearance volume (reciprocating engine measurement). The volume of the cylinder of a reciprocating engine when the piston is at the top of its stroke.

cleared approach (air traffic control). ATC authorization for an aircraft to execute any standard or special instrument approach procedure for an airport. Normally, an aircraft will be cleared for a specific instrument approach procedure.

"Cleared as filed" (air traffic control). A statement meaning the aircraft is cleared to proceed in accordance with the route of flight filed in the flight plan.

"Cleared for (type of) approach" (air traffic control). ATC authorization for an aircraft to execute a specific instrument approach to an airport.

"Cleared for approach" (air traffic control). ATC authorization for an aircraft to execute any standard or special instrument approach for that airport.

"Cleared for takeoff" (air traffic control). ATC authorization for an aircraft to depart. This clearance is based on known traffic and known physical airport conditions.

"Cleared for the option" (air traffic control). ATC authorization for an aircraft to make a touch-and-go, low approach, missed approach, stop-and-go, or full-stop landing at the discretion of the pilot. This clearance is normally used in flight training, to allow the instructor to evaluate the student's performance under changing situations.

"Cleared through" (air traffic control). ATC authorization for an aircraft to make intermediate stops at specified airports without refiling a flight plan while en route to the clearance limit.

"Cleared to land" (air traffic control). ATC authorization for an aircraft to land. This clearance is based on known traffic and known physical airport conditions.

clear ice (meteorology). Transparent ice that forms on an aircraft in smooth layers when the aircraft is flying through freezing rain or supercooled clouds. Clear ice, also called glaze ice, forms fastest when the drops of water are large, such as those found in cumuloform clouds.

clearing an engine (gas turbine engine operation). The act of clearing combustible gases from the inside of a gas turbine engine after an aborted start. The engine is rotated with the starter so the compressor can force fresh air through the engine and carry all the dangerous vapors out the tail pipe.

clearing turns (flight maneuver). Ninety-degree turns made in each direction before flight maneuvers to ensure that the flight area is free of other aircraft.

clear of the runway (air traffic control). A phrase used to describe the position of a taxiing aircraft approaching a runway when at a point in which all parts of the aircraft are held short of the applicable runway holding position marking. A pilot or controller may consider an aircraft exiting or crossing a runway to be clear of the runway when all parts of the aircraft are beyond the runway edge and there are no restrictions to its continued movement beyond the applicable runway holding position marking.

clearway. *14 CFR Part 1:*

"(1) For turbine engine powered airplanes certificated after August 29, 1959, an area beyond the runway, not less than 500 feet wide, centrally located about the extended centerline of the runway, and under the control of the airport authorities. The clearway is expressed in terms of a clearway plane, extending from the end of the runway with an upward slope not exceeding 1.25 percent, above which no object nor any terrain protrudes. However, threshold lights may protrude above the plane if their height above the end of the runway is 26 inches or less and they are located to each side of the runway.

(2) For turbine engine powered airplanes certificated after September 30, 1958, but before August 30, 1959, an area beyond the takeoff runway extending no less than 300 feet on either side of the extended centerline of the runway, at an elevation no higher than the elevation of the end of the runway, clear of all fixed obstacles, and under the control of the airport authorities."

Cleco fastener. A patented spring-type fastener used to hold metal sheets until they can be permanently riveted together. A special pair of Cleco pliers pulls the spreader from between the jaws of a Cleco fastener so the jaws will pull together enough for them to pass through the rivet holes drilled in the metal. When the fastener is installed, the pliers release the spreader, which forces the jaws out against the metal and pulls the sheets tightly together.

clevis. A U-shaped fitting which has matching holes in the arms of the U. A clevis pin or clevis bolt is passed through the holes to fasten a control cable to a control horn or to fasten a push-pull rod to a bell crank.

clevis bolt. A special bolt used to attach a clevis to a control horn or bell crank so the clevis is free to move. Clevis bolts have a short threaded section separated from the shank of the bolt by a shallow groove. The head of a clevis bolt is slotted so it can be turned with a screwdriver, but the slot is so shallow very little torque can be applied. A thin nut is used on a clevis bolt, and this nut should not be tightened enough to keep the clevis from moving freely on the device to which it is connected.

clevis pin. A flathead pin used to attach a clevis to a control horn. The clevis pin is inserted through the holes in the clevis and the control horn, a washer is placed on the shank of the clevis pin, and the clevis pin is secured with a cotter pin passed through the hole in its shank.

climate (meteorology). The meteorological conditions, including temperature, precipitation, and wind that characteristically prevail in a region or area.

climatological forecast (meteorology). A forecast based solely upon the climatological statistics for a region rather than the dynamical implications of the current conditions.

climatology (meteorology). The study of climate.

climbing blade (helicopter operation). The blade of a helicopter rotor that is in track when checked on the ground or in a hover, but rises above the other blade in forward flight.

climb gradient. The actual measure of altitude gained for each 100 feet of horizontal travel of an aircraft, expressed as a percentage.

climb-out. The portion of flight operation between takeoff and the initial cruising altitude.

climb-out speed. *14 CFR Part 1:* "With respect to rotorcraft, means a referenced airspeed which results in a flight path clear of the height-velocity envelope during initial climbout."

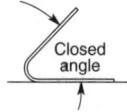

"Climb to VFR" (air traffic control). ATC authorization for an aircraft to climb to VFR conditions within a control zone when the only weather limitation is restricted visibility. The aircraft must remain clear of clouds while climbing to VFR.

clinometer. A device made of a curved, liquid-filled, glass tube, with a black glass ball inside it. A clinometer shows the relationship between the object on which it is mounted and a line perpendicular to the earth's surface. A clinometer is built into a turn and slip indicator and a turn coordinator to show the relationship between the rate of turn and the angle of bank used to make the turn.

clock (electronic equipment). A pulse generator in a piece of electronic equipment used to synchronize the timing of switching circuits. In a digital computer, the clock determines the speed of the CPU.

clockwise rotation. Rotation of an object in the same direction the hands of a clock move.

closed angle (sheet metal fabrication). An angle formed in sheet metal which has been bent through more than 90°. When a piece of sheet metal is bent through 135°, it forms a closed angle of 45°.

closed assembly time. The time elapsing between the assembly of glued joints and the application of pressure.

closed angle

closed-center hydraulic system. A hydraulic system in which the selector valves are installed in parallel with each other. When no unit is being actuated, fluid circulates from the pump back to the reservoir without flowing through any of the selector valves.

closed-center selector valve. A type of flow-control valve used to direct pressurized fluid into one side of an actuator, and at the same time, direct the return fluid from the other side of the actuator to the fluid reservoir. Closed-center selector valves are connected in parallel between the pressure manifold and the return manifold.

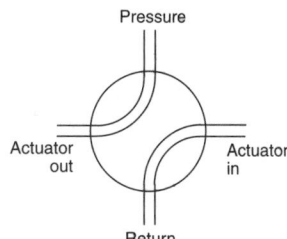

closed-center selector valve

closed-circuit voltage. The voltage of an electrical circuit, measured when a load is connected and current is flowing.

closed-loop control. A type of control in which part of the output is fed back to the input. This allows the input to continually compare the command signals with the output, showing the extent to which the commands have been complied with.

closed low (meteorology). A low pressure area that may be completely encircled by an isobar or contour line.

closed runway. A runway that is unusable for aircraft operations.

closed traffic. Successive operations involving takeoffs and landings or low approaches where the aircraft does not exit the traffic pattern.

close-grain wood. Wood in which the annual rings are small and close together. In close-grain wood there is very little difference in the texture of the spring wood and the summer wood, the light and dark stripes in the wood.

close parallels (airport configuration). Two parallel runways whose extended centerlines are separated by at least 3,400 feet, but less than 4,300 feet. Precision runway monitoring (PRM) systems are available that permit simultaneous independent ILS approaches.

close-quarter iron. A small handheld iron with an accurately calibrated thermostat. This iron is used for heat-shrinking polyester fabrics in areas that would be difficult to work with a large iron.

close-tolerance bolt. A special bolt used in aircraft construction in which the shank is ground to a tolerance of +0.000, −0.0005 inch. Close-tolerance bolts are identified by a triangle around the mark on the bolt head that identifies the material of which the bolt is made. The shank of a close-tolerance bolt is not cadmium plated, but it is kept from rusting by a coating of wax or grease.

close-tolerance bolt

cloud (meteorology). A collection of tiny droplets of water suspended, or floating, in the air. A cloud forms when invisible water vapor in the air condenses and becomes droplets of visible liquid water.

cloud amount (meteorology). The amount of sky estimated to be covered by a specified cloud type or level (partial cloud amount) or by all cloud types and levels (total cloud amount).

cloud bank (meteorology). A generally well-defined mass of cloud observed at a distance. It covers an appreciable portion of the sky on the horizon, but does not extend overhead.

cloudburst (meteorology). A term used to describe an extremely heavy rain.

cloud detection radar (meteorology). A vertically-directed radar used to detect cloud bases and tops.

cloud height (meteorology). The height of the cloud base above local terrain.

cloud point (petroleum specification). The temperature to which a petroleum product must be cooled for the wax it contains to begin to solidify and separate out into tiny crystals. These tiny crystals cause the material to appear cloudy.

cloud streets (meteorology). Parallel rows of cumulus clouds. Each row can be as short as 10 miles or as long as 100 miles or more.

clove hitch. A knot used to make individual spot ties for securing a bundle of electrical wires in an aircraft. A clove hitch is actually two half hitches around the wire bundle secured with a square knot.

clubhead (malformed rivet). A rivet whose bucked head is slanted rather than flat. This is caused by the bucking bar being tilted when the rivet was driven.

club propeller. A short, stubby propeller used for testing an aircraft engine after it has been overhauled. Club propellers impose the correct load on the engine, and they move the maximum volume of cooling air through the cylinder fins.

cluster weld (aircraft construction). A welded joint in an aircraft steel-tube fuselage made where a number of tubes meet at a common point.

clutch. A component in a machine that connects or disconnects parts while they are moving. Clutches may be actuated by mechanical levers, hydraulic actuators, centrifugal force, or electromagnetism.

clutter (radar operation). The reception and visual display of radar returns caused by precipitation, chaff, terrain, numerous aircraft targets, or other phenomena.

coalesce. To come together, or unite, to form a whole unit. In a water separator, such as used in an air-cycle air conditioning system, tiny droplets of water suspended in the air are forced to coalesce, or join together, to form large drops of water that separate from the air.

coalescent bag (air conditioning system component). A porous bag in the water separator of an air-cycle air conditioning system which traps water from the air.

Coanda effect (aerodynamics). A stream of air flowing over a curved surface will follow the curvature of the surface. As the surface drops away from the stream of air, the Coanda effect causes the air to speed up, and according to Bernoulli's principle, when the velocity of the air increases, its pressure decreases.

C

coastal fix. A navigation aid or intersection where an aircraft transitions between the domestic route structure and the ocean route structure.

coast-down check (gas turbine engine maintenance check). A check of the length of time needed for a gas turbine engine to coast to a complete stop after the fuel is shut off when the engine is operating at its idle speed. The measured coast-down time is compared with the time specified in the engine operations manual to determine the condition of the engine.

coated cathode (electron tube component). A cathode of an electron tube which is covered with a material that emits a great many electrons when it is heated.

coating (of balloon fabric). A thin synthetic added to the surface of balloon fabric to lessen porosity and ultraviolet-light damage.

coaxial. Rotating about the same axis. Coaxial rotors of a helicopter are mounted on concentric shafts in such a way that they turn in opposite directions to cancel torque.

coaxial cable (electrical cable). A type of two-conductor electrical cable in which a center conductor is held rigidly in the center of a braided shield which serves as the outer conductor. The term coaxial cable comes from the fact that the two conductors are coaxial—they have the same center. Coaxial cable, or coax, as it is normally called, is used for attaching radio receivers and transmitters to their antenna.

coaxial propellers. Propellers of a multiengine airplane mounted on concentric propeller shafts. The engines are mounted side-by-side and drive the propeller shafts through gears. Coaxial propellers, turning in opposite directions, allow the torque produced by one propeller to counteract the torque caused by the other.

coaxial rotors (helicopter rotors). A rotor system in which two rotors are mounted on the helicopter, on concentric shafts, in such a way that they turn in opposite directions— their torques cancel.

coaxial shafts. Two or more shafts that have the same axis—they are concentric with each other. The hands of an analog watch are mounted on coaxial shafts.

cobalt. A hard, brittle, metallic chemical element. Cobalt's symbol is Co, its atomic number is 27, and its atomic weight is 58.93. Cobalt is used as an alloying element in permanent magnets.

cobalt chloride. A dye used with silica-gel in a dehydrator to indicate the presence of moisture. When cobalt chloride is dry, it is deep blue in color, but when it absorbs water, it turns pink. If a dehydrator element is blue, the component it protects is dry. But if moisture gets into it, the silica-gel absorbs some of the moisture, and the cobalt chloride turns pink.

COBOL (computer language). A high-level computer language whose command signals are similar to English commands. The acronym COBOL is taken from COmmon Business Oriented Language.

cock. The British term for a valve used to stop or control the flow of fluid in a fluid line.

cockpit. The portion of an aircraft or a spacecraft from which the flight crew controls the vehicle.

cockpit display of traffic information (CDTI). The display and user interface for information about air traffic within approximately 80 miles. It will typically combine and show traffic data from TCAS, TIS-B, and ADS-B. Depending on features, the display may also show terrain, weather, and navigation information.

cockpit resource management (CRM). Techniques designed using cockpit human resources that reduce and manage pilot errors which do occur. Errors are going to happen in a complex system with error-prone humans; therefore good technique must be learned to reduce risk. *See also* crew resource management.

Code of Federal Regulations (CFR). The codification of the general and permanent rules published in the Federal Register by the executive departments and agencies of the Federal Government. For example, the FAA-written "Title 14 of the Code of Federal Regulations" is established by law to provide for the safe and orderly conduct of flight operations and to prescribe airmen privileges and limitations.

code markings (aircraft plumbing). Markings on fluid lines made with colored tape on which words and geometric symbols are used to identify the type of fluid carried in the lines.

codes, transponder. The number assigned to a particular multiple-pulse reply signal transmitted by a radar beacon transponder.

coefficient. A dimensionless number used as a measure of some property or characteristic. For example, a coefficient of friction is a number used to indicate the relative amount of friction between different materials.

coefficient of coupling (transformer characteristic). A measure of the amount of coupling that exists between the two windings of a transformer. If all the expanding and contracting lines of magnetic flux from one winding cut across all the turns of the other winding, the coefficient of coupling is unity, 1.0, or 100%.

coefficient of drag (aerodynamic parameter). A dimensionless number used in the formula for finding the induced drag of an airfoil as it relates to the angle of attack.

coefficient of friction. A dimensionless number used to show the ratio of the amount of force needed to move a body parallel to the surface on which it is resting to the amount of force needed to move the body perpendicular to the surface.

coefficient of lift (aerodynamic parameter). A dimensionless number relating the amount of aerodynamic lift produced by an airfoil to its angle of attack.

coefficient of linear expansion. A number relating the change in the length of an object to the change in its temperature. The coefficient of linear expansion is expressed in such terms as fractions of an inch per degree Celsius.

coefficient of thermal expansion. The ratio of change in length, area, or volume of a material to the change in its temperature. It is expressed in such terms as fractions of an inch per degree Celsius.

coercive force (magnetism). A magnetic force used to remove magnetism from a magnetized object. The polarity of a coercive force is opposite to that which magnetized the object.

coffin corner. The flight condition in which any increase in airspeed will induce high speed Mach buffet and any decrease in airspeed will induce low speed Mach buffet.

cog belt. A flexible belt used to drive one shaft from another. The inside of the belt is crossed with a series of teeth which mate with teeth around the outside of the drive and driven wheels. A cog belt is used for timing and for transmitting force where there must be no slippage.

cognitive domain (psychology). A grouping of levels of learning associated with mental activity which range from knowledge through comprehension, application, analysis, and synthesis to evaluation.

cognitive theory (psychology). Focuses on what is going on inside the student's mind. Learning is not just a change in behavior; it is a change in the way a student thinks, understands, or feels.

coherent light. Light made up of a single frequency of electromagnetic radiation.

cohesion. A force which causes a material to stick to itself. Cohesion differs from adhesion, which is a force that causes a material to stick to some other material.

coil (electrical component). A device made of several turns of wire wound around a core. A coil is used to add inductance to an electrical circuit.

C

coil assembly (magneto component). An assembly in a magneto that consists of a soft iron core around which is wound a primary coil and a secondary coil. The secondary coil is wound on top of the primary coil.

coil form. The spool or tubing over which an electrical coil is wound.

coil spring. A spring made of hardened steel wire wound in the form of a spiral. Coil springs may be used to apply force or to absorb shock or vibration. Short, open coil springs are used to cushion compressive loads, and tightly wound coil springs are used to absorb tensile loads. Coil springs can be used to measure force because their deflection is directly proportional to the applied force.

coin dimpling (sheet metalworking). A process of preparing holes in sheet metal to receive flush rivets. The metal in the area to be dimpled is heated, and a coining die is pressed into it. The pressure of the die in the softened metal gives the dimpled hole sharp edges that provide a good fit for the countersunk rivet heads.

coin pressing (riveting process). A method of countersinking a rivet hole using a countersink rivet as the male dimpling die. The rivet is placed through the rivet hole in the thin sheet metal and is driven into a female die with a flush rivet set in a pneumatic rivet gun.

coin tap (composites). A test for delamination in a laminated composite. The edge of a coin is tapped lightly over the suspect area and the sound made by the coin is noted. A delaminated area is usually indicated by a dull thudding sound.

coke (lubricating oil contaminant). A solid carbon residue left when all the volatile parts of a mineral oil have been removed by heat. Coke in an engine is a contaminant, and it must be removed.

coking (lubrication system problem). A buildup of coke in the lubrication system of either a reciprocating engine or a gas turbine engine. If the engine is shut down before it has had time to cool properly, oil trapped in some of the hot locations will get so hot it will decompose into a hard, solid carbon deposit, coke.

col (meteorology). The areas on a weather map that indicate the point of highest pressure between two lows and the lowest pressure between two highs.

cold. A relative condition that indicates the lack of heat energy.

cold air funnel (meteorology). A weak tornado that forms in a cold air mass.

cold air mass (meteorology). An extensive body of air in which the temperature is lower than that of the air surrounding it.

cold bending (sheet metalworking). A method of working sheet metal in which the metal is bent without heating it. Some types of metal such as thin sheets of aluminum and magnesium alloys are normally bent cold, but other metals, especially thick sections of steel, are heated red-hot before they are bent.

cold-cathode vacuum tube. A vacuum tube, or electron tube, whose cathode is made of a material that emits (gives off) electrons at normal room temperature. Cold-cathode vacuum tubes do not have filaments, or heaters.

cold chisel. A metal-cutting tool made by grinding a sharp edge onto a flattened portion of a hardened steel rod. A cold chisel is used to cut metal when the metal is cold.

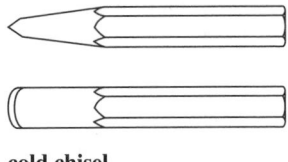

cold chisel

cold circuit (electrical circuit). An electrical circuit that is not energized—not connected to a source of electrical power.

cold-cranking amps (battery rating). A measure of the capacity of a battery when it is supplying a high rate of current, such as it would if it were being used to crank a cold engine. The cold-cranking amps discharge rate is similar to the five-minute discharge rate that specifies the number of ampere-hours of capacity the battery has when it is discharged at a rate that will drop its cell voltage to a specified low value in five minutes.

The ampere hour capacity of a battery at its five-minute discharge rate is much lower than its capacity at the other discharge rates. The actual capacity at this rate is given in the specifications the manufacturer issues for each battery.

cold-cranking simulation (lubricating oil specification). A method used for specifying the characteristics of a lubricating oil at low temperature. Oils that have been rated by this test are identified by the letter W (standing for Winter) in their designation. For example, SAE 15W50.

cold cylinder test (air-cooled engine maintenance test). A maintenance test used to identify the cylinder in an air-cooled engine which is not firing. When a cylinder is not firing, the temperature of the exhaust stack near the head is colder than the temperature measured at the same place on a cylinder that is firing normally. Handheld temperature gages, called magic wands, can be used to find the cold cylinder, but on most small engines the cold cylinder can be located by feel.

cold dimpling (sheet metal work). A method of preparing a hole in sheet metal to receive flush rivets. A male dimpling die forces the metal around the rivet hole into a female die to form a depression into which the rivet head fits. A countersunk-head rivet fits into a dimpled hole in such a way that the top of the head is flush with the surface of the metal.

cold downslope winds (meteorology). A strong movement of cold air flowing downslope on the lee sides of mountains. The cold dense air tends to increase the velocity of the wind.

cold drawing. A method of reducing the diameter of a wire or tube by drawing it through a series of progressively smaller dies without the wire or tube being heated.

cold flow (condition of fluid hoses). A deep, permanent deformation of a flexible hose, caused by pressure applied by the hose clamps.

cold forming (metal working). A forging operation in which the metal is worked while cold. Cold forming allows a high degree of dimensional accuracy.

cold front (meteorology). Any nonoccluded front which moves in such a way that cold air replaces warmer air.

cold front occlusion (meteorology). An occlusion that occurs when the air in a fast-moving cold front is colder than the air ahead of a slow-moving warm front. The cold air replaces the cool air and forces the warm front aloft.

cold heading (metal working). A cold forming process that increases the cross-sectional area of a metal by forcing it into a die.

cold inflation (hot air balloon operation). Forcing cold air into a balloon envelope to give it some shape and allow the air to be heated with the heater.

cold junction (thermocouple junction). The reference junction of a thermocouple. A thermocouple is a generator of electrical current made of two dissimilar metal wires connected into a loop. The ends where the two wires are joined are called junctions. The amount of current flowing in a thermocouple is determined by the difference in the temperature of the two junctions: the cold, or reference, junction, and the hot, or measuring, junction.

cold light. Light that has little or no radiation in the infrared range. Cold light produces almost no heat.

cold-rolled steel. Low-carbon steel that has been passed through rollers while it was cold.

cold rolling (metal working). A process by which sheet metal is work hardened by passing it back and forth through a pair of rollers while it is cold. This strain hardening decreases the thickness of the metal and makes it both harder and stronger.

cold section (gas turbine engine). The portion of a gas turbine engine ahead of the combustion section. The cold section includes the inlet duct or ducts, compressor, and diffuser.

cold soak. The effect of the exposure of equipment such as an aircraft engine to low temperatures (usually, below-freezing) for an extended period of time. A cold-soaked engine requires preheating before use, as lubricants have thickened, metal has become brittle, and tolerances have diminished.

In glider operations, a self-launch glider's engine (or a glider's sustainer engine) can become cold-soaked to the point where an in-flight engine start can be difficult or impossible to perform. This can occur due to long-term exposure to cold such as after a long soaring flight at altitudes with cold temperatures, for example, as in high-altitude wave soaring during the winter.

cold-solder joint (electrical wiring). A soldered connection in electrical wiring in which the wires were moved before the solder solidified. A cold-solder joint has a granular appearance, little physical strength, and a high electrical resistance. Cold-solder joints are undesirable and must be reheated to melt the solder. The solder must then be allowed to solidify completely before the joint is moved.

cold spark plug. A spark plug with a short path for the heat to travel between the nose core insulator and the shell. A cold spark plug carries the heat away from the nose core, so it can operate in a high-compression engine without the nose core becoming too hot. Too hot a nose core can cause preignition in the cylinder.

cold stream (gas turbine engine). The British term for the fan discharge in a turbofan engine.

cold-tank lubrication system (gas turbine engine lubrication system). A turbine engine lubricating system in which the oil cooler is in the scavenge subsystem. The oil leaves the engine, passes through the cooler, and then goes into the supply tank.

cold weld. Fusion between two pieces of metal obtained by pressure without the application of external heat.

cold working (metalworking). A method of increasing the strength and hardness of metal without the use of external heat. Cold working is done by hammering the metal, bending it back and forth, or pulling it through dies.

coleopter. A concept of a flying machine in which the wing is built in the form of a venturi tube. The engine and propeller are mounted inside the tube-shaped wing.

collar. A ring, or round flange, made as a part of a shaft or installed on it to either restrain movement or hold something in place.

collective pitch control (helicopters). The flight control of a helicopter that changes the pitch of all the rotor blades at the same time. Movement of the collective control increases or decreases the lift produced by the entire rotor disk.

collector (transistor electrode). The electrode in a bipolar transistor from which conventional current leaves the transistor. The collector is the electrode in the transistor symbol on the same side of the base line as the emitter, but it does not have the arrowhead.

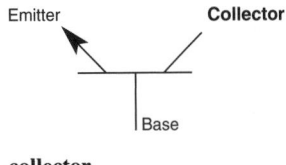

collector

collector ring (electrical equipment). Rings mounted on the rotor shaft of an electrical machine to carry current into and out of the rotating winding. Collector rings are made of a conductive material such as copper or brass, and brushes normally made of a carbon compound ride on them to carry the current into and out of the rotor winding. Collector rings are also called slip rings.

collector ring (reciprocating engine exhaust system). A type of exhaust system used on radial engines. A collector ring is a corrosion-resistant steel manifold connected to the exhaust ports of all the cylinders. Exhaust gases, collected from the cylinders, are dumped overboard at one location through a tail pipe.

collimated light. Light which has been passed through a collimator lens so all the rays are parallel, rather than converging or diverging.

collimator. An instrument which produces parallel rays of light.

collision hazard (traffic control). A condition, event, or circumstance that could induce an occurrence of a collision or surface accident or incident.

collodion. Cellulose nitrate used as a film base for certain aircraft dopes.

colocate. To place two facilities at the same location. In radio navigation, VOR (very-high-frequency omnirange navigation) facilities may be colocated with TACAN (tactical air navigation) facilities. The combination of these facilities is called a VORTAC station.

color. The characteristic of light caused by the different wavelengths of the electromagnetic energy that make up the light. Violet light has the shortest wave lengths, and red, the longest.

color code. A method of using marks of different colors to identify materials. Some electrical resistors and capacitors have color codes to show their value and tolerances. Bungee shock cords use color codes to indicate the year and quarter of the year in which they were made. Color codes are used to identify the type of steel in steel bars and rods. Colored bands are used around aircraft plumbing to identify the fluid being carried in the line.

color temperature. The temperature to which a perfect blackbody radiator would have to be heated to produce the same color as the source of light being measured. Color temperature is measured in degrees Kelvin (°K).

color tempering. A method of removing some of the brittleness from a piece of steel being heat-treated. The steel part is heated red-hot and quenched in water, oil, or brine. A portion is then polished bright, and the part is reheated to a temperature indicated by the color of the oxide that forms on its surface. When the correct color of oxide forms, the heating is stopped, and the metal is again quenched.

color wheel. A device used for mixing paints which shows the primary colors and the various colors that can be made by mixing them. A color wheel helps visualize the results you will get when you mix different colors of paint.

combinational logic (digital electricity). Digital circuitry which incorporates gates whose logic outputs are determined by the logic states of the inputs. Combinational logic differs from sequential logic, in whose gates the states of the outputs are determined by the previous logic state of the inputs.

combination chuck (machine tool component). A four-jaw chuck used to hold a piece of material in a lathe. The jaws of a combination chuck can be moved in or out as a unit, or each of the jaws can be moved separately.

combination compressor (gas turbine engine component). A type of gas turbine engine compressor which has both an axial-flow and a centrifugal stage. Inlet air first passes through the low-pressure axial-flow compressor and then flows into the high-pressure centrifugal compressor. The centrifugal compressor builds up the pressure of the air high enough for efficient operation in the combustors.

C

combination inertia starter (reciprocating engine starter). An inertia starter for a large reciprocating engine that allows the flywheel to be brought up to speed by either an electric motor or a hand crank.

combination set (layout and measuring tool). A layout and measuring tool that consists of a 12-inch, hardened-steel rule with three heads held onto the rule by clamps. One head is a stock head, which converts the rule into a square for measuring 90° and 45° angles. The stock head also has a bubble level and a scriber. A protractor head can be attached to the rule and be set to measure any angle between the rule and the bottom of the head. The third head is the center head in which one edge of the rule bisects the two arms of the head which are 90 degrees apart. When the two arms are held against a circular object, the edge of the rule passes across the object's center.

combination ski (aircraft ski). A type of aircraft ski that can be used on snow or ice, but also allows the use of the wheels for landing on runways. Also called wheel skis.

combination wrench (mechanic's hand tool). A mechanic's hand tool which has a box-socket wrench on one end and an open-end wrench on the other. Both ends normally fit the same size nut or bolt.

combined center-RAPCON (CERAP) (air traffic control). An air traffic control facility which combines the functions of an ARTCC and a radar approach control facility.

combustibles. Materials that are capable of being ignited and burned.

combustion. A chemical reaction in which a material, called the fuel, combines with oxygen so rapidly that a large amount of energy is released in the form of heat and light. Combustion and burning mean essentially the same thing.

combustion chamber (reciprocating engine component). The portion of the cylinder of a reciprocating engine in which the fuel-air mixture is burned.

combustion heater. A type of cabin heater used in some aircraft. Gasoline from the aircraft fuel tanks is burned in the heater.

combustion liner (gas turbine engine component). The perforated steel inner liner that fits into the combustion chamber of a gas turbine engine. Combustion air and cooling air both flow through the combustion liner, and fuel is sprayed into the liner and burned. The combustion liner can be removed from the engine for inspection and maintenance.

combustion section (turbine engine component). The section of a turbine engine in which the fuel-air mixture is burned. The combustion heats and expands the air, which then passes through the engine and spins the turbines.

combustion starter (turbine engine starter). A small self-contained gas turbine engine. This little engine has a centrifugal compressor, reverse-flow combustor and a free turbine which drives the main engine compressor through a clutch and a series of reduction gears.

combustor (gas turbine engine component). The section of a gas turbine engine in which the fuel is injected, mixed with air and burned. The intense heat from the combustion expands the air flowing through the combustor and directs it out through the turbine.

There are a number of types of combustors, but all have an outer liner and a thin-wall perforated inner liner, in which the combustion takes place. In addition to the air used in the combustion process, a large amount of cooling air flows through the combustor to keep the heat from damaging its thin walls. Combustors are also called combustion chambers or burners.

combustor drain valve (gas turbine engine component). A spring-loaded valve in the bottom of the combustor outer case to drain fuel from the combustor after an aborted start. The combustor drain valve is spring-loaded to its open position, and burner pressure holds it closed when the engine is operating.

combustor efficiency (gas turbine engine). The ratio of the amount of heat energy released by burning the fuel in a gas turbine engine to the amount of heat energy in the fuel.

comfort zone. The range of temperature, humidity, and air movement most suitable for human enjoyment and well-being.

coming-in speed (electrical component). The speed an electrical machine, such as a generator or magneto, must be turned for it to produce its rated output. In a magneto, the coming-in speed is the lowest speed at which the magneto produces enough voltage to fire all the spark plugs consistently.

comma cloud. A synoptic scale cloud pattern with a characteristic comma-like shape, often seen on satellite photographs associated with large and intense low-pressure systems.

command bars. A flight director display that presents roll and pitch instructions (generally V-shaped visual cues) to help the pilot maintain the flight path/flight track to the selected point. The pilot keeps the airplane symbol aligned with the command bars on the flight director, or centered on the FD crossbars (e.g., in older Cessna units).

commercial air tour. A flight conducted for compensation or hire in an airplane or helicopter where a purpose of the flight is sightseeing. Among other factors, the FAA may consider the following in determining whether a flight is a commercial air tour: whether there was a holding out to the public of willingness to conduct a sightseeing flight for compensation or hire; whether the person offering the flight provided a narrative that referred to areas or points of interest on the surface below the route of the flight; the area of operation, route, or how often the flight is offered; the inclusion of sightseeing flights as part of a travel arrangement package; or whether the flight in question would have been canceled based on poor visibility of the surface below the route of the flight.

commercial operator (aircraft operator). Anyone, except an air carrier, who engages in the carriage of persons or property in an aircraft for compensation or hire.

   14 CFR Part 1: "A person who, for compensation or hire, engages in the carriage by aircraft in air commerce of persons or property, other than as an air carrier or foreign air carrier or under the authority of Part 375 of this title. Where it is doubtful that an operation is for 'compensation or hire,' the test applied is whether the carriage by air is merely incidental to the person's other business or is, in itself, a major enterprise for profit."

commercial fastener. A fastener manufactured to published standards and stocked by manufacturers or distributors. The material, dimensions and finish of commercial fasteners conform to the quality level generally recognized by manufacturers and users as commercial quality.

commercial pilot. A pilot who has completed the Federal Aviation Administration's requirements for the commercial certificate, including a minimum of 250 hours of flight time and passing a knowledge exam and flight test. Commercial pilots are authorized to carry passengers or cargo for compensation or hire under certain conditions.

common-base amplifier (transistor amplifier). A transistor amplifier in which the base of the transistor is connected in such a way that it is in both the input and output circuits.

common-collector amplifier (transistor amplifier). A transistor amplifier in which the collector of the transistor is connected in such a way that it is in both the input and output circuits.

common-emitter amplifier (transistor amplifier). A transistor amplifier in which the emitter of the transistor is connected in such a way that it is in both the input and output circuits.

common fraction (mathematics). A fraction written in the form of one number above another. The number on the bottom is the denominator, indicating the number of parts into which the whole is divided, and the top number is the numerator, indicating the number of parts being considered.

C

common point (air traffic control). A significant point over which two or more aircraft will report passing or have reported passing before proceeding on the same or diverging tracks. To establish/maintain longitudinal separation, a controller may determine a common point not originally in the aircraft's flight plan and then clear the aircraft to fly over the point.

common route (air traffic control). (1) That segment of a North American Route between the inland navigation facility and the coastal fix. (2) Typically the portion of a RNAV STAR between the en route transition end point and the runway transition start point; however, the common route may only consist of a single point that joins the en route and runway transitions.

common traffic advisory frequency. *See* CTAF.

communications (electronic). The branch of science or technology that changes information into electrical impulses and transmits it from one location to another. At the destination, the electrical impulses are changed back into some form of audible or visual output.

communications receiver. A radio receiver designed and built primarily for receiving voice or coded radio transmissions. Communications receivers have good selectivity and sensitivity but they do not receive music with a great deal of fidelity.

communications satellite. A man-made satellite that orbits the earth at an altitude of 22,300 miles (35,900 kilometers), appearing at this altitude to remain stationary over a given location. Communications satellites receive radio and television transmissions from earth stations and re-transmit them. Three satellites in essentially the same orbit are able to cover almost the entire earth with the signals they re-transmit.

community aerodrome radio station (CARS). A ground station established by the Government of the Northwest Territories or the Government of the Yukon Territory to provide advisory services to aircraft and a communications service for the safe movement of aircraft.

commutation (electrical machine). The process by which DC voltage is taken from an armature that has had AC voltage induced into it.

commutator (electrical machine component). A mechanical rectifier mounted on the armature shaft of a DC generator or motor. It consists of a cylindrical arrangement of insulated copper bars connected to the armature coils. Carbon brushes ride on the copper bars to carry current into or out of the commutator, providing a unidirectional current from a generator or a reversal of current in the coils of a motor.

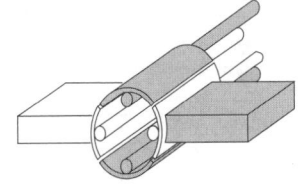

commutator

commuter operation. Any scheduled operation conducted by any person operating aircraft with a frequency of operations of at least five round trips per week on at least one route between two or more points according to the published flight schedules. A commuter operation applies only to (1) airplanes, other than turbojet-powered airplanes, having a maximum passenger-seat configuration of 9 seats or less, excluding each crewmember seat, and a maximum payload capacity of 7,500 pounds or less; or (2) rotorcraft.

comparator (electronic circuit). An electronic circuit that compares two signals and produces a third signal that indicates whether the first two are the same or different.

compartment (structural component). An enclosed area, or space, in an aircraft structure. An engine compartment is an enclosed area in which the engine is mounted.

compass (drafting instrument). An instrument used to draw circles or portions of a circle. A compass is made of two legs, hinged in the center. One leg is fitted with a sharp point to hold it at the center of the circle, and the other leg can be fitted with a lead holder or ink pen to draw the circle.

compass (navigation instrument). A navigation instrument that indicates the direction to the earth's magnetic north pole. The simplest compasses use a small permanent magnet mounted on a pivot and free to turn. It aligns itself with the magnetic lines of flux that extend across the earth from the magnetic north pole to the magnetic south pole.

compass card (magnetic compass component). A drum-like scale, marked in degrees, from 0° to 360°, fastened around the float in an aircraft magnetic compass. The magnets align the float with the earth's magnetic field, and the compass card, which is read opposite a fixed lubber line, shows the pilot the direction the nose of the aircraft is pointed relative to magnetic north.

compass compensation. A maintenance procedure that corrects a magnetic compass for deviation error. The aircraft is aligned on a compass rose, and the compensating magnets in the compass case are adjusted to get the compass to align with the direction marked on the rose. After the deviation error is minimized on all headings, a compass correction card is filled out and mounted on the instrument panel next to the compass. Compass compensation is also called compass swinging.

compass correction card. A small card mounted near the magnetic compass to show the pilot the amount of deviation error for each heading.

compass course (navigation). A true course corrected for variation and deviation errors.

compass fluid. A highly refined, water-clear petroleum product similar to kerosine, used to damp the oscillations of magnetic compasses.

compass heading (navigation). Magnetic heading plus or minus deviation. It is the compass indication needed to make good the desired course.

compass locator (electronic navigation facility). A low-power, low- or medium-frequency (L/MF) radio beacon installed at the site of the outer or middle marker of an instrument landing system (ILS). Compass locators can be used for navigation at distances of approximately 15 miles or as is authorized in the approach procedure. The outer compass locator (LOM) is installed at the site of the outer marker of an instrument landing system, and the middle compass locator (LMM) is installed at the site of the middle marker.

compass north. The direction to which the magnets in an aircraft compass actually point. The magnetic field with which the compass magnets align is the combination of the earth's magnetic field and local magnetic fields. These local fields are caused by magnetized parts of the aircraft and by electrical current flowing in the aircraft structure and in wires.

compass rose. A graduated circle painted on a ramp or taxiway of an airport. Compass roses are laid out at a location where local magnetic fields are minimum, and where traffic will not interfere with aircraft using the rose to have their compasses swung (compensated).

The graduations of the compass rose are laid out with reference to magnetic north, and they are marked every thirty degrees.

To compensate the compass, the aircraft is taxied over the compass rose so it lines up with the directional marks of the rose. The compensating

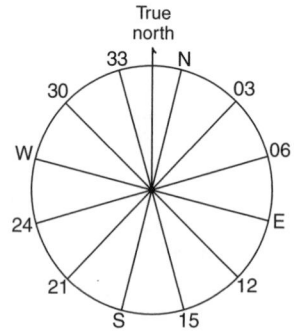

compass rose

magnets in the compass are adjusted to cause the compass to agree with the direction the aircraft is pointed.

A compass rose is also the name of a small circle graduated in 360° increments printed on some navigational charts to show the amount of compass variation at different locations on the chart.

compass saw. A small handsaw having a thin, tapered blade, used to cut circles and curves. A keyhole saw is a form of compass saw.

compass swinging. *See* compass compensation.

compass turns. Turns made, using the magnetic compass for heading reference. When making compass-only turns, you must compensate for lead or lag created by acceleration and deceleration errors in order to roll out on the desired heading.

compensated cam (magneto component). The type of cam used to open the breaker points in a magneto installed on a high-performance radial engine. The master and link rod arrangement used in a radial engine causes the pistons in the different cylinders to be a different linear distance from the top of their stroke for the same angular displacement of the crankshaft relative to top dead center. A compensated cam has one lobe for each cylinder, and these lobes are not all the same. The difference in the lobes causes the breaker points to open when the piston in each cylinder is the same linear distance from the top of its stroke.

compensated fuel pump. A vane-type, engine-driven fuel pump that has a diaphragm connected to the pressure-regulating valve. The chamber above the diaphragm is vented to the carburetor upper deck where it senses the pressure of the air as it enters the carburetor. The diaphragm allows the fuel pump to compensate for altitude changes and keeps the carburetor inlet fuel pressure a constant amount higher than the carburetor inlet air pressure.

compensating cam (turbine-engine-powered helicopter control). A cam in the engine control system of a turbine-engine-powered helicopter that coordinates the engine power with the position of the collective-pitch control stick.

compensating relief valve (reciprocating engine lubrication system component). A type of oil pressure relief valve used in some of the larger aircraft engines. When the oil is cold, two springs hold the pressure relief valve on its seat. But when the oil warms up, a thermostatic valve directs oil against a piston in the relief valve. This oil disables one spring and allows the oil pressure to be controlled by only one spring. The initial high oil pressure forces the thick, cold oil through the engine and assures that all the bearings are lubricated when the oil is cold.

compensating winding (electrical generator). A series winding in a compound-wound DC generator. The coils of the compensating winding are embedded in the faces of the field poles, and their magnetic fields assist the fields from the interpoles to effectively cancel the field distortion caused by armature current.

compensator port (aircraft brake master cylinder component). A small hole between a hydraulic brake master cylinder and the reservoir. The first movement of the piston in the master cylinder covers the compensating port and traps fluid between the master cylinder piston and the brake wheel cylinders to apply the brakes. When the brake is released, the piston uncovers the compensator port, and if any fluid has been lost from the brake, the reservoir will refill the master cylinder. A restricted compensator port may cause the brakes to drag or slow their release.

compiler (computer programming). A program that converts a high-level language that is easy for a programmer to use into machine language that can be used by the computer.

complementary angles. The complement of an angle is 90° minus the angle. For example, 30° is the complement of 60°: 90° – 60° = 30°. An angle of 30° and an angle of 60° are complementary angles; their sum is 90°. The two acute angles in a right triangle are always complementary angles.

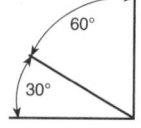

complementary angles

complementary colors. Two colors of light, which, when added in the proper proportion, produce white light.

complex airplane. An aircraft with flaps, retractable landing gear and a constant speed propeller.

complex circuit (electrical circuit). A circuit that contains a number of components, some of which are connected in series and others in parallel.

complex number (mathematics). A number which contains real numbers and imaginary numbers. *See* real number.

"comply with restrictions" (air traffic control). An ATC instruction that requires an aircraft to be vectored back onto an arrival or departure procedure to comply with all altitude and/or speed restrictions depicted on the procedure. This term may be used in lieu of repeating each remaining restriction that appears on the procedure.

Component Maintenance Manual (CMM). A maintenance manual created by component manufacturers.

composite. Something made up of different materials combined in such a way that the characteristics of the resulting material are different from those of any of the components.

composite fan blades (turbofan engine component). A conceptual idea for turbofan blades to be composed of graphite fibers.

composite flight plan (air traffic control). A flight plan that specifies VFR operation on one portion of the flight and IFR operation on another.

composite propeller blade. A propeller blade made of a number of materials such as metal, graphite, glass, or aramid fibers, and foam.

composite route system (air traffic control). An organized oceanic route structure, incorporating reduced lateral spacing between routes, in which composite separation is authorized.

composite separation (air traffic control). A method of separating aircraft in a composite route system where, by management of route and altitude assignments, a combination of half the lateral minimum specified for the area concerned and half the vertical minimum is applied.

composite structure. A type of aircraft structure made of plastic resins reinforced with strong, lightweight filaments. Fiberglass, carbon, Kevlar®, and boron are materials used for composite structure. Composite materials combine high strength and rigidity with light weight.

composition resistor (electrical component). A resistor made of a mixture of carbon and an insulating material. The mixture is molded inside a protective insulation with a wire lead extending radially from each end. The ohmic value of the resistor is determined by the percentage of insulating material in the mixture, and the physical size determines the amount of heat the resistor can dissipate. The resistance, in ohms, is marked by a series of colored bands around one end.

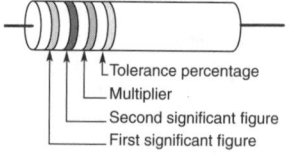

composition resistor

compound (chemical). *See* chemical compound.

compound curve. A curve formed in more than one plane. The surface of a sphere is a compound curve.

compound gage. A pressure gage used to measure the pressure in the low side of an air conditioning system. A compound gage is calibrated from zero to 30 inches of mercury, negative, and from zero to about 150-pounds-per-square-inch positive pressure.

compound lever. A series of levers connected in such a way that the output of one lever is used as the input of another. Compound levers are used to multiply force.

compound-wound generator (electrical generator). An electrical generator which has both a series and a shunt field winding.

compound-wound motor (electric motor). An electric motor which has both a series and a shunt field winding. A series motor has a high starting torque, but poor speed control. A shunt motor has a low starting torque, but good speed control. A compound motor has some of the good characteristics of both types of motors.

comprehensiveness (in teaching/learning process). The degree to which a test measures the overall objective.

compressed air. Air whose pressure has been increased above that of the ambient, or surrounding, air by some form of mechanical compressor.

compressibility. The ability of the material to be reduced in volume by the application of pressure. Air is a compressible fluid, and soft rubber is a compressible solid.

compressibility burble (high-speed flight). The separated air flow over the top surface of an airfoil caused by a shock wave.

compressibility effect. The sudden increase in the total drag of an airfoil in transonic flight caused by formation of shock waves on the surface.

compressibility error (flight instrument error). The airspeed indicator error caused by compression of the air at the forward end of the pitot tube. This compression is caused by the pitot tube moving through the air at a speed greater than the speed of sound.

compressible flow (aerodynamics). The flow of a fluid in which the density of the fluid varies. Compressible flow is encountered in supersonic flight.

compressible fluid. A fluid to which energy can be added by compressing, or squeezing it into a smaller volume. Gases are compressible fluids.

compression (physical force). A resultant of two forces acting in the same plane, but in opposite directions, toward each other. A compression, or compressive, force tries to mash the ends of an object together.

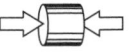

compression

compression failure. A type of structural failure caused by the application of too much compressive stress. Compression failure causes the material to buckle or collapse.

compression fastener (structural component). A fastener whose primary function is to resist forces which tend to compress it.

compression ignition. The form of ignition used in diesel engines. Air inside the cylinder of the engine is compressed, and the compression heats the air enough that when fuel is sprayed into it, the fuel ignites and burns.

compression ignition engine. A form of reciprocating engine which uses heat produced by compressing the air in the cylinder to ignite the fuel. A diesel engine is a compression-ignition engine. The piston, moving upward in the cylinder, compresses and heats the air. When the piston is near the top of its stroke, fuel is sprayed into the hot air, and it ignites and burns.

compression molding (plastics manufacturing process). A method of molding thermosetting resins. A mold is opened and heated, and resin is put in it. The mold is then closed, and pressure is applied. The resin flows under pressure and completely fills the cavity of the mold. The mold is kept closed and heated until the resin is completely cured.

compression ratio (reciprocating engine parameter). The ratio of the volume of a cylinder of a reciprocating engine with the piston at the bottom of its stroke to the volume of the cylinder with the piston at the top of its stroke.

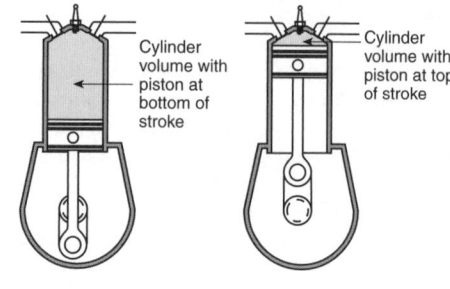

Cylinder volume with piston at bottom of stroke

Cylinder volume with piston at top of stroke

compression ratio

compression ratio (turbine engine parameter). The ratio of the pressure of the air at the discharge of a turbine engine compressor to the pressure of the air at the inlet.

compression rib (aircraft structural member). A special rib used in a Pratt truss airplane wing to take the place of a separate compression strut. A compression rib has strong cap strips and webs designed to withstand compressive loads.

compression rings (reciprocating engine piston rings). The top rings used on reciprocating engine pistons to seal the piston in the cylinder so the upward-moving piston can compress the air in the cylinder. Compression rings also transfer heat from the piston into the cylinder wall. *See* illustration for scraper rings.

compression spring. A form of spring which resists a force trying to compress it, or squeeze it together. Open coil springs are often used as compression springs.

compression stress. A type of stress that tries to squeeze the ends of an object closer together. A compression stress is also called a compressive stress.

compression strut (airplane wing structural member). A heavy structural member, often in the form of a steel tube, used to hold the spars of a Pratt truss airplane wing apart. A compression strut opposes compressive loads between the spars put there by the tensile loads from the drag and anti-drag wires.

compression test (reciprocating engine maintenance test). A maintenance test performed on a reciprocating engine to determine the ability of the cylinders to hold air pressure. A cylinder will fail a compression test if an excessive amount of air leaks past the piston rings, or if any air leaks past the intake or exhaust valve.

compression tester (differential). A maintenance tool used to determine the functional condition of a reciprocating engine cylinder. A regulated air pressure of 80 psi is directed into the cylinder through a calibrated orifice, and the pressure is measured on both sides of the orifice. The difference between the indications on the two gages is the pressure drop across the orifice. This drop is caused by air leaking past the piston rings or the valves. Typically, a cylinder should hold 75% of the air pressure applied to it. Therefore the cylinder pressure gage should read at least 60 psi when the input pressure gage reads 80 psi.

compression wave (high-speed aerodynamics). A shock wave which forms on the surface of an airfoil moving through the air at a speed greater than the speed of sound.

compression wood. The defect in wood which causes it to have a high specific gravity and the appearance of an excessive growth of summerwood. In most species, there is little difference between the color of the springwood and summerwood. Any material containing compression wood is unsuited for aircraft structural use and must be rejected.

compressive load (compressive stress). A physical load, or stress, which tries to squeeze together the ends of the object on which it acts.

compressive strength. The ability of an object to resist a compressive load. Compressive strength resists the force that tries to squeeze the ends of an object together.

compressor (air conditioning system component). The component in a vapor-cycle cooling system in which the low-pressure refrigerant vapors, after they leave the evaporator, are compressed to increase both their temperature and pressure before they pass into the condenser. Increasing the temperature of the refrigerant allows it to give up some of its heat energy to the air flowing through the condenser. Some compressors are driven by electric motors, others by hydraulic motors and, in the case of many light airplanes, are belt driven from the engine.

compressor (gas turbine engine component). The section of the gas turbine engine whose components increase the pressure of the air flowing through it.

compressor blade (gas turbine engine component). A rotating airfoil installed on the disk of a compressor in a gas turbine engine. A compressor blade adds energy to the air as it moves through the engine.

compressor bleed air (gas turbine engine). Air that is tapped off from a turbine engine compressor and used for anti-icing the inlet ducts and cooling the turbine inlet guide vanes and first stage turbine blades. Bleed air may also be dumped to relieve internal pressure and prevent a compressor stall. Compressor bleed air may also be used for such airframe functions as pressurization and the operation of some of the components in the pneumatic system. *See* customer bleed air.

compressor case (gas turbine engine component). The outer housing of the compressor section of a gas turbine engine. In an engine using an axial-flow compressor, the stator vanes are mounted in the compressor case.

compressor disk (gas turbine engine component). The inner section of a compressor wheel that makes up a stage of compression in an axial-flow compressor. The disk mounts on the compressor shaft, and the rotor blades mount around the periphery of the disk. There is one compressor disk for each stage of compression.

compressor efficiency (turbine engine component efficiency). The ratio of energy output to energy input.

compressor front frame (turbine engine component). The component in an axial-flow turbine engine that supports the stator vane casing and the forward end of the compressor rotor shaft. It directs the air flow into the first stage of the compressor.

compressor hub (turbine engine component). The component in an axial-flow compressor to which the compressor blades attach.

compressor pressure ratio (gas turbine engine parameter). The ratio of the pressure of the air at the compressor discharge to the pressure at the compressor inlet.

compressor stage (gas turbine engine). The components in an axial-flow compressor which consist of one set of rotor blades and the following set of stator blades. Axial-flow compressors have a number of stages of compression. Each stage consists of rotor blades to increase the velocity of the air and stator blades to convert the velocity energy into pressure.

compressor stall (gas turbine engine operating condition). A condition in a turbine engine axial-flow compressor in which the angle of attack of one or more blades becomes excessive and the smooth airflow through the compressor is disrupted. When only a few blades stall, the effect is minimal and is noticed by a fluttering or rumbling sound. When the entire compressor disk stalls, the effect can be a serious slowing down of the air through the engine. This can result in a loud explosive noise with a resulting RPM fluctuation and a serious increase in exhaust gas temperature. A compressor stall can occur if the airflow through the engine is restricted while the compressor RPM is high.

compressor stall-margin curve (gas turbine engine operation). A gas turbine engine operating curve which shows the relationship between the compression ratio of the engine and the mass airflow that must be maintained through the engine.

compressor surge (gas turbine engine operating condition). A severe compressor stall across the entire face of the compressor. Compressor surges occur when there is a complete stoppage of airflow, or a reversal of flow through the compressor. A compressor surge can cause a flameout or, if it is severe enough, can cause structural damage.

compulsory reporting points (air traffic control). Reporting points which must be reported to ATC. Compulsory reporting points are shown on IFR charts as solid triangles.

computer (electronic). A device that receives data, processes it, and then uses it in some type of output device. There are two types of electronic computers, digital and analog.

computer-aided design (CAD). Using a computer in the design of a product.

computer-aided design drafting (CADD). Using a computer in the design and drafting process.

computer-aided engineering (CAE). Using a computer in the engineering of a product.

computer-aided manufacturing (CAM). Using a computer in the manufacturing of a product.

computer-assisted instruction (CAI). Instruction in which the instructor is responsible for the class and uses the computer to assist in the instruction.

computer-based training (CBT). The use of the computer as a training device. CBT is sometimes called computer-based instruction (CBI); the terms and acronyms are synonymous and may be used interchangeably.

computer graphics. Drawing with the use of a computer.

computer navigation fix. A point used to define a navigation track for an airborne computer system such as GPS or FMS.

concave surface. A surface that is curved inward with the outer edges higher than the center.

concave surface

concentration cell corrosion. A form of corrosion on metal alloys caused by a potential difference in the electrolyte, rather than by a potential difference caused by a galvanic couple within the metal. The potential difference in the electrolyte may be caused by a concentration of either oxygen or metallic ions.

concentric. Having the same center.

concentric circles. Circles which have the same center.

concurrent lines. Lines which pass through a common point. The perpendicular bisectors of the three sides of a triangle all pass through the same point, and these bisectors are concurrent lines.

condensation. The process in which a material is changed from one form, or state, into a denser state. For example, water can exist in its vapor state, as steam, and by the process of condensation, the steam can be changed into liquid water.

condensation level (meteorology). The height at which a rising parcel or layer of air would become saturated if it were lifted adiabatically—lifted with heat neither added to it nor taken from it.

condensation nuclei (meteorology). Small particles in the air on which water vapor condenses or sublimates.

condensation trail (meteorology). Cloud-like streamers often seen behind aircraft flying in clear, cold air. Condensation trails are usually called contrails or vapor trails.

condenser (air conditioning system component). The component in a vapor-cycle air conditioning system in which the refrigerant gives up the heat it picked up as it passed through the evaporator. This heat is given up to the air flowing through the fins around the condenser tubing. When the refrigerant gives up its heat, it changes state, or condenses from a gas into a liquid.

C

condenser (electrical component). An old term for a capacitor. *See* capacitor.

con-di duct. The British name for a convergent-divergent duct. *See* convergent-divergent duct.

"condition" (lesson preparation, teaching/learning process). The second part of a performance-based objective which describes the framework under which the skill or behavior will be demonstrated.

conditionally unstable air (meteorology). Unsaturated air that will be unstable if it becomes saturated. Unstable air rises because it is warmer than the air surrounding it.

condition lever (turboprop engine control). An engine control used with a turboprop engine to control the pitch of the propeller for the flight operating range, the alpha range, of operation.

conductance (electrical parameter). A measure of the ability of a device to conduct electricity. The symbol for conductance is G, and it was once measured in mhos (ohm spelled backward), but it is now measured in siemens.

conduction (thermal). A method of heat transfer by direct contact in which heat energy moves from a higher energy level to a lower level by direct contact. A hand touching a hot stove will be burned because heat energy from the stove is transferred by conduction.

conductive coating (electrically conductive material). A finish applied to a nonconductive material to lower the electrical resistance of its surface. A conductive coating on an aircraft component prevents the buildup of static electricity on its surface.

conductivity (electrical characteristic). The ability of a material to allow electrons to move freely between its atoms.

conductivity (thermal characteristic). The ability of a material to transfer heat by allowing heat energy to pass from one molecule to another within the material.

conductor (electrical). A material whose outer shell (valence shell) electrons are held in the atom with a weak force and are therefore able to be moved from one atom to another with a small amount of electrical pressure. Most conductors have three or fewer valence electrons.

conductor (thermal). A material that is able to transfer heat easily and directly to another material by conduction. Most metals are good thermal conductors, while wood, paper, cloth, and many plastic materials are poor conductors—they are insulators.

conduit (electrical component). A tube or duct used to enclose and protect electrical wiring. Rigid conduit is usually made of thin-wall aluminum tubing, and flexible conduit is made of metal braid.

cone. A solid shape formed by rotating a right triangle about one of the legs which forms the right angle.

cone bottoming (propeller installation problem). A condition in the installation of a propeller on a splined shaft when either the front or rear cone contacts an obstruction that prevents the cone seating properly inside the propeller hub.

cone clutch. A type of clutch used to engage and disengage a component from a drive unit. The part of the clutch attached to the drive unit is a smooth internal cone, and the drive element of the clutch is made in the form of an external cone that mates exactly with the drive cone. Most cone clutches use a friction liner between the two surfaces. Oil pressure applies a force that wedges the two cones tightly together to engage the clutch, and a spring disengages the clutch by forcing the cones apart when the oil pressure is released.

cone of confusion (radio navigation). A cone-shaped volume of airspace directly above a VOR station where no signal is received. The CDI fluctuates when the aircraft in is the cone of confusion.

cone of silence (radio navigation). A location directly above the antenna of a four-course, low-frequency radio range in which the signals from the antennas cancel and no signal is received. The cone of silence can be identified by the signal building up in volume just before it disappears.

confidence maneuver (Pilot/Controller Glossary). A maneuver consisting of one or more turns, a climb or descent, or other maneuver to determine if the pilot in command (PIC) is able to receive and comply with ATC instructions.

configuration. (1) The general arrangement of the wings, empennage, and landing gear of an airplane. Examples: low-wing monoplane, biplane, V-tail, tricycle landing gear. (2) A term used to reference the position of the landing gear and flaps for a given flight condition. When the aircraft is in the landing configuration, the landing gear is down and locked, and the flaps are lowered.

configuration deviation list (CDL). The aircraft source document listing for operation of an aircraft with parts and/or combinations of parts permitted to be missing, and the associated performance reductions and other limitations, as determined and presented in the Airplane Flight Manual. Often used in conjunction with the minimum equipment list (MEL). As defined in FAA Order 8900.1, certified aircraft intended for use under 14 CFR Parts 121 or 135 may be approved for operations with missing secondary airframe and engine parts, upon approval of the CDL under an amendment to the type certificate.

configuration, maintenance, and procedures (CMP) document. A document that typically is published and maintained by the airplane manufacturer and approved by the FAA, which contains minimum configuration, operating, and maintenance requirements, hardware life-limits, and master minimum equipment list (MMEL) constraints necessary for an airplane-engine combination to meet ETOPS ("extended operations") type design requirements. The requirements in the CMP are established by the FAA at the time of initial ETOPS type design approval of the airplane-engine combination.

Airplane manufacturers may continue to release CMP revisions beyond the basic revision level required for ETOPS. The CMP revision levels required for specific airplane-engine combinations are typically listed in the front of the CMP or may be controlled through issuance of customized CMP documents.

confined area (air traffic control). An area where the flight of an aircraft is limited in some direction by terrain or the presence of obstructions, natural or man-made.

conflict alert (air traffic control). The function of an automated air traffic control system which alerts radar controllers of existing or pending situations which the program recognizes as requiring immediate attention and/or action.

conflict resolution (air traffic control). The resolution of potential conflicts between aircraft that are radar identified and in communication with ATC by ensuring that radar targets do not touch. Pertinent traffic advisories shall be issued when this procedure is applied.

conformance (air traffic control). The condition established when an aircraft's actual position is within the conformance region constructed around that aircraft at its position, according to the trajectory associated with the aircraft's current plan, which at a given time is determined by the simultaneous application of the lateral, vertical, and longitudinal conformance boundaries for the aircraft at the position defined by time and aircraft's trajectory.

conformance region (air traffic control). A volume of airspace, bounded laterally, vertically, and longitudinally, within which an aircraft must be at a given time in order to be in conformance with the current plan trajectory for that aircraft. At a given time, the conformance region is determined by the simultaneous application of the lateral, vertical, and longitudinal conformance bounds for the aircraft at the position defined by the time and the aircraft's trajectory.

conformity inspection (aircraft inspection). A physical comparison of a component or modification to the engineering drawings and specifications to verify that the component or modification conforms to the data.

congeal. To change from a freely flowing liquid into a liquid too viscous, or stiff, to flow.

congealed oil. Oil that has become too viscous, or thick, to flow because of its low temperature or because of contamination. Congealed oil is too stiff to act as a proper lubricant for an aircraft engine.

conifer (wood nomenclature). A tree that bears cones. The technical meaning of the term softwood is wood that comes from a conifer, or cone-bearing tree.

coning (helicopter rotor). *See* blade coning angle.

coning angle (helicopter rotor blade parameter). The angle formed between the plane of rotation of a helicopter rotor blade when it is producing lift, and a line perpendicular to the rotor shaft. The degree of the coning angle is determined by the relationship between the centrifugal force acting on the blades and the aerodynamic lift produced by the blades.

conn. To steer or control the direction of a ship or aircraft.

connecting rod (reciprocating engine component). The rigid rod that connects the pistons in a reciprocating engine to the throws of the crankshaft.

consensus standard. A standard developed through industry consensus for the purpose of certificating light-sport aircraft, applying to aircraft design, production, and airworthiness. It includes, but is not limited to, standards for aircraft design and performance, required equipment, manufacturer quality assurance systems, production acceptance test procedures, operating instructions, maintenance and inspection procedures, identification and recording of major repairs and major alterations, and continued airworthiness.

conservation of energy (physical law). The law of conservation of energy states that energy can neither be created nor destroyed, but it can be changed from one form into another.

CONSOL (CONSOLAN). A low-frequency, long-distance navigational aid used principally for transoceanic navigation.

console (aircraft controls). The portion of the cockpit of an aircraft in which many of the operating controls are located. The control console is normally in the form of a pedestal that extends out from the instrument panel between the seats for the pilot and copilot.

constant (mathematical). A number or symbol that has a fixed value for a given condition. An example of a constant useful in aviation maintenance is the relationship between the circumference of a circle and its diameter. This constant has a value of 3.1416 and is commonly known by the Greek letter pi (π).

constantan. A copper-nickel alloy used as the negative lead of a thermocouple for measuring cylinder head temperature in a reciprocating engine. Either iron or copper may be used as the positive lead for the thermocouple.

constant-current charge (battery charging). A method of restoring the charge to a storage battery by connecting it across a source of direct current that can be maintained at a constant value by varying the voltage as the state of charge progresses. The ideal charging current is about 7% of the ampere-hour capacity of the battery.

constant differential mode (aircraft pressurization). The mode of pressurization in which the cabin pressure is maintained a constant amount higher than the outside air pressure. The maximum differential pressure is determined by the structural strength of the aircraft cabin.

constant-displacement pump (fluid pump). A pump that moves a constant volume of fluid with each rotation. Gear pumps, gerotor pumps, vane pumps, and some types of piston pumps are constant-displacement pumps. Some form of pressure regulator or relief valve must be used with a constant-displacement pump when it is driven by the aircraft engine.

constant-force spring. A form of helical coil spring wound in such a way that it always produces a constant restorative force, regardless of the amount it is displaced.

constant-pressure chart (meteorology). A weather chart showing a constant-pressure surface. It may contain analysis of height, wind, temperature, humidity, and/or other elements.

constant-pressure cycle of energy release. The cycle of energy transformation used by a gas turbine engine. *See* Brayton cycle.

constant-speed drive (AC generator drive). *See* CSD.

constant-speed propeller. A type of propeller used on an airplane to hold the engine at a constant RPM as the air load on the propeller changes. A centrifugal governor senses the engine RPM, and if it increases above that for which the governor is set, the pitch of the propeller blades will increase. This increased blade angle increases the air load on the propeller, and the engine slows down. If the RPM drops below that for which the governor is set, the propeller pitch will decrease, and the decreased air load allows the engine to speed back up to its on-speed condition.

constant-voltage charge (batteries). A method of charging aircraft batteries in which a constant voltage is placed across the battery while it is being charged. When a battery is discharged, its voltage is low and the charging current is high. But as the battery becomes charged, its voltage rises and the charging current decreases. When the battery voltage is the same as the voltage of the charging source, no more charging current flows. Aircraft generators charge the batteries with a constant-voltage charge.

constant-voltage power supply (electronic power supply). A regulated power supply that maintains a constant output voltage as the electrical load varies.

constant-volume cycle of energy release. The cycle of energy transformation used by a reciprocating engine. *See* Otto cycle.

constrained-gap igniter (gas turbine engine igniter). A type of igniter used in a gas turbine engine ignition system. The center electrode is set back into the insulator so the spark jumps out past the end of the igniter. Constrained-gap igniters do not protrude into the combustion liner, so they run cooler than annular-gap igniters.

constructivism (psychology). A philosophy of learning founded on the premise that, by reflecting on experiences, students construct their own understanding of the environment.

contact (engine starting command). The term used between a person hand-propping an aircraft engine and the person in the cockpit. When the person is ready to spin the propeller, he or she calls "contact." The person in the cockpit turns on the fuel, slightly opens the throttle, applies the brakes, and replies "contact," and then turns the ignition switch to BOTH. The propeller is then pulled through to start the engine.

contact approach (air traffic control). An approach in which an aircraft on an IFR flight plan, having an air traffic control authorization, operating clear of clouds with at least one mile flight visibility and a reasonable expectation of continuing to the destination airport in those conditions, may deviate from the instrument approach procedure and proceed to the destination airport by visual reference to the surface.

contact cement. A type of adhesive that is spread on both surfaces to be joined and allowed to dry. The dried contact cement is not sticky to touch, but when the two coated surfaces are brought into contact with each other, they bond tightly together.

contact cooling (meteorology). The loss of heat from warm air to colder air or ground beneath it.

contact flying. Flight in which the attitude of the aircraft is maintained and its navigation is done by visual reference to the horizon and to the ground over which the aircraft is flying.

contactor (electrical control device). A heavy-duty, remotely operated switch used to control electrical circuits carrying large amounts of current.

contaminant. An impurity that pollutes. Dirt and water are contaminants that pollute aircraft fuel.

contaminated runway (air traffic control). A runway is considered contaminated whenever standing water, ice, snow, slush, frost in any form, heavy rubber, or other substances are present. A runway is contaminated with respect to rubber deposits or other friction-degrading substances when the average friction value for any 500-foot segment of the runway within the available landing distance falls below the recommended minimum friction level, and the average friction value in the adjacent 500-foot segment falls below the maintenance planning friction level.

contamination. The polluting of a substance by an impurity.

conterminous United States. The 48 adjoining states and the District of Columbia. These states are also called the contiguous United States.

continental control area (air traffic control). The airspace of the 48 contiguous states, the District of Columbia, and Alaska, excluding the Alaska peninsula west of Long. 160°00'00" W, and above 14,500 feet MSL, but not including:

1. Airspace less than 1,500 feet above the surface of the earth or,
2. Prohibited and restricted areas other than the restricted areas listed in 14 CFR Part 71.

continental United States. The 49 states located on the continent of North America and the District of Columbia.

"continue" (air traffic control). An air traffic control (ATC) instruction that is followed by another word or words to clarify what is expected of the pilot. For example: "continue taxi," "continue descent," or "continue inbound".

continuity (electrical circuit condition). A condition in which something is complete or unbroken. An electrical circuit is said to have continuity when current can flow from one end of the circuit to the other.

continuity light (electrical test equipment). A simple piece of test equipment used to check an electrical circuit for continuity. A continuity light consists of a flashlight battery and a bulb, connected in series with test leads used to complete the circuit. The test leads are connected to the ends of an electrical circuit. If the circuit is continuous (there are no breaks, or opens, in the circuit) the light will illuminate. If the circuit is not continuous (there is an open, or a break, in it), the light will not illuminate. Continuity lights are sometimes called bug lights because they are used to find the "bugs" in a circuit. More elaborate continuity testers have buzzers in addition to the light. The buzzer allows a circuit to be checked without having to watch the tester.

continuity tester. A troubleshooting tool that consists of a battery, a light bulb, and test leads. The test leads are connected to each end of the conductor under test, and if the bulb lights up, there is continuity. If it does not light up, the conductor is open.

continuous airworthiness inspection program. An inspection program that is part of a continuous airworthiness maintenance program approved for certain large airplanes (to which 14 CFR Part 125 is not applicable), turbojet multiengine airplanes, turbopropeller-powered multiengine airplanes, and turbine-powered rotorcraft.

continuous airworthiness maintenance program (CAMP). A progressive-type maintenance program that complies with Part 121 and 135 operations, and with the fractional ownership operations as outlined in 14 CFR Part 91 (Subpart K). CAMP is an FAA-approved program and is run in a manner similar to progressive inspections for general aviation aircraft, but is regulated in a way specifically tailored to for-hire aviation operations.

continuous casting (metal casting). A method of casting metal in which the ingot is continuously cooled and pulled as it is being poured. Continuous casting produces ingots whose length is not determined by the length of a mold.

continuous-duty ignition system (gas turbine engine). A type of secondary ignition system for a gas turbine engine. This system is used during takeoff and landing, as well as in flight when weather conditions are such that could cause an engine to flame out. The continuous-duty system keeps one igniter plug firing.

continuous-duty rating (electrical machinery). The rating of an electrical machine which specifies the amount of electrical load the machine can carry for an indefinite period of time.

continuous-duty solenoid. A solenoid-type switch designed to be kept energized by current flowing through its coil for an indefinite period of time. The battery contactor in an aircraft electrical system is a continuous-duty solenoid. Current flows through its coil all of the time the battery is connected to the electrical system.

continuous-element fire detection system. A fire and overheat detection system in which a gas-releasing element and a pressure switch are sealed in a stainless steel tube installed so it surrounds the compartment being protected. If the tube is exposed to a fire or an overheat condition, the element releases gas and closes the pressure switch. This actuates the fire warning system.

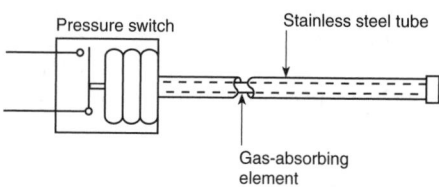

continuous element fire detection system

continuous filament (composites). A single, flexible, small-diameter fiber of indefinite length.

continuous-flow oxygen system. A system of aviation breathing oxygen in which a metered amount of oxygen flows continuously into the mask. A rebreather-type mask is used with a continuous-flow system. The simplest form of continuous-flow oxygen systems regulates the flow by a calibrated orifice in the outlet to the mask, but most systems use either a manual or automatic regulator to vary the pressure across the orifice proportional to the altitude being flown.

continuous gusset (wing rib bracing). A brace made of thin plywood used to reinforce the glue joints of all the upright and diagonal braces used in a wooden wing rib. The continuous gusset runs the full length of the rib, rather than being made in the form of small separate gussets at each joint.

continuous ignition system (turbine ignition system). An ignition system that can be turned on and used continuously when the need arises.

continuous-loop fire detection system. A type of fire detection system which uses two conductors, separated by a thermistor material, formed into a continuous loop that surrounds the area being

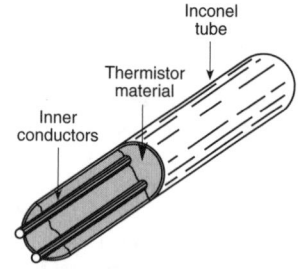

continuous-loop fire detection system element

protected. A thermistor is an electrical insulator at normal temperature, but becomes a conductor when heated. When a fire occurs, the thermistor conducts electricity and completes the fire warning circuit. This turns on the fire warning light and starts the fire warning horn or bell.

continuous magnetic particle inspection. A method of magnetic particle inspection in which the part is inspected while the magnetizing current is flowing either through the material or through a coil, or solenoid around the part.

continuous wave radio transmission. *See* CW.

contour (meteorology). A line drawn on a constant-pressure chart to show the pattern of points of equal pressure. These lines are similar to the contours shown on a topographical relief map that show lines of equal height.

contour (radar meteorology). A line on a radar scope that shows the areas of equal radar echo intensity.

contouring circuit (radar meteorology). A circuit which displays multiple contours of echo intensity simultaneously on the plan position indicator or range-height indicator scope.

contour map. A map of a geographical area which has lines drawn on it that connect points of equal elevation.

contrail. The long visible trail resembling a cloud left behind some airplanes as they fly at high altitude. Contrails form when water vapor from the hot engine exhausts condense and freeze into tiny ice crystals. These crystals reflect light from the sun and form the visible track across the sky.

contrarotating. Rotating in opposite directions.

contrarotating propellers. Two propellers mounted on concentric shafts and turning in opposite directions. The two propellers are driven by either a single engine or two engines coupled together, and their opposite rotation counteracts the effect of torque caused by the engines driving the propellers.

control. A mechanism or system used to regulate or guide the operation of a machine or organization.

control and performance (instrument flying). A method of attitude instrument flying in which one instrument is used for making attitude changes, and the other instruments are used to monitor the progress of the change.

control area (air traffic control). Airspace designated as Colored Federal Airways, VOR Federal Airways, control areas associated with jet routes outside the continental control area (14 CFR §71.161), additional control areas (14 CFR §71.163), control area extensions (14 CFR §71.165), and area low routes. Control areas do not include the continental control area, but unless otherwise designated, they do include the airspace between a segment of a main VOR Federal Airway and its associated alternate segments, with the vertical extent of the area corresponding to the vertical extent of the related segment of the main airway.

control cable (aircraft control system component). A steel cable used to connect the cockpit control to the flight control surfaces of an aircraft. *See* aircraft control cable.

control circuit (electrical circuit). An electrical circuit used to control other circuits in an electrical device or system. Control circuits include sensors and measuring devices. The output current in a control circuit is low, usually just enough to actuate the devices that control the main load current of the device or system.

control column (airplane control system). The control in the cockpit of an airplane on which the control wheel is mounted. Rotation of the control wheel operates the ailerons, and back-and-forth movement of the control column moves the elevators up or down.

Control Display Unit. *See* CDU.

control grid (electron tube component). The grid in an electron tube to which the signal to be amplified is applied. The voltage on the control grid controls the amount of electron flow allowed between the cathode and the anode, or plate, of the tube.

control horn (aircraft control system component). The arm on a control surface to which the control cable or push-pull rod attaches to move the surface.

controllability. The characteristic of an aircraft that allows it to change its flight attitude in response to the pilot's movement of the cockpit controls.

controllable-pitch propeller (aircraft propeller). A propeller whose blade pitch angle can be changed in flight. Takeoff is made with a low blade angle (low pitch) that allows the engine to develop its maximum power. When the airplane is set up for cruise flight, the pitch of the blades is increased so the propeller advances farther through the air each revolution of the engine. This allows the engine to operate at a slower, more economical speed. A controllable-pitch propeller and a constant-speed propeller are similar, the main difference being the control. The pitch of a constant-speed propeller is controlled by a governor, and the pitch of a controllable-pitch propeller is controlled by a manually actuated valve or switch.

controlled airport. An airport that has an operating control tower.

controlled airspace (air traffic control). Airspace designated as a continental control area, control area, control zone, terminal control area, transition area, or positive control area within which some or all aircraft may be subject to air traffic control.

14 CFR Part 1: "An airspace of defined dimensions within which air traffic control service is provided to IFR flights and to VFR flights in accordance with the airspace classification. *Note:* Controlled airspace is a generic term that covers Class A, Class B, Class C, Class D, and Class E airspace."

controlled departure time programs (air traffic control). The flow control process in which aircraft are held on the ground at the departure airport when delays are projected to occur in either the en route system or the terminal of intended landing. The purpose of controlled departure time programs is to reduce congestion in the air traffic system or to limit the duration of airborne holding in the arrival center or terminal area. A CDT is a specific departure slot shown on the flight plan as an expected departure clearance time (EDCT).

controlled diffusion compressor blade (turbine engine compressor blade). A design of compressor blade used in some of the modern axial-flow gas turbine engines. The leading edge is thicker than that of the conventional circular arc blade. Controlled diffusion blades minimize transonic drag rise and prevent separation of the air over their surface. The thicker leading edges erode far less than the leading edges of circular arc blades.

controlled firing areas. Special use airspace wherein activities are conducted under conditions so controlled as to eliminate hazards to nonparticipating aircraft and to ensure the safety of persons and property on the ground.

controlled flight into terrain (CFIT). A situation where a mechanically normally functioning airplane is inadvertently flown into the ground, water, or an obstacle. There are two basic causes of CFIT accidents; both involve flight crew situational awareness. One definition of situational awareness is an accurate perception by pilots of the factors and conditions currently affecting the safe operation of the aircraft and the crew. The causes of CFIT are the flight crews' lack of vertical position awareness or their lack of horizontal position awareness in relation to terrain and obstacles.

controlled time of arrival (air traffic control). The original estimated time of arrival adjusted by the air traffic control system command center ground delay factor.

control locking device (aircraft control system). A device used to lock the flight-control surfaces of an aircraft in their neutral position when the aircraft is on the ground.

C

Control locking devices normally have some type of warning flag to direct attention to the fact that they are installed or engaged. This prevents their being left in place when the aircraft is readied for flight.

control panel. The panel in an aircraft cockpit that contains the flight and engine instruments and switches for the operation of the aircraft systems.

controlled firing area *(14 CFR Part 1).* A controlled firing area is established to contain activities, which if not conducted in a controlled environment, would be hazardous to nonparticipating aircraft.

controlled rectifier. *See* SCR silicon controlled rectifier.

controller (air traffic). A person authorized to provide air traffic service, specifically enroute and terminal control personnel.

controller pilot data link communications (CPDLC). A two-way digital very high frequency (VHF) air/ground communications system that conveys textual air traffic control messages between controllers and pilots.

control pressure (aircraft controls). The amount of physical exertion needed to be applied on the control column in order to achieve the desired aircraft attitude.

control rod (aircraft control system component). A rigid rod normally made of aluminum alloy tubing used to actuate flight controls from the cockpit. Control rods are often called push-pull rods because of the method of their actuation.

control rod (nuclear reactor). A rod used to control the amount of activity in a nuclear reactor. It may be a fuel rod or a neutron-absorbing rod.

control sector (air traffic control). An airspace area of defined horizontal and vertical dimensions for which a controller or group of controllers has air traffic control responsibility, normally within an air route traffic control center or an approach control facility.

control slash (air traffic control). A radar beacon slash representing the actual position of the associated aircraft. Normally, the control slash is the one closest to the interrogating radar beacon site. When ARTCC radar is operating in the narrow-band (digitized) mode, the control slash is converted to a target symbol.

control snubber (boosted aircraft control system component). A device in a hydraulically boosted aircraft control system that cushions the movement of a control at the end of its travel.

control stick (aircraft control system component). A vertical stick in the cockpit of an airplane with which the pilot operates the ailerons and elevators. Side-to-side movement of the stick moves the ailerons, and back-and-forth movement moves the elevators. Most modern airplanes use control wheels, rather than control sticks.

control surface (airplane flight controls). Aerodynamic surfaces which can be moved from the cockpit of an airplane to cause the airplane to rotate about its three axes. The primary control surfaces are the ailerons, elevators, and rudder.

control touch. The ability to sense the action of the airplane and its probable actions in the immediate future, with regard to attitude and speed variations, by sensing and evaluating varying pressures and resistance of the control surfaces transmitted through the cockpit flight controls.

control tower. A terminal facility that uses air/ground communications, visual signaling, and other devices to provide ATC services to aircraft operating in the vicinity of an airport or on the movement area. Authorizes aircraft to land or take off at the airport controlled by the tower or to transit the Class D airspace area regardless of the flight plan or weather conditions. May also provide radar or non-radar approach control services.

control wheel (aircraft control system component). A wheel-like control in an airplane cockpit used by the pilot to move the ailerons and elevators. Rotation of the wheel moves the ailerons, and back-and-forth or in-and-out movement moves the elevators. Because the wheel does not rotate in a complete circle, most aircraft control wheels are not round, but are, rather, only segments of a wheel.

control yoke. The movable column on which an airplane control wheel is mounted. The yoke may be moved in or out to actuate the elevators, and the control wheel may be rotated to actuate the ailerons.

control zone (air traffic control). Controlled airspace which extends upward from the surface and terminates at the base of the continental control area. Control zones that do not underlie the continental control area have no upper limit. A control zone may include one or more airports. It is normally a circular area with a radius of five statute miles from the center of the airport and may include any extensions necessary for instrument approach and departure paths.

control zone (ICAO). A controlled airspace extending upwards from the surface of the earth to a specified upper limit.

convection (meteorology). Predominantly vertical movement of the atmosphere that results in mixing the atmospheric properties. Convection differs from advection, which is the horizontal movement of the atmosphere.

convection (heat transfer). A method of heat transfer within a fluid by means of vertical currents. Heat is absorbed in the bottom layer of the fluid by conduction, and this heat decreases the density of the fluid. The less dense fluid rises and forces the cooler, more dense fluid down.

convection cooling (electronic equipment cooling). Heat released from electronic equipment warms the air surrounding it. The warm air rises and escapes from the housing through outlet openings. Cooler air is drawn into the housing through the inlet openings replaces the warm air.

convection current. The vertical movement of molecules of a fluid in a container that is being heated. The warmed fluid rises and forces the cold fluid down.

convective cloud (meteorology). *See* cumuliform.

convective condensation level (meteorology). The lowest level at which condensation will occur as a result of convection due to surface heating. When condensation occurs at this level, the layer between the surface and the CCL will be thoroughly mixed, the temperature lapse rate will be dry adiabatic, and the mixing ratio will be constant.

convective instability (meteorology). The state of an unsaturated layer of air whose lapse rates of temperature and moisture are such that, when the air is lifted adiabatically until the layer becomes saturated, spontaneous convection will occur.

convective lifting (meteorology). Vertical movement of heated air. When a parcel of air is heated, it becomes less dense and begins to rise above the cooler, denser air surrounding it.

convective SIGMET (weather advisory). A weather advisory concerning convective weather significant to the safety of all aircraft. Convective SIGMETs are issued for:
1. Severe thunderstorms with surface winds of 50 knots or greater or hail at the surface with a diameter of $3/4$-inch or greater
2. Tornadoes
3. Embedded thunderstorms
4. Line of thunderstorms
5. Thunderstorms with very heavy precipitation and severe turbulence affecting 40% or more of an area of at least 3,000 square miles.

conventional current (electrical current). An imaginary flow of electricity said to go from the positive terminal of an electrical source to its negative terminal. The actual movement within an electrical circuit is that of electrons and is called electron current. The arrowhead in a semiconductor diode symbol points in the direction of conventional current, while electron current moves in the opposite direction.

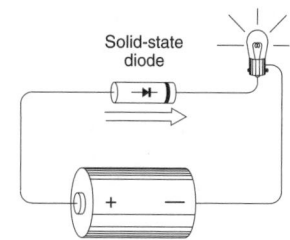

conventional current

conventional landing gear (airplane landing gear). The type of airplane landing gear with the main wheels ahead of the center of gravity and a small wheel supporting the tail when the airplane is on the ground. A conventional landing gear requires a great deal of pilot skill to keep the airplane from ground looping (accidentally turning around) when it is moving at a fast speed on the ground. The other type of landing gear, which is now the most commonly used, is the tricycle landing gear. The two main wheels are behind the center of gravity, and the auxiliary wheel supports the aircraft nose.

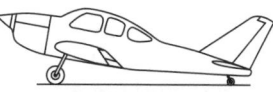

conventional landing gear

conventional tail (empennage configuration). An airplane tail design with the horizontal stabilizer mounted at the bottom of the vertical stabilizer. This is correctly called an inverted cruciform tail. Other types of empennage are: T-tail, with the horizontal stabilizer above the vertical surface, and V-tail, in which two surfaces forming a V provide both longitudinal and vertical stability and control.

converge. To draw closer together and eventually to meet. Converging lines are lines which, if continued, will meet and cross one another.

convergence (meteorology). The condition that exists when the distribution of winds within a given area is such that there is a net horizontal inflow of air into the area. In convergence at lower levels, the removal of the resulting excess air is accomplished by upward movement. Clouds and precipitation are likely to occur in areas of low-level convergent winds.

convergence zone (meteorology). A geographical area over which two air masses move back and forth. Weather conditions in a convergence zone can drastically change from moment to moment as fronts form and dissipate.

convergent-divergent duct. A duct that has a decreasing cross section in the direction of flow (convergent) until a minimum area is reached. After this point, the cross section increases, or becomes divergent. Convergent-divergent ducts are called CD ducts, or in the United Kingdom, con-di ducts.

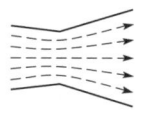

convergent-divergent duct

convergent-divergent exhaust duct (gas turbine engine exhaust duct). An exhaust duct used on the engine of a supersonic aircraft. The cross-sectional area of the duct decreases in the direction of the gas flow until it is small enough that the gases passing through this area travel at the speed of sound. Beyond this point of minimum area, the duct enlarges so the gases can be further speeded up above the speed of sound.

convergent-divergent inlet duct (supersonic airplane component). A form of duct, or passage, used for the inlet air to supersonic airplane engines. The forward section of the duct is convergent (it becomes smaller in the direction of the airflow). The air entering the duct at a supersonic speed is slowed to a speed of Mach one by a shock wave in the narrowest part of the duct. Beyond this point, the area of the duct increases—becomes divergent. The air, now traveling slower than the speed of sound, is further slowed, and its pressure increases.

convergent duct. A duct, or passage, whose cross-sectional area decreases in the direction of fluid flow.

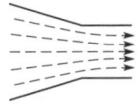

conversion coating (aircraft finishing system component). A chemical solution used to form an airtight oxide or phosphate film on the surface of aluminum or magnesium parts. The conversion coating prevents air reaching the metal and keeps it from corroding.

convergent duct

convertaplane (aircraft design). A type of heavier-than-air aircraft able to rise and descend vertically. The convertaplane rises vertically by using rotors similar to those on a helicopter. But, when it is in the air, the rotors can be tilted forward to produce thrust to pull the convertaplane through the air as a fixed-wing aircraft.

converter (electrical machine). A rotating electrical machine that changes, or converts, alternating current into direct current. A converter is usually a form of motor-generator, in which an AC motor drives a DC generator.

convex surface. A surface that is curved outward with its outer edges lower than the center.

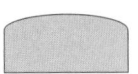

coolant. A fluid used to remove heat from a component or a system. A mixture of ethylene glycol and water is normally used as a coolant in liquid-cooled aircraft engines.

convex surface

cooling fins. Thin ribs that extend outward from a surface to carry heat from the surface into the air flowing through the fins.

The cylinders of air-cooled aircraft engines are finned to increase their surface area, so a maximum amount of heat can be transferred from the cylinder into the air.

cooling vent. A vent in the side or top of the balloon envelope that opens to release hot air and automatically closes after the release of air.

cooperative aircraft. An aircraft that is being tracked by air traffic control (ATC) or an aircraft that has an electronic means of identification (i.e., a transponder) aboard.

cooperative or group learning. An instructional strategy which organizes students into small groups so that they can work together to maximize their own and each other's learning.

coordinated flight. Application of all appropriate flight and power controls to prevent slipping or skidding in any flight condition.

coordinated turn. Turn made by an aircraft where the horizontal component of lift is equal to the centrifugal force of the turn.

coordinated universal time (UTC). Time corrected for the seasonal variations in the earth's rotation about the sun. Coordinated universal time is also known as universal time coordinated (thus UTC), Greenwich mean time (GMT), and Zulu time.

coordinates (air traffic control). The intersection of lines of reference, usually expressed in degrees/minutes/seconds of latitude and longitude, used to determine a position or location.

coordination fix (air traffic control). The fix in relation to the facilities which will hand off, transfer control of an aircraft, or coordinate flight progress data. For terminal facilities, the coordination fix may also serve as a clearance for arriving aircraft.

COP. *See* changeover point.

copal resins. Hard, natural resins that come from trees grown in the East Indies, South America, and Africa. Copal resins are soluble in alcohol, linseed oil, and turpentine, and are used in the manufacture of some types of aircraft finishes.

copilot (aircraft flight crewmember). A person who assists the pilot in flying an aircraft, but is not in command of the aircraft.

coping saw. A small, wood-cutting handsaw that uses a replaceable blade only about $\frac{1}{8}$-inch wide. The blade is held under tension in the jaws of a U-shaped frame that has a handle in line with the blade. Coping saws are used to cut curves in thin wood.

copper. A ductile, malleable, reddish-brown, metallic chemical element. Copper's symbol is Cu, its atomic number is 29, and its atomic weight is 63.546. Copper is one of our most important nonferrous metals. It is heavy, ductile, and malleable and has excellent electrical and thermal conductivity. Copper is used as a pure metal and as an alloy for other metals. One of copper's widest uses is in the manufacture of electrical wire.

copper brazing. A method of brazing in which copper is used as the filler metal. Steel parts to be brazed are put together with as little space as possible between them. Copper is melted along the edges of the steel parts, and as the molten copper wets the steel, capillary action pulls the molten copper between the steel parts. When the copper cools, it solidifies and forms a tight bond between the steel parts.

copper-constantan thermocouple. A thermocouple combination used to measure temperatures up to about 300°C. Copper forms the positive element, and constantan, the negative.

copper crush gasket. A copper gasket used to form a leakproof seal between components that operate at a high temperature. The gasket is made of a hollow copper ring formed around a ring of asbestos. When the component to be sealed is tightened down on the gasket, the asbestos compresses, and the surfaces press into the soft copper and form a leakproof seal.

copper loss (electrical loss). Energy loss caused by heat produced when current flows through the windings of an electric motor.

copper-oxide rectifier (electrical component). A rectifier that allows electrons to pass in one direction, but opposes their flow in the opposite direction. An oxide film is formed on a disk of copper, and a disk of lead is pressed tightly against the oxide. A barrier exists between the copper and the copper oxide that allows electrons to pass from the copper through the oxide to the lead; but they cannot pass from the lead through the oxide and the barrier to the copper.

copperweld (electrical wire). A high-strength electrical conductor made by plating a steel wire with copper. Copperweld is used for high-voltage transmission line, and for certain types of radio antenna where high strength is more important than maximum conductivity.

cord body (tire construction). Diagonal layers of rubber-coated nylon cord fabric oriented at opposite angles to each other. These plies provide the strength of a tire.

core (composites). The central component of a composite sandwich to which the face plies or skins are bonded.

core airflow. Air drawn into the engine for the gas generator.

core crush (composites). A collapse, distortion, or compression of the core of a composite sandwich.

core depression (composites). A gouge or indentation in the core material of a composite sandwich.

core engine (gas turbine engine). The gas generator portion of a gas turbine engine. The core engine consists of the portion of the compressor used to supply air for the operation of the engine, the diffuser, the combustors, the turbine nozzle, and the stages of the turbine used to drive the compressor. The core engine provides the high-velocity gas used to drive the fan and any free turbines that provide power for propellers, rotors, pumps, or generators.

core orientation (composites). The orientation of the ribbon direction of the honeycomb material used as the core of a composite sandwich. *See* ribbon direction.

core separation (composites). The breaking of the cells in a honeycomb core.

core speed sensor (gas turbine engine instrument component). The tachometer used to measure the speed of the high-pressure compressor (N_2) of a two-spool gas turbine engine.

core splicing (composites). Bonding together two segments of the core of a composite sandwich.

Coriolis effect (helicopter rotor condition). The change in rotor blade velocity to compensate for a change in the distance between the center of mass of the rotor blade and the axis of rotation of the blade as the blades flap in flight.

Coriolis force (meteorology). A force which acts on a particle while it is moving along a path in a plane that is being rotated. For example, when wind blows along a path over the surface of the earth from the poles toward the equator, the rotation of the earth causes the wind to deflect to the right in the northern hemisphere and to the left in the southern hemisphere. It is the Coriolis force that causes the circular movement of the winds. It is also the Coriolis force that causes water to swirl in a spiral as it drains out the bottom of a bowl.

Coriolis illusion. The illusion of rotation or movement in an entirely different axis, caused by an abrupt head movement, while in a prolonged constant-rate turn that has ceased to stimulate the brain's motion-sensing system.

cork. The tough, resilient, lightweight bark of the cork oak tree. Cork was used in some of the older aircraft as a thermal insulating material.

cornice brake (sheet metalworking tool). A large shop tool used to make straight bends across a sheet of metal. The sheet of metal is clamped in the brake, and a heavy steel leaf is lifted to bend the metal. The distance between the clamping jaw and the hinge line of the leaf determines the radius of the bend. Cornice brakes are often called leaf brakes.

corona (meteorology). A prismatically colored circle or arc of a circle with the sun or moon at its center. The color of a corona changes from blue inside to red outside, which is opposite to that of a halo. Coronas vary in size and are much smaller than the fixed size of a halo. Coronas form in middle clouds, which are composed of water droplets, and halos form in cirriform clouds, which are composed of ice crystals.

corona (electrical discharge). A discharge of electricity that appears as a bluish-purple glow on the surface of a conductor when the voltage on the conductor exceeds a certain critical value. Corona is caused by the ionization of the gases surrounding the conductor.

corona loss. Power loss caused by ionization of the gas surrounding a high-voltage conductor.

corposant (meteorology). Another name for Saint Elmo's fire. This is a visible electrical discharge from pointed objects when the air is highly charged electrically.

corrected altitude. Indicated altitude shown on an aircraft altimeter corrected for non-standard temperature of the air. The correction is based on the estimated difference between the existing temperature and the standard atmospheric temperature. Corrected altitude is an approximation of true altitude.

C

"correction" (air traffic control). A term used in pilot–controller communications to indicate that an error has been made in the transmission and that the correct version will follow.

correlation. A basic level of learning where the student can associate what has been learned, understood, and applied with previous or subsequent learning.

correlation box (helicopter engine control unit). A component in the reciprocating engine controls for a helicopter that automatically increases and decreases the amount of throttle opening as the collective pitch control is raised or lowered. The final adjustment of the power must be done by the twist grip, because the correlation box does not adjust for nonstandard atmospheric conditions.

corrosion. An electrolytic action which takes place within a metal or on its surface. The metal reacts with an electrolyte, and part of the metal is changed into a porous salt. This salt absorbs and holds water in contact with the metal and causes more corrosion to form.

corrosion inhibiting primer (aircraft finishing system component). A primer which prevents, or at least slows, the formation of corrosion in the metal it covers.

corrosion inhibitor. A material used to stop or slow the action of corrosion. To protect aluminum and magnesium alloys from corrosion, a tight, continuous oxide film is deposited on the surface. This film acts as a corrosion inhibitor.

corrosion prevention compound (reciprocating engine preservative). A special oil that has little tendency to run off of a surface on which it is sprayed. Corrosion prevention compound is sprayed into the cylinders of a reciprocating engine when it is to be stored. This compound forms an airtight seal over the surface of the metal and keeps air and moisture away from the surface. When air and moisture cannot reach the metal, corrosion or rust cannot form on it.

corrosion-resistant steel. Steel alloyed with nickel and chromium, to increase its resistance to corrosion or rust. Corrosion-resistant steel is also called stainless steel.

corrugate. To form ridges or waves in a piece of material to increase its rigidity.

corrugated fastener (wood fastener). A small strip of corrugated steel ground on one edge to form a series of sharp points. Corrugated fasteners are driven into butt joints in wood to fasten the pieces together.

corrugated sheet metal. Sheets of metal that have been made more rigid by forming a series of parallel ridges or waves in their surfaces.

cosecant (trigonometric function). The trigonometric function which is the ratio of the length of the hypotenuse of a right triangle to the length of the side opposite an acute angle.

cosine (trigonometric function). The trigonometric function which is the ratio of the length of the side adjacent to an acute angle in a right triangle to the length of the hypotenuse.

cosmic ray. A stream of electrons and hydrogen atom nuclei that comes from outer space, penetrates the earth's atmosphere, and strikes the earth from all directions. Cosmic rays travel at the speed of light.

cotangent (trigonometric function). The trigonometric function which is the ratio of the length of the side adjacent to an acute angle in a right triangle to the length of the side opposite the angle.

cotter pin. A split metal pin used to safety a castellated or slotted nut to a bolt. The cotter pin, which is also called a cotter key, is passed through the slots in the nut and the hole drilled through the shank of the bolt. The ends of the pin are spread back over the end of the bolt and the side of the nut to prevent the nut turning on the bolt.

cotton braid. A fabric tube made of loosely woven cotton thread. Cotton braid is used to encase bungee shock cord and certain types of rubber hose.

cotton staple. The natural fibers in cotton. Grade-A cotton fabric used for covering an aircraft is made of long-staple cotton.

coulomb. A unit of electrical charge equal to 6.28 billion billion (6.28 x 10^{18} or 6,280,000,000,000,000,000) electrons. One ampere of electrical flow is equal to the flow of one coulomb per second.

counterbore (machine tool). A special cutting tool used to enlarge the diameter of a hole for a certain depth. A counterbore has a pilot, or guide pin, the size of the hole, and the cutting edges are perpendicular to the axis of the tool. A counterbore enlarges the hole for a certain depth and produces a smooth, flat bottom to form a seat for a bolt head or nut.

counterboring (machining operation). The process of enlarging the entrance of a hole to a specified diameter and depth using a counterbore or a similar cutting tool.

counterelectromotive force. *See* CEMF.

counter-rotating propellers. Propellers on wing-mounted engines that turn in opposite directions. When flying at a high angle of attack, the descending propeller blade has a higher angle of attack than the ascending blade and the half of the propeller disk with the descending blade produces more thrust than the half with the ascending blade. On an airplane equipped with counter-rotating propellers the descending blades on both engines are near the aircraft centerline and neither engine is a critical engine. *See* critical engine.

countersink (metalworking tool). A metal-cutting tool used to chamfer (bevel) the edges of a hole so the head of a countersunk rivet will be flush, or even, with the surface of the metal.

countersink (*verb*). To prepare a rivet hole for a flush rivet by beveling the edges of the holes with a cutter of the correct angle.

countersunk-head rivet. A rivet whose cone-shaped head fits into a beveled hole in the metal. When the rivet is driven, the top of the manufactured head is flush with the surface of the metal.

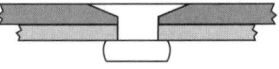

countersunk-head rivet

counterweight. A concentrated mass used to balance a weight or a load. Counterweights are used on the movable control surfaces of an airplane to prevent the surface from fluttering in high-speed flight.

counterweight (reciprocating engine crankshaft). A heavy weight fastened to one of the throws of a crankshaft to balance the assembly of the crankshaft, connecting rods, and pistons.

coupled ailerons and rudder (airplane flight controls). A control system in which the ailerons and rudder are coupled with interconnect springs. The coupling allows them to work together to counteract adverse yaw. The coupling can be overridden to slip the aircraft.

coupled approach (air traffic control). An instrument approach performed by the aircraft autopilot which is receiving position information and/or steering commands from onboard navigation equipment. In general, coupled nonprecision approaches must be discontinued and flown manually at altitudes lower than 50 feet below the minimum descent altitude, and coupled precision approaches must be flown manually below 50 feet AGL.

course (flight planning). The intended direction of flight, measured in the horizontal plane in degrees clockwise from north.

Course Deviation Indicator. *See* CDI.

course of training. A complete series of studies leading to attainment of a specific goal, such as a certificate of completion, graduation, or an academic degree.

C

course reversal (air traffic control). This maneuver is required when it is necessary to reverse direction to establish the aircraft inbound on an intermediate or final approach course. Components of the required procedure are depicted in the plan view of the instrument approach plate and the profile view. The maneuver must be completed within the distance and at the minimum altitude specified in the profile view.

covalent bond. A type of linkage between atoms in a chemical compound in which an electron is shared by two atoms. The sharing of the electron holds the atoms together. Two atoms of hydrogen share electrons with one atom of oxygen to form one molecule of water, a stable chemical compound.

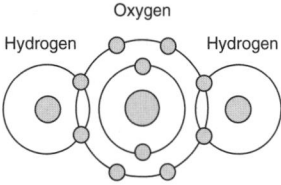

covalent bond

Coverite surface thermometer. The registered trade name for a small surface-type bimetallic thermometer used to calibrate the temperature of an iron used to heat-shrink polyester fabrics.

cowl flaps (reciprocating engine cooling system component). Movable flaps located at the exit of the cowling that houses an air-cooled aircraft engine. Opening or closing the cowl flaps controls the amount of air flowing through the cowling, and this in turn controls the amount of heat removed from the engine cylinders.

cowling (aircraft component). The removable cover which encloses an aircraft engine.

CPU (central processing unit). The portion of a computer that contains the main storage, the arithmetic-logic-unit, or ALU, and special register groups. The CPU performs arithmetic and logic functions, controls the processing of instructions, and furnishes timing signals for other computer functions.

crab (aircraft flight condition). Aircraft flight in which the nose of the aircraft is pointed into the wind, while the flight path over the ground is partially across the wind. An airplane is crabbed into the wind to keep it from drifting off the runway when making an approach for a crosswind landing.

crack (material defect). A partial separation in a piece of material caused by vibration, overloading, or internal stresses.

crack arrester (aircraft structure). A small hole drilled in the end of a crack to prevent the crack continuing. Drilling this hole is called stop-drilling the crack. A crack in a piece of metal will continue to grow as long as the stresses concentrated at the end of the crack are greater than the tensile strength of the metal. A hole drilled at the end of a crack spreads these stresses out over the entire circumference of the hole, rather than allowing them to concentrate at the extremely small area of the end of the crack.

cracked gasoline. A hydrocarbon fuel (gasoline) manufactured by heating crude petroleum products under pressure, usually in the presence of a catalyst. The heavier hydrocarbons in the crude oil are broken down by the cracking process into products that are distilled into gasoline.

cradle (maintenance fixture). A supporting fixture used to hold an aircraft structure while it is being repaired or stored. The cradle is padded so it will not damage the lightweight aircraft structure placed in it.

crankcase (reciprocating engine component). The housing which encloses the crankshaft, camshaft, and many of the accessory drive gears of a reciprocating engine. The cylinders mount on the crankcase, and the engine is attached to the airframe by the crankcase.

crankpin (reciprocating engine crankshaft component). The portion of a crankshaft to which the connecting rod is attached. The force produced by the expanding gases pushing on the piston is applied to the crankpin by the connecting rod. The crankpin travels in a circular path and causes the crankshaft to rotate.

crankshaft (reciprocating engine component). The central component of a reciprocating engine, a high-strength, alloy steel shaft with hardened and polished bearing surfaces that ride in bearings in the crankcase. Offset throws are formed on the crankshaft on which crankpins are ground and polished. Connecting rods, driven by the pistons, ride on the crankpins and change the in-and-out motion of the pistons into rotation of the crankshaft. The propeller of an airplane or the rotor system transmission of a helicopter is driven by the crankshaft.

crankshaft runout (reciprocating engine dimension). The amount a crankshaft is bent. Runout is checked by supporting the crankshaft in V-blocks or rollers and mounting a precision dial indicator so its arm rides around the end of the crankshaft as it is rotated. As the shaft is turned, the dial indicator shows the amount, usually in thousandths of an inch, the shaft is bent, or the amount it is run out.

crankshaft throw (reciprocating engine term). The offsets of an engine crankshaft to which the connecting rods attach. Each throw has a hardened and polished crank pin on which the connecting rod big-end bearing rides.

crater (welding bead component). A recess, or dip, in the puddle of molten metal in the flame of a gas welding torch or in the arc used for electric welding.

craze (transparent plastic damage). A series of tiny cracks in the surface of a piece of transparent plastic material.

crazing. A form of heat damage that occurs in a transparent thermoplastic material. Crazing appears as a series of tiny, hairlike cracks in the surface of the plastic. If a material is heated nonuniformly, one side will expand more than the other, and the stresses caused by the uneven expansion produce the crazing. Crazing destroys the strength of the material and makes it difficult to see through.

creep (gas turbine engine component defect). A condition of permanent elongation of a turbine blade. Creep causes the turbine blades to actually grow in length when they are acted on by high temperature and high centrifugal loading.

creeper (shop tool). A flat board with low wheels on it. A mechanic can lie on a creeper while working under the fuselage or under a low wing of an airplane.

crepe masking tape. A form of paper tape which is crinkled, with one side coated with a pressure-sensitive adhesive. Crepe masking tape is used to prepare a surface for painting. The crinkles allow the tape to lie flat when it is used to mask a curved line.

Crescent wrench. The registered trade name for an adjustable open-end wrench. Because of its popular use, the name Crescent wrench has become accepted as the generic name for this type of wrench. A Crescent wrench has one fixed jaw and one adjustable jaw. The adjustable jaw moves in and out, parallel to the fixed jaw. The jaws form a parallel opening that is offset by about 15° from the axis of the wrench handle.

crest (thread nomenclature). The peak, or top, of a machined thread.

crest clearance (thread nomenclature). The distance, measured perpendicular to the axis of a threaded component, between the crest of a thread and the root of its mating thread.

crew chief. A crewmember who is assigned the responsibility of organizing and directing other crewmembers.

crewmember (aircraft flight crew). A person aboard an aircraft for the purpose of operating the aircraft in flight. *14 CFR Part 1:* "A person assigned to perform duty in an aircraft during flight time."

crew resource management (CRM). The application of team management concepts in the flight deck environment. It was initially known as "cockpit resource management," but as CRM programs evolved to include cabin crews, maintenance personnel and others, the more descriptive phrase has been adopted. Pilots of small aircraft, as well as crews of larger aircraft, also must make effective use of all available resources—human resources, hardware, and information—basically, all groups routinely working with the cockpit crew who are involved in decisions required to operate a flight safely. These groups include, but are not limited to: pilots, dispatchers, cabin crewmembers, maintenance personnel, and air traffic controllers. CRM is one way of addressing the challenge of optimizing the human/machine interface and accompanying interpersonal activities.

crimping (sheet metal fabrication procedure). Shortening a piece of sheet metal by forming small pleats or corrugations in its surface. A formed metal angle may be bent into a curve by crimping the edge of one of its legs.

crimping tool (electrical wiring tool). A special tool used to install crimp-on terminals on the ends of electrical wires. The tool is designed to exert enough pressure that the barrel of the terminal is squeezed into the strands of the wire to form a strong, low-resistance attachment.

crimp-on terminals (electrical wire terminals). Terminals which are attached to the end of an electrical wire for the purpose of connecting the wire to a terminal strip or component, or for splicing the wires. The terminals are attached to the wire ends by squeezing the terminal into the strands of the wire. No solder is used.

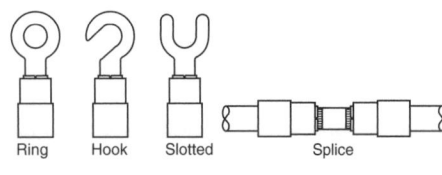

Ring   Hook   Slotted   Splice

crimp-on terminals

crinkle finish. A type of finish formed by a special paint in which the surface dries in a series of wrinkles. The paint used to make a crinkle finish contains special ingredients that cause the surface to partially dry before the paint below the surface dries. As the subsurface paint dries, it shrinks and pulls the surface into a series of wrinkles. Crinkle finish is used on instrument panels to give a tough, attractive finish that does not reflect light.

"criteria" (lesson preparation, teaching/learning process). The third part of a performance-based objective—descriptions of standards that will be used to measure the accomplishment of the objective.

criterion referenced testing. A system of testing where students are graded against a carefully written, measurable standard, or criterion, rather than against each other.

critical altitude (aircraft reciprocating engine specification). The maximum altitude under standard atmospheric conditions at which an aircraft reciprocating engine can deliver its rated horsepower.

14 CFR Part 1: "The maximum altitude at which, in standard atmosphere, it is possible to maintain, at a specified rotational speed, a specified power or a specified manifold pressure. Unless otherwise stated, the critical altitude is the maximum altitude at which it is possible to maintain, at the maximum continuous rotational speed, one of the following:

(1) The maximum continuous power, in the case of engines for which this power rating is the same at sea level and at the rated altitude.

(2) The maximum continuous rated manifold pressure, in the case of engines, the maximum continuous power of which is governed by a constant manifold pressure."

critical angle of attack (aerodynamics). The highest angle of attack at which air passes over an airfoil in a smooth flow. At angles of attack greater than the critical angle, the air burbles, or flows in a disturbed pattern, and lift is lost. The critical angle of attack is sometimes called the stalling angle of attack.

critical areas (radio navigation). Areas where disturbances to the ILS localizer and glideslope courses may occur when surface vehicles or aircraft operate near the localizer or glideslope antennas.

critical compression ratio (compression-ignition engine). The lowest compression ratio of a compression-ignition engine that allows a specific fuel to be ignited by compression ignition.

critical coupling (electrical transformers). The coupling between the windings of a transformer that transfers the maximum amount of energy. Critical coupling is also known as optimum coupling.

critical engine (aircraft operation). The engine of a multiengine airplane which would cause the most difficulty in maintaining control if it failed in a critical condition of flight, such as on takeoff. *14 CFR Part 1:* "The engine whose failure would most adversely affect the performance or handling qualities of the aircraft."

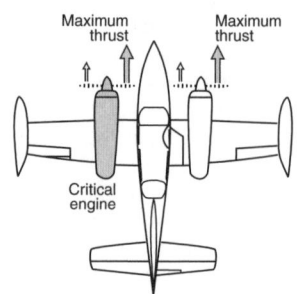

critical engine

critical field length (flight operation). The balanced field length as it applies to a particular airplane. The critical field length is calculated for each individual airplane to meet the balanced field length criteria.

critical height (flight operation). The minimum height above aerodrome level to which an approach to landing by an aircraft can safely be continued without visual reference to the ground.

critical Mach number (aerodynamics). The flight Mach number at which there is the first indication of air flowing over any part of the structure at a speed of Mach one, the local speed of sound.

critical part. The part in an assembly or component whose failure would prevent the assembly or component functioning as it should.

critical pressure (reciprocating engine fuel). The highest pressure of the fuel-air mixture inside the cylinder of a reciprocating engine that allows the mixture to burn evenly, rather than explode, or detonate.

critical RPM range (engine operating condition). A range of engine RPM in which the natural vibratory frequency of the engine-propeller combination is excited. Continued operation in the critical range, which is marked on the tachometer dial with a red arc, can cause destructive vibration.

critical strain (material strength). The amount of strain required for a material to reach its yield point. *See* yield point.

critical stress area (aircraft structure). An area in an aircraft structure that either has been exposed to an excess of stress or would cause the maximum amount of strength loss if it were damaged.

critical temperature (reciprocating engine fuel). The temperature inside the cylinder of a reciprocating engine that will cause the fuel to explode, rather than burn evenly when it is ignited.

critical temperature of a metal (heat treatment). The temperature at which the internal structure of a metal takes on a crystalline form.

CRM. *See* crew resource management.

crocus cloth. An abrasive cloth that has a fine, dark red iron oxide bonded to its surface. Crocus cloth is used for polishing hard metal surfaces.

cross (fix) at (altitude) (air traffic control). Instructions from ATC for an aircraft operating under instrument flight rules to cross a specified fix at a specified altitude. Instructions may also be given to cross the specified fix at or above a given altitude, or at or below a certain altitude.

cross [fix] at or above [altitude] (air traffic control). A term used by ATC when an altitude restriction at a specified fix is required. It does not prohibit the aircraft from crossing the fix at a higher altitude than specified; however, the higher altitude may not be one that will violate a succeeding altitude restriction or altitude assignment.

cross-bleed (gas turbine engine air starting system). An air ducting system used in a multiengine turbojet airplane in which compressor bleed air from one engine can be directed to another engine where it can be used to operate its air starter.

cross-check. The first fundamental skill of instrument flight, also known as "scan,"—the continuous and logical observation of instruments for attitude and performance information.

cross coat (aircraft finishing system). A double coat of aircraft finishing material in which the second coat is sprayed over the first coat at right angles to it, before the solvents in the first coat have evaporated from it.

cross-country flight. A flight conducted by a person who holds a pilot certificate which includes a landing at a point other than the point of departure, and involves the use of dead reckoning, pilotage, or other navigation system to navigate to the landing point.

cross-country time (flight training). Time tracked for the purpose of meeting the aeronautical experience requirements for a pilot certificate or instrument rating. A flight which includes a point of landing that was at least a straight-line distance of more than 50 nautical miles from the original point of departure (25 nautical miles for a Sport Pilot applicant, 15 nautical miles for a powered parachute pilot, and 25 nautical miles for an instrument-helicopter rating), and involves the use of dead reckoning, pilotage, or other navigation system to navigate to the landing point.

crosscut saw. A form of wood saw having short, sharp, knife-like teeth. A crosscut saw is used to cut wood across its grain.

crossed-control stall (flight training). A demonstration maneuver used to show the effect of improper control technique and to emphasize the importance of using coordinated control pressures when making turns.

cross-feed system (aircraft fuel system). An arrangement of the fuel system plumbing of a multiengine aircraft that allows any of the engines to operate from any of its fuel tanks. The cross-feed system also allows fuel to be transferred from one side of the aircraft to the other side to maintain balance in flight.

cross-feed valve (fuel system component). A valve in a fuel system that allows any engine of a multiengine aircraft to draw fuel from any fuel tank. Cross-feed systems are used to allow a multiengine aircraft to maintain a balanced fuel load.

cross-filing (metal cutting). A method of cutting metal with a file in which the file is moved endwise over the work. Cross-filing is different from draw-filing, in which the file is moved sideways across the work.

cross-firing (reciprocating engine ignition system malfunction). A malfunction in which high voltage in the distributor jumps between the terminals and causes the wrong spark plug to fire.

"Cross [fix] at [altitude]" (air traffic control). A phrase used by ATC when a specific altitude restriction at a specified fix is required.

"Cross [fix] at or above [altitude]" (air traffic control). A phrase used by ATC when an altitude restriction at a specified fix is required. It does not prohibit the aircraft from crossing the fix at a higher altitude than specified; however, the higher altitude must not be one that will violate a succeeding altitude restriction or altitude assignment.

"Cross [fix] at or below [altitude]" (air traffic control). A phrase used by ATC when a maximum crossing altitude at a specific fix is required. It does not prohibit the aircraft from crossing the fix at a lower altitude; however, the aircraft must be at or above the minimum IFR altitude.

cross-flow valve (landing gear system component). An automatic flow-control valve installed between the gear-up and gear-down lines of the landing gear of some large airplanes. When the landing gear is released from its uplocks, its weight causes it to fall faster than the hydraulic system can supply fluid to the gear-down side of the actuation cylinder. The crossflow valve opens and directs fluid from the gear-up side into the gear-down side. This allows the gear to move down with a smooth motion.

cross-hatching (mechanical drawings). A method of using angled, parallel lines to show that a section of a drawing has been cut away. Different arrangements of the cross-hatch lines are used to identify the material of which the part is made.

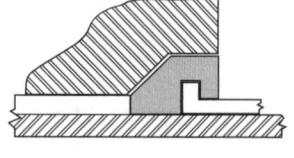

cross hatching

crossing restriction. A directive issued or published by air traffic control that instructs the pilot to cross a given waypoint at a specified altitude, and sometimes at a specified airspeed.

cross linking (composites). The setting-up of chemical links between polymer molecular chains. When extensive, as in most thermosetting resins, cross-linking makes one infusible supermolecule of all the chains.

cross member (structural component). An auxiliary member of a primary aircraft structure. Cross members are installed between the major lengthwise structural members (longerons and spars) to separate them and to carry stresses other than the primary stresses.

cross modulation. *See* cross talk.

crossover (helicopter rotor system). A condition in which helicopter rotor blades track on the ground and in a hover, but one blade flies higher than the other in flight.

crossover tube (gas turbine engine component). A small tube that connects the burner cans in a multiple-can combustor. Crossover tubes carry flame from one can to the other when the engine is being started.

cross-ply laminate (composites). Any filamentary laminate that is not uniaxial. In some references, the term cross-ply is used to designate only those laminates in which the laminae are at right angles to one another, while the term "angle-ply" is used for all others.

cross-sectional view (mechanical drawing). An auxiliary view of an aircraft drawing used to show the cross-sectional shape or the construction of part of a structure or component.

cross talk (electronic system). An undesirable condition, also known as cross modulation, in which the output from one system or part of a system is fed over into another system. The output contains the signal that has been fed into it as well as the desired signal. Cross talk occurs when signals on one channel or circuit are unintentionally fed over so they appear on another channel or in another circuit.

crosswind (aviation operations). A wind blowing across the flight path of an aircraft. When an aircraft is flying in a crosswind, correction must be made to keep it from being blown from its desired flight path.

crosswind component (aircraft operation). The wind component, measured in knots, at 90° to the longitudinal axis of a runway.

crosswind correction. Correction applied in order to maintain a straight ground track during flight when a crosswind is present.

crosswind landing (aircraft operation). A landing made in a direction across, or nearly perpendicular to, the direction from which the wind is blowing.

crosswind landing gear (airplane landing gear). A type of landing gear installed on some tailwheel airplanes to make crosswind landings easier for the pilot. In a crosswind landing gear, the two main wheels are equipped with a spring-loaded cam that allows them to be turned away from their normal position which is parallel to the fuselage of the airplane. When an airplane, crabbed into the wind for a crosswind landing, touches down, the wheels automatically turn at an angle to the fuselage so they roll straight down the runway while the fuselage is pointed into the wind.

crowfoot wrench. A very short open-end or box-end wrench with a square drive hole that allows it to be mounted on an extension which may be turned by a flex, or breakover, handle. A crowfoot wrench is used to turn a nut in a location where it cannot be reached and turned with any other kind of wrench.

crown line (balloons). A line attached to the top of most balloons to assist in the inflation and deflation of the envelope. Sometimes referred to as "apex line" or "top handling line."

CRT (cathode-ray tube). A display tube used in oscilloscopes, digital computers, and television receivers. An electron gun emits a stream of electrons that is attracted to a positively charged inner surface of the face of the tube. Acceleration grids and focusing grids speed the movement of the electrons and shape the beam into a pinpoint size. Electrostatic or electromagnetic forces caused by deflection plates or coils move the beam over the face of the tube. The inside of the face is treated with a phosphor material that emits light when the beam of electrons strikes it.

crucible. A container made of a material that can be heated to a very high temperature. Materials to be melted are put into the crucible and heated to the temperature needed to melt them. Certain types of high-grade steel are made in crucibles.

crucible steel. A high grade of steel produced by melting scraps of iron and steel in a graphite crucible and adding the correct amounts of alloying elements and fluxes. The metal is boiled to remove the volatile oxides, and after the slag is removed, the molten steel is cast into ingots.

crude oil. Petroleum in the condition it is in when taken from the ground.

cruise (air traffic control). When used in an ATC clearance, the term cruise means that the pilot may conduct flight at any altitude from the minimum IFR altitude up to and including the altitude specified in the clearance. The pilot may level off at any intermediate altitude within the block of airspace. Climb or descent within the airspace may be made at the discretion of the pilot. However, once the pilot starts descent and verbally reports leaving an altitude in the block, he may not return to that altitude without additional ATC clearance.

cruise (aircraft flight condition). A flight condition that allows an aircraft to operate smoothly and efficiently for a long period of time.

cruise clearance. An ATC clearance issued to allow a pilot to conduct flight at any altitude from the minimum IFR altitude up to and including the altitude specified in the clearance. Also authorizes a pilot to proceed to and make an approach at the destination airport.

cruise climb (air traffic control). A climb technique employed by aircraft usually at a constant power setting, resulting in an increase of altitude as the aircraft weight decreases.

cruise power (engine power setting). The power setting for an aircraft engine during cruise flight that will obtain the best fuel flow and performance.

cruising altitude. An altitude or flight level maintained during en route level flight.

cruising level (ICAO). A level maintained during a significant portion of a flight.

crush gasket. A form of gasket made of thin copper, formed around a core of asbestos. When the component being sealed by this gasket is screwed tightly into its housing, the gasket is crushed so it conforms to the two surfaces and provides a leakproof seal.

cryogenic gyroscope. A form of gyroscope which uses a spherical rotor made of niobium. The rotor is suspended in a magnetic field and is operated at a cryogenic (extremely low) temperature. At this temperature the niobium acts as a superconductor.

cryogenic liquid. A liquid which boils at temperatures of less than about 110°K (–163°C) at normal atmospheric pressures. Liquid nitrogen and liquid oxygen are commonly used cryogenic liquids.

cryogenics. The branch of science or engineering that deals with technical operations involving very low temperatures; temperatures near absolute zero.

crystal (frequency control device). A piece of quartz or Rochelle salt which has piezo-electric characteristics. A piezoelectric crystal produces a voltage between two of its opposite surfaces, or faces, when it is bent or compressed. A crystal also distorts when a voltage is placed across two of its opposite faces. All physical objects have a natural resonant frequency at which they vibrate most easily. A piezoelectric crystal will, when it is placed in an electrical circuit and excited with a pulse of electrical energy, vibrate at its resonant frequency. As the crystal vibrates, it produces an AC voltage whose frequency is the same as the resonant frequency of the crystal.

crystal-controlled oscillator. An electronic oscillator which produces alternating current from direct current. The frequency of the AC is determined by the resonant frequency of a piezoelectric crystal in the oscillator circuit.

crystal diode. A form of electronic check valve. A crystal diode uses a semiconductor material which allows electrons to pass in one direction, but prevents their flowing in the opposite direction. A crystal diode is made of either silicon or germanium which has areas doped with impurities that make P-areas and N-areas.

crystal diode

crystal earphones. Earphones in which alternating current distorts a piezoelectric crystal. The crystal is attached to a diaphragm in such a way that, as the crystal distorts, the diaphragm produces changes in air pressure (sound waves). The sound waves duplicate the changes in the alternating current.

crystal filter (electronic circuit). An electronic filter which opposes a certain band of frequencies, but allows all frequencies on either side of the band to pass. A crystal filter attenuates, or decreases the value of, AC signals whose frequencies are near the resonant frequency of the crystal in the filter circuit.

crystalline (physical structure). A type of molecular structure in which the molecules of a material are arranged in a definite pattern throughout the material. This pattern of molecular arrangement is called a crystal lattice.

crystal microphone (aircraft radio component). A microphone used for aircraft radio transmissions in which sound pressure waves distort a piece of piezoelectric crystal.

A diaphragm in the microphone is attached to a crystal of Rochelle salt or other piezoelectric material in such a way that, when sound waves vibrate the diaphragm, it distorts the crystal. When the crystal vibrates, it produces a voltage across two of its opposite faces that changes in exactly the same way the sound pressure changes.

crystal oscillator. *See* crystal-controlled oscillator.

crystal oven. A device inside a piece of sensitive electronic equipment that holds the temperature of a frequency-controlling crystal constant. The crystal is kept at a constant temperature inside the oven to prevent change in its physical characteristics and thus in the frequency of the alternating current it produces.

crystal transducer. A device that uses a piezoelectric crystal to change mechanical pressure or vibrations into electrical signals. When a piezoelectric crystal is physically distorted, a potential difference is created across its faces. Crystal transducers are also called piezoelectric transducers.

C

CSD (constant-speed drive). A component used with either aircraft gas turbine or reciprocating engines to drive AC generators. The speed of the output shaft of the CSD is held constant while the speed of its input shaft varies. The CSD holds the speed of the generator constant and thus the frequency of the AC it produces, as the engine speed varies through its normal operating range.

C-stage (composites). The final stage in the reaction of certain thermosetting resins in which the material is relatively insoluble and infusible. Certain thermosetting resins in a fully cured adhesive layer are in this stage.

CTAF (common traffic advisory frequency). A frequency designated for the purpose of carrying out airport advisory practices while operating to or from an uncontrolled airport. The CTAF may be a UNICOM, MULTICOM, FSS, or tower frequency, and it is identified in the appropriate aeronautical publications.

CTF (centrifugal twisting force). The force acting about the longitudinal axis of a propeller blade which tries to rotate the blade to a low-pitch angle. *See* CTM.

CTM (centrifugal twisting moment). The force moment, acting about the longitudinal axis of a propeller blade, which tries to rotate the blade toward a low-pitch angle. As the engine rotates the propeller, centrifugal force tries to flatten the blade so all of its mass rotates in the same plane. Centrifugal twisting moment (CTM) opposes aerodynamic twisting moment (ATM), but normally CTM is the greater. The resultant of these two twisting moments is a force on a rotating propeller that tries to move the blades toward a low-pitch angle.

CT message (air traffic control). An expected departure clearance time (EDCT) generated by the air traffic control system command center (ATCSCC) to regulate traffic at arrival airports. Normally, a CT message is automatically transferred from the traffic management system computer to the National Airspace System enroute computer and appears as an EDCT.

cube (geometric figure). A solid geometric figure which has six square sides. All the angles in a cube are right angles (90° angles), and all of the sides have the same length.

cube (mathematical power). The third power of the number. It is the value obtained when the number is multiplied by itself two times. The cube of three (33) is 27. We find this by multiplying three by itself two times: $3 \cdot 3 \cdot 3 = 27$.

cube root (mathematical term). The inverse of the cube of a number. The inverse of a number is one, divided by the number. The cube root of 27 ($\sqrt[3]{27}$) is 3. This is the same as 27 raised to the $^{1}/_{3}$ power.

cuff (propeller component). A thin, sheet metal, airfoil-shaped covering over the shank of a propeller blade. Cuffs force air through the cowling of an air-cooled engine to improve its cooling.

cuff (wing leading edge components). Specially shaped pieces of sheet metal attached to the leading edge of the wing to increase the camber, or curvature, of the airfoil to improve the slow-flight characteristics of the wing.

cumuliform (meteorology). A term used to describe all convective clouds which exhibit vertical development. Cumuliform clouds are distinguished from stratiform clouds, which have no vertical development.

cumulonimbus (meteorology). Heavy, dense cumuliform clouds with considerable vertical development in the form of massive towers. Cumulonimbus develop from cumulus clouds, and the tops of the towers, which are often in the shape of an anvil or massive plume, extend upward for many thousands of feet. Lightning, thunder, and often hail accompany a cumulonimbus; and virga, precipitation, and low, ragged clouds, called scud, often form under their dark base. Cumulonimbus occasionally produce tornadoes or waterspouts.

cumulonimbus mamma (meteorology). A cumulonimbus cloud having protuberance-like pouches, or udders, hanging on their underside. Cumulonimbus mamma clouds normally indicate the presence of severe turbulence.

cumulus (meteorology). A cloud in the form of individual detached, dense, and well-defined domes or towers. Cumulus clouds develop vertically in the form of rising mounds whose bulging upper parts often resemble a cauliflower. The sunlit parts of these clouds are mostly a brilliant white, while their bases, which are nearly always horizontal, are relatively dark.

cumulus congestus. A cumulus cloud of significant vertical extent and usually displaying sharp edges. In warm climates, these sometimes produce precipitation. Also called towering cumulus, these clouds indicate that thunderstorm activity may soon occur.

cumulus stage (meteorology). The initial stage of a thunderstorm characterized by updrafts and a cumulus growing to a towering cumulus (Tcu). Sometimes referred to as "cumulus congestus."

Cuno filter (fluid filter). The registered trade name for a type of edge filter used in aircraft engines and hydraulic systems. The Cuno filter element is made of a stack of thin metal disks separated by thin spacers. Fluid flows between the disks, and contaminants in the fluid are trapped and held on the edges of the disks. The disks are rotated so the spacers can scrape away the contaminants, which collect in a low point in the filter housing until they can be removed.

cup point (threaded fastener). The end of a threaded fastener made in the form of an open cup. The end of the fastener is formed in the shape of a cone with its point cut off and the end drilled with a cone-shaped depression. The contact area of a cup-point fastener is a circular ridge which makes a slight depression in the surface onto which it is tightened. Cup points are used for set screws.

cup washer. A form of lock washer made of spring steel formed into the shape of a cup. When the nut is tightened on a cup washer, the washer compresses, and its spring action holds pressure between the threads in the nut and those in the bolt. This pressure prevents vibration from loosening the nut.

cure (plastic resin condition). A step in the manufacture of parts made from plastic resins. The components of the resin are mixed, and heat produced in the resin or heat applied externally causes the resin to cure, or change into a compound different from that of its components.

cure temperature (composites). The temperature to which a cast, molded, or extruded product, a resin-impregnated reinforcement or adhesive is subjected for curing.

cure time (plastic resin). The amount of time needed for a plastic resin to change from a liquid into a solid.

curing agent (composites). A catalytic or reactive agent that brings about polymerization when it is added to a resin.

curium. A silvery, metallic, synthetic, radioactive chemical element. Curium's symbol is Cm, and its atomic number is 96.

currency (time requirement). Meeting the legal requirements to exercise the pilot certificate, usually requiring a certain number of hours of flight time over a given period of time.

current (electricity). A term used to describe the flow of electricity. Electron current is the flow of electrons in a circuit. They move through a circuit from the negative terminal of the source of electrical energy to its positive terminal. Conventional current is an assumed flow of electricity which travels from positive to negative. It was only after the discovery that it is the negative electrons that actually move in an electrical circuit that the concept of electron current was developed. Previous to this discovery, many texts were written using the positive to negative direction of flow. For this reason, positive to negative flow is called conventional current. Current is measured in amperes, with one ampere being the rate of flow of one coulomb per second. *See* coulomb.

current amplifier (electronic circuit). An electronic amplifier in which the current in its output circuit is greater than the current in its input circuit.

current density. The ratio found by dividing the total amount of current flowing through a conductor, in amperes, by the cross-sectional area of the conductor, in square inches. Current density is measured in amperes per square inch.

current electricity. The form of electricity which makes use of the heat and/or the magnetic field produced when electrons flow in a conductor.

current-fed antenna (radio transmitting antenna). A center-fed radio transmitting antenna that is half a wavelength long.

current flight plan (ICAO). The flight plan including changes, if any, brought about by subsequent clearances.

current induction. An electrical current being induced into, or generated in, any conductor that is crossed by lines of flux from any magnet.

current limiter (generator control component). A device in the control system of a DC generator which reduces the output voltage or removes the generator from the electrical system any time it produces more than its rated current. Some current limiters are a type of slow-blow fuse in the generator output circuit which removes the generator from the electrical system if its output becomes excessive. Other current limiters reduce the generator output voltage if it tries to put out more than its rated current.

current-limiting resistor (electrical circuit). A resistor used to limit the maximum amount of current allowed to flow in a circuit. A current-limiting resistor is often installed in series with a fuse to limit the maximum amount of current that can flow before the fuse heats up enough to melt and open the circuit.

current plan (air traffic control). The ATC clearance an aircraft has received in response to its filed flight plan, and is expected to fly, which shows on the controller's terminal display for the selected aircraft. *See also* trial plan.

current regulator. A device or circuit in the output of an electrical power source that maintains a constant output current. If the load demands more current, the regulator raises the output voltage. If the load demands less current than that for which the regulator is set, the regulator lowers the output voltage.

current transformer. An electrical transformer used for measuring or control purposes. The primary winding of a current transformer is installed in series with the electrical load, and the voltage produced in the transformer secondary winding is proportional to the amount of load current.

curriculum. A set of courses in an area of specialization offered by an educational institution. A curriculum for a pilot school usually includes courses for the various pilot certificates and ratings.

cursor mode. The function offered by the FMS/RNAV that allows data entry into an avionics unit such as the FMS and RNAV.

Curtiss Jenny (Curtiss JN4-D airplane). A World War I training airplane powered by a Curtiss OX-5 engine. It was widely available after the war and helped introduce aviation to the general public.

curvic coupling (turbine engine component). A type of coupling used to join a series of axial-flow compressor disks or axial turbine wheels to each other. The coupler consists of a series of radial, gear-like teeth on the faces of two mating flanges. Curvic couplings provide a positive engagement with no slippage.

cusp. A pointed end.

customer bleed air (gas turbine engine). Air bled from one of the stages of the engine compressor and used for some function other than the operation of the engine. These functions include pressurization, deicing, anti-icing, air conditioning, and engine starting.

cut-away. A model of an object that is built in sections so it can be taken apart to reveal the inner structure.

cutaway drawing (mechanical drawing). A drawing which shows the inside construction or contents of an object, as well as the outside of the object. A part of the outside of the object is cut away to show the inside.

cutoff. The point in which a system ceases to operate because a defined cutoff condition has been reached.

cutout switch (electrical component). A switch inside a piece of electrical equipment that opens the circuit when a certain operating condition is reached.

cut threads. Threads that have been formed on a rod by removing part of the metal with a cutting tool. Cut threads are different from rolled threads, which have been formed on a rod by rolling the rod between grooved dies.

cutting fluid (machine tool operation). A fluid, often an emulsion of oil and water, poured over a metal while it is being drilled or turned on a lathe. Cutting fluid carries away some of the heat caused by friction, lubricates the surface being cut, prevents rust, and flushes chips away from the cutting edge of the tool.

cutting plane (mechanical drawing). A line on a mechanical drawing used to indicate the location from which an auxiliary view is made.

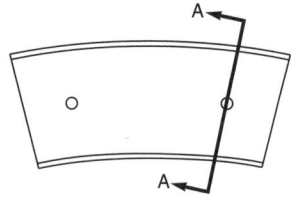

cutting plane

cutting speed (machine tools). The speed of the relative motion between a cutting tool and the work being cut. It is important that the correct cutting speed be used when cutting or drilling metal to get the smoothest cut and the longest life of the cutting or drilling tool.

cutting torch. An oxy-gas torch which has a preheating flame to get the metal red-hot before it is cut. When the metal is sufficiently hot, a jet of oxygen is blown through the center of the flame. This oxidizes, or burns, through the metal and produces a smooth cut.

CVFP (charted visual flight procedure approach). An approach authorized for a radar-controlled aircraft on an IFR flight plan, but operating in VFR conditions. When authorized by ATC, the aircraft may proceed to the airport of intended landing via visual landmarks and altitudes depicted on a charted visual flight procedure.

CW (continuous wave radio transmission). A method of transmitting radio-frequency electromagnetic energy in the form of long and short spurts that may be considered to be dashes and dots. The electromagnetic energy radiates from a transmitting antenna, and this is picked up at some distant location by a receiving antenna. The long and short spurts of energy are converted into letters and numbers according to the International Morse code.

cyanide. Any of the various salts of hydrogen cyanide which contain a CN (carbon and nitrogen) group. One of the best known cyanide compounds is sodium cyanide, NaCN, which is used in metal heat treatment. Sodium cyanide is extremely poisonous.

cyaniding (metal heat treatment). A type of case hardening of steel done by heating the metal in a bath of molten cyanide salts. Carbon and nitrogen are absorbed from the salts into the surface of the steel. After the steel has been in the salts for the correct length of time, it is removed and quenched.

cyanoacrylate adhesive. An instant adhesive that has excellent bonding properties.

C

cybernetics. The science of systems and controls as they pertain to the relationship between living beings and automatic machines.

cycle. A complete series of events or operations that recur regularly. The last event ends at the same place the first begins, and as soon as the last event is completed, the first is ready to begin again.

cycle per second. A measure of frequency of a recurring event. One cycle per second is called one hertz (Hz).

cyclic feathering. The mechanical change of the angle of incidence, or pitch, of individual rotor blades independently of other blades in the system.

cyclic pitch control (helicopter rotor control). The control in a helicopter that allows the pilot to change the pitch of the rotor blades individually, at a specific point in their rotation. The cyclic pitch control allows the pilot to tilt the plane of rotation of the rotor blades to change the direction in which the lift produced by the rotor disk acts. Tilting the plane of the rotor controls the direction the helicopter moves.

cycling. Operating a device or a system through its entire range of actuation several times. A retractable landing gear is cycled when it is raised and lowered several times, to check its operation and to remove air from its operating fluid.

cyclogenesis (meteorology). Any development or strengthening of cyclonic circulation in the atmosphere. Cyclonic circulation is counterclockwise in the northern hemisphere and clockwise in the southern hemisphere.

cyclone (meteorology). An area of low atmospheric pressure which has a closed circulation. In the northern hemisphere the circulation is counterclockwise, and in the southern hemisphere it is clockwise.

Because cyclonic circulation and relatively low atmospheric pressure usually coexist, the terms cyclone and low are often used interchangeably. Also, because cyclones are often accompanied by inclement and sometimes destructive weather, they are frequently referred to as storms. Tropical cyclones are called hurricanes or typhoons, and cyclones that form in the higher latitudes are called barometric depressions.

cyclonic flow (meteorology). The term for the counterclockwise flow of gradient winds in the Northern Hemisphere around low pressure areas.

cyclostrophic wind (meteorology). The horizontal wind velocity for which the centripetal acceleration exactly balances the horizontal pressure force.

cyclotron (nuclear accelerator). An accelerator in which positively charged particles such as protons and deutrons are accelerated (sped up) by a constant-frequency alternating electric field synchronized with their movement. The particles are held in a spiral path in a constant magnetic field as they speed up.

cyclic feathering (helicopter rotor). The change of the angle of incidence, or pitch, of individual rotor blades independently of other blades in the system.

cylinder (reciprocating engine component). The component in a reciprocating engine which houses the piston and valves. The cylinders form the combustion chambers of the engine.

cylinder (geometric shape). A solid form whose ends are circular and whose sides are parallel. The volume of a cylinder is found by the formula:

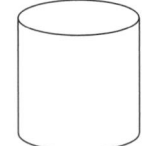

cylinder

$$V = 0.7854 \cdot D^2 \cdot H$$
$$V = \text{Cylinder volume in cubic inches}$$
$$0.7854 = \text{A constant } \pi \div 4$$
$$D = \text{Cylinder diameter, or bore in inches}$$
$$H = \text{Cylinder height, or stroke in inches}$$

cylinder baffles (reciprocating engine component). Thin sheet metal covers fastened around the fins on the cylinders of an air-cooled engine. The baffles force cooling air to flow through the fins so it can pick up heat from the cylinder and carry it away from the engine.

cylinder barrel (reciprocating engine component). The high-strength steel tube in which the piston moves up and down in a reciprocating engine. The cylinder barrel of an air-cooled engine has fins cut onto its outer surface to remove heat, and it screws into the cylinder head to form the cylinder assembly.

cylinder bore (reciprocating engine dimension). The inside diameter of the cylinder barrel.

cylinder flange (reciprocating engine component). A heavy flange machined around the base of an air-cooled cylinder barrel, slightly below the bottom cooling fin. Holes are drilled in the cylinder flange so the cylinder can be mounted on studs in the engine crankcase.

cylinder head (reciprocating engine component). The part of a reciprocating engine cylinder that forms the combustion chamber. Most modern reciprocating engines have the intake and exhaust valves and the spark plugs in the cylinder heads.

cylinder head temperature (reciprocating engine instrumentation). The temperature of the cylinder head of an air-cooled reciprocating engine. Both cylinder head temperature and oil temperature are used to monitor the operating condition of air-cooled aircraft reciprocating engines.

cylinder honing (reciprocating engine overhaul). A final finishing operation for the walls of a plain or nitrided steel cylinder. The surface is roughened in a specified crosshatch pattern to make it hold lubricating oil. The surface roughness is measured in microinches RMS.

cylinder pad (reciprocating engine component). The portion of the crankcase of a reciprocating engine to which the cylinders bolt. Studs stick through the machined surface of the pad, and the cylinder bolts to the studs.

cylinder skirt (reciprocating engine component). The portion of the cylinder of an aircraft engine that protrudes into the crankcase. The skirt is the portion of the cylinder barrel below the cylinder flange.

Delta

DA. *See* decision altitude.

Dacron. The registered trade name for polyester fibers manufactured by the E. I. DuPont de Nemours & Company. Cloth woven from Dacron fibers is used as a covering material for aircraft structure.

dado head (woodworking tool). A multibladed circular saw having two blades mounted on an arbor with a chipper between them. A dado head is used to cut a flat-bottomed groove in wood.

dado plane (woodworking tool). A hand plane with a narrow blade. Dado planes are used to cut flat-bottom grooves in wood.

Dalton's law. The gas law which states that there will always be the same number of molecules of gas in a container when the gas is held at a uniform pressure and temperature. Dalton's law explains the partial pressure of the gases which make up the air in our atmosphere.

damp, or dampen (*verb*). To decrease the amplitude of an oscillating or reciprocating motion.

damped oscillations. Oscillations whose amplitude decreases with time. The oscillations of an airplane that has positive static stability and positive dynamic stability are damped oscillations.

damper, or dampener (vibration damper). A device used to dampen vibrations or oscillations or to bring a vibrating body to a stop with a minimum of oscillations.

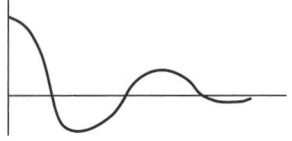

damped oscillation

damper-type fire valve (combustion heater component). An automatic valve that closes off the air supply to a combustion heater if a fire or over-temperature condition occurs.

A spring-loaded, butterfly-type damper valve is installed in the air inlet duct to the heater, and it is held open by fusible links. If an over-temperature condition occurs, the links will melt, and the damper valve will shut off the air to the heater. The fire will go out.

damper valve. A butterfly-type valve in an air duct. This valve is a round plate mounted on a shaft sticking through the duct. When the damper is open, it is parallel with the duct, and the air flows around it. When it is closed, the valve plate is almost perpendicular to the duct, and no air can flow past it.

damping action. The decrease in the amplitude of oscillations with time.

damping tube (instrument component). A short length of capillary tubing at the rear of a manifold pressure gage which protects the instrument from damage caused by an engine backfire. The sudden surge of pressure caused by a backfire is considerably reduced by the restriction of the capillary.

danger area (ICAO). An airspace of defined dimensions within which activities dangerous to the flight of aircraft may exist at specified times.

Note: The term "danger area" is not used in reference to areas within the United States or any of its possessions or territories.

Daniell cell (electrical energy). A form of standard cell used for measuring voltage by comparison. A Daniell cell produces an accurate voltage of 1.1 volts with a copper electrode in a copper sulfate solution and a zinc electrode in a zinc sulfate solution. The two solutions are separated by a porous membrane.

dark adaptation. Physical and chemical adjustments of the eye that make vision possible in relative darkness.

dark current (photoelectric device). The current which flows in a photoelectric device, such as a photodiode or phototransistor, when no light is falling on the light-sensitive junction.

Darlington amplifier (electronic circuit). A type of transistor amplifier in which two bipolar transistors are connected in such a way that the emitter of the input transistor is connected directly to the base of the output transistor. The collectors of both transistors are connected together. A Darlington amplifier is a double emitter-follower amplifier.

D'Arsonval meter (electrical measuring instrument). One of the most widely used types of direct-current measuring instruments. In a D'Arsonval meter, a small coil carrying the current to be measured is mounted on pivots and suspended in the field of a permanent magnet. A pointer is attached to the coil, and the rotation of the coil is restrained by two calibrated hairsprings.

Current flowing through the coil produces a magnetic field that reacts with the field of the permanent magnet, and the coil rotates against the opposition of the hairsprings. The greater the current flowing through the coil, the stronger its magnetic field and the farther the coil rotates. A pointer attached to the coil moves across a scale calibrated in amps, milliamps, or microamps. D'Arsonval meters can be connected into circuits with multiplier resistors or shunts and can be used to measure voltage, current, or resistance.

dart leaders (meteorology). In the sequence of events that create a flash of lightning, secondary-occurring "dart leaders" follow the initial "stepped leader" electrons along the conducting path to the ground, encouraging repeat strokes after the initial one.

dashpot. A pneumatic or hydraulic dampener used to cushion or slow down mechanical movements. A loose-fitting piston moves back and forth in a cylinder which contains a fluid, either liquid or air. The piston is connected to the component whose movement is to be damped. The component can move slowly with little opposition if the fluid is given time to move from one side of the piston to the other, but the dashpot restrains fast movement because of the time it takes to transfer the fluid from one side of the piston to the other. A shimmy damper used on the nose wheel of a tricycle-gear airplane is a form of dashpot.

data. A term that refers to all the facts available about a situation or project. Data can be accumulated and changed into a form usable in a computer. The computer then processes the data to produce records and projections. The word data is actually the plural form of datum, but it is often used as though it were singular.

database (computer operation). The body of information available on any particular subject. All Airworthiness Directives issued by the Federal Aviation Administration are contained in a database. This allows a person performing an inspection on an aircraft to access, or tap into, this database and get a list of all of the ADs that pertain to the particular aircraft, its engines, and components.

database field (computers). The collection of characters needed to define one item of information.

database identifier. A specific geographic point in space designated on an aeronautical chart and in a navigation database for identification purposes only; these are officially set by the controlling state authority or derived by the chart publisher. They have no navigational function and should not be used in filing flight plans or when communicating with ATC.

database record (computers). A single line of computer data made up of the fields necessary to define fully a single useful piece of data.

data block. *See* alphanumeric display.

data bus. A wire or group of wires used to move data within a computer system.

data link weather service. *See* broadcast weather service.

data plate (identification plate). A small tag, usually made of metal, that is attached to a component. It provides the name of the manufacturer, model number, part number, serial number, and other important information.

data-plate performance (gas turbine engine performance). Performance specifications of a gas turbine engine that were determined in the manufacturer's test cell when the engine was calibrated. This information, recorded on the engine data plate includes the engine speed at which a specified EPR is attained. When trimming the engine, the technician uses this data as the goal.

datum. A reference from which measurements are made. For example, mean sea level is a datum for measuring true altitude, and the freezing point of pure water is a datum for measuring temperature.

datum (aircraft location). An imaginary vertical reference plane or line chosen by the aircraft manufacturer from which all arms used for weight and balance computation are measured.

Davis wing (aerodynamics). A relatively thick, narrow-chord wing used on some airplanes. A Davis wing has a relatively low drag and a stable center of pressure, and it develops lift at low angles of attack. The B-24 Liberator bomber of World War II used the Davis wing.

daybeacons (marine navigation). Unlighted beacons.

daylight. The period of time in any day when the center of the sun's disc is less than 6 degrees below the horizon, and, in any place where the sun rises and sets daily, may be considered to be the period commencing one half hour before sunrise and ending one half hour after sunset.

daymarks. In marine navigation, these are conspicuous markings or shapes that serve as visual aid to daytime navigation. They can be painted rocks or prominent landmarks but the most common are boards, attached to posts, of certain shape and color to delineate channel boundaries.

DC electricity (direct current electricity). Electricity in which the electrons flow in the same direction all of the time. Electricity produced by chemical cells, solar cells, and thermocouples is DC electricity.

DC alternator. The electrical generation device that has replaced the generator on practically all modern automobiles and light airplanes. Excitation current from the aircraft battery flows through the voltage regulator into the rotor coil through brushes and slip rings to produce a multiple-pole rotating magnetic field. This rotating field cuts across the three-phase output windings in the stator to produce an alternating current whose amount is determined by the alternator speed and the amount of excitation current supplied by the voltage regulator. A six-diode, three-phase rectifier changes the AC into DC before it leaves the alternator.

DC amplifier (electronic amplifier). An electronic amplifier which can amplify direct-current signals and alternating current signals having a very low frequency.

DC generator (electrical machine). An electrical machine that converts mechanical energy into DC electricity. A conductor is moved through a magnetic field, and the mechanical energy used to move the conductor is changed into electrical energy. Almost all generators of this type produce alternating current, and some type of rectifier is used to change the AC into DC before it leaves the generator.

DC motor (electrical machine). An electric motor that operates on direct current.

DC power. The product of current and voltage. DC power is measured in watts.

D-check. *See* maintenance checks.

dead. A term used in technology to mean the absence of motion.

deadbeat. The condition of a free-swinging device when it comes to rest without overshooting its at-rest position. A pointer on a highly damped measuring instrument is said to be deadbeat when it changes its indication from one point to another without overshooting its final indication. It does not oscillate back and forth over its final position.

dead center (machine tool). A pointed device mounted in the tailstock of a lathe. The dead center is used to support the work being turned. The dead center does not turn with the work.

dead-center position (reciprocating engine). The position of the piston in a reciprocating engine in which the wrist pin, the crank pin, and the center of the crankshaft are all in a straight line. There are two dead-center positions: TDC (top dead-center) and BDC (bottom dead-center).

When the crankshaft is in either of the dead-center positions, the piston has stopped moving and is reversing its direction of travel.

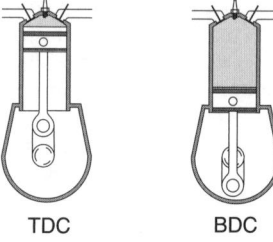

TDC   BDC

dead-center position

dead engine (aircraft engine). An engine which has been shut down in flight and is no longer operating.

deadhead. A return trip made by a commercial aircraft in which no cargo or persons are carried for hire.

deadhead transportation. Transportation of a flightcrew member as a passenger or non-operating flightcrew member, by any mode of transportation, as required by a certificate holder, excluding transportation to or from a suitable accommodation. All time spent in deadhead transportation is duty and is not rest. For purposes of determining the maximum flight duty period in Table B of 14 CFR Part 117, deadhead transportation is not considered a flight segment.

dead reckoning navigation (aircraft navigation). A method of navigating an aircraft in which the direction and speed of movement of the aircraft are determined by graphically computing the effect of the wind on the aircraft. A flight computer is used to plot the true airspeed and true heading against the wind direction and velocity to find the true course, or track, and the ground speed of the aircraft.

deadrise angle (float design). The angle of rise in the "V" design of the float or hull.

dead room (acoustic testing). A room or chamber used to test acoustic devices. The floor, walls, and ceiling of the dead room are treated in such a way that they prevent the reflection of sound energy. Dead rooms are also called anechoic rooms or anechoic chambers.

dead short (electrical circuit condition). A short circuit in an electrical device in which there is an absolute minimum of resistance across the source of electrical energy.

dead-stick landing (aircraft maneuver). A landing made by an aircraft when the engine is producing no power.

dead-weight tester (instrument calibration equipment). A device used to produce an accurate amount of pressure to calibrate pressure-measuring instruments. Oil pressure built up in the tester is applied to a cylinder fitted with a free-floating piston. This piston has an accurately known area and is loaded with an accurately known weight.

The amount of pressure needed to raise the piston is found by dividing the weight being lifted by the area of the piston. This pressure is applied to the gage being calibrated, and the gage is adjusted to read this amount.

D

deaerator chamber (gas turbine engine lubrication system component). A chamber in the lubrication system of a gas turbine engine in which the return oil from the engine collects before it is returned to the reservoir. Any air in the oil is allowed to escape while the oil is in this chamber.

debarkation. The removal of cargo or passengers from an aircraft.

debooster (aircraft brake component). A component in a power brake system between the power brake control valve and the wheel cylinder.

The debooster lowers the pressure of the fluid going to the brake and increases its volume, allowing the brakes to be applied more smoothly and released more quickly than they could be if system pressure went directly into the brakes.

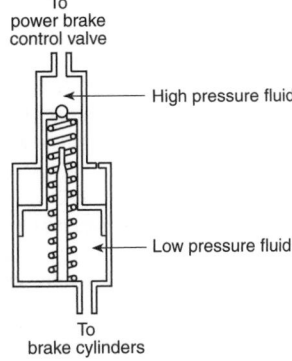

debooster

debonding. Separation of the bond between the skin laminates and the core of a composite structure.

debugging. The process of troubleshooting a piece of electronic hardware or software to find any faults that would prevent the equipment operating as it should.

deca, or deka. The metric prefix that means ten. The prefix deca or deka is often used before such terms as meter (decameter, or dekameter) or liter (decaliter, or dekaliter).

decade. A relationship between any two values that have a numerical ratio of 10:1.

decade resistance box (electrical test equipment). A piece of precision electrical test equipment containing two or more sets of precision resistors mounted on ten-position rotary selector switches. A typical decade resistance box may have one switch with resistors having values of between 0.1 and 0.9 ohm and another switch with resistors having values of between 1.0 and 9.0 ohms. A third switch may have resistors with values of between 10.0 and 90.0 ohms. By the proper positioning of the three switches, any value of resistance between 0.1 ohm and 99.9 ohms may be selected.

decalage. The difference in the angles of incidence between the two wings of a biplane. If the upper wing has a greater angle of incidence than the lower wing, the decalage is positive. If the lower wing has the greater angle of incidence, the decalage is negative.

decarbonizer. A solvent used to soften carbon deposits that have formed on metal surfaces. Carbon formed on engine parts because of the coking action of oil is hard and is baked onto the surface of the metal. It must be softened with a decarbonizer before it can be removed. Some decarbonizers are used cold, and others are heated to make them act faster.

decay (condition of vibrations). To gradually decrease the amplitude of vibrations. A damped oscillation is one in which the amplitude of the oscillations decay, or become less with time. *See* damped oscillation.

decay (wood defect). The breakdown, or decomposition, of the structure of wood fibers. Wood that shows any indication of decay must be rejected for aircraft structure.

Decca navigation system. A long-range, hyperbolic navigation system that allows a navigator to establish a line of position by measuring the phase difference between a master signal and three slave signals. These medium-frequency continuous-wave signals are transmitted simultaneously from a land-based master station and three slave stations.

decelerate. To decrease the speed of a moving object; to slow it down.

deceleration. The amount the velocity of an object, measured in feet per second, is decreased by a force during each second it is acted upon by that force. Deceleration is normally expressed in terms of feet per second, per second (fps^2).

deceleration check (engine performance check). A check made while retarding the throttle from an acceleration check. The engine RPM should decrease smoothly and evenly with little or no tendency for the engine to afterfire.

deceleration error. *See* acceleration error (magnetic compass error).

deceleration segment. A planned portion of a descent designed to permit the aircraft to slow to meet a terminal-area speed restriction, crossing restriction, or other speed restriction.

deci. The metric prefix that means one tenth. For example, a deciliter is one tenth of a liter.

decibel (acoustic measurement). The basic unit of sound intensity equal to one tenth of a bel. For practical purposes, one decibel (abbreviated dB) is the lowest amount of sound pressure that can be heard by a normal human ear. Sounds above about 130 decibels normally cause pain.

decibel (electrical measurement). A measurement of the ratio of two electrical powers. One decibel is equal to ten times the logarithm of the ratio of the two powers. *See* bel.

DECIDE model (psychology). A tool used in making good aeronautical decisions which is six-step process intended to provide the pilot with a logical way of approaching decision making:
1. Detect. The decision maker detects the fact that change has occurred.
2. Estimate. The decision maker estimates the need to counter or react to the change.
3. Choose. The decision maker chooses a desirable outcome (in terms of success) for the flight.
4. Identify. The decision maker identifies actions which could successfully control the change.
5. Do. The decision maker takes the necessary action.
6. Evaluate. The decision maker evaluates the effect(s) of his/her action countering the change.

deciduous. A type of tree that sheds its foliage at the end of the growing season. Hardwoods come from deciduous trees.

decimal digit. Any of the Arabic numerals 0, 1, 2, 3, 4, 5, 6, 7, 8, and 9.

decimal fraction. A proper fraction whose denominator is a number which is a power of ten. The value of the denominator is not written, but it is indicated by the position of the decimal point. One digit to the right of the decimal point means that the denominator is 10 ($0.1 = \frac{1}{10}$); two digits to the right of the decimal shows the denominator is 100 ($0.01 = \frac{1}{100}$), and three digits indicates 1,000 ($0.001 = \frac{1}{1,000}$).

decimal number system. The system of numbers using ten as its base. The digits in the decimal number system are 0, 1, 2, 3, 4, 5, 6, 7, 8, and 9. In a multidigit number, the position of the digit shows its value. Each position has a value ten times that of the position immediately to its right. For example, the number 5,286 is the same as 5,000 $(5 \cdot 1,000) + 200 (2 \cdot 100) + 80 (8 \cdot 10) + 6 (6 \cdot 1)$.

decimal point. A dot which separates a whole number from its decimal fraction. In the United States, the decimal point is placed at the bottom of the number, as in 14.2. In European countries, the dot for the decimal point is raised to the center of the number, as in 14·2.

decision altitude/decision height (ICAO). A specified altitude or height (A/H) in the precision approach at which a missed approach must be initiated if the required visual reference to continue the approach has not been established.

decision height (DH) (aircraft operation). *14 CFR Part 1:* "The height at which a decision must be made, during an ILS or PAR instrument approach, to either continue the approach or to execute a missed approach."

D

deck (float component). The top of a seaplane float, which can serve as a step or walkway, and where bilge pump openings, hand-hole covers, and mooring cleats are typically located.

deck angle. The angle of the cart's lower frame (from the front wheel to the rear wheels) relative to the landing surface.

declination (navigation). The error in the indication of a magnetic compass caused by the magnetic north pole not being at the same location as the geographic north pole.
In aerial navigation, declination is called variation. *See* variation.

decoder (radar). The device used to decipher signals received from air traffic radar beacon transponders and display them as select codes.

decompose. To separate into basic components, or elements. When electric current passes through water (a chemical compound), the water decomposes into its two chemical elements, hydrogen and oxygen.

decompression (cabin environmental control system). The inability of the airplane's pressurization system to maintain its designed pressure differential. This can be caused by a malfunction in the pressurization system or structural damage to the airplane.

decompression sickness. A condition where the low pressure at high altitudes allows bubbles of nitrogen to form in the blood and joints causing severe pain. Also known as the bends.

decontamination. The process of removing contamination from a body or a mechanism. Radiological decontamination is the process of removing or neutralizing radioactive contaminants from a person or a structure.

decouple. To disconnect two components that are joined together, or to isolate one electrical circuit from another.

dedicated computer. A small digital computer, often built into an instrument or control device, that contains a built-in program to perform a specific function. A digital autopilot is a dedicated computer to control an aircraft. It does not perform any other function.

de-energize. To disconnect an object from its source of power.

deep cycling (nickel-cadmium battery servicing). A maintenance procedure used with nickel-cadmium batteries to equalize all the cells. The battery is completely discharged, all of the cells are shorted, and the battery is allowed to stand in its shorted condition for a specified period of time. Then, the battery is recharged to 140% of its ampere hour capacity.

deep discharge (batteries). A maintenance procedure for discharging a battery that removes all the electrical energy from the battery before it is recharged. When a battery is deep discharged, it is discharged at a specified rate until its voltage is down to a certain value, and then all the terminals of all the cells are connected with shorting straps and left shorted for a specified period of time. Deep discharging puts all the cells in a battery in the same condition, ready to receive a new charge.

deepening (meteorology). A decrease in the central pressure of a pressure system. This term is usually applied to a low rather than to a high, but technically it is acceptable in either case.

deep-vacuum pump. A vacuum pump capable of removing almost all the air from an air conditioning system. A deep-vacuum pump can reduce the pressure inside the system to a few microns.

defect. A flaw, damage, or imperfection in a component or a piece of material that requires a repair or replacement of the part.

defective. Faulty, or not operating as it should.

defense mechanisms. Subconscious ego-protecting reactions to unpleasant situations.

deferred item (minimum equipment list). An item on the minimum equipment list that is not operating.

deflation (pneumatic component procedure). The release of air from a pneumatic component.

deflation panel (balloon component). A panel at the top of the balloon envelope that is deployed at landing to release all hot air (or other lifting gas) from the envelope. A parachute top is a form of deflation panel.

deflator cap. A cap for a tire, strut, or accumulator air valve that, when screwed onto the valve, depresses the valve stem and allows the air to safely escape through a hole in the side of the cap.

deflecting-beam torque wrench (precision hand tool). A calibrated wrench which indicates the amount of torque being applied to a nut or bolt. This is done by measuring the amount the beam of the wrench deflects when the torque is being applied.

deflecting-beam torque wrench

According to Hooke's law of elasticity, the beam will deflect the same amount each time a given amount of torque is applied by the wrench. The indication of the amount of torque is read by the position of a pointer attached to the drive of the wrench, over a fixed scale fastened to the beam of the wrench.

defense visual flight rules. *See* DVFR.

degauss. To demagnetize an object, or to neutralize a magnetic field. Magnetic recording tape is erased by degaussing it.

degeneration (negative electrical feedback). Feedback of an electrical signal from the circuit output to the circuit input, with a phase opposite the phase of the signal on the input. Degeneration stabilizes the output of a circuit, decreases circuit distortion, and improves the frequency response of the circuit.

degradation (of a structural material or part). The alteration of the material properties in alloys, composites, or other manufactured aircraft parts or structures, which may result from environmental exposure, deviations in manufacturing, or from repeated loading or thermal pressures. Deterioration such as this can affect properties such as a material's strength, modulus (the stiffness to density ratio), or coefficient of expansion (or, the amount a material is expected to expand or change dimension, upon exposure).

degreaser. A chemical solution used to remove oil and grease from a part. Stoddard solvent and naphtha are two popular degreasers used in aircraft maintenance shops.

dehumidify. To decrease the amount of moisture (water vapor) in the air. Dehumidifying is often done by installing a small cooling system in the room to cause moisture to condense on its coils. Water vapor is removed from the air and changed into liquid water.

dehydrator. A material that removes some of the moisture from the air inside a component. Some dehydrators use silica gel to absorb the moisture. The silica gel crystals may be colored with an indicator dye that changes its color from blue to pink when the crystals absorb moisture.

dehydrator plug (reciprocating engine preservative device). A transparent plastic tube filled with a desiccant agent, such as silica gel, and an indicator, such as cobalt chloride. One end of the tube is sealed, and the other end is fitted with a perforated plug and threaded so that it can be screwed into a spark plug hole. When the air inside the cylinder is dry, the indicator dye is blue, but if moisture gets into the cylinder, it is absorbed by the silica gel, and the indicator changes its color to pink.

deice. The act of removing ice accumulation from an aircraft structure.

deicer. A system or component used to remove ice from a surface. Deicers must not be confused with anti-icers, which prevent the formation of ice. Deicers remove ice after it has formed.

D

deicer boots (aircraft deicing component). Inflatable rubber boots attached to the leading edges of the wings and empennage of an airplane. Compressed air is pumped into tubes in the boots to inflate them in a timed sequence. Ice is allowed to form over these boots while they are deflated, and when they inflate, they break the ice from the surface, and the airflow carries it away.

deicing fluid. A fluid that is heated and sprayed onto an aircraft being prepared for takeoff in conditions of freezing temperature and snow. Most deicing fluids contain a form of glycol, with thickeners added to hold the glycol to the surface. These fluids remove the ice and then stick to the surface and prevent the formation of more ice.

deka, or deca. The metric prefix that means ten. The prefix deka or deca is often used before such terms as meter (dekameter, or decameter) or liter (dekaliter, or decaliter).

delamination. A separation of the layers of a laminated material. Plywood is made up of layers, or laminations, of wood glued together. When the glue weakens, the layers can separate and the plywood is said to be delaminated. Delamination of bonded composite materials causes the materials to lose strength.

delay assignment (DAS) (air traffic control). A type of hold instruction to aircraft pilots or dispatchers from ATC, mostly for takeoffs but also used for landings, based on logistics in the ATC traffic management computer program. ATC assigns delays to aircraft according to the program's parameters, calculated in 15-minute increments. DAS information appears as a table in the traffic flow management system (TFMS).

"Delay indefinite [reason, if known] expect further clearance [time]" (air traffic control). A phrase used by ATC to inform a pilot when an accurate estimate of the delay time and the reason for the delay cannot immediately be determined. Such delays could be a disabled aircraft on the runway, terminal or center area saturation, or weather below landing minimums.

delay time (air traffic control). The amount of time an arriving aircraft must lose to cross the meter fix at the assigned meter fix time. This is the difference between actual calculated landing time (ACLT) and the vertex time of arrival (VTA).

delivery air duct check valve (pressurization system component). An isolation valve at the discharge side of the air turbine that prevents the loss of cabin pressurization through a disengaged cabin air compressor.

delta (Δ). One of the Greek letters which has a common usage in technology to mean a change in something. A small change is indicated by the lowercase letter delta (δ), and a larger change is shown by the use of a triangle, the uppercase letter delta (Δ).

delta airplane. An airplane with a triangular-shaped wing. A delta wing has an extreme amount of sweepback on its leading edge and a trailing edge that is almost perpendicular to the longitudinal axis of the airplane.

Δ CG (delta CG). A change in the center of gravity of an aircraft.

delta connection (electrical wiring connection). A type of connection used for three-phase alternating-current generators, motors, and transformers. Two of the phase windings are in series, across the third phase winding.

The term delta connection comes from the symbol for this type of connection, which is drawn in such a way that it shows the windings arranged in the form of a triangle, or delta. The current flowing between any two leads in a delta-connected circuit is 1.73 times the current flowing in any single winding.

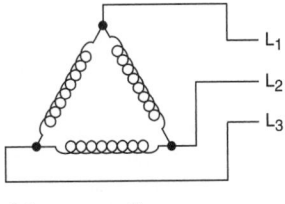

delta connection

delta hinge (helicopter rotor hinge). A hinge at the root of a helicopter rotor blade. The axis of the delta hinge lies in the plane of rotation of the blade, and allows the blade to flap up or down to equalize the lift produced by the rotor system as the helicopter moves through the air.

delta iron. The molecular arrangement in iron at temperatures between 1,392°C and 1,538°C. Pure iron melts at 1,538°C.

Δ P (delta P). Differential pressure.

delta wing (airplane wing configuration). A wing having a triangular shape—an extreme amount of sweepback on the leading edge and a trailing edge that is almost perpendicular to the longitudinal axis of the airplane. Delta wings are used on some supersonic airplanes.

demagnetize. To remove the magnetism from a piece of magnetized material. When a piece of material is magnetized, all the magnetic domains are aligned, or oriented in the same direction. When it is demagnetized, the magnetic domains are knocked out of alignment, and their magnetic fields cancel so there is no overall magnetic field.

demand oxygen system (breathing oxygen system). An oxygen system installed in an aircraft and used by the flight crew when flying at high altitude. The demand system meters oxygen from the regulator to the mask only when the user inhales, and the flow of oxygen is shut off during exhale. A demand oxygen system is much more economical of the oxygen supply than a continuous-flow system.

demodulate (telecommunications). To remove the modulation from a telecommunicated signal. When computer data is transmitted by telecommunications, it is changed into audible tones, or modulated, so it will pass it over the telephone lines. At the receiving computer, the data is demodulated (the modulation is removed), and the data is changed back into its digital form.

demodulation (radio signal). The production inside a radio receiver of an audio-frequency AC signal that follows the modulation on a radio-frequency carrier. Audio-frequency information or music is used to change the amplitude or frequency of the RF carrier wave in the radio transmitter. When the modulated carrier is picked up by the receiver, it is demodulated. Changes in the amplitude or frequency of the carrier produce an audio-frequency AC that follows these changes.

demonstration-performance method. An educational presentation in which an instructor first shows the student the correct way to perform an activity and then has the student attempt the same activity.

demonstration stalls (flight instruction maneuver). A stall that a flight instructor should demonstrate for a student pilot to instruct them how to avoid the situation leading the stall. Instructors should teach demonstration stalls to all students, but students should not practice them, especially when flying solo.

demulsibility. The ability of an oil-water emulsion to separate into its components of water and oil.

demulsifier. A chemical, physical, or electrical system that either breaks down a liquid-in-liquid emulsion or keeps such an emulsion from forming.

denatured alcohol. Ethyl, or grain, alcohol that has been treated with some type of additive to make it unfit for humans to drink.

denier. A measure of the fineness of the yarns in a fabric.

denim. A tough, heavy-duty fabric used for making work clothing. Denim is woven with colored threads for the warp (the threads that run the length of the fabric) and white threads for the fill (the threads that run across the fabric).

denominate number. A number that has a unit of measurement with it. Three inches, six minutes, and 360 degrees are all denominate numbers.

denominator (mathematical term). The part of a common fraction below the line. The denominator shows the number of parts the whole unit is divided into. In the common fraction $^9/_{16}$, the denominator is 16. The whole unit is divided into 16 equal parts, and this fraction uses only nine of them.

density. A measure of the amount of mass in a unit volume. An example is the amount of mass in a cubic foot, cubic inch, or cubic centimeter. Density is usually expressed in such units as pounds per cubic foot or grams per cubic centimeter.

density altitude. The altitude in standard air at which the density is the same as that of the existing air. Density altitude is found by using a computer or chart to correct pressure altitude for nonstandard air temperature. Density altitude is used for computing the performance of an aircraft and its engines.

density ratio (σ). The ratio of the density of the air at a given altitude to the density of the air at sea level under standard conditions.

dent. A depression (usually smooth) in the surface of a material caused by the part being struck or pressed on by some outside object. A dent, unlike a gouge, removes none of the material.

departure center (air traffic control). The ARTCC having jurisdiction for the airspace that generates a flight to the impacted airport.

departure control (air traffic control). The function of an approach control facility that provides air traffic control service for departing IFR and, under certain conditions, VFR aircraft.

departure end of runway (DER). The end of the runway that is opposite the landing threshold. It is sometimes referred to as the stop end of runway.

departure procedure (DP). Preplanned IFR ATC departure, published for pilot use, in textual and graphic format.

departure sequencing program (air traffic control). A program designed to assist in achieving a specified interval over a common point for departures.

departure time. The time at which an aircraft becomes airborne.

depletion area (semiconductor term). The area on either side of the junction in a semiconductor device in which the majority carriers have been pulled away and ionic charges left. When the junction is forward-biased, the depletion area is very small. But when the junction is reverse-biased, the depletion area is large.

depolarization (electrochemical cell condition). Removal of the hydrogen gas which forms on the positive material inside an electrochemical cell by absorbing it into one of the materials mixed with the electrolyte. If the cell is not depolarized, the hydrogen gas will form an insulation on the positive material and increase the internal resistance of the cell.

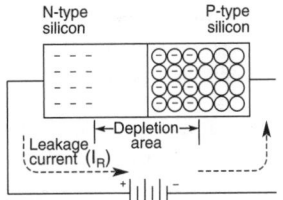

depletion area

deposition. *See* sublimation.

depreservation. The clean up and inspection of an aircraft part when it is to be put into service after it has been prepared for storage.

depression (meteorology). An area of low pressure, also called a low, or a trough. The term depression is usually applied to a certain stage in the development of a tropical cyclone, but it also applies to migratory lows and troughs and to upper-level lows and troughs that are only weakly developed.

depth gage. An instrument used to measure the depth of a hole or groove. The measuring scale protrudes from the center of a flat blade. The blade is laid across the top of the hole or groove, and the measuring scale is pushed to the bottom. The amount the scale sticks out of the blade is the depth of the hole or groove. Depth gages are used to measure the depth of the tread on aircraft tires.

depth micrometer. A precision measuring instrument which uses a standard micrometer caliper head mounted in a flat-ground bar. The distance the spindle sticks out of the bar is read in thousandths of an inch. Depth micrometers are used to measure the depth of machined grooves.

derate. To reduce the power output allowed for an engine or the voltage or current allowed for an electrical component. Derating is done to extend the life or reliability of a device. Newly designed aircraft engines are quite often placed in service with a lower power rating than they are designed to produce—they are derated. As operational experience is gained, the rated power is increased.

derichment (fuel metering system operation). A condition in the fuel metering system of a large reciprocating engine in which the fuel-air mixture is leaned out, or deriched, when antidetonation injection (ADI) fluid is injected into the engine. If the mixture were not leaned, the addition of the ADI fluid would enrich the mixture so much the engine could not produce its maximum power.

"descend via" (air traffic control). In ATC–pilot communications, a "descend via" clearance instructs the pilot to follow the altitudes published on a STAR. The pilot is not authorized to leave the last assigned altitude unless specifically cleared to do so. If ATC amends the altitude or route to one that is different from the published procedure, the rest of the charted descent procedure is canceled and ATC will assign any further route, altitude, or airspeed clearances, as necessary.

descent (aircraft flight condition). A decrease in altitude.

descent speed adjustments (air traffic control). Speed decrease calculations made to determine an accurate vertex time of arrival (VTA). These calculations start at the transition point and use arrival speed segments to the vertex.

"description of a skill or behavior" (lesson preparation, teaching/learning process). The first part of a performance-based objective set for a student lesson that explains the desired outcome of the instruction in concrete terms that can be measured. *See also* performance-based objective.

desiccant. A material, such as silica gel, that is able to absorb moisture from the air. When precision equipment is stored, bags of silica gel are packed with it. The silica gel absorbs moisture from the air and prevents the moisture damaging the equipment.

In pneumatic power systems, the high-pressure compressed air passes through a desiccant which absorbs all the moisture in the air. If moisture were left in the air, it would freeze when the air expands and its temperature drops.

designated examiner. A person authorized by the FAA to conduct a pilot proficiency test or a practical test for an airman certificate or rating issued under this part, or a person who is authorized to conduct a knowledge test.

designated intersection (navigational location). A point on the surface of the earth over which two or more designated position lines intersect. The position lines may be magnetic bearings from NDBs, radials from VHF/UHF aids, centerlines of designated airways, air routes, localizers and DME distances.

designated pilot examiner (DPE). An individual designated by the FAA to administer practical tests to pilot applicants.

design load. The maximum load a component is designed to carry. The design load is made up of the actual load the component is expected to encounter, plus a factor of safety.

design maneuvering speed (V$_A$). The maximum speed for maneuvers at which full application of the primary flight controls cannot overstress the airframe. If during flight, rough air or severe turbulence is encountered, reduce the airspeed to maneuvering speed or less to minimize stress on the airplane structure.

desired course. A predetermined desired course direction to be followed, measured in degrees from true north (true desired course), or measured in degrees from local magnetic north (magnetic desired course).

desired track (navigation). The planned or intended track between two waypoints. It is measured in degrees from either magnetic or true north. The instantaneous angle may change from point to point along the great circle track between waypoints.

destructive testing. A method of testing that results in the destruction of the part being tested. Destructive testing is normally an engineering procedure, used to determine the ultimate strength of a device or part, and to identify its weakest point.

detachable part. A part of a component which can be removed without damaging the component.

detail drawing (aircraft mechanical drawing). A drawing that contains enough information to allow a component to be fabricated.

detailed inspection. A thorough examination of an item including disassembly. The overhaul of a component is considered to be a detailed inspection.

detail view (drawing). A view which shows only a part of an object but in greater detail and to a larger scale than the principal view.

detector (electronic component). A rectifier in an electronic circuit. The term detector is normally used for a rectifier that changes modulated radio-frequency alternating current into pulsating direct current whose amplitude varies in the same way as the modulation on the original AC.

detent. A spring-loaded pin or tab that enters a hole or groove when the device to which it is attached is in a certain position. Detents are used on fuel selector valves to provide a positive means of identifying the position in which the valve is fully on and fully off.

detergent. A synthetic cleaning material. A detergent is similar to soap in its ability to emulsify oil and hold dirt and other solid or semi-solid contaminants. Unlike soap, a detergent is composed of man-made chemicals, rather than organic matter such as animal or vegetable fat.

detergent oil. A type of mineral oil to which metallic-ash-forming detergents have been added. Detergent oil is not generally used in aircraft engines because of its tendency to loosen carbon deposits from the engine parts. These loosened deposits can plug oil passages inside the engine.

determiners (psychology). In test items, words which give a clue to the answer. Words such as "always" and "never" are determiners in true–false questions. Since absolutes are rare, such words usually make the statement false.

detonation (reciprocating engine condition). An explosion or uncontrolled burning inside the cylinder of a reciprocating engine. Detonation occurs when the pressure and temperature inside the cylinder become higher than the critical pressure and temperature of the fuel, and may be caused by using fuel that has a lower octane rating or performance number than is specified for the engine.

The pressure rise inside the cylinder caused by the fast-moving flame front can heat and compress the unburned fuel-air mixture enough for it to explode, or release its energy faster than the engine can accept it. This causes a rapid rise in cylinder pressure, excessive cylinder head temperature, and a decrease in engine power. Detonation is often confused with preignition but is not the same. *See* preignition.

DETRESFA (distress phase) (ICAO). The code word used to designate an emergency phase wherein there is reasonable certainty that an aircraft and its occupants are threatened by grave and imminent danger or require immediate assistance.

deuterium. An isotope of hydrogen which has one proton and one neutron in the nucleus. A normal atom of hydrogen has one proton, but no neutrons in its nucleus.

Deutsch rivet. A type of hollow-shank, high-strength blind rivet. The rivet is put into the hole in the structure, and a tapered pin is driven into the hollow shank. The pin expands the rivet so serrations on the outside of the shank press into the sides of the hole and hold the rivet firmly in place.

developed width of a part (sheet metal layout). The width of the sheet metal cut to form a part. If an angle, with legs of one inch and two inches, is to be formed of sheet metal, the developed width of the metal will be less than three inches. This is because the metal does not go to the mold lines of the angle, but goes

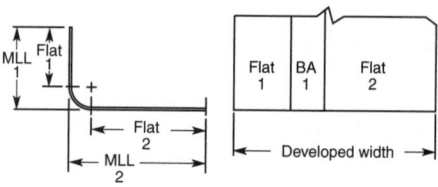

developed width

around the corner in the bend radius. The developed width of the metal is the sum of the flats plus the bend allowance. This is less than the sum of the mold line lengths (MLL).

developer (dye penetrant inspection). A powder used to pull a penetrating dye out of a defect in a part being inspected by the dye-penetrant inspection method. The part is soaked in the penetrant. Then, all the penetrant is washed from its surface and the surface is covered with the developer. The developer pulls any penetrant that has seeped into a defect to the surface where it shows up as a visible mark.

deviations (flight operations). Any break from the planned flight route.

deviation (magnetic compass error). An error in the indication of a magnetic compass, caused by local magnetic fields within the aircraft. Deviation error, which is different on each heading, is minimized by the technician compensating, or swinging, the compass. A compass must be compensated so the deviation error on any heading is no greater than 10 degrees.

dew. Water that condenses out of the air and forms on the ground and on objects that are cooler than the air. Dew usually forms at night when the ground cools as heat leaves it by radiation.

Dewar flask. A special container used to store liquid oxygen and liquid nitrogen. A Dewar flask has an inner and an outer container, with the space between them evacuated to form a vacuum. This serves as a thermal insulator and minimizes the amount of heat allowed to enter the container. The two surfaces within the evacuated area are silvered to reflect heat away from the container walls.

dewaxed oil. A petroleum oil from which some of the solid hydrocarbons, or waxes, have been removed in the refining process.

DEWIZ (distant early warning identification zone). An air defense identification zone (ADIZ) over the coastal waters of Alaska.

dew point. The temperature below which air can no longer hold water in its vapor state. At the dew point temperature, the relative humidity is 100% and water vapor condenses out of the air and forms visible water—dew.

DF (direction finder) (navigation system component). A radio receiver equipped with a direction-sensing antenna used to take bearings on a radio transmitter. Specialized radio direction finders are used in aircraft as navigation aids. Others are ground-based, primarily to obtain a fix on a pilot requesting orientation assistance or to locate downed aircraft. A location fix is established by the intersection of two or more bearing lines plotted on a navigational chart, using either two separately located direction finders to obtain a fix on an aircraft or by a pilot plotting the bearing indications of his DF on two separately located ground-based transmitters, both of which can be identified on his chart.

UDFs receive signals in the ultrahigh frequency radio broadcast band, VDFs in the very high frequency band, and UVDFs in both bands. ATC provides DF service at those air traffic control towers and flight service stations listed in the Airport/Facility Directory and the DOD/FLIP IFR En Route Supplement.

DF approach procedure (air traffic control). An emergency approach procedure used under conditions when no other instrument approach procedure can be executed.

DF fix. The geographic location of an aircraft obtained by the use of one or more direction finders.

DF guidance (air traffic control). Headings provided an aircraft by a ground facility using direction finding equipment. DF headings, if followed, will lead the aircraft to a predetermined location.

DF steer. *See* DF guidance.

DH. *See* decision height.

diac (semiconductor device). A semiconductor used as a triggering device for a triac. A diac acts in much the same way as two zener diodes installed back to back, with one forward biased and the other reverse biased. No current can flow through the diac until the breakdown voltage of the reverse-biased diode is reached. When this breakdown voltage is reached, the diac immediately turns on and allows the gate current for the triac to flow.

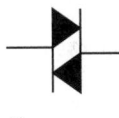

diac

diagonal cutting pliers. A type of wire cutters commonly used by aircraft maintenance technicians. The short, strong jaws are ground so they cut the wire by a chiseling action, rather than by shearing.

diagram. A line drawing used to represent a system or process. A diagram can be used to trace a flow of electrons, fluid, or components in a manufacturing process.

dial (instrument face). The face of an instrument on which calibration numbers are printed. The indication of the instrument is read as the number on the dial to which the pointer is pointing.

dial-indicating torque wrench (precision hand tool). A type of deflecting-beam torque wrench that uses a dial indicator to measure the amount the beam deflects. The dial of the indicator is graduated in foot-pounds, inch-pounds, or meter-kilograms of torque, rather than units of beam deflection.

dial indicator. A precision measuring instrument that uses a compound lever arrangement to amplify the movement of a stylus. The amount the stylus moves, in thousandths of an inch, is read on a circular dial.

diamagnetic material. A material which has a magnetic permeability of less than one, less than that of a vacuum. A diamagnetic material is repelled by a magnet and will try to align itself across the lines of magnetic flux, rather than along them.

diameter (dimension of a circle). The length of a line that touches the circumference of a circle in two places and passes through its center. The diameter of a circle is twice its radius.

diamond. An extremely hard, almost colorless form of pure carbon. Some diamonds reflect light so well they are used as gems, and low-grade diamonds are hard enough to be used as industrial cutting tools.

diamond chisel (metal-cutting tool). A metal-cutting chisel whose cutting edge is in the shape of a diamond. A diamond chisel is used to cut V-shaped grooves in metal.

diamond-point cutting tool (machine tool). A cutting tool used for machining hard metal. The cutting edge of the tool is an industrial diamond.

diamond-point dressing tool (machine tool). A tool used to smooth the surface of an abrasive grinding wheel. An industrial diamond is mounted in the tool, which is clamped in the tool rest in such a way that the diamond can be moved across the face of the abrasive wheel. The diamond wears away any roughness on the wheel and produces a smooth surface.

dibromodifluoromethane (fire extinguishing agent). A colorless, heavy liquid fire extinguishing agent. Dibromodifluoromethane is also known as Halon 1202.

dichromate solution. A solution of potassium or sodium dichromate used to form a hard, airtight film on the surface of magnesium parts to prevent corrosion.

dichromate treatment (corrosion protection). A corrosion-preventive treatment for magnesium alloys. A tight oxide film is formed on the surface of a magnesium alloy when it is treated with a solution of potassium or sodium dichromate.

die (metal-cutting tool). A cutting tool used to cut threads on the outside of a piece of round stock.

die (permanent mold). A permanent mold used to cast parts from metal or plastic resin. Material in its plastic state is forced into the die under pressure.

die casting. A method of forming metal parts by forcing metal in its plastic state into a high-strength die, using a large amount of force. Die-cast parts have more strength than parts cast by pouring the molten metal into a mold.

dielectric. An insulating material that can store electrical energy in an electrostatic field. The valence electrons in a dielectric material can be pulled away from their atom only with a strong electrical force, but the orbits of these electrons can be distorted by an electric field. Electrical energy is stored in this distorted field. Glass and ceramics are examples of good dielectrics.

dielectric constant. A number used to indicate the ease with which a particular dielectric material concentrates lines of electrostatic force. A vacuum is used as the reference and is assigned a dielectric constant of one. The dielectric constant of air is very near that of a vacuum; it is 1.0006. Mica allows the lines of electrostatic force to pass much more easily, and it has a dielectric constant of 7. The dielectric constant of the insulating material in a capacitor determines its capacity.

dielectric heating. A process used to heat certain types of nonconductive plastic materials. The material to be heated forms the dielectric, or insulator, of a capacitor, and two metal electrodes act as the plates. Alternating current with a frequency of between 20 and 80 megahertz is placed across the plates.

The material between the plates is heated by the dielectric losses caused by the friction of the molecules moving under the influence of the rapidly changing electrostatic field. Dielectric heating is used to seal bags made of vinyl film and to cure certain types of plastic resins.

dielectric loss. Electrical energy converted into heat in a dielectric material. Dielectric loss occurs when the material is subjected to a rapidly changing electrostatic field. Power is lost, and heat is produced.

dielectric strength. The maximum amount of voltage that can be placed across a dielectric material without it breaking down and conducting. Dielectric strength is normally measured in volts per millimeter of thickness.

diesel engine. A form of compression-ignition reciprocating heat engine. In a diesel engine, the fuel-air mixture inside the cylinder is ignited by the heat of compression rather than by an electric spark. The air inside the cylinder is heated as it is compressed and, when the piston is near the top of its stroke, the air is very hot. A fuel injector sprays a very fine mist of fuel into the hot air and the fuel ignites and burns. Heat added by the burning fuel expands the air and pushes the piston down.

diesel fuel. A hydrocarbon fuel used in a compression-ignition engine. Diesel fuel, obtained by fractional distillation of crude oil, is the fraction that distills off just after kerosine.

D

dieseling (reciprocating engine malfunction). A condition in which an aircraft reciprocating engine tries to run after the ignition is turned off. Dieseling normally occurs when the engine is overheated. Carbon particles inside the cylinders become incandescent and ignite the fuel-air mixture in the cylinder and keep the engine running.

difference. The amount by which one quantity is greater or less than another. The answer in a subtraction problem is called the difference.

differential aileron travel (airplane control system). The difference between the upward and downward travel of an aileron. An aileron moves a greater number of degrees upward than downward to counteract adverse yaw. The downward-moving aileron produces both induced and parasite drag, but the upward-moving aileron produces only parasite drag. To prevent the combined drag causing the nose of the airplane to start to move toward the down aileron, the up aileron travels a greater distance, producing enough additional parasite drag to overcome the induced drag caused by the down aileron. *See* adverse yaw.

differential amplifier (electronic amplifier). An amplifier with two inputs and one output. The signal on the output is an amplification of the difference between the signals on the two inputs.

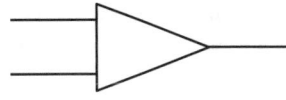

**differential
amplifier**

differential coil. A coil wound in such a way that its magnetic field opposes the field produced by another coil.

differential compression check (reciprocating engine maintenance check). A maintenance check used to determine the condition of the piston rings and the valves in the cylinders of a reciprocating engine. An air pressure regulator holds a constant pressure of 80 psi on the input side of a calibrated orifice. The output side of the orifice is connected to the cylinder through an adapter screwed into a spark plug hole.

Air flowing into the cylinder, to replace that which leaks past the piston rings and valves, causes a pressure drop across the orifice. The amount of leakage is indicated by the difference in the readings of the two pressure gages on the tester.

The sound of leaking air heard at the carburetor air inlet indicates a leaking intake valve. A leaking exhaust valve is indicated by the sound being heard at the exhaust tail pipe. Worn piston rings are indicated by the sound of leaking air being heard at the crankcase breather.

differential compression tester (reciprocating engine test equipment). Test equipment consisting of an air pressure regulator, two pressure gages with a calibrated restrictor orifice between them, and a shutoff valve. A regulated pressure of 80 psi is directed into the cylinder being tested, and the pressure drop across the orifice indicates the amount of air leaking past the piston rings or valves. A cylinder in good condition should hold at least 75% of the air supplied through the tester. With 80 psi on the input pressure gage, the cylinder pressure gage should indicate at least 60 psi.

differential global positioning system (DGPS). A system that improves the accuracy of global navigation satellite systems (GNSS) by measuring changes in variables to provide satellite positioning corrections.

differential heating (metallurgy). A thermal gradient that exists in a metal that induces stresses. It is caused by uneven application of heat or by uneven heat transfer.

differentially compounded electric motor. An electric motor having both series and shunt field windings. The two windings are connected in such a way that the magnetic field produced by the shunt winding opposes the field produced by the series winding.

differential pressure. A single pressure which is the difference between two opposing pressures. The resultant of a 12 psi pressure opposing a 32 psi pressure, is a 20 psi differential pressure. This is expressed as 20 psid.

differential-pressure range of aircraft cabin pressurization. The range of cabin pressurization in which the controller maintains a constant difference between the pressure of the air inside the structure and the pressure of the air outside the structure. The amount of differential pressure allowed is determined by the strength of the aircraft structure.

differential screw. A compound screw arrangement. A differential screw changes the separation between two parts by the amount of difference in the pitch of the two screw threads. If the coarse screw increases the space 0.050 inch for each revolution, and the fine screw decreases the space 0.0357 inch for each revolution, one revolution of the differential screw will increase the space by 0.0143 inch.

differential screw

differential-voltage reverse-current relay (aircraft electrical system component). A reverse-current relay installed with a high-current aircraft generator. The reverse-current relay closes to connect the generator to the battery when the generator voltage is a specified amount higher than the voltage of the battery. Reverse-current relays used with smaller generators connect the generator to the battery when the generator produces a specific voltage, regardless of the voltage of the battery.

differentiating circuit (electronic circuit). An electronic circuit whose output is proportional to the rate of change of the signal in the input circuit.

diffuser (gas turbine engine component). A duct installed in the compressor outlet in a turbine engine to reduce the velocity of the air leaving the compressor and increase its pressure.

diffusion (light). The scattering of light rays as they pass through a translucent material or as they bounce off a rough surface. These light rays are disturbed from their straight path, and they travel out in all directions. Diffused, or scattered, light forms very weak shadows or no shadows at all.

diffusion welding. A form of welding in which the surfaces to be joined are melted and pressed together. The edge of one surface diffuses into the edge of the other.

digital ATIS (D-ATIS). An alternative method of receiving ATIS reports by aircraft equipped with datalink services capable of receiving information in the cockpit over their Aircraft Communications Addressing and Reporting System (ACARS) unit.

digital circuits. Electronic circuits which operate as switches or gates. There are only two digital conditions, and these represent logic one and logic zero. These two values may be represented by high and low voltage levels, or on and off conditions. Digital circuits containing the appropriate gates can be made to perform arithmetic and logic operations.

digital computer. A digital electronic device that contains a central processing unit (CPU), an input, an output, and some memory units. Digital computers are used to process numbers or words and to control many different types of electrical and mechanical devices.

digital data (digital information). Data in one of only two conditions: zero or one, off or on, false or true, low or high. Digital data differs from analog data in that it does not have any in-between conditions.

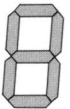

digital display. A series of alphanumeric characters that may be formed by segments made visible, usually by light-emitting diodes (LED) or liquid crystal displays (LCD). The segments are selected by a dedicated digital computer to form the appropriate character.

The most widely used numerical display is made of seven segments arranged to form the numeral eight (8). By selectively energizing two or more segments, any numeral between zero (0) and nine (9) may be formed.

digital
display

digital elevation model (DEM). A digital representation of ground surface topography or terrain.

digital multimeter. An electrical test instrument that can be used to measure voltage, current, and resistance. The indication is in the form of a liquid crystal display in discrete numbers.

digital readout (instrument indication method). Information shown on an indicating instrument in the form of digits. A digital readout differs from an analog readout, which displays information by the position of a pointer over a calibrated dial.

digital target (radar display). A computer-generated symbol representing an aircraft's position, based on a primary return or radar beacon reply, shown on a digital display.

digital terminal automation system (DTAS). A system where digital radar and beacon data is presented on digital displays and the operational program monitors the system performance on a real-time basis.

digital voltmeter. A voltage measuring instrument that displays the voltage in discrete numbers, rather than by the position of a needle over a calibrated dial.

digitize. To change an analog value into a digital value. Mechanical movement can be followed by allowing the movement to change the amount of resistance in a variable resistor. This is an analog change.

The analog change can be digitized with an analog-to-digital (A-to-D) converter, which changes the analog values into combinations of voltage and no voltage (one and zero) that can be used in a digital computer.

digitized image. A modified image picked up by a miniature TV camera in the end of a fiber optic probe. This image is converted into a digital electronic signal that eliminates unwanted portions of the viewed area and allows the desired image to be enhanced for clearer viewing.

digitized target (air traffic control). A computer-generated indication shown on an analog radar display resulting from a primary radar return or a radar beacon reply.

dihedral (airplane rigging measurement). The positive angle formed between the lateral axis of an airplane and a line which passes through the center of the wing or the horizontal stabilizer. Dihedral is used to increase the lateral stability of an airplane.

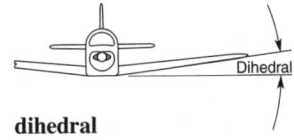

dihedral

diluent. A material used to thin, or dilute, a concentrated material without changing its basic characteristics. A weak solution contains a large amount of diluent. Paint thinner is a diluent used to make paint less viscous so it can be sprayed or brushed more easily. The diluent evaporates after the paint is applied.

diluter-demand oxygen system. A popular type of breathing oxygen system in which oxygen is metered to the mask where it is diluted with cabin air by an airflow-metering aneroid assembly which regulates the amount of air allowed to dilute the oxygen on the basis of cabin altitude.

As the aircraft goes to higher altitude, the amount of cabin air metered into the oxygen is automatically decreased until at about 34,000 feet, the cabin air is entirely shut off and the regulator sends 100% oxygen to the mask.

Continued

diluter-demand oxygen system. *Continued*
      The oxygen and air flow to the mask only when the wearer inhales, but the regulators have an emergency position which allows the pilot to manually bypass the demand function and sends a continuous flow of 100% oxygen to the mask.

dilution air (diluter-demand oxygen system). In a diluter-demand oxygen system, oxygen is metered to the mask as a function of the altitude. Below the altitude that requires 100% oxygen, ambient air (dilution air) is proportionally mixed with the oxygen.

dimension. A measurement used to describe the size of an object. The basic dimensions of an object are its L (length), W (width), and H (height).

dimensional inspection. One step in the overhaul of a piece of equipment. In a dimensional inspection, all the moving parts are measured with precision instruments, such as micrometer calipers, to determine if their dimensions are within the tolerances allowed by the manufacturer for the part to be serviceable.

dimension line (mechanical drawings). A light solid line on a machine drawing. A dimension line is drawn between extension lines that indicate the beginning and the end of a dimension. A dimension line has an arrowhead at each end and a break in its middle where the dimension and the tolerance are written.

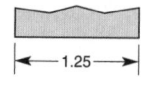

dimension line

dimmer (electric lights). A circuit or device used to decrease the intensity of an electric light. A dimmer may decrease the voltage supplied to the light by adding resistance, as is done with a rheostat. Or it may shorten the time electrons flow in each cycle of alternating current as is done with an SCR, a silicon controlled rectifier.

dimming relay (lighting system component). A relay that automatically dims the cockpit warning lights when the position lights are illuminated.

dimpling (sheet-metalworking procedure). The treatment of a hole in a piece of sheet metal for the installation of a countersunk rivet or screw. The metal is placed over a female dimpling die, and a male die is driven into it. The dies press the edges of the hole down so the head of the countersunk rivet or screw will be flush with surface of the metal.

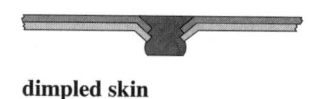

dimpled skin

diode (electrical component). A two-element electrical device. A diode contains an anode and a cathode and acts as an electron check valve. Electrons can pass from the cathode to the anode, but they cannot pass from the anode to the cathode. A diode may be either a vacuum tube or a semiconductor device.

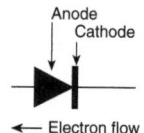

semiconductor diode

dioxide. A chemical compound which contains two atoms of oxygen. Carbon dioxide contains one atom of carbon and two atoms of oxygen (CO_2).

DIP (integrated circuit packaging). The abbreviation for dual in-line package. Different types of integrated circuits and switches are mounted in DIPs, which are standardized with regard to size, pin spacing, and the distance between the two rows of pins.

dip (magnetic compass characteristic). The angle formed between a compass magnet aligned with the earth's magnetic field and the horizontal plane. Dip is caused by the vertical component of the earth's magnetic field, and to correct for dip, a weight is often put on one end of the magnet to keep it horizontal. This weight is the cause of two errors found in aircraft magnetic compasses: acceleration error and northerly turning error. *See* acceleration error and northerly turning error.

dipcoating (insulation application). A method of electrically insulating the handles of certain tools, such as pliers, that are used in electrical work. The handles are dipped into a liquid plastic resin. The resin that sticks to the handle hardens and forms a comfortable, attractive, nonconductive grip.

diplexer (aircraft radio component). A coupling system used with an aircraft radio antenna. A diplexer allows two different transmitters to use the same antenna.

diplex operation (communications operation). A method of communicating which allows transmission and reception of two signals at the same time. Diplex operation uses a single antenna or a single carrier.

dipole antenna (radio antenna). A straight-wire, half-wavelength, center-fed radio antenna. The length of each of the two poles of the antenna is approximately one quarter of the wavelength of the frequency for which the antenna is designed.

dip soldering. The method of soldering component leads to a printed circuit board. The ends of the component leads pass through holes in the printed circuit board and stick out through the bottom. The board is floated on the top of a bath of molten solder, and the solder joins the component leads to the printed conductors.

dipstick. A gage, made in the form of a thin metal rod, used to measure the level of a liquid in a reservoir. The dipstick is pushed into the reservoir until it contacts a built-in stop; then it is removed and visually inspected. The level of the liquid in the reservoir is indicated by the amount of the dipstick wet by the liquid. A dipstick is the normal method used for measuring the amount of lubricating oil in the sump of an engine and the amount of hydraulic fluid in a reservoir.

direct (flight operation). Straight-line flight between two navigation fixes.

direct air carrier. A person who provides or offers to provide air transportation for passengers or cargo under 14 CFR Part 121 or 135 and who has control over the operational functions performed in providing that transportation. A person may not operate as a direct air carrier unless he or she (1) is a citizen of the United States; (2) obtains an Air Carrier Certificate; and (3) obtains operations specifications that prescribe the authorizations, limitations, and procedures under which each kind of operation must be conducted.

direct altitude and identity readout (DAIR). The DAIR system is a modification of the AN/TPX-42 interrogator system. The DAIR detects, tracks, and predicts secondary radar aircraft targets. Targets are displayed by means of computer-generated symbols and alphanumeric characters depicting flight identification, altitude, ground speed, and flight plan data. The DAIR system is capable of interfacing with ARTCCs.

direct-arc furnace (metallurgy). A type of electric furnace used to melt metal. The metal is placed in a container lined with a material that can withstand extremely high temperatures, and a carbon rod is lowered to contact the metal. Electrical current is then forced to flow between the rod and the metal. While current is flowing, the rod is slowly pulled away, and as it breaks contact, an intensely hot arc forms between the rod and the metal. This arc melts the metal.

direct control (rotorcraft). A system of rotorcraft control in which the rotor disk is tilted by changing the pitch of the rotor blades individually at a specific point in their rotation. *See* cyclic pitch control.

direct-cranking electric starter (reciprocating engine starter). A high-torque DC motor used to crank a reciprocating engine for starting.

direct current (DC). *See* DC electricity.

direct indication (attitude indicator). The true and instantaneous reflection of aircraft pitch-and-bank attitude by the miniature aircraft, relative to the horizon bar of the attitude indicator.

directional antenna (radio antenna). An antenna which radiates stronger signals in one direction than in others.

directional gyro. A flight instrument used in airplanes and helicopters, using a gyro-stabilized compass card to show the direction in which the nose of the aircraft is pointed. A directional gyro does not align itself with magnetic north, and it must be set to point to magnetic north either by hand or by driving it with some form of magnetic compass.

directionally solidified (turbine blade manufacturing). A method of manufacturing turbine blades in which the blades are cast and removed from the casting furnace in such a way that all of the crystals in the metal form columnar grains extending along the length of the blade.

directional stability (aircraft stability). The stability of an aircraft about its vertical axis. Directional stability causes an aircraft to return to straight flight after it has been disturbed by a yawing or side-slipping action.

direction finder. *See* DF.

"directly behind" (air traffic control). A phrase used in ATC–pilot communications to describe an aircraft's position during operation when it is following the actual flight path of the lead aircraft over the surface of the earth, except when ATC applies wake turbulence separation criteria.

direct question (in teaching/learning process). In the context of a classroom and how the instructor engages student participation in a guided discussion, this is a question used for follow-up purposes and directed at a specific individual.

direct shaft turbine (turbine engine type). A turboshaft engine in which the compressor and power section are mounted on a common driveshaft.

direct user access terminal system (DUATS). A system that provides current FAA weather and flight plan filing services to certified civil pilots, via a personal computer, modem, and telephone access to the system. Pilots can request specific types of weather briefings and other pertinent data for planned flights.

dirigible. A large, steerable, cigar-shaped, self-propelled lighter-than-air craft. Dirigibles are made of a rigid truss structure covered with fabric. Gas bags inside the structure contain the lifting gas, which may be either hydrogen or helium.

discrimination (in teaching/learning process). The degree to which a test distinguishes the differences between students.

disbond (composites). A lack of proper adhesion in a bonded joint. This may be local or may cover a majority of the bond area. It may occur at any time in the cure or subsequent life of the bond area and may arise from a wide variety of causes.

disc area (helicopter parameter). The total area swept by the main rotor of a helicopter.

discharge indicator disk (fire extinguishing system). Fire extinguishing system discharge indicating disks are mounted on the outside of the aircraft to show either manual discharge of the containers, or automatic discharge overboard due to a thermal condition. A blown-out yellow disk shows that the system was discharged normally. When the system is discharged because of an overheat condition, the red discharge disk will be blown out.

disc loading (helicopter parameter). The ratio found by dividing the gross weight of a helicopter by the total area of its rotor disk.

discontinuity. In nondestructive inspection, any interruption in the normal physical structure or configuration of a part. A discontinuity may or may not affect the usefulness of a part.

discreet. Having good judgment. A discreet action is one that gives the desired results without being showy or calling attention to itself.

discrete. Separate, not continuous. A discrete change is made in a number of separate steps, rather than in a continuous, smooth movement.

discrete code (air traffic control). As used in the air traffic control radar beacon system (ATCRBS), a discrete code is any one of the 4096 selectable Mode 3/A aircraft transponder codes except those ending in zero zero. Examples of discrete codes are 0010, 1201, 2317, and 7777.

Nondiscrete codes, such as 0100, 1200, and 7700, are normally reserved for radar facilities that are not equipped with discrete decoding capability and for other purposes such as emergencies (7700) and VFR aircraft (1200).

discrete component (electrical components). A device such as an individual resistor or capacitor. Discrete components have been replaced in many modern circuits with integrated circuits in which a number of individual components are built into a single integrated circuit (IC) chip.

discrete frequency (radio communications). A separate radio frequency for use in direct pilot-controller communications in air traffic control which reduces frequency congestion by controlling the number of aircraft operating on a particular frequency at one time. Discrete frequencies are normally designated for each control sector in enroute/terminal ATC facilities and are listed in the A/FD and the DOD FLIP IFR Enroute Supplement.

discriminator (frequency modulated radio circuit). A circuit in a frequency modulated (FM) radio receiver that changes deviations in the frequency of the carrier into amplitude variations of the audio-frequency output. The audio-frequency output, used to operate a speaker, is a duplicate of the modulating signal in the transmitter.

disengage. To disconnect, or release one device or component from another.

dish antenna (radio equipment antenna). A shallow, concave, circular reflector used with a radio antenna, actually with the shape of a parabola. Signals from a transmitter are received in the dish and are reflected in such a way that they concentrate at a point from which they are picked up and carried into the receiver. Signals picked up by a dish are highly directional.

disk brake. A popular type of nonservo brake used on aircraft. *See* multiple disk brake and single disk brake.

disk sander (power tool). A power tool consisting of a rotating disk covered with an abrasive material. The part to be sanded, or abraded, is held against the disk, and the abrasive wears it away.

dispersant. A material or substance used to keep something dispersed, or suspended, in something else. Ashless Dispersant (AD) oil contains a dispersant that keeps all the contaminants picked up by the oil dispersed until it passes through filters where the contaminants are trapped. If the oil did not have the dispersant, the contaminants would settle out and plug passages inside the engine.

displaced threshold. The beginning of the usable portion of a runway that is located at a point other than the designated beginning of the runway.

displacement position (seaplane floats). The attitude of a seaplane when its entire weight is supported by the buoyancy of the floats, as it is when at rest or during a slow taxi. Also called the idling position.

display tube (electrical instruments). A cathode-ray tube used to display information. Cathode-ray oscilloscopes and computer video monitors use display tubes.

dissimilar-metal corrosion. Corrosion that forms where two different types of metals are in contact with each other. The severity of the corrosion is determined by the relative location of the metals in the electrochemical series. *See* electrochemical series.

dissipate. To scatter, or disperse. Smoke from a smokestack blown by the wind is dissipated, or scattered, into the atmosphere.

dissipate (power). To use something up. When electrons flow through a resistor, power is dissipated, and the resistor gets hot. The resistor dissipates power by converting it into heat.

dissipating stage (meteorology). Downdrafts characterize the dissipating stage of a thunderstorm cell and the storm dies rapidly. When rain has ended and downdrafts have abated, the dissipating stage is complete.

dissipation trail (distrail) (meteorology). A rift in clouds caused by the heat of exhaust gases from an aircraft flying in a cloud layer that is both thin and relatively warm. The exhaust sometimes warms the air to the extent that it is no longer saturated and that part of the cloud evaporates.

dissolve. To become a liquid and form a mixture with another liquid. When grains of solid sugar are put into a glass of water, the sugar dissolves. It becomes a liquid and mixes with the water.

dissolved acetylene gas. Acetylene gas which has been dissolved, or absorbed, in liquid acetone. Acetylene gas becomes unstable when it is held under pressure of more than about 15 psi, but if it is dissolved in acetone, it can be safely held under a pressure of more than 250 psi.

dissymmetry of lift (helicopter flight condition). The unequal lift produced across the rotor disk of a helicopter moving through the air. The advancing blade, the blade whose tip is moving in the same direction the helicopter is flying, has a speed equal to its own speed plus the speed of the helicopter. The retreating blade, the blade whose tip is moving in the opposite direction, is traveling at a speed equal to its own speed less the speed of the helicopter. Since aerodynamic lift is determined by the speed of the airfoil through the air, the advancing blade produces more lift than the retreating blade.

Dissymmetry of lift is compensated by allowing the blades to flap. As the lift produced by the advancing blade increases, it flaps upward, decreasing its angle of attack, and thus its lift. As the lift produced by the retreating blade decreases, it flaps downward, increasing both its angle of attack and the lift it produces.

distance available (ALD). Available landing distance is that portion of a runway available for landing and roll-out for aircraft cleared for land-and-hold-short operation (LAHSO). This distance is measured from the landing threshold to the hold-short point.

distance circle. *See* reference circle.

distance measuring equipment. *See* DME.

distillate. A liquid obtained by condensing the vapors boiled off a material when it is heated in the process of distillation.

distillation. A process by which components of a liquid mixture are separated. Crude oil, for example, is a source of many hydrocarbon fuels and lubricants which are obtained by the process of distillation.

The crude oil is heated to a specific temperature and some vapors are driven off, and these vapors are cooled until they condense into a liquid. The temperature of the oil is increased and more vapors are driven off and condensed.

Butane, gasoline, kerosine, diesel fuel, furnace oil, lubricating oil, and tar all have different boiling points and are all produced by distilling crude oil.

distilled water. Water that has been purified by distillation. The water is boiled to convert it into water vapor, and the vapor is condensed into liquid water. Minerals and other contaminants in the liquid water do not stay with the water when it is changed into a vapor. They are removed by the process of distillation.

distractors. Incorrect response options on a multiple-choice test item.

distress (air traffic control). A condition of being threatened by serious and/or imminent danger, and of requiring immediate assistance.

distress frequencies (radio communications). Frequencies for radio transmission recognized by most nations as universal frequencies for distress, or emergency, purposes. In the low-frequency band, 500 kilohertz is the distress frequency. In the VHF (very high frequency) band, it is 121.5 megahertz, and in the UHF (ultra high frequency) band, it is 243.0 megahertz. These distress (or emergency) frequencies are continuously monitored by many military and commercial radio operators.

distributed pole motor. A type of electric motor whose stator windings are wound in a series of slots in the motor frame. A distributed pole motor is different from a salient pole motor whose field windings are wound around separate pole shoes that project inward from the frame toward the rotor.

distributor (magneto ignition system component). A high-voltage rotary selector switch used in an aircraft engine magneto to direct high-voltage electrical energy from the magneto coil secondary winding to the spark plugs at the time they should fire. The rotor of the distributor is gear-driven from the crankshaft.

distributor block (magneto ignition system component). The insulated block in a high-voltage magneto distributor to which the ignition leads attach. The distributor rotor passes near fixed contacts inside the distributor block, and the high-voltage current jumps from the rotor to the contact, then out the correct ignition lead to the spark plug. Distributor blocks are made of a plastic material having an extremely high dielectric strength.

distributor finger (magneto ignition system component). A term for a magneto distributor rotor. The finger, or rotor, is the device inside a distributor that picks up the high voltage from the magneto coil and directs it to the terminal inside the distributor block to which the ignition lead for the correct spark plug is attached.

distributor valve (Hamilton Standard Hydromatic propeller component). A valve which screws into the end of the propeller shaft on which a Hydromatic propeller is mounted. For all normal operations of the propeller, including feathering, the distributor valve acts only as an oil passage. But when the propeller is being unfeathered, the distributor valve shifts and directs high-pressure oil to the side of the piston in the propeller dome that moves the blades toward their unfeathered position.

distributor valve (pneumatic deicer system component). A rotary selector valve in a pneumatic deicer system. The distributor valve, installed between the air pump and the deicer boots, sequences the inflation and deflation of the boots to break the ice that has formed on the leading edges of the wings and tail surfaces. Air flowing over the surface gets under the broken ice and blows it away.

disturbance (meteorology). An area in which weather, wind, pressure, etc., show signs of cyclonic development.

disuse. A theory of forgetting that suggests a person forgets those things that are not used.

ditching. An emergency landing of an aircraft in water.

dither signal (automatic control signal). An oscillating, or alternating, signal sent into the servo motors of an automatic pilot. The dither signal does not produce rotation of the motor when there is no directional signal. But, as soon as the directional signal is sent to the motor, the dither signal adds to it and helps overcome the effect of friction or hysteresis.

diurnal. Daily. This term applies to a cycle complete within a 24-hour period and which recurs every 24 hours.

diurnal effects (meteorology). A daily variation in temperature, moisture, wind, cloud cover, etc., especially pertaining to a cycle completed within a 24-hour period.

dive (flight maneuver). A steep descending flight path.

dive brake (glider flight control). A secondary flight control that extends from both the upper and lower surfaces of the wing of a glider to increase drag.

dive flaps (airplane auxiliary control surfaces). Surfaces on either the wings or fuselage of an airplane that can be extended in flight to create enough parasite drag to keep the airplane from reaching an excessive speed in a dive. Dive flaps, also called speed brakes or dive brakes, are designed to produce a minimum amount of pitch change when they extend.

divergence (meteorology). A condition that exists when the distribution of winds within a given area is such that there is a net horizontal flow of air outward from the region. In divergence at lower levels, the resulting movement of air away from the surface is compensated for by subsidence of air from aloft. The air is heated and the relative humidity is lowered, making divergence a warming and drying process. Low-level divergent regions are areas in which clouds and precipitation are unlikely to form. Divergence is the opposite of convergence.

divergent duct (fluid flow passage). A duct, or passage, whose cross-sectional area increases in the direction of fluid flow. When fluid flows through a divergent duct at a subsonic rate, its velocity decreases, and its pressure increases.

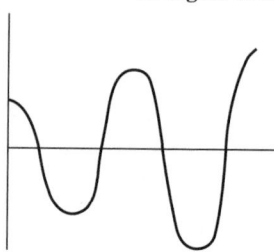

divergent duct

divergent oscillation. Oscillations whose amplitude increases with time. The oscillations of an airplane that has positive static stability but negative dynamic stability are divergent oscillations.

diverse vector area (air traffic control). That area, in a radar environment, in which a prescribed departure route is not the only suitable route to avoid obstacles. The area in which random radar vectors below the minimum vectoring altitude/minimum IFR altitude (MVA/MIA), established in accordance with the terminal instrument procedures (TERPS) criteria for diverse departures, obstacles and terrain avoidance, may be issued to departing aircraft.

divergent oscillation

diversion (DVRSN) (air traffic control). A flight that is required to land at other than its original destination for reasons beyond the control of the pilot or company, such as in periods of significant weather.

dividend (mathematical term). The number in a division problem that is to be divided. The components of the problem 36 ÷ 3 = 12 are: 36 is the dividend, 3 is the divisor, and 12 is the quotient.

dividers (layout tool). A sheet metal layout tool that looks much like a drafting compass. Dividers are used to lay out circles or arcs of a circle and to divide a line into equal spaces.

diving blade (helicopter rotor blade). The blade of a helicopter rotor that flies increasingly lower in the blade path as RPM or power increases.

division. The process of finding how many times one number (the divisor) is contained in another number (the dividend).

divisor (mathematical term). The number in a division problem that is used to go into, or to divide, the dividend. The dividend is divided by the divisor. *See* dividend.

DME (distance measuring equipment). A pulse-type electronic navigation system that shows the pilot, by an instrument-panel indication, the number of nautical miles between the aircraft and a ground station. The DME transmitter in the aircraft transmits a specific pulse of electrical energy. This pulse is received by the ground station and retransmitted on another frequency. When the pulse is received back in the aircraft, the time used for its travel to the ground station and back is converted into terms of nautical miles to the station. DME is a portion of the military TACAN (Tactical Air Navigation) system.

DME arc. A flight track that is a constant distance from the station or waypoint.

DME fix. A geographic location determined by reference to a navigational aid which provides distance and azimuth information. The direction of a DME fix is specified in degrees magnetic from the facility, and the distance from the facility is given in nautical miles.

DME separation. Air traffic control spacing of aircraft in terms of nautical miles as determined by reference to distance measuring equipment.

dock (aircraft maintenance facility). An area in which the proper scaffolds and work platforms can be put around an aircraft so it can be inspected or repairs can be made.

dock (seaplane operation). *(verb)* To secure a seaplane to a permanent structure fixed to the shore. *(noun)* The platform or structure to which the seaplane is secured.

DOD. Department of Defense.

DOD (domestic object damage). Damage to the components in the gas path of a turbine engine caused by the failure of parts within the engine itself.

DOD commercial air carrier evaluator. A cockpit evaluator qualified by the Air Mobility Command Survey and Analysis Office who is performing the duties specified in Public Law 99-661 when flying on an air carrier that is contracted or pursuing a contract with the U.S. Department of Defense (DOD).

DOD FLIP (Department of Defense Flight Information Publication). A publication put out by the Department of Defense and used for flight planning, en route, and terminal operations.

doghouse (mark on a turn and slip indicator dial). A mark on the dial of a four-minute turn and slip indicator that has the shape of a doghouse.

The inside edge of the doghouse is located one needle width away from the edge of the center reference mark on the dial, so a turn in which the needle aligns with the doghouse, a two-needle-width turn, is a standard rate, three degrees per second, turn. A one-needle-width turn on a turn and slip indicator which has doghouses on the dial is a four minute, or $1^{1}/_{2}$-degree-per-second turn.

dog point (threaded fastener). The point of a threaded fastener cut in the form of a cylinder. The length of the dog point is about one half of the diameter of the bolt, and its diameter is slightly less than the diameter of the bolt at the bottom of the threads. A dog point is used as a pilot, or guide, when assembling parts.

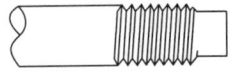

dog point

doldrums (meteorology). The equatorial belt of calm or light and variable winds between the two tradewind belts.

dolly (shop tool). Any of several types of wheeled platforms used in a maintenance shop to move or store heavy aircraft or engine components.

dolly block (sheet metalworking tool). A hardened steel block having a smooth, curved surface. Dolly blocks are used to back up a mallet when hand-forming sheet metal into compound curves.

dolphin flight (glider flight). In glider flight, glides can often be extended and average cross-country speeds increased by flying faster in sink, and slower in lift without stopping to circle.

domain (magnetic term). Clumps of molecules in a piece of ferromagnetic material that change their magnetic alignment as a group, rather than as individual molecules.

domestic airspace (air traffic control). Airspace which overlies the continental land mass of the United States plus Hawaii and U.S. possessions. Domestic airspace extends to 12 miles offshore.

domestic object damage. *See* DOD.

domestic operation. Any scheduled operation conducted by any person operating: (1) a turbojet-powered airplane; (2) an airplane with more than 9 passenger seats, excluding each crewmember seat; or (3) an airplane with a payload capacity of more than 7,500 pounds, when operating at locations as defined in 14 CFR §110.2. These locations are defined as: (1) between any points within the 48 contiguous states of the U.S. or the District of Columbia; (2) operations solely within the 48 contiguous states of the U.S. or the District of Columbia; (3) operations entirely within any state, territory, or possession of the United States; or (4) when specifically authorized by the Administrator, operations between any point within the 48 contiguous States of the U.S. or the District of Columbia and any specifically authorized point located outside the 48 contiguous States of the U.S. or the District of Columbia.

Domestic Reduced Vertical Separation Minimum (DRVSM). Additional flight levels between FL 290 and FL 410 to provide operational, traffic, and airspace efficiency.

donor atom (semiconductor material). Atoms of pentavalent elements (elements having five valence electrons) used to dope silicon or germanium for making semiconductor diodes or transistors. A donor atom has more electrons than needed for the covalent bonds within the material and donates these extra electrons to acceptor atoms.

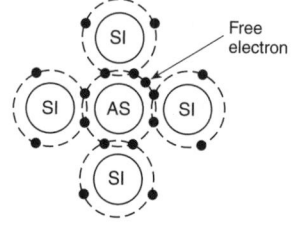

donor atom

donor impurity (semiconductor component). Any of the chemical elements with five valence electrons used to dope silicon or germanium to produce N-type semiconductor material. Phosphorus, arsenic, and antimony are commonly used as donor impurities.

dope (aircraft finishing material). A finishing material used to shrink cotton or linen fabric and make it airtight and weatherproof. Dope is made of a cellulose film base mixed with suitable solvents, thinners, and plasticizers.

doped-in panel (aircraft fabric repair). A repair made to a fabric-covered aircraft wing in which an entire panel of fabric from the leading edge to the trailing edge, between one or more ribs, is replaced. The new fabric is attached to the old fabric by doping it in place, rather than sewing it in, but it is attached to the structure by rib stitching.

doped-on fabric repair. A repair to a small damaged area in an aircraft fabric covering in which the patch is doped to the old fabric, rather than sewed in place.

dope proofing (aircraft finishing procedure). The treatment of a structure to be covered with fabric to keep the solvents in the dope from softening the protective coating on the structure.

dope-proof paint (aircraft finishing material). A type of finish applied over a varnished surface to be covered with fabric and doped. The dope-proof paint prevents the solvents in the dope from softening the varnish.

dope roping (aircraft finishing problem). A condition of aircraft dope being brushed onto a surface that causes the dope to form a stringy, uneven surface, rather than flowing out smoothly. Dope roping is caused by the dope being too cold when it is brushed on.

doping (semiconductor manufacturing). The process of adding small amounts of certain elements as impurities to a semiconductor element to alter its electrical characteristics.

Doppler effect. The apparent rise in the pitch, or frequency, of a sound as its source approaches the hearer, and the decrease in pitch as the source moves away.

Doppler radar. An electronic system used to detect the speed of a moving vehicle. Speed is measured by computing the change in frequency of an electronic signal bounced back from the vehicle. This change in frequency is related to the speed the vehicle is moving toward or away from the source of the signal.

Doppler VOR (DVOR). A radio navigation system in which the carrier is amplitude modulated by the reference signal and frequency modulated by the variable signal. The Doppler Principle states that there is a change in frequency of a signal received when the distance between the source and receiver changes. When the distance decreases, the frequency increases. The opposite is true when the distance increases.

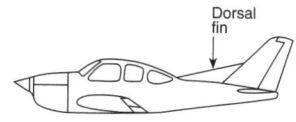

dorsal fin (aircraft surface). A fixed vertical fin extending from the top of the fuselage to the leading edge of the vertical fin. Dorsal fins are used to increase the directional stability of an airplane.

dorsal fin

double-acting actuator (fluid power actuator). A linear fluid power (hydraulic or pneumatic) actuator that uses fluid to move the piston in both directions. A single-acting actuator, by contrast, uses fluid to move the piston in one direction and some other type of force, such as a spring, to move it in the opposite direction.

double-acting hand pump. A hand-operated fluid pump that moves fluid during both strokes of the pump handle.

double-backed tape (adhesive tape). A type of adhesive tape with adhesive on both sides.

double-cut file. A file with two series of parallel cutting teeth. These teeth cross each other at an angle.

double-cut file

double-cut saw. A saw with teeth that cut on both the forward and return stroke.

double-entry centrifugal compressor. A form of centrifugal air compressor with vanes on both sides of the rotor. Air is taken into both faces of the rotor and discharged from its periphery.

double flare (rigid fluid line component). A flare made on a piece of rigid tubing in which the tubing in the flare is doubled back on itself to produce two thicknesses of metal in the flare. A double flare is acceptable in aircraft fluid systems on soft aluminum tubing having an outside diameter no larger than $3/8$ of an inch.

double gimbal (instrument component). A type of mount used for the gyro in an attitude instrument. The axes of the two gimbals are at right angles to the spin axis of the gyro, allowing free motion in two planes around the gyro.

double-loop rib stitching (aircraft fabric attachment). A type of stitch used to attach fabric to an aircraft structure in which the rib-stitching cord is wrapped around the rib two times to form a double loop before the knot is tied.

double magneto (reciprocating engine component). An aircraft engine magneto that uses a single rotating magnet to supply the magnetic flux for two magneto circuits. A double magneto has two coil assemblies, two sets of breaker points, and two distributors, but only one rotating magnet and one cam.

doubler (sheet-metal structural component). A piece of sheet metal used to strengthen and stiffen an aircraft skin at the location some component is to be attached. A doubler is normally riveted to the inside of the aircraft skin where a radio antenna is mounted.

double-row radial engine (reciprocating engines). A radial engine with two rows of cylinders whose pistons are connected to a single crankshaft. The crankshaft of a double-row radial engine has two throws, 180° apart. The master rod for the front row of cylinders attaches to one throw, and the master rod for the rear row of cylinders attaches to the other throw. Most double-row radial engines have either 14 or 18 cylinders.

double-shear loading (riveted joint). A riveted joint that contains two shear planes. The total shear strength of the joint is approximately twice the shear strength of a joint with a single-shear load.

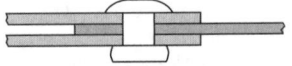

double-shear loading

double spread (adhesive application). The application of a layer of adhesive to each of the two surfaces being bonded together.

double-tapered wing (aerodynamic shape). A wing tapered in both planform and thickness. The planform of a wing is its shape as seen from above, looking down on it, and thickness is the shape as seen from the front, looking aft.

double-throw switch. An electrical switch with three positions, CIRCUIT 1, OFF, and CIRCUIT 2. A single-pole, double-throw (SPDT) switch can select one of three conditions in a single circuit, and a double-pole, double-throw (DPDT) switch can select one of three conditions in two circuits with the movement of a single control.

dovetail (type of fitting attachment). A method of attaching or joining parts in which the ends to be joined are shaped in the form of the spread-out tail of a dove. The rotor blades of some turbine engine compressors are attached to the disk by a dovetail joint. The periphery of the disk is cut with a series of triangular-shaped slots, and the blade roots are made with a dovetail-shaped end that fits into the slots in the disk. The dovetail method of blade attachment holds the blades firmly against centrifugal force, dampens vibration, and compensates for the effect of temperature change.

dovetailing (woodworking). A method of joining pieces of wood to form the sides of a box or drawer. The ends of one piece of wood are cut with triangular-shaped cutouts that look like the spread-out tail of a dove. These cutouts are called the mortises. The other piece of wood is cut with tenons that are shaped so they exactly fit into the mortises. When the tenons are fitted into the mortises, they form a solid joint.

dowel. A round wooden peg used to fasten pieces of wood together without the use of metal fasteners. Holes are drilled into each of the pieces to be joined, and a short dowel is pressed into the holes to hold the pieces together.

dowel rod. A round piece of wood used to make dowels for holding pieces of wood together.

Dow metal. The registered trade name for a series of magnesium alloys produced by the Dow Chemical Corporation.

downburst (meteorology). A strong downdraft which induces an outburst of damaging winds on or near the ground. The sizes of downbursts vary from one-half mile or less to more than 10 miles. An intense downburst often causes widespread damage. Damaging winds, lasting from five to 30 minutes, could reach speeds as high as 120 knots.

downdraft (meteorology). A relatively small-scale downward current of air. Downdrafts are often observed on the lee side of large objects that restrict the smooth flow of the air or in precipitation areas in or near cumuliform clouds.

downdraft carburetor. A carburetor that mounts on the top of a reciprocating engine. Air entering the engine flows downward through the carburetor.

downlocks (aircraft landing gear component). Mechanical locks used to hold a retractable landing gear in its down position. Downlocks prevent the landing gear from accidentally retracting when there is no hydraulic pressure on the actuating cylinder.

downslope wind (meteorology). A wind directed down a slope, often used to describe winds produced by processes larger in scale than the slope.

downswell (seaplane operation). In seaplane flight, motion in the same direction a swell is moving.

downtime (aircraft operation). Any time during which an aircraft is out of commission and not able to be operated.

D

downwash (aerodynamics). Air forced down by aerodynamic action below and behind the wing of an airplane or rotor of a helicopter. Aerodynamic lift is produced when air is deflected downward. The upward force on the aircraft is the same as the downward force on the air. When the mass of air in the downwash is equal to the weight of the aircraft forcing it down, the aircraft rises.

downwash angle (aerodynamics). The angle formed between the direction of air movement as it approaches an airfoil and its direction as it leaves. An airfoil produces lift by deflecting air downward. The upward component of lift is equal to the downward component created by the mass of the downwashed air.

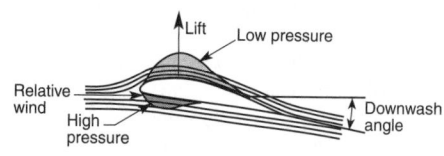

downwash angle

downwind. The direction measured relative to the way the wind is blowing. Downwind means the direction in which the wind is moving.

downwind landing (aircraft operation). A landing in which the aircraft is moving in the same direction the wind is blowing. Normal landings are made into the wind, or upwind, allowing the wind to slow the ground speed of the aircraft. When an aircraft lands into the wind, its ground speed is its airspeed minus the speed of the wind. When it lands downwind, its speed over the ground is equal to its airspeed plus the speed of the wind.

downwind leg (airport flight pattern). A flight path parallel to the landing runway in the opposite direction of landing.

DP. *See* departure procedure.

DPDT switch (double-pole, double-throw electrical switch). A type of electrical switch with six terminals. It can be used to select any one of three conditions in two separate circuits. *See* double-throw switch.

DPDT switch

DPE. *See* designated pilot examiner.

DPST switch (double-pole, single-throw electrical switch). A type of electrical switch having four terminals. It can select either of two conditions in two separate circuits. *See* double-throw switch.

DPST switch

draft of a mold. The taper in the sides of a part cast in a mold. Draft makes it easy to remove the solidified part from the mold.

draftsman. A person who uses the process of mechanical drawing to make plans or sketches of machinery or structures. A draftsman functions differently from an artist in that the draftsman uses templates and other mechanical devices to assure technical accuracy of the drawing. Drawings made by an artist are normally done freehand, and they convey thoughts and impressions, rather than objective representation of specific details.

drag (aerodynamic parameter). An aerodynamic force acting in the same plane as the relative wind striking an airfoil. Two basic types of drag act on an aircraft in flight: induced drag and parasite drag.

Induced drag is caused by the same factors that produce lift, and its amount varies inversely as the airspeed. As the airspeed decreases, the angle of attack must increase, and this increases the induced drag.

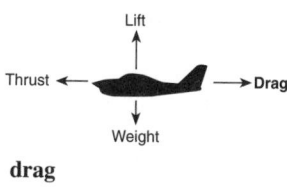

drag

Parasite drag is caused by the friction of air moving over the structure, and its amount varies directly as the airspeed. The higher the airspeed, the greater the parasite drag.

drag (helicopter rotor blade movement). Fore-and-aft movement of the tip of a helicopter rotor blade in its plane of rotation.

drag brace (helicopter rotor component). An adjustable brace used to adjust the blade alignment of a semirigid helicopter rotor. Drag braces resist movement of the blade about its lead-lag hinge.

drag brace (landing gear component). A brace which supports an aircraft landing gear against loads trying to force the landing gear backward.

drag chute (aircraft operation). A small parachute attached to the rear of an airplane structure. The drag chute can be deployed (opened) after the airplane touches down on landing to help it slow down.

drag coefficient (aerodynamics). A dimensionless number used to find the amount of induced drag produced by an airfoil. The drag coefficient is determined by the shape of the airfoil section and by the angle of attack. The coefficient of drag for any airfoil section increases as the angle of attack increases.

drag curve. A graphed representation of the amount of drag experienced by an aircraft at various airspeeds, showing the combined forces of parasite, profile, and induced drag. Understanding the drag curve can provide valuable insight into the various performance parameters and limitations of the aircraft. Pilots use the information from this graph to find the maximum endurance and range of the aircraft. The drag curve also illustrates the two regions of command: the region of normal command, and the region of reversed command.

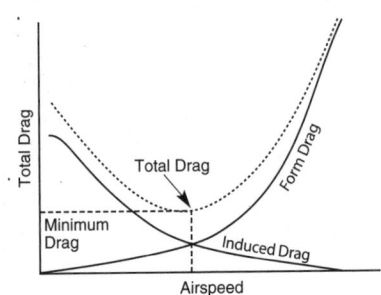

drag curve

dragging brakes (aircraft brake malfunction). A condition in which the brakes do not fully release when pressure is removed from the brake pedal. The brakes are partially applied all the time, which causes excessive lining wear and heat. Dragging brakes can cause serious overheating, and may be caused by a malfunction in the brake master cylinder or by warped disks.

drag hinge (helicopter rotor component). A hinge in the rotor system of a helicopter that allows the individual blades to move back and forth in their plane of rotation. This movement helps minimize vibration. The drag hinge is also called the lead-lag hinge.

drag landing (balloon flight). A high-wind landing where the balloon drags across the ground after the deflation panel has been opened.

drag line (balloon operation). A gas balloon term used to describe a large, heavy rope, deployed at landing, which orients the balloon (and rip panel) to the wind, and transfers weight from the balloon to the ground, creating a landing flare.

drag wire (aircraft structure). A structural wire inside a Pratt truss airplane wing between the spars. Drag wires run from the front spar inboard, to the rear spar at the next bay outboard. Drag wires oppose forces that try to drag a wing backward. Each drag wire is crossed by an antidrag wire.

drain (electronics). The electrode in a field effect transistor (FET) through which load current flows. Load current flowing from the source to the drain is controlled by the amount of voltage applied to the gate. The drain of an FET corresponds to the collector in a bipolar transistor.

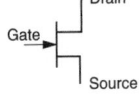

drain

drainage wind (meteorology). A mountain wind that often continues down the more gentle slopes of canyons and valleys.

D

drain can (jet aircraft component). A container in a jet aircraft engine compartment used to collect the fuel which drains from the main fuel manifold when the engine is shut down.

drain hole (aircraft structure). A small hole in the lowest part of an aircraft structure, used to ventilate the inside of the structure and to drain any water which collects in this area.

drain plug. A removable plug in the lowest point of a liquid container. The plug is removed to drain the liquid.

drain valve (fuel tank component). A valve in the bottom of a fuel tank that allows water and sediment, that has collected in the tank, to be drained.

drape (textile characteristic). The ability of a woven fabric to conform to a contoured shape.

draw filing. A method of cutting metal or plastic with a hand file by moving the file crosswise over the work. Draw filing produces a very smooth finish.

drawing number (aircraft drawing). The number assigned to an aircraft drawing, which is located in the title block in the lower right-hand corner of the drawing. Drawing numbers often become the part number for the part made from the drawing.

drawknife. A woodworking tool consisting of a sharp blade with two handles, one at either end of the blade, mounted at right angles to the blade. A drawknife is pulled across the work to shave off part of its surface or to make its edges round.

draw set (riveting tool). A metalworking hand tool used to draw sheets of metal closely together before they are riveted. A draw set is a steel bar with a hole drilled in one end to fit loosely over the shank of a rivet. The rivet is put through the holes in the sheets of metal, and the draw set is placed over the rivet shank. Then the rivet head is tapped lightly with the rivet set. This procedure draws the sheets of metal closely together before the rivet is actually driven.

drift (navigation). The term used in navigation for the sideways movement of an aircraft caused by the wind. Drift must be corrected for by heading the aircraft slightly into the direction from which the wind is blowing.

drift angle (aircraft flight). The angular difference between the direction an aircraft is headed in flight and the direction it actually moves over the ground.

drift correction. Correction that is applied to counter the effects of wind on an aircraft's flight and ground track.

driftdown (flight procedure). A procedure by which an airplane with one or more inoperative engines, and the remaining engines producing maximum continuous thrust (MCT), and while maintaining a specified speed (usually best L/D x 1.01%), descends to the altitude at which the airplane can maintain altitude and begin to climb (this altitude is defined as driftdown height).

drifting snow (meteorology). Snow particles picked up from the surface by the wind and carried to a height of less than six feet.

drift magnet (electrical instrument component). A small permanent magnet used in some electrical indicating instruments to pull the instrument pointer off the scale when the instrument is not energized.

drift punch. A pin punch with a long straight shank and a flat end. A drift punch is used to drive a shaft out of its hole.

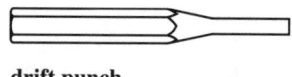

drift punch

drift sight (aircraft navigation instrument). A navigational instrument used in an aircraft when it is being navigated by dead reckoning. The drift sight measures the angle between the direction the aircraft is pointed and the direction it is moving over the ground.

drill (rotary cutting tool). A pointed rotary cutting tool rotated under pressure in a drill press or with a handheld drill motor to cut a hole in a piece of solid material. A drill is correctly called a twist drill.

drill and practice method. A time-honored training delivery method based on the learning principle that connections are strengthened with practice.

drill bushing. A hardened steel bushing installed in an assembly fixture. A piece of metal to be assembled is clamped in the fixture, and a twist drill is guided by the bushing to drill a hole at the correct location. The hardened metal prevents the bushing being worn by the drill.

drill chuck (machine tool component). A three-jaw clamp attached to the spindle of a drill press or the shaft of a drill motor to hold a twist drill centered. The jaws of the chuck may be tightened on the drill with a chuck key or Allen wrench, and some chucks are designed to be tightened by hand.

drilling burrs (sheet metal working). Sharp, ragged edges left around a hole after it has been drilled.

drill jig (metal fabrication tool). A device for guiding a drill to make a precise and correctly positioned hole.

drill motor. An electric or pneumatic motor that drives a chuck which holds a twist drill. The best drill motors produce high torque, and their speed can be controlled.

drill press. A power tool used for drilling holes in metal or wood. The drill press consists of a motor-driven spindle on which is mounted a drill chuck that holds a twist drill. The material to be drilled is placed on a steel table under the spindle, and the spindle is forced down, causing the drill to cut into the material.

drill rod (metallurgy). A rod of steel having a carbon content of at least 0.85%.

drip loop (electrical wiring). A half loop of wire at the cable entrance of an exposed junction box. The final section of the cable runs upward, preventing water entering the box.

drip pan. A shallow metal pan placed under the engine of an aircraft when it is in the hangar to catch any oil that might drip from it.

drip-stick fuel gage (fuel quantity indicator). A type of visual fuel-quantity indicator used on large aircraft to measure the amount of fuel in a tank. The drip stick, which is normally locked in the tank in its up position, is unlocked and slowly pulled down from the bottom of the tank. The bottom of the drip stick is watched until the first drips of fuel come from it. At this point, the top of the drip stick is level with the top of the fuel in the tank. Marks on the outside of the drip stick at the point it leaves the tank show the amount of fuel in the tank.

drive coupling (engine component). A shock-absorbing coupling used between the accessory drive in an engine and an accessory that is subject to torsional vibrations. A safety link designed to shear if the accessory should freeze, or jam, is usually incorporated as a part of a drive coupling.

drive fit (mechanical fit). A tight fit between mating parts of a mechanism in which one part fits inside another. In a drive fit, the hole is smaller than the part that fits into it, and force must be used to assemble the parts. A drive fit is also called an interference fit.

drive gear. The gear attached to the power source in a gear train. The drive gear meshes with and drives the driven gear. If the drive gear is smaller than the driven gear, the driven gear turns slower than the drive gear.

driven gear. The gear in a gear train that meshes with and is driven by the drive gear.

driver (electronic circuit). A piece of electronic equipment in a circuit that supplies input power to an output circuit or device.

driver head (threaded fastener). A type of bolt or screw head that is either slotted or fitted with a recess. A driver head makes it possible to drive the fastener with some form of screwdriver, rather than with a wrench.

drivescrew. A form of self-tapping screw that has no screwdriver slot nor recess in its head. Drivescrews are used to attach nameplates to an engine crankcase and to plug holes in a tubular steel structure through which preservative oil has been pumped. Drivescrews are installed by driving them in place with a hammer.

drizzle (meteorology). Very small droplets of water that appear to float with the air currents while falling in an irregular path. Drizzle differs from rain, which falls in a comparatively straight path, and fog, whose droplets remain suspended in the air.

drogue. Any of several types of devices used to slow or stabilize a body moving through water or air. A drogue parachute is a small parachute which can be opened behind an airplane to slow or stabilize it in flight.

A drogue is also the funnel-shaped device on the end of an inflight refueling hose. The drogue stabilizes the hose and allows the aircraft being refueled to connect its probe into the fueling line.

A sea anchor, which is a canvas bucket with a small opening in its bottom, is also a drogue. A sea anchor is used to stabilize and control the movement of a boat or seaplane.

drone. A pilotless airplane used for target practice or for research in conditions that would be dangerous for a manned aircraft. Drones are remotely controlled by radio from a mother aircraft or from a ground station.

droop (turbine engine fuel control condition). A progressive decrease in RPM with load in an engine whose speed is governed with a flyweight-type governor. As the load is increased, the pilot valve drops down to meter more fuel. The lower position of the valve decreases the compression of the speeder spring and allows the flyweights to assume an onspeed position at a lower RPM.

droop compensator (helicopter turbine engine control). A linkage between the collective pitch control and the turbine speed governor that adjusts for the increased load the rotor places on the engine, as collective pitch is increased. The droop compensator prevents the rotor speed decreasing as the load is applied.

droop restraint (helicopter rotor system). A mechanical device that limits the amount the blades of a helicopter rotor can droop when the rotor is turning at a slow speed, and there is not enough centrifugal force to overcome the effect of gravity on the blades.

drop cloth. A piece of canvas or plastic used to cover the floor or objects on the floor when walls and ceilings are being painted. The drop cloth prevents paint from dripping on areas where it should not be.

drop forging. A method of forging steel parts by forcing semi-molten metal into a die by a heavy blow from a drop hammer. The grain structure of a drop-forged part gives it more strength than a cast part.

drop hammer. A large metalworking machine that uses heavy matched dies to form compound curves in sheet metal. The sheet of metal to be formed is placed over a female die, and a heavy, matching male die is raised above it and dropped into the female die, forming the metal into the shape of the dies. Drop hammers are also used to forge semimolten metal in a die.

drop line (balloon operation). A rope or webbing, which may be deployed by the pilot to the ground crew to assist in landing or ground handling a balloon.

drop-out voltage (electrical relays). The minimum voltage needed to keep an electrical relay energized. When the voltage drops below this value, the relay automatically de-energizes. Electromagnetism holds the relay energized, and a spring de-energizes it when the voltage producing the electromagnetism is below the drop-out voltage.

dropping resistor (electric circuit). A resistor in an electrical circuit used to drop voltage. For example, if a 12-volt light bulb is used in a 24-volt electrical system, a dropping resistor must be installed in series with the bulb to drop 12 volts. This allows only 12 volts across the bulb.

dropsonde (meteorology). An instrument pack and radio transmitter dropped by parachute from an aircraft to measure conditions of the atmosphere through which it passes. This information is continuously transmitted to meteorologists on the ground.

drop tank (fuel tank for military aircraft). An externally mounted fuel tank used on some military aircraft. Fuel is used from the drop tank first, and then the entire tank is dropped from the aircraft to get rid of the weight and the drag.

dross. The impurity that forms on the surface of molten metal. Dross is composed of the oxides produced by the reaction of oxygen in the air with the hot metal.

drum brake. A form of friction brake used on some airplanes. A drum brake is composed of two curved shoes which have a heat-absorbing friction material bonded to their outer surface. These shoes are pressed outward against the inside of a cylindrical drum that rotates with the wheel. The brake is applied by hydraulic pressure or mechanical leverage forcing the shoes out against the drum, and a spring pulls them away from the drum when the brake pedal or handle is released.

dry adiabat. A line on a thermodynamic chart representing a rate of temperature change at the dry adiabatic lapse rate.

dry adiabatic lapse rate (meteorology). The rate of decrease of temperature with altitude when unsaturated air is lifted adiabatically—that is, lifted without the addition to, or loss of, any heat energy. The dry adiabatic lapse rate is 3°C (5.4°F) per thousand feet.

dry adiabatic process (meteorology). (1) An adiabatic process in a hypothetical atmosphere in which no moisture is present. (2) An adiabatic process in which no condensation of its water vapor occurs and no liquid water is present. *See* adiabatic process (meteorology).

dry air (standard atmosphere). Air that contains no water vapor. Dry air is used as an atmospheric standard. Dry air weighs 0.07651 pound per cubic foot under standard sea-level conditions of 59°F (15°C) and a barometric pressure of 14.69 pounds per square inch or 29.92 inches of mercury.

dry air pump. *See* dry-type air pump.

dry-bulb temperature. Temperature measured by a thermometer not affected by the evaporation of water. Relative humidity is measured by finding the difference between wet-bulb and dry-bulb temperature. The thermometer that measures wet-bulb temperature has a wick around its sensitive end. This wick is saturated with water, and air blown across it evaporates the water. The evaporation causes the wet-bulb temperature to be lower than the dry-bulb temperature, and the amount lower is determined by the humidity, or the amount of water vapor in the air.

dry-cell battery. A common term used for a single cell of a carbon-zinc battery. A dry cell is not totally dry. Its electrolyte is a moist paste, and it is sealed to retain its moisture.

dry-charged battery. A lead-acid storage battery that has been fully charged by the manufacturer. Before the battery is shipped, all the electrolyte is drained out of it, and the cells are all sealed. Before the battery is placed in service, it is filled with electrolyte having the proper specific gravity, and the battery is given a freshening charge (a charge that brings its voltage up to the proper value).

dry-chemical fire extinguisher. A type of handheld fire extinguisher which uses a dry chemical, such as sodium bicarbonate, as the extinguishing agent. The dry chemical is normally forced out of the extinguisher by compressed nitrogen.

dry fiber (composites). A condition in which fibers are not fully encapsulated by resin during pultrusion. *See* pultrusion (composites).

dry ice. Solidified carbon dioxide. Dry ice sublimates, or changes from a solid directly into a gas, at a temperature of −110°F (−78.5°C), without passing through the liquid state. Dry ice is used as a refrigerant and as a means of chilling mechanical parts when they are being assembled with an interference fit.

drying oil. An oil used in paints and varnishes. The oil, usually cottonseed or linseed oil, is mixed in the paint or varnish. When it is exposed to air, the oil oxidizes and forms a hard, dry film.

dryline (meteorology). A boundary that separates a moist air mass from a dry air mass. In spring and early summer over western Texas, into the Plains States, and for some distance eastward, the dryline is a favored spawning area for squall lines and tornadoes.

dry rot. A type of decay found in seasoned wood. Dry rot is caused by fungi in the wood which change the normal fibers into a soft material that becomes a powder. Wood with dry rot has no structural strength.

dry-sump engine. An engine in which the lubricating oil supply is carried in a reservoir, or tank, that is not part of the engine. Both gas turbine and reciprocating engines can have dry-sump lubricating systems.

dry-sump system (engine lubrication system). A type of lubrication system used on both reciprocating and turbine engines. The oil is held in an external tank, drawn from the tank and circulated through the engine by an engine-driven pressure pump. After lubricating the engine, the oil drains into a integral sump from which it is picked up and returned to the oil tank by a scavenger pump.

dry-type air pump (engine accessory). An engine-driven air pump that uses carbon vanes, rather than steel vanes.

Dry-type pumps require no lubrication, but the vanes are extremely susceptible to damage from solid airborne particles. These pumps must therefore be operated with filters in their inlet.

dry wash (aircraft maintenance). A method used to remove airport film, dust, and small accumulations of dirt and soil from an aircraft structure when the use of liquids is neither desirable nor practical.

dual-beam oscilloscope. A cathode-ray oscilloscope with two electron beams which produce two traces on the screen at the same time. Dual-beam oscilloscopes may be used to observe the signals on the input and the output of a portion of a circuit at the same time.

dual controls (aircraft flight controls). Two sets of fully functioning flight controls in an aircraft. Dual controls allow the aircraft to be flown from either the left or right seat. All aircraft whose certification requires a pilot and copilot must be equipped with fully functioning dual controls.

dual flight. Flight time that is received and logged as training time. Dual flight time must be endorsed by a certified flight instructor.

dual ignition. An ignition system of an aircraft reciprocating engine that has two of every critical unit, including two spark plugs in each cylinder. Dual ignition provides safety in the event of one system malfunctioning, but more important, igniting the fuel-air mixture inside the cylinder at two locations provides more efficient expansion of the air in the cylinder.

dual indicator (aircraft instrument). An aircraft instrument in which two instrument mechanisms move pointers across a single dial. Many engine instruments installed in multiengine aircraft are dual indicators. For example, the oil pressure for both engines may be indicated on a single instrument. There are two separate indicator mechanisms and two pointers, but only one instrument case and one dial.

dual magneto. A magneto having a single rotating magnet and cam, but two sets of breaker points, two coils, two condensers, and two distributors. A dual magneto is considered to be the equivalent of two separate ignition systems for an aircraft engine.

dual rotor system (helicopter rotor system). A system of helicopter rotors in which there are two main rotors driven by coaxial drive shafts. The rotors turn in opposite directions so their torques counteract each other.

dual-spool gas-turbine engine. An axial-flow turbine engine that has two independent compressors, each driven by its own stage or stages of turbines. The high-pressure, or N_2, compressor is speed governed by the fuel control, but the low-pressure, or N_1, compressor is not governed but seeks its own best speed as the ambient air density changes.

DUATS. *See* direct user access terminal system.

duckbill pliers (mechanic's hand tools). A special type of pliers used to twist safety wire. Duckbill pliers have long handles and wide, flat jaws with serrations to grip the wire, but they do not have jaws for cutting the wire.

duct (air conditioning and heating component). A thin-wall tube installed in an aircraft to carry heated or cooled air for distribution at the proper locations.

ducted-fan engine (aircraft engine). A form of aircraft engine in which a propeller or fan is enclosed in a specially shaped shroud, or duct. A ducted-fan engine has a high degree of propulsive efficiency.

duct heater. A thrust augmentation system similar to an afterburner in which fuel is added to the fan discharge air and burned.

ductility (metal characteristic). The property of a material that allows it to be drawn into a thin section without breaking. Because copper has a great deal of ductility, it is possible to draw it into very fine wires.

duct losses (gas turbine engine losses). A decrease in pressure of the air flowing into a gas turbine engine caused by friction.

due regard (air traffic control). A phase of flight in which an aircraft commander of a state-operated aircraft assumes responsibility to separate his/her aircraft from all other aircraft, and assures that an appropriate monitoring agency assumes responsibility for search and rescue actions. Commanders operating under "due regard" must do so under at least one of the following conditions: (a) in visual meteorological conditions (VMC); (b) within radar surveillance and radio communications of a surface radar facility; (c) be equipped with airborne radar that is sufficient to provide separation between his/her aircraft (and any other aircraft he/she may be controlling), and other aircraft; or (d) operate within Class G airspace. The pilot and controller should concur regarding the intent of the pilot and the status of the flight before the aircraft leaves the ATC frequency.

dummy load. A noninductive, high-power resistor that can be connected to a transmission line in place of the antenna. The transmitter can be operated into the dummy load without transmitting any signal.

dump chute (aircraft fuel system component). A specially shaped duct, or tube, used to carry fuel away from the aircraft when it is dumped from the fuel tanks. Some large aircraft are permitted to take off with a greater weight than they are allowed to have when they land. However, if such an aircraft must make an emergency landing before it has burned off enough fuel to reduce its weight to its legal landing weight, it must dump enough fuel to get rid of this excess weight. The dump chute is designed to carry the fuel away from the aircraft so it will not be ignited by the engine exhaust or by static electricity.

duo-servo brakes (type of aircraft shoe brakes). A form of shoe brake that uses the weight of the aircraft to wedge the shoes tightly against the drum when the aircraft is rolling either forward or backward.

duplexer (radio communication device). A device that isolates the receiver from the transmitter while permitting them to share a common antenna.

duplex fuel nozzle (gas turbine engine component). A type of fuel nozzle that discharges its fuel into the combustor, or burner, at two different rates and flow patterns; one for low airflow and the other for high airflow. These flow patterns determine the shape of the flame inside the burner and both flow patterns keep the flame centered in the burner so it will not touch the thin metal of which the burner is made.

duplex operation (electronic communications). A method of communications in which each end can simultaneously transmit and receive. Communication by telephone is duplex operation. Duplex operation by radiotelephone requires the use of two frequencies.

durability. A measure of engine life. Durability is normally measured in hours of time between overhauls, or TBO.

dural (structural material). *See* duralumin.

duralumin. The trade name for one of the original alloys of aluminum, magnesium, manganese, and copper. Duralumin, which is the same as modern 2017 aluminum alloy, was first used by the Germans to build the Zeppelins of World War I. The term dural, which was at one time used for almost all the high-strength aluminum alloys, was taken from the name duralumin.

dust (meteorology). Fine particles of dry matter suspended in the atmosphere.

dust devil (meteorology). A small, vigorous whirlwind, usually of short duration. Dust devils are made visible by dust, sand, and debris picked up from the ground.

duster. *See* dust storm.

dust storm (meteorology). An unusual, frequently severe weather condition in which strong winds and dust-filled air cover an extensive area.

Dutchman shears (mechanic's hand tool). A common name for compound-action sheet metal shears. Dutchman shears come in three types: those that cut straight, those that cut to the right, and those that cut to the left.

Dutch roll (flight condition). An undesirable, low-amplitude oscillation about both the yaw and roll axes that affects many swept wing airplanes. Dutch roll is minimized by the use of a yaw damper.

duty cycle. A schedule that allows a device to operate for a given period of time, with a cooling down period required before the device can be operated again.

D-value (meteorology). The difference, shown on a constant-pressure chart, between the actual height and the standard atmospheric height of a constant-pressure surface. D-value is the algebraic difference between true altitude and pressure altitude.

DVFR (defense visual flight rules). Rules applicable to flights within an air defense identification zone (ADIZ) conducted under visual flight rules as defined in 14 CFR Part 91.

DVFR flight plan (air traffic control). A flight plan filed for a VFR aircraft which intends to operate in airspace within which the ready identification, location, and control of aircraft are required in the interest of national security.

dwell angle (battery ignition system). The number of degrees the distributor cam rotates between the time the breaker points close and the time they open. This determines the amount of time current flows in the primary winding of the ignition coil.

dwell chamber (turbine engine lubrication system component). A chamber in a turbine engine oil tank into which the scavenged oil is returned. Entrapped air can separate from the oil in this chamber before it is picked up by the pressure pump.

dwell time (penetrant inspection). The length of time a penetrant is allowed to remain on the surface of a part being inspected. The dwell time is determined by the temperature of the part and the size of the suspected defect.

dye. A colored substance used to add a more or less permanent color to another object. Dyes are added to aviation gasoline to give each grade an identifying color. Dyes are also used to add an attractive color to the oxide film that forms when aluminum alloys are anodized.

dye penetrant inspection. A method of nondestructive inspection used to detect surface defects in metal or plastic parts. The part to be inspected is soaked in a penetrating liquid for a specified period of time, and then all the penetrant is washed from its surface. The surface is then covered with a developing powder that pulls the penetrant from any defects that extend to the surface of the part. The penetrant plainly shows up on the powder-covered surface, outlining the defect.

dynafocal engine mount (reciprocating engine mount). A special type of mount for an aircraft engine in which straight lines that pass through the engine mount bolts intersect at the center of gravity of the engine and propeller assembly. Dynafocal engine mounts absorb much of the torsional vibration caused by the engine.

dynamic (air traffic control). Continuous review, evaluation, and change to meet demands.

dynamic balance. The balance of a rotating object, such as a wheel or propeller spinner. The condition of dynamic balance is checked with the object rotating. If an unbalanced condition causes vibration, the balancing equipment shows the amount of weight and the location of the weight needed to stop the vibration. Wheels and tires, as well as propellers, are dynamically balanced.

dynamic braking (electrical braking). Braking of an electric motor done by switching the power leads of the motor from the source of power to an electrical load. The electrical load consumes power which is changed to a mechanical force that opposes the rotation of the motor armature.

dynamic damper (reciprocating engine component). Heavy weights mounted on some of the cheeks of a reciprocating engine crankshaft to absorb torsional vibrations. The weights are attached to the cheek by small pins that ride in larger holes in the weights. This arrangement allows the weights to rock back and forth as the crankshaft rotates. It is this rocking motion that absorbs the torsional vibrations of the engine.

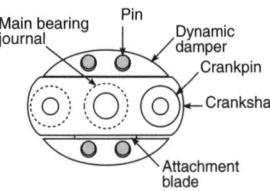

dynamic damper

dynamic hydroplaning (braking condition). A condition that exists when landing on a runway surface with standing water deeper than the tread depth of the tires. When the brakes are applied, there is a possibility that the wheel will lock up and the tire will ride on the surface of the water, much like a water ski. When the tires are hydroplaning, directional control and braking action are virtually impossible. An effective anti-skid system can minimize the effects of hydroplaning.

dynamic load (aircraft structural load). The apparent weight of an entire loaded aircraft. The apparent weight is the actual weight of the aircraft multiplied by the load factor, which is the increase in weight caused by acceleration.

For example, an aircraft in a properly coordinated 60° banked turn has a load factor of two. This means that if the loaded aircraft weighs 3,000 pounds, its dynamic load in a coordinated 60° banked turn is two times 3,000 pounds, or 6,000 pounds.

dynamic magnetic variation (navigation database fix error). A field in a "fix record" that contains only a computer model-calculated value instead of a measured value in the record for a waypoint. *See also* fix record.

dynamic microphone. A type of microphone in which sound pressure vibrates a cone on which is mounted a coil of wire. The coil vibrates in a magnetic field, and a voltage is produced in the coil. The frequency and waveform of the voltage is similar to that of the sound waves that vibrated the cone.

dynamic pressure, q (aerodynamic parameter). The pressure a moving fluid would have if it were stopped. Dynamic pressure is measured in pounds per square foot.

dynamic restrictions (air traffic control). Those restrictions imposed by the local facility on an "as needed" basis to manage unpredictable fluctuations in traffic demands.

dynamic rollover (helicopter operation). The tendency of a helicopter to roll over on landing. If one gear is on the ground and the helicopter pivots around that point, it will continue to roll when a critical angle is exceeded.

dynamic stability (aerodynamics). The stability that causes an aircraft to return to a condition of straight and level flight after it has been disturbed from this condition. When an aircraft is disturbed from straight and level flight, its static stability starts it back in the correct direction; but it overshoots, and the corrective forces are applied in the opposite direction. The aircraft oscillates back and forth on both sides of the correct condition, with each oscillation smaller than the one before it. Dynamic stability is the decreasing of these restorative oscillations.

dynamite. An explosive made by mixing nitroglycerine with a material such as sawdust, flour, or starch, and some type of oxygen-supplying salt.

dynamometer (electrical measuring instrument). An electrical measuring instrument that measures current and voltage at the same time and displays the results as electrical power. The instrument pointer moves over the dial an amount proportional to the product of the current and the voltage.

The current being measured flows through two series current coils and produces a fixed electromagnetic field whose strength is proportional to the amount of current. The voltage being measured forces current to flow through a movable voltage coil and produces a magnetic field proportional to the amount of voltage.

The pointer, mounted on the movable coil, is restrained by two calibrated hairsprings. The amount of its rotation is proportional to the strength of the two magnetic fields, and this makes the movement of the pointer proportional to the amount of power being measured.

dynamometer (mechanical measuring instrument). A device used to measure the amount of torque being produced by a rotating machine. The rotating machine is loaded with either an electric generator or a fluid pump whose output is measured and converted into units of mechanical power. A dynamometer measures the torque the machine produces at a specific RPM, and this data is converted into brake horsepower.

dynamotor (electrical machine). An electrical machine that converts low-voltage DC into high-voltage DC. The dynamotor has two armatures on its single rotating shaft, and these armatures turn inside of two sets of field coils. One set of field coils and one armature is for a low-voltage DC motor, and the other set of field coils and armature are for a high-voltage DC generator. A dynamotor is also called a rotary converter.

dyne. A unit of force in the centimeter-gram-second system of units. One dyne is the amount of force needed to cause a mass of one gram to accelerate one centimeter per second, each second it is acted on. One dyne is equal to $2.248 \cdot 10^{-6}$ pounds.

dynode (electronic component). One of a series of electrodes within a photomultiplier tube. Each dynode is more positively charged than its predecessor. Secondary emission occurs at the surface of each dynode.

dysprosium. A soft, silvery, rare-earth metallic chemical element. Dysprosium's symbol is Dy, its atomic number is 66, and its atomic weight is 162.50.

Dysprosium is used in nuclear research.

Dzus fastener (aircraft cowling fastener). A patented fastener used to secure aircraft cowling and inspection plates. A slotted stud is forced down over a piece of spring steel wire and is locked in place by turning the stud a quarter of a turn. This forces the wire into a cam-shaped groove in the stud.

Echo

EADI (electronic attitude director indicator). A colored multifunction display flight instrument that shows pitch and roll attitude indications along with flight director commands, localizer and glide slope indications, selected airspeed, ground speed, automatic flight control system and autothrottle modes, and radio altitude and decision height. An EADI is used in conjunction with an EHSI. *See* EHSI.

Early ETOPS. ETOPS-type design approval obtained without gaining non-ETOPS service experience on the ETOPS-certified candidate airplane-engine combination.

early warning radar (defense radar). Long-range radar that scans the sky in all directions to detect enemy aircraft and/or missiles. Detection and warning occur early enough to allow fighters to intercept and destroy the threat before it reaches its target.

earplug (hearing protector). A device made of rubber or some type of soft plastic worn in the ear canal to prevent loud noises damaging the delicate mechanism in the ear. Earplugs or other types of hearing protectors must be worn when working on most jet aircraft flight lines to prevent hearing loss.

earth (electrical connection). Earth is the term used in the United Kingdom for the electrical reference called "ground" in the United States.

earth ground (electrical equipment). An electrical connection to a metal cold-water pipe or metal rod driven into the ground. The neutral conductor in a three-wire, single-phase electrical installation normally connects to earth ground.

earth induction compass (navigation instrument). A form of navigation instrument which gets its directional reference from lines of magnetic flux of the earth cutting across the windings of a flux valve mounted in the aircraft.

The output of the flux valve is used to drive the pointer of the radio magnetic indicator (RMI) or some other type of direction indicator.

earth's magnetic field. The magnetic lines of flux that leave the north magnetic pole and travel over the surface of the earth and re-enter it at the south magnetic pole.

EARTS (enroute automated radar tracking system). An automated radar and radar beacon tracking system. It functions much the same as terminal ARTS IIIA, except that it is capable of employing both short-range and long-range radars, it uses full digital radar displays, and has a fail-safe design.

Easy-Out (hand tool). The registered trade name for a type of screw extractor (a tool used to remove broken screws or studs from their holes). An Easy-Out is made of hardened steel and has a tapered, left-hand spiral. A hole is drilled in the broken shank of the screw, and the Easy-Out is screwed into it by turning it to the left. The spiral wedges tightly into the broken screw and allows the Easy-Out to unscrew it from its hole.

ECAM (electronic centralized aircraft monitor). An electronic instrument system that monitors the functions of the entire aircraft and displays the information on two color multifunction displays in the aircraft cockpit. The left-hand display shows the status of the systems, and the right-hand display shows diagrams and additional information about the system shown on the left-hand display.

eccentric. Two or more circular objects turning in the same plane, but having different centers.

eccentric bushing (airplane rigging component). A special bushing used between the rear spar of certain cantilever airplane wings and the wing attachment fitting on the fuselage. The portion of the bushing that fits through the hole in the spar is slightly offset from that which passes through the holes in the fitting. By rotating the bushing, the rear spar may be moved up or down to adjust the root incidence of the wing.

eccentric cam. A circular cam mounted on a shaft, with its center different from the center of the shaft. As the shaft rotates about its axis, the outside of the eccentric rises and falls, changing rotary motion into linear motion.

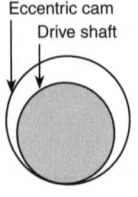

Eccentric cam
Drive shaft

eccentric cam

ECCM (electronic counter-countermeasures). Tactics used in military aircraft to reduce the effectiveness of the countermeasures used by the enemy against electronic countermeasures.

echo (radar meteorology). An image formed on a radarscope by energy reflected or scattered from a target.

ECM (electronic countermeasures). Tactics used in military aircraft to evade or deceive enemy radar. Chaff, made of strips of metal foil or metalized glass fibers, is released to form a large radar return to decoy the enemy radar away from the true target.

Electromagnetic radiation over a wide band of frequencies can prevent the enemy receiving radio transmissions. This form of ECM is called jamming.

economizer system (fuel metering system). The system in a carburetor or fuel injection system that meters additional fuel to the engine when the throttle is wide open. This additional fuel removes some of the heat from the cylinders when the engine is producing maximum power.

Economizer systems, also called power-enrichment systems, allow the engine to operate with an economical fuel-air mixture for all conditions except full power.

E-core (electric transformer core). The core of a transformer on which the windings, or coils, are mounted. The core is made of thin sheets (laminations) of soft iron or silicon steel cut in the shape of the letter E. The coils are placed over the legs of the core, and the opening is closed with strips of the same material cut in the shape of the letter I.

eddy (meteorology). A local irregularity of wind in a larger scale wind flow. Small-scale eddies produce turbulent conditions.

eddy current (induced electrical current). Current induced in the core of a transformer or the armature core of a motor or generator by current flowing in the winding. Eddy currents cause a power loss and are minimized by making the core of thin soft-iron laminations insulated from each other by a thin coat of varnish. Eddy currents can also be induced in a conductor by a moving or nonuniform magnetic field.

eddy current damping. Decreasing the amplitude of oscillations by the interaction of magnetic fields. In the case of a vertical-card magnetic compass, flux from the oscillating permanent magnet produces eddy currents in a damping disk or cup. The magnetic flux produced by the eddy currents opposes the flux from the permanent magnet and decreases the oscillations.

eddy current inspection (nondestructive inspection method). A form of nondestructive inspection used to locate faults in a metal part. Eddy currents are induced into the part being inspected and also into a similar part known to be sound. The presence of a defect is indicated by a difference in the amount of current needed to induce the eddy current in the two parts.

eddy current losses (electrical machinery). The loss of electrical power caused by eddy currents induced into the cores of transformers and the armatures of generators and motors. This lost power produces heat.

edge distance (sheet metal measurement). The distance from the center of a bolt hole or rivet hole to the edge of the metal sheet.

edge-grain wood. Wood that has been sawed from the tree in such a way that the edges of its grain are visible in the wide part of the plank. Edge-grain wood is also called quarter-sawed wood.

edge thickness (sheet metal measurement). The thickness of the edge of a sheet of material.

EDM (electric-discharge machining). A method of machining complex contours in a piece of metal by allowing a controlled electric arc to erode, or eat away, the metal. Electric-discharge machining (EDM) is used to form the dies used for certain types of plastic molding.

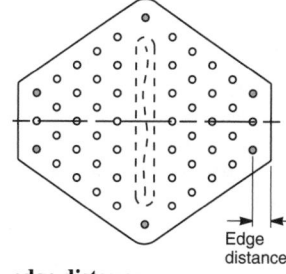

edge distance

eductor. A form of jet pump used to pick up one liquid and mix it with another. Eductors are used in some aircraft fuel systems to remove fuel from a vent-drain tank and return it to the main tank. Fuel from the boost pump flowing through the eductor produces a low pressure that pulls fuel from the vent-drain tank and carries it back into the main tank.

EEC (electronic engine control). An electronic fuel control for a gas turbine engine. The EEC senses the power-lever angle (PLA), engine RPM, bleed valve, and variable stator vane position, and the various engine pressures and temperatures. It meters the correct amount of fuel to the nozzles for all flight conditions to prevent turbine overspeed and overtemperature.

EFAS. *See* enroute flight advisory service.

EFC. *See* expect further clearance.

EFD. *See* electronic flight display.

effect, law of (in learning process). Thorndike's principle of learning that says the learning effect is strengthened when accompanied by a pleasant or satisfying feeling, and that learning is weakened when associated with an unpleasant feeling.

effective value (AC electricity). The value of sine wave alternating current needed to produce the same amount of heat as this value of direct current. The effective value of sine wave AC is 0.707 time its peak value. This means that AC having a peak value of one amp will produce as much heat as $1/\sqrt{2}$, or 0.707 amp of direct current.

Effective value, also called root mean square, or rms, value of alternating current is found by: (1) squaring all the instantaneous values of the current or voltage in one alternation; then (2) averaging these values; and then (3) finding the square root of this average. Most AC voltmeters are calibrated to show the effective value of the voltage they measure.

effective voltage. A measure of AC voltage that is 0.707 times the maximum instantaneous voltage. It is also called rms (root mean square) voltage.

efficiency. A measure of the effectiveness of a system or device. Efficiency is found by dividing the output of the device by its input, and it is usually expressed as a percentage. If the output of a device is exactly the same as its input, the device has an efficiency of 100%. If its output is only one half of its input, its efficiency is 50%.

effort arm. The distance on a lever between the fulcrum and the point of application of the force or weight.

EFIS (electronic flight instrument system). A complete electronic flight instrumentation system that includes the EICAS (engine indicating and crew alerting system) and the ECAM (electronic centralized monitoring) system. *See* EICAS and ECAM.

E-gap angle (magneto measurement). The position of the rotating magnet in a magneto when the breaker points are timed to open. The E-gap (efficiency gap) angle is several degrees of magnet rotation beyond the magnet's neutral position. At this point the magnetic field stress is the greatest, and the change in flux is the greatest, inducing the maximum voltage in the secondary winding.

E-glass (composites). Electrical glass; the borosilicate glass most often used for the glass fibers in conventional reinforced plastics.

EGT (exhaust gas temperature). The temperature of the gases as they leave the cylinder of a reciprocating engine or the turbine of a gas turbine engine.

EGT indicating system (gas turbine engine). An indicating system used with a gas turbine engine to measure the temperature of the exhaust gases as they enter the tail pipe, after passing through the turbine. The turbine inlet, a point just before the exhaust gases enter the turbine, is the most critical location inside a gas turbine engine with regard to temperature. But it is very difficult to measure the temperature at this location.

The temperature of the gases after they have passed through the turbine is easy to measure, and this temperature relates to that of the gases at the turbine inlet. The EGT system consists of a number of thermocouples connected in parallel and arranged around the tail pipe so they measure the average temperature of the exhaust gases.

EGT indicating system (reciprocating engine). A system for measuring the exhaust gas temperature (EGT) of a reciprocating engine to give the pilot an indication of the efficiency with which the fuel-air mixture inside the cylinders is burning. A thermocouple mounted in the exhaust stack just a few inches from the cylinder measures the temperature of the exhaust gases as they leave the cylinder.

The fuel-air mixture that produces the highest EGT contains 15 parts of air to one part of fuel, by weight. The pilot can lean the fuel-air mixture while watching the EGT indicator until the EGT peaks (reaches its highest point and then starts back down). When the temperature peaks, the engine is burning a fuel-air mixture of 0.067 (an air-fuel ratio of 15:1). By enriching the mixture (adding more fuel) until the temperature drops a specified amount, the pilot knows the fuel-air mixture is correct to develop the most efficient operation without danger of detonation.

EGT indicator. A thermocouple-type instrument that shows the temperature of the gas leaving the exhaust valve of a reciprocating engine or in the tail cone of a turbine engine. EGT of a reciprocating engine is measured by a chromel-alumel thermocouple probe inserted into one or more exhaust pipes near the cylinder. EGT of a turbine engine is measured by averaging the output of a series of chromel-alumel thermocouples connected in parallel and arranged around the tail cone just aft of the last stage of turbine.

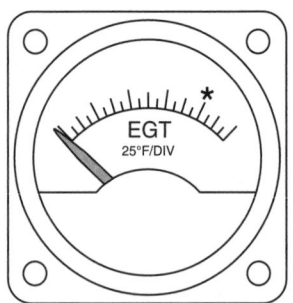

EGT indicator

EHSI (electronic horizontal situation indicator). An electronic flight instrument that displays navigation information on a multicolor display. An EHSI is used in conjunction with an EADI.

The information displayed on an EHSI include: magnetic track, aircraft heading, ground speed, distance to go, VOR course, wind speed and direction, ILS display, and a visual display of the flight plan. *See* EADI.

EICAS (engine indication and crew alerting system). An electronic instrument system for modern turbine-powered aircraft that senses engine parameters and displays them on one of two multicolor display units on the instrument panel.

The EICAS evaluates changes in any of the parameters and, based on programmed limits, warns the flight crew of any changes that could signal an impending problem. Only vital information is shown at all times, but any of the sensed parameters are automatically displayed when they fall outside of their allowable range of operation.

eight-harness satin (composites). A weave for composite fabric that is to be draped over complex shapes with a high degree of smoothness. Each warp thread passes over one fill thread and under seven. *See* satin-weave fabric.

eights around pylons (flight training maneuver). A ground-track maneuver in which the airplane flies a figure-eight pattern, maintaining a constant radius around two points, or pylons. The objective is to learn to correct for wind drift.

einsteinium. A synthetic, radioactive chemical element produced by neutron bombardment of uranium in cyclotrons. Einsteinium whose symbol is Es, and its atomic number is 99 was first discovered in the debris of a nuclear explosion.

ejection seat (military aircraft component). A type of seat installed in a military aircraft that may be shot out of the aircraft with a powder charge in the event of an inflight emergency.

ejector (jet pump). A form of jet pump used to pick up a liquid and move it to another location. Ejectors are used in an aircraft fuel system to assure that the compartment in which the boost pumps are mounted is kept full of fuel. Part of the fuel from the boost pump flowing through the ejector produces a low pressure that pulls fuel from the main tank and forces it into the boost-pump sump area.

elasticity. The ability of a material to be elongated, or stretched, by pulling on it, and to return to its original size and configuration after the force causing the elongation is removed.

elastic limit (material strength). The maximum amount of tensile load, in pounds per square inch, a material is able to withstand without being permanently deformed. Any time a material is loaded to less than its elastic limit and the load is released, the material will return to its original size and configuration. When loaded beyond its elastic limit, it will deform and not return to its original condition.

Elastic Stop Nut. The registered trade name of a special type of self-locking nut. A collar of fiber whose inside diameter is slightly smaller than the diameter of the threads on which the nut is screwed is swaged into a recess in the end of the nut. Forcing the threads into the fiber prevents vibration loosening the nut.

elastomer. A material, such as synthetic rubber, that can be stretched at room temperature to at least twice its original length. When it is released, it will return to its original size and shape.

elastomeric bearing. A type of bearing used for oscillating loads where complete rotation is not needed. An elastomeric bearing is made of alternate layers of an elastomer, a rubber-like material, and metal, bonded together. Elastomeric bearings can be designed to take radial loads, axial loads, or torsional loads.

E-layer (atmosphere). An ionized layer of the atmosphere existing at an altitude of between 60 and 75 miles (100 to 120 kilometers) above the earth. Radio waves bounce off the E-layer. The effect of the E-layer is most noticeable in the daytime, and to a lesser degree at night.

elbow (fluid line fitting). A type of fitting used to join two pieces of tubing at an angle of 90°.

Elcon connector (battery connector). The registered trade name for a special type of connector used to connect a high-output battery to an aircraft electrical system. The connector is held tightly to the two battery terminals by pressure exerted by a hand screw.

electret. A dielectric (insulating) material that is permanently polarized. Electret is made by heating a material such as barium titanate ceramic or carnauba wax and holding it in a strong electric field as it cools. The electric field surrounding electret is much like the magnetic field surrounding a piece of magnetized steel.

electret microphone. An acoustic transducer, a device that changes sound pressure into an electrical signal. A diaphragm made of a thin foil of electret is placed next to a metal-coated backplate. Sound pressure picked up by the microphone vibrates the diaphragm and, as the electric field cuts across the metal plate, it generates a voltage. The waveform of this voltage is a copy of the waveform of the sound that vibrated the diaphragm to produce it.

electrical bonding. The process of connecting the structural parts of an aircraft together with conductors to keep them all at the same electrical potential. Bonding prevents sparks caused by static electricity from jumping between the parts and causing radio interference.

electrical bus (electrical system component). A distribution point in an electrical system to which the battery and generator are connected, and from which the electrical loads receive their power.

electrical charge. Electrical energy stored on the surface of an object. This charge is produced by the accumulation of electrons in one area and a shortage, or deficiency, of electrons in another area.

electrical diagram. A line drawing using schematic symbols to show the relationship of all the components in an electrical system.

electrical energy. Energy possessed by a material or device because of an unequal distribution of electrons. Chemical energy, mechanical energy, heat energy, and light energy can all be converted into electrical energy.

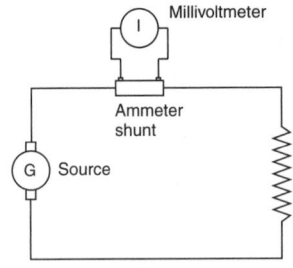

electrical diagram

electrical generator. A machine that converts mechanical energy into electrical energy. Mechanical energy is used to move conductors through a magnetic field, and voltage is induced into them as they cut across the lines of magnetic flux.

electrical insulator. A material that offers a large amount of opposition to the flow of electrons. Glass, most types of plastic, ceramics, and a vacuum are examples of electrical insulators.

electrically suspended gyroscope. A gyroscope whose rotor is supported in either an electrostatic or electromagnetic field, rather than in conventional bearings. The gyroscope spins with an absolute minimum of friction while it is supported in either of these fields.

electrical potential. The electrical force caused by a deficiency of electrons in one location and an excess of electrons in another. Electrical potential is measured in volts.

electrical resistance welding. A method of welding thin sheets of metal by clamping them tightly together and passing electric current through them. The heat produced by the current melts the metal, and the

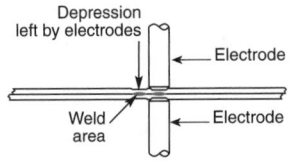

electrical resistance welding

pressure forces the molten metal from the two sheets together. Spot welding and seam welding are both types of electrical resistance welding.

electrical shield. A housing made of a conductive material such as copper or aluminum that encloses an electrical circuit. The shield picks up stray electrical energy radiated from the circuit and carries it to ground so it cannot interfere with any other electrical or electronic equipment.

The ignition systems used on almost all aircraft reciprocating engines are electrically shielded by enclosing the entire system in a conductive covering that is electrically grounded to the engine.

electrical short (electrical system fault). An unwanted connection that provides a low-resistance path across an electrical circuit. Electrons flow through the short to ground without passing through the load.

electrical steel. An alloy of low-carbon steel that contains up to about 5% silicon. Electrical steel in the form of thin laminations is used for the cores of transformers and armatures of electrical motors and generators.

electrical strain gage. A device used to measure the amount of physical strain (deformation caused by a stress) in a piece of material. A strain gage is made of very fine wire mounted between two pieces of tissue paper, about the size of a postage stamp. The strain gage is bonded (glued) to the material in which the strain is to be measured, and the two ends of the wire are connected into a sensitive resistance-measuring bridge circuit.

When the material on which the strain gage is mounted is under a tensile stress, the wire in the strain gage stretches—it becomes longer and thinner, and its resistance increases. When the material is under a compressive stress, the wire becomes shorter and larger in diameter, and its resistance decreases. The change in resistance is proportional to the amount of strain in the material, and the amount of strain is proportional to the amount of stress causing it.

electrical strength. The maximum amount of electrical pressure (voltage) that can be placed across an insulator before it breaks down and allows electrons to flow through it.

electrical symbols. Standardized graphic symbols that have been agreed upon as representing various components in electrical schematic diagrams.

electrical zero (synchro system). A specific position of the rotor inside the stator of a synchro (a remotely controlled position indicating system). Electrical zero is used as a reference position for meshing gears and installing indicator pointers.

electric drill motor. A series-wound, alternating-current motor used to drive a chuck which holds a twist drill. The motor is geared down so that it furnishes a high torque to the chuck.

electric inertia starter (reciprocating engine starter). A type of starter for large aircraft reciprocating engines. A series-wound electric motor spins a heavy flywheel to store energy. When the flywheel is spinning at a high speed, the motor is disconnected, and the flywheel is connected to the engine crankshaft through a series of reduction gears and a slip clutch.

electricity. A force caused by electrons moving from one atom to another. A deficiency of electrons is called a positive charge, and an excess of electrons is called a negative charge. The difference in electrical charges causes electrical pressure. When electrical pressure forces electrons to move in a conductor, heat is produced, and a magnetic field surrounds the conductor.

electroacoustic transducer. A device that changes either variations in sound pressure into variations of electrical pressure (voltage), or variations in voltage into variations of sound pressure. Microphones and speakers are both examples of electroacoustic transducers.

electrochemical series. A list of metals arranged according to their electrode potential. Metals highest in the list give up electrons to all metals below them. When corrosion occurs, the metal highest in the series will be the one that is corroded, or eaten away.

The electrochemical series is also known as the electromotive series.

1. Magnesium
2. Zinc
3. Cadmium
4. 2075-T6 aluminum alloy
5. 2024-T3 aluminum alloy
6. Mild Steel
7. Lead
8. Tin
9. Copper
10. Stainless steel
11. Silver
12. Nickel
13. Chromium
14. Gold

electrochemistry. The aspects of chemistry that deal with electron potentials within the different chemical elements.

electrode. A conductor, or part of an electrical component through which electrons flow to or from an external circuit. The carbon rod and zinc can are electrodes in a carbon-zinc battery. The emitter, base, and collector are the electrodes in a bipolar transistor.

electrode potential. A voltage existing within an alloy of metals or in any type of electrochemical cell. The electrode potential is caused by chemical differences of the materials involved, and it causes electrons to flow within the material any time there is a conductive path between the different materials.

electrodynamic damping (electrical meter damping). The decreasing amplitude of pointer oscillation of an electrical meter, caused by the generation of a voltage in the moving coil as it oscillates back and forth in the field of a permanent magnet. Energy used to produce current in the moving coil decreases the energy causing the oscillations.

electrodynamics. The aspect of electricity that deals with electrons in motion. This includes the effects of magnetism and induction. The other aspect of electricity is electrostatics, which deals with electrical charges caused by electrons that are stationary.

electrogalvanizing. The process of electrolytically depositing a layer of zinc on sheets of steel.

electrohydraulic. Hydraulic control which is electrically actuated.

electroluminescence. The emission of light caused by the application of a strong electrical field to certain materials. It is not caused by the heating effect of the electricity.

electrolysis. The process in which the chemical composition of a material is changed by passing electrical current through it. When DC electricity passes through water, the water breaks down into its two chemical constituents, hydrogen and oxygen. Hydrogen bubbles form on the negative electrode, and oxygen bubbles form on the positive electrode.

electrolyte. A chemical solution, either a liquid or a gas, that conducts electrical current by releasing ions (unbalanced atoms) that unite with oppositely charged ions on the electrodes. Negative ions, atoms having an excess of electrons, move through the electrolyte to the positive electrode. Positive ions, atoms having a deficiency of electrons, move to the negative electrode.

A lead-acid battery uses an electrolyte of sulfuric acid and water. When the battery is being charged, negative sulfate ions from the plates join positive hydrogen ions in the water and form sulfuric acid. When the battery discharges, negative sulfate ions leave the electrolyte and go to both plates. Positive hydrogen ions left from the sulfuric acid join negative oxygen ions from the positive plate and form water.

The condition of charge of a lead-acid battery can be determined by measuring the specific gravity of the electrolyte with a hydrometer. The specific gravity shows the amount of acid in the electrolyte.

electrolytic capacitor. A capacitor that uses metal foil for the electrodes and an extremely thin film of metallic oxide, a nonconductor, as the dielectric. Two sheets of metal foil separated by a piece of porous paper impregnated with an electrolyte are the plates. The dielectric is an oxide film formed on the surface of one of the plates.

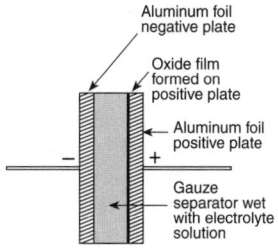

electrolytic capacitor

The capacity of a capacitor is inversely proportional to the thickness of the dielectric—the thinner the dielectric, the greater the capacity. And, since the oxide film is extremely thin, an electrolytic capacitor has a large capacity for its physical size.

One major disadvantage of an electrolytic capacitor is its low DC working voltage compared with that of other types of capacitors. The thin oxide film can be easily punctured by a high voltage. An oxide film on a piece of metal acts as a rectifier. Electrons can pass from the metal through the film into the electrolyte. But they cannot pass from the electrolyte through the film to the metal.

Because of this rectifying action, electrolytic capacitors must never be used in AC circuits, and they must be installed in a DC circuit with their anode, the terminal marked with a plus sign, connected to the positive voltage.

electrolytic dissociation. The reduction of certain chemical compounds into their composite elements by passing electricity through them. When electrical current passes through water, it dissociates into hydrogen and oxygen.

electromagnet. A magnet produced by electrical current flowing through a coil of wire. The coil of an electromagnet is normally wound around a core of soft iron. This soft iron has an extremely low retentivity so it releases the material being picked up as soon as current stops flowing through the coil.

electromagnetic emission (electronic communications). The radiation of electromagnetic energy for communications. There are six types of amplitude-modulated emission classified by international agreement. These are:

A0. Unmodulated continuous-wave
A1. Telegraphy, or pure continuous wave
A2. Modulated telegraphy
A3. Telephony
A4. Facsimile
A5. Television

electromagnetic induction. The transfer of electrical energy from one conductor to another that is not electrically connected. This transfer is done by a changing magnetic field produced by current flowing in one conductor cutting across the other conductor. As the lines of flux expand and collapse across the conductor, a voltage is induced in it.

electromagnetic interference. *See* EMI.

electromagnetic radiation. One method by which energy is transmitted from one location to another. Radio and television signals, for example, reach us by electromagnetic radiation. When electric and magnetic fields oscillate back and forth at a high enough frequency, they extend out into space in the form of waves. These waves may be absorbed (received) at some distant point. Very little energy transmitted by electromagnetic radiation is lost, or used up, by the space between the point from which it is sent and the point at which it is received. Energy from the sun reaches the earth by electromagnetic radiation, and only a very small amount of this energy is lost in the empty space between the sun and the earth.

electromagnetic vibrator. A device that interrupts a flow of direct current and changes it into pulsating DC. An electromagnetic vibrator consists of an electrical relay whose contacts are held closed by a spring and opened by the pull of the electromagnetic coil. The contacts and coil are connected in series across a source of direct current.

When current flows through the coil, the magnetic field pulls the contacts open and stops the current. When the current stops flowing, the spring closes the contacts and current begins to flow again. The contacts vibrate between open and closed as long as the vibrator is connected to a source of direct current.

electromagnetic waves. Vibrations of electric and magnetic fields that move at the speed of light. Electromagnetic waves radiate out at right angles to the direction of their wave motion.

electromagnetism. The magnetic field surrounding a current-carrying conductor. The strength of the field is determined by the amount of current flowing in the conductor.

electromechanical frequency meter. A type of instrument that uses the resonant frequency of a vibrating metal reed to measure the frequency of alternating current.

Metal reeds having different lengths are vibrated by electromagnetism produced by the alternating current. The reed whose resonant frequency is the same as that of the AC will vibrate with the greatest amplitude, and the resonant frequency of this reed is shown on a calibrated scale on the face of the instrument. An electromechanical frequency meter is also called a vibrating-reed frequency meter.

electromotive force. *See* EMF.

electron. The negatively charged part of an atom of which all matter is made. Electrons circle around the nucleus of an atom in orbits, or shells, and electrons of certain atoms can be forced out of their outer shell and caused to move from one atom to another to produce a flow called electron current.

electron beam. A thin stream of electrons all moving in the same direction under the influence of electrical or magnetic fields. Electron beams may be focused and directed by these fields. When an electron beam strikes certain phosphors, electroluminescence is produced and the phosphor glows. This is the way the image is formed on a television screen and on the face of a cathode-ray tube.

electron-beam welding. A method of welding metal by the heat produced when a high-speed stream of electrons strikes the metal. Electron-beam welding is used in applications in which the heat must be concentrated at the point the weld is being made.

electron current. The movement of electrons through a circuit from the negative terminal of the power source to its positive terminal.

Electron current moves in the direction opposite the direction of the arrowheads in the symbol for a semiconductor diode. These symbols are drawn to follow conventional current, an imaginary flow considered to be from positive to negative. Electron current is the actual movement of electrons.

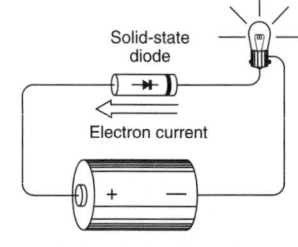

electron current

electron drift. The relatively slow movement of individual electrons through a conductor. Electron drift is not the same as electron flow, or electron current.

electron gun. An electron-emitting cathode in a cathode-ray tube. Grids associated with the cathode accelerate, control, and focus the beam of electrons to form a spot of the desired size on the face of the tube.

electronic. Relating to the application of the flow of free electrons through semiconductor devices and across a vacuum.

electronic emission. The discharge of electrons from a material. Electrons are held tightly in their atoms, but certain kinds of outside energy can cause them to move from one atom to another. When heat energy causes electrons to leave, the emission is called thermal emission. When the electrons are moved out of their atoms by light energy, the emission is called photoemission.

electronic flight bag (EFB). An electronic display system intended primarily for cockpit or cabin use that can display a variety of aviation data or perform basic calculations (e.g., performance data, fuel calculations, etc.). Some of these functions were traditionally accomplished using paper references or were based on data provided to the flight crew by an airline's "flight dispatch" function.

electronic flight display (EFD). For the purpose of standardization, any flight instrument display that uses an LCD or other image-producing system, e.g., cathode ray tube (CRT), etc.

electronic flight instruments. Flight instruments that use electronic devices to prepare and/or present information such as airspeed, attitude, altitude, and position.

electronic horizontal situation indicator (EHSI). An electronically generated HSI display, either CRT or LCD type, indicating all standard HSI functions on a video screen instead of using mechanical components.

electronic leak detector (air conditioning system servicing tool). An electronic oscillator whose frequency changes if refrigerant gas is picked up in its sensor tube. The sensor tube is held below a suspected leak, and if any refrigerant is leaking, the sound produced by the oscillator will change from a low tone to a high-pitched squeal. Electronic leak detectors can detect a leak as small as a few parts of refrigerant gas in a million parts of air.

electronic learning (e-learning). Any type of education that involves an electronic component such as the Internet, a network, a stand-alone computer, CD/DVDs, video conferencing, websites, or e-mail in its delivery.

electronic oscillator. An electronic circuit that converts DC electricity into AC electricity.

electronics. The study and use of the movement of free electrons. In electricity, we normally think of the movement of electrons only through conductors; but in electronics, we also consider the movement of electrons through materials that are not always conductors. Electrons can be caused to flow through a vacuum and through semiconductor materials such as silicon and germanium.

electronic voltmeter. A special type of electronic instrument used to measure voltage. Electronic voltmeters use electron tubes or solid-state components, such as field-effect transistors (FET), to amplify the voltage being measured before it is read by the indicating instrument. An electronic voltmeter has a much higher input impedance than a nonelectronic meter, and it can measure AC voltages having a wider range of frequencies.

electron volt (eV). The unit of energy that is acquired by an electron when it passes through a potential difference of one volt in a vacuum. One electron volt is equal to approximately $1.602 \cdot 10^{-19}$ volt.

electron-pair bond. Bonding of the atoms within a crystal by the sharing of valence electrons.

electron spin. The rotation of an electron about its own axis. Electron spin is not the same as the rotation of an electron about the nucleus of its atom.

electron transit time. The length of time required for an electron to travel between two points in an electronic device. While this time appears to be extremely short, it is an important factor in designing high-speed electronic computers.

electron tube. The correct term for an electronic component which normally goes by the name of vacuum tube or valve. An electron tube is a form of electron control valve. Electron tubes have a heated cathode that emits electrons and an anode, or plate, connected to a high positive voltage that attracts the electrons. The flow of electrons between the cathode and the anode is controlled by the voltage on one or one more grids placed between the cathode and anode. The cathode and its heater, the grids, and the anode, are all housed inside a glass or metal envelope from which all the oxygen has been removed. The envelope may be left with a vacuum, or it may be filled with an inert gas.

electroplating. A method of coating one kind of metal with another. Cadmium is often plated on steel to make it corrosion resistant, and chromium can be plated on steel to make it hard and wear resistant. The steel is connected to the negative terminal of a direct current power supply, the cadmium or chromium is connected to the positive terminal, and both metals are immersed in an electrolyte.

Ionized atoms of cadmium or chromium in the electrolyte are deposited on the steel, and these atoms are replaced from the cadmium or chromium electrode.

electropolishing. The production of a smooth finish on a piece of metal by submerging it in a suitable electrolyte and making it the anode in an electrolytic process. The surface roughness is electrolytically removed.

electrostatic charge. An electrical charge that can exist on the plates of a capacitor or on an insulated object. A negative electrostatic charge is caused by an accumulation of electrons, and a positive charge is caused by a lack of electrons.

electrostatic deflection. A method of controlling the position of a beam of electrons on the face of a cathode-ray tube. The beam of electrons that forms the trace on a cathode-ray tube may be deflected to the correct position on the screen by electrostatic charges on plates placed above and below the beam, and on each side of the beam.

If, for example, the top plate is given a positive charge, and the bottom plate a negative charge, the electrons in the beam (all electrons are negative) will deflect away from the lower plate toward the upper plate. The beam will deflect upward.

electrostatic energy. Energy stored by an electric stress in the dielectric of a capacitor when two opposing electrical charges act across the dielectric. When a battery is connected across the two plates of a capacitor, electrons are pulled from one plate and forced into the other. When all the electrons that can be moved by the battery have been moved, the capacitor is charged and no more current flows. The battery can be disconnected, but electron pressure still remains between the plates. This voltage across the dielectric (the voltage on the plates) is caused by electrostatic energy.

electrostatic field. The space between two bodies that have opposite electrical charges. Lines of electrostatic force are considered to leave the negatively charged body and enter the body having the positive charge. The strength of the electrostatic field is determined by the number of electrons that make up the charge, and by the square of the distance separating the bodies.

electrostatics. The aspect of electricity that deals with electrical charges caused by electrons that are stationary, or not moving. Electrodynamics is the aspect of electricity that deals with electrons in motion.

element of threat (in learning process). A perception factor describing how a person is unlikely to easily comprehend an event if feeling threatened since most of the person's effort is focused on the threat itself.

elevator (airplane control). The horizontal, movable control surface in the tail section, or empennage, of an airplane. The elevator is hinged to the trailing edge of the fixed horizontal stabilizer. Moving the elevator up or down, by fore-and-aft movement of the control yoke or stick, changes the aerodynamic force produced by the horizontal tail surface.

elevator downspring. A spring in the elevator control system that produces a mechanical force that tries to lower the elevator, and thus the nose of the airplane. In normal flight this spring force is overcome by the aerodynamic force from the elevator trim tab. But in slow flight with an aft CG position, the trim tab loses its effectiveness and the downspring lowers the nose to prevent a stall.

elevator illusion (physiology). The feeling of being in a climb or descent, caused by the kind of abrupt vertical accelerations that result from up or downdrafts.

elevator trim stall (flight condition). A stall that occurs when full power is applied to an airplane configured with excessive nose-up trim. Positive control of the airplane is lost resulting in a stall. This type of stall usually occurs during a go-around procedure from a normal landing approach or a simulated forced landing approach, or immediately after takeoff.

elevon (airplane control surface). A combination elevator and aileron. Elevons are installed on the trailing edge of a delta wing or a flying wing airplane. Fore-and-aft movement of the control yoke causes the elevons to operate together. This causes the airplane to rotate about its lateral, or pitch, axis.

Movement of the stick or control wheel to the right or left causes the elevons to move differentially. The left elevon moves up and the right elevon moves down. Differential movement of the elevons causes the airplane to rotate about its longitudinal, or roll, axis.

ellipse. A figure formed when a plane cuts across the axis of a cylinder at an angle other than a right angle.

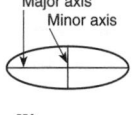

ellipse

ellipsoid of revolution (mathematics). A figure that is generated when an ellipse is rotated about one of its axes.

ELT (emergency locator transmitter). A small self-contained radio transmitter carried in an aircraft. If the aircraft crashes, the force of the impact automatically sets the transmitter into operation, transmitting a series of down-sweeping tones on the two emergency frequencies of 121.5 and 243.0 megahertz. Searchers who receive the signal from the ELT are able to locate the wreckage by using radio direction finding equipment.

emergency (air traffic control). A distress or an urgency condition.

emergency descent (flight maneuver). A maneuver for descending as rapidly as possible to a lower altitude or to the ground for an emergency landing. The need for this maneuver may result from an uncontrollable fire, a sudden loss of cabin pressurization, or any other situation demanding an immediate and rapid descent.

emergency frequency. A frequency used by aircraft in distress to gain ATC assistance. 121.5 MHz is an international emergency frequency guarded by flight service stations and some military and civil aircraft.

emery paper. An abrasive paper made by bonding a layer of emery dust (pulverized corundum or aluminum oxide) to one side of a sheet of flexible paper. Emery paper is used to polish or clean metal surfaces.

emery wheel. An abrasive wheel made by molding a mixture of emery (pulverized corundum or aluminum oxide) and a suitable binder into the form of a wheel. Emery wheels mounted on an arbor and turned by an electric motor can be used to grind metal and shape or sharpen steel tools.

EMF (electromotive force). The force that causes electrons to move from one atom to another within an electrical circuit. An EMF is the difference in the electrical pressure, or potential, that exists between two points, and can be produced by converting mechanical, chemical, light, or heat energy into electrical energy. The basic unit of electromotive force is the volt.

EMI (electromagnetic interference). Interference of radio reception by the radiation of electromagnetic energy from a piece of electronic equipment, or from conductors carrying high-frequency alternating current.

emitter (bipolar transistor component). The electrode in a bipolar transistor (PNP or NPN transistor) that compares with the cathode in an electron tube. In the symbol for a bipolar transistor, the emitter is the electrode with the arrowhead.

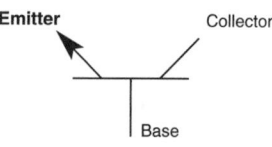

emitter

empennage (airplane structure). The tail section of an airplane. The empennage stabilizes the airplane in flight and causes it to rotate about its vertical and lateral axes. An inverted cruciform empennage consists of a fixed vertical fin with a movable rudder attached to its trailing edge, and a fixed horizontal stabilizer with a movable elevator hinged to its trailing edge on both sides of the fuselage.

Another type of empennage, the V-tail, has only two fixed and two movable surfaces, arranged in the shape of the letter V. These two surfaces stabilize the airplane and rotate it about its two axes in the same way as the three fixed and three movable surfaces.

emphasis error (instrument flying). An error caused by paying too much attention to a particular instrument during the cross-check, instead of relying on a combination of instruments necessary for attitude and performance information.

empty-field myopia (physiology). Induced nearsightedness associated with flying at night, in instrument meteorological conditions and/or reduced visibility. With nothing to focus on, the eyes automatically focus on a point just slightly ahead of the airplane.

empty weight (aircraft specification). The weight of the airframe, engines, and all items of operating equipment that have fixed locations and are permanently installed in the aircraft. Empty weight includes optional and special equipment, fixed ballast, full reservoirs of hydraulic fluid, engine lubricating oil, and the unusable fuel, but does not include occupants, baggage, or cargo.

empty-weight center of gravity (aircraft specification). The center of gravity of an aircraft when it contains only the items specified in aircraft empty weight.

empty-weight center of gravity range (aircraft specifications). The distance between the allowable forward and aft empty-weight CG limits. When EWCG limits are given for an aircraft, and the empty-weight CG falls within these limits, it is not possible to legally load the aircraft so that its operational CG will fall outside its operational CG limits.

EMSAW (enroute minimum safe altitude warning). A function of the NAS Stage A enroute computer. This function aids the controller by alerting him when a tracked aircraft is below, or is predicted to go below, a predetermined minimum IFR altitude.

emulsion. A suspension of small globules of one material in another, when the two materials will not mix. Oil and water will not mix, but they can be formed into an emulsion. An emulsion will separate into its components when it is allowed to sit.

emulsion-type cleaner. A chemical cleaner used to loosen dirt, grease, oxides, and carbon deposits from the surface of an aircraft. Solvents are mixed with water and a petroleum product, such as naphtha. An emulsifying agent is used to form an emulsion with these products that do not normally mix.

The cleaner is sprayed on the dirty surface and allowed to remain long enough to penetrate the surface contamination and reach the metal. Then it is washed off with hot water or steam.

EM wave. *See* electromagnetic wave.

enamel. A type of finishing material that flows out to form a smooth surface. Enamel is normally made of a pigment suspended in some form of resin. When the resin hardens, it leaves a smooth, protective surface that may have either a glossy or a velvet finish. Polyurethane enamel is an exceptionally durable, chemical-resistant finish used on modern aircraft.

encapsulate. To completely cover, or encase, something. An electrical component is encapsulated when it is completely covered with, or embedded in, a plastic material.

enclosed relay (electrical component). An electrical relay in which both the coil and the contacts are enclosed in a protective housing. Enclosed relays are used in aircraft for the main battery contactor and for the starter relay.

encode. To convert analog information, such as the degrees of rotation of a shaft, into a digital code.

encoding altimeter (aircraft flight instrument). A special type of pressure altimeter used to send a signal to the air traffic controller on the ground, showing the pressure altitude the aircraft is flying. Pressure altitude is the altitude shown on the altimeter when its barometric scale is adjusted to the standard sea level pressure of 29.92 inches of mercury, or 1013.2 millibars.

The altimeter provides a signal showing the altitude in one-hundred-foot increments to the radar beacon transponder. The transponder sends this information in coded form to the ground radar, where it shows up on the radar screen in numbers beside the radar return from the aircraft.

endothermic action. A chemical action in which heat energy is absorbed.

endurance (aircraft specification). The length of time an aircraft can remain in the air. The power produced by the engines and the flight conditions can be regulated to give the aircraft the greatest speed, the greatest range, or the greatest endurance.

end voltage (battery servicing term). The cell voltage of an aircraft battery agreed upon by the battery manufacturing industry to indicate when a battery is discharged. A closed-circuit voltage of one volt per cell is the end voltage of a nickel-cadmium aircraft battery. When the cell voltage gets down to one volt, the battery is considered to be discharged.

energizing brake. A brake that uses the momentum of the aircraft to increase its effectiveness by wedging the shoe tightly against the brake drum. Energizing brakes are also called servo brakes. A single-servo brake is energizing only when moving in the forward direction, and a duo-servo brake is energizing when the aircraft is moving either forward or backward.

energy. The capacity for performing work. Something that changes, or tries to change, matter. There are two basic types of energy: potential, or stored energy, and kinetic energy, associated with motion. Common forms of energy are: chemical, electrical, light, and heat. We are able to convert energy between these different forms, but can neither create nor destroy energy.

engaged. A system mode or function that is actively performing its function.

engine analyzer (trouble detection instrument). A portable or permanently installed instrument used to detect, locate, and identify engine operating abnormalities such as those caused by a faulty ignition system, detonation, sticking valves, poor fuel injection, etc.

engine-driven air pump. A vane-type positive-displacement air pump that is mounted on the accessory section of an engine and driven by the accessory gears.

engineered performance standards. *See* EPS.

engine gage unit (reciprocating engine instrument). A single panel-mounted instrument case that contains three engine instruments. An oil pressure gage, oil temperature gage, and fuel pressure gage are mounted in the same case so the pilot can see at a glance these vital engine conditions. Some engine gage units have a cylinder head temperature gage in place of the fuel pressure gage.

engine logbook (aircraft record). A record book in which all the operating time, maintenance that has been performed, and the inspection status of an aircraft engine are recorded.

engine mount. The part of an aircraft structure designed to support the engine. Vibration isolators are normally included as part of the engine mount assembly.

engine nacelle (aircraft structure). The compartment on a multiengine aircraft in which the engine is mounted. The engine nacelle for a turbojet engine that mounts on the fuselage or below the wing is often called an engine pod.

engine oil sump (engine component). The low point in an aircraft engine where lubricating oil collects and is stored or transferred to an external oil tank. A removable sump attached to the bottom of the crankcase of a reciprocating engine is often called an oil pan.

engine performance. The way an engine operates with regard to such parameters as the engine power settings, fuel and oil consumption, and manifold pressure.

engine pressure ratio. *See* EPR.

engine ratings. FAA-established information included in the engine type certificate data sheet of ratings and limitations based on the specified operating conditions and any other information found necessary for safe operation of the engine.

engine stations (gas turbine engine). A method of identifying various locations in a gas turbine engine for ease of describing pressures and temperatures. Station designations are different for different types of turbine engines, and stations can be subdivided using decimal numbers. The following station designations are used for a typical dual-rotor turbofan engine:

Station	Location
AM	Ambient conditions ahead of the engine
1	Tip of nose cone
2	Fan or low-pressure compressor inlet
3	High-pressure compressor inlet
4	Combustor inlet
5	High-pressure turbine inlet
6	Low-pressure turbine inlet
7	Turbine discharge
8	Turbine duct discharge
9	Exhaust nozzle discharge

engine trimming (gas turbine engine operation). A maintenance procedure in which a turbine engine fuel control is adjusted. The idling speed and the high-end performance are adjusted to cause the engine to produce the required EGT or EPR at the RPM specified by the engine manufacturer.

enhanced flight visibility (EFV) *(14 CFR Part 1).* The average forward horizontal distance, from the cockpit of an aircraft in flight, at which prominent topographical objects may be clearly distinguished and identified by day or night by a pilot using an enhanced flight vision system. *See* enhanced flight vision system.

enhanced flight vision system (EFVS) *(14 CFR Part 1).* An electronic means to display the forward external scene topography (the natural or man-made features of a place or region especially in a way to show their relative positions and elevation) through the use of imaging sensors, such as a forward looking infrared, millimeter wave radiometry, millimeter wave radar, low light level image intensifying.

Enhanced Traffic Management System (ETMS). An automation system developed for the FAA that tracks, anticipates, and manages the flow of air traffic throughout U.S.

airspace. It integrates real-time flight and weather data from multiple sources, presenting information graphically in a highly adaptable format.

enrich (fuel metering term). To make a fuel-air mixture richer. The fuel-air mixture ratio may be adjusted to vary the amount of fuel mixed with the air used in the engine. When the amount of fuel metered into the engine is increased without increasing the air, the mixture is enriched.

enroute air traffic control services. Air traffic control service provided for aircraft operating on IFR flight plans between departure and terminal areas. This service is normally provided by the air route traffic control centers (ARTCC).

enroute automated radar tracking system. *See* EARTS.

enroute automation system (EAS) (air traffic control). The complex integrated environment consisting of situation display systems, surveillance systems and flight data processing, remote devices, decision support tools, and the related communications equipment that form the heart of the automated IFR air traffic control system. The EAS interfaces with automated terminal systems and is used in the control of en route IFR aircraft.

enroute descent (flight operations). Descent from enroute cruising altitude which takes place along the route of flight.

enroute facilities ring. A circle depicted in the plan view of IAP charts to designate NAVAIDs, fixes, and intersections that are part of the enroute low altitude airway structure.

enroute flight advisory service (EFAS). This service, also known as flight watch, is designed to provide, upon pilot request, timely weather information pertaining to the type of flight, intended route of flight, and altitude.

enroute high-altitude charts. Aeronautical charts for enroute instrument navigation (IFR) in the high-altitude stratum. Information includes the portrayal of jet routes, identification and frequencies of radio aids, selected airports, distances, time zones, special use airspace, and related information.

enroute low-altitude charts. Aeronautical charts for enroute instrument navigation (IFR) in the low-altitude stratum. Information includes the portrayal of airways, limits of controlled airspace, position identification and frequencies of radio aids, selected airports, minimum en route and minimum obstruction clearance altitudes, airway distances, reporting points, restricted areas, and related data.

enroute minimum safe altitude warning. *See* EMSAW.

enroute obstacle clearance areas. Obstacle clearance areas for enroute planning are identified as primary, secondary, and turning areas, designed to provide obstacle clearance route protection width for airways and routes.

enroute spacing program (ESP) (air traffic control). An ATC computer program designed to fit departing traffic into a densely packed overhead system, while maintaining the required in-trail spacing of aircraft in enroute flight.

enroute transition. (1) Conventional STARs/SIDs. The portion of a SID/STAR that connects to one or more en route airway/jet route. (2) RNAV STARs/SIDs. The portion of a STAR preceding the common route or point, or for a SID the portion following, that is coded for a specific en route fix, airway or jet route.

entrained air. Air trapped in a liquid, forming an emulsion with it. When lubricating oil passes through an engine, it picks up large quantities of air, and this entrained air increases the volume of the oil, making it less effective as a lubricant.

Entrained air must be removed from the oil by a deaerator system, an air-oil separator, before it is sent back through the engine.

entrained water. Water held in suspension in the fuel carried in an aircraft fuel tank. Entrained water does not cause many problems on airplanes powered with reciprocating engines, but it does cause serious problems with turbine-powered aircraft. This is because turbine-powered aircraft fly at much higher altitude, where the air is so cold the entrained water condenses out and freezes on the fuel filters. This ice shuts off the flow of fuel to the engines. The fuel used in many turbine-powered aircraft is treated with an anti-icing agent which mixes with and lowers the freezing point of the water condensed from the fuel in the tanks.

entropy. A measure of the capacity of a thermodynamic system to undergo a spontaneous change. Entropy varies with the change in the ratio of the increment of heat taken in to the absolute temperature at which it is absorbed.

envelope (balloon component). The fabric portion of a balloon that contains hot air or gas.

envelope method of covering an airplane. A method of covering an airplane by slipping a machine-sewed fabric envelope over the structure. After the envelope is slipped over the structure, the opening is hand-sewed closed, or the fabric is otherwise fastened to the structure. The fabric covering for the wings is laced to each of the ribs, and the fabric is shrunk.

environmental control systems (aircraft system). The systems in an aircraft that make it possible for the human occupants to function at high altitude. Environmental control systems include supplemental oxygen, air conditioning, heaters, and pressurization systems.

environmental stress cracking (ESC). The premature initiation of cracking and embrittlement of a plastic due to the simultaneous action of stress and strain and contact with specific fluids.

Eonnex (aircraft fabric). The registered trade name for an aircraft fabric woven from polyester fibers.

EP (extreme pressure) lubricant. A lubricant that reacts with iron to form iron chlorides, sulfides, or phosphides on the surface of a steel part. These compounds reduce wear and damage to surfaces that are in heavy rubbing contact. EP lubricants are specially suited for lubricating gear trains.

epicyclic gear train. An arrangement of gears in which one or more gears travel around the circumference of another. An example of an epicyclic gear train is the planetary gear arrangement used to reduce the speed of the propeller shaft of a geared aircraft engine.

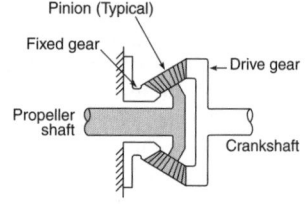

epicyclic gear train

One system of planetary gears uses a spur-type sun gear mounted rigidly in the nose section of the engine, and a ring gear with internal teeth driven by the crankshaft. The propeller shaft is mounted on a spider having several arms. Each arm of the spider carries a planetary gear that meshes with and rides between the sun gear and the ring gear.

As the planetary gears travel around the sun gear, they turn the spider and the propeller shaft, in the same direction as the crankshaft, but at a slower speed.

epitaxial layer (transistor construction). A layer of semiconductor material whose crystalline orientation is the same as that of the substrate on which it is grown.

epoxy. A flexible, thermosetting polyether resin that has wide application as a matrix for composite materials and as an adhesive that bonds many different types of materials. Epoxy is noted for its durability and chemical resistance.

epoxy primer. A two-component finishing material that is mixed and sprayed over a steel or aluminum alloy aircraft structure. Epoxy primer provides a tough, chemical-resistant covering for the metal to protect it from corrosion and to provide a good bond for a topcoat system. Epoxy primers are not used in many of the high-volume production lines because of the time needed for them to cure properly.

epoxy resin. A flexible, thermosetting resin used as a chemical-resistant coating. Epoxy resins can be reinforced with fiberglass or filaments of boron or carbon to make high-strength structural materials.

EPR (engine pressure ratio). The pressure measurement used as an indication of the amount of thrust being developed by an axial-flow gas turbine engine. EPR is the ratio between the compressor inlet total pressure and the turbine discharge total pressure.

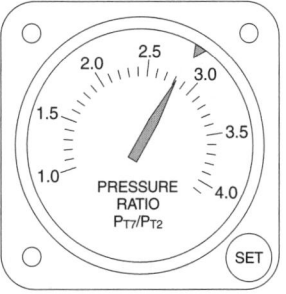

EPR rated engine (gas turbine engine rating). A gas turbine engine whose rated thrust is expressed in terms related to its engine pressure ratio (EPR).

EPS (engineered performance standards) (air traffic control). A mathematically derived runway capacity standard. EPS's are calculated for each airport on an individual basis and reflect that airport's aircraft mix, operating procedures, runway layout, and specific weather conditions. EPS's do not give consideration to staffing, experience levels, equipment outages, and in-trail restrictions as does the airport acceptance rate (AAR).

EPR indicator

equalization (battery servicing operation). A procedure used with nickel-cadmium batteries to bring all the cells to exactly the same state of charge. The battery is completely discharged and all the cells are shorted and allowed to stand for several hours with the shorting straps in place. Then the battery is given a constant-current charge to restore 140% of its ampere-hour capacity.

equalizer circuit (aircraft generator system). A circuit used in a multiengine generator system that causes the generators to share the electrical load equally. A low-resistance shunt, called an equalizing resistor, is installed between each generator and ground so all the current produced by the generator flows through it. The voltage drop across the equalizing resistors is sensed by the voltage regulators to control the output of the generators.

When one generator carries more than its share of the load, the voltage drop across its equalizing resistor is greater than that across the resistors of the other generators. The voltage regulators sense this difference and decrease the voltage of the generator carrying the greater part of the load, and in this way force the other generators to carry their share.

equalizing resistor. A large resistor in the ground circuit of a heavy-duty aircraft generator through which all of the generator output current flows. The voltage drop across this resistor is used to produce the current in the paralleling circuit that forces the generators to share the electrical load equally.

equator (balloon and LTA term). The widest diameter of the envelope.

equilibrium. A condition that exists within a body when the sum of the moments of all of the forces acting on the body is equal to zero. In aerodynamics, equilibrium is when all opposing forces acting on an aircraft are balanced (steady, unaccelerated flight conditions).

equipment ground (electrical equipment). A connection inside a piece of electrical equipment between a metal part that does not carry current and the earth ground. Equipment ground is carried out of the equipment through a green wire connected to the round pin in the standard three-pin electrical plug. The function of equipment ground is to reduce the possibility of electrical shock.

equipment list (aircraft documentation). A list of all the equipment approved for installation on a particular aircraft. An equipment list itemizing the approved equipment installed on the aircraft must be kept current and with the aircraft records.

equipment suffix. *See* aircraft equipment suffix.

equi-time point. The point on the route of flight where the flight time to each of two selected airports, considering wind, is equal.

equivalent airspeed. Calibrated airspeed corrected for errors caused by the compressibility of the air inside the pitot tube. Calibrated airspeed is the airspeed shown on the airspeed indicator, corrected for errors caused by the instrument installation.

   14 CFR Part 1: "The calibrated airspeed of an aircraft corrected for adiabatic compressible flow for the particular altitude. Equivalent airspeed is equal to calibrated airspeed in standard atmosphere at sea level."

equivalent circuit (electronics). The result of the reduction of a complex circuit into a simpler form. Any complex circuit consisting of impedances can be redrawn (reduced) to a basic equivalent circuit containing a power source and a single impedance representing total impedance.

equivalent flat-plate area (aerodynamics). The area of a flat surface perpendicular to the direction of motion of the body that produces the same opposition to the airflow as the streamlined body.

equivalent resistance (electrical circuit). The resistance of a single resistor that is the same as that of several resistors connected in a circuit.

erbium. A soft, malleable, silvery, rare-earth chemical element. Erbium's symbol is Er, its atomic number is 68, and its atomic weight is 167.26. Erbium is used in metallurgy and nuclear research.

erosion. The process in which a material is worn away by a scraping or abrading action.

error chain. A series of mistakes that may lead to an accident or incident. Two basic principles generally associated with the creation of an error chain are: (1) one bad decision often leads to another; and (2) as a string of bad decisions grows, it reduces the number of subsequent alternatives for continued safe flight. Aeronautical decision making is intended to break the error chain before it results in an accident or incident.

escape velocity. The speed a flight vehicle must reach in order to escape from the gravitational field of the earth. The escape velocity on the earth is about seven miles per second. Because of the smaller gravitational field on Mars, a vehicle leaving Mars would have an escape velocity of only slightly more than three miles per second.

ESFC (equivalent specific fuel consumption). A measure of the efficiency of a turboprop engine. It is the number of pounds of fuel burned per hour to produce one equivalent shaft horsepower (ESHP) and is found by dividing the fuel flow, in pounds per hour, by the ESHP.

ESHP (equivalent shaft horsepower). A measure of the power produced by a turboprop engine. ESHP is the sum of the shaft horsepower delivered to the propeller and the thrust horsepower produced by the exhaust gas. The approximate amount of thrust horsepower can be found by dividing the static thrust by 2.6.

established (air traffic control). To be stable or fixed on a route, route segment, altitude, heading, etc.

estimated ceiling (meteorology). A ceiling classification applied when the ceiling height has been estimated by the observer. The term *estimated* also applies when the ceiling has been determined by some other method, but because of the specified limits of time, distance, or precipitation conditions, a more descriptive classification cannot be applied.

estimated elapsed time (ICAO). The estimated time required to proceed from one significant point to another.

estimated off-block time (ICAO). The estimated time at which the aircraft will commence movement associated with departure.

Estimated Position Error (EPE). A measure of the current estimated navigational performance. Also referred to as Actual Navigation Performance (ANP).

estimated time en route. *See* ETE.

estimated time of arrival. *See* ETA.

ETA (estimated time of arrival) (air traffic control). The time the flight is estimated to arrive at the gate, for scheduled operators, or at the actual runway for nonscheduled operators.

etch. To chemically eat away part of a material. The surface of clad aluminum alloy sheet must be etched to microscopically roughen it before it is painted so the primer can bond tightly to it.

ETE (estimated time en route) (air traffic control). The estimated flying time from departure point to destination (lift-off to touchdown).

ethanol. Alcohol made from cereal grains such as corn.

ether. A volatile, highly flammable liquid that may be used to prime the cylinders of an aircraft engine for starting under extremely cold conditions.

ethylene dibromide. A colorless poisonous liquid, $BrCH_2CH_2Br$, added to aviation gasoline to minimize lead fouling of the spark plugs. Tetraethyl lead improves the antidetonation characteristics of aviation gasoline, but it leaves lead deposits inside the spark plugs. Ethylene dibromide combines with the lead before it solidifies and changes it into volatile lead bromides, which pass out with the exhaust gases.

ethylene glycol. A form of alcohol used as a coolant for liquid-cooled aircraft engines and as an anti-icing agent. It is also used in automobile engines as a permanent antifreeze.

ETOPS. *See* extended operations (ETOPS).

ETOPS significant system. An airplane system, including the propulsion system, that if fails or malfunctions could adversely affect the safety of an ETOPS flight, or the continued safe flight and landing of an airplane during an ETOPS diversion. Each ETOPS significant system is either an ETOPS group 1 significant system or an ETOPS group 2 significant system. An ETOPS group 1 significant system: (1) has fail-safe characteristics directly linked to the degree of redundancy provided by the number of engines on the airplane; (2) is a system, the failure or malfunction of which could result in an in-flight shutdown, loss of thrust control, or other power loss; (3) contributes significantly to the safety of an ETOPS diversion by providing additional redundancy for any system power source lost as a result of an inoperative engine; and (4) is essential for prolonged operation of an airplane at engine inoperative altitudes. An ETOPS group 2 significant system is an ETOPS significant system that is not an ETOPS group 1 significant system.

europium. A silvery-white, soft, malleable, rare-earth chemical element. Europium's symbol is Eu, its atomic number is 63, and its atomic weight is 151.96. Europium is used as a dopant for laser technology and as an absorber of neutrons in nuclear research.

eutectic. An alloy or solution whose composition gives it the lowest possible melting point. Solder, for example, is an alloy of lead and tin. Lead has a melting point of 327°C, and tin melts at 232°C. When tin and lead are combined in an alloy of 63 parts of tin and 37 parts lead, the alloy is eutectic, and it melts at a temperature of 188°C.

evacuated bellows (pressure instrument reference). A stack of metal bellows used as a reference for measuring atmospheric pressure. These bellows, made of circularly corrugated bronze disks, have nearly all the air pumped out of them.

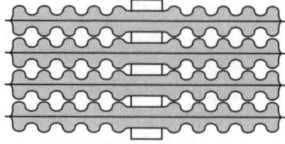

evacuated bellows

The pressure of the atmosphere compresses the bellows against their inherent spring action, and changes in atmospheric pressure can be measured by measuring the changes in the thickness of the bellows stack.

evacuation (refrigeration system servicing). A procedure in servicing vapor-cycle cooling systems in which a vacuum pump is used to remove all of the air from the system. Evacuation removes all traces of water vapor that could condense out, freeze, and block the system.

evaporation. The physical change of state of a material from a liquid into a gas.

evaporative cooling. *See* steam cooling.

evaporator (air condition system component). The component in a vapor-cycle air conditioning system in which the refrigerant absorbs heat from the aircraft cabin. The refrigerant in the evaporator coils is a liquid in the form of tiny droplets. Warm air from the cabin blows through the fins on the coils, and heat from this air is absorbed by the refrigerant, changing the droplets of liquid into a vapor. The heat used to make this change is taken from the air and as a result the air passing through the evaporator is cooled.

exceedance condition. A condition in which a parameter sensed by the EICAS exceeds the limits for which it is programmed. *See* EICAS.

exciter (electrical generator). A device used to generate DC electricity to produce electro-magnetism in the field of an alternator or generator.

exclusive OR gate (logic gate). A digital logic device having two or more inputs and only one output. There is a logic high on the output when one and only one input has a logic high.

exclusive OR gate

"Execute missed approach" (air traffic control instruction). An instruction issued to a pilot on an instrument approach, directing him to continue inbound to the missed-approach point and then to execute the missed-approach procedure, as described on the Instrument Approach Procedure Chart or as previously assigned by ATC.

exercise, law of (in learning process). Thorndike's principle of learning that emphasizes exercise as having a strengthening effect on learning; practice is necessary for understanding and remembering what has been learned. Exercise is most effective and meaningful when the skill is learned within the context of a real-world application of the concept.

exerciser jack (aircraft landing gear maintenance tool). A hydraulic jack placed under the landing gear shock absorber while it is being filled with oil. The jack moves the piston in and out of the shock absorber cylinder while it is being filled, to work all the air out of the oil.

exfoliation corrosion. An advanced form of intergranular corrosion that forms in extruded metal parts. Exfoliation corrosion causes the metal to separate along its layer-like grain structure.

exhaust. The rear opening of a turbine engine exhaust duct. The nozzle acts as an orifice, the size of which determines the density and velocity of the gases as they emerge from the engine.

exhaust back pressure (reciprocating engine parameter). The pressure in the exhaust system of a reciprocating engine that opposes the flow of exhaust gases as they are forced out of the cylinders when the exhaust valve is open.

exhaust cone (turbine engine component). The fixed conical fairing centered in the exhaust stream immediately aft of the last-stage turbine wheel. It prevents turbulence and prevents the hot gases from circulating over the rear face of the turbine wheel.

exhaust contrails. A visible trail of condensed water vapor (a cloud), formed in the cold atmosphere by the addition of water vapor from aircraft engine exhaust gases.

E

exhaust gas analyzer (reciprocating engine maintenance tool). An instrument used to analyze the chemical composition of the exhaust gas released by a reciprocating engine. One type of analyzer measures the conductivity of the exhaust gas and indicates the ratio of fuel and air in the mixture that produced the exhaust gas. An exhaust gas temperature (EGT) system is not the same as an exhaust gas analyzer.

exhaust gas temperature. *See* EGT.

exhaust gas temperature indicating system (gas turbine engine). *See* EGT indicating system (gas turbine engine).

exhaust gas temperature indicating system (reciprocating engine). *See* EGT indicating system (reciprocating engine).

exhaust manifold (reciprocating engine component). The arrangement of exhaust pipes that attach to the cylinders of an aircraft engine to collect the exhaust gases and carry them outside of the engine cowling.

exhaust nozzle (gas turbine engine component). The opening in the tail pipe of a gas turbine engine through which the exhaust gases leave the engine. The area of the exhaust nozzle is critical, as it affects the back pressure on the turbine, and this in turn affects the engine RPM, the exhaust gas temperature, and the thrust the engine produces. Some gas turbine engines use variable-area exhaust nozzles.

exhaust stacks (reciprocating engine component). Short pipes that carry the exhaust gases from the cylinder into the surrounding air. Also called exhaust pipes.

exhaust stroke (reciprocating engine). The stroke in the operating cycle of a reciprocating engine in which the piston is moving away from the crankshaft and the exhaust valve is open. Burned gases are forced out of the cylinder during the exhaust stroke.

exhaust valve (reciprocating engine component). The valve in a reciprocating engine cylinder through which exhaust gases leave.

exit guide vanes (gas turbine engine component). Stationary airfoils at the discharge end of an axial-flow compressor. As the air passes through the compressor, the rotating vanes give the air a swirling, or rotational, motion. The exit guide vanes straighten it out so the air leaves the compressor in an axial direction, parallel to the length of the engine.

exitation (electrical generator). Current supplied to the field coils of a generator to create the magnetic field used to produce a flow of electrons.

exothermic action. A chemical action in which heat energy is released.

expanded plastic. A plastic resin whose volume has been increased by bubbles of gas which are generated when the constituents of the plastic are mixed. Expanded plastic is also known as foamed plastic.

expanded-scale meter (electrical meter). A current-measuring analog electrical indicator whose needle deflection is not uniform over its entire scale. The amount of deflection for a given input is increased for certain ranges of indication. Expanded-scale meters are used when small changes in the upper limit of the value being measured are important.

expanded service volume (air traffic control). When ATC or a procedures specialist requires the use of a NAVAID beyond the limitations specified for standard service volume, an ESV may be established. *See* standard service volume.

expander-tube brake (aircraft brake). A type of lightweight, nonenergizing, hydraulically operated aircraft brake. A synthetic rubber tube is installed around the brake housing mounted on the landing gear axle, and blocks of brake lining material are held pressed against the expander tube with flat metal springs. The brake drum, mounted inside the wheel, rotates around the linings.

When the brake pedal is depressed, hydraulic fluid is forced into the tube. The tube expands and forces the brake blocks against the rotating brake drum. This force applies enough friction to the drum to slow the rotation of the wheel.

expansion reamer (metal-cutting tool). A precision cutting tool used to smooth the inside of a drilled hole and enlarge it to an accurately specified dimension. The diameter of the hole cut by an expansion reamer can be increased a few thousandths of an inch by adjusting a wedge inside the blades to move them outward.

expansion turbine (air-cycle air conditioning system component). A small turbine in an air-cycle cooling system that extracts energy from compressed air as it drives a compressor. Bleed air containing a large amount of energy is taken from the turbine-engine compressor. This hot air passes through a primary heat exchanger where it gives up some of its energy. It is then taken into a compressor driven by the expansion turbine. Here its pressure and temperature are both increased. This air then passes through a secondary heat exchanger where it gives up more of its energy and its temperature is dropped. From here it flows into the expansion turbine that drives the compressor, using up much of its remaining energy.

After leaving the turbine, it expands into the air conditioning ducts. Having lost most of its energy through the heat exchangers and the expansion turbine, the air is now cold.

expansion wave (high-speed aerodynamics). The change in pressure and velocity of a supersonic flow of air as it passes over a surface, which drops away from the flow. As the surface drops away, the air tries to follow it. In changing its direction, the air speeds up to a higher supersonic velocity, and its static pressure decreases.

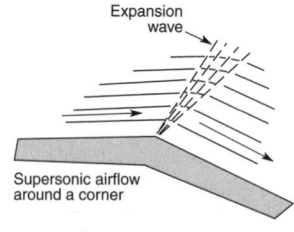

Supersonic airflow around a corner

expansion wave

There is no change in the total amount of energy as the air passes through an expansion wave, and so there is no noise as there is when air passes through a shock wave.

"Expect (altitude) at (time) or (fix)" (air traffic control). A portion of an instrument departure clearance, to provide a pilot with an altitude to be used in the event of two-way radio communication failure.

expect departure clearance time (EDCT) (air traffic control). The runway release time assigned to an aircraft in a traffic management program and shown on the flight progress strip as an EDCT. *See* ground delay program.

"Expect departure clearance (time)" (air traffic control). The time an operator can expect a gate release. This is used in the Fuel Advisory Departure (FAD) program.

"Expect further clearance (time)" (air traffic control). The time a pilot can expect to receive clearance beyond a clearance limit.

"Expect further clearances via (airways, routes, or fixes)" (air traffic control). This phrase is used by air traffic controllers to inform a pilot of the routing he may expect if any part of the route beyond a short range clearance limit differs from that filed.

"Expedite" (air traffic control). A warning used by air traffic controllers when prompt compliance is required in order to avoid the development of an imminent situation.

E

expendable parts (maintenance supply). Fast-moving consumable items, usually with a unit cost of $50.00 or less. Expendable parts include nuts, bolts, gaskets, abrasives, and glues.

expendable weight (aircraft operation). The part of an aircraft load that is used in flight. The fuel carried in an aircraft is an expendable weight. It is used up as the flight progresses.

experimental category. A type of special airworthiness certificate issued to operate an aircraft that does not have a type certificate or does not conform to its type certificate and is in a condition for safe operation. This certificate is also issued to operate a primary category kit-built aircraft assembled without the supervision or quality control of the production certificate holder. Special airworthiness certificates in the experimental category may be issued for various purposes including research and development; showing compliance with regulations; crew training; exhibition; air racing; market surveys or demonstrations; and operating amateur-built, kit-built, or light-sport aircraft. An aircraft with a special airworthiness certificate in the experimental category may not be used for compensation or hire.

experimental license (aircraft certification). A license issued by the Federal Aviation Administration that allows an aircraft to be flown for the purpose of proving its design and construction in order to qualify for a regular license. The FAA puts certain restrictions on experimental aircraft. These restrictions apply to the crew allowed to fly in the aircraft and where it can be flown.

experimental light-sport aircraft (ELSA). An aircraft issued an experimental certificate under 14 CFR Part 21.

explode. To make a violent change in the chemical composition of a material. Usually an explosion is accompanied by a loud noise and the release of light and heat. When a mixture of gasoline fumes and air in a closed container is ignited, it explodes. In the explosion, the gasoline and air change into carbon dioxide and water and produce a loud noise, light, and heat.

exploded-view drawing. A drawing showing all of the parts spread out to show their relative location in the component.

explosion-proof motor (electric motor). An electric motor totally enclosed in a housing. Explosive gases cannot get into the housing to explode, and sparks produced inside the housing cannot ignite gases on the outside.

explosion-proof switch (electrical component). A special electrical switch enclosed in a housing that prevents the sparks which occur when the contacts separate from igniting any explosive gases that may be on the outside of the housing.

explosive atmosphere. Atmosphere (air) which holds explosive vapors or certain types of powder that can be ignited. Dust and particles of powdered metal are easily ignited, and atmosphere which contains these contaminants can become dangerously explosive.

explosive bolt. A special bolt with an explosive charge built into it. This is a remotely operated charge that causes the bolt to fail and release its hold. Explosive bolts are used to allow stages of rockets to separate, and to release droppable fuel tanks from an airplane.

explosive decompression (aircraft operation). A condition that can occur in a pressurized aircraft when part of the structure fails and releases the pressure inside the cabin at an explosive rate.

explosive rivet (special aircraft fastener). A type of blind rivet with a hollow end, filled with an explosive charge, and sealed with a plastic cap. The rivet is slipped into the prepared hole, and a rivet set containing an electric heater is held against the head of the rivet. The heat ignites the explosive charge, and the end of the rivet swells out, clamping the sheets tightly together.

exponent (mathematics). A number written above and to the right of a mathematical expression, called the base. An exponent tells the number of times the base is to be used as a factor (a part of the problem). In the expression 4^2, the exponent is 2. The base 4 is to be used two times; it is to be multiplied by itself. $4^2 = 4 \cdot 4 = 16$.

extend. To move something to the limit of its travel. When a retractable landing gear is moved from its retracted position to a position that allows the airplane to land on it, the landing gear has been extended—it has been moved to the extent of its travel.

extended operations (ETOPS). An airplane flight operation, other than an all-cargo operation in an airplane with more than two engines, during which a portion of the flight is conducted beyond the engines' time threshold identified in 14 CFR Part 121 or Part 135, an operation guideline that is determined using an approved one-engine-inoperative cruise speed under standard atmospheric conditions in still air.

extended over-water operation. *14 CFR Part 1:*
"(1) With respect to aircraft other than helicopters, an operation over water at a horizontal distance of more than 50 nautical miles from the nearest shoreline; and
(2) With respect to helicopters, an operation over water at a horizontal distance of more than 50 nautical miles from the nearest shoreline and more than 50 nautical miles from an offshore heliport structure."

extension lines (mechanical drawing). Thin lines on an aircraft drawing that extend out from an object to show the location from which dimensions are taken. Dimension lines show the distance between the extension lines.

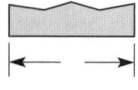

extension lines

exterior angle. The angle between one side of a polygon and an extension to an adjacent side. The sum of the exterior angles of any polygon regardless of the number of sides, is always 360°.

external combustion engine. A form of heat engine in which the fuel is burned to release its heat energy outside the engine. A steam engine is a form of external combustion engine. Fuel is burned outside the engine to heat water and change it into steam. The steam is then fed into the cylinder or through the turbine of the engine where it expands and performs work.

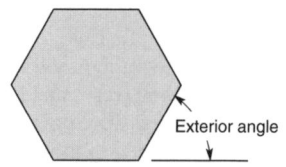

exterior angle

external load. A load carried by a helicopter outside of the aircraft itself. External loads are normally carried by slings suspended below the helicopter. *14 CFR Part 1:* "A load that is carried, or extends, outside the aircraft fuselage."

external-load attaching. *14 CFR Part 1:* "The structural components used to attach an external load to an aircraft, including external-load containers, the backup structure at the attachment points, and any quick-release device used to jettison the external load."

external tooth lock washer. A form of thin, spring-steel lock washer. The inside of the washer fits around the bolt or screw, and the outside is notched to form teeth, each of which is twisted. When the nut is screwed down tight against the washer, the twisted teeth flatten out, and their spring action holds the nut tight against the threads of the screw and prevents its backing off. An external-tooth lock washer is also called a Type-B shakeproof lock washer.

extra-flexible control cable. Aircraft control cable made up of seven strands of wire with each strand containing 19 individual wires. Extra-flexible cable, normally called 7 by 19 cable, is used in all locations where the cable must pass over a pulley.

extra-flexible control cable

extratropical low (meteorology). Any cyclone that is not a tropical cyclone. It usually refers to the migratory frontal cyclones found in the middle or high latitudes.

extreme pressure (EP) lubricant. A lubricant that reacts with iron to form iron chlorides, sulfides, or phosphides on the surface of a steel part. These compounds reduce wear and damage to surfaces in heavy rubbing contact. EP lubricants are specially suited for lubricating gear trains.

extrusion. A form of structural material made by passing metal heated to its plastic state through specially shaped dies. The extruding process is used to make long, continuous lengths of such structural shapes as angles and channels.

eye (meteorology). The roughly circular area of calm or relatively light winds and comparatively fair weather at the center of a well-developed tropical cyclone. Wall clouds mark the outer boundary of the eye.

eyebolt. A bolt having a blade-like head with a hole in it. An eyebolt is used to attach a cable to a structure.

eyebolt

eyebrow lights. Small lights placed in a shield over the two top corners of an instrument installed in an aircraft instrument panel. Eyebrow lights illuminate the dial of the instrument, but do not shine in the pilot's eyes.

eye wall (meteorology). The region immediately outside of the eye of a tropical cyclone; an area of vigorous tall/deep clouds, heavy rainfall, and the strongest observed winds.

Foxtrot

FA. *See* area forecast.

FAA (Federal Aviation Administration). The division within the Department of Transportation of the United States government that has the responsibility of promoting safety in the air, by both regulation and education. Aircraft and the airmen who operate them are licensed by the FAA, and the FAA maintains the airways along which the aircraft fly. The FAA is headed by a civilian, the Administrator of Federal Aviation.

FAA Form 337. The *Major Repair and Alteration* form that must be completed when a major repair or major alteration has been completed on an FAA-certificated aircraft or engine.

FAA Inspector. An FAA employee who can administer practical and proficiency tests and issue pilot certificates.

FAA Knowledge Exam. The exam administered by the FAA as a prerequisite for airman certification, confirming the required knowledge needed before progressing to the practical exam. Pilot and mechanic applicants are required to pass the FAA Knowledge Exam before they can be issued FAA certificates or ratings.

FAASTeam. *See* Federal Aviation Administration Safety Team.

FAASTeam program manager. The person who designs, implements, and evaluates the FAASTeam within the FAA flight standards district office (FSDO) area of responsibility.

FAASTeam representative. A volunteer within the aviation community who shares technical expertise and professional knowledge as a part of the FAASTeam.

fabric. A cloth produced by interlacing two yarns at right angles to each other.

fabricate. A term that means to build or to manufacture something.

fabrication. The process of assembling parts to make a complete unit or structure.

fabric punch test (aircraft maintenance test). A maintenance test performed by a technician to determine the condition of the fabric used to cover an aircraft. A special spring-loaded punch with a sharp point is pressed into the fabric, and the amount of force needed to cause the punch to make a specific size hole in the fabric is measured. The stronger the fabric, the more force is needed to make the hole.

A color-coded scale is used to indicate the condition of the fabric. Green means the fabric is good, yellow means that the strength of the fabric is questionable, and red means that the fabric is too dead to pass an airworthiness test. A fabric punch test is not an absolute indication of the strength of the fabric, but it is quick and accurate enough to determine the basic condition of the fabric.

fabric punch tester. A device used to determine the relative strength of the fabric covering on an aircraft. The tester can give a general idea of the strength without cutting a sample of the fabric or removing the finish.

fabric repair (aircraft repair). A repair to the fabric used to cover an aircraft. A repair, when properly done, must restore the strength and tautness the fabric had before it was damaged.

fabric test (balloon fabric). A test of the envelope fabric for tensile strength, tear strength, and/or porosity. Fabric tests are specified by each balloon manufacturer.

face (propeller nomenclature). The surface of a propeller that strikes the air first as the propeller rotates. The face of a propeller corresponds to the bottom of an airplane wing.

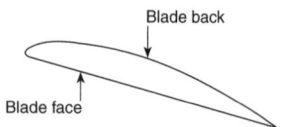

propeller blade face

faceplate (lathe component). A heavy steel disk mounted on and turned by the headstock of a metalworking lathe. Work to be turned on the lathe can be mounted on the faceplate.

face shield. A transparent shield used to cover your face when working with anything that could get into your eyes or with anything that could damage your face. Face shields are made of transparent plastic and are attached to a band worn around your head. Face shields should be worn when working with metal-cutting tools that are likely to throw chips, when using a grinding wheel, and when servicing an air conditioning system with liquid refrigerant.

face-to-face bearing installation. Ball bearings designed to take thrust loads that are applied to a shaft in both directions. Two sets of bearings are installed on the shaft in such a way that one set carries thrust loads in one direction, and the other set carries the loads in the opposite direction.

fading (radio reception). The decrease in strength of a received radio signal.

facsimile. A means of communications in which a graphic document is scanned and the image converted into digital data which is transmitted over telephone lines or by radio waves. At the receiving end, the data is processed in a printer, and a paper copy of the original document is produced.

factor of safety (aircraft structure). The ratio of the breaking strength of a structure to the maximum load that will ever be applied to it. If a structure is designed to carry a load of 2,000 pounds, but there will never be a load of more than 1,000 pounds applied to it, the structure has a factor of safety of two.

FAD (fuel advisory departure). Procedures used to minimize engine running time for aircraft destined for an airport experiencing prolonged arrival delays.

FADEC (full-authority digital electronic control). A digital electronic fuel control for a gas turbine engine that functions during all engine operations, hence "full-authority." It includes the electronic engine control (*See* EEC), functions with the flight management computer (*See* FMC), and schedules the fuel to the nozzles in such a way that prevents overshooting of power changes and over-temperature conditions. FADEC furnishes information to the engine instrument and crew alerting system (*See* EICAS).

fading of brakes. The decrease in the amount of braking action that occurs with some types of brakes that are applied for a long period of time. True fading occurs with overheated drum-type brakes. As the drum is heated, it expands in a bell-mouthed fashion. This decreases the amount of drum in contact with the brake shoes and decreases the braking action.

A condition similar to brake fading occurs when there is an internal leak in the brake master cylinder. The brakes are applied, but as the pedal is held down, fluid leaks past the piston, and the brakes slowly release.

FAF. *See* final approach fix.

Fahnstock clip (electrical connector). A type of spring clip used to temporarily connect a wire into an electrical circuit. Some batteries have Fahnstock clips for connecting wires to their terminals.

Fahrenheit temperature. Temperature measured on a scale that uses 32° as the point at which pure water freezes, and 212° as the point at which pure water boils under standard atmospheric pressure. There are 180 equal graduations between the freezing and boiling points of water. Absolute zero (the point at which molecular motion stops) is $-460°F$.

faildown. The substitute display or backup instrument mode available if the primary component fails. For example, in some systems the multi-function display (MFD) can substitute for the primary flight display (PFD) if the PFD fails. The PFD information "fails down" to the MFD. In other systems, the substitute for the PFD might be the conventional standby instruments and the standby or secondary navigation CDI.

fail-hardover (automatic flight control malfunction). A type of failure of an automatic flight control system that produces a steady signal which drives the controls to the extreme end of their travel and holds them there. Hardover failure can result in a crash, and to prevent it, automatic flight control systems have some method of releasing or overpowering the control if such a condition occurs.

F

fail-safe control. A type of control that automatically puts the controlled device in a safe condition if the control system should fail.

faired curve. A smooth curve that has no sharp changes in its direction.

fairing. A part of a structure or machine whose primary purpose is to produce a smooth surface or a smooth junction where two surfaces join.

fairlead (aircraft control system). A plastic or wooden guide used to prevent a steel control cable from rubbing against an aircraft structure.

fall wind (meteorology). A cold wind blowing downslope. Fall wind differs from a foehn (*See* foehn) in that the air is initially cold enough to remain relatively cold despite the heating from the compression it received during its descent.

false horizon. Inaccurate visual information for aligning the aircraft caused by various natural and geometric formations that disorient the pilot from the actual horizon.

false lift. *See* uncontrolled lift.

false rib (airplane structural component). A short, partial rib used in a truss-type airplane wing to improve the shape of the leading edge of the airfoil. False ribs, also known as nose ribs, extend back only as far as the front spar.

false spar. A short, partial wing spar behind the rear spar, used to support the aileron hinges.

false start (gas turbine engine operation). A condition in which the fuel-air mixture inside a gas turbine engine ignites and burns, but the RPM does not build up high enough for the engine to continue to run without help from the starter. A false start, also called a hung start, is caused by the starter not turning the engine fast enough for it to start properly.

fan blade shingling (turbofan engine damage). A type of damage in which the midspan shrouds on the fan blades overlap, shingle fashion, rather than touching with face-to-face contact. Fan blade shingling is caused by a sudden stoppage of the fan, or by an overspeed condition.

fan-in (digital electronic circuit). The number of inputs connected to a single digital logic circuit.

fan marker (electronic navigation equipment). A highly directional radio signal transmitted vertically upward from a transmitter located along a navigational radio range. The output of the fan marker is heard only when the aircraft is directly above the transmitter, and this allows the pilot to know his exact location.

fan-out (digital electronic circuit). The number of parallel loads connected to a single logic circuit.

fan pressure ratio (turbofan engine parameter). The ratio of the fan discharge pressure to the fan inlet pressure.

FAP (final approach point) (air traffic control). The point, applicable only to a nonprecision approach with no depicted FAF (such as an on-airport VOR), where the aircraft is established inbound on the final approach course from the procedure turn, and where the final approach descent may be commenced. The final approach point serves as the final approach fix and identifies the beginning of the final approach segment.

FAR (Federal Aviation Regulations). Regulations established by the Federal Aviation Administration (FAA), which govern the operation of aircraft, airways, and airmen. Compliance with FARs is mandatory. When directly referencing individual parts and sections of the FARs, the designation "14 CFR" is used, which stands for "Title 14 of the Code of Federal Regulations."

farad (electrical unit). The basic unit of capacitance. One farad is the amount of capacitance that allows a charge of one coulomb to be stored under a pressure of one volt. The farad is too large for most practical circuits, so the microfarad (one millionth of a farad) and the picofarad (one millionth of a millionth of a farad) are the most generally used values of capacitance.

Faraday's law of electrolysis. The amount of any substance dissolved or deposited in electrolysis is proportional to the total electrical charge passed.

Faraday's law of electromagnetic induction. The electromotive force induced in a circuit by a changing magnetic field is determined by the rate of change of the magnetic flux linking the circuit.

fast file (flight plan filing). A method of filing a flight plan by telephone. The flight plan is tape recorded and transcribed for transmission to the appropriate air traffic control facility.

fatal injury. Any injury that results in death within 30 days of the accident.

fatigue (metal condition). A condition existing in a metal which causes it to lose some of its strength. Fatigue occurs when the metal is subjected to a series of stress reversals, such as happens when the metal is repeatedly bent back and forth.

fatigue crack (metal failure). A crack caused by stress reversals in a piece of metal. Vibration is one of the main sources of the stress reversals that cause fatigue cracks.

fatigue failure (material strength). The tendency of a material to fracture under continued repetition of stress at levels considerably lower than its ultimate static strength.

fatigue limit (material strength). The maximum value of an applied alternating stress which a test piece can withstand indefinitely.

fatigue resistance (metal characteristic). The ability of a material to withstand vibration and repeated stress reversals without damage.

fatigue strength (material strength). The maximum cyclic stress a material can withstand for a given number of cycles before failure occurs.

FATO. *See* Final Approach and Takeoff Area.

fault (electrical circuit defect). Typical faults are: an open circuit (a broken wire), a short circuit (an uninsulated portion of the wire making a connection it should not make), or a grounded circuit (a connection made to ground where there should be no connection).

faying surface (sheet metal structure). The portion of a lap joint in a sheet metal structure where two sheets of metal overlap. Moisture can be trapped in the faying surface, and it can cause corrosion if this area is not adequately protected.

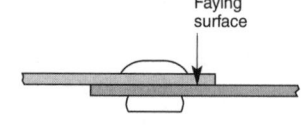

Faying surface

faying surface

FCC (Federal Communications Commission). A governmental board whose responsibility is the regulation of all interstate electrical communications and all foreign electrical communications that originate in the United States. The FCC is made up of seven commissioners appointed by the President of the United States, under the Communications Act of 1934.

FCC (flight control computer). A portion of the automatic flight control system (*see* AFCS) that has inputs from the aircraft control surfaces and the engine controls, and outputs to the engine indicating and crew alerting system (*see* EICAS) and the flight management computer (*see* FMC).

FD. *See* flight director.

FDC NOTAM. A flight data center (FDC) notice to airmen (NOTAM) that is regulatory in nature and published every 28 days in the Notices to Airmen Publication (NTAP) by the United States NOTAM office (USNOF). FDC NOTAMs are considered regulatory because they deal with airspace, airways, instrument approach procedures, and aeronautical charts. *See also* NOTAM.

FDI. *See* Flight Director Indicator.

FDR (flight data recorder). A sealed recording instrument installed in transport aircraft that makes a continuous record of the flight altitude, airspeed, heading, accelerations, and voices and noises heard on the flight deck. The flight recorder, called a "black box," is installed in a fireproof housing and is mounted in the tail of the aircraft where it is least likely to be destroyed in a crash.

feather (helicopter rotor blade movement). Rotation of a helicopter rotor blade about its pitch-change axis.

featheredge. A thin, sharp edge on a piece of material, left as the material is worn away by abrasion.

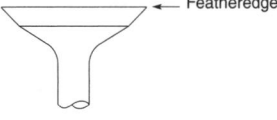

feathering (helicopter rotor blade). The action which changes the pitch angle of helicopter rotor blades by rotating them about their feathering axis.

featheredge

feathering axis (helicopter rotor blade). The axis about which the pitch angle of a rotor blade is varied. The feathering axis is the same as the spanwise axis.

feathering propeller (aircraft propeller). A propeller whose blades can be moved to an extremely high pitch angle of approximately 90° so they face directly into the airstream and produce no aerodynamic forces. If an engine fails in flight, the aerodynamic forces acting on the propeller will cause it to continue to turn, or windmill.

A windmilling propeller produces enough drag on a multiengine aircraft to cause extreme control difficulties, and it can easily lead to a crash. To decrease the drag, the propeller blades can be feathered. Because a feathered propeller does not turn the engine, a damaged engine is prevented from destroying itself.

feathering solenoid (propeller control). A solenoid switch used to initiate feathering of a Hydromatic propeller. Momentarily depressing the feathering switch energizes the feathering solenoid which allows current to flow to the feathering pump motor until the propeller is completely feathered.

feathering switch (Hamilton Standard Hydromatic propeller component). A locking, solenoid-operated switch used in the feather-motor circuit for a Hydromatic propeller. When the feathering switch button is momentarily depressed, a holding coil holds the switch closed until the feathering pump sends enough oil into the propeller dome to feather the blades. The pump continues to build up oil pressure until a cutout switch in the governor opens the circuit for the holding coil. The switch then opens the circuit and the feathering pump stops running.

federal airway. (1) Airspace corridor based on a centerline that extends from one NAVAID intersection to another. Federal airways are 4 miles each side of the centerline. (2) Class E airspace areas that extend upward from 1,200 feet to, but not including, 18,000 feet MSL, unless otherwise specified.

Federal Aviation Administration. *See* FAA.

Federal Aviation Administration Safety Team (FAASTeam). An organization promoting safety standards and the reduction of aircraft-related accidents. Each of the eight FAA flight standards regions has a dedicated FAASTeam office.

Federal Aviation Regulations. *See* FAR.

Federal Communications Commission. *See* FCC.

feedback. A process in an electrical circuit or control system in which some energy from the output of the system or circuit is fed back into the input. If the energy being fed back is in phase with the input signal, the feedback is positive and the output is increased. But if it is fed back out of phase with the input signal, the feedback is negative and the output is decreased. A control system using feedback is called a closed-loop system. The feedback closes the loop.

feeder facilities. NAVAIDs used by ATC to direct aircraft to intervening fixes between the enroute structure and the initial approach fix.

feeder fix (air traffic control). The fix depicted on instrument approach procedure charts which establishes the starting point of a feeder route.

feeder route (air traffic control). A route depicted on instrument approach procedure charts to designate routes for aircraft to proceed from the enroute structure to the initial approach fix (IAF).

feedthrough capacitor. A capacitor used to carry a conductor through a panel or bulkhead. The outer conductor of the capacitor is connected to the case, and the inner conductor is connected to terminals that extend from both ends of the capacitor. Feedthrough capacitors used in some aircraft magnetos minimize breaker point arcing and also decrease the radio interference caused by electrical energy radiated from the ignition switch lead.

feedthrough connector. A type of electrical connector used to carry a group of conductors through a bulkhead or panel. Feedthrough connectors do not have wires fastened to them, but rather they allow cables on both sides of the bulkhead to be connected through them. Sealed feedthrough connectors carry circuits through the bulkheads of pressurized aircraft.

feeler gage (precision tool). A type of measuring tool consisting of strips of precision-ground steel of accurately measured thickness. Feeler gages are used to measure the distance between close-fitting parts, such as the clearances in a mechanical system or the distance by which moving contacts are separated.

fence (aerodynamics). A stationary vane that extends chordwise, from the leading edge to the trailing edge, across upper surface of the wing of a high-speed airplane. Fences prevent the air from flowing spanwise along the wing.

Fenestron tail rotor (helicopter component). A shrouded tail rotor that has a number of small blades rotating in a protective shroud. A Fenestron rotor is more effective than a conventional tail rotor because its shroud aids in directing the air through the blades and it protects the rotor and ground personnel from damage.

Fenwal fire detection system. A patented spot-type fire detection system installed in an aircraft. This system uses individual thermal switches connected between two insulated conductors. An open circuit in either of the two conductors will not prevent the system from detecting a fire, but it will keep it from indicating good when the test switch is closed.

fermium. A synthetic, metallic, radioactive chemical element. Fermium's symbol is Fm, its atomic number is 100, and it has mass numbers ranging between 248 and 257. Fermium was first discovered as debris from a hydrogen bomb explosion, and it is now made in nuclear reactors.

ferrite. A material used as a core for many electromagnetic components. Ferrite is made of powdered metal sintered and molded into the proper shape. Sintering is a process in which powdered metal is heated but not quite melted, and then squeezed together. Ferrite has a high permeability, it easily accepts lines of magnetic flux, but it has such a high resistance that eddy current losses are very low.

ferrite steel. Alpha iron into which some carbon has been dissolved. It exists at temperatures below its critical temperature.

ferromagnetic material. A material that contains iron and has a high magnetic permeability. Ferromagnetic materials can be magnetically saturated (all the magnetic domains aligned in the same direction). They have good retentivity; they retain a large amount of their magnetism when the magnetizing force is removed.

ferrous metal. Any metal that contains iron and has magnetic characteristics. Magnetic characteristics include the ability to be magnetized and to be attracted by a magnet.

ferrule. A metal ring or cap used to reinforce or protect the end of a tube or tool handle. Ferrules are also used to form electrical contacts on the end of an insulating tube. *See* ferrule resistor.

ferrule resistor (electrical component). A type of resistor that has metal ferrules, or bands, around each end so it can be mounted in a standard fuse clip.

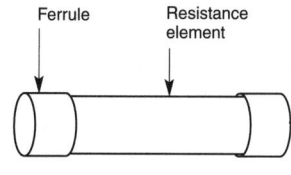

ferrule resistor

ferrule terminals (electrical fuse component). The terminals on each end of a tubular fuse. Ferrule terminals are short, closed, metal caps that slip over the ends of a glass tube that contains a fuse link. The ferrule terminals are held in fuse clips.

ferry flight. A flight for the purpose of returning an aircraft to base, delivering an aircraft from one location to another, or moving an aircraft to and from a maintenance base. Ferry flights, under certain conditions, may be conducted under terms of a special flight permit.

ferry permit. A special flight permit issued by the Federal Aviation Administration that allows an unlicensed aircraft to be flown from its present location to another location where it can be repaired, inspected, or otherwise prepared for licensing.

FET (field effect transistor). A high-impedance semiconductor device in which the flow of load current between the source and drain is controlled by variations in voltage on the gate, rather than current, as is done with a bipolar transistor.

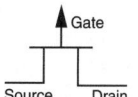

field-effect transistor

Load current flowing between the source and the drain, through a semiconductor channel, is switched and regulated by the effect of an electric field exerted by the voltage on the gate. An FET is sometimes called a unipolar transistor.

fetch (seaplane term). An area where wind is generating waves on the water surface. Also the distance the waves have been driven by the wind blowing in a constant direction without obstruction.

FHP (friction horsepower). The amount of horsepower used to turn the crankshaft, pistons, gears, and accessories in a reciprocating engine and to compress the air inside the cylinders.

fiberglass. Thin fibers of glass used to reinforce plastic resins in the manufacture of strong, lightweight structural components. The glass fibers have diameters between 0.005 mm and 0.2 mm (0.0002 inch and 0.008 inch).

fiber locknut (self-locking nut). A type of self-locking nut used on a bolt that is subject to vibration—it cannot, however, be used on a bolt that is subject to rotation. A collar of resilient, or springy, fiber is locked into the end of the threads in the nut. The hole in the fiber is slightly smaller than the major diameter of the threads on the bolt on which it fits. When the nut is screwed onto the bolt, the threads press, but do not cut, into the fiber and cause so much friction that the nut cannot vibrate loose from the bolt. A fiber locknut can be reused as long as a wrench is needed to turn it onto the bolt.

fiber optics. The branch of technology that deals with the transmission of light through long, slender, flexible fibers of glass or transparent plastic material. Transparent fibers arranged in a compact bundle have the ability to transmit an image from one end to the other, even if the bundle is bent around a corner.

Fiber optic borescopes are used to inspect the inside of a structure without requiring any major disassembly. These instruments may be fitted with a light source to illuminate the inside of the device being inspected, and a camera to make a permanent record of what is seen through the eyepiece.

fidelity. The accuracy with which an amplifier reproduces the signal applied to its input.

field (electrical). A space across which electrical lines of force exist.

field (magnetic). A space across which magnetic lines of force exist.

field cleaning (turbine engine maintenance procedure). Cleaning the compressor blades, casings, and inlet guide vanes of a turbojet engine by spraying them with an emulsion-type cleaner, followed by a rinse with distilled or demineralized water. Field cleaning is done while the engine is motored by the starter or operated at a low RPM.

field coil (electrical machine). A coil of insulated wire wound around a laminated steel pole shoe in an electrical motor or generator. Each motor or generator has two or more field coils that may be connected either in parallel or in series with the armature.

Direct current flowing through the field coils of a generator produces magnetic flux which induces a voltage in the conductors of the armature as they pass in front of the pole shoes. The amount of voltage induced in the armature is determined by the strength of the magnetic field. A voltage regulator is normally used to control the amount of current flowing in the field coils, and thus the strength of the magnetic field.

In a motor, torque is produced by the reaction between the magnetic flux produced by current flowing in the field coils and the flux produced by current flowing through the armature coils.

field effect transistor. *See* FET.

field elevation. The highest point of an airport's usable runways measured in feet from mean sea level.

field excitation (aircraft generator). Direct current supplied to the field coils of a generator to produce the magnetic field in which the armature rotates. DC generators are normally self-excited. This means that the field excitation current comes directly from the armature. Self-excited generators depend upon residual magnetism in the field frame to produce the initial excitation current as soon as the generator begins to turn.

field frame (generator component). The steel housing of a generator in which the field coils are mounted. The field frame provides a low reluctance path for the magnetic flux from the field coils, and it retains enough magnetism, when the generator is not operating, to start the generator producing current. This magnetism is called residual magnetism.

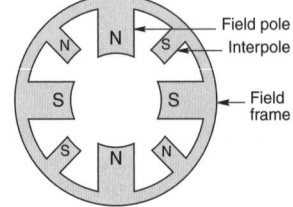

field frame

field maintenance (aircraft maintenance). Maintenance performed on an aircraft when it is away from its regular maintenance base or out of the maintenance dock. Field maintenance is limited, as much as possible, to minor replacement operations.

field strength meter (electrical measuring device). An electrical instrument used to measure the strength of the electromagnetic field radiated from a radio transmitting antenna.

filament (electron tube component). The heater in an electron tube. The filament is a small piece of flat resistance wire mounted inside a tube-like cathode. Electrons flowing through the filament cause it to glow red-hot, and this heats the cathode. The heat speeds up the molecular movement in the cathode enough that electrons are emitted from its surface. Electron tube filaments are heated with low-voltage AC or with low-voltage batteries.

file (air traffic control). Used in conjunction with flight plans to indicate that a flight plan has been submitted to ATC.

file (metal-cutting tool). A handheld cutting tool used to remove a small amount of metal by pushing the tool across the metal surface. A file is made of very hard, high-carbon steel, and has rows of teeth cut across its face at an angle to the length of the file.

file (double cut)

Files with a single set of teeth are called single-cut files, and a file having a second set of teeth that cross the first set is called a double-cut file. The teeth on a file vary from very fine to coarse. A file with the finest teeth is said to have a dead-smooth cut; next in coarseness is a smooth cut, then a second cut, a bastard cut, and finally a coarse cut.

filed enroute delay (air traffic control). A preplanned delay at points along the route of a flight which requires special flight plan filing and handling techniques. Filed enroute delays may be terminal area delays, special use airspace delays, or aerial refueling delays.

filed flight plan. A flight plan as filed with an air traffic service (ATS) unit by the pilot or his/her designated representative without any subsequent changes or clearances.

filiform corrosion. A thread-, or filament-like corrosion which forms on aluminum skins beneath a dense paint film. Filiform corrosion gets its name from the fact that it grows in shape of a thread, or a filament.

filler material (plastic resin component). A material mixed into a plastic resin to give body to the resin. Powdered chalk and microballoons are two commonly used filler materials.

filler neck (fluid reservoir component). A cylindrical tube extending from a fluid reservoir to a location that is convenient to fill the reservoir. Some hydraulic reservoirs and fuel tanks are installed inside an aircraft structure in a location where servicing is difficult. A filler neck is installed on these reservoirs to allow them to be filled from outside the aircraft.

filler plug (flush-skin repair component). A plug of sheet metal installed in a flush-skin repair to bring the surface of the repair even with the skin being repaired. The strength of the repair is in the doubler inside the structure, and the filler plug is used only to make the surface aerodynamically smooth.

filler rods (welding). Long pieces of wire that are melted into a weld to provide additional material to strengthen the weld. Filler rods are usually called welding rods.

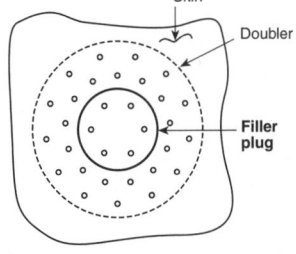

filler plug

filler valve (oxygen system component). A valve in an oxygen system through which oxygen from the storage bottles is put into the system. Filler valves normally incorporate a restriction that prevents the system from being filled too quickly. If they were filled too quickly, enough heat could be built up to cause an explosion.

fillet (aircraft structure). A fairing used to give shape, but not strength, to an object. A fillet produces a smooth junction where two surfaces meet. Fillets are often used to produce a smooth, aerodynamically clean junction between the wing and the fuselage of an airplane.

filling (meteorology). An increase in the central pressure of a meteorological pressure system. Filling, which is the opposite of deepening, is more commonly applied to a low, rather than a high.

fillister-head screw. A machine screw whose head has a rounded top, straight sides, and a flat bearing surface. Fillister-head screws often have holes drilled through the head so they can be safetied with safety wire.

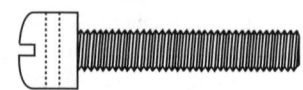

fillister-head screw

fill threads (aircraft fabric). Threads woven across the width of a piece of fabric, from one selvage edge to the other. Fill threads are also called woof, or weft, threads.

film strength (lubricant characteristic). The measure of the ability of a lubricant to maintain a continuous film without breaking down under mechanical pressure.

filter (electrical circuit). A tuned electrical circuit that will pass certain frequencies or bands of frequencies while attenuating others. *See* band-pass filter, band-reject filter, high-pass filter, and low-pass filter.

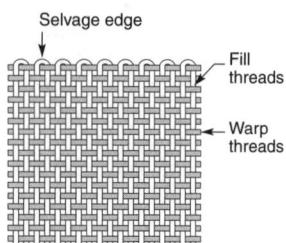

fill threads

filter (fluid filter). A component in a system that traps and holds contaminants carried in the fluid flowing through the system. Aircraft fuel systems, lubrication systems, and hydraulic systems all use filters.

filter capacitor (electronic component). An electrolytic capacitor connected in parallel with the output of a DC power supply. The capacitor has a low impedance for any ripple that may be superimposed on the DC output, and the ripple is passed to ground, while the DC is not affected.

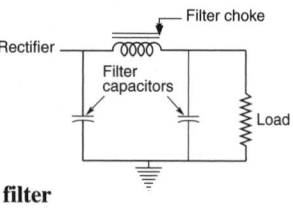

filter

filter choke (electronic component). An iron-core inductor installed in series with the output of a DC power supply. The filter choke impedes, or opposes, any ripples or portions of alternating current that are superimposed on the DC output.

fin (aircraft structural component). A fixed vertical aerodynamic surface used to provide directional stability to an aircraft.

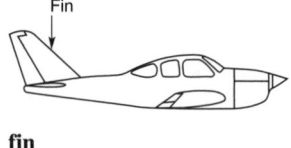

fin

final (air traffic control). The point at which an aircraft is on the final approach course or is aligned with a landing area.

final approach (aircraft flight operation). The portion of an aircraft flight just before landing. The aircraft is aligned with the runway and is on a descending flight path.

final approach and takeoff area (FATO). The FATO is a defined heliport area over which the final approach to a hover or a departure is made. The touchdown and lift-off area (TLOF) where the helicopter is permitted to land is normally centered in the FATO. A safety area is provided around the FATO.

final approach course (aircraft flight operation). A straight-line extension of a localizer, a final approach radial, or a runway center line, all without regard to distance.

final approach fix (FAF) (instrument flying). The fix from which the IFR final approach to an airport is executed, and which identifies the beginning of the final approach segment. An FAF is designated on government charts by a Maltese cross symbol for nonprecision approaches, and a lightning bolt symbol for precision approaches.

final approach-IFR (air traffic control). The flight path of an aircraft which is inbound to an airport on a final instrument approach course, beginning at the final approach fix or point, and extending to the airport or the point where a circle-to-land maneuver or a missed approach is executed.

final approach point. *See* FAP.

final approach segment (ICAO). That segment of an instrument approach procedure in which alignment and descent for landing are accomplished.

final controller (air traffic control). The controller providing information and final approach guidance during precision approach radar (PAR) and airport surveillance radar (ASR) approaches utilizing radar equipment.

final guard service. A value added service provided in conjunction with LAA/RAA only during periods of significant and fast changing weather conditions that may affect landing and takeoff operations.

final leg. The leg of a traffic pattern on a descending flight path starting from the completion of the base-to-final turn and extending to the point of touchdown.

final monitor aid (air traffic control). A high-resolution color display that is equipped with the controller-alert system hardware/software which is used in the precision runway monitor (PRM) system. The display includes alert algorithms providing the target predictors, a color-change alert when a target penetrates or is predicted to penetrate the no transgression zone (NTZ), a color-change alert if the aircraft transponder becomes inoperative, synthesized voice alerts, digital mapping, and like features contained in the precision runway monitoring (PRM) system.

final monitor controller. ATC specialist assigned to radar monitor the flight path of aircraft during simultaneous parallel and simultaneous close parallel ILS approach operations.

final takeoff speed. *14 CFR Part 1:* "The speed of the airplane that exists at the end of the takeoff path in the enroute configuration with one engine inoperative."

fineness ratio. The ratio of the length of a streamlined body to its maximum diameter. In a helicopter rotor it is the thickness of the airfoil as a percentage of its chord length.

fine-wire spark plug (aircraft reciprocating engine component). A type of spark plug used in aircraft engines that have problems with lead fouling the plugs. The electrodes are made of small-diameter platinum or iridium wire which leaves the firing end of the spark plug open so the gases inside the cylinder can scavenge the lead compounds before they solidify and foul the plug.

finger brake (sheet metal shop tool). Another term for a box brake. *See* box brake.

finger patch (welded structural repair). A type of patch welded over a cluster in a welded truss-type aircraft fuselage. The patch covers and reinforces damaged areas of the tubes and has fingers that extend out along each of the tubes in the cluster.

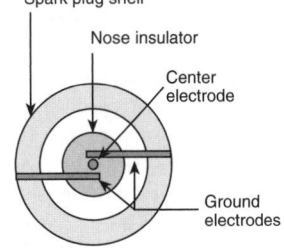

fine-wire spark plug

finger screen (fuel system filter). A coarse-mesh, small-diameter screen made in the shape of a finger. A finger screen is installed in the end of the outlet line inside a fuel tank to prevent large contaminants from restricting the flow of fuel from the tank. Small contaminants and water that pass through the finger screen are trapped in finer screens and filters further along in the fuel system.

finishing tape. Another name for surface tape. *See* surface tape.

finish turning (metal machining). A step in the machining of a metal part in which the part is turned to its correct dimension and given its final smoothness.

FIR. *See* flight information region.

fire detection system (aircraft fire warning system). A system in an aircraft that warns the flight crew of the presence of a fire in any of the engines, the cargo area, or the wheel wells.

fire extinguisher. A device, either handheld or installed in an aircraft, that directs a fire extinguishing agent onto a fire.

fire extinguishing agent. A chemical used to extinguish a fire. A fire extinguishing agent can extinguish a fire by reducing the temperature of the fuel to a value below its kindling point, by excluding oxygen from the fire, or by preventing the oxygen combining with the fuel. Carbon dioxide, water, Halon 1211, and Halon 1301 are fire extinguishing agents used in aircraft fire protection systems.

fire point (chemical characteristic). The lowest temperature at which the fumes of a volatile liquid (a liquid that evaporates easily) will ignite and continue to burn when a small flame is passed above its surface.

fireproof. *14 CFR Part 1:*
"(1) With respect to materials and parts used to confine fire in a designated fire zone, means the capacity to withstand at least as well as steel in dimensions appropriate for the purpose for which they are used, the heat produced when there is a severe fire of extended duration in that zone; and
(2) With respect to other materials and parts, means the capacity to withstand the heat associated with fire at least as well as steel in dimensions appropriate for the purpose for which they are used."

fireproof structure. A structure built of noncombustible materials and designed so it cannot be destroyed by fire.

fire-pull handle. The handle in an aircraft cockpit that is pulled at the first indication of an engine fire. Pulling this handle disconnects the generator from the electrical system, shuts off the fuel and hydraulic fluid to the engine, and closes the compressor bleed air valve. The fire extinguisher agent discharge switch is uncovered, but it is not automatically closed.

fire resistant. *14 CFR Part 1:*
"(1) With respect to sheet or structural members means the capacity to withstand the heat associated with fire at least as well as aluminum alloy in dimensions appropriate for the purpose for which they are used; and
(2) With respect to fluid-carrying lines, fluid system parts, wiring, air ducts, fittings, and powerplant controls, means the capacity to perform the intended functions under the heat and other conditions likely to occur when there is a fire at the place concerned."

fire-resistant structure. A structure that is able to resist fire or exposure to high temperature for a specified period of time without being destroyed or structurally damaged.

fire sleeve. A protective covering wrapped around flexible hoses installed in the engine compartments of an aircraft. A fire sleeve does not increase the service temperature of the hose, but it protects the hose from direct fire long enough to allow appropriate action to be taken.

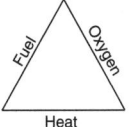

fire triangle. A graphic display of the three components that must be present for a fire. These components are: fuel, oxygen, and heat.

firewall (aircraft structural component). A bulkhead made of a fire-proof material used to separate the engine compartment from the rest of the aircraft.

fire triangle

firewall shutoff valve (aircraft fluid system component). A valve located on the airframe side of the engine firewall that will completely shut off the flow of fuel, oil, or hydraulic fluid to the engine in the case of an engine compartment fire.

F

fire zone. An area in an aircraft designated by the aircraft manufacturer as requiring a fire detection and/or fire extinguishing system.

firing order (reciprocating engine). The sequence in which the cylinders of a reciprocating engine fire in a normal cycle of operation.

firmer chisel (wood-cutting tool). A type of woodworking chisel having a thin, flat blade.

firmware (computer operations). A computer program stored in read-only memory (ROM). Programs are stored in ROM when they are used repeatedly; such as, for example, the operating procedures in dedicated computers.

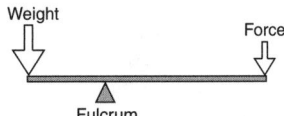

first-class lever. A lever in which the fulcrum is located between the force and the weight. The force and the weight try to rotate the lever in opposite directions.

first-class lever

first gust (meteorology). The leading edge of a spreading downdraft, called a plow wind, in front of an approaching thunderstorm.

fir-tree attachment. A method of attaching turbine blades into the turbine wheel. The root of the blade is shaped like a notched-edge Christmas tree which fits loosely in a similar-shaped slot in the periphery of the wheel. When the engine is cold, the blades are loose, but as the engine heats up, the blades tighten in the wheel.

fisheyes (finishing system defect). A type of finishing system defect in which small, local areas of the finish do not cure properly. These small areas resemble the eyes of a fish.
    Fisheyes are caused by small specks of wax or silicone material on the surface when the finish was sprayed on, or by contaminants that fell on the finish before it cured.

fishmouth splice (welded tubular structure). A type of splice used in a welded steel tubular structure, in which the end of a tube, whose inside diameter is the same as the outside diameter of the tube being spliced, is cut in the shape of a V, or fishmouth, and is slipped over the smaller tube and welded. A fishmouth splice has more weld area than a butt splice, and it allows the stresses from one tube to transfer gradually into the other tube.

fission. *See* nuclear fission.

fishtail (aircraft flight maneuver). A method of decreasing the speed of an airplane during its approach for landing. Airplanes without flaps can be slowed down and kept on a relatively straight flight path by alternately skidding the airplane to the left and then to the right, by using the rudder while keeping the wings level with the control stick or wheel. Side and forward slips are used more often than fishtailing for slowing an airplane.

fitting. An attachment device that is used to connect components to an aircraft structure.

five-hour rating (battery capacity rating). The ampere-hour rating of a battery when current is taken from it at a rate that will discharge it in five hours. A 20-ampere-hour battery will supply four amps of current for five hours, but if it is discharged at a higher rate, its ampere-hour capacity will be less. The five-hour rating is the rating most generally used for aircraft storage batteries.

five-minute rating (battery capacity rating). The ampere-hour rating of a battery when current is taken from it at such a high rate that the battery will be discharged in five minutes. The high current drawn from a battery causes the ampere-hour capacity to be much less at its five-minute rating than it is at its five-hour rating. The five-minute rating gives an indication of the way the battery will respond under the load placed on it by the engine starter.

fix (aircraft navigation). A geographical position determined by visual references to the surface, by reference to one or more radio NAVAIDs, by celestial plotting, or by other navigational methods.

fixation. A psychological condition in which the pilot fixes attention on a single source of information and ignores all other sources.

fix balancing (air traffic control). A process whereby aircraft are evenly distributed over several available arrival fixes. Fix balancing reduces delays and controller workload.

fixed fire-extinguishing system. A fire-extinguishing system installed in an aircraft.

fixed landing gear (aircraft landing gear). A nonretractable landing gear. A fixed landing gear cannot be retracted into the aircraft structure to decrease the wind resistance.

fixed-pitch propeller (aircraft propeller). A type of propeller used on aircraft when low cost and simplicity are more important than efficient performance. The blades of a fixed-pitch propeller are set at one pitch angle which cannot be changed. Up through World War II, most fixed-pitch propellers were made of laminated birch, but since that time, most have been made of forged aluminum alloy.

The pitch angle of a fixed-pitch propeller is a compromise between that which allows the engine to turn fast enough to produce the maximum horsepower for takeoff, and that which moves the aircraft through the air a maximum distance for each revolution, giving the best fuel economy and speed.

fixed shaft turboprop engine. A turboprop engine in which the gas producer spool is directly connected to the output shaft.

fixed slot (high-lift device). A fixed, nozzle-shaped opening near the leading edge of a wing that ducts air onto the top surface of the wing. Its purpose is to allow flight at a higher angle of attack before a stall occurs.

fixed-wing aircraft. An airplane or glider whose wing is rigidly attached to the structure. The term fixed-wing is used to distinguish these aircraft from rotary-wing aircraft, such as helicopters and autogiros.

fix record (airborne navigation database data). A database record used in an airborne navigation database that describes a specific location on the face of the earth, such as a NAVAID, waypoint, intersection, or airport.

FL. *See* flight level.

flag (on flight instruments) (Pilot/Controller Glossary). A warning device incorporated into certain airborne navigation and flight instruments to indicate when instruments are inoperative or otherwise not operating satisfactorily, or signal strength or quality of the received signal falls below acceptable values.

flag alarm (instrument warning device). A warning device incorporated in certain airborne navigation and flight instruments indicating that instruments are inoperative or otherwise not operating satisfactorily, or that signal strength or quality of the received signal falls below acceptable values.

flag operation. Any scheduled operation conducted by any person operating: (1) a turbojet-powered airplane; (2) an airplane with more than 9 passenger seats, excluding each crewmember seat; or (3) an airplane with a payload capacity of more than 7,500 pounds, when operating at locations as defined in 14 CFR §110.2. These locations are defined as: (1) between any point within the State of Alaska or the State of Hawaii or any territory or possession of the United States and any point outside the State of Alaska or the State of Hawaii or any territory or possession of the United States, respectively; (2) between any point within the 48 contiguous states of the U.S. or the District of Columbia and any point outside the 48 contiguous states of the U.S. and the District of Columbia; or (3) between any point outside the U.S. and another point outside the U.S.

flameout (gas turbine engine operation). A condition in the operation of a gas turbine engine in which the fire in the engine unintentionally goes out. If too much fuel is sprayed into the combustors, the fire will go out, and this is called a rich flameout. If there is too little fuel, the fire will go out, and this is called a lean flameout.

flameout pattern (air traffic control). An approach normally conducted by a single-engine military aircraft experiencing loss or anticipated loss of engine power or control. The standard overhead approach starts at a relatively high altitude over a runway (high key) followed by a continuous 180° turn to a high, wide position (low key), followed by a continuous 180° turn to final. The standard straight-in pattern starts at a point that results in a straight-in approach with a high rate of descent to the runway. Flameout approaches terminate in the type of approach requested by the pilot (normally full stop).

flameout, simulated. A practice approach by a jet aircraft (normally military) at idle thrust to a runway. The approach may start at a runway (high key) and may continue on a relatively high and wide downwind leg with a continuous turn to final. It terminates in landing or low approach.

flame resistant. *14 CFR Part 1:* "Not susceptible to combustion to the point of propagating a flame, beyond safe limits, after the ignition source is removed."

flame spraying. A process in which molten metal is deposited on a surface. A wire of the metal to be deposited is fed into an oxy-acetylene flame and melted. The molten metal is blown by a stream of high-pressure air onto the surface to be coated.

Pure aluminum can be sprayed onto steel to prevent corrosion, and metal can be sprayed onto an insulating material to make the surface electrically conductive.

flame tubes (turbine engine component). Small-diameter metal tubes that connect can-type combustors to carry the ignition flame to all of the combustion chambers.

flammable. Easily ignited. Flammable replaces the older term inflammable which can be misinterpreted to mean not flammable. *14 CFR Part 1:* "With respect to a fluid or gas, means susceptible to igniting readily or to exploding."

flammable liquid. A liquid that gives off combustible vapors (vapors that are easily ignited). Gasoline is an example of a flammable liquid.

flange. A ridge that protrudes from a device and is used for attaching something to the device, or for connecting two objects together. The propeller shaft of most modern aircraft engines is fitted with a flange on which the propeller mounts.

The end of the propeller shaft is formed into a flat plate (the flange) whose face is perpendicular the propeller shaft. The propeller is held on this flange with high-strength steel bolts.

flanged propeller shaft

flap (helicopter rotor blade movement). Up-and-down movement of the tip of a helicopter rotor blade.

flaperon (aircraft control). Controls used on some swept wing airplanes that serve as both ailerons and wing flaps. The flaperons on both wings can be lowered together to increase the lift and drag of the wings. This is the flap function. The flaperons can also be moved differentially: one moves up, while the other moves down. This is the aileron function.

flap extended speed. *14 CFR Part 1:* "The highest speed permissible with wing flaps in a prescribed extended position."

flap overload valve. A valve in the flap system of an airplane that prevents the flaps being lowered at an airspeed which could cause structural damage. If the pilot tries to extend the flaps when the airspeed is too high, the opposition caused by the airflow will open the overload valve and return the fluid to the reservoir.

flapper valve. A form of hinged check valve that allows fluid to flow through it in one direction only. Fluid can flow in the direction which forces the valve off its seat, but it cannot flow in the direction which forces the flapper against its seat.

flapping (helicopter rotor blade). The vertical movement of a helicopter rotor blade about its delta, or flapping, hinge.

flapping hinge (helicopter rotor). The hinge with its axis parallel to the rotor plane of rotation. The flapping hinge permits the rotor blades to flap up or down to equalize the lift, or rotor thrust, between the advancing-blade half and the retreating-blade half of the rotor disk.

flaps (airplane control surfaces). Auxiliary controls built into the wings of an airplane. Flaps can be extended, or lowered, to change the airfoil shape of the wing to increase both its lift and drag. When the flaps are fully extended, the drag is increased so the airplane can descend at a steep angle without building up excessive airspeed. Partially lowering the flaps increases the lift so the airplane can fly at a slower airspeed. *See* plain flap, split flap, slotted flap, Fowler flap, and triple-slotted flap.

flare (aircraft flight maneuver). The last flight maneuver made by an airplane in a successful landing. The airplane is slowed down in preparation for landing, and it descends along a gradually sloping flight path that brings it to the end of the runway. When the airplane is over the end of the runway, just a few feet above the surface, the pilot flares by gently pulling back on the control wheel.

   Flaring increases the angle of attack and allows the airplane to settle onto the runway with the slowest forward speed and the least vertical speed. Flaring is sometimes called rounding out.

flare (aircraft safety equipment). A safety device that was at one time carried in most airplanes that flew at night. A flare is a magnesium candle supported by a small parachute. If it was necessary for an airplane to make an emergency landing at night, the pilot released a flare, and as it left the airplane, it automatically ignited. The burning magnesium made a bright light that allowed the pilot to see the ground and make a reasonably safe landing. The parachute lowered the flare slowly enough that it was completely burned out before it reached the ground.

flare (rigid fluid lines). A cone-shaped expansion on the end of a piece of rigid fluid line tubing. The fitting to which the flared tubing attaches has a cone-shaped end that exactly mates with the flare, and when the tubing nut is tightened onto the fitting, the flare and the flare cone form a fluid-tight seal. Tubing used in automotive fluid lines is flared at an angle of 45°, and tubing used in aircraft fluid lines is flared at an angle of 37°.

flareless fitting (fluid lines). A type of fitting used on a fluid line that forms its seal without being flared. Flareless fittings use a compression sleeve around the end of the tube. The sleeve fits into a recess in the fitting, and when the nut is tightened, the sleeve is forced tightly between the tube and the fitting, making a fluid-tight seal.

flaring block (maintenance tool). A hinged double bar with holes corresponding to the outside diameter of various sizes of tubing. These holes are countersunk with a 37° taper (45° for automotive flares) to form the outside support against which the flare is formed. The tube is inserted in the correct hole and the bars clamped together. A flaring cone is forced into the end of the tube to form the flare.

flashback (welding problem). A problem in oxy-gas welding in which the flame burns back into the mixing chamber of the torch. A clogged or overheated tip can cause the flame to disappear from the tip and burn back into the mixing chamber.

A flashback is always accompanied by a shrill hissing or squealing, and the flame does not reappear at the tip as it does with a backfire. Flashback is extremely dangerous, and if the fuel gas, the acetylene or hydrogen, is not turned off at the regulator, the fire can burn back through the hose and cause an explosion.

flasher (electric lights). An automatic switch installed in a light system to turn the lights on and off in a definite sequence. Flashers may be operated by a thermal switch, or they may have a motor that drives a selector switch.

In a thermally operated switch, the current used in the lights passes through a strip of bimetallic material and heats it. When the strip gets hot, it warps and separates the contacts, opening the circuit. Current stops flowing, and the lights go out. When the strip cools, it snaps back to its original shape and closes the contacts, and the lights turn back on.

flashing off (finishing system). A step in the curing process of a finishing system. The finishing material is thinned with a solvent to get the proper viscosity for spraying. When the finish is sprayed on the surface, it is shiny because of the solvents. These solvents evaporate very soon and leave the surface of the finish dry to the touch, but it is not completely cured. The evaporation of the thinning solvents is called flashing off.

flashing the field (generator maintenance). A maintenance procedure for an aircraft generator that restores residual magnetism to the field frame. DC generators get their field excitation current from the armature, and the field frame must retain a small amount of permanent magnetism to furnish the magnetic field to begin producing current in the armature. As soon as current begins to flow in the armature, it excites the field.

If the field frame loses its residual magnetism, it must be restored before the generator can produce current. This residual magnetism is restored by flashing the field. A battery is momentarily connected to the field coil so current flows through it in its normal direction for a few seconds. This current magnetizes the field frame.

flash line (molded products). The raised line along the surface of a molded part caused by the molten material flowing into the space formed by the slightly rounded edges of the two halves of the mold.

flashover (reciprocating engine ignition system fault). An ignition system problem in which the high voltage in the magneto distributor jumps to the wrong terminal. Flashover causes the wrong spark plug to fire, and this reduces the engine power and produces vibration and excessive heat.

Flashover is often caused by moisture inside the distributor, but it also occurs when flying at high altitude where the air inside the distributor does not have enough density to act as an effective dielectric. Physically large distributors, low-tension ignition systems, and pressurized distributors have been used to prevent flashover.

flash plating (metal finishing). The deposit of an extremely thin coating of metal on a surface. A flash coating is only thick enough to give color to the surface.

flash point (petroleum specification). The temperature to which a material must be raised for it to ignite, but not continue to burn, when a flame is passed above it.

flash resistant. *14 CFR Part 1:* "Not susceptible to burning violently when ignited."

flat-compounded generator. A compound-wound generator (a generator that has both a series and a parallel, or shunt, winding) in which the effect of the two fields are balanced so they hold the output voltage constant from a no-load condition to the maximum load the generator can produce. *See* overcompounded generator and undercompounded generator.

flat file (metal-cutting hand tool). A common type of file used to smooth the edges or surface of a piece of metal or hard plastic. A flat file is tapered toward the tip in width and slightly tapered in thickness. It has two sets of teeth arranged diagonally across the surface in opposite directions (double cut), on both sides and a single row of teeth along both edges.

flat grain wood. Wood that has been sawed in such a way that the annual rings form an angle of less than 45° to the face of the piece.

flathead pin. A high-strength steel pin with a flat head on one end and a hole for a cotter pin on the other end. A flathead pin, called a clevis pin, is used to connect a clevis to an eyebolt or control horn.

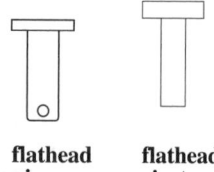

flathead rivet. An AN442 rivet used on the inside of an aircraft structure where it is not exposed to the airflow. Flathead rivets are often used because they are easy to install with automatic riveting machines.

flathead pin **flathead rivet**

flat lacquer (finishing material). A type of lacquer that dries with a flat, or nonglossy, surface. Flat lacquer is used for painting instrument panels and any part of an aircraft that must not reflect light.

flat pattern layout. The pattern for a sheet metal part that has the material used for each flat surface, and for all of the bends marked out with bend-tangent lines drawn between the flats and bend allowances.

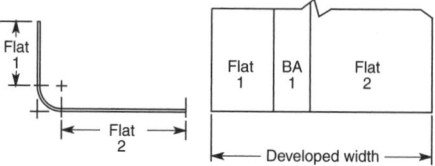

flat pattern layout

flat pitch. A propeller configuration in which the blade chord is aligned with the direction of rotation.

flat-rated engine. A turboprop engine whose allowable output power is less than the engine is physically capable of producing. Below a specific density altitude, the engine is limited by the amount of torque the airframe can tolerate. Above this altitude, the engine is limited by the exhaust gas temperature.

flat spin (aircraft maneuver). An aircraft maneuver in which the aircraft is autorotating (being pulled around by aerodynamic forces) as it descends, with one wing flying, and the other actually stalled. In a normal spin, the aircraft is pitched steeply nose down, but since it is descending, it has a very high angle of attack. Recovery is made by moving the control wheel forward (the elevators down). This decreases the angle of attack and allows the stalled wing to begin flying again, and the airplane stops spinning.

In a flat spin, the angle of attack cannot be lowered enough, even with full-down elevators to bring the wing out of its stalled condition. Flat spins are caused by the center of gravity of the aircraft being too far aft, allowing centrifugal force to flatten the spin. Very few aircraft can recover from an unintentional flat spin.

flat washer. A disk of metal with a hole in its center. A flat washer, also called a plain washer, is used under the head of a bolt to provide a bearing surface. It can also be used under a nut to make a surface for the nut to turn against so that it will not dig into the material contacted by the nut.

flaw. An imperfection in a material, often concealed, that impairs soundness.

fleet weight (aircraft operation). The average weight of aircraft of the same model that have the same equipment installed. Operations under 14 CFR Part 121 and 135 may use fleet weight, rather than having to weigh each individual aircraft.

Fleming's rule for direction of magnetic flux. Place the fingers of the right hand around a current-carrying conductor in such a way that the thumb points in the direction of conventional current flow (from positive to negative). The fingers encircle the wire in the same direction as the lines of flux.

Fleming's rule for electric generators. This is the rule for determining the direction of current flow in a wire caused by the wire passing through a magnetic field. Hold the right hand with the thumb, first finger, and second finger extended so that they are at right angles to each other. When the first finger points in the direction of the lines of magnetic flux (from the north pole to the south pole), and the thumb points in the direction the wire is moving through the field, the second finger points in the direction of conventional current flow (from positive to negative).

Fleming's rule for electric motors. The rule for determining the direction of movement of a current-carrying conductor in a magnetic field. Hold the left hand with the thumb, first finger, and second finger extended so that they are at right angles to each other. When the first finger points in the direction of the lines of magnetic flux (from the north pole to the south pole), and the second finger points in the direction of conventional current flow (from positive to negative), the thumb points in the direction the conductor will move.

flexibility. The characteristic of a material that allows it to be repeatedly bent within its elastic limits and still return to its original condition each time the bending force is removed.

flexible control cable (aircraft control system component). A steel cable used to connect the cockpit controls to the control surfaces. Flexible cable is made up of seven strands of wire, with each stand being made up of seven individual wires. This is called 7 x 7 cable. Extra-flexible cable has seven strands, with each strand made of 19 wires, and nonflexible cable is made of either seven or 19 solid wires wound into a cable.

flexible control cable

flexible suspension (balloon component). Balloon basket suspension consisting of steel or fiber cables without rigid structure.

flicker vertigo. A disorientating condition caused by flickering light off the blades of the propeller.

"Flight check" (air traffic control). A call-sign prefix used by FAA aircraft engaged in flight inspection/certification of navigational aids and flight procedures.

flight computer. A circular slide rule or electronic calculator used to determine wind correction angle, fuel consumption, airspeed, and other performance calculations during flight planning.

flight configuration. Adjustments to the aircraft control surfaces (including flaps and landing gear) in a manner that will achieve a specified attitude.

flight controller (automatic pilot component). The command unit of an automatic pilot. The human pilot is able to control the flight of the aircraft when the automatic pilot is engaged by using the controls on the flight controller.

flightcrew member. *14 CFR Part 1:* "A pilot, flight engineer, or flight navigator assigned to duty in an aircraft during flight time."

flight data recorder. *See* FDR.

flight deck (aircraft compartment). The compartment in a large aircraft in which all the flight, engine, communications, and navigation controls are located.

flight director. An electronic flight calculator that analyzes the navigation selections, signals, and aircraft parameters. It presents steering instructions on the flight display in the form of command bars or crossbars, which the pilot uses to position the nose of the aircraft over or to follow.

flight director indicator (FDI). One of the major components of a flight director system, the FDI provides steering commands that the pilot (or the autopilot, if coupled) follows.

flight director system (aircraft automatic flight control system). An automatic flight control system in which the commands needed to fly the aircraft are computed by the system, shown on a flight instrument, and followed by the human pilot. In an automatic pilot, these same commands are sent to servos that move the flight controls.

flight engineer. A flightcrew member of a large aircraft who is responsible for the mechanical operation of the aircraft and its engines. His or her duties include monitoring the engines, the electrical systems, the fuel system, and the environmental control system.

flight idle (gas turbine engine operation). An engine speed that produces a minimum amount of flight thrust. Flight idle RPM is usually in the 70% to 80% RPM range.

flight information region (FIR) (air traffic control). An airspace of defined dimensions within which flight information service and alerting service are provided.

flight information service. A service provided by the FAA for the purpose of giving advice and information useful for safe and efficient conduct of flights.

flight information service-broadcast (FIS-B). A ground broadcast service provided through the FAA's Universal Access Transceiver (UAT) "ADS-B Broadcast Services" network. The FAA FIS-B system provides pilots and flight crews of properly equipped aircraft with a cockpit display of certain aviation weather and flight operational information.

flight inspection (air navigation aids). Inflight investigation and evaluation of navigational aids to determine whether they meet established tolerances.

flight level. A measure of altitude used by aircraft flying above 18,000 feet. Flight levels are indicated by three digits representing the pressure altitude in hundreds of feet. An airplane flying at flight level 360 is flying at a pressure altitude of 36,000 feet. This is expressed as FL360. *See* pressure altitude.

   14 CFR Part 1: "A level of constant atmospheric pressure related to a reference datum of 29.92 inches of mercury. Each is stated in three digits that represents hundreds of feet. For example, flight level 250 represents a barometric altimeter indication of 25,000 feet; flight level 255, an indication of 25,500 feet."

flight line (airport area). The area of an airport in which aircraft are parked while they are being prepared for flight. Flight lines are also called ramps or tarmacs.

flight management systems. *See* FMS.

flight management system procedure (air traffic control). An arrival, departure, or approach procedure developed for use by aircraft with a slant (/)E or slant (/)F equipment suffix.

flight manual (aircraft documentation). An FAA-approved manual that must be in an aircraft any time it flies. The flight manual contains information regarding speed limitations, weight and balance, allowable maneuvers, engine operating limits, and other limitations that apply to the specific aircraft.

flight path. The line, course, or track along which an aircraft is flying or is intended to be flown.

flight patterns (flight operations). Basic maneuvers, flown by reference to the instruments rather than outside visual cues, for the purpose of practicing basic attitude flying. The patterns simulate maneuvers encountered on instrument flights such as holding patterns, procedure turns, and approaches.

flight plan. Specific information related to the intended flight of an aircraft. A flight plan is filed with an FAA flight service station or an air traffic control facility. *14 CFR Part 1:* "Specified information, relating to the intended flight of an aircraft, that is filed orally or in writing with air traffic control."

flight plan area (air traffic control). The geographical area assigned by regional air traffic divisions to a flight service station for the purpose of search and rescue for VFR aircraft, issuance of NOTAMs, pilot briefing, inflight services, broadcast, emergency services, flight data processing, international operations, and aviation weather services. Three letter identifiers are assigned to every flight service station and are annotated in Airport/Facilities Directories (A/FDs) and FAA Order 7350.6 as tie-in-facilities.

flight plan equipment codes. *See* aircraft equipment suffix.

flight recorder. A general term applied to any instrument or device that records information about the performance of an aircraft in flight or about conditions encountered in flight. Flight recorders may make records of airspeed, outside air temperature, vertical acceleration, engine RPM, manifold pressure, and other pertinent variables for a given flight.

flight recorder (ICAO). Any type of recorder installed in the aircraft for the purpose of complementing accident/incident investigation.

flight review. An industry-managed, FAA-monitored currency program designed to assess and update a pilot's knowledge and skills; a review of flying skills and aviation knowledge conducted by a flight instructor required for all certificated pilots every 24 months in order to retain pilot-in-command privileges. A flight review consists of at least 1 hour of flight training and 1 hour of ground training.

flight service station. *See* FSS.

flight simulation training device (FSTD). *See* flight training device (FTD) and flight simulator.

flight simulator. A training device that duplicates the flight characteristics of an aircraft. The simulator looks like the flight deck or cockpit of a specific aircraft. All the controls and instruments are computer driven, and they duplicate those in the aircraft. The controls have the same feel, and the instruments give the same indications as those in the real aircraft. Flight simulators allow many different types of emergency situations to be simulated under safe conditions, so flight crews will know how to respond when a real emergency occurs.

flight standards district office. *See* FSDO.

flight strips (air traffic control). Paper strips containing instrument flight information, used by ATC when processing flight plans.

flight test. Flight for the purpose of investigating the flight or operational characteristics of an aircraft or aircraft component, or evaluating an applicant for a pilot certificate or rating.

flight time (aircraft records). *14 CFR Part 1:* "The time from the moment the aircraft first moves under its own power for the purpose of flight until the moment it comes to rest at the next point of landing. ('Block-to-block' time.)"

flight training device (FTD). A full-sized replica of the instruments, equipment, panels, and controls of an aircraft, or set of aircraft, in an open flight deck area or in an enclosed cockpit.

flight visibility. *14 CFR Part 1:* "The average forward horizontal distance, from the cockpit of an aircraft in flight, at which prominent unlighted objects may be seen and identified by day and prominent lighted objects may be seen and identified by night."

flight watch (air traffic control). A shortened term for use in air-ground contacts on the frequency of 122.0 MHz to identify the flight service station providing enroute flight advisory service (EFAS).

flint lighter (welding equipment). A device used to light an oxy-gas welding torch. The lighter consists of a small piece of flint that can be rubbed against a piece of rough, hardened steel. A metal cup behind the steel prevents the flame from reaching out and burning anything as the torch is being lit.

flip-flop (digital electronic building block). A digital building block having two stable states, used to store information. A flip-flop is made of two cross-coupled NAND or NOR gates that act as a latch. The output of each gate is applied to the input of the other.

float chamber (carburetor component). The component of a float-type carburetor in which a float-actuated needle valve maintains the fuel at a constant level, slightly below the outlet of the discharge nozzle. *See* float-type carburetor.

floated battery. A storage battery permanently installed across the output of a generator. The generator carries the normal electrical load and keeps the battery fully charged at all times. The battery supplies current to help the generator when the electrical load is unusually high.

floating. A condition during landing in which the airplane does not settle to the runway due to excessive airspeed.

floating ground (electrical equipment). *See* chassis ground.

floating waypoints. Representative of airspace fixes at a point in space not directly associated with a conventional airway. In many cases they may be established for such purposes as ATC metering fixes, holding points, RNAV-direct routing, gateway waypoints, etc.

floatplane. A seaplane equipped with separate floats to support the fuselage well above the water surface.

floats (seaplane component). The components of a floatplane's landing gear that provide the buoyancy to keep the airplane afloat.

floats-on-skids (helicopter landing gear). A type of helicopter float that sits on top of the fully functional skids. During water operations, the floats support the weight of the aircraft, and on hard surfaces the skids support the weight of the aircraft.

float-type carburetor. A type of carburetor used on reciprocating engines in which the fuel-metering force is produced between a fixed fuel level and a variable negative air pressure that is produced by a venturi. The venturi pressure varies with the amount of air flowing into the engine. This variable fuel-metering force acting across a fixed-size jet meters the correct amount of fuel into the air.

flock. Pulverized wool or cotton fibers mixed with an adhesive. Flock can be sprayed on metal to produce a velvet-like protective finish. It can also be bonded to wire screen and used as a filtering element for certain types of air filters.

flooded engine (aircraft engine condition). A reciprocating engine that has too much fuel in its cylinders for it to start, or a turbine engine that has so much fuel in its combustors that it would create a fire hazard or a hot start if the fuel were ignited.

floor load limit (structural limitation). The maximum weight a floor can sustain per square inch/foot as provided by the manufacturer.

flow chart. A diagram that uses special symbols connected by arrows or lines to indicate the sequence of step-by-step procedures that must be followed to accomplish a given task. Flow charts are used to design a computer program and to explain processes that take place in manufacturing.

flow control (air traffic control). Measures designed to adjust the flow of traffic into a given airspace, along a given route, or bound for a given airport in order to ensure the most effective utilization of the airspace.

flow-control valve (fluid power system component). A fluid power valve that controls the direction or amount of fluid flow. Most fluid power systems use both flow-control and pressure-control valves. Check valves and selector valves are examples of flow-control valves.

flow divider (turbine engine component). A component in a turbine engine fuel system that routes all of the fuel to the primary nozzles or primary orifices when starting the engine and when the RPM is low. When the engine speed builds up, the flow divider shifts and opens a passage to send the majority of the fuel to the secondary nozzles or orifices.

flow divider (reciprocating engine component). The valve in an Precision Airmotive RSA fuel injection system that divides the fuel from the fuel control unit and distributes it equally to all of the cylinders. The flow divider in an RSA fuel injection system compares with the manifold valve in a Teledyne-Continental system.

flow indicator (aircraft oxygen system). An indicator visible to the wearer of an oxygen mask that shows when oxygen is flowing into the mask.

fluctuate. To swing back and forth or to shift a value between a high and a low limit.

fluctuating arc (electric arc welding condition). A malfunction in an electric arc welding system that causes the arc to vary its intensity. A fluctuating arc is caused by an inadequate electrical ground.

F

fluid. A form of material whose molecules are able to flow past one another without destroying the material. Gases and liquids are both fluids. Fluids tend to conform to the shape of their container.

fluidics. The branch of technology that uses a flow of fluids through specially shaped ducts and nozzles to sense, measure, and control a physical condition. Fluidics does not involve the use of moving mechanical parts.

fluid mechanics. The branch of science and technology that deals with forces produced by fluids, either gaseous or liquid. Hydraulics is the branch of fluid mechanics that deals with forces produced by incompressible fluids (liquids). Pneumatics is the branch of fluid mechanics that deals with forces produced by compressible fluids (gases).

fluid ounce. A unit of liquid volume which is equal to $\frac{1}{16}$-liquid pint, or 1.8 cubic inches.

fluid power. The transmission of force by the movement of a fluid.

fluid power systems. Mechanical systems that transfer energy from one location to another by the use of fluids. Hydraulic systems transfer energy by the use of noncompressible fluids, such as oil and water. Pneumatic systems transfer energy by the use of a compressible fluid, such as air.

fluorescence. The emission of electromagnetic radiation, especially in the frequency of visible light, stimulated in a substance by the absorption of incident radiation and persisting only so long as the stimulating radiation is continued.

fluorescent lamp. A tubular electric lamp in which ionized mercury vapor causes a fluorescent coating inside the tube to glow.

fluorescent penetrant inspection. A form of nondestructive inspection used to detect surface faults in either ferrous or nonferrous metals or in nonporous, nonmetallic materials. The part to be inspected is thoroughly cleaned and soaked in a penetrating liquid that contains a fluorescent dye. After the part has soaked for a specified period of time, all the penetrant is washed off its surface, and it is dried. The part is then covered with a developer, a chalk-like powder, that pulls the penetrant out of any cracks or faults into which it has seeped. The part is then inspected under an ultraviolet light that causes any penetrant pulled from a fault to show up as a bright spot or line on the surface.

fluorescent pigment. Pigment used in a paint which can absorb either visible or nonvisible electromagnetic radiation and release it as energy of the desired wavelength. Fluorescent pigments are used for painting pointers and numbers on instrument dials. When ultraviolet light strikes the fluorescent pigment, the dial and pointers glow with a highly visible light.

fluorine. A pale yellow, highly corrosive, poisonous, gaseous, halogen chemical element. Fluorine's symbol is F, its atomic number is 9, and its atomic weight is 18.998. Fluorine is reactive with most other elements, and it is used extensively in industrial compounds.

fluoroscope. An instrument used for nondestructive inspection. A fluorescent screen is used in place of photographic film, to display the shadows which form when X-rays penetrate the structure being inspected.

flush patch (aircraft sheet metal repair). A type of sheet metal repair that leaves a perfectly smooth surface. The reinforcement for the patch is mounted inside the structure, and the hole left where the damaged material was removed is filled with a filler plug. All rivets used for the repair are flush rivets. *See* illustration for filler plug.

flush rivet. An MS20426 aircraft solid rivet that has a countersunk head. The hole for the rivet is prepared by either countersinking or dimpling. When the rivet is driven, its head is flush with the surface of the metal. Flush rivets are used to produce an aerodynamically smooth surface.

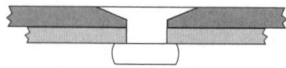

flush rivet

flute. A groove cut into a cylindrical object. A twist drill is a type of tool having cutting edges on its end and flutes cut in the form of a spiral running the length of the drill. Lubricant can be fed to the cutting edge through the flutes, and chips move up through the flutes to keep the hole clean.

flutter (flight condition). Rapid and uncontrolled oscillation of a flight control surface on an aircraft caused by a dynamically unbalanced condition. Flutter normally causes the loss of the control surface and a crash.

flux (magnetism). Lines of magnetic flux are the same as lines of magnetic force.

flux (soldering flux). A material used to prepare a metal so it will accept solder. There are two basic types of flux used with soft solder: acid and resin. Muriatic acid, a form of hydrochloric acid, is used to prepare steel for soldering. The acid cleans the metal by removing oxides from the surface, and etches, or roughens, the surface of the cleaned metal so the solder will stick to it.

Resin is used as a flux for soldering copper wires. The wires must be clean and the joint mechanically sound. When the joint is heated, the resin, which melts at a lower temperature than the solder, flows out ahead of the solder. The flux covers the metal, preventing oxygen reaching the heated metal and forming oxides.

Acid must never be used for soldering any type of electrical equipment because of the difficulty of removing the acid after the soldering is completed. Unless every trace of the acid is removed, corrosion will form.

flux density (magnetism). The number of lines of magnetic flux in a unit of area.

flux gate. *See* flux valve.

flux valve (earth induction compass component). A special transformer that receives a directional signal from the earth's magnetic field and directs it into an amplifier and then into a gyro-stabilized compass indicator. A flux valve is also called a flux gate.

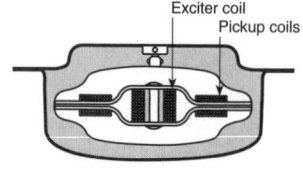

flux valve

fly-by waypoint. A fly-by waypoint requires the use of turn anticipation to avoid overshoot of the next flight segment.

fly-by-wire (flight control system). A method of control used by some modern aircraft in which control movement or pressures exerted by the pilot are directed into a digital computer where they are input into a program tailored to the flight characteristics of the aircraft. The computer output signal is sent to actuators at the control surfaces to move them the optimum amount for the desired maneuver.

fly cutter (hole-cutting tool). An adjustable hole cutter turned in a drill press. The cutting tool is set so its distance from the center of the pilot drill is exactly that needed for the radius of the hole. The pilot drill cuts the center hole, and the cutting tool is fed very slowly into the metal. The cutting tool can be reversed in the holder so the edge of the hole being cut will be either straight or beveled.

"Fly heading...degrees" (air traffic control). Instructions issued by ATC to a pilot directing him to turn to and continue in a specific compass direction.

flying boat. An airplane whose fuselage is built in the form of a boat hull to allow it to land and takeoff from water. Most flying boats have small floats mounted out near the wing tips to support the wing when the aircraft is at rest on the water. In the past, flying boats were a popular form of large airplane for long distance flights, but their inefficiency caused them to become almost extinct after the end of World War II, when there were land airports with long runways scattered throughout the world.

flying wing. A type of heavier-than-air aircraft that has no fuselage or separate tail surfaces. The engines and useful load are carried inside the wing, and movable control surfaces on the trailing edge provide both pitch and roll control.

fly-over waypoint. A fly-over waypoint precludes any turn until the waypoint is overflown and is followed by an intercept maneuver of the next flight segment.

flyweights (speed sensors). Speed sensors used in many types of governors and speed-control devices. A typical flyweight is an L-shaped arm, pivoted at the center, and mounted on a spinning plate. There are usually two or three flyweights mounted on the same plate. A control rod is held against the flyweight by a control, or speeder, spring.

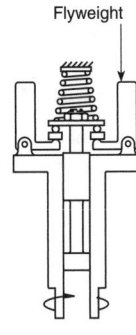

Flyweight

When the plate is not spinning, the speeder spring holds the control rod down, and the toes of the flyweights rest against the plate. This is called the underspeed condition.

When the plate is spinning and the pressure of the speeder spring is weak, centrifugal force causes the flyweights to sling out and lift the control rod. This is called the overspeed condition.

When the centrifugal force on the flyweights exactly balances the compressive force of the speeder spring, the flyweights stand straight up, and the control rod is in a middle position. This is called the onspeed condition.

flyweight

flywheel. A heavy wheel used to smooth the pulsations in a drive system. A reciprocating engine delivers its power in a series of pushes as each cylinder, in turn, goes through its power stroke. A heavy flywheel stores kinetic energy from each power stroke and gives it back by keeping the engine turning between power strokes. An airplane engine does not need a flywheel, because the propeller serves the same purpose.

flywheel effect (electronic circuit). One of the characteristics of an LC circuit, a circuit that contains both inductance and capacitance. If a class-C amplifier supplies an LC circuit with short pulses of energy at the proper time, the magnetic field around the inductor will build up and decay, and the capacitor will charge and discharge.

The LC circuit acts as a flywheel, and a continuous flow of alternating current is maintained between the inductor and capacitor, even though the energy is supplied in short pulses. Energy stored in the electromagnetic and electrostatic fields is supplied to the circuit during the time it is not being supplied by the amplifier.

FM (radio modulation). *See* frequency modulation.

FMC (flight management computer). An electronic flight instrumentation system that allows the flight crew to initiate and implement a given flight plan and monitor its execution.

FMS (flight management systems) (air traffic control). A computer system that uses a large data base to allow routes to be preprogrammed and fed into the system by means of a data loader. The system is constantly updated with respect to position accuracy by reference to conventional navigation aids. The sophisticated program and its associated data base insures that the most appropriate aids are automatically selected during the information update cycle.

foamed plastic. A synthetic resin filled with millions of tiny bubbles. Foamed plastic is lightweight and resilient (soft and pliable) and is used as a packing material and a thermal (heat) insulator. Foamed plastic is sometimes called expanded plastic.

foaming (lubrication system malfunction). A condition in a lubrication system in which oil passing through the engine picks up air which causes thousands of tiny bubbles to form. Foaming oil does not lubricate efficiently, neither does it adequately pick up heat. Foam is removed from the lubricating oil by passing the oil through a deaerator system.

foam rubber. A form of rubber filled with millions of tiny air bubbles. These bubbles were beaten into the latex before it was vulcanized.

FOD (foreign object damage). Damage to the components in the gas path of a turbine engine that is caused by ingesting objects that are not part of the engine. Technicians tools carelessly left in the intake ducts as well as debris from the runways or taxiways can cause FOD when the engine is being run on the ground. In flight, the ingestion of ice and birds can cause FOD.

foehn (meteorology). Warm, dry downslope wind whose warmness and dryness is caused by adiabatic compression upon descent. Foehns are characteristic of mountainous regions. *See* adiabatic process, Chinook, Santa Ana.

fog (meteorology). An obscuration to visibility caused by water droplets that are small enough to remain suspended in the air. Fog differs from drizzle in that it does not fall to the surface, and it differs from cloud only because it extends all the way down to the surface.

foil. A form of metal rolled out into very thin sheets. Foil is normally thought of as a sheet of metal with a thickness of less than 0.15 millimeter (0.006 inch).

folded fell seam (machine-sewed fabric seam). A type of machine-sewed seam in which the edges of the fabric are folded back and a double row of stitches used to form the seam. The stitches pass through three thicknesses of material.

folded fell seam

follow-up question (in teaching/learning process). In the guided discussion method of presenting instructional material, a follow-up question is used by an instructor to get a classroom discussion back on track if it strays from a main point, or to get the students to more thoroughly explain their responses to the instructor's lead-off questions.

follow-up signal. A signal in an autopilot system that nulls out the input signal to the servo when the correct amount of control surface deflection has been reached.

footcandle (illumination). The amount of illumination on a surface when all points are one foot from a uniform light source of one candela, the amount of light produced by one international candle.

foot-pound (measurement of torque). The amount of torque produced when one pound of force is applied one foot from the point of rotation.

foot-pound (measurement of work). The basic measure of work in the English gravitational system. One foot-pound is the amount of work done by one pound of force when it causes a movement of one foot in the direction of its application. One foot-pound is equal to 1.355818 joules.

foot-poundal (measurement of work). The basic measure of work in the English absolute system. One foot-poundal is the amount of work done when one poundal of force causes a movement of one foot in the direction of its application. One foot-poundal is equal to 0.0421 joule. The difference between a foot-pound and a foot-poundal is that foot-pounds use a measure of weight, and foot-poundals use a measure of mass.

$$\text{Mass} = \frac{\text{Weight}}{32.2}$$

force. Energy brought to bear on an object that causes or tries to cause it to change its direction or speed of motion.

forced landing (aircraft operation). An unscheduled landing caused by a malfunction in an aircraft or engine, or by improper flight planning or operation.

forceps. A type of instrument or small tool used to grasp or hold objects. Most forceps have a ratchet mechanism that allows them to be locked onto the object they are holding.

forebody length (float dimension). The distance from the step, to the bow of a float or flying boat hull.

fore flap (control component). The section of a triple-slotted flap that is closest to the wing. *See* triple-slotted flap.

F

forehand welding. Welding in which the torch is pointed in the direction the weld is progressing.

foreign air carrier. *14 CFR Part 1:* "Any person other than a citizen of the United States, who undertakes directly, by lease or other arrangement, to engage in air transportation."

foreign air commerce. *14 CFR Part 1:* "The carriage by aircraft of persons or property for compensation or hire, or the carriage of mail by aircraft, or the operation or navigation of aircraft in the conduct or furtherance of a business or vocation, in commerce between a place in the United States and any place outside thereof; whether such commerce moves wholly by aircraft or partly by aircraft and partly by other forms of transportation."

foreign air transportation. *14 CFR Part 1:* "The carriage by aircraft of persons or property as a common carrier for compensation or hire, or the carriage of mail by aircraft, in commerce between a place in the United States and any place outside of the United States, whether that commerce moves wholly by aircraft or partly by aircraft and partly by other forms of transportation."

foreign object damage (FOD). Damage to a gas turbine engine caused by an object sucked into the engine while it is running. Debris from runways or taxiways can cause foreign object damage during ground operations, and the ingestion of ice and birds can cause FOD in flight.

forge, forging. A method of forming metal parts by heating the metal to a plastic state (nearly, but not quite melted) and hammering it to shape.

forge welding. A method of welding in which the two ends of the metal to be joined are heated until they are almost, but not quite, melted. The ends are placed together and hammered until they flow together and become one piece.

forklift. A self-propelled machine used to lift heavy weights and move them from one location to another. A forklift has two long steel fingers that can be slid under a pallet on which the load is placed. The fingers can then be raised to lift the load off the floor and move it.

formal lecture. An oral presentation where the purpose is to inform, persuade, or entertain with little or no verbal participation by the listeners.

formation flight. Flight of more than one aircraft which, by prior arrangement between the pilots, operate as a single aircraft with regard to navigation and position reporting.

form drag. Parasite drag that is caused by the form of the object passing through the air.

former (aircraft structural member). An aircraft structural member used to give a fuselage its shape. The truss structure of an aircraft fuselage provides the necessary strength, but its cross section is usually square or triangular and does not have the clean aerodynamic shape needed for streamlining.

Formers of wood or light metal are attached to the truss, and stringers (lightweight strips of metal or wood) are placed over the formers to give the fuselage its shape. All of this structure is covered with fabric or thin sheet metal.

A monocoque fuselage carries most of its stresses in its outside skin whose shape is produced by formers to which the skin is attached. Formers that divide a fuselage into compartments are called bulkheads.

form factor (electrical inductor characteristic). The ratio of the length of a coil of wire to its diameter. Form factor is one of the characteristics that affect the inductance of a coil.

forming block (sheet-metal forming tool). A block of hardwood around which sheet metal parts are formed.

forward bias (semiconductor operating condition). A condition of operation of a semiconductor device, such as a transistor or a diode, in which a positive voltage is connected to the P-type material, and a negative voltage is connected to the N-type material. When the device is forward-biased, the barrier voltage is minimum, and the maximum amount of current can flow through it.

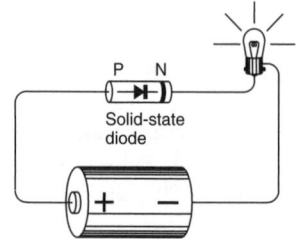

forward-biased diode

forward center of gravity limit (aircraft weight and balance). The most forward location on an aircraft allowed for its loaded center of gravity.

forward current (semiconductor characteristic). Current that flows across the junction in a semiconductor device when it is forward-biased.

forward-fan engine (aircraft gas turbine engine). A turbofan engine with some of its low-pressure compressor blades extended. These extended blades act as a fan and force air around the outside of the gas-generator portion of the engine. Most modern turbofan engines are forward-fan engines.

forward slip (flight maneuver). A crossed-control maneuver used to dissipate altitude without increasing the aircraft's speed. The direction of flight is not changed when the aircraft is slipped. *See* side slip.

forward voltage drop (semiconductor characteristic). The voltage drop across a semiconductor device when forward current is flowing through it.

forward wing. *14 CFR Part 1:* "A forward lifting surface of a canard configuration or tandem-wing configuration airplane. The surface may be a fixed, movable, or variable geometry surface, with or without control surfaces."

fouled spark plug (malfunctioning ignition system component). A spark plug that is unable to fire because of contamination in its firing-end cavity. Oil, soot, silicon deposits, or lead deposits can build up in the firing end until they provide a bridge that allows the voltage to leak off before it can build up high enough to jump across the gap between the electrodes.

four-corner post configuration (air traffic control). An arrangement of air traffic pathways in a terminal area that brings incoming flights over fixes at four corners of the traffic area, while outbound flights depart between the fixes, thus minimizing conflicts between arriving and departing traffic.

four-harness satin (composites). A weave for composite fabric that is more pliable than plain weave and is easier to conform to curved surfaces common in reinforced plastics. In this weave pattern each warp thread passes under one fill thread and over three. *See* satin-weave fabric.

four-stroke cycle. A constant-volume cycle of energy transformation that has separate strokes for intake, compression, power, and exhaust. *See* Otto cycle.

four-stroke-cycle reciprocating engine. A form of reciprocating engine which has an intake and an exhaust valve in each cylinder. Four strokes of the piston (two in and two out) are needed to change chemical energy in the fuel into mechanical energy at the rotating crankshaft.

During the intake stroke, the piston moves inward, with the intake valve open and the exhaust valve closed. A mixture of fuel and air is pulled into the cylinder through the carburetor.

On the compression stroke, the piston moves outward with both valves closed. This compresses the fuel-air mixture. Near the end of the compression stroke, the spark plug fires and ignites the compressed fuel-air mixture.

The burning fuel heats and expands the air inside the cylinder, and the expanding air forces the piston inward on the power stroke. Near the end of the power stroke, the exhaust valve opens.

During the exhaust stroke, the piston moves outward with the exhaust valve open. As the piston moves outward, it forces the burned gases from the cylinder, and the cylinder is prepared for another cycle of operation.

Fowler flap (airplane secondary flight control). A type of wing flap which moves out of the trailing edge of a wing on tracks. Fowler flaps increase both the wing area and camber which increases the lift and drag produced by the wing. They allow the wing to produce its lift at a slower airspeed so less runway is required for takeoff and landing.

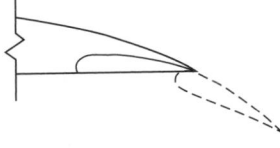

Fowler flap

FPD (freezing point depressant). A chemical compound added to a liquid to lower its freezing temperature. FPDs are used in the fluid sprayed on an aircraft to deice it before flight.

FPM. Feet per minute.

fraction. A number written in the form N/D in which N is the numerator and D is the denominator. For example, $^5/_{16}$ is a fraction.

fractional distillation. The procedure used for separating the various components from a physical mixture of liquids. Crude oil is a mixture of many different types of hydrocarbon fuels which can be separated by carefully raising its temperature. The first products to be released, those having the lowest boiling points, are some of the gaseous fuels; then gasoline, kerosine, diesel fuel, heavy fuel oils, lubricating oils, and finally, tar and asphalt.

fractus (meteorology). Clouds in the form of ragged, irregular shreds, appearing as if they were torn. Fractus clouds of the cumulus family are called fractocumulus, and those in the stratus family are called fractostratus.

francium. An extremely unstable, radioactive chemical element. Francium's symbol is Fr, and its atomic number is 87. The most stable of francium's isotopes is Fr 223, which has a half-life of 21 minutes.

frangible. Breakable, or easily broken.

free balloon. A lighter-than-air device that is free to rise in the air. A free balloon is used in weather observations to find the height of the base of the lower layer of clouds. A rubber balloon is filled with helium until it has a specified diameter, and it is released into the air. The rate of rise of this balloon is known, and the time between its release and its disappearance into the clouds is measured. This time determines the height of the base of the clouds.

free electrons. Electrons that are not bound to any particular atom. They are free to move about from one atom to another in a material. A semiconductor material having a large number of free electrons is called an N-type material.

free fit (threaded fastener). A loose fit between moving parts, used when accuracy of movement is not important. A nut that turns easily over the threads of a screw or bolt is said to have a free fit.

free flight. A method of air traffic management designed to enhance the safety, capacity, and efficiency of the NAS. Under this system, air traffic control is expected to move gradually from a highly structured system based on elaborate rules and procedures to a more flexible system that allows pilots, within limits, to change their route, speed, and altitude, notifying the air traffic controller of the new route.

free-running multivibrator (electronic oscillator). A form of oscillator that produces a square-wave output. It uses two transistors arranged in a circuit in such a way that when one transistor begins to conduct (when it turns on), it turns the other transistor off. When the second transistor turns off, it feeds a signal to the first transistor that turns it off. When the first transistor turns off, it turns the second one on.

A free-running multivibrator has no stable condition, and because of this, it is called an astable (no stable condition) oscillator.

free turbine (gas turbine engine component). A turbine or stage of turbines in a gas turbine engine that is not used to drive the compressor in the gas-generator section of the engine. A free turbine may be used to drive the reduction gears for the propeller in a turboprop engine, or the transmission and a rotor of a helicopter. Free turbines are also used in industrial turbine engines to drive pumps or generators. Free turbines are sometimes referred to as free power turbines.

free wheeling unit (helicopter component). A component part of the transmission or power train of a helicopter which automatically disconnects the main rotor from the engine when the engine stops or slows below the equivalent RPM of the rotor.

freeze calculated landing time (air traffic control). A dynamic parameter number of minutes prior to the meter fix calculated time of arrival for each aircraft when the TCLT is frozen and becomes an ACLT (i.e., the VTA is updated and consequently the TCLT is modified as appropriate until FCLT minutes prior to meter fix calculated time of arrival, at which time updating is suspended and an ACLT and a frozen meter fix crossing time (MFT) is assigned).

freeze/frozen (air traffic control). An ATC description used in reference to (1) aircraft arrivals that have been assigned an actual calculated landing time (ACLT), and (2) the list displaying ACLTs of aircraft arrivals.

freeze horizon (air traffic control). The time or point at which an aircraft's STA becomes fixed and no longer fluctuates with each radar update. This setting insures a constant time for each aircraft, necessary for the metering controller to plan his/her delay technique. This setting can be either in distance from the meter fix or a prescribed flying time to the meter fix.

freeze speed parameter (air traffic control). A speed adapted for each aircraft to determine fast and slow aircraft. Fast aircraft freeze on parameter FCLT and slow aircraft freeze on parameter MLDI.

freezing. The process in which a liquid is changed into a solid by the removal of heat energy. When enough heat energy is removed from liquid water, it freezes, or turns into solid water (ice).

freezing level (meteorology). The level in the atmosphere at which the temperature is 0°C (32°F).

freezing point. The temperature at which a liquid changes into a solid. In petroleum specifications, freezing point is the temperature at which solids, such as wax crystals, separate from a hydrocarbon fuel as it is cooled.

freezing rain (meteorology). Rain that falls through air whose temperature is lower than 0°C. It is supercooled but remains in its liquid form. It freezes upon contact with objects on the ground or in the air.

French fell seam (machine-sewed fabric seam). A type of machine-sewed seam in which the edges of the two pieces of fabric are folded together, and a double row of stitches passes through four thicknesses of the material.

French fell seam

Freon. The registered trade name for a fluorinated hydrocarbon compound used as a refrigerant and a fire extinguishing agent. There are a number of Freon compounds identified with numbers. Each compound having different characteristics. Freon-12 has been the most commonly used refrigerant in aircraft air conditioning systems, but because of environmental considerations it is being phased out and replaced by R-134a which is more environmentally friendly.

frequency. The number of complete cycles of a recurring event that take place in one unit of time.

frequency converter (electronic circuit). A circuit which changes the frequency of alternating current. Alternating current with a frequency of 1,000 hertz, for example, can be changed to 200 hertz by combining it with an AC signal having a frequency of 1,200 hertz. When alternating currents having these two frequencies are combined, or mixed, two more alternating currents are produced: one having a frequency which is the sum of the two, 2,200 hertz, and the other a frequency which is the difference between the two—in this case, 200 hertz, the desired frequency.

frequency divider (electronic circuit). An electronic circuit whose output has a frequency that is an exact divisor of the frequency at the input. If a signal of 100 kilohertz is placed on the input of a frequency divider that divides by two, the frequency at the output will be 50 kilohertz.

frequency doubler (electronic circuit). An electronic circuit whose output is resonant at the second harmonic of the input signal. The frequency of the second harmonic of an alternating current is exactly two times the frequency of the input AC. The output frequency of the frequency doubler is two times that of the input.

frequency meter (electrical measuring instrument). An electrical instrument that measures the frequency of an alternating current and shows this frequency directly on its dial. One commonly used type of frequency meter is a vibrating reed-type instrument. A series of metal reeds of different lengths is excited by the AC, and the reed that vibrates with the greatest amplitude is resonant at the frequency of the AC. The frequency at which each reed is resonant is marked beside each reed.

frequency modulation (radio communications). One method of putting an audio frequency signal on a radio frequency carrier. Rather than the AF signal changing the amplitude of the carrier, as is done in amplitude modulation (AM), the AF signal changes the frequency of the carrier by an amount determined by the amplitude of the audio signal. The amplitude of the frequency-modulated carrier is clipped so static caused by electrical interference causes a minimum of distortion.

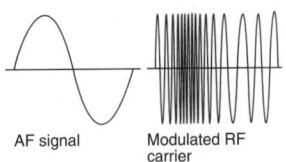

AF signal   Modulated RF
                carrier

frequency modulation

frequency multiplier (electronic circuit). An electronic circuit whose output has a frequency that is a multiple of the frequency of the input signal. Frequency doublers and triplers are commonly used frequency multipliers.

frequency synthesizer (electronic circuit). An electronic circuit used to produce alternating current having an accurately controlled frequency. One type of frequency synthesizer uses a crystal-controlled oscillator to produce a single accurate frequency. Frequency multipliers and dividers change the crystal frequency into the required frequencies.

fresh annual inspection. A term used frequently when selling aircraft. It means that the aircraft has recently had an annual inspection.

freshening charge (battery servicing). A constant-voltage charge given to dry-charged batteries to get them ready for installation. Most lead-acid batteries are shipped from the manufacturer in a dry-charged state. The battery was charged at the factory, the electrolyte was drained, and the cells were sealed.

Continued

freshening charge (battery servicing). *Continued*

When the battery is ready to be put into service, electrolyte having the proper specific gravity is poured into the cells, and the battery is given a constant-voltage freshening charge. The battery is considered ready for service when the specific gravity of the electrolyte does not change in three hours of charging.

fretting. A type of mechanical damage to the surface of an object. Fretting is caused by one object rubbing against another and wearing part of it away.

fretting corrosion. A form of corrosion between two surfaces which have a slight amount of relative motion between them. The protective oxide coating that forms on aluminum or magnesium alloys is rubbed away by the movement of the parts. New oxides must be continually formed to replace those that are worn away and these oxides act as an abrasive to further damage the metal.

friction. Opposition to the relative movement between two objects.

friction brake. A mechanism used with a rotating wheel or shaft in which friction is used to slow its rotation.

friction clutch. A device used to connect a motor to a mechanical load. A plate or cone on the load is driven by a mating device on the motor. A lining made of a material that causes a good deal of friction separates the two surfaces, and a spring forces the surfaces and lining tightly together, allowing the motor to drive the load. The spring force can be released to disconnect the motor from the load.

friction drag. The portion of parasitic drag on a body resulting from viscous shearing stresses over its wetted surface.

friction error (instrument indications). The error caused by friction in an instrument mechanism. The amount of friction error is found by reading the instrument, vibrating it, and then reading it again. The difference between the two indications is the amount of friction error.

friction horsepower (reciprocating engine specification). The amount of horsepower used to turn the crankshaft, pistons, gears and accessories in a reciprocating engine, and to compress the air in the cylinders. The brake horsepower actually delivered to the output shaft of the engine is the total horsepower developed by the engine, less the friction horsepower.

friction level classifications (for a runway surface). The levels of friction value in three classifications, which are allowed for the runway pavement surface as measured by FAA-qualified "continuous friction measurement equipment" (CFME). The CFME friction values are a guideline for evaluating the surface friction deterioration of runway pavements, as well as for identifying the appropriate corrective actions required for safe aircraft operations. The three classification levels are minimum, maintenance planning, and new design/construction (per Advisory Circular 150/5320-12).

friction-lock Cherry rivet. A type of self-plugging blind rivet in which a stem with a tapered end is pulled through the hollow rivet shank. The tapered end swells the shank to pull the sheets of metal being joined tightly together. Continued pulling breaks the stem and leaves it wedged tightly inside the shank. Friction holds the stem in the rivet shank, but it can vibrate out. For this reason friction-lock rivets cannot be used to replace solid rivets on a size-for-size basis. *See* Cherry rivet.

friction loss. The loss of mechanical energy in a mechanism caused by friction changing mechanical energy into heat.

friction measurement (runway condition). A measurement of the friction characteristics of the runway pavement surface, using continuous self-watering friction measurement equipment in accordance with the specifications, procedures, and schedules contained in AC 150/5320-12, *Measurement, Construction, and Maintenance of Skid-Resistance Airport Pavement Surfaces.*

friction tape. A type of electrical insulating tape that was commonly used in the past, but is being replaced by more effective types of tape. Friction tape is a cloth tape impregnated with a black, sticky, tar-like material.

friction welding. A method of joining thermoplastic materials by rubbing the mating surfaces together while applying a large amount of pressure. Heat caused by the friction softens the material, and the pressure fuses the softened edges together.

Frise aileron (airplane control). A type of aileron used for lateral control of an airplane. The hinge line of a Frise aileron is set back from the leading edge so a portion of its surface is ahead of the hinge line. When the aileron is raised, to lower the wing on which it is mounted, the portion ahead of the hinge line protrudes below the wing and causes parasite drag. This parasite drag counteracts the induced drag produced on the opposite wing when its aileron is lowered. Frise ailerons minimize adverse yaw.

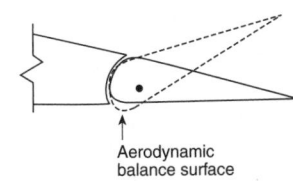

Aerodynamic
balance surface

Frise aileron

front (meteorology). A surface, interface, or transition zone of discontinuity between two adjacent air masses having different densities. More simply, a front is the boundary between two different air masses.

frontal zone (meteorology). A front or zone with a marked increase-of-density gradient. The term frontal zone is used because fronts are not truly a "surface" of discontinuity, but, rather, a "zone" of rapid transition of meteorological elements.

frontogenesis (meteorology). The initial formation of a front or frontal zone.

frontolysis (meteorology). The dissipation of a front or frontal zone.

front-surface mirror. A mirror with the reflective material on its front surface, rather than on the back.

front-to-back ratio (semiconductor characteristic). A rough measurement of the condition of a semiconductor diode. When the resistance of the diode is measured with an ohmmeter, it should have a high resistance one way (the junction is reverse-biased), but when the leads are reversed, the resistance should be low (the junction is forward-biased). A high front-to-back ratio normally indicates a good diode.

frost (meteorology). Ice crystal deposits formed by sublimation when the temperature and dew point are below freezing.

frustrum. The portion of a cone or a cone-shaped solid from which the top has been removed. The top and the bottom of the frustrum are parallel surfaces, with the top surface smaller than the bottom.

FSDO (Flight Standards District Office). An FAA field office serving an assigned geographical area, staffed with Flight Standards personnel who serve the aviation industry and the general public on matters relating to the certification and operation of air carrier and general aviation aircraft. FSDO activities include general surveillance of operational safety, certification of airmen and aircraft, accident prevention, investigation, enforcement, etc.

FSS (flight service station). Air traffic control facilities which provide these services:
- Pilot briefing
- Enroute communications
- VFR search and rescue services
- Assistance to lost aircraft and aircraft in emergency situations
- Relay ATC clearances
- Originate Notices to Airmen
- Broadcast aviation weather and NAS information

Continued

FSS (flight service station). *Continued*
- Receive and process IFR flight plans
- Monitor NAVAIDs

Some flight service stations perform these services in addition:
- Provide Enroute Flight Advisory Service (Flight Watch)
- Take weather observations
- Issue airport advisories
- Advise Customs and Immigration of transborder flights

FTD. *See* flight training device.

fuel. Any material that can be burned to release its energy. Gasoline, kerosine, coal, wood, and natural gas are all forms of fuel.

fuel-air mixture ratio. The ratio of the number of pounds of fuel to the number of pounds of air in the mixture burned, in an internal combustion engine.

fuel boost pump (aircraft fuel system component). An auxiliary fuel pump used in an aircraft fuel system to provide fuel pressure for starting the engine, for use as an emergency backup in case the fuel pump fails, and to transfer fuel from one tank to another.

fuel cell (electrical device). A type of electrical cell that converts chemical energy directly into electrical energy. The electrical energy is produced by a chemical reaction between an electrolyte and a liquid or gaseous fuel.

fuel control unit (gas turbine engine). The fuel metering device for a gas turbine engine that senses the variables of power lever position, pressure, speed, and temperature in the engine. The fuel control unit then meters the correct amount of fuel to be sent to the burners for the existing conditions.

fuel dumping. Airborne release of usable fuel, a procedure used by aircraft in certain emergency situations in order to either lighten the aircraft's weight or to reduce risk of fire. Used before a return to the airport shortly after takeoff, or before landing short of the aircraft's intended destination (an emergency landing). Also referred to as a fuel jettison. (*Note:* this term does not refer to the dropping of fuel tanks.)

fuel dump system (aircraft fuel system). *See* fuel jettison system.

fuel evaporation ice (carburetor ice). A type of carburetor ice that forms in the throat of a float-type carburetor when the discharged fuel evaporates and lowers the temperature of the air passing through the carburetor. As the air is cooled, water vapor condenses into liquid water and freezes. *See* carburetor ice.

fuel flow. The rate at which fuel flows in a fuel metering system. Fuel flow is normally expressed in terms of pounds per hour.

fuel flowmeter (aircraft instrument). An instrument used to show the rate of fuel flowing to an engine. Fuel flowmeters used with modern fuel-injected reciprocating engines are actually pressure gages that measure the pressure drop across the injector nozzles. A popular flowmeter for turbine engines uses a small turbine in the fuel line to the fuel control unit that measures the rate of fuel flow. It converts this flow rate into an electrical signal and sends it to an indicator in the instrument panel.

fuel flow transmitter (powerplant instrument). A device in the fuel line between the engine-driven fuel pump and the carburetor that measures the rate of flow of the fuel. The flowmeter transmitter converts the flow rate into an electrical signal and sends it to an indicator in the instrument panel.

fuel grade (aviation gasoline characteristic). A system of rating aviation gasoline according to its antidetonation characteristics. This is based on the older system of octane rating or performance number in which the higher the number, the more resistant the fuel is to detonation.

fuel heater (turbojet airplane fuel system component). A form of fuel-air heat exchanger in which heat is taken from the compressor bleed air and put into the fuel before it flows through the fuel filter. At high altitude, the temperature is so low that water entrained in the fuel precipitates out and freezes on the fuel filter. The fuel heater warms the fuel enough to prevent the water freezing.

fuel injection manifold valve (reciprocating engine component). The valve used in a reciprocating engine fuel injection system that takes fuel from the fuel control unit and distributes it to the various injection nozzles. The manifold valve provides a metering force for conditions of low fuel flow, and also provides a positive fuel shutoff when the engine is shut down. By shutting off the fuel at the manifold valve, the lines to the injector nozzles are kept full of fuel.

F

fuel injection system (reciprocating engine). A form of fuel metering system for a recip- rocating engine that injects the fuel directly into the cylinder, rather than mixing it with the air before it is taken in through the intake valve. There are two types of fuel injection systems in use, the direct injection system and the continuous-flow injection system.

The direct injection system, such as is used in a diesel engine, sprays the fuel into the cylinder under high pressure. The fuel is atomized by the spray for better combustion.

The continuous-flow fuel injection system used on many of the modern horizontally opposed aircraft engines is not a true injection system. It meters the fuel and delivers it under a low pressure to the outside of the intake valve. This fuel, along with the necessary air for combustion, is pulled into the cylinder when the intake valve opens.

fuel jettison system. The portion of an aircraft fuel system that allows fuel to be dumped from the tanks to lower the landing weight so a safe landing can be made. Some aircraft are certificated with a higher takeoff weight than is allowed for landing. If an emergency requires such an airplane to return for a landing before enough fuel is used from the tanks to lower the weight enough for landing, fuel may be dumped.

Boost pumps in the fuel tanks move the fuel from the tank into a fuel manifold. From the fuel manifold it flows away from the aircraft through dump chutes in each wing tip. The dumped fuel evaporates and is diluted by the air, so it causes no danger to people on the ground. Fuel jettison systems are designed and constructed in such a way that they are free from fire hazards.

fuel load. The expendable part of the load of the aircraft. Fuel load includes only the fuel that is usable in flight.

fuel management system or function. An advanced avionics system that assists the pilot in managing fuel by considering fuel flow, airspeed, and winds to help predict remaining fuel at each waypoint along the programmed route, total endurance, and the viability of alternative routings or diversions. Stand-alone systems may integrate the output data into the FMS/RNAV or provide a discreet display, while the fuel management function is an integral portion of the FMS/RNAV system. In either instance, the fuel data management goals are similar.

fuel nozzle (gas turbine engine component). The nozzle in a gas turbine engine combustor through which the fuel is discharged. The spray pattern from the fuel nozzle is such that the flame is always centered in the burner so it will not overheat it.

fuel-oil heat exchanger (gas turbine engine component). A heat exchanger used on turbine engines to take heat from the engine oil and put it into the fuel. The fuel flows through tubes that pass through the hot engine oil. Heat from the oil enters the fuel and raises its temperature, and at the same time, the temperature of the oil is lowered.

fuel pump (fuel system component). An engine-driven or electrical pump that moves fuel from the fuel tank to the fuel metering system.

fuel range ring. A graphical depiction of the point at which an aircraft is predicted to exhaust its fuel reserves or reach a point at which only reserve fuel remains.

"Fuel remaining" (air traffic control). A phrase used by either pilots or controllers that relates to the fuel remaining on board until actual fuel exhaustion. When transmitting such information in response to either a controller question or pilot initiated cautionary advisory to air traffic control, pilots will state the *approximate number of minutes* the flight can continue with the fuel remaining. All reserve fuel *should be included* in the time stated, as should an allowance for established fuel gage system error.

fuel selector valve. The valve in an aircraft fuel system that allows the pilot to select the fuel tank that feeds the engine or engines.

fuel shut-off valve (fuel system component). A valve that shuts off the fuel supply to the engine.

fuel siphoning. Unintentional release of fuel from an aircraft, caused by overflow, puncture, loose tank caps, etc.

fuel system (aircraft system). The system of components that includes tanks, fuel lines, valves, pumps, and pressure and flow indicators that stores fuel and delivers it to the fuel metering system in adequate quantities at the proper pressure and flow rate for all normal flight conditions.

fuel tank vent (fuel system component). A vent in the top of the fuel tank that allows the air pressure above the fuel in the tank to remain the same as outside pressure as altitude changes. Reduced pressure in the tank caused by ineffective venting could reduce the rate of fuel flow to the engine and cause the fuel tank to collapse.

fuel totalizer. A fuel quantity indicator that gives the total amount of fuel remaining on board the aircraft on one instrument. The totalizer adds the quantities of fuel in all of the tanks.

fulcrum. The point about which a lever balances.

full-bodied (finishing system component condition). Not thinned.

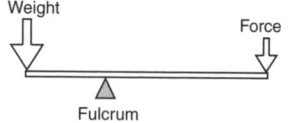

fulcrum

full flight simulator (FFS). A replica of a specific type or make-model-series aircraft cockpit. An FFS includes the assemblage of equipment and computer programs necessary to represent aircraft operations in ground and flight conditions, a visual system providing an out-of-the-cockpit view, a system that provides cues at least equivalent to those of a three-degree-of-freedom motion system, and the full range of capabilities of the systems installed in the device as described in 14 CFR Part 60 and the qualification performance standards (QPS) for a specific FFS qualification level.

full-register position (aircraft magneto timing). The position of the rotating magnet in an aircraft magneto in which the poles of the magnet are aligned with the pole shoes. The maximum number of lines of flux pass from the magnet through the core of the coil when the magnet is in its full-register position.

full-rich (fuel metering system condition). The position of the mixture control in the fuel metering system of a reciprocating engine that meters the maximum amount of fuel to the engine.

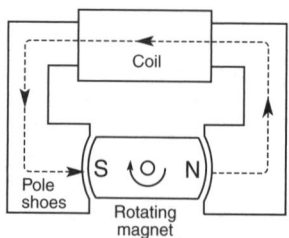

full-register position

full-scale drawing (mechanical drawing). A drawing of a part drawn to the full size of the part.

full-throttle altitude (aircraft performance). The highest altitude at which maximum engine power output is available. Above this altitude, the horsepower of the engine will be less than its rated horsepower.

full-wave rectifier (electronic circuit). A type of rectifier circuit used to change alternating current into direct current that uses both the positive and negative alternation of the AC.

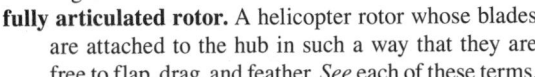

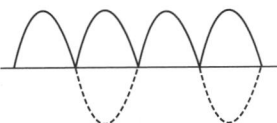

full-wave rectification

F

fully articulated rotor. A helicopter rotor whose blades are attached to the hub in such a way that they are free to flap, drag, and feather. *See* each of these terms.

functional test. A test given to a component or system to determine whether or not it functions as it should. A functional test is not a quantitative test.

fundamental frequency (vibration frequency). Vibration of a mechanical object that has the lowest frequency and the highest amplitude. The fundamental frequency is called the first harmonic, or the fundamental harmonic, of the frequency.

fundamental skills. Pilot skills of instrument cross-check, instrument interpretation, and aircraft control.

fundamental wavelength (radio communications). The length of the wave of the fundamental frequency of an electromagnetic radiation. In a radio antenna, the fundamental wavelength is the wavelength of the lowest frequency to which the antenna is resonant.

fungicidal paste (aircraft fabric covering material). A paste containing an agent that kills the spores of fungus and mildew. This fungicidal paste is added to the dope used for the first coat applied to cotton or linen fabric.

fungus (*plural* fungi). Any of several types of plant life that include yeasts, molds, and mildew.

funnel cloud (meteorology). A tornado, or vortex cloud, extending downward from the parent cloud, but not reaching the ground.

fuse (electrical component). An electrical circuit protection device that consists of a strip of low-melting-point metal that will melt and open the circuit when an excessive amount of current flows through it. In many modern aircraft electrical systems, fuses have been replaced with resettable circuit breakers.

fuse

fuse (hydraulic component). A hydraulic flow control valve that automatically closes when a given amount of fluid has passed, or when an excessive pressure drop occurs across the valve. Hydraulic fuses prevent the loss of all of the fluid in the event of a broken line.

fuse holder (electrical component). A device that holds a tubular fuse and makes connections to both its ends. A panel-mounted fuse holder makes it easy to replace a blown fuse.

fuselage (aircraft component). The body, or central structural component of an airplane. The passengers and flight crew are housed in the fuselage, and the wings and tail attach to it. In most single-engine airplanes, the engine and landing gear attach to the fuselage.

fuselage center line. A line parallel to the longitudinal axis of an airplane that divides the fuselage into symmetrical halves.

fuselage station (location in an aircraft structure). The location along the longitudinal axis of an aircraft that is a given number of inches ahead of or behind the datum, or reference plane.

fuse link (electrical component). A strip of low-melting-point metal used in an electrical fuse to protect a circuit. The amount of current that can flow through the fuse link before it melts and opens the circuit is determined by the size of the fuse link and the type of metal of which it is made.

fusible alloy. A metal alloy that is capable of being melted by heat. Strips of fusible alloy are used in electrical fuses to melt and open the circuit when a specified amount of current passes through them.

fusible plug (aircraft wheel component). A safety plug used in an aircraft wheel that mounts a tubeless tire. The plug has a hole drilled through it, and this hole is filled with a low-melting-point alloy. If a wheel is overheated by the excessive use of the brakes during an aborted takeoff, the alloy in the plug will melt and deflate the tire. This prevents the air pressure in the tire building up high enough to cause an explosion.

fusion. *See* nuclear fusion.

G *or* **Gs (measure of gravity).** A measure of the force of gravity. One G is a force equal the weight of an object.

GADO (general aviation district office). An FAA field office serving a designated geographical area, staffed with Flight Standards personnel who have responsibility for serving the aviation industry and the general public on all matters relating to the certification and operation of general aviation aircraft. Many GADOs have been replaced by FSDOs. *See* FSDO.

gadolinium. A silvery-white, malleable, ductile, metallic, rare-earth chemical element. Gadolinium's symbol is Gd, its atomic number is 64, and its atomic weight is 157.25. Gadolinium is highly magnetic, especially at low temperatures, and is used as an absorber of neutrons in nuclear reactors and as an alloying element for other metals.

gage (measuring instrument). A gage (also spelled gauge) is a measuring instrument. There are many different types of gages. A pressure gage is used to indicate the amount of pressure being applied to a fluid. A depth gage is used to measure the distance between the edge of a hole or groove and its bottom. A thickness gage (often called a feeler gage) is used to measure the clearance between close-fitting parts of a machine.

gage (rivet). The distance between rows of rivets in a multirow seam. Gage is also called transverse pitch.

gage block (precision tool). A precision-ground block of hardened and polished steel used as the standard for precise linear measurements in most manufacturing processes, and to check the accuracy of micrometer calipers. The dimensional accuracy of a gage block is normally measured in millionths of an inch.

gage pressure. Pressure referenced from the existing atmospheric pressure. Engine oil pressure and hydraulic pressure are normally measured as gage pressure. If gage pressure is measured in pounds per square inch, it is spoken of as so many psig.

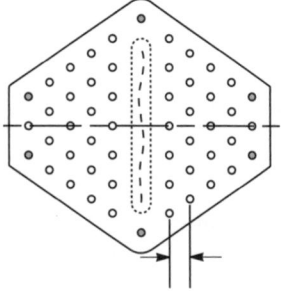

gage (rivet)

Two other commonly used types of pressure are differential pressure (psid), which is the difference between two pressures, and absolute pressure (psia), which is referenced from zero pressure (a vacuum).

gain (electrical). An increase in the power of an electrical signal produced by an amplifier.

galena. A bluish-gray crystal that is primarily lead sulfide (PbS). It is the main ore from which lead is obtained. Galena is one of the crystals used in the early days of radio experimentation. When a crystal of galena is in contact with a fine-pointed wire called a cat whisker, it acts as a rectifier and can be used as a detector for radio signals picked up on an antenna.

galling. A form of damage to the mating surfaces of moving metal parts. When localized high spots rub against each other, they become heated by friction enough to weld together, and as they continue to move, the welded areas pull apart and destroy some of the surface.

gallium. A rare, metallic chemical element that melts at approximately 30°C. Gallium's symbol is Ga, its atomic number is 31, and its atomic weight is 69.72. Gallium is used as a doping agent in the manufacture of semiconductors.

gallon, Imperial. A unit of liquid measurement used in the United Kingdom. One Imperial gallon is the volume occupied by ten pounds of pure water under specified conditions of temperature and pressure. One imperial gallon is equal to 277.4 cubic inches, 4.55 liters, or 1.201 U.S. gallons.

gallon, U.S. A unit of liquid measurement used in the United States of America. One U.S. gallon is equal to 231 cubic inches, 128 fluid ounces, 3.785 liters, or 0.832 imperial gallon.

galvanic action. Electrical pressure within a substance which causes electron flow because of the difference of electrode potential within a material.

galvanic corrosion. A form of corrosion that occurs between two metals having different locations in the electrolytic, or galvanic, series. *See* galvanic series. Corrosion can take place any time two metals are covered with an electrolyte. The amount of corrosion is determined by the difference in the location of the two metals in the galvanic series. The more active metal (the metal highest in the galvanic series) acts as the anode in the electrolytic process, and is eaten away. The more noble metal is not affected.

galvanic couple. A pair of unlike metals that produce an electrical potential when they are covered with an electrolyte. Copper and zinc form a commonly used galvanic couple. When a piece of copper and a piece of zinc are covered with the same electrolyte, a voltage is produced between them. The zinc, being the less noble of the two metals, forms the anode. Electrons leave the zinc and travel to the copper. The copper is the positive terminal of the galvanic couple, and the zinc is the negative terminal.

galvanic generation of electricity. The production of electricity by chemical action. Electricity produced by dry-cell batteries and storage batteries are examples of galvanic production of electricity.

galvanic grouping. The arrangement of metals in a series according to their electrode potential difference.

galvanic series. A list of metals arranged in the order of their chemical activity. The metals are listed in their order of activity with the more active (least noble) metal being the anode in an electrolytic action.

galvanizing. A form of corrosion protection for steel parts in which the surface of the steel is covered with a coating of zinc. The zinc may be applied by hot dipping or by electroplating.

galvanometer. An instrument used to measure electrical current. A galvanometer measures the amount of current flowing in a circuit by measuring the interaction between two magnetic fields. One field is produced by a permanent magnet, and its strength is fixed. The other field, an electromagnetic field, is produced by current flowing through a moving coil, and its strength is determined by the amount of current being measured. The moving coil is restrained by a calibrated hairspring in such a way that its deflection is proportional to the amount of current flowing through it.

gamma iron. The molecular arrangement of iron at temperatures between 911°C and 1,392°C.

gamma rays. A form of electromagnetic radiation that results from nuclear fission. Gamma rays have the ability to penetrate solid material, and they are used in the radiographic method of nondestructive inspection.

ganged tuning (electronic circuitry). The process of tuning two or more circuits with a single control.

Most Active
(Least Noble)

Zinc
Cadmium
Iron
Lead
Tin
Nickel
Brass
Copper
Bronze
Monel
Silver
Gold
Platinum

Least Active
(Most Noble)

galvanic series

garnet paper. An abrasive and polishing paper made by coating one side of a sheet of flexible paper with a layer of crushed garnet.

gas. The physical state of matter in which a material takes the shape of its container and expands to fill the entire container. Oxygen and nitrogen are two chemical elements that are gases at normal room temperature and pressure. The air we breathe is a physical mixture of gases, primarily nitrogen and oxygen.

gas discharge tube (electron tube). A gas-filled diode electron tube used in a high energy capacitor-discharge ignition system for a turbine engine. The discharge tube blocks all electron flow until the voltage across its electrodes builds up to the ionization voltage of the gas inside the tube. When this voltage is reached, the gas ionizes and the tube conducts, discharging the capacitor through the high-voltage transformer.

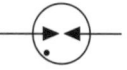

gas discharge tube

G

gaseous breathing oxygen (aviator's breathing oxygen). Oxygen approved for use in an aircraft. Practically all water vapor has been removed and it is at least 99.5 percent pure.

gaseous fuel. A mixture of flammable gases used for fuel.

gas-filled tube (electron tube). An electron tube whose envelope is filled with an inert gas, such as argon. The inert gas prevents the heated elements from oxidizing.

gas generator (gas turbine engine). The basic gas turbine engine consisting of the compressor, diffuser, combustor, and turbine. The gas generator, also called the core engine, is the part of a turbine engine that produces the hot, high-velocity gases. The gas generator does not include the inlet duct, fan section, free power turbines, or the tail pipe.

gasket. A seal between two stationary objects. A gasket is usually made of a soft material so it can conform to the surfaces of the two parts and form a leakproof seal. A gasket is similar to a packing, except a packing is used when there is relative motion between the parts being sealed.

gasoline. A liquid hydrocarbon fuel obtained from the distillation of crude oil. Gasoline is the most commonly used fuel for aircraft reciprocating engines and automobile engines.

gas path (turbine engines). The path air follows as it passes through a gas turbine engine.

gassing (battery condition). A condition that occurs near the end of the charging cycle of lead-acid storage batteries. Hydrogen and oxygen are released as free gases, hydrogen at the negative plate, and oxygen at the positive plate.

gas tungsten arc welding. *See* GTAW.

gas turbine engine. An internal combustion engine in which energy is released from the fuel in a constant-pressure cycle. Air is taken into the engine and compressed by either an axial-flow or a centrifugal compressor. The compressed air then passes into the combustion chambers where fuel is sprayed into a continuously burning fire. The burning fuel heats and expands the air which then flows through a turbine, where some of the energy is extracted to turn the compressor. The energy remaining in the gases leaving the engine causes the exhaust velocity to be greater than that of the air entering the engine, and this acceleration produces thrust. Some gas turbine engines use additional stages of turbines to extract energy from the hot gases to drive such devices as fans, propellers, rotors, generators, or pumps. Gas turbine engines are far superior to reciprocating engines, with regard to their weight-to-horsepower ratio.

gas welding. A method of joining metals by melting them and allowing the molten metal from the two pieces to flow together. The heat used to melt the metal is provided by burning a mixture of fuel gas and oxygen. The two most generally used fuel gases are acetylene and hydrogen.

gate (electrode of a semiconductor device). The electrode in a silicon controlled rectifier (SCR), triac, or field effect transistor (FET), to which trigger pulses of electrical energy are applied to cause a flow of electrons between the other electrodes.

gate hold procedures (aircraft operation). Procedures at selected airports to hold aircraft at the gate or other ground locations whenever departure delays exceed or are anticipated to exceed five minutes.

gate-type check valve. A type of one-way valve that uses a swinging gate, or flapper, to control the flow of fluid. Gate-type check valves are used in multiengine aircraft vacuum systems to isolate one of the pumps if it should fail.

gateway fix (navigation). A navigational aid or fix where an aircraft transitions between the domestic route structure and the oceanic route airspace.

gauge. *See* gage.

gauss. The unit of magnetic flux density in the centimeter-gram-second system of metric measurement. One gauss is a flux density of one line of flux (one maxwell) per square centimeter.

Gay Lussac's law. *See* Charles's law.

GCA (ground controlled approach) (air traffic control). A radar approach system operated from the ground by air traffic control personnel transmitting instruction to the pilot by radio. The approach may be conducted with surveillance radar (ASR) only or with both surveillance and precision approach radar (PAR).

Usage of the term GCA by pilots is discouraged except when referring to a GCA facility. Pilots should specifically request a PAR approach when a precision radar approach is desired or request an ASR, or surveillance, approach when a nonprecision radar approach is desired.

gear. A special wheel with notched teeth on its periphery. Gears transmit power from one shaft to another without slippage by meshing the teeth of the gear on one shaft with the teeth of the gear on the other. Gears are used to reverse the direction of shaft rotation and to gain mechanical advantage.

gear and pinion mechanism. A mechanical force amplifying system that uses two gears of different sizes. The smaller gear, the pinion, meshes with and turns faster than the larger gear. The ratio between the number of teeth on the pinion and the number on the large gear determines the mechanical advantage of the mechanism.

gear backlash. The amount of clearance between the teeth of two meshed gears. It is very important that the correct amount of gear backlash be maintained when meshing gears. If there is no backlash, the teeth cannot be properly lubricated, and the gears will wear excessively. If there is too much backlash, the load is not properly transmitted from one tooth to the other.

Gear backlash is measured by holding one gear still and measuring, with a dial indicator, the amount the meshing gear can move back and forth. Service manuals for equipment using gears specify the amount of gear backlash required.

gear-driven supercharger (aircraft reciprocating engine component). An air compressor driven by gears from the crankshaft of a reciprocating engine. Power is taken from the engine to drive the supercharger, but the increase in power produced by compressing the intake air more than compensates for the loss. Gear-driven superchargers are not as efficient as turbochargers, because the power used to drive a turbocharger would otherwise be wasted.

geared-fan engine (aircraft gas turbine engine). A type of turbofan engine using a set of reduction gears between the first stage of the gas generator compressor and the fan. By using reduction gears, the fan can turn slowly enough that its tip speed is held below the speed of sound. And at the same time, the gas generator compressor can turn at speeds high enough for it to be efficient.

geared propeller (aircraft engine). A propeller on an aircraft engine that is driven from the crankshaft through a set of reduction gears. The engine is allowed to operate at a speed at which it is most efficient, and the propeller turns slowly enough that its tips do not exceed the speed of sound.

gear preload. The amount of pressure applied in a gear system to keep the gears meshed.

gear-type pump. A type of power-driven pump used to move such fluids as fuel and oil. A gear-type pump is a constant-displacement pump using two meshing spur gears, mounted in a close-fitting housing.

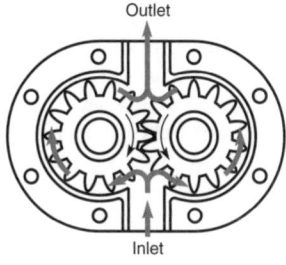

gear-type pump

Fluid is taken into the housing where it fills the space between the teeth of the gears, and it is carried around the housing as the gears rotate. On the discharge side of the pump, the gear teeth mesh, and the fluid is forced out of the pump.

gel coat (composites). A polyester material that is applied to a mold surface and becomes an integral part of the finished product. It is used to make fiberglass reinforced plastic parts and for repairs to existing gel-coated parts.

gelled cell (batteries). A type of lead-acid battery cell that has a gelling agent added to the electrolyte to make it nonspillable. Gelled-cell batteries are used for portable operations.

gel time (composites). The period of time from initial mixing of liquid reactants with a resin to the point when gelation occurs as defined by a specific test method.

genemotor (electrical machine). A type of electrical machine used to change low-voltage direct current from a storage battery into high-voltage DC for operating some types of communications equipment. A genemotor has two armatures on a single shaft. One armature and one set of field coils are for the DC motor. The other armature and set of field coils are for the high-voltage generator. Genemotors are also called dynamotors.

general aviation. A term used to describe the total field of aviation operation other than the military and the airlines. General aviation includes business flying (corporate, or executive), agricultural aviation, personal flying for sport or pleasure, flight schools, and flying clubs. The manufacturers of the aircraft and the maintenance facilities that service them are also a part of general aviation.

general aviation district office. *See* GADO.

General Aviation Airworthiness Alerts. Documents furnished by the FAA to technicians alerting them of problems that have been found in specific models of aircraft, and reported on Malfunction and Defect Reports. Airworthiness Alerts suggest corrective action, but compliance with the suggestion is not mandatory. Alerts include items that have been reported to be significant, but which have not been fully evaluated at the time the material went to press. *See* Malfunction and Defect Report.

general gas law. A single law that combines the laws of Boyle and Charles to explain the relationship between the volume, the absolute pressure, and absolute temperature of a gas. The general gas law is expressed in a formula as:

$$\frac{P_1 V_1}{T_1} = \frac{P_2 V_2}{T_2}$$

P_1 = initial absolute pressure
P_2 = final absolute pressure
V_1 = initial volume
V_2 = final volume
T_1 = initial absolute temperature
T_2 = final absolute temperature

generator (electrical machine). A device that converts mechanical energy into electrical energy by rotating coils of wire through a magnetic field. As the conductors in the coils cut across the lines of magnetic flux, a voltage is generated that causes current to flow.

generator field (A-circuit). A generator circuit in which the voltage regulator is installed between the shunt field and ground.

generator field (B-circuit). A generator circuit in which the voltage regulator is installed between the shunt field and the armature.

generator series field. A set of heavy field windings in a generator connected in series with the armature. The magnetic field produced by the series windings is used to change the characteristics of the generator.

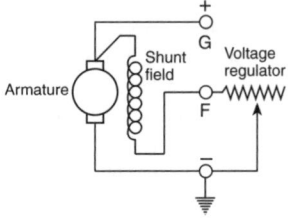

generator field A-circuit

generator shunt field. A set of field windings in a generator connected in parallel with the armature. Varying the amount of current flowing in the shunt field windings controls the voltage output of the generator.

geodetic construction (aircraft structure). A form of stressed skin construction in which the stresses are carried in a portion of the structure made up of strips of metal or wood that cross to form a diamond-shaped lattice. Geodetic structure was used for aircraft construction in the past, but has been replaced to a great extent by monocoque structure, which is similar to geodetic except it uses solid sheets of thin metal, rather than the lattice structure.

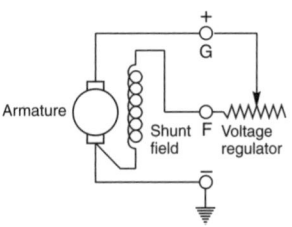

generator field B-circuit

geographic poles (navigation). Either end of the axis about which the earth rotates. All of the meridians of longitude cross at the north and south geographic poles. The north pole is located at latitude 90° north and the south pole is located at latitude 90° south. Directions measured from the geographic poles are true directions.

GEO map (air traffic control). The digitized map markings associated with the ASR-9 radar system.

geopotential of the tropopause. The point in the standard atmosphere where the temperature stops dropping and becomes constant. This is the tropopause, or the dividing line between the troposphere and the stratosphere.

geostrophic wind (meteorology). Wind resulting from the balance between the Coriolis force and the pressure gradient force. They flow at a constant speed along straight line contours/isobars.

germanium. A brittle, crystalline, gray-white, metallic chemical element. Germanium's symbol is Ge, its atomic number is 32, and its atomic weight is 72.59. Germanium is in the same chemical family as carbon, silicon, tin, and lead, and is obtained from the residue left when lead and zinc are refined electrolytically. Germanium is widely used in the manufacture of semiconductor devices.

German silver. An alloy of copper, zinc, and nickel. German silver is also called nickel silver.

gerotor pump (fluid pump). A form of constant displacement gear pump that uses an external-tooth drive gear that meshes with and drives an internal-tooth gear that has one more space for a tooth than there are teeth on the drive gear. Both gears turn inside a close-tolerance housing.

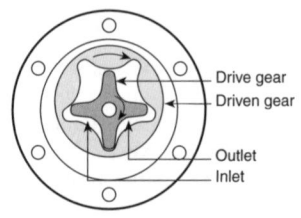

gerotor pump

As the gears rotate, fluid flows between the teeth that are beginning to unmesh, and the fluid is carried around the pump as this space continues to open up. On the discharge side of the pump, the teeth begin to mesh, and as the space between the teeth becomes smaller, fluid is forced out of the pump.

getter. A small piece of alkaline metal placed inside an electron tube (vacuum tube) when it is manufactured. When the tube is completed and the air evacuated from it, current is passed through the getter which raises its temperature enough to melt it, causing it to react with any oxygen left inside the tube. The silvery deposit often seen inside the glass tube envelope is the residue from the getter.

GHz (gigahertz). One billion (1,000,000,000) cycles per second.

giga. The metric prefix that means billion.

gigacycle. *See* GHz (gigahertz.)

gilbert. A unit of magnetomotive force. One gilbert is equal to the force produced by an electromagnet of 0.7957 ampere-turn. The constant 0.7957 is found by dividing 10 by 4 π.

gill-type cowl flap (reciprocating engine cowling component). A small flap located at the rear of the cowling for a reciprocating engine. Opening the cowl flap increases the amount of cooling air flowing through the engine by decreasing the pressure at the point the air leaves the engine compartment.

gimbal. A type of support that allows an object, such as a gyroscope, to remain in an upright condition when its base is tilted. Gyroscopes used in certain aircraft flight instruments are mounted in gimbals. Some in single gimbals, and others in double gimbals. The gyro in a turn and slip indicator is mounted in a single gimbal, and it senses rotation only about the vertical axis of the aircraft. The gyro in an attitude gyro instrument is mounted in a double gimbal, and it senses rotation about both the lateral and the longitudinal axes.

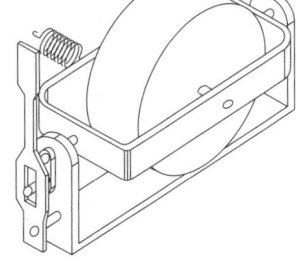

gimbal (single)

gimbal ring. A type of support that allows an object, such as a gyroscope, to remain in an upright condition when its base is tilted.

gimlet point (threaded fastener). A threaded, cone-shaped point on self-tapping sheet metal screws that are installed through holes in several sheets of thin sheet metal.

glass cloth. Cloth woven from glass fibers. Glass cloth can be impregnated with a thermosetting resin and cured in a mold to produce complex-shaped aircraft structural components.

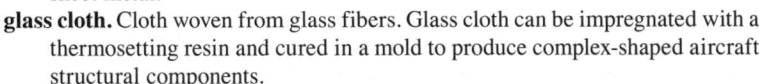

gimlet point

glass cockpit. An aircraft instrument system that uses a few multicolor cathode-ray-tube displays to replace a large number of mechanically actuated instruments.

glass fiber. A filament, or thread, of glass, usually less than one-thousandth of an inch (25 micrometers) in diameter. Glass fibers, woven into cloth or packed together into a mat, are used for thermal and acoustical insulation and for reinforcing plastic resins to make various types of molded products.

glassy water (seaplane operation). Flat, calm, mirror-like water conditions, perhaps the most deceptive that a seaplane pilot will experience and frequently the most dangerous for seaplane operation. It inhibits depth perception during landing and adds significant drag during takeoff.

glaze (aircraft brake malfunction). A hard, glass-like coating that forms on the brake disk surface. The friction caused by the glazed surface is not uniform, and when the brakes are applied, they grab and release at such a high rate that they chatter or squeal. The glazed surface must be removed from a disk for the braking to be effective.

glaze ice (meteorology). Ice that forms when large drops of water strike a surface whose temperature is below freezing. Glaze ice is clear and heavy.

glide (aircraft flight maneuver). A flight maneuver in which an aircraft descends at a gradual angle without the use of engine power.

glidepath angle (GPA). The angular displacement of the vertical guidance path from a horizontal plane that passes through the reference datum point (RDP). This angle is published on approach charts (e.g., 3.00°, 3.20°, etc.). GPA is sometimes referred to as vertical path angle (VPA).

"Glide path...(on/above/below)" (air traffic control). Information provided by ATC to a pilot making a PAR (precision approach radar) approach regarding the position of the aircraft relative to the descent profile. *See* glide slope.

glider (type of aircraft). An aircraft having no engine, which is capable of free flight only while it is descending through the air. Gliders are launched by towing them behind an airplane, pulling them into the air with an automobile, or shooting them into the air with a catapult. High-performance gliders are called sailplanes.

14 CFR Part 1: "A heavier-than-air aircraft, that is supported in flight by the dynamic reaction of the air against its lifting surfaces and whose free flight does not depend principally on an engine."

glide ratio (aircraft performance). The ratio of the forward distance traveled to the vertical distance an aircraft descends when it is operating without power. For example, if an aircraft descends 1,000 feet while it travels through the air for a distance of two miles (10,560 feet), it has a glide ratio of slightly more than 10:1.

glide slope (electronic navigation system). A portion of an Instrument Landing System (ILS). The glide slope is a radio beam extending upward at angle of approximately 2$\frac{1}{2}$° from the approach end of an instrument runway. The glide slope provides the vertical path for the aircraft to follow when making an ILS approach along the localizer path. The horizontal needle of the cross-pointer indicator (the ILS indicator) shows the pilot the relative position of the aircraft as it descends along the glide slope. The glide slope is sometimes called the glide path.

glide slope indicator

glide slope (GS) function. The autopilot function that manipulates the pitch of the aircraft to track a glideslope signal or APV guidance during a precision approach.

glide slope intercept altitude. The minimum altitude of an intermediate approach segment prescribed for a precision approach which ensures obstacle clearance.

glide speed for range (flight operation). The airspeed that results in an angle of attack that gives the maximum lift/drag ratio.

glint (radar operation). A distorted radar signal which varies in amplitude from pulse to pulse. A glint is caused by the radar beam being reflected by some rapidly moving object.

G-loads. Loads imposed on an airframe due to inertia (centrifugal force). 1G load factor represents the weight of the actual aircraft. 2G represents twice the aircraft's actual weight.

global circulation system (meteorology). The worldwide air circulation pattern determined by variations in insulation, combined with the Coriolis effect due to the earth's rotation. It is a major controlling factor of the world's weather patterns.

global navigation satellite system (GNSS). An umbrella term adopted by the International Civil Aviation Organization (ICAO) to encompass any independent satellite navigation system used by a pilot to perform onboard position determinations from the satellite data.

global positioning system (GPS). A navigation system using a constellation of between 24 and 32 satellites in orbit around the Earth. Each satellite transmits precise microwave signals that enable a GPS receiver to determine its location, speed, direction, and the current time.

global positioning system steering (GPSS). The autopilot function that receives signals directly from the GPS/FMS/RNAV to steer the aircraft along the desired track to the active waypoint set in the GPS receiver.

glow-discharge tube (electronic device). A glass electron tube containing a gas under a low pressure. A high voltage across two electrodes in the tube ionizes the gas, and when electrons flow through the ionized gas, it glows. The type of gas determines the ionization voltage and the color of the glow. Since the ionization voltage remains constant regardless of the amount of current, glow-discharge tubes can be used to produce a reference voltage in a voltage regulator circuit.

glow-plug igniter (turbine engine ignition component). A low-voltage turbine engine igniter used on some of the smaller engines. It consists of a coiled resistance element, whose inner end is connected to an insulated pin to which the lead from the DC ignition exciter is connected. The outer end of the coil is grounded to the igniter body. Current flowing through the resistance element heats it until it glows orange-yellow, and air flowing through the coil produces a streak of flame that ignites the fuel-air mixture in the combustor.

GLS. *See* GPS landing system.

glue. A general term used for an adhesive material.

glue joint (wood aircraft construction). A joint or connection made between two pieces of wood by an adhesive, or glue, rather than any type of mechanical fastener. The wood is prepared by shaping it so the grains in the two pieces are parallel, and the surfaces to be glued are perfectly smooth and clean. The glue is spread evenly over either one or both surfaces, and the surfaces are pressed together and held by clamps until the glue dries. A correctly made glue joint is stronger than the wood itself.

Glyptal. The registered trade name for an insulating varnish used to insulate certain types of electrical machinery.

GNSS. *See* global navigation satellite system.

go, no-go gage. A type of measuring device used to determine whether or not the dimensions of an object being measured are within allowable limits. A go, no-go gage can be used to determine if a hole is of the correct size. If the hole is at least as large as the minimum diameter allowed, the "go" part of the gage will fit into it, and if it is no larger than the maximum diameter allowed, the "no-go" part of the gage will not fit into it.

"Go ahead" (air traffic control). The phrase used by air traffic controllers meaning "proceed with your message." This phrase is not to be used for any other purpose.

"goals and values" (in learning process). A factor that describes how a person's perception of an event depends on beliefs. Motivation toward learning is affected by how much value a person puts on education. Instructors who have some idea of the goals and values of their students will be more successful in teaching them.

"Go around" (air traffic control). Instructions for a pilot to abandon his approach to landing.

go-around power or thrust setting. The maximum allowable inflight power or thrust setting identified in the performance data.

gold. A soft, yellow, heavy, corrosion-resistant chemical element. Gold's symbol is Au, its atomic number is 79, and its atomic weight is 196.967. Gold is a good thermal and electrical conductor, and because of its resistance to corrosion, it is often plated onto critical electrical contacts and slip rings.

goldbeater's skin. A thin, flexible material made by treating the outside membrane of the large intestine of cattle. Goldbeater's skin is used to separate sheets of gold foil as they are being hammered (beaten) until they are thinned into gold leaf. Many thousands of goldbeater's skins were joined together to form the gas bags that held the lifting gas for the huge lighter-than-air dirigibles and Zeppelins.

gold leaf. Pure gold that has been rolled or beaten into extremely thin sheets. Gold leaf is usually about one microinch (1×10^{-6} inch) thick. Gold foil is similar to gold leaf, but is thicker.

Gold Seal Flight Instructor Certificate. Flight Instructor Certificates with distinctive gold seals are issued by the FAA to instructors who currently meet certain qualifications. These certificates are intended to identify instructors who have high personal qualifications and who have good records as active flight instructors.

gondola. Portion of a gas balloon that carries the pilot, passengers, cargo, ballast, and instruments.

goniometer. An instrument used to measure angles. The goniometer used in an automatic direction finder (ADF) uses the output of a fixed loop antenna to sense the angle between a fixed reference, usually the nose of the aircraft, and the direction from which the radio signal is being received. An electronic goniometer measures the angle by comparing radio signals picked up on a nondirectional antenna with signals picked up on a directional antenna.

gore (parachute component). A single triangular-shaped panel in the canopy of a parachute. The canopy is made by sewing the gores together to form a large circular canopy. Shroud lines are sewed along the seams that join the gores.

gouge. A defect in the form of a groove or deep scratch in an otherwise smooth surface.

governing range. The range of the amount of pitch that a propeller governor can control during flight.

governor. A control used to cause certain types of equipment to operate at a desired speed. A governor has a sensor to measure the speed, a datum from which the speed is referenced, and a control to adjust the speed so it agrees with the datum.

GPS (global positioning system). An electronic navigation system in which the position of the aircraft is determined by the angular relationship between the aircraft and a series of orbiting satellites.

GPS overlay approach. A conventional nonprecision approach procedure that can be flown using RNAV equipment.

GPS landing system (GLS). An instrument approach with lateral and vertical guidance with integrity limits (similar to barometric vertical navigation, or Baro VNAV). Sometimes referred to as the "global landing system."

GPSS. *See* global positioning system steering.

GPS stand-alone approach. A nonprecision approach procedure based solely on the use of the global positioning system and an IFR-certified FMS/RNAV unit using GPS signals.

GPU (ground power unit). A piece of aircraft ground support equipment that includes a motor-generator and an air compressor. The GPU can be connected to an aircraft on the ground to supply electrical power and compressed air for system operation when the engines are not operating.

GPWS. *See* ground proximity warning system.

grab test (balloon fabric test). A test, as specified by balloon manufacturers, to determine the tensile strength of envelope fabric.

grade-A cotton fabric (aircraft structural material). Cloth made of long-staple cotton, used to cover certain types of aircraft structures. Grade-A cotton fabric has between 80 and 84 threads per inch in both warp and fill, and new grade-A fabric has a minimum tensile strength of 80 pounds per inch.

gradient (meteorology). A change in value per unit of a second parameter. Such terms as pressure gradient (inches of mercury per thousand feet) and temperature gradient (degrees Celsius per thousand feet) are commonly used in meteorology.

gradient wind (meteorology). A theoretical wind that flows at a constant speed along curved contours/isobars.

grain (wood characteristic). The direction, size, and arrangement of the fibers in a piece of wood.

grain boundary (metallurgy). The lines inside a piece of metal formed by the surfaces of the grains. Intergranular corrosion forms along the grain boundaries in metal that has been improperly heat-treated in such a way that the grains have become enlarged. The hardness of a metal is determined by the size of the grain. The smaller the grain, the harder the metal.

gram. A unit of mass in the metric system. One gram is equal to $1/1000$ of a kilogram or about 0.035 ounce and is the weight of one cubic centimeter of water at its maximum density.

gram-centimeter (unit of work). A unit of work in the centimeter-gram-second gravitational system. One gram-centimeter is the amount of work done when a force of one gram causes a movement of one centimeter in the direction the force is applied.

graphic plan display (GPD) (air traffic control). A view available with URET that provides a graphic display of aircraft, traffic, and notification of predicted conflicts.

graphite. A soft, black form of carbon that normally has a greasy feel. Graphite, also known as black lead, is used as a dry lubricant and also as the "lead" in a pencil. Structural graphite is used in composite structure because of its strength and stiffness.

graphite fibers. An advanced composite fiber made by drawing filaments of carbon at a high temperature and in a controlled atmosphere. Graphite fibers are very strong and stiff.

graupel (meteorology). Also called soft hail or snow pellets, these are white, round or conical ice particles $1/8$ to $1/4$ inch diameter. They often form as a thunderstorm matures and indicate the likelihood of lightning.

graveyard spiral (flight maneuver). An inadvertent flight maneuver that can develop when flying without reference to a natural or instrument horizon. An inherently stable airplane, if left to its own devices, will eventually develop into a coordinated, constant-rate descending spiral. Because the maneuver is coordinated, the pilot has no sensation of turning. The airspeed builds up and the altitude decreases. The natural instinct is to come back on the stick or wheel. This only exacerbates the situation. This is called a graveyard spiral because, before the common use of turn coordinators or turn and slip indicators, many pilots were killed in the ensuing crash.

gravitational acceleration. The acceleration (speeding up) of a freely falling object caused by the attraction of the mass of the earth. If an object is allowed to fall freely in a vacuum, it will accelerate at a rate of 32.2 feet per second, or 980.7 centimeters per second, each second it falls.

gravity. The force of attraction between objects. The force of gravity is directly proportional to the mass of the objects (the greater the mass, the stronger the pull of gravity), and inversely proportional to the square of the distance between the objects (the farther apart the objects, the weaker the pull of gravity).

G

Gray code (binary number code). A binary number system in which only one bit changes in each successive binary word. The Gray code is used for optical encoders that translate degrees of shaft movement into a binary signal.

Decimal	Binary	Gray
0	0000	0000
1	0001	0001
2	0010	0011
3	0011	0010
4	0100	0110
5	0101	0111
6	0110	0101
7	0111	0100
8	1000	1100
9	1001	1101
10	1010	1111
11	1011	1110
12	1100	1010
13	1101	1011
14	1110	1001
15	1111	1000

Gray code

great circle (aerial navigation). A circle formed on the surface of a sphere in such a way that the plane of the circle passes through the center of the sphere. All meridians of longitude on the earth's surface are great circles, but the equator is the only parallel of latitude that is a great circle.

great circle course (navigation). The route between two points on the earth's surface measured along the shorter segment of the circumference of the great circle on which the two points are located. A great circle course establishes the shortest distance over the surface of the earth between any two terrestrial points.

green run (aircraft manufacturing operation). The first time an engine is run in the process of aircraft manufacturing or major overhaul.

Greenwich mean time. Mean solar time at the 0° meridian, the meridian of longitude that passes through the Royal Observatory in London, England. Greenwich mean time (GMT) is also known as Zulu time and Universal time.

greige (pronounced gray). The unshrunk condition of a polyester fabric as it is removed from the loom. The material has not been bleached, dyed, or shrunk.

grid (electron tube component). The electrodes in an electron tube between the cathode and the anode. Grids are used to control the amount, the shape, and the velocity of the stream of electrons between the cathode and the anode.

grid dip meter (electrical measuring instrument). An electronic instrument used to find the resonant frequency of an inductive-capacitive (LC) tuned circuit. The grid dip meter contains a variable-frequency oscillator and an indicating instrument. The probe of the grid dip meter is held near the circuit being examined, and the oscillator is tuned until the meter dips. The frequency produced by the oscillator when the meter dips is the resonant frequency of the circuit.

grid navigation. A navigation system devised for use in areas in close proximity to the north pole.

grinder (power tool). A power tool using an electric motor to drive an abrasive wheel. Grinders are used to sharpen tools and to grind away or shape metal parts.

grinding wheel (maintenance shop tool). A motor-driven abrasive wheel that is used to grind away the surface of certain metals, primarily steel or iron.

grip length (threaded fastener specification). The thickness of material a fastener is designed to fasten, or hold together. The grip length of a bolt is the length of the unthreaded portion of the shank.

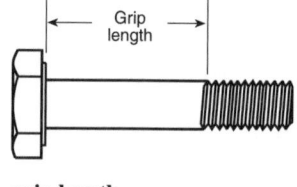

grip length

grip range (special rivet specification). The difference between the minimum and maximum thickness of material a special rivet can be used to fasten.

grit blasting. Another name for abrasive blasting. *See* abrasive blasting.

grommet (protective device). A rubber or plastic ring used to cover the edges of a hole in thin sheet metal. When wires or tubes pass through a hole in a piece of thin sheet metal, the edges of the hole should be protected with a grommet so the sharp metal cannot damage them.

gross navigation error (GNE). In the North Atlantic area of operations, a gross navigation error is a lateral separation of more than 25 NM from the centerline of an aircraft's cleared route, which generates an Oceanic Navigation Error Report. This report is also generated by a vertical separation if you are more than 300 feet off your assigned flight level.

gross thrust (turbine engine specification). The thrust produced by a turbojet or turbofan engine when the engine is static, or not moving. The air is considered to have no inlet velocity, and the velocity of the gas leaving the engine is considered to be the acceleration factor. Gross thrust includes the thrust generated by the momentum of the outgoing gases and the thrust resulting from the difference between static pressure at the nozzle and ambient pressure.

G

gross weight (aircraft specification). The loaded weight of an aircraft. Gross weight includes the total weight of the aircraft, the weight of the fuel and oil, and the weight of all the load it is carrying.

ground (electrical reference point). A reference point in an electrical system from which all voltage measurements are made. In an aircraft electrical system, the negative terminal of the battery is normally connected to the aircraft structure, and this acts as the ground. In household and industrial electrical power systems, one lead connects to the earth, which serves as the ground. In the United Kingdom ground is spoken of as "earth."

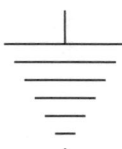

ground symbol

ground-adjustable propeller. A type of aircraft propeller whose blade pitch angle can be adjusted when the engine is not running. The adjustment requires loosening the blades in the hub.

ground adjustable trim tab (secondary flight control). A small, fixed, metal tab that is attached to the trailing edge of a rudder, elevator, or aileron. It may be bent to deflect the air leaving the surface to produce an aerodynamic force that moves the surface on which it is attached to trim the aircraft for straight and level flight at a desired airspeed.

ground-based transceiver (GBT). The ground-based transmitter/receiver (transceiver) receives automatic dependent surveillance-broadcast messages, which are forwarded to an air traffic control facility for processing and display with other radar targets on the plan position indicator (radar display).

ground-boosted engine (reciprocating engines). An aircraft reciprocating engine with a built-in supercharger that boosts the sea-level rated horsepower of the engine.

ground clutter (radar reception). A pattern produced on the radarscope by ground returns which may degrade other radar returns in the affected area.

ground communication outlet (GCO). An unstaffed, remotely controlled, ground/ground communications facility. Pilots at uncontrolled airports may contact ATC and FSS via VHF to a telephone connection to obtain an instrument clearance or close a VFR or IFR flight plan. They may also get an updated weather briefing prior to takeoff. The GCO system is intended to be used only on the ground.

ground control (traffic control position). The operating position in a control tower that provides clearances and instructions for the movement of airport traffic and the pertinent information to all traffic within the airport perimeter.

ground controlled approach. *See* GCA.

ground crew (aircraft operation). The group of people who service and maintain an aircraft when it is on the ground. The ground crew prepares the aircraft for flight and services it after its return from flight.

ground delay (air traffic control). The amount of delay attributed to ATC, encountered prior to departure, usually associated with a controlled departure time (CDT) program.

ground delay program (GDP). A traffic management process administered by the ATCSCC; when aircraft are held on the ground. The purpose of the program is to support the TM mission and limit airborne holding. It is a flexible program and may be implemented in various forms depending upon the needs of the AT system. Ground delay programs provide for equitable assignment of delays to all system users.

grounded-base amplifier (transistor amplifier). *See* common-base amplifier.

grounded-collector amplifier (transistor amplifier). *See* common-collector amplifier.

grounded-emitter amplifier (transistor amplifier). *See* common-emitter amplifier.

ground effect (aerodynamics). An increase in lift of an aerodynamic flying machine (airplane or helicopter) flying very near the ground. This additional lift is caused by an effective increase in angle of attack without the accompanying increase in induced drag and is caused by the deflection of the downwashed air. Ground effect disappears when the flying machine is about a half wing span or half rotor span above the surface.

ground fog (meteorology). A fog that conceals less than six tenths of the sky and is not a part of the cloud base.

ground idle (gas turbine engine operating specification). The engine speed normally used for operating a gas turbine engine on the ground so it produces the minimum amount of thrust. Ground idle is normally in the range of 60% to 70% of the maximum RPM.

ground loop (aircraft operation). A sharp, uncontrolled change in direction of an airplane on the ground. Tail wheel-type airplanes are highly subject to ground looping because their center of gravity is behind the point at which the main wheels contact the ground.

ground loop (electrical condition). A condition of unwanted current flow in a circuit that uses shielded wire (wire encased in a braided metal cover). The purpose of the shielding is to intercept and carry to ground electrical energy radiated from the wires inside the shielding.

If the shielding is connected to the ground at more than one point, it is possible for current to flow out one connection, through the ground, and back into the shielding through another connection. This current flowing in the shielding can interfere with delicate electrical signals in the shielded wire. To prevent ground loops, the shielding is grounded at one point only.

ground plane (radio antenna component). A reflector used with a vertically polarized, quarter-wavelength radio antenna. Horizontal arms or a flat metal plane that sticks out at least a quarter wavelength from the base of the antenna reflects the signal.

ground potential (electrical circuit condition). An electrical condition in which there is no voltage difference, or potential, between a point at ground potential and the ground point in the circuit.

ground power unit. *See* GPU.

ground proximity warning system (GPWS). A system designed to determine an aircraft's clearance above the earth. It provides limited predictability about aircraft position relative to rising terrain.

ground track. The aircraft's path over the ground when in flight.

ground weather surveillance radar system. Any ground-based facility equipped to gather information about significant weather across a wide area.

ground reference maneuvers (flight training maneuver). Ground reference maneuvers and their related factors are used in developing a high degree of pilot skill. Although most of these maneuvers are not performed as such in normal everyday flying, the elements and principles involved in each are applicable to performance of the customary pilot operations. They aid the pilot in analyzing the effect of wind and other forces acting on the airplane and in developing a fine control touch, coordination, and the division of attention necessary for accurate and safe maneuvering of the airplane.

ground resonance (helicopter operation). Destructive vibration that occurs with a helicopter, usually on landing. If the helicopter touches down rough and unevenly, the shock can throw a load into the lead-lag hinges of the rotor blades and cause the blades to oscillate (move back and forth) about this hinge.

If the frequency of this oscillation is the same as the resonant frequency of the fuselage, the energy will cause the helicopter to strike the ground hard with the opposite skid or wheel. This will increase the energy and cause more severe contact with the ground. If corrective action is not taken immediately, either lifting the helicopter or placing it firmly on the ground, ground resonance can destroy it.

ground-return circuit (electrical circuit). An electrical circuit using the ground or the structure of a vehicle as one of its conductors. Almost all automobiles and aircraft use ground-return electrical systems. One of the terminals of the battery, usually the negative terminal, is connected directly to the framework of the vehicle.

One wire is used to connect the components to the positive terminal of the battery, and another wire connects the component to the structure. The return current from the component flows back to the battery through the structure.

ground speed (aircraft navigation). The speed at which an aircraft is moving over the ground. When an aircraft is flying, its speed through the air is its airspeed. The air moves over the ground and carries the aircraft with it, so the ground speed is the vector sum of the airspeed and the direction of flight of the aircraft, combined with the speed and direction of the air movement over the ground (the wind speed and direction).

If the air is moving in the same direction the aircraft is flying, the ground speed is equal to the airspeed plus the speed of the air movement. If the wind is blowing in the direction opposite that which the aircraft is flying, the ground speed is equal to the airspeed minus the speed of the wind. When the wind is blowing at an angle to the flight path, the ground speed is found by adding the airspeed and the wind speed as vectors.

ground stop (GS) (air traffic control). The GS is a process that requires aircraft that meet a specific criteria to remain on the ground. The criteria may be airport specific, airspace specific, or equipment specific; for example, all departures to San Francisco, or all departures entering Yorktown sector, or all Category I and II aircraft going to Charlotte. GS's normally occur with little or no warning.

ground support equipment (aircraft operations). All the equipment needed to service and maintain aircraft on the ground. Ground support equipment includes such equipment as tugs to move the aircraft and auxiliary power units to provide electrical power and compressed air when the engines are not running.

ground visibility. *14 CFR Part 1:* "Prevailing horizontal visibility near the earth's surface as reported by the United States National Weather Surface or an accredited observer."

ground wave (radio transmission). The component of a transmitted electromagnetic wave that travels from the transmitting antenna along the surface of the earth.

growler. A piece of electrical test equipment used to check armatures in DC motors and generators for open or shorted turns in the windings. The armature to be tested is placed on the growler, and the AC power is turned on. The growler acts as the primary of a transformer and the armature as the secondary. A voltmeter is used to measure the voltage induced into the armature windings. A growler gets its name from the growling noise made when an armature is being tested.

GS. *See* glide slope.

GTAW (gas tungsten arc welding). A method of electric arc welding in which the electrode in the torch is a fine, nonconsumable tungsten wire. The arc is enveloped in a flow of an inert gas such as argon or helium. GTAW was formerly called heli-arc welding.

guarded switch (type of electrical switch). A special switch whose operating control is inside a guard that must be raised before the switch can be actuated. Guarded switches are used for circuits that must not be accidentally operated.

gudgeon pin (reciprocating engine component). The British name for the wrist pin in a reciprocating engine. *See* wrist pin.

guided discussion method (in learning process). An educational presentation typically used in the classroom where the topic to be covered by a group is introduced and the instructor participates only as necessary to keep the group focused on the subject.

guide vanes (turbine engine component). Fixed, curved steel vanes that direct the air flowing into the first stage rotor blades of an axial-flow compressor. The vanes impart a swirling motion to the air and direct it into the compressor at the optimum angle.

GUMP. An acronym used by a pilot for a pretakeoff check to be sure that none of the most important items are missed:

G — Gasoline (The correct fuel tank should be selected for takeoff.)

U — Undercarriage (The landing gear selector should be in the down position and the indicator lights show that the gear is locked down.)

M — Mixture (The mixture control should be in the correct position for takeoff.)

P — Propeller (The propeller pitch control should be in the low-pitch, high RPM position for takeoff.)

guncotton. A highly explosive form of cellulose nitrate made by treating cotton fibers with nitric and sulfuric acids. Guncotton is used in making the film base of nitrate dope.

G-unit. A measure of the force of gravity. One G-unit is the force acting on an object caused by the gravitational pull of the earth. High-performance aircraft have an instrument called an accelerometer to show the pilot the number of G-units acting on the aircraft during any flight maneuver.

Gunk. The registered trade name of a type of liquid decarbonizer used to remove soft carbon deposits from metal parts.

gusset. A small plate attached to two or more members of a truss structure to strengthen the truss.

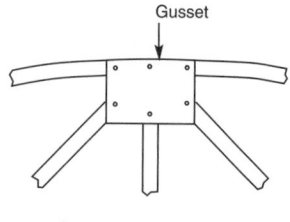

Gusset

gusset

gust (wind). A temporary increase in the speed of the wind. A gust lasts for a very short period of time, and it is usually followed by a wind whose speed is lower than normal.

gust front (meteorology). A boundary that separates a cold downdraft of a thunderstorm from warm, humid surface air. Air tends to be cool and gusty behind the gust front.

gust lock (aircraft control systems). A ground lock for aircraft controls, used to prevent the wind damaging the control surfaces by knocking them against their stops. Gust locks may either be built-in features of the control system or external locks that are slipped between the movable surface and the fixed structure. All gust locks are required to have some kind of warning device to indicate to the pilot that they are installed or engaged.

gustnadoes (meteorology). Cold air being forced out from under an advancing storm swirls at the storm's head (gust front). The result is a gustnado that lasts for a relatively short period of time. These phenomenon appear as a dust whirl or debris cloud that look very similar to a horizontal tornado.

gust penetration speed. The speed that gives the greatest margin between the high and low Mach speed buffets.

"GWPS". *See* ground proximity warning system (GPWS)

gyro. *See* gyroscope.

gyrocompass. A form of navigation instrument that uses a gyroscope as a stable reference for a direction-seeking pickup. The direction-seeking pickup of a gyrocompass lines up with the magnetic field of the earth just as an ordinary magnetic compass, but the gyroscope keeps it from oscillating.

gyrocopter. A trademark applied to gyroplanes designed and produced by the Bensen Aircraft Company.

gyrodyne. *14 CFR Part 1:* "A rotorcraft whose rotors are normally engine driven for takeoff, hovering, and landing, and for forward flight through part of its speed range, and whose means of propulsion, consisting usually of conventional propellers, is independent of the rotor system."

gyro horizon (aircraft flight instrument). A gyroscopic flight instrument that gives the pilot an artificial reference for the pitch and roll attitude of the aircraft. A gyroscope with an erection system that keeps it perpendicular to the earth's surface controls a bar that remains parallel with the horizon. By referring to this instrument, the pilot can keep the aircraft level when the natural horizon is not visible.

gyroplane (type of aircraft). A type of rotorcraft whose main rotors are not connected to the engine except for the initial spin-up. Aerodynamic forces cause the main rotor to spin during normal flight. An autogiro is a form of gyroplane.

14 CFR Part 1: "A rotorcraft whose rotors are not engine driven, except for initial starting, but are made to rotate by action of the air when the rotorcraft is moving; and whose means of propulsion, consisting usually of conventional propellers, is independent of the rotor system."

gyroscope. A rapidly spinning wheel with its weight concentrated about its rim. Gyroscopes have two basic characteristics that make them useful: rigidity in space and precession. Because of its rigidity in space, the spinning gyroscope does not tilt its axis of rotation as the earth rotates.

Precession is the characteristic that causes the gyroscope to react to an applied force at a point 90° away from the point of application, in the direction of its rotation. Gyroscopes are used in both attitude and rate indicating flight instruments. *See* rigidity in space and gyroscopic precession.

gyroscopic precession. A characteristic of a gyroscope that causes it to react to an applied force as though the force were applied at a point 90° in the direction of rotation, from the actual point of application.

Precession is the characteristic used in rate gyros. A rate gyro will precess, or lay over in its gimbal, an amount proportional to the rate at which the gimbal is rotated. Rate gyros are the heart of turn and slip indicators and turn coordinators. The rotor of a helicopter acts in much the same way as a gyroscope and is affected by gyroscopic precession.

gyroscopic turn indicator. A rate-type flight instrument used to show the pilot the rate at which the aircraft is rotating about its vertical axis. Both turn and slip indicators and turn coordinators are gyroscopic turn indicators.

Hotel

HAA (height above airport) (air traffic control). The height of the minimum descent altitude above the published airport elevation. HAA is published in conjunction with circling minimums.

hacksaw. A handheld saw using a narrow, fine-tooth, replaceable blade, held under tension in a metal frame. Hacksaw blades used for cutting metal and other hard materials are designed to cut only on the forward movement of the blade. The blade should be lifted from the work on its return stroke.

hafnium. A brilliant, silvery, metallic chemical element. Hafnium's symbol is Hf, its atomic number is 72, and its atomic weight is 178.49. Hafnium has an extremely high melting point (above 2,000°C) and is used in the manufacture of filaments for incandescent lamps.

hail (meteorology). A form of precipitation which comes from cumulo nimbus clouds. Hail forms when drops of water are carried by up-currents of air inside the cloud to a level where the temperature is low enough that the water freezes into pellets of ice.

Near the top of the cloud, the ice pellets are thrown from the up-current and fall into the warmer air below. They pick up more water and are again carried upward. Each trip up and down allows the ice pellets, called a hailstones, to gain another layer of ice. This process continues until the hail is too heavy to stay in the cloud. Some hailstones grow large enough to cause severe damage to people, property, or animals on the ground.

hair hygrometer. An instrument used to measure the humidity of the air. The sensitive element in a hair hygrometer is a bundle of human hair held under a slight tension by a spring. The length of the hair expands or contracts as the humidity in the air changes. This change in length moves a pointer over a calibrated scale.

hairline crack. A tiny crack visible on the surface of a piece of material.

hairspring. A flat, spirally wound spring used to provide a restraint for rotary motion of a shaft. Hairsprings are used in D'Arsonval-type electrical instruments to provide a calibrated restraint for the moving coil and to carry current into and out of the coil. Hairsprings are also used in spring-powered clocks and watches to regulate the movement of the balance wheel.

HAL (height above landing) (air traffic control). The height above a designated helicopter landing area used for helicopter instrument approach procedures.

halation (cathode-ray tube). A form of distortion that causes a blurred image of the trace on a cathode-ray display tube. The blurring is caused by reflection from the back of the fluorescent coating when the coating is too thick.

half-duplex operation (communications). A type of communications in which signals can be sent in either direction, one direction at a time, but cannot be sent in both directions at the same time.

half hitch. A type of knot used for lacing wire bundles together. The bundle is tied with two half hitches secured with a square knot.

half-life. A measure of the rate of decay of radioactive material. In one half-life, the material decays, or loses one half of its radioactivity. In the next half-life interval, the material loses one half of that which is left. The half-life of various types of radioactive materials varies from a few microseconds (millionths of a second) up to billions of years.

half-round file. A metalworking or woodworking file that has one flat side. The other side is convex—thicker in the center than at the edges.

half-sectional view (technical illustration). A view of a component in which one half of it is cut away to show the inside. The other half is not cut away, and it shows the outside.

half view (aircraft drawing). A mechanical drawing used to show a symmetrical object. The center line of the object is shown, and break lines indicate that only one half of the object is shown.

half-wave antenna (radio antenna). A radio antenna whose electrical length is one half of the wavelength of the frequency for which the antenna is tuned.

half-wave rectifier (electrical circuit). A form of electrical circuit that changes alternating current into pulsating direct current. One rectifier, either a semiconductor diode or a diode electron tube, is used to block the flow of one half of the AC wave while allowing the other half to pass through. Half-wave rectifiers are inefficient and do not produce smooth direct current. However, they are used where economy of components is important and pulsations in the output are of no concern.

half-wave rectification

Hall-effect generator (electronic device). An electronic device which uses a thin wafer of semiconductor material to measure the intensity of a magnetic field. Control current flowing through the generator produces a Hall-effect voltage whose direction is perpendicular to the current, and whose intensity is proportional to both the control current and the strength of a magnetic field. The direction of the magnetic field passing through the generator is perpendicular to both the current and the voltage.

halo (atmospheric phenomenon). A prismatically colored or whitish circle or arc of a circle, with the sun or moon at its center. Coloration of a halo changes from red inside to blue outside, which is opposite to the coloration of a corona. *See* corona.

A halo is fixed in size and has an angular diameter of 22° (common) or 46° (rare). Halos are characteristic of clouds composed of ice crystals and are useful in telling the difference between cirriform (ice) clouds and lower clouds, which are composed of liquid water.

halo (cathode-ray oscilloscope). A bright ring around the spot produced by a beam of electrons striking the fluorescent coating in a cathode-ray tube. The halo is caused by light reflecting from the back side of the phosphorescent screen.

halogen. Any of the five chemical elements in Group VII of the periodic table of chemical elements. Fluorine, chlorine, bromine, iodine, and astatine are the halogens.

halogenated hydrocarbon. A hydrocarbon compound in which one or more of the hydrogen atoms have been replaced with an atom of one of the halogen elements, such as fluorine, chlorine, or bromine.

Halon 1211. A halogenated hydrocarbon fire-extinguishing agent that is used in many of the HRD (high-rate discharge) fire-extinguishing systems for powerplant protection. The technical name for Halon 1211 is bromochlorodifluoromethane.

Halon 1301. A halogenated hydrocarbon fire-extinguishing agent that is one of the best for extinguishing cabin and powerplant fires. It is highly effective and is the least toxic of the extinguishing agents available. The technical name for Halon 1301 is bromotrifluoromethane.

hammer. A handheld tool used for pounding. A hammer has a heavy, hard steel head mounted across the end of its handle. There are a number of types of hammer heads. Claw hammers have claws on one side of the head for removing nails. Ball peen hammers have a ball on one side of the head for forming heads on rivets. Cross peen and straight peen hammers have a wedge on one side of their head for shaping sheet metal.

hammer welding. A form of forge welding in which the edges of two pieces of metal are heated red-hot and then pounded together with a hammer.

handbook. A manual that describes an operation or a system of operations. A handbook normally contains specific rather than general information, and is usually prepared in a format that allows it to be kept at the point it is to be used. For example, a handbook on the operation of a piece of machinery should be kept with the machinery, rather than in a library or office.

hand-cranked inertia starter (reciprocating engine starter). A starter for a large aircraft reciprocating engine that uses a hand crank to store energy in a spinning flywheel. The crank drives the flywheel through a high-ratio gear system to spin it at a high speed and store a great deal of kinetic energy. When the flywheel is spinning, the hand crank is removed and the flywheel is coupled, through a slip clutch, to the engine crankshaft. There is enough energy in the spinning flywheel to turn the engine fast enough for it to start. Many electric-inertia starters have provisions for spinning the flywheel with a hand crank when there is no electrical power available for starting.

H

hand drill. A hand-operated tool used to turn a twist drill. The twist drill is mounted in a drill chuck which is turned with a set of bevel gears driven by a hand crank.

hand forming (sheet metal forming). A method of forming sheet metal parts by using a soft-faced hammer to shrink or stretch the metal. The metal may be formed over forming blocks or dies, or it may be shaped by hammering it into a sandbag.

handling line. A line, usually $\frac{1}{4}$– to $\frac{1}{2}$–inch diameter rope, attached to a balloon envelope or basket, used by the pilot or ground crew to assist in the ground handling, inflation, landing, and deflation of the balloon.

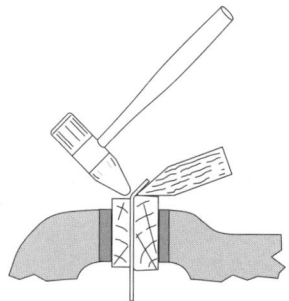

hand forming

hand-off (air traffic control). An action taken to transfer the radar identification of an aircraft from one controller to another if the aircraft will enter the receiving controller's airspace and radio communications with the aircraft will be transferred.

hand-operated bending tool (tubing bending tool). A tool used to bend thin-wall tubing without it collapsing. The tubing is bent around a deep-grooved radius block, using a sliding bar with a matching groove.

hand propping. Starting an aircraft engine by rotating the propeller by hand.

hand pump (hydraulic system component). A device used in a hydraulic system to move fluid. Most hand pumps are of the piston type, in which movement of the pump lever, or handle, moves a piston inside the pump. Some hand pumps are single-acting, which means that they move fluid only during one stroke of the handle. No fluid is moved during the return stroke. Other hand pumps are double-acting, which means that they move fluid during both strokes of the handle. Most aircraft hydraulic systems that use an engine-driven or electric motor-driven hydraulic pump have a hand pump as a backup in case the power pump fails.

hand rivet set (sheet metal tool). A rivet set, or die, that may be clamped in a vice. The manufactured head of a rivet is placed in the cup of the set and the shank of the rivet is upset with a hammer and a flat punch.

hand signals. Signals used by ramp personnel to communicate with pilots and crewmembers for the safe operation of aircraft on the ground.

hand tools. A general name for all of the handheld tools a technician uses when performing aircraft maintenance.

hangar. A building used to house aircraft.

hangar queen. A term used for an aircraft whose maintenance has a very low priority. It is worked on when no more profitable project is available for the maintenance crew.

hangar rash. Scrapes, bends, and dents in an aircraft structure that are caused by careless handling, usually when the aircraft is being moved inside the hangar.

hang glider. A motorless heavier-than-air aircraft deriving its lift from surfaces that remain fixed in flight, designed to carry not more than two persons and having a launch weight of 100 pounds or less.

hard (physical condition of a material). Compact, solid, and difficult to bend or deform.

hardboard. A composition material made by bonding sawdust and chips of wood with an adhesive under heat and pressure.

hard bronze. A high-strength copper alloy made of 88% copper, 7% tin, 3% zinc, and 2% lead.

hard-drawn copper wire. Copper wire that has not been annealed after it was formed by pulling it through dies. Pulling the wire through dies reduces its diameter to the desired size. It also work hardens the wire and increases its tensile strength.

hardenability (metals). The ability of a metal to be hardened by either heat treatment or cold-working.

hardened steel. Steel that has been heated red-hot and then quenched in brine, water, or oil. Hardened steel is strong but brittle.

hardener (plastic resin component). A material used with a plastic resin to improve its hardening.

hardening (metal heat treatment). A step in the heat treatment of metal in which the metal is made hard but brittle. Most ferrous metals (metals containing iron) are hardened by heating them to a specified temperature and then quenching them in oil, water, or brine. Other metals can be hardened only by cold-working them: by rolling them between steel rollers or by bending or hammering them.

hard-facing. A method of increasing the hardness of the face of a steel tool to keep it from being worn away in normal use. Hard-facing is done by welding, plating, or spraying a hard material, such as a carbide, on the surface of the tool.

hard landing (aircraft operation). An airplane landing in which enough forces have been transmitted into the structure to have likely caused damage.

hardness. The ability of a material to resist being scratched. Hardness is measured using the Mohs scale, which rates the hardness of a material by comparing it with ten minerals that have been given Mohs hardness values from one to ten. These minerals range from talc, whose Mohs hardness is one, through gypsum, calcite, fluorite, apatite, orthoclase, quartz, topaz, corundum, to diamond. Diamond has a Mohs hardness of ten.

hardness test. A test that can be made of either metallic or nonmetallic materials to determine their physical condition. A cone- or a ball-shaped tool is forced into the surface of the material, and the diameter or depth of the penetration caused by a given amount of force is measured. The diameter or depth of the penetration is related to the hardness and the strength of the material. *See* Rockwell hardness tester and Brinell hardness test.

hard rubber. Rubber that has been vulcanized under high temperature and pressure to make it hard. Hard rubber is used as an electrical insulator and for the handles of many different types of tools.

hardware. A general term for all of the small components, such as nuts, bolts, screws, and washers used to assemble an aircraft or aircraft engine.

hardware (computer operation). The physical equipment used in computer operation.

hardwood. Wood from a broadleaf tree that sheds its leaves each year.

hard X-rays. X-rays that have a great deal of penetrating power. The penetrating power of X-rays is determined by the amount of voltage applied to the anode of the X-ray tube. The higher the voltage, the harder the X-ray (the greater its penetrating power).

harmonic. A vibration whose frequency is an even multiple of another vibration. The first harmonic of a 400-Hz vibration has a frequency of 400 Hz. The frequency of the first harmonic is the same as the fundamental frequency. The second harmonic has a frequency of 800 hertz, and the third harmonic has a frequency of 1,200 hertz.

harness (electrical). A bundle of wires routed through an aircraft structure, connecting electrical components to each other and to the power bus.

Hartley oscillator. A popular electronic oscillator circuit which uses a tapped coil in parallel with a capacitor to determine the frequency of the AC the circuit produces. Energy from the collector of a transistor, or the plate of a vacuum tube, passes through one half of the coil and induces a voltage in the other half. This induced voltage is applied to the base of the transistor, or the grid of the vacuum tube, with a polarity that causes the circuit to oscillate, or produce alternating current.

Hasteloy. The registered trade name of a family of nickel-base alloys used to make turbine blades capable of operating at high temperatures.

HAT (height above touchdown) (air traffic control). The decision height or minimum descent altitude above the highest runway elevation in the touchdown zone (first 3,000 feet of the runway). HAT is published on instrument approach charts in conjunction with all straight-in minimums. *See* decision height, MDA (minimum descent altitude).

hat channel (metal construction). A type of formed or extruded structural material having the cross-sectional shape of a hat. Hat channels are attached to flat sheets of metal to stiffen them and give them rigidity.

"Have numbers" (air traffic control). A phrase used by pilots to inform ATC that they have received runway, wind, and altimeter information only.

hazardous attitudes (in decision-making). Attitudes on the part of the pilot that can lead to poor decision making and actions that involve unnecessary risk. Pilots must examine decisions carefully to ensure they have not been influenced by such attitudes.

hazardous inflight weather advisory service. *See* HIWAS.

hazardous weather information (air traffic control). A meteorological summary that contains information which is considered significant and is not included in a current hazardous weather advisory broadcast. This includes:
- Significant meteorological information (SIGMET/WS)
- Convective significant meteorological information (convective SIGMET/WST)
- Urgent pilot weather reports (urgent PIREP/UUA)
- Center weather advisories (CWA)
- Airmen's meteorological information (AIRMET/WA)
- Isolated thunderstorms that are rapidly developing and increasing in intensity
- Low ceilings and visibilities that are becoming widespread

haze (meteorology). An obstruction to visibility caused by fine dust or salt particles dispensed through a portion of the atmosphere. The particles are so small they cannot be felt or individually seen with the naked eye. Haze is distinguished from fog by its bluish or yellowish tinge.

head angle (countersunk fastener dimension). The included angle formed between the sides of the head of a countersunk rivet or screw.

head eccentricity (rivet dimension). The amount of difference between the center of the shank of a rivet and the center of its head.

heading. The direction in which the longitudinal axis of an aircraft is pointed, usually expressed in degrees clockwise from true, magnetic or compass north.

heading bug. A marker on the heading indicator that can be rotated to a specific heading for reference purposes or to command an autopilot to fly that heading.

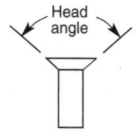

head angle

heading function. The flight director/autopilot function that steers the aircraft along a specified magnetic heading.

heading indicator. A gyroscopic flight instrument that gives the pilot an indication of the heading of the aircraft.

headless fastener. A type of friction-held fastener used to join mechanical parts. Neither end of the fastener is enlarged to form a head. A roll pin is an example of a headless fastener. *See* roll pin.

head of pressure. The pressure exerted by a column of fluid that is caused by the height of the column.

headphone (audio system). A small receiver, or earphone, mounted on a band worn over the head. Most headphones have two receivers mounted in soft cups so one can be comfortably worn over each ear.

head pressure of a fluid. The pressure exerted by a column of fluid caused by the height of the column.

head-up display. *See* HUD.

head-up guidance system (HGS). A system which projects critical flight data on a display positioned between the pilot and the windscreen. In addition to showing primary flight information, the HUD computes an extremely accurate instrument approach and landing guidance solution, and displays the result as a guidance cue for head-up viewing by the pilot. *See* HUD.

head wind (aircraft flight). A wind which blows from the direction the aircraft is flying. The ground speed of an aircraft (the speed the aircraft is moving over the ground) is less than the speed through the air by the velocity of the head wind.

headwork (in decision-making). Required to accomplish a conscious, rational thought process when making decisions.

hearth furnace. A type of furnace used to melt iron and steel. The metal is melted by passing hot gases over the charge of metal on the floor, or hearth, of the furnace.

heat. A form of energy that affects the speed of movement of the molecules of which a material is made. The more heat energy in a material, the faster its molecules move, and the amount of heat energy in a material determines its physical condition. Water that contains very little heat energy is a solid, ice. When heat is added to ice, the ice melts and becomes liquid water. Additional heat added to the liquid water causes it to boil, and it becomes water vapor (steam).

Our chief source of heat energy is the sun. Heat energy from the sun reaches the earth by radiation, and it is stored in plants and animals in the form of chemical energy. This chemical energy can be changed back into heat energy by the use of various types of machines.

heat engine. A form of mechanical device that converts heat energy into mechanical energy. The two most widely used types of heat engines for aircraft are reciprocating engines and turbine engines.

heater (electron tube). A small strip of resistance wire mounted inside a tubular cathode in an electron tube. Low-voltage AC flowing through the heater causes it to get red-hot. This heats the cathode enough for it to emit, or give off, electrons.

heat dissipation. The loss of heat.

heat exchanger. A device used to exchange heat from one medium to another. Radiators, condensers, and evaporators are all examples of heat exchangers. Heat always moves from the object or medium having the greatest level of heat energy to a medium or object having a lower level. Air-to-air, air-to-liquid, liquid-to-air, and liquid-to-liquid heat exchangers are commonly used with aircraft engines.

heating element (electrical heater). A coil or a piece of resistance wire connected across a source of electrical energy. The resistance of the element is high enough that current flowing through it produces enough heat to cause it to glow red-hot.

heat lamp. A form of incandescent lamp that produces a maximum of infrared radiation (heat) with a minimum of visible light rays. Heat lamps are used for curing resins, drying paint, keeping food warm, and applying heat to parts of the human body.

heat load (air conditioning system). The amount of heat that must be added to or taken away from the inside of an aircraft cabin, during a specified unit of time, to keep the temperature of the cabin constant.

heat of compression (physics). Heat that is introduced into a gas by its compression.

heat pump. A device that moves heat from one location to another. An air conditioning system is a form of heat pump. Heat from inside the aircraft cabin is absorbed by a liquid refrigerant. When the refrigerant absorbs the heat, it evaporates, or changes into a gas. The gas is then compressed, and the compression raises its temperature higher than that of the outside air.

The compressor forces the hot gas through the condenser, located outside the aircraft. Here, the gas transfers some of its heat to the outside air and condenses back into a liquid. Heat in this way is pumped from inside the aircraft cabin to the air outside the aircraft.

heat-shrinkable fabric. Certain inorganic fabrics used to cover aircraft structure. The fabric used for this purpose is sold in its unshrunk state and is put on the structure so that it is taut, but not tight. After it is secured to the structure with a special adhesive, it is shrunk to the correct tautness by ironing it with an electric iron or blowing it with a special heater/blower.

After the fabric has the correct tautness, it is coated with a nontautening dope. Organic fabrics, such as cotton and linen, are not heat-shrinkable and are shrunk on the structure with a shrinking-type dope.

heat sink. A piece of heavy metal on which such electrical components as power transistors are mounted. Heat from the component is transferred into the heat sink by conduction, and from there it is dissipated into the surrounding air. A silicone grease may be spread between the component and the heat sink to help transfer the heat. Many heat sinks on which high-power components are mounted have fins to increase their cooling area.

heat treatment (metal). A process by which certain types of metal are hardened or softened by heat. Most metals containing iron can be hardened by heating them to a high temperature and quenching them in water, brine (a solution of salt and water), or oil. These same metals can be softened by heating them to a high temperature and allowing them to cool slowly in an oven. Copper cannot be hardened with heat. When copper is heated red-hot and quenched in water, it becomes soft. Metals that cannot be hardened with heat can be work hardened by bending, hammering, rolling, or stretching. However, most of these metals can be softened by heating them and cooling them slowly.

heat treatment (plastic resins). A process used to strengthen cemented joints in thermoplastic resins. After the cemented joint is completed, the material is held at an elevated temperature (not high enough to distort the material) for a specified period of time. The heat causes solvents concentrated in the joint to diffuse (to spread evenly) throughout the material. This diffusion decreases the concentration of the solvents in the joint and increases its strength.

Heaviside layer (atmosphere). A layer of ionized particles that surrounds the earth at a height of about 55 to 85 miles above the surface. The Heaviside layer is also called the Kennelly Heaviside layer and the E-region of the atmosphere. The Heaviside layer reflects relatively long, low-frequency radio waves.

heavy ends (petroleum refining). The components of crude petroleum that have the highest boiling points. In the process of fractional distillation, the lighter products boil off first and are condensed. The heavy ends are the parts of the petroleum that boil off last.

heavy hydrogen. Isotopes of hydrogen having one or two neutrons in the nucleus. Isotopes with one neutron are called deuterium ^{2}H, and isotopes with two neutrons are called tritium ^{3}H.

heavy water. A compound of hydrogen and oxygen containing a larger proportion of deuterium (an isotope of hydrogen with one neutron in the nucleus) than normally occurs in water.

hecto. The metric prefix that means one hundred (1×10^2). Hecto is used as a prefix, as in hectometers (100 meters), hectoliters (100 liters), etc.

hedge-hop (aircraft flight). To fly an aircraft very near the surface of the earth. This flight is below the level of many obstructions on the ground, and the aircraft must be pulled up to pass over these obstructions. Hedge-hopping is both dangerous and illegal in all except a few special instances, such as agricultural application.

heel of a bend (rigid fluid lines). The outside of a bend. The metal in the heel of a bend in rigid tubing has been stretched and is thinner than in other parts of the tubing.

height above airport. *See* HAA.

height above landing. *See* HAL.

height above touchdown. *See* HAT.

height band (sailplane flight). The altitude range in which the thermals are strongest on any given day. Remaining within the height band on a cross-country flight should allow the fastest average speed.

height-to-length ratio (water navigation). The ratio between the swell height to the length between two successive crests (swell length).

height-velocity envelope (helicopter operation). A chart produced by the manufacturer of a helicopter showing the conditions of airspeed related to height that produces conditions unsafe for an autorotative landing.

Heliarc welding. A name used for inert-gas arc welding. There are two basic types of Heliarc welding: TIG (tungsten inert-gas) welding and MIG (metal inert-gas) welding. TIG welding uses a small-diameter nonconsumable tungsten rod as the electrode from which the arc jumps to the metal being welded. MIG welding uses a consumable soft steel rod as an electrode. This rod melts and adds metal to the molten pool to reinforce the weld.

helical potentiometer (electrical component). A multi-turn potentiometer, or variable resistor. The resistance element is made in the form of a spiral, or helix, and the wiper is moved over the element by turning a multi-turn screw. Most helical potentiometers require ten turns of the screw to move the wiper from one end of the resistance element to the other.

helical spline. A spline that twists, or winds, around the periphery of a shaft. Helical splines are used to change linear motion of the device that rides on the splines into rotary motion of the shaft on which the splines are cut. They are also used to change rotary motion of the shaft into linear motion of the device that rides on it.

Helical splines are cut onto the shaft of some aircraft engine starter motors to move the starter gear into mesh with the flywheel gear (linear motion) when the starter shaft is spun (rotary motion).

helical spring. A coil spring wound in the form of a spiral, or helix. Helical springs can be wound in such a way that they can absorb either tensile or compressive loads.

Heli-Coil insert. The registered trade name for a special helical insert used to restore threads that have been stripped from a hole. The

helical compression spring

damaged threads are drilled out, and new threads are cut with a special oversize tap. A stainless steel coil of wire whose cross section is in the shape of a diamond is screwed into the hole and left there to serve as the new threads.

Heli-Coil inserts are also used to provide durable threads in soft metal castings. Some spark plug holes in cast-aluminum cylinder heads are fitted with Heli-Coil inserts to minimize the wear caused by repeated removal and installation of the spark plugs.

helicopter. A heavier-than-air flying machine that is supported in the air by aerodynamic lift produced by an engine-driven rotor. Since the rotor is engine driven, a helicopter does not need forward motion through the air for the rotor to produce lift.

14 CFR Part 1: "A rotorcraft that, for its horizontal motion, depends principally on its engine-driven rotors."

Helicopter Emergency Medical Service (HEMS) Weather Display. A product of the Aviation Digital Data Service, this computer program gives weather information, both realtime and forecast, for 5-kilometer square areas nationwide. It can be viewed and downloaded at www.weather.aero/HEMS.

helipad. A small designated area, usually with a prepared surface, on a heliport, airport landing/takeoff area, apron/ramp, or movement area used for takeoff, landing, or parking of helicopters.

heliport. *14 CFR Part 1:* "An area of land, water, or structure used, or intended to be used, for the landing and takeoff of helicopters."

heliport reference point (HRP). The geographic center of a heliport.

helium. A colorless, odorless, tasteless, inert gaseous chemical element. Helium's symbol is He, its atomic number is 2, and its atomic weight is 4.0026. Because helium will not combine with other chemical elements, it is used to force oxygen away from the molten metal in certain types of arc welding, and to fill some types of electron tubes to prevent oxygen from contacting the hot filaments. Because of its lightness and because it will not burn, helium is used to inflate lighter-than-air aircraft.

helix. A screw-like, or spiral, curve.

henry. The basic unit of inductance. One henry, H, is the amount of inductance needed to produce an electromotive force of one volt, when the current in the inductor changes at the rate of one ampere per second.

heptane. A liquid organic hydrocarbon compound, $CH_3(CH_2)_5CH_3$. Heptane, which has a very low critical pressure and temperature, is used as the low reference fuel (octane zero) in determining the octane rating of a reciprocating engine fuel.

heptode (electron tube). An electron tube, or vacuum tube, that has seven active electrodes. The electrodes in a heptode are the anode, the cathode, the control grid, and four special purpose grids, such as a screen grid, suppressor grid, and beam-forming grids.

hermaphrodite calipers. Calipers having one sharp-pointed leg, similar to that used on dividers, and one leg of an outside caliper. Hermaphrodite calipers are used to scribe a mark along a piece of material a specific distance from the edge.

hermetic seal. An airtight seal used to protect components or devices from the effect of moisture in the air. To achieve a hermetic seal, air is pumped out of the container or displaced by a dry inert gas, such as nitrogen, and the container is sealed so no moisture can get into it.

herringbone gear. A gear whose teeth are cut across its face in the shape of a V. A herringbone gear is similar to two helical gears whose teeth run in opposite directions, mounted side-by-side on the shaft.

hermaphrodite calipers

hertz. The term used for the frequency of any cyclic repetition. One hertz, Hz, is one cycle of events each second.

Hertz antenna (radio antenna). An ungrounded, half-wave antenna whose resonant frequency is determined by its distributed capacity. This capacity, and therefore its resonant frequency, is determined by the antenna length.

heterodyne. To mix two electrical or acoustic signals having different frequencies so they produce two new signals whose frequencies are different from either of the two original signals. If a signal with a frequency of 1,000 hertz is mixed with a signal having a frequency of 800 hertz, two new frequencies are produced: the sum of the two frequencies, 1,800 hertz, and the difference between the two, 200 hertz.

heterodyne-type frequency meter. An instrument used to determine the frequency of alternating current. The frequency of an accurately calibrated internal oscillator is varied and compared with the frequency being measured. When the two frequencies are mixed, a third frequency, called the beat frequency, is produced. This beat frequency is the difference between the two.

   The variable frequency is changed until the beat frequency disappears. When it disappears, the frequency being measured is the same as that being produced by the oscillator.

heterogeneous mixture. A physical mixture of dissimilar ingredients. Concrete is a heterogeneous mixture of sand, gravel, and portland cement.

hexadecimal number system. A number system that uses 16 as its base. The values from 0 through 9 are represented by the numerals 0 through 9, and values from 10 through 15 use the letters A through F. Hexadecimal numbers can easily be converted into binary numbers for use in a computer. Values of up to decimal 255 or binary 1111 1111 can be expressed by using only two hexadecimal digits, FF.

Decimal	Hex	Binary	Decimal	Hex	Binary
0	0	0000	8	8	1000
1	1	0001	9	9	1001
2	2	0010	10	A	1010
3	3	0011	11	B	1011
4	4	0100	12	C	1100
5	5	0101	13	D	1101
6	6	0110	14	E	1110
7	7	0111	15	F	1111

hexagon. A closed, plane figure that has six sides.

hexagon head bolt. A bolt whose head has six sides (a hexagon). A hex-head bolt can be turned with an open-end wrench or with either a six-point or a 12-point socket wrench. The six flat sides of a hex-head bolt allow the wrench to be repositioned more often than could be done with a square-head bolt, and this makes for easier installation and removal.

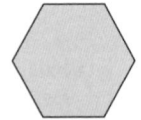

hexagon

hexode (electron tube). A form of electron tube having six active electrodes. The electrodes are the cathode, the anode, the control grid, and three other grids that serve special functions in controlling the passage of electrons between the cathode and the anode.

Hg. Abbreviation for mercury, from the Latin *hydrargyrum.*

hidden line (aircraft drawing). A medium-weight line made up of short dashes that shows a surface of a part that is not visible in the view shown.

hidden surface (aircraft drawing). Any surface on an object that cannot be seen in the view depicted by a drawing. A hidden surface is represented in outline form by a hidden line, a series of medium-weight dashes.

"hierarchy of human needs" (behavioral studies). A listing by Abraham Maslow of needs, from the most basic to the most fulfilling: physiological, security, belonging, esteem, cognitive and aesthetic, and self-actualization.

high (meteorology). An area of high barometric pressure with its attendant system of anticyclonic winds, winds that circulate in a clockwise direction in the northern hemisphere and counterclockwise in the southern hemisphere.

high altitude redesign (HAR). A level of nonrestrictive routing service for aircraft that have all waypoints associated with the HAR program in their flight management systems or RNAV equipage.

high blower (aircraft engine supercharger condition). The condition of supercharging of a reciprocating engine in which a two-speed, single-stage internal supercharger is operating at its high-speed ratio. This ratio is normally about ten times the speed of the crankshaft.

high-bypass turbofan engine. A turbofan engine in which the fan moves more than four times as much air as is moved by the core engine compressor. This type of engine is said to have a bypass ratio of more than 4:1.

high-carbon steel. Steel that contains at least 0.50% carbon. High-carbon steel can be hardened to increase its strength, but this causes it to become brittle.

high-frequency communications. Radio communications using frequencies between three and 30 megahertz. HF communication is used between aircraft and ground facilities in over water operations.

high-impedance voltmeter. A voltmeter whose meter movement requires very little current for full-scale deflection. Most high-impedance voltmeters have a sensitivity of at least 20,000 ohms per volt, and when a very-high-impedance voltmeter is needed, vacuum-tube or FET voltmeters are used. The sensitivity of these meters is measured in megohms per volt. High-impedance voltmeters do not load the circuit, which would give erroneous reading when voltage is measured across a high resistance.

high-level airspace. All airspace that is within the National Airspace System at or above 18,000 feet MSL.

high-level airway. In the controlled high-level airspace, a prescribed track between specified radio aids to navigation that is designated "J," along which ATC service is provided.

high-level language (computer language). A computer language whose instructions are terms similar to those used in normal communications. Statements in the high-level language entered into the computer produce a series of machine-language instructions the computer can understand. BASIC, FORTRAN, COBOL, and PASCAL are examples of high-level languages.

high-lift device (aircraft component). Any component used to increase the lift produced by an aircraft wing. High-lift devices include leading edge flaps, slots, slats, trailing edge flaps, and boundary layer control systems. High-lift devices allow the wing to reach a higher angle of attack and thus produce more lift, before the airflow over its surface separates and the wing stalls.

high metal ion concentration cell corrosion. Corrosion that results from a concentration of metallic ions in the electrolyte. The area of high concentration of metallic ions is the cathode of the cell.

high-pass filter (electronic circuit). A type of electronic filter that passes, with little opposition, alternating current above a certain frequency. A high-pass filter blocks direct current, and blocks or reduces the amplitude of all alternating current having a frequency lower than that for which it is designed.

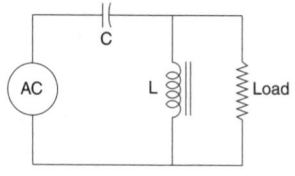

high-pass filter

high-performance aircraft. An aircraft with an engine of more than 200 horsepower, has a controllable pitch propeller and retractable landing gear, or is turbine powered.

high-potential test (ignition lead test). A test used to determine whether or not the insulation around certain shielded wires in an ignition system can withstand the high voltage they carry without leaking an excessive amount of current to ground. A high potential (high voltage) is placed between the center conductor and the metal shield around the outside of the insulation. An indicator light glows if the leakage current between the two conductors is excessive. A high-potential test is often called a high-pot test.

high-pressure compressor (gas turbine engine component). The second-stage compressor in a dual-spool gas turbine engine. The high-pressure compressor, called the N_2 compressor, is the one that is rotated by the starter for starting, and the one whose RPM is controlled by the fuel control.

high-pressure oxygen system. An oxygen system installed in an aircraft in which gaseous oxygen is carried in steel bottles under a pressure of between 1,800 and 2,000 pounds per square inch.

high-pressure turbine (gas turbine engine component). The stage, or stages, of turbines used to drive the high-pressure (N_2) compressor in a two-spool, axial-flow gas turbine engine.

high-Q circuit (electronic circuit). An electronic circuit having a high ratio of circuit impedance to resistance. Q is a measure of the efficiency of a reactive circuit.

high-rate discharge (battery operation). Discharge of a battery at the highest rate it is likely to encounter in service. This is also called the cold-cranking discharge rate.

high-resistance connection (electrical circuit). A connection in an electrical circuit which has an excessive amount of resistance. High-resistance connections are caused by corrosion, loose fasteners, and cold-solder joints.

high-speed steel. Steel alloys used to make metal-cutting tools. These alloys retain their strength and hardness when operating at high temperatures.

high-speed taxiway [ICAO: rapid exit taxiway]. A long-radius taxiway designed and provided with lighting or marking to define the path of aircraft traveling at high speed (up to 60 knots) from the runway center to a point on the center of a taxiway. A high-speed taxiway is also referred to as a long-radius exit or turn-off taxiway and is designed to expedite aircraft turning off the runway after landing, thus reducing runway occupancy time.

high-strength steel. Steel whose tensile strength can be increased by proper heat treatment to between 50,000 and 100,000 pounds per square inch.

high-tension magneto (reciprocating engine ignition system). A self-contained ignition system used with a spark-ignition reciprocating engine. A high-tension magneto contains an alternating current generator that produces a flow of primary current, and a set of breaker points that interrupts this current the instant the spark is needed.

When the primary current stops flowing, its magnetic field collapses. The collapsing lines of flux cut across many thousands of turns of wire in the secondary winding of the built-in magneto coil and induces a high voltage into it. The distributor, which is a high-voltage selector switch, directs the high voltage from the magneto coil to the proper spark plug for ignition.

high unmetered fuel pressure. The pressure in a Teledyne-Continental fuel injector pump that is adjusted by the variable orifice.

high vacuum. An absolute pressure of between 1 x 10^{-3} and 1 x 10^{-6} millimeters of mercury.

highway in the sky (HITS). A graphically intuitive pilot interface system that provides an aircraft operator with all of the attitude and guidance inputs required to safely fly an aircraft in close conformance to air traffic procedures.

hinge. A form of fastener that allows one connected piece to rotate with respect to the other. Hinges are used to connect a door to the edge of an opening in a compartment or bulkhead. The hinges allow the door to swing, or rotate, open or closed. Ailerons are attached to a wing trailing edge with hinges so they can rotate with respect to the wing surface.

Hipernik. The registered trade name for a magnetic alloy made of 50% iron and 50% nickel.

Hi-Shear rivet. A patented, high-strength, pin-type fastener used in aircraft construction. Hi-Shear rivets are often used in place of bolts in strong, lightweight structure. The pin of a Hi-Shear rivet has a thin, flat head on one end and a groove around its shank at the other end. The pin is pressed through a tight-fitting hole in the pieces of metal to be joined, and a soft steel or aluminum alloy collar is slipped over its grooved end.

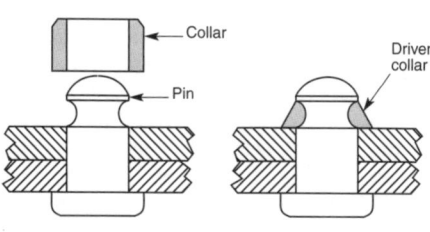

Hi-Shear rivet

A swaging tool forces the collar into the groove and pulls the head of the rivet tight against the metal through which it is installed.

HIWAS (hazardous inflight weather advisory service) (air traffic control). Continuously recorded hazardous inflight weather forecasts broadcast to airborne pilots over selected VOR outlets defined as HIWAS broadcast areas.

HIWAS broadcast area. A geographical area of responsibility including one or more HIWAS outlet areas assigned to an AFSS/FSS for hazardous weather advisory broadcasting.

HIWAS outlet area. An area defined as a 150 NM radius of a HIWAS outlet, expanded as necessary to provide coverage.

hoar frost (meteorology). White ice crystals that form when the air is moist and the surface is cold. They are deposited on the ground or exposed objects. Hoar frost is often seen on cold, clear autumn nights.

Hobbs meter. The registered trade name of an operating-time indicator used with reciprocating engines to show the number of hours the engine has operated. The Hobbs meter consists of a clock that is actuated by an engine oil pressure switch. When the engine is producing oil pressure, the clock runs, but when oil pressure is lost at engine shutdown, the clock stops.

hoist load, maximum permissible (helicopter specification). The maximum external load that is permitted for a helicopter to carry. This load is specified in the POH.

hold in lieu of procedure turn. A hold in lieu of procedure turn is established over a final or intermediate fix when an approach can be made from a properly aligned holding pattern. The hold in lieu of procedure turn permits the pilot to align with the final or intermediate segment of the approach and/or descend in the holding pattern to an altitude that will permit a normal descent to the final approach fix altitude.

hold, or holding, procedure (air traffic control). A predetermined maneuver which keeps aircraft within a specified airspace while awaiting further clearance from air traffic control.

"Hold for release" (air traffic control). A phrase used by ATC to delay an aircraft for traffic management reasons; i.e., weather, traffic volume, etc. Hold for release instructions (including departure delay information) are used to inform a pilot or a controller (either directly or through an authorized relay) that an IFR departure clearance is not valid until a release time or additional instructions have been received.

holding coil (electrical relay). An auxiliary coil in an electrical relay. Current flowing through the holding coil keeps the relay energized after the control current that caused the relay to close has stopped flowing through the main coil.

holding fix (navigation). A specified fix identifiable to a pilot by NAVAIDs or visual reference to the ground, used as a reference point in establishing and maintaining the position of an aircraft while holding.

holding pattern. A racetrack pattern involving two turns and two legs used to keep an aircraft within a prescribed airspace with respect to a geographic fix. A standard pattern uses right turns; nonstandard patterns use left turns.

holding point (ICAO). A specified location, identified by visual or other means, in the vicinity of which the position of an aircraft in flight is maintained in accordance with air traffic control clearances.

holding relay. An electrical relay whose coil is in series with its contacts. The contacts are closed by sending a pulse of current through the coil, and the contacts remain closed until the current flowing through them is interrupted.

hold-short point (air traffic control). A point on the runway beyond which a landing aircraft with a land and hold short (LAHSO) clearance is not authorized to proceed. The hold-short point may be located prior to an intersecting runway, taxiway, predetermined point, or approach/departure flight path.

hold-short position lights (air traffic control). Flashing in-pavement white lights located at specific hold-short points.

hold-short position marking (air traffic control). The painted runway marking located at the hold-short point on all land and hold short (LAHSO) runways.

hold-short position signs (air traffic control). Red and white holding position signs located alongside the hold-short point.

hole (semiconductor device). A concept used to explain the action that takes place in a semiconductor material. A hole is a location in a covalent atomic bond where there should be an electron, but where there is none.

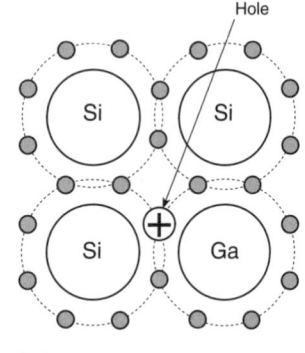

hole

Holes are the mobile charges in a piece of P-type semiconductor material, and since they are located where an electron (a negative charge) should be, they act as positive charges. *See* acceptor atom.

hole finder (sheet metal hand tool). A hand tool used in sheet metalwork that allows a technician to locate a rivet hole in a new sheet metal skin so the hole will be directly in line with a hole already existing in the structure being repaired.

The tool consists of a drill guide directly in line with a pilot pin and space for the undrilled skin to slip between the guide and the pin. The tool is slipped over the edge of the skin and the pilot pin inserted in the existing rivet hole. A hole drilled through the drill guide is directly in line with the existing rivet hole.

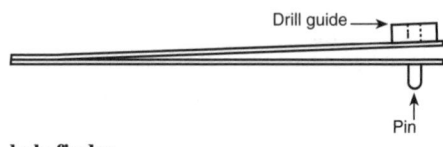

hole finder

hollow drill. A drill with a hole through its center. Air or liquid lubricant can be pumped through a hollow drill into the hole being drilled, to make it easier for the drill to cut, and to remove chips from the hole.

holmium. A relatively soft, malleable, stable, rare-earth chemical element. Holmium's symbol is Ho, its atomic number is 67, and its atomic weight is 164.93. Holmium has a melting point of about 1,500°C.

homebuilt aircraft. Aircraft that are built by individuals as a hobby rather than by factories as commercial products. Homebuilt, or amateur-built, aircraft are not required to meet the stringent requirements imposed on the manufacturer of FAA-certificated aircraft.

homing (aircraft flight). Flight toward a NAVAID without a wind correction being applied. This is done by adjusting the aircraft heading to maintain a relative bearing of zero degrees between the NAVAID and the nose of the aircraft.

homing (ICAO). The procedure of using the direction-finding equipment of one radio station with the emission of another radio station, where at least one of the stations is mobile, and whereby the mobile station proceeds continuously towards the other station.

hone. A fine abrasive stone. Hones are used to sharpen cutting tools and to smooth a surface by wearing away surface roughness.

honeycomb (structural material). A type of material used as the core for laminated structural panels. Honeycomb may be made from aluminum foil, fiberglass cloth, or paper. It is made with a series of hexagonal (six-sided) compartments joined together in such a way that they look much like the comb produced by the honeybee.

honeycomb

Honeycomb has almost no strength against side loads, but it has an exceptional strength against loads applied in line with its openings. Honeycomb material is sliced to the proper thickness and bonded between face sheets of thin sheet metal or fiberglass reinforced plastic resin. Laminated honeycomb material is rigid, strong, and lightweight.

honing. A method of removing a very small amount of material from a metal surface by abrading the surface with a fine stone. Honing is used to produce a smooth finish on a surface, or to produce a sharp edge on a knife or chisel.

honing (cylinder wall treatment). Scratching the surface of the cylinder wall with an abrasive stone to produce a series of grooves of microscopic depth and uniform pattern. The honed pattern holds oil to lubricate the cylinder walls.

Hooke's law. A basic law of physics that deals with the relationship between stress and strain. Hooke's law explains that the strain within a material (the amount the material deforms) is directly proportional to the amount of stress that causes the deformation. This is true only until the material reaches its elastic limit.

When the stress that strains a material within its elastic limit is removed, the material will return to its original size and shape. But, if the material is strained beyond its elastic limit, it will not return to its original size and shape, but will be permanently deformed.

hook rule. A steel scale with a projection off of one end of the scale at the zero position. A hook rule is used to measure to the edge of a piece of material that has a radius on its edges.

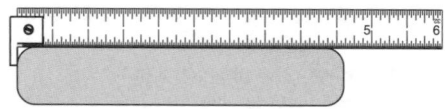

hook rule

hook spanner. A type of wrench used to turn a splined shaft. Some hook spanners have a hinged hook that allows them to be used on shafts of different diameters.

hopper. A funnel-shaped container with an opening in the top for loading and a smaller opening in the bottom for dumping. Hoppers are used to store the abrasive in an abrasive blaster. The abrasive is loaded in through the large opening, and it feeds out as needed through the small opening.

hopper-type oil tank (reciprocating engine oil tank). An oil tank, or reservoir, in which there is a hopper around the outlet from the tank. When oil dilution is being used, the diluted oil fills the hopper before the engine is shut down. Then, when the engine is started, the diluted oil is the first used. This diluted oil helps start the engine in cold weather. As soon as the oil begins to warm up, oil around the outside of the hopper feeds into the engine.

horizon. The line we see that forms an apparent boundary between the earth and sky.

horizontal component of lift (HCL) (aerodynamics). A component of flight that works along with the vertical component in turning flight, HCL is the lift that acts horizontally and in opposition to inertia (centrifugal force). The horizontal component of lift creates a force directed inward toward the center of rotation, which is known as centripetal force. *See also* vertical component of lift.

horizontally opposed engine (reciprocating engine). A reciprocating engine in which the cylinders are arranged in two banks separated by 180°, with the cylinders and crankcase mounted in the aircraft so they are flat. The cylinders are staggered, with one bank slightly ahead of the other. Staggering the cylinders allows each piston to be connected to a separate throw of the crankshaft. Horizontally opposed engines are called flat engines.

horizontal needle of the cross-pointer indicator (aircraft instrument). The horizontal needle of the cross-pointer indicator of the Instrument Landing System (ILS) shows the pilot the vertical position of the aircraft as it descends along the glide slope for an instrument approach.

If the horizontal needle is above the center mark, or doughnut, the aircraft is below the glide slope, and the pilot should fly upward. If the needle is below the doughnut, the aircraft is too high and should descend. The glide slope is sometimes called the glide path. *See* illustration for glide slope.

horizontal plane. A horizontal plane is one that is perpendicular to the gravitational field of the earth.

horizontal situation indicator. *See* HSI.

horizontal stabilizer (airplane control). The fixed horizontal surface on the tail of a conventional airplane. The horizontal stabilizer is usually adjustable in flight to vary the down-load produced by the tail. This allows the airplane to fly hands-off at any desired airspeed.

horse latitudes. The region between the trade winds and the prevailing westerlies, where the winds are often light or calm.

horsepower. A measure of mechanical power equal to 33,000 foot-pounds of work done in 1 minute, 550 foot-pounds of work done in 1 second, or 746 watts of power. One metric horsepower is equal to 75 meter-kilograms per second or 0.9863 English horsepower.

horseshoe magnet. A permanent magnet formed in the shape of the letter U, the shape of a horseshoe. The poles of a horseshoe magnet are close together, and the magnetic flux between them is concentrated.

hose. A flexible fluid line. A hose may have threaded fittings installed in its ends for attachment to other fittings, or it may be slipped over a piece of rigid tubing and secured with hose clamps.

hot bond repair (composites). Repair made using a hot-patch bonding machine to cure and monitor the curing. These machines typically include a heater and a vacuum source.

hot-blow forming (sheet metal forming). A method of forming sheet metal by forcing it into a die with argon gas whose pressure is computer-controlled to maintain the correct rate of strain of the metal.

hot corrosion (turbine engine damage). A term used for a localized, accelerated corrosion attack caused by the presence of a salt layer on the metal. This may be seen on the blades and vanes of gas turbines which are generally made of nickel- or cobalt-base alloys.

hot dimpling (sheet metal construction process). A process used to dimple, or indent, the hole into which a flush rivet is to be installed. Some metals, such as magnesium and the harder aluminum alloys, cannot be dimpled cold because they are likely to crack. These metals must be hot dimpled.

Hot dimpling equipment consists of a pair of electrically heated dies with a pilot that goes through the rivet hole. The pilot is passed through the hole, and the heated dies are pressed together. The dies heat the metal enough to soften it and force it into the shape of the die. This is the proper shape for the rivet head.

hot forming (metal forming process). Hot forming operations include forging, extruding, hot upsetting, piercing, shearing, and any other operations involving cutting or deforming metal at relatively high temperatures.

hot junction (thermocouple junction). The junction in a thermocouple that is exposed to the temperature to be measured. *See* thermocouple house thermal (meteorology).

hot section (gas turbine engine). The portion of a gas turbine engine that operates at high temperature. The hot section includes the combustors, the turbine, and the exhaust system of the engine.

hot section inspection (gas turbine engine maintenance procedure). The inspection of the hot section of a gas turbine engine.

hot spark plug (reciprocating engine ignition component). A spark plug with a long path for heat to travel from the nose core insulator to the spark plug shell. Because the heat must travel a long distance before it is transferred into the cylinder head, the nose core stays quite hot. Hot spark plugs are used in low-powered engines because a cold spark plug would not get hot enough to burn the contaminants out of its firing-end cavity. If these contaminants are not burned out, they will foul the spark plug and prevent it from firing properly.

hot stamping. A method of marking plastic materials, cloth, or paper by using heated metal dies. The heated dies force molten metal leaf (extremely thin sheets of metal) into the surface of the material.

hot start (gas turbine engine). A condition in which a gas turbine engine starts, but its internal temperature rises high enough to damage the engine. Any time an engine has a hot start, it must be given a special inspection to determine if any damage has been done.

hot streaking (turbine engine malfunction). A hot section malfunction in which the flame penetrates through the entire turbine system and into the tail pipe.

hot-tank lubrication system (gas turbine engine). A lubrication system of a gas turbine engine in which the oil cooler is in the pressure portion of the system. Hot oil returns directly from the engine into the tank without being cooled.

hot valve clearance (radial reciprocating engine specification). The clearance between the valve stem and the rocker arm of a radial engine when the engine is operating at its normal temperature. The hot, or running, clearance is much greater than the cold clearance, and it is measured only when adjusting the valve timing. After the timing is properly adjusted, using the hot clearance, all of the valves are set to the much smaller cold clearance.

hot wire. The common term used for a wire connected to the source of electrical power.

hot-wire ammeter. An ammeter used for measuring high-frequency alternating current. The current flows through a fine wire held under a slight tension, and the heat produced by the current causes the wire to expand and increase its length. As the wire lengthens, it moves a pointer across the dial to show the amount of current flowing through the wire.

hot-wire anemometer. A form of windspeed indicator in which the wind whose speed being measured passes over a wire heated by an electrical current. The amount of heat the moving air removes from the wire is proportional to the wind speed.

hot-wire cutter. A cutter used to shape blocks of Styrofoam. The wire is stretched tight between the arms of a frame and heated by electrical current. The hot wire melts its way through the foam.

hourmeter (aircraft instrument). An instrument installed in many aircraft to show the actual number of hours the engine has operated. The hourmeter is an electrical clock that starts when the engine oil pressure builds up, and runs until the engine is shut down and the oil pressure drops to zero.

house thermal (glider operations). A "house thermal" is one that frequently forms in the same or similar location. In locating thermals for soaring flight it is worth noting where thermals were found previously, as some areas tend to be consistent thermal sources.

housing. An enclosure used to hold or protect a mechanical or electronic device.

hover (helicopter operation). A condition of helicopter flight in which the machine holds a fixed position over the earth. When a helicopter is hovering, it is not moving in any direction relative to the terrain below it.

hover check (helicopter operation). A stabilized hover of a helicopter or VTOL aircraft used to conduct a performance/power check prior to hover taxi, air taxi, or takeoff.

hovering ceiling (helicopter flight). The maximum altitude at which a helicopter can support itself without forward motion. Hovering ceiling is normally given in two figures: in ground effect (IGE) and out of ground effect (OGE).

hovering in ground effect (helicopter operation). A helicopter hovering in ground effect (IGE) is in flight, but it is not moving over the ground, and it is flying at a height equal to or less than the span of its rotor above the surface. A helicopter can hover in ground effect at a higher density altitude than it can hover out of ground effect.

hovering out of ground effect (helicopter operation). A helicopter hovering out of ground effect (OGE) is in flight, but it is not moving over the ground, and it is flying at a height above the ground greater than the span of its rotor.

hover taxi (helicopter operation). Movement of a helicopter or VTOL aircraft above the surface and in ground effect, at airspeeds of less than approximately 20 knots.

"How do you hear me?" (radio communications). A question relating to the quality of the transmission or to determine how well the transmission is being received.

HRD fire extinguisher (high-rate-discharge). A fire extinguisher that carries the extinguishing agent in a sealed sphere or cylinder. When the agent-discharged switch is closed, a powder charge drives a cutter through a frangible disk and releases the agent. The entire contents of the container are emptied in much less than a second.

HSI (horizontal situation indicator). An electronic flight and navigation instrument that shows the pilot the proper changes to make in directional flight. An HSI shows the pilot the relationship of the aircraft to the VOR radial or ADF bearing, the magnetic direction, the desired course and heading, and also the relationship of the aircraft to the glide slope.

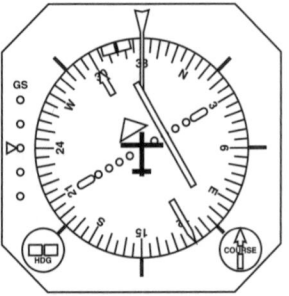

horizontal situation indicator

hub of a propeller. The portion of a propeller that attaches to the propeller shaft of the engine. The propeller blades fasten into the hub.

HUD (head-up display). A special type of flight instrumentation that allows the pilot of an aircraft to watch the instruments while looking ahead of the aircraft for the approach lights or the runway. Head-up displays increase the safety of flight during the transition from instrument flight to visual flight during a landing.

hue (color characteristic). The characteristic of light, caused by its wavelength, that gives a color its name. Red, blue, and green are hues.

human factors. The study of the way people interact with their environments. In the case of general aviation, it is the study of the way pilot performance is influenced by such issues as the design of cockpits, the function of the organs of the body, the effects of emotions, and the interaction and communication with the other participants of the aviation community, such as other crewmembers and air traffic control personnel.

human nature. The general psychological characteristics, feelings, and behavioral traits shared by all humans; that is, the qualities common to humanity and the elements that are a basic part of the life of all humans, distinguishing it from other animal life. These qualities and elements help explain the motivations and attitudes in people's behavior and how they learn in a setting such as flight training.

humidity. A term used to indicate the presence of water vapor, or moisture, in the air.

hung start (gas turbine engine operation). An improper start of a gas turbine engine in which the engine starts, but fails to accelerate to a self-sustaining speed. *See* false start.

hunting (automatic flight control system). An undesirable condition in an automatic flight control system in which the system oscillates back and forth on either side of a stable condition. The control system seeks, or hunts for, its stable condition, but each time it approaches it, it overshoots and must seek it again.

hunting (helicopter rotor). The oscillation of a helicopter rotor blade back and forth about its lead-lag hinge as the blade is rotating.

hurricane (meteorology). A violent tropical cyclone caused by air flowing into a low-pressure area. Winds blow in a hurricane at a speed of 74 miles per hour (64 knots) or greater. This is a Beaufort force 12 (the highest force). Hurricanes bring rain, thunder, and lightning, as well as devastating winds. In the northern hemisphere, the air in a hurricane moves in a counterclockwise direction, while in the southern hemisphere, it moves in a clockwise direction.

hybrid compressor engine. A gas turbine engine that has both centrifugal and axial-flow compressors.

hybrid computer. A computer that has both analog and digital circuits and functions.

hybrid spark plug. A fine-wire spark plug that has a platinum center electrode and iridium ground electrodes.

hydraulic actuator. The component in a hydraulic system that converts hydraulic pressure into mechanical force. The two main types of hydraulic actuators are linear (cylinders and pistons) and rotary (hydraulic motors).

hydraulic brake. An aircraft brake in which the friction is applied to the wheel by a hydraulically actuated unit. The friction is produced in a disk brake when the rotating disk is clamped tightly between friction linings held in a hydraulically operated clamp.

hydraulic fluid. The fluid used in a hydraulic system to transmit a force from one location to another. The fluid can drive a rotary or linear actuator to move flight controls, retract or extend landing gear, or apply brakes.

hydraulic fuse. A device in a hydraulic system that automatically shuts off the flow of fluid if a line should break. There are two types of hydraulic fuses: one type shuts off the flow after a given volume of fluid flows, and the other type shuts off the flow any time the rate of flow becomes excessive.

hydraulic lock (reciprocating engine condition). A condition in which oil drains into the lower cylinders of an engine and leaks past the piston rings to fill the combustion chamber. If this oil is not removed before the engine is started, it can cause serious damage.

The propellers on all radial, inverted V-, and inverted in-line engines must be pulled through by hand before they are cranked with the starter to be sure that none of the cylinders have hydraulic lock.

hydraulic motor. A hydraulic actuator that converts fluid pressure into rotary motion. Hydraulic motors have an advantage in aircraft installations over electric motors, because they can operate in a stalled condition without the danger of a fire. Hydraulic motors may be of the gear, piston, or vane type.

hydraulic power pack. A small, self-contained hydraulic system that consists of a reservoir, pump, selector valves, and relief valves. The power pack is removable from the aircraft as a unit to facilitate maintenance and service.

hydraulic pump. A fluid-power pump used to force fluid through a hydraulic system. Hydraulic pumps may be engine driven, or they may be operated by an electric motor or by hand.

hydraulic reservoir. The container in a hydraulic system that holds the hydraulic fluid. Reservoirs used on some aircraft that fly at high altitude are pressurized to ensure a positive flow of fluid to the pumps.

hydraulics. The branch of science or technology that deals with the transmission of power through an incompressible fluid, such as oil or water.

hydraulic system. A fluid power system that transmits power or force through an incompressible fluid, such as oil. A complete hydraulic system contains a reservoir to hold the fluid, a pump to move the fluid, valves to control the flow of fluid, and actuators to produce the mechanical force. All of the components are connected together with either rigid or flexible fluid lines.

hydraulic valve lifter (reciprocating engine component). A hydraulic device in the valve train of certain aircraft reciprocating engines. When the cam follower is on top of a cam lobe, the intake or exhaust valve is held open by a cushion of oil inside the valve lifter. A specific amount of this oil leaks out while the valve is open, and when the valve closes, a spring pushes the piston up and oil is pulled into the lifter to replace that which was lost. The continual leakage and replenishment of the oil in the hydraulic valve lifter keeps all clearance out of the valve operating system.

hydrocarbon. An organic compound which contains only carbon and hydrogen. The vast majority of fossil fuels such as gasoline and turbine-engine fuel are hydrocarbons.

hydrodynamic forces. Forces relating to the motion of fluids and the effects of fluids acting on solid bodies in motion relative to them.

hydrodynamic lift. For seaplanes, the upward force generated by the motion of the hull or floats through the water. When the seaplane is at rest on the surface, it is supported by a hydrostatic force, but as it moves through the water, hydrodynamic lift begins to support its weight.

hydrodynamics. The branch of science or technology that deals with forces produced by incompressible fluids in motion.

hydrofoils. Flat or airfoil-shaped plates attached to struts below the hull of a hydrofoil watercraft.

hydrofoil vessel. A watercraft with a conventional hull which supports it when it is still or moving at a slow speed, but when traveling at a high speed, hydrodynamic lift produced by hydrofoils below the hull lifts the vessel out of the water, greatly decreasing the drag and allowing the vessel to travel at a higher speed.

hydrogen. A colorless, highly flammable, lighter-than-air, gaseous chemical element. Hydrogen's symbol is H, its atomic number is 1, and its atomic weight is 1.00794. Hydrogen is the lightest of all of the chemical elements.

An atom of hydrogen has one proton and no neutrons in its nucleus, and spinning around this nucleus is only one electron. A molecule of hydrogen gas is made up of two atoms of hydrogen (H_2). Hydrogen gas is colorless, tasteless and lighter than air. It is used as a fuel gas for welding.

hydrogen bomb. A nuclear weapon in which two light elements such as deuterium and tritium are forced together under extreme conditions of heat and pressure. When two of the light nuclei join together to form a heavier nucleus (this is called atomic, or nuclear, fusion), a tremendous amount of heat is released. A hydrogen bomb is far more powerful than the original atomic bomb.

hydrogen brazing. A form of brazing in which hydrogen is used as the fuel gas.

hydrogen embrittlement. A condition in which certain types of metal become brittle from absorbing hydrogen while they are being electroplated.

H

hydrogen peroxide. A heavy, colorless, unstable liquid used as a bleaching agent, an antiseptic, and a fuel for liquid-propellant rocket engines.

hydrological cycle. The continuous circulation of water within the Earth's hydrosphere driven by solar radiation.

hydrolysis. The change in a chemical substance caused by water.

hydromechanical. Any device that combines fluid pressures with mechanical actions to achieve a desired result. In a hydromechanical fuel control used for a turbine engine, hydraulic servos are used in conjunction with mechanical linkages.

hydrometeor (meteorology). A general term for particles of liquid water or ice, such as rain, fog, frost, etc., formed by modification of water vapor in the atmosphere. The term hydrometeor also applies to sea spray or blowing snow, which are water or ice particles lifted from the earth by the wind.

hydrometer. An instrument used to measure the specific gravity of a liquid. A float-type hydrometer consists of a specially weighted float with a graduated stem above the weight. The specific gravity, or density, of the liquid determines the amount the float sinks, and the number on the stem even with the surface of the liquid is the specific gravity of the liquid.

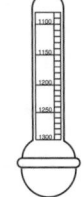

hydrometer

hydroplaning. A condition that can exist when a high-speed airplane is landed on a water-covered runway. High-speed airplanes use relatively narrow, high-pressure tires that, when the brakes are applied, try to lock up and skid on the surface of the water in much the same way a water ski rides on the surface. A hydroplaning tire can develop enough heat to ruin it. Effective anti-skid brake systems prevent hydroplaning.

hydropneumatic. Equipment that uses both hydraulic and pneumatic forces. Certain types of control systems use pneumatic inputs to operate hydraulic valves. A pneumatic input requires very little power, and it can control a hydraulic output that produces a great deal of force.

hydro-ski. A hydrofoil mounted below the hull of a flying boat. As the flying boat begins to move through the water, hydrodynamic lift produced by the hydro-ski lifts the hull out of the water. When the hull is out of the water, the drag is decreased, and the flying boat can quickly accelerate to takeoff speed.

hydrosorb (landing gear component). A hydraulic shock absorber used with a bungee shock cord landing gear to prevent rebound.

hydrostatic testing (gas cylinder test). A type of test required for cylinders used to carry compressed gases. The cylinder is filled with water under a pressure higher than that of the gas it is to carry, and this pressure is held for a specified length of time. Cylinders are hydrostatically tested rather than being tested with compressed air because, if the cylinder should fail, the incompressible water will not cause an explosion, as would occur if a cylinder filled with compressed air should fail.

When oxygen cylinders are hydrostatically tested for installation in an aircraft, they are filled with water and pressurized to $\frac{5}{3}$ of their working pressure. Standard-weight cylinders (DOT 3AA) must be hydrostatically tested every five years, and lightweight cylinders (DOT 3HT) must be tested every three years.

hydroxide. A chemical compound consisting of a metal, usually a base, or a nonmetal, usually an acid, and a negative hydroxyl ion (OH). Hydroxides are found in both organic and inorganic chemicals. Some of the more familiar hydroxides are sodium hydroxide (NaOH) and potassium hydroxide (KOH).

hygrograph (meteorology). The record produced by a continuous-recording hygrometer.

hygrometer. An instrument used to measure the amount of moisture in the air to determine its humidity.

hygroscopic material. A material that absorbs moisture from the air. Silica gel is a hygroscopic material used to protect delicate equipment from damage caused by moisture in the air. When bags of silica gel are placed in the equipment, any moisture in the air is absorbed by the silica gel, and the air is kept dry.

hyperbola (mathematical curve). A plane curve traced by a point that moves in such a way that the difference of its distance from two fixed points, called foci, remains constant.

hyperbolic navigation system. A system of electronic navigation in which a master and a remotely located slave station transmit a signal simultaneously. The difference between the time the signals from the two stations are received in an aircraft is carefully measured and plotted on a chart of hyperbolic curves. This information gives a line of position along which the aircraft is located.

An electronic computer determines the position by plotting lines of position from two sets of stations. The aircraft is located at the latitude and longitude the lines cross.

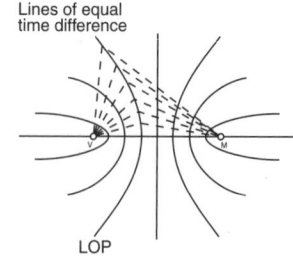

Lines of equal time difference

LOP

hyperbolic navigation system

hyper engines. A series of experimental high-performance aircraft engines built with U.S. Army and Navy financing in the early 1930s. The goal of these engines, which had been unattainable up to that time, was to develop one horsepower for each cubic inch of piston displacement.

hypersonic engine. An engine designed to operate at speeds above Mach 5.00.

hypersonic flight. Flight at air speeds greater than five times the local speed of sound, more than Mach 5.0.

hyperventilation. A breathing problem caused by too little carbon dioxide in the lungs. Hyperventilation causes a person to breathe too rapidly, and this results in dizziness and may even lead to unconsciousness.

hypotenuse (mathematics). The side of a right triangle opposite the right angle.

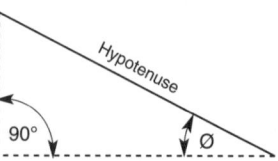

Hypotenuse

90°

∅

hypotenuse of a right triangle

hypoxia. A physiological condition in which a person is deprived of the needed oxygen. The effects of hypoxia normally disappear as soon as the person is able to breathe air that contains sufficient oxygen.

Histotoxic. The inability of the cells to effectively use oxygen. Plenty of oxygen is being transported to the cells that need it, but they are unable to make use of it.

Hypemic. A type of hypoxia that is a result of oxygen deficiency in the blood, rather than a lack of inhaled oxygen. It can be caused by a variety of factors. Hypemic means "not enough blood."

Hypoxic. This type of hypoxia is a result of insufficient oxygen available to the lungs. A decrease of oxygen molecules at sufficient pressure can lead to hypoxic hypoxia.

Stagnant. A type of hypoxia that results when the oxygen-rich blood in the lungs isn't moving, for one reason or another, to the tissues that need it.

hysteresis. A condition in which a physical action lags behind its cause. A spring is often slow to return to its original length when the load is removed. This slow return is caused by friction within the material of which the spring is made. This internal friction causes hysteresis.

H

hysteresis error (instrument indication error). An instrument error that causes a difference in the readings of an instrument when the indicated values are increasing, compared with the readings at the same point when the values are decreasing. Hysteresis error is caused by internal friction in the instrument mechanism.

hysteresis loop (magnetic materials). A curve showing the way flux density in a magnetic material varies with the magnetizing force applied to it. The shape of a hysteresis loop gives an indication of the magnetic characteristics of the material.

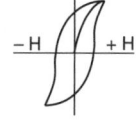

hysteresis loop

IA (Inspection Authorization). An authorization issued by the Federal Aviation Administration to certain licensed and experienced aviation maintenance technicians that allows them to perform annual and progressive inspections. This authorization also allows them to approve aircraft for return to service after certain types of major repairs and major alterations.

IAF (initial approach fix) (air traffic control). The fixes depicted on the instrument approach procedure charts that identify the beginning of the initial approach segment(s).

IAP (instrument approach procedure). A series of predetermined maneuvers for the orderly transfer of an aircraft under instrument flight conditions from the beginning of the initial approach to a landing or to a point from which a landing may be made visually.

IAS (indicated airspeed). The speed an aircraft is moving through the air as is shown on the airspeed indicator, before any corrections for errors or nonstandard conditions are made.

I-beam. A piece of structural material having a cross-sectional shape that resembles the letter "I." I-beams used in aircraft structure may be extruded or built up from aluminum alloys, or they may be made of wood. Wooden I-beams may be either built up of several pieces of wood or shaped by removing some of the wood from the sides of the beam with a router.

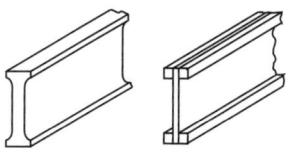

I-beams (wooden)

IC (integrated circuit). A combination of electronic components built onto a single substrate of semiconductor material. Transistors, diodes, capacitors, and resistors are all built onto a tiny chip and mounted in a protective package that allows the circuit to connect with other components or devices. Logic gates, rectifiers, amplifiers, microprocessors, and semiconductor memory circuits can all be built as integrated circuits. The development of integrated circuits has made miniature electronics possible.

ICA. *See* initial climb area.

ICAO (International Civil Aviation Organization). A specialized agency of the United Nations whose objective is to develop the principles and techniques of international air navigation and to foster planning and development of international civil air transport. The term ICAO is normally pronounced as a single word (eye-kay-o), rather than using the entire name or the initials.

icebox rivet (aircraft fastener). A solid aircraft rivet made of 2017 or 2024 aluminum alloy. These rivets are too hard to drive in the condition they are received from the manufacturer, and they must be heat-treated to soften them. They are heated in a furnace and then quenched in water. Immediately after quenching, they are soft, but within a few hours at room temperature, they become quite hard. Hardening can be delayed for several days by immediately placing the rivets in a subfreezing icebox and holding them at this low temperature until they are used.

ice bridging. A spark plug failure that occurs when a reciprocating engine is started in extremely cold weather. When a cylinder fires, the fuel-air mixture is converted into carbon dioxide and water vapor. The water vapor condenses on the spark plug electrodes and forms ice that bridges the electrode gap and prevents the plug firing until the ice is melted. This normally requires removing the spark plugs from the engine.

ice crystals (meteorology). A type of precipitation composed of unbranched ice crystals in the form of needles, columns, or plates. Ice crystals normally have a slight downward motion and may fall from a cloudless sky.

ice fog (meteorology). An obstruction to visibility caused by tiny ice crystals, rather than the tiny droplets of water that make up ordinary fog. Ice fog occurs at very low temperatures and may cause a halo.

ice light (aircraft light). A light mounted on the fuselage of an airplane in such a way that it shines on the leading edge of the wing. This light allows the pilot to check for the buildup of ice on the wing while flying through icing conditions at night.

ice needles (meteorology). A long, thin ice crystal with a hexagonal cross section.

ice pellets (meteorology). Small, transparent or translucent, round or irregularly shaped pellets of ice. Ice pellets may be hard grains that rebound on striking a hard surface or may be pellets of snow encased in ice.

ice. The solid state of water. If enough heat is removed from liquid water to drop its temperature to 0°C (32°F), the molecules moving about in the water will slow down enough that the water will change from a liquid into a solid. This solid form of water is called ice.

icing (meteorology). Ice forming on an aircraft. Classifications of icing are: clear, rime, and glaze.

icing, mixed (meteorology). Ice that forms on a surface when drops very in size, or when liquid drops are intermingled with snow or ice particles.

ident (air traffic control). A request by ATC for a pilot to activate the radar beacon transponder identification feature.

ident feature (radar beacon transponder). The special feature in the Air Traffic Control Radar Beacon System (ATCRBS) equipment used to immediately distinguish one displayed beacon target from other beacon targets.

identification zone. An airspace of defined dimensions extending upwards from the surface of the earth within which certain rules apply for the security control of air traffic.

IDG (integrated drive generator). An AC generator installed on turbine engines. An IDG incorporates a brushless, three-phase AC generator and a constant-speed drive in a single component.

idiot light. A warning light, whose proper name is nondiscrete indicator, used instead of an indicating instrument. Some aircraft have "idiot lights" rather than ammeters, to alert the pilot when the generator is not producing adequate voltage. Other idiot lights indicate such conditions as low oil pressure and cabin heater malfunctions.

idle cut-off (reciprocating engine fuel metering system). The position of the mixture control in a reciprocating engine fuel metering system that shuts off all fuel to the cylinders. Most aircraft engine fuel metering systems have a mixture control that allows the pilot to adjust the fuel-air mixture ratio to compensate for changes in air density as the aircraft goes up in altitude. When this mixture control is placed in the idle cut-off position, all fuel is shut off to the cylinders and the engine stops running.

idle mixture (reciprocating engine fuel metering system). The fuel-air mixture ratio used by an aircraft engine while it is operating at its idle speed. The uneven distribution of the fuel-air mixture to the cylinders at idle speed requires the idle mixture ratio to be richer than that required for best burning.

idle mixture adjustment (reciprocating engine fuel metering system adjustment). Adjusting the fuel-air mixture metered to the engine at idle speed.

idler gear (gear train). A gear used to reverse the direction of rotation of another gear without changing its speed of rotation. An idler gear does not add nor take away mechanical advantage from the gear train.

idler pulley (belt-drive system). A pulley in a belt-drive system used to adjust the tension on the belt that joins a drive pulley with a driven pulley. The idler pulley does not change the direction of rotation of either pulley, nor does it change the speed relationship between the pulleys.

idle speed. The lowest speed at which an engine operates smoothly when it is not carrying any type of mechanical load. Idle speed is measured in revolutions per minute (RPM).

idle thrust (gas turbine engine). The thrust produced by an aircraft gas turbine engine when the power control lever is pulled back to the idle stop. *14 CFR Part 1:* "The jet thrust obtained with the engine power control lever set at the stop for the least thrust position at which it can be placed."

idling current (electronic equipment). Current flowing in an electronic circuit when there is no input signal requiring the system to act. Idling current, also called quiescent current, is normally much less than the operating current of the system.

idling position (seaplane floats). *See* displacement position (seaplane floats).

IFF (identification, friend or foe). An electronic identification system that is the forerunner of the modern radar beacon transponder used by air traffic controllers to identify specific aircraft. IFF, developed in the latter part of World War II, is an electronic pulse system in which interrogation pulses of electrical energy are transmitted from a ground station and received in the aircraft.

If the airborne equipment is set to respond with the proper code, the IFF identifies the aircraft as friendly. But if the equipment does not reply with the correct code, the ground station is alerted to the fact that the indications received on its radarscope may be caused by a foe, or enemy. The principles of IFF equipment apply to other pulse navigation systems, especially aircraft radar beacon transponders and distance measuring equipment (DME).

IFIM (International Flight Information Manual). A publication designed primarily as a pilot's preflight planning guide for flights into foreign airspace and for flights returning to the U.S. from foreign locations.

"If no transmission received for [time]" (air traffic control). A phrase used by ATC in radar approaches to prefix procedures which should be followed by the pilot in event of lost communications.

IFR (instrument flight rules). Rules and regulations established by the Federal Aviation Administration to govern flight under conditions in which flight by outside visual reference is not safe. Instrument flight rules govern the flight of aircraft along the federally-controlled airways and airports, and this flight is directed and controlled by operators on the ground. Flight according to instrument flight rules depends upon flying by reference to instruments in the cockpit, and navigation is done by reference to electronic signals.

IFR aircraft (air traffic control). An aircraft conducting flight in accordance with instrument flight rules.

IFR conditions. *14 CFR Part 1:* "Weather conditions below the minimums allowed for flight under visual flight rules."

IFR military training routes (air traffic control). Routes used by the Department of Defense and associated Reserve and Air Guard units for the purpose of conducting low-altitude navigation and tactical training in both IFR and VFR weather conditions below 10,000 feet MSL at airspeeds in excess of 250 knots IAS.

IFR over-the-top. *14 CFR Part 1:* "With respect to the operation of aircraft, means the operation of an aircraft over-the-top on an IFR flight plan when cleared by air traffic control to maintain 'VFR conditions' or 'VFR conditions on top'."

IFR takeoff minimums and departure procedures (air traffic control). Minimums listed in 14 CFR Part 91, prescribing standard takeoff rules for certain civil users. At some airports, obstructions or other factors require the establishment of nonstandard takeoff minimums, departure procedures, or both, to assist pilots in avoiding obstacles during climb to the minimum en route altitude. Those airports are listed in NOS/DOD Instrument Approach Charts (IAPs) under a section entitled "IFR Takeoff Minimums and Departure Procedures." The NOS/DOD IAP chart legend illustrates the symbol used to alert the pilot to nonstandard takeoff minimums and departure procedures.

When departing IFR from such airports or from any airports where there are no departure procedures, SIDs or ATC facilities available, pilots should advise ATC of any departure limitations. Controllers may query a pilot to determine acceptable departure directions, turns, or headings after takeoff. Pilots should be familiar with the departure procedures and must assure that their aircraft can meet or exceed any specified climb gradients.

IFWP. Intermediate Fix Waypoint.

IGFET (insulated gate field effect transistor). A field-effect transistor whose gate is insulated from the channel by a layer of silicon oxide.

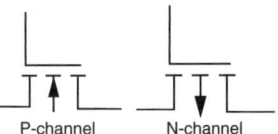

P-channel   N-channel

insulated gate field effect transistor (IGFET)

igniter (gas turbine engine component). A component in a gas turbine engine used to ignite the fuel-air mixture when the engine is being started. Some igniters resemble spark plugs used in reciprocating engines, while others are glow plugs heated yellow-hot with electrical current.

igniter (hot-air balloon). A welding striker, piezo sparker, matches, or other means used to ignite the balloon pilot flame.

ignition (heat engine operation). The procedure by which the temperature of a portion of the fuel-air mixture in the engine is raised high enough for the hydrocarbon fuel to begin combining with the oxygen in the air. This heat is normally provided by an electrical spark.

ignition harness (reciprocating engine ignition system component). The complete set of high-tension cables, terminals, and connectors used to carry high voltage from the magnetos to the various spark plugs in the engine.

ignition timing (reciprocating engine). The timing of the ignition spark with respect to the piston position in the cylinder of a reciprocating engine. For the most power to be produced, the fuel-air mixture must be ignited while the piston is still moving upward on the compression stroke. This allows time for the burning mixture to produce its maximum push on the piston just as it starts down on the power stroke.

The correct piston position for ignition varies with the speed of the engine, and the ignition timing on automobile engines is variable; but nearly all aircraft engines have fixed timing. The spark occurs at the same position of the piston regardless of the engine conditions. Fixed timing is a performance compromise, but fixed-timing ignition systems are less complicated than variable-timing systems.

ignitron (electrical component). A special high-current rectifier tube. In each cycle of operation of an ignitron tube, an ignitor dips into a pool of mercury, and as it is withdrawn, it creates an arc which produces ionized mercury vapor that conducts a large amount of current.

I-head cylinder (reciprocating engine). The cylinder of a reciprocating engine with both the intake and exhaust valves mounted in the head. I-head cylinders are also called valve-in-head cylinders.

IHP (indicated horsepower). The theoretical horsepower a reciprocating engine is developing. The horsepower an engine actually delivers to its output shaft is called brake horsepower (BHP). A large amount of power is used to rotate the engine and compress the air in the cylinders. This power is called friction horsepower (FHP). Indicated horsepower is the sum of the brake horsepower and the friction horsepower: IHP = BHP + FHP.

illumination. Light energy that falls on a given surface area.

illustrated parts list (service information). An exploded view of an assembly in which all of the component parts are laid out so each can be identified. Each part is coded with a letter or number, and a table is included with the drawing, giving the name and correct number for each part and the quantity of the parts needed for the assembly.

illustrated talk (in learning process). An oral presentation in which the speaker relies heavily on visual aids to convey ideas to the listeners.

ILS (instrument landing system). A special type of electronic guidance system used to allow aircraft to land when the ceiling and visibility are too low for a safe visual approach to the runway. An ILS is made up of four basic parts: the localizer, glide slope, marker beacons, and approach lights. The localizer produces a narrow electronic path extending out along the center line of the instrument runway, to direct the pilot laterally as he approaches the runway.

The glide slope produces a narrow electronic path extending upward from the approach end of the instrument runway at an angle of approximately three degrees. The glide slope directs the pilot vertically as the aircraft approaches the end of the runway.

The marker beacons produce highly directional radio signals to identify the position of the aircraft along the localizer path. When the aircraft is directly over a marker beacon, a distinctive tone is received on the radio, and a colored light on the instrument panel flashes the proper code.

The approach lights are a series of high-intensity lights located along the approach path to help the pilot transition from flying by instruments to flying by visual reference as the aircraft breaks out of the overcast.

ILS categories. Categories of instrument flight allowed at airports equipped with the following types of instrument landing systems:

ILS Category I. An ILS approach procedure which provides for approach to a height above touchdown of not less than 200 feet and with runway visual range of not less than 1,800 feet.

ILS Category II. An ILS approach procedure which provides for approach to a height above touchdown of not less than 100 feet and with runway visual range of not less than 1,200 feet.

ILS Category IIIA. An ILS approach procedure which provides for approach without a decision height minimum and with runway visual range of not less than 700 feet.*

ILS Category IIIB. An ILS approach procedure which provides for approach without a decision height minimum and with runway visual range of not less than 150 feet.*

ILS Category IIIC. An ILS approach procedure which provides for approach without a decision height minimum and without runway visual range minimum.*

ILS PRM approach. An instrument landing system (ILS) approach conducted to parallel runways whose extended centerlines are separated by less than 4,300 feet and the parallel runways have a Precision Runway Monitoring (PRM) system that permits simultaneous independent ILS approaches.

---

* Effective July 2012, the FAA removed the definitions of ILS Category IIIa, IIIb, and IIIc operations; they are outdated and no longer used for aircraft certification or operational authorization.

IMC (instrument meteorological conditions) (air traffic control). Meteorological conditions expressed in terms of visibility, distance from cloud, and ceiling less than the minimums specified for visual meteorological conditions.

IMEP (indicated mean effective pressure). The average pressure existing inside the cylinder of a reciprocating engine during its power stroke. IMEP, expressed in pounds per square inch, is a measured pressure which contrasts with brake mean effective pressure, BMEP, which is a computed pressure. The horsepower found when IMEP is used in the horsepower formula is indicated horsepower, IHP.

"Immediately" (air traffic control). A term used by ATC when such action compliance is required to avoid an imminent situation.

immersion heater. An electrical heater used to heat liquids by immersing (submerging) the heater in the liquid.

immiscible. Not able to mix. Liquids are immiscible if they will not mix with each other. Water and oil are immiscible. If a bottle containing both water and oil is agitated, the oil and water will form an emulsion. But when the bottle sits for a while without further agitation, the oil and water will separate, the oil rising to the top of the water.

impact extrusion. A form of extrusion made by forcing cold metal through a die by striking it a hard blow. This blow comes from a punch driven at a high velocity.

impact ice. Ice that forms on an aircraft flying through freezing rain or other visible moisture when the air temperature is in the freezing range (between 0° and –15°C). Impact ice forms on the leading edges of the wing and tail surfaces and disturbs the smooth flow of air over these surfaces. Impact ice also forms on the engine inlet air filters and can stop an engine functioning unless inlet air is taken from an alternate source. Impact ice forming on the inlet air duct of a jet engine can break off and be pulled through the engine, causing severe damage to the compressor blades.

impact pressure. Pressure resulting when moving air is stopped. Impact pressure picked up by a pitot tube is called pitot pressure.

impact wrench. A power-driven tool used to install and remove nuts, bolts, and screws. The torque delivered to the fastener by an impact wrench is in a series of sharp blows or impacts.

impedance (Z). The total opposition to the flow of alternating current caused by the combined effect of resistance, capacitance, and inductance in a circuit. Impedance (Z) is found by adding, as vectors, the resistance (R) of the circuit with the combined values of the inductive reactance (X_L) and capacitive reactance (X_C) in the circuit. If the capacitive reactance is larger than the inductive reactance, the formula for impedance is:

$$Z = \sqrt{R^2 + (X_C - X_L)^2}$$

If the inductive reactance is larger than the capacitive reactance, the formula for impedance is:

$$Z = \sqrt{R^2 + (X_L - X_C)^2}$$

impedance coupling (electronic circuits). A method of using a transformer to join, or couple, stages of an electronic device, such as an amplifier. The impedance of the primary winding of the coupling transformer is the same as the output impedance of the first stage, and the impedance of the secondary winding is the same as the input impedance of the following stage. Impedance coupling is primarily used in circuits carrying audio-frequency AC because of the limited bandwidth of the coupling transformer.

impedance matching (electronic circuits). The process of matching the impedance of a source of electrical power with the impedance of the load using the power. For maximum power transfer to occur, the impedance of the source and the impedance of the load should be the same. Transformers can be used to match impedance. The following formula is used to relate the impedance ratio to the turns ratio:

$$\frac{N_P}{N_S} = \sqrt{\frac{Z_P}{Z_S}}$$

N_P = number of turns in the primary winding
N_S = number of turns in the secondary winding
Z_P = impedance of the primary winding
Z_S = impedance of the secondary winding

impedance matching transformer. A transformer used in an electronic circuit to match the impedance of the load to the impedance of the source of electrical energy.

impedance triangle. A graphic method of showing the relationship existing between resistance, reactance, and impedance in an AC circuit. An impedance triangle is a right triangle, with the horizontal side representing the circuit resistance and the vertical side representing the combined capacitive and inductive reactance in the circuit. The hypotenuse represents the circuit impedance.

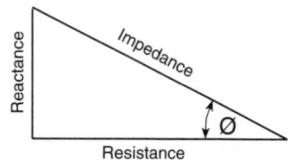

impedance triangle

The angle formed between the hypotenuse and the horizontal side is the phase angle (ø) of the circuit, the number of electrical degrees the current leads or lags the voltage.

impeller (centrifugal pump). A vaned wheel used to move and add energy to a fluid. The fluid enters the center of the impeller and is thrown outward by centrifugal force. As the fluid leaves the impeller, it is collected in a diffuser where it is slowed and its pressure is increased.

Impellers can move either liquids or gases. Some applications are: moving cooling fluid through a reciprocating engine, compressing the air before it goes into the carburetor of a reciprocating engine, and compressing the air in a gas turbine engine.

imperial gallon. A measure of volume used in the United Kingdom for liquid or dry substances. One imperial gallon is equal to 4.545 liters or 1.2 U.S. gallons.

impingement starter (gas turbine engine starter). The simplest type of starter used to start a gas turbine engine. A stream of compressed air, directed against the turbine blades or onto the centrifugal compressor, spins the compressor fast enough to start the engine.

implode. To burst inwardly. Electron tubes, such as the cathode-ray tubes used in television sets and computer displays, have the air evacuated from them so the pressure of the air outside the tube is much greater than the pressure inside the tube. If the glass envelope of the tube cracks, outside air will rush violently onto the tube and the tube will implode.

improper fraction (mathematics). A common fraction in which the numerator, the number above the line, is greater than the denominator, the number below the line.

impulse coupling (magneto component). A spring-loaded coupling between a magneto and an aircraft reciprocating engine that causes the magneto to produce a hot and late spark for starting the engine. The rotating magnet in a magneto must be turned at a fast rate to produce a hot spark, but when the engine is being started, the magneto turns slowly. Arms inside the impulse coupling contact stop pins in the magneto housing and hold the magnet while the crankshaft turns. A heavy, flat spring winds up as the crankshaft continues to turn, with the magnet held stationary. When the crankshaft turns about thirty degrees past the point at which ignition normally occurs, a cam forces the arms

Continued

impulse coupling (magneto component). *Continued*
off the stop pins, and the spring spins the magnet at a fast rate. When the magnet spins, it produces a hot spark. And since the spark occurs late, the piston is moving downward, preventing the engine kicking back. As soon as the engine is running normally, counterweights on the arms sling outward and hold the arms in, away from the stop pins. This keeps the impulse coupling disengaged so it has no effect on the ignition timing for normal engine operation.

impulse-reaction turbine (gas turbine engine component). A type of turbine in which hot, high-velocity gases produce an aerodynamic force as well as an impulse force as they move the turbine blades in the direction needed to spin the turbine wheel.

impulse turbine (gas turbine engine component). A form of turbine that is rotated by air striking bucket-shaped turbine blades. An impulse turbine changes the direction of the air flowing through it. The energy that causes this change in direction spins the turbine. An impulse turbine does not produce a pressure drop across the blade as the reaction turbine does.

impurity (semiconductor material). A chemical element added to silicon or germanium to give it specific electrical characteristics. Arsenic, phosphorus, and antimony are pentavalent elements, elements having five electrons in their valence shell. When these elements are used as impurities, they form N-type material because there are more electrons than are needed to form covalent bonds within the material. Atoms of N-type material are called donor atoms.

Aluminum, boron, gallium, and indium are elements having only three electrons in their valence shell, and when used as impurities with silicon or germanium, produce P-type materials. P-type materials have fewer electrons than are needed to form covalent bonds, and they accept electrons from other materials. Atoms of P-type materials are called acceptor atoms.

inadvertent instrument meteorological conditions (IIMC). In flight, this refers to unintentionally entering weather conditions not favorable for visual operations—that is, IMC—and is considered an emergency situation. *See also* instrument meteorological conditions (IMC).

inboard. The direction in an aircraft toward its center line.

incandescent. Glowing because of intense heat. Carbon particles inside the cylinder of a reciprocating engine can absorb enough heat from the burning gases to become incandescent, or glow. These incandescent particles are the cause of preignition.

incandescent lamp. A form of electric lamp in which a white-hot, incandescent filament produces light. The filament is enclosed in a glass bulb from which all the air has been removed and replaced with an inert gas, such as argon. The inert gas replaces oxygen so the filament does not burn up when it becomes white-hot. Incandescent lamps produce a large amount of heat as well as light.

INCERFA (ICAO). A situation in which there is uncertainty as to the safety of an aircraft and its occupants.

inch of mercury, in. Hg. A unit for measuring absolute pressure. One inch of mercury is the amount of pressure needed to support a column of mercury one inch (2.54 centimeters) high. Standard atmospheric pressure will support a column of mercury 29.92 inches high.

inch-pound (measure of torque). A measure of torque, or the rotation that is caused by a force of one pound acting one inch from the center of rotation.

inch-pound (measure of work). A measure of work accomplished when a force of one pound moves an object a distance of one inch.

inch-pounds. *See* torque.

incidence board (airplane rigging tool). A triangular board used when rigging the incidence in the wing of an airplane. The airplane is leveled, the incidence board is held along the bottom of one of the wing root ribs, and a level is held against the bottom of the board. When the bottom of the board is level, the wing is set to the correct angle of incidence. *See* angle of incidence.

incident. An occurrence other than an accident, associated with the operation of an aircraft, which affects or could affect the safety of operations.

inclined plane. One of the basic machines used to gain mechanical advantage. The other basic machines are the lever and the wheel. A loading ramp which is a plane surface forming an angle with the horizon is an inclined plane. A force of only 100 pounds is needed to roll a 400-pound drum of oil up onto the bed of a truck, three feet high, if the drum is rolled up a ramp 12 feet long.

inclinometer. An instrument used to measure the attitude of an aircraft relative to the horizontal. An inclinometer is usually made of a curved glass tube, partially filled with a clear liquid and holding a black glass ball. The curved tube is mounted in line with either the lateral or longitudinal axis of the aircraft, so the ball is in the center when the aircraft is level. When the aircraft tilts, the ball remains at the low point of the tube and shows the number of degrees the aircraft is tilted.

inclinometer

inclusion (metal casting defect). A defect in a metal casting caused by nonmetallic impurities, such as carbon or sand trapped in the molten metal when it was poured into the mold. An inclusion weakens the casting and makes proper machining difficult.

incoherent light. Light whose vibrations do not have any consistent phase relationship.

incompressible fluid. A liquid used in a fluid power system. A hydraulic system uses an incompressible fluid, such as oil, while a pneumatic system uses a compressible fluid, such as air.

Inconel. The registered trade name for an alloy of chromium and iron. Inconel, which is similar to stainless steel but cannot be hardened by heat treatment, is used for aircraft engine exhaust system components.

incursion. Entry into something. Runway incursion occurs when an aircraft taxies onto a runway.

indefinite ceiling (meteorology). A ceiling classification denoting vertical visibility into a surface-based obscuration.

index point (weight and balance). A location specified by the aircraft manufacturer from which arms used in weight and balance computations are measured. Arms measured from the index point are called index arms.

indicated airspeed. *14 CFR Part 1:* "The speed of an aircraft as shown on its pitot static airspeed indicator, calibrated to reflect standard atmospheric adiabatic compressible flow at sea level uncorrected for airspeed system errors."

indicated altitude. The altitude above mean sea level shown on a pressure altimeter when the local altimeter setting is adjusted into the barometric scale. The altimeter setting is the barometric pressure existing at the reporting station, corrected to the value it would have if the station were located at sea level.

Indicated altitude is used by all aircraft flying below 18,000 feet. At higher altitudes, aircraft use pressure altitude, in which the barometric scale is adjusted to standard sea-level barometric pressure of 29.92 inches of mercury, or 1013.2 millibars.

indicating fuse holder. A type of electrical fuse holder that shows when a fuse has blown and opened the circuit. A small neon bulb is installed in the fuse holder, in parallel with the fuse. The resistance of a good fuse is so low that when current flows through it, there is not enough voltage drop across it to illuminate the bulb.

But if the fuse blows and opens the circuit, the entire system voltage is dropped across the neon bulb, and it illuminates. The bulb does not allow enough current to flow to damage the circuit.

indicating instrument. An instrument that shows in a visual form the value it is sensing. There are two basic types of indicating instruments: instruments that give their indication in an analog form, and instruments that have a digital readout. An analog instrument has a dial and one or more pointers. The position of the pointer on the dial is an analog, or representation, of the value the indicator is sensing. A digital instrument uses numbers to indicate the value it is sensing. An ordinary clock is a form of analog indicating instrument. The number of degrees the hands have moved past their straight-up position relates to the number of hours, minutes, or seconds that have passed since noon or midnight. A digital clock uses just numbers to indicate the seconds, minutes, and hours that have passed since noon or midnight.

indirect indication (instrument indication). The indication of aircraft pitch and bank attitude by instruments other than the attitude indicator.

indirect light. Light that falls on an object after it has been reflected from a nonlight-producing object.

indirectly heated cathode (vacuum tube component). A cathode in a vacuum tube that is heated by a filament which is not a part of the cathode. The cathode is made in the form of a metal tube whose surface is coated with a material that emits electrons when it is heated. The filament, a small resistance-wire heater inside the cathode, heats it but does not touch it. Indirectly heated cathodes allow the filament to be heated with alternating current without causing the hum that would be present if the AC passed through the cathode itself.

indium. A soft, malleable, silvery-white, metallic chemical element. Indium's symbol is In, its atomic number is 49, and its atomic weight is 114.82. Indium is used as a plating over silver in making mirrors and as a component in semiconductors.

induced current. Electrical current produced in a conductor when it is cut, or crossed, by changing lines of magnetic flux. Induced current always flows in the opposite direction to the current that produced the magnetic flux.

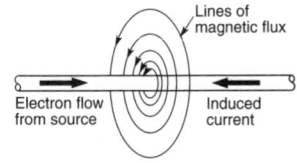

induced current

induced drag (aerodynamics). Aerodynamic drag produced by an airfoil when it is producing lift. The amount of induced drag is determined by the shape and the area of the airfoil, the angle of attack, the air density, and the speed of the air moving over the airfoil.

induced flow (helicopter aerodynamics). The mass of air forced down by rotor action. Most of the induced flow passes through the rotor disc.

induced voltage. Voltage generated in a conductor when it is cut, or crossed, by lines of magnetic flux. There are three ways a conductor can be cut by lines of magnetic flux: (1) The conductor can be held stationary and the magnetic field moved back and forth across it. (2) The conductor can be moved back and forth through a stationary magnetic field. (3) Both the conductor and the magnetic field can be held stationary, but the magnetic field can be produced by alternating current, which constantly changes its direction and strength.

inducer (turbine engine component). Rotating inlet guide vanes installed on the center of a centrifugal compressor to pick up the inlet air and direct it at the correct angle into the impeller blades.

inductance. The electrical characteristic of a conductor which causes a voltage to be produced when it is cut, or crossed, by lines of magnetic flux. The basic unit of inductance is the henry. *See* henry.

inductance bridge (electrical measuring instrument). A bridge-type precision instrument used to measure an unknown inductance by comparing its inductive reactance at a specific frequency with that produced at the same frequency by an accurately known inductance.

induction compass. *See* earth induction compass.

induction furnace. An electric furnace in which the metal to be melted is heated by the induction of high-frequency electromagnetic energy.

induction heating. A method of heating an electrically conductive material by inducing alternating current into it. The rapidly reversing current causes the material to get hot.

induction icing. A type of ice in the induction system that reduces the amount of air available for combustion. The most commonly found induction icing is carburetor icing.

induction manifold. The part of the engine that distributes intake air to the cylinders.

induction motor. A type of alternating current motor in which the line voltage is connected across stationary windings in the motor housing. The rotor of an induction motor is made in the form of a "squirrel cage." Bars of copper or aluminum are embedded in slots in a laminated soft-iron core, and are welded to heavy copper or aluminum plates on each end of the core. There is no electrical connection to the rotor.

The stator winding serves as the primary of a transformer, and the bars and end plates of the rotor act as the secondary. Current induced into the rotor bars causes a magnetic field that reacts with the field of the stator, and this reaction causes the rotor to turn. The magnetic field of the stator of a single-phase induction motor does not rotate, but rather it pulses on and off. A separate start winding is wound in the stator to produce a rotating field for starting a single-phase motor. The phase of the current in the start winding is shifted by a capacitor or inductor so that it is different from the phase of the current in the run winding. This shifted phase produces a rotating magnetic field.

As soon as the rotor is turning at the correct speed, the start winding is automatically disconnected, and the inertia of the heavy rotor keeps it spinning in the pulsing magnetic field produced by the run winding. Three-phase induction motors do not need separate start windings, because the three separate phase windings produce a rotating magnetic field.

induction period (aircraft finishing system condition). The period of time after a catalyzed material, such as an epoxy or polyurethane, is mixed before it is ready to be sprayed onto the surface of the aircraft. The induction period allows the material to begin its curing action before it is applied.

induction system (aircraft reciprocating engine system). The entire system in an aircraft reciprocating engine that carries air into the engine cylinders. The induction system consists of the air filter, carburetor heater or alternate air valve, the turbocharger, and all the piping used to carry this air into the cylinders.

induction vibrator (reciprocating engine ignition system component). An electrical relay connected in such a way that it chops up direct current and produces pulsating DC. The pulsating DC is sent through the primary winding of the magneto coil where it induces a high voltage in the secondary winding. This high voltage causes a spark to jump across the gap in a spark plug. Induction vibrators are used with magnetos to produce a hot spark for starting the engine when the magneto is turning slowly.

induction welding. A method of welding in which the metal is melted by heat generated by alternating current induced into the metal.

inductive circuit. An alternating current circuit in which the inductive reactance is greater than the capacitive reactance. Changes in the current flowing in an inductive circuit lag behind changes in the voltage.

inductive kick. A pulse of high voltage produced across a coil when current flowing through it is interrupted. When direct current flows through a coil, a magnetic field surrounds each turn of wire, and this magnetic field is sustained as long as the current flows. When the current is interrupted, the magnetic field instantly collapses, and the lines of magnetic flux cut across each turn of the coil. This collapsing field induces a short-duration pulse of voltage into the coil that is many times greater than the original voltage. This pulse of high voltage is called an inductive kick, or a transient voltage spike.

inductive reactance. An opposition to the flow of alternating current or changing direct current, caused by inductance in the circuit. Inductive reactance, whose abbreviation is X_L, is measured in ohms, and it decreases the amount of current flowing in a circuit. Resistance is also measured in ohms, and it too decreases the current, but resistance uses power and produces heat, while inductive reactance does not.

Inductive reactance is caused by the generation of an induced voltage whose polarity is opposite to that of the voltage causing it. The induced voltage opposes some of the applied voltage, and because there is less voltage available to force current through the circuit, less current flows. Inductive reactance increases as both the frequency of the alternating current and the inductance of the circuit increase. The formula for inductive reactance is:

X_L = $2 \pi fL$
X_L = Inductive reactance in ohms
2π = A constant, 6.28
f = Frequency in hertz
L = Circuit inductance in henries

inductive time constant. The amount of time, in seconds, needed for current flowing in an inductive circuit to reach 63.2% of its maximum value. The inductive time constant, in seconds, may be found by dividing the circuit inductance, in henries, by the circuit resistance, in ohms:

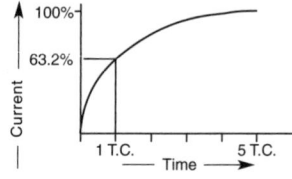

$$TC = \frac{L}{R}$$

inductive time constant

TC = Time constant in seconds
L = Inductance in henries
R = Resistance in ohms

inductive tuning. A method of selecting the frequency to which a radio-frequency circuit is resonant by changing the inductance in a tuned circuit. The resonant frequency of an L-C circuit (a circuit that contains both inductance and capacitance) can be changed by changing the amount of either the inductance or the capacitance. The inductance is normally changed by moving a powdered iron slug into or out of the coil. Moving the slug into the coil increases the inductance, and pulling the slug out of the coil decreases the inductance.

inductor. A coil of wire used to produce inductance in an electrical circuit. The amount of inductance is determined by the number of turns of wire in the coil, by the ratio of the diameter of the coil to its length, and by the type of material used as the core of the coil. Inductance is measured in henries, millihenries, or microhenries.

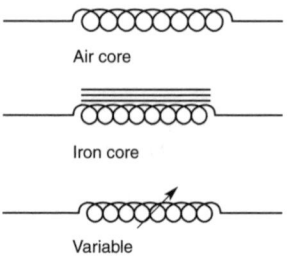

Air core

Iron core

Variable

inductors

industrial diamond. A diamond that is not of gem quality, but because of its hardness, is used as an industrial cutting tool.

inert-gas shielded-arc welding. A form of electric arc welding in which the arc is formed inside a shield of inert gas, such as argon or helium. The inert gas drives all the oxygen away from the arc and prevents oxides from forming in the molten metal.

inert gas. A gas that has a stable atomic structure. Its valence shell neither tries to gain nor lose electrons. An inert gas has no tendency to unite with other elements to form chemical compounds. Helium, neon, argon, krypton, xenon, and radon are inert gases.

inertia. A characteristic of all matter that causes an object to try to remain in its present condition. If the object is at rest, not moving, its inertia tries to keep it at rest. But if it is moving, its inertia tries to keep it moving—in the same direction, and at the same speed.

inertial navigation system (navigation system). A computer-based navigation system that tracks the movement of an aircraft by signals produced by onboard accelerometers. The initial location of the aircraft is entered into the computer, and all movement of the aircraft is sensed and used to keep the position updated. An INS does not require any inputs from outside signals. *See* INS.

inertia starter (reciprocating engine starter). A type of starter used on some large reciprocating engines. Energy is stored in a spinning flywheel by an electric motor or a hand crank. When enough energy has been put into the flywheel, it is coupled to the crankshaft, and turns it fast enough for the engine to start.

inertia switch. An electrical switch actuated by a sudden change in the velocity of the object on which it is mounted. An inertia switch is built into an emergency locator transmitter (ELT) installed in an aircraft. If the aircraft crashes, the inertia switch automatically closes and starts the ELT transmitting.

inflammable. Easily ignited. Because the prefix "in" quite often means "not able to," the word inflammable could be thought to mean "is not easy to ignite." Because of this possibility for misunderstanding, the word inflammable has been replaced in many instances with the word "flammable."

in-flight shutdown (IFSD) (ETOPS usage only). Describes when an engine ceases to function (when the airplane is airborne) and is shut down, whether self-induced, initiated by the flight crew, or caused by an external influence. The FAA keeps track of IFSDs for all causes in order to log the number and types of failure in ETOPS flight; including flameout, internal failure, flight crew-initiated shutdown, foreign object ingestion, icing, inability to obtain or control desired thrust or power, and cycling of the start control, however briefly, even if the engine operates normally for the remainder of the flight.

inflight weather advisory. *See* weather advisory.

information request. A request originated by an FSS for information concerning an overdue VFR aircraft.

infrared guidance. A method of guidance used on some missiles that causes the missile to seek and home on a source of infrared radiation.

infrared lamp. A form of incandescent lamp whose filament temperature is lower than that used to produce ordinary white light. The light produced by an infrared lamp has a large portion of its electromagnetic energy in the infrared range.

infrared radiation. Invisible electromagnetic radiation whose wavelength is between 7,800 and 1,000,000 angstroms, just slightly longer than the longest wavelength of visible light. Infrared radiation is used for heating.

infrasonic frequencies. Frequencies of vibration lower than those in the audible range. Infrasonic frequencies were formerly called subsonic frequencies.

ingest. To take something in. A gas turbine engine, for example, ingests a large volume of air in its normal operation.

ingot. A large block of metal that was molded as it was poured from the furnace. Ingots are further processed into sheets, bars, tubes, or structural beams.

in-ground effect (IGE) hover (rotorcraft). *See* hovering in ground effect (helicopter operation).

inhibitive film (corrosion protection). A hard, airtight oxide coating deposited on the surface of aluminum or magnesium alloys. Both aluminum and magnesium alloys corrode easily when their surfaces are covered with an electrolyte such as water or moist air. To protect against corrosion, an inhibitive oxide film is deposited on the surface to keep all oxygen and moisture away from the metal. Inhibitive films may be deposited by either chemical or electrolytic action.

initial approach fix. *See* IAF.

initial approach segment (ICAO). That segment of an instrument approach procedure between the initial approach fix and the intermediate approach fix or, where applicable, the final approach fix or point.

initial climb. The stage of a climb that begins when the airplane leaves the ground and a pitch attitude has been established to climb away from the takeoff area.

initial climb area (ICA). An area beginning at the departure end of runway (DER) to provide unrestricted climb to at least 400 feet above DER elevation.

initialization (computer operation). The process by which a computer is prepared to run a program. All the addresses, counters, and switches are set to their proper position for starting.

injection molding. A method of forming both thermoplastic and thermosetting resins. Soft resin is injected under pressure, into the cavity of a mold and allowed to cure. The mold is then opened to remove the part.

injection pump (compression-ignition engine component). A high-pressure fuel pump used on a compression-ignition reciprocating engine. The injection pump forces a measured amount of fuel as an atomized spray into the combustion chamber of the engine. The high-pressure, high-temperature air in the cylinder ignites the atomized fuel as it leaves the injector nozzle.

inland navigation facility. A navigation aid on a North American Route at which the common route and/or the noncommon route begins or ends.

inlet duct (turbine engine powered aircraft component). The portion of the aircraft ahead of the engine compressor that takes the air into the aircraft and directs it into the engine at the correct speed and direction.

inlet guide vanes (gas turbine engine component). Stationary vanes located in front of the first stage of the compressor in an aircraft gas turbine engine. The purpose of the inlet guide vanes is to direct the air into the first stage of the compressor at the proper angle for the most efficient compression. Most inlet guide vanes are fixed, but in some engines, their angle can be changed by hydraulic actuators controlled by the fuel control unit. Movable guide vanes direct the air into the compressor at the correct angle as the operating conditions inside the engine change.

inlet spike (supersonic aircraft inlet air duct). A sharp-pointed spike in the inlet air duct of a supersonic aircraft. This spike forms an oblique, or angled, shock wave inside the inlet duct as it passes through the air. Air entering the first-stage compressor of a gas turbine engine must flow at a speed below the speed of sound, and when the airplane is flying faster than sound, the air must be slowed before it enters the compressor.

When air passes through the oblique shock wave, it slows down, but is still moving faster than the speed of sound. Just inside the inlet duct, a second shock wave, this time a normal shock wave, is produced. This normal shock wave is at right angles to the airflow, and air passing through it is slowed to a speed below the speed of sound.

in-line engine (reciprocating engine). A reciprocating engine in which all the cylinders are arranged in a straight line. In an in-line engine, the piston in each cylinder is connected to a separate throw of the crankshaft.

V-engines are a form of inline engine having two banks of cylinders mounted on the crankcase, with an angle of between 45 and 90 degrees between the banks. Two pistons, one in a cylinder in each bank, connect to each throw of the crankshaft.

inner marker (instrument landing system component). A marker beacon used with an ILS Category II precision approach. It is located between the middle marker and the end of the ILS runway.

Inner markers transmit a radiation pattern keyed with six dots per second and indicate both aurally and visually that, if the aircraft is on the glide path, it is at the designated decision height (DH)—normally 100 feet above the touchdown zone elevation on the CAT II approach.

inner tube. An airtight rubber tube used inside a pneumatic tire to hold the air that inflates the tire. Some tires do not use inner tubes, because the tire itself forms an airtight seal with the wheel.

inoperative. Not functioning, or not working. A device or circuit is inoperative when it is not working or not able to be used.

inoperative components. Higher minimums are prescribed when the specified visual aids are not functioning; this information is listed in the Inoperative Components Table found in the U.S. Terminal Procedures Publications.

in phase. A condition in which two vibrations or changing electrical signals pass through zero at the same time, going in the same direction. To be in phase, both signals or vibrations should reach their positive and negative peak values at the same time.

input capacitance. The capacitance across the input terminals of an electrical circuit. It is the capacitance "seen" by the input device.

input circuit (electronic equipment). The circuit through which the input signal or input information is introduced into a piece of electronic equipment. The input circuit of an amplifier, for example, must supply whatever power is needed by a microphone, and it must have an input impedance that matches the impedance of the microphone.

input impedance. The impedance across the input terminals of an electronic circuit or device. The input impedance must be matched with the impedance of the component that provides the input signal.

input transformer. An electrical transformer used to feed an alternating current signal from a pickup device into the input stage of an electronic system. The input transformer isolates the pickup device from the input circuit and matches the impedance of the two devices. *See* impedance matching.

inrush current (electrical machines). The large amount of current that flows into an electrical machine when the switch is first closed. When an electric motor is connected to a power source, a high rate of current begins to flow. This inrush current causes the rotor to begin to turn, and as it turns, it produces a back voltage, or counter EMF, that opposes the source voltage. Since the CEMF opposes the source voltage, the net voltage (the voltage that actually forces the current through the motor) drops, and the current flowing into the motor decreases to a value much lower than the inrush current.

Incandescent light bulbs also cause a high inrush current. The resistance of the light bulb filaments is low when they are cold, but as soon as current flows through them, they get hot, and their resistance increases. The current drops below that of the inrush current as the filament resistance increases.

INS (inertial navigation system). A form of computerized long-range navigation system that is entirely independent of outside signals. The exact latitude and longitude of the aircraft is entered into the computer before takeoff, and accelerometers and gyros produce input signals that continually update the computer as the aircraft moves through the air.

The latitude and longitude of the destination and of way points along the route are entered into the computer, and the INS works with the course deviation indicator (CDI) and the horizontal situation indicator (HSI) to direct the autopilot or the human pilot to fly the correct course to the chosen waypoint or destination.

inside calipers (measuring device). A hinged measuring device similar to a pair of dividers. The difference between inside calipers and dividers is that the ends of the caliper's legs are bent outward so they are at right angles to the legs. Inside calipers are used to measure the inside diameter of a hole. The legs of the calipers are placed in the hole and spread until the points just touch the outside edges. The calipers are then taken from the hole and the distance between the points measured with a steel scale.

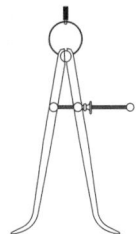

inside
calipers

inside micrometer. A precision measuring instrument used to measure the inside diameter of a cylinder or hole in increments of a thousandth of an inch or less. The body of an inside micrometer is the same as that used on an outside micrometer caliper. The ends of the thimble and the spindle are rounded, and when the zero mark on the thimble is lined up with the zero index on the sleeve, the end of the spindle and the end of the thimble are exactly two inches apart, and the spindle will move out of the thimble for exactly one inch. Extensions can be fastened into the end of the spindle to measure diameters greater than three inches.

insight (in learning process). The mental relating and grouping of associated perceptions into meaningful wholes. Creating insight in students is one of an instructor's major responsibilities, so they can understand how each factor or change of factors in a process can affect all the others.

insolation (meteorology). Incoming solar radiation falling upon the earth and its atmosphere.

Inspection Authorization. *See* IA.

inspection door (aircraft component). A small hinged cover installed over an opening in an aircraft structure. These openings allow the inspection of the inside of the aircraft.

inspection plate (aircraft component). A plate or panel used to cover an inspection opening in an aircraft structure. Inspection plates in nonstressed portions of the structure may be held in place with a few machine screws or self-tapping sheet-metal screws, but inspection plates in a highly-stressed portion of the structure are held in place with a large number of high-strength structural screws.

instability (meteorology). A general term used to indicate various states of the atmosphere in which spontaneous convection will occur when prescribed criteria are met. Instability of the air indicates turbulence.

installation drawing (aircraft drawing). A drawing used to show the way subassemblies are put together to make a complete assembly. A bill of materials included with an installation drawing gives the name and part number of all the components used to connect the subassemblies. Dimensions are not normally given on an assembly drawing, but where dimensions are needed, they are shown on the detail drawings for the parts listed in the installation drawing.

installation error (static air system error). An error in any of the instruments connected to the aircraft static air system, caused by the static air source not being located in an area in which the air is absolutely still (static). Installation error affects the airspeed indicator, altimeter, and vertical speed indicator, and it changes as the angle of attack of the aircraft changes.

instantaneous rate of climb indicator (aircraft flight instrument). A type of vertical speed indicator that compensates for the lag inherent in these instruments. When the aircraft pitches at the beginning of a climb or descent, two accelerometer-actuated air pumps inside the instrument case send a change of air pressure into the indicating bellows to start the pointer moving in the correct direction. As soon as the aircraft actually begins changing altitude, the change in static air pressure actuates the instrument mechanism.

instantaneous vertical speed indicator (IVSI). A flight instrument that assists in interpretation by instantaneously indicating the rate of climb or descent at a given moment with little or no lag, as is experienced with a vertical speed indicator (VSI).

instructional aids. Devices that assist an instructor in the teaching-learning process. They are supplementary training devices, and are not stand-alone or self-supporting.

Instructions for Continued Airworthiness (maintenance manual). A manual published by an aircraft manufacturer specifying procedures for inspection, maintenance, repair, and mandatory replacement times for life-limited parts.

instrument. *14 CFR Part 1:* "A device using an internal mechanism to show visually or aurally the attitude, altitude, or operation of an aircraft or aircraft part. It includes electronic devices for automatically controlling an aircraft in flight."

instrument approach procedure (air traffic control). A series of predetermined maneuvers for the orderly transfer of an aircraft under instrument flight conditions from the beginning of the initial approach to a landing or to a point from which a landing may be made visually. An instrument approach procedure is prescribed and approved for a specific airport by competent authority.

instrument approach procedure (ICAO). A series of predetermined maneuvers by reference to flight instruments with specified protection from obstacles from the initial approach fix, or where applicable, from the beginning of a defined arrival route to a point from which a landing can be completed and thereafter, if a landing is not completed, to a position at which holding or en route obstacle clearance criteria apply.

Instrument Approach Procedures Charts. Aeronautical charts that portray the aeronautical data required to execute an instrument approach to an airport. These charts depict the procedures, including all related data, and the airport diagram. Each procedure is designated for use with a specific type of electronic navigation system, such as NDB, TACAN, VOR, ILS, and RNAV.

instrument approach waypoint. Fixes used in defining RNAV instrument approach procedures, including the feeder waypoint (FWP), the initial approach waypoint (IAWP), the intermediate waypoint (IWP), the final approach waypoint (FAWP), the runway waypoint (RWY WP), and the airport waypoint (APT WP), when required.

instrument clamp. A cylindrical metal clamp attached to the back of an instrument panel aligned with the hole through which an instrument fits. The instrument is installed from the front of the panel by sliding it through the hole and the clamp and tightening the clamp by means of a screw on the front of the panel.

instrument departure procedure (DP). A preplanned instrument flight rule (IFR) air traffic control departure procedure printed for pilot use in graphic and/or textual form. DPs provide transition from the terminal to the appropriate enroute structure.

instrument flight. A flight made solely by reference to the cockpit instruments during low visibility or bad weather.

instrument flight rules. *See* IFR.

Instrument Landing System. *See* ILS.

instrument meteorological conditions. *See* IMC.

instrument panel (aircraft component). A panel in the cockpit of an aircraft that holds all the indicating instruments used to show the condition of the aircraft and its engines.

instrument procedure with vertical guidance (IPV). Satellite or Flight Management System (FMS) lateral navigation (LNAV) with computed positive vertical guidance based on barometric or satellite elevation. This term has been renamed APV.

instrument proficiency check (IPC). An evaluation ride based on the instrument rating practical test standard which is required to regain instrument flying privileges when the privileges have expired due to lack of currency.

instrument runway. A runway equipped with electronic and visual navigation aids for which a precision or nonprecision approach having straight-in landing minimums has been approved.

instrument shunt. An electrical shunt used with a millivoltmeter to measure current. The shunt is a low-resistance precision resistor, installed in a circuit in such a way that the circuit current flows through it. The millivoltmeter is connected across the shunt to measure the voltage dropped across it.

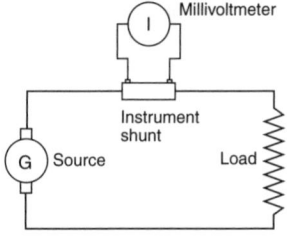

instrument shunt

The indication on the millivoltmeter is directly related to the amount of current flowing through the shunt, and because of this, it is possible to calibrate the dial of the millivoltmeter directly in amps or milliamps.

instrument takeoff. Using the instruments rather than outside visual cues to maintain runway heading and execute a safe takeoff.

instrument weather conditions (IMC). Weather that includes reduced visibility and cloud ceilings that require a pilot to fly by reference to his or her cockpit instruments.

insulating tape (electrical tape). An adhesive-backed flexible tape used as a temporary insulation over wire terminals and wire splices. This tape is usually made of a polyvinylchloride material. One side of the tape is coated with an adhesive, and the tape is wound over areas of bare wire to insulate it.

insulation (thermal). A material used to prevent the transfer of heat by conduction. Thermal insulation, for example, keeps hot air ducts from overheating the structure through which they are routed.

insulation blanket (turbine engine aircraft component). A layer of fireproof insulating material used to keep heat from the tail pipe of a gas turbine engine from damaging the aircraft structure. Insulation blankets are usually quilted, to allow the maximum amount of insulating material to be used and at the same time make the blanket easy to install and hold in place.

insulation resistance. The DC resistance of an electrical insulating material. Resistance specifications normally list the amount of leakage current allowed for a given applied voltage.

insulation strength. A measure of the amount of electrical stress an insulation can withstand before it breaks down and conducts. Insulation strength is measured in volts-per-unit of insulation thickness, normally in volts-per-mil (0.001 inch).

insulator (electrical). A material whose outer shell electrons (valence electrons) are so tightly bound to the atom that they resist any force that tries to move them from one atom to another. Glass, mica, paper, ceramics, and certain types of plastic materials are used as insulators in electrical and electronic equipment.

intake valve (reciprocating engine component). The valve in the cylinder of a reciprocating engine through which the fuel-air mixture passes as it enters the combustion chamber.

integer. A whole number, or counting number. Integers include negative numbers, positive numbers, and zero.

integral fuel tank (aircraft fuel tank). A fuel tank that is formed by sealing off part of the aircraft structure and using it to hold fuel. An integral wing tank is called a "wet wing" and is used because it is lighter than a bladder-type fuel tank. The only way to repair an integral fuel tank is by replacing damaged sealant and making riveted repairs, as is done with any other part of the aircraft structure.

Integrated Airman Certification and Rating Application (IACRA). An online application system that allows for the issuance of student, private, and commercial pilot certificates without generating paperwork; the certificate application and approval is performed through the use of electronic "signatures."

integrated circuit. A tiny chip or wafer of silicon on which is etched, imprinted, or diffused electronic components such as transistors, diodes, capacitors and resistors with their interconnections.

integrated flight instruction. A technique of flight instruction where students are taught to perform flight maneuvers by reference to both the flight instruments and to outside visual references from the time the maneuver is first introduced. Handling of the controls is the same regardless of whether flight instruments or outside references are being used.

integrating circuit. An electronic circuit whose output is determined by the sum of all of its inputs.

integrity (navigation instruments). The ability of a system to provide timely warnings to users when the system should not be used for navigation.

intensity (in learning process). A principle of learning in which a dramatic or exciting learning experience is likely to be remembered longer than a boring experience. Students will learn more when they experience the real thing than when they are merely told about the real thing.

intensity control (cathode-ray tube). The control for a cathode-ray tube that regulates the quantity of electrons in the beam that strikes the phosphorescent screen inside the cathode-ray tube. The intensity of the electron beam determines the amount of light produced by the screen.

interactive video. Software that responds quickly to certain choices and commands made by the user. A typical system consists of a compact disk, a computer, and video technology.

intercooler (reciprocating engine installation component). An air-to-air heat exchanger installed between a turbosupercharger and the carburetor. Intercoolers decrease the temperature of the compressed air to prevent detonation.

A turbosupercharger compresses the air before it enters the fuel metering system of a reciprocating engine, and when it is compressed, it becomes too hot to be used. Before it enters the induction system, it is cooled by passing it through an intercooler.

intercostal. A structural member used in a stressed-skin structure to stiffen the skin between the bulkheads or other major structural components. An intercostal does not carry stresses from the skin into the structure supporting the skin.

intercylinder baffles (reciprocating engine component). Pieces of thin sheet metal installed between the cylinders of an air-cooled aircraft engine to force air to flow through the fins on the cylinders.

interelectrode capacitance. The capacitance between the electrodes in an electron tube (vacuum tube). A capacitor is simply two conductors separated by an insulator, or dielectric. The electrodes in an electron tube are the conductors, and the vacuum is the dielectric. High-frequency signals can feed back from one electrode to another through the interelectrode capacitance inside a tube. To prevent this feedback, neutralizing circuits must be used.

interelement capacitance. The capacitance inside a bipolar transistor caused by the junction between the P-material and the N-material.

interference (in learning process). (1) A theory of forgetting based on the idea that a person forgets something because a certain experience overshadows it, or the learning of similar things has intervened. (2) Barriers to effective communication caused by physiological, environmental, and psychological factors outside the direct control of the instructor. The instructor must take these factors into account in order to communicate effectively.

interference angle (poppet valve dimension). The difference between the angles at which the valve seat and the valve face are ground. Normally the valve seats are ground with between 0.5° and 1° greater angle than the valve face. This allows the face to touch the seat with a line contact that provides the best sealing.

interference drag (aerodynamic drag). Parasite drag caused by air flowing over one portion of the airframe interfering with the smooth flow of air over another portion.

interference fit. A type of fit used when assembling certain mechanical devices. To create an interference fit, a hole is made smaller than the part that fits into it. The material containing the hole is heated to expand the hole, and the object to fit in the hole is chilled to shrink it. The parts are easily assembled when one is hot and the other is cold, but when they reach the same temperature, the fit is so tight they will not loosen in service.

intergranular corrosion. A type of corrosion which forms along the boundaries of the grains inside a piece of metal alloy. Stress corrosion and exfoliation corrosion are types of intergranular corrosion.

interlock. A form of automatic safety control. An interlock in a device can prevent an action from occurring until the device is ready for the action. An interlock can be installed on the door of a compartment so the door cannot be opened when the equipment inside the compartment is operating. When the door is opened, the interlock switch automatically turns the power off and discharges any high-voltage capacitors inside the housing.

intermediate approach segment. *See* segments of an instrument approach procedure.

intermediate approach segment (ICAO). That segment of an instrument approach procedure between either the intermediate approach fix and the final approach fix or point, or between the end of a reversal, race track or dead reckoning track procedure and the final approach fix or point, as appropriate.

intermediate fix (IF) (air traffic control). The turning point of an instrument approach between the departure and arrival fix. The fix that identifies the beginning of the intermediate approach segment of an instrument approach procedure. The fix is not normally identified on the instrument approach chart as an intermediate fix (IF).

intermediate fix/initial approach waypoint (IF/IAWP). The waypoint where the final approach course of a T approach meets the crossbar of the T. When designated (in conjunction with a TAA) this waypoint will be used as an IAWP when approaching the airport from certain directions, and as an IFWP when beginning the approach from another IAWP.

intermediate frequency (radio receiver). A single frequency of alternating current produced inside a superheterodyne radio receiver. A superheterodyne receiver circuit is efficient because most of its amplification is done with a single intermediate frequency, rather than with a wide band of frequencies.

A local oscillator inside the receiver produces an alternating current whose frequency is always a constant amount different from the radio-frequency signal being received. When the local oscillator signal is mixed with the received signal, two other frequencies are produced: One frequency is the sum of the two, and the other is the difference between the two. Filters allow only the signal whose frequency is the difference between the two to be amplified. This is the intermediate frequency, the IF.

intermediate frequency transformer (radio receiver component). An interstage coupling transformer used in a superheterodyne radio receiver. Both the primary and secondary windings of the IF transformer are tuned to the intermediate frequency. *See* intermediate frequency. The output winding of the IF transformer feeds the input of the IF amplifier with a signal whose frequency is that to which the IF transformer is tuned.

intermediate landing. On the rare occasion that this option is requested, it should be approved. The departure center, however, must advise the ATCSCC so that the appropriate delay is carried over and assigned at the intermediate airport. An intermediate landing airport within the arrival center will not be accepted without coordination with and the approval of the ATCSCC.

intermittent-duty relay or solenoid. An electrically operated relay or solenoid that must be de-energized (the power to its operating coil must be turned off) at intervals to keep the coil from overheating. Starter relays and relays used to operate motors that run for only a short period of time can be intermittent-duty relays. Intermittent-duty relays cannot be used as master battery relays or light relays that must be energized for long periods of time.

intermittent fault. A fault which occurs in a system or circuit only at certain times and under certain conditions. Intermittent faults often do not follow a consistent pattern, and their cause is usually difficult to determine.

intermittent load (electrical load). An electrical load that is not continuously applied to the circuit. The landing gear retraction motor and the flap operating motor are both intermittent loads in that neither of them are operated continuously.

internal combustion engine. A form of heat engine in which the fuel and air mixture is burned inside the engine to heat and expand the air so it can perform work.

internal control lock (aircraft control system component). A device used to lock the flight controls of an aircraft so they cannot be damaged by the wind. Internal locks hold the control stick or wheel and the rudder pedals, rather than clamping the control surfaces themselves.

internally wrenching bolt. A special type of bolt having a large, cylindrical head with a flat top and a hexagonal socket cut into it. Internally wrenching bolts are used for high-strength and high-temperature applications.

internal resistance (batteries). Opposition to the flow of current caused by the plates of a battery. The internal resistance of a lead-acid storage battery increases as the battery becomes discharged, and current flowing through the higher resistance causes a voltage drop that lowers the closed-circuit voltage of the battery.

internal supercharger (reciprocating engine component). A gear-driven centrifugal air pump installed inside a reciprocating engine. Fuel and air are mixed in the carburetor, and the mixture is compressed by the internal supercharger before it is distributed to the cylinders.

internal supercharger drain valve (reciprocating engine component). A pressure-operated valve in the bottom of the internal supercharger section of a reciprocating engine that is open when the pressures inside and outside the supercharger housing are the same. Excess fuel can drain from the engine through this valve if the engine is flooded during the starting procedure.

internal timing (aircraft magneto operation). Correctly meshing the gears and adjusting the breaker point clearance in an aircraft magneto so the breaker points begin to open when the rotating magnet is in the correct position relative to the pole shoes, in its E-gap position. When a magneto is correctly timed internally, it produces the hottest spark.

international airport. An airport having customs service for passengers arriving from foreign countries.

international airport (ICAO). Any airport designated by the Contracting State in whose territory it is situated as an airport of entry and departure for international air traffic, where the formalities incident to customs, immigration, public health, animal and plant quarantine and similar procedures are carried out.

International Civil Aviation Organization. *See* ICAO.

international date line. The 180° meridian of longitude. The international date line is on the opposite side of the earth from the prime meridian, which passes through Greenwich, England.

International Field Offices (IFO). International version of the Flight Standards District Office (FSDO).

international flight information manual (IFIM). A publication designed primarily as a pilot's preflight planning guide for flights into foreign airspace and for flights returning to the U.S. from foreign locations.

International Morse Code. A group of dot and dash combinations which have been agreed upon internationally to represent the letters of the alphabet, numbers, and certain punctuation symbols. Morse code is used for some types of radio communications, and for the code identifiers of VOR and VORTAC stations, and the localizer in an instrument landing system. *See* International Phonetic Alphabet and Morse Code in Appendix 4.

International Phonetic Alphabet. An internationally agreed upon system of code words identifying the letters of the alphabet and numbers. The words in the phonetic alphabet have been carefully chosen so that people of all language backgrounds can pronounce them. *See* International Phonetic Alphabet and Morse Code in Appendix 4.

international standard atmosphere (ISA). Also known as a standard day. A representative model of atmospheric air pressure, temperature, and density at various altitudes for reference purposes. At sea level, the ISA has a temperature of 59°F or 15°C and a pressure of 29.92 in. Hg or 1013.2 millibars.

International System of Units. The system of metric units agreed upon by the General Conference on Weights and Measures. The International System of Units, abbreviated SI, is based on the following units: meter, kilogram, second, ampere, candela, degrees Kelvin, hertz, radian, newton, joule, watt, coulomb, volt, ohm, farad, tesla, and weber.

Internet. An electronic network that connects computers around the world.

interphone system. A system for communication between crew members of an aircraft. Interphone communications are normally conducted using the same microphone and earphones or speakers used for radio communications. A selector switch is positioned in such a way that the interphone signals do not enter the radio transmitter circuits.

interplane struts (biplane component). Struts located between the two wings of a biplane, usually near the wing tips. Interplane struts attach to the front and rear wing spars and are normally N-shaped or I-shaped.

interpolate. To determine a value in a series between two known values.

interpole (electrical machine component). A field pole in a compound-wound generator used to minimize armature reaction. Armature reaction is the distortion of the magnetic field produced by the field coils caused by the magnetic field produced by current flowing in the armature. The amount of armature reaction varies with the armature current. Armature reaction causes a voltage across the commutator segments shorted by the brushes, and this produces sparks.

Interpoles are located between each of the regular field poles, and the interpole coils are in series with the armature so all the armature current flows through them. The magnetic fields produced by the interpole coils cancel the distortion caused by the armature field, and the brushes short across segments of the commutator where there is no potential difference and therefore no sparking.

inter-rib bracing (fabric-covered wing component). Bracing between the ribs of a fabric-covered wing made of reinforcing tape wrapped around the rib cap strips midway between the spars. Inter-rib bracing holds the ribs in the correct position until they are laced to the fabric.

interrogator (radar). A ground-based surveillance radar beacon transmitter-receiver which normally scans in synchronization with a primary radar. The interrogator transmits discrete radio signals which continuously request a reply from all transponders using the selected mode. The received replies are mixed with the primary radar returns and displayed on the same PPI (plan position indicator radarscope).

intersecting runways. Two or more runways which cross or meet within their lengths.

intersection. (1) A point defined by any combination of courses, radials, or bearings of two or more navigational aids. (2) Used to describe the point where two runways, a runway and a taxiway, or two taxiways cross or meet.

intersection departure (air traffic control). A takeoff or proposed takeoff on a runway from an intersection.

interstage transformer (electronic device). A transformer used to couple two stages of an electronic device. An interstage transformer prevents the flow of direct current from one stage to the other, and it matches the output impedance of one stage with the input impedance of the following stage.

interstate air commerce. *14 CFR Part 1:* "The carriage by aircraft of persons or property for compensation or hire, or the carriage of mail by aircraft, or the operation or navigation of aircraft in the conduct or furtherance of a business or vocation, in commerce between a place in any State of the United States, or the District of Columbia, and a place in any other State of the United States or the District of Columbia; or between places in the same State of the United States through the airspace over any place outside thereof; or between places in the same territory or possession of the United States, or the District of Columbia."

interstate air transportation. *14 CFR Part 1:* "The carriage by aircraft of persons or property as a common carrier for compensation or hire, or the carriage of mail by aircraft in commerce:
(1) Between a place in a State or the District of Columbia and another place in another State or the District of Columbia.
(2) Between places in the same State through the airspace over any place outside that State; or
(3) Between places in the same possession of the United States;
Whether that commerce moves wholly by aircraft or partially by aircraft and partly by other forms of transportation."

intertropical convergence zone (meteorology). The boundary zone between the trade wind system of the northern and southern hemispheres. It is characterized in maritime climates by showery precipitation, with cumulonimbus clouds sometimes extending to great heights.

intrastate air transportation. *14 CFR Part 1:* "The carriage of persons or property as a common carrier for compensation or hire, by turbojet-powered aircraft capable of carrying thirty or more persons, wholly within the same state of the United States."

Invar. The registered trade name for an alloy of 63.8% iron, 36% nickel, and 0.2% carbon. Invar has a high relative resistance and a very low coefficient of thermal expansion. Invar is used for wire-wound resistors.

inverse peak voltage. The peak, or maximum, voltage applied across a rectifier during the half cycle of alternating current when the rectifier is not conducting.

inverse ratio. A ratio of the reciprocals of two quantities.

inverse square law. A law of physics that applies to several natural conditions, such as the strength of a magnetic field, the amount of light falling on a surface, and the intensity of sound pressure. When referring to the strength of a magnetic field, the inverse square law states that the strength of the field varies inversely (the strength decreases as the distance increases) as the square of the distance between the pole and the point at which the strength is measured. For example, if we double the distance (make it two times as great), the magnetic strength is decreased to a value of one-fourth its original strength. One-fourth is the inverse square of two.

inverse voltage (electrical rectifier). The voltage applied to a rectifier during the half cycle in which it does not conduct.

inversion (meteorology). An increase in temperature with height. An inversion is a reversal of the normal decrease in temperature with height in the troposphere.

inversion illusion (physiology). The feeling that the aircraft is tumbling backwards, caused by an abrupt change from climb to straight-and-level flight while in situations lacking visual reference.

inverted engine (reciprocating engine). An in-line or V-type reciprocating engine installed in an aircraft with the crankshaft and crankcase above the cylinders.

inverted
inline engine

inverted spin (aircraft flight maneuver). An acrobatic flight maneuver in which an aircraft spins in an inverted attitude.

inverter (electrical component). An electrical component which changes direct current into alternating current. A rotary inverter is a form of motor-generator unit in which a DC motor drives an AC generator. A static inverter is a solid-state oscillator-amplifier combination.

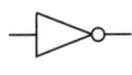

inverter

inverter (logic device). A logic device with one input and one output. The logic state of the output is always opposite that of the input. An inverter is sometimes called a negator, or a NOT function.

invert. To turn something upside down.

iodine. A lustrous, grayish-black, corrosive, poisonous chemical element. Iodine's symbol is I, its atomic number is 53, and its atomic weight is 126.9044. Iodine is used as a germicide, an antiseptic, and a component in dyes.

ion. An atom with an imbalance between its electrons and its protons. A balanced atom has the same number of protons (positive electrical charges) in its nucleus as it has electrons (negative electrical charges) surrounding the nucleus. If a balanced atom loses an electron, it becomes a positive ion. If it gains an extra electron, it becomes a negative ion.

ion engine. A form of reaction engine that produces forward thrust by the rearward ejection of a stream of ionized particles. Ion engines using ionized particles produced by nuclear reaction have been proposed for space flight.

ionic charges. Electrical charges within a semiconductor diode that result when the mobile charges are pulled away from the PN junction in the diode. When the free electrons in the N-material are drawn away from the junction, a positive ionic charge is left. And when the holes in the P-material are drawn away from the junction, a negative ionic charge is left. It is the ionic charges in a semiconductor diode that produce the barrier voltage.

ionize. The process of making positive ions by freeing electrons from balanced atoms or molecules. The electrons freed from the atoms travel to other atoms or molecules and become part of them.

ionosphere. A region of electrically charged particles (ions) extending upward from about 30 miles above the surface of the earth. The ionosphere is composed of a number of layers that vary in the amount of ionization, with the lower layers not ionized as heavily as the higher layers. The names of the layers of the ionosphere, beginning at the lower layer, are:

D region

E region (the Kennelly Heaviside layer)

F1 region

F2 region

Heliosphere

Protonosphere

Magnetosphere

IRAN (aircraft inspection). A type of aircraft inspection in which the aircraft is inspected and any needed repairs are made. IRAN stands for "inspect and repair as necessary."

IRBM (intermediate-range ballistic missile). A ballistic missile with a range of between 200 and 1,500 miles. *See* ballistic missile.

IR drop. The decrease in electrical pressure caused by electrons flowing through a resistance. The amount of IR drop, expressed in volts, is found by multiplying the current (I), in amps, by the resistance (R), in ohms.

iridium. A very hard, brittle, highly corrosion-resistant, whitish-yellow, metallic chemical element. Iridium's symbol is Ir, its atomic number is 77, and its atomic weight is 192.2.

Iridium is used for electrical contacts and as an alloying agent in high-temperature metals. Spark plugs having fine-wire electrodes made of iridium are used in engines in which lead-fouling is a problem.

Irish linen (aircraft fabric). A strong organic fabric made from the fibers of the flax plant. Irish linen is approved as a direct replacement for grade-A cotton fabric as a covering material for aircraft structures.

iron. A silvery-white, lustrous, malleable, ductile, metallic chemical element. Iron's symbol is Fe, its atomic number is 26, and its atomic weight is 55.847. Iron is an important structural metal in the form of steel (iron with controlled amounts of carbon and other elements).

iron carbide. The form in which carbon exists in steel. The amount of iron carbide and its distribution in the metal determine the hardness of the steel.

iron-constantan thermocouple. A thermocouple combination used to measure temperatures up to about 410°C. Iron forms the positive element, and constantan, the negative. Iron-constantan thermocouples are generally used to measure cylinder head temperature on reciprocating engines.

iron-core coil. A type of inductor wound around a core of laminated iron sections. Iron has a much higher permeability than air, and an iron-core coil has a greater inductance than an equivalent size air-core coil.

iron-core transformer (electrical component). A transformer with the coils wound over a core of laminated soft iron. The soft iron core concentrates the lines of magnetic flux and increases the inductance of the coil. The laminations decrease the eddy current losses in the core.

iron-vane meter movement (AC ammeter). The mechanism in an AC ammeter whose pointer is attached to a soft iron vane and restrained by a calibrated hairspring. The vane is rotated by the magnetic field produced by the unknown current flowing through a surrounding coil. The greater the current, the stronger the magnetic field and the greater the pointer deflection.

irreversible controls (aircraft controls). Controls in an aircraft operated by a boost system. Cockpit controls move the control surfaces, but aerodynamic forces on the control surfaces cannot feed back into the cockpit controls.

"I say again" (air traffic control). A phrase used in verbal ATC communications to indicate that the message will be repeated.

isobar (meteorology). A line on a weather map that shows equal or constant barometric pressure.

isobaric range of cabin pressurization. The range of cabin pressurization in which cabin pressure is maintained at a constant level (a constant cabin altitude), rather than allowing it to change with flight altitude. Most cabin pressurization systems operate in the isobaric range up to the altitude at which the cabin differential pressure is the maximum allowed by the aircraft structure. Then the system automatically shifts to the constant-differential mode, which keeps a constant pressure difference between the pressure of the air inside the cabin and the air outside the cabin.

isoecho (radar meteorology). A circuit in a weather radar that reverses signal strength above a specified intensity level. An iso echo circuit causes a void on the scope in the most intense portion of an echo when the maximum intensity is greater than the specified level.

isogonic lines. Lines drawn across aeronautical navigational charts that connect points having the same magnetic variation. Isogonic means "the same angle."

isoheight (meteorology). A line on a weather chart showing equal height. An isoheight is the same as a contour.

isohumes (meteorology). Lines of equal relative humidity.

isolation mount (shock-absorbing engine mount). A type of mount that supports the engine on steel-backed rubber pads. These pads isolate the engine from the airframe and prevent vibrations damaging the structure.

isolation transformer (electrical component). An electrical transformer used to isolate a piece of electrical equipment from the power line. An isolation transformer has the same number of turns in its secondary winding as it has in its primary. This one-to-one turns ratio causes the output voltage and current to be the same as that of the input.

An isolation transformer electrically isolates equipment connected to its secondary winding from the power line. This isolation prevents the danger of electrical shock when working on the equipment.

isoline (meteorology). A line on a chart showing an equal value of a variable quantity. Weather maps use isobars (lines of equal pressure), isotherms (lines of equal temperature), isoshears (lines of equal wind shear), and isotachs (lines of equal, or constant, wind speed).

isometric drawing. A drawing made in such a way that it has no visual perspective. Equal distances on the object are equal distances on the drawing.

iso-octane. A flammable, colorless hydrocarbon liquid $(CH_3)_2CHCH_2C(CH_3)_3$, used as a component of aviation gasoline and as the datum for rating the antidetonation characteristics of gasoline. The high critical pressure and temperature of iso-octane make it resistant to detonation.

isopleth (meteorology). A line connecting points of constant or equal value.

isopropyl alcohol. A colorless liquid used in the manufacture of acetone and its derivatives and as a solvent and anti-icing agent.

isoshear (meteorology). A line on a weather chart showing equal values of wind shear.

isotach (meteorology). A line on a weather chart showing equal, or constant, wind speed.

isotherm (meteorology). A line on a weather chart showing equal, or constant, temperature.

isothermal (meteorology). This term relates to equal, or constant, temperature with respect to a variable, such as space or time. When referring to the relationship between temperature and height, isothermal is the same as zero lapse rate.

isothermal change. A physical change that takes place within a material in which heat energy is added to or taken from the material as needed to keep its temperature constant.

isothermal forming (sheet metal forming). A method of forming sheet metal by using heated dies of metal or ceramic.

isotope. A special atom of an element having the same number of protons as an ordinary atom, but with more than the normal number of neutrons. An isotope of an element has the same atomic number as a normal atom, but because of the additional neutrons, it has a greater atomic weight.

I^2R (electrical power). Power dissipated in an electrical circuit computed by multiplying the square of the current by the circuit resistance.

I^2R loss (electrical power). The power lost in an electrical device, such as a transformer. This power loss is caused by the current flowing through the component resistance.

ITT (Interstage Turbine Temperature). The temperature of the gases flowing inside a gas turbine engine between the high-pressure and the low-pressure turbine wheels.

IVSI. *See* instantaneous vertical speed indicator.

I

jack (electrical connection). A socket into which a plug can be pushed to make an electrical connection. Jacks are often used on the front of electrical test equipment to make temporary connections for test leads. Some of the more commonly used types of jacks are phone jacks, miniature jacks, microphone jacks, and banana plug jacks.

jack (mechanical equipment). A tool used to lift an aircraft or other types of equipment off the floor. Jacks can be operated in several ways: by hydraulic pressure built up by a self-contained pump, by shop air pressure, by mechanical screw threads, or by a ratcheting lever that locks on each stroke.

jacket (gas turbine engine component). A shroud or metal blanket used to insulate a portion of the hot section of a gas turbine engine. The jacket keeps heat from damaging the aircraft structure.

jack pad. A fixture that attaches to the structure of an aircraft to fit the jack that is used to raise the aircraft for weighing or servicing.

jackscrew. A hardened steel rod with strong threads cut into it. A jackscrew may be rotated by hand or with a motor to apply a force or to move an object.

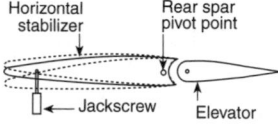

jackscrew

jagged edge. A sharp and irregular edge on a piece of metal, wood, or plastic material.

jam acceleration (gas turbine engine operation). Rapid movement of the power control lever of a gas turbine engine which calls for maximum acceleration of the engine.

jamming (radar and radio). Electronic or mechanical interference used to disrupt the display of aircraft on radar or the transmission/reception of radio communications or navigation information.

jam nut. A thin nut screwed down on top of a regular nut to lock it onto the bolt. The jam nut keeps the regular nut from backing off. A jam nut is sometimes called a check nut.

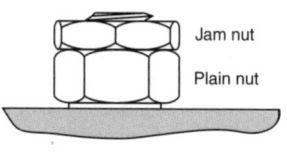

jam nut

JAN specifications (joint Army–Navy). Specifications for technical equipment that have been established by a joint board of the United States Army and Navy. These specifications describe the equipment in detail. They are usable for civilian equipment as well as for equipment built specifically for the military.

JATO (jet assisted takeoff). A system of auxiliary thrust used for heavily loaded aircraft to assist their takeoff. JATO units are small rocket engines fastened to the aircraft structure when a difficult takeoff is to be made. The JATO units are fired the moment the aircraft rotates for takeoff, and the boost from the rocket engines provides the additional thrust needed to get the aircraft airborne. JATO is more properly called RATO for Rocket Assisted TakeOff.

javelin. The streamlined wood or metal rod that is secured at the intersection of the landing and flying wires of a biplane. Javelins prevent the wires from vibrating in flight.

jerry can. A flat-sided five-gallon can, used for carrying fuel. Jerry cans are made so they stack together and fit in special racks on vehicles.

jet (fuel metering system component). A special threaded plug with a specifically designed hole drilled through it. The diameter and length of the hole and the approach angles to the hole determine the amount of fuel that can flow through the jet for a given pressure drop across it.

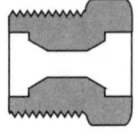

jet

Jet-A fuel (gas turbine engine fuel). A kerosine-type fuel used in most commercially operated jet-propelled aircraft. Jet-A is similar to military JP-5 fuel. Its flash point is between 110° and 150°F, and its freezing point is −40°F.

Jet-A1 fuel (gas turbine engine fuel). A kerosine-type fuel similar to Jet-A fuel except that it contains additives that decrease its freezing point to −58°F. Jet-A1 fuel is used in aircraft that remain at high altitudes for long periods of time. Jet-A1 fuel is similar to NATO JP-8 fuel.

jet assisted takeoff. *See* JATO.

Jet-B fuel (gas turbine engine fuel). A gasoline-type fuel used in most military jet-propelled aircraft. Jet-B fuel has a flash point of 0°F and a freezing point of −76°F. Jet-B fuel is similar to the military JP-4 fuel.

jet blast. Jet engine exhaust (thrust stream turbulence).

JetCal analyzer (gas turbine engine test equipment). The registered trade name for a piece of test equipment used to check the engine RPM and various temperatures and pressures inside an operating gas turbine engine. A JetCal also checks the accuracy of the instruments installed in the aircraft.

jet fuel. Fuel designed and produced to be used in aircraft gas turbine engines.

jet nozzle (gas turbine engine component). The opening at the rear of the exhaust duct of a gas turbine engine. A jet nozzle is also called an exhaust nozzle.

jet-powered airplane. An aircraft powered by a turbojet or turbofan engine.

jet propulsion. A method of propulsion by thrust produced as a relatively small mass of air is accelerated through a large change in velocity.

jet pump (aircraft fuel system). A form of fluid pump that produces a low pressure by moving fluid at a high velocity through a venturi. A jet pump can be used to remove vapor from fuel before it enters a fuel control unit. Some of the fuel from the main fuel pump is returned to the tank through a venturi (the jet pump). The venturi is connected to the top of the chamber in which the vapors collect. The low

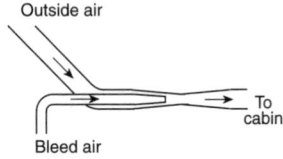

jet pump

pressure at the throat of the venturi pulls the vapors out of the chamber and returns them with the fuel back to the tank.

jet pump (environmental control system). A special venturi in a line carrying air from certain areas in an aircraft that need an augmented flow of air through them. High-velocity compressor bleed air is blown into the throat of a venturi where it produces a low pressure that pulls air from the area to which it is connected. Jet pumps are often used in the lines that pull air through galleys and toilet areas.

jet route. A route designated to serve flight operations from 18,000 feet MSL, up to and including flight level 450. The routes are referred to as "J" routes, with numbers to identify the designated route.

jet silencer. A noise suppressor used with a gas turbine engine. A jet silencer does not actually silence a jet engine; rather, it converts some of the low-frequency vibrations into higher frequency vibrations that are more easily dissipated as they mix with the surrounding air.

jet stream (meteorology). A high-velocity narrow stream of winds usually found near the upper limit of the troposphere. The jet stream normally blows from west to east, and the winds in the stream may reach velocities of up to 250 miles per hour.

jet stream axis (meteorology). Sometimes called jet axis. The axis of maximum wind speed in a jet stream.

jet stream cirrus (meteorology). Cirrus specifically associated with vertical motion with respect to the jet stream, which gives a visual indication of the existence and direction of the jet stream across the sky.

jettison. To drop something from an aircraft or space craft in flight. Fuel is jettisoned when it is dumped from the aircraft fuel tanks to lower the weight of the aircraft to a weight approved for landing.

jet wake. The stream of hot, high-velocity gases that come from the exhaust of a gas turbine engine.

jewel bearing. A cup-type bearing in which a hardened steel pivot rides. Jewel bearings used in many types of indicating instruments are normally made of an extremely hard glass.

jeweler's file. A small, fine-cut metalworking file used by instrument technicians to repair aircraft instruments. Jeweler's files are available in many shapes.

jeweler's rouge. A very fine, dark red abrasive made of ferric oxide. Jeweler's rouge is used for polishing hard metal surfaces.

JFET (junction field effect transistor). A high-imped-ance semiconductor device that controls the flow of electrons between its source and drain by a voltage placed on its gate. The function of a JFET is similar to that of a bipolar transistor, except the control is a small change in voltage rather than a small change in current.

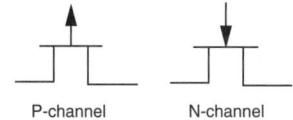

P-channel   N-channel

junction field effect transistor

jig (manufacturing fixture). A strong, heavy framework used to hold a component while it is being assembled. Parts are assembled in jigs to assure their interchangeability. Airplane wings, for example, are assembled in jigs, and any wing having a given part number can be interchanged with another wing having the same part number.

If the parts were not assembled in a jig, they might look the same, but they would probably not interchange; the bolt holes would likely not line up.

jigsaw. A type of saw that uses a very narrow blade moved back and forth across the work being cut. A jigsaw is used to cut small-radius curves in wood, metal, or plastic.

Jo-bolt (special aircraft fastener). A patented, high-strength structural fastener used where strength requirements are high. The Jo-bolt is passed through a close-tolerance hole, and a sleeve is pulled up over its tapered shank to form a blind head inside the structure.

joggle (sheet metal). A small offset near the edge of a piece of sheet metal.

It allows one sheet of metal to overlap another sheet while maintaining a flush surface.

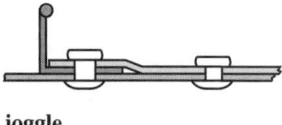

joggle

Johansson block. An accurately ground gage block used as a reference in precision machining operations. A Johansson block (Jo block) is usually ground to an accuracy of at least 0.000 01 inch (0.25 micrometer).

Johnson bar (aircraft controls). A type of brake control used on some early airplanes. A Johnson bar is a long handle located between the pilot's and copilot's seats, easily accessible to both.

Pulling straight back on the Johnson bar applies both brakes equally. Pulling the bar back diagonally applies the brake on the side to which the bar is pulled.

joint en route terminal system (JETS). An automated ATC system that displays digitally on a radar console altitude information on airplanes with Mode C transponder capability.

jointer (woodworking tool). A woodworking power tool used to smooth the edges of a board or piece of wood.

joule. A measure of work in the kilogram-meter-second system of units. One joule is the amount of work done when a force of one newton moves an object one meter in the direction in which the force is applied. A joule is also known as a newton-meter. One joule is equal to 0.1020 meter-kilogram, or 0.7375 foot-pound of work.

journal (bearing surface). A hardened and polished surface on a rotating shaft that rides in a plain bearing. The bearing journal provides a smooth bearing surface and wears very little.

joystick (airplane control). An old name for the control stick used to control an airplane. Movement of the joystick to the front or back moves the elevators to control the pitch of the airplane. Movement from side to side moves the ailerons to rotate the airplane about its longitudinal axis (to roll the airplane).

The term joystick has been changed to control stick or, more simply, to just "stick."

JP-4 (gas turbine engine fuel). JP-4 is a mixture of hydrocarbons. It is a flammable transparent liquid with clear or straw color. Its freezing point is −77°F (−60°C) and its flash point temperature is 0°F (−18°C). It was formerly the standard fuel for military jet aircraft and is basically equivalent to commercial Jet-B.

JP-5 (gas turbine engine fuel). JP-5 is a kerosine based jet fuel with a minimum flash point of 60°C, and a freezing point of −46°C. It was developed for the U.S. Navy for use in aircraft operated from aircraft carriers where the risk from fire is particularly great. JP-5 is similar to the newer JP-8.

JP-7 (gas turbine engine fuel). JP-7 is a jet fuel developed by the U.S. Air Force for use in supersonic aircraft because of its high flashpoint and thermal stability. It is the fuel used in the Pratt & Whitney J58 engines, installed in the Lockheed SR-71 Blackbird. JP-7 is a mixture composed of hydrocarbons, and it includes additives to increase its lubricating properties, an oxidizing agent to make it burn better, and it contains a compound which aids in disguising the radar signature of the exhaust. JP-7 has low vapor pressure and high thermal oxidation stability and is to operate over a wide range of temperatures, from near freezing of high altitudes to the high temperature of airframe and engine parts with which it comes in contact.

JP-8 (gas turbine engine fuel). JP-8 is a kerosine-based jet fuel, adopted in by the U.S. government as a replacement for JP-4 because it is less flammable and less hazardous. It contains icing and corrosion inhibitors, lubricants, and antistatic agents, and has better safety and combat survivability. JP-8 is the equivalent of commercial Jet-A.

judgment (psychology). The mental process of recognizing and analyzing all pertinent information in a particular situation, a rational evaluation of alternative actions in response to it, and a timely decision on which action to take.

jumper (electrical circuit). A short wire used to temporarily connect two points in an electrical circuit. Jumpers are normally used to temporarily bypass a portion of a circuit for test purposes and for troubleshooting.

jump seat. A removable seat that can be set up between, and slightly behind, the pilot's and copilot's seats in an airplane. A flight mechanic (flight engineer) or observer riding in the jump seat can watch the instruments and can operate some of the auxiliary controls.

junction (thermocouple). The point in a thermocouple at which the dissimilar metals join. A thermocouple has two junctions: the hot, or measuring, junction, and the cold, or reference, junction.

junction box (electrical equipment). A box in which electrical wires can be joined and the junction of the wires protected from damage. Junction boxes are normally made of metal or fiberglass-reinforced plastic.

junction field effect transistor. *See* JFET.

junction transistor. A semiconductor device made of three layers of doped silicon or germanium. In an NPN junction transistor, layers of N-material are used as the emitter and collector. Between the two layers of N material is a very thin layer of P-material, which acts as the base. Electrons flowing between the emitter and base control the electrons flowing between the emitter and collector.

A PNP junction transistor is like an NPN transistor except that the base is made of N-material between an emitter and collector of P-material. *See* illustration for bipolar transistor.

jury strut (airplane structure). A small strut that connects the center of the main wing struts of a strut-braced monoplane to the wing spar. A jury strut stiffens the main struts to prevent their vibrating.

justifiable aircraft equipment. Any equipment necessary for the operation of the aircraft. It does not include equipment or ballast specifically installed, permanently or otherwise, for the purpose of altering the empty weight of an aircraft to meet the maximum payload capacity.

J

Kilo

K. The abbreviation for the unit of measurement in the metric system equal to one thousand. K stands for kilo. In computer use, K is a measure equal to the number two, raised to its tenth power (2^{10}), and this is equal to 1,024. A computer with a memory of 64K has a memory that can actually store 65,536 bits of information.

kaolin. A fine, white clay used for making ceramic materials and as a filler for certain types of plastic resins.

katabatic wind (meteorology). Any wind blowing downslope. Fall winds, foehns, chinooks, and Santa Anas are katabatic winds.

K-band (aircraft radar). A type of radar that operates in the frequency range from approximately 10.9 to 36.0 gigahertz. The wavelength of K-band radar is between about 2.73 to 0.83 centimeters.

keel (seaplane structure). The main longitudinal structural member extending along the center line of the bottom of a seaplane hull or float.

keeper (magnet). A piece of soft iron placed across the poles of a magnet when the magnet is not being used. Magnetic energy is used to force lines of flux through the air between the poles, and the loss of this energy partially demagnetizes the magnet.

The amount of energy used is determined by the reluctance (the opposition to the passage of the lines of flux) of the material between the poles. The soft iron keeper has a very low reluctance compared with air, and when the lines of flux travel through the keeper rather than through the air, less energy is used, and the magnet self-demagnetizes less.

Kelvin bridge (resistance measuring instrument). A form of precision resistance-measuring instrument which is a modification of the Wheatstone bridge. A Kelvin bridge minimizes the effect of lead and contact resistance and is used for accurate measurements of low resistances.

Kelvin temperature (absolute temperature). Temperature measured from absolute zero on a scale using the same divisions as are used in the Celsius system. Water freezes at 273°K and boils at 373°K.

Kennelly-Heaviside layer (atmospheric layer). A layer of ionized particles in the atmosphere at an altitude of between 100 and 120 kilometers above the surface of the earth. Some radio waves cannot penetrate these particles, and they bounce back to the earth. The Kennelly-Heaviside layer is also called the Heaviside layer and the E-layer.

kerf. The slit (the narrow slot, or opening) made by a saw blade as it cuts through wood, metal, or plastic, or by a cutting torch as it cuts through metal.

kerosine (petroleum product). A light (specific gravity of about 0.8), almost colorless hydrocarbon liquid obtained from crude oil by the process of fractional distillation. Kerosine is used as a fuel for lamps and stoves and as a base for turbine engine fuel, and is commonly called coal oil.

The name kerosine was originally spelled kerosene, but the "ene" ending wrongly implied that kerosine is made of unsaturated compounds (compounds having atoms bound together with more than one bond). To keep the spelling of the name from giving the wrong idea of the chemical composition of the material, the spelling was changed in 1957 by petroleum chemists to kerosine.

Ketts saw (sheet-metal cutting tool). A power-operated saw used for cutting various thicknesses of metal sheet. The metal is cut with a small-diameter circular saw blade mounted in the head of this handheld tool.

Kevlar. A patented synthetic aramid fiber noted for its flexibility and light weight. It is to a great extent replacing fiberglass as a reinforcing fabric for composite aircraft construction.

key (telegraph). A form of electrical switch used to break a continuous wave of radio-frequency alternating current into a series of dots and dashes for use in continuous wave (CW) radio transmission. The key allows the operator to send the dots and dashes in the sequence needed to transmit information by Morse code.

key (*verb*). To initiate an action by depressing a key or a button.

keyhole saw. A small handsaw with a stiff, tapered blade. The blade of a keyhole saw can start its cut through a small hole drilled in the material. A keyhole saw is a form of compass saw.

keyway. A lengthwise groove cut in the outside of a shaft. A similar keyway cut into the side of the hole in the hub that fits on the shaft is aligned with the keyway on the shaft, and a rectangular piece of metal called a key locks the keyways together, preventing the hub turning on the shaft.

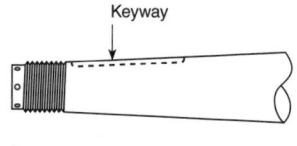

Keyway

keyway

K-factor (sheet metal layout). A factor used in sheet metal work to determine the setback for other than a 90° bend. K-factors are found in charts in most sheet metal working handbooks.

Setback = K · (bend radius + metal thickness).

For bends of less than 90°, the value of K is less than 1; for bends greater than 90°, the value of K is greater than 1.

kHz. The abbreviation for kilohertz (1,000 cycles per second).

KIAS. Knots indicated airspeed.

kickback (reciprocating engine operation). A condition of engine operation in which the engine tries to run backward when it is being started. Kickback is caused by the ignition spark occurring while the piston is moving slowly upward on the compression stroke. Since the piston is moving slowly, the pressure from the expanding gases is applied to the piston before it passes over top center of the compression stroke. Kickback is prevented by timing the ignition so the starting spark occurs late.

kick-in pressure (hydraulic system operation). The pressure at which an unloading valve causes a hydraulic pump to direct its fluid into the system manifold.

kick-out pressure (hydraulic system operation). The pressure at which an unloading valve shuts off the flow of fluid into the system pressure manifold and directs it back to the reservoir under a much reduced pressure.

kilo (k). The metric prefix that means 1,000. A kilogram is one thousand grams, a kilometer is one thousand meters, and a kilohertz is one thousand cycles per second.

kilogram. One of the commonly used units in the metric system for measuring mass. One kilogram is the mass of one thousand cubic centimeters of pure water. In the International Bureau of Standards in Paris, France, there is a cylinder of platinum having a mass of exactly one kilogram. It is known as the standard kilogram.

kilomega (kM). A term that has, in the past, been used to represent the quantity 1,000,000,000 or 1×10^9. The prefix giga is now used in place of kilomega.

kilovolt (kV) (electrical measurement). Electrical pressure equivalent to 1,000 volts.

kilovolt-amperes reactive (kVAR) (electrical measurement). A measure of reactive power. *See* reactive power (electrical power).

kindling temperature. The temperature to which a material must be heated for it to combine with oxygen from the air and burn. The kindling temperature of a material is also called its ignition temperature, or its kindling point.

kind of operation (for a certificate holder). One of the various operations (for example, domestic, flag, supplemental, commuter, or on-demand) a certificate holder is authorized to conduct, as specified in its operations specifications.

kinematic viscosity. The ratio of the absolute viscosity of a fluid to its density. Kinematic viscosity is measured in centistokes.

kinesthesia. The sensations from receptors in muscles, tendons, and joints by which movements are detected or perceived; by "feel."

kinetic energy. Energy in an object caused by its motion. Kinetic energy is equal to one half the mass of the body times the square of its speed.

$$E_K = \frac{M \cdot V^2}{2}$$

kink (form of metal damage). A sharp bend or twist in a piece of wire, tubing, or sheet metal.

Kirchhoff's current law. One of the basic laws of electrical circuits, stating that the sum of the current flowing away from any point in an electrical circuit is equal to the sum of the current flowing to that point.

Kirchhoff's voltage law. One of the basic laws of electrical circuits stating that the algebraic sum of all of the voltage drops in any closed circuit is equal to zero. Another way to think of this is that the sum of all the voltage drops in a circuit is equal to the sum of the voltage sources in the circuit.

K

kirksite. A Zinc based alloy used for dies for forming sheet metal and for molding plastics.

kite (form of flying machine). A captive flying machine made of a lightweight framework covered with paper or cloth. The kite is tethered to the ground and is held up by aerodynamic lift produced as air flows over its surface. *14 CFR Part 1:* "A framework, covered with paper, cloth, metal, or other material, intended to be flown at the end of a rope or cable, and having as its only support the force of the wind moving past its surfaces."

kiting. Taxiing a powered parachute on the ground with the wing inflated and overhead.

klystron (electronic component). An electron tube used as an oscillator or amplifier of microwave energy.

K-monel. An alloy of nickel, copper, and aluminum. K-monel is nonmagnetic, heat-treatable, corrosion resistant, and has high strength.

knife-edge. A device having a sharp edge of hardened steel that resembles the edge of a knife. Knife-edges are used as fulcrums in many types of precision balancing instruments.

knife switch (electrical component). A type of electrical switch having a movable blade (the knife) for one of the terminals and two contacts that are spring-loaded together for the other terminal. When the blade is between the contacts, the switch is closed, and current flows in the circuit. When the blade is lifted from the contacts, the switch is open, and no current flows. Knife switches are seldom used in aircraft electrical circuits.

knock (reciprocating engine operation). A loud rattling noise inside the cylinders of a reciprocating engine caused by shock waves produced by detonating fuel. The fuel-air mixture burning inside a cylinder is supposed to move across the face of the piston with a smooth flame front. But if the wrong type or wrong amount of fuel is used, the fuel-air mixture ahead of the flame front gets so hot it explodes. The explosion, called detonation, causes shock waves and produces a tremendous amount of pressure in the cylinder. The resultant stresses can damage the engine.

knot (measure of speed). A measure of speed used in aerial navigation. One knot is equal to one nautical mile per hour.

One knot   =   1.151 statute miles per hour
　　　　 =   1.688 feet per second
　　　　 =   1.852 kilometers per hour
　　　　 =   0.5144 meters per second

knot (wood). A hard, usually round section of a tree branch embedded in a board. The grain of the knot is perpendicular to the grain of the board. Knots decrease the strength of the board and must be avoided where strength is needed.

knowledge. Information that humans are consciously aware of and can articulate.

knowledge exam. A multiple-choice test used by the FAA to assure that applicants have the required aeronautical knowledge for the certificate and/or rating they seek. This test must be passed with a grade of 70% or higher before being allowed to take to the practical test or checkride.

"Known traffic" (air traffic control). When used as part of an ATC clearance, this means aircraft whose altitude, position, and intentions are known to ATC.

knuckle pin (radial engine component). A short, high-strength, polished steel pin that connects a link rod in a radial engine to the master rod. A radial engine has only one throw on the crankshaft for each row of cylinders. Only one connecting rod (the master rod) goes around the throw of the crankshaft and connects one piston to the crankshaft.

The pistons in the other cylinders are connected to the master rod by link rods (articulated rods), and the link rods are connected to the master rod with knuckle pins.

knurl. A type of finish used on the handle of some metal tools to keep the handle from slipping in your hands. Knurling is done by pressing a special tool against the handle while it is being turned in a lathe.

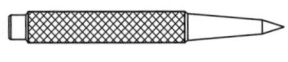

knurled handle

Kollsman window. The barometric scale window of a sensitive altimeter. *See* barometric scale.

Koroseal lacing. A plastic lacing material that is available in round or rectangular cross sections and is used for holding wire bundles and tubing together. It holds tension on knots indefinitely and is impervious to petroleum products.

kraft paper. A tough brown wrapping paper, like that used for paper bags.

Krueger flaps (aircraft flight control). A form of leading-edge flap used on the wings of some high-performance airplanes. When a Krueger flap is retracted into the wing, the leading edge has the shape that allows efficient high-speed flight.

When the airplane is prepared for landing or takeoff, the Krueger flaps are extended, and they deflect the airflow into the trailing-edge flaps. The combination of leading-edge and trailing-edge flaps allows the airplane wing to develop its needed lift at the lowest possible airspeed.

krypton. A colorless, odorless, tasteless, inert, gaseous chemical element. Krypton's symbol is Kr, its atomic number is 36, and its atomic weight is 83.80. Krypton is used to fill fluorescent lamps.

LAAS (low altitude alert system). An automated function of the ground radar that alerts the controller when a Mode C transponder-equipped aircraft on an IFR flight plan is below a predetermined minimum safe altitude.

labyrinth seal. A type of air and/or oil seal used around the main-shaft bearings in a gas turbine engine. The seal consists of a series of rotating blades that almost contact the seal land. A small amount of air flows between the seal and the land and prevents oil flowing past the seal.

lacing cord (aircraft fabric covering material). A strong cotton, linen, or synthetic fiber string used to lace fabric to an aircraft structure. Lacing cord is also called rib-stitching cord.

"lack of common experience" (in teaching/learning process). In communication, a difficulty which arises because words have different meanings for the source and the receiver of information due to their differing backgrounds.

lacquer (finishing material). A material used to decorate and protect a surface. Lacquer is made of a film base, solvents, plasticizers, and thinners. The film base forms a tough film over the surface when it dries. The solvents dissolve the film base so it can be applied as a liquid. The plasticizers give the film base the needed resilience, and the thinners dilute the lacquer so it can be applied with a spray gun.

Lacquer is sprayed on the surface as a liquid, and as soon as the solvents and the thinner evaporate, the film base remains as a tough, decorative coating.

lag. The delay that occurs before an instrument needle attains a stable indication.

lagging (lubrication system component). A type of insulation wrapped around some of the lines in an aircraft engine lubrication system to keep it from losing heat in the oil to the outside air.

lagging current (electrical current). Current flowing in an AC circuit that has more inductive reactance than capacitive reactance. Voltage changes occur in an inductive circuit before current changes, and the current is said to lag the voltage.

LAHSO (land-and-hold-short operations) (air traffic control). Operations which include simultaneous takeoffs and landings and/or simultaneous landings when a landing aircraft is able and is instructed by the controller to hold short of the intersecting runway/taxiway or designated hold-short point. Pilots are expected to promptly inform the controller if the hold-short clearance cannot be accepted.

LAHSO-dry. Land-and-hold-short operations on runways that are dry.

LAHSO-wet. Land-and-hold-short operations on runways that are wet (but not contaminated).

lambert (luminance). The unit of luminance (photometric brightness) that is the same as $1/\pi$ (0.3183) candela per square centimeter.

laminar flow (aerodynamics). A type of airflow over an airfoil in which the air passes over the surface in smooth layers with a minimum of turbulence. With most airfoils, there is a layer of air adjacent to the surface that flows in a random fashion, even sometimes reversing its direction of flow. This is called the boundary layer.

A laminar-flow airfoil is designed in such a way that the boundary layer has a minimum thickness, and nearly all the air flows in smooth layers. Laminar flow of the air decreases the drag produced by the airfoil.

laminated core (electrical machinery). The core of an electrical transformer made up of a stack of thin sheets, or laminations, of soft iron or a special highly permeable steel, insulated from each other by an oxide or varnish coating.

Eddy currents are induced into the cores of transformers by alternating current flowing in the windings surrounding them, and these eddy currents produce heat and cause electrical losses. The high resistance of the laminated core opposes the flow of eddy current and minimizes the losses.

laminated plastic material. A type of reinforced plastic resin made by laminating, or stacking together, layers of cloth, paper, or wood that are impregnated with plastic resin. The layers of the material are forced together by pressure, and the resin is cured with heat.

laminated wood. A type of wood product made by gluing together several thin strips of wood. In laminated wood, the grain of all the pieces runs in the same direction. A wooden propeller is made of several pieces of hardwood laminated together.

lampblack. A form of almost pure carbon made by burning oil or coal in an atmosphere in which there is not enough oxygen for complete combustion. Lampblack is used for making brushes for electric motors and generators, for the graphite in lead pencils, for the pigment in paint, and for mixing with rubber for making tires.

land (reciprocating engine piston component). The portion of a piston between the ring grooves.

land (splined shaft). The portion of a splined shaft between the grooves.

land-and-hold-short operations. *See* LAHSO.

"land as soon as possible" (air traffic control). A phrase used in ATC–pilot communications that means to land without delay at the nearest suitable area, such as an open field, at which a safe approach and landing is assured.

"land as soon as practical" (air traffic control). A phrase used in ATC–pilot communications indicating that the landing site and duration of flight are at the discretion of the pilot. Extended flight beyond the nearest approved landing area is not recommended.

land breeze (meteorology). A coastal breeze blowing from land to sea. Land breezes, which normally blow at night, are caused by a temperature difference when the sea surface is warmer than the adjacent land. Land breezes alternate with sea breezes, which blow inland during the day when the sea surface temperature is cooler than the land.

lander (space vehicle). A space vehicle designed to land on a celestial body, such as the moon or one of the planets.

"land immediately" (air traffic control). A phrase used in ATC–pilot communications that means the urgency of the landing is paramount. The primary consideration is to ensure the survival of the occupants. Landing in trees, water, or other unsafe areas should be considered only as a last resort.

landing area (air traffic control). Any locality either on land, water, or structures, including airports/heliports and intermediate landing fields, which is used, or intended to be used, for the landing and takeoff of aircraft. Landing areas may or may not have facilities for the shelter and servicing of aircraft, or for receiving or discharging passengers or cargo.

landing direction indicator. A device which visually indicates the direction in which landings and takeoffs should be made. Wind cones, wind socks, and tetrahedrons are commonly used landing direction indicators.

landing distance available (ICAO). The length of runway which is declared available and suitable for the ground run of an aeroplane landing.

landing flaps (airplane secondary control surfaces). An airplane control surface used to increase the camber, or curvature, of the wing airfoil. This increases both the lift and the drag produced by the wing.

By increasing the lift, the airplane can be landed at a slower airspeed, and by increasing the drag, the airplane can descend at a steeper angle without building up excessive airspeed. Some landing flaps increase the area of the wing as well as the camber. *See* plain flap, split flap, slotted flap, Fowler flap, and triple-slotted flap.

landing gear (aircraft component). The part of an aircraft structure that supports the aircraft when it is not flying. For operation from runways and dry ground, the landing gear uses wheels. Operation from snow and ice is done with skis, and operation from water is done with a landing gear using floats.

Wheeled landing gear is by far the most common, and there are two basic types: tricycle and tail wheel-type. The tail wheel-type landing gear is often called a conventional landing gear. In a tricycle landing gear, two main wheels are located behind the center of gravity, and a third wheel, nearly as large as the main wheels, is located near the nose of the aircraft. In a tail wheel-type landing gear, the two main wheels are ahead of the center of gravity, and a much smaller wheel is located at the tail of the aircraft.

Landing gear can be either fixed so it is always extended in the airstream or retractable. Retractable landing gear can be folded into the wing or fuselage when the aircraft is off the ground, reducing the drag caused by air flowing over the structure.

landing gear extended speed. *14 CFR Part 1:* "The maximum speed at which an aircraft can be safely flown with the landing gear extended."

landing gear operating speed. *14 CFR Part 1:* "The maximum speed at which the landing gear can be safely extended or retracted."

landing gear position indicating system. A system required on all aircraft having retractable landing gear to show the pilot the position of the landing gear. The most commonly used system on modern aircraft is a series of lights. When all three wheels are down and locked, three green lights appear on the instrument panel. A red light indicates that the landing gear is in transit. It has been released by the up-locks, but it has not yet locked down.

landing gear warning system. A warning system used in an aircraft with retractable landing gear, to warn the pilot of an unsafe landing gear condition. A red light indicates that any of the wheels are in an unsafe condition, and an aural warning system sounds a horn if any of the wheels are not down and locked when the throttles are retarded for landing.

landing light (aircraft component). A high-intensity spotlight mounted on an aircraft and aimed in such a direction that it shines on the runway when the aircraft is on the final approach for landing.

landing minimums, IFR (aircraft operation). The minimum visibility prescribed for landing a civil aircraft while using an instrument approach procedure. The minimums apply with other limitations set forth in 14 CFR Part 91 with respect to the minimum descent altitude (MDA) or decision height (DH) prescribed in the instrument approach procedures.

landing roll. The distance from the point of touchdown to the point where the aircraft can be brought to a stop or can exit the runway.

landing sequence. The order in which aircraft are positioned for landing.

landing/takeoff area. Any locality, either on land, water, or structures, including airports/heliports and intermediate landing fields, which is used, or intended to be used, for the landing and takeoff of aircraft. A landing/takeoff area is not required to have facilities for shelter, servicing, and receiving or discharging passengers or cargo.

landing weight (aircraft specification). The maximum weight an aircraft is allowed to have for landing. Landings put far more stress into an aircraft structure than takeoffs, and therefore large aircraft that fly for long distances are allowed to have a greater weight for takeoff than for landing.

Airplanes approved for a greater takeoff weight than landing weight must have some method of jettisoning enough fuel to bring the weight down to the allowable landing weight if the aircraft should have to land before enough fuel has been consumed by the engines.

landing wires (airplane structural components). Brace wires used to support the weight of the wings during landing and when they are not producing lift. The landing wires of a biplane run from the center section of the upper wing to the interplane strut on the lower wing.

landplane. An airplane with a wheeled landing gear that enables it to operate from a hard surface, rather than from water or snow.

lanthanum. A soft, silvery-white, malleable, ductile, metallic, rare-earth chemical element. Lanthanum's symbol is La, its atomic number is 57, and its atomic weight is 138.91. Lanthanum is used as an element in making glass for special lights.

lap belt. A name sometimes given to a seat belt or safety belt used to hold a person seated in an aircraft. A lap belt passes across a person's lap.

lap joint. A type of joint made between two pieces of material in which one piece is lapped over the other and the two fastened together. Lap joints are used to join sheets of metal by welding, riveting, or bolting. Lap joints are also used for joining sheets of wood, paper, or cloth with adhesives.

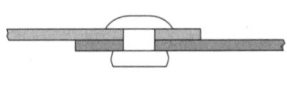

lap joint

lapping (machining operation). A method of producing a close fit between two metal parts by rubbing them together with a very fine abrasive lapping compound between them. The fit of a lapped joint is checked by removing all the lapping compound and lightly coating one of the surfaces with Prussian blue transfer dye. The parts are reassembled and rubbed together. If the parts fit as they should, the Prussian blue will transfer evenly to the part that was not covered. If not enough blue transfers, more lapping is required.

lapping compound. A very fine abrasive paste used to wear away a metal surface to make it smooth, and to assure a perfect fit between two machined surfaces. Lapping compound is similar to valve-grinding compound.

laps (metal defects). A type of metal defect produced in the rolling mill. Ridges or bulges on the surface of the metal are folded over and forced down into the metal as it is being rolled. Laps decrease the strength of the metal.

lapse rate (meteorology). The rate of decrease of an atmospheric variable with height. Lapse rates often refer to a decrease in temperature with height.

lap winding (electrical armature). A method of connecting the armature coils in a DC generator or motor. The ends of each coil on the armature are connected to the next adjacent commutator segment, and the coils lap over each other. Lap winding differs from wave winding in which the ends of the coils are attached to segments on the opposite side of the commutator.

large aircraft. *14 CFR Part 1:* "Aircraft of more than 12,500 pounds, maximum certificated takeoff weight."

large calorie (C). A unit of heat energy. One large calorie, also called a kilocalorie, is the amount of heat energy needed to raise the temperature of one kilogram of water one degree Celsius. One large calorie is equal to 1,000 small calories.

large scale integration (LSI) (digital electronics). A method of miniaturization of electronic circuit components, in which 100 or more gates are built into a single integrated circuit (IC) chip. LSI techniques lower the cost per gate of logic components.

LASCR (light-activated silicon controlled rectifier). A semiconductor device having two P-sections and two N-sections. Light falling on the LASCR produces gate current that triggers it into a state of conduction.

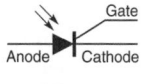

LASCR

laser. A coined word meaning Light Amplification by Stimulated Emission of Radiation. A laser changes incoherent light, light whose vibrations do not have any consistent phase relationship, into coherent light, light whose vibrations are all in phase.

The light beam from a laser is highly concentrated, very narrow, and has an extremely high intensity. High-power lasers produce a great deal of heat in an extremely small area, and laser technology is opening new doors in all aspects of science.

laser memory (computer memory). A method of storing a large amount of digital information permanently and inexpensively on a disk similar to but smaller than a phonograph record. A high-power laser (*see* laser) burns extremely small pits into the reflective surface of a disk to write, or record, digital data on the disk. The information stored on the disk is read by the reflection or the lack of reflection of a low-power laser shone on the surface. A reflection is read as a logic one, and a space where there is no reflection, an area caused by a pit, is read as a logic zero.

The fact that billions of bits can be stored on a relatively small disk makes laser memory an inexpensive method of storing video programs.

laser printer. A type of printer used to produce a hard copy of the information being processed by a computer. A laser (*see* laser) shines a series of dots of light in a matrix pattern onto the surface of the paper as it moves in front of the print head, and each dot of light leaves the paper with an electrostatic charge.

A dust of metallic powder, called toner, is blown across the paper, and some of it sticks to the charged areas. None, however, sticks to the uncharged portion of the paper. The paper with the powder sticking to the charged areas passes over a heater, which fuses, or melts, the powder into the paper to form a permanent image.

laser ring gyro. A device that can replace mechanical gyroscopes in aircraft by using laser light to detect motion. A laser ring gyro has no moving parts and consequently has no precession due to friction.

laser tachometer. A highly accurate tachometer that shines a laser beam on the rotating element and senses the reflection from a reflective tape or contrasting mark. The reflected laser beam is converted into electrical pulses which are counted and displayed on a monitoring instrument.

laser welding. A method of welding by the heat produced by a laser beam. The high-intensity, concentrated heat allows the welding of exotic alloys that cannot be welded by other methods.

last assigned altitude. The last altitude/flight level assigned by ATC and acknowledged by the pilot.

last-chance filter (gas turbine engine component). An oil filter installed in the lubricating system of a gas turbine engine just ahead of the jets that spray oil onto the bearings. These filters trap any contaminants that get past the main system filters and prevent the oil jets becoming clogged. Last-chance filters cannot be serviced during normal engine maintenance. They are cleaned only when the engine is disassembled for overhaul.

latching relay (locking relay). A relay that, once energized, remains in its energized condition after the current stops flowing in its coil. When the relay is energized, the contacts are locked in the energized position by a mechanical latch. A mechanical release must be actuated to allow the relay to return to its de-energized condition. Latching relays are being replaced to a great extent by solid-state flip-flop circuits.

latent heat. Heat added to a material which changes its physical state, but does not change its temperature. When a pan of water is put on a hot stove and heat is added to it, its temperature rises—but in standard conditions, only until it reaches 100°C. Heat which changes the temperature of water is called sensible heat. If additional heat is added to the water, it will boil away, or change from liquid water into water vapor, but its temperature will not change. Heat added to water after it begins to boil is called latent heat—more correctly, latent heat of evaporation, or latent heat of vaporization. When water vapor is cooled until it condenses into liquid water, the latent heat which caused the evaporation is given up by the water and absorbed by the surrounding air.

latent heat of condensation. Heat released during the change of state that occurs when water vapor changes into liquid water.

latent heat of fusion. Heat absorbed during the change of state that occurs when solid water (ice) changes into liquid water.

latent heat of sublimation. Heat absorbed during the change of state that occurs when ice changes directly into water vapor without passing through the liquid state.

latent heat of vaporization. Heat absorbed during the change of state in which liquid water is changed into water vapor.

lateral axis of an airplane. An imaginary line passing through the center of gravity of an airplane and extending across the airplane parallel to a line joining the wing tips. The lateral axis is also called the pitch axis, and movement of the elevators rotates an airplane about its lateral axis.

lateral axis

lateral balance (aircraft stability). Balance around the longitudinal, or roll, axis of an aircraft.

lateral navigation (LNAV). A function of area navigation (RNAV) equipment which calculates, displays, and provides lateral guidance to a profile or path.

lateral offset moment (helicopter operation). The moment, in pound-inches (lb-in), of a force that tends to rotate a helicopter about its longitudinal axis. The lateral offset moment is the product of the weight of the object and its distance from butt line zero. Lateral offset moments that tend to rotate the aircraft clockwise are positive, and those that tend to rotate it counterclockwise are negative.

lateral precision performance with vertical guidance (LPV). A type of approach with vertical guidance (APV) based on WAAS, published on RNAV (GPS) approach charts. This procedure takes advantage of the precise lateral guidance available from WAAS. The minima is published as a decision altitude (DA).

lateral separation (air traffic control). The lateral spacing of aircraft at the same altitude by requiring operation on different routes or in different geographic locations.

lateral stability (aircraft stability). The stability of an airplane about its longitudinal axis, the axis passing through an airplane from nose to tail. If an airplane is disturbed from level flight so that one wing drops, lateral stability returns it to a level-flight attitude.

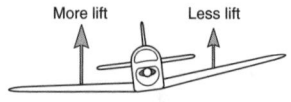

lateral stability

When a wing drops, the airplane begins to slip to that side, and the lift produced by the lowered wing increases. At the same time, the lift produced by the raised wing decreases. This uneven lift, caused by lateral stability, returns the airplane to level flight.

lateral vibration (helicopter operation). Vibration of a helicopter which causes the rotor to move back and forth in a lateral plane. Lateral vibration is often caused by an out-of-balance main rotor.

lathe (machine tool). A metalworking or woodworking power tool used to change the shape or size of cylindrically shaped objects. The material to be shaped is clamped horizontally in a chuck and is rotated. The unclamped end of the material is steadied by the lathe tail stock. Cutting tools are fed into the material from the side to remove unwanted material.

latitude. The angular measurement of distance on the surface of the earth, north and south of the equator. Latitude is measured in degrees, minutes, and seconds, and parallels of latitude cut the earth into imaginary parallel slices. The equator, which is zero degrees latitude, forms a belt around the center of the earth. The north pole is 90° north latitude, and the south pole is 90° south latitude.

launching pad (rocket operation). A smooth, debris-free, nonflammable area from which rockets are fired to launch them.

launch weight (ultralight flight). The total weight of a hang glider or an ultralight airplane when it is ready for flight. It includes any equipment, instruments and the maximum quantity of fuel and oil that it is designed to carry but does not include the weight of any float equipment (to a maximum of 75 lbs), the weight of the occupant or the weight of any parachute installation.

law of conservation of energy. One of the basic laws of physics stating that energy can be neither created nor destroyed, but it can be changed from one form into other forms. Regardless of the form or forms into which the energy is changed, the total amount of energy always remains the same.

lawrencium. A synthetic, radioactive chemical element. Lawrencium's symbol is Lr, and its atomic number is 103. One of the isotopes of lawrencium has a mass number of 257 and a half-life of eight seconds.

layer (meteorology). With regard to sky cover, layers refer to clouds or other obscuring phenomena whose bases are at approximately the same level. The layer may be continuous or composed of detached elements. The term layer does not imply that a clear space exists between the layers or that the clouds or obscuring phenomena composing them are of the same type.

lay line (flexible hose). A colored line that runs the length of a piece of flexible hose. A lay line is used to indicate whether or not the hose was twisted during installation. If the lay line spirals around the hose, the hose is twisted.

lay-up (composite structure). The placement of the various layers of resin-impregnated fabric in a mold in the process of manufacturing a piece of laminated composite material.

lazy eight (flight maneuver). A maneuver designed to develop perfect coordination of controls through a wide range of airspeeds and altitudes so that certain accuracy points are reached with planned attitude and airspeed. In its execution, the dive, climb, and turn are all combined, and the combinations are varied and applied throughout the performance range of the airplane.

L-band radar. Airborne radar which operates in the frequency range of 0.39 to 1.55 gigahertz. The wavelength of L-band radar is between 77 and 19 centimeters.

LC circuit (electrical circuit). An alternating current circuit containing both inductance (L) and capacitance (C). An LC circuit is considered to have no resistance. In a purely capacitive circuit, changes in current lead changes in voltage by 90°. In a purely inductive circuit, current changes lag 90° behind voltage changes. Because the effects of capacitance and inductance are 180° apart, the total opposition to the flow of current in an LC circuit is the difference between the capacitive and the inductive reactances.

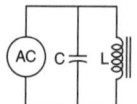

LC parallel circuit

LCD (liquid crystal display). A type of visual display used in digital watches, computers, calculators, and some of the newer aircraft instruments. An extremely thin layer of a normally transparent liquid crystal material is sealed between two sheets of glass. The outsides of the two pieces of glass are coated with an electrically conductive oxide. The oxide coating on one side of the glass is etched to form the segments of letters and numbers, and each segment is connected by a printed circuit lead to a connector at the edge of the display.

The back of the display is covered with a reflecting material, and a piece of transparent polarizing material is placed over the display to polarize the light passing through it. When light is polarized, all its waves vibrate in the same plane.

When a voltage is placed between the oxide coatings on the two sides of the display, the molecules in the liquid crystal material arrange themselves in such a way that the polarized light cannot pass through them. The liquid crystal material under the segment having voltage on it shows up as though it were black against the reflected background.

LCR circuit (electrical circuit). An alternating current circuit containing inductance (L), capacitance (C), and resistance (R). The total opposition to the flow of current in an LCR circuit is the circuit impedance (Z), which is the vector sum of the total reactance (the difference between the inductive and the capacitive reactances), and the resistance. *See* impedance.

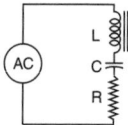

LCR series circuit

LDA (localizer-type directional aid). A NAVAID used for nonprecision instrument approaches, with utility and accuracy comparable to a localizer. An LDA is not a part of a complete ILS and is not aligned with the runway.

L/D$_{MAX}$. The maximum ratio between total lift (L) and total drag (D). This point provides the best glide speed. Any deviation from the best glide speed increases drag and reduces the distance you can glide.

L/D or lift/drag ratio (aerodynamic parameter). A measure of efficiency of an airfoil. L/D is the ratio of the lift to the total drag, or the coefficient of lift to the coefficient of drag at a specified angle of attack. The lift/drag ratio is commonly called the L-over-D ratio.

lead. A soft, malleable, ductile, bluish-white, dense, metallic chemical element. Lead's symbol is Pb, its atomic number is 82, and its atomic weight is 207.19. Lead is used in the manufacture of soft solder, type metal, plates for lead-acid batteries, and radiation shielding.

lead-acid battery. A popular form of storage battery used in automobiles and airplanes. The positive plate of a fully charged lead-acid battery is made of lead peroxide, and the negative plate is pure lead. The electrolyte is a solution of sulfuric acid and water. When a lead-acid battery discharges, both plates change into lead sulfate, and some of the acid in the electrolyte changes into water.

Passing electrical current through a lead-acid battery from its negative terminal to its positive terminal reverses the chemical action which took place as the battery discharged, and the battery becomes charged again. In the charging process, sulfate ions are driven from the plates back into the electrolyte.

lead-off question (in learning process). A question used by an instructor in the guided discussion method to open up an area for discussion and get it started.

leading current (electrical current). Current flowing in an AC circuit that has more capacitive reactance than inductive reactance. Current must flow into a capacitive circuit before voltage can build up across it; therefore, in a capacitive circuit, the current leads the voltage.

leading edge. The edge of a moving object that reaches a point in space or time ahead of the rest of the object. In an airplane wing or a helicopter rotor, the leading edge is the part of the wing or rotor the moving air touches first. In a pulse of electrical energy, the leading edge is the first part of the pulse that moves away from the quiescent, or at-rest, state.

leading edge devices (airplane secondary control devices). High lift devices which are found on the leading edge of the airfoil. The most common types are fixed slots, movable slats, and leading edge flaps.

leading-edge flap (aerodynamic control). A type of aerodynamic control surface, used on some airplanes to increase the lift produced by the wing. Part of the leading edge bends downward to increase the camber (the curvature) of the airfoil. Increasing the camber increases the pressure difference across the wing, which in turn increases the lift. Leading-edge flaps are used for both takeoff and landing, to increase the lift at low airspeed.

lead-lag hinge (helicopter rotor system). The hinge in the root of a helicopter rotor blade that allows the blade tip to move back and forth in its plane of rotation. Movement about the lead-lag hinge is called drag, and this movement is opposed by drag dampers. A lead-lag hinge is also called an alpha hinge.

L

lead of a screw thread. The linear distance from the apex of one screw thread to the apex of the next thread. Lead is also the distance the screw advances in one complete rotation.

lead radial. The radial at which the turn from the DME arc to the inbound course is started.

leaf brake (sheet metal shop tool). A large bending tool used to make straight bends across a sheet of metal. The metal to be bent is clamped between a flat lower jaw and an upper jaw fitted with a radius bar having the proper bend radius. A heavy leaf, mounted on a hinge, folds up to bend the metal over the radius bar. A leaf brake is also called a cornice brake.

leaf spring. A flat spring hinged at one end and arched in the center. The load is applied to the center of the arch and is absorbed as the spring alternately straightens out and returns to its arched shape.

leakage (electrical). Electrical current that passes through an insulator which is supposed to stop all flow. The amount of leakage is determined by the dielectric strength of the insulator and the amount of voltage, or electrical pressure, across the insulator.

leakage current (semiconductor characteristic). The flow of minority carriers in a semiconductor device when the junction is reverse-biased. Both high voltage and high temperature cause electrons to break out of their bonds and leave holes. These electrons and holes are attracted to the junction, where they recombine and cause a small amount of current to flow. Leakage current increases as the temperature of the device increases.

leakage flux (magnetism). Magnetic flux that does not pass directly between the poles of a magnet. Leakage flux does no useful work.

lean blow out. *See* lean flameout.

lean flameout (gas turbine engine operation). A condition in which the flame inside a gas turbine engine goes out because there is not enough fuel for the amount of air flowing through the engine. Turbine engine fuel controls are designed to measure the air flowing through the engine and adjust the fuel flow so a lean flameout, or lean die-out, cannot occur. A lean flameout is also called a lean die-out.

lean mixture. A fuel-air mixture that contains more than 15 parts of air to 1 part of fuel, by weight.

leans, the. A physical sensation caused by an abrupt correction of a banked attitude entered too slowly to stimulate the motion sensing system in the inner ear. The abrupt correction can create the illusion of banking in the opposite direction.

learning. A change in behavior as a result of experience.

learning plateau. A learning phenomenon where progress appears to cease or slow down for a significant period of time before once again increasing.

learning style. Preferred way(s) by which people learn. Common learning styles include visual, auditory, and kinesthetic (tactile, or hands-on). Learning skills can be loosely grouped into physical and cognitive styles.

learning theory. A body of principles advocated by psychologists and educators to explain how people acquire skills, knowledge, and attitudes.

least significant bit. *See* LSB.

least significant digit. *See* LSD.

Leclanche cell (batteries). Another name for a carbon-zinc cell. An ordinary carbon-zinc flashlight battery is an example of a Leclanche cell. The negative terminal is the zinc can that forms the outside shell, and the positive terminal is a carbon rod supported inside the can by the electrolyte.

The electrolyte is a moist paste of sal ammoniac (ammonium chloride), with manganese dioxide mixed in it to absorb the hydrogen bubbles which form on the carbon rod as the battery is used.

lecture method. An educational presentation usually delivered by an instructor to a group of students with the use of instructional aids and training devices. Lectures are useful for the presentation of new material, summarizing ideas, and showing relationships between theory and practice.

LED (light emitting diode). An optoelectronic device that emits visible light when electrons pass through it. P and N impurities are mixed with such chemical compounds as indium phosphide, gallium arsenide, and zinc selenide to form a P-N junction.

LED light emitting diode

When the P-N junction is reverse-biased (the negative terminal of the voltage source is connected to the P-material), no electrons flow, and the LED remains dark. But when the diode is forward-biased (the negative terminal of the voltage source connected to the N-material), electrons flow through the LED, and it emits light.

lee side. The side of an island or mountain away from the direction from which the wind is blowing. The lee side is the side sheltered from the wind.

leeward. Downwind, or the downwind side of an object.

lee wave (meteorology). Any stationary wave disturbance caused by a barrier in a fluid flow. In the atmosphere, when sufficient moisture is present, lee waves are evidenced by lenticular clouds on the lee side of mountain barriers. Lee waves are also called mountain waves or standing waves.

left-hand rule for electric motors. The rule for determining the direction of movement of a current-carrying conductor in a magnetic field. Hold the left hand with the thumb, first finger, and second finger extended so they are at right angles to each other. When the first finger points in the direction of the lines of magnetic flux (from the north pole to the south pole), and the second finger points in the direction of conventional current flow (from positive to negative), the thumb points in the direction the conductor will move. This is also known as Fleming's rule for electric motors.

left-hand rule for generators. Arrange the fingers of your left hand in such a way that the thumb, forefinger, and second finger are at right angles to each other. The thumb points in the direction the conductor in the armature is moving, the first finger points in the direction the magnetic flux passes over the conductors (the flux leaves the north pole and enters the south pole), and the second finger points in the direction the electrons are flowing in the armature conductors (from negative to positive).

left-hand rule for the direction of magnetic flux. Grasp a conductor with your left hand in such a way that the thumb points in the direction electrons are moving (from the negative terminal of the power source to the positive terminal). Your fingers encircle the conductor in the same direction as the lines of magnetic flux.

left-hand rule for the polarity of an electromagnet. Grasp the coil of an electromagnet in such a way that the fingers encircle the coil in the same direction electrons are flowing (from the negative terminal of the power supply to the positive terminal). The thumb points to the north pole of the electromagnet formed by the coil.

left-hand thread. The threads on a bolt or screw which are cut in such a direction that they wind in a counterclockwise direction. A left-hand thread is turned to the left, to screw it in.

left-right indicator (navigation instrument). The course-deviation indicator used with a VOR navigation system. *See* VOR.

legs of a right triangle. The two sides of a right triangle which are joined by the right angle.

LEMAC (leading edge of the mean aerodynamic chord). A reference for many of the aerodynamic measurements used in aircraft design and operation. When the CG of an airplane is given in % MAC, LEMAC is specified in inches from the datum to allow weight and balance computations to relate % MAC to the datum. *See* MAC.

lenticular cloud (meteorology). A species of cloud whose elements have the form of more or less isolated, generally smooth lenses or almonds. Lenticular clouds most often appear in formations on the lee side of a mountain peak as a result of lee waves, and they remain nearly stationary with respect to the terrain.

Lenticular clouds are an indicator of extreme turbulence.

Lenz's law (electrical law). The electrical law explaining induced current. Lenz's law states that the current induced in a conductor cut by lines of magnetic flux flows in the direction opposite to that of the current which produced the lines of flux.

lesson plan. An organized outline for a single instructional period. It is a necessary guide for the instructor in that it tells what to do, in what order to do it, and what procedure to use in teaching the material of a lesson.

level (horizontal condition of a body). A flat, horizontal surface of a body is said to be level when all points on the surface are perpendicular to a line which points directly toward the center of the earth.

level (spirit level, or bubble level). An indicating device used to show a level condition. A curved glass tube is almost, but not completely, filled with a clear liquid, and since the tube is not entirely full, there is a small air bubble in the liquid. This bubble, being much lighter than the liquid, always rises to the highest point in the tube.

The curved tube is mounted in a long straight bar, or housing, in such a way that the bubble rises to the center of the tube when the housing is perpendicular to the pull of gravity (perpendicular to a line pointing to the center of the earth).

leveling lugs (aircraft component). Brackets or other structural devices installed in an aircraft in such a way that when the aircraft is in its level-flight attitude, a straightedge placed across the lugs will be level.

leveling means (aircraft specification). The method specified by the aircraft manufacturer to determine the level-flight attitude of an aircraft. The leveling means may require the use of a spirit level or a plumb bob.

level of free convection (meteorology). The level at which a parcel of air lifted dry-adiabatically until it becomes saturated, and then moist-adiabatically would become warmer than its surroundings in a conditionally unstable atmosphere.

lever. A rigid bar, free to pivot, or rotate about a point called the fulcrum with an input force applied to one point, and an output force taken from another point. The lever, one of the simple machines like the wheel, screw, and inclined plane, can be used to change a force or the speed of movement.

The action of a lever is determined by the placement of the fulcrum and by the distance between the fulcrum and the points the force is put into and taken from the lever. *See* first-class lever, second-class lever, and third-class lever.

levitate. To suspend an object in the air in such a way that it appears to disobey the law of gravity. A magnetic body can be levitated by suspending it in a strong magnetic field.

Leyden jar. One of the earliest examples of an electrical capacitor. A Leyden jar is a glass container with a liner of metal foil pressed against its inside surface and a coating of metal foil on the outside of the jar. When a source of DC electricity is connected across the two pieces of foil, electrostatic energy is stored in the glass (the dielectric of the capacitor).

liaison aircraft. A type of light military aircraft made popular during World War II because of its ability to land and takeoff from unimproved terrain. Liaison aircraft have been replaced by helicopters.

licensed empty weight. The empty weight that consists of the airframe, engine(s), unusable fuel, and undrainable oil plus standard and optional equipment as specified in the equipment list. Some manufacturers used this term prior to GAMA standardization.

life-limited part. An aircraft part whose service life is limited to a specified number of operating hours or operating cycles.

life-support systems. Systems in an aircraft which make it possible for the occupants to operate in an environment that does not support life. Oxygen systems and pressurization systems are examples of life-support systems.

lift (aerodynamic force). An aerodynamic force caused by air flowing over a specially shaped surface called an airfoil. The airfoil is curved in such a way that the air flowing over the upper surface finds the surface falling away from it. The air is being pressed onto the surface by the air

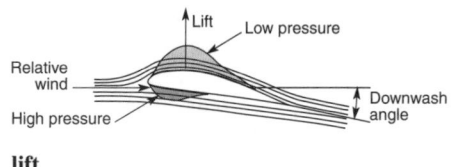

lift

above it, and in order for it to remain on the surface, it must speed up. As the air speeds up, its pressure drops, and the air above it flows down to fill the low-pressure area.

The air below the airfoil finds the surface rising into its flow path, and this slows the air. As the air slows down, its pressure rises, and it forces the surrounding air away from it. The combination of the low pressure pulling air down to the airfoil and the high pressure forcing air away from the airfoil causes the air to be deflected downward. When an airfoil forces air downward, a force equal to the weight of the deflected air forces the airfoil upward. This force is called lift.

lift coefficient (aerodynamic parameter). A dimensionless number used in the formula for aerodynamic lift that varies with the shape of the airfoil and the angle of attack. The lift coefficient (C_L) is obtained from wind tunnel data and is plotted on a set of airfoil characteristic curves.

lift fan. A special type of turbofan engine installed on an aircraft in such a way that it can be pivoted to direct its thrust in a vertical direction. Lift fans are used on some types of V/STOL (vertical, or short takeoff and landing) aircraft.

lifting body (aerodynamic shape). The shape of the fuselage of an aircraft that produces lift. Such a device can fly without wings.

lifting condensation level (meteorology). The level at which a parcel of unsaturated air lifted dry-adiabatically becomes saturated.

lift-off. The act of becoming airborne as a result of the wings lifting the airplane off the ground, or the pilot rotating the nose up, increasing the angle of attack to start a climb.

lift wires (airplane structural components). Wires installed between the wings of a biplane to support the wings against the forces of lift. Lift wires run from the inboard end of the lower wing to the interplane struts on the upper wing. Lift wires are also called flying wires.

light. The portion of the electromagnetic spectrum that produces waves visible to the naked eye. The wavelengths of visible light range from 3,800 to 7,800 Angstroms.

light-activated silicon controlled rectifier (LASCR) (electronic component). A semiconductor device having two P-sections and two N-sections. Light falling on the LASCR produces gate current that triggers it into a state of conduction.

light aircraft. As defined by the Federal Aviation Administration, a light aircraft is one having a maximum certificated takeoff weight of less than 12,500 pounds.

light chopper (optoelectronic device). An optoelectronic device that interrupts a beam of light being shone on a photoelectric cell. The chopper changes the steady DC output of the photoelectric cell into pulsating DC that can be easily amplified.

lighted airport. An airport with runway and obstruction lighting available.

light-emitting diode. *See* LED.

light ends (petroleum products). The portions of a petroleum product that boil off first in the process of fractional distillation. Butane is an example of one of the light ends of petroleum fuel.

lightening hole (aircraft structure). A hole cut in a piece of structural material to get rid of weight, or lighten the structure, without losing any strength. A hole several inches in diameter may be cut in a piece of metal at a point where the metal is not needed for strength; for example, in the web of a wing rib. The edges of the hole are flanged (bent outward) to give the metal rigidity. A piece of metal with flanged lightening holes is more rigid than the metal before the lightening holes were cut.

lighter-than-air aircraft. A device sustained in the air by aerostatic lift. Balloons and dirigibles are examples of lighter-than-air aircraft made of materials that are heavier than air, but are filled with a gas (or with hot air) that is less dense than the surrounding air.

When a gas-filled aircraft displaces a greater weight of air than it weighs, aerostatic lift is produced, and the aircraft rises into the air. *14 CFR Part 1:* "Aircraft that can rise and remain suspended by using contained gas weighing less than the air that is displaced by the gas."

light gun (air traffic control). A hand-held directional light signaling light device used for controlling traffic operating in the vicinity of the airport and on the airport movement area. It emits a brilliant narrow beam of white, green, or red light as selected by the tower controller. The color and type of light transmitted is used to approve or disapprove anticipated pilot action when radio communication is not available.

Color and Type	Aircraft on the ground	Aircraft in the Air
Steady green	Cleared for takeoff	Cleared to land
Flashing green	Cleared for taxi	Return for landing
Steady red	Stop	Give way to other aircraft and continue circling
Flashing red	Taxi clear of runway in use	Airport unsafe, do not land
Flashing white	Return to starting point on airport	Not applicable
Alternating red and green	Exercise extreme caution	Exercise extreme caution

light gun signals

lightning (atmospheric condition). A bright flash of light in the atmosphere caused by a discharge of electricity from one cloud to another or between a cloud and the earth. Lightning is actually an extremely large spark.

lightplane (type of airplane). A simple, single-engine airplane, used for training or non-commercial flying.

light sensitive diode (semiconductor device). A semiconductor diode whose ability to conduct in a forward direction is determined by the amount of light falling on the PN junction.

light sensitive diode

light-sport aircraft (LSA). A fixed-wing (airplane), powered parachute, weight-shift control (trike), gyrocopter, lighter-than-air, or glider aircraft certified to meet the LSA criteria. These criteria include: a maximum takeoff weight of not more than 1,320 pounds for an aircraft not intended for water operation, a maximum airspeed of not more than 120 knots, a maximum stalling speed of not more than 45 knots, no more than 2 seats, no more than 1 reciprocating engine, and fixed landing gear, propeller, or rotor, and nonpressurized cabin.

light-up (turbine engine operation). Engine start in a turbine engine.

light year. The distance traveled by light in one year. The light year is a unit of measurement commonly used in discussing astronomy and is equal to 5.879 trillion (5.879 x 10^{12} miles).

lime grease. A semisolid lubricant made by mixing oil with calcium carbonate. Lime grease is more suitable for use around water than grease having a sodium carbonate base.

limitations. Restrictions placed on a balloon by its manufacturer. Examples are maximum envelope temperature and maximum gross weight. *See also* operating limitations.

limit load (aircraft operation). The maximum load, expressed in terms of positive or negative Gs (one G is equal to the weight of the aircraft) an aircraft can sustain before structural damage occurs. The load limit varies with the design of the aircraft. For example; the maximum limit load of a normal category airplane must be not less than 3.8G positive and 1.52G negative.

limit switch (electrical switch). A precision electrical switch, used to turn a mechanism on or off when some part of the mechanism reaches a specific position or location. Limit switches are actuated by a very short movement of the actuating control, and they actuate at exactly the same position of the control each time.

Lindberg fire detection system. A type of aircraft fire detection system that detects either a fire or a general overheat condition. The detector element consists of a sealed, stainless steel tube filled with a material that absorbs gas when it is cool and releases it when it is heated. This tube is fitted with a pressure-actuated switch that initiates a fire warning signal when the tube is heated and releases enough gas to close the switch.

linear accelerometer. An accelerometer that measures the rate of change of motion in a straight line.

linear actuator (fluid power system component). A device which uses a piston moving inside a cylinder to change hydraulic or pneumatic pressure into linear (straight line) motion.

linear amplification (electronic amplification). Amplification of a signal in which the amplitude of the output is directly proportional to the amplitude of the input.

linear change. A change in which the output is directly proportional to the input.

linear control (electrical control). A device that changes its controlling function by the same increments throughout its complete range of movement. A potentiometer can be made in the form of linear control. The resistance of a linear potentiometer changes the same amount for each degree of rotation of its control shaft.

linear integrated circuit (electronic component). An integrated circuit (IC) whose output changes directly as the input changes. Linear ICs are often called analog ICs. Some of the more commonly used linear ICs are voltage regulators, comparators, sense amplifiers, and linear amplifiers.

linear operation. An operation in which the output of a device is directly proportional to its input. If the value of the input increases by ten percent, the output will increase its value by ten percent.

linear taper (electrical resistance). The change in resistance of a potentiometer that varies directly with the number of degrees of rotation of the potentiometer shaft.

line boring. A method of assuring that all of the bearing cavities for a crankshaft or camshaft are in correct alignment. A boring bar extends through the crankcase and cuts the inside diameters of all the bearing cavities so they are concentric.

lineholder. A flightcrew member who has an assigned flight duty period and is not acting as a reserve flightcrew member.

line loss (electrical power). Electrical power lost in the process of moving current through a transmission line.

line maintenance (aircraft maintenance). Maintenance that can be done without having to take the aircraft into a hangar or maintenance dock. Troubleshooting, minor repairs, systems servicing, and the removal and replacement of many components are classified as line maintenance.

linen. A type of cloth made from yarn spun from fibers of the flax plant. Linen has been used for centuries as a fine cloth for clothing, and at one time was popular as a fabric for covering airplane structures.

line-of-sight radio reception. A characteristic of certain radio signals that causes them to act in the same way as light. These signals travel in straight lines and cannot bend around obstructions. Very-high-frequency (VHF) and ultra-high-frequency (UHF) communications are line-of-sight transmissions which require a clear path between the transmitting and receiving antennas. The reception distance of VHF and UHF signals is dependent upon the altitude of the aircraft above the transmitting antenna.

line oriented flight training (LOFT). A program in flight crew training to facilitate the transition from the simulator to line flying for airline pilot trainees. It consists of a training course with representative flight segments of the operator's route, which include normal operating procedures from push back at one airport to arrival at another, and abnormal and emergency flight operations.

line-overs. A dangerous situation in which the suspension line goes over the top of the powered parachute's wing instead of going straight from the wing to the riser system. This condition will prevent proper inflation of the wing.

lines of flux (magnetism). Invisible lines of magnetic force that pass between the north and south poles of a magnet.

line twist. Occurs when the powered parachute suspension lines on both sides of the wing are spiraled together. Flying with a line twist is unsafe; the wing is unairworthy until it is corrected.

"line up and wait" (LUAW) (air traffic control). A phrase used by ATC to instruct a pilot to taxi onto the departure runway to line up and wait. It is not authorization for takeoff, but is used when takeoff clearance cannot immediately be issued because of traffic or other reasons.

line voltage (electrical power system). The voltage measured at the power line which supplies power to a piece of electrical equipment. In an installation using alternating current, this voltage is the effective, or rms, value of the AC.

line-voltage regulator (electrical system component). A piece of electronic equipment, used to stabilize the line voltage supplied to a piece of electrical or electronic equipment. Circuits in the line-voltage regulator increase the output voltage when the load current increases to prevent the output voltage dropping. And they decrease the voltage when the load decreases, preventing the output voltage rising above the regulated value.

link. On a webpage, a reference to data that a user can click on to be directed to information on other webpages or documents posted on the Internet. They are usually identified by their appearance in a different format (font color, underlining), or as a button (picture or icon) communicating access to additional information or a new webpage.

link rod (radial reciprocating engine component). The rod in a radial engine that connects one of the piston wrist pins to a knuckle pin on the master rod. Link rods are also called articulated rods. *See* articulated connecting rod.

linseed oil. Oil obtained from the seed of the flax plant. Linseed oil is used as a drying agent in some types of enamel, and as a rust preventive coating inside steel tubing used in welded aircraft structure.

liquid. One of the three physical forms of matter: solid, liquid, and gas. A liquid takes the shape of its container, but does not expand to fill the entire container. Water and gasoline are examples of liquids.

liquid air. Air that has been changed into its liquid state by lowering its temperature below the boiling points of oxygen and nitrogen (the main constituents of air). Liquid air is an extremely cold, faintly bluish, transparent liquid. For air to remain in its liquid state, it must be stored in a special insulated container. If liquified air is allowed to boil, the first gas released is nitrogen, and then, when the nitrogen has all boiled away, the oxygen turns into a gas. Both nitrogen and oxygen are produced commercially by boiling liquid air.

liquid-cooled engine (reciprocating engine). A reciprocating engine that uses a liquid, such as water or ethylene glycol, to remove excess heat. Much of the heat energy in the fuel burned in an engine is wasted and must be carried away from the engine, or it will cause damage.

In a liquid-cooled engine, the liquid coolant circulates around the cylinders in jackets and absorbs heat. This absorbed heat is carried outside the engine in the coolant, and as the coolant passes through a radiator (a liquid-to-air heat exchanger), the unwanted heat is given up to the outside air.

liquid cooling (engine cooling). The removal of unwanted heat from an aircraft engine by transferring it into a liquid and then passing the heated liquid through a liquid-to-air heat exchanger (radiator) to transfer the heat into the surrounding air.

liquid crystal. A type of liquid whose molecules can be arranged by electrical charges in such a way that polarized light cannot pass through a film of the liquid. Liquid crystal is used in the displays for calculators, clocks, watches, and in the new generation of aircraft instruments.

liquid lock. *See* hydraulic lock.

liquid nitrogen. Nitrogen that has been changed into its liquid state by lowering its temperature. Nitrogen remains in its liquid state under standard atmospheric pressure when its temperature is kept at −195°C (78°K) or lower.

liquid oxygen, LOX. Oxygen that has been changed into its liquid state by lowering its temperature. LOX remains a liquid if its temperature is kept at −183°C (90°K) or lower.

Lissajous figures. Figures formed on the screen of a cathode-ray oscilloscope that show the relationship between the frequency of sine wave signals being applied to the horizontal and vertical inputs. If the frequency and phase of the two sine wave signals are the same, the Lissajous figure will be in the shape of a circle. If the frequency of the sine wave signal applied to the vertical input is two times that of the signal applied to the horizontal plates, the Lissajous figure will be shaped like a figure eight (8).

liter. A metric unit of volume. One liter is the volume of one kilogram of pure water at a temperature of 4°C under standard atmospheric conditions. One liter is equal to 1,000 cubic centimeters, and it is the same as 1.0567 quarts in the English system of measurement.

lithium. A soft, silvery, highly reactive, alkali-metal chemical element. Lithium's symbol is Li, its atomic number is 3, and its atomic weight is 6.939. Lithium is the lightest of the metals, and it is used as an ingredient in batteries and as an alloying agent for other metals.

lithium cell (primary electrical cell). A lightweight, high-energy primary electrical cell, useful because of its long shelf life. A lithium cell uses lithium metal as its negative electrode and a gas dissolved in an electrolyte as its positive electrode. Lithium cells produce an open-circuit voltage of between 2.8 and 3.6 volts, which is about twice the open-circuit voltage of most other primary cells.

lithium grease. A semisolid lubricant made of lithium salts and fatty acids. Lithium grease is highly water resistant and is useful for low-temperature lubricating applications.

lithometeor (meteorology). The general term for dry particles suspended in the atmosphere. Lithometeors include dust, haze, smoke, and sand.

lithosphere. The outer crust of the earth. The lithosphere is made mostly of rock and is considered to extend down for about 50 miles.

litmus. A water-soluble powder that changes its color when acted on by an acid or a base (alkali). Litmus turns red when it is acted on by an acid and blue when acted on by a base.

litmus paper. An indicator paper, used to determine whether a solution is acidic or basic (alkaline). Litmus paper is made by soaking a piece of absorbent paper in a solution of litmus powder dissolved in water. When blue litmus paper is wet with an acid solution, it turns red, and when red litmus paper is wet with an alkaline solution, it turns blue.

Litzendraht wire (litz wire). A special type of conductor, used for carrying high-frequency alternating current. Litz wire is made of fine strands of insulated wire, woven together in such a way that any individual strand occupies, at some time, every position in the cross section of the conductor. This special type of construction gives litz wire its low opposition to the flow of high-frequency AC.

live center (machine tool component). A sharp-pointed center that fits into the headstock of a lathe and turns with it. The material to be turned is mounted between the live center and the dead center and is turned by a lathe dog that clamps the material and turns with the faceplate.

LMM. *See* locator middle marker.

LNAV. Lateral (azimuth) navigation guidance. A type of navigation associated with nonprecision approach procedures or en route navigation.

LNAV/VNAV. Lateral navigation/vertical navigation minimums provided for RNAV systems that include both lateral and vertical navigation (e.g., WAAS avionics approved for LNAV/VNAV, certified barometric VNAV with IFR approach certified GPS). Procedure minimums altitude is published as DA (decision altitude).

load (electrical). A device that uses electrical power. A load converts electrical energy into some other form of energy: mechanical, heat, light, or chemical.

load bank (electrical component). A heavy-duty electrical resistor, used to dissipate large amounts of electrical energy. Load banks are used to discharge storage batteries for servicing them and to dissipate large amounts of current when loading a generator as is done with a reciprocating engine dynamometer.

load cell (electronic weighing system component). A component in an electronic weighing system that contains strain gages. When an aircraft is weighed, the load cells are placed between the jacks and the jack pads on the aircraft, and the aircraft is raised by the jacks. The weight of the aircraft compresses the load cells, and the compression changes the resistance of the strain gages. The change in this resistance is converted into units of weight the load cell is supporting.

load factor (aircraft structure). The ratio of the amount of load imposed on an aircraft structure to the weight of the structure itself. Load factors imposed on an aircraft in flight are measured by accelerometers and are expressed in terms of G-units (gravity units).

14 CFR Part 1: "The ratio of a specified load to the total weight of the aircraft. The specified load is expressed in terms of any of the following: aerodynamic forces, inertia forces, or ground or water reactions."

loading chart (weight and balance). A chart designed to graphically calculate the loaded center of gravity and show whether or not it is within allowable limits. Another type of loading chart calculates moments for each station.

loading graph (weight and balance). A graph of load weight and load moment indexes. Diagonal lines for each item relate the weight to the moment index without having to use mathematics.

loading schedule (weight and balance). A procedure used to ensure that an aircraft is properly loaded and will not exceed approved weight and balance limitations during operation.

load manifest (weight and balance). A record concerning the loading of an aircraft. It contains information such as the number of passengers, the total weight of the loaded aircraft, the maximum allowable takeoff weight for that flight, the center of gravity limits, the center of gravity of the loaded aircraft, the registration number of the aircraft or flight number, the origin and destination and identification of crew members and their crew position assignments.

load matching network (electrical circuit). An electrical circuit used to match the input impedance of an electrical load to the output impedance of a power circuit, such as an amplifier.

loadmeter (electrical instrument). A type of ammeter installed between the generator output and the main bus in an aircraft electrical system. Loadmeters are calibrated in percentage of the generator's rated output, rather than in amperes.

LOC. *See* localizer.

local action (battery discharge). The gradual self discharge of a battery on storage caused by internal chemical action.

local airport advisory (air traffic control). A service provided by flight service stations or the military at airports not serviced by an operating control tower. This service consists of providing information to arriving and departing aircraft concerning wind direction and speed, favored runway, altimeter setting, pertinent known traffic, pertinent known field conditions, airport taxi routes and traffic patterns, and authorized instrument approach procedures. This information is advisory in nature and does not constitute an ATC clearance.

local area augmentation system (LAAS). A differential global positioning system (DGPS) that improves the accuracy of the system by determining position error from the GPS satellites, then transmitting the error, or corrective factors, to the airborne GPS receiver.

localizer (instrument landing system). The portion of an instrument landing system (ILS) that directs the pilot of an aircraft down the center line of the instrument runway for the final approach in an instrument landing. The localizer transmits two signals, one modulated with a 90-hertz tone, and the other with a 150-hertz tone. These two signals are transmitted from highly directional antennas so they overlap along the center line of the runway by two and a half degrees. The vertical needle of the cross-pointer indicator in the aircraft responds to these two signals. When the aircraft is flying along a path lined up with the center line of the runway, the needle is centered. When the aircraft moves to one side of the center line or the other, the signal for the side it is on is the stronger, and the needle swings over to show the side of the runway over which the airplane is flying.

localizer course (ICAO). The locus of points, in any given horizontal plane, at which the DDM (difference in depth of modulation) is zero.

localizer offset (air traffic control). An angular offset of the localizer from the runway extended center line in a direction away from the no transgression zone (NTZ) that increases the normal operating zone (NOZ) width. An offset requires a 50-foot increase in the decision height (DH) and is not authorized for CAT II and CAT III approaches.

localizer performance with vertical guidance (LPV). An instrument approach that combines WAAS lateral and vertical guidance. This approach has minimums similar to an ILS but is limited to areas where terrain is not a challenge. Approach minimums as low as 200 feet HAT and $1/2$ SM visibility are possible, even though LPV is still considered a semi-precision, not a precision, approach. However, like precision approaches (such as an ILS approach), LPVs have a decision altitude (DA).

localizer-type directional aid (air traffic control). A NAVAID used for nonprecision instrument approaches, with utility and accuracy comparable to a localizer but not a part of a complete ILS and not aligned with the runway.

localizer usable distance. The maximum distance from the localizer transmitter at a specified altitude as verified by flight inspection, at which reliable course information is continuously received.

local Mach number. The Mach number of any isolated, or localized, flow of air over an aircraft structure. Because of the shape of the aircraft structure, the local Mach number is often higher than the flight Mach number of the aircraft. Shock waves normally form on an aircraft structure when the air passing over the structure reaches a speed of Mach one, the speed of sound.

local oscillator (radio receiver circuit). An electronic oscillator in a superheterodyne radio receiver. A superheterodyne receiver is highly selective because it selects an extremely narrow band of frequencies and rejects all frequencies on either side.

A radio-frequency (RF) signal is picked up by the receiver and mixed with a signal produced by the local oscillator, which is tuned with the same tuning control used to select the RF signal. Since both the local oscillator and the RF signal are tuned at the same time, the frequency of the local oscillator is always the same number of kilohertz or megahertz different from the RF, regardless of the frequency of the RF.

The difference frequency between the received RF and the frequency produced by the local oscillator is filtered and amplified through the remaining stages of the receiver. This frequency is called the intermediate frequency, the IF.

local traffic (air traffic control). Aircraft operating in the traffic pattern or within sight of the tower, aircraft known to be departing or arriving from flight in local practice areas, or aircraft executing practice instrument approaches at the airport.

locator (ICAO). An LF/MF nondirectional beacon used as an aid to final approach.

locator middle marker (LMM). Nondirectional radio beacon (NDB) compass locator, collocated with a middle marker (MM).

locator outer marker (LOM). NDB compass locator, collocated with an outer marker (OM).

lockbolt (structural fastener). A type of fastener that may be used where high strength is required in major structural components. The lockbolt consists of a stump and a collar. The stump, which has a number of locking grooves around the end of its shank, is inserted into a prepared hole, often with an interference fit. A collar made, of a crushable material is placed over the grooved end of the stump. The head of the lockbolt is supported with a heavy bucking bar and the collar is swaged down into the grooves with a special swaging set in a rivet gun.

There is also a blind lockbolt that has a long grooved shank with a shear groove. The lockbolt is put through the hole and the collar is slipped over the shank. A special pulling-tool is clamped over the grooves and, as it is pulled, a die forces the collar into the locking grooves. Continued pulling breaks the stem at the shear groove.

locked-rotor current (electric motor specification). The steady-state current flowing through the windings of an electric motor when the rotor is held in a locked position with the rated voltage applied to it. Locked-rotor current is much higher than the running current, because as soon as the rotor begins to turn, it generates a counter-electromotive force that opposes the source voltage and decreases the running current.

lockout debooster (brake system component). A component in an aircraft power brake system, used to reduce the pressure between the brake control valve and the wheel cylinder. A lock-out debooster shuts off the flow of fluid to the wheel cylinder if the line should break. *See* debooster.

lock ring (safety device). A retaining ring used to prevent a shaft moving lengthwise out of a hole. A groove is cut around the outside of the shaft, and the spring steel lock ring grips the groove and holds the shaft in place.

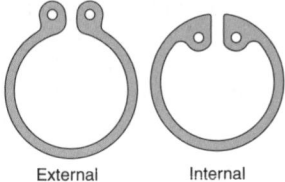

External   Internal

lock ring

A lock ring is made in the shape of an open circle, with tabs at both of its ends so a pair of special lock ring pliers can be used to expand the ring enough for it to slip over the shaft. When the ring is over the groove, the pliers are released, and the spring action of the lock ring holds it tight in the groove. Lock rings are made for both external and internal grooves.

lockstitch (aircraft fabric covering). A type of stitch used to prevent an entire hand-sewed seam loosening if the thread should break at any point. When making a sewed-in patch to aircraft fabric, the patch is sewed in using a baseball stitch. At every eight to ten stitches, the seam is locked with a modified seine knot.

lock tab (mechanical locking device). A type of mechanical lock, used to prevent a nut from loosening on a shaft. A locking hole or keyway is cut in the shaft and the internal tab on the lock ring is slipped into it. The nut is screwed down onto the shaft and tightened to the proper torque; then one or more of the external locking tabs are bent up against the flats of the nut to keep it from backing off and becoming loose.

lockwire. A term used for safety wire. Lockwire is soft brass, stainless steel, or galvanized low-carbon steel wire, used to safety fasteners so they will not loosen by vibration. Lockwire is passed through holes in the fasteners and twisted, then secured to a hole in an adjacent fastener or to a hole in the structure. Twisted lockwire should always pull on the fastener in the direction that tries to tighten it.

lodestone. A natural magnetic iron oxide. Lodestones were discovered in ancient times and were the first devices to be used as a magnetic compass. The term lodestone comes from "leading stone."

log (record). A record kept of activities, with entries made as they occur. In the field of aviation, a log is kept by pilots to record flight time. A log is kept on every airframe, engine, propeller, and rotor, to show the amount of time in service and to record all the maintenance that has been done on each device.

logarithm. The exponent used to indicate the power to which a base number must be raised to obtain a given number. In the expression $6^4 = 1{,}296$, the base number is 6, and 4 is the power to which 6 must be raised to get 1,296. Four is the logarithm of 1,296 to the base 6.

logarithmic curve. A mathematical curve plotted in such a way that the coordinate of any point varies as the logarithm of the other coordinate.

Horizontal coordinate	Vertical coordinate
0	0
2^1	2
2^2	4
2^3	8
2^4	16
2^5	32
2^6	64
2^7	128
2^8	256

logbook (pilot's record book). A register book that lists a pilot's flight time, instructor endorsements, and completed training topics.

logic. The branch of science that deals with the principles used in truth tables. Logic has become of major importance, with the introduction of digital electronics and especially digital computers. Electronic logic uses Boolean algebra, which allows a person to set up conditions using such operators as AND, OR, NOT, IF, ONLY IF, or THEN. By using these conditions and answering them with YES or NO that can be produced by a switch being open or closed, logic conclusions can be reached.

Electronic logic circuits use gates which are combinations of switches with a single output, but with one or more inputs. For any given combination of logic conditions (yes or no, one or zero) on the inputs, there can be one and only one logic condition on the output. The most commonly used logic gates are the AND gate, the OR gate, and the NOT gate (an inverter). See the definitions for each of these gates.

logic circuit. An electronic circuit that operates according to the fundamental laws of logic.

logic decision. A decision based on logic. This is the type of decision made by a digital computer when there are two possible conditions or alternatives.

If a computer is instructed to count ten items and then turn off the power to a motor, it will count one item and then ask for a logic decision to be made: "Have ten items been counted?" If the answer is NO, the computer will make the logic decision to count again. After the tenth item has been counted and the computer asks the question "have ten items been counted?" the answer is now YES, and the computer will make the logic decision to turn off the power to the motor.

A decision point where the computer is asked to make a logic decision is shown on a flowchart as a diamond.

logic flowchart. A graphic way to show the flow of information through a computer program. An oval shape shows the point at which the program starts or stops. A rectangular box is an information box that explains something. A box shaped like a parallelogram is a point where data is put into the program or taken from it. A diamond-shaped box is a decision point at which a logic decision must be made.

logic functions (logic gates). Some of the logic functions, or gates, most frequently used in digital computers are: AND, OR, NOT, NOR, NAND, and EXCLUSIVE OR. *See* definitions of each of these terms.

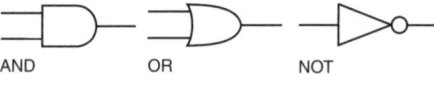

AND   OR   NOT

logic gates

logic one. One of the two conditions (zero and one) used when working with digital electronic equipment. A logic one represents a YES or a TRUE condition, and it is produced by a closed switch or by the presence of a voltage.

logic probe. An electronic instrument that determines the logic level, or state, (0 or 1) at specific points in a digital circuit.

logic state. The logic condition of a conductor in a piece of digital electronic equipment— that is, whether the conductor is carrying a logic zero or a logic one.

logic zero. One of the two conditions (zero and one) used when working with digital electronic equipment. A logic zero represents a NO or a FALSE condition, and it is produced by an open switch or by no voltage.

LOM. *See* locator outer marker.

lomcovàk (aerobatic maneuver). A family of high-precision maneuvers in which the gyroscopic action of the propeller works with the aerodynamic forces to cause the airplane to tumble end over end and rotate about all three of its axes.

longeron (aircraft structural component). The main longitudinal, load-bearing members of a truss-type aircraft fuselage.

long-call reserve (in flight operations). This describes a situation in which a flightcrew member, prior to beginning the rest period required by 14 CFR §117.25, is notified by the certificate holder to report for a flight duty period following the completion of the rest period.

longitude (navigation). The angular east-west measurement of location on the earth's surface. The surface of the earth is divided by 360 meridians, or lines of longitude, that pass through both the north and south poles. The meridian passing through the Royal Observatory at Greenwich, near London, England, is 0° longitude and is called the prime meridian. On the opposite side of the earth is the 180° meridian. Longitude east of the prime meridian is called east longitude, and that west of the prime meridian is called west longitude.

longitudinal axis of an aircraft. An imaginary line through an aircraft from nose to tail, passing through its center of gravity. The longitudinal axis is also called the roll axis of the aircraft. Movement of the ailerons rotates an airplane about its longitudinal axis. *See* axes of an aircraft.

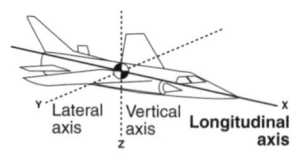

Y Lateral axis   Vertical axis   **Longitudinal axis**   x   z

longitudinal axis

longitudinal balance (aircraft stability). Balance around lateral, or pitch, axis of an aircraft.

longitudinal magnetization. A method of magnetizing a part for magnetic particle inspection. Current flows through a solenoid, or coil, that encircles the part so the lines of magnetic flux pass lengthwise through it. Longitudinal magnetism makes it possible to detect faults that extend across the part.

longitudinal separation (air traffic control). The longitudinal spacing of aircraft at the same altitude by a minimum distance expressed in units of time or miles.

longitudinal stability (aircraft stability). The tendency of an airplane to remain level about its lateral axis. (The lateral axis passes through the center of gravity and extends outward parallel to the span of the wing.) Longitudinal stability, also called pitch stability, is provided by a downward aerodynamic load on the horizontal tail surface. The center of gravity, which does not change with airspeed, causes the airplane to rotate nose-down about its lateral axis. The tail load, which does change with airspeed, is located behind the center of gravity, and it causes the airplane to rotate nose-up about its lateral axis.

If the nose pitches down, the airspeed builds up, and the downward tail load increases. This brings the nose back to a level flight attitude. If the nose pitches up, the airspeed slows down, and the tail load decreases. The center of gravity causes the nose to return to a level flight attitude.

longitudinal wave. Waves within an elastic material in which the particles in motion move back and forth, parallel to the direction the wave is traveling.

long-range communication system. A system that uses satellite relay, data link, high frequency, or other approved communication system which extends beyond line of sight.

long-range navigation system. An electronic navigation system that is approved for use under instrument flight rules as a primary means of navigation and has at least one source of navigation input, such as inertial navigation system, global positioning system, Omega/very low frequency, or LORAN C.

long-term memory. The portion of the brain that stores information that has been determined to be of sufficient value to be retained. In order for the information to be retained in long-term memory, it must have been processed or coded in the working memory.

loom (electrical wiring). A type of flexible, braided insulating material put over a wire or a bundle of wires to protect it against physical damage caused by heat or abrasion.

loop (aircraft maneuver). A flight maneuver in the vertical plane in which an airplane passes successively through a climb, inverted flight, dive, and then returns to normal flight.

loop (electrical circuit). A complete path in an electrical circuit through which current flows from one terminal of the power source back to the opposite terminal.

loop antenna (radio direction finding). A type of directional antenna, used with radio direction finding equipment to determine the direction to the station transmitting the signal the loop is receiving. Loop antennas must be used with a sense antenna to show the side of the loop on which the transmitting antenna is located.

loopstick antenna. A type of radio antenna made of a number of turns of wire wound around a rod of powdered iron. The powdered iron increases the permeability of the core of the coil and increases the radio signal picked up by the coil.

LORAN (electronic navigation system). A type of electronic navigation system, used by aircraft and ships. The name LORAN comes from LOng RAnge Navigation. LORAN is a low-frequency pulse navigation system based on latitude and longitude coordinates. Hyperbolic lines of position are determined by measuring the difference in the time of reception of synchronized pulse signals from two fixed transmitters. LORAN A operates in the 1750-1950 kHz frequency band. LORAN C and D operate in the 100-110 kHz frequency band. LORAN is being phased out and replaced by GPS as the primary electronic navigation system for aircraft.

loss of separation (aircraft traffic control). An occurrence or operation that results in less than prescribed separation between aircraft, or between an aircraft and a vehicle, pedestrian, or object.

lost communications. Loss of the ability to communicate by radio. Aircraft in this condition are sometimes referred to as NORDO (no radio). Standard pilot procedures for lost communications are specified in 14 CFR Part 91.

lost-wax casting. A method of casting such components as turbine blades. A highly polished internal cavity is made in the die, having the exact inverse shape of the finished part, and a special molten wax is injected into it to completely fill the cavity. When the wax solidifies, it is removed from the die.

Several of the wax patterns are assembled on a wax gating tree, which is then dipped into a liquid ceramic slurry a number of times until a ceramic coat about a quarter of an inch thick builds up. The resulting ceramic mold is fired at a temperature of about 1,000°C, which melts the wax out and prepares the mold for the next steps. The extremely hot mold is filled with the blade alloy which has been melted in an induction furnace. After the metal has cooled, the mold is removed and the blades are cleaned and inspected.

louver. A slotted opening in a structure, used for the passage of cooling air. Louvers are often fitted with vanes to control the amount of air flowing through them.

low (meteorology). An area of low barometric pressure, with its attendant system of winds. A low is also called a barometric depression or cyclone.

low altitude airway structure. The network of airways serving aircraft operations, up to, but not including, 18,000 feet MSL.

low-altitude alert system. *See* LAAS.

low approach. An approach over an airport or runway following an instrument approach or a VFR approach, including the go-around maneuver in which the pilot intentionally does not make contact with the runway.

low blower (supercharger operation). The operation of a two-speed supercharger at its low impeller speed.

low-bypass engine. A turbofan engine whose bypass ratio is less than 2:1. *See* bypass ratio.

low-frequency radio waves. Electromagnetic waves with frequencies between 30 and 300 kilohertz. Low-frequency radio waves have wavelengths between 10,000 and 1,000 meters.

low-lead 100-octane aviation gasoline. A type of aviation gasoline having an octane rating of 100, but containing a maximum of two milliliters of tetraethyl lead per gallon. Normal, or high-lead, 100-octane aviation gasoline is allowed to have as much as 4.6 milliliters of lead per gallon, and this additional lead fouls the spark plugs of engines designed to use fuel with a lower lead content. Low-lead 100-octane aviation gasoline is dyed blue to distinguish it from normal 100-octane aviation gasoline which is dyed green.

low-level air route. In the low-level airspace, a route extending upwards from the surface of the earth and within which ATC service is not provided.

low-level airspace. All airspace within the National Airspace System below 18,000 feet MSL.

low-oxygen concentration cell corrosion. Corrosion that forms between the lap joints of metal and under labeling tape, tabs or placards that trap and hold moisture. Moisture on the surface of the metal absorbs oxygen from the air, and the extra oxygen causes the water to attract electrons from the metal to form negative hydroxide ions. Moisture trapped in the lap joints does not have any extra oxygen and therefore does not form any negative ions. Since the metal in the lap joints has not given up any electrons, it is more negative than the metal around it, and it becomes the anode in a corrosion cell and forms a salt of the metal—it corrodes.

low-pass filter (electronic filter). A type of electronic filter that passes all frequencies of alternating current below a certain frequency, but blocks or attenuates all higher frequencies.

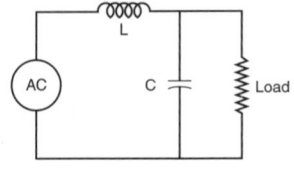

low-pass filter

low-pressure compressor (gas turbine engine component). The first-stage compressor in a dual-spool gas turbine engine. The low-pressure compressor is called the N_1 compressor and its speed is not governed. It seeks its own best speed as the atmospheric conditions change so it can furnish the optimum mass of air to the inlet of the second-stage compressor.

low-pressure oxygen system. A gaseous oxygen system in which the oxygen is carried in steel cylinders under a pressure of approximately 450 psi. Low-pressure oxygen systems were used in military aircraft during World War II, but these systems have been replaced by high-pressure systems or liquid oxygen (LOX) systems.

low-tension ignition system. A type of magneto ignition system designed for reciprocating engines that operate at high altitude. The coil in a low-tension magneto has only one winding, the one that compares with the primary coil in a high-tension magneto. A carbon-brush-type distributor directs the low voltage from the magneto to the proper cylinder.

Each spark plug has its own step-up transformer, to change the low distributor voltage to the high voltage needed to jump the gap in the spark plug. Low-tension ignition systems are not popular today because most aircraft that fly at high altitudes are turbine powered.

low unmetered fuel pressure. The pressure in a Teledyne-Continental fuel injector pump that is adjusted by the relief valve.

LOX. The abbreviation for liquid oxygen. *See* liquid oxygen.

LPV. *See* localizer performance with vertical guidance.

LR circuit (electrical circuit). An alternating current circuit containing inductance (L) and resistance (R). The total opposition to the current in an LR circuit is impedance (Z), which is the vector sum of the inductive reactance and the resistance.

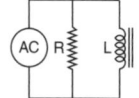

LR parallel circuit

LRU (line replaceable unit). Components in an aircraft that are designed so that they can be replaced as a unit while the aircraft is on the flight line.

LSA. *See* light sport aircraft

LSB (least significant bit). The bit in a binary number that has the lowest place value. The LSB is the bit on the extreme right.

LSD (least significant digit). The digit in a decimal number that has the lowest place value. The LSD is the digit on the extreme right.

LSI (large scale integration). A method of miniaturization of electronic circuit components, in which 100 or more gates are built into a single integrated circuit (IC) chip. LSI techniques lower the cost per gate of logic components.

LTA. lighter-than-air

lubber line. The reference line used in a magnetic compass or directional gyro, to indicate the nose of the aircraft. The heading of the aircraft is shown as the degrees on the card or dial of the instrument opposite the lubber line.

lubricant. A natural or synthetic material used to reduce the friction between parts in sliding contact with each other. Even parts that seem to be smooth actually have microscopically rough surfaces. When one rough surface slides over another, the surfaces lock and oppose the movement (this is called friction). A lubricant between the surfaces holds them apart, and they slide over a film of the lubricant, rather than over each other. Lubricants may be in the form of a dry powder (powdered graphite or molybdenum), a liquid (oil), or a semi-liquid (grease).

Lucite. The registered trade name for a transparent acrylic resin. Lucite is a thermoplastic resin, used for windshields and side windows of some aircraft.

luminance. The amount of light emitted or scattered by a surface. Luminance is measured in lamberts.

luminescence. The production of light by some method other than incandescence (light emitted because of high temperature). Luminescence may be caused by friction, chemical action, or electrical charges, and regardless of the method of luminescence, the light produces little or no heat.

luminous paint. A type of paint having components that cause it to emit light, or glow in the dark. Radium was, at one time, the main component in luminous paint. But because of its harmful characteristics, it has been replaced by other materials. Luminous paint is used on instrument dials and pointers to make them visible in the dark.

lutetium. A silvery-white, rare-earth chemical element. Lutetium's symbol is Lu, its atomic number is 71, and its atomic weight is 174.97. Lutetium is the heaviest of the rare-earth elements and is used in nuclear technology.

lye. A strong alkaline solution made of potassium hydroxide or sodium hydroxide.

MAA (maximum authorized altitude). A published altitude representing the maximum usable altitude or flight level for an airspace structure or route segment. MAA is the highest altitude on a Federal airway, jet route, area navigation low or high route, or other direct route for which an MEA is designated in 14 CFR Part 95, at which adequate reception of navigation aid signals is assured.

MAC (mean aerodynamic chord). The chord of an imaginary airfoil that has the same aerodynamic characteristics as the actual airfoil. The length of the MAC is given for many aircraft, and the CG is expressed in percent of the mean aerodynamic chord (% MAC).

Mach compensating device. A device that alerts the pilot of inadvertent excursions beyond the aircraft's certified maximum operating speed.

Mach cone. The cone-shaped shock wave produced by a sharp-pointed object moving through the atmosphere at a speed greater than the speed of sound.

machine bolt. The common name for a hex-head bolt.

machine language (computer operation). A language, made up of zeros and ones, that is usable by a digital computer. Machine language is difficult to write into a computer, so compilers and assemblers are used. A compiler is a special program that converts a high-level language that is easy for a programmer to use, into machine language that can be used by the computer. An assembler converts assembly language programs into machine language the computer can use.

machine screw. A blunt-end screw with uniform threads that can be screwed into a tapped hole or a nut. A machine screw is turned with a screwdriver and may have a round, flat, truss, oval, or fillister head.

machine-sewn seams (aircraft fabric covering). Seams in aircraft fabric made with a sewing machine. French fell, folded fell, and plain overlap are the seams most generally used.

machining. The process of removing material by turning, planing, shaping, milling, or otherwise cutting with machine-operated tools. Lathes, milling machines, shapers, and planers are the most commonly used machine tools.

machinist. A person skilled in the use of such metalworking machine tools as lathes, shapers, planers, and milling machines.

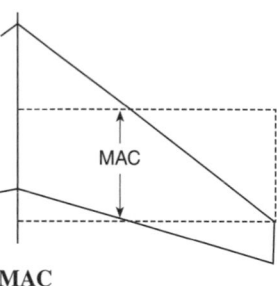

MAC

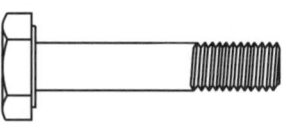

machine bolt

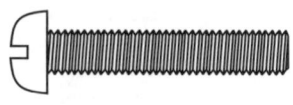

machine screw

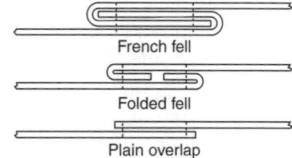

French fell

Folded fell

Plain overlap

machine-sewn seams

M

Machmeter. A flight instrument that indicates the flight Mach number of an aircraft. The mechanism inside a Machmeter includes a bellows that measures the difference between pitot pressure and static pressure. It also contains an aneroid that modifies the output of the differential pressure bellows to correct for the changes in altitude.

Mach number. A measurement of speed based on the ratio of the speed of the aircraft to the speed of sound under the same atmospheric conditions. An airplane flying at Mach 1 is flying at the speed of sound. *14 CFR Part 1:* "The ratio of true airspeed to the speed of sound."

Mach technique (ICAO). A control technique used by air traffic control whereby turbojet aircraft operating successively along suitable routes are cleared to maintain appropriate Mach numbers for a relevant portion of the enroute phase of flight. The principal objective is to achieve improved utilization of the airspace and to ensure that separation between successive aircraft does not decrease below the established minimums.

Mach tuck (aerodynamics). A flight condition that can occur when operating a swept wing airplane in the transonic speed range. Under certain conditions a shock wave forms in the root portion of the wing and causes the air behind it to separate. This shock-induced separation causes the center of lift to move aft. At the same time, the disturbed air causes the horizontal stabilizer to lose some of its effectiveness. The airplane develops a nose-down pitch, or tucks under. *See* shock stall.

mackerel sky (meteorology). A condition of cloud coverage of the sky consisting of rows of altocumulus or cirrocumulus clouds. These clouds look like the pattern of scales on a mackerel fish.

magamp. *See* magnetic amplifier.

magnesium. A light, silvery-white, malleable, ductile, metallic chemical element. Magnesium's symbol is Mg, its atomic number is 12, and its atomic weight is 24.312. Magnesium burns with an intense white light, and because of this, it is used for making flares. Magnesium's light weight makes it useful as a structural material, but it has disadvantages. It corrodes easily, and vibration causes it to crack.

Magnesyn. The registered trade name for a remote indicating system, used in certain aircraft instruments. A Magnesyn transmitter consists of a permanent-magnet rotor, free to rotate inside a toroidal coil. The magnet is rotated by the physical movement being measured. The indicator contains a small permanent magnet on a shaft, free to rotate inside a toroidal coil. A pointer is also mounted on the shaft.

The toroidal coils in the transmitter and indicator are tapped in such a way that they form delta windings. The cores of these coils are rings of soft iron, and the two coils are connected in parallel and excited, or powered, with 26-volt, 400-hertz alternating current.

The AC alternately saturates and demagnetizes the soft iron cores, so the magnetic flux from the permanent-magnet rotors is alternately accepted and rejected by the cores. This changing flux cuts across the windings of the coils and induces a voltage in them. The relationship between the voltage induced in each section of the windings is determined by the position of the rotor inside the transmitter coil. Since the two coils are in parallel, the voltage induced by the flux from the magnet is the same in both coils, and the small permanent magnet rotor in the indicator follows the movement of the larger magnet in the transmitter.

magnet. A piece of material or a device that has the ability to attract pieces of iron or steel and to generate an electrical voltage in a wire passing near it. A piece of ferrous metal (metal containing iron) contains billions of tiny magnetic fields, called magnetic domains. When the metal is not magnetized, these domains lie in a random fashion, and their fields cancel each other, so the metal has no overall magnetic field.

But when the metal is magnetized, the domains are aligned so all the north poles point in one direction, and all the south poles point in the opposite direction. The metal now has a magnetic field. Invisible lines of magnetic flux leave the north pole of the magnet and travel by the easiest path to the south pole. These lines leave and enter the magnet at right angles to the surface. A magnet attracts pieces of iron or steel (ferrous metals), and if a wire is moved through the lines of magnetic flux between the poles, electrons are forced to flow in it.

There are two basic types of magnets: permanent magnets and electromagnets. Permanent magnets are pieces of metal with the magnetic domains in alignment. The metal used as a permanent magnet has a high retentivity; therefore it keeps, or retains, its magnetism.

Electromagnets are made of a coil of wire wound around a core of soft iron. When direct current flows through the coil, the domains in the soft iron line up, and the core becomes a strong magnet. Iron has very low retentivity, however, and as soon as the current stops flowing in the coil, the domains in the iron core lose their alignment, and the iron is no longer a magnet.

magnetic amplifier (magamp). A type of electrical control transformer in which a small amount of current flowing in the control winding determines the amount of load current allowed to flow in the load winding. Direct current flowing through the bias and control windings of the magamp varies the magnetic saturation of the core, and the condition of saturation determines the permeability of the core. Varying the permeability of the core varies the amount of inductive reactance opposing the AC flowing in the load winding. Magnetic amplifiers are also called magamps and saturable reactors.

magnetic bearing (navigation). The direction to or from a radio transmitting station measured relative to magnetic north.

magnetic brake (electric motor component). A type of friction brake that automatically releases when current flows through the motor windings. As soon as current to the motor is shut off, a spring forces a stationary friction disk against a disk that rotates with the motor armature. The friction prevents the armature turning. An electromagnet pulls the stationary disk away from the rotating disk when current flows in the motor.

magnetic bubble memory (digital computers). A method of storing information for use in a digital computer. Tiny areas of magnetism can be formed in a thin film of magnetic garnet crystal. These tiny areas, or bubbles, can be moved about within the film to change the logic conditions they represent. Magnetic bubble memory allows an extremely large amount of digital information to be stored in an exceedingly small area.

magnetic chuck. A special work surface used with certain types of metal-machining tools. An electromagnetic force holds the material being machined tightly to the surface.

magnetic circuit. The complete path in an electrical machine that is followed by lines of magnetic flux. Lines of flux leave the north pole of the magnet, flow through all the circuit components, and re-enter the magnet at its south pole. In a motor or generator, the magnetic circuit is made up of the pole shoes, the armature core, the field frame, and the air gaps between the pole shoes and the armature.

magnetic circuit breaker. An electrical component that opens a circuit any time excessive current flows. A magnetic field is produced by current flowing through the circuit breaker, and the strength of the field is proportional to the amount of current. When more current flows through the circuit breaker than it is rated to carry, the magnetic field becomes strong enough to snap open a set of contacts and break, or open, the circuit.

magnetic compass. An instrument that gives the pilot an indication of the direction between the aircraft and the earth's north magnetic pole. The instrument consists of a pair of small magnets suspended on a pivot and attached to a compass card that is graduated in 360 degrees clockwise from North. Long marks are used for each 10° and short marks for each 5°. Every third long mark is replaced with a number represented the number of degrees from North with the last digit omitted. The number 3 represents 30°, 12 is 120°, and 33 is 330°.

magnetic compass errors. There are four basic magnetic compass errors; variation, deviation, turning error, and acceleration error. *See* variation, deviation, northerly turning error, and acceleration error.

magnetic course (navigation). A desired flight path referenced from magnetic north. A true course measured on a navigational chart is referenced to the geographic north pole but a magnetic compass points to the magnetic north pole. The angular difference between a true course and a magnetic course is called variation.

magnetic deviation (navigation). A form of compass error caused by local magnetic fields in the aircraft interacting with the magnetic field of the earth. Deviation error is minimized by counteracting the interfering magnetic fields by adjusting small compensating magnets that are built into the compass housing. This compensating procedure is called "swinging the compass." Deviation error differs with each heading of the aircraft.

magnetic dip. *See* dip (magnetic compass characteristic).

magnetic-drag tachometer. An instrument used in an aircraft to show the rotational speed of the engine crankshaft. A flexible shaft, or cable, turned at one-half crankshaft speed, spins a permanent magnet inside the tachometer.

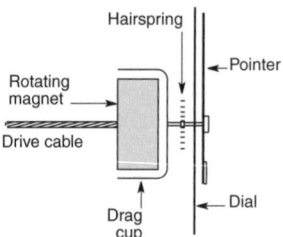

magnetic-drag tachometer

An aluminum drag cup rides over the spinning magnet, but does not touch it. A pointer shaft is mounted on the center of the cup, and the tachometer pointer is pressed onto the end of the shaft. A flat, coiled hairspring attached to the shaft holds the cup against a stop so the pointer rests on zero when the magnet is not spinning.

When the engine is running, the magnet spins, and its lines of flux cut across the aluminum drag cup and generate a voltage in it. This voltage causes eddy currents to flow in the aluminum cup where they produce a magnetic field. The magnetic field caused by the eddy currents opposes the field of the spinning magnet. The faster the magnet spins, the more the cup is pushed against the restraint of the hairspring.

Most magnetic-drag tachometers incorporate an hourmeter, similar to the odometer in an automobile speedometer. The hourmeter is a gear-driven counter which counts the revolutions of the drive shaft and displays the number of hours the engine has run on the hourmeter wheels. The hours shown are correct only at a specific RPM, which is normally the cruising speed of the engine. This speed is stamped on the tachometer case.

magnetic drain plug (engine lubrication system component). A drain plug in the sump of either a reciprocating engine or a gas turbine engine. Two small permanent magnets built into the drain plug attract and hold ferrous metal chips or shavings that may be in the lubricating oil. Metal on the drain plug is an indication of internal engine failure.

Some magnetic drain plugs in gas turbine engines have the two magnets connected into an electrical warning system. When bits of metal short across them, a circuit is completed, and a warning light is turned on to show that metal particles are loose in the engine.

magnetic field. The invisible, but measurable, force surrounding a permanent magnet or current-carrying conductor. This field is produced when the orbital axes of the electrons of the atoms in the material are all in alignment. When a piece of iron or steel is held in the magnetic field, it is pulled toward the magnet, and when a conductor passes through a magnetic field, current is induced into it.

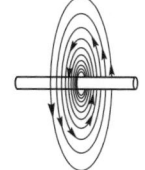

magnetic field

magnetic flux. Invisible lines of force passing between the poles of a magnet. These invisible lines are considered to leave the north pole of a magnet and enter its south pole, and they always follow the path of least resistance. Lines of flux form complete loops through the magnet and across the gap between the poles, and the loops never cross one another. When an electrical conductor cuts across the lines of magnetic flux, a voltage is produced that causes current to flow in it.

magnetic flux density. The number of lines of magnetic flux per unit of area. Magnetic flux density is measured in gausses. One gauss is equal to one line of flux (one maxwell) per square centimeter.

magnetic flux valve. A type of magnetometer using coils of wire as the transmitting portion of a synchronous repeating system, conventionally used to stabilize and correct a slaved gyroscopic heading (azimuth) indicator by sensing changes in the earth's magnetic field.

magnetic heading (navigation). The direction an aircraft is pointed with respect to magnetic north. Magnetic north is the direction to the magnetic north pole, rather than the geographic north pole.

magnetic hysteresis. The characteristic of a magnetic material that causes it to retain some magnetism after the magnetizing force is removed. In order to remove all the magnetism from a part, it must be demagnetized with a force opposite to the one that magnetized it.

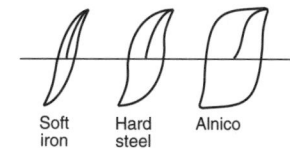

Soft iron   Hard steel   Alnico

magnetic hysteresis loops

Soft iron has very little hysteresis. This means that as soon as a magnetizing force is removed, iron becomes almost demagnetized. Hard steel, on the other hand, has a large amount of hysteresis, and a strong force is needed to demagnetize it.

magnetic north. The earth has the properties of a huge magnet. The magnetic north pole is the location on the earth's surface where the lines of magnetic flux leave, and the magnetic south pole is the point they return. A freely floating magnet will align with this flux and the north-seeking end will point to the magnetic north pole. This is magnetic north.

magnetic north pole. The location on the earth near the north geographic pole to which compass magnets point. The earth is a huge magnet spinning about its axis in space. Lines of magnetic flux leave the earth at its magnetic north pole and enter at its magnetic south pole, a location near its south geographic pole. Magnetic compasses align with this magnetic flux, with one end pointing to the magnetic north pole.

magnetic particle inspection (nondestructive inspection method). A method of inspecting ferrous metal components for cracks and other types of flaws. The part being inspected is magnetized and then flooded with iron oxide suspended in a light oil much like kerosine. Any flaw, either on the surface or slightly below the surface, forms a north and a south pole, and the iron oxide attracted to these poles helps locate the flaw. The iron oxide is often treated with a fluorescent dye, and the inspection is conducted in a darkened booth. When an ultraviolet light (black light) is shone on the part, the treated iron oxide shows up as a brilliant line.

M

magnetic poles. The locations on a magnet at which the lines of flux leave and enter. All magnets have both a north pole and a south pole. The lines of flux leave the magnet at right angles to the face of the north pole and enter at right angles to the face of the south pole.

magnetic saturation. The condition in which all the magnetic domains in a piece of magnetized material are lined up in the same direction. When a piece of unmagnetized iron or other magnetizable material is held in a magnetic field, increasing the magnetizing force increases the magnetism. But when all the domains are aligned in the same direction, increasing the magnetizing force no longer increases the strength of the magnet. The magnet is said to be saturated.

magnetic shunt (electrical measuring instrument component). A piece of soft iron placed across the air gap in a magnet used in an electrical measuring instrument to vary the amount of magnetic flux across the gap. The permeability of soft iron is much higher than that of air (flux can pass through iron much easier than it can pass through air), and the flux passes through the iron, rather than crossing the air gap. The position of the magnetic shunt is changed to calibrate the instrument.

magnetic variation (navigation). A compass error caused by the difference in the locations of the earth's geographic north pole and its magnetic north pole. All navigation charts and maps are drawn with reference to the geographic north pole, and all magnetic compasses point to the magnetic north pole. These two locations are not the same, and they are only in alignment along the agonic line. At any particular location on the surface of the earth, the variation error is the same for all headings. Variation is called declination in land navigation. *See* agonic line, isogonic lines.

magnetic wind direction. The direction from which the wind is blowing as measured clockwise from magnetic north.

magnetism. A property possessed by certain materials that causes them to attract or repel other materials having this same property. Magnetism also causes electrical current to flow in a conductor when it is moved across the lines of magnetic flux extending out from the magnet.

magnet keeper. A piece of soft iron placed across the poles of a horseshoe permanent magnet when the magnet is not in use. The permeability of the soft iron is much greater than that of the air between the poles, and by keeping the flux concentrated, the flux loss is minimized and the magnet is prevented from becoming demagnetized.

magneto (reciprocating engine ignition system component). The source of high-voltage electrical energy, used to produce the spark to ignite the fuel-air mixture inside the cylinders of a reciprocating engine. A magneto contains a small alternating-current generator with a set of breaker points to interrupt the current the instant the spark is needed.

Current produced by the AC generator flows through the primary winding of a step-up transformer, the magneto coil, and this current causes lines of magnetic flux to expand out across the many turns of wire in the secondary winding of the coil. When the breaker points open, the primary current immediately stops flowing, and the magnetic field instantly collapses, cutting across the secondary winding and producing a high voltage in it. A capacitor, installed across the breaker points, prevents arcing as the points open.

A magneto also incorporates a distributor, or high-voltage selector switch, to direct the high voltage to the correct spark plug.

magnetometer. An instrument used to measure and plot the strength and direction of the earth's magnetic field. Magnetometers are often towed behind low-flying airplanes to find deposits of magnetic minerals by noting the change in the direction of the local magnetic field. These aerial surveys are referred to as MAD (magnetic anomaly detection) surveys.

magnetomotive force (mmf). A force that produces a magnetic field. The magnetomotive force caused by current flowing in a coil of wire is determined by both the amount of current and the number of turns of wire.

The gilbert is the unit of magnetomotive force, with one gilbert being the amount of mmf needed to cause one maxwell (one line of magnetic flux) to flow through a magnetic circuit having a reluctance (the opposition to the passage of magnetic flux) of one unit. One gilbert is also the amount of mmf produced by 0.7957-ampere turn. The constant 0.7957 is 10 divided by four π.

magneto safety check (aircraft reciprocating engine operation check). A check made by the pilot of an aircraft to determine that the ignition switch is operating properly. The engine is idled, and the ignition switch is momentarily placed in the OFF position. The engine should stop firing, but the switch is returned to the BOTH position before the engine stops turning. This safety check ensures that both magnetos are grounded when the switch is in the OFF position.

magnetosphere. The outer layer of the earth's atmosphere. The magnetosphere starts about a thousand miles above the earth and is the beginning of interplanetary space. The magnetic field of the earth traps charged particles in the magnetosphere.

magnetostriction. The characteristic of certain ferromagnetic materials (magnetic materials containing iron) that causes them to change their physical size when they are subjected to a magnetic field. Magnetostriction is used in some types of transducers (devices that change electrical signals into physical movement).

If a bar of magnetostrictive material is used as the core of a coil through which alternating current is flowing, the changing magnetic field produced by the AC causes the magnetostrictive bar to change its size enough that it will vibrate an object attached to it.

M

magnetron. A special electron tube used to produce high-power electromagnetic energy in the ultrahigh and superhigh frequency ranges. Magnetron tubes are used in airborne radar equipment.

magnet wire. The common name for small diameter, varnish-insulated, annealed copper wire. Magnet wire is used for winding coils for electromagnets, transformers, motors, and generators.

magnitude of a force. A quantitative measure of the amount of a force.

Magnus effect (fluid mechanics). The lifting force, or pressure differential, that is produced when air flows over a rotating cylinder or sphere. The Magnus effect causes a baseball to curve or a golf ball to slice.

main gear. The wheels of an aircraft's landing gear that support the major part of the aircraft's weight.

main landing gear. The landing gear that carries the majority of the weight of an aircraft on the ground. The main landing gear is usually supported with an auxiliary nose wheel or tail wheel.

main rotor. *14 CFR Part 1:* "The rotor that supplies the principal lift to a rotorcraft."

"maintain" (air traffic control). In ATC–pilot communications concerning altitude/flight level, this term means to remain at the specified altitude/flight level. The phrase "climb and" or "descend and" normally precedes "maintain" and the altitude assignment; for example, "descend and maintain 5,000." Concerning other ATC instructions, the term is used in its literal sense, e.g., "maintain VFR."

maintenance. The upkeep of equipment. Mechanical and electrical equipment must be periodically inspected, to be sure it performs as it was designed and built to perform. When it begins to fail, correct maintenance will usually prevent the problem becoming major. In addition to inspection, maintenance includes adjustments, lubrication, and the replacement of parts to keep the equipment operating as it should. *14 CFR Part 1:* "Inspection, overhaul, repair, preservation, and the replacement of parts, but excludes preventive maintenance."

maintenance checks (letter checks). A classification of maintenance inspections or checks used in airline operation.

A-check. A thorough visual inspection and an operational check of all major systems of the airframe and engine.

B-check. A complete A-check and a more detailed check of certain systems specified for the particular aircraft.

C-check. Complete A and B checks with more in-depth inspection of certain systems. A C-check may include a flight check.

D-check. The most in-depth inspection of the aircraft. It requires removal of such components as engines and landing gear.

maintenance manual. A set of detailed instructions issued by the manufacturer of an aircraft, engine, or component that describes the way maintenance of the device should be performed. Maintenance manuals for certificated aircraft and their components are approved by the Federal Aviation Administration and may be used as approved data when making repairs.

maintenance planning friction level. *See* friction level classifications.

maintenance release. A release, signed by an authorized inspector or AMT, signifying that an aircraft has been approved for return to service after certain maintenance functions have been completed. It is also a statement made by an Approved Repair Station in lieu of a Form 337 that approves a product for return to service after a major repair.

major alteration (aircraft alteration). *14 CFR Part 1:* "An alteration not listed in the aircraft, aircraft engine, or propeller specifications—
(1) That might appreciably affect weight, balance, structural strength, performance, powerplant operation, flight characteristics, or other qualities affecting airworthiness; or
(2) That is not done according to accepted practices or cannot be done by elementary operations."

major axis of an ellipse. A line passing through the two focuses of an ellipse. *See* ellipse.

major diameter (threaded fastener). The diameter of the threads of a bolt or screw measured at the crests (the tops) of the threads.

majority carriers (semiconductor material). The main electrical carriers within a semiconductor material. The majority carriers in P-type material are holes, and in N-type material, electrons.

major overhaul (engine overhaul). The disassembly, cleaning, and inspection of an engine and the repair and replacement of all parts that do not meet the manufacturer's specifications. After all of the inspections and repairs are made, the engine is reassembled and tested according to the manufacturer's instructions. Major overhaul restores an engine to a serviceable condition, and it normally operates as though it were new.

major repair (aircraft maintenance). *14 CFR Part 1:* "A repair:
(1) That, if improperly done, might appreciably affect the weight, balance, structural strength, performance, powerplant operation, flight characteristics, or other qualities affecting airworthiness; or
(2) That is not done according to accepted practices or cannot be done by elementary operations."

make-before-break switch (electrical switch). A type of two-pole switch that, when switching from one circuit to another, makes contact with the second circuit before it breaks contact with the first.

make/model. The manufacturer and model of a specific aircraft.

"Make short approach" (air traffic control). A phrase used by ATC to inform a pilot to alter his traffic pattern so as to make a short final approach.

male connector (electrical connector). The half of an electrical connector that contains pin-type contacts that complete circuits by sliding into sockets (female connectors).

malfunction. The improper operation of a component or system.

Malfunction and Defect Report (M & D Report). A small postcard-like form used by repair stations, maintenance shops, and technicians to report to the FAA a defect or unacceptable condition discovered in an FAA-certificated component. Information gathered on M & D reports allows the FAA to identify and track weaknesses in certificated products that could create a safety problem. M & D reports provide the basis for the General Airworthiness Alerts and subsequent Airworthiness Directives.

malleability. The ability of a material to be stretched or shaped by rolling or hammering it. Malleable materials do not crack when they are formed in this way. Gold and lead have a high degree of malleability. Both can be shaped into almost any desired form by hammering or beating them.

mallet. A type of hammer whose head has the shape of a cylinder. Mallet heads are usually made of a soft material such as wood, plastic, fiber, leather, or a soft metal, such as brass or lead.

mammatus (meteorology). A cellular pattern of pouches that hangs underneath the base of a cloud, often a cumulus or cumulonimbus.

M

mandatory altitude (air traffic control). An altitude depicted on an Instrument Approach Procedure Chart requiring the aircraft to maintain altitude at the depicted value.

mandatory block altitude (air traffic control). An altitude depicted on an instrument approach chart with two altitude values underscored and overscored. Aircraft are required to maintain altitude between the depicted values.

mandrel (machine tool). A tapered shaft or spindle that fits into a hole. A mandrel is used to support and center a device or piece of material so it can be machined in a lathe or balanced on a balancing machine.

mandrel (tube bending machine). A long steel rod with a rounded end that is inserted into a piece of thin-wall metal tubing when it is being bent in a tube-bending machine. The rounded end of the rod is held at the point the bend is started to keep the tubing from flattening as it is bent.

mandrel (propeller balancing component). A precision steel bar on which a propeller is mounted for balancing. The mandrel is placed across two perfectly level knife-edge plates and the propeller is allowed to rotate until it stops with its heavy point at the bottom.

maneuverability. *See* controllability.

maneuvering altitude. An altitude above the ground that allows a sufficient margin of height to permit safe maneuvering.

maneuvering area (flight operations). That part of an airport intended for the taking off and landing of aircraft and for the movement of aircraft associated with takeoff and landing. It excludes the aprons.

maneuvering speed (aircraft specification). The maximum speed at which the flight controls can be fully deflected without damage to the airplane structure.

manganese. A silvery, brittle, metallic chemical element. Manganese's symbol is Mn, its atomic number is 25, and its atomic weight is 54.938. Manganese is used as an alloy for steel to increase its strength, hardness, and wear resistance.

manganese dioxide. A chemical compound used as a depolarizer in carbon-zinc batteries. Hydrogen gas forms in bubbles on the carbon rod when electrons flow to it from the zinc can. If these bubbles are allowed to remain on the rod, they will insulate it from the electrolyte and shut off the flow of electrons. Manganese dioxide absorbs the hydrogen gas, allowing the electrolyte to remain in contact with the carbon rod and keep the electrons flowing.

Manganin. The registered trade name for an alloy of copper, manganese, and nickel. Manganin is used for wire-wound resistors because its resistance changes very little as its temperature changes.

manifold absolute pressure. *See* MAP.

manifold (hydraulic system component). The portions of an aircraft hydraulic system to which the selector valves are connected. Selector valves receive pressurized fluid from the pressure manifold and route return fluid from the actuators to the return manifold and then to the reservoir.

manifold (reciprocating engine exhaust system component). A chamber connected to the exhaust ports on the cylinders of an engine. All the cylinders empty their exhaust gases into the manifold from which they are carried overboard through the muffler and tail pipe.

manifold cross-feed fuel system. A type of fuel system commonly used in large transport-category aircraft. All fuel tanks feed into a common manifold, and the dump chutes and the single-point fueling valves are connected to the manifold. Fuel lines to each engine are taken from the manifold.

manifold pressure. *14 CFR Part 1:* "Absolute pressure as measured at the appropriate point in the induction system and usually expressed in inches of mercury."

manifold pressure gage. A pressure gage that measures the absolute pressure inside the induction system of a reciprocating engine. When the engine is not operating, this instrument shows the existing atmospheric pressure.

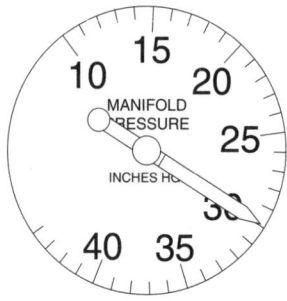

manifold valve. *See* flow divider.

manometer. An instrument used to measure low values of air pressure. A manometer consists of a long glass tube mounted in front of a calibrated scale. The tube is filled with a liquid, and air pressure forces the liquid up in the tube where its height is measured against the scale.

manifold pressure gage

Different ranges of pressure can be measured by using different liquids: water is used for low pressure, ethylene dibromide for medium pressure, and mercury for higher pressure. Differential pressure can be measured by forming the tube into the shape of the letter U and applying the two pressures to the two ends of the tube.

man-portable air-defense systems (MANPADS). Lightweight, shoulder-launched missile weapon systems designed for the purpose of bringing down aircraft or attacking ground targets. Although these weapons have limited range and their accuracy is affected by poor visibility and adverse weather, they can be used anywhere on land or sea where there is unrestricted visibility to the target and as such are a potential threat to airborne aircraft.

manual depressurization valve (aircraft pressurization system component). A manual back-up for the automatic cabin pressure outflow valve. If the automatic outflow valve should malfunction, the cabin pressure can be controlled with the manual depressurization valve.

manufactured rivet head. The head of a rivet that was formed when the rivet was manufactured. The head formed when the rivet is driven is called the shop head. Rivets used in aircraft construction have several different shapes of manufactured heads. The most common are: the universal head (MS20470), the 100° countersunk head (MS20426), the round head (AN 430), and the flat head (AN 442).

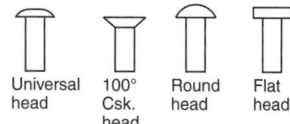

manufactured rivet heads

manufacturer's maintenance or service manual. A document issued by the manufacturer of an aircraft, engine, or component and approved by the FAA that details procedures to be followed for the maintenance of the specific device.

manufacturing. The process in which raw materials are changed into finished and usable products. An aircraft is manufactured when the raw aluminum, iron, copper, and organic chemicals are changed into the finished product.

MAP (manifold absolute pressure). The absolute pressure of the fuel/air mixture inside the induction system of a reciprocating engine, usually measured in inches of mercury. The manifold pressure of a nonsupercharged engine can never be higher than the pressure of the surrounding air, but supercharging can increase the manifold pressure above that of the atmosphere.

MAP (missed approach point) (air traffic control). A point prescribed in each instrument approach at which a missed approach procedure shall be executed if the required visual reference does not exist.

M

Marconi antenna (radio antenna). A quarter-wavelength, vertically polarized antenna, normally used for transmitting and receiving radio communications in the higher frequency bands. Aircraft communications in the very-high-frequency (VHF) band normally uses a Marconi antenna whose length is one fourth of the wavelength of the center frequency to be transmitted.

One conductor from the transmitter is connected to the quarter-wave antenna, and the other conductor is connected to the metal structure of the aircraft on which the antenna is mounted. This metal structure serves as a quarter-wavelength reflector. A Marconi antenna is nondirectional (it radiates its signal equally well in all directions).

mare's tail (meteorology). A cirrus cloud with a curve on one end and a long flowing tail on the other.

marginal VFR (MVFR). Weather conditions with a ceiling of 1,000 to 3,000 feet and/or visibility 3 to 5 miles inclusive.

margin identification. The top and bottom areas on an instrument approach chart that depict information about the procedure, including airport location and procedure identification.

marine grommet (aircraft fabric covering component). A small plastic or metal reinforcing ring attached to the fabric covering at low points in the structure and at the trailing edges of the wing and tail surfaces. Grommets are used to reinforce the drain or vent holes cut in the fabric at these locations. A marine grommet, also called a seaplane grommet, differs from ordinary grommets because of a shield placed over the hole. This shield keeps the spray during takeoff and landing from getting into the structure.

marker beacon (radio navigation equipment). A low-powered, 75-MHz, fixed-frequency radio transmitter that directs its signal vertically upward in a small, fan-shaped pattern. Marker beacons are located along the flight path used when approaching an airport for landing, and are identified by their modulation frequency and keying code. When received by compatible airborne equipment, marker beacons indicate to the pilot, both aurally and visually, when the aircraft is directly over the facility.

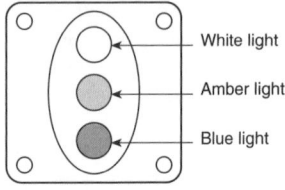

White light

Amber light

Blue light

marker beacon lights

When the aircraft is directly above the outer marker the pilot hears a series of 400-hertz dashes and the blue light illuminates in the series of dashes. Over the middle marker, the amber light illuminates in a series of alternate dots and dashes and the aural tone is a series of 1,300-hertz dots and dashes. The inner marker is identified by the white light illuminating in a series of dots and a series of 3,000-hertz dots is heard by the pilot.

married needles (helicopter operation). The needles (pointers) of a dual tachometer indicator installed in a helicopter are said to "married" when one needle is exactly on top of the other. One needle is driven by a tachometer generator on the engine and the other by a generator on the transmission that senses the speed of the rotor. When the rotor-drive clutch is fully engaged and there is no slippage, the needles are married.

Martin clip (fabric covering component). A patented wire clip used to attach aircraft fabric to the wing ribs. A Martin clip is long piece of spring steel wire with a series of hooks bent into it at each location the

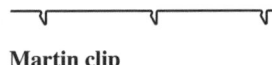

Martin clip

fabric should be attached to the rib cap strip. The hooks are pressed through small slits in the reinforcing tape and the fabric and through elongated holes in the rib cap strips. The hooks lock the clip in the holes and pull the fabric tight against the cap strip. The use of Martin clips rather than rib stitching saves a tremendous amount of time when covering an aircraft surface.

masking material (aircraft finishing). Masks are used to prevent the finishing materials coming into contact with a surface. Masks are made of such materials as thin metal, fiberboard, paper, or masking tape.

masking tape. Paper tape with a pressure-sensitive adhesive on one side. Masking tape has a wrinkled texture so it will lie smoothly around a curve, and the adhesive is easily removed from a properly prepared surface. Masking tape is used to fasten paper to parts of a surface being painted, to prevent the paint from reaching certain areas.

Masonite. The registered trade name for a type of fiberboard. Masonite is made by exploding wood chips in a steam gun to break them into long, individual fibers. These fibers are bonded together with lignin (a natural adhesive in the original wood) to make a smooth, grainless sheet of material that can be used for insulation, partitions, etc.

mass. The amount of matter, or material, in an object. To find the mass of an object, divide its weight, in pounds, by 32.2. The constant, 32.2, is derived from the fact that a freely falling object is accelerated by the force of gravity 32.2 feet per second each second it falls.

$$\text{Mass} = \frac{\text{Weight}}{32.2}$$

mass flow rate. The product of fluid density and its linear velocity. The symbol for mass flow rate is the letter G.

massive-electrode spark plug. A type of spark plug used in aircraft reciprocating engines. A massive-electrode spark plug has three or four nickel-alloy ground electrodes surrounding the insulated center electrode. Massive-electrode spark plugs provide reliable ignition under normal operating conditions, but are replaced with fine-wire spark plugs in conditions where lead fouling is a problem.

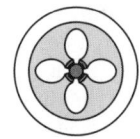

massive-electrode spark plug

mass production. A method of producing large numbers of identical objects by the use of specialized jigs and fixtures. In the process of mass production, the manufacturing procedure is broken down into small steps that can be performed by automatic machinery or that can be done quickly and repeatedly by unskilled workers. Mass production of interchangeable parts has made the manufacture of complex equipment possible and economical.

mast (rotorcraft component). The component that supports the main rotor.

mast bumping (rotorcraft). The action of an underslung rotor head when it strikes the mast.

master cylinder (hydraulic brake system component). The cylinder in an aircraft hydraulic brake system whose piston is moved by the pilot. When the piston is pressed into the master cylinder, hydraulic fluid is forced into the wheel cylinder, applying the brake.

master rod (radial reciprocating engine component). The only rod in a radial engine that connects a piston directly to the crankshaft. The crankshaft of a radial engine has only one throw for each row of cylinders, and the large end of the master rod rides on the journal of this throw. The small end of the master rod is connected through a wrist pin to one piston. The pistons in all the other cylinders in that row attach to link rods (articulated rods) that connect to the master rod through knuckle pins.

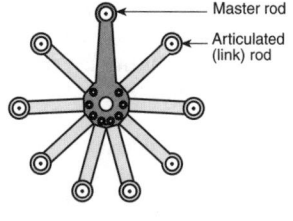

master rod

master switch (aircraft electrical system). A single switch that controls electrical power to all the circuits in an aircraft electrical system. When the master switch (a form of safety switch) is off, no circuit can be energized.

master tank (hot-air balloon). The propane tank, usually tank number one, that offers all appropriate services, such as liquid, vapor, and backup system.

mat (reinforced plastic component). A pack of loose glass fibers that can be impregnated with a plastic resin to strengthen parts being formed in a mold.

matching transformer (electrical component). An electrical transformer with a turns ratio between its coils that matches the impedance of the load to the impedance of the source of electrical power. The impedance of the primary winding of the transformer is the same as the output impedance of the source, and the impedance of its secondary winding is the same as the impedance of the load. The maximum amount of power can be transferred in an electrical circuit when the impedance of the source matches the impedance of the load.

matching-type test item. A test item in which the student is asked to match alternatives on one list to related alternatives on a second list. The lists may include words, terms, illustrations, phrases, or sentences.

matrix (composite materials component). The material that bonds the fibers together and carries the stresses into the fibers in a piece of advanced composite structure. Resins are the most widely used matrix material.

matter. Anything that has mass and takes up space. Matter may exist as a solid, liquid, or gas, and all matter has both physical and chemical properties.

mature stage of a thunderstorm (meteorology). The most intense phase of a thunderstorm. It begins when the first drop of precipitation hits the ground and is characterized by high clouds with an anvil top.

maximum allowable gross lift. The maximum amount of weight that a balloon may lift under standard conditions. This is usually a part of the balloon's design criteria and can be found on the type certificate data sheet for that particular balloon.

maximum allowable takeoff power. The maximum power an engine is allowed to develop for a limited period of time; usually about one minute. For example, especially in the case of go-arounds, the instant the pilot decides to go around, full or maximum allowable takeoff power must be applied smoothly and without hesitation, and held until flying speed and controllability are restored.

maximum allowable zero-fuel weight (aircraft specification). The maximum weight authorized for an aircraft that does not include the weight of the fuel.

maximum altitude. An altitude depicted on an instrument approach chart with an over-scored altitude value, at or below which aircraft are required to maintain altitude.

maximum authorized altitude (air traffic control). A published altitude representing the maximum usable altitude or flight level for an airspace structure or route segment. It is the highest altitude on a Federal airway, jet route, area navigation low or high route, or other direct route for which an MEA is designated in 14 CFR Part 95, at which adequate reception of navigation aid signals is assured.

maximum engine overtorque. The maximum torque of the free power turbine rotor assembly, the inadvertent occurrence of which, for periods of up to 20 seconds, will not require rejection of the engine from service or any maintenance action other than to correct the cause. This applies to turbopropeller and turboshaft engines incorporating free power turbines for all ratings except one-engine-inoperative (OEI) ratings of two minutes or less.

maximum landing weight (aircraft specification). The greatest weight an aircraft is allowed to have when it lands. A takeoff places much less strain on an aircraft structure than a landing, and many aircraft that fly for long distances are allowed to takeoff with a greater weight than they are allowed to have for landing. If an aircraft leaves with its maximum takeoff weight and must return for landing before it has burned off enough fuel to get down to its allowable landing weight, it must be able to dump part of its fuel load.

maximum payload capacity. For an aircraft for which a maximum zero fuel weight is prescribed in FAA technical specifications, this is the maximum zero fuel weight when subtracting empty weight, all justifiable aircraft equipment, and the operating load (minimum flightcrew, foods and beverages, and supplies and equipment related to foods and beverages, but not including disposable fuel or oil). For all other aircraft, maximum payload capacity is the maximum certificated takeoff weight of the aircraft, minus the empty weight, all justifiable aircraft equipment, and operating load (minimum fuel load, oil, and flightcrew). Details regarding the allowance for the weight of the crew, oil, and fuel are found in 14 CFR §110.2.

maximum ramp weight (GAMA). Maximum weight approved for ground maneuver. It includes weight of start, taxi, and runup fuel.

maximum takeoff weight (aircraft specification). The maximum allowable weight at the start of the takeoff run. The aircraft may be initially loaded to a greater weight to allow for fuel burnoff during ground operation. The takeoff weight for a particular flight may be limited to a lesser weight when runway length, atmospheric conditions, or other variables are adverse.

maximum taxi weight. Maximum weight approved for ground maneuvers. This is the same as maximum ramp weight.

maximum weight (aircraft specification). The maximum authorized weight of the aircraft and all of its equipment as specified in the TCDS (Type Certificate Data Sheets) for the aircraft.

maximum wind axis (meteorology). A line on a constant-pressure chart which denotes the axis of maximum wind speeds at that constant-pressure surface.

maximum zero fuel weight. The maximum authorized weight of an aircraft without fuel. This is the sum of the basic operating weight, BOW, and the payload.

maxwell (unit of magnetic flux). The unit of magnetic flux in the centimeter-gram-second system of measurements. One maxwell is equal to one line of magnetic flux. One maxwell gives a magnetic induction of one gauss per square centimeter.

mayday. The international call for help, used with voice radio transmission. The term "mayday" comes from the French word *m'aidez* (help me), pronounced "mayday" in English. Mayday is used in voice transmission in the same way the letters SOS are used in code transmission.

MB. *See* magnetic bearing.

MCA (minimum crossing altitude). The lowest altitude at certain fixes at which an aircraft must cross when proceeding in the direction of a higher minimum en route IFR altitude (MEA).

MCW (modulated continuous wave). A type of radio code transmission in which the carrier wave is modulated with a continuous audio-frequency tone. Code is sent by transmitting the modulated carrier in short and long pulses, or bursts. The short pulses are called dots, and the long pulses are called dashes. Modulated continuous wave code differs from continuous wave (CW) code in that a beat-frequency oscillator is not needed in the receiver for MCW to be heard.

M

MDA (minimum descent altitude). *14 CFR Part 1:* "The lowest altitude, expressed in feet above mean sea level, to which descent is authorized on final approach or during circle-to-land maneuvering in execution of a standard instrument approach procedure, where no electronic glide slope is provided."

MEA (minimum enroute IFR altitude). The lowest published altitude between radio fixes which ensures acceptable navigational signal coverage and meets obstacle clearance requirements between those fixes. The MEA prescribed for a federal airway or segment thereof, area navigation low or high route, or other direct route applies to the entire width of the airway, segment, or route between the radio fixes defining that airway, segment, or route.

mean. A term used for the middle-point, or median. Mean sea level is the midpoint between the highest and lowest level of the sea. Mean values are used when measuring from a reference that moves, or changes, between specific limits.

mean aerodynamic chord. *See* MAC.

mean camber. A line that is drawn midway between the upper and lower camber of an airfoil section. The mean camber determines the aerodynamic characteristics of the airfoil.

Mean camber line

mean camber

mean sea level. *See* MSL.

mean solar day. The time it takes the earth to rotate about its axis, with respect to the mean location of the sun. The length of a mean solar day is 24 hours, 3 minutes, and 56.555 seconds.

mean wind (meteorology). Wind direction and speed as determined from a sample reading every second over the last two minutes.

measured ceiling (meteorology). A ceiling classification applied when the ceiling value has been determined by instruments or the known heights of unobscured portions of objects other than natural landmarks.

mechanic. A person skilled in repairing mechanical devices. The Federal Aviation Administration issues a license for aircraft mechanics with two ratings applicable: airframe and powerplant. *See* A & P mechanic *and* AMT (Aviation Maintenance Technician).

mechanical advantage. The increase in force or speed produced by a mechanical device, such as the lever, pulley, gears, or hydraulic cylinder. These devices increase speed or force, but they cannot produce work. The force needed to lift a weight may be reduced, or the speed at which an object moves may be changed. But if mechanical losses are discounted, the amount of work (force times distance) taken from the device is the same as the amount of work put into it.

mechanical blockage thrust reverser (gas turbine engine component). A type of thrust reverser that uses a pair of clamshell doors set into the tail cone of the engine to deflect the exhaust gases forward when the pilot wants to slow the aircraft.

mechanical efficiency (reciprocating engines). The ratio of the amount of brake horsepower delivered to the output shaft of a reciprocating engine to the amount of indicated horsepower produced in the cylinders of the engine.

mechanical energy. The energy possessed by an object because of its motion (kinetic energy) or its stored energy of position (potential energy).

mechanical properties of metals. Properties used as measurements to show the way metals behave under a load. These properties include strength, hardness, toughness, elasticity, plasticity, brittleness, ductility, and malleability.

Mechanic Certificate. A certificate issued under 14 CFR Part 65, *Certification: Airmen other than Flight Crewmembers,* to a person who demonstrates the required experience, knowledge, and skills. This certificate must be accompanied by either an Airframe or Powerplant rating or both.

MEDEVAC. A term used to request ATC priority handling for a medical evacuation flight based on a medical emergency in the transport of patients, organ donors, organs or other urgently needed life-saving medical material.

median (mathematics). The number, in a series, that has as many numbers below it as there are above it. In the series of numbers 1, 2, 3, 4, 5, 6, 7 the median is 4. There are three numbers below 4 and three numbers above it.

medical certificate. *14 CFR Part 1:* "Acceptable evidence of physical fitness in a form prescribed by the Administrator."

medium banked turn. Turn resulting from a degree of bank (approximately 20 to 45 degrees) at which the aircraft remains at a constant bank.

medium-bypass turbofan engine. A turbofan engine with a bypass ratio of between 2:1 and 4:1. This means that the fan moves two to four times as much air as the core engine.

medium frequency (radio transmission frequency). The portion of the band of frequencies of electromagnetic radiation between 300 kilohertz and 3 megahertz. Commercial radio broadcasting uses the medium frequency band.

medium-scale integration (MSI). An integrated circuit chip having between 10 and 100 gates or gate-equivalent circuits.

mega (M). The metric prefix that means one million, 1,000,000, or 10^6.

megahertz (MHz). A frequency of one million cycles per second.

Megger. The registered trade name for a high-voltage, high-range ohmmeter. A Megger has a built-in, hand-turned generator, to produce the high voltage needed to measure the resistance. Meggers are used to measure insulation resistance and the resistance between components and electrical ground.

megohmmeter. An instrument used to measure very high values of resistance such as found in materials normally considered to be insulators. Megohmmeters use a high voltage to force current through the material and a sensitive indicator to measure the extremely small current that results.

MEK (methyl-ethyl-ketone). A volatile organic chemical solvent that is soluble in water and is used as a solvent for vinyl and nitrocellulose films. MEK is an efficient solvent for removing oily contaminants from ignition system components and for cleaning and preparing surfaces for priming or painting. MEK's chemical formula is $CH_3COC_2H_5$.

MEL. *See* minimum equipment list.

melt. To change the physical state of a material from a solid to a liquid. A material melts when it absorbs enough heat to change from a solid into a liquid.

melting point. The temperature at which a material changes from a solid into a liquid because of the heat it has absorbed.

memory (in learning process). The ability of people and other organisms to store and use information, consisting of three main stages: encoding (initial perception and registration of information), storage (retention of encoded information over time), and retrieval (processes involved in using stored information).

mendelevium. A radioactive chemical element in the actinide series. Mendelevium's symbol is Md, and its atomic number is 101. Mendelevium is made by bombarding lighter elements with light nuclei accelerated in cyclotrons.

meniscus. The shape of the top of a column of liquid caused by surface tension. Water wets the inside of a glass tube, and capillary action pulls the water up the sides of the tube. Surface tension causes the meniscus of water to be concave. Mercury does not wet the glass, so surface tension causes mercury to have a convex meniscus.

When reading a barometer or manometer using a column of liquid in front of a calibrated scale, read the height of the column at a point tangent to the meniscus rather than from the edge of the liquid on the glass.

meniscus lens (optics). A simple lens having one concave and one convex side. If the convex side has a longer focal length than the concave side, the lens is a diverging lens. But if the concave side has the longer focal length, the lens is a converging lens.

mensuration. The act of measuring or computing lengths, areas, volumes, and angles of various geometric shapes or quantities.

Mercator projection (navigation). The projection used for map making in which the meridians of longitude and parallels of latitude are straight, parallel lines. The distance between each meridian of longitude is the same, but the parallels of latitude are close together near the equator and become increasingly farther apart as they near the poles. The shape and size of land masses near the poles are greatly distorted on a map drawn on a Mercator projection.

mercerize. A treatment given to cotton thread to make it strong and lustrous. The thread is stretched while it is soaked in a solution of caustic soda. Mercerized thread has a sheen similar to silk, it is stronger and more pliable than untreated thread, and it accepts dye more readily.

mercury. A silvery-white, poisonous, metallic chemical element that is liquid at room temperature. Mercury's symbol is Hg, its atomic number is 80, and its atomic weight is 200.59. Mercury is heavy (more than 13 times as heavy as water), is a good conductor of electricity, and readily unites with other chemical elements. It is used in thermometers to measure temperature by the amount it expands or contracts as temperature changes. It is also used in barometers to determine the pressure of the atmosphere by measuring the height of the column of mercury the atmospheric pressure supports.

M

mercury barometer. An instrument used to measure atmospheric pressure. A glass tube about one meter long, with one end closed and the other end open, is filled with mercury, and the open end is submerged in a bowl, or cistern, of mercury. The mercury in the tube will drop down, leaving a vacuum above the mercury in the closed end.

Atmospheric pressure pressing down on the mercury in the bowl holds the mercury up inside the tube. The height of the top of the mercury in the tube above the level of the mercury in the bowl is an accurate measure of the amount of pressure produced by the weight of the atmosphere. Standard atmospheric pressure at sea level holds the mercury up in the tube to a height of 760 millimeters, or 29.92 inches.

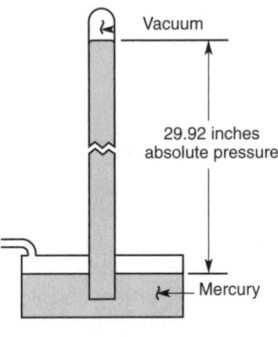

mercury barometer

mercury cell (electrical battery). A type of primary electrical cell (a cell that cannot be recharged). A mercury cell uses zinc for its anode (positive terminal), mercuric oxide for the cathode (negative terminal), and potassium hydroxide for the electrolyte. A mercury cell has a longer life than either an alkaline cell or a carbon-zinc cell, and its low internal resistance allows it to hold a constant output voltage until it is almost completely discharged.

mercury oxide cell. A nonrechargeable electrochemical battery, a primary cell. The anode material is pure powdered zinc and the cathode material is mercuric oxide. The electrolyte is a paste of potassium hydroxide in water. The case of the mercury oxide battery is nickel plated and acts as the positive terminal, or cathode, of the cell.

mercury switch. A form of electrical switch using mercury in a glass tube as a conductor. Two wires are brought into the glass tube in such a way that they are near each other, but do not touch. When the tube is tilted in such a way that mercury sealed in the tube covers the ends of the two wires, the switch is closed and current flows through the mercury. When the tube is tilted in the opposite direction, the mercury moves away from the wires, the switch is open, and no current flows.

mercury thermometer. A form of liquid thermometer. A glass tube having an extremely small inside diameter is attached to a small reservoir completely filled with mercury. The volume of mercury in the reservoir is determined by its temperature. As the mercury absorbs heat, it expands and rises inside the tube. A temperature scale is marked alongside the tube, and, since the height of the mercury in the tube relates to the temperature of the mercury in the reservoir, the level of the top of the column of mercury can be marked to indicate the temperature.

mercury vapor lamp. A form of electric-arc lamp. An arc is formed inside a transparent tube between two electrodes in an atmosphere of mercury vapor. Mercury-vapor lamps produce a bluish-green light containing a large amount of ultraviolet radiation.

mercury vapor rectifier (electrical component). A type of electrical component, used to change alternating current into direct current. Drops of liquid mercury inside an evacuated glass tube are changed into mercury vapor by heat from a built-in filament. Mercury vapor can be ionized by a low voltage of one polarity, but it must have an extremely high voltage of the opposite polarity to ionize it. This makes it a good rectifier. Mercury rectifiers have a small voltage drop across them when they are conducting, and they are efficient conductors of large amounts of current in high-voltage circuits.

meridian (navigation). An imaginary great circle on the surface of the earth that passes through the North and South geographic poles. The reference, or prime, meridian passes through the Royal Observatory in Greenwich, England, and the meridians are numbered in degrees east and west to the 180° meridian, which is the international date line.

mesopause (meteorology). The top of the mesosphere and the base of the thermosphere.

mesoscale (meteorology). A term that refers to features with spatial dimensions of one-tenth to 1 nautical mile and lasting for seconds to minutes.

mesoscale convective complex (MCC). A large mesoscale convective system, generally round or oval-shaped, which normally reaches peak intensity at night.

mesoscale convective system (MCS). A large cluster of thunderstorms with horizontal dimensions on the order of 100 miles. MCS's are sometimes organized in a long line of thunderstorms (e.g., a squall line) or as a random grouping of thunderstorms. Individual thunderstorms within the MCS may be severe.

mesosphere. The portion of the earth's atmosphere extending from about 45 to 55 kilometers (28 to 34 miles) up to about 80 to 95 kilometers (50 to 59 miles). The mesosphere begins at the top of the stratosphere, and in the mesosphere, the temperature generally decreases with altitude.

metal. A fusible, ductile, lustrous material. Fusible means it can be melted, ductile means its shape can be changed by drawing or stretching, and lustrous means it reflects light evenly without sparkling. Nearly all metals are good conductors of electricity and heat, and all metals readily lose electrons to form positive ions.

metal fatigue. The progressive, localized, and permanent structural damage that occurs within a metal when it is subjected to repeated cyclic or fluctuating strains. The stresses causing these strains may be much less than the static yield strength of the material.

M

metal-film resistor (electrical component). A type of electrical resistor made by depositing an extremely thin film of metal on a ceramic form. The thickness and type of metal film determines the resistance and the power-dissipating ability of the resistor.

metal foil (electrical capacitor component). A very thin sheet of metal used as an electrode in electrolytic capacitors. The use of foil allows a large-area electrode to be contained in a small physical space.

metal-ion concentration-cell corrosion. A type of concentration-cell corrosion that forms in the metal skin of an aircraft along the edges of a lap joint where moisture can be trapped. When trapped water absorbs oxygen from the air, it attracts electrons from the metal and forms negative hydroxide ions. When electrons are taken from the metal, positive metallic ions are left, and these positive ions collect in the stagnant moisture trapped between the skins in the lap joint. The positive ions attract electrons from the metal along the edges of the lap joint and cause the metal to unite with the hydroxide ions in the moisture to form a salt. This salt is corrosion.

metallic pigment. Thin flakes of aluminum or copper that are mixed with a liquid vehicle to serve as the pigment for paint. When the paint is applied to a surface, these tiny flakes spread out to form a solid, opaque covering.

metallic ring test (test for bonded-structure delamination). A very simple test for delamination in a bonded structural component. The material is tapped with a coin, and the sound is noted. If the sound is a clear metallic ringing, the material is good, and there is no delamination. But if the tapping produces a dull thudding noise, there is a good possibility that the laminations of which the material is made have begun to separate.

metallizing. (1) The application of molten metal onto the surface of any solid base material by spraying or by vacuum evaporation. (2) The replacing of fabric covering of an airplane structure with thin sheet metal.

metallurgy. The area of materials science and engineering that relates to the physical and chemical behavior of metallic elements, their intermetallic compounds and their mixtures, or alloys.

metal oxide rectifier. A form of electrical rectifier that operates on the principle that electrons can flow from a base metal through a film of oxide, but cannot flow through the oxide into the base metal. Copper oxide and selenium oxide rectifiers have both been used in the past, but they have been replaced, to a great extent, by silicon or germanium semiconductor diode rectifiers.

metal oxide semiconductor capacitor. *See* MOS capacitor.

metal oxide semiconductor field effect transistor. *See* MOSFET.

metal spinning. A method of forming sheet metal. A disk of metal is clamped in a lathe in front of a male die whose shape is that of the inside of the part to be spun. The lathe is turned at a high speed, and the metal is forced against the die with a wooden tool.

metal spraying. A method of covering a material with a coating of metal. The metal to be used for the coating is melted and sprayed out with hot, high-velocity compressed air. Metal spraying is used to cover a steel part with aluminum to prevent corrosion, and it can also be used to cover a nonconductive material, such as wood or paper, with metal to make it electrically conductive.

METAR (aviation routine weather report). Observation of current surface weather reported in a standard international format.

metastable compound. A chemical compound that is stable under some conditions, but unstable under others.

meteor. A small particle of solar matter that is visible only as it becomes incandescent (glows because of its extremely high temperature). The high temperature is caused by friction as the meteor falls through the earth's atmosphere. Meteors are made of metal or rock or a combination of metal and rock. They are often called "shooting stars" or "falling stars," and millions of burned-out particles of meteors fall on the earth each day as dust.

meteorological impact statement (air traffic control). *See* MIS.

meteorological visibility. A main category of visibility which includes the subcategories of prevailing visibility and runway visibility. Meteorological visibility is a measure of horizontal visibility near the earth's surface, based on sighting of objects in the daytime or unfocused lights of moderate intensity at night.

meteorology. The branch of science that deals with the physical properties of the atmosphere. Meteorology deals with the way weather conditions develop and change.

meter. The basic unit of length measurement in the metric system. One meter is equal to one ten-millionth of the distance between the equator and the earth's north pole. The length of the standard meter is marked on a special bar of platinum alloy deposited in Paris, France. One meter is equal to 1,650,763.73 wavelengths of the orange light emitted when an electric arc passes through krypton gas. One meter is also equal to 39.37 inches, and in the metric system the meter can be changed into millimeters, centimeters, and kilometers by dividing or multiplying by units of ten.

meter fix arc (air traffic control). A semicircle of area, equidistant from a meter fix and usually located at low altitude relatively close to the meter fix, used to help controllers calculate a meter time and determine appropriate sector meter list assignments for aircraft not on an established arrival route or assigned a meter fix.

meter fix time/slot time (air traffic control). A calculated time to depart the meter fix in order to cross the vertex at the actual calculated landing time (ACLT). This time reflects descent speed adjustment and any applicable time that must be absorbed prior to crossing the meter fix.

metering (air traffic control). A method of time-regulating arrival traffic flow into a terminal area so as not to exceed a predetermined terminal acceptance rate.

metering airports (ATC term). Airports adapted for metering and for which optimum flight paths are defined. A maximum of 15 airports may be adapted.

metering fix, or meter fix (air traffic control). A fix along an established route from over which aircraft will be metered prior to entering terminal airspace. Normally, this fix should be established at a distance from the airport which will facilitate a profile descent 10,000 feet above airport elevation or above.

metering jet. A precision orifice used to restrict the flow of a fluid. The diameter and length of the orifice, and the approach and departure angles to and from the orifice, all determine the amount of fluid that can flow under a given pressure drop across the orifice. *See* illustration for calibrated orifice.

metering pin. A flow control device in a metering orifice, used to vary the amount of fluid that can flow through it. The area of the orifice with the pin fully in it determines the minimum amount of fluid that can flow, and the area of the jet with the pin all the way out determines the maximum amount of flow. The shape, or contour, of the metering pin determines the amount of fluid that can flow with the pin in any position other than full in or full out.

metering position(s) (air traffic control). Controller plan view displays and main display monitors, and associated "D" positions, which have been adapted for display of a metering position list. A maximum of four plan view displays (PVDs) may be adapted. An ATC metering position keeps track of when aircraft will be allowed to takeoff, in such a way that time-regulates the traffic flow. *See also* metering.

metering position list (air traffic control). An ordered list of data on aircraft arrivals for a selected metering airport shown on a metering position plan view display or main display monitor.

metering valve (balloon operation). A valve on a balloon heater that can be set to allow propane to pass through at a specific rate.

meter-kilogram. The amount of work done when one kilogram of force acts through a distance of one meter.

meter list display interval (MLDI) (air traffic control). A dynamic parameter that controls the number of minutes prior to the flight plan calculated time of arrival at the meter fix for each aircraft that the "tentative calculated landing time (TCLT)" is frozen and becomes an "actual calculated landing time (ACLT)." In this ATC computer process, the vertex time of arrival (VTA) is updated and consequently the TCLT is modified as appropriate until frozen, at which time updating is suspended and an ACLT is assigned. When frozen, the flight entry is inserted into the arrival sector's meter list for display on the sector plan view display (PVD) or main display monitor. MLDI is used if the filed true airspeed is less than or equal to the freeze speed parameters (FSPD).

methanol (wood alcohol). A poisonous liquid alcohol, formed by the distillation of wood pulp. Methanol is used as a fuel, a solvent, and an antifreeze agent.

methylene chloride. A chemical compound, CH_2Cl_2, that has a very high volatility and the ability to dissolve a wide range of organic compounds. It is used as the volatile agent in pressure type oil temperature indicators and as active element in some paint strippers. It must be used with caution because of its potential risk of causing cancer, and of its adverse effects on the heart, central nervous system and liver.

METO power (maximum except takeoff power). A rating for aircraft reciprocating engines. METO power is the maximum power allowed to be continuously produced by an engine. Takeoff power is usually limited to a given amount of time, such as one minute or five minutes.

metric horsepower. A unit of power equal to 75 meter-kilograms of work per second. One metric horsepower is also equal to approximately 753.5 watts of power.

metric prefixes. The metric system operates on the basis of each unit being a multiple of ten times the base unit. Each value, or multiple of ten, has its own prefix name. The prefixes most commonly used in electrical and electronic work are:

Tera ....10^{12}
Giga..10^9
Mega..10^6
Kilo ....10^3
Milli ....10^{-3}
Micro ....10^{-6}
Nano..10^{-9}
Pico ....10^{-12}

MFD (multi-function display). A computer screen (LCD or CRT) that electronically displays navigational information such as GPS moving maps, airport data, weather information, terrain proximity, and aircraft engine and systems information, replacing several analog-type indicators.

MH. *See* magnetic heading.

MHA (minimum holding altitude) (air traffic control). The lowest altitude prescribed for a holding pattern which assures navigational signal coverage and communications and meets obstacle clearance requirements.

mho. A unit of electrical conductance; it has been replaced by the siemen. One mho (one siemen) is the amount of conductance that allows an electrical pressure of one volt to cause a continuous flow of one ampere of current. The mho is the reciprocal, or opposite, of the ohm.

MHz (megahertz). 1,000,000 cycles per second.

MIA (minimum IFR altitudes). Minimum altitudes for IFR operation as prescribed in 14 CFR Part 91. These altitudes are published on Aeronautical charts and prescribed in 14 CFR Part 95 for airways and routes, and in 14 CFR Part 97 for standard instrument approach procedures. If no applicable minimum altitude is prescribed in 14 CFR Parts 95 or 97, the following minimum IFR altitude applies:

1. In designated mountainous areas: 2,000 feet above the highest obstacle within a horizontal distance of five statute miles from the course to be flown.

2. Other than mountainous areas: 1,000 feet above the highest obstacle within a horizontal distance of five statute miles from the course to be flown.

3. As otherwise authorized by the Administrator or assigned by ATC.

mica. A transparent mineral of the silicate family that can be separated into thin sheets. Mica is a very good thermal and electrical insulator. Thin sheets of mica are used as the dielectric in capacitors and as insulators for electric irons and heaters.

Micarta. The registered trade name for a thermosetting phenolic-resin-impregnated cloth. Micarta is used as an electrical insulator, as a chemical-resistant covering for tables and work surfaces, and for pulleys and cable guides in aircraft control systems.

mice (gas turbine engine components). Small restrictors placed in the tail pipe of a gas turbine engine to change the exhaust nozzle area. Changing the area of the exhaust nozzle affects the trim conditions of the engine.

micro. The metric prefix that means one millionth, $^1/_{1,000,000}$, or 0.000 001 of a unit. Micro-farads, microhenries, microwatts, and micrograms are all commonly used terms having this prefix. Micro is also generally used as a prefix to mean something is unusually small; for example, microelectronics, microbiology, and microgroove.

microammeter. An electrical current measuring instrument sensitive enough to measure a flow as small as a few microamperes (millionths of an ampere).

microballoons. Hollow, microscopic-size spheres of hardened phenolic resin. Microballoons add body with very little weight to a resin used as a filler. The resin is mixed with the proper amount of accelerator, and then sufficient microballoons are added to give the resin enough body to be an effective filler.

microbarograph (meteorology). An aneroid barograph designed to record atmospheric pressure changes of very small magnitudes.

microbes. Extremely small living plant and animal organisms, including bacteria, mold, and algae. The term more often used for this is *micro-organisms.*

microbial contaminants. A scum inside the fuel tanks of turbine-engine-powered aircraft caused by micro-organisms that feed on the fuel and live in water that has condensed from the fuel. This scum clogs fuel filters, lines, and fuel controls and holds water in contact with the aluminum alloy fuel tank structure causing severe corrosion.

microbiological corrosion. Microbiological corrosion is the deterioration of materials caused directly or indirectly by bacteria, algae, molds or fungi; singly or in combination.

microburst (meteorology). A localized, extremely high-intensity column of descending air. Microbursts have such extreme downward velocity that any aircraft, when flying slow near the ground, as during takeoff and landing, can be slammed into the ground before it is able to fly out of it.

microcircuit (electronic component). A small electronic device having a large number of equivalent circuit elements made onto a single substrate, or layer of supporting material. An IC chip is an excellent example of a microcircuit, as it contains many equivalent components and many separate circuits, all in an extremely small package.

microcomputer. An electronic computer consisting of a central processing unit (CPU), input and output devices, and some memory capacity. Microcomputers are smaller and slower than either mini-computers or mainframe computers.

microelectronics. The branch of electronics working with integrated circuits (ICs) and with extremely small circuit components.

micro-enroute automated radar tracking system (MEARTS). An automated radar tracking system capable of employing both short-range and long-range radars.

microfarad. A unit of capacitance equal to one millionth of a farad. The microfarad, abbreviated μf, mf, or mfd, is equal to 1×10^{-6} farads, or 1,000,000 (1×10^6) picofarads.

microfiche. A photographic method of record storage in which information to be stored is photographed and printed on sheets of photographic film called fiche. Different formats, ranging from 24 pages to 288 pages of information, can be printed on a single fiche. Microfiche is read in an enlarging machine, called a reader, that displays the page of information on a screen that looks much like a television screen. Some readers have a built-in printer that can produce a full-size printed copy of the information.

microfilm. A photographic method of record storage in which the information to be stored is photographed, one page at a time, on a long roll of 35-millimeter film. The film, called microfilm, is put into a reader which projects the image on the back of a translucent screen that looks much like a television screen. The image of the page shows up in a size that is larger than the original page.

microinches rms. A measure used for cylinder wall surface roughness. One microinch is equal to one millionth of an inch (0.000 001 inch). If a cylinder wall is required to have a roughness of 20 microinches rms (20 μin rms), the highest and lowest deviation from the average surface is 20 millionths of an inch.

Micro-Mesh. A patented graduated series of cloth-backed cushioned sheets which contain abrasive crystals. Micro-Mesh is used for polishing and restoring transparency to acrylic plastic windows and windshields.

micrometer (unit of length). A unit of length equal to one millionth of a meter. A micrometer is also called a micron.

micrometer caliper. A precision measuring instrument in which the spindle moves in and out a specific amount for each revolution of the thimble. The amount the thimble turns, as shown on a scale engraved on the thimble, determines the amount the spindle moves. Micrometer calipers are built into instruments used to measure outside and inside dimensions and the depth of grooves.

micrometer-setting torque wrench (precision hand tool). A type of hand-operated torque wrench in which the wrench handle snaps when the preset torque on the wrench drive is reached. The preset value of torque is determined by the compression of a spring in the wrench handle, and this compression is adjusted by screwing the handle onto the wrench body. The body and handle are marked in the same way as the spindle and thimble of a micrometer caliper.

micro-microfarad. A unit of capacitance equal to one millionth of a millionth (1×10^{-12}) of a farad. The term micro-microfarads has been changed to picofarads.

micron (linear measurement). A unit of linear measurement equal to one millionth of a meter (0.000 001 or 1×10^{-6} meter), one thousandth of a millimeter, or 0.000 039 inch. A micron is also called a micrometer (micro meter).

micron (pressure measurement). The amount of pressure exerted by a column of mercury one micrometer (one millionth of a meter) high, under standard conditions. One micron of pressure is equal to 0.001 millimeter of mercury (1×10^{-6} meter of mercury) at 0°C.

micron (filter specification). A unit used to measure the effectiveness of a hydraulic filter and to identify the size of particles that are trapped by filters. One micron is a micrometer, or one millionth of a meter. It is 0.000 039 inch.

Micronic filter. The registered trade name for a type of fluid filter whose filtering element is a specially treated cellulose paper formed into vertical convolutions, or wrinkles. Micronic filters prevent the passage of solids larger than about 10 microns, and they are normally replaced with new filters rather than being cleaned.

micro-organism. An organism, normally bacteria or fungus, of microscopic size.

microphone. An acoustic transducer. A microphone changes sound pressure variations into electrical signals.

microprocessor. A small central processing unit (CPU) for a microcomputer. A microprocessor is built into a single integrated circuit chip, and it includes the arithmetic-logic unit (ALU), the control unit, and the necessary registers that serve as the computer memory.

microscope. An optical instrument used to magnify the size of an extremely small image. A compound microscope uses an objective lens to magnify the image of an object to form the primary image. An eyepiece lens (ocular lens) further magnifies the primary image. A compound microscope may have several different strengths of objective lenses mounted on a turret, so that different magnifications can be made.

microsecond. A unit of time equal to one millionth of a second.

microshaver. A metal-cutting tool used to shave the head of a countersunk rivet, so that it is perfectly flush with the surface of the metal in which it is installed. The depth the microshaver cuts is adjusted with a micrometer-type scale.

Microswitch. The registered trade name for a precision electrical switch, used as a limit switch. Microswitches are actuated by very small and precise movement of the actuator and are used to control the movement of mechanical devices.

microwave landing system. *See* MLS.

microwaves. A general classification of electromagnetic radiation having wavelengths between 0.3 and 30 centimeters. These wavelengths correspond to frequencies between one and 100 gigahertz (1×10^9, and 100×10^9 hertz).

Microwave radiation falls between infrared waves and radio waves, and many of the principles which apply to the transmission of light also apply to the transmission of microwave radiation. Microwaves used in communications are transmitted from antennas mounted in dish-shaped reflectors and are concentrated and aimed in much the same way as a beam of light.

middle marker (ILS system component). A marker beacon that defines a point along the glideslope of an ILS. It is normally located at or near the point of decision height (ILS Category I). It is keyed to transmit alternate dots and dashes at the rate of 95 dot/dash combinations per minute on a 1300 Hz tone which is received aurally and visually by compatible airborne equipment.

mid-RVR. The runway visual reference, RVR, readout values obtained from sensors located midfield of the runway.

MIG welding (metal inert gas welding). A form of electric arc welding in which the electrode is an expendable wire. MIG welding is now called GMA (gas metal arc) welding.

mil. A unit of length equal to $^1/_{1,000}$ inch (0.001 inch). Mil is short for milli-inch.

mildew. A gray or white fungus growth that forms on organic matter. Mildew forms on cotton and linen aircraft fabric and destroys its strength.

mildewcide. A material used to kill mildew before it destroys organic materials, such as cotton or linen fabric or leather. Cotton and linen fabric are both used to cover aircraft structure, and unless they are protected by a mildewcide, they soon lose their strength. A mildewcide is mixed in the first coat of clear dope applied to these fabrics.

mild steel. Steel containing between 0.05 and 0.25 percent carbon. Mild steel is used for applications where high strength and light weight are not required.

mile. A unit of distance in the English system of measurement. One statute mile is equal to 5,280 feet. One nautical mile is one minute of arc of a great circle of the earth, and is equal to approximately 6,080 feet.

mileage break (ATC term). A point on a route where the leg segment mileage ends, and a new leg segment mileage begins, often at a route turning point.

miles-in-trail (MIT) (air traffic control). The specific number of miles (stated in NM) required between aircraft that meet a specific criteria, which may be separation, airport, fix, altitude, sector, or route specific. MIT are used to apportion traffic into manageable flows, as well as provide space for additional traffic (merging or departing) to enter the flow of traffic. Normally this is in the same stratum associated with the same destination or route of flight. *See also* minutes-in-trail (MINIT).

military airspace management system (MAMS). A Department of Defense system to collect and disseminate information on the current status of special use airspace. This information is provided to the Special Use Airspace Management System (SAMS). The electronic interface also provides SUA schedules and historical activation and utilization data.

"military authority assumes responsibility for separation of aircraft" (air traffic control). An ATC phrase describing a condition in which the military services involved assume responsibility for separation between participating military aircraft in the ATC system. It is used only for required IFR operations specified in Letters of Agreement (LOA) or other appropriate FAA or military documents.

military landing zone. A landing strip used exclusively by the military for training. A military landing zone does not carry a runway designation.

military operations area (MOA). A MOA is airspace established outside of Class A airspace area to separate or segregate certain nonhazardous military activities from IFR traffic and to identify for VFR traffic where these activities are conducted.

military standards (MS). *See* MIL standards.

military training route (MTR). Airspace of defined vertical and lateral dimensions established for the conduct of military training at airspeeds in excess of 250 KIAS.

M

milli, m. The metric prefix meaning one thousandth of a unit, $^{1}/_{1,000}$, 0.001, or 1×10^{-3}. Millimeters, milliliters, milliohms, milligrams, and millivolts are commonly used terms having this prefix.

milliammeter. An instrument that measures electrical current in units of thousandths of an ampere.

millibar. A measure of pressure in the metric system that is equal to one thousandth of a bar. One bar is a pressure of 14.5 psi, or 29.52 in. Hg. (10^5 pascals or 10^5 newtons per square meter), and one millibar is equal to a pressure of 1,000 dynes per square centimeter, 0.014 69 psi, or 0.029 52 in. Hg. Standard sea level pressure equal to 1,013.2 millibars.

milling machine. A type of metalworking machine tool. The work to be machined is fastened to a movable table, and the table moves to feed the work into a rotating tool called a milling cutter.

millivoltmeter. An electrical instrument that measures voltage in units of millivolts (thousandths of a volt).

MIL standards. A group of standard specifications used by the United States Military services to describe the products they buy. MIL standards are known and used by most manufacturers to keep parts standardized and interchangeable.

mindset (in aeronautical decision making). The pilot's current inclination or intention affects his or her decision making in flying, and preconceived ideas can influence the outcome of events. For example, having a mindset to expect improving weather conditions can lead to increased risk-taking regarding a flight. This is due to an inability to recognize and cope with changes in the situation that are different from those anticipated or planned, such as not noticing deteriorating weather or conditions that warrant a new course. Therefore the pilot should be aware of having any set notions or attitudes about conditions before planning a flight, because just as physical fatigue and illness will directly affect judgment, so too will attitude management, stress management, risk management, personality tendencies, and situational awareness.

minicomputer (digital computer). A small- to medium-size digital computer. There is no clear-cut distinction between a small minicomputer and one of the larger microcomputers, but generally speaking, a minicomputer is faster and can be expanded more than a microcomputer.

minimum altitude. An altitude depicted on an instrument approach chart with the altitude value underscored. Aircraft are required to maintain altitude at or above the depicted value.

minimum controllable airspeed (V_{MC}). The lowest airspeed at which an airplane is controllable with one engine developing takeoff power and the propeller on the other engine windmilling. V_{MC} is marked on an airspeed indicator with a red radial line.

minimum crossing altitude. *See* MCA.

minimum descent altitude. *See* MDA.

minimum drag (aerodynamics). The point on the total drag curve where the lift-to-drag ratio is the greatest. At this speed, total drag is minimized.

minimum enroute IFR altitude. *See* MEA.

minimum equipment list (MEL). A list developed for larger aircraft that outlines equipment that can be inoperative for various types of flight including IFR and icing conditions. This list is based on the master minimum equipment list (MMEL) developed by the FAA and must be approved by the FAA for use. It is specific to an individual aircraft make and model.

minimum friction level (runway specification). The friction level specified in Advisory Circular 150/5320-12 ("Measurement, Construction, and Maintenance of Skid Resistant Airport Pavement Surfaces") that represents the minimum recommended wet pavement surface friction value for any turbojet aircraft engaged in LAHSO. This value will vary with the particular friction measurement equipment used.

"Minimum fuel" (air traffic control). A statement indicating that an aircraft's fuel supply has reached a state where, upon reaching the destination, it can accept little or no delay. This is not an emergency situation, but merely indicates that an emergency situation is possible should any undue delay occur.

minimum fuel for weight and balance. Minimum fuel is the amount of fuel necessary for one half hour of operation at the rated maximum-continuous power setting of the engine and, for weight and balance purposes, is $^1/_{12}$ gallon per METO (maximum-except-takeoff) horsepower. It is the maximum amount of fuel which could be used in weight and balance computations when low fuel might adversely affect the most critical balance conditions. To determine the weight of the minimum fuel in pounds, divide the METO horsepower by 2. When computing the adverse loaded center of gravity conditions of an aircraft, if the fuel pulls the center of gravity into the correct range, the minimum fuel must be used.

minimum holding altitude. *See* MHA.

minimum IFR altitudes (air traffic control). Minimum altitudes for IFR operations as prescribed in 14 CFR Part 91. These altitudes are published on aeronautical charts and prescribed in Part 95 for airways and routes, and in Part 97 for standard instrument approach procedures.

minimum level flight speed (rotorcraft). The speed below which a gyroplane, whose propeller is producing maximum thrust, loses altitude.

minimum navigation performance specification airspace (MNPSA). Designated airspace in which MNPS procedures are applied between MNPS certified and equipped aircraft. Under certain conditions, nonMNPS aircraft can operate in MNPSA. However, standard oceanic separation minima is provided between the nonMNPS aircraft and other traffic. Currently, the only designated MNPSA is described as follows: (1) between FL285 and FL420; (2) between latitudes 27°N and the North Pole; (3) in the east, the eastern boundaries of the CTAs Santa Maria Oceanic, Shanwick Oceanic, and Reykjavik; and (4), in the west, the western boundaries of CTAs Reykjavik and Gander Oceanic and New York Oceanic excluding the area west of 60°W and south of 38°30'N.

minimum navigation performance specifications. *See* MNPS.

minimum obstruction clearance altitude. *See* MOCA.

minimum off-route altitude (MORA). An altitude which provides 2,000 feet of terrain clearance in mountainous areas and 1,000 feet in nonmountainous regions. You can fly an off-airway route using the MORA and be assured of terrain clearance.

minimum reception altitude. *See* MRA.

minimum safe altitudes (MSA). MSAs are published for emergency use on IAP charts. For conventional navigation systems, the MSA is normally based on the primary omnidirectional facility on which the IAP is predicated. For RNAV approaches, the MSA is based on the runway waypoint (RWY WP) for straight-in approaches, or the airport waypoint (APT WP) for circling approaches. For GPS approaches, the MSA center will be the Missed Approach Waypoint (MAWP).

minimum safe altitude warning. *See* MSAW.

minimum sector altitude (ICAO). The lowest altitude which may be used under emergency conditions which will provide a minimum clearance of 300 m (1,000 feet) above all obstacles located in an area contained within a sector of a circle of 46 km (25 NM) radius centered on a radio aid to navigation.

minimum sink airspeed (glider operation). The airspeed, as determined by the performance polar, at which the glider will achieve the lowest sink rate. That is the glider will lose the least amount of altitude per unit of time at minimum sink airspeed.

M

minimums, weather. Weather condition requirements established for a particular operation or type of operation; e.g., IFR takeoff or landing, alternate airport for IFR flight plans, VFR flight, etc.

minimums section. The area on an IAP chart that displays the lowest altitude and visibility requirements for the approach.

minimum vectoring altitude. *See* MVA.

minor alteration (aircraft alteration). *14 CFR Part 1:* "An alteration other than a major alteration." *See* major alteration.

minor axis of an ellipse. A chord of an ellipse that passes through its center and is perpendicular to the major axis. *See* ellipse.

minor diameter (threaded fastener). The diameter of a threaded fastener measured at the roots of the threads.

minority carriers (semiconductor material). The mobile charges within semiconductor materials that are not the majority carriers. In N-type material, holes are the minority carriers, and in P-type material, electrons are the minority carriers. Leakage current in a reverse-biased junction is actually the flow of minority carriers.

minor repair (aircraft maintenance). *14 CFR Part 1:* "A repair other than a major repair." *See* major repair.

minuend (mathematical term). The number from which another number, called the subtrahend, is to be subtracted. In the subtraction problem, $8 - 3 = 5$, eight is the minuend, three is the subtrahend, and five is the difference.

minus. A term that means a negative value, or a value less than zero. Minus values are indicated by using a short dash in front of the value (-4). A minus sign (the short dash) is used in electricity to indicate a negative condition, one in which there is an excess of electrons.

minute (angular measurement). An angle equal to one sixtieth of a degree. A complete circle is made up of 360 degrees, or 21,600 minutes.

minute (time). A unit of time equal to one sixtieth of an hour, or sixty seconds.

minutes-in-trail (MINIT) (air traffic control). The number of minutes' duration of a specified interval, which is required between successive aircraft. It is normally used in a non-radar environment, or when transitioning to a non-radar environment, or if additional spacing is required due to aircraft deviating around weather. Using the MINIT method, this time interval remains the same—it does not fluctuate with altitude. *See also* miles-in-trail (MIT).

mirror image. A duplicate of an object which is like the original object in all ways except that one side is the reverse of the other: the left side is on the right, and the right side is on the left. This term is taken from the image we see formed in a mirror. When we face a mirror, the image we see has its right side on the left and its left side on the right.

MIS (meteorological impact statement). An unscheduled planning forecast describing conditions expected to begin within 4 to 12 hours which may impact the flow of air traffic in a specific center's (ARTCC) area.

miscible. Capable of being dissolved into, or blended with, another material. Oil is highly miscible in gasoline, but only slightly miscible or not miscible at all in water.

misfire (explosive charge). A condition in which an explosive charge fails to ignite, or to fire.

missed approach (air traffic control). A maneuver conducted by a pilot when an instrument approach cannot be completed to a landing. The route of flight and altitude are shown on instrument approach procedure charts. A pilot executing a missed approach prior to the missed approach point (MAP) must continue along the final approach to the MAP.

missed approach holding waypoint (MAHWP). An approach waypoint sequenced during the holding portion of the missed approach procedure that is usually a fly-over waypoint, rather than a fly-by waypoint.

missed approach point. *See* MAP.

missed approach procedure (ICAO). The procedure to be followed if the approach cannot be continued.

missed approach waypoint (MAWP). An approach waypoint sequenced during the missed approach procedure that is usually a fly-over waypoint, rather than a fly-by waypoint.

mist. Droplets of a liquid which are so small they float, or remain suspended, in the air. The droplets making up the atmospheric condition we call mist are larger than the droplets making up haze and smaller than those making up fog.

mist coat. A very light coat of metal primer. A mist coat is so thin that the metal is still visible, but the primer makes pencil marks easy to see.

miter (woodworking). To cut the edges of boards or surfaces in such a way that they match, or fit together.

miter box. A device that holds a piece of wood and a saw, so the saw can cut the wood at an angle to form a mitered joint. The wood used in a picture frame is cut in a miter box so that the ends match, forming a right angle and leaving no gap.

miter square (woodworking tool). A small, adjustable T-square used for marking the ends of wood strips to be cut at an angle other than a right angle. Some miter squares have the blade rigidly set at an angle of 45° to the head, and others have an adjustable blade that can be set at any angle relative to the head.

mixed-exhaust engine (gas turbine engines). A type of turbofan engine in which the exhaust from the gas generator mixes with the air from the fan that bypasses the gas generator. These two flows mix before they leave the exhaust system of the engine.

mixed ice. A mixture of clear ice and rime ice.

mixed number. A number that contains both an integer and a fraction.

mixer (electronic circuit). An electronic circuit used in a superheterodyne radio receiver. When two electrical signals having different frequencies are fed into a mixer, the mixer output will contain four signals: Signals having the two original frequencies, a signal whose frequency is the sum of the two original frequencies, and one whose frequency is the difference between the two original frequencies. The output of the mixer is directed into a filter circuit which selects the difference frequency for use in subsequent stages as the intermediate frequency, or IF.

mixing ratio (meteorology). The ratio by weight of the amount of water vapor in a volume of air to the amount of dry air. Mixing ratio is usually expressed as grams per kilogram (g/kg).

mixture. A combination of substances held together by physical rather than chemical means. The constituents of a mixture retain all their own chemical properties and mixtures do not have to be combined in definite proportions, as is required for chemical compounds. Sweetened tea is a mixture of tea and sugar, and concrete is a mixture of sand, gravel, and cement.

mixture control (reciprocating engine control). A control installed in a reciprocating-engine-powered aircraft that allows the pilot to vary the fuel-air mixture ratio while the engine is running.

A reciprocating engine requires the proper amount of fuel to be mixed with the air on the basis of the weight of the air. But most fuel-metering systems measure the fuel on the basis of the volume, not the weight, of the air entering the engine. The density (weight per unit volume) of the air decreases as the aircraft goes up in altitude, and the pilot must be able to decrease the amount of fuel metered into the less dense air. This adjustment is made with the mixture control.

M

MLS (microwave landing system). An instrument landing system operating in the microwave spectrum which provides lateral and vertical guidance to aircraft having compatible avionics equipment. An MLS approach procedure provides for an approach to a height above touchdown (HAT) of not less than 200 feet and a runway visual range (RVR) of not less than 1,800 feet. It is categorized as MLS Category I, II, or III depending on the installation and equipment associated with the specific procedure.

MM (middle marker). A marker beacon that defines a point along the glide slope of an instrument landing system (ILS), normally located at or near the point of decision height (ILS Category I). The middle marker is keyed to transmit alternate dots and dashes keyed at the rate of 95 dot-dash combinations per minute, with a 1,300-Hz tone which is received aurally and visually by compatible airborne equipment.

MNPS (minimum navigation performance specifications) (air traffic control). A set of standards which require aircraft to have a minimum navigation performance capability in order to operate in MNPS designated airspace. In addition, aircraft must be certified by their State of Registry for MNPS operation.

MOA. *See* military operations area.

mobile charges (semiconductor materials). Electrical charges that move about within a semiconductor material. Holes are positive mobile charges, and they drift within the material toward a negative electrical charge. Electrons are negative mobile charges, and they drift within the material toward a positive electrical charge.

Mobius strip. A one-sided surface twisted in the form of a loop. A Mobius strip, or Mobius loop, is made by taking a long strip of material, holding one end stationary, twisting the other end 180°, and then joining the two ends.

MOCA (minimum obstruction clearance altitude) (air traffic control). The lowest published altitude in effect between radio fixes on VOR airways, off-airway routes, or route segments which meets obstacle clearance requirements for the entire route segment and which assures acceptable navigational signal coverage only within 25 statute (22 nautical) miles of a VOR.

mock-up. A full-sized imitation of a real device. Mock-ups of complex and costly devices, such as aircraft and space vehicles, are built to assure that all the different systems and components will work properly when they are installed in the actual vehicle. Mock-ups can also be a portion of a complete device used as a training aid. In this regard, the control system and instruments of an aircraft or spacecraft can be made into a mock-up, so flight crews can be trained before the actual vehicle is ready for flight.

mode A (transponder operation). The specific pulse spacing of radio signals, coded by letter A, which are transmitted or received by ATCRBS (radar) components. Mode A is equivalent to military Mode 3 and is the "location only" mode of a transponder; used in air traffic control.

mode awareness. The pilot's ability to monitor how system settings are configured throughout the flight.

mode C (transponder operation). The specific pulse spacing of radio signals, coded by letter C, which are transmitted or received by ATCRBS (radar) components. Mode C is for altitude reporting and used in air traffic control. Also, the "ALT" position on the transponder function switch by which, if an encoding altimeter is installed, Mode C will transmit the aircraft altitude to the ground radar facility.

mode C intruder alert (air traffic control). A function of certain air traffic control automatic systems designed to alert radar controllers to existing or pending situations between a tracked target (known IFR or VFR aircraft) and an untracked target (unknown IFR or VFR aircraft) that requires immediate attention or action.

model (in aviation education). A representative copy of a real object which can be life-size, smaller, or larger than the original, effective for instructional use in explaining aircraft and equipment function.

modem. A MOdulator-DEModulator used to connect two computers by way of telephone lines. Digital information from one computer is changed into tones for transmission over the phone lines. This is the function of the modulator. At the receiver end, the tones are changed back into digital information for the other computer to process. This is called demodulation.

mode SSR (or, SSR mode) [ICAO]. For ICAO operations, the specific pulse spacings of the interrogation signals transmitted by an interrogator. The different codes used (Modes A, B, C, D) are specified in Annex 10.

modification. An alteration or change made to the basic design of a product or component. If the basic design of an airplane calls for the installation of a particular engine, the change of the design so another engine can be installed is a modification of the original design.

modify. To change something. If a schedule requiring something to be done every six days is changed to require it to be done every ten days, the schedule has been modified.

modular engine construction (gas turbine engines). The method of construction used on most modern gas turbine engines. The engine is made up of several modules, or units, that can be removed and replaced or serviced independent of the rest of the engine.

modular maintenance. A form of maintenance used on many types of complex machinery and equipment. Modular equipment is made in units (modules) that can be removed and replaced with another module in a minimum of time and with a minimum of equipment. The malfunctioning module can then be taken to a facility in which specialists using sophisticated equipment can isolate the problem and fix it. Modern turbine engines and most sophisticated electronic equipment are made to allow for modular maintenance.

modular structure. A structure built in standard units, or modules.

M

modulate (radio communications). In radio communications, to modulate means to change some characteristic, such as amplitude, frequency, or phase of an alternating current wave. A radio-frequency (RF) wave having a constant amplitude can be amplitude modulated (AM) by an audio-frequency (AF) voltage changing the amplitude of the RF wave in the same way the amplitude of the AF signal varies. The changes in voltage of the modulated RF wave can be used to produce a varying AF voltage. This process is called demodulation.

modulated light. Light whose intensity is changed by an audio-frequency AC voltage. When modulated light shines on a photoelectric cell, the output of the cell changes in the same way as the intensity of the modulated light.

modulator (electronic circuit). The circuit in a radio transmitter that modulates the carrier, or places information (data) on the signal being transmitted.

moiré. An independent pattern formed when two regular geometric patterns are superimposed (one placed on top of the other), with the one on top not exactly lined up with the one on the bottom. A moiré pattern is formed when a piece of transparent film having a series of closely spaced straight lines is placed at a slight angle over a print of the same size lines with the same spacing.

moist adiabatic lapse rate (meteorology). *See* saturated-adiabatic lapse rate.

moisture. Water contained in a mass of air. The water may be in the form of vapor, or it may be tiny droplets of haze, mist, or fog.

moisture separator (pneumatic system component). A component in a high-pressure pneumatic system that removes most of the water vapor from the compressed air. When the compressed air is used, its pressure is dropped, and this pressure drop causes a drop in temperature. If any moisture were allowed to remain in the air, it would freeze and block the system. The separation is normally done by centrifugal action of the air that slings the moisture out into an area where it can be collected and drained when the system is shut down.

mold line (sheet metal layout). A line used in the development of a flat pattern for a formed piece of sheet metal. The mold line is an extension of the flat side of a part beyond the radius. The mold line dimension of a part is the dimension made to the intersection of mold lines and is the dimension the part would have if its corners had no radius.

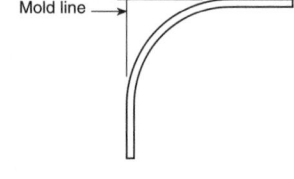

mold line

mold point. The intersection of two mold lines of a part. Mold line dimensions are made between mold points.

mold release agent. A lubricant used to coat a mold in which plastic resin is formed. Resin does not stick to the release agent, and the part can be taken from the mold when the resin has cured. A mold-release agent is also called a parting agent.

molecule. The smallest particle of a substance that retains all the properties of the substance. A molecule is made up of one or more atoms.

molybdenum. A hard, gray, metallic chemical element. Molybdenum's symbol is Mo, its atomic number is 42, and its atomic weight is 95.95. One of the main uses of molybdenum is as an alloying agent for steel. Molybdenum increases the toughness of steel and makes it easy to weld and machine.

moment. A force that causes or tries to cause an object to rotate. The moment of a lever is the distance, in inches, between the point at which a force is applied and the fulcrum, or the point about which a lever rotates, multiplied by the force, in pounds. Moment is expressed in inch-pounds.

Moment = distance · force

In weight and balance, a moment that causes a nose-down condition is a negative moment, and one that causes a nose-up condition is a positive moment.

moment arm (physics). The distance from a fulcrum to the applied force.

moment index (weight and balance). A moment divided by a constant, such as 10, 100, 1,000, or an even larger number. The use of a moment index allows weight and balance computations to be made using smaller numbers, and this decreases the chance for errors.

moment index envelope (weight and balance). A graphical representation of the forward and aft CG limits of an airplane using weight and moment indexes. If a horizontal line representing the weight of the aircraft and a vertical line representing its total moment index (the moment divided by a reduction factor) intersect within the envelope, the aircraft weight and balance conditions are within allowable limits.

moment limits vs. weight envelope. An enclosed area on a graph of three parameters. If the intersection of the diagonal line representing the moment/100 crosses the horizontal line, representing the weight, at the vertical line representing the CG location, in inches aft of the datum falls within the envelope, the aircraft is loaded within its weight and CG limits.

moment of inertia (rotational inertia). A measurement related to torque that concerns to the ease or difficulty of starting or stopping the rotation of an object. The moment of inertia of an object is the sum of all the masses making up the object multiplied by the square of the distance of each mass from the axis of rotation.

$$MI = \frac{mr^2}{4}$$

MI = Moment of Inertia
m = mass of object
r = radius of object from axis of rotation

momentum. A force caused by the inertia of a moving body trying to keep the body moving in the same direction, at the same speed or, if the body is at rest, trying to keep it at rest. The momentum of a body is the product of its mass times its velocity.

Monel. The registered trade name for a corrosion-resistant alloy made of 67% nickel, 30% copper, and 3% aluminum or silicon.

monitor (air traffic control). When used with communications transfer, means to listen on a specific frequency and stand by for instructions. Under normal circumstances, monitoring does not establish communications.

monitor alert (MA) (air traffic control). A function of the traffic flow management system (TFMS) that provides traffic management personnel with a tool for predicting potential capacity problems in individual operational sectors. The MA indicates that traffic management personnel need to analyze a particular sector for actual activity and determine the required action(s), if any, needed to control the demand. A monitor alert parameter (MAP) is designated for each operational sector in increments of 15 minutes, to aid in processing the MAs.

monkey wrench. A common name for a form of adjustable wrench. A monkey wrench has one fixed jaw and one movable jaw, with the opening between the jaws at right angles to the length of the handle. The jaws of a monkey wrench are smooth, rather than toothed like the jaws of a pipe wrench.

monocoque (aircraft structure). A single-shell type of aircraft structure in which all of the flight loads are carried in its outside skin. Modern aircraft have skins made of aluminum alloy, formed into compound curves, and riveted together into a structure that resembles an eggshell. There is a minimum of structure inside a monocoque skin.

monolithic casting. A type of casting in which the object is cast or formed as a single piece. A large and complex object cast with one pouring of the molten metal into a mold is a monolithic casting. Monolithic castings have no seams or joints.

M

monoplane (type of airplane). An airplane having only one main supporting wing. Up through the 1920s, most airplanes were biplanes (airplanes having two wings) because of the ease of bracing. But as engineering knowledge increased, engineers were able to make monoplanes of sufficient strength. The lower drag of a monoplane makes it more efficient than a biplane.

monopropellant (rocket fuel). A type of propellant used for rocket engines in which the fuel and the oxidizer are both parts of a single substance.

monorail. A type of transportation system using a single rail to carry the cars or other objects moved along the system. Many industrial factories use a monorail above the production line to move heavy equipment along the line.

monospar wing (aircraft structure). A form of airplane wing structure which uses only one spar, or main spanwise structural member, to carry the loads.

monostable. Having only one stable mode of operation. Any time a monostable device is disturbed from its stable condition, it automatically returns to it.

monostable multivibrator (electronic circuit). A type of electronic oscillator that has two conditions. It is stable in one of these conditions and tries to remain in this condition, but a special signal can cause it to shift to the other. As soon as the signal is removed, it automatically returns to its first condition.

monsoon (meteorology). A wind that in summer blows from the sea to a continental interior, bringing copious amounts of rain. In the winter this wind blows from the interior to the sea, resulting in sustained dry weather.

moor. To secure or tie the seaplane to a dock, buoy, or other stationary object on the surface.

mooring (in balloon operations). Operation of an unmanned balloon secured to the ground by lines or controlled by anything touching the ground. *See* 14 CFR Part 101.

mooring cleat (aircraft float component). A metal fitting with projecting ends to which a rope can be fastened.

Morse code. A standardized code of dots and dashes used to transmit information over wires or by radio, using continuous wave (CW) or modulated continuous wave (MCW) radio-frequency energy. The various letters and numbers are made up of combinations of long and short pulses of energy. The long pulses are called dashes, and the short pulses are called dots. *See* International Phonetic Alphabet and Morse Code in Appendix 4.

mosaic/multi-sensor mode (radar mode). The mode that accepts positional data from multiple radar or ADS-B sites. Targets are displayed from a single source within a radar sort box according to the hierarchy of the sources assigned.

MOS capacitor (metal oxide semiconductor capacitor). A capacitor that uses a semiconductor material as one plate, a thin film of silicon oxide as the dielectric, and a tiny spot of metal plated on the oxide as the other plate. MOS capacitors used as temporary storage devices in a digital computer are called dynamic RAMs (random access memories).

MOSFET (metal-oxide silicon field-effect transistor). A semiconductor device that consists of P-type source and drain regions diffused into a substrate of N-type silicon. A substrate is the supporting material on which an integrated circuit chip is built. The source and drain are on either side of a narrow channel of N-material, and an insulating layer of silicon oxide is deposited over the substrate so it covers the source, the drain, and the channel between them. A gate connection is formed between the source and the drain, and it is insulated from them by the oxide film.

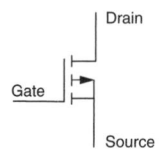

MOSFET

A control voltage applied to the gate causes the material in the channel to act as though it were P-type material, and electrons flow from the source to the drain without having to cross a P-N junction. The source and drain of a MOSFET serve the same functions as the emitter and collector of a bipolar transistor. However, the source and drain can be interchanged, while the emitter and collector of a bipolar transistor cannot.

mothball (equipment storage). A term used for the preservation of equipment or machinery. When something is mothballed, it is sealed so moisture cannot get into it. Desiccant materials (materials that absorb moisture) are packed inside the equipment to absorb moisture from the air sealed in it, and the outside is covered with whatever type of protection is appropriate. Airplanes and ships that have been declared surplus by the military are often mothballed and stored in case they are ever needed again.

mother board (electronic equipment). A printed circuit board used in modern electronic equipment to supply power and to carry electrical signals to other printed circuit boards that are plugged into it.

motion. Movement, the process in which objects change their position or location.

motivation (in learning process). A need or desire that causes a person to act. Motivation can be positive or negative, tangible or intangible, subtle or obvious.

motor (*verb*). The act of rotating a turbine engine using the starter with the ignition system deactivated. An engine is motored to force air through it to purge it of fuel fumes.

mountainous area/region (air traffic control). An area of defined lateral dimensions above which special rules concerning minimum en route altitudes apply.

mountain wave (meteorology). A standing wave or lee wave on the lee, or downwind, side of a mountain barrier.

mouth, of a balloon envelope. The bottom, open end of a hot air balloon envelope. Also called the "throat."

movable slat. A movable auxiliary airfoil on the leading edge of a wing. It is closed in normal flight but extends at high angles of attack. This allows air to continue flowing over the top of the wing and delays airflow separation.

movement area (air traffic control). The runways, taxiways, and other areas of an airport/ heliport which are utilized for taxiing, hover taxiing, air taxiing, takeoff, and landing of aircraft, exclusive of loading ramps and parking areas.

movement area (ICAO). That part of an aerodrome to be used for the takeoff, landing and taxiing of aircraft, consisting of the maneuvering area and the apron(s).

moving-coil meter movement (electrical instrument). An instrument that measures the current flowing through a coil mounted and free to rotate within a magnetic field. The deflection of the coil is proportional to the amount of current flowing through it. Moving-coil meters are normally called D'Arsonval meters.

moving map. A graphical depiction of the aircraft's position, the route programmed into the FMS/RNAV, surrounding geographical features, and any other information about the immediate flight environment such as traffic and weather that may be available from other avionics systems.

moving target indicator. *See* MTI.

moving-vane meter movement (electrical instrument). A meter movement that uses the magnetic repulsion of the like poles created in two iron vanes by current flowing through a coil of wire. This is the most commonly used movement for measuring alternating current. This is also called a moving-iron meter movement.

MRA (minimum reception altitude). The lowest altitude at which an airway intersection can be determined.

MSA (minimum safe altitude). The minimum altitude specified in 14 CFR Part 91 for various aircraft operations, or altitudes depicted on approach charts which provide at least 1,000 feet of obstacle clearance for emergency use within a specified distance from the navigation facility upon which a procedure is prescribed. These altitudes are:

1. *Minimum Sector Altitudes:* Altitudes depicted on approach charts which provide at least 1,000 feet of obstacle clearance within a 25-mile radius of the navigation facility upon which the procedure is predicated.

    Sectors depicted on approach charts must be at least 90° in scope. These altitudes are for emergency use only and do not necessarily ensure acceptable navigational signal coverage.

2. *Emergency Safe Altitudes:* Altitudes depicted on approach charts which provide at least 1,000 feet of obstacle clearance in nonmountainous areas and 2,000 feet in designated mountainous areas within a 100-mile radius of the navigation facility upon which the procedure is based and normally used only in military procedures.

MSAW (minimum safe altitude warning). A function of the ARTS III computer that aids the controller by alerting him when a tracked Mode C-equipped aircraft is below, or is predicted by the computer to go below, a predetermined minimum safe altitude.

MSB (most significant bit). The bit in a binary number that has the highest place value. The MSB is the bit on the extreme left.

MSD (most significant digit). The digit in a decimal number that has the highest place value. The MSD is the digit on the extreme left.

MSDS (material safety data sheets). Documents relating to hazardous materials that contain information on health precautions, flammability, ventilation requirements, and information for health professionals in case of an accident. MSDS are furnished with all hazardous materials and are required by law to be available to all personnel working with the material.

MS flareless fittings. Fluid-line fittings that form their seal with a ferrule around the tubing rather than with a flare.

MSL (mean sea level). The datum used as a reference for measuring elevations throughout the United States. It is the average height of the surface of the sea for all stages of tide. When the letters MSL are used with an altitude, it means that the altitude measured from mean, or average, sea level.

MTBF (mean time between failures). A statistical measure of the average length of time between successive system failures.

MTI (moving target indicator). An electronic device which causes a radar scope to show only targets which are in motion. An MTI is a partial remedy for ground clutter.

MTR (military training routes). Airspace of defined vertical and lateral dimensions, established for the conduct of military training at airspeeds in excess of 250 knots IAS.

muff (heater). A thin sheet metal shroud that wraps around the exhaust stack or the muffler of a reciprocating engine to pick up heat. Ventilating air blows through the muff and carries the heat it picks up into the cabin.

mule (hydraulic power supply). An auxiliary power supply that can be connected to an aircraft to supply fluid under pressure to the hydraulic system when the engines are not operating. Mules supply hydraulic pressure to an aircraft to perform the landing gear retraction test when the aircraft is up on jacks.

multi-cell thunderstorm. A group or cluster of individual thunderstorm cells in varying stages of development. These storms are often self-propagating and can last for several hours.

MULTICOM (air traffic control). A mobile service not open to public correspondence, used to provide communications essential to conduct the activities being performed by or directed from private aircraft.

multi-engine aircraft. An aircraft with two or more engines.

multi-function display. *See* MFD.

multimedia. A combination of more than one instructional medium. This format can include audio, text, graphics, animations, and video. In recent usage, multimedia implies a computer-based presentation.

multimeter (electrical test equipment). An electrical measuring instrument that uses a single current-measuring meter and the necessary components to measure several ranges of voltage, current, and resistance. The different functions and ranges are selected by switches or by jacks into which test leads are plugged. Multimeters are often called VOMs, because they are able to measure volts, ohms, and milliamps. Multimeters with a digital readout are called DVOMs.

multiple-can combustor (turbine engine component). A combustor used in a gas turbine engine that consists of a series of individual burner cans, each of which consists of an inner liner and an outer case. The individual cans are arranged around the periphery of a centrifugal compressor. The hot gases flow directly from the cans into the turbine.

multiple-choice-type test item. A test item consisting of a question or statement followed by a list of alternative answers or responses.

multiple-disk brake. A form of aircraft brake in which a series of metal or carbon disks keyed to slots inside the wheel rotate between a series of fixed disks keyed to the axle on which the wheel is mounted. Pistons in a series of hydraulic cylinders produce a force that clamps the rotating disks between the fixed disks. This produces enough friction to slow or stop the aircraft on which the brake is installed.

multiple runways (air traffic control). The utilization of dedicated arrival runway(s) for departures and a dedicated departure runway(s) for arrivals, when feasible to reduce delays and enhance capacity.

multiplex (method of communications). Multiplex transmission is a method of two-way communications in which both stations can transmit at the same time on the same frequency or on the same line. Normal telephone communications is an example of multiplex communications. Both parties can talk on the same line at the same time.

multiplicand (mathematics). The number in a multiplication problem that is multiplied by another number. In the problem 4 · 2 = 8, the number four is the multiplicand.

multiplication. The process of repeated addition.

multiplier (mathematics). The number in a multiplication problem that is used to multiply another number. In the problem 4 · 2 = 8, the number two is the multiplier.

multiplier resistor. A resistor in series with a voltmeter mechanism used to extend the range of the basic meter or to allow a single meter to measure several ranges of voltage.

multispar wing (aircraft structure). A type of airplane wing construction that uses several small spars extending along the span of the wing to carry the structural loads. Multiple small spars carry the load better and weigh less than the two larger spars used in many aircraft wings.

multivibrator (electronic circuit). A type of oscillator in which there are two active devices (transistors or electron tubes) which alternate in conducting. Multivibrators may be free running, bistable, or monostable. A free-running multivibrator automatically switches back and forth between the devices and continues to do this as long as power is supplied.

In a monostable multivibrator, one device is normally conducting, but a pulse on its base or grid will switch it off and the other one on. As soon as the pulse is removed, the conduction is switched back to the first.

In a bistable multivibrator, either device conducts equally well. A pulse on the base or grid of the first device turns it off and causes the second one to conduct until it receives a pulse on its base or grid. It then turns off, and conduction reverts back to the first.

mumetal. An alloy having a high magnetic permeability used to make magnetic shields. Mumetal is an alloy of 14% iron, 5% copper, 1.5% chromium, and 79.5% nickel.

muriatic acid. A form of commercial hydrochloric acid (HCl). One of the popular uses for muriatic acid is as a flux for cleaning metal in preparation for soldering.

mushing. A flight condition caused by slow speed where the control surfaces are marginally effective.

mushroomed head (damaged tool head). A damaged head on a chisel or punch caused by hammering on the tool. Mushroomed heads are dangerous, because a piece of the metal can be easily broken off and cause injury. A mushroomed head must be ground off of a tool as soon as it forms.

mutual induction. The cause of a voltage being induced in one circuit by a changing current in another circuit when there are no electrical connections between the two. Changing current causes lines of magnetic flux to expand and contract. When this changing flux cuts across the conductors in another circuit, mutual induction causes a voltage to be induced in it.

MVA (minimum vectoring altitude) (air traffic control). The lowest MSL altitude at which an IFR aircraft will be vectored by a radar controller, except as otherwise authorized for radar approaches, departures, and missed approaches. The altitude meets IFR obstacle clearance criteria, and it may be lower than the published minimum en route altitude (MEA) along an airway or J-route segment. It may be utilized for radar vectoring only upon the controller's determination that an adequate radar return is being received from the aircraft being controlled. Charts depicting minimum vectoring altitudes are normally available only to the controllers and not to pilots.

Mylar. The registered trade name for a polyester film widely used as an electrical insulator and as a packaging material. Mylar is also used as a film on which high-quality ink drawings can be made.

Mylar capacitor. A nonelectrolytic capacitor that uses strips of metal foil as the plates and Mylar film as the dielectric.

M

N₁. A symbol representing the rotational speed of the low-pressure compressor in a dual-spool gas turbine engine. In common usage, the low-pressure compressor is often called the N_1 compressor.

N₂. A symbol representing the rotational speed of the high-pressure compressor in a dual-spool gas turbine engine. In common usage, the high-pressure compressor is often called the N_2 compressor.

N₃. A symbol representing the rotational speed of the high-pressure compressor in a triple-spool gas turbine engine.

NACA (National Advisory Committee for Aeronautics). This organization was dedicated to the technical development of aviation and was superseded in October of 1958 by NASA, the National Aeronautics and Space Administration.

NACA cowling (reciprocating engine cowling). A long-chord ring cowling whose trailing edge fairs smoothly into the fuselage or engine nacelle. NACA cowlings are used on the vast majority of modern radial engine installations.

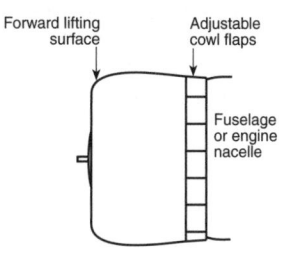

NACA cowling

The cooling air rams into the open front of the cowling and exits through an annular slot at the rear. This slot is often covered with adjustable cowl flaps to control the amount of cooling air allowed to flow through the engine. The airfoil shape of the cowling produces a forward aerodynamic force that more than compensates for the cooling drag of the engine.

nacelle. An enclosed compartment in an aircraft in which an engine is mounted. Most multiengine propeller-driven airplanes have engine nacelles mounted on the leading edge of the wings far enough out that the propellers clear the fuselage. Multiengine jet-propelled airplanes often have their engines mounted in nacelles on the sides of the fuselage between the wing and the tail, or in nacelles hanging below the wings. Nacelles in which jet engines are mounted are often called pods.

NACO. *See* AeroNav.

nailing strip. A method of applying pressure to the glue in a scarf joint repair in a plywood skin. A strip of thin plywood is nailed over the glued scarf joint with the nails extending into a supporting structure beneath the skin. The strip is installed over vinyl sheeting to prevent it sticking to the skin. When the glue is thoroughly dry, the nailing strip is broken away and the nails removed.

NAND gate (logic gate). A NOT AND logic gate having two or more inputs and one output. The output is a logic zero (NOT one) if all of the inputs are logic one. The symbol for a NAND gate is the same as for an AND gate, followed by a small circle to show that the output is inverted. (Its logic condition is changed.)

NAND gate

nano. The metric prefix meaning one billionth (1×10^{-9}) of a unit.

nanovoltmeter. An extremely sensitive voltmeter that can measure voltages as low as one nanovolt (one thousandth of a microvolt).

nap (fabric). The ends of the fibers in a fabric. Certain steps in the finishing of fabric materials cause the nap to stick up. This is called "raising the nap." When an aircraft structure is covered with cotton or linen fabric, the first coat of dope raises the nap. This nap must be carefully removed by sanding to get a smooth finish.

naphtha (aliphatic naphtha). A petroleum product whose boiling point is between that of gasoline and kerosine. Aliphatic naphtha is used as a cleaning solvent and as an ingredient in certain finishing materials.

naphtha (aromatic naphtha). A solvent produced from coal tar. Aromatic naphtha is used as a blending agent for changing the performance characteristics of gasoline. It has a softening effect on rubber goods, such as flexible hoses and diaphragms used in pumps and fuel metering components.

narcosis. A condition of deep stupor or unconsciousness produced by a drug or other chemical substance.

narrowing grinding (reciprocating engine valve seat grinding). The grinding away of part of the top edge of the valve seat in the cylinder of a reciprocating engine. Narrowing decreases the contact area between the valve face and the valve seat.

NAS. *See* national airspace system.

NASA. National Aeronautics and Space Administration. *See* NACA.

NAS specifications (National Aircraft Standards). Specifications established by the National Aircraft Standards Committee for the design and construction of components. Parts conforming to these standards are identified with a number preceded by the initials NAS. Included are system components shared jointly with the military.

NAS stage A (air traffic control). The enroute ATC system's radar, computers and computer programs, controller plan view displays (PVDs/radar scopes), input/output devices, and the related communications equipment which are integrated to form the heart of the automated IFR air traffic control system. This equipment performs flight data processing (FDP) and radar data processing (RDP). It interfaces with automated terminal systems and is used in the control of enroute IFR aircraft.

National Aeronautical Charting Office (NACO). *See* AeroNAV.

national airspace system (NAS). The common network of U.S. airspace; air navigation facilities, equipment and services, airports or landing areas; aeronautical charts, information and services; rules, regulations and procedures, technical information, and manpower and material.

National Beacon Code Allocation Plan airspace (air traffic control). Airspace over United States territory located within the North American continent between Canada and Mexico, including adjacent territorial waters and extending outward to approximately the boundaries of the oceanic control areas or Flight Information Regions (FIR).

national defense airspace. Airspace established as necessary in the interest of national defense and in which the flight of civil aircraft is restricted or prohibited when such aircraft cannot be identified, located, and controlled with available facilities in those areas. National defense airspace is established by the FAA Administrator in consultation with the Secretary of Defense through a regulation or order issued under 49 U.S.C. 40103(b)(3).

National Flight Data Center. *See* NFDC.

National Flight Data Digest (air traffic control publication). A daily (except weekends and Federal holidays) publication of flight information appropriate to aeronautical charts, aeronautical publications, Notices to Airmen, or other media, serving the purpose of providing operational flight data essential to safe and efficient aircraft operations.

National Route Program (NRP). A set of rules and procedures designed to increase the flexibility of user flight planning within published guidelines.

national search and rescue plan (air traffic control). An interagency agreement which provides for the effective utilization of all available facilities in all types of search and rescue missions.

National Security Area (NSA). Consist of airspace of defined vertical and lateral dimensions established at locations where there is a requirement for increased security and safety of ground facilities. Pilots are requested to voluntarily avoid flying through the depicted NSA. When it is necessary to provide a greater level of security and safety, flight in NSAs may be temporarily prohibited. Regulatory prohibitions are disseminated via NOTAMs.

National Transportation Safety Board (NTSB). A U.S. independent federal agency responsible for investigations of accidents involving aviation, highways, waterways, pipelines, and railroads in the United States. The NTSB is charged by Congress to investigate every civil aviation accident in the United States.

natural aging (metal heat treatment). A step in the heat treatment of aluminum alloys in which the metal is removed from the quench bath and allowed to gain its full strength at room temperature. In artificial aging, the metal is held at an elevated temperature for it to gain its full strength in a shorter period of time.

naturally aspirated engine (reciprocating engine). A reciprocating engine that uses atmospheric pressure to force the charge of fuel-air mixture into the cylinders. A naturally aspirated engine differs from a supercharged engine that uses a mechanical air compressor to increase the pressure of the air and force the fuel-air mixture into the cylinders.

natural numbers. Positive integers (numbers, such as 1, 2, 3, 4, 5, etc.). Natural numbers are also called counting numbers. Zero, negative numbers, and fractions are not natural numbers.

nautical mile (NM). A measure of distance used in air and sea navigation. One nautical mile is equal to the length of one minute of latitude along the earth's equator. One nautical mile is nominally considered to be 6,080 feet, or 1,853.2 meters. However, when the United States accepted the metric system in 1959, the nautical mile was officially set as 6,076.115 feet.

nautical twilight. The period of time before sunrise and after sunset when the sun is not more than 12° below the horizon.

NAVAIDs (navigational aids). Any visual or electronic device, airborne or on the surface, which provides point-to-point guidance information or position data to aircraft in flight. Electronic NAVAIDs have been installed around airports and along airways to help pilots navigate without reference to visual features of the terrain. Very-high-frequency OmniRange navigation equipment (VOR), Instrument Landing Systems (ILS), and Distance Measuring Equipment (DME) are examples of NAVAIDs.

NAVAID classes. Classification of navigational aids according to their operational uses. The three classes are: T – Terminal, L – Low altitude, and H – High altitude.

NAV/COM. Navigation and communication radio.

navigable airspace. *14 CFR Part 1:* "Airspace at and above the minimum flight altitudes prescribed by or under this chapter, including airspace needed for safe takeoff and landing."

navigational aid. Any visual or electronic device airborne or on the surface that provides point-to-point guidance information or position data to aircraft in flight.

navigational gap. A navigational course guidance gap, referred to as an MEA gap, describes a distance along an airway or route segment where a gap in navigational signal coverage exists. The navigational gap may not exceed a specific distance that varies directly with altitude.

navigation database. The information stored in the FMS/RNAV; it contains most of the time-sensitive navigational information found on en route and procedural charts.

navigation function. An autopilot function that allows you to track the route programmed in the FMS/RNAV or navigation receiver, such as a VOR radial.

navigation lights (aircraft). Colored lights on an aircraft used at night to show the direction the aircraft is moving. A red light is installed on the left wing tip, a green light is on the right wing tip, and a white light is installed on the tail of the aircraft.

navigation reference system (NRS). The NRS is a system of waypoints developed for use within the United States for flight planning and navigation without reference to ground based navigational aids. The NRS waypoints are located in a grid pattern along defined latitude and longitude lines. The initial use of the NRS will be in the high altitude environment in conjunction with the High Altitude Redesign initiative. The NRS waypoints are intended for use by aircraft capable of point-to-point navigation.

navigation specification (ICAO). A set of aircraft and flight crew requirements needed to support performance-based navigation operations within a defined airspace. There are two kinds of navigation specifications: An RNP specification, which is based on area navigation that includes the requirement for performance monitoring and alerting, designated by the prefix "RNP" (e.g., RNP 4, RNP APCH); and an RNAV specification based on area navigation that does not include the requirement for performance monitoring and alerting, designated by the prefix "RNAV" (e.g., RNAV 5, RNAV 1).

N-channel FET (semiconductor device). A field-effect transistor in which the resistive area between the source and drain is made of N-type semiconductor material.

NDB (nondirectional beacons). A L/MF or UHF radio beacon transmitting nondirectional signals. The pilot of an aircraft equipped with direction finding equipment can determine his bearing to or from the NDB and home on or track to or from the station.

needle and ball indicator (aircraft flight instrument). An old name for a turn and slip indicator. *See* turn and slip indicator.

needle bearings. A type of anti-friction bearing. Needle bearings are made of a series of relatively long, small-diameter rollers (the needles) made of hardened steel. The needles ride between two hardened and polished steel races. One race is pressed into the housing, and the other race is pressed onto the rotating shaft. Needle bearings are effective for radial loads only.

needle valve. A fluid control valve that uses a long tapered needle to control the amount of fluid that can flow through an orifice. The needle valve can be moved into or out of the orifice. When the needle is completely in the orifice, the fluid flow is minimum, and when it is completely out of the orifice, the flow is limited by the size of the orifice. When the needle is neither fully in nor fully out, its position controls the effective size of the orifice and thus the amount of fluid allowed to flow.

"Negative" (air traffic control). A term used by ATC to mean "no," or "permission not granted," or "that is not correct."

negative (electrical condition). A condition in which there are more electrons (negative charges) than there are protons (positive charges). A negative condition is indicated by a minus sign (–) in front of the value. For example, –6 volts is negative six volts.

negative acceleration. A term meaning deceleration, or slowing down. Negative acceleration is a decrease in speed with time and is expressed in such terms as feet per second, per second or meters per second, per second.

negative angle of attack. The angle of attack that produces a downward aerodynamic force. The horizontal stabilizer on an airplane is mounted in such a way that in straight and level flight, it has a negative angle of attack. This allows it to produce a downward force to give the airplane longitudinal stability. *See* angle of attack (α).

negative buoyancy. The tendency for an object to sink if it is heavier than the fluid it displaces.

negative charge (electrical charge). An unbalanced electrical condition caused by there being more electrons than there are protons.

"Negative contact" (air traffic control). A term used by pilots to inform ATC that the previously issued traffic is not in sight, or they are unable to contact ATC on a particular frequency.

negative dihedral (airplane stability). The downslope of airplane wings, or the downward angle formed between the wings and the lateral axis of an airplane. Negative dihedral, also called cathedral, increases the maneuverability of the airplane while decreasing its lateral stability.

negative feedback (electronic circuit condition). A condition in an electronic circuit in which a part of the output signal is fed back into the input 180° out of phase with the input signal. Negative feedback decreases circuit amplification and also circuit distortion. It makes the output signal a truer copy of the input signal.

negative ion. An unbalanced atom having more electrons spinning around the nucleus than there are protons in the nucleus.

negative logic (digital electronics). A type of logic used in some digital electronic circuits. In negative logic, the lower of two voltage levels represents the condition of one, or yes, while the higher voltage represents the condition of zero, or no.

negative moment. A moment, or rotational force, that causes a body to rotate in a counterclockwise direction.

negative number. A number less than zero. It is a number preceded by a minus sign.

negative pressure. Gage pressure less than the atmospheric pressure from which it is measured. Negative pressure is sometimes called suction, or vacuum.

negative pressure relief valve (aircraft pressurization system component). A valve in an aircraft cabin pressurization system that prevents the pressure inside the cabin ever becoming lower than the pressure of the air outside of the cabin.

N

negative resistance. A condition in which an increase in voltage across a device causes a decrease in current through it. Under certain operating conditions, a tunnel diode shows negative resistance (the more voltage across it, the less current through it).

negative stagger (aircraft structure). The vertical alignment of the wings of a biplane in which the lower wing is ahead of the upper wing. Most biplanes have positive stagger, in which the upper wing is ahead of the lower wing. But the distinctive appearance of the classic Beech Model 17, called the Staggerwing Beechcraft, is due to its negative stagger.

negative static stability (aircraft stability). The type of static stability which causes an aircraft, once disturbed from a condition of rest, to move further from its condition of rest. Negative static stability is also called static instability.

negative temperature coefficient. A decrease in a value, such as resistance or capacitance, with an increase in the temperature. A thermistor is a semiconductor material with a large negative temperature coefficient of resistance. Its resistance decreases greatly as its temperature increases. This makes thermistors valuable in fire detection systems.

negative terminal (batteries). The terminal of a battery from which electrons leave.

negative torque sensing system (propeller feathering system). The portion of a propeller feathering system that senses the torque being produced by the engine. If an engine fails in flight, its torque drops off drastically. The NTSS senses this loss of torque and sends a signal to the propeller feathering system. The propeller then automatically feathers. The blade pitch increases until the blades are parallel with the air passing over them. Feathering the propeller stops the engine rotation and reduces the drag.

negative vorticity (meteorology). Vorticity caused by anticyclonic turning. Negative vorticity is associated with downward motion of the air.

neodymium. A bright, silvery, rare-earth chemical element. Neodymium's symbol is Nd, its atomic number is 60, and its atomic weight is 144.24. Neodymium is used for coloring glass and in laser technology.

neon. An inert gaseous chemical element. Neon's symbol is Ne, its atomic number is 10, and its atomic weight is 20.183. Neon is widely used in electric signs in which neon gas in glass tubes is ionized. The ionized gas glows with a reddish-orange light.

neon bulb. A type of glow lamp made of two insulated electrodes inside a glass envelope filled with neon gas. Neon gas does not conduct electricity until the voltage across the electrodes rises to the ionization, or firing, voltage of the neon. When this voltage is reached, the neon gas ionizes and conducts. Electrons flowing through the ionized gas cause it to glow with a reddish-orange light. The gas continues to glow until the voltage across the electrodes drops to a value lower than its ionization voltage.

neon-bulb oscillator (electronic circuit). A relaxation oscillator using a neon bulb to produce oscillation. The bulb is installed in parallel with a capacitor. When DC voltage is applied to the circuit through a resistor, the voltage across the bulb and capacitor rises until the ionization voltage of the bulb is reached. As soon as the neon gas ionizes, it short-circuits the capacitor, and the voltage drops to the deionization voltage, at which time conduction stops. The waveform of a neon-bulb oscillator is a sawtooth.

neoprene. A type of synthetic rubber made from petroleum. Neoprene is superior to natural rubber and other synthetic rubbers because of its resistance to damage from petroleum products.

neptunium. A silvery, metallic, naturally radioactive chemical element. Neptunium's symbol is Np, its atomic number is 93, and its atomic weight is 237.0482. Neptunium is found as a trace element in uranium ores and is produced synthetically in nuclear reactions.

net thrust (turbine engine specification). The thrust produced by a turbojet or turbofan engine in which the acceleration factor is the difference between the velocity of the incoming air and the velocity of the exhaust gases leaving the engine. Net thrust is actually the change in momentum of the mass of air and fuel passing through the engine.

net weight (weight and balance). The weight of the aircraft less any tare weight (the weight of any chocks or other devices used to hold the aircraft on the scales).

neutral axis (structures). The neutral axis of a piece of material being bent is a plane within the material along which there is no stress. The neutral axis is located approximately halfway (actually 44.5% of the thickness of the material) from the inside of the bend. The material on the outside of the bend is under a tensile stress, and that on the inside is under a compressive stress. There is no stress along the neutral axis.

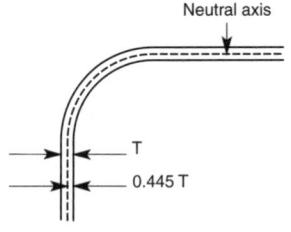

neutral axis

neutral buoyancy (balloon flight). A condition wherein a balloon weighs exactly the same as the air it displaces and is neither ascending nor descending.

neutral conductor (electrical power system). A conductor in both three-wire single-phase, and Y-connected three-phase electrical systems in which the voltage is the same between it and any of the other conductors. The neutral conductor in a three-wire single-phase system is normally grounded with 110 volts between either line and the neutral conductor, and 220 volts between the two lines. In a Y-connected, three-phase

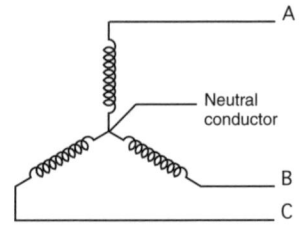

neutral conductor

system, there is normally 120 volts between any of lines and the neutral conductor and 208 volts between any two of the lines.

neutral flame (oxygas welding). A flame that uses the chemically correct ratio of fuel gas and oxygen. A neutral flame in an oxyacetylene torch has an almost white, rounded inner cone and an envelope of light blue flame. Too much oxygen changes a neutral flame into an oxidizing flame, and the inner cone becomes pointed. Too much acetylene changes a neutral flame into a carburizing, or reducing, flame, and a feather appears around the inner cone.

neutralization (electronic circuit). The use of external circuit devices to cancel, or neutralize, the effect of interelectrode capacitance in an electron tube.

neutral line. *See* neutral axis (structures).

neutral plane (electrical machine). An imaginary line perpendicular to the lines of magnetic flux passing between the field poles of an electric motor or generator. If the brushes are mounted along this neutral plane, the segments of the commutator they short across have the same electrical potential, and there will be no sparking at the brushes.

neutral position of the rotating magnet (aircraft magneto). The position of the rotating magnet in an aircraft magneto in which the poles of the magnet are directly between the pole shoes in the magneto housing. When the magnet is in its neutral position, no magnetic flux flows through the core of the magneto coil.

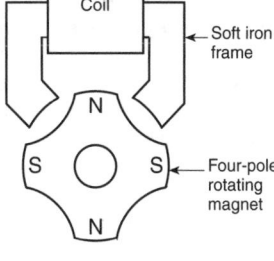

neutral static stability (aircraft stability). A condition of static stability in which an aircraft, if disturbed from its condition of rest, will neither attempt to deviate farther from this condition nor to return to its original condition.

neutral position

neutron. A particle in the nucleus of an atom which has mass, but no electrical charge. A neutron has about the same mass as a proton, and it adds weight to the atom, but does not affect its chemical behavior. Neutrons serve as a "cement" to hold the protons in the nucleus of an atom.

newton. a unit of force in the metric system. One newton is the amount of force needed to cause a mass of one kilogram (1,000 grams) to accelerate at a rate of one meter per second each second the force acts on it. One newton is equal to 100,000 dynes, or $2.248 \cdot 10^{-1}$ pound.

Newton's first law of motion. The law of physics which describes inertia. An object at rest will try to remain at rest, and a moving object will try to keep moving in the same direction, at the same speed, unless it is acted upon by an outside force.

Newton's metal. A low-melting-point metal used for the fusible links in an automatic sprinkler systems. Newton's metal, which is made of 50% bismuth, 31% lead, and 19% tin, melts at 95° Celsius.

Newton's second law of motion. The law of physics concerning acceleration. The amount of acceleration imparted to an object by a force is directly proportional to the amount of force acting on it, and inversely proportional to the mass of the object. The greater the force, the greater the acceleration, and the greater the mass, the less the acceleration.

Newton's third law of motion. The law of physics relating to action and reaction. For every action, there is an equal and opposite (equal amount and opposite direction) reaction.

Next Generation Air Transportation System (NextGen). This refers to the ongoing, wide-ranging transformation of the systems in place within the National Airspace System (NAS). NextGen represents an evolution from a ground-based system of air traffic control to a satellite-based system of air traffic management.

Next Generation Radar (NEXRAD) system. A network of Weather Surveillance Radar-1988 Doppler (WSR-88D) sites situated throughout the U.S. as well as selected overseas sites. The NEXRAD system is a joint venture of U.S. government departments, and the agencies with control over it are the NWS, the Air Force Weather Agency (AFWA), and the FAA. Convection and precipitation data collected from WSR-88D returns are used to prepare weather radar products that can be supplied to the cockpit via a broadcast weather service.

NEXRAD. *See* Next Generation Radar system.

NFDC (National Flight Data Center). A facility in Washington, D.C., established by the FAA to operate a central aeronautical information service for the collection, validation, and dissemination of aeronautical data in support of the activities of government, industry, and the aviation community. The information is published in the *National Flight Data Digest.*

NFDD (National Flight Data Digest). A daily publication of flight information appropriate to aeronautical charts, aeronautical publications, Notices to Airmen, or other media serving the purpose of providing operational flight data essential to safe and efficient aircraft operations.

nibble (data processing term). A grouping of four bits of digital data. Two nibbles form a byte (eight bits of digital data).

nibbler. A sheet-metal-working tool. A nibbler uses a reciprocating punch to remove metal as it moves back and forth. The punch takes away only a small bite of metal each stroke.

Nichrome. The registered trade name for an alloy of nickel and chromium. Nichrome wire, whose resistance is about 65 times that of copper, is used for making electrical heater elements and precision wire-wound resistors.

nickel. A silvery, hard, ductile, magnetic, metallic chemical element. Nickel's symbol is Ni, its atomic number is 28, and its atomic weight is 58.71. Nickel is used for plating, as an alloy in steel, and for making batteries.

nickel-cadmium battery. A form of storage battery in which nickel hydroxide is the active element in the positive plates, and cadmium hydroxide is the active element in the negative plates. The electrolyte is potassium hydroxide and water. The cells of a nickel-cadmium battery have a closed-circuit voltage of approximately 1.25 volts, and they maintain this voltage until they are almost completely discharged. Nickel-cadmium batteries have a low internal resistance and are ideally suited for such high-current applications as starting gas turbine engines.

nickel silver. An alloy of copper, zinc, and nickel. Nickel silver is also called German silver.

night. *14 CFR Part 1:* "The time between the end of evening civil twilight and the beginning of morning civil twilight, as published in the American Air Almanac, converted to local time."

night vision. The ability of the human eye to detect objects at night. The rods and cones function in daylight and in moonlight, but in the absence of normal light, the process of night vision is placed almost entirely on the rods.

nimbostratus (meteorology). A principal cloud type, gray colored and often dark. The appearance of nimbostratus clouds is often diffused by more or less continuously falling rain or snow, which in most cases reaches the ground. Nimbostratus clouds are normally thick enough to blot out the sun.

niobium. A silvery, soft, ductile, metallic chemical element. Niobium's symbol is Nb, its atomic number is 41, and its atomic weight is 92.906. Niobium is used as an alloying element for steel and as a metal used in superconductivity research.

nipple (pipe fitting). A short piece of pipe, threaded on both ends.

nitrate dope (aircraft finishing material). A finishing material whose film base is made of a cellulose material dissolved in nitric acid. Nitrate dope has good encapsulating properties, but it is being replaced by cellulose acetate butyrate (CAB) dope, because it is far more flammable than CAB dope.

nitride (metal surface treatment). A compound of nitrogen and a metal. Reciprocating engine cylinders are often nitrided by forming aluminum nitride on the inside of the cylinder bore to provide a hard, wear-resistant surface.

nitriding. A method of case hardening steel. The steel to be case hardened is placed in a retort (a sealed, high-temperature furnace) and heated to a specified high temperature while it is surrounded by ammonia gas (NH_3). The ammonia breaks down into nitrogen and hydrogen, and the nitrogen unites with some of the alloying agents in the steel to form an extremely hard surface.

Nitriding, which is used to harden crankshaft bearing surfaces and cylinder walls, is done at a lower temperature than other forms of case hardening, and it does not warp the parts being hardened.

nitrogen. A colorless, odorless, tasteless, inert, gaseous chemical element. Nitrogen's symbol is N, its atomic number is 7, and its atomic weight is 14.0067. Nitrogen makes up about 78% of the volume of the earth's atmosphere and is used as an ingredient in fertilizers and explosives.

nitrogen charging (balloon operation). A technique of adding nitrogen gas to propane tanks to increase the fuel pressure. It is used in place of heat to control propane pressure in hot air balloons during cold weather.

NM. nautical mile.

NOAA. National Oceanic and Atmospheric Administration.

nobelium. A radioactive, synthetic chemical element in the actinide series. Nobelium's symbol is No, its atomic number is 102, and its atomic weight is 254.

noble. Inactive or inert. In the electrochemical series of metals, the metal in a combination that does not corrode is the more noble.

noble gas. Another name for inert gas. The noble (inert) gases are helium, neon, argon, krypton, xenon, and radon.

noctilucent clouds (meteorology). Clouds of unknown composition which occur at great heights, probably around 75 to 90 kilometers. They resemble thin cirrus, but usually have a bluish or silvery color, although sometimes orange to red.

nocturnal inversion (meteorology). This term is used interchangably with *radiational inversion*; a temperature inversion that develops during the night as a result of radiational cooling of the surface. Because the immediate surface (lower boundary layer) cools much more rapidly during radiational cooling conditions than the air just above (upper boundary layer), a temperature inversion can be created overnight, but typically erodes quickly after sunrise.

nodal suspension system (helicopter rotor suspension system). A method of vibration dampening, used in certain Bell helicopters to reduce the vibration of the main rotor system.

no-further-input prediction. A technique to help pilots maintain awareness of how advanced avionics systems are configured, and of the likely future behavior of the aircraft. No-further-input predictions are made by considering what the aircraft will do if the pilot makes no further entries or commands.

no-gyro approach (air traffic control). A radar approach or vector provided by ATC to an aircraft in case of a malfunctioning gyro compass or directional gyro. Instead of providing the pilot with headings to be flown, the controller observes the radar track and issues control instructions such as "turn right/left" or "stop turn," as appropriate.

noise (electronic equipment). Any unwanted electrical interference. Noise may come from static electricity or from signals fed into the circuit by inductive or capacitive coupling from other circuits.

noise abatement (flight operation procedure). Specific operational procedures that airports develop that will help limit aircraft noise while operating over nearby areas. This information is provided to pilots, operators, air carriers, air traffic facilities, and other special groups.

no-load current (electrical transformer current). Current flowing in the primary winding of a transformer connected to a source of AC voltage when no current is flowing in the secondary winding. No-load current is also called excitation current, or idling current.

Nomex. A patented nylon material that is used to make the honeycomb core for certain types of aircraft structural sandwich-type materials. Nomex is also used to make fire-resistant fabrics.

nominal value. A stated value that may be different from an actual value. For example, an electrical resistor may have a nominal resistance of 1,000 ohms, with a tolerance of plus or minus ten percent. Its nominal value is 1,000 ohms, but its actual value may be anywhere between 900 and 1,100 ohms.

nomogram. A graph that typically consists of three sets of data. Knowledge of any two sets of data enables the reader to determine the third set.

nonabrasive (material characteristic). The characteristic of a material that keeps it from scratching another material when it is rubbed against it.

nonapproach control tower (air traffic control). A control tower that authorizes aircraft to land or takeoff at the airport controlled by the tower or to transit the Class D airspace. The primary function of a nonapproach control tower is the sequencing of aircraft in the traffic pattern and on the landing area. Nonapproach control towers also separate aircraft operating under instrument flight rules clearances from approach controls and centers. They also provide ground control services to aircraft, vehicles, personnel, and equipment on the airport movement area.

nonaqueous developer (dye penetrant inspection component). A dye penetrant developer that is suspended in a volatile solvent and applied with a spray gun or an aerosol can. The developer forms a slightly translucent white coating that shows up a fault as a brilliant line when its capillary action pulls penetrant from the fault.

nonatomizing spray gun (paint spray gun). A type of spray gun that propels the material in a solid stream, rather than in the form of tiny droplets.

noncommon carriage. An aircraft operation for compensation or hire that does not involve making flights available to the public via advertising or other publicly communicated means.

noncommon route/portion. That segment of a North American route between the inland navigation facility and a designated North American terminal.

noncomposite separation (air traffic control). Air traffic separation in accordance with minimums other than the composite separation minimum specified for the area concerned.

non-cooperative aircraft. Aircraft that are not being tracked by ATC, or that do not have an electronic means of identification (such as a transponder) aboard, or that are not operating such equipment due to malfunction or deliberate action.

nondestructive inspection. Any type of inspection that does not damage the system or component being inspected. X-ray is a system of nondestructive inspection that allows the inside of a device to be inspected without its having to be opened or in any way damaged.

nondestructive testing (NDT). A preventative maintenance test procedure that can detect hidden defects without damage to the part being inspected. Methods of NDT include X-ray, gamma ray, ultrasonic, magnetic particles, eddy current, and dye penetrant.

nondimensional number. A pure number which has no dimensional value assigned to it. Ratios, such as Mach numbers and Reynolds numbers, are examples of nondimensional numbers.

nondirectional antenna (radio antenna). A radio antenna that receives or transmits signals from all directions with equal strength.

nondirectional beacon (air traffic control). *See* NDB.

nonenergizing brakes. *See* nonservo brakes.

nonferrous metal. A metal that does not contain iron.

nonflexible control cable. Steel aircraft control cable made of either 7 or 19 strands of solid wire. Nonflexible cable can be used only for installations in which the cable does not pass over pulleys.

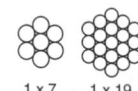

1 x 7   1 x 19

nonflexible control cable

noninductive load (electrical load). An electrical load that does not have any inductance. Its opposition to current is caused by resistance and/or capacitance.

noninductive winding (electrical machine). A two-part winding made in such a way that the magnetic field produced by one part cancels the field produced by the other. When the magnetic fields cancel each other, there is no opposition caused by inductance. All the opposition is caused by resistance.

nonlinear scale (indicating instrument scale). A scale on an indicating instrument in which the numbers are grouped close together at one end and spread out at the other end.

nonlinear system. A system whose output does not change in the same proportion as the input. If the output voltage of a system changes as the square of the input voltage, the system is nonlinear.

nonmagnetic material. Any material that cannot be magnetized nor is attracted to a magnet. Wood, paper, and most plastics are nonmagnetic, and aluminum, brass, and most nonferrous metals are nonmagnetic.

nonmovement area (air traffic control). Taxiways and apron (ramp) areas not under the control of air traffic.

nonporous. The state of a material having no pores or openings through which liquids or gases can seep. Glass is an example of a nonporous material.

nonprecision approach procedure. *14 CFR Part 1:* "A standard instrument approach procedure in which no electronic glide slope is provided."

nonradar. Precedes other terms and generally means without the use of radar, such as:

   a. *Nonradar Approach.* Used to describe instrument approaches for which course guidance on final approach is not provided by ground-based precision or surveillance radar. Radar vectors to the final approach course may or may not be provided by ATC. Examples of nonradar approaches are VOR, NDB, TACAN, and ILS/MLS approaches.

   b. *Nonradar Approach Control.* An ATC facility providing approach control service without the use of radar.

   c. *Nonradar Arrival.* An aircraft arriving at an airport without radar service or at an airport served by a radar facility and radar contact has not been established or has been terminated due to a lack of radar service to the airport.

   d. *Nonradar Route.* A flight path or route over which the pilot is performing his/her own navigation. The pilot may be receiving radar separation, radar monitoring, or other ATC services while on a nonradar route.

   e. *Nonradar Separation.* The spacing of aircraft in accordance with established minima without the use of radar; e.g., vertical, lateral, or longitudinal separation.

N

nonradar separation (ICAO). The separation used when aircraft position information is derived from sources other than radar.

nonrepairable damage. Damage to an aircraft or component that cannot be repaired. This type of damage requires the part to be replaced.

non-restrictive routing (NRR). Portions of a proposed route of flight where a user can flight plan the most advantageous flight path with no requirement to make reference to ground-based NAVAIDs.

nonrigid airship. A form of steerable lighter-than-air aircraft that uses the pressure of the gas to maintain the shape of the envelope. A blimp is an example of a nonrigid airship.

non-RNAV DP. A departure procedure in which the ground track is based on ground-based NAVAIDs and/or dead reckoning navigation.

nonscheduled airline. An airline that carries passengers or cargo for hire, but does not operate according to a regular or published schedule.

nonsequencing mode (avionics). The FMS/RNAV navigation mode that does not automatically sequence between waypoints in the programmed route. The nonsequencing mode maintains the current active waypoint indefinitely, and allows the pilot to specify desired track to or from that waypoint.

nonservo brakes (aircraft brakes). Brakes that do not use the weight of the aircraft to increase the friction. Disk brakes and expander tube brakes are examples of nonservo brakes.

nonskid brakes. Aircraft power brakes that do not lock up and allow a tire to skid. Wheels equipped with nonskid brakes have a wheel-speed sensor in their hub that measures the rate at which the wheel decelerates (slows its rotation). If the wheel decelerates at a rate that shows a skid is beginning, the nonskid valve between the power brake control valve and the wheel cylinder is signaled to release the hydraulic pressure to the brake until the wheel begins to speed up. Then the valve automatically reapplies the pressure. A wheel equipped with a nonskid brake is held on the edge of a skid, but a skid is not allowed to develop. Nonskid brakes are also called antiskid brakes.

nonspecular. Nonreflecting. Nonspecular lacquer is used to finish the deck of an aircraft fuselage ahead of the cockpit so light reflections will not impair the pilot's vision.

nontautening dope. Aircraft dope that causes almost no shrinkage of the fabric on which it is applied. Nontautening dope is used on polyester fabric after it has been shrunk with heat.

nontowered airport. An airport without air traffic control; pilots fly into and out of these airport using standard operating procedures to avoid one another.

nonvolatile memory (digital computer memory). Memory in which the stored data is not lost when power to the computer is turned off. ROM (Read Only Memory) is nonvolatile, while RAM (Random Access Memory) is volatile.

no procedure turn (NoPT). A term used along with the appropriate course and altitude to denote that the procedure turn is not required.

NoPT. *See* no procedure turn.

NORDO. Aircraft in which no radio equipment is installed.

NOR gate (logic gate). A NOT OR logic gate that has two or more inputs and one output. The output is logic zero (NOT one) when the signal on any one of the inputs is logic one. The symbol for a NOR gate is the symbol for an OR gate, followed by a small circle, to show that the output of the gate is inverted. (Its logic condition is changed.)

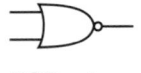

NOR gate

normal (geometry). Normal, in geometry, means perpendicular. A line is normal to another line if it is perpendicular to it, and it is normal to a curve if it is perpendicular to a line tangent to the curve at the point the line intersects it.

normal (meteorology). The value of an element averaged for a given location over a period of years and recognized as a standard.

normal axis. *See* vertical axis of an aircraft.

normal category aircraft. An aircraft certificated under 14 CFR Part 23 that is not certificated in the utility, acrobatic, or commuter category.

normal heptane. A hydrocarbon, C_7H_{16}, that has a very low critical pressure and temperature. Normal heptane is used as the low reference in measuring the anti-detonation characteristics of aviation gasoline.

normalize (steel heat treatment). A process of strain-relieving steel that has been machined, welded, or worked in any way that leaves it in a strained condition. The steel is heated to a specified temperature, usually red-hot, and then allowed to cool in still air to room temperature.

normalizing (turbonormalizing). A turbocharger that maintains sea-level pressure in the induction manifold at altitude.

normally aspirated engine (reciprocating engine). *See* naturally aspirated engine.

normally closed (NC) relay. A relay whose contacts are held closed by a spring. The contacts are opened by the magnetic pull of an electromagnet.

normally open (NO) relay. A relay whose contacts are held open by a spring. The contacts are closed by the magnetic pull of an electromagnet.

normal operating speed (aircraft performance specification). The level-flight speed of an aircraft at its design altitude, with the engine operating at no more than 75% of its rated horsepower.

normal operating zone. *See* NOZ.

normal refraction (radar technology). Refraction of a radar beam under normal atmospheric conditions. The normal radius of curvature of the beam is about four times the radius of the curvature of the earth.

normal shock wave (aerodynamics). A shock wave that forms ahead of a blunt object moving through the air at the speed of sound. The shock wave is perpendicular (normal) to the air approaching the object. Air passing through a normal shock wave is slowed to a subsonic speed, and its static pressure is increased. *See* shock wave.

norm-referenced testing (in teaching process). System of testing in which students are ranked against the performance of other students.

North American route. A numerically coded route preplanned over existing airway and route systems to and from specific coastal fixes serving the North Atlantic. North American Routes consist of the following:

    a. *Common Route/Portion.* That segment of a North American Route between the inland navigation facility and the coastal fix.

    b. *Noncommon Route/Portion.* That segment of a North American Route between the inland navigation facility and a designated North American terminal.

    c. *Inland Navigation Facility.* A navigation aid on a North American Route at which the common route and/or the noncommon route begins or ends.

    d. *Coastal Fix.* A navigation aid or intersection where an aircraft transitions between the domestic route structure and the oceanic route structure.

North American route program (NRP). The NRP is a set of rules and procedures which are designed to increase the flexibility of user flight planning within published guidelines.

northerly turning error (magnetic compass error). An error inherent in an aircraft magnetic compass. The float on which the compass magnets are mounted is unbalanced to compensate for the vertical component of the earth's magnetic field, and it is this unbalanced condition that causes northerly turning error.

    When a turn is made from either an easterly or westerly heading toward the north, the heavy end of the float causes the compass to overshoot the heading, and when turning toward the south, to lag behind the turn. Northerly turning error is also called dip error.

northern domestic airspace (NDA). All airspace within the Canadian Domestic Airspace that lies north of a line that, specifically defined by regulation, begins at the Alaska/Canada border on the Arctic Ocean and, more or less, extends southward through Yellowknife to Churchill and thence northeast to Frobisher and the Atlantic Ocean.

north mark. A beacon data block sent by the host computer to be displayed by the ARTS on a 360° bearing at a locally selected radar azimuth and distance. The north mark is used to ensure correct range/azimuth orientation during periods of CENRAP.

North Pacific (air traffic control). An organized route system between the Alaskan west coast and Japan.

north pole of a magnet. The pole of a magnet from which the lines of magnetic flux are considered to leave. The north pole is actually the north-seeking pole. When a magnet is suspended so it is free to rotate, it will turn until its north pole points to the magnetic north pole of the earth.

nose cone (rocket component). The forwardmost, usually separable section of a rocket or guided missile that is shaped to offer minimum aerodynamic resistance and often bears protective cladding against heat.

nose gear (aircraft landing gear). The wheel under the forward end of the fuselage of an aircraft equipped with a tricycle landing gear.

nose-gear centering cam. A cam in the shock strut that causes the wheel of a retractable nose gear to straighten fore-and-aft when the strut is fully extended. When the aircraft takes off and the strut extends, the wheel straightens so it can be retracted into the wheel well.

nose heavy (stability condition). A condition in which the center of lift of an airplane wing is behind the aircraft center of gravity. This creates a tendency for the aircraft to nose down.

nose rib (airplane wing component). A partial wing rib that extends back only to the front spar. Nose ribs, also called false ribs, are installed between each full rib to support the leading edge and give the wing its correct aerodynamic shape.

nose section (aircraft reciprocating engine component). The forward section of an aircraft reciprocating engine crankcase that contains the thrust bearing and propeller reduction gears.

NOTAM (Notice to Airmen). A notice containing information (not known sufficiently in advance to publicize by other means) concerning the establishment, condition, or change in any component (facility, service, or procedure of, or hazard in the National Airspace System), the timely knowledge of which is essential to personnel concerned with flight operations.

notch sensitivity. A measure of the loss of strength of a material caused by the presence of a notch, or V-shaped cut.

NOT gate (logic gate). A NOT gate is an inverter. A NOT gate has one input and one output, and the logic condition at the output is always opposite the logic condition at the input. The symbol for a NOT gate is a triangle (the symbol for a buffer), followed by a small circle to show that the output is inverted. *See* inverter.

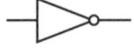

NOT gate

Notice to Airmen. *See* NOTAM.

Notice to Airmen Publication. *See* NTAP.

no transgression zone. *See* NTZ.

now wind (meteorology). Wind direction and speed as determined from a sample reading every second and averaged over the last five seconds.

NOZ (normal operating zone) (air traffic control). The operating zone within which aircraft flight remains during normal independent simultaneous parallel ILS approaches.

nozzle. A tapered end of a duct through which fluid flows. The area of a converging nozzle decreases in the direction the fluid is flowing, and when fluid flows through a converging nozzle at a subsonic speed, it speeds up. The area of a diverging nozzle increases in the direction the fluid is flowing, and when fluid flows through a diverging nozzle at a subsonic speed, it slows down.

nozzle diaphragm (gas turbine engine component). The ring of stationary vanes directly ahead of the turbine wheel. The vanes in the nozzle diaphragm form a series of convergent ducts which accelerate the air as it leaves the combustors and direct it into the turbine blades at the angle that gives the turbine its maximum efficiency. The nozzle diaphragm is also called the turbine inlet guide vanes. *See* turbine inlet guide vanes.

nozzle guide vanes. *See* turbine inlet guide vanes.

NPN transistor. A bipolar transistor made of three pieces of semiconductor material (silicon or germanium) joined together. The emitter and collector are made of N-type material, and the base, which is sandwiched between them, is made of P-type material.

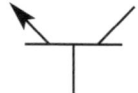

NPN transistor

NRP. *See* National Route Program.

NSA. *See* National Security Area.

N-struts (airplane wing struts). Interplane struts installed between the upper and lower wings of a biplane near the wing tips. N-struts get their name from the fact that the three pieces of these struts are arranged in the shape of the letter N.

NTAP (Notice to Airmen Publication). A publication issued every four weeks, designed primarily for the pilot, which contains current NOTAM information considered essential to the safety of flight as well as supplemental data to other aeronautical publications. The contraction NTAP is used in NOTAM text.

NTSB. *See* National Transportation Safety Board.

N-type semiconductor material. A semiconductor element, such as silicon or germanium, doped with an element having more electrons in its valence shell than are needed to complete the covalent bonds within the material. There are electrons in N-type material that are free to move about. Silicon and germanium are doped with a pentavalent element, such as arsenic or phosphorus, to make N-type material.

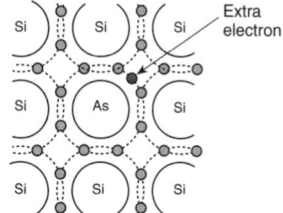

N-type silicon

NTZ (no transgression zone). A 2,000-foot-wide zone, located equidistant between parallel runway final approach courses in which flight is not allowed.

nuclear energy. Energy released when neutrons are knocked out of the nuclei of certain materials. Neutrons bind the protons together in the nucleus of an atom, and when neutrons are knocked out, the protons are then able to leave the nucleus. As they leave, they release great amounts of energy in the form of heat and light.

nuclear fission. The breaking apart of the nucleus of an atom by striking the nucleus with a neutron. If a neutron strikes the nucleus with enough force, it splits the nucleus and creates atoms of different materials. Nuclear fission releases a tremendous amount of heat and light.

nuclear fusion. A method of energy release in which a heavier nucleus is formed by fusing two lighter nuclei. When the lighter nuclei fuse, a large amount of energy is released.

nuclei. A plural form of nucleus; an alternate plural form is nucleuses.

nucleonics. The branch of science and technology that deals with nuclear energy and its applications.

nucleus of an atom. The core (center portion) of an atom. The nucleus contains one or more protons (positive charges), and all nuclei except that of hydrogen contain one or more neutrons. Neutrons have mass but no electrical charge.

nuisance alert. A term used to describe a "false alarm" provided by an avionics system designed to detect surrounding hazards such as proximate traffic and terrain.

null balance. A method of setting one voltage exactly equal to another. When no current flows between the two voltages, as indicated by a sensitive current-measuring instrument, the two voltages are exactly the same. The voltages have nulled out, or cancelled, each other.

null detector (electrical instrument). An instrument used to measure a value by comparing it with a known variable value. The known value is compared with the unknown and is changed until the null detector determines that there is no difference between the two. The known value is now exactly the same as that of the unknown.

null position (automatic direction finder). The position of an ADF loop antenna when the signal being received is canceled in the two sides of the loop, and the signal strength is the weakest.

numbers. Terms used to assign a value or an order to something. Cardinal numbers, such as 1, 2, and 3, tell how many. They assign a value to something. One engine, 2 wrenches, 3 airplanes are examples of cardinal numbers being used to assign values.

Ordinal numbers, such as first, second, and third, tell us the order in which something occurs. The first day, the second order, or the third time are examples of the use of ordinal numbers.

numerator (mathematics). The part of a common fraction above the line; the denominator is the part of the fraction below the line. The numerator shows the number of parts of the denominator that are used. In the fraction $\frac{9}{16}$, nine is the numerator. The whole unit is divided into 16 equal parts (the denominator), and we are using only nine of these parts.

numerical control. A digital control system. Numerical control (digital control) is used with production machine tools to machine complex parts with more precision than can be done with an analog control system.

numerical weather prediction (meteorology). Forecasting by digital computers solving mathematical equations. Numerical weather prediction is used extensively in weather services throughout the world.

numerous targets vicinity (location) (air traffic control). A traffic advisory issued by ATC to advise pilots that targets on the radar scope are too numerous to issue individually.

nun buoys (nautical navigation markings). Cone shaped buoys painted red and marked with even numbers that increase as you return from the open sea. They mark the right side of the channel for an inbound vessel.

nut (threaded fastener). A small metal collar, usually having a hexagonal (six-sided) shape. The hole in the nut is threaded so that it can be screwed onto a bolt. Bolts and nuts are used to fasten two or more pieces of material together. The bolt is installed in holes drilled through the pieces, and a nut is screwed onto the bolt to clamp the pieces together.

nutation. The slow back-and-forth rocking of the axis of a spinning body. A gyroscope, a spinning top, and even the earth, as it spins, have a slight nutation.

nutplate (aircraft fastener). A special form of nut that can be riveted to an aircraft structure. Screws can be driven into a nutplate without having to hold the nutplate with a wrench.

NWS. National Weather Service.

nylon. The name of a family of synthetic materials that are part of the polymer chain. Nylon is used for making cloth and rope and for such molded parts as wheels, gears, and pulleys. Nylon is strong, lightweight, and resistant to most chemicals.

Oscar

OALT (operational acceptable level of traffic) (air traffic control). An air traffic activity level associated with the designed capacity for a sector or airport. The OALT considers dynamic changes in staffing, personnel experience levels, equipment outages, operational configurations, weather, traffic complexity, aircraft performance mixtures, transitioning flights, adjacent airspace, hand-off/point-out responsibilities, and other factors that may affect an air traffic operational position or system element. The OALT is normally considered to be the total number of aircraft that any traffic functional position can accommodate for a defined period of time under a given set of circumstances.

objectivity (in teaching/learning process). The characteristics of a good test wherein the scoring and grading can be based on single-answer responses, to avoid reflecting the biases of the person grading the test.

oblique angle. An angle that is neither a right angle (a 90° angle) nor a straight line (a 180° angle). An oblique angle can be either an acute angle (an angle of less than 90°) or an obtuse angle (an angle of more than 90°).

oblique photography. A type of aerial photography in which photographs are taken with the camera pointed at an angle, rather than straight down, as is done in aerial mapping.

oblique shock wave (aerodynamics). A shock wave that forms on a sharp-pointed object moving through the air at a speed greater than the speed of sound. Air passing through an oblique shock wave is slowed down, but not to a subsonic speed, and its static pressure is increased. *See* illustration for shock wave.

oblique triangle. A closed three-sided, plane (flat) figure that does not contain any right angles (90° angles).

oblique triangle

oblique view. A view that is similar to an isometric view except with two of the three drawing axes always at right angles to each other.

oblong shape. A shape that is neither square nor round, but can be either an elongated (stretched) square or circle. An oblong circle is called an ellipse, and an oblong square is called a rectangle.

obscuration (meteorology). A term meaning that the sky is hidden by surface-based obscuring phenomena and vertical visibility is restricted overhead.

obscuration aloft (weather report). Denotes a nonsurface-based obscuring phenomena.

obscuring phenomena (meteorology). Any dry particles or particles of liquid water other than clouds. Obscuring phenomena may be either surface-based or aloft.

observation aircraft. Aircraft used by the military to fly behind enemy lines and observe the movement of troops or the effects of artillery fire.

OBS mode (avionics). The name for the nonsequencing mode on some FMS/RNAV units. *See* nonsequencing mode.

obsolete. Out of date or no longer in use because of being replaced with something newer.

obstacle (air traffic control). An existing object, object of natural growth, or terrain at a fixed geographical location or which may be expected at a fixed location within a prescribed area, with reference to which vertical clearance is or must be provided during flight operation.

obstacle clearance altitude/height. The lowest altitude above the elevation of the relevant runway threshold or above the airport elevation used in establishing compliance with appropriate obstacle clearance criteria.

obstacle clearance surface (OCS). An inclined surface associated with a wide area augmentation system or an approach with vertical guidance glidepath angle. The separation between this surface and the vertical path angle at any given distance from the ground point of intercept defines the minimum required obstruction clearance at that point.

obstacle departure procedure (ODP). (1) A procedure that provides obstacle clearance. ODPs do not include ATC-related climb requirements. (2) A preplanned IFR departure procedure printed for pilot use in textual or graphic form to provide obstruction clearance via the least onerous route from the terminal area to the appropriate en route structure.

obstacle free zone (OFZ) (air traffic control). A three dimensional volume of airspace which provides protection for the transition of aircraft to and from the runway. The OFZ clearing standard precludes taxiing and parked airplanes and object penetrations, except for frangible NAVAID locations that are fixed by function. Additionally, vehicles, equipment, and personnel may be authorized by air traffic control to enter the area using the provisions of FAA Order 7110.65, *Air Traffic Control*, paragraph 3-1-5. The runway OFZ, and where applicable, the inner-approach OFZ and the inner-transitional OFZ, comprise the OFZ.

obstacle identification slope (OIS). A departure procedure is structured to provide at least 48 feet per NM of clearance above objects that do not penetrate the obstacle slope, which is based on a 40 to 1 ratio, the equivalent of a 152-foot per NM slope.

obstacle identification surface (OIS). The slope integrated into a departure procedure that is designed to provide at least 48 feet per NM of clearance above objects that do not penetrate the obstacle slope, using a 200 feet per NM climb. The slope, known as the obstacle identification surface, is based on a 40 to 1 ratio, which is equivalent to a 152-foot per NM slope. The design of the departure assumes an initial climb of 200 feet per NM after crossing the departure end of the runway (DER) at a height of at least 35 feet above the ground.

obstruction (in airspace). Any object/obstacle exceeding the obstruction standards specified by 14 CFR Part 77, Subpart C, which are used to determine obstructions to air navigation that may affect the safe and efficient use of navigable airspace and the operation of planned or existing air navigation and communication facilities. Such facilities include air navigation aids, communication equipment, airports, federal airways, instrument approach or departure procedures, and approved off-airway routes. An obstruction can be an object of natural growth; terrain; permanent or temporary construction; or an alteration of an existing structure.

obstruction clearance limit (OCL) (ICAO). The height above the aerodrome elevation below which the minimum prescribed vertical clearance cannot be maintained either on approach or in the event of a missed approach.

obstruction light (airport lighting). A light or one of a group of lights, usually red or white, frequently mounted on a surface structure or natural terrain to warn pilots of the presence of an obstruction.

obtuse angle. An angle of more than 90°, yet less than 180°. An obtuse angle may be called an open angle.

obtuse angle

obtuse triangle. A triangle that contains an obtuse angle (an angle greater than 90°). *See* illustration for oblique triangle.

occluded front (meteorology). A composite of two fronts. An occluded front forms when a cold front overtakes a warm front or a quasi-stationary front.

ocean display and planning system (air traffic control). An automated digital display system that provides flight data processing, conflict probe, and situation display for oceanic air traffic control.

oceanic airspace (air traffic control). Airspace over the oceans of the world, considered international airspace, where oceanic separation and procedures per ICAO are applied. Responsibility for the provisions of air traffic control service in this airspace is delegated to various countries, based generally upon geographic proximity and the availability of the required resources.

oceanic navigational error report. A report filed when an aircraft exiting oceanic airspace has been observed by radar to be off course. ONER reporting parameters and procedures are contained in FAAO 7110.82, Monitoring of Navigational Performance In Oceanic Areas.

oceanic published route (air traffic control). A route established in international airspace and charted or described in flight information publications such as Route Charts, DOD En Route Charts, Chart Supplements, NOTAMs, and Track Messages.

oceanic transition route. An ATS route established for the purpose of transitioning aircraft to/from an organized track system.

O-condition (sheet metal temper condition). Fully annealed. A fully annealed aluminum alloy sheet is said to be in its O-condition.

octagon. A plane (flat), closed, eight-sided figure. In a regular octagon, all sides have the same length, and all of the angles are the same.

octahedron. A solid form that has eight plane (flat) surfaces.

octal number system. A system of numbers based on eight units (zero through seven). Octal numbers are used in digital electronics to make long strings of zeros and ones more manageable. One octal digit replaces three binary digits.

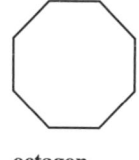

octagon

Decimal	Octal	Binary
0	0	000
1	1	001
2	2	010
3	3	011
4	4	100
5	5	101
6	6	110
7	7	111

octane rating (reciprocating engine fuel rating). The system used to rate the ability of a reciprocating-engine fuel to resist detonation. The higher the octane number, the more resistant the fuel is to detonation. The fuel being rated is run in a test engine whose compression ratio can be varied. This ratio is changed until the fuel detonates, or explodes inside the cylinder, rather than burning as it should. The engine is left with the compression ratio that caused the fuel to detonate, and a fuel composed of a mixture of iso-octane, a fuel that resists detonation, and heptane, a fuel prone to detonate, is fed to the engine.

The ratio of the two fuels is varied until the engine detonates as it did with the fuel being rated. When the performance with the two fuels is matched, the ratio of the octane to heptane is noted, and the fuel is rated with the percentage of octane used. If a mixture of 80% octane and 20% heptane causes the engine to perform as it did with the fuel being rated, the fuel is given an octane number of 80. At one time aviation gasoline was given a dual rating such as 80/87. The first number represented its antidetonation rating with a lean, cruise fuel-air mixture, and the higher number, its rating with a rich, takeoff mixture. Fuel with antidetonation characteristics better than that of iso-octane is rated in performance numbers. *See* performance numbers.

octave. An interval of audible vibrations spanning eight full tones above or below another. A tone, in this regard, is a sound with a distinct pitch.

odd harmonics. The odd multiples of a fundamental frequency. For example, frequencies that are three, five, seven, and nine times that of a fundamental, or original, frequency are odd harmonics of the frequency.

odometer. The portion of an automobile speedometer that indicates the distance traveled.

ODP. *See* obstacle departure procedure.

oersted. A unit of magnetic intensity in the centimeter-gram-second system of measurement. One oersted is the amount of magnetic intensity equal to one gilbert per square centimeter, and this is 79.577 ampere-turns per meter.

off-airport (in UA operations). Any location that is used to launch or recover an unmanned aircraft (UA), but that is not considered an airport. An example of an off-airport location is an open field.

off-airway routes. The FAA prescribes altitudes governing the operation of aircraft under IFR for off-airway routes in a similar manner to those on federal airways, jet routes, area navigation low or high altitude routes, and other direct routes for which an MEA is designated.

off course (air traffic control). A term used to describe a situation where an aircraft has reported a position fix or is observed on radar at a point not on the ATC-approved route of flight.

off-idle mixture (aircraft fuel metering system adjustment). The fuel-air mixture ratio produced by a fuel metering system during the time the engine is transitioning from its idle RPM to a speed at which fuel is metered through the main metering system.

off-route obstruction clearance altitude (OROCA) (air traffic control). An off-route altitude which provides obstruction clearance with a 1,000-foot buffer in nonmountainous terrain areas and a 2,000-foot buffer in designated mountainous areas within the United States. This altitude may not provide signal coverage from ground-based navigational aids, air traffic control radar, or communications coverage.

off-route vector (air traffic control). A vector by ATC which takes an aircraft off a previously assigned route. Altitudes assigned by ATC during such vectors provide required obstacle clearance.

offset parallel runways. Staggered runways having center lines which are parallel.

offset rivet set (sheet-metalworking tool). A rivet set, used in a pneumatic rivet gun, in which the cup that fits the manufactured head of the rivet is offset from the center line of the rivet set shank. Offset rivet sets are used to drive rivets in a location where a straight set cannot be used.

offset screwdriver. A screwdriver whose blade is perpendicular to the handle. Offset screwdrivers are used to turn screws where there is not enough clearance to allow the use of a regular screwdriver.

offset throw (crankshaft design). Crank arms on a reciprocating engine crankshaft. The arms, or throws, to which the connecting rods and pistons are attached are offset from the center of the crankshaft to move the pistons in and out of the cylinder. The amount of the offset determines the stroke of the engine.

offshore/control airspace area. That portion of airspace between the U.S. 12 NM limit and the oceanic CTA/FIR boundary within which air traffic control is exercised. These areas are established to provide air traffic control services. Offshore/Control Airspace Areas may be classified as either Class A airspace or Class E airspace.

off-the-shelf item. A standard production item. An off-the-shelf computer program, for example, is a standard program that can be bought and used, rather than having a custom program written.

OFZ (obstacle free zone) (air traffic control). A three dimensional volume of airspace which provides protection for the transition of aircraft to and from the runway. The OFZ clearing standard precludes taxiing and parked airplanes and object penetrations, except for frangible NAVAID locations that are fixed by function. Additionally, vehicles, equipment, and personnel may be authorized by air traffic control to enter the area using the provisions of FAA Order 7110.65, *Air Traffic Control*, paragraph 3-1-5. The runway OFZ, and where applicable, the inner-approach OFZ and the inner-transitional OFZ, comprise the OFZ.

ohm (Ω). The standard unit of electrical resistance. One ohm is the resistance of a column of mercury weighing 14.4521 grams, formed into a column of uniform cross section and a length of 1,006.3 centimeters. This standard resistance is measured with the mercury having a temperature of 0°C. More practically, one ohm is the amount of resistance that will cause a voltage drop of one volt when one ampere of current flows through it.

Ohm's law. The law that explains the relationship between the flow of electrons (current), electrical pressure (voltage), and the opposition to flow (resistance). According to Ohm's law, the amount of current flowing in a circuit is directly proportional to the circuit voltage and inversely proportional to the circuit resistance.

ohmmeter. An electrical measuring instrument that measures the resistance in a circuit or component and shows its value in ohms. An ohmmeter determines the value of an unknown resistance by measuring the current flowing through it when the voltage across it is known.

ohms-per-volt (voltmeter sensitivity). A measure of the sensitivity of a voltmeter, found by dividing one by the amount of current (in amperes) needed to deflect the pointer of the meter full scale.

$$\text{Ohms per volt} = \frac{1}{\text{Full-scale current (amps)}}$$

For example, a meter that requires one milliamp (0.001 amp) of current for full-scale pointer deflection has a sensitivity of 1,000 ohms per volt.

$$\text{Ohms per volt} = \frac{1}{0.001} = 1,000$$

The greater the ohms-per-volt, the more sensitive the meter.

oil analysis. A method of measuring the contents in parts per million of various chemical elements in a sample of oil. A sample of the oil is burned in an electric arc, and the resulting light is analyzed with a spectroscope which identifies the chemical elements in the oil and gives an indication of the amount of each element.

oil can (sheet metal problem). A condition in which a flat piece of sheet metal is stretched so it snaps in and out between rows of rivets, in the same way the bottom of an oil can snaps in and out.

oil circuit breaker. A protection device for electrical circuits that carry large amounts of current. The housing containing the current-carrying contacts is filled with oil which quenches the arc that forms as the contacts open. Quenching the arc prevents damage to the contacts when they open a circuit carrying a large amount of current.

oil control ring (reciprocating engine component). One of the cast-iron rings installed in grooves around a piston. The oil control ring is installed in the groove below the compression rings (top rings), and it is usually made in several sections. The oil control ring controls the amount of oil allowed to flow between the piston and the cylinder wall. Excess oil is drained back into the crankcase through holes drilled through the piston in the ring groove.

oil-cooled transformer (electrical transformer). An electrical transformer whose core and coils are immersed in oil. The oil circulates through the transformer and carries heat from the core and windings to the housing. Air flowing around the housing removes this heat. The housings for small oil-cooled transformers have a smooth outer surface, but the housing of larger units is sometimes finned to assist in carrying away heat.

oil cooler (reciprocating engine component). An air-oil heat exchanger, used to remove excess heat from the lubricating oil. If the oil is too hot as it leaves the engine, it flows through the oil cooler, where it gives up the excess heat to the air flowing through or around the tubes in the cooler. The cooled oil then returns to the engine oil sump or to the oil tank.

oil-damped bearing (gas turbine component). A type of roller bearing installation in a gas turbine engine in which the outer race is installed in an oil damper compartment whose inside diameter is a few thousandths of an inch larger than the outside diameter of the outer race. Oil under pressure fills the oil damper compartment and allows the bearing to compensate for sight misalignment and to absorb vibrations of the shaft.

oil dilution (reciprocating engine operation). A method of treating the lubricating oil to make it possible to start a reciprocating engine when the temperature is very low. When the oil gets cold, it becomes thick and hard to move, making it difficult for the starter to turn the engine over fast enough for it to start. Before shutting the engine down, enough gasoline from the fuel system is mixed with the lubricating oil to dilute it, so the starter can turn the engine over when the oil is cold. When the engine starts and the oil warms up, the gasoline evaporates from it. The oil is not damaged by diluting it. Oil dilution is no longer needed because multiviscosity oil is thin enough at low temperature to allow the engine to start.

oil filter (lubrication system component). A device in the lubrication system of either a reciprocating engine or a gas turbine engine that removes contaminants suspended in the oil.

oil hardening (metal heat treatment). A method of hardening steel by heating it red-hot and then quenching it in a bath of oil. Oil cools the steel more slowly than either water or brine and gives it a uniform hardness.

oilite bushing. A type of self-lubricating bushing. Oilite bushings are made of a porous bronze material impregnated with oil. They can be pressed into holes to decrease the resistance to shafts turning in the holes. When a shaft turns in an oilite bushing, it produces heat that brings the oil to the surface and provides lubrication between the bushing and the shaft.

Oilite bushings must never be washed, as washing removes the oil.

oil jet (lubricating system component). A small nozzle which directs a stream of lubricating oil to a specific point to be lubricated. Oil jets are used to direct oil to bearings and gears.

oil pan (reciprocating engine component). The removable lower part of the crankcase of a reciprocating engine. Engine lubricating oil is collected and stored in the pan and is taken from the pan by the pressure pump and forced through passages in the engine. Gravity then drains the oil back into the pan. An oil pan is commonly called an oil sump.

oil pressure indicator (aircraft engine instrument). An instrument used to show the pilot or flight engineer the pressure of the lubricating oil being delivered to the engine bearings.

oil scraper ring (reciprocating engine component). Another name for an oil wiper ring. *See* oil wiper ring.

oil screen (lubricating system component). A fine-mesh wire screen used inside an engine lubricating system to trap contaminants suspended in the lubricating oil. A screen is not as effective as a filter, and many engines use both screens and filters.

oil seal (engine component). A type of seal used in an engine to prevent oil leaking from the engine around a rotating shaft.

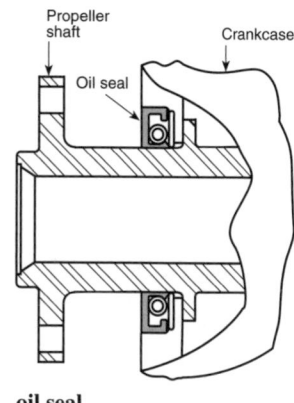

oil seal

oil separator. A device used to remove oil from the air discharged from an oil-lubricated air pump. A wet, vane-type air pump is lubricated and sealed by a small amount of engine oil flowing through the pump. This oil must be removed before the air can be used.

An oil separator contains a series of baffles over which the pump-discharge air must pass. Any oil in the air sticks to the baffles and drains to the bottom of the separator housing, and from here it is returned to the engine crankcase. Air from which the oil has been removed leaves the separator from a connection above and beyond the baffles.

oil slinger. A ridge around a rotating shaft on the engine side of an oil seal. The slinger throws much of the oil away from the shaft, back into the engine crankcase, before it reaches the oil seal.

oil sump (engine lubricating system component). An engine component designed to hold the lubricating oil. In a wet-sump engine, the entire supply of oil is held in the sump. In a dry-sump engine, the sump is small and holds the oil only until the scavenger pump can move it into an external oil tank.

oil tank pressurizing valve (turbine lubricating system component). A check valve in the oil tank vent system that maintains an air pressure of between 3 and 6 psi on the oil. This pressure assures a positive flow of oil to the engine-driven oil pump at all altitudes.

oil temperature indicator (aircraft engine instrument). An engine instrument that shows the pilot or flight engineer the temperature of the oil as it enters the engine.

oil temperature regulator (reciprocating engine component). The device used to keep the temperature of the oil entering the engine within allowable limits. This type of regulator controls the temperature by directing hot oil through the core of the oil cooler and cold oil around the cooler or between the core and the shell.

oil wiper ring (reciprocating engine component). One of the cast-iron rings installed in the grooves around a piston. The oil wiper ring is the bottom ring on a piston, and its purpose is to direct oil up between the piston and the cylinder wall for lubrication and sealing. The amount of oil allowed to remain between the piston and the cylinder wall is determined by the oil control ring. *See* oil control ring.

OIS. *See* obstacle identification surface.

oleo strut (aircraft shock absorber). A type of hydropneumatic (oil-air) shock absorber used on aircraft landing gear. The shock of the landing impact is absorbed by oil flowing through a metering orifice (restricting hole). The smaller shocks from taxiing are taken up by a cushion of compressed air.

OM. Outer marker of the ILS.

Omega navigation system. A worldwide, electronic, hyperbolic navigation system. A master and one or more slave stations transmit a CW (continuous wave) signal simultaneously on the same VLF (very-low-frequency) carrier. The receiving aircraft measures the phase difference between these signals as they are received, and plots, on a hyperbolic chart, the line of position on which this phase difference can occur. The lines of position from two Omega stations cross at the location of the aircraft.

O

omission error (flight training). In instrument training: failing to anticipate significant instrument indications following attitude changes; for example, concentrating on pitch control while forgetting about heading or roll information, resulting in erratic control of heading and bank.

OMNI (electronic navigation system). A term used for the VOR, Very-high-frequency Omni-Range, navigation system. *See* VOR.

omni bearing selector (electronic navigation instrument). A component in the VOR system on which the pilot selects the radial from the VOR station along which he wishes to fly. The omni bearing selector (OBS) shifts the phase of the reference signal inside the instrument, so the needle on the course deviation indicator (CDI) will center when the aircraft is on the selected radial.

omnidirectional antenna (radio antenna). A type of radio antenna that has the same field strength in all horizontal directions. An omnidirectional antenna is also called a nondirectional antenna.

omnidirectional microphone. A microphone that picks up sounds equally well from all directions around it. An omnidirectional microphone is also called a nondirectional microphone.

onboard lightning detection systems. An onboard weather detection system that senses electrical discharges suggestive of the presence of thunderstorm cells.

onboard weather radar. An onboard system capable of detecting significant masses of precipitation. The primary use of weather radar is to aid the pilot in avoiding thunderstorms and their associated hazards.

on-condition maintenance (aircraft maintenance). A type of aircraft maintenance in which parts are replaced only when their condition is such that they appear to be no longer airworthy. On-condition maintenance differs from life-limited maintenance, in which a part is replaced at the end of a specified number of operational hours or operational cycles, regardless of its apparent condition.

on course (air traffic control). Term used to indicate that an aircraft is established on the route centerline, or used by ATC to advise a pilot making a radar approach that his/her aircraft is lined up on the final approach course.

on-course indication (air traffic control). An indication on an instrument which provides the pilot a visual means of determining that the aircraft is located on the center line of a given navigational track, or an indication on a radarscope that an aircraft is on a given track.

on-demand operation. Any operation for compensation or hire that is (1) passenger-carrying conducted as a public charter (per 14 CFR Part 380) in which departure time and location are negotiated with the customer and that is any of the following types of operations: common carriage, noncommon carriage, or rotorcraft; or (2) is scheduled passenger-carrying conducted with a frequency of less than five round trips per week, on at least one route between two or more points according to published flight schedules, in airplanes (other than turbojet-powered) with a maximum passenger-seat configuration of 9 seats or less and a maximum payload capacity of 7,500 pounds or less, or in rotorcraft; or (3) all-cargo operations conducted with airplanes having a payload capacity of 7,500 pounds or less, or with rotorcraft.

one-hundred-and-eighty-degree ambiguity (navigation system error). An error inherent in some types of radio direction finding equipment in which the equipment cannot distinguish whether the signal being received is ahead of the aircraft or behind it. Automatic direction finding (ADF) equipment solves this problem by using a sense antenna.

one-hundred-hour inspection (aircraft maintenance inspection). An inspection required by 14 CFR §91.409 for FAA-certificated aircraft that are operated for hire, or are used for flight instruction for hire. A 100-hour inspection is similar in content to an annual inspection, but it can be conducted by an aircraft mechanic who holds an Airframe and Powerplant rating, but does not have an Inspection Authorization. A list of the items that must be included in an annual or 100-hour inspection is included in 14 CFR Part 43, Appendix D.

one-minute weather. The most recent one-minute updated weather broadcast received by a pilot from an uncontrolled airport ASOS/AWOS.

one-shot rivet gun (sheet-metal working tool). A hard-hitting air hammer, used to drive large, solid aluminum alloy rivets. A one-shot rivet gun hits the rivet with a single hard blow each time the trigger is pulled. This is different from the action of an ordinary rivet gun, which delivers a continuous series of blows as long as the trigger is held down.

    Aluminum alloy rivets are strain hardened by repeated hammering, and they can become so brittle they crack. To prevent this, they can be driven with a single hard blow from a one-shot rivet gun.

one-to-one vibration (rotorcraft). A low frequency vibration having one beat per revolution of the rotor. This vibration can be either lateral, or vertical.

on-speed condition (propeller governor condition). The condition of a propeller governor when the engine is turning at the speed selected by the governor. The centrifugal force acting on the flyweights in the governor is exactly balanced by the compression of the speeder spring.

OODA loop. A model for aeronautical decision making based on the concept of a recurring cycle (or loop) of "observe, orient, decide, act." It is a standard description of decision-making cycles that provides immediate feedback throughout the process. Using the OODA loop, it is possible to have multiple decision-making cycles in progress and in different stages of completion.

open angle (sheet metal forming). An angle in which sheet metal is bent less than 90°.

open-assembly time (adhesive consideration). The amount of time allowed to elapse between the spreading of an adhesive on the surfaces to be joined and the time the surfaces are clamped together.

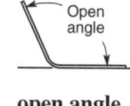

open angle

open-center hydraulic system. A fluid power system in which the selector valves are arranged in series with each other. Fluid flows from the pump through the center of all of the selector valves, back into the reservoir when no unit is being actuated.

open-center selector valve (hydraulic system component). A type of selector valve that functions as an unloading valve as well as a selector valve. All open-center selector valves are installed in series, and when no unit is being actuated, fluid from the pump flows through the centers of all of the valves and returns to the reservoir.

    When a unit is selected for actuation, the center of the selector valve is shut off and the fluid from the pump goes through the selector valve into one side of the actuator. Fluid from the other side of the actuator returns to the valve and goes back to the reservoir through the other selector valves. When the actuation is completed, the selector valve is placed in its neutral position. Its center opens, and fluid from the pump flows straight through the valve, unloading the pump.

open circuit (electrical circuit condition). A condition in which there is no complete path for electrons to flow from one terminal of the source of electrical energy to the other terminal.

open-circuit voltage. The voltage of a battery measured when it is supplying no current to the circuit. Open-circuit voltage is higher than closed-circuit voltage because there is no voltage drop across internal resistance of the battery.

open-end wrench (mechanic's hand tool). A hand tool used by mechanics to turn nuts and bolts. The jaws of the wrench are in the form of a slot with parallel sides that fit the nut or the bolt head. These jaws are usually offset from the axis of the handle by about 15°.

open-hearth furnace. A furnace used for melting metals. Pig iron and scrap metal are placed in a shallow hearth within the furnace and are melted by heat supplied by a direct flame and from radiation from the walls and ceiling of the furnace.

open wiring (aircraft electrical system installation). Electrical wiring installation in which the wires are tied together in bundles and clamped to the aircraft structure rather than being enclosed in conduit.

operate. *14 CFR Part 1:* "Use, cause to use or authorize to use aircraft, for the purpose (except as provided in §91.13 of this chapter) of air navigation including the piloting of aircraft, with or without the right of legal control (as owner, lessee, or otherwise)."

operate time (electrical relay). The time measured from the instant a relay control switch closes until the relay contacts are fully open or fully closed.

operating center of gravity range (weight and balance). The distance between the forward and rearward CG limits indicated in the pertinent aircraft specifications or TCDS.

operating cycle (turbine engine operation). One complete series of events in the operation of a gas turbine engine that consists of starting the engine, taking off, landing, and shutting the engine down.

operating limitations. Specifications published by aircraft manufacturers to define limitations on maneuvers, flight load factors, speeds, and other limits. They are presented in the aircraft in the form of placards and printed in the limitations section of the aircraft flight manual.

operating pressures (fluid mechanics). The pressure range experienced in a hydraulic or pneumatic system during normal operation.

operating weight (weight and balance). The empty weight of the aircraft plus the weight of the required crew, their baggage and other standard items such as meals and potable water.

operational amplifier (electronic circuit). A two-input linear amplifier, often built into a single integrated circuit (IC) chip. The output is an amplification of the difference between the signals on the two inputs. An operational amplifier is commonly called an op-amp.

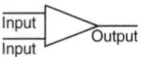

operational amplifier

operational CG (weight and balance). The center of gravity of an aircraft when it is loaded for flight.

operational checks (aircraft operation). The inspection of a system to determine if it is operating within normal limits specified by the manufacturer.

operational control. *14 CFR Part 1:* "With respect to a flight, means the exercise of authority over initiating, conducting or terminating a flight."

operational pitfalls (psychology). Classic behavioral traps into which pilots have been known to fall. Pilots, particularly those with considerable experience, as a rule, always try to complete a flight as planned, please passengers, and meet schedules. The basic drive to meet or exceed goals can have an adverse effect on safety, and can impose an unrealistic assessment of piloting skills under stressful conditions. These tendencies ultimately may bring about practices that are dangerous and often illegal, and may lead to a mishap. A pilot will develop awareness and learn to avoid many of these operational pitfalls through effective ADM training.

operation raincheck. A program designed to familiarize pilots with the ATC system, its functions, responsibilities and benefits.

operations specifications (OpsSpecs). A published document providing the conditions under which an air carrier and operator for compensation or hire must operate in order to retain approval from the FAA.

operator (of an aircraft). Any person who causes or authorizes the operation of an aircraft, such as the owner, lessee, or bailee of an aircraft.

opposed-type engine. A reciprocating engine with two banks of cylinders directly opposite each other with a crankshaft in the center. The pistons of both cylinder banks are connected to the single crankshaft. Although the engine can be either liquid-cooled or air-cooled, the air-cooled version is used predominantly in aviation. It can be mounted with the cylinders in either a vertical or horizontal position.

opposite direction aircraft (air traffic control). Aircraft are operating in opposite directions when (1) they are following the same track in reciprocal directions; or (2) their tracks are parallel and the aircraft are flying in reciprocal directions; or (3) their tracks intersect at an angle of more than 135°.

opposite side (mathematics). The side of a triangle opposite the angle being referenced. In the illustrated triangle, the solid line shows the side opposite the angle Ø.

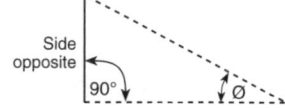

opposite side of a right triangle

optical coupler. An optoelectronic device used to couple electronic circuits by using electromagnetic radiation, either visible or invisible. The input circuit contains some form of light source, usually a light-emitting diode (LED). The intensity of the light is determined by the amount of current flowing in the input circuit.

The output circuit contains a photodiode, phototransistor, or light-dependent resistor. The light source and light sensor are mounted in a light-tight housing, so the light emitted by the source striking the sensor controls the output of the coupled circuit.

optical illusion (physiology). A misleading visual image of features on the ground associated with landing, which causes a pilot to misread the spatial relationships between the aircraft and the runway.

optical micrometer (precision measuring instrument). A precision instrument, used to measure the depth of scratches and other surface damage to a piece of material. The lens of the instrument is focused on the undamaged surface which is used as a reference, and then it is focused at the bottom of the damage. The amount the lens must be moved to change the focus is converted into a measure of the depth of the damage.

optical pyrometer (temperature measuring instrument). An instrument used to measure the temperature of molten metal inside a furnace. A piece of resistance wire extends across the optical path of the instrument, and current through the wire is increased until its heat causes the wire to glow. The user of the instrument looks at the molten metal in the furnace through the instrument, and while watching it, increases the current through the resistance wire until it glows with exactly the same color as the molten metal. The indicator on the instrument converts the amount of current flowing through the resistance wire into terms of the temperature of the molten metal.

optional equipment (installed aircraft equipment). Equipment approved for installation in an aircraft, but not required to be installed. Several types of communications and navigation radio equipment and different types of instruments are included in the optional equipment list.

option approach (air traffic control). An approach requested and conducted by a pilot which will result in either a touch-and-go, missed approach, low approach, stop-and-go, or a full-stop landing.

optoelectronic device. An electronic device that produces, modulates, or senses electromagnetic radiation in the ultraviolet, visible light, or infrared portions of the energy spectrum.

optoelectronics. The branch of electronics that deals with the relationships between electrical current and light. Optoelectronics makes use of light-emitting and light-sensitive devices.

orange peel (finishing system problem). Roughness caused by the surface of a finishing material drying before the material below the surface. The rough surface may be caused by using the wrong viscosity finishing material, the wrong amount of air pressure on the spray gun, or incorrect setting of the spray gun controls. It can also be caused by holding the spray gun an incorrect distance from the surface being sprayed.

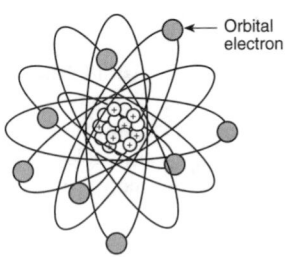

orbital electron. An electron spinning in an orbit around the nucleus of an atom. The term orbital electron is used to distinguish these electrons from free electrons moving from one atom to another.

orbital electron

ordinal number. Ordinal numbers indicate position in a series or order such as first, second, and third. They tell us the order in which something occurs. The first day, the second order, or the third time are examples of the use of ordinal numbers.

ordinate. The vertical line (vertical coordinate, or Y-axis) drawn on a graph. Variable quantities are measured by the scale to which the ordinate is drawn. The horizontal coordinate (X-axis) on a graph is called the abscissa.

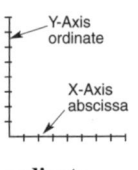

ordinate

organic brake lining. Brake linings that are made of carbon-based compounds, usually reinforced with some type of synthetic fibers. They have replaced linings that contain asbestos because of its health hazard.

organic fabric (aircraft fabric). Natural-fiber fabrics used for covering aircraft structures. Long-staple cotton and linen are the two most widely used organic fabrics.

organized track system (air traffic control). A series of ATS routes which are fixed and charted; i.e., CEP, NOPAC, or flexible and described by NOTAM; i.e., NAT TRACK MESSAGE.

OR gate (logic gate). A logic gate having two or more inputs and one output. An OR gate has a logic one on its output when there is a logic one on any one of its inputs. There are two kinds of OR gates: INCLUSIVE OR, and EXCLUSIVE OR. An INCLUSIVE OR gate has a logic one on its output any time one or more of its inputs are at logic one. An EXCLUSIVE OR gate has a logic one on its output when one and only one of its inputs is at logic one.

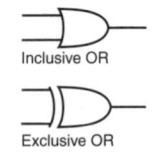

OR gates

orientation. Awareness of the position of the aircraft and of oneself in relation to a specific reference point.

orifice. A hole. When the word orifice is used, the hole is considered to have special characteristics. The orifice in a carburetor jet, for example, has a specific diameter, length, and approach and departure angles.

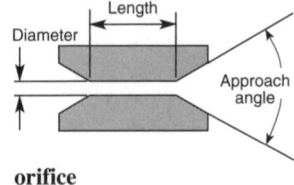

orifice

orifice check valve (fluid power system component). A special check valve used in a hydraulic or pneumatic system, to allow full flow of fluid in one direction but a restricted flow in the opposite direction.

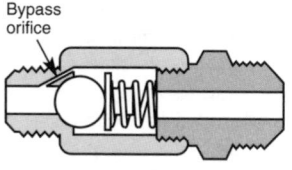

Bypass orifice

orifice check valve

O-ring. A type of seal used in fluid-power system components. An O-ring is a ring-shaped seal with a round cross section, made of a resilient material. An O-ring fits into a groove to form a seal between two parts.

O-rings are two-way seals; they seal in either direction. They can be used as either packings between moving parts or gaskets between parts having no relative motion.

ornithopter. A type of flying machine that has been proposed since the days of Leonardo daVinci (around 1500 AD), but has never been built in a practical form. An ornithopter is supposed to support itself in the air by moving the air with flapping wings.

OROCA. *See* off-route obstruction clearance altitude.

orographic. A term pertaining to mountains or anything caused by mountains. Examples are orographic clouds, orographic lift, and orographic precipitation.

orographic lifting (meteorology). Occurs when an air mass is forced from a low elevation to a higher elevation as it moves over rising terrain.

oronasal oxygen mask. A type of oxygen mask that covers only the mouth and nose of the wearer. An oronasal mask is distinguished from the full face mask, which covers the entire face as well as the eyes of the person wearing it.

orphaned airplane. An airplane that is no longer in production and is no longer supported by its manufacturer. Parts and information for its maintenance are usually difficult to obtain.

orthographic projection (graphics). A method of showing all the sides of an object by projecting straight lines from the object to the drawing surface. An orthographic projection of a solid object requires six separate views: top, bottom, right and left sides, front, and back.

oscillate. To swing back and forth. A pendulum is useful as a timing device because it oscillates with a definite period, or length of time required for each cycle of oscillation.

oscillator (electronic circuit). An electronic circuit that converts direct current into alternating current. The component values in an oscillator can be chosen to produce AC with any desired frequency and with any desired waveform.

oscillograph. An electronic instrument that produces a permanent record of the values of electrical current as it changes with time. Transducers produce electrical signals that relate to the mechanical movement being measured. These signals are recorded on a time base in such a way that they produce a graphic record of the way the mechanical movement changes with reference to time.

oscilloscope. An electrical measuring instrument that displays, on the face of a cathode-ray tube, the way an electrical value changes with time. A high-velocity beam of electrons strikes a phosphorescent coating on the inside of the cathode-ray tube face and produces a visible glow. The beam is swept from side to side by a time-controlled oscillator and deflected up and down by the electrical value being measured.

osmium. A bluish-white, hard, metallic chemical element. Osmium's symbol is Os, its atomic number is 76, and its atomic weight is 190.2. Osmium is used as a hardener for platinum to increase its wearing ability.

otolith organ. An inner ear organ that detects linear acceleration and gravity orientation.

O

Otto thermodynamic cycle. The constant-volume cycle of energy transformation used in a reciprocating engine. Fuel and air are drawn into the cylinder as the piston moves to the bottom of its stroke. The fuel-air mixture is then compressed as the piston moves upward in the cylinder, and when the piston is near the top of its stroke, the mixture is ignited and burns. The burning mixture heats and expands the air inside the cylinder and forces the piston down, performing useful work. The piston then moves back up, forcing the burned gases out of the cylinder. The pressure inside the cylinder varies throughout the cycle, but all events take place in the same location.

"Out" (air traffic control). A term used in air traffic control to indicate that the conversation is ended and no response is expected.

outer area (air traffic control). Nonregulatory airspace surrounding designated Class C airspace airports in which ATC provides radar vectoring and sequencing on a full-time basis for all IFR and participating VFR aircraft. The normal radius is 20 nautical miles, with some variations based on site-specific requirements. The outer area extends outward from the primary Class C airspace airport and extends from the lower limits of radar/radio coverage up to the ceiling of the approach control's delegated airspace, excluding the Class C charted area and other airspace as appropriate.

outer compass locator (LOM). A compass locator installed at the site of the outer marker of an instrument landing system. *See* outer marker.

outer fix (air traffic control). A general term used within ATC to describe fixes in the terminal area, other than the final approach fix. Aircraft are normally cleared to these fixes by ARTCC or an approach control facility, and aircraft are normally cleared from these fixes to the final approach fix or final approach course.

outer fix arc (air traffic control). A semicircle area, usually about a 50–70 mile radius from a meter fix located at high altitude, which is used by controllers to calculate outer fix times and determine appropriate sector meter list assignments for aircraft on established arrival routes that will traverse the arc.

outer fix time (air traffic control). A calculated time to depart the outer fix in order to cross the vertex at the actual calculated landing time (ACLT). The time reflects descent speed adjustments and any applicable delay time that must be absorbed prior to crossing the meter fix.

outer marker (OM). A marker beacon at or near the glideslope intercept altitude of an ILS approach. It is keyed to transmit two dashes per second on a 400-Hz tone, which is received aurally and visually by compatible airborne equipment. The OM is normally located four to seven miles from the runway threshold on the extended centerline of the runway.

outflow boundary (meteorology). A mesoscale cold front. Outflow boundaries primarily originate from thunderstorms. *See* mesoscale.

outflow valve (aircraft pressurization system component). The valve in an aircraft pressurization system that controls the pressure inside the aircraft cabin. More air than needed is pumped into the cabin, and the outflow valve controls the air allowed to escape to maintain the pressure in the cabin at the correct level. Operation of the outflow valve is controlled by the cabin pressure regulator.

outlook briefing (flight planning). This type of briefing is provided for planning purposes only for a flight with a departure time of 6 or more hours away. It provides initial forecast information that is limited in scope due to the timeframe of the planned flight.

out-of-ground-effect (OGE) hover (rotorcraft). Hovering at a height greater than one rotor diameter above the surface. Because induced drag is greater while hovering out of ground effect, it takes more power to hover OGE.

out-of-phase. A condition of cyclic values in which two waves do not pass through zero at the same time.

out-of-rig (aircraft flight condition). A condition of aircraft rigging that prevents hands-off flight. When an aircraft is properly rigged and flown in still air at the correct power setting, it will maintain its altitude and heading without the pilot touching the controls. But, if it is out-of-rig, it will not hold its altitude nor its heading.

out-of-round (condition of physical wear). The condition of a circular object when its wear is not uniform around its circumference. Wear changes its shape from circular to oblong.

out-of-track (helicopter rotor condition). A condition of a helicopter rotor in which the blade tips do not follow the same path in their rotation.

out-of-trim (flight condition). A flight condition in which an aircraft does not fly straight and level, hands off. It is caused by improper adjustment of the trim controls.

output power (electronic circuit). The power an electronic circuit delivers to its load.

output transformer (electronic component). An audio-frequency transformer, used between the last stage of an audio-frequency amplifier and a speaker. The impedance of the amplifier's output stage is usually quite high, and the impedance of a speaker is low. For the maximum amount of power to be transferred from the amplifier to the speaker, the impedance of the amplifier must match that of the speaker, and this matching is done with an output transformer.

outside air temperature (OAT). The temperature of the ambient air through which an aircraft is flying.

outside calipers. A measuring device having two inwardly curved, hinged legs. The calipers are closed until the points of the legs just touch the outside of the device to be measured, and the distance between the two points is measured with a steel scale.

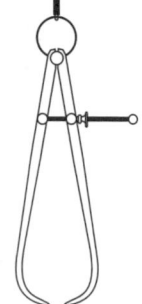

outside
calipers

out time (composites). The total amount of time a prepreg material is out of the freezer and exposed to room temperature.

"Over" (air traffic control). A term used in air traffic control to indicate "My transmission is ended; I expect a response."

overbalance (control surface balance condition). The static balance condition of a control surface in which the area behind the fulcrum is lighter than the area ahead of the fulcrum. The trailing edge rises above the fulcrum.

overboost (reciprocating engine operation). A condition of excessive manifold pressure in a reciprocating engine. Overboosting occurs when the supercharger is operated at too high a speed.

overcompounded generator (electrical generator). An electrical generator which has both a series and a shunt field with the effect of the series field being greater than that of the shunt field. The output voltage tends to increase as the electrical load increases.

overcompounded motor (electric motor). A compound-wound motor (a motor having both a series and a shunt field) in which the series field has the greater effect on the motor characteristics. The shunt, or parallel, field attempts to hold the speed of the motor constant as the load changes, but the series field causes the motor to speed up as the load increases.

In a flat compounded motor, the effects of the two fields cancel, and the motor speed remains relatively constant as the load changes. In an overcompounded motor, the series winding has the greater effect, and the motor tries to speed up as the load increases.

overcontrol (flight condition). The application of a greater amount of control movement than is needed for the desired result.

overcurrent protection device. A device in an alternator or generator control system that reduces the output voltage when excessive current flows.

overhang (meteorology). A radar term indicating a region of high reflectivity at the middle and upper levels above an area of weak reflectivity at low levels. The overhang is found on the inflow side of a thunderstorm (normally the south or southeast side).

overhaul (maintenance procedure). The maintenance procedure in which a device is disassembled to the extent needed to determine the condition of all its parts. Each part is inspected, and, if damaged or excessively worn, it is repaired or replaced. The device is then reassembled and tested, and if it functions as it should, is returned to service.

overhead-cam engine (type of reciprocating engine). A reciprocating engine in which the camshaft is located in the cylinder head. The valves are opened by rocker arms that are actuated by the cam lobes. The valves of engines that have the camshaft in the crankcase are actuated by pushrods and rocker arms.

overhead maneuver (traffic entry maneuver). A series of predetermined maneuvers prescribed for aircraft, often in formation for entry into the VFR traffic pattern and to proceed to a landing. An overhead maneuver is not an IFR approach procedure. An aircraft executing an overhead maneuver is considered VFR and the IFR flight plan is cancelled when the aircraft reaches the initial point approach portion of the maneuver.

overhead question. In the guided discussion method, a question directed to the entire group in order to stimulate thought and discussion from the entire group. An overhead question may be used by an instructor as the lead-off question.

overhead-valve engine (type of reciprocating engine). A reciprocating engine in which the intake and exhaust valves are located in the cylinder head. This type of engine is also called a valve-in-head engine.

overheat warning system (fire warning system). A type of warning system that warns the flight crew that an engine nacelle or wheel well is too hot for normal operation, but there is no localized high temperature that indicates the presence of a fire.

overinflation valve (aircraft wheel component). A valve used in some large aircraft wheels that mount tubeless tires. The valve opens and relieves the excess pressure if the tire is accidentally overinflated.

overload. A load in excess of that designed for a system or structure.

overlying center (air traffic control). The ARTCC facility that is responsible for arrival/departure operations at a specific terminal.

overpower. To use more power than required for the purpose of achieving a faster rate of airspeed change.

overrunning clutch. A type of clutch that couples a drive element with a driven element. When the drive element is being rotated, the driven element rotates with it. But when the driven element is being rotated by an outside force, the drive element does not turn. Overrunning clutches are used in some types of aircraft engine starters. The starter rotates the engine through the clutch, but when the engine starts and turns faster than the starter motor, the clutch prevents the engine driving the starter.

overrunning, weather pattern. A relatively warm air mass is in motion above another air mass of greater density at the surface. Embedded thunderstorms sometimes develop in such a pattern.

overseas air commerce. *14 CFR Part 1:* "The carriage by aircraft of persons or property for compensation or hire, or the carriage of mail by aircraft, or the operation or navigation of aircraft in the conduct or furtherance of a business or vocation, in commerce between a place in any State of the United States, or the District of Columbia, and any place in a territory or possession of the United states; or between a place in a territory or possession of the United States, and a place in any other territory or possession of the United States."

overseas air transportation. *14 CFR Part 1:* "The carriage by aircraft of persons or property as a common carrier for compensation or hire, or the carriage of mail by aircraft, in commerce:

(1) Between a place in a State or the District of Columbia and a place in a possession of the United States; or

(2) Between a place in a possession of the United States and a place in another possession of the United States; whether that commerce moves wholly by aircraft or partly by aircraft and partly by other forms of transportation."

overshoot (flight operation). A landing approach in which an aircraft is still airborne as it passes the touchdown point chosen by the pilot.

overshooting tops (meteorology). A dome-like protrusion above the anvil of a thunderstorm, representing a very strong updraft; hence a higher potential for severe weather exists with that storm. A persistent, large overshooting top (or anvil dome) often is present with a supercell.

oversize stud (aircraft hardware). A special stud used to replace a standard stud that has worn its hole oversize. The thread pitch and type are the same as those of the standard stud, but the diameter of the oversize stud is greater.

overspeed condition (propeller governor condition). The condition in which an engine is turning at a speed greater than that selected by the governor. The upward force produced by the governor flyweights is greater than the downward force of the speeder spring, and the governor causes the pitch of the propeller to increase to reduce the engine speed.

overtemperature (engine operation). A condition in which an engine has reached a temperature above that approved by the manufacturer, or any exhaust temperature that exceeds the maximum allowable for a given operating condition or time limit. Overtemperature can cause internal damage to an engine.

overtemperature warning system. A warning system similar in many ways to a fire warning system, but differing in that it initiates the warning signal at a lower temperature than needed for a fire warning. A high temperature in a small area initiates a fire warning, but a lower temperature over a larger area indicates an overtemperature condition.

over-the-top. *14 CFR Part 1:* "Above the layer of clouds or other obscuring phenomena forming the ceiling."

overtone. A whole-number multiple of the frequency of a vibration. An overtone is the same as a harmonic. *See* harmonic.

overtorque (engine operation). A condition in which a turboprop or turboshaft engine has produced more torque than the manufacturer recommends, or where the engine torque has exceeded the maximum allowable for a given operating condition or time limit. Overtorque can cause internal damage to an engine.

overvoltage protector (electrical circuit component). A component used to protect electrical circuits from surges of high voltage that could cause damage. A sensor monitors the voltage and, if it becomes excessive, the overvoltage protector opens the circuit to protect the components.

oxidation. The chemical action in which a metallic element is united with oxygen. Electrons are removed from the metal in this process.

oxide (chemical compound). A chemical compound, such as aluminum oxide (Al_2O_3), that is composed of oxygen and another element, in this case, aluminum.

oxidizing flame (oxygas welding). An oxygas welding flame in which more oxygen is supplied to the torch than is needed for a neutral flame. An oxidizing flame is identified by a sharp-pointed inner cone and a hissing noise made by the torch.

oxyacetylene. A controlled mixture of oxygen and acetylene gas that is used produces a flame temperature in the range of 5,700°F to 6,300°F. Oxyacetylene gas is used for welding and cutting metal, principally steel.

oxygas welding. A form of welding in which a fuel gas, such as acetylene or hydrogen, is mixed with oxygen in the mixing chamber of a torch. When these gases are burned, they produce the large amount of heat needed to melt the metal so it can be welded.

oxygen. A colorless, odorless, tasteless, gaseous chemical element that makes up about 21% of the earth's atmosphere. Oxygen's symbol is O, its atomic number is 8, and its atomic weight is 15.9994. Oxygen will not burn, but it supports combustion and combines chemically with all other elements except the inert gases. Oxygen is absolutely necessary to support human and animal life.

oxygen concentration cell corrosion. Corrosion that occurs when some of the electrolyte on a metal surface is partially confined (such as between faying surfaces or in a deep crevice). Metal in this confined area corrodes more rapidly than other metal surfaces of the same part outside this area. *See* concentration cell corrosion.

oxygen starvation (hot air ballooning). The condition inside a balloon envelope where all available oxygen has been consumed by the heater flame and additional burning is impossible since propane must have oxygen to burn. In extreme cases, the blast flame and pilot light flame will extinguish after a long burn or series of burns and may not relight until the envelope has "breathed" additional air.

ozone. An unstable form of oxygen. A molecule of ozone contains three atoms of oxygen (O_3), rather than two, as in a molecule of oxygen gas (O_2). Ozone is blue in color, and it smells much like chlorine. Ozone, which is produced by passing an electric spark through oxygen, is a powerful oxidizing agent and is used as a bleach and in the treatment of industrial wastes. Ozone is harmful to rubber products.

ozone layer (atmospheric science). An atmospheric layer that contains a high proportion of oxygen that exists as ozone (O_3). It acts as a filtering mechanism against incoming ultraviolet radiation. It is located between the troposphere and the stratosphere, around 9.5 to 12.5 miles (15 to 20 kilometers) above the earth's surface.

ozonosphere. The layer of the earth's atmosphere that extends from about 20 to 30 miles above the earth. The ozonosphere has a high concentration of ozone that absorbs ultraviolet radiation from the sun.

pack carburizing (metal heat treatment). A method of case hardening the surface of a steel part without hardening the inside and making it brittle. The part to be case hardened is packed in a fire-clay container and entirely surrounded with a special ground-up charcoal. The container is sealed and put into a furnace and heated to a temperature greater than 910°C. At this temperature, the iron takes on a crystalline form called gamma iron. The heated charcoal releases carbon monoxide, and since it cannot escape, it combines with the gamma iron and forms an extremely hard surface. The depth to which the carbon penetrates the steel is determined by the length of time it is held at this high temperature.

packing. A seal used between surfaces in which there is relative movement. When there is no movement between the surfaces, a gasket is used to provide the seal.

page. Any one of a collection of information displays that appear on the FMS/RNAV unit. Every page has a title and presents information related to a particular navigation topic (e.g., airport elevation, runways, communication frequencies). Pages are usually arranged in divisions called "chapters," which group pages of similar information by topic (e.g., airports, approaches, VORs).

paint. A covering applied to an object or structure to protect it and improve its appearance. Paint consists of a pigment suspended in a vehicle such as oil or water. When the vehicle, which can be thinned for best application, dries by evaporation or curing, the pigment is left as a film on the surface.

paint dryer. A component, usually an oil, added to a paint to improve its drying characteristics.

paint stripper. A material used to remove paint from a surface. Paint stripper contains very strong solvents in a wax-like vehicle which prevents the solvents from evaporating before they can soak into the paint film.

Most paint strippers soften a lacquer film, so it can be wiped off. But rather than softening a film of enamel, the stripper penetrates it and causes it to swell. When the film swells, it wrinkles and breaks away from the surface on which it is applied. The wrinkled enamel is then scrubbed from the surface or washed off with steam or hot water.

palladium. A soft, ductile, steel-white, tarnish-resistant metallic chemical element. Palladium's symbol is Pd, its atomic number is 46, and its atomic weight is 106.4. Palladium is used in the manufacture of electrical contacts, jewelry, and surgical instruments.

Pal nut. The registered trade name for a thin, pressed-steel nut which has a shallow cup-shaped bottom surface. A Pal nut is screwed down over the top of a plain nut to lock the nut onto a stud. When the Pal nut is tightened, the bent-up threads are forced down, so they hold pressure on the plain nut and prevent its vibrating loose.

pan-pan (urgency signal). The international radio-telephony urgency signal. When repeated three times, pan-pan indicates uncertainty or alert, followed by the nature of the urgency.

pancake landing (aircraft operation). A landing in which the aircraft is flared out (leveled off) several feet above the surface of the ground. As the aircraft loses its forward speed and aerodynamic lift, it drops to the ground in a flat attitude.

panhead screw (aircraft hardware). A machine screw or sheet metal screw that has a large-diameter head that is slightly crowned, or rounded, on top.

pants (airplane wheel covers). A commonly used name for the streamlined wheel covers installed on some fixed landing gear airplanes.

paper capacitor (electrical component). A type of capacitor made of two strips of metal foil for its plates and strips of waxed paper for its dielectric. Leads are attached to the metal foil, and the foil and waxed paper are formed into a tight, compact roll. The entire roll is then encapsulated in a plastic resin. A mark or line around one end of a paper capacitor identifies the lead attached to the outside layer of foil.

panhead sheet metal screw

PAPI. *See* precision approach path indicator.

PAR (precision approach radar). A type of radar used at an airport to guide an aircraft through the final stages of landing. The radarscope has two plots: one showing the position of the aircraft along an extended center line of the runway, and the other showing the position of the aircraft as it descends along the glide slope to the runway. The radar operator directs the pilot to change heading or adjust the descent rate to keep the aircraft on a path that allows it to touch down at the correct spot on the runway.

parabola. A curve formed by points that are an equal distance from a straight line and from a fixed point.

parabolic microphone. An extremely sensitive microphone mounted at the focus of a parabolic sound reflector. The reflector is aimed at the source of sound to be picked up, and the parabolic surface reflects the sound waves, concentrating them at the microphone.

parabolic reflector (light reflector). A light reflector whose surface is made in the form of a parabola. The filament producing the light is located at the focus of the parabola, and the light is reflected from the parabolic surface as a beam of parallel rays.

parachute. A large umbrella-shaped device, made of lightweight cloth, used to slow an object falling through the air. Parachutes are folded into a pack and worn by a person who jumps from an aircraft. When the pack is opened, the parachute canopy is pulled out by the air and opens. The parachute creates so much drag that the wearer descends at a rate slow enough to prevent injury when contact is made with the ground. Cargo parachutes are used to lower equipment at locations where it is impractical for airplanes or helicopters to land.

   14 CFR Part 1: "A device used or intended to be used to retard the fall of a body or object through the air."

parachute top (hot air balloon). A deflation system wherein the deflation port is sealed with a disc of balloon fabric shaped like a parachute. Lines attached to the edge of the parachute disc gather into a single line that may be pulled down by the pilot in the basket.

parafoil. *See* ram-air wing.

par-al-ketone. A heavy waxlike grease, used to protect cables, bolts, and other types of fittings from rust and corrosion when they are exposed to water. Par-al-ketone is also used to protect metal objects that are to be stored for long periods of time.

parallax. An optical (viewing) error caused by an object appearing to be in different locations when it is viewed from different angles. Parallax causes a pointer-type instrument to give an inaccurate indication unless it is viewed from directly above the pointer. Moving your head as you read the dial can give different indications. Precision instruments have a mirror built into the dial to prevent parallax error. When reading such an instrument, move your eye until the pointer is directly over its reflection. When viewed from this position there is no parallax.

parallax error (optical phenomenon). A characteristic of airplanes that have side-by-side seats, where the pilot is seated to one side of the longitudinal axis about which the airplane rolls. This makes the nose appear to rise when making a left turn and to descend when making right turns, a common error among students and experienced pilots.

parallel access (digital computers). A method of accessing data from a computer in which all bits of the data are transferred at the same time. Parallel access is different from serial access, in which the data is transferred one bit at a time.

parallel bus system (electrical power system). An electrical power system in which all of the operating generators are connected to a single power bus.

parallel electrical circuit. A circuit in which the components are connected in such a way that there is more than one complete path for electrons to pass from the negative terminal of the power source back to its positive terminal.

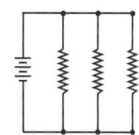

parallel circuit

parallel ILS approaches (air traffic control). Approaches to parallel runways by IFR aircraft which, when established inbound toward the airport on the adjacent final approach courses, are radar-separated by at least two miles.

paralleling circuit. A circuit in a multiengine aircraft electrical system that causes the generators or alternators to share the electrical load equally.

paralleling generators (aircraft electrical system operation). The procedure in which the output voltages of the generators in a multiengine aircraft electrical system are adjusted so that they share the electrical load equally. If one generator carries more than its share of the load, its output voltage is decreased and the output of the other generators is increased until all share the load equally.

paralleling relay. A relay in a multiengine aircraft electrical system that controls a flow of control current which is used to keep the generators or alternators sharing the electrical load equally. The relay opens automatically to shut off the flow of paralleling current any time the output of either alternator or generator drops to zero.

parallel lines. Lines that run in the same direction and are at all points separated by the same distance. Parallel lines never cross.

parallel offset route (air traffic control). A parallel track to the left or right of the designated or established airway/route. Normally associated with area navigation (RNAV) operations.

P

parallel operation (computer operation). Data transfer by moving digital words (groups of bits) all at one time. Parallel operation is much faster than serial operation, in which the bits are moved one at a time, but it requires much more complex circuitry.

parallel resonant circuit (electronic circuit). A circuit consisting of an inductor and capacitor connected in parallel. The impedance, or the total opposition to the flow of current, of a parallel resonant circuit is maximum at the frequency to which the circuit is resonant. A parallel resonant circuit is called a tank circuit.

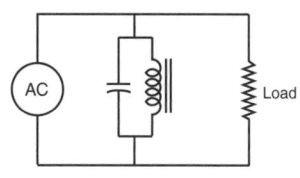

parallel resonant circuit

parallel runways. Two or more runways at the same airport whose center lines are parallel. In addition to runway number, parallel runways are designated as L (left) and R (right) or, if three parallel runways exist, L (left), C (center), and R (right).

parallels of latitude. Imaginary lines on the surface of the earth parallel to the equator. Parallels of latitude are used as north and south reference lines for map making and navigation. The equator is the 0° parallel of latitude, the geographic north pole is located at 90° north latitude, and the geographic south pole is located at 90° south latitude.

parallel-wound motor. A DC electric motor whose field coils are connected in parallel with the armature. A parallel-wound motor has a low starting torque, but it operates at a relatively constant speed.

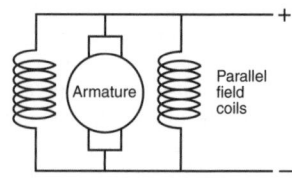

parallel-wound motor

paramagnetic material. A material whose permeability is greater than that of a vacuum (permeability of one) but less than that of a ferromagnetic material. The permeability of a paramagnetic material does not change as the magnetizing force applied to it changes. Some alloys of nickel and titanium are paramagnetic.

parameter. A quantity whose value determines characteristics or behavior. Temperature, pressure, and humidity are parameters of the atmosphere.

parasite drag (aerodynamic drag). A form of aerodynamic drag caused by friction between the air and the surface over which it is flowing. Parasite drag increases as the velocity of the air increases.

parasol wing airplane. An airplane with a single main wing mounted on struts above the fuselage. The struts between the wing and the fuselage are called cabane struts.

parcel (meteorology). A volume of air small enough to contain uniform distribution of its meteorological properties, and large enough to remain relatively self-contained and respond to all meteorological processes. No specific dimensions have been defined for a parcel; however, the order of magnitude of one cubic foot has been suggested.

Parco lubrizing. A chemical treatment for steel that reduces wear on moving parts. The steel surface is converted into a nonmetallic, oil absorptive phosphate coating. The part is vapor degreased and immersed in a solution of water and Parco Lubrite®. After a specified dwell time, it is rinsed with water and finally soaked in water-soluble oil. The phosphate coating absorbs and retains the oil.

parent metal (welding). The metal being welded. This term is used to distinguish it from the metal of the welding rod.

Parkerizing (corrosion protection). The registered trade name for a process in which a steel part is covered with a hard oxide film that prevents oxygen reaching the metal. The oxide film is formed by soaking the steel in a solution of phosphoric acid and manganese or zinc dioxide.

Parker-Kalon screw. The registered trade name for a self-tapping sheet metal screw, often called a PK screw. Parker-Kalon screws, made of hardened steel and having sharp, coarse threads, are used to hold thin sheets of metal together. As the screw is turned through matching holes in the thin metal, the threads clamp the sheets tightly together. *See* illustration for panhead screw.

parking brake. A brake system used to keep an aircraft from rolling when it is parked. The parking brake holds pressure on the brake system when there is no operator at the controls.

Part 61 (14 CFR). A section of aviation regulations describing pilot training at flight schools, including subject matter and flight-time minimums. Most flight schools train their students according to Part 61.

Part 141 (14 CFR). A section of aviation regulations describing training at flight academies, such as universities. Because of the intensive, structured nature of these training programs, students are permitted lower minimum flight-time requirements than at Part

61 schools. The material covered is identical, since all student pilots must meet the performance criteria published in the FAA Practical Test Standards.

partial obscuration (meteorology). A designation of sky cover when part of the sky is hidden by surface-based obscuring phenomena.

partial-panel instrument flight. Instrument flight by reference to only a limited number of flight instruments. Partial-panel flight uses the airspeed indicator, turn and slip indicator, or turn coordinator, and clock to keep the aircraft straight and level and to maneuver it. Partial-panel flight assumes the attitude gyro and horizontal situation indicator (or gyro horizon and directional gyro) to be inoperative.

partial pressure (gas pressure). The percentage of the total pressure of a mixture of gases produced by each of the individual gases in the mixture. The atmosphere surrounding the earth is a mixture of gases of which nitrogen makes up about 78% and oxygen 21%. If the pressure of the atmosphere is 29.92 inches (760 mm) of mercury, the partial pressure of the nitrogen is 78% of this, or 23.33 inches (592.8 mm) of mercury, and the partial pressure of the oxygen is 21% of the total or 6.28 inches (159.6 mm) of mercury.

particulates. Tiny solid particles which remain suspended in a gas.

parting compound (composition materials fabrication). A material spread on a mold before plastic resin is put into it. The parting compound keeps the resin from sticking to the mold. Parting compound is sometimes called a parting agent.

parting film. A layer of thin plastic material that is placed between a composite lay-up and the heating blanket. It prevents the blanket sticking to the fabric.

part number (aircraft parts identification). The number assigned by the aircraft manufacturer to identify a particular aircraft part. The part number is normally the same as the drawing number for the part.

parts list (aircraft drawing). A list of all items and their part numbers that are included on an assembly drawing. A parts list is also called a Bill of Materials.

Parts Manufacturer Approval. *See* PMA.

pascal. The unit of pressure in the metric system that is produced when one newton of force acts uniformly over an area of one square meter. One pascal is equal to $14.503 \cdot 10^{-5}$ (0.000 145 03) psi. The kilopascal (kPa) is easier to manipulate. 1 kPa = 1,000 Pa = 0.14503 psi. The pascal is named after the French mathematician Blaise Pascal, who was born in 1623.

Pascal's law (physics law). A basic law of physics which states that pressure built up in an enclosed container of fluid is transmitted equally and undiminished to all parts of the container, and this pressure acts at right angles to the walls of the container.

passenger-carrying operation. Any aircraft operation carrying any person, unless the only persons on the aircraft are those identified in 14 CFR §121.583(a) or §135.85, as applicable. An aircraft used in a passenger-carrying operation may also carry cargo or mail in addition to passengers.

passenger mile. A measure of the amount of travel provided by an airline, steamship line, or railroad. One passenger mile is the carriage of one passenger for one mile.

passivation (corrosion protection). A method of protecting aluminum or magnesium alloys from corrosion. Passivation consists of forming a hard, tight oxide film on the surface of the metal by chemical action.

passive component (electrical component). A component that produces no gain in an electrical circuit. Resistors, capacitors, and inductors are passive components. Active components are such devices as transistors and electron tubes that do produce current or voltage gain.

passive electrical circuit. An electrical circuit that does not contain any source of electrical energy. A passive circuit depends upon an active circuit for its power.

P

passive satellite. A satellite that reflects but does not amplify or change communications signals from the ground or other satellites.

passive sonar. An acoustic underwater detection system that listens for the sound produced by underwater objects. Passive sonar does not transmit signals to search for submerged objects.

patent certificate. A legal document giving a person the exclusive right to own a particular device. When a person invents something, the rights of ownership are protected by patenting the device. A search is made by the patent office to be sure no one has patented the same device at an earlier time. If no earlier patent is recorded, the person applying for the patent is issued a patent certificate.

pattern (flight operation). A published description of the flight paths aircraft must follow when approaching an airport for landing and when leaving the airport after taking off. All aircraft following the same flight pattern minimizes the danger of inflight collision.

pattern (metal molding). A model used to form the mold into which molten metal is poured to cast a metal part. Patterns are usually made of wood, and are made with allowance for the dimensional changes that take place when the metal cools and turns into a solid from its molten state.

pattern altitude. The common altitude used for aircraft maneuvering in the traffic pattern. Usually 1,000 ft. above the airport surface.

PATWAS (Pilots Automatic Telephone Weather Answering Service). A continuous telephone recording containing current and forecast weather information for pilots.

PAVE. The four fundamental risk elements: the Pilot, the Aircraft, the enVironment, and External pressures.

pawl (ratchet device). A driving or holding link used in a ratchet mechanism. The pawl allows a ratchet wheel to turn in one direction, but keeps it from turning in the opposite direction.

payload. The amount of load carried by a vehicle over and above the load necessary for the operation of the vehicle. Payload is actually the amount of revenue-producing load an aircraft can carry.

P-band radar. Radar that operates in the frequency range between 225 and 390 megahertz. At this frequency, the wavelengths of the pulses of energy are between 133.3 and 76.9 centimeters.

PCB (plenum chamber burning). A method of thrust augmentation used on engines with vectored nozzles. Fuel injected into the fan discharge air is burned to increase thrust.

P-channel field effect transistor. A field effect transistor having a source, drain, and channel of P-material formed on a substrate of N-material. *See* field effect transistor.

P-channel field effect transistor

peak current (alternating current value). The greatest amount of current flowing in one alternation of alternating current. Peak current can be measured with an oscilloscope by measuring the distance between the zero-current level and the point of the greatest deviation (the greatest distance from the zero-current line).

peak inverse voltage (PIV). The highest peak value of reverse voltage a rectifying diode can withstand before it breaks down and conducts. A semiconductor diode does not normally conduct when it is reverse-biased (the anode negative and the cathode positive). But if too high a reverse voltage is placed across the diode, it will break down and conduct.

peak-to-peak voltage (alternating current value). Voltage measured with a cathode-ray oscilloscope between the peak negative value and the peak positive value.

peak voltage (alternating current value). The greatest momentary voltage in an alternating current circuit. In sine wave AC, the peak voltage is 1.414 times the effective, or rms, value of the voltage. *See* effective value of AC.

peak voltage. The AC voltage measured from zero voltage to the peak of either alternation.

pedestal grinder (machine tool). A type of electric motor-driven grinding wheel mounted on a pedestal, rather than on a bench.

peel ply (composite materials fabrication). A layer of porous fabric used in the lay-up of a composite material that vents the excess resin and prevents the bagging material from sticking to the part. The peel ply is removed after the resin has cured.

peel strength (composites). The adhesive bond strength, expressed in pounds per inch of width, and obtained by a stress applied in a peeling mode.

peen. To flatten or round-over the end of a rivet or shaft by a series of light hammer blows around its edge.

pencil compass (drawing instrument). A drawing instrument made in the shape of a pair of dividers. One leg has a sharp point that forms the center of a circle or arc, and the other leg holds a pencil or a piece of pencil lead that marks the circumference of the circle or the arc.

pendular action (rotorcraft). The lateral or longitudinal oscillation of the fuselage due to it being suspended from the rotor system.

pendulum. A weight suspended on a rod or cable from a fixed point, free to swing back and forth. The period of a pendulum, the time required for one complete swing, is determined by its length. A pendulum is used as the regulating device in a clock because the period of a fixed-length pendulum is always the same. The clock spring or weights add a tiny bit of energy to the pendulum each time it swings, and by adding as much energy as the pendulum loses because of friction, the pendulum can be kept swinging.

pendulum valves (pneumatic gyro horizon component). Gravity-operated air valves mounted on the bottom of the gyro housing in a gyro horizon instrument. Air used to spin the gyro leaves the housing through these valves. If the gyro should tilt, the size of the holes covered by the valves changes, and the exhausting air produces a force that causes the gyro to erect.

penetrant dwell time. The length of time a part is left in the penetrant when preparing it for inspection by the fluorescent or dye penetrant method. The hotter the part and the longer the penetrant dwell time, the smaller the fault that will be detected.

penguin trainer (early training aircraft). A type of training aircraft used by the French in the early stages of World War I. The engines in these aircraft were not powerful enough to produce flight, but the student was able to develop enough feel of the controls to allow an effective transition to a flyable aircraft.

pentagrid converter (electron tube). A mixer tube used in a superheterodyne radio receiver. A pentagrid converter tube has five grids, a cathode, a plate, and a filament. The incoming radio-frequency signal is applied to the signal grid, and a signal from a local oscillator is applied to the oscillator grid. The two signals mix and form two additional signals. The frequency of one is the sum of the two, and the frequency of the other is the difference between the two. The other three grids in the pentagrid tube are: two screen grids and one suppressor grid.

pentavalent element. A chemical element with five electrons in its valence shell. Nitrogen, arsenic, antimony, and bismuth are pentavalent elements.

pentode (electron tube). A vacuum tube with five active electrodes. A pentode tube has a cathode, a control grid, a screen grid, a suppressor grid, and a plate, or anode.

percentage. Used to express a number as a fraction of 100. Using the percentage sign (%), 90 percent is expressed as 90%.

perceptions. The basis of all learning, perceptions result when a person gives meaning to external stimuli or sensations. Meaning derived from perception is influenced by an individual's experience and many other factors.

percussive welding. A method of electric arc welding, used to attach studs to metal plates. A large amount of electrical energy is stored in capacitors and released through the stud. This produces a high current density between the stud and the plate. The high current density ionizes the air and allows an arc to form between the stud and the plate. The arc melts the end of the stud and the area of the surface of the plate where the stud is to be attached. The stud is pressed into the molten metal to complete the weld.

perfect dielectric. A dielectric (insulator) that, when an electric field is removed, returns to the circuit all the energy used to establish the field. A perfect dielectric has absolutely no conductivity—its resistance is infinite. The only known perfect dielectric is a vacuum.

perforate. To punch a series of holes in a material. Paper is often perforated with a series of tiny holes in a straight line, so it will tear evenly along the perforations.

performance-based navigation (PBN) (ICAO). Area navigation based on performance requirements for aircraft operating along an air traffic service (ATS) route, on an instrument approach procedure or in a designated airspace. Performance requirements are expressed in navigation specifications (RNAV specification, RNP specification) in terms of accuracy, integrity, continuity, availability, and functionality needed for the proposed operation in the context of a particular airspace concept.

performance-based objective. A statement of purpose for a lesson or instructional period that includes three elements: a description of the skill or behavior desired of the student, a set of conditions under which the measurement will be taken, and a set of criteria describing the standard used to measure accomplishment of the objective.

performance chart. A chart published by an aircraft manufacturer that predicts an aircraft's performance under specific conditions.

performance envelope. A term that refers to the capabilities of an aircraft design in terms of speed, altitude and maneuverability. When an aircraft is pushed, for example, by diving it at a speed higher than the manufacturer allows, it is said to be flown "outside the envelope" which is considered dangerous.

performance maneuvers (flight training maneuvers). Maneuvers that are useful in developing a high degree of pilot skill. Most of these maneuvers are not performed during everyday flying, but they aid the pilot in analyzing the forces acting on the airplane and in developing a fine control touch, coordination, and division of attention for accurate and safe maneuvering of the airplane.

performance number (reciprocating engine fuel specification). The antidetonation rating of a fuel which has a higher critical pressure and temperature than iso-octane (a rating of 100). Iso-octane which has been treated with varying amounts of tetraethyl lead is used as the reference. Aviation gasoline antidetonation ratings above 100 are called performance numbers.

period (oscillation). The length of time needed for one complete cycle of oscillation to take place.

periodic. Repeated at regular time intervals. Any event repeated regularly, with the same amount of time between the events, is said to be a periodic event.

periodic inspection (aircraft inspection). A maintenance inspection that must be performed on a regular or recurring basis. Annual and 100-hour inspections are both periodic inspections.

periodic table of chemical elements. A table listing all the chemical elements, arranged in horizontal rows and vertical columns to show the similarities of the properties of the elements. *See* Appendix 2.

periodic vibration. A vibration having a regularly recurring waveform. Vibrations in the form of sine waves, square waves, or sawtooth waves are examples of periodic vibrations.

peripheral equipment (computer equipment). Components in a computer system that may be attached to the computer. Peripherals consist of display units, storage devices, and such input/output devices as keyboards and printers.

Permalloy. The registered trade name of an alloy of iron and nickel. Permalloy has a high magnetic permeability and is used in the manufacture of permanent magnets.

permanent ballast (aircraft balance). A weight permanently installed in an aircraft to bring its center of gravity into allowable limits.

permanent echo (radar return). Radar signals reflected from fixed objects on the earth's surface; objects such as buildings, towers, and terrain that under certain conditions may be used to check radar alignment. Permanent echoes are distinguished from ground clutter by being definable locations rather than large areas.

permanent magnet. A piece of magnetizable material, such as hard steel, that has been exposed to a strong magnetizing force. This force aligns the spin axes of the electrons surrounding the atoms of the material, and thus the magnetic domains within it. When the material is removed from the magnetic field, it is magnetized and the domains remain in alignment until a strong demagnetizing force is applied.

permanent magnet speaker. The type of speaker used in small radios and tape players. The magnetic field in which the voice coil moves is produced by a small permanent magnet.

permanent mold. A reusable metal mold, used for making complex castings. Castings made in permanent molds can be made thinner than those made by sand casting.

permanent-mold casting. A casting made in a reusable metal mold. Many aircraft engine crankcases are cast in permanent-molds because their walls can be made thinner than similar walls made by sand casting.

permanent set (mechanical deformation). A permanent deformation in a material that has been strained beyond its elastic limit. According to Hooke's law, a material deforms, or strains, in proportion to the amount of stress put on it, and when the stress is removed, the material will return to its original shape and size. This is true until the elastic limit of the material is reached. If the elastic limit of the material is exceeded, the material will not return to its original condition; rather it will take a permanent set.

permeability (μ). A measure of the ease with which lines of magnetic flux can pass through a material. The permeability of a material is found by dividing the flux density (B), in lines per square inch, by the magnetizing force (H), in ampere-turns per inch, needed to produce this flux density.

$$\mu = \frac{B}{H}$$

Air is used as the reference, and it is assigned a permeability of one. Pure iron has a permeability of about 200,000.

persistence (cathode-ray oscilloscope characteristic). A measure of the length of time the phosphor dot on the surface of a cathode-ray tube will glow after the beam of electrons passes on. A long-persistence tube leaves a definite trace of the pattern of the beam after the beam has moved on. In a short-persistence tube, the electron beam leaves very little trace of its passage.

persistence forecast (meteorology). A forecast that the future weather condition will be the same as the present condition.

person. *14 CFR Part 1:* "An individual, firm, partnership, corporation, company, association, joint-stock association, or governmental entity. It includes a trustee, receiver, assignee, or similar representative of any of them."

personal computer-based aviation training devices (PCATD). A device using software that can be displayed on a personal computer to replicate the instrument panel of an airplane. A PCATD must replicate a type of airplane or family of airplanes and meet the virtual control requirements specified in Advisory Circular 61-126.

personality. The embodiment of personal traits and characteristics of an individual that are set at a very early age and are extremely resistant to change.

perspective view. A view of an object in which parallel lines do not appear parallel, but converge at a vanishing point off of the drawing.

petrolatum-zinc dust compound (abrasive compound). A special abrasive compound, used inside an aluminum terminal that is being swaged onto an aluminum electrical wire. As the terminal is compressed, the zinc dust abrades the oxide from the wires, and the petrolatum prevents oxygen reaching the wire, so no more oxides can form.

petroleum. The family of flammable materials obtained from crude oil by the process of distillation. Butane, propane, gasoline, naphtha, kerosine, diesel fuel, furnace oil, lubricating oil, marine fuel, road oil, tar, and asphalt are all petroleum products.

petroleum fractions. The various components of a hydrocarbon fuel which are separated by boiling them off at different temperatures in the process of fractional distillation.

P-factor (aerodynamics). The asymmetrical thrust produced by a propeller when the airplane is flying at a high angle of attack. The downward moving propeller blade has a greater angle of attack than the blade moving upward, and the thrust produced by the half of the propeller disk having the downward moving blade is greater than the thrust produced by the other half.

PFD. *See* primary flight display.

pH. A measure of acidity or alkalinity of a solution. Solutions with pH values less than 7 are acidic. A solution with a pH of 7 is neutral, and solutions with pH values greater than 7 are alkaline.

phantom line (mechanical drawing). A line used on a mechanical drawing to show the location of a part that is not visible in the view shown, but is used as a reference. A phantom line is a thin line made up of a series of an alternate long dash and two short dashes.

— — — — — —

phantom line

phase (alternating current relationship). The angular relationship between voltage and current in an electrical circuit. Voltage and current are in phase when they both pass through zero, moving in the same direction at the same time. If changes in current occur before changes in the voltage, the current is leading the voltage. But if changes in the current occur after changes in the voltage, the current is lagging the voltage, or the voltage is leading the current.

phase angle (alternating current electricity). The number of electrical degrees between the time an AC voltage passes through zero, going in a positive direction, and the time the current passes through zero going in the same direction. If it were possible for a circuit to be purely inductive, having neither capacitance nor resistance, the voltage would lead the current by 90°. This circuit would have a phase angle of 90°.

phased array antenna (radio antenna). A complex antenna which consists of a number of elements. A beam of energy is formed by the superimposition of the signals radiating from the elements. The direction of the beam can be changed by varying the relative phase of the signals applied to each of the elements.

phase inverter (electronic circuit). An electronic circuit that inverts the phase of a signal. Phase inverters change the phase of a signal by 180° to make it usable for the input of one side of a push-pull amplifier.

phase lock (electronic circuit). A method of adjusting the phase of one electronic oscillator, so it follows that of another oscillator. The phase of the two signals is compared, and a resultant signal is produced. This resultant signal is used to adjust one oscillator to bring its output exactly into phase with the other.

phase modulation (PM). A method of modulating a sine-wave carrier, so its phase is changed by an amount proportional to the instantaneous value of the modulating voltage.

phase-reversal protection. A circuit or device used in a three-phase alternating current system that interrupts the power if reversal of the phase rotation should occur.

phase-rotation indicator. An indicator, consisting of two lamps, used to indicate the direction of phase rotation of a three-phase alternating current generator. One lamp is bright and the other dim if the phase rotation is A-B-C. If the phase rotation is A-C-B, the condition of the lamps reverses. The first lamp will be dim and the second will be bright.

phase sequence, or phase rotation. The sequence with which the output phases of a three-phase generator are connected to the load. Reversing the phase sequence of a generator from A-B-C to A-C-B prevents the generator being synchronized with the others on the bus.

phase shift. The difference in time between similar points of an output and an input wave. If the input and the output waves pass through zero at the same time, going in the same direction, the waves are in phase. But if the circuit shifts the phase, the output will either lead or lag the input.

phase shifter (electronic circuit). A circuit that shifts the phase of an alternating current signal. A phase shifter causes the output signal to either lead or lag the input signal.

phenol-formaldehyde resin. One of the oldest of thermosetting plastic resins. Phenol-formaldehyde resin, called phenolic resin, has high strength and good chemical and electrical resistance and is low in cost. It may be reinforced with cloth or paper to make molded plastic objects.

phenolic plastic. A plastic material made of a thermosetting phenol-formaldehyde resin, reinforced with cloth or paper. Phenolic plastic materials are used for electrical insulators and control pulleys.

Phillips screw. A type of recessed-head screw designed to be driven with a power screwdriver. The recess in the head of a Phillips screw is in the form of a cross, with the sides of the recess tapered and the bottom of the recess nearly flat.

A Reed and Prince screw is similar to a Phillips screw, but the edges of the recess in a Reed and Prince screw are straight, rather than tapered, and the bottom of the recess is sharp. *See* Reed and Prince screw.

Phillips screw

P

phonetic alphabet. A list of standard words used for each letter in the alphabet. The use of a standard phonetic alphabet ensures that the letters are not misunderstood during radio transmission. *See* International phonetic alphabet.

phosgene gas. A highly toxic, colorless gas, with an unpleasant odor. Phosgene is formed when certain halogen compounds, such as Freon or carbon tetrachloride, are passed through a flame.

phosphate-ester hydraulic fluid. A synthetic hydraulic fluid used in many high-performance aircraft hydraulic systems. Phosphate-ester hydraulic fluid is fire-resistant and is used in place of petroleum-base hydraulic fluid. It is identified by the military specifications number MIL-H-8446.

phosphate film (corrosion protection). A dense, airtight film formed on the surface of aluminum or magnesium alloy to prevent oxygen or electrolyte reaching the surface and causing oxidation or corrosion.

phosphor coating. *See* phosphorescent paint.

phosphorescent paint. Paint that absorbs energy from natural or ultraviolet light and radiates visible light. Phosphorescent paint continues to glow for some time after the excitation is removed, and for this reason it is used on dials and hands of clocks, watches, and aircraft instruments so they can be seen in the dark. Phosphorescent paint has replaced radium paint for instrument marking because of the poisonous nature of radium.

phosphorus. A highly reactive, poisonous, nonmetallic chemical element. The symbol for phosphorus is P, its atomic number is 15, and its atomic weight is 30.98. Phosphorus is used in the manufacture of matches, explosives, and fertilizer.

photocathode. An electrode in an electron tube that releases electrons when exposed to light. Photocathodes are used in television cameras to convert light energy into electrical energy.

photochemistry. The branch of chemistry that deals with the effects of light on chemical reactions.

photoconductive cell. A photoelectric device that changes its resistance as the amount of light striking it changes. When the cell is in total darkness, its resistance is maximum, and as light falls on it, its resistance decreases. Photoconductive cells using either cadmium sulfide or cadmium selenide as the active elements are called light-dependent resistors (LDRs), and one of their uses is in photographic light meters.

photodiode. A semiconductor diode whose conduction characteristics change when its PN junction is exposed to light. A photodiode in total darkness acts as an open circuit; no current can flow.

photodiode

photoelectric characteristics. The characteristics of a material that change when the material is exposed to light. Some materials (photovoltaic materials) produce a voltage when exposed to light, and others (photoconductive materials) change their resistance when exposed to light.

photoelectricity. Electricity produced by light. When light strikes certain types of semiconductor materials (for example, selenium and cadmium oxides), light energy is absorbed into the material, and electrons are forced to move through it. This movement of electrons is photoelectricity.

photoelectric material. A material that emits electrons when light shines on it. Some of the alkaline metals, such as cesium, lithium, and rubidium, are photoelectric.

photoemissivity. The characteristic of a material that causes it to emit electrons when it is exposed to light.

photofet. A junction field effect transistor in which the gate-to-channel junction acts as a photodiode. The light sensitivity of a photofet is about ten times as great as that of an ordinary phototransistor.

photon. A massless particle of an electromagnetic field. A photon, which is also called a quantum of light, has both energy and momentum.

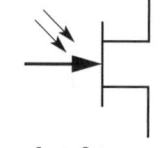

photofet

photonegative characteristics. The characteristics of a material that cause its resistance to increase when light shines on it.

photophone. A device that changes variations of light intensity into sound. A beam of light can be modulated by the output of a microphone. If this modulated light beam is shone on a photoelectric cell, its output current will duplicate the current produced by the microphone.

photo reconnaissance (air traffic control). Military activity that requires locating individual photo targets and navigating to the targets at a preplanned angle and altitude. Photo reconnaissance normally requires a lateral route width of 16 nautical miles and an altitude range of 1,500 feet to 10,000 feet AGL.

photoresistor. A semiconductor device that acts as a variable resistor whose resistance is determined by the amount of light shining on it through a built-in lens. The resistance of a photoresistor increases as the amount of light shining on it increases.

photoresistor

photothyristor. A light-activated silicon controlled rectifier (LASCR). Light falling on the gate-cathode junction triggers the LASCR into conduction.

phototransistor. A junction transistor in which emitter-collector current flows when light shines on the reverse-biased collector-base junction. A small window in the housing allows light to shine on the junction and control the current. Phototransistors produce a current gain and are often used in place of photodiodes.

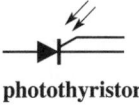

photothyristor

photovoltaic cell. A solid-state electrical component that produces a voltage when it is exposed to light.

phugoid oscillation. Oscillations of an aircraft about its pitch, or lateral, axis (*along* its longitudinal axis). These oscillations consist of long-term, low-amplitude climbs and dives, with little or no change in the angle of attack.

physical organism. A perception factor that describes a person's ability to sense the world around them.

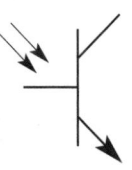

phototransistor

physics. The branch of natural science that deals with the interaction between matter and energy in the fields of: acoustics, optics, heat, mechanics, electricity, magnetism, radiation, atomic structure, and nuclear phenomena.

pi (π). The mathematical constant 3.1415927... .

Pi, usually written with the Greek letter π, is an irrational number, a number that cannot be expressed as an even ratio of any two integers. Pi is the ratio of the length of the circumference of a circle to the length of its diameter.

photovoltaic cell

piano hinge. A continuous hinge consisting of hinge sections fastened to both the fixed and movable bodies. A piece of hard spring-steel wire passes through holes in the two sections to act as the hinge pin.

P

PIBAL (pilot balloon observation). A method of winds-aloft observation by visually tracking a pilot balloon.

PIC. *See* pilot in command.

pick (balloon operation). (1) Of balloon envelopes, stuffing the envelope into its storage back after a flight. (2) Of balloon cold inflation, filling the envelope nearly full of cold air with a very large fan.

pickling. The treatment of a metal surface with an acid to remove surface corrosion.

pico. The metric prefix meaning one millionth of a millionth (1 x 10^{-12}). A picofarad, for example, is one millionth of a millionth of a farad. Pico was at one time called micro-micro.

picofarad. One millionth of a millionth of a farad. 10^{-12} or 0.000 000 000 000 1 farad.

pictorial diagram. A diagram of a wiring or plumbing installation in which sketches of the actual component, rather than symbols, are used to represent components.

piezoelectric crystal. A thin square of quartz or Rochelle salt that has the characteristic of producing a voltage across its opposite faces when it is physically distorted. The physical resonant frequency of the crystal makes it useful as a component in an oscillator to maintain a constant electrical frequency. When the crystal is shocked with a pulse of electrical energy, it vibrates at its resonant frequency. As it

piezoelectric crystal

vibrates, it produces a voltage across its faces that varies at the same frequency as the crystal vibrates.

piezoelectric effect. The ability of certain crystalline materials, such as quartz and Rochelle salt to produce an alternating electric charge across their faces when they are bent, twisted or hit with a hard object. Conversely, when an alternating current charge is placed across the faces, the material will vibrate.

piezoelectricity. Electricity produced when certain crystalline materials, such as quartz or Rochelle salt, are deformed (bent or twisted) by pressure.

piezoelectric spark generator (hot air balloon component). A device used to ignite the pilot light in the burner. Pressing the button on the small handheld generator causes a spring-loaded hammer to hit a piezoelectric crystal. This produces a high voltage which causes current to jump across a small spark gap and ignite the gas. *See* piezoelectric effect.

piezoelectric transducer. An electrical device that uses a crystal to change mechanical movement into an electrical signal. Crystal phonograph pickups and crystal microphones are examples of piezoelectric transducers.

pi (π) filter. An electronic filter used to prevent electromagnetic energy produced in an ignition exciter from feeding back into the aircraft electrical system. The filter is made of an inductor with a capacitor on its input and its output. The name is derived from the fact that the three components on a schematic diagram resemble the Greek letter pi (π).

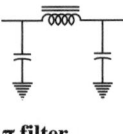

π filter

pig iron. Crude iron as it is reduced from iron ore in a blast furnace and molded in rough blocks called pigs. Pig iron has a high carbon content.

pigment (paint constituent). A material ground into a fine powder and dispersed evenly through the vehicle of a finishing material such as paint or enamel. Pigment gives the finishing material its color.

pigtail (electrical component). A piece of wire protruding from a component, such as a resistor or a capacitor, that allows the component to be installed in an electrical circuit.

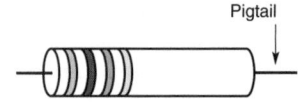

Pigtail

pigtail

pilot (aircraft operator). The person who operates the flight controls of an aircraft in flight.

pilotage (navigation). A method of navigation in which a pilot proceeds from checkpoint to checkpoint by visual reference to objects on the ground.

pilot balloon (meteorology). A small, black, spherical balloon used to determine the speed and direction of winds in the upper air. The rate of ascension of the balloon is known so its altitude can be determined, and it is followed with a theodolite to determine the speed and direction of the wind.

pilot balloon observation (PIBAL). A method of winds aloft observation by visually tracking a pilot balloon.

pilot briefing (air traffic control). A service provided by a flight service station (FSS) to assist pilots in flight planning. Briefing items may include weather information, NOTAMs, military activities, flow control information, and other items as requested.

pilot briefing information. The current format for charted IAPs issued by NACO. The information is presented in a logical order facilitating pilot briefing of the procedures. Charts include formatted information required for quick pilot or flight crew reference located at the top of the chart.

pilot chute. A small parachute attached to the canopy of the main parachute and used to pull it from the pack, so it can open.

pilot-controlled lighting (PCL). Lighting at selected uncontrolled airports that the pilot may control by using the radio. This is done by selecting a specified frequency and clicking the radio microphone.

pilot error. Means that an action or decision made by the pilot was the cause of, or contributing factor which led to an accident or incident. This definition also includes failure of the pilot to make a decision or take action.

pilot hole. A small hole punched or drilled in a piece of sheet metal to locate a rivet hole. Pilot holes are smaller than the rivet hole, but are large enough to allow sheet metal fasteners to be used to assemble the parts. When the parts are assembled and temporarily fastened together, a drill of the proper size for the rivet is passed through both pieces of metal. This method of assembly assures the rivet holes will line up properly.

pilot-in-command (PIC). The pilot responsible for the operation and safety of an aircraft during a flight. This is the person who has the final authority for operation and safety, and who has been designated as pilot-in-command before or during the flight. This person holds the appropriate category, class and type rating (if appropriate), for the conduct of the flight.

pilot-induced oscillation (PIO). Rapid oscillations caused by the pilot's overcontrolled motions. PIOs usually occur on takeoff or landings with pitch sensitive gliders, and in severe cases can lead to damage or loss of control.

pilot light (electrical equipment component). A small indicator light on a piece of electrical equipment illuminated all the time power is supplied to the equipment. Pilot lights are a reminder to turn the equipment off when it is not being used.

Pilot Proficiency Award Program. An FAA program designed to provide pilots with the opportunity to establish and participate in a personal recurrent training program, and also to participate in an awards program. Also known as the WINGS program.

pilot report, or pilot weather report (PIREP). A report of meteorological phenomena encountered by aircraft in flight.

Pilots Automatic Telephone Weather Answering Service. *See* PATWAS.

"Pilot's discretion" (air traffic control). A phrase that, when used in conjunction with altitude assignments, means that ATC has offered the pilot the option of starting climb or descent whenever he wishes and conducting the climb or descent at any rate he wishes. The pilot may temporarily level off at any intermediate altitude. However, once an altitude has been vacated, he may not return to that altitude.

Pilot's Operating Handbook. *See* POH.

pinch-off voltage (FET specification). The amount of reverse voltage required on the gate of a field effect transistor to decrease the source-to-drain current to some specified low value.

pint contacts (electrical connectors). Contacts in one half of an electrical connector, made in the form of metal pins. These pins, called male contacts, fit into sockets, female contacts, in the other half of the connector. Pin contacts are normally used on the half of the connector in the "cold" part of the circuit, the part not connected to the source of power.

PIN diode (semiconductor device). A semiconductor diode having a layer of P-silicon and a layer of N-silicon. Between these two layers is a thin layer of undoped silicon called intrinsic silicon. PIN diodes are used in high-frequency switching circuits because of their ability to turn on and off at an extremely fast rate.

pinhole (balloon operation). Any small hole in a balloon envelope smaller than the maximum dimensions allowed for airworthiness.

pinhole (finishing system). A small hole in the film of aircraft finishing material left by a bubble. The bubble migrated to the surface of the material and burst after the material had dried too much to flow into the resulting hole.

pinion. A small gear that meshes with a larger gear, a sector of a gear, or a toothed rack.

pin jack (electrical connector). A single female connector that accepts and holds a small metal pin attached to the end of a wire or a test lead. Pin jacks are used on test equipment to attach test leads to the instrument.

pinked-edge fabric (aircraft fabric). Aircraft fabric having a series of small V-cuts along its edge made by cutting the fabric with pinking shears. Pinked-edge fabric does not ravel.

pinked-edge tape. Cloth tape whose edges have small V-shaped notches cut along their length. The pinked edges prevent the tape from raveling.

pinking shears. Special fabric-cutting scissors that produce a series of small V-shaped notches where the fabric is cut. These notches keep the edges of the fabric from raveling.

pin knot cluster. A group of knots, all having a diameter of less than approximately $1/16$ inch.

pinouts (electronic circuit diagram). Identification of each of the external connections of an integrated circuit chip.

pin punch. A long punch with straight sides. A pin punch can be passed through bolt holes in a piece of equipment to temporarily hold its pieces together until they can be bolted. A pin punch can also be used to drive bolts, rivets, or pins from tight-fitting holes.

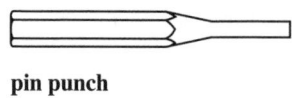

pin punch

pin spanner. A special type of wrench used to turn ring-shaped nuts. Thin, ring-shaped nuts are used on cylinders and rods as mechanical stops and locking nuts. These nuts are turned with a pin spanner whose pins fit into small holes in the outer circumference of the nut.

pint. A unit of liquid measurement. One pint is equal to $1/8$ U.S. gallon, $28\,7/8$ cubic inches, or approximately 4.73×10^{-4} cubic meters.

pip (cathode ray tube indication). The display of a received pulse on the screen of a cathode-ray tube. A pip is also called a blip.

pipe threads. The type of thread cut on the outside of an iron or steel pipe. Pipe threads are tapered approximately $1/16$-inch to the inch to form a tight, leakproof seal when the pipe is screwed into a fitting or coupling.

PIREP. *See* pilot report.

piston. A sliding plug in an actuating cylinder used to convert pressure into force and then into work.

piston (reciprocating engine component). A movable plug inside the cylinder of a reciprocating engine that moves up and down to compress the fuel-air mixture and to transmit the force from the expanding gases in the cylinder to the crankshaft. The piston is

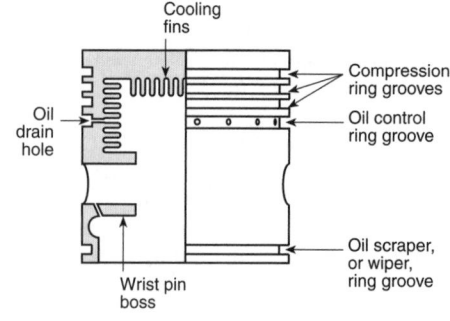

piston

sealed in the cylinder by cast-iron piston rings and connected to the crankshaft through a connecting rod.

piston displacement (reciprocating engine specification). The total volume, in cubic inches, cubic centimeters, or liters swept by all of the pistons of a reciprocating engine as they move in one revolution of the crankshaft.

piston engine (heat engine type). One of the common terms used for a reciprocating engine.

piston pin (reciprocating engine component). The hardened and polished steel pin used to connect the piston of a reciprocating engine to the connecting rod. Piston pins are also called wrist pins and gudgeon pins.

piston ring grooves (reciprocating engine). The grooves on the outside of the piston into which the piston rings fit. *See* piston rings (reciprocating engine component).

piston rings (reciprocating engine component). Metal rings, usually made of cast iron, that fit into grooves around the outside of a reciprocating-engine piston. Piston rings form a seal between the piston and the cylinder wall to prevent the high-pressure air in the cylinder from leaking out.

piston skirt (reciprocating engine). That part of the piston between the first ring groove above the wrist pin hole, and the bottom (open end) of the piston. The skirt forms a bearing area in contact with the cylinder wall.

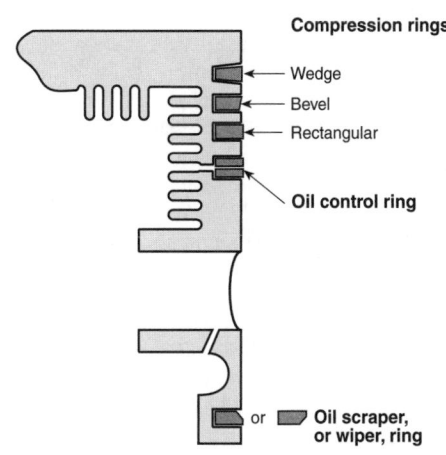

piston rings

piston-type pump (fluid pump). A mechanical pump which moves fluid by pistons moving back and forth in the pump cylinders. In an axial-piston pump, the cylinders are arranged parallel to the pump axis, and in a radial-piston pump, the cylinders radiate out perpendicular to the axis.

pit (corrosion). A pocket of chemical salts that forms on the surface of a metal when it corrodes.

pitch (aircraft maneuver). Rotation of an aircraft about its lateral axis.

pitch (rivet layout dimension). The distance between the centers of adjacent rivets installed in the same row.

pitch (sound vibrations). The auditory perception of a sound based on a relative scale of frequency of vibration.

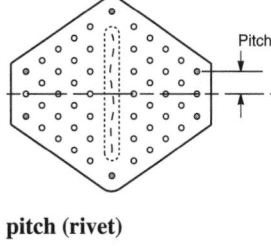

pitch (rivet)

pitch (thread dimension). The linear distance, measured parallel to the length of a threaded fastener, between corresponding points on two adjacent threads.

pitch angle (helicopter rotor blade). The angle between the chord line of a rotor blade and the reference plane of the main rotor hub, or the plane of rotation of the rotor.

pitch angle (propeller specification). The angle between the chord line of a propeller blade and the plane of rotation.

pitch attitude. The attitude of an aircraft relative to its longitudinal axis. Pitch attitude serves as a visual reference for the pilot to maintain or change airspeed.

pitch axis (aircraft axis). The lateral axis of an aircraft that extends from wing tip to wing tip and passes through the center of gravity. This is the axis about which the aircraft pitches. *See* axes of an aircraft.

pitch distribution (propeller specification). The gradual twist in the propeller blade from shank to tip.

pitch pocket (wood defect). Cavities filled with pitch that appear in the growth rings of a piece of wood.

pitch point. A fix/waypoint that serves as a transition point from a departure procedure or the low-altitude ground-based navigation structure into the high-altitude waypoint system.

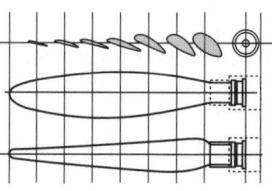

pitch distribution

pitot pressure. Ram air pressure used to measure airspeed. The pitot tube faces directly into the air flowing around the aircraft. It stops the air and allows the pressure caused by its movement to be measured.

pitch setting. *14 CFR Part 1:* "The propeller blade setting as determined by the blade angle measured in a manner, and at a radius, specified by the instruction manual for the propeller."

pitot-static system. A system that powers the airspeed altimeter and variometer by relying on air pressure differences to measure glider speed, altitude, and climb or sink rate.

pitot-static tube. A combination pickup used to sample pitot pressure (ram air pressure) and static pressure (still air pressure). These two pressures, taken from outside a moving aircraft, are combined to measure airspeed. Pitot pressure is picked up through an open-end tube that sticks directly into the airstream, and static pressure is picked up through small holes or slots in the side of the pitot-static tube, or through flush ports on the side of the aircraft. Also called pitot-static head.

pitot tube. An open-end tube that points directly into the air flowing over an aircraft structure. The pitot tube samples the pressure of the ram air. This pressure is taken into the airspeed indicator where it is compared with static air pressure to produce the airspeed indication.

pitting corrosion. A type of corrosion that forms on the surface of metal as small, localized pits filled with the salts of corrosion.

pivotal altitude. A specific altitude at which, when an airplane turns at a given ground speed, a projecting of the sighting reference line to a selected point on the ground will appear to pivot on that point.

PK screw. *See* Parker-Kalon screw.

placard. A notice placed on an aircraft in plain sight of the appropriate crew member to give information pertinent to the operation of the aircraft. Operations limitations as well as maintenance specifics are often displayed by placards.

plain bearing. A bearing made of a material, such as lead or babbitt, that has a low coefficient of friction. Plain bearings can support only loads applied in a direction perpendicular to their surface, and are used as crankshaft bearings in most reciprocating engines.

plain flap (aircraft secondary control). A type of wing flap in which a part of the wing trailing edge inboard of the aileron is hinged to fold downward in flight to change the camber of the wing.

plain nut. A form of hexagonal nut that has no provisions for locking it onto a bolt or stud.

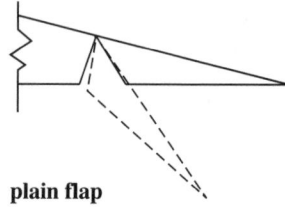

plain flap

plain overlap seam (aircraft fabric seam). A type of
machine-sewed seam used to join two pieces of aircraft fabric. The edge of one piece of fabric overlaps
the edge of the other, and one or two rows of stitches
are used to join the pieces. In a plain overlap seam,
the thread passes through two layers of fabric.

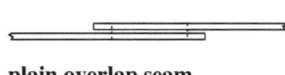

plain overlap seam

plain rib (airplane wing rib). A wing rib used to give the wing its airfoil shape. Plain ribs
are also called former ribs.

plain ski (landing gear component). A type of aircraft ski that can only be used on snow
or ice, as compared to combination skis, which also allow the use of the skiplane's
wheels for landing on runways.

plain washer (aircraft hardware). A disk of metal with a hole in its center. Plain washers
are used to provide a smooth surface on which a nut can ride, and to fill the space
between a surface and the nut to adjust for the grip length of a bolt.

plain-weave fabric. Fabric in which each warp thread passes over one
fill thread and under the next. Plain-weave fabric normally has the
same strength in both warp and fill directions.

plan area. The area of a surface as viewed from the top.

plane of rotation (helicopter rotor). The plane in which the rotor blades
travel. The plane of rotation is perpendicular to the rotor shaft, which
is the axis of rotation of the rotor blades.

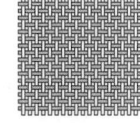

**plain-weave
fabric**

plane of symmetry (aircraft layout). An imaginary vertical plane that
passes through the longitudinal axis of an aircraft and divides the
aircraft into two symmetrical halves.

planer. A woodworking power tool used to smooth the surfaces of a piece of wood.

planetary electrons. Electrons that circle around the nucleus of an atom in rings, or shells.

planetary gear system. A system of gears that changes the speed of rotation of a shaft, but
does not change its direction of rotation. The sun gear is mounted on the crankshaft
and is surrounded by and meshes with a set of planetary gears mounted on a carrier,
or spider, that is part of the propeller shaft. The planetary gears also mesh with and
rotate inside the fixed ring gear. When the sun gear turns, the planetary gear spider
rotates inside the ring gear and turns the propeller shaft at a speed slower than that of
the crankshaft.

   The ratio between the speeds of the crankshaft and the propeller shaft is found by
dividing the sum of the teeth on the ring gear and the sun gear by the number of teeth
on the sun gear. Neither the number of teeth on the planetary gears nor the number of
planetary gears rotating around the sun gear enters into the computation for the gear
ratio.

planform (aeronautical engineering). The shape or form of a wing as viewed from above.
The planform of a wing determines its aerodynamic efficiency and its stall progression.

planing position (seaplane operation). The attitude of a seaplane when its weight is
supported by a combination of hydrodynamic and aerodynamic lift, as it is during
high-speed taxi or just prior to takeoff. This position produces the least amount of water
drag. It is also called the step position, or being "on the step."

plan position indicator. *See* PPI.

plans display (air traffic control). A display available in ATC's user request evaluation tool
(URET) that provides detailed flight plan and predicted conflict information in textual
format for requested current plans and all trial plans. *See also* current plan, trial plan.

Plante cell (electrochemical cell). A type of lead-acid cell in which the active material is
electrochemically formed on lead plates rather than being applied as a prepared paste.

P

plan view (aeronautical charts). The overhead view of an approach procedure on an instrument approach chart. The plan view depicts the routes that guide the pilot from the en route segments to the IAF.

plan view (aircraft drawing). The top view of an object in an orthographic projection.

plaque (battery component). Powdered nickel used as a base for the active elements in both the positive and negative plates of an aircraft nickel-cadmium battery. Plaque is forced by heat and pressure to bond to a nickel wire mesh screen to form the plates for the battery.

plasma. A completely ionized gas, consisting of equal numbers of positive ions and free electrons. Plasma is electrically neutral.

plasma arc welding. A method of welding in which the metal is heated by an electric arc whose temperature has been greatly intensified by the injection of a gas. The plasma arc becomes a jet of high current density that produces temperatures of up to 60,000°F (33,316°C). One of the chief advantages of plasma arc welding is the concentration of this extreme heat which allows parts to be welded with a minimum of distortion.

plasma engine. An engine having applications for space travel. Neutral plasma, accelerated and directed by external magnetic fields, interacts with the magnetic fields produced by current flowing through the plasma.

plasma generator. A device, such as an electric arc chamber, that generates an extremely large amount of heat and changes neutral gases into plasma.

plasma torch. A torch in which plasma gas is injected into an electric arc formed between two electrodes in a chamber. The stream of hot gases leaves the torch at an extremely high speed through an orifice in the negative electrode. This high-velocity, high-temperature stream can be used for welding, cutting, or spraying molten metal. The temperature produced by a plasma torch can be as high as 60,000°F.

plastic (material condition). The condition in which a material is capable of being shaped or formed. A material in its plastic condition is normally in a semi-solid state.

plasticizer (finishing material constituent). Materials used in a lacquer finishing system to give the film flexibility and resilience.

plastic range (material science). The stress range in which a material will not fail when subjected to the action of a force, but will be permanently deformed.

plastics. The generic name for any of the organic materials produced by polymerization. Plastics can be shaped by molding or drawing.

Plastic Wood. The registered trade name for a form of wood filler made of wood fibers mixed with a synthetic resin. Plastic wood is used to fill cracks and holes in wood. When it hardens, it can be worked with ordinary woodworking tools and can be finished to match the wood it is used to fill.

plate (electron tube component). The anode of an electron tube. A high positive voltage on the plate attracts electrons from the cathode. This flow of electrons is controlled by the voltage on grids located between the cathode and the plate.

plate current (electron tube current). Current that flows between the cathode and plate in an electron tube.

plate glass. A thick, flat, high-quality sheet of glass. Plate glass is used for windows where strength and undistorted vision are necessary.

plate power supply (electron tube equipment). A high-voltage, positive DC power supply for electronic equipment using electron tubes (vacuum tubes). Plate power supplies are usually called B+ power supplies.

plate resistance (electron tube specification). A dynamic value found by dividing the change in plate voltage by the change in plate current caused by the voltage change. No conditions other than the voltage and current are allowed to change when making this measurement.

plate saturation (electron tube condition). The condition in an electron tube in which the plate, or anode, is attracting all of the electrons being emitted by the cathode.

plating (metal surface treatment). The process in which a thin coating of one metal is electrolytically deposited on the surface of another. Cadmium and chromium are used to plate steel parts to protect the steel from corrosion. Chromium also makes the surface of the steel resistant to wear.

platinum. A heavy, silvery-white, metallic chemical element that is resistant to nearly all acids. Platinum's symbol is Pt, its atomic number is 78, and its atomic weight is 195.09. Because platinum is able to withstand extremely high temperatures, it is used as the electrodes in some fine-wire spark plugs. Platinum's appearance is pleasing, and it is so durable it is used for jewelry.

platinum fine-wire spark plug (reciprocating engine component). An aircraft spark plug whose electrodes are made of small-diameter platinum wire. Platinum spark plugs are especially suited for use in reciprocating engines whose fuel contains a large amount of tetraethyl lead. Tetraethyl lead produces lead oxides inside the firing-end cavity of a spark plug, and enough of this oxide can build up to foul the spark plug, preventing its firing.

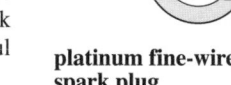

platinum fine-wire spark plug

Fine-wire platinum electrodes allow the firing-end cavity to be open enough that the gases containing the lead are blown out, preventing the formation of the lead buildup. Platinum can operate at such high temperatures that any lead deposits which form on the electrodes will immediately burn off.

play. A term commonly used to mean relative movement between parts. There is said to be play in the controls of an aircraft if the control surfaces can be moved without the cockpit controls moving.

P-lead (aircraft ignition system component). The commonly used term for the wire that connects the primary circuit of an aircraft magneto to the ignition switch. A magneto is turned off by grounding its P-lead.

plenum chamber. An enclosed chamber in which air can be held at a pressure slightly higher than that of the surrounding air. Plenum chambers are used with a gas turbine engine to stabilize the pressure of the air before it enters a double-entry centrifugal compressor.

Plexiglas. The registered trade name for a transparent acrylic plastic material used for aircraft windshields, canopies, and side windows.

pliers. A form of gripping hand tool having two pivoted handles and two notched, or serrated, jaws. Common slip-joint pliers are used to hold small objects and to cut and bend wire.

plowing position (seaplane operation). A nose-high, powered taxi characterized by high water drag and an aftward shift of the center of buoyancy. The weight of the seaplane is supported primarily by buoyancy, and partially by hydrodynamic lift.

plow wind (meteorology). A straight-line, spreading downdraft in front of a thunderstorm. A plow wind is also called a first gust.

plumb. A condition of being straight up and down, or vertical.

plumb bob. A pointed weight with a string attached to a hole in line with its point. When the string is fastened to an object, the point of the plumb bob is directly below the point of attachment, and a freely hanging plumb bob always points directly toward the center of the earth. Anything that aligns with the string attached to the plumb bob is said to be plumb.

plumbing. A term referring to all of the tubing and hoses used to connect the hydraulic and pneumatic system components in an aircraft; also the tubing and hoses that carry fuel and lubricating oil.

plumb line. The string to which a plumb bob is attached.

plutonium. A naturally radioactive, silvery, metallic chemical element used as a nuclear fuel. Plutonium's symbol is Pu, its atomic number is 94, and the mass number of its most stable isotope is 244.

ply (composites). (1) A thin layer of material bonded to one or more additional thin layers. (2) A strand of yarn made by twisting together two or more strands.

ply rating (tire rating). A rating used for aircraft and automobile tires to indicate their relative strength. The ply rating does not indicate the actual number of plies of fabric in the tire; rather, it indicates the number of plies of cotton fabric needed to produce the same strength as the actual plies.

plywood. A form of manufactured wood product made of thin layers (plies) of wood veneer glued together. The grain of each alternate ply of veneer runs at 90° or 45° to the plies next to it. Plywood is strong, lightweight, rigid, and relatively inexpensive.

PMA (Parts Manufacturer Approval). An approval, granted by the FAA under 14 CFR Part 21, that allows a person to produce a modification or replacement part for sale for installation on a type-certificated product.

PMB (plastic media blasting). A method of removing paint from an aircraft surface by dry-blasting it with tiny plastic beads.

pneumatic. Operation of a part or system by the use of compressed air, or by gas under pressure.

pneumatic altimeter. A form of aneroid barometer whose dial is calibrated in feet or meters, rather than units of pressure. A pneumatic altimeter has a barometric scale that can be adjusted to any desired reference pressure, and the pointers of the instrument measure the difference between the existing pressure and this reference pressure in terms of feet or meters.

When the local altimeter setting is set on the barometric scale, the altimeter shows indicated altitude. When standard sea level pressure of 29.92 inches of mercury or 1013.2 millibars is set on the barometric scale, the altimeter shows pressure altitude.

Another type of altimeter is an absolute (radar or radio) altimeter. It measures the actual distance between an aircraft and the terrain below it by measuring the time needed for an electrical signal to pass from the aircraft to the ground and back to the aircraft. *See* radio altimeter.

pneumatic drill motor (air drill). A small, handheld air turbine fitted with a chuck to hold a twist drill. The housing in which the turbine is mounted has a trigger-actuated air valve that controls the speed of the turbine by controlling the amount of air flowing through it. Pneumatic drill motors are used in aircraft manufacture and maintenance because they are safer than electric drill motors, and they give the operator excellent control of the drill speed. Pneumatic drill motors do not overheat when they are stalled.

pneumatics (fluid power). The branch of fluid power systems that uses a compressible fluid to transfer energy.

PN junction (semiconductor device). The surface in a semiconductor diode or transistor between the P-material and the N-material. When the PN junction is forward-biased (positive voltage to the P-material), holes in the P-material and free electrons in the N-material drift to the junction. Here they combine by the free electrons filling the holes. A maximum number of electrons flow across a forward-biased PN junction. When the PN junction is reverse-biased (positive voltage to the N-material), the holes and free electrons are drawn away from the junction and very few electrons cross it.

PNP transistor (semiconductor device). A bipolar transistor made of P-type and N-type silicon or germanium. The base, made of N-type material, is between a collector and an emitter, both made of P-type material. A very small current flow in the emitter-base circuit controls a much larger flow of current between the emitter and collector.

PNP transistor

pogonip (meteorology). A type of fog, composed of suspended particles of ice.

POH (Pilot's Operating Handbook). An FAA-approved document published by the airframe manufacturer that lists the operating conditions for a particular model of aircraft. Engine operating parameters are included in the POH.

POI. *See* principal operations inspector.

pointer (analog instrument). The thin strip of metal or small rod moved by an analog instrument mechanism over a calibrated scale. The position of the pointer over the scale shows the value of the measurement being made. Instrument pointers are sometimes called hands or needles.

point-in-space approach (rotorcraft). A type of helicopter instrument approach procedure to a missed approach point more than 2,600 feet from an associated helicopter landing area.

point out. *See* radar point out.

point-to-point (PTP). A level of NRR service for aircraft that is based on traditional waypoints in their FMS's or RNAV equipage.

point-to-point wiring (electronic component assembly). A method of assembling components in an electronic device. The components are mounted on a chassis, and wires are routed from the pins on one component to the pins on another and soldered. Components built with printed circuit boards and integrated circuit chips have, to a great extent, replaced components made with point-to-point wiring.

poise. A unit of viscosity measurement in the centimeter-gram-second system. One poise is equal to one dyne-second per square centimeter. Centipoise is a more commonly used value, and one centipoise is equal to 0.01 poise.

polar air (meteorology). An air mass with characteristics developed over high latitudes, especially within the subpolar highs. Continental polar air (cP) has cold surface temperatures, low moisture content, and, especially in its source regions, great stability in its lower layers. It is shallow in comparison with Arctic air. Maritime polar (mP) air initially possesses similar properties to those of continental polar air, but as it passes over warmer water, it becomes unstable, with a higher moisture content.

polar easterlies (meteorology). The rather shallow, irregular, and diffuse easterly winds located poleward of the subpolar low pressure belt.

polar front (meteorology). A semipermanent, semicontinuous front, separating air masses of tropical and polar origins.

polarity. The possession or manifestation of two opposing characteristics. A battery has polarity because one terminal has an excess of electrons and the other a deficiency. A magnet has polarity because the lines of magnetic flux leave one pole and return to the other.

polarized capacitor (electronic component). A capacitor that can be used only in a DC circuit. When using a polarized capacitor, attention must be paid to the polarity of the voltage to which it is connected. Most electrolytic capacitors are polarized and are marked so they can be correctly installed in a circuit. If a polarized capacitor is incorrectly installed, enough current can flow through it to destroy it.

polarized light. Light in which all of the electromagnetic energy is vibrating in the same plane.

P

polarized receptacle (electrical wiring receptacle). An electrical receptacle whose sockets are arranged in such a way that its mating plug can be inserted in only one way. Nonpolarized receptacles for house wiring have two flat sockets of the same size, and a plug can be inserted with either pin fitting into either socket.

Polarized receptacles used in modern house wiring have three sockets. A round socket is connected to the earth ground, and the socket for the common wire (the white wire) is wider than the socket for the "hot" wire (the black wire).

polar track structure (air traffic control). A system of organized routes between Iceland and Alaska that overlie Canadian MNPS Airspace.

pole shoes (electrical machine component). Inward extensions from the field frame of an electric motor or generator around which the field coils are mounted. The pole shoes are fastened to the field frame to form a very low reluctance path for the lines of magnetic flux. The pole shoes are shaped in such a way that the density of the flux across the air gap between the pole shoe and the armature is uniform.

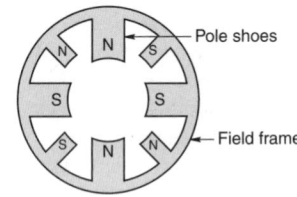

pole shoes

poles of a magnet. The locations on a magnet where the lines of magnetic flux leave and where they enter. In a ferromagnetic metal, groups of atoms whose electrons have their spin axes in alignment are called magnetic domains. When all of the domains are aligned in the same direction, the material is magnetized.

All magnets, regardless of their size, have two poles, a north pole and a south pole. Lines of magnetic flux leave the magnet at its north pole and return through its south pole. All the lines of flux leave and enter the poles at right angles to the surface.

polonium. A naturally radioactive, metallic chemical element produced by bombarding bismuth or lead with neutrons. Polonium's symbol is Po, its atomic number is 84, and the mass number of its most stable isotope is 209.

polyconic projection (map projection). A projection used for laying out the grid of latitude and longitude for a chart or map. In a polyconic projection, the parallels of latitude are represented by arcs of a circle whose center is the north or south pole. The meridians of longitude are straight lines radiating from the poles.

polyester fibers. A synthetic fiber made by the polymerization process, in which tiny molecules are united to form a long chain of molecules. Polyester fibers are woven into fabrics that are known by their trade names of Dacron, Fortrel, and Kodel. Polyester film and sheet are known as Mylar and Celenar.

Cloth woven of polyester fibers for use as an aircraft covering material is sold under such trade names as Poly Fiber, Eonnex, and Ceconite. This cloth is shrunk on the structure with heat, rather than with shrinking dope.

polyester resin (reinforced plastic component). A thermosetting resin serving as the matrix for much of the fiberglass cloth and mat used to make parts for aircraft composite construction.

polyethylene plastic material. A lightweight, chemical-resistant, thermoplastic material. Polyethylene resins are used for making sheets of protective covering material and containers for liquids.

Poly-Fiber® (aircraft covering material). A proprietary system for covering an aircraft structure. It uses a heat-shrinkable polyester fabric and an all-vinyl system of finishing materials. It is stronger, lighter, and longer lasting than a doped cotton system.

polymerization. A chemical reaction in which several small molecules join together to form larger molecules. The larger molecules are made up of repeating structural units of the original molecules. Polymerization often causes liquid materials to change into a jelly.

polymer paint. A water-based paint that contains vinyl or acrylic resins. When the water evaporates, it leaves a waterproof film of the plastic resin.

polyphase alternating current. Alternating current electricity produced by more than one set of generator windings. The most commonly used polyphase electricity has three phases.

polyphase electric motor. An induction motor designed to operate on two-phase or three-phase alternating current.

polystyrene (composites). A synthetic resin made by polymerization of styrene. It is used as a fabric lamination and for molded or extruded plastic components. It is a good electrical insulator.

polyurethane enamel. A two-part, chemically cured, finishing material that contains a high percentage of solids. Polyurethane enamel requires a long time to flow out, and this long flowing-out time gives the finish a "wet" look. Polyurethane enamel is highly resistant to mechanical abrasion and chemical action.

polyvinyl chloride (thermoplastic resin). A thermoplastic resin used to make transparent tubing for insulating electrical wires. Polyvinyl chloride (PVC) tubing is used for carrying low-pressure air to aircraft instruments.

pontoon (aircraft landing gear component). A float that can be attached to a land airplane to allow it to operate from water. Two pontoons are often installed on a land plane to convert it into a float plane.

poor judgment chain (psychology). A term used in aeronautical decision making referring to a series of mistakes that may lead to an accident or incident. Two basic principles generally associated with the creation of a poor judgment chain are: (1) One bad decision often leads to another; and (2) as a string of bad decisions grows, it reduces the number of subsequent alternatives for continued safe flight. ADM is intended to break the poor judgment chain before it can cause an accident or incident.

pop-out floats (helicopter component). Helicopter floats that are stored deflated on the skids or in compartments along the lower portion of the helicopter, and deployed in the event of an emergency landing on water. Compressed nitrogen or helium inflates the floats very quickly.

poppet valve (reciprocating engine component). A T-shaped valve with a circular head. Poppet valves are used to cover the intake and exhaust openings in the cylinder head of a reciprocating engine. The valves are held closed with one or more coil springs and are opened by a cam lobe or rocker arm pushing on the end of their stem.

porcelain. A high-grade, translucent ceramic material having a hard, glazed finish. Porcelain is used for dishes, vases, and high-strength electrical insulators. It was used as the insulator in some early aircraft spark plugs.

poppet valve

porosity. The condition of a material that has many tiny openings, or pores, in its surface. These pores allow liquids or gases to seep (pass slowly) through the material. Cast iron and certain types of wood are porous, while glass and hard steel are not. They have very little porosity.

porous chrome plating. A method of treating the walls of aircraft reciprocating engine cylinders that hardens them and increases their ability to hold lubricants. Worn cylinder barrels may be ground so their bore is straight and round. Then hard chromium is electroplated on the walls to a depth that brings the diameter of the cylinder bore back to its original dimension.

Continued

porous chrome plating. *Continued*

The surface of the hard chrome plating resembles a maze of spiderwebs, with thousands of tiny, interconnected cracks. After the correct depth of chromium has been deposited, the electroplating current is reversed, and the tiny cracks enlarge enough to hold oil.

Porous chrome plating provides a hard, wear-resistant surface over which the piston rings ride. The oil trapped in the tiny grooves furnishes lubrication to minimize piston ring and cylinder wall wear and helps the rings seal.

porpoising (flight condition). An unstable flight condition in which an aircraft continually oscillates along its longitudinal axis. Porpoising is caused by the aircraft possessing neutral dynamic longitudinal stability.

port side. The left side of an aircraft or ship, as viewed when looking forward.

position and hold (air traffic control). Used by ATC to inform a pilot to taxi onto the departure runway in takeoff position and hold. It is not authorization for takeoff. It is used when takeoff clearance cannot immediately be issued because of traffic or other reasons.

position error (aircraft instrument error). An error in the indication of flight instruments connected to the static air system (altimeter, airspeed indicator, and vertical speed indicator). This error is caused by the air at the entrance to the static system not being absolutely still. The amount of position error changes with the angle of attack or airspeed of the aircraft and is usually greatest at low airspeeds when the angle of attack is the highest.

position lights. Another name for the navigation lights mounted on the wings and tail of an aircraft. *See* navigation lights.

position line (aircraft drawings). A line used to show the extreme position to which a part can be moved.

position report (air traffic control). A report over a known location as transmitted by an aircraft to ATC.

position symbol (radar indication). A computer-generated indication shown on a radar display to indicate the mode of tracking.

positive angle of attack (aerodynamics). The condition in which the leading edge of the chord line of the wing is above the line representing the relative wind. A positive angle of attack produces an upward thrust.

positive charge (electrical charge). An unbalanced electrical condition caused by a deficiency of electrons. A positive charge can be produced by chemical cells, photocells, and thermocouples.

positive control. *14 CFR Part 1:* "Control of all air traffic, within designated airspace, by air traffic control."

positive control area. *See* PCA.

positive course guidance (PCG). A continuous display of navigational data that enables an aircraft to be flown along a specific course line (e.g., radar vector, RNAV, ground-based NAVAID).

positive-displacement pump (fluid pump). A type of fluid pump that moves a specific amount of fluid each time it rotates. Since the pump is always moving fluid, some form of relief valve must be used to relieve pressure when the system cannot use the fluid as fast as the pump moves it. Gear pumps, gerotor pumps, and vane pumps are examples of positive-displacement pumps.

positive dynamic stability. The tendency over time for an aircraft to return to a predisturbed state.

positive electrical charge. An electrical condition in which an object has a deficiency of electrons. In an electrochemical cell, electrons are attracted from one terminal to the other. The terminal from which the electrons were removed is left with a positive charge.

positive feedback (electronic amplifier). A condition in an electronic amplifier in which part of the amplified signal is fed back from the output to the input. Positive feedback, also called regenerative feedback, is used to reinforce the input signal.

positive ion. An atom that has become electrically unbalanced by losing one or more electrons. Since there are more protons in the nucleus than there are electrons surrounding the nucleus, the atom has a positive charge.

positive logic (digital electronics). The form of logic in which the more positive voltage represents a logic one and the less positive voltage or zero voltage represents a logic zero.

positive number. A number greater than zero.

positive static stability (aircraft stability). The production of a force that causes an aircraft to return to a condition of straight and level flight after it has been disturbed from this condition.

positive temperature coefficient. The change of a value, such as resistance, capacitance, or physical length, with temperature in such a way that the value increases as the temperature increases.

positive terminal (electrical power source). The terminal of a source of electrical energy through which electrons return to the source after they have passed through the external circuit.

positive vorticity (meteorology). Vorticity caused by cyclonic turning. Positive vorticity is associated with upward motion of the air.

positron. An unstable atomic particle. A positron has the same mass and spin characteristics as an electron, but it has a positive electrical charge. (An electron has a negative electrical charge.)

post cure (composites). The exposure of certain resins to higher than normal curing temperatures after the initial cure cycle. This second stage is necessary to attain the complete cure and the desired mechanical properties of the resins involved.

potable water. Water carried in an aircraft for the purpose of drinking.

potassium. A soft, silvery-white, lightweight, alkali metal chemical element. Potassium's symbol is K, its atomic number is 19, and its atomic weight is 39.102. Potassium salts are important in the manufacture of soaps and grease.

potential barrier (semiconductor characteristic). The voltage in a semiconductor device on either side of a PN junction. Free electrons from the N-material migrate across the junction to fill some of the holes in the P-material. This migration causes a positive potential at the edge of the N-material, and a negative potential at the edge of the P-material.

potential barrier

The potential barrier, sometimes called the potential hill, blocks any forward current flow across the junction until the forward voltage is higher than that of the potential barrier. The potential barrier in a silicon device is approximately 0.7 volt and approximately 0.3 volt in a germanium device.

potential difference. A difference in electrical pressure. A potential difference exists when one component, or point, has an excess of electrons (a negative charge) and another has a deficiency of electrons (a positive charge). Potential difference is measured in volts.

potential drop. A drop in voltage in an electrical circuit caused by current flowing through a resistance. The amount of potential drop, which is also called a voltage drop or an IR drop, is determined by both the current and the resistance.

potential energy. Energy possessed by an object because of its position, configuration, or the chemical arrangement of its constituents.

potential instability (meteorology). The state of an unsaturated layer or column of air in the atmosphere with a wet-bulb potential temperature (or equivalent potential temperature) that decreases with elevation. Also called convective instability, or thermal instability.

potentiometer (electrical measuring instrument). An electrical instrument that measures the voltage of a source without taking current from it. The unknown voltage is compared with an adjustable voltage that can be accurately measured. When no current flows between the two voltage sources, they are exactly the same.

potentiometer

potentiometer (variable resistor). A variable resistor with three terminals, or connections. One connection is made to each end of the resistance element, and a third connection is made to a wiper that can be moved over the resistance element. The position of the wiper determines the amount of resistance used in the circuit.

pot life (resin specification). The length of time a resin will remain workable after the catalyst has been added. If a catalyzed material is not used within its usable pot life, it must be discarded and a new batch mixed.

potted circuit. An electrical circuit in which all the components are protected by encapsulating them in an insulating potting compound.

potting compound. A liquid plastic resin poured over electrical components in a potted circuit. The potting compound cures into an insulating, rubber-like solid that protects the parts from moisture and physical damage.

pound. A commonly used measure of weight or mass in the English system. One pound is equal to approximately 0.454 kilogram.

poundal. A measure of force in the English system. One poundal is the amount of force needed to cause a mass of one pound to accelerate at the rate of one foot per second each second it is acted upon.

pound-inches. *See* work.

pour point (petroleum product specification). The lowest temperature at which a material will pour without assistance.

powdered-iron core (electrical component). A highly permeable core used in some electrical coils. The core is made of fine particles of powdered iron, mixed with a suitable binder, and molded into the needed shape. Powdered-iron cores have a high permeability and low eddy current losses.

powder metallurgy. A sintering process for making various parts out of metal powder. The metal powder is compacted in a closed metal cavity, or die under pressure. This compacted material is placed in an oven and sintered in a controlled atmosphere at high temperatures. The metal powders coalesce and form a solid. Powder metallurgy is useful in making parts that have irregular curves, or recesses that are hard to machine. *See* sintered metal.

power (electrical). The product of the applied voltage and the current in a DC circuit. In an AC circuit, power is the product of the applied voltage and only that portion of the current in phase with the voltage. The basic unit of electrical power is the watt, the amount of power used when one ampere of current is forced through an electrical load under a pressure of one volt. One mechanical horsepower is equal to 746 watts of electrical power.

power (exponent). A shorthand method of indicating how many times a number, called the base, is multiplied by itself. For example, in the number 43, 3 is the power, or exponent, and 4 is the base. That is, 43 is equal to $4 \times 4 \times 4 = 64$.

power (mechanical). The time rate of doing work. Power is found by dividing the amount of work done, measured in foot-pounds, by the time in seconds or minutes used to do the work.

$$\text{Power} = \frac{\text{Force} \cdot \text{Distance}}{\text{Time}}$$

Power can be expressed in terms of foot-pounds of work per minute, horsepower, or watts. One horsepower is equal to 33,000 foot-pounds of work per minute, 550 foot-pounds of work per second, or 746 watts. One metric horsepower is equal to 75 meter-kilograms of work per second or 0.9863 English horsepower.

power amplifier (electronic circuit). An electronic amplifier designed to produce a gain in power (the product of current and voltage), rather than just voltage.

power assurance check (gas turbine engine maintenance check). A test run made of a gas turbine engine to determine the way its performance compares with its performance when it was new or freshly overhauled.

power brake control valve (aircraft brake system component). The valve operated by the pilot of a large aircraft to meter hydraulic system pressure into the brakes to apply them. The power brake control valve meters pressure into the brake cylinders proportional to the amount of force the pilot exerts on the brake pedals.

power brakes. Aircraft brakes that use the main hydraulic system to supply fluid for the brake actuation. Aircraft that require a large amount of fluid for their brake actuation normally use power brakes, and the volume of fluid sent to the brakes is increased by the use of deboosters. *See* debooster.

power control system (aircraft flight control system). A type of control system in which normal operation of the flight controls causes hydraulic or pneumatic actuators to assist in moving the control surfaces. This reduces the force needed by the pilot. An irreversible power control system is a type of system that does not allow forces on the flight control surfaces to be fed back to the cockpit control.

power control valve (hydraulic system component). A hand-operated hydraulic pump unloading valve. When the valve is open, fluid flows from the pump to the reservoir with little opposition. To actuate a unit, the selector valve is turned to select the desired actuation and the power control valve is manually closed. Pressurized fluid flows to the unit, and when actuation is completed, the power control valve automatically opens.

power density (radar meteorology). The amount of radiated energy per unit cross-sectional area in a radar beam.

powered-lift. *14 CFR Part 1:* "A heavier-than-air aircraft capable of vertical takeoff, vertical landing, and low speed flight that depends principally on engine-driven lift devices or engine thrust for lift during these flight regimes and on nonrotating airfoil(s) for lift during horizontal flight."

powered parachute. *14 CFR Part 1:* "A powered aircraft comprised of a flexible or semi-rigid wing connected to a fuselage so that the wing is not in position for flight until the aircraft is in motion. The fuselage of a powered parachute contains the aircraft engine, a seat for each occupant and is attached to the aircraft's landing gear."

P

power-enrichment system (fuel metering system). A subsystem in a carburetor or fuel injection system used on a reciprocating engine. This system enriches the fuel-air mixture when the engine is operating at full power. The mixture ratio used for cruise power is adjusted to give the most economical operation, but when the engine develops full power, enough heat is released to cause damage. The power enrichment system meters additional fuel when the throttle is wide open. This fuel absorbs the excess heat. A power-enrichment system is also called an economizer system.

power factor (electrical value). The ratio of the actual power to the apparent power in an alternating current circuit. Actual power, measured by a wattmeter, is the product of the circuit voltage and only that portion of the current in phase with the voltage. Apparent power is the product of the circuit voltage and the total circuit current. Power factor is also the ratio of the circuit resistance to the circuit impedance, and is the cosine of the phase angle.

power frequencies (electrical power). The frequency of alternating current used to provide electrical power. In the United States, 60 hertz is the most commonly used power frequency. In other parts of the world, 50-hertz AC is used. Aircraft AC electrical systems use 400 hertz as the power frequency.

power lever (turbine engine control). The lever used to actuate the fuel control unit on an aircraft turbine engine. The power lever programs the unit to supply the amount of fuel needed for the operation called for by the pilot. The fuel control delivers this fuel only when all of the conditions in the engine are such that allow it to take the fuel without stalling or flaming out.

power loading (aircraft performance). The ratio found by dividing the maximum weight of the aircraft by the brake horsepower produced by all the engines.

power of a number (mathematics). The number of times a number is multiplied by itself. The power is indicated by an exponent, a small superscript number such as the 3 in 4^3. For example, $4^3 = 64$. This is the same as $4 \cdot 4 \cdot 4 = 64$.

power-off accuracy approaches (flight training maneuver). Approaches and landings made by gliding with the engine idling, through a specific pattern to a touchdown beyond and within 200 feet of a designated line or mark on the runway. The objective is to instill in the pilot the judgment and procedures necessary for accurately flying the airplane, without power, to a safe landing.

power overlap (reciprocating engine parameter). The number of degrees of crankshaft rotation during which more than one cylinder is on its power stroke.

powerplant (aircraft component). The complete installation of an aircraft engine, propeller, and all accessories needed for its proper functioning.

powerplant rating (FAA rating). The rating associated with an FAA-issued aircraft mechanic license that allows the holder to inspect, repair, and maintain the engine and propeller of an FAA-certificated aircraft.

power recovery turbine (reciprocating engines). A small turbine installed in the exhaust system of a reciprocating engine. Its purpose is to extract some of the energy from the exhaust gas that would otherwise be lost. The output shaft of the turbine is coupled through a hydraulic clutch to the engine crankshaft.

power section (reciprocating engine component). The section of the crankcase of a radial engine to which the cylinders are attached.

powers of ten (mathematics). A handy mathematical tool in which very large and very small numbers are changed to numbers between 1 and 10 with a superscript (exponent) to show the number of places to move the decimal point. Powers of ten is another name for scientific notation. Numbers greater than 1 have a positive exponent, and numbers smaller than 1 have a negative exponent.

powers of ten (mathematics). *Continued*

$$10^0 = 1$$
$$10^1 = 10$$
$$10^2 = 100$$
$$10^3 = 1,000$$
$$10^4 = 10,000$$
$$10^5 = 100,000$$
$$10^6 = 1,000,000$$

power stroke (reciprocating engine operation). The stroke in the operating cycle of a reciprocating engine in which both of the valves are closed, the fuel-air mixture has been ignited and burned, and the piston is being forced downward by the expanding gases. Work is done in a reciprocating engine only during the power stroke.

power supply (electrical component). A circuit or device that changes alternating current at the power-line voltage into direct current of the required voltage. Many power supplies include a voltage regulator circuit that holds the output voltage constant as the load current changes.

power transformer (electrical component). The transformer in an electrical power supply that changes the line voltage into the voltages needed for the circuits using the power supply.

PPC. Powered parachute.

PPI (plan position indicator). A radar indicator in which the returns from the targets appear as bright spots at the locations they would have on a circular or fan-shaped map of the area being scanned. The range of the target is indicated by the distance of the spot from the center of the scope, and the bearing of the target is indicated by the radial angle between the spot and a vertical reference line. Some radar antenna rotate, and their PPI scopes are circular. Other antenna oscillate, and their PPI scopes are fan shaped.

power stroke

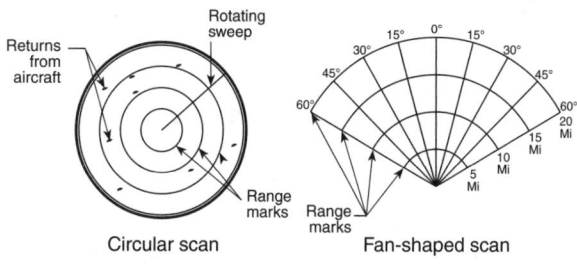

plan position indicator

practical exam (flight test). The "driver's test" a new pilot takes in the airplane to earn a pilot certificate. Also known as a "checkride."

practical slip limit. The maximum slip an aircraft is capable of performing due to rudder travel limits.

practical test standards (PTS). An FAA published list of standards that must be met for the issuance of a particular pilot certificate or rating. FAA inspectors and designated pilot examiners use these standards when conducting pilot practical tests and flight instructors should use the PTS while preparing applicants for practical tests.

practice instrument approach (air traffic control). An instrument approach procedure conducted by a VFR or an IFR aircraft for the purpose of pilot training or proficiency demonstrations.

praseodymium. A soft, silvery, malleable, ductile, rare-earth, metallic chemical element. Praseodymium's symbol is Pr, its atomic number is 59, and its atomic weight is 140.91. Praseodymium is used in the manufacture of colored glass and as an alloy with other metals.

Pratt truss. A type of truss structure in which the longitudinal members are separated by vertical members that carry only compression loads, and diagonal members that carry only tensile loads. Most fabric-covered airplane wings are built with a Pratt truss. The wing spars are the main structural members, the compression struts or compression ribs carry only compressive loads, and the drag and anti-drag wires carry only tensile loads.

preamplifier (electronic circuit). An electronic circuit that amplifies an extremely weak input signal to a value strong enough to be used in other amplifiers. Preamplifiers used in some sound systems have provisions for mixing inputs from more than one microphone and for equalizing the sounds by amplifying some frequencies more than others.

prearranged coordination (air traffic control). A facility's standardized procedure that describes the process by which one controller allows an aircraft to penetrate or transit another controller's airspace in a manner that ensures standard separation without individual coordination for each aircraft.

precession (gyroscopic characteristic). One of the two basic characteristics of a gyroscope. The other basic characteristic is rigidity in space. Precession causes a force applied to a spinning gyroscope to be felt, not at the point the force is applied, but at a point 90° in the direction of rotation from that point.

precious metal. Metals that are valuable because they are scarce. Gold, silver, and platinum are examples of precious metals.

precipitable water (meteorology). The amount of liquid precipitation that would result if all water vapor in a sample of air were condensed.

precipitation (meteorology). Any or all forms of water particles, whether liquid or solid, that fall from the atmosphere and reach the surface. Precipitation is a major class of hydrometeor and is distinguished from cloud and virga in that it reaches the surface.

precipitation fog (meteorology). This fog forms as precipitation falls into drier air below the cloud and the liquid droplets evaporate into water vapor. The water vapor cools and at dew point, it condenses and fog forms.

precipitation heat treatment. A method of increasing the strength of heat-treated aluminum alloy. After the aluminum alloy has been solution-heat-treated by heating and quenching, it is returned to the oven and heated to a temperature lower than that used for the initial heat treatment. It is held at this temperature for a specified period of time and then removed from the oven and allowed to cool slowly. Precipitation heat treatment is also known as artificial aging.

precipitation-induced downdraft (meteorology). Downdrafts that are the result of precipitation beginning which drags the air downward, causing a downdraft.

precipitation intensity. *See* precipitation radar weather descriptions.

precipitation radar weather descriptions (air traffic control). The precipitation intensity descriptors a controller provides to pilots when interpreting radar weather returns. When the intensity levels can be determined, they are described as: LIGHT (< 30 dBZ), MODERATE (30 to 40 dBZ), HEAVY (> 40 to 50 dBZ), or EXTREME (> 50 dBZ). Controllers issue (where the capability exists) radar-observed precipitation intensity when using a weather and radar processor (WARP), or ground-based digital radars with weather capabilities. When precipitation intensity information is not available, the intensity will be described as UNKNOWN.

All weather areas displayed on ATC radar are referred to as "precipitation" because even though some systems can estimate levels of intensity, the type of precipitation (whether rain, hail, or snow) cannot be detected by radar. Furthermore, existing radar systems cannot detect turbulence, but there is a direct correlation between the degree of turbulence as well as other weather features associated with thunderstorms and the displayed weather radar precipitation intensity.

precipitation static (radio interference). A form of radio interference caused by rain, snow, or dust particles hitting the antenna and inducing a small radio-frequency voltage into it.

precision approach. *14 CFR Part 1:* "A standard instrument approach procedure in which an electronic glide slope is provided, such as ILS and PAR."

precision approach path indicator (PAPI). Similar to the VASI but consisting of one row of lights in two- or four-light systems. A pilot on the correct glide slope will see two white lights and two red lights. *See* visual approach slope indicator.

precision approach procedure. A standard instrument approach procedure in which an electronic glideslope/glidepath is provided; e.g., ILS, MLS, and PAR.

precision approach radar. *See* PAR.

precision approach radar (ICAO). Primary radar equipment used to determine the position of an aircraft during final approach, in terms of lateral and vertical deviations relative to a nominal approach path, and in range relative to touchdown.

precision obstacle free zone (POFZ). An 800-foot-wide by 200-foot-long area centered on the runway centerline adjacent to the threshold designed to protect aircraft flying precision approaches from ground vehicles and other aircraft when ceiling is less than 250 feet, or visibility is less than $\frac{3}{4}$ statute mile (or runway visual range is below 4,000 feet).

precision runway monitor (PRM). Provides air traffic controllers with high precision secondary surveillance data for aircraft on final approach to parallel runways that have extended centerlines separated by less than 4,300 feet. High resolution color monitoring displays are required to present surveillance track data to controllers along with detailed maps depicting approaches and no transgression zone.

precision switch (electrical component). A snap-action switch that requires a very small amount of movement for its actuation. The amount of movement needed is the same each time the switch is actuated. Precision switches are used in position-indicating circuits and as limit switches to start or stop an action any time a mechanical device reaches a specific position.

pre-departure clearance (PDC). An application with the Terminal Data Link System that provides clearance information to subscribers, through a service provider, in text to the cockpit or gate printer.

predictive wind shear (PWS) alert system. A self-contained system used onboard some aircraft to alert the flight crew to the presence of potential wind shear. PWS systems typically monitor 3 miles ahead and 25 degrees left and right of the aircraft's heading at or below 1,200 feet AGL. Departing flights may receive a wind shear alert after they start the takeoff roll and may elect to abort the takeoff. Aircraft on approach receiving an alert may elect to go around or perform a wind shear escape maneuver.

predrilling (sheet metal fabrication). The use of small holes drilled in sheet metal parts to locate rivet holes. Replacement skin panels purchased from an aircraft manufacturer have all the rivet holes predrilled in all of the proper locations with holes smaller than that needed for the rivet. The replacement panel is put place and a drill of the correct size for the rivet is passed through the hole in the original skin and through the predrilled hole in the new skin.

P

preferential departure route (PDR). A specific departure route from an airport or terminal area to an en route point where there is no further need for flow control. It may be included in an instrument departure procedure or a preferred IFR route.

preferential routes (air traffic control). Preferential routes are adapted in ARTCC computers to accomplish inter/intrafacility controller coordination and to ensure that flight data is posted at the proper control positions.

Locations having a need for these specific inbound and outbound routes normally publish such routes in local facility bulletins, and their use by pilots minimizes flight plan route amendments. When the workload or traffic situation permits, controllers normally provide radar vectors or assign requested routes to minimize circuitous routing. Preferential routes are usually confined to one ARTCCs area and are referred to by the following names or acronyms:
• Preferential departure route (PDR).
• Preferential arrival route (PAR).
• Preferential departure and arrival route (PDAR).

preferred IFR routes (air traffic control). Routes established between busier airports to increase system efficiency and capacity. Preferred IFR routes normally extend through one or more ARTCC areas and are designed to achieve balanced traffic flows among high density terminals. IFR clearances are issued on the basis of these routes except when severe weather avoidance procedures or other factors dictate otherwise. Preferred IFR routes are listed in the Airport/Facility Directory.

If a flight is planned to or from an area having such routes but the departure or arrival point is not listed in the A/FD, pilots may use that part of the preferred IFR route which is appropriate for the departure or arrival point that is listed. Preferred IFR routes are correlated with SIDs and STARs and may be defined by airways, jet routes, direct routes between NAVAIDs, waypoints, NAVAID radials/DME, or any combination of these items. *See* SID, STAR.

preferred runway. When there is no active runway, the preferred runway is considered to be the most suitable operational runway taking into account such factors as: the runway most nearly aligned with the wind; noise abatement or other restrictions which prohibit the use of certain runways; ground traffic and runway conditions.

preferred values (electrical components). A series of values for resistors and capacitors, selected by the Electronic Industries Association (EIA) and the military services. The steps between the values are chosen, so the difference between any two steps is essentially the same percentage as the difference between any other two steps. The use of preferred values allows the most complete coverage of the needed values, with a minimum number of components.

preflight inspection (aircraft inspection). An inspection of an aircraft performed by the pilot or flight engineer before the aircraft is approved for flight. The purpose of a preflight inspection is to assure that the aircraft is in a safe condition for the flight being proposed.

preformed cable (aircraft control cable). A type of steel cable used in aircraft control systems. Preformed cable is made up of seven bundles (strands) of wires wound together to form the complete cable. Each strand is formed into a spiral (preformed) before the cable is wound. Because each strand is preformed, the cable does not spread out when it is cut.

preheating (engine operation). The heating of an aircraft engine, battery and cockpit instruments prior to start up in cold weather operations.

preignition (reciprocating engine malfunction). Ignition of the fuel-air mixture inside the cylinder of an engine before the normal spark occurs. Preignition can be caused by an incandescent piece of carbon or by any other sharp edge or point inside the cylinder that gets red-hot.

preoiling (engine installation). A step in the installation of a new or overhauled engine in an aircraft. Lubricating oil is pumped through the oil passages in the engine, so all the bearing surfaces will be flooded with oil when the engine starts.

preparation (in teaching/learning process). The first step of the teaching process, consisting of determining the lesson's scope, objectives, and goals to be attained. This portion also includes making certain all necessary supplies are on hand. When using the telling-and-doing technique of flight instruction, this step is accomplished prior to the flight lesson.

prepreg (preimpregnated fabric). A type of composite material in which the reinforcing fibers are encapsulated in an uncured resin. Prepreg must be kept refrigerated to prevent the resin curing before it is used. Prepreg materials are cut to size and shape and laid up with the correct ply orientation, and the entire component is cured with heat and pressure.

preprogrammed course reversal. A course reversal (commonly called a "procedure turn") that appears as part of an instrument approach procedure that has been loaded into the FMS/RNAV. Many FMS/RNAV units automatically attempt to perform the course reversal procedure when it is encountered. Others require the pilot to manually navigate the depicted procedural track or to use the heading mode to fly the depicted track.

preprogrammed holding pattern (preprogrammed hold). A hold that is published as part of an instrument procedure (e.g., approach, missed approach) that has been loaded into the FMS/RNAV. Some FMS/RNAV units automatically enter and fly the holding procedure when it is encountered. Others must be flown around the depicted holding pattern, usually by changing the heading (bug). Some units require switching to the nonsequencing (OBS) mode so the active waypoint remains set to the designated holding fix.

prerotation (gyroplane operation). The spinning of the rotor to a sufficient rpm prior to flight.

presentation (in teaching/learning process). The second step of the teaching process, which consists of delivering information or demonstrating the skills that make up the lesson. The delivery could be by either the lecture method or demonstration-performance method. In the telling-and-doing technique of flight instruction, this is the segment in which the instructor both talks about and performs the procedure.

press brake (production sheet-metal tool). A form of sheet-metal bending tool in which a long, straight male die whose bottom edge has the correct bend radius is pressed down onto a sheet of metal placed over a female die containing a long V-shaped groove. The male die is usually forced down by energy stored in a large flywheel.

press fit. An interference fit between machine parts. The hole into which a part is to fit is slightly smaller than the part itself, and the two can be assembled only by pushing the part into the hole with a press.

press-to-test light (indicator light). A type of indicator light used in an aircraft. The bulb may be tested by pressing on the top of the light fixture to complete a circuit to ground. If the bulb is good, the light will illuminate.

pressure. A measure of force applied uniformly over a given unit of surface area. Pressure is normally expressed in such terms as pounds per square inch or grams per square centimeter.

pressure altimeter. Another name for a pneumatic altimeter. *See* pneumatic altimeter.

pressure altitude. The altitude in standard atmosphere at which the pressure is the same as the existing pressure. Because a pneumatic altimeter operates solely on pressure, pressure altitude is the uncorrected altitude indicated by an altimeter when its barometric scale is adjusted to standard sea-level pressure of 29.92 inches of mercury, or 1013.2 millibars.

pressure carburetor (reciprocating engine component). A fuel metering device that meters fuel to a reciprocating engine on the basis of the mass of air flowing into the engine. The pressure forcing the fuel through the metering jet is determined by the difference between two air-metering forces: the low pressure produced at the throat of a venturi, and the high pressure of the air as it rams into the carburetor. These two air pressures act on a diaphragm to control a fuel pressure regulating system that varies the pressure drop across the fuel metering jet as a function of the mass of air flowing into the engine.

pressure casting. A method of casting metal parts in which molten or plastic metal is forced into permanent molds under pressure.

pressure cooling (reciprocating engine cooling). A method of air-cooling an engine in which the cylinders are enclosed in tight-fitting shrouds. The cowling is divided into two compartments by baffles and seals, with half of each cylinder in each compartment. Ram air is directed into one compartment, and the pressure in the other is decreased by air flowing over a flared exit or adjustable cowl flaps. The pressure difference across the cylinders causes cooling air to be drawn through the fins to remove the unwanted heat.

pressure-demand oxygen system. A type of oxygen system used by aircraft that fly at very high altitude. This system functions as a diluter-demand system below about 40,000 feet. Above this altitude, the regulator furnishes the mask with 100% oxygen under pressure to force the oxygen into the lungs, rather than depending on the low pressure produced when the wearer of the mask inhales to pull in the oxygen. *See* diluter-demand oxygen system.

pressure-fed spray gun (paint spraying device). A paint spray gun in which the material being sprayed is fed to the gun under pressure from a pressure pot or pressure cup. Pressure-fed spray guns are used when a large quantity of material is to be sprayed, or when the material is too heavy or too viscous to be picked up by a suction-fed spray gun.

pressure fueling (aircraft fueling). The method of fueling used by almost all transport aircraft. The fuel is put into the aircraft through a single underwing fueling port. The fuel tanks are filled to the desired quantity and in the sequence selected by the person conducting the fueling operation. Pressure fueling saves servicing time by using a single point to fuel the entire aircraft, and it reduces the chances for fuel contamination.

pressure gradient (meteorology). The rate of decrease of pressure per unit distance at a fixed time.

pressure gradient force (meteorology). Pressure differences that create a force which drives the wind.

pressure-injection carburetor (reciprocating engine fuel metering device). A multibarrel pressure carburetor used on large radial and V-engines. The fuel is metered on the basis of the mass of the air flowing into the engine and is sprayed under pressure into the eye, or center, of the internal supercharger impeller.

pressure jump (meteorology). A sudden significant increase in station pressure.

pressure manifold (fluid power system component). The portion of a fluid power system from which the selector valves receive their pressurized fluid.

pressure plate (aircraft disk brake component). A strong, heavy plate used in multiple-disk brakes that receives the force from the brake cylinders and changes it into a squeezing action on the brake disks to produce the friction that slows the aircraft when the brakes are applied.

pressure pot (paint spray equipment). A container that holds the paint material to be sprayed under a controlled air pressure. The material is forced by the air pressure to the spray gun, where it is mixed with atomizing air and sprayed onto the surface being painted.

pressure ratio controller (turbosupercharger control). The control in a turbosuper-charger system that works in parallel with the absolute pressure controller to maintain a specified upper deck pressure after the engine has reached its critical altitude.

pressure reducing valve (fluid power system component). A valve in a fluid power system that reduces the pressure of a liquid or gas from a high value to a fixed lower value.

pressure regulator (fluid power system component). A control valve in a fluid power system that reduces the pressure of a liquid or gas from a high value to a lower value that can be adjusted by the operator. After being set, the output pressure remains constant as the input pressure changes, within limits.

pressure relief valve (fluid power system component). A valve that relieves all pressure above a given amount. In a hydraulic system, the pressure is relieved back to the inlet side of the pump, and in a pneumatic system, it is relieved to the outside air.

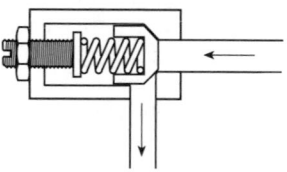

pressure relief valve (oxygen system component). A valve in an oxygen system that relieves the pressure if the pressure reducing valve should fail.

pressure relief valve

pressure switch. A switch used to turn an electrical device on or off when a specified fluid pressure is reached. Some hydraulic systems have a pressure switch that senses the hydraulic system pressure. When the pressure drops to a low value, called the cut-in pressure, the switch closes and turns the hydraulic pump on. When the pump brings the pressure up to a higher value, called the cut-out pressure, the pressure switch turns the pump off.

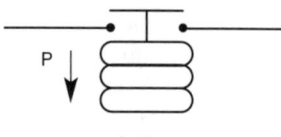

pressure switch

pressure transducer. A type of pressure measuring device that produces an electrical signal proportional to the pressure being measured.

pressure vessel (aircraft structure). The portion of the structure of a pressurized aircraft that is sealed and pressurized in flight. Normally, only the area housing the occupants and some of the baggage areas are included in the pressure vessel.

pressurization. A form of climate control of an aircraft. An air compressor increases the pressure of the air inside the cabin of a high-flying aircraft to a value that allows the occupants to breathe normally. Without pressurization, supplemental oxygen would be needed when flying above an altitude of about 10,000 feet.

pressurization controller (cabin pressurization system component). The component in a cabin pressurization system that allows the flight crew to select the desired cabin altitude and cabin rate of climb. The cabin altitude increases until the maximum allowable pressure differential between cabin and ambient pressure is reached, then the controller maintains this differential as the aircraft altitude continues to increase.

pressurized aircraft. An aircraft in which the cabin area is sealed off and pressurized with air from a cabin supercharger. Passengers and crew need supplemental oxygen when the air pressure gets much below that found at an altitude of about 10,000 feet.

To preclude the need of supplemental oxygen when flying at high altitude, the air pressure in the cabin can be increased to a pressure that compares with an altitude of about six to eight thousand feet. Humans are comfortable at this pressure.

pressurized ignition system (aircraft reciprocating engine). A type of ignition system used on reciprocating engines of aircraft that fly at high altitude. The low air pressure at high altitude allows the high voltage inside an unpressurized distributor to jump to the wrong electrode. To prevent this, the distributor can be pressurized with compressed air from the engine supercharger. This higher-density air is a good enough insulator to prevent the high voltage from jumping to the wrong electrode.

pressurizing and dump valve (turbine engine fuel system component). A valve used in a turbine engine fuel system equipped with duplex fuel nozzles. When the demand for fuel is low, fuel flows through the primary manifold, but when the demand is high, the pressurizing valve opens and directs fuel into the secondary fuel manifold as well. When the engine is shut down, the dump valve drains the fuel from the manifolds. *See* duplex fuel nozzles.

prestretching (control cable manufacturing process). A step in the manufacture of aircraft control cable assemblies. After the terminals are installed on the cables, a load of 60% of the cable breaking strength is applied and held for a specified length of time. Prestretching prepares the cable for installation in the aircraft.

pretest (psychology). A criterion-referenced test constructed to measure the knowledge and skills that are necessary to begin the course. Pretests also may be used to determine the student's current level of knowledge and skill in relation to the material that will be presented in the course. The pretest measures whether or not the student has the prerequisite knowledge and skills necessary to proceed with the course of instruction.

prevailing easterlies (meteorology). The broad current or pattern of persistent easterly winds in the tropics and in polar regions.

prevailing torque. The torque required to turn a threaded fastener before it contacts the surface it is intended to hold.

prevailing visibility (meteorology). The greatest horizontal visibility which is equaled or exceeded throughout half of the horizon circle. The half of the horizon circle need not be a continuous half.

prevailing westerlies (meteorology). The dominant west-to-east motion of the atmosphere, centered over the middle latitudes of both hemispheres.

prevailing wind (meteorology). The direction from which the wind blows most frequently.

preventive maintenance. Maintenance procedures followed to keep a piece of equipment working properly. Changing the oil, cleaning the spark plugs, cleaning the fuel and oil strainers, and checking or replacing hose connections are examples of reciprocating engine preventive maintenance. *14 CFR Part 1:* "Simple or minor preservation operations and the replacement of small standard parts not involving complex assembly operations."

prick punch. A sharp-pointed punch used to mark a location when laying out metal parts. A prick punch makes only a small mark on the surface of the metal, just large enough to accurately position a center punch.

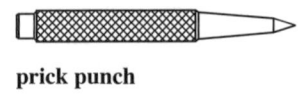

prick punch

primacy. A principle of learning in which the first experience of something often creates a strong, almost unshakable impression. The importance to an instructor is that the first time something is demonstrated, it must be shown correctly since that experience is the one most likely to be remembered by the student.

primary air (gas turbine engine). The air that flows through the combustors of a gas turbine engine and is used in the combustion process.

primary and supporting (flight instrument classification). A method of attitude instrument flying using the instrument that provides the most direct indication of attitude and performance.

primary cell (electrochemical cell). An electrochemical cell that changes chemical energy into electrical energy. A primary cell cannot be recharged, and it must be replaced when it becomes discharged. A carbon-zinc battery, such as used in a flashlight, is an example of a primary cell.

primary circuit (magneto ignition system). The circuit in a magneto ignition system in which the primary current flows. Primary current is produced when lines of flux from the rotating magnet cut across the turns of wire in the primary winding of the magneto coil. At the instant the primary current is greatest, a set of breaker points opens the circuit and the flow stops immediately. The magnetic field caused by the primary current collapses, cuts across the many turns of wire in the secondary winding of the coil, which is wound around the primary winding, and induces a high voltage in it.

The primary circuit includes the primary winding of the coil, the breaker points, a condenser, and an ignition switch. The breaker points, condenser, and switch are in parallel with each other and in series with the coil.

primary flight controls (aircraft controls). The flight controls that cause an aircraft to rotate about its three axes. In an airplane, the primary flight controls are the ailerons, elevators, and rudder.

primary flight display (PFD). A computer screen (LCD or CRT) that electronically displays flight information. The PFD replaces the round dial altimeter, airspeed indicator, attitude gyro, heading indicator, vertical speed indicator, and turn coordinator.

primary frequency (radio communications). The radio frequency assigned to an aircraft as a first choice for air-ground communication.

primary fuel (gas turbine engine). Fuel that flows from the nozzles in a gas turbine engine under conditions of low airflow.

primary instruments (flight instrument classification). The instruments that provide the most pertinent and essential information during a flight.

primary radar. Radar in which the beam from the transmitter bounces off a target and is returned to the same antenna and directed to the receiver.

primary radar target. An analog or digital target, exclusive of a secondary radar target, presented on a radar display.

primary structure (aircraft structure). The portion of the structure of an aircraft that would seriously disable the aircraft if it were to fail. The primary structure includes such items as the wings, controls, and engine mounts.

primary wave (meteorology). The first wave crest of a mountain wave system. It features a roll or rotor cloud with one or more lenticulars above.

primary winding (ignition system component). The winding in a magneto or ignition coil between the source of voltage and the breaker points. The primary winding is normally made of comparatively large diameter wire and has a small number of turns, typically about 200.

primary winding (transformer winding). The winding of a transformer connected across the power line. The primary winding is the input winding.

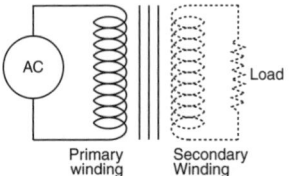

primary winding transformer

primer (finishing system component). A component in a finishing system that provides a good bond between the surface and the material used for the topcoats.

primer (reciprocating engine component). A small, hand-operated pump, used to spray gasoline into the induction system for starting the engine.

primer-surfacer (finishing system component). A type of primer used in a finishing system to provide a good bond between the surface and the topcoat material. A primer-surfacer has enough body to be sanded smooth to cover minor roughness of the surface being finished.

priming pump (fuel system component). A small hand-operated pump, normally mounted on the instrument panel, that allows the pilot to pump a small amount of gasoline directly into the intake manifold near the cylinder heads. This provides a rich mixture for starting the engine.

principal base of operations. The primary operating location of a certificate holder as established by the certificate holder.

Principal Maintenance Inspector (PMI). The FAA inspector responsible for overseeing all maintenance issues relative to a specific operator, to include input on training programs, OpSpecs, MEL requests, etc.

principal operations inspector (POI). A person assigned to scheduled air carriers and operators for compensation or hire to work directly with the companies to coordinate FAA operating approval.

printed circuit (PC). An electrical circuit in which the conductors joining the components are made of conductive strips bonded onto the surface of an insulating board. A thin sheet of copper or other conducting material is bonded to a sheet of fiberglass-reinforced resin, and the desired pattern of conductors is drawn on the copper. All of the unwanted copper is chemically etched away, and only the desired conductors are left. The component leads are assembled through holes in the PC board and soldered to the copper conductors. PCs have almost completely replaced the older point-to-point wired circuits.

print tolerance (aircraft drawings). A general tolerance that can be applied to parts where the dimensions are not critical. Where a tolerance is not shown on a dimension line, the print tolerance applies.

priority valve (fluid power system component). A type of flow-control valve used in a fluid power system that causes the components to operate in the correct sequence. Priority valves are used in an aircraft hydraulic system to cause the landing gear doors to open fully before the uplocks release the landing gear.

private airport. An airport that is privately owned and not available for use by the public without prior permission. Private airports are depicted on aeronautical charts for emergency and landmark purposes.

private pilot. A pilot who has completed the FAA's requirements for the private pilot certificate, including a minimum of 40 hours of flight time, passing a knowledge exam, and flight test or check ride.

PRM (precision runway monitor) (air traffic control). A monitor that provides air traffic controllers with high-precision secondary surveillance data for aircraft on final approach to closely spaced parallel runways. High-resolution color monitoring displays present surveillance track data to controllers, along with detailed maps depicting approaches and the no transgression zone.

problem-based learning. Learning accomplished through lessons that present problems encountered in real life, which forces students to reach real-world solutions.

procedure turn (air traffic control). The maneuver prescribed when it is necessary to reverse direction to establish an aircraft on the intermediate approach segment or final approach course. The outbound course, direction of turn, distance within which the turn must be completed, and minimum altitude are specified in the procedure. However, unless otherwise restricted, the point at which the turn may be commenced and the type and rate of turn are left to the discretion of the pilot.

procedure turn (ICAO). A maneuver in which a turn is made away from a designated track followed by a turn in the opposite direction to permit the aircraft to intercept and proceed along the reciprocal of the designated track.

procedure turn inbound. The point of a procedure turn maneuver at which course reversal has been completed and an aircraft is established inbound on the intermediate approach segment or final approach course. A report of "procedure turn inbound" is normally used by ATC as a position report for separation purposes.

process annealing (metal heat treating). An annealing process used to treat work-hardened parts made out of low-carbon steels (<0.25% carbon). This makes the parts soft enough to undergo further cold working without fracturing.

product (mathematics). The answer in a multiplication problem.

Production Certificate. A certificate issued under 14 CFR Part 21 that allows a certain certificated aircraft, aircraft engine, or appliance to be manufactured by the specified facility.

profile descent (air traffic control). An uninterrupted descent (except where level flight is required for speed adjustment; e.g., 250 knots at 10,000 feet MSL) from cruising altitude or flight level to the interception of a glideslope or to a minimum altitude specified for the initial or intermediate approach segment of a nonprecision instrument approach. The profile descent normally terminates at the approach gate where the glideslope or other appropriate minimum altitude is intercepted.

profile drag (aerodynamic drag). Aerodynamic drag caused by friction between the air and the surfaces of an aircraft over which it is flowing. Profile drag is one of the forms of parasite drag.

profile tip (turbine engine compressor blade tip). An axial-flow compressor blade whose tip thickness is reduced to give it a higher resonant frequency so it will not be subject to the vibrations that would affect a blade with a squared tip. The profile tip also provides a more aerodynamically efficient shape for the high-velocity air that is moved by the blade. Profile tips often touch the housing and make a squealing noise as the engine is shut down. For this reason, profile tips are sometimes called squealer tips.

profile view. Side view of an IAP chart illustrating the vertical approach path altitudes, headings, distances, and fixes.

profilometer. A precision measuring instrument used to measure the depth of the hone marks in the surface of an aircraft engine cylinder wall.

prognostic chart (meteorology). A chart showing expected or forecast weather conditions. Prognostic charts are generally referred to as prog charts.

program (computer operation). A series of step-by-step instructions that tells a computer exactly how it is to receive data, store it, process it, and deliver it to the user.

program flowchart (computer operation). A chart of the steps taken in the execution of a program by a computer. Symbols are used in the flowchart to show the beginning and the end of the program, data input and output points, and decision points.

programmable calculator. An electronic calculator controlled by a program stored in its memory. A programmable calculator is a versatile instrument that allows the use of different programs to solve many different types of problems.

programmable read-only memory. *See* PROM.

progressive inspection (aircraft maintenance inspection). An inspection that may be used in place of an annual or 100-hour inspection. It has the same scope as an annual inspection, but it may be performed in increments so the aircraft does not have to be out of service for a lengthy period of time.

progressive taxi (air traffic control). Precise taxi instructions given to a pilot unfamiliar with the airport or issued in stages as the aircraft proceeds along the taxi route.

prohibited area. *14 CFR Part 1:* "Designated airspace within which flight of aircraft is prohibited."

PROM (programmable read-only memory). An integrated circuit memory device for a digital computer. Read-only memory is stored in PROM as a series of logic zeros and ones, by burning out certain diodes in it. Once the PROM is programmed, it cannot be changed. There is an erasable, programmable read-only memory (EPROM) that can be erased by exposing it to ultraviolet light. It can then be reprogrammed by using a special programmer.

promethium. A radioactive, rare-earth chemical element used as a source of beta rays. Promethium's symbol is Pm, its atomic number is 61, and the mass number of its most stable isotope is 145.

prominent obstacle. An obstacle that (1) stands out beyond the adjacent surface of surrounding terrain and immediately projects a noticeable hazard to aircraft in flight; (2) is not characterized as low and close in, whose height is no less than 300 feet above the departure end of takeoff runway (DER) elevation, is within 10 NM from the DER, and that penetrates that airport/heliport's diverse departure obstacle clearance surface (OCS); and/or (3) is beyond 10 NM from an airport/heliport that requires an obstacle departure procedure (ODP) to ensure obstacle avoidance.

prony brake. An instrument used to measure the amount of horsepower an engine or motor is delivering to its output shaft. The engine is operated at a specified RPM, and a brake is applied to its output shaft. The amount of torque applied to the brake is measured, and this, with the RPM, is converted into brake horsepower. Dynamometers have replaced prony brakes for measuring brake horsepower.

propane. A colorless and odorless gas used as a heat source for hot-air balloons. Ethyl mercaptan is added to propane to give it a detectable odor.

propeller. A rotating airfoil driven by an airplane engine to produce thrust to pull or push an airplane through the air. *14 CFR Part 1:* "A device for propelling an aircraft that has blades on an engine-driven shaft and that, when rotated, produces by its action on the air, a thrust approximately perpendicular to its plane of rotation. It includes control components normally supplied by its manufacturer, but does not include main and auxiliary rotors or rotating airfoils of engines."

propeller anti-icer. A system that spreads a mixture of alcohol and glycerin along the propeller blades when the aircraft is flying in icing conditions. The alcohol and glycerin prevent water reaching the metal of the propeller blade and freezing on it.

propeller blade angle. The angle between the propeller chord and the propeller plane of rotation. It is measured at a specified blade station.

propeller blade tipping (wooden propeller component). Thin sheet metal tipping on the blades of a wooden propeller. The metal reinforces the thin tips and prevents damage to the wood by water, sand, and rocks thrown into the propeller.

propeller blast. The volume of air accelerated behind a propeller-producing thrust.

propeller brake. A friction brake used on some free-turbine turboprop engines to prevent the propeller windmilling in flight after it has been feathered and to prevent it from rotating when the engine is ground idling.

propeller cones. Tapered metal cones placed over a splined propeller shaft to hold the propeller centered on the shaft. A single-piece bronze cone is used as the rear cone and it slips over the shaft and contacts the thrust bearing retainer nut that is screwed onto the propeller shaft. The front cone is a two-piece, chrome-plated steel, matched set. It contains a groove into which a flange on the propeller retaining nut fits. When the retaining nut is tightened, the propeller hub is squeezed between the two cones which centers it on the shaft.

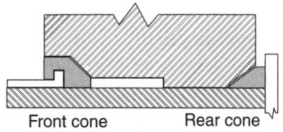

Front cone   Rear cone

propeller cones

propeller effective pitch. The actual distance a propeller moves through the air in one revolution. Effective pitch is the geometric pitch minus the slip. *See* propeller geometric pitch, propeller slip.

propeller efficiency. The ratio of the thrust horsepower produced by the engine-propeller combination to the brake horsepower delivered to the propeller shaft.

propeller end (aircraft engine nomenclature). The end of a reciprocating engine to which the propeller is attached.

propeller geometric pitch. The distance the propeller would move forward in one complete revolution if it were turning in a solid.

propeller hub. The central component of a propeller. It is mounted on the engine propeller shaft and all of the blades are secured in it. The pitch-change mechanism is contained in the hub of a controllable or constant-speed propeller.

propeller lever. The control on a free power turbine turboprop that controls propeller speed and the selection for propeller feathering.

propeller protractor. *See* universal propeller protractor.

propeller/rotor modulation error (helicopter operation). Certain propeller RPM settings or helicopter rotor speeds can cause the VOR course deviation indicator (CDI) to fluctuate as much as ±6°. Slight changes to the RPM setting will normally smooth out this roughness.

P

propeller shaft. The shaft on which the propeller is mounted. On a direct-drive engine, the propeller mounts on the end of the engine crankshaft. On a geared engine, the propeller is mounted on a separate shaft which is part of the reduction gear system.

Before and during World War II tapered shafts were used on most of the smaller engines and splined shafts were used on all of the larger engines. Almost all modern engines except some of the very largest turboprop engines are equipped with flanged propeller shafts.

propeller slip. The difference between the geometric pitch of the propeller and its effective pitch. *See* propeller effective pitch, propeller geometric pitch.

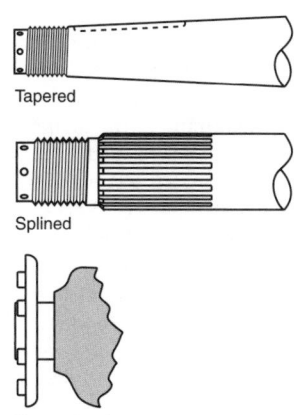

Tapered

Splined

Flanged

propeller shafts

propeller synchronization. The function of keeping the RPM of all the engines in a multiengine aircraft exactly the same. One engine is used as the master engine, and the speed of each of the other engines, called slave engines, is compared to it. The propeller governor on each slave engine is automatically adjusted, to change the pitch of its propeller to maintain an RPM the same as that of the master engine.

propeller thrust. The forward aerodynamic force produced by a propeller as it accelerates a large mass of air rearward.

proper fraction (mathematics). A common fraction in which the numerator is smaller than the denominator.

Propfan engine. The trade name registered by Hamilton Standard for an ultrahigh-bypass turbine engine. *See* UHB engine, and UDF engine.

proportion. A proportion is a statement of equality between two or more ratios. The example of A is to B as C is to D can be represented A:B = C:D or A/B = C/D.

proportional control. A type of control in which the magnitude of the corrective action (the output) is directly proportional to the magnitude of the error (the input signal). An autopilot controls an airplane by proportional control. If a wing drops slightly (the error), the autopilot servo causes the proper aileron movement to smoothly return the aircraft to level flight.

proposed boundary crossing time (PBCT) (ATC term). Each center has a PBCT parameter for each internal airport. Proposed internal flight plans are transmitted to the adjacent center if the flight time along the proposed route from the departure airport to the center boundary is less than or equal to the value of PBCT or if airport adaptation specifies transmission regardless of PBCT.

proposed departure time (air traffic control). The time a scheduled flight will depart the gate for scheduled operators, or the actual runway-off time for nonscheduled operators. For expected departure clearance time (EDCT) purposes, the air traffic control system command center (ATCSCC) adjusts the proposed departure time for scheduled operators to reflect the runway-off time.

propulsive efficiency. A measure of the effectiveness with which an aircraft engine converts the fuel it burns into useful thrust, and is the ratio of the thrust horsepower produced by a propeller to the torque horsepower of the shaft turning the propeller. The more nearly the speed of the aircraft is to the speed of the exhaust jet or propeller wake, the less kinetic energy is lost in the jet or wake, and the higher the propulsive efficiency.

propwash. A commonly used term for the air blown back from an airplane by the propeller.
In the early days of aviation, one of the ways of hazing a fledgling mechanic was to send him across the airport "to get a bucket of propwash."

protactinium. A rare, radioactive chemical element in the actinide group. Protactinium's symbol is Pa, and its atomic number is 91. The most common isotope of protactinium, Pa 231, has a half-life of more than 32,000 years.

protected airspace. The airspace on either side of an oceanic route/track that is equal to one-half the lateral separation minimum except where reduction of protected airspace has been authorized.

proton. The positively charged particles in the nucleus of an atom.

prototype device. A working model of a device usually made by hand. The prototype of an aircraft is built to prove the design or design concept. After all of the design "bugs" are worked out of the prototype, production tooling is set up, and production models are built. The production models are quite similar to, but not exactly like the prototype.

protractor. An instrument used to measure angles.

protruding head rivet (aircraft structural component). An aircraft rivet whose head protrudes, or sticks up, above the surface of the metal it is used to join. The universal head rivet (MS20470) is the most commonly used protruding head rivet in modern aircraft construction.

Universal head   Round head   Flat head

protruding-head rivets

provisional airport. An airport approved by the FAA Administrator for use by a certificate holder for the purpose of providing service to a community when the regular airport used by the certificate holder is not available.

PRT (power recovery turbine). A turbine driven by the exhaust gases from several cylinders of a reciprocating engine. Energy extracted from the exhaust gases by the turbine is coupled, through a fluid clutch, to the engine crankshaft.

Prussian blue dye. A type of industrial dye used to measure the amount of contact between mating parts. One of the surfaces to be mated is given a light coat of Prussian blue dye, and the parts are assembled. During the assembly, one part is moved slightly with respect to the other. The parts are then disassembled, and the amount of dye transferred from one part to the other gives an indication of the amount of physical contact between the two parts.

p-static. *See* precipitation static.

psychrometer (meteorological instrument). An instrument used to measure the amount of water vapor in the air. Two thermometers are used to measure the air temperature. One thermometer has a cloth wick around its sensitive end, and this wick is dipped in water and air is blown across it.

The difference in temperature shown on the wet-bulb thermometer and the dry-bulb thermometer is an indication of the amount of cooling done by the evaporating water. The amount of cooling is inversely proportional to the amount of water vapor in the air.

psychomotor domain (psychology). A grouping of levels of learning associated with physical skill levels which range from perception through set, guided response, mechanism, complex overt response, and adaptation to origination.

P-time. *See* proposed departure time.

PTS. *See* practical test standards.

P-type semiconductor material. A semiconductor material, either silicon or geranium, that has been doped with a few parts per million of an impurity atom having three electrons in its valence shell. Boron, aluminum, gallium, and indium are elements used to dope silicon and germanium to make P-type material.

public aircraft. *14 CFR Part 1:* "Aircraft used only in the service of a government, or a political subdivision. It does not include any government-owned aircraft engaged in carrying persons or property for commercial purposes."

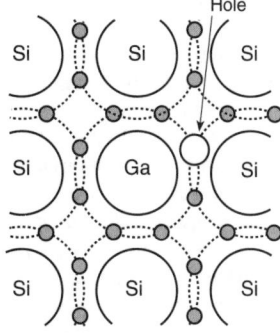

P-type silicon

public aircraft. As per 49 CFR Part 830, an aircraft used only for the U.S. government, or an aircraft owned and operated (except for commercial purposes) or exclusively leased for at least 90 continuous days by a government other than the U.S. government. "Public aircraft" does not include a government-owned aircraft transporting property for commercial purposes nor a government-owned aircraft transporting passengers other than: transporting (for other than commercial purposes) crewmembers or other persons aboard the aircraft whose presence is required to perform, or is associated with the performance of, a governmental function such as firefighting, search and rescue, law enforcement, aeronautical research, or biological or geological resource management; or transporting (for other than commercial purposes) persons aboard the aircraft if the aircraft is operated by the Armed Forces or a U.S. intelligence agency *(see* 49 CFR §830.2*).*

public aircraft operator. An operator that is a government entity or otherwise qualifies for public aircraft operation, according to federal regulations. *See also* public aircraft.

public airport. An airport that is available to the aviation public.

published route. A route for which an IFR altitude has been established and published; e.g., federal airways, jet routes, area navigation routes, specified direct routes.

puckers (composites). Local areas on prepreg where material has blistered and pulled away from the separator film or release paper.

pulley (aircraft control system component). A grooved wheel around which a steel control cable passes. Pulleys are used to change the direction of movement of a control cable.

pull test (aircraft fabric test). A test to measure the strength of the fabric used to cover an aircraft. A strip of fabric exactly one inch wide is cut from the aircraft and all of the dope removed from it. This strip is put into a tensile tester and pulled until it breaks. The number of pounds of pull required to break the strip is the strength of the fabric in pounds per inch.

pull-up resistor (digital electronic device). A resistor used in electronic logic circuits. Pull-up resistors may be found at inputs to logic systems so that a definite logic level is asserted if an external device is disconnected. Pull-up resistors may also be used at the interface between two different types of logic devices, possibly operating at different power supply voltages.

pulsating direct current. A flow of electrons that varies in its rate of flow, but does not change its direction of flow. A rectifier changes alternating current into pulsating direct current.

pulsating DC

pulse (electrical energy). A sudden change in voltage in an electrical circuit, lasting only a short period of time. A pulse can be either an increase or decrease in the voltage, and can be used as a bit of information transmitted in the circuit.

pulse (radar technology). A brief burst of electromagnetic radiation emitted by a radar. A pulse has a very short time duration.

pulse amplifier. A wide-band electrical amplifier used to increase the voltage of a square wave of alternating current or pulsating direct current. An effective pulse amplifier does not change the waveform of square-wave pulses of energy.

pulse counter. An electronic circuit that measures the number of pulses of electrical energy it receives in a given interval of time.

pulse-echo method of ultrasonic inspection. A form of nondestructive inspection used to detect the presence of internal damage or faults in a piece of aircraft structure. Pulses of ultrasonic energy are introduced into the material being inspected, and the time required for these pulses to travel through the material and return to the transducer is measured. If there is a fault in the material, the pulses will bounce off it, rather than traveling all the way to the rear surface of the material. This short travel time indicates the presence of a fault.

pulse generator (electronic test equipment). An electronic device that produces a series of pulses of electrical energy. These pulses have an accurately controlled pulse width, pulse spacing, pulse amplitude, and pulse repetition rate.

pulse-jet engine. A type of air-breathing reaction engine that was used during World War II to power jet-propelled missiles. Fuel is sprayed into the combustion chamber and ignited. The air is thus heated, and as it expands, it closes the one-way shutter valve in the front of the engine and exits the engine through the nozzle at the rear. As soon as the pressure inside the combustion chamber decreases, air enters through the shutter valve and more fuel is ignited. The thrust is produced in a series of pulses.

pulse length (radar technology). The dimension of a radar pulse. It may be expressed as the time duration or the length in linear units. The linear dimension of a pulse is equal to time duration multiplied by the speed of propagation, which is approximately the speed of light.

pultrusion (composites). The process of producing materials for composite components in which the reinforcing fibers are passed through a thermosetting resin, a preshaper, and a die to give the material its final shape.

pumice. A very fine abrasive powder used to polish metal surfaces.

pump control valve (hydraulic system component). A control valve in a hydraulic system that allows the pilot to manually direct the output of the hydraulic pump back to the reservoir when no unit is being actuated.

punch test (aircraft fabric). A test of the strength of aircraft fabric that can be performed on the aircraft with a minimum of damage to the fabric. A special tester with a sharp-pointed, spring-loaded punch is pressed into the fabric, and the amount of force needed for the punch to penetrate the fabric is measured. A punch test does not give a truly accurate indication of the strength of the fabric, but it is sufficiently accurate to tell whether or not the fabric strength is above a minimum value.

Pureclad. A registered trade name for clad aluminum alloy sheets.

purge (air conditioning system maintenance). The maintenance procedure in which all of the moisture and air is removed from a cooling system by flushing the system with a dry gaseous refrigerant.

P

push-button switch (electrical switch). A type of electrical switch actuated by a push button. The button must be pushed each time the switch is to be opened or closed.

pusher configuration. A propeller configuration in which the propeller shaft faces the rear of the aircraft. Thrust produced by the propeller pushes the aircraft, rather than pulling it.

pusher powerplant. A powerplant whose propeller is mounted at the rear of the airplane and pushes, rather than pulls, the airplane through the air.

pusher propeller (aircraft propeller). A propeller installed on an aircraft engine whose propeller shaft faces the rear of the aircraft. Thrust produced by the propeller pushes the aircraft, rather than pulling it.

push fit. A fit between pieces in a mechanical assembly that is close enough to require the parts to be pushed together. A push fit is looser than a press fit, but closer than a free fit.

push-pull amplifier (electronic circuit). A type of electronic amplifier with two output circuits whose output voltages are equal but 180° out of phase with each other. A push-pull amplifier is also called a balanced amplifier.

push-pull rod (aircraft control system component). A stiff rod in an aircraft control system that moves a control surface by either pushing or pulling on it.

pushrod (reciprocating engine component). A stiff rod or hollow tube used to open the intake and exhaust valves of a reciprocating engine. One end of the pushrod rides in the cam follower, and the other end fits in a socket on one end of a rocker arm. When the cam follower rides up on the cam lobe, the pushrod transmits this movement to the rocker arm, and the rocker arm pushes the valve off its seat.

PVC (polyvinylchloride). A thermoplastic resin used to make transparent tubing for insulating electrical wires.

PV diagram (reciprocating engine relationship). A diagram showing the relationship between the volume of a cylinder and the pressure during a cycle of engine operation.

pylon (jet aircraft component). The structure which holds an engine nacelle or pod to the wing or fuselage of a jet-propelled aircraft.

pyrometer. An instrument used to measure high temperatures. Pyrometers usually begin measuring at temperatures above about 600°C.

Pythagorean theorem (mathematics). The statement that the square of the length of the hypotenuse of a right triangle is equal to the square root of the sum of the squares of the lengths of the other two sides.

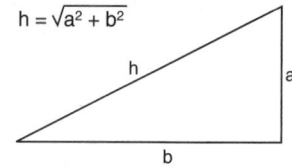

Pythagorean theorem

Quebec

Q-band radar. Radar that operates in the frequency band from 36 to 46 gigahertz. At this frequency, the wavelength of the energy is between 0.834 and 0.652 centimeter.

QEC assembly (engine maintenance unit). An engine change assembly (quick engine change) that allows an aircraft engine to be changed with the least amount of downtime. The engine is mounted on the engine mounts, all of the accessories and the propeller are mounted on the engine, and the cowling is installed. The QEC assembly essentially contains everything forward of the firewall.

Q-factor of a coil. A measure of the quality factor of the coil. Q is the ratio of the inductive reactance of a coil to its resistance, both measured in ohms.

$$Q = \frac{X_L}{R}$$

QNE. The barometric pressure used for the standard altimeter setting (29.92 inches Hg.).

QNH. The barometric pressure as reported by a particular station.

Q route. "Q" is the designator assigned to published RNAV routes used in the U.S.

quadrant (aircraft controls). The housing in an aircraft cockpit on which the engine control levers are mounted. The top of the quadrant is in the shape of a quarter of a circle, and the control levers stick out radially from the quadrant.

quadrant (air traffic control). A quarter part of a circle, centered on a NAVAID, oriented clockwise from magnetic north as follows: NE quadrant 000° – 089°, SE quadrant 090° – 179°, SW quadrant 180° – 269°, and NW quadrant 270° – 359°.

quadrant (mathematics). One of the four parts of a plane formed by the system of rectangular coordinates. The four quadrants are numbered with Roman numerals. I is the upper right-hand quadrant, II, the upper left-hand. III is the lower left-hand, and IV, the lower right-hand quadrant.

quadrantal error. The error in an automatic direction finder system installation caused by the metal in the aircraft. The quadrantal error is different in each of the four quadrants (front right, front left, rear left, rear right).

quadratic equation (mathematics). An algebraic equation that contains both the first and second powers of the unknown quantity, as well as a constant term. An example of a quadratic equation is:
$$ax^2 + bx + c = 0$$

quadrilateral. A plane (flat), closed polygon with four sides. Squares, rectangles, parallelograms, and trapezoids are all forms of quadrilaterals.

quadrivalent element (chemical element). A chemical element with four electrons in its valence shell. Carbon, silicon, germanium, tin, and lead are quadrivalent elements.

quality control. A system of control in a manufacturing company that is responsible for the quality of the product produced by the company. The inspection department is normally a part of the quality control department.

quantum theory. The theory which states that an atom or molecule does not absorb energy in a continuous and even fashion. Energy is absorbed in steps (quanta), with the amount of energy in each step being related to the frequency of the energy.

quart. A unit of volume measurement. One quart is equal to: two pints; one-fourth U.S. gallon; 57.75 cubic inches; 9.46×10^{-4} cubic meters.

Q

quartersawn wood. Wood sawn from a tree in such a way that the annual rings cross the plank at an angle of greater than 45°.

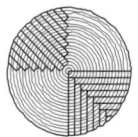

quarter-sawn wood

quarter-wave antenna. A radio antenna whose length is one quarter of the wavelength of the frequency for which the antenna is used.

quartz. A mineral (silicon dioxide) found in nature as a hexagonal (six-sided) crystal. Quartz has piezoelectric characteristics, as it produces a voltage when it is bent or pressed, and it changes its shape when a voltage difference exists across two of its faces.

quartz crystal. A thin slab of quartz, used to control the frequency of an electronic oscillator. A quartz crystal vibrates at its natural resonant frequency when it is excited with a pulse of electrical energy. As the crystal vibrates, it produces an alternating current whose frequency is determined by the physical dimensions of the crystal.

quartz glass. A type of glass made from pure quartz. Quartz glass does not filter out ultraviolet rays.

quartz-iodine lamp. An incandescent lamp with a tungsten filament and a quartz envelope. The envelope is filled with iodine vapor that reacts with the vaporized tungsten to prevent the tungsten vapors from darkening the quartz envelope.

quartz lamp. A mercury-vapor lamp enclosed in a transparent housing made of quartz, rather than glass. Quartz resists heat better than glass and allows ultraviolet rays to pass through, rather than absorbing them as glass does.

quartz oscillator. An electronic oscillator whose frequency is determined by the resonant frequency of a quartz crystal.

quartz pressure transducer. A precision instrument that senses pressure changes by the change in frequency of a quartz oscillator. When the quartz crystal controlling the frequency of the oscillator is acted on by the pressure being measured, the oscillator frequency changes. The amount of frequency change is proportional to the amount of pressure being measured.

quasi-stationary front (meteorology). A front which moves at a speed of less than five knots.

quenching (metal heat treatment). A process in the heat treatment of metal. The metal is heated to a specified temperature and then removed from the furnace and submerged in oil, brine, or water. The effect of quenching is different for different types of metal. Steel is hardened by quenching, and copper is softened by quenching.

quick-break fuse. A tubular fuse, used to protect a circuit containing an inductive load. If enough current flows to melt the fuse link, a spring pulls the melted ends apart by a distance great enough to prevent an arc from forming.

quick-break switch. An electrical switch with its contacts mounted on a spring. The contacts snap open quickly, even when the switch control is moved slowly. Quick-break switches are used to control circuits containing inductive loads. If the switch contacts were opened slowly, the inductance in the circuit would keep current flowing across the contacts as they separate. This would form an arc and damage the contacts.

quick-change gearbox (machine tool). A gearbox containing a cluster of gears, mounted on a machine tool such as a lathe. These gears allow the speed ratio between the drive motor and the work to be changed easily.

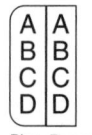

Plug Receptacle

quick-disconnect connector (electrical wire component). A type of wire connector used in aircraft electrical systems. The wires terminate inside an insulated plug with pins or sockets that mate with the opposite type of terminals in a similar plug. The two halves of the connector push together and are held tight with a special nut.

quick-disconnect connector

quick-disconnect coupling (fluid lines). A fluid line coupling that automatically seals the line when it is disconnected. Hydraulic pumps are normally connected into the hydraulic system with quick-disconnect couplings. This allows the pump to be removed for maintenance without air getting into the system. External hydraulic power sources can be connected into the system through quick-disconnect couplings.

quick engine change assembly (QECA). A quick engine change kit completely assembled on a quick engine change stand with the engine and all accessories, less the propeller for reciprocating engines.

quick look (air traffic control). A feature of the en route automation system (EAS) and automated radar terminal system (ARTS) that provides the controller with the capability to display full data blocks of tracked aircraft from other control positions.

quicksilver. Another name for mercury. *See* mercury.

quiescent current. Current flowing in an electronic circuit when there is no signal on the input.

quill shaft (generator coupling). A type of shaft used to couple an intermittent load, such as a generator to an engine. A quill shaft is a long, thin, hardened steel shaft with splines on each end. One end splines into the engine and the other end splines into the generator. When an electrical load is suddenly applied to the generator, the quill shaft absorbs the load by twisting. This prevents the load being applied to the gear train of the engine as a sudden shock.

quill shaft (torsional vibration damper). A form of torsional vibration damper used between the engine crankshaft and the propeller reduction gears. The quill shaft is a hardened steel shaft with splines on both ends. One end splines into the crankshaft and the other end into the drive gear of the propeller reduction gear system. Torsional vibration is absorbed by the twisting of the quill shaft.

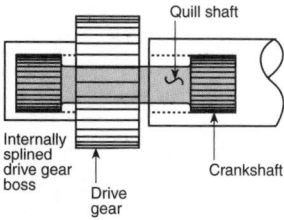

quill shaft

quotient (mathematics). The answer found when one number is divided by another.

RA. *See* resolution advisory.

rabbet. A groove cut near the edge of a piece of wood that allows another piece to fit into it to form a joint.

rabbet plane. A woodworking plane whose blade extends to the outside edge of the body of the plane. A rabbet plane is used to cut a rabbet (groove) in the face of a piece of wood.

rabbit, the (airport lighting). A high-intensity flasher system installed at many large airports. The flashers consist of a series of brilliant blue-white bursts of light flashing in sequence along the approach lights, giving the effect of a ball of light traveling towards the runway.

race (bearing). A hardened and polished steel surface on which antifriction bearings roll. The races for ball bearings are grooves. For tapered roller bearings, the races are cones, and for needle bearings, the races are flat rings.

rack-and-pinion (gear arrangement). An arrangement of gears in which rotary motion of the pinion (a small spur gear) is changed into linear motion of the rack. The rack is a straight piece of metal with teeth cut into one of its sides. The teeth of the pinion mesh with the teeth of the rack, and as the pinion rotates, it moves the rack. The rack and pinion may also be designed in such a way that movement of the rack rotates the pinion.

rack-and-pinion actuator (fluid power actuator). A form of rotary actuator in which the fluid acts on a piston on which a rack of gear teeth is cut. As the piston moves, it rotates a pinion gear which is mated with the teeth cut in the rack.

radar. An electronic device which, by measuring the time interval between transmission and reception of radio pulses and correlating the angular orientation of the radiated antenna beam or beams in azimuth and/or elevation, provides information on range, azimuth, and/or elevation of objects in the path of the transmitted pulses. Radar, an acronym for RAdio Detecting And Ranging, was developed as a military system during World War II.

A pulse of high-frequency electrical energy is transmitted from a highly directional antenna. The pulse travels until it strikes an object, then bounces back and is received by the antenna. The return pulse causes a bright spot to appear on the screen of a cathode-ray tube.

Radar is used for detecting precipitation, for navigation, and for detecting obstructions to flight. Simplified radar is used for measuring the speed of vehicles on our highways.

radar advisory (traffic advisory). The provision of advice and information based on radar observations.

radar altimeter. *See* radio altimeter.

radar altitude. The altitude of an aircraft determined by a radar-type radio altimeter. It is the actual distance between the aircraft and the nearest terrain feature.

radar approach (air traffic control). (1) The controller provides vectors while monitoring the progress of the flight with radar, guiding the pilot through the descent to the airport/heliport or to a specific runway. (2) An instrument approach procedure that uses Precision Approach Radar (PAR) or Airport Surveillance Radar (ASR). (3) [ICAO] An approach, executed by an aircraft, under the direction of a radar controller.

R

radar approach control facility. A terminal ATC facility that uses radar and nonradar capabilities to provide approach control services to aircraft arriving, departing, or transiting airspace controlled by the facility.

radar arrival. An aircraft arriving at an airport served by a radar facility and in radar contact with the facility.

radar attenuation. The absorption or reflection of radar signals by a weather cell, preventing that radar from detecting any additional cells that might lie behind the first cell.

radar beacon transponder. A type of radar used to identify aircraft flying along controlled airways. Ground radar at the airways traffic control center transmits a pulse of electromagnetic energy. When this pulse is received by the transponder, it replies with a special coded pulse. The coded reply is received by the ground radar and displayed on the controller's radar scope to show the location of the aircraft. An encoding altimeter directs the transponder to use a code that shows the altitude the aircraft is flying. This altitude shows up as numbers beside the return on the radar screen.

radar beam. A beam of focused electromagnetic energy radiated by radar. It is similar to a flashlight or searchlight beam, except that the frequency of the electromagnetic energy is beyond the visible range.

radar clutter (ICAO). The visual indication on a radar display of unwanted signals.

radar contact. A term used by ATC to inform an aircraft that it is identified on the radar display and radar flight following will be provided until radar identification is terminated. Radar service may also be provided within the limits of necessity and capability.

"Radar contact lost" (air traffic control). A phrase used by ATC to inform a pilot that radar data used to determine the aircraft's position is no longer being received or is no longer reliable, and radar service is no longer being provided. The loss may be attributed to several factors, including the aircraft merging with weather or ground clutter, the aircraft operating below radar line of sight coverage, the aircraft entering an area of poor radar return, failure of the aircraft transponder, or failure of the ground radar equipment.

radar environment (air traffic control). The airspace area within which radar coverage is available (depending upon existing equipment), and ATC radar services can be provided to flights operating in that area. Within the radar environment, radar coverage is possible, but not guaranteed.

radar flight following. The observation of the progress of radar identified aircraft, whose primary navigation is being provided by the pilot, while the controller retains and correlates the aircraft identity with the appropriate target displayed on the radar scope.

radar identification (air traffic control). The procedure for ascertaining that an observed radar target is the radar return from a particular aircraft.

radar identified aircraft (air traffic control). An aircraft that has its position correlated with an observed target or symbol on the radar display.

radar mile. The time in microseconds needed for a pulse of radar energy to travel a distance of one nautical mile and return to the radar receiver. One radar mile is approximately 12.4 microseconds.

radar point out (air traffic control). Refers to the action taken by a controller to transfer the radar identification of an aircraft to another controller when not transferring radio communications.

radar required. A notation displayed on charts and approach plates and included in FDC NOTAMs to alert pilots that segments of either an instrument approach procedure or a route are not navigable because of either the absence or unusability of a NAVAID. The pilot can expect to be provided radar navigational guidance while transiting segments labeled with this term.

radar route. A flight path or route over which an aircraft is vectored. Navigational guidance and altitude assignments are provided by ATC.

radar service. Services based on the use of radar provided by a controller to a pilot of a radar-identified aircraft: (1) radar monitoring—radar flight-following of aircraft, whose primary navigation is being performed by the pilot, to observe and note deviations from its authorized flight path, airway, or route; (2) radar navigational guidance—vectoring aircraft to provide course guidance; (3) radar separation—spacing of aircraft in accordance with established minima.

radar service terminated. A term used by ATC to inform a pilot that he/she will no longer be provided any of the services that could be received while in radar contact.

radarsonde observation (radar meteorology). A weather observation in which winds are measured by radar tracking a balloon-borne target.

radar summary chart. A chart produced 35 minutes past each hour and depicts a collection of radar weather reports. This chart displays areas and type of precipitation, intensity, coverage, echo top, and cell movement. In addition, an area of severe weather is plotted if they are in effect when the chart is valid.

radar surveillance. The radar observation of a given geographical area for the purpose of performing some radar function.

radar traffic advisories. Advisories issued to alert pilots of known or observed radar traffic which may affect their intended route of flight.

radar vector. A navigational heading assigned by ATC to a pilot.

radar vectoring (ICAO). Provision of navigational guidance to aircraft in the form of specific headings, based on the use of radar.

radar weather report (SD). A report issued by radar stations at 35 minutes after the hour, or as needed for special reports. Radar weather reports provide information on the type, intensity, and location of the echo tops of the precipitation.

radial (electronic navigation term). A line of radio bearing radiating outward from a very-high-frequency omnirange (VOR) navigation facility. There are 360 radials radiating out from each VOR, and each radial is named for the number of degrees clockwise from magnetic north that the radial leaves the facility.

radial bearing load. The load on a bearing that is perpendicular to the shaft on which the bearing is mounted. Centrifugal loads are radial loads.

radial engine. A form of reciprocating engine that was at one time very popular for use on aircraft. The cylinders are arranged radially around a small central crankcase. Radial engines have an exceptionally good power-to-weight ratio, but they have so much frontal area that they cause an excessive amount of aerodynamic drag and are not efficient for modern high-speed airplanes.

R

radial-inflow turbine. A type of turbine that uses a wheel similar to the wheel of a centrifugal air compressor. The hot exhaust gases that drive the turbine flow in through its outer rim and out its center. Radial-inflow turbines are used to drive the compressors in turbochargers for reciprocating engines.

radial lead (electrical component). The lead of an electrical component, such as a resistor or capacitor, that protrudes from the side of the component (it radiates outward). The other type of lead used on these components is an axial lead, which sticks out straight from the center of the end of the component.

radial outflow compressor (type of turbine engine compressor). This is another name for a centrifugal compressor. The air being compressed is drawn into the center of the compressor and thrown outward by centrifugal force, where it passes through the diffuser and then into the compressor manifold.

radial ply tire. A tire in which the body chords run straight across the tire. A belt of metal or synthetic cords is placed between the radial cords and the tread.

radian. A measure of angular displacement. One radian is the angle formed by the arc of a circle whose length is equal to the radius of the circle. A complete circle (360°) contains two π (6.28318) radians, and one radian is equal to 360° divided by 6.28318, or 57.2958°.

radiant energy. Energy transmitted in the form of waves of electromagnetic radiation. Light, heat, and radio-frequency electrical energy are forms of radiant energy.

radiant heat. Heat transmitted in the form of waves of electromagnetic radiation, rather than by conduction or convection. The heat we receive from the sun is a form of radiant heat.

radiation (electromagnetic). The transfer of energy in the form of electromagnetic waves through either air or the vacuum of space. *See* electromagnetic radiation.

radiation (heat transfer). The method of heat transfer by electromagnetic wave action.

radiation fog (meteorology). Fog that forms on a clear, calm night when the surface of the earth is cooled by radiation until the temperature of the air near the surface is below its initial dew point.

radiation shield (gas turbine engine component). A layer of aluminum built into the insulation blanket used around the hot section and exhaust of a gas turbine engine. The radiation shield prevents heat being radiated from the engine into the aircraft structure.

radical sign (mathematics). The mark in the shape of the letter V with a tail on it. A radical sign placed in front of and extending over a number shows that a root should be extracted from the number. If there is no number in the V-part of the radical sign, the square root of the number is indicated. Any number written in the V of the radical sign shows which root of the number is to be taken.

radioactivity. A property or characteristic of certain unstable chemical elements in which they lose some of their neutrons. As they lose neutrons, they change into stable isotopes of the element or into atoms of other elements having different chemical properties.

radio. A device used for audio communication of audible signals encoded in electromagnetic waves, and to transmit radio signals (transmitter), to receive radio signals (receiver), or both; also refers to a flight service station (e.g., "Seattle Radio" is used to call Seattle FSS).

radio altimeter. A type of absolute altimeter that measures the height of an aircraft above the terrain. A pulse of radio-frequency energy is transmitted downward from the aircraft. This pulse strikes the ground and is reflected back up to the aircraft where it is received. The time used by the pulse in traveling from the aircraft to the ground and back is changed into feet or meters and is displayed before the pilot. Radio altimeters are sometimes called radar altimeters.

radio control. Control of some type of mechanical device by electrical signals transmitted from a remote location.

radio-frequency alternating current. Alternating current whose frequency is between about 10 kilohertz (10 x 10^3 hertz) and 100 gigahertz (100 x 10^9 hertz). Radio-frequency alternating current is used for various types of communications and navigation.

radio-frequency choke. An inductor (coil) with enough inductive reactance at radio frequencies to block the flow of RF alternating current. Either air or a slug of powdered iron may be used as the core of a radio-frequency choke.

radio-frequency oscillator. An electronic oscillator that changes direct current electricity into alternating current whose frequency is in the radio-frequency (RF) spectrum.

radio-frequency spectrum. The classification of frequencies of electromagnetic radiation usable for communications. The bands of radio-frequency radiation used for communications and their commonly used names are:

Frequency Range	Band Name
3 – 30 kHz	Very Low Frequency (VLF)
30 – 300 kHz	Low Frequency (LF)
300 – 3,000 kHz	Medium Frequency (MF)
3 – 30 MHz	High Frequency (HF)
30 – 300 MHz	Very High Frequency (VHF)
300 – 3,000 MHz	Ultrahigh Frequency (UHF)
3 – 30 GHz	Superhigh Frequency (SHF)
30 – 300 GHz	Extremely High Frequency (EHF)

radio-frequency transformer. A transformer usable with alternating current in the radio-frequency (RF) spectrum. Most RF transformers have an air core.

radiographic inspection. A type of nondestructive inspection using X-rays and gamma rays to determine the condition of an aircraft structure at locations which could not otherwise be inspected without disassembly. Radiographic energy is passed through the structure and it exposes a photographic film or excites a fluorescent screen. Faults show up because their density is different from that of sound material.

radio magnetic indicator (RMI). An aircraft navigational instrument coupled with a gyro compass or similar compass that indicates the direction of a selected NAVAID and indicates bearing with respect to the heading of the aircraft.

radio marker beacon. A low-power, single-frequency (75-MHz), highly directional radio transmitter located at an important aviation navigation fix. The signal from a radio marker beacon is received only when the aircraft is directly above the transmitting antenna.

radiosonde. A device consisting of a group of meteorological instruments and a radio transmitter carried to a high altitude by a weather balloon. The instruments in the radiosonde measure the air pressure, temperature, and humidity and transmit this information to weather stations on the ground.

radio telegraphy. The method of radio communications in which information is transmitted by long and short spurts of radio-frequency energy. Radio telegraphy normally uses the International Morse Code. *See* International Morse Code in Appendix 4.

radio transmitter. An electronic device that transmits information by means of electromagnetic waves. The transmitter consists of an oscillator, a modulator, and an amplifier. The oscillator produces a carrier wave of the proper radio frequency. The modulator impresses the information to be transmitted onto the carrier, and the modulated carrier wave is amplified and delivered to an antenna from which it radiates into space.

R

radio wave. An electromagnetic wave (EM wave) with frequency characteristics useful for radio transmission.

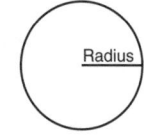

radius

radium. A radioactive chemical element, used as a source of neutrons in medicine and industrial radiography. Radium's atomic number is 88, and its symbol is Ra. Its most abundant, naturally occurring isotope has a mass number of 226 and a half-life of 1,620 years.

radius (mathematics). A straight line joining the center of a circle with a point on its circumference. The radius is one half of the diameter of the circle.

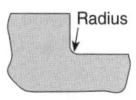

radius. The rounded edges of a component that forms a smooth curved intersection between the bottom and sides of a groove.

radius

radius bar (sheet-metal brake component). A bar, having an accurately ground radius on its edge, used with a sheet-metal brake. The metal bent in the brake is formed around the radius bar to give the bend the correct radius.

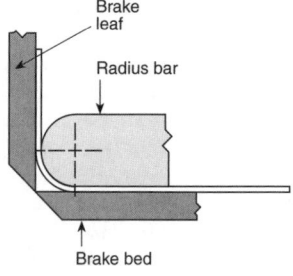

radius bar

radius dimpling (sheet-metal forming). A method of cold-forming the edges of a hole in a piece of sheet metal so it can be riveted with flush rivets. A cone-shaped male die fits into the rivet hole and forces the metal down into a depression in a female die. The edges of a radius-dimpled hole are rounded, rather than sharp, as they are in a coin-dimpled hole.

radius gage. A precision measuring tool consisting of a number of thin steel blades used to find the radius of a curved surface. Each blade is shaped with an inside and an outside radius of a specific size with the radius of the curve marked on the gage. Different gages are tried, until the gage is found that exactly fits the curvature of the surface.

radius of turn. The amount of horizontal distance an aircraft uses to complete a turn.

radome. A strong, electrically transparent housing, used to enclose a radar antenna and protect it from the wind and weather.

rag wing. A term commonly used to describe an airplane with fabric covered wings.

RAIM. *See* receiver autonomous integrity monitoring.

rain. A form of liquid water which falls from the atmosphere. The drops of water forming rain are usually more than a half-millimeter in diameter. Precipitation having smaller droplets than that of rain is called drizzle.

rain bands (meteorology). Lines of thunderstorms surrounding the center of a hurricane, which give hurricanes their spiral appearance, and produce rain.

rain gage. An instrument used to collect and measure the amount of rain which has fallen at a given location.

rain shadow (meteorology). A dry region leeward or behind a mountain with respect to the prevailing wind direction, due to moist air masses rising over a mountain range or large mountain, and cooling/condensing as rain or snow, thereby falling on the windward side or top of the mountain.

rain shower. *See* shower.

ram air pressure. Pressure produced when moving air is stopped. Ram air pressure is the same as pitot pressure.

ram air temperature rise (high speed aerodynamics). The increase in temperature created by the ram compression on the surface of an aircraft traveling at a high rate of speed through the atmosphere. The rate of increase is proportional to the square of the speed of the object.

ram-air wing. An airfoil designed with an aerodynamic cell structure which is inflated by the wind, forming a classic wing cross-section that generates lift. Also known as a parafoil.

ram drag. The loss of thrust produced by a turbojet or turbofan engine that is caused by increasing the velocity of the air entering the engine. The amount of ram drag is the difference between gross thrust and net thrust.

ramjet engine. The simplest type of air-breathing reaction engine. The air enters the front of the engine at a high velocity and fuel is sprayed into it and ignited. The air entering the front of the engine forms a barrier that forces the expanding gases to leave through the nozzle at the rear. The energy added by the burning fuel accelerates the air and produces a forward thrust. Ramjet engines are used in some military unmanned aircraft that are initially boosted to a speed high enough for the engine to function.

ramp (aircraft service area). A paved area on an airport, usually around the hangars where aircraft can be parked. Most ramps have provision for securing aircraft so they will not be blown away by strong winds. Ramps are also called aprons and tarmacs.

ramping (seaplane operation). The use of a ramp that extends under the water surface as a means of getting the seaplane out of the water and onto the shore. The seaplane is typically driven under power onto the ramp, and slides partway up the ramp due to inertia and engine thrust.

ram pressure. Pressure produced when a moving fluid is stopped.

ramp weight. The total weight of a loaded aircraft. The ramp weight includes all the fuel, and it is greater than the takeoff weight by the weight of the fuel that will be burned during the taxi and run-up operations. Ramp weight is also called taxi weight.

ram recovery (gas turbine engine parameter). The slight increase in thrust produced by a gas turbine engine, caused by the increase in air density as the air is rammed into the inlet duct by the forward movement of the aircraft.

ram-recovery speed. The speed at which the ram effect caused by the forward movement of the aircraft increases the air pressure at the compressor inlet until it is the same as that of the ambient air.

random altitude (air traffic control). An altitude inappropriate for direction of flight and/or not in accordance with FAA-O-7110.65, Para 4-5-1, Vertical Separation Minima.

random route (air traffic control). Any route not established or charted/published, or not otherwise available to all users.

random RNAV routes (air traffic control). Direct routes, based on area navigation capability, between waypoints. They are defined in terms of latitude/longitude coordinates, degree-distance fixes, or off-sets from established routes/airways at a specified distance and direction.

range-height indicator (RHI) scope. A radar indicator scope displaying a vertical cross-section of targets along a selected azimuth.

range markings. Colored marks on an aircraft instrument dial that identify certain ranges of operation as specified in the aircraft maintenance or flight manual and listed in the appropriate aircraft Type Certificate Data Sheets or Aircraft Specifications. Color-coding directs attention to approaching operating difficulties. These ranges and colors are the most generally used:

Red radial line — do not exceed.

Green arc — normal operating range.

Yellow arc — caution range.

Blue radial line — used on airspeed indicators to show best single-engine rate-of-climb speed.

White arc — used on airspeed indicators to show flap operating range.

range resolution (radar technology). The ability of radar to distinguish between targets along the same azimuth, but at different ranges.

ranging signals. Signals transmitted from the GPS satellite, these allow the aircraft's receiver to determine range (distance) from each satellite.

Rankine temperature (absolute temperature scale). The absolute temperature which uses the same increments as the Fahrenheit scale. All molecular activity stops at 0°R; water freezes at 492°R and boils at 672°R. *See* temperature.

rapid decompression (cabin pressurization). The almost instantaneous loss of cabin pressure in aircraft with a pressurized cockpit or cabin.

rapid descent. A relatively fast loss of altitude. Rapid descent is a subjective term, but is usually meant to describe a descent of more than 500 fpm.

R

rarefying. Decreasing the pressure of air.

rasp (woodworking tool). A coarse-toothed tool, similar to a file used for cutting wood. A rasp has individual cutting points, rather than lines of teeth, as on a file.

ratchet. A device that allows rotation of a wheel or handle in one direction, but prevents its turning in the opposite direction. A ratchet assembly consists of a toothed wheel and a pawl. The pawl is a lever that rides over the teeth when the wheel is turned in one direction, but engages the teeth to prevent the wheel turning in the opposite direction. Most ratchets have a method of reversing the pawl so the ratchet will work in either direction.

ratchet coupling. A coupling between two rotating shafts that allows one shaft to drive the other, but will not allow the driven shaft to rotate the drive shaft.

ratchet handle (mechanic's hand tool). A handle that has a ratchet built into its head, and used to drive a socket wrench. Back-and-forth movement of the handle causes the socket to rotate in one direction. By reversing the pawl in the ratchet head, the same back-and-forth movement of the handle will rotate the socket in the opposite direction.

rated 30-second OEI (one engine inoperative) power (rotorcraft turbine engines). According to 14 CFR Part 33, this is the approved brake horsepower for continuation of OEI flight operation, developed under static conditions at specified altitudes and temperatures within the operating limitations established for a rotorcraft engine. Such continuous flight operation after the failure or shutdown of one engine in multi-engine rotorcraft, can be extended for up to three periods of use of no longer than 30 seconds each in any one flight. This must be followed by mandatory inspection and prescribed maintenance action.

rated 2-minute OEI (one engine inoperative) power (rotorcraft turbine engines). According to 14 CFR Part 33, this is the approved brake horsepower for continuation of OEI flight operation, developed under static conditions at specified altitudes and temperatures within the operating limitations established for a rotorcraft engine. Such continuous flight operation after the failure or shutdown of one engine in multi-engine rotorcraft, can be extended for up to three periods of use, of no longer than 2 minutes each in any one flight. This must be followed by mandatory inspection and prescribed maintenance action.

rated continuous OEI (one engine inoperative) power. *14 CFR Part 1:* "With respect to rotorcraft turbine engines, means the approved brake horsepower developed under static conditions at specified altitudes and temperatures within the operating limitations established for the engine under Part 33 of this chapter, and limited in use to the time required to complete the flight after the failure of one engine of a multiengine rotorcraft."

rated horsepower (aircraft engine specification). The horsepower the engine manufacturer guarantees an engine will produce under specified conditions.

rated maximum continuous augmented thrust. *14 CFR Part 1:* "With respect to turbojet engine type certification, means the approved jet thrust that is developed statically or in flight, in standard atmosphere at a specified altitude, with fluid injection or with the burning of fuel in a separate combustion chamber, within the engine operating limitations established under Part 33 of this chapter, and approved for unrestricted periods of use."

rated maximum continuous power. *14 CFR Part 1:* "With respect to reciprocating, turbopropeller, and turboshaft engines, means the approved brake horsepower that is developed statically or in flight, in standard atmosphere at a specified altitude, within the engine operating limitations established under Part 33, and approved for unrestricted periods of use."

rated maximum continuous thrust. *14 CFR Part 1:* "With respect to turbojet engine type certification, means the approved jet thrust that is developed statically or in flight, in standard atmosphere at a specified altitude, without fluid injection and without the burning of fuel in a separate combustion chamber, within the engine operating limitations established under Part 33 of this chapter, and approved for unrestricted periods of use."

rated takeoff augmented thrust. *14 CFR Part 1:* "With respect to turbojet engine type certification, means the approved jet thrust that is developed statically under standard sea level conditions, with fluid injection or with the burning of fuel in a separate combustion chamber, within the engine operating limitations established under Part 33 of this chapter, and limited in use to periods of not over 5 minutes for takeoff operation."

rated takeoff power. *14 CFR Part 1:* "With respect to reciprocating, turbopropeller, and turboshaft engine type certification, means the approved brake horsepower that is developed statically under standard sea level conditions, within the engine operating limitations established under Part 33, and limited in use to periods of not over 5 minutes for takeoff operation."

rated takeoff thrust. *14 CFR Part 1:* "With respect to turbojet engine type certification, means the approved jet thrust that is developed statically under standard sea level conditions, without fluid injection and without the burning of fuel in a separate combustion chamber, within the engine operating limitations established under Part 33 of this chapter, and limited in use to periods of not over 5 minutes for takeoff operation."

rated thrust (aircraft engine specification). The amount of thrust the manufacturer of a gas turbine engine guarantees the engine will produce under certain specified conditions.

rated 30-minute OEI (one engine inoperative) power. *14 CFR Part 1:* "With respect to rotorcraft turbine engines, means the approved brake horsepower developed under static conditions at specified altitudes and temperatures within the operating limitations established for the engine under Part 33 of this chapter, and limited in use to a period of not more than 30 minutes after the failure of one engine of a multiengine rotorcraft."

rated 2$^1\!/_2$-minute OEI (one engine inoperative) power. *14 CFR Part 1:* "With respect to rotorcraft turbine engines, means the approved brake horsepower developed under static conditions at specified altitudes and temperatures within the operating limitations established for the engine under Part 33 of this chapter, and limited in use to a period of not more than 2$^1\!/_2$ minutes after the failure of one engine of a multiengine rotorcraft."

rate gyro. An instrument which measures the rate of rotation of an object about an axis. A spinning gyroscope precesses, or tilts, when it is rotated in a plane at right angles to its own spin axis. The amount the gyroscope tilts is proportional to the rate at which it is rotated about an axis at right angles to both its spin axis and the axis of its precession (the axis about which it tilts). Rate gyros are used in turn and slip indicators and turn coordinators.

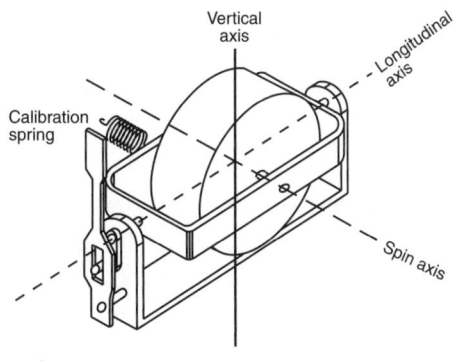

rate gyro

rate-of-climb indicator (aircraft instrument). An instrument used to show the pilot the rate at which the aircraft is climbing or descending. A rate-of-climb indicator is a pressure instrument that compares the pressures inside and outside a metal capsule inside the instrument case. Static pressure is directed into the instrument case and also into the capsule, but to get into the capsule, the air must flow through a calibrated orifice (a tiny hole of a specific size).

When the aircraft is not changing altitude, the pressure inside the capsule is the same as that inside the instrument case. But when the aircraft is climbing or descending, the orifice causes the pressure inside the capsule to change more slowly than the pressure inside the case. This lag in the pressure change causes the capsule to expand or collapse until the pressure equalizes. The amount of expansion or collapse is measured, and it indicates on the instrument dial as the number of feet-per-minute climb or descent. Rate-of-climb indicators are also called vertical-speed indicators.

rate-of-temperature-rise fire detector. A type of fire detection system that uses a series of thermocouples to detect a fire condition by the rate at which the temperature being monitored rises. A series of thermocouples is placed in the area being protected, and a reference thermocouple in the area is insulated so its temperature always changes slowly. When the overall temperature rise is slow enough that the insulated thermocouple remains at the same temperature as the measuring thermocouples, no signal is sent to the fire warning system. But if a fire occurs and the measuring thermocouple gets hot before the insulated reference thermocouple, a voltage is produced that causes a current to flow and actuate the fire warning system.

rate of turn. The amount of time it takes for an aircraft to turn a specified number of degrees.

rate of yaw. The rate, usually expressed in degrees per second, at which an aircraft rotates about its vertical axis.

rating. *14 CFR Part 1:* "A statement that, as a part of a certificate, sets forth special conditions, privileges, or limitations."

ratio. A relationship between two quantities. A ratio of two to one (2:1) is a relationship in which the first quantity is two times as large as the second.

ratiometer indicator mechanism. A direct current indicating instrument in which the pointer deflection is proportional to the ratio between the current flowing in a reference coil and that flowing in the measuring coil.

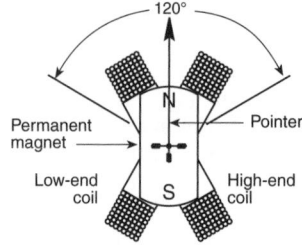

ratiometer

RATO (rocket assisted takeoff). RATO is a method of assisted takeoff that can be used by a heavily loaded airplane when taking off from a high-altitude airport. Auxiliary boost rockets, attached to the airframe, are ignited at the critical time during takeoff to provide the needed additional thrust.

rattail file. A long, narrow, tapered, round file. Rattail files are used for filing a radius in the corner of a cutout.

rawhide mallet. A soft-face mallet whose head is made of a tightly wound roll of rawhide. Rawhide mallets are used to form soft sheet metal and to pound parts that must not be damaged by hitting them with a hard hammer.

rawinsonde observation (radar meteorology). A combined winds aloft and radiosonde observation. Winds are determined by tracking the radiosonde by radio direction finder or radar. Also called a rawin.

RB. *See* relative bearing.

RBI. *See* relative bearing indicator.

RC circuit (electrical circuit). An electrical circuit that contains both resistance and capacitance.

RCO. *See* remote communications outlet.

RC time constant. *See* capacitive time constant.

RDF (radio direction finding). A method of locating a radio transmitter by using radio receivers equipped with directional antennas. The station to be located is received by two or more RDF stations, and the bearings (the direction from the receivers to the transmitter) are plotted on a chart. The transmitting antenna is located at the point the bearings from all of the RDF stations cross.

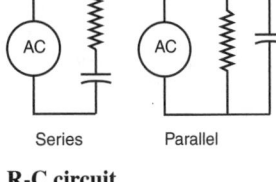

Series   Parallel

R-C circuit

reach (spark plug design feature). The length of the threads on a spark plug shell. The reach needed by a spark plug is determined by the thickness of the cylinder head into which the spark plug screws. The end of the spark plug should be flush with the inside of the cylinder head. A long-reach 18-mm aircraft spark plug has a reach of $^{13}/_{16}$-inch; a short-reach 18-mm spark plug has a reach of $^{1}/_{2}$-inch.

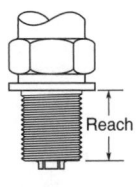

reach

reactance (X). Opposition to the flow of alternating current caused by capacitance and inductance in the circuit. Reactance opposes the flow of alternating current without using any power.

Reactance caused by capacitance is called capacitive reactance, its symbol is X_C, and it is measured in ohms. Capacitive reactance causes the current in the circuit to lead the voltage.

Reactance caused by inductance is called inductive reactance, and its symbol is X_L. Inductive reactance is also measured in ohms, and it causes the current in a circuit to lag behind the voltage.

reaction. A response to an action that occurs in a direction opposite to the action. The recoil produced when a gun is fired is an example of reaction. When the powder in the cartridge burns, the resulting gas forces the bullet out the barrel. The action forcing the bullet from the barrel causes an opposing reaction that pushes back on the gun with exactly the same amount of force.

reaction engine. A form of heat engine that produces thrust by heating a mass of air inside the engine and discharging it at a high velocity through a specially shaped nozzle. The amount of thrust is determined by the mass of the air and by the amount it is accelerated. Reaction engines which include rocket engines are commonly called jet engines.

reaction turbine. A type of turbine wheel turned by an aerodynamic force produced by the turbine blades. This force is similar to the lift produced by an aircraft wing. The blades of a reaction turbine are small airfoils mounted on the periphery of the turbine wheel in such a way that they form converging ducts that accelerate the hot gases passing through them. The high-velocity gas flowing over the reaction turbine blades produces a pressure difference between the top and bottom of the blade. This pressure difference produces a force which rotates the turbine wheel.

reactive current (electrical current). Current flowing in an alternating current circuit that is not in phase with the voltage.

reactive metal. A metal that reacts readily with oxygen to form an oxide. Aluminum and magnesium are both reactive metals.

reactive power (electrical power). Wattless power in an alternating current circuit. Reactive power, the power consumed in the inductive and capacitive reactances in the circuit, is expressed in volt-amps reactive (VAR) or in kilovolt-amps reactive (KVAR).

R

reactor (electrical circuit). A small coil installed in an alternating current circuit to furnish inductive reactance to cancel some of the capacitive reactance in the circuit. Reactors normally have very little resistance.

"Read back" (air traffic control). A phrase used by ATC to mean "repeat my message back to me."

reader (microfiche system). An optical instrument used to read the information recorded on a microfiche. The microfiche is placed on the reader and moved around to position the correct image in front of the lens. The magnified image is projected onto a screen so the operator can read it. Some microfiche readers have a built-in printer that makes a hard copy of the projected image. This type of reader is called a reader-printer.

readiness, law of (in learning process). Thorndike's principle of learning that maintains that the eagerness and single-mindedness of a person toward learning affect the outcome of the learning experience.

real number. Numbers that include positive numbers, negative numbers, and zero.

real power (electrical power). The power in an alternating current circuit that actually produces work. Real power (true power) is measured in watts and is the product of the circuit voltage and only the current in phase with this voltage. Real power can be found by multiplying the apparent power, the product of the total voltage and the total current, by the power factor, the percent of the total current in phase with the circuit voltage.

ream (metalworking process). To enlarge a hole and smooth its sides. If a hole in a piece of metal is to be fitted with a close-tolerance part, it is usually drilled slightly undersize and cut to the correct diameter with a reamer.

reamed fit. The fit of a shaft in a hole in which the hole is drilled undersize and cut with a reamer to the correct diameter. Reamed holes have smooth walls and a consistent diameter.

reamer (metal-cutting tool). A cutting tool used to produce a smooth surface on the inside of a drilled hole. A reamer has several sharp cutting edges that cut away the rough surface left by the drill.

rebreather oxygen mask. A type of mask used with a continuous-flow oxygen system. Oxygen continuously flows into the bottom of the loose-fitting rebreather bag on the mask, and the wearer of the mask exhales into the top of the bag. The first air exhaled contains some oxygen, and this air goes into the bag first. The last air to leave the lungs contains little oxygen, and it is forced out as the bag is filled with fresh oxygen. Each time the wearer of the mask inhales, the air first exhaled, along with fresh oxygen, is taken back into the lungs, or rebreathed.

rebuilt engine. A used engine that has been completely disassembled, inspected, repaired as necessary, reassembled, tested, and approved in the same manner and to the same tolerances and limits as a new engine, using either new or used parts. The parts used in a rebuilt engine must conform to all production drawings, tolerances, and limits for new parts or be of approved oversize or undersize dimensions allowed for a new engine.

According to 14 CFR §91.421, a rebuilt engine is considered to have no previous operating history and may be issued a zero-time logbook. Only the engine manufacturer or an agent approved by the manufacturer can rebuild an engine and issue a zero-time record.

receiver. In communication, the listener, reader, or student who takes in a message containing information from a source, processes it, reacts with understanding, and changes behavior in accordance with the message.

receiver autonomous integrity monitoring (RAIM). (1) A system used to verify the usability of the received GPS signals and warns the pilot of any malfunction in the navigation system. This system is required for IFR-certified GPS units. (2) A technique whereby a civil GNSS receiver/processor determines the integrity of the GNSS navigation signals without reference to sensors or nonDoD integrity systems other than the receiver itself, achieved by a consistency check among redundant pseudorange measurements.

receiver-dryer (vapor-cycle cooling system component). The component in the high side of a vapor-cycle cooling system that serves as a reservoir for the liquid refrigerant. The receiver-dryer contains a desiccant that absorbs any moisture that may be in the refrigerant.

receiver-transmitter (RT). The component in a radio altimeter system that receives and transmits a signal from the antennas, which is interpreted by the RT unit into height above terrain information. This HAT is then displayed on the radio altimeter system indicator (if the system includes one).

receiving controller (air traffic control). A controller/facility receiving control of an aircraft from another controller/facility.

recency in flight instruction (psychology). A principle of learning that states that things most recently learned are best remembered. Conversely, the further a student is removed timewise from a new fact or understanding, the more difficult it is to remember.

reciprocal. Opposite. If the heading of an aircraft is 270°, its reciprocal heading is 090° (the heading in the opposite direction). The reciprocal of a number is the number one, divided by the number. The reciprocal of two is one-half, one divided by two ($1 \div 2$ or $\frac{1}{2}$).

reciprocating engine. A type of heat engine that changes chemical energy in fuel and air into mechanical energy. A mixture of fuel and air is drawn into a cylinder as a close-fitting piston moves downward.

The valve through which the fuel-air mixture entered the cylinder closes, and the piston moves up, compressing the mixture. As the piston nears the top of its stroke, the compressed mixture is ignited, and it burns. The burning gases heat the air in the cylinder, and as it expands, it pushes the piston downward.

The reciprocating piston is connected to a crankshaft throw by a connecting rod. As the piston moves up and down in the cylinder, the connecting rod rotates the crankshaft.

reciprocating saw (metal-cutting tool). A saw that cuts metal as its blade moves back and forth across the work. Pressure is applied to the blade only on its forward stroke, and the blade is lifted from the work on its return stroke.

reclaimed oil (petroleum product). Used lubricating oil that has been processed to remove the impurities.

recombination (semiconductor device). The action in a semiconductor device that occurs when a free electron fills a hole. The hole and the free electron disappear at the same time.

recommended altitude (instrument flight). An altitude value of advisory nature, depicted on an instrument approach chart with the altitude value neither underscored nor overscored.

reconformance (air traffic control). The automated process of bringing an aircraft's current plan trajectory into conformance with its track.

rectangle. A plane, four-sided, closed figure with four right angles. The opposite sides of a rectangle are parallel, but all four sides do not necessarily have the same length. If all sides of a rectangle are the same length, the rectangle is called a square.

rectangle

rectification. The conversion of alternating current into direct current by means of a rectifier.

rectification (electrical welding). A condition in AC electric arc welding in which oxides on the surface of the metal act as a rectifier and prevent electrons flowing from the metal to the electrode during the half cycle when the electrode is positive.

rectifier (electrical circuit). An electrical circuit that changes alternating current into direct current. A rectifier circuit uses one or more rectifier devices, such as semiconductor diodes, vacuum-tube diodes, or metal-oxide rectifiers. These devices act as electron check valves, allowing electrons to flow during one alternation of the AC, but opposing their flow during the next alternation.

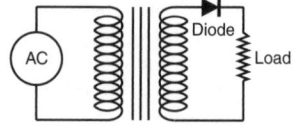

rectifier (half wave)

recurrent training (flight training). Annual or semi-annual training used to refresh a pilot's knowledge and skills in a variety of flight situations, including inflight emergencies.

recurring Airworthiness Directive (aircraft maintenance document). An Airworthiness Directive that must be complied with on an aircraft or aircraft engine on a scheduled basis. For example, certain inspections must be performed on a part every so many hours until the part is replaced.

red brass. A copper alloy containing 85% copper, 5% zinc, 5% tin, and 5% lead.

red line. On gauges used in aircraft, "red line" refers to the airspeed limit-line shown on an ASI that indicates the "never-exceed speed" (or VNE); it can also refer to any limit-line on instrument gauges that cautions against going beyond the "red line" indication.

In balloon operations: also called the "vent line," this refers to the rope line (usually red-colored) that controls the functioning of the deflation port (or parachute valve) to release a controlled amount of hot air from the top of a balloon envelope; it may also refer to the limit-line on the envelope temperature gauge (or pyrometer) that indicates "maximum envelope temperature allowed."

red-line condition. A maximum allowable condition. This term is derived from the fact that the maximum allowable condition is normally marked on an indicating instrument with a red radial line. Airspeed, engine RPM, and various engine temperatures all have specified red-line conditions.

red rust. A product of corrosion which results from atmospheric oxidation of iron or steel surfaces.

reduced vertical separation minimums (RVSM). RVSM airspace is where air traffic control separates aircraft by a minimum of 1,000 feet vertically between flight level (FL) 290 and FL 410 inclusive. RVSM airspace is special qualification airspace; the operator and the aircraft used by the operator must be approved by the FAA. Air traffic control notifies operators of RVSM by providing route planning information.

reducing flame (gas welding). *See* carburizing flame.

reduction factor (weight and balance). A constant which, when divided into a moment, results in an index. Reduction factors of 100, 1,000, and 10,000 are used to simplify weight and balance computations.

reduction gear train. A gear arrangement in which the output shaft turns more slowly than the input shaft. A reduction gear train is used to increase the torque produced by a motor.

Reed and Prince screw. A form of recessed head screw that can be driven with a power screwdriver. The cross cut into the head of a Reed and Prince screw has straight sides, and the bottom of the recess is a sharp V.

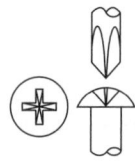

reed valve. A simple check valve that allows fluid to flow in one direction, but blocks its flow in the opposite direction. The reed is a flat piece of flexible material, often spring steel, fastened by one of its edges to one side of a hole. Fluid flowing from the side of the hole

Reed & Prince screw

opposite the reed forces it off its seat, and the fluid flows through the hole. When fluid tries to flow through the hole from the side on which the reed is mounted, it forces the reed tightly against the hole, and no fluid can flow. Reed valves are used in some types of simple air compressors and pulse jet engines.

reference circle (instrument approach chart). The circle depicted in the plan view of an IAP chart that typically has a 10 NM radius, within which the elements are drawn to scale. This is also known as distance circle.

reference datum (GAMA). An imaginary vertical plane from which all horizontal distances are measured for balance purposes.

reference designator. A designator used in schematics and printed circuit board layouts to label components. Reference designators are commonly alphanumeric; they consist of a letter indicating the general category of the component followed by a number.

reference dimensions. Dimensions on installation drawings that shows the dimensions necessary for the location of specific parts with relation to the other parts.

reference junction (thermocouple junction). One of the two junctions in a thermocouple system. The voltage produced by a thermocouple is determined by the difference in the temperature of the two junctions. By holding the temperature of the reference junction constant, the voltage produced by the system is determined by the temperature of the measuring junction.

reference landing speed (V_{REF}). The speed of the airplane, in a specified landing configuration, at the point where it descends through the 50-foot height in the determination of the landing distance.

reference pressure (pneumatic systems). A pressure that is used as a standard or datum from which another pressure is measured. For example, static air pressure is used in an airspeed indicator as a reference pressure to correct the ram, or pitot, pressure for altitude and temperature changes.

refining (petroleum production). The process in which a material, such as crude oil, is broken down into its constituent parts.

reflector (light). A polished surface used to reflect light. When light strikes a reflector it changes its direction. The angle of reflectance at which the light leaves the surface is exactly the same as the angle at which it arrived at the surface, the angle of incidence. By using the proper shape reflector, the light can be formed into a beam.

refraction (radar technology). The bending of a radar beam by variations in atmospheric density, water vapor content, and temperature.

refrigerant. A chemical compound used in a refrigerator or air conditioning system to absorb heat, then carry it to another location where it is given up to the outside air.

refrigerant-12. The refrigerant that was formerly widely used in aircraft vapor-cycle air cooling systems. Refrigerant-12 (R-12) is the name generally used for dichlorodifluoromethane, which is sold under such registered trade names as Freon-12, Genetron-12, and Ucon-12. R-12 is being replaced by R-134a, which is more environmentally friendly.

regeneration (electronic amplification). A method of increasing the gain of an amplifier by feeding part of the amplified signal back into its input in phase with the input signal. If too much energy is fed back into the input, the amplifier will oscillate and produce an unwanted signal, often in the form of a whistle, or squeal. Regeneration is also called regenerative feedback or positive feedback.

regenerative braking (electrical braking). A method of slowing the rotating armature of an electric motor. When the brake control switch is moved to the STOP position, it removes power from the motor and connects the armature across an electrical load. As long as the armature is rotating, it produces electrical current, and power is required to force this current through the load. This power taken from the rotating armature causes it to slow down.

R

regional airline. A commuter airline that serves smaller cities and brings passengers to larger hub airlines.

region of reverse command (flight condition). Flight at an airspeed, or angle of attack, lower than that which produces the maximum endurance. Below this speed, an increase in power will actually result in a lower airspeed. This is generally known as "flying behind the power curve." Decreasing the angle of attack allows the airspeed to increase without increasing the power or thrust.

regions of command. The "regions of normal and reversed command" refers to the relationship between speed and the power required to maintain or change that speed in flight.

registration certificate (aircraft document). A document issued by the FAA which shows the name and address of the owner of the aircraft. The registration certificate must be displayed in the aircraft at all times.

regular airport. An airport used by a certificate holder in scheduled operations which is listed in its operations specifications.

regulated power supply (electrical power supply). An electrical device that changes line-voltage alternating current into direct current with the required voltages. The regulator circuit causes the voltage to remain constant as the load current varies.

regulator tube (electron tube voltage regulator). A gas-filled, glow-discharge electron tube. A regulator tube is installed in parallel with the load across the output of a DC power supply. The regulator tube maintains a constant voltage across its terminals, even as the current flowing through it changes.

reheat system. The British name for afterburner. *See* afterburner.

Reid vapor pressure. The amount of pressure that must be exerted on a liquid to keep it from vaporizing. The vapor pressure of a liquid is affected by its temperature, and the Reid vapor pressure of a liquid is specified at 100°F.

REIL. *See* runway end identifier lights.

reinforce. To strengthen something by adding additional structural components or by using additional material.

reinforced shell. *See* semimonocoque structure.

reinforcing tape (aircraft fabric covering component). A narrow strip of woven fabric material placed over the fabric at the points it is being attached to the aircraft structure with ribstitching cord. The reinforcing tape carries a large amount of the load and prevents the fabric from tearing at the stitches.

rejuvenation (aircraft finishes). The process of restoring resilience to an old dope film on a fabric-covered aircraft. When aircraft dope is exposed to the sun for several years, the plasticizers migrate from it, and the dope film become brittle and cracks. Rejuvenator, which is a mixture of strong solvents and plasticizer, is sprayed over the old dope. The solvents penetrate the dope, and the plasticizer restores resilience to the dope film.

rejuvenator (aircraft finishing material). A finishing material used to restore resilience to an old dope film. Rejuvenator contains strong solvents to open up the dried-out dope film and plasticizers to restore resilience to the old dope.

relative (or resultant) airflow (RAF) (helicopter aerodynamics). The velocity vector of the airflow approaching the blades. The relative airflow is dependent on a number of component flows, e.g., induced flow, flow due to rotor rpm, and others.

relative bearing (RB) (navigation). The number of degrees measured clockwise between the heading of the aircraft and the direction from which the bearing is taken.

relative bearing indicator (RBI). Also known as the fixed-card ADF, zero is always indicated at the top of the instrument and the needle indicates the relative bearing to the station.

relative humidity. The ratio of the amount of water vapor in the air to the amount of water vapor the air can hold at its present temperature.

relative motion. Motion of one object with reference to another. One object can be moving and the other object still, or both objects may be moving, but at different rates, or directions.

relative vorticity (meteorology). Vorticity of the air relative to the earth, disregarding the component of vorticity resulting from the earth's rotation.

relative wind. The direction the wind strikes an airfoil.

relaxation oscillator. A type of electronic oscillator that changes direct current into pulsating DC with a sawtooth waveform. A capacitor is charged through a resistor to produce a slow rise in voltage. At a specified voltage, the gas in a gas-filled electron tube becomes ionized and conducts. The capacitor immediately discharges through this ionized gas.

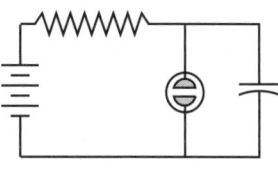

relaxation oscillator

The frequency of oscillation is determined by the values of the capacitor and the resistor and by the ionization voltage of the gas in the tube. *See* sawtooth waveform.

relay (electrical component). An electrically operated switch. One switch contact is mounted on a movable steel arm, the armature, which is held away from the fixed contact by a spring. When current flows through the electromagnetic coil of the relay, it pulls the armature down and causes the movable contact to press tightly against the fixed contact, closing the switch.

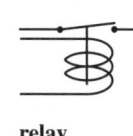

relay

Relays are used to remotely control a large amount of current by using a small amount of control current flowing through the relay coil. Relays are being replaced in many types of electrical equipment with solid-state components that do the same job, but have no moving parts.

relay question (in learning process). A student's question that the instructor redirects to another student.

release film (composites). A thin layer of plastic material that is used to prevent a resin from adhering to a mold while it is being cured.

release time (air traffic control). A departure time restriction issued to a pilot by ATC (either directly or through an authorized relay) when necessary to separate a departing aircraft from other traffic.

release time (ICAO). Time prior to which an aircraft should be given further clearance or prior to which it should not proceed in case of radio failure.

reliability. The ability of an aircraft engine to perform its designed functions under widely varying operating conditions.

relief hole (sheet metal fabrication). A hole drilled at the point at which two bend lines meet in a piece of sheet metal. When a piece of sheet metal is formed into a pan, a square is cut from the corners of the sheet, and the sides are bent upward. The metal where the two bends meet will usually buckle and crack. To prevent this cracking, a relief hole whose diameter is approximately twice the radius of the bend is drilled at the point the two bends meet. This relief hole spreads the stresses so the metal does not crack.

relief map. A three-dimensional map in which mountains and valleys are formed so they show the way the land actually looks.

relief tube. A urinal installed in some special-purpose aircraft.

relief valve. A pressure-control valve that relieves any pressure over the amount for which it is set. Pressure relief valves are used in both hydraulic and pneumatic systems to prevent damaging high pressures that could be caused by a malfunctioning pressure regulator, or by thermal expansion of fluid trapped in portions of the system.

R

reluctance. Opposition to the passage of lines of magnetic flux through a material. Reluctance in a magnetic circuit compares with resistance in an electrical circuit.

remainder (mathematics). The number left in a mathematical problem when one number is subtracted from another. The remainder is also the number left in a division problem when the divisor does not go into the dividend an even number of times.

remanufactured engine. An aircraft engine that has been completely rebuilt by the original engine manufacturer or by a facility approved by them. A remanufactured engine is considered to be a zero-time engine and is usually given the same warranty as a new engine.

The term "remanufactured" does not have any official meaning to the FAA, but it is often used to mean the same as the FAA term "rebuilt." *See* rebuilt engine.

remote airport advisory (RAA). A remote service that may be provided by facilities not located on the landing airport, but which have a discrete ground-to-air communication or tower frequency when the tower is closed. RAA may have automated weather reporting with voice available to the pilot at the landing airport, and a continuous ASOS/AWOS data display, other direct reading instruments, or manual observation available to the AFSS specialist.

remote airport information service (RAIS). A temporary service provided by facilities not located on the landing airport, but which have communication capability and automated weather reporting available to the pilot at the landing airport.

remote communications air/ground facility. An unmanned VHF/UHF transmitter/receiver facility used to expand ARTCC air/ground communications coverage and facilitate direct contact between pilots and controllers.

remote communications outlet (RCO). An unmanned communications facility remotely controlled by air traffic personnel. RCOs serve flight service stations. Also called a remote transmitted receiver (RTR) when serving a terminal ATC facility. An RCO or RTR may be UHF or VHF and will extend the communication range of the air traffic facility.

remote control. Control of an object from a location different from that of the device being controlled. Remote control can be accomplished by fluid power, by electrical current carried through wires, or by signals transmitted by radio or light.

remote scope (radar meteorology). A slave radarscope remotely operated from a weather radar.

Rene metal. The registered trade name for a series of high-strength, high-temperature, nickel-chromium alloys, used in the manufacture of gas turbine engines.

repair. A maintenance procedure in which a damaged component is restored to its original condition or at least to a condition that allows it to fulfill its design function.

repairman license (Federal Aviation Administration license). A license issued by the Federal Aviation Administration under 14 CFR Part 65 to a specialist in some form of aircraft maintenance who is employed by a certificated repair station or airline. The repairman certificate (license) is valid only as long as the repairman is employed by the company for which the certificate was issued.

Repair Station. A certificated maintenance facility approved by the FAA to perform certain specific maintenance functions. These facilities are certificated under 14 CFR Part 145.

repeating decimal (mathematics). The decimal equivalent of a fraction in which the denominator does not go into the numerator an even number of times. The fraction $\frac{1}{3}$ gives a repeating decimal: 0.3333333... .

"Report" (air traffic control). A term used by ATC to instruct pilots to advise ATC of specific information, such as "Report passing Hamilton VOR."

reporting point. *14 CFR Part 1:* "A geographic location in relation to which the position of an aircraft is reported."

repression (human factors). A defense mechanism whereby a person places uncomfortable thoughts, or things he or she can't cope with, into inaccessible areas of the unconscious mind. In Freudian theory, some forgetting of learned information is caused by repression. A person is more likely to forget information that is unpleasant or produces anxiety.

repulsion. A mechanical force that tries to move objects apart. There is a force of repulsion between like magnetic poles, between electrical charges of the same polarity, and between parallel wires carrying current in the same direction.

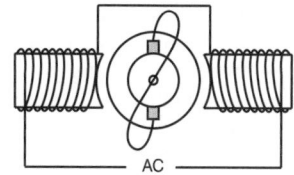

repulsion motor (electric motor). A type of AC motor in which the source current is supplied to the stator winding, and current is induced into the rotor windings. The rotor windings end at copper bars on a

repulsion motor

commutator, and brushes pick up rotor current. The brushes are connected together so they short-circuit some of the rotor windings.

Rotor current flowing through the short-circuited coils produces a magnetic field whose axis is at an angle to the magnetic field in the stator. Because the two magnetic fields are at an angle to each other, they repel, or push away from, each other.

The brushes of a repulsion motor are usually mounted on a control that allows them to be rotated with reference to the stator field. Moving the brushes controls the direction of rotation and the speed of a repulsion motor.

request full route clearance. A term used by pilots to request that the entire route of flight be read verbatim in an ATC clearance. Such request should be made to preclude receiving an ATC clearance based on the original filed flight plan when a filed IFR flight plan has been revised by the pilot, company, or operations prior to departure.

required equipment (aircraft equipment). Equipment required by the FAA to be installed in an aircraft for it to be considered airworthy. All FAA-certificated aircraft must carry an up-to-date equipment list, itemizing all of the required equipment.

required navigation performance (RNP). A statement of the navigational accuracy and performance necessary for operation within a defined airspace. RNP requires that an aircraft flying through certain airspace navigate within certain pre-set tolerances. RNP airspace is a generic term designating airspace, route(s), leg(s), operation(s), or procedure(s) where minimum required navigational performance (RNP) criteria have been established. RNP equipped aircraft can fly to lower approach minimums, have greater confidence with aircraft separation and fly repeatable curved course.

rescue coordination center (RCC). A search and rescue (SAR) facility equipped and manned to coordinate and control SAR operations in an area designated by the SAR plan. The U.S. Coast Guard and the U.S. Air Force have responsibility for the operation of RCCs.

rescue co-ordination center (ICAO). A unit responsible for promoting efficient organization of search and rescue service and for coordinating the conduct of search and rescue operations within a search and rescue region.

reserve flightcrew member. A flightcrew member who is required by the certificate holder to be available to receive an assignment for duty.

reservoir. A container in which liquid is stored. The tank in a hydraulic system is called a reservoir because it stores fluid until it is needed to actuate some component in the system.

residual charge (capacitor). The electrical charge left on the plates of a capacitor after its initial discharge.

R

residual fuel and oil (aircraft specification). Another term for unusable fuel and undrainable oil. Residual fuel and oil are considered to be part of the empty weight of an aircraft.

residual magnetic flux. The magnetic flux left in a piece of iron or steel after the magnetizing force is reduced to zero. Soft iron can hold very little residual magnetic flux, but hard steel and certain alloys hold a large amount of residual magnetic flux.

residual magnetic particle inspection. A form of magnetic particle inspection for small steel parts that have a high degree of retentivity. The part is magnetized, then removed from and inspected away from the magnetizing machine.

residual magnetism (electric generator). The magnetism that remains in the field frame of a generator when no current is flowing in the field coils. It is residual magnetism that produces the initial current when a generator begins to turn. As soon as the current produced by the residual magnetism begins to flow in the field coils, the field strength increases and more current is produced.

residual risk (risk assessment, aeronautical decision making). Some types of hazard or risk cannot be known, and are only identified subsequently when a mishap occurs. In risk assessment, those risks that cannot be assessed as to their manageability in flight or whether they can be reduced through prior action, end up being passed on to the pilot (or the person attempting risk management for a certain flight) as residual risk. (*See also* acceptable risk, unacceptable risk.)

residual voltage (generator voltage). The voltage produced in a generator armature when there no current is flowing in the field windings. Residual voltage is produced when the armature rotates in the permanent magnetism in the generator field frame. If this permanent magnetism is lost and no residual voltage is produced, it can be restored by flashing the field. *See* flashing the field.

resilient sealant. A sealing compound that hardens to the consistency of rubber. It does not get brittle.

resin (natural). A natural, translucent, solid or semisolid material, produced from the sap of certain trees or plants. Resins are soluble in organic solvents, such as ether, but are not soluble in water. Resins are used in the manufacture of varnishes, inks, and certain types of plastics.

resin rich (composites). A localized area in a composite lay up that is filled with resin but lacks sufficient reinforcing fiber.

resin starved (composites). A localized area in a composite lay up that lacks sufficient resin to thoroughly wet the reinforcing fiber.

resin transfer molding (RTM) (composites). A molding process in which catalyzed resin is introduced into an enclosed mold into which the fiber reinforcement has been placed. The cure is normally accomplished without external heat. RTM combines relatively low tooling and equipment costs with the ability to mold large structural parts.

resistance, R (electrical characteristic). The characteristic of an electrical circuit that opposes the flow of electrons. When electrons flow through a resistance, power is used, voltage is dropped, and, generally, heat is produced. The amount of resistance in a circuit is measured in ohms, with one ohm being the amount of resistance needed to produce a one-volt drop when one amp of current flows through it.

resistance decade (electronic equipment). A piece of electronic test equipment consisting of several precision resistors and selector switches. By connecting the resistance decade into a circuit and setting the selector switches in the proper positions, any required amount of resistance can be put into a circuit.

The resistance decade gets its name from the increments of resistance that can be selected. One switch can select resistances between 0.0 ohm and 0.9 ohm, in ten steps (a decade of steps) of 0.1 ohm each. The next switch can select resistances between 1.0 and 9.0 ohms. The other switches can select between 10.0 and 90.0, 100.0 and 900.0, and 1,000 and 9,000 ohms. With five switches, any amount of resistance between 0.1 ohm and 9,999.9 ohms can be put into a circuit.

resistance furnace. A type of furnace used for making alloys of certain metals. The heat that melts the metal is produced by passing a large amount of electrical current through it.

resistance thermometer. A type of electrical temperature-measuring instrument that uses a resistance bulb as its temperature-sensing element. The resistance bulb contains a length of small diameter nickel wire, wound on a mica form and enclosed in a thin stainless steel tube. The resistance of the nickel wire increases as its temperature increases. The resistance bulb is installed in a Wheatstone bridge circuit in such a way that current flowing through the indicating instrument changes as the resistance of the bulb changes.

resistance welding. A form of electrical welding used for joining thin sheets of metal. The metal to be welded is pressed together by the electrodes of the welding machine, and low-voltage current is passed through the metal. Heat caused by the current softens the metal, and pressure on the electrodes forces the softened metal together. The current is stopped, but the pressure is held on the electrodes until the softened metal hardens. Spot welding and seam welding are types of resistance welding.

resistance wire. Wire made of such alloys as Manganin or Nichrome. This wire has a high resistance and is used to make precision, wire-wound resistors and electric heater elements.

resistive circuit (electrical circuit). An electrical circuit in which all of the opposition to the flow of electrons is caused by circuit resistance. In a resistive circuit, the current and voltage are in phase.

resistivity (electrical characteristic). The amount of resistance for a given volume of material or for a given amount of surface area. Resistivity is the reciprocal (the opposite) of conductivity.

resistor (electrical component). A component used to place a specific amount of resistance in an electrical circuit.

resistor color code. A color code used to show the amount of resistance and the resistance tolerance of a composition resistor. Three or four colored bands are placed around one end of the resistor. The band nearest the end of the resistor indicates the first significant digit in the resistance. The second band is for the second significant digit. The third band shows the number of zeros to add to the two significant digits. The fourth band shows the tolerance of the resistance in percentage of the nominal value. *See* resistor color code illustration.

resistor spark plug (ignition system component). A shielded aircraft spark plug with a built-in carbon resistor between its terminal end and center electrode. Shielded ignition leads have a metal braid around the insulator, and this braid, with the insulator and conductor, acts as a capacitor and stores electrical energy.

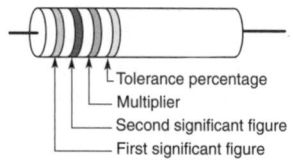

Tolerance percentage
Multiplier
Second significant figure
First significant figure

Color	Number	%Tolerance
Black	0	
Brown	1	
Red	2	
Orange	3	
Yellow	4	
Green	5	
Blue	6	
Violet	7	
Gray	8	
White	9	
Gold		5%
Silver		10%
No color		20%

resistor color code

When the spark jumps the gap in the spark plug, the energy stored in the lead capacity causes the spark to continue after the fuel is ignited. This prolonged spark needlessly wears away the spark plug electrodes. The built-in resistor causes enough opposition to this current to reduce the spark duration and increase the life of the spark plug electrodes.

resolution (radar technology). The ability of radar to show discrete targets separately. The better the resolution, the closer two targets can be to each other and still be detected as separate targets.

resolution advisory (RA) (air traffic control). A display indication given to the pilot by the traffic alert and collision avoidance system (TCAS II) recommending a maneuver to increase vertical separation relative to an intruding aircraft. Positive, negative, and vertical speed limit advisories constitute the resolution advisories. A resolution advisory is also classified as corrective or preventive.

resonance (electrical). The condition in an electrical circuit in which the inductive reactance and the capacitive reactance are equal. The reactances are determined by the frequency, and a circuit is resonant for a very narrow band of frequencies.

resonance (mechanical). The frequency of vibration of a mechanical system or device at which the vibration has the greatest displacement. The physical dimensions of an object determine the frequency at which it is resonant.

resonance method of ultrasonic inspection. A method of nondestructive inspection for internal faults in a piece of material. A pulse of ultrasonic energy of known frequency and intensity is induced into the material, and the vibration produced by this energy is displayed on an oscilloscope. There is a definite change in the vibration pattern if the wave of energy passes over a fault within the material.

resonant circuit (electrical circuit). A tuned electrical circuit that contains both capacitance and inductance. By adjusting the amount of capacitance or inductance, the circuit can be tuned (its resonant frequency can be changed).

resonant frequency (alternating current). The frequency of alternating current that produces the same inductive reactance and capacitive reactance in a circuit. Capacitive reactance decreases as the frequency increases, but the inductive reactance increases with the frequency. At only one frequency, the resonant frequency (F_r), the inductive reactance, and capacitive reactance are the same.

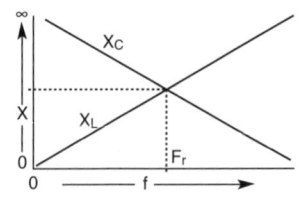

resonant frequency

resonant frequency (mechanical vibration). The frequency at which a mechanical object vibrates, or oscillates, with the maximum amplitude for the amount of energy used to produce the vibration. The resonant frequency of an object is sometimes called its natural frequency.

respirator. A device worn over the mouth and nose of a person working in an atmosphere of dangerous gases or contaminated air. Some respirators supply oxygen or clean air for the wearer, while others simply filter the contaminants from the air.

response (in teaching/learning process). A possible answer to a multiple-choice test item. The correct response is often called the keyed response, and incorrect responses are called distractors.

restricted area. *14 CFR Part 1:* "Airspace designated under Part 73 of this chapter within which the flight of aircraft, while not wholly prohibited, is subject to restriction."

restricted area (ICAO). An airspace of defined dimensions, above the land areas or territorial waters of a State, within which the flight of aircraft is restricted in accordance with certain specified conditions.

restrictor (fluid-flow system component). An orifice installed in a fluid flow system to decrease the amount of fluid allowed to flow under a specific amount of pressure.

resultant flux (aircraft magneto flux). The total magnetic flux that cuts across the secondary winding of the magneto coil. Resultant flux is the combination of the permanent magnet flux and the flux produced by current flowing in the primary winding of the coil.

resultant relative wind. Airflow from rotation that is modified by induced flow.

resultant vector. A single vector which is the sum of two or more vectors.

"Resume normal speed" (air traffic control). A phrase used by ATC to advise that previously issued speed control (controller assigned or as part of a published procedure) restrictions are deleted. This statement does not relieve the pilot of those speed restrictions which are applicable to 14 CFR §91.117.

"Resume own navigation" (air traffic control). A phrase used by ATC to advise a pilot to resume his own navigation responsibility. This is issued after completion of a radar vector or when radar contact is lost when the aircraft is being radar vectored.

retard. To slow something down or cause it to operate later than it normally does. In a reciprocating engine, the spark that ignites the fuel-air mixture inside the cylinders must be timed so the burning gases produce the greatest amount of push on the piston. When the engine is started, the pistons move slowly, and the spark must be delayed until the pistons begin to move downward. The spark for starting must be retarded.

retard breaker points (aircraft magneto component). An extra set of breaker points installed in aircraft magnetos equipped with the "Shower of Sparks" starting system. When the ignition switch is moved to the START position, a second set of breaker points is connected in parallel with the normal breaker points. These points open later than the normal points, and the spark does not occur inside the cylinder until the engine has rotated far enough beyond its normal firing position for these retard points to open.

retarded sparks. The timing of the firing of the spark plugs used to start a reciprocating engine. The sparks for starting occur later in terms of crankshaft rotation than those used for normal operation. Retarding the sparks prevent the engine from kicking back when it is being started.

retarder (finishing system component). A special thinner used in some types of finishing material, such as lacquer, to slow its drying time. When lacquer or dope dries too fast, the evaporation of the solvents often drops the temperature of the surrounding air enough that moisture condenses out of the air onto the wet finish. This causes the finish to blush, or become dull and porous.

Retarder, added to the lacquer or dope before it is sprayed onto the surface, keeps it from drying too fast. When it dries slowly, the temperature does not drop enough to condense moisture out of the air.

retention in flight instruction (psychology). The ability to recall what has been learned. There are five principles which are generally accepted as having a direct application to remembering; praise, recall, favorable attitudes, learning with all of the senses and meaningful repetition.

retentivity (magnetism). The ability of a magnetizable material to retain the alignment of the magnetic domains after the magnetizing force has been removed. Hard steel normally has a high retentivity, while soft iron and electrical steel both have very low retentivity.

retort. A vessel used to distill a material. The material to be distilled is put into the retort and boiled. Vapors from the boiling material are picked up from the top of the retort and cooled enough for them to condense back into a liquid. The liquid is collected from the retort in a suitable container.

retrace line (cathode-ray tube). The line followed by the beam of electrons in a cathode-ray tube after it ends one line and returns to the start of the next line. Retracing is also called flyback.

retract. To draw back or draw up. The landing gear of most modern airplanes can be retracted, or drawn up into the wing or fuselage.

R

retractable landing gear (aircraft landing gear). The type of landing gear that can be folded up into the structure when the aircraft is off the ground. A fixed (nonretractable) landing gear produces a large amount of drag when the aircraft is flying at a high speed. To reduce this drag, the landing gear is retracted, or folded up into the structure.

retraction test (aircraft landing gear). A part of a 100-hour or annual inspection of an aircraft. The aircraft is raised off the floor with jacks, and the retractable landing gear is operated through its retraction and extension cycle. It is checked for its operating time and for any indication of improper operation.

retread (tires). To apply new tread to a tire. The tread wears off most airplane tires long before the tire carcass is damaged or worn out, so for economical operation, the tire can be retreaded. The remaining tread is ground off and the carcass inspected. If it is in good condition, a new tread can be put on and vulcanized. A properly retreaded tire is as serviceable as a new tire, and it costs much less.

retreating blade (helicopter rotor blade). The blade of a helicopter rotor moving in the direction opposite to that in which the helicopter is flying. The blade on the opposite side of the helicopter is called the advancing blade.

retreating blade stall. The stall of a helicopter rotor disc that occurs near the tip of the retreating blade. A retreating blade stall occurs when the helicopter airspeed is high and the retreating blade airspeed is low. This results in a high angle of attack, which causes the stall.

retrofit. A part made by a manufacturer, to be installed on a device that is no longer in production. If a new engine is developed that improves the performance of an older aircraft, a retrofit can be made to install the new engine on the older aircraft. When a retrofit part is produced, it is often sold as a kit which includes the new part and all of the necessary hardware and instructions.

return manifold (fluid power system). The portion of a fluid power system through which the fluid is returned to the reservoir.

return stroke (meteorology). The intense luminosity that propagates upward from earth to cloud base in the last phase of each lightning stroke of a cloud-to-ground discharge.

return to service (aircraft maintenance operation). An aircraft is returned to service when it completes a test flight by an appropriately certified pilot. A certificated mechanic or authorized inspector must approve an aircraft for return to service after it has been inspected, repaired, or altered.

revalidate. To make something valid again. Certain licenses and certificates are valid for a definite length of time. After this time has lapsed, the holder of the license or certificate must take some specified action or pass some type of test to revalidate the license.

reverse-biased junction (semiconductor device). A voltage placed across the PN junction in a semiconductor device, with the positive voltage connected to the N-material and the negative voltage to the P-material. When the PN junction in a diode or a transistor is reverse-biased, the depletion area is enlarged so electrons cannot cross the junction to flow in the external circuit.

reverse current (semiconductor device). Current in a semiconductor device that flows across a PN junction when the junction is reverse-biased. Reverse current is the movement of minority carriers in the semiconductor material. Also called leakage current, it increases with the temperature of the device.

reverse-current relay (generator control device). A normally open, magnetically closed switch in the output circuit of a DC generator, between the generator and the battery. When the generator voltage is lower than that of the battery, a spring holds the reverse-current relay contacts open, and the generator is not connected to the battery. As soon as the generator voltage rises above that of the battery, an electromagnet in the relay closes the contacts and connects the generator to the battery. The more current flowing from the generator to the battery, the tighter the contacts are pulled together. When the generator voltage drops below that of the battery, reverse current flows from the battery to the generator. When reverse current flows, the magnetic field holding the contacts closed is cancelled, and a spring pulls the relay contacts open. This disconnects the generator from the battery. If a DC generator control circuit did not incorporate a reverse-current relay, the battery would discharge through the generator when the generator voltage was lower than that of the battery.

reverse-flow combustor (gas turbine engine component). A type of turbine engine combustor in which the air flowing from the compressor follows an S-shaped pattern and enters the combustor at its rear end. As the air flows forward through the combustor, fuel is sprayed into it and burned. The burning fuel heats and expands the air. After the hot gases leave the combustor, they complete the S-turn and flow rearward, through the turbine. Reverse-flow combustors allow the engine to be shorter than it could be if straight-through combustors were used.

reverse-polarity welding. DC electric arc welding in which the electrode is positive with respect to the work.

reverse question (in learning process). A question used in response to a student's question. Rather than give a direct answer to the student's query, the instructor returns the question to the same student to answer.

reverse riveting. A method of driving a rivet by supporting the manufactured head in a hand rivet set and upsetting the shank with a flat punch and hammer or a flush set in a rivet gun. *See* hand rivet set.

reverse sensing (electronic navigation). The condition in which the VOR needle indicates the reverse of normal operation. This occurs when the aircraft is headed toward the station with a FROM indication or when the aircraft is headed away from the station with a TO indication.

reverse thrust. A condition in which jet thrust is directed forward during landing to increase the rate of deceleration.

reversible-pitch propeller (airplane propeller). An aircraft propeller whose blades can be moved to a pitch angle that produces reverse thrust. Reversible-pitch propellers are used to decrease the length of the landing roll needed by the airplane.

review and evaluation (in teaching/learning process). The fourth and last step in the teaching process consisting of a review of all material and an evaluation of the students. In the telling-and-doing technique of flight instruction, this step consists of the instructor evaluating the student's performance while the student performs the required procedure.

revision block (aircraft drawing). An area on an aircraft drawing, usually in the lower right-hand corner, where a record is made of the number of the revision of the part shown in the drawing.

revolved section (aircraft drawing). A detailed view of a part cut from one of the main views of the drawing and revolved to show its cross section.

Reynolds number (fluid mechanics). A dimensionless number used to determine the flow characteristics of a fluid passing over a body. Reynolds number (RN) is determined by the velocity of the fluid, the distance the fluid travels over the body, and the kinematic viscosity of the fluid. Kinematic viscosity is the absolute viscosity of the fluid divided by its density.

$$RN = \frac{Vx}{\nu}$$

V = Velocity in feet per second
x = Distance from leading edge in feet
ν = kinematic viscosity in square feet per second

RF. Radio frequency.

RF energy. Radio frequency energy. Electromagnetic energy with a frequency high enough that it will radiate from any conductor through which it is flowing.

RFI (radio-frequency interference). Interference with the operation of radios, televisions, and other types of electronic equipment caused by electromagnetic radiation. RFI is caused by spurious (unwanted and unintentional) radiation of electromagnetic energy. Improperly filtered amateur radio transmitters, radio-frequency electrical heaters, and certain types of medical equipment cause radio-frequency interference.

rheostat (electrical component). A variable resistor having two connections to install it in a circuit. The resistance element of a rheostat is made either of wire wound on a circular insulating card or of a carbon compound molded onto a disk. A wiper moves across the resistance element to change the amount of resistance put into the circuit. A rheostat is similar to a potentiometer except that the potentiometer has three connections rather than two.

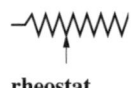

rheostat

rhetorical question (in teaching/learning process). Generally, a question asked for a purpose other than to obtain a reply. It can be a question asked to stimulate group thought. Normally answered by the instructor, rhetorical questions are more commonly used in lecturing than in guided discussions.

RHI (range-height indicator) scope (radar meteorology). A radar indicator scope that displays a vertical cross section of targets along a selected azimuth.

rhodopsin. The photosensitive pigments that initiate the visual response in the rods of the eye.

rhomboid. A plain, four-sided, closed figure in which the opposite sides are parallel, and the adjacent sides have different lengths. None of the angles in a rhomboid are right angles (90° angles).

rhomboid

rhumb line (navigation). A line drawn on a navigational chart that crosses all the meridians of longitude at the same angle.

rib (aircraft structure). The part of an aircraft wing structure that gives the wing its aerodynamic cross section. Sheet metal or fabric covers the ribs and gives the wing its airfoil shape.

ribbon direction (honeycomb material). The direction in a piece of honeycomb material that is parallel to the length of the strips of material that make up the core.

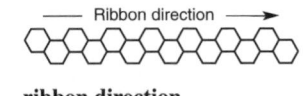

ribbon direction

ribbon parachute. A parachute whose canopy is made of a series of cloth tapes that resemble ribbons. A ribbon parachute has less opening shock than a solid-canopy parachute because of the air escaping between the ribbons.

rib lacing. *See* rib stitching.

rib stitching (aircraft fabric covering). A method of attaching fabric to the structure of an aircraft by sewing it with a strong waxed string called rib-stitching cord. The cord is passed around the wing ribs, through the top and bottom fabric, and over a reinforcing tape. Each stitch is locked with a modified seine knot.

rib stitching cord. *See* lacing cord.

rib tread (tire tread). A series of circumferential grooves cut into the tread of a tire. A rib tread pattern provides superior traction and directional stability on hard-surfaced runways.

rich flameout (gas turbine engine operation). A condition in which the flame in a gas turbine engine goes out because of an overly rich fuel-air mixture. For fuel to burn in a turbine engine, it must be mixed with air in a ratio of between 8 and 18 parts of air for 1 part of fuel, by weight. If there is either more fuel or more air than this in the mixture, the flame will go out.

rich mixture (fuel-air mixture). An air-fuel mixture that contains less than 15 parts of air to 1 part of fuel, by weight.

ridge (meteorology). An elongated area of relatively high atmospheric pressure. Ridges are usually associated with, and most clearly identified as, areas of maximum anticyclonic curvature of the wind flow.

riffle file. A hand file with its teeth formed on the outside of a curved surface that resembles the bowl of a spoon.

rigging (aircraft maintenance). Adjustment of the wings and tail surfaces of an aircraft to give it the proper flight characteristics.

rigging load (control cable specification). The tension applied to an aircraft control cable when it is being rigged. This tension must take into consideration the cable size and the ambient temperature.

rigging pins (aircraft maintenance devices). Special pins installed in holes in an aircraft control system to hold the components in a specified position when the controls are being rigged and the control cable tension adjusted.

right angle. An angle of ninety degrees (90°).

right-hand rule for electric generators. The rule for determining the direction of current flow in a wire passing through a magnetic field. Hold the right hand with the thumb, first finger, and second finger extended so they are at right angles to each other. When the first finger points in the direction of the lines of magnetic flux (from the north pole to the south pole), and the thumb points in the direction the wire is moving through the field, the second finger will point in the direction of current flow (from positive to negative). This is also known as Fleming's rule for electric generators.

right-hand rule for the direction of magnetic flux. Place the fingers of the right hand around a current-carrying conductor in such a way that the thumb points in the direction of conventional current flow (from positive to negative). The fingers will encircle the wire in the same direction as the lines of flux. This rule is also known as Fleming's rule for the direction of magnetic flux.

right-hand threads. Threads that cause a screw or threaded component to advance, or screw in, when it is turned in a clockwise direction. Most aircraft threaded components have right-hand threads.

right triangle. A triangle that contains one right (90°) angle.

rigid airship. A form of lighter-than-air flying machine. A rigid airship has a framework of aluminum alloy covered with fabric. The lifting gas is held inside the rigid framework in separate ballonets.

The German Zeppelins of World War I, the British R-100 and R-101, as well as the U.S. Navy's Los Angeles, Shenandoah, Akron and Macon and the German Graf Zeppelin and Hindenburg, are examples of rigid airships.

rigid conduit. Aluminum alloy tubing used to house electrical wires in areas where they are subject to mechanical damage.

rigidity in space. The characteristic of a gyroscope that prevents its axis of rotation tilting as the earth rotates. This characteristic is used for attitude gyro instruments.

rigid rotor (helicopter rotor). A helicopter rotor attached in its hub so its only freedom of movement is that of changing the blade pitch angle. The blades of a rigid rotor have no hinges that allow them to flap or drag.

rigid tubing (fluid power systems component). Thin-wall tubing made of stainless steel, aluminum alloy, or copper, used in aircraft plumbing. Rigid tubing can be used to join components only where there is no relative movement. If there is relative movement, flexible hose must be used.

rime ice. A type of ice which forms on an aircraft flying through visible moisture (as in a cloud) when the air temperature is below freezing. Rime ice is made of ice crystals and is rough and milky looking. Rime ice not only adds weight to the aircraft, but since it is rough, it disturbs the airflow over the wing and tail surfaces and destroys lift.

ring cowl (reciprocating engine cowling). A type of cowling used to cover an aircraft radial engine. A ring cowl surrounds the cylinder heads and decreases the aerodynamic drag caused by the cylinders and improves the flow of cooling air through the cylinder fins. Ring cowls are also called speed rings, or more properly, Townend rings, after their inventor, English physicist H.L. Townend. *See* illustration for Townend ring.

ring gear. One of the gears in a planetary gear system. The teeth are on the inside of the ring gear, and the planetary gears mounted on pins fastened to the spider-like output shaft mesh with and ride between the inside the ring gear and the outside of the sun gear. The ring gear can be either rigidly mounted in the gear housing, or it can be driven by the input shaft, depending upon the gear ratio of the system. If the ring gear is rigidly mounted, the sun gear is driven by the input shaft.

ring grooves (reciprocating engine piston). The grooves around a piston into which the piston rings are installed. *See* piston rings (reciprocating engine component).

ringworms (fabric defect). A series of circular cracks in the dope film on a fabric-covered aircraft. Ringworms appear when a blunt object presses against the fabric that is covered with a dope film that has become brittle because its plasticizers have dried out. Ringworms can be removed by rejuvenating the dope. *See* rejuvenation.

rip panel (free balloon component). A panel in the gas bag of a free balloon that can be opened by pulling the rip cord to dump gas from the balloon.

ripple filter (electronic filter). An electronic filter installed in a DC power supply. The ripple filter decreases the amplitude of the ripple remaining when alternating current is rectified.

ripple frequency. The frequency of the ripple in the output of a rectifier circuit. In a full-wave rectifier, the ripple frequency is twice the frequency of the alternating current. In a half-wave rectifier, the ripple frequency is the same as that of the AC.

ripsaw. A woodcutting saw with large, chisel-shaped teeth. A ripsaw is used to cut wood in the direction of its grain.

riser. One of several straps that attach the cart of a powered parachute to the suspension lines. Sometimes referred to as "V lines," risers are the intermediate link between the suspension lines and the aircraft.

rise time (electrical pulses). The length of time (usually measured in picoseconds or nanoseconds) needed for the leading edge of an electrical pulse to rise from 10% to 90% of its final value. The rise time of a pulse relates to the steepness of the leading edge of the pulse.

risk (aeronautical decision making). Future uncertainty caused by an existing hazard; the impact or result of a hazard to flight that is not eliminated or controlled.

risk elements (in ADM). The four fundamental risk factors that must be taken into consideration in ADM: the pilot, the aircraft, the environment, and external pressures. *See* PAVE.

risk elements (psychology). There are four fundamental risk elements: the pilot, the aircraft, the environment, and the type of operation that comprise any given aviation situation.

risk management (psychology). The part of the decision making process which relies on situational awareness, problem or hazard recognition, and good judgment to reduce risks associated with each flight. It is a practical approach to managing uncertainty and is used to control, eliminate, or reduce the hazard to fall within parameters of acceptability. *See also* acceptable risk.

rivet. A small pin-type fastener, used to fasten pieces of sheet metal together. Most aircraft rivets are made of aluminum alloy and are driven cold. The rivet is slipped through holes in the material being fastened, and a heavy steel bucking bar is held against the end of the shank. The head of the rivet is hammered with a rivet gun (an air hammer). The bucked head, or shop head, that is formed when the rivet is driven, is flat on top, and its sides are rounded.

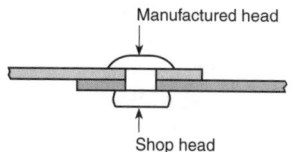

rivet

rivet cutter (mechanic's hand tool). A special type of cutter used to cut aircraft solid rivets to the required length. The jaws of the cutter are ground so the cut end of the rivet shank is flat.

rivet gage. The distance between rows of rivets in a riveted aircraft structure.

rivet gun (aircraft sheet metalworking tool). A handheld air hammer that drives a rivet set with a series of sharp blows. A rivet set, with a recess the shape and size of the head of the rivet being driven, is held in the rivet gun with a spring-type retainer. The rivet set is pressed against the head of the rivet, and a heavy polished-steel bucking bar is held against the end of the rivet shank. The blows on the head of the rivet upset the shank and cause it to swell out and form the bucked, or shop, head.

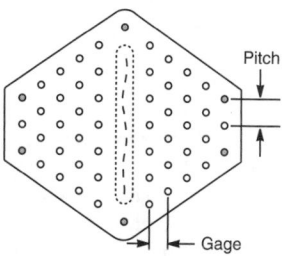

rivet gage and pitch

rivet pitch. The distance between the center of adjacent rivets in the same row in a riveted aircraft structure. *See* illustration for rivet gage.

rivet set. A tool used to drive aircraft rivets. A rivet set is a piece of hardened steel with a recess the shape of the rivet head in one end. The other end of the rivet set fits into the rivet gun. The rivet gun vibrates the rivet set and hammers the rivet against a heavy steel bucking bar held against the end of the rivet shank.

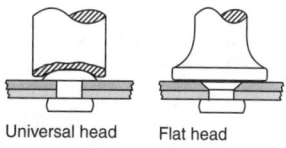

rivet set

Rivnut. A patented fastener used to install threads in thin sheet metal. A Rivnut is a blind rivet with an internally threaded hollow shank. The Rivnut is slipped through a hole drilled in the thin sheet metal, and its shank is collapsed by pulling it with a special pulling tool screwed into the threads. Rivnuts were developed by the B.F. Goodrich Company to install deicer boots on airplane wings.

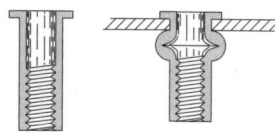

Rivnut

RL circuit (electrical circuit). An electrical circuit that contains both resistance and inductance.

RLC circuit (electrical circuit). An electrical circuit that contains resistance, inductance, and capacitance.

RMI (radio magnetic indicator). An electronic navigation instrument that combines a magnetic compass
with an automatic direction finder (ADF). The card
of the RMI acts as gyro-stabilized magnetic compass, and shows the magnetic heading the aircraft is
flying. A pointer gives the relative bearing between
the nose of the aircraft and the radio station being
received on the navigation radio.

rms (root mean square). *See* root mean square.

RNAV. *See* area navigation.

RNAV approach. An instrument approach procedure
that relies on aircraft area navigation equipment for
navigational guidance.

**RMI (radio
magnetic indicator)**

RNAV (GPS) approach. An approach procedure based
on GPS signals for guidance.

RNAV DP. A departure procedure developed for RNAV-equipped aircraft whose ground
track is based on satellite or DME/DME navigation systems.

RNAV system, suitable. An area navigation (RNAV) system that meets the required
performance established for a type of operation (e.g. IFR) and is appropriately fitted
for operation over the route to be flown in terms of any performance criteria (including accuracy) established by the air navigation service provider for certain routes (e.g.
oceanic, ATS routes, and IAPs). An RNAV system's suitability is dependent upon the
availability of ground and/or satellite navigation aids that are needed to meet route
performance criteria that may be prescribed in route specifications to navigate the aircraft along the route to be flown. Information on suitable RNAV systems is published
in FAA guidance material (such as Advisory Circulars).

RNAV waypoint. *14 CFR Part 1:* "A predetermined geographical position used for route or
instrument approach definition or progress reporting purposes that is defined relative
to a VORTAC station position."

RNP. *See* required navigation performance.

ROAB. A radiosonde observation.

road reconnaissance. Military activity requiring navigation along roads, railroads, and
rivers. Reconnaissance route/route segments are seldom along a straight line and
normally require a lateral route width of 10 NM to 30 NM and an altitude range of
500 feet to 10,000 feet AGL.

robot. A form of automated machine, used to replace a human operator in some tasks that
are dangerous or highly repetitive. Robots can be programmed to sense certain conditions and act in the correct way for the conditions that exist.

robotics. The branch of science or technology that deals with the design, application,
construction, and maintenance of robots.

rocker arm (reciprocating engine component). A pivoted arm on the cylinder head of a
reciprocating engine. The pushrod forces one end of the rocker arm up, and as the other
end moves down, it forces the intake or exhaust valve off its seat.

rocker box. The enclosed part of a reciprocating engine cylinder head that houses the valve
mechanism.

rocket. A flight vehicle propelled by expanding gases produced when the fuel combines
with oxygen carried in the vehicle. Rocket engines can use either liquid or solid fuel,
and they are not dependent upon oxygen in the atmosphere. Rockets are used to launch
orbiting satellites.

14 CFR Part 1: "An aircraft propelled by ejected expanding gases generated in the engine from self-contained propellants and not dependent on the intake of outside substances. It includes any part which becomes separated during the operation."

rocket engine. A form of reaction engine whose fuel and oxidizer contain all of the oxygen needed for the release of heat energy. The released heat expands the gases which are ejected at a high velocity from a nozzle at the rear of the rocket. Rocket engines can operate in outer space where there is no atmosphere.

rocketsonde (meteorology). A type of radiosonde launched by a rocket which makes its measurements during a parachute descent. Rocketsondes are capable of obtaining soundings to a much greater height than is possible by balloon or aircraft.

rocking shaft (aircraft instrument component). A shaft used in the mechanism of a pressure-measuring instrument to change the direction of movement by 90° and to amplify the amount of movement.

Rockwell hardness tester. A precision testing machine, used to measure the hardness of a material. A diamond pyramid or hardened steel ball is pressed by an accurately calibrated force into the surface of the material being tested. The depth to which the pyramid or ball penetrates the surface is measured with a dial indicator. The greater the depth of penetration, the softer the material.

rock wool. A form of insulating material made by blowing a high-velocity stream of air through molten rock. Rock wool is fireproof, and the dead air space it contains makes it a good thermal insulator.

roentgenology. The branch of science dealing with the use of X-rays.

roger (radio communications term). A term meaning "I have received all of your last transmission." This statement should not be used to answer a question requiring a yes or no answer.

roll (aircraft flight maneuver). Rotation of an aircraft about its longitudinal axis.

roll cloud (meteorology). A dense and horizontal roll-shaped cloud located on the lower leading edge of a cumulonimbus, or less often on a rapidly developing cumulus. Roll clouds indicate the presence of turbulence.

roller bearing. A form of antifriction bearing that supports the load on hardened steel cylinders rolling between two hardened and polished races. Roller bearings are used for radial loads, rather than thrust loads.

roller bearings, straight. A type of nonfriction bearing used where the bearing is subjected to radial loads only. They are often used in high power aircraft engines for the crankshaft main bearings and in other applications where radial loads are high.

R

roll-out RVR (runway visual range). The RVR readout values obtained from sensors located nearest the rollout end of the runway.

roll pin. A press-fit pin used as a pivot in certain types of machinery. A roll pin is made of spring steel sheet rolled into a small, open-sided cylinder. When a roll pin is pressed into a hole slightly smaller than its outside diameter, it squeezes together to fit into the hole. The spring action trying to expand the pin to its normal diameter holds it tightly in the hole.

roll threading. A method of forming threads on a bolt or rod by rolling the material to be threaded between grooved rollers. No material is removed when the threads are rolled, as it is when they are cut.

RONLY. The notation on a flight plan that the aircraft has a radio receiver only, no transmitter.

root (mathematics). A number which, when multiplied by itself a specified number of times, will produce a given number.

root (propeller blade nomenclature). The portion of a propeller blade that secures the blade in the hub.

root mean square (rms) (alternating current value). A value used to measure the heating effect of sine-wave alternating current. The rms value is found by dividing one alternation of the AC into an infinite number of instantaneous values. Each instantaneous value is squared (multiplied by itself), and all of the squares are averaged to find the average, or mean, square. The square root is taken of this mean square.

The rms value of sine wave alternating current is 0.707 time the peak value of one alternation. One ampere rms has a peak value of 1.414 ($\sqrt{2}$) amps and produces the same amount of heat as one amp of direct current. The rms value is also called the effective value.

Roots-type air compressor. A positive-displacement air pump that uses two intermeshing figure-8-shaped rotors to move the air.

rosette weld. A method of securing one steel structural tube inside another. Small holes are drilled in the outer tube, and the inner tube is welded to it around the circumference of the holes. Rosette welds are used to prevent the inner tube moving inside the outer tube. This type of weld gets its name from the fact that the finished welds look like small roses.

rosin. A reddish-brown, translucent material left in the process of distilling turpentine from the sap of pine trees. Rosin is used in the manufacture of paints, inks, adhesives, and as a flux for soldering.

rosin-core solder. A type of solder used for electrical and electronic work. Rosin-core solder is made in the form of a hollow metal wire, filled with rosin. When the solder melts, the rosin flows out to cover the metal and keep oxygen away from the surface, preventing the formation of oxides. Solder using synthetic rosin for the core is called resin-core solder.

rosin joint (bad solder connection). The common term for a bad connection made when soldering electrical wires. Rosin core or resin core solder is used for this type of work, and it is possible for the melted flux to hold the wires together without the solder wetting the wires and making a secure joint. A rosin joint can be prevented by having the wires perfectly clean, and hot enough to melt the solder before the solder is allowed to touch the wires.

rotable parts (maintenance supply). High usage, locally repairable components such as aircraft wheels, tires, avionics assemblies, propellers, and built-up engines.

rotary actuator. A fluid-power actuator whose output is rotary movement. A hydraulic motor is a rotary actuator.

rotary breather (turbine engine component). A small engine-driven slinger located in the lubrication vent subsystem. The oil leaving the engine-accessory gear box contains some air, and the slinger separates the oil from the air. The deareated oil is then returned to the gear box sump.

rotary radial engine. A form of reciprocating engine used in some early airplanes because of its light weight. In a rotary radial engine, the crankshaft is attached to the airframe and the crankcase, cylinders, and propeller rotate. Rotary radial engines were popular up through World War I.

rotary switch. An electrical switch capable of selecting any of several circuits. Contacts around the periphery of an insulating wafer connect to all of the circuits to be selected. The common lead is connected to a wiper that makes connection with the contacts, one at a time. This wiper is turned by a shaft through the center of the wafer. By turning the shaft, the wiper is moved to complete the selected circuit Rotary

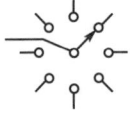

rotary switch

switches may have several wafers stacked on one shaft to control several circuits at the same time.

rotary wing. A classification of aircraft that is sustained in the air by a rotating airfoil (a rotor) rather than a fixed airfoil, or wing. Helicopters and gyroplanes are examples of rotary-wing aircraft.

rotating combustion (RC) engine. *See* Wankel engine.

rotation. That portion of the takeoff of an airplane equipped with a tricycle landing gear in which the airplane has gained enough speed for the nose wheel to be lifted to increase the angle of attack and thus the lift. The rotation speed is identified as the V_R speed.

rotational velocity, Vr (helicopter aerodynamics). The velocity of the air flowing across a helicopter rotor blade caused by the rotation of the blade. Vr varies with the blade station and the rotor RPM.

rotator vent. *See* turning vent.

rote learning. A basic level of learning in which the student has the ability to repeat back something learned, with no understanding or ability to apply what was learned.

rotometer. A form of flow measuring instrument. A rotometer is made of a tapered glass tube holding a metal indicator float. The fluid whose flow rate is to be measured enters the bottom of the rotometer and flows upward, lifting the float. The taper inside the tube causes the pressure drop across the rotometer to remain constant as the rate of flow changes. Rotometers can be used to measure the flow rate of either gases or liquids.

rotor (axial-flow compressor component). The moving part of an axial-flow compressor. The rotor is made of a series of disks, containing the compressor blades, that rotate between stages of fixed stator vanes. Air is moved through the engine by the aerodynamic action of the rotor blades.

rotor (DC alternator component). The rotating component in a DC alternator. The rotor contains a field coil mounted between two hard steel plates with interlacing fingers around their periphery. These fingers form the poles for the rotating magnetic field. Excitation current is fed into the field coil through brushes riding on two smooth slip rings.

rotor (meteorology). A turbulent air circulation under mountain-wave crests, to the lee side and parallel to the mountains creating the wave. Glider pilots use the term rotor to describe any low-level turbulent flow associated with mountain waves.

rotor brake (helicopter rotor component). A brake used to stop the rotation of the rotor when a helicopter is being shut down. The rotor brake may be actuated by either a mechanical or a hydraulic mechanism.

R

rotor cloud (meteorology). A turbulent cloud formation found on the lee of some large mountain barriers. The air in the cloud rotates about an axis parallel to the range, and rotor clouds indicate the possibility of violent turbulence.

rotorcraft. A heavier-than-air aircraft whose aerodynamic lift is produced by a set of rotating airfoils called rotors. Helicopters and autogiros are types of rotorcraft. *14 CFR Part 1:* "A heavier-than-air aircraft that depends principally for its support in flight on the lift generated by one or more rotors."

rotorcraft-load combination. *14 CFR Part 1:* "The combination of a rotorcraft and an external-load, including the external-load attaching means.

Rotorcraft-load combinations are designated as Class A, Class B, Class C, and Class D, as follows:

(1) Class A rotorcraft-load combination means one in which the external load cannot move freely, cannot be jettisoned, and does not extend below the landing gear.

Continued

rotorcraft-load combination. *Continued*

(2) Class B rotorcraft-load combination means one in which the external load is jettisonable and is lifted free of land or water during the rotorcraft operation.

(3) Class C rotorcraft-load combination means one in which the external load is jettisonable and remains in contact with land or water during the rotorcraft operation.

(4) Class D rotorcraft-load combination means one in which the external load is other than a Class A, B, or C and has been specifically approved by the Administrator for that operation."

rotor disc area. *See* disc area.

rotor force (gyroplane aerodynamics). The aerodynamic forces acting on the rotor of a gyroplane. It is comprised of rotor lift and rotor drag.

rotor streaming (meteorology). A phenomenon that occurs when air flowing across a mountain is sufficient for wave formation, but decreases with altitude above the mountain. The air downstream of the mountain breaks up and becomes turbulent, similar to a rotor, but no lee waves form above the mountain.

round file. *See* rattail file.

round off (mathematics). The mathematical process in which some of the least significant digits of a number are deleted. The rule for rounding off: If the first digit in the discarded part is 5 or greater, increase the lowest digit in the part being saved by one. If the first digit in the discarded part is less than 5, leave the saved part as it is.

roundout (aircraft landing). A slow, smooth transition from a normal approach attitude to a landing attitude, gradually rounding out the flightpath to one that is parallel with the runway, and within a very few inches above.

route (air traffic control). A defined path, consisting of one or more courses in a horizontal plane, which aircraft traverse over the surface of the earth.

route action notification (air traffic control). A user request notification tool (URET) alert to the controller that a preferential route (such as PAR/PDR/PDAR) has been applied to the flight plan. *See also* preferential routes, and user request notification tool (URET).

router (metal or woodcutting tool). A wood- or metal-working power tool, used to cut grooves in a surface, or to cut the core from a honeycomb material. A router consists of a high-speed motor spinning a tool whose cutting edges are on its side. A guide is used to control the depth to which the cutting tool can penetrate the material being routed.

route segment. *14 CFR Part 1:* "A part of a route. Each end of that part is identified by:

(1) A continental or insular geographical location; or

(2) A point at which a definite radio fix can be established."

route segment (ICAO). A portion of a route to be flown, as defined by two consecutive significant points specified in a flight plan.

routine inspection. A visual examination or check of an item in which no disassembly is required.

roving (textile materials). A lightly twisted roll or strand of textile material. Fiberglass roving is used in place of fiberglass mat, to reinforce plastic resins molded into certain structural shapes.

RPM (revolutions per minute). A measure of rotational speed. One RPM is one revolution made in one minute.

rubber cement. An adhesive used to fasten sheets of paper together. Rubber cement is made of unvulcanized rubber dissolved in an organic solvent.

rubidium. A soft, silvery-white, reactive, alkali-metal chemical element. Rubidium's symbol is Rb, its atomic number is 37, and its atomic weight is 85.47. Rubidium ignites spontaneously in air and reacts violently with water. It is used in the manufacture of photocells and electron tubes.

rudder (airplane control surface). The movable control surface mounted on the trailing edge of the vertical fin of an airplane. The rudder is moved by foot-operated pedals in the cockpit, and movement of the rudder rotates the airplane about its vertical axis.

rudder pedals (flight controls). The controls that allow the pilot to yaw the aircraft. In an airplane, the rudder pedals move the rudder and produce an aerodynamic force that causes the airplane to rotate about its vertical axis. In a helicopter, the rudder pedals, more accurately called the anti-torque pedals, control the pitch of the tail rotor to increase or decrease its thrust to rotate the helicopter about its vertical axis.

ruddervator (airplane controls). Control surfaces on an airplane that combine the functions of the rudder and the elevators. Ruddervators are the movable surfaces in a V-tail empennage. Moving together, they act as elevators, rotating the airplane about its lateral axis. Moving differentially, they act as the rudder to rotate the airplane about its vertical axis.

rule of sixty (navigation). A rule of thumb that states for 60 miles of flight, each degree of drift will cause the aircraft to be one mile off course.

run (paint defect). A defect in a paint film caused by the paint attempting to flow off the surface. Runs are caused by the application of too much paint.

run-in (engine operation). A time of controlled operation of a new or freshly overhauled aircraft engine that allows the moving parts to wear together. The operating conditions of pressures, temperatures, and vibration are carefully monitored during the run-in. After the run-in is completed, the lubricating oil is drained and examined for the presence of metallic particles.

running fit. A fit between parts of a mechanism that allows them to move relative to each other.

runout check (dimensional inspection). A check made of a rotating shaft to determine its straightness. The shaft is supported on its main bearing journals in a set of V-blocks and is rotated while a dial indicator rests on the portion of the shaft being checked. The dial indicator measures the amount the shaft is bent.

run up (engine operation). A procedure in which an aircraft engine is operated on the ground to determine its condition and performance.

runway (aviation operation). A defined rectangular area on a land airport prepared for the landing and takeoff run of aircraft along its length. Runways are normally numbered in relation to their magnetic direction rounded off to the nearest ten degrees, such as Runway 01 or Runway 25.

runway centerline lights. Runway lighting that consists of flush centerline lights spaced at 50-foot intervals beginning 75 feet from the landing threshold.

runway centerline markings (RCLM). The runway centerline identifies the center of the runway and provides alignment guidance during takeoffs and landings. The centerline consists of a line of uniformly spaced stripes and gaps.

runway condition reading. Numerical decelerometer readings relayed by air traffic controllers at USAF and certain civil bases for use by the pilot in determining runway braking action. These readings are routinely relayed only to USAF and Air National Guard Aircraft.

runway edge lights. A component of the runway lighting system that is used to outline the edges of runways at night or during low visibility conditions. These lights are classified according to the intensity they are capable of producing.

runway end identifier lights (REIL). This system consists of a pair of synchronized flashing lights, located laterally on each side of the runway threshold, to provide rapid and positive identification of the approach end of a runway.

R

runway gradient. The average slope, measured in percent, between two ends or points on a runway. Runway gradient is depicted on government aerodrome sketches when the total runway gradient exceeds 0.3%.

runway heading. The magnetic direction that corresponds with the runway centerline extended, not the painted runway number. When cleared to "fly or maintain runway heading," pilots are expected to fly or maintain the heading that corresponds with the extended centerline of the departure runway. Drift correction shall not be applied; e.g., Runway 4, actual magnetic heading of the runway centerline 044, fly 044.

runway hotspots. Locations on a particular airport that historically have hazardous intersections. Hot spots alert pilots to a possible lack of visibility at certain points or the fact that the tower may be unable to see particular intersections. Pilots need to be aware that these hazardous intersections exist and be increasingly vigilant when approaching and taxiing through them. Pilots are typically notified of these areas by a Letter to Airmen or by accessing the FAA Office of Runway Safety.

runway incursion. An occurrence at an airport involving an aircraft, vehicle, person, or object on the ground that creates a collision hazard or results in a loss of separation with an aircraft that is taking off, intending to take off, landing, or intending to land.

runway in use/active runway/duty runway. Any runway or runways currently being used for takeoff or landing. When multiple runways are used, they are all considered active runways.

runway markings. *See* airport marking aids.

runway overrun (military aviation term). A stabilized or paved area beyond the end of a runway, of the same width as the runway plus shoulders, centered on the extended runway centerline.

runway profile descent. An IFR ATC arrival procedure to a runway published for pilot use in graphic and/or textual form which may be associated with a STAR and provides routing. May depict crossing altitudes, speed restrictions, and headings to be flown from the enroute structure to the point where the pilot will receive clearance for and execute an instrument approach procedure. May apply to more than one runway if so stated on the chart.

runway safety area. A defined surface surrounding the runway that is prepared, or suitable, for reducing the risk of damage to airplanes in the event of an undershoot, overshoot, or excursion from the runway. The dimensions of the RSA vary and can be determined by using criteria from AC 150/5300-13, "Airport Design."

runway safety program (RSP). A program designed to create and execute a plan of action that reduces the number of runway incursions at the nation's airports.

runway temperature. Temperature of the air just above a runway, ideally at engine and/or wing height. Runway temperature is useful for determining density altitude when computing engine and aircraft performance.

runway threshold markings. Markings that help identify the beginning of the runway that is available for landing. Runway threshold markings come in two configurations, consisting of either eight longitudinal stripes of uniform dimensions disposed symmetrically about the runway centerline, or a number of stripes related to the runway width. In some instances, the landing threshold may be displaced.

runway transition. In conventional STARs/SIDs, the portion of a STAR/SID that serves a particular runway or runways at an airport. In RNAV STARs/SIDs, defines a path(s) from the common route to the final point(s) on a STAR; or, the common route that serves a particular runway or runways at an airport for a SID.

runway use program. A noise abatement runway selection plan designed to enhance noise abatement efforts with regard to airport communities for arriving and departing aircraft. These plans are developed into runway use programs and apply to all turbojet aircraft 12,500 pounds or heavier; turbojet aircraft less than 12,500 pounds are included only if the airport proprietor determines that the aircraft creates a noise problem. Runway use programs are coordinated with FAA offices, and safety criteria used in these programs are developed by the Office of Flight Operations.

runway visibility (meteorology). The meteorological visibility along an identified runway, determined from a specified point on the runway. Runway visibility may be determined by a transmissometer or by an observer.

runway visibility value (RVV). The visibility determined for a particular runway by a transmissometer. A meter provides a continuous indication of the visibility (reported in miles or fractions of miles) for the runway. RVV is used in lieu of prevailing visibility in determining minimums for a particular runway.

runway visual range (RVR). The range over which the pilot of an aircraft on the centerline of a runway can see the runway surface markings or the lights delineating the runway or identifying its centerline.

rust. A red oxide that forms on ferrous metal (metal that contains iron). Rust has no strength, it is porous, and it continues to eat the metal until it is completely destroyed. Rust can be prevented by keeping all oxygen away from the metal, by painting it, or by coating it with a film of oil or grease.

ruthenium. A hard, white, acid-resistant, metallic chemical element. Ruthenium's symbol is Ru, its atomic number is 44, and its atomic weight is 101.07. Ruthenium is used as an alloying agent for platinum and palladium and is also used in the manufacture of electrical contacts.

RVR (Runway Visual Range). An instrumentally derived horizontal distance a pilot should see down the runway from the approach end. RVR is based on either the sighting of high-intensity runway lights or on the visual contrast of other objects, whichever yields the greatest visual range.

RVV. *See* runway visibility value.

R

Sierra

SA. *See* selective availability.

saber saw. An electrically operated, handheld jigsaw. A saber saw uses a short, stiff blade, motor driven in a reciprocating (in-and-out) fashion.

sacrificial corrosion. A form of corrosion in which an active material is used as the anode in the corrosion process to protect a less active material. The anode is sacrificed to save the cathode.

Steel parts are often plated with cadmium to sacrificially protect them from corrosion. If the coating of cadmium is scratched through to expose the steel, a corrosion cell is formed between the cadmium and the steel. The cadmium, being more anodic (more chemically active) than the steel, will be changed into a salt and it, rather than the steel, will corrode.

saddle gusset. A piece of plywood glued to an aircraft structural member. The saddle gusset has a cutout to hold a backing block or strip tightly against the skin to allow a nailing strip to be used to apply pressure to a glued joint in the skin.

saddle-mount oil tank (gas turbine engine component). A type of lubricating oil tank used with a gas turbine engine. A saddle-mount tank is shaped in such a way that it fits around the curvature of the engine compressor case in much the same way a saddle fits a horse.

SAE (Society of Automotive Engineers). A professional organization that formulates standards for the automotive and aviation industries.

safety alert (air traffic control). An alert issued by ATC to aircraft under their control if ATC is aware that the aircraft is at an altitude which, in the controller's judgment, places it in unsafe proximity to terrain, obstructions, or other aircraft. The controller may discontinue the issuance of further alerts if the pilot advises he is taking action to correct the situation or has the other aircraft in sight.

safety belt. A belt installed in an aircraft to hold the occupants tight in their seat. Safety belts are also called seat belts or lap belts.

safety factor (structural design). The ratio of the maximum load a structure is designed to support, to the maximum load it will ever be required to support. If a beam is expected to support a maximum load of 10,000 pounds and is designed in such a way that it can support 20,000 pounds, it has a safety factor of two.

safety gap (magneto ignition system). A location inside a high-tension magneto in which a portion of the metal housing is close enough to the high-voltage terminal to prevent the secondary voltage building up high enough to damage the coil insulation. The spark plug normally provides the gap for the spark to jump, but if a lead is off a spark plug, the secondary voltage could build up high enough to damage the coil insulation. Rather than the voltage building up this high, it jumps the safety gap.

safety glass. A type of glass that does not leave jagged fragments when it breaks. Safety glass may be made by laminating a layer of resilient transparent plastic material between two sheets of glass. This type of safety glass will break, but all of the pieces stick to and are held by the center plastic layer. Another form of safety glass is tempered glass that breaks into small grains, rather than into sharp pieces.

S

safety logic system (air traffic control). A software enhancement to airport surface detection equipment (ASDE-3, ASDE-X, and ASDE-3X) that predicts the path of aircraft landing and/or departing, and/or vehicular movements on runways. Visual and aural alarms are activated when the safety logic projects a potential collision. The Airport Movement Area Safety System (AMASS) is a safety logic system enhancement to the ASDE-3. The safety logic system for ASDE-X and ASDE-3X is an integral part of the software program.

safety logic system alerts (air traffic control). Alerts generated by the safety logic system of airport surface detection equipment, categorized into five types: Alert, false alert, nuisance alert, valid non-alert, and invalid non-alert. An "alert" is an actual situation involving two real safety logic tracks (aircraft/aircraft, aircraft/vehicle, or aircraft/other tangible object) that the system has predicted will result in an imminent collision. A "false alert" is an alert generated by one or more false surface-radar targets that are interpreted as real tracks by the system. A "nuisance alert" is generated by a known situation or approved operation that is not considered unsafe (e.g., LAHSO). A "valid non-alert" occurs in a situation in which the system software correctly determines that an alert is not required based on the design specifications and current safety logic parameters. An "invalid non-alert" occurs when the system software does not issue an alert when one is required.

safety valve (pressure system component). A pressure relief valve used on containers holding a compressible fluid under pressure. If the pressure inside the container becomes excessive, the safety valve will pop off its seat and relieve the excess pressure.

safety wire. Soft wire used to secure fasteners (bolts, pins, and clips) so they will not vibrate loose in operation. Safety wire (also called lockwire) is made of galvanized low-carbon steel, annealed stainless steel, or brass.

safety wiring (maintenance procedure). A method of securing a threaded device so it cannot accidentally turn. Bolts, screws, and turnbuckles are often safetied by passing soft steel or brass wire through holes in them, twisting the wire, and attaching it to the structure in such a way that it pulls in the direction to tighten the fastener.

sail back (seaplane operations). A maneuver during high wind conditions (usually with power off) where floatplane movement is controlled by water rudders and/or opening and closing cabin doors.

sailing (seaplane operations). Using the wind as the main motive force while on the water.

sailplane (aircraft type). A high-performance glider. Sailplanes normally have a high-aspect-ratio wing, are lightweight, and very strong. Sailplanes glide so well that they ride upward on rising air currents. They can stay airborne for hours and can travel long distances.

Saint Elmo's fire (meteorology). A discharge of static electricity often seen on airplanes flying through stormy weather. Static electricity from the clouds collects on the airplane structure and discharges from sharp points in the form of visible light.

sal ammoniac. A name commonly used for ammonium chloride. Ammonium chloride is one of the components of the moist-paste electrolyte used in carbon-zinc flashlight batteries.

salient pole (electrical machine). A field pole of an electrical generator or motor that has its own pole shoe protruding radially inward from the field frame. A field coil is wound around this pole shoe. Salient poles are often used instead of distributed poles which do not have separate pole shoes.

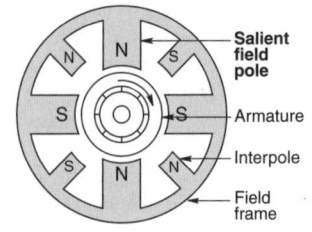

salient pole

salt. A product of a chemical reaction in which a metal displaces the hydrogen in an acid. If sulfuric acid (H_2SO_4) reacts with sodium hydroxide (NaOH), sodium sulfate (Na_2SO_4) and water (H_2O) are produced. Sodium sulfate is a salt. The food seasoning called "salt" is sodium chloride (NaCl).

samarium. A pale gray, rare-earth, metallic chemical element. Samarium's symbol is Sm, its atomic number is 62, and its atomic weight is 150.35. Samarium is used in laser technology and as an ingredient in infrared-absorbing glass.

same direction aircraft (air traffic control). Aircraft that are following the same track in the same direction; aircraft with parallel tracks and flying in the same direction; or aircraft with tracks that intersect at an angle of less than 45 degrees.

sandbag (sheet-metal-working tool). A heavy canvas or leather bag filled with sand. A sandbag is used to shape sheet metal parts by forming a depression in the sand and hammering the metal into it with a soft-face mallet.

sand casting (metal forming). A method of casting metal parts in a mold made of sand. A pattern that duplicates the part to be molded is made of wood and is covered with a special casting sand that contains a resin to bind it together.

The mold is separated along a special parting line, and the pattern is removed. The mold is put back together, and the cavity is poured full of molten metal. When the metal cools, the sand is broken away from the molded part. Sand casting is less expensive than permanent-mold casting.

sanding coat (finishing system). A coat of heavy-bodied surfacer material sprayed over a surface to be painted. After the sanding coat has thoroughly dried, it is sanded to give a smooth surface over which the subsequent coats of finishing material are applied.

sandpaper. An abrasive paper made by bonding grains of sharp sand to the surface of a piece of paper. Sandpaper is used for abrading (wearing away) rough surfaces or unwanted material.

sandwich construction. A type of laminated structure used where high strength, light weight, and rigidity are required. One commonly used type of sandwich construction is made of a fiberglass or metal honeycomb core bonded between two sheets of resin-impregnated fiberglass or metal.

sandwich structure (composites). A composite material composed of a lightweight core (usually honeycomb or foam) to which two relatively thin, dense, high-strength, functional or decorative skins are bonded.

Santa Ana (meteorology). A hot, dry, foehn wind, generally from the northeast or east, occurring west of the Sierra Nevada Mountains, especially in the pass and river valley near Santa Ana, California.

SAR. *See* search and rescue.

satellite. An object that rotates in an orbit around a larger object. Today, man-made satellites rotate in orbits around the earth for the purposes of observation and communication.

satellite ephemeris data. Data broadcast by the GPS satellite containing very accurate orbital data for that satellite, atmospheric propagation data, and satellite clock error data.

satin-weave fabric. Fabric in which the warp threads pass under one fill thread and over several more. Satin-weave fabrics are used when the lay-up must be made over complex shapes.

satin weave

saturated reactor (electrical component). A type of electrical transformer whose core permeability is varied to control the current flowing in its secondary winding. A control winding carrying direct current is wound over the transformer core. When no current flows through the control winding, the permeability of the core is high, and the transformer has enough inductive reactance to decrease the secondary current.

When maximum current flows in the control winding, its magnetic field saturates the core with a steady magnetic flux. This flux decreases the permeability of the core so much that the changing flux caused by the secondary current does not affect the core. There is less inductive reactance, so the secondary current has less opposition, and it increases.

saturate (meteorology). To combine to such an extent that there is no more tendency to combine. Dry air absorbs water vapor. But when the air becomes saturated, it will not absorb any more. The amount of water the air can hold before becoming saturated depends upon its temperature.

saturated adiabatic lapse rate (meteorology). The rate of decrease of temperature with altitude as saturated air is lifted with no gain or loss of heat from outside sources. The saturated adiabatic lapse rate varies with temperature, being greatest at low temperature.

saturated air (meteorology). Air that cannot hold any more water vapor and has a relative humidity of 100 percent.

saturated vapor. The condition of the vapor above a liquid that will not allow any more of the liquid to evaporate.

saturated vapor pressure. The static pressure of a vapor when the vapor phase of some material is in equilibrium with the liquid phase of that same material.

saturation (meteorology). The condition of the atmosphere when the actual water vapor present in the air is the maximum the air can hold at the existing temperature.

saturation current (electron control current). The plate current flowing in an electron tube circuit when all of the electrons emitted from the cathode are attracted to the plate. In a transistor circuit, saturation current is the current flowing between the emitter and collector when an increase in the forward bias between the base and emitter causes no further increase in the emitter-collector current.

sawtooth waveform. The waveform of voltage produced by a relaxation oscillator. The voltage across the capacitor in a relaxation oscillator rises relatively slowly because it flows through the series resistor. But, when the voltage rises to the ionization potential of the gas discharge tube, the tube fires and the voltage across the capacitor drops off immediately. The slow rise and rapid fall produce a sawtooth-shaped voltage wave. *See* relaxation oscillator.

sawtooth waveform

"Say again" (air traffic control). A phrase used by ATC to request a repeat of the last transmission. This usually specifies the transmission or the portion that was not understood or received, such as "Say again all after Abram VOR."

"Say altitude" (air traffic control). A phrase used by ATC to ascertain an aircraft's specific altitude or flight level. When the aircraft is climbing or descending, the pilot should state the indicated altitude rounded off to the nearest 100 feet.

Saybolt universal viscosity. A measure of the viscosity (resistance to flow) of a lubricating oil. The number of seconds needed for 60 milliliters of the liquid, at a specified temperature, to flow through a calibrated orifice is measured and is called the Saybolt Seconds Universal (SSU) viscosity of the liquid.

The viscosity number used for commercial aviation engine lubricating oil relates closely to the SSU of the oil at 210°F. Aviation 80 engine oil has an SSU viscosity at 210°F of 79.2, and Aviation 100 oil has an SSU viscosity of 103.0 at the same temperature.

"Say heading" (air traffic control). A phrase used by ATC to request an aircraft heading. The pilot should state the actual heading of the aircraft.

S-band radar. Radar that operates in the frequency band between 1,550 and 5,200 megahertz. In this frequency band, the wavelengths are between 19.35 and 5.77 centimeters.

SBT. *See* scenario-based training.

scale effect (aerodynamics). The variation of the aerodynamic characteristics of a wind tunnel model with Reynolds Number. It is extremely important in correlating wind tunnel test data of scale models with the actual flight characteristics of the full size aircraft. *See* Reynolds Number.

scale model. A copy of something made in the same proportions as the original, but of a smaller size. When an airplane is designed, a scale model is built and tested in a wind tunnel. The model has the same shape as the actual aircraft, but it is much smaller. It is a scaled-down copy of the real thing.

scalene triangle. A closed, three-sided, plane (flat) figure that has no two sides of the same length, nor are any of the angles the same.

scaling from a print. The measuring of a distance on a blueprint by using a ruler or scale. This is not an acceptable practice, as the paper shrinks or stretches. All dimensions and tolerances must be clearly indicated on the drawing so that there is no need for scaling.

scan (instrument flying). The first fundamental skill of instrument flight, also known as "cross-check"; the continuous and logical observation of instruments for attitude and performance information.

scandium. A silvery-white, very lightweight, rare-earth, metallic chemical element. Scandium's symbol is Sc, its atomic number is 21, and its atomic weight is 44.956. A radioactive isotope of scandium is used in petroleum exploration.

scarfed patch. A type of patch made to a thin plywood structure. The damaged area is cleaned out and the edges of the hole tapered, with the length of the taper about 12 times the thickness of the plywood. Temporary backing blocks support the area while the patch is glued in place. A scarfed patch is the most difficult to make, but it is the preferred patch for aircraft plywood skins.

scarf joint (woodworking). A joint in a wood structure in which the ends to be joined are cut in a long taper, normally 12:1, and fastened together by gluing. A glued scarf joint makes a strong splice, because the joint is made along the side of the wood fibers rather than along their ends.

scavenge. A term that means to collect and remove something that has been used. In a turbine engine lubrication system, the scavenge subsystem collects the oil after it has lubricated the bearings and gears and returns it to the oil tank.

S

scavenge oil system. The subsystem in the lubrication system of a gas turbine engine that collects the oil after it has lubricated the bearings and gears and returns it to the oil tank.

scavenger pump (lubrication system). A pump in a dry sump lubrication system that picks up the oil after it passes through the engine and returns it to the oil tank. Scavenger pumps have a larger capacity than pressure pumps, because the oil being returned is hot and contains air. Both conditions increase its volume.

scenario-based training (SBT). A training method that uses a highly structured script of real-world experiences to address aviation training objectives in an operational environment.

scheduled maintenance. The individual maintenance tasks that are performed according to the maintenance time limitations (maintenance schedule).

scheduled operation. Any common carriage passenger-carrying operation for compensation or hire conducted by an air carrier or commercial operator for which the certificate holder or its representative offers in advance the departure location, departure time, and arrival location. It does not include any passenger-carrying operation that is conducted as a public charter operation under 14 CFR Part 380.

scheduled time of arrival (STA)(air traffic control). An STA is the desired time that an aircraft should cross a certain point (landing or metering fix), taking other traffic and airspace configuration into account. An STA time shows the results of the scheduler that has calculated an arrival time according to parameters such as optimized spacing, aircraft performance, and weather.

schematic diagram. A diagram of an electric or fluid power system in which the components are represented by symbols, rather than drawings or pictures of the actual devices. Schematic diagrams are used for troubleshooting.

Schrader valve. A spring-loaded service valve used in an air conditioning system. A Schrader valve is much like the valve used to put air into a tire.

scientific notation (mathematics). A mathematical time saver used when working with very large and very small numbers. When using scientific notation, all numbers are changed into a positive number between one and 10 by moving the decimal point and attaching the number ten, raised to the power showing the number of places the decimal has been moved.

A negative (minus) number is used if the decimal was moved to the right, and a positive number is used if it is moved to the left. Using this system, $1,000 = 1 \cdot 10^3$, and $0.001 = 1 \cdot 10^{-3}$.

scimitar shape. The shape of the blades of the propellers mounted on an unducted-fan engine. The name is taken from the shape of a curved Asian sword that has its edge on the convex side.

scissors (landing gear component). A name commonly used for landing gear torque links. *See* torque links.

score (mark). A scratch across a piece of material made to cause the material to break along the line. When a piece of glass is to be cut with a glass cutter, it is scored by scratching through its surface with the cutter. When the glass is bent, all of the stresses concentrate in the scored line, and the glass breaks along the line.

SCR (silicon controlled rectifier). A reverse-blocking triode thyristor that can be triggered into conduction in only one direction. The three terminals of an SCR are the anode, the cathode, and the gate.

An SCR blocks electron flow in both directions until a pulse of electrical energy of the proper polarity is applied to the gate. The SCR will then conduct electrons in its forward direction, between its cathode and its anode. A conducting SCR will continue to conduct until the voltage across the anode and cathode is removed or until its polarity is reversed. *See* thyristor.

scramjet (supersonic combustion ramjet). A special type of ramjet engine whose fuel can be ignited while the vehicle is moving at a supersonic speed. *See* ramjet engine.

scraper ring (reciprocating engine component). The bottom ring on a piston of a reciprocating engine. The scraper ring, also called a wiper ring, scrapes the oil from the cylinder wall and pumps it into the space between the piston and the cylinder.

screeching (gas turbine engine operation). A condition of combustion instability in a gas turbine engine or afterburner. The combustion produces a shrill, high-pitched noise.

screech liner (turbine engine afterburner component). Screeching is a shrill, high pitched noise caused by combustion instability as the tremendous amount of heat is released in an afterburner. A screech liner that fits into the inner wall of an afterburner duct is corrugated and perforated with thousands of small holes. It minimizes the screeching by absorbing, or damping, some of the pressure fluctuations.

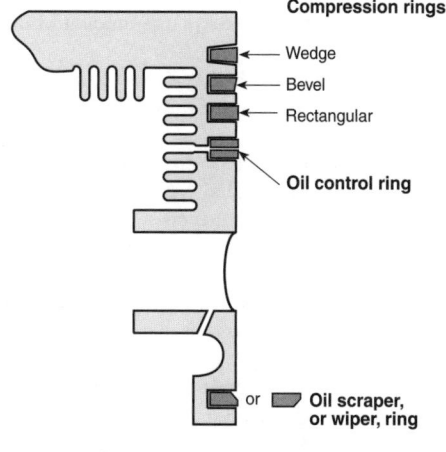

scraper ring

screeding tool. A tool used when working with plastic resins, to spread the resin evenly over a surface and level it. Screeding tools are often made of some form of polyvinylchloride plastic material that releases the resin, making the tool easy to clean.

screen grid (electron tube component). The grid in an electron tube between the control grid and the plate (anode). The screen grid has a positive voltage on it slightly lower than the voltage on the plate. The steady positive voltage on the screen grid minimizes voltage feedback from the plate to the control grid through the interelectrode capacitance.

screwdriver. A hand tool used to install or remove screws. The bit of a screwdriver may be in the form of a straight, flat-edged blade, or it may be fluted to fit into a recessed-head screw. A screwdriver has a handle on its shank in line with the blade, but on the opposite end. The bit of the screwdriver fits into the slot or recess in the head of the screw, and the handle is twisted to turn the screw.

screw-pitch gage. A set of thin metal blades with a series of V-shaped notches cut along one edge of each blade. The notched edge of each gage is compared with the thread being checked until one is found that exactly meshes with it. The number marked on the gage that fits the threads shows the number of threads per inch in the nut or on the bolt.

scriber. A sharp-pointed tool used to scribe (mark) lines on metal.

scud (meteorology). A commonly used term for small patches of low clouds that often form below a heavy overcast.

scuffing. A severe type of damage to moving parts caused when one metal part moves across another without sufficient lubricant between them. Enough heat is generated by friction to cause the high points of the surfaces to weld together, and continued movement tears, or scuffs, the metal.

scupper (fuel tank component). A recess around the filler neck of an aircraft fuel tank. Any fuel spilled when the tank is being filled collects in the scupper and drains to the ground through a drain line, rather than flowing into the aircraft structure.

SDF. *See* simplified directional facility.

S

sea anchor. An open-bottom canvas bucket towed behind a boat or seaplane in the water. A sea anchor causes a large amount of drag and is used to reduce the drift and to aid in maneuvering the vessel.

sea breeze (meteorology). A coastal breeze blowing from sea to land. Sea breezes are caused by the temperature difference when the land surface is warmer than the sea surface.

sea breeze front (meteorology). The leading edge of the intrusion of cooler, more moist marine air associated with a sea breeze.

sea fog (meteorology). A type of advection fog that forms when air that has been lying over a warm land surface moves over a colder water surface.

seal. A component used to prevent fluid leaking between two surfaces. If there is relative movement between the surfaces, the seal is called a packing. If there is no movement between the surfaces, it is called a gasket.

sea lane. A designated portion of water outlined by visual surface markers for and intended to be used by aircraft designed to operate on water.

sealant. A heavy liquid or paste spread between two surfaces to form a seal. Sealant may be used with a gasket or, in some instances, instead of a gasket.

sea level. The average level of the surface of the sea. Sea level is the mid position between the level of the water at low tide and the level at high tide.

sea-level-boosted engine. A reciprocating engine that has had its sea-level rated horsepower increased by supercharging. This is the same as a ground-boosted engine.

sea-level engine. *14 CFR Part 1:* "A reciprocating aircraft engine having a rated takeoff power that is producible only at sea level."

sea-level pressure (meteorology). The atmospheric pressure that exists at mean (average) sea level. Sea-level pressure can be measured directly, by stations located at sea level, or determined from charts showing the station pressure and temperature taken at stations not at sea level. Sea-level pressure is used as a common reference for analysis of surface pressure patterns.

seam welding (electrical resistance welding). A form of electrical resistance welding in which small metal wheels are used as the electrodes. These wheels roll over the metal, and the current is conducted through the metal from the wheel on one side to the wheel on the other side. Heat caused by the current flowing through the resistance of the metal softens the metal, and pressure between the wheels forces the softened metal in the two pieces to flow together.

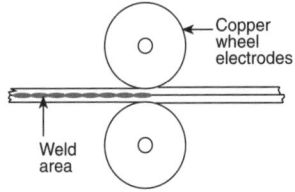

seam welding

Seam welding is similar to spot welding, except that the weld is a continuous line, rather than individual spots. Fuel tanks are usually seam welded, rather than spot welded.

seaplane. An airplane that can operate from water, rather than land. Some seaplanes are landplanes with the wheels removed and floats installed. A flying boat is a type of seaplane whose fuselage is similar to the hull of a boat. Sponsons (a type of stub wing near the water line) or wingtip floats keep the flying boat relatively level while it is in the water.

search and rescue (SAR). A service that seeks missing aircraft and assists those found to be in need of assistance. It is a cooperative effort using the facilities and services of available Federal, state and local agencies. The U.S. Coast Guard is responsible for coordination of search and rescue for the Maritime Region, and the U.S. Air Force is responsible for search and rescue for the Inland Region. Information pertinent to search and rescue should be passed through any air traffic facility or be transmitted directly to the Rescue Coordination Center by telephone.

search and rescue facility. A facility responsible for maintaining and operating a search and rescue (SAR) service to render aid to persons and property in distress. It is any SAR unit or other operational activity which can be usefully employed during an SAR Mission; e.g., a Civil Air Patrol Wing, or a Coast Guard Station.

sea smoke. Same as steam fog.

seasoned lumber. Lumber that has been dried, in a kiln or in some other way, and has had its moisture content reduced to a specified low amount.

sea state condition number. A standard scale ranging from 0–9 that indicates the height of waves.

seaward. The direction away from shore.

secant (mathematics). The trigonometric function of a right triangle which is the ratio of the length of the hypotenuse to the length of the side adjacent to an acute angle.

second (unit of angular measurement). One-sixtieth part of a minute of angular measurement. Three hundred and sixty degrees, 21,600 minutes, or 1,296,000 seconds makes up a complete circle.

second (unit of time). The basic unit of time in both the English and the metric systems of measurement. Sixty seconds is equal to one minute, 60 minutes (3,600 seconds) is one hour, and 24 hours (86,400 seconds) is one day, or the amount of time needed for one complete revolution of the earth.

secondary. A condition in which something has a level of importance just below that which is most important.

secondary air (gas turbine engines). Air which has passed through a gas turbine engine compressor and is used for cooling. Secondary air is not used in the combustion process.

secondary cell (batteries). A battery which can be recharged after it has been discharged. The action in which chemical energy is changed into electrical energy is reversible. This means that electrical energy from a battery charger can be changed into chemical energy to recharge the cell.

secondary color. A color produced by combining two primary colors in equal proportions. Green is a secondary color made by mixing equal amounts of two primary colors, yellow and blue.

secondary controls of an airplane. Controls that modify the effect of the ailerons, rudder, and elevators of an airplane, and do not in themselves cause rotation of the airplane about any of its three axes. Wing flaps, trim tabs, servo tabs, spring tabs, and antiservo tabs are examples of secondary controls.

secondary current (electrical current). Current that flows in the secondary winding of a transformer. Secondary current in a magneto ignition system is the high-voltage current induced in the secondary winding of the magneto coil. It is this secondary current that flows through the distributor and produces the spark at the spark plug.

secondary emission (electron tubes). Emission of electrons in an electron tube from an electrode other than the cathode. Secondary emission takes place when electrons traveling at a high velocity strike the anode (plate) and knock other electrons from it. When secondary emission is a problem, a suppressor grid is installed near the anode. A negative voltage on the suppressor grid suppresses the secondary emission by forcing the electrons that have been knocked from the anode, back onto it.

secondary fuel (gas turbine engine fuel metering). The main flow of fuel from the fuel nozzles inside a gas turbine engine. Primary, or pilot, fuel is used for starting the engine and for low-speed operation. Secondary fuel allows the engine to produce its maximum power.

S

secondary radar. Radar which responds to pulses of energy transmitted from an interrogator. The response is transmitted on a frequency different from that which was received.

secondary radar target. A target derived from a transponder return presented on a radar display.

secondary standard. A unit of length, weight, voltage, capacitance, time, or other value that is compared with a primary standard to determine its accuracy. Secondary standards are working standards. A clock, for example, is used as a secondary standard for measuring time, and it is calibrated by comparing it to the time signal transmitted by radio station WWV. In this example, the signal transmitted by station WWV is used as the primary standard.

secondary surveillance radar (SSR). A radar system that requires complementary aircraft equipment (transponder). *See* air traffic control radar beacon system (ATCRBS).

secondary voltage. The voltage in an alternating current circuit produced across the secondary winding of a transformer.

secondary winding (electrical transformer). The transformer winding connected to the electrical load. The winding connected to the source of electrical energy is called the primary winding. If the secondary winding has more turns than the primary winding, the transformer is a step-up transformer.

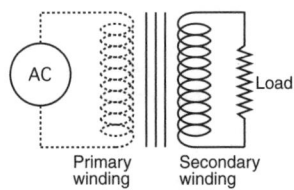

Primary
winding

Secondary
winding

secondary winding

secondary winding (magneto coil). The winding in a magneto or ignition coil that connects to the distributor rotor. The secondary winding is normally made of very small-diameter wire and has a large number of turns, typically about 20,000.

second-class lever. A lever in which the fulcrum is at one end, and the lifting force is at the other. The weight force is between the lifting force and the fulcrum. A wheelbarrow is an example of a second-class lever.

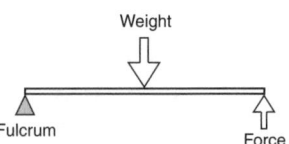

second-class lever

second in command. *14 CFR Part 1:* "A pilot who is designated to be second in command of an aircraft during flight time."

sectional chart. An aeronautical chart drawn to a scale of 1:500,000 (one inch is equal to eight statute miles). Sectional charts are designed for visual navigation of slow- or medium-speed aircraft. Topographic information on these charts feature the portrayal of relief and a judicious selection of visual checkpoints for VFR flight. Aeronautical information includes visual and radio aids to navigation, airports, controlled airspace, restricted areas, obstructions, and related data.

sectional view (aircraft drawing). A detail view in an aircraft drawing that shows the inside of a part. A view of the main drawing is cut with a cutting plane, and the sectional view is drawn to show the shape and construction of the piece along this cutting plane.

sectioning (aircraft drawing). The use of cross-hatching to indicate the type of material used in a sectional view of a part on an aircraft drawing.

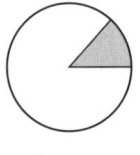

sector (part of a circle). A part of a circle bounded by two radii and the arc that lies between them.

sector gear. A piece of a gear wheel that contains the hub and a portion of the rim with the teeth. A sector gear, which is used where only a small amount of angular movement is needed, usually meshes with

sector

and drives a small pinion gear. The shaft of the pinion gear can turn several revolutions, while the shaft of the sector gear is turning through only a few degrees.

sector list drop interval (air traffic control). A parameter, in number of minutes after the meter fix time, indicating when arrival aircraft will be deleted from the arrival sector list. *See also* metering and meter time fix.

sector visibility (meteorology). Meteorological visibility within a specified sector of the horizon circle.

security notice (SECNOT) (air traffic control). A request originated by the Air Traffic Security Coordinator (ATSC) for an extensive communications search for aircraft involved, or suspected of being involved, in a security violation. A SECNOT will include the aircraft identification, search area, and expiration time. The search area, as defined by the ATSC, could be a single airport, multiple airports, a radius of an airport or fix, or a route of flight. Once the expiration time has been reached, the SECNOT is considered to be cancelled.

security services airspace (air traffic control). Areas established through the regulatory process or by NOTAM, issued by the FAA Administrator under 14 CFR §§99.7, 91.141, and 91.139, which specify that ATC security services are required (i.e., ADIZ or temporary flight rules areas).

sediment. Contaminants that settle to the bottom of a reservoir or container.

see and avoid. When weather conditions permit, pilots operating IFR or VFR are required to observe and maneuver to avoid other aircraft.

seesaw rotor (helicopter rotor). Another name for a semirigid rotor. A semirigid rotor is a helicopter rotor whose blades can rotate about their feathering axis, but there are no separate flapping hinges. The rotor pivots on the mast in much the same way a seesaw pivots on its fulcrum.

segment (part of a circle). The part of a circle formed by a chord (a line passing across the circle and touching the circumference at two points) and the arc between the two points.

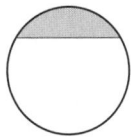

segment

segmented circle. A visual indicator around a windsock or tetrahedron designed to show the traffic pattern for each runway. Segmented circles are used at airports without operating control towers, and which have some runways with right-hand traffic patterns and others with left-hand patterns.

segmented-rotor brake (multiple-disk brake). A heavy-duty, multiple-disk brake used on large, high-speed aircraft. Stators, surfaced with a material that retains its friction characteristics at high temperatures, are keyed to the axle. Rotors, keyed into the wheels, rotate between each pair of stators. The rotor disks are made in segments to aid in dissipation of heat and to prevent their warping.

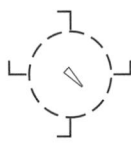

segmented circle

segments, of an instrument approach procedure. An instrument approach procedure may have as many as four separate segments depending on how the approach procedure is structured: (1) The initial approach segment between the initial approach fix and the intermediate fix or the point where the aircraft is established on the intermediate course or final approach course; (2) the intermediate approach segment between the intermediate fix or point and the final approach fix; (3) the final approach segment between the final approach fix or point and the runway, airport, or missed approach point; and (4) the missed approach segment between the missed approach point or the point of arrival at decision height and the missed approach fix at the prescribed altitude.

seize (equipment failure). A type of failure in which parts stick or jam because of friction, pressure, or excessive temperature.

Selcal system. Selective calling system. Each aircraft operated by an airline is assigned a particular four tone audio combination for identification purposes. A ground station keys the signal whenever contact with that particular aircraft is desired. The signal is decoded by the airborne selcal decoder and the crew alerted by the selcal warning system.

selection-type test items. Test items that require the student to choose from two or more alternatives provided. True/false, matching, and multiple-choice type questions are examples of selection-type test items.

selective availability (SA). A method by which the Department of Defense (DOD) can, in the interest of national security, create a significant clock and ephemeris error in the satellites, resulting in a navigation error.

selective plating. A method of electroplating only a portion of a metal part. The portion not to be plated is masked with a nonconductive material, and only the unmasked area accepts the electroplating.

selectivity (radio reception characteristic). The ability of a radio receiver to separate the signals it receives. Selectivity is a very important characteristic of a communications receiver because of the large number of transmissions in a narrow band of frequencies. The better the selectivity of a receiver, the narrower the band of frequencies it amplifies.

selector switch. A multi-pole switch used to connect a single conductor to any one of several other conductors. *See* rotary switch.

selector valve (fluid power system component). A flow control valve used in hydraulic systems to direct pressurized fluid into one side of an actuator, and at the same time direct return fluid from the other side of the actuator back to the reservoir. There are two basic types of selector valves: open-center valves and closed-center valves. The four-port closed-center valve is the most frequently used type. *See* closed-center selector valve and open-center selector valve.

selenium. A steel-gray, highly toxic, nonmetallic chemical element. Selenium's symbol is Se, its atomic number is 34, and its atomic weight is 78.96. Selenium, which is in the sulfur family, has the useful characteristic of changing its resistance as light falls on it. In the dark, selenium's resistance is high, but in the bright light, its resistance is low.

selenium rectifier. A type of rectifier using a cadmium and selenium junction to control the flow of electrons. When a layer of selenium is deposited on an aluminum base, and a cadmium alloy plate is pressed against the selenium, a barrier is formed between the selenium and the cadmium. Electrons can easily pass through this barrier from the cadmium, through the selenium to the aluminum, but they cannot pass through the barrier in the opposite direction.

self-accelerating speed (turbine engine condition). The speed attained by a gas turbine engine during start-up that allows it to accelerate to its normal idling speed without assistance from the starter.

self-aligning bearing. A type of bearing used on a control rod end that functions properly, even though the control rod does not move at right angles to the surface to which it is attached. One of the most commonly used self-aligning bearings is the spherical bearing. The bearing surface has the shape of a sphere with a hole drilled through it. The two sides of the sphere perpendicular to the hole are ground flat so it can be attached to the component to be moved by the control rod. The control rod end has a socket into which the sphere fits, and the sphere rotates on a film of grease. The rod end can be out of alignment by a few degrees without affecting the operation of the bearing. Self-aligning bearings are used in control rods installed in helicopter rotor systems.

self-centering chuck (machine tool component). A type of chuck used on a drill motor or lathe that has all its jaws connected in such a way that they move together. When a drill or piece of work is placed in the chuck and the jaws tightened, all of the jaws move inward together and hold the drill or the work centered in the chuck.

self-concept (in learning process). A factor that affects a person's ability to perceive and be receptive to experience. One's self-image, whether it is positive or negative, has great influence on the process of perception; if the image of self is favorable, a person tends to be receptive to experiences and learn new things easily. But a negative concept of self can inhibit the perceptual process and cause a tendency to reject additional experience and learning.

self-demagnetization. The process in which the magnetic fields surrounding a piece of magnetized material try to demagnetize it. If a permanent magnet sits for a long period of time, it will partially self-demagnetize. But if a keeper, a piece of soft iron, is placed across its poles, the lines of magnetic flux will not spread out from the poles, and the magnet will self-demagnetize far less than if no keeper were used.

self-excited generator. An electrical generator whose field coils are supplied with current produced in the armature. The voltage regulator for a self-excited generator is a variable resistor in the field circuit between the armature and the field coils or between the field coils and ground. When the resistance in the field circuit decreases, the field current increases, and the generator output voltage increases. Most aircraft generators are self-excited, but DC alternators are not.

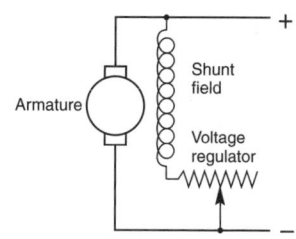

self-excited generator

self-extinguishing. A combustible material is said to be self-extinguishing if it burns when it is exposed to a flame or to a high temperature, but the burning process automatically stops as soon as the flame or source of high temperature is removed.

self-healing capacitor. An electrolytic capacitor with the ability to automatically restore the oxide film dielectric to the plate if the film is ever punctured by too high a voltage.

self-induction. The characteristic of an electrical conductor that causes a counter electromotive force (CEMF, or back voltage) to be built up in it by alternating current flowing through it. The expanding and collapsing magnetic field caused by the alternating current cuts across the conductor and induces the CEMF in it. The polarity of the self-induced voltage is always opposite that of the voltage in the original circuit.

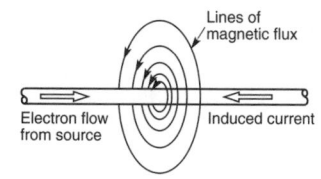

self induction

self-launch glider. A glider equipped with an engine so it can be launched under its own power. When the engine is shut down, a self-launch glider displays the same characteristics as a nonpowered glider.

self-locking nut. A type of nut with a built-in locking device that makes the nut tightly grip the threads of the bolt. This locking device may be a fiber collar, with a hole slightly smaller than the major diameter of the bolt threads, or it may be a portion of the threads in the nut that is slightly out of phase with its main threads. A self-locking nut must be turned onto a bolt with a wrench and grip the bolt threads tightly enough that vibration will not cause it to loosen or back off.

self-tapping screw. A type of screw with sharp threads that cut their own matching threads when screwed into soft metal, wood, or plastic. Self-tapping screws are especially suited for holding together sheets of thin metal, and for this reason, they are often called sheet-metal screws, or PK screws, after Parker-Kalon, one of their major manufacturers.

self-tapping sheet metal screw

Selsyn system. The registered trade name for a DC synchro system. Mechanical movement of the transmitter shaft moves a two-arm wiper across a tapped, circular, variable resistor. Direct current enters the transmitter through the arms of the wiper and flows through the resistor out to the indicator. Here, the current flows into three sections of a coil wound around a ring-shaped core. A small permanent magnet on the pointer shaft is free to rotate inside the indicator coil.

As the wipers move across the transmitter resistor, the current in the three sections of the indicator coil change. The changing current changes the magnetic field produced by the coil so the magnet to which the pointer is attached moves in exactly the same way as the shaft in the transmitter.

selvage edge (fabric). The woven edge of fabric used to prevent the material unraveling during normal handling. The selvage edge, which runs the length of the fabric parallel to the warp threads, is normally removed from materials before they are used in composite construction.

semi. A prefix meaning partially or part (usually half) of something. A semicircle is half of a circle, and a semiannual event is something that takes place every half year (twice in a year).

semiautomatic operation. An operation that is partially automatic. Some manual input is needed to start the operation, but once started, it completes its cycle of operation with no further input.

semiconductor. A material whose electrical conductivity is between that of an insulator and a conductor. The electrical properties of a semiconductor are caused by its atomic structure and by the way the material has been processed.

Valence electrons are the electrons in the outer shell of an atom, and the number of valence electrons is the important characteristic of the atomic structure of a semiconductor material. Silicon and germanium, the two chemical elements most often used for semiconductor devices, both have four valence electrons.

An important step in the production of semiconductor materials is that of "doping," which is the addition of minute amounts of other chemical elements, called impurity elements, which have either three or five valence electrons. Just a few parts per million of these impurity elements cause the semiconductor material to act as either a conductor or an insulator, depending upon the polarity of the voltage placed across it.

semiconductor diode. A two-element, solid-state electron check valve made of silicon or germanium, doped with appropriate impurities. Electrons can either flow through a semiconductor diode or not flow through it depending upon the polarity of the voltage across it.

When the diode is forward-biased, with the positive voltage connected to the anode, and the negative voltage to the cathode, electrons flow through it. But, when it is reverse-biased, with the negative voltage connected to the anode, electrons do not flow through it.

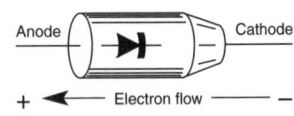

semiconductor diode

semiconductor integrated circuit. A complex electronic circuit made on a single chip of semiconductor material. Passive components, such as resistors and capacitors, and active components such as transistors are formed by several layers of conducting and insulating materials. These components are connected together to form such complete circuits as gates and amplifiers.

semiconductor memory (computer memory). A computer memory in which data is stored in semiconductor devices, such as flip-flop circuits and capacitors. Flip-flops are normally used for static storage and capacitors for dynamic storage. Static storage is used for ROM (read-only memory), in which data is programmed when the chip is manufactured. Data can be read from it, but no new data can be written into it. ROM is nonvolatile, meaning that the data remains in ROM even when all computer power is turned off.

Dynamic storage is used for RAM (random-access-memory). Data can be both written into RAM and read from it, and this data can be changed as needed. The data stored in a dynamic RAM (D-RAM) is volatile. This means that all data is lost when computer power is shut off. The data in a D-RAM must be continually refreshed (the charge renewed) as the charge (the data) leaks off.

semiconductor transducer. A piezoelectric crystal that converts input energy of one form, such as pressure, into output energy of another, such as an electrical signal.

semicircular canal. An inner ear organ that detects angular acceleration of the body.

semimonocoque structure (aircraft structure). A form of stressed skin structure used in the construction of aircraft. Most of the strength of a semimonocoque structure is in the skin, but the skin is supported on a substructure of formers and stringers that gives the skin its shape and increases its rigidity.

semirigid rotor (helicopter rotor). A type of helicopter rotor that allows the pitch of the blades to be changed by rotating the blades about their feather axis (the axis that extends along the length of the blade). The blades cannot flap up and down individually, but the entire rotor can flap as a unit. It is free to teeter (rock back and forth) about the mast.

sender (fuel quantity measuring system). The part of a fuel quantity measuring system located at the tank to measure the level of the fuel in the tank. In most simple systems, the sender is a variable resistor mounted outside the tank with a wire arm protruding into the tank. A float mounted on the arm rides on the top of the fuel, and the arm is connected to the wiper of the variable resistor. As the level of fuel in the tank changes, the position of the arm on the variable resistor changes. The fuel quantity gage on the instrument panel measures the current flowing through the variable resistor and translates this current into the amount of fuel in the tank.

sense antenna (automatic direction finder antenna). A type of nondirectional radio antenna used with an automatic direction finder. The sense antenna picks up signals with equal strength from all directions. An ADF system uses two antennas—a loop antenna and a sense antenna. The loop antenna is highly directional; the strength of the signal it picks up changes with the direction between the antenna and the station. But the signal strength is the same if the station is in front of the antenna or behind it.

The signals picked up by both the loop antenna and the sense antenna are fed into the same equipment, and as the two signals mix, they form a pattern that allows the ADF system to measure the exact direction between the loop antenna and the station being received. Using the sense antenna eliminates the problem of 180° ambiguity. It allows the system to distinguish whether the station is in front of the antenna or behind it.

S

sensible heat. Heat energy added to a material that causes it to change its temperature, but not its physical state. The other kind of heat is latent heat, which causes a material to change its physical state but not its temperature.

When a pan of water is put on a hot stove, sensible heat enters it until the water reaches a temperature of 100°C (under standard conditions). At this temperature, the water begins to boil, or change its physical state from liquid to gas without increasing its temperature. Heat added to the water after it begins to boil is called latent heat.

sensitive altimeter. A form of multipointer pneumatic altimeter with an adjustable barometric scale that allows the reference pressure to be set to any desired level. Sensitive altimeters have a high degree of mechanical amplification in their movement. The small amount of movement of the expanding bellows inside the instrument is multiplied enough to rotate one of the pointers completely around the dial for a pressure change equivalent to only one thousand feet of altitude. This is approximately one inch of mercury.

sensitive relay (electrical component). An electromagnetically operated switch whose operating coil requires very little current to close the switch contacts. Sensitive relays are used in photoelectric and thermocouple circuits. The very small current produced by a photocell or thermocouple operates the relay, and the relay contacts control enough current to operate other equipment. Sensitive relays are being replaced today with solid-state devices that do the same job, but have no moving parts.

sensitivity (radio receiver specification). A measure of the signal strength needed to produce distortion-free output. The output must not have any excessive noise (unwanted electrical signal) in it, and the output must be electrically identical to the input, except for its higher voltage. A radio receiver with a high sensitivity can produce a usable output from a very weak, or faint, input signal.

sensitivity time control (radar technology). A radar circuit designed to correct for range attenuation so the echo intensity on the scope is proportional to reflectivity of the target regardless of range.

sensor (automated equipment). The component in a piece of automated equipment affected by some physical condition. The sensor sends signals into the equipment so it will operate in the correct manner. An automatic cowl flap actuation system has a temperature sensor affected by the cylinder head temperature. This sensor sends signals to the cowl flap motor. If the cylinder head temperature is too low, the motor closes the cowl flaps, and if the temperature is too high, the motor opens them. A photoelectric cell is a form of sensor. It is affected by the amount of light or by the color of the light.

sensory register. The portion of the brain that receives input from the five senses. The individual's preconceived concept of what is important determines how the register prioritizes the information for passing it on to the rest of the brain for action.

separation (air traffic control). The spacing of aircraft to achieve their safe and orderly movement in flight and while landing and taking off.

separation minima (air traffic control). The minimum longitudinal, lateral, or vertical distances by which aircraft are spaced through the application of air traffic control procedures.

sequence valve (fluid power system component). A type of flow control valve that allows one system to fully operate before another system begins its operation. Sequence valves are used in aircraft hydraulic systems to cause the wheel well doors to open fully before the landing gear is released from its uplocks.

sequencing mode. The FMS/RNAV mode that automatically sequences along the waypoints in the programmed route. The sequencing mode alerts the pilot to upcoming waypoints, and offers guidance to each successive waypoint in the route.

sequential logic devices. Digital memory devices that have several inputs and several outputs. The combination of bits at the outputs is determined by the bits on the inputs and the bits that were previously on the inputs.

SER. *See* start end of runway.

serial number. An identification number assigned sequentially to items which have the same part number.

serial operation (computer operation). Data transfer by moving bits sequentially, one at a time, rather than simultaneously, as is done by parallel operation. Series operation is much slower than parallel operation, but it requires far less complex circuitry.

series circuit. A type of circuit in either an electrical or a fluid power system in which all of the components are connected in such a way that they provide only one path from the source of current or fluid flow, through all of the components, and back to the source.

series-parallel circuit (electrical circuit). A type of electrical circuit in which some of the components are connected in series, and others are connected in parallel.

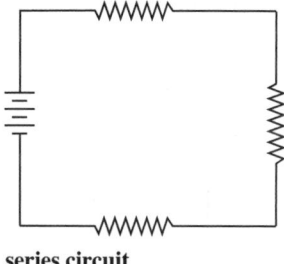

series circuit

series resonant circuit. A resonant AC electrical circuit that contains a capacitor and an inductor connected in series. At the resonant frequency of the circuit, the inductive reactance and the capacitive reactance are the same. But they are 180° out of phase, and they cancel each other. The only opposition to the flow of AC in a series resonant circuit is caused by the circuit resistance.

series-wound generator (electrical generator). A form of electrical generator in which the field coils are connected in series with the armature. Series-wound generators are not commonly used to supply power for aircraft electrical systems because of the difficulty in controlling the output voltage.

series-parallel circuit

series-wound motor (electric motor). A commutator-type electric motor that has the field coils connected in series with the armature. A series-wound motor has a high starting torque, but if it is not operated with a mechanical load connected to it, it will accelerate to a speed that will destroy it. Starter motors for both reciprocating engines and gas turbine engines are series-wound.

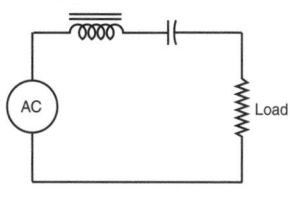

series resonant circuit

serious injury. An injury that: (1) Requires hospitalization for more than 48 hours, commencing within 7 days from the date of the injury was received; (2) results in a fracture of any bone (except simple fractures of fingers, toes, or nose); (3) causes severe hemorrhages, nerve, muscle, or tendon damage; (4) involves any internal organ; or (5) involves second- or third-degree burns, or any burns affecting more than 5 percent of the body surface.

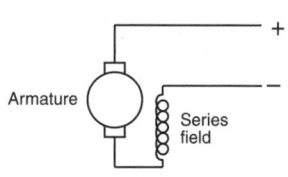

series-wound generator

serrations. A series of teeth or notches, usually along the cutting edge of a knife or a saw.

service (air traffic control). A generic term that designates functions or assistance available from or rendered by air traffic control. For example, Class C service would denote the ATC services provided within a Class C airspace area.

serviceable (physical condition). The condition of a piece of equipment that allows it to be returned to service or to be installed in an operating aircraft.

serviceable limits. One type of limits included in a reciprocating engine overhaul manual. If a part measures outside of the new-parts limits, but within the serviceable limits, it will likely not wear to the point of causing engine failure within the next TBO interval.

service bulletin (maintenance information). A bulletin issued by the manufacturer of an aircraft, engine, or component that describes a service procedure the manufacturer recommends to make the device safer or to improve its service life.

service ceiling (aircraft performance). The highest altitude at which an aircraft can maintain a steady rate of climb of 100 feet per minute.

service life. The length of time a piece of equipment can reasonably be expected to operate in a satisfactory manner.

service manual (maintenance information). A manual written by the manufacturer of an aircraft, engine, or component that describes the way the device should be serviced and maintained. The service manual for an FAA-certificated aircraft is approved by the FAA, and it serves as approved data for making repairs.

servo (automatic pilot component). A component in an automatic flight control system that actually moves the flight control. There are servos in each of the primary controls: the ailerons, elevators, and rudder. The automatic pilot senses when a flight correction is needed, and it sends a signal to the servo to move the control surface in the proper direction to make the correction.

servo altimeter. A type of pneumatic altimeter in which the bellows moves an electrical pickup whose signal is amplified enough for it to drive a servo motor. The servo motor moves the drums and pointer in the display.

servo amplifier. An electronic amplifier in an autopilot system that increases the signal from the autopilot enough that it can operate the servos that move the control surfaces.

servo brake. A type of wheel brake that uses the momentum of the aircraft to increase the friction applied by the brake. The brake drum is a hollow cylinder, turned by the wheel that rides over the brake shoes.

Brake linings, made of a material with a high coefficient of friction, are bonded to the surface of steel brake shoes and are pressed against the inside of the drum by the piston in a hydraulic brake cylinder. When the brakes are not being applied, a spring holds the shoes away from the drum. When the pilot depresses the brake pedal, hydraulic fluid forces the piston out and moves the shoe against the drum. The shoe is mounted in such a way that when it contacts the rotating drum, friction wedges it tightly against the drum. Movement of the aircraft increases the friction produced by the brake.

servo feedback. A type of automatic control system in which part of the output is fed back into the input to help control the action. In an automatic pilot system, an attitude sensor detects a wing dropping and generates an error signal that causes the servo to move the aileron down.

A servo feedback signal is sent from the aileron to the attitude sensor, indicating that corrective action is being taken. The attitude sensor progressively cancels its error signal as the deflected aileron brings the wings back to a level attitude. By the time the wings are level, the error signal is eliminated and the aileron is no longer deflected.

servo loop. *See* servo feedback.

servomechanism. A type of control system in which a small signal or small force is used to control a much larger force. In a hydraulic servomechanism, a sensor detects that some type of output movement is needed. A control valve directs hydraulic fluid into a hydraulic actuator, and the movement takes place. A feedback sensor compares the amount the actuator moves with the amount of movement the original sensor called for, and when the actuator has moved the correct amount, the selector valve is shut off.

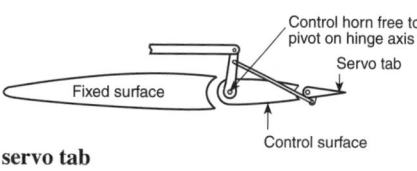

servo tab

servo tab (aircraft controls). A small movable tab built into the trailing edge of an aircraft primary control surface. A servo tab is actuated by the cockpit control, and it moves in the direction opposite to the direction the primary surface is to move. The servo tab produces an aerodynamic force that moves the surface on which it is mounted.

servo-type carburetor. A type of carburetor or continuous-flow fuel injection system that uses the pressure drop across a servo bleed orifice (a metering jet) to control the amount of metered fuel allowed to flow to the cylinders. The servo system adjusts for changes in inlet fuel pressure so the pressure of the fuel sent to the cylinders is proportional only to the amount of air being drawn into the cylinders.

sesquiplane (type of airplane). A biplane in which one wing, usually the lower wing, has an area less than one-half the area of the other wing.

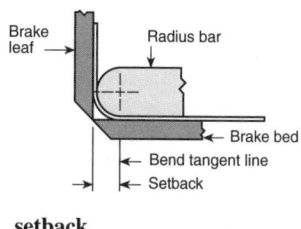

setback

setback (sheet metal layout). A measurement used in sheet metal layout. Setback is the distance the jaws of a brake must be set back from the mold line to form a bend. Setback for a 90° bend is equal to the inside radius of the bend, plus the thickness of the metal being bent. For a bend of other than 90°, a factor called a K-factor must be used. *See* K-factor.

setscrew. A headless screw used to prevent relative movement between a wheel and a shaft. A hole is drilled through the hub boss of the wheel, and it is tapped so a setscrew can be screwed through it and tightened against the shaft. The set screw prevents the wheel turning on the shaft.

settling with power (helicopter operation). An operation of a helicopter in which the main rotor is operating in its own downwash. The flow of air through the center portion of the rotor disk is upward, and the flow through the outer portion of the disk is downward, as it should be. Settling with power is more correctly called "operating in the vortex ring."

severe weather avoidance plan. *See* SWAP.

severe weather forecast alerts. Preliminary messages issued in order to alert users that a severe weather watch bulletin (WW) is being circulated by the SPC (Storm Prediction Center). *See* severe weather watch bulletin (WW).

severe weather watch bulletin (WW). An aviation weather report from the Storm Prediction Center in Norman, OK, that identifies areas of possible severe thunderstorms or tornado activity. WW messages are unscheduled and issued as required. A preliminary message called a severe weather forecast alert (AWW) is issued to alert airmen a bulletin is forthcoming.

S

sewed-in panel repair (aircraft fabric repair). A repair to a fabric-covered airplane wing in which a section of fabric extending from the leading edge to the trailing edge between two or more ribs is replaced by sewing the new fabric to the old. All the seams are reinforced with surface tape.

sewed-patch repair (fabric covering repair). A repair to a damaged fabric-covered structure that cannot be repaired by closing with stitches. The damaged area is removed and a piece of new fabric is used to replace the removed fabric. It is sewed by hand with baseball stitches. After the patch is in place it is shrunk with dope and the seams covered with surface tape.

sextant (navigation instrument). An optical instrument used in celestial navigation to measure the angle between the horizon and a line to one of the navigational stars. By finding this angle and referring to the appropriate tables in a nautical almanac for the exact time the observation was made, the observer can determine his latitude and longitude.

Seyboth fabric tester (aircraft fabric tester). A type of tester used to determine the condition of the fabric installed on an aircraft. A specially shaped, spring-loaded, sharp-pointed plunger is pressed into the fabric until a shoulder around the point contacts the fabric. The amount of force required to press the shoulder to the fabric is measured on a colored scale in the handle of the tester. Weak fabric requires very little force to press the shoulder against the fabric, and it shows up as a red band. Airworthy fabric requires enough force to compress the spring that the indicator moves up to one of the green bands.

A Seyboth test does not indicate the strength of the fabric in pounds per inch, but it is sufficiently accurate to distinguish between fabric that is either definitely good or definitely bad.

S-glass (composites). A glass that contains magnesia, alumina, and a silicate. It is used as a fiber in fiberglass cloth where high strength is required.

shaded-pole motor (AC electric motor). A type of alternating current induction motor used for light-duty, constant-speed loads, such as fans, blowers, and tape players. A coil excited by single-phase alternating current is wound around a laminated steel frame, and a squirrel-cage rotor is mounted in bearings attached to the frame. Shading coils made of one or two bands of heavy copper are installed around diagonally opposite pole shoes, the part of the frame around the rotor.

Current induced into the shading coils by the AC in the exciter coil demagnetizes the part of the pole shoe around which it is wound. The AC alternately magnetizes and demagnetizes the corners of the pole shoes, producing a rotating magnetic field which the squirrel-cage rotor follows. Shaded-pole motors have a relatively constant speed, but their torque is quite low.

shaft axis (helicopter design). The line consistent with the rotor shaft (mast). Only when the plane of rotation is exactly perpendicular to the shaft axis will the axis of rotation coincide with the shaft axis.

shaft horsepower. The horsepower actually available at a rotating shaft.

shaft runout (engine overhaul measurement). The amount the end of the crankshaft of an aircraft reciprocating engine is bent. Shaft runout is measured by mounting the shaft in a set of V-blocks and holding the arm of a dial indicator against the edge of the shaft at its end. When the shaft is rotated, the pointer of the dial indicator shows the amount the shaft is bent or out of round.

shaft turbine (gas turbine engine). A turboshaft engine that uses most of the energy extracted from the burning fuel to drive an output shaft. Turboshaft engines are used to power helicopter rotors.

shake (wood defect). Longitudinal cracks in a piece of wood, usually between two annual rings.

shallow banked turn. A turn less than approximately 20 degrees; the aircraft's inherent lateral stability often acts to level the wings unless the pilot maintains the bank.

shank of a drill. The smooth part of the body of a twist drill that fits into the drill chuck. The three basic parts of a twist drill are the shank, the body (the flutes), and the point.

shaving (metal-cutting operation). An operation in which thin layers of metal are removed from the outer surface of the device being shaved.

shear. To cut by causing the parts to slide over each other.

shear failure (structural failure). The failure of a riveted or bolted joint in which the fastener, rather than the material being joined, fails. The fasteners (rivets or bolts) shear off, rather than the material tearing at the fastener hole. A joint should be designed so it will fail in shear rather than in bearing. When a joint fails in shear, only the fasteners must be replaced; but if it fails in bearing, the torn material must be repaired.

shear nut. A thin nut used on a clevis bolt to hold the bolt in place. Shear nuts are used when the fastener on which they are screwed is loaded in shear only. They do not have enough threads to allow their use for a tensile load.

shear pin. A pin used to protect a piece of equipment by intentionally shearing if the equipment should seize. A shear pin is used in the drive shaft of some engine-driven pumps. If the pump should seize, the shear pin will break and allow the shaft to turn, but the pump is protected from further damage.

shears (cutting tools). A type of cutting tool used to cut sheet metal, paper, or cloth. Shears are similar to scissors, except that they are usually larger and more powerful. Power shears, used to cut thick sheets of metal, are driven by an electric motor.

shear section. A necked-down section of an engine-driven pump shaft designed to shear if the pump should seize. When the shear section breaks, the drive can continue to turn without causing further damage to the pump or the engine.

shear strength (sheet metal construction). The strength of a riveted joint in a sheet metal structure in which the rivets shear before the metal tears at the rivet holes. A properly designed riveted joint will fail in shear. The rivets will shear before the metal tears at the rivet holes.

shear stress. A type of stress that tries to slide an object apart.

shear wave (mechanical vibration). A vibrational wave within an elastic material in which the material changes its shape without changing its volume.

sheave. A grooved wheel used as a pulley. A sheave can be used to change the direction a cable must be pulled to move a weight and it can also be used to increase the force applied to a weight. If a sheave is attached to a weight, the amount of force needed to lift the weight is only one half the weight. But the cable will have to be pulled twice the distance the weight is lifted.

S

sheet metal. Metal that has been rolled into sheets whose thickness is less than 0.25 inch. Metal whose thickness is greater than 0.25 inch is called metal plate.

sheet metal layout. The drawing or pattern used to cut a piece of sheet metal. The layout includes marks to locate all of the bend tangent lines and the center marks for all of the holes to be drilled.

shelf cloud (meteorology). A low-level, horizontal, wedge-shaped arcus cloud associated with a convective storm's gust front (or occasionally with a cold front).

shelf life. The normal length of time an object or material can be expected to keep its usable characteristics if it is stored and not used. Many products, such as batteries, rubber seals, shock cord, and certain types of finishing materials, have a date stamped on them. This date relates to the shelf life. If these products are not used by the date stamped on them, there is a possibility that they will not function as they should.

shell (atomic structure). The outer structure of an atom formed by electrons having the same energy level as they spin around the nucleus. The K shell is nearest the nucleus. The L shell is next and, depending on the number of electrons, an atom can also have M, N, O, P, and Q shells.

shell-type transformer. A type of electrical transformer encased in a steel shell. The shell completely surrounds the winding and keeps magnetic lines of flux from radiating out from the transformer.

SHF (Superhigh Frequency). Electromagnetic energy with a frequency between 3 and 30 gigahertz ($3 \cdot 10^9$ and $30 \cdot 10^9$ hertz). The SHF band is used for weather and doppler radar.

shielded-arc welding. A form of arc welding in which the arc and the metal being welded are shielded, or covered, with an inert gas or with melted flux that keeps air away from the molten metal in the weld.

shielded cable. An electrical cable of one or more insulated conductors enclosed by a shield that may be composed of braided strands of copper (or other metal), a nonbraided spiral winding of copper, or a layer of metal tape.

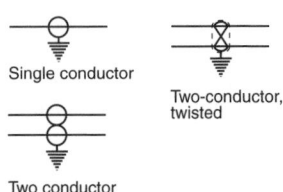

shielded conductors

shielded conductor (electrical conductor). Insulated electrical wire enclosed in a conducting braid, usually made of tinned copper. The braid is grounded so any electromagnetic radiation picked up by the braid is carried to ground. This prevents interference with the signal being carried in the conductor.

shielded ignition cable (reciprocating engine ignition system component). A type of ignition cable used to carry high voltage from the magneto distributor to the spark plug. Shielded ignition cable is used in aircraft installations where the electromagnetic radiation from the high-voltage spark plug leads could cause radio interference.

The spark plug leads are enclosed in a metal braid. One end of the braid is connected to a terminal in a shielded spark plug, and the other end is connected to the magneto distributor. Any radio-frequency energy that radiates from the wire when the spark is jumping the gap in the spark plug is picked up by the braid and carried to ground, rather than radiating into space and causing radio interference.

shielded spark plug (reciprocating engine ignition system component). A spark plug entirely enclosed in a steel housing. A shielded ignition lead terminates with an insulated connector that fits into an insulated cavity inside the spark plug. The nut on the end of the ignition lead screws onto the spark plug barrel. Electromagnetic energy released when the spark jumps the gap in the spark plug is picked up by the metal in the spark plug and the shielded ignition lead, and is carried to ground preventing it from causing radio interference.

shielded wire. Electrical wire enclosed in a braided metal jacket. Electromagnetic energy radiated from the wire is trapped by the braid and carried to ground.

shielding. A metal braid that encloses wires which carry high-frequency alternating current or high-voltage DC that has radio-frequency energy superimposed on it. The shielding intercepts any electromagnetic radiation and carries it to the engine structure so it will not interfere with any installed electronic equipment.

shim. A thin piece of material used to fill a space between two objects or to level an object. Thin metal shims are used in some bevel gear systems to adjust the gear preload, and behind some bearing inserts to adjust the clearance between the bearing and the shaft.

shimmy. Abnormal, and often violent, vibration of the nose wheel of an airplane. Airplane nose wheel installations must be loose enough to allow them to be steered, but if they are too loose, they will shimmy. Shimmying is prevented by a shimmy damper. *See* shimmy damper.

shimmy damper (aircraft landing gear component). A small hydraulic shock absorber installed between the nose wheel fork and the nose wheel cylinder which is attached to the aircraft structure. The piston inside the shimmy damper cylinder is free to move back and forth when it is moved slowly enough to allow fluid to transfer from one side of the piston to the other through a restrictor. Slow movement of the piston allows the nose wheel to pivot so the aircraft can be steered on the ground. But, the restrictor slows the flow of fluid inside the cylinder and prevents the piston from moving back and forth as fast as it would if the nose wheel were shimmying.

shock absorber (aircraft landing gear component). A device in an aircraft landing gear that absorbs the shock which occurs when an aircraft touches down on landing. The most commonly used shock absorber is the oleo (oil and air) shock strut. The initial landing impact is taken up by oil transferring from one chamber inside the shock absorber to another through a metering orifice. The much smaller shocks that occur when the aircraft is taxiing are taken up by a cushion of compressed air.

shock cool. Rapid cooling of a piston engine by suddenly retarding the throttle while the engine is hot and the outside air is cold. Shock cooling causes the cylinders to shrink around the pistons and cause serious cylinder wall scuffing.

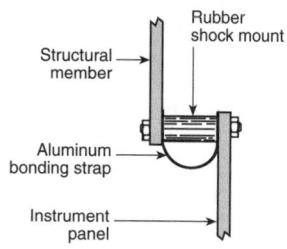

**shock mount
(instrument panel)**

shock mount. A type of vibration isolator used between a moving vehicle and a component sensitive to vibration. Shock mounts allow the component a certain degree of free movement, but absorb the high-frequency vibrations that are so destructive to delicate mechanisms.

shock stall (high-speed aerodynamics). A type of stall that affects some airplanes as they fly in the transonic speed range. In the transonic range, some air flowing over the aircraft surface is moving faster than the speed of sound, while other air is moving at a speed slower than the speed of sound.

When a shock wave forms on the upper surface of a wing, it gets in the way of the air flowing behind it, and this air breaks away from the wing surface. The shock wave causes the wing to stall. Shock stalls can cause control problems as an airplane is passing from subsonic flight into supersonic flight.

shock strut. *See* shock absorber.

shock wave. A pressure wave formed in the air as an object, such as a flight vehicle, passes through the air at a speed greater than the speed at which sound can travel. As the vehicle moves through the air, it creates disturbances, and sound waves spread out in all directions from the disturbance. Since the vehicle is flying faster than the sound waves are moving, they build up and form a shock wave at the front and the rear of the vehicle. As air passes through a shock wave, it slows down and its static pressure increases. The energy in the air is decreased. *See* oblique shock wave and normal shock wave.

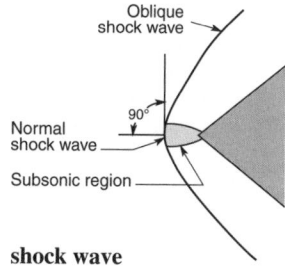

shock wave

shop head (rivet head). The head of a solid rivet which is formed when the shank is upset.

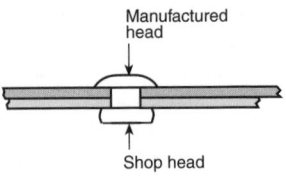

shop head

Shore Scleroscope. A form of hardness tester used to determine the hardness of such material such as rubber, metal, or plastic. A metal weight is dropped through a glass tube onto the surface of the material being tested, and the height of the rebound of the weight is measured. The harder the material, the higher the weight will bounce.

short circuit (electrical circuit). An electrical circuit in which there is a fault that causes electrons to flow across a portion of the circuit that should act as an insulator. The electrons find a short path to ground. Fuses and circuit breakers protect the circuit from damage that could be caused by excess current flowing through a short circuit.

short-field landing. Landing technique that becomes necessary when you have a relatively short landing area or when an approach must be made over obstacles that limit the available landing area.

shorting switch. A type of make-before-break switch. A make-before-break switch is a multipole switch in which one circuit is completed before another circuit is opened. A shorting switch is used in circuits that must never operate, even for a microsecond, without an electrical load being connected.

short range clearance. A clearance issued to a departing IFR flight which authorizes IFR flight to a specific fix short of the destination while air traffic control facilities are coordinating and obtaining the complete clearance.

short stacks (reciprocating engine exhaust system). The exhaust system of an aircraft reciprocating engine made of short pipes that direct the exhaust gases from each individual cylinder of the engine away from the aircraft.

short takeoff and landing aircraft (STOL). An aircraft which, at some weight within its approved operating weight, is capable of operating from a STOL runway in compliance with the applicable STOL characteristics, airworthiness, operations, noise, and pollution standards.

short takeoff and vertical landing (STOVL). The ability of some aircraft to take off from a short runway, and land vertically (i.e., with no runway).

short wave (radio waves). Waves of electromagnetic radiation that are shorter than 60 meters, or about 197 feet. The frequencies used for short-wave radio communications are above about five megahertz.

shot peening (metal treatment). A method of strengthening the surface of a metal part by blasting it with steel shot. The blows from the steel shot produce a compressive stress on the surface of the metal which must be overcome by a tensile stress of a greater intensity before the tensile stress can cause the surface of the metal to crack.

shoulder bolt. A special type of fastener used to prevent damage to a structure that could be caused by squeezing the surfaces together when the nut is tightened on the bolt. The diameter of the shank is larger than the diameter of the threaded portion of the bolt. The length of a shoulder bolt is chosen so its shank is the same length as the thickness of the material being fastened together.

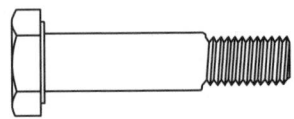

shoulder bolt

shoulder-wing airplane. A monoplane in which the wing is mounted near the top of the fuselage, but not on the top. The classifications of a monoplane with regard to the placement of the wing are: low-wing, midwing, shoulder-wing, high-wing, and parasol-wing.

show. A term meaning to demonstrate, confirm, validate, or substantiate something. In legal documents it means to plead or allege. *14 CFR Part 1:* "Unless the context otherwise requires, means to show to the satisfaction of the Administrator."

shower (meteorology). Precipitation from a cumuliform cloud. Showers are characterized by the suddenness of beginning and ending, by the rapid change of intensity, and usually by the rapid change in the appearance of the sky. Showery precipitation may be in the form of rain, ice pellets, or snow.

Shower of Sparks ignition system (aircraft reciprocating engine ignition system). The registered trade name for a type of magneto ignition system. When the ignition switch in a Shower of Sparks ignition system is placed in the START position, the primary circuit of the right magneto is grounded, and pulsating direct current from a vibrator flows into the primary winding of the left magneto to ground through a set of retard breaker points. When the crankshaft turns far enough for the retard points to open, the pulsating DC in the primary winding induces a high voltage in the secondary winding of the left magneto. This high voltage causes the spark plugs connected to the left magneto to produce a "shower of sparks."

show-type finish (aircraft finish). A type of finish put on some aircraft that are built for show. A show-type finish is usually made up of many coats of dope or lacquer, with much sanding and rubbing of the surface between coats.

shrink fit. An interference fit between pieces of an assembly. The hole into which a part is to fit is enlarged by heating it, and the piece to fit into the hole is shrunk by chilling it. The two pieces are assembled while their temperatures are different. Then, when they reach the same temperature, the fit is so tight no relative movement can take place between the parts.

shrinking blocks (sheet metalworking tool). A pair of wooden blocks used to clamp a sheet of metal to keep it from buckling when it is hammered with a mallet to shrink it.

shrink-wrapping. A method used to protect products from damage while they are being displayed for sale. The material to be shrink-wrapped is covered with a thin film of transparent thermoplastic material. Heat is applied, and the film shrinks to form a smooth protective cover.

shroud (air-cooled engine component). A sheet-metal cover placed over an air-cooled engine to pick up and force cooling air through the cylinder fins to remove heat from the engine.

shrouded-tip turbine blades (gas turbine engine component). A type of turbine blade with a T-shaped tip. The tips of the blades touch each other to form a ring around the turbine wheel to support the blades.

shunt (electrical instrument component). A precision resistor installed in parallel with a voltage measuring instrument to measure the amount of current flowing in a circuit. Load current flows through the shunt and produces a voltage drop proportional to the amount of current flowing through it.

A millivoltmeter whose dial is calibrated in amps is used to read the voltage drop across the shunt. The standard shunt used with aircraft ammeters produces a voltage drop of 50 millivolts when the shunt's rated current flows through it.

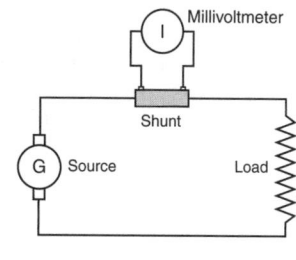

shunt

shunt circuit (electrical circuit). A parallel circuit, or a circuit in which there are more than one path for electrons to flow.

shunt ohmmeter. A type of ohmmeter used for measuring very low values of resistance. Voltage across the meter is adjusted until the meter pointer deflects full scale. Then, the unknown resistor is connected in parallel (in shunt) with the meter. The resistance of the unknown resistor is indicated by the decrease in the current flowing through the meter.

shunt winding. Field coils in an electric motor or generator that are connected in parallel with the armature.

shunt-wound generator. An electrical generator whose field windings are connected in shunt (parallel) with the armature winding. Most aircraft generators are shunt-wound, because their output voltage can be controlled by varying the amount of current flowing through the shunt-connected field winding.

shunt-wound motor. A commutator-type electric motor in which the field windings are connected in shunt (parallel) with the armature. Shunt-wound motors do not have a large amount of starting torque, but they operate at a relatively constant speed, and they do not need to have a mechanical load connected to them to prevent them from overspeeding. Shunt-wound motors are used for blowers and other low-torque applications.

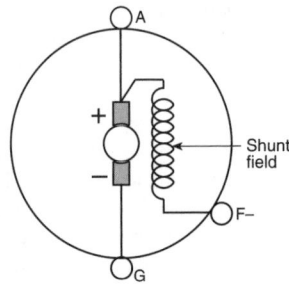

shunt-wound generator

shut-off valve (fluid power system component). A valve used in a fluid power system to shut off the flow of fluid.

shuttle valve (fluid power system component). A type of automatic selector valve installed in a critical portion of a fluid power system. Fluid for normal operation of the system flows through the shuttle valve into the actuating cylinder. But if the normal system pressure fails, emergency fluid pressure can be directed into the actuator through the shuttle valve. Shuttle valves are used in aircraft landing gear and brake systems to allow compressed air to be used to extend the landing gear or apply the brakes if the normal hydraulic system should fail.

SI. The universal abbreviation for the International System of Units. *See* International System of Units.

SID. *See* standard instrument departure.

SID (Standard Instrument Departure) charts. Aeronautical charts designed to expedite clearance delivery and facilitate transition between takeoff and enroute operations.

sidebands (radio transmission). The bands of frequencies on either side of the carrier frequency in amplitude modulated (AM) radio transmission. The bandwidth of a transmitted radio signal includes the carrier frequency (the frequency produced by the oscillator in the transmitter) and the frequencies of both the lower and the upper sidebands.

The frequency of the lower sideband is the carrier frequency minus the highest audio frequency used to modulate the carrier. The frequency of the upper sideband is the carrier frequency plus the highest audio frequency used to modulate the carrier.

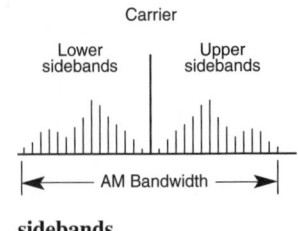

sidebands

side slip (airplane flight maneuver). A flight maneuver in which the airplane is banked while the rudder keeps it on a straight heading. This crossed-control condition causes the airplane to move sideways toward the low wing.

sidestep maneuver (air traffic control). A visual maneuver accomplished by a pilot at the completion of an instrument approach to permit a straight-in landing on a parallel runway not more than 1,200 feet to either side of the runway to which the instrument approach was conducted.

sidestick controller. A cockpit flight control used on some of the fly-by-wire equipped airplanes. The stick is mounted rigidly on the side console of the cockpit, and pressures exerted on the stick by the pilot produce electrical signals that are sent to the computer that flies the airplane.

sidetone (radio transmission). The audio-frequency signal fed back from the microphone of a radio transmitter into the earphones connected to the radio receiver. Sidetones allow a person to hear the signal as it is being transmitted.

siemens. A unit of electrical conductance. The siemens has replaced the older measurement called a mho. One siemens is the amount of electrical conductance that allows an electromotive force of one volt to move a flow of electrons of one ampere (one coulomb per second). One siemens is the reciprocal of one ohm.

sight glass (air conditioning system component). A small window in the high side of a vapor-cycle cooling system. Liquid refrigerant flows past the sight glass, and if the charge of refrigerant is low, bubbles will be seen. There are no bubbles in the refrigerant of a fully charged system.

sight glass (liquid-level indicator). A transparent tube on the outside of a reservoir or tank connected to the bottom of the container. The level of the liquid in the sight glass is the same as that in the container, and it gives a visual indication of the level of liquid in the reservoir.

sight line (sheet-metal layout). A line, drawn on a sheet-metal layout, one bend radius from the bend tangent line. The sight line is placed so it is directly below the nose of the radius bar in a leaf brake. When the metal is clamped in this position, the bend tangent line is at the correct position for the beginning of the bend.

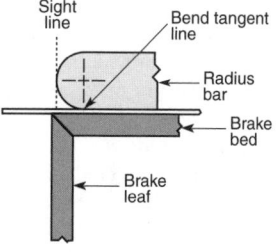

sight line

SIGMET (significant meteorological information). A weather advisory issued concerning weather significant to the safety of all aircraft. SIGMET advisories cover severe and extreme turbulence, severe icing, and widespread dust or sandstorms that reduce visibility to less than three miles.

SIGMET (ICAO). Information issued by a meteorological watch office concerning the occurrence or expected occurrence of specified enroute weather phenomena which may affect the safety of aircraft operations.

signal generator (electronic test equipment). A piece of electronic test equipment that produces an electrical signal having a specified voltage, frequency, and waveform. Signal generators are used for troubleshooting and calibrating electrical and electronic equipment.

signal-strength meter (radio receiver component). A meter connected into the automatic volume control (AVC) circuit in a radio receiver. A signal-strength meter is calibrated in decibels (dB) or in "S" units and is used to provide an indication of the strength of the signal being picked up by the receiver.

signal-to-noise ratio (radio reception). The ratio of received signal strength to the background noise. This is a measure of the readability of the received signal.

signal tracer (electronic test equipment). A piece of electronic test equipment used to trace a signal through each stage of a piece of electronic equipment. Troubleshooting of malfunctioning equipment is simplified by comparing the waveform of the signal at each stage with the waveform that should be at that stage.

signed numbers. A signed number can be either a positive or negative number. A positive number is a number greater than zero. A negative number is a number less than zero.

significant digits. The digits of a decimal number, beginning at the first nonzero digit and extending to the right to include all of the digits needed to give the required accuracy. One-half expressed as a decimal fraction with one significant digit is 0.5. If greater accuracy is required, this same value can be expressed with three significant digits as 0.500.

significant meteorological information. *See* SIGMET.

significant point (air traffic control). A point, whether a named intersection, NAVAID, fix derived from a NAVAID(s), or geographical coordinate expressed in degrees of latitude and longitude, which is established for the purpose of providing separation, as a reporting point, or to delineate a route of flight.

significant weather prognostic chart. A chart that presents four panels showing forecast significant weather and forecast surface weather.

silica. Silicon dioxide (SiO_2), as it occurs in nature.

silica gel. A form of extremely porous silica used as a desiccant. Silica gel, packaged in porous paper bags, is stored inside delicate instruments and electronic equipment that could be damaged by moisture. Moisture in the air is absorbed and held by the silica gel.

silicon. A dark brown, tetravalent (having four valence electrons), nonmetallic crystalline chemical element. Silicon's symbol is Si, its atomic number is 14, and its atomic weight is 28.086. Silicon is the second most abundant chemical element in nature (oxygen is the most abundant). Because of the ease with which silicon unites with oxygen to form silicon dioxide (sand and quartz), it is never found in nature in its pure state. Silicon is used to make semiconductor diodes, transistors, and all forms of integrated circuit devices.

silicon carbide. An abrasive that is often ground into small particles and bonded to sheets of paper or cloth or formed into grinding wheels for use on power grinders.

silicon controlled rectifier (SCR). A semiconductor electron control device. An SCR blocks current flow in both directions until a pulse of positive voltage is applied to its gate. It then conducts in its forward direction, while continuing to block current in its reverse direction.

silicone. A group of semi-inorganic polymers that have good thermal stability, are chemically inert, water repellent, and are good lubricants. Silicone products are available as liquids, solids, and semisolids. They are used in the manufacture of adhesives, lubricants, sealants, and electrical insulators.

silicone rubber. An elastomeric material made from silicone elastomers. Silicone rubber is compatible with fluids which attack other natural or synthetic rubbers.

silicon glaze (spark plug contaminant). A form of contamination on aircraft spark plugs that can lead to engine failure. Silica is found in sand and dust, and if a carburetor air filter leaks and allows sand or dust to get into the engine, the silica can form a hard, glasslike deposit on the nose core insulators of the spark plugs. Silicon glaze is an insulator at low temperatures, and will not cause a spark plug to show up as bad on a tester. But when the spark plug gets hot, the silicon glaze becomes conductive, and short circuits the high voltage to ground before it builds up high enough to jump the gap between the electrodes.

silicon solar cell. A special type of semiconductor device made of P-type silicon doped with boron and N-type silicon doped with arsenic. When light strikes the PN junction, electrons flow through the load circuit from the N-silicon to the P-silicon.

silicon steel. An alloy steel that contains between 0.5% and 4.5% silicon. Silicon steel in sheet form is used for laminations to make up the core of electrical transformers.

silver. A lustrous white, ductile, malleable, metallic chemical element. Silver's symbol is Ag, its atomic number is 47, and its atomic weight is 107.870. Silver has the highest thermal and electrical conductivity of any metal, and it is used in electrical contacts and printed circuits. One of the primary industrial uses of silver is in photography.

silver brazing. A form of brazing in which the filler metal is a silver-base alloy. *See* brazing.

silvered-mica capacitor. A high-voltage capacitor that uses thin sheets of mica as the dielectric. Both sides of the mica are electrolytically coated with silver. This silver forms the plates of the capacitor.

silver solder. An alloy of copper, silver, and zinc. The melting point of silver solder is lower than that of silver, but higher than that of lead-tin solder (soft solder).

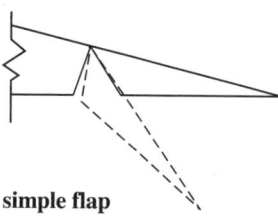

simple flap

simple flap (airplane flap). A type of wing flap installed on some of the smaller airplanes. A portion of the trailing edge of the wing inboard of the ailerons can be folded downward in flight to increase the camber of the wing. This increases both the lift and the drag the wing produces. *See* plain flap.

simple fraction (mathematics). A mathematical fraction with whole numbers for both its numerator and its denominator. An example of a simple fraction is $\frac{3}{4}$. Fractions that are not simple fractions are called complex fractions. An example of a complex fraction is:

$$\frac{1}{2}\Big/\frac{3}{4}$$

simple machine. Any of the basic, or elementary, mechanical devices from which all machines are built. Simple machines include the wheel and axle, the lever, and the inclined plane.

simple motion. Motion along a straight line, a circular path, or a helix.

simplex. Transmission and reception on the same frequency.

simplex communications. A method of communications in which one station transmits while the other receives, then the second station transmits and the first receives. Simplex communications differs from duplex communications, such as telephone, in which both stations can transmit and receive at the same time.

simplex fuel nozzle (gas turbine engine component). A type of fuel nozzle in a gas turbine engine in which all of the fuel is fed to the nozzle through a single fuel manifold.

simplified directional facility (SDF). A NAVAID used for nonprecision instrument approaches. The final approach course is similar to that of an ILS localizer except that the SDF course may be offset from the runway, generally not more than 3°, and the course may be wider than the localizer, resulting in a lower degree of accuracy.

simulate. To copy something or to make something that represents or acts like something. When a person is learning to fly an airplane, the flight instructor simulates every emergency situation the student is likely to encounter. By experiencing these simulated emergencies under controlled conditions, the student will know how to act if the real emergency ever occurs.

simulated flameout. A practice approach by a jet aircraft (normally military) at idle thrust to a runway, with the purpose of simulating a flameout. The approach may start at a runway (high key) and may continue on a relatively high and wide downwind leg with a continuous turn to final. It terminates in landing or low approach.

simulator. A device used for training or research that duplicates a piece of complex equipment. Flight simulators duplicate the cockpit of an airplane. All of the controls and instruments are connected to a computer that gives the operator the feel and the indications that would exist under actual flight conditions in a real aircraft. Emergency and unusual conditions can be simulated and practiced in the simulator far more safely and economically than can be done in the real aircraft.

simultaneous ILS approaches. An approach system permitting simultaneous ILS/MLS approaches to airports having parallel runways separated by at least 4,300 feet between centerlines. Integral parts of a total system are ILS/MLS, radar, communications, ATC procedures, and appropriate airborne equipment.

sine (trigonometric function). The sine of an angle is the ratio of the length of the side of a right triangle opposite the angle, to the length of the hypotenuse (the side opposite the right angle). Sine is abbreviated *sin*.

sine wave. The waveform of a periodically reversing vibration produced by a rotating machine in which the instantaneous values of the wave are the peak value multiplied by the sine of the angle through which the rotating element has turned.

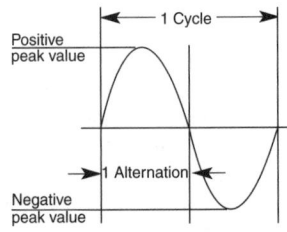

sine wave

sine-wave alternating current. Alternating current whose waveform is that produced by a rotary generator. The instantaneous value of sine-wave voltage is found by multiplying its peak value by the sine of the angle through which the rotor of the generator has turned.

For example, when the rotor has turned 30° from the position in which it produces zero voltage, the instantaneous voltage is one-half the peak voltage (the maximum voltage it can produce). The sine of 30° is 0.5, or one-half. When the rotor has turned 45°, the instantaneous voltage is 0.707 time the peak voltage. The sine of 45° is 0.707. When all of the instantaneous values of sine-wave alternating current are plotted, a smooth sine curve results.

single-acting actuator (fluid power system). A type of actuator in a fluid power system that uses fluid under pressure to move it in one direction, but a spring to return it. Hydraulic brakes use single-acting actuators to move the brake shoes out against the rotating drum. Hydraulic pressure moves the shoes out, but a spring pulls them back when the brake pedal is released.

single-action hand pump. A hand-operated fluid pump that moves fluid only during one stroke of the pump handle. One stroke pulls the fluid into the pump, and the other forces the fluid out.

single-axis autopilot (aircraft flight control systems). A simple automatic flight control system that controls the airplane only about its longitudinal, or roll, axis. The autopilot sensor detects any change in either roll or yaw and sends a signal to the aileron servos to produce a roll that counteracts the original roll. Single-axis autopilots are sometimes called wing levelers.

single-cut file (metal-cutting file). A file that has a single row of teeth extending across its face at an angle of between 65° and 85° to the length of the file.

single-cut file

single direction routes. Preferred IFR routes sometimes depicted on high altitude enroute charts, which are normally flown in one direction only.

single-disk brake. An aircraft brake in which a single steel disk rotates with the wheel and rides between two or more pads, or linings. These linings are mounted in the jaws of a stationary clamp which is closed by hydraulic pressure. When the brake is applied, the disk is clamped tightly between the linings, and the resulting friction slows the aircraft and converts energy of motion of the aircraft into heat.

single engine absolute ceiling. The altitude at which a twin-engine airplane can no longer climb with one engine inoperative.

single engine service ceiling. The altitude at which a twin-engine airplane can no longer climb at a rate greater than 50 fpm with one engine inoperative.

single-face repair (bonded structure repair). The repair to a piece of laminated structural material in which the damage extends through only one face of the material and partly into the core.

single flare (rigid tubing flare). A flare made on a piece of rigid tubing in which there is only one thickness of the tubing material in the flare.

single frequency approach (SFA). A service provided under a letter of agreement to military single-piloted turbojet aircraft which permits use of a single UHF frequency during approach for landing. Pilots are not normally required to change frequency from the beginning of the approach to touchdown, but pilots conducting an enroute descent are required to change frequency when control is transferred from the ARTCC to the terminal facility. The abbreviation "SFA" in the DOD FLIP IFR Supplement under "Communications" indicates this service is available at an airport.

single-loop rib stitching (aircraft fabric attachment). A method of attaching the fabric to the wing of an airplane in which only one loop of rib-stitching cord passes around the rib in each stitch.

single piloted aircraft (air traffic control). A military turbojet aircraft possessing one set of flight controls, tandem cockpits, or two sets of flight controls but operated by one pilot.

single-pilot resource management (SRM). The ability of a pilot to effectively manage all resources to ensure a successful flight outcome.

single-point fueling (aircraft fueling). A method of filling multiple fuel tanks in large aircraft from a single fueling point. The fuel hose is attached to the fueling station in the aircraft, and the correct tank valves are opened. Fuel flows into the tank until either the correct level is reached or the tank is full. Then, fuel to that tank is automatically shut off. Single-point fueling is fast, efficient, and safe, and it is used on almost all transport-type aircraft.

single-point grounding (electrical grounding). A method of grounding an electrical circuit by connecting all of the wires that go to ground to a single point on the equipment chassis. When single-point grounding is used, there is very little current flow in the chassis, and the interference from magnetic fields in the chassis is avoided.

single-servo brake (aircraft brake). A type of brake installed on some aircraft that uses the momentum of the rotating wheel to wedge the brake shoe tightly against the brake drum when the aircraft is moving in a forward direction. A double-servo (duo-servo) brake produces a wedging action between the shoes and the drum, whether the aircraft is moving forward or backward. A nonservo brake does not produce a wedging action in either direction.

single-shaft turboprop engine. A turboprop engine in which the propeller reduction gears are driven by the same shaft which drives the compressor for the gas generator.

single-shear rivet loading. A joint in which the two sheets of metal are riveted together. The rivet is subjected to only a single shear load as the sheets try to slide past one another.

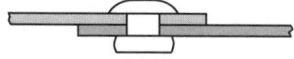

single-shear rivet loading

single-sideband radio transmission. A type of radio transmission in which only one of the sidebands of the signal is transmitted. The other sideband and the carrier wave are suppressed.

single-spool turbine engine (gas turbine engine). A gas turbine engine that has only one rotating mass. The compressor is directly connected to the turbine, and everything rotates at the same speed. A twin-spool turbine engine has a low-pressure compressor driven by one turbine and a high-pressure compressor driven by another. The two compressors are linked only by the air that flows through them, and they turn at different speeds.

single spread (adhesive application). A method of adhesive application in which the adhesive is spread on only one of the two surfaces being joined.

single-throw switch. An electrical switch that has only two conditions, ON or OFF. In one direction of the operating control, the contacts are open (OFF). Moving the control to the opposite position closes the contacts (ON). A single-pole, single-throw (SPST) switch can select one of the two conditions in one circuit, and a double-pole, single-throw (DPST) switch can select one of the two conditions in two circuits with the movement of a single control.

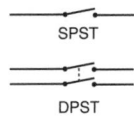

single-throw switches

sintered metal. A type of molded metal in which powdered metal is pressed together and molded into the desired shape while it is cold. Then the molded metal is heated to form it into a strong cohesive material.

sintered plate (battery component). A plate of a nickel-cadmium battery made of powdered metal that has been heated and molded to form a strong, cohesive material. Sintered material is used because its granular structure gives it a large surface area.

sintering. A process in which powdered metal is heated but not quite melted and then squeezed together.

sinusoidal curve. *See* sine wave.

siphon. A device used to move a liquid from a container, over an edge higher than the level of the liquid, down to a lower level. A curved tube is put into the liquid, and some form of mechanical force is applied to start the liquid flowing through the tube. A suction is often put on the end of the tube to start the liquid flowing. When the flow is started, atmospheric pressure forces the liquid from the higher container into the tube, and the weight of the liquid flowing through the tube to the lower level keeps the liquid flowing.

sister keelsons. Structural members in the front portion of floats lying parallel to the keel and midway between the keel and chines, adding structural rigidity and adding to directional stability when on the water.

Sitka spruce. A tall, straight spruce tree that grows on the northern Pacific coast of North America. Sitka spruce wood is strong, lightweight, and straight grained, and is used as the reference to which all other aircraft structural woods are compared.

situational awareness (psychology). The accurate perception and understanding of all the factors and conditions within the four fundamental risk elements that affect safety before, during, and after the flight.

sizing (textile materials). A filler put into some types of fabric or paper to fill the pores and make the material smooth and stiff. Starch is often put into cloth as a sizing so it will stay smooth when it is ironed.

skeg (seaplane float component). A robust extension of the keel behind the step which helps prevent the seaplane from tipping back onto the rear portion of the float.

sketch. A rough drawing made to illustrate a part or principle. Sketches are made according to regular mechanical drawing practices, but they are usually made without the use of drawing instruments, and they show only a minimum of detail.

skew-T chart (or skew-T/log-P diagram). In meteorology, this is a type of thermodynamic diagram used for the plotting of radiosonde soundings. The temperature and dew point soundings presented on a skew-T give a profile of the atmosphere from a point on the ground to about the 100 mb level, showing atmospheric stability, moisture content, and winds versus altitude. These charts can help a pilot assess the stability or instability of the atmosphere. *See also* thermodynamic diagram.

skid (aircraft flight maneuver). A flight maneuver in which the aircraft is turned without using a steep enough angle of bank. Centrifugal force caused by the turning aircraft is not opposed by enough inward lift (from banking), and the aircraft skids out from its curved flight path away from its direction of turn. A skid is the opposite of a slip. In a slip, the angle of bank is too steep for the rate of turn, and the aircraft slides to the inside of the turn.

skid shoes (helicopter landing gear component). Plates attached to the bottom of skid landing gear protecting the skid.

skids-on-floats (helicopter float design). A type of helicopter float design where the rigid portion of the landing gear rests on the floats. The floats support the whole weight of the helicopter in water or on hard surfaces.

skill knowledge. Knowledge reflected in motor or manual skills and in cognitive or mental skills that manifests itself in the doing of something.

skills and procedures. The procedural, psychomotor, and perceptual abilities used to control a specific aircraft or its systems. Skills and procedures are the stick and rudder, or airmanship abilities, that are gained through conventional training, are perfected, and become almost automatic through experience.

skin. The outside covering of an aircraft airframe.

skin antenna (aircraft antenna). A type of flush antenna (an antenna even with the surface of the aircraft skin). A part of the metal skin of the aircraft is electrically isolated by an insulating material and is used as the antenna conductor. Skin antennas are used on many high-speed aircraft.

skin effect (radio-frequency electrical energy). The cause of the unequal distribution of radio-frequency alternating current throughout a conductor. AC at radio frequencies tends to have a greater current density (more current flow) on the surface of a conductor than it does near the center. Because of skin effect, some conductors used to carry high radio-frequency AC are hollow tubes.

skin friction (aerodynamic drag). A type of aerodynamic drag caused by air flowing over the surface of the aircraft. Skin friction is a component of parasite drag.

skin radiator. A type of radiator used on some of the liquid-cooled racing airplanes. The radiator is made of two thin sheets of brass, slightly separated so the heated coolant can flow between them. A skin radiator may be mounted on the surface of the wing, the sides of the fuselage, or on the floats of seaplanes. Air flowing over the smooth surface of the radiator removes heat from the coolant.

skip distance (radio transmission characteristic). The distance from a radio transmitting antenna to the point on the surface of the earth the reflected sky wave first touches after it has been bounced off the ionosphere.

ski plane. An airplane whose wheeled landing gear has been replaced with skis so it can operate from snow or ice. Some types of skis require the wheels to be removed, and others can be installed without removing the wheels. Retractable skis have a slot in their bottom surface so they can be pulled up enough for the wheel to protrude below the ski, enabling the airplane to land on a hard surface on its wheels.

skipping (seaplane operation). Successive sharp bounces along the water surface caused by excessive speed or an improper planing attitude when the seaplane is on the step.

skip welding. A method of welding thin material. Skip welding is done in a series of short beads, with a space between each bead about as long as one of the beads. After the first series of beads is made, a second series is made between each of the first ones. Skip-welded material is less likely to warp than material welded with one continuous bead. Skip welding is sometimes called step welding.

ski tuck (flight problem). When skis are not rigged properly or a pilot exceeds recommended airspeeds, a ski can tuck down and give the momentary downward rotation of the nose of the aircraft.

skull-cap spinner (propeller spinner). A small, conical, streamlined cover retained by a bracket attached to the hub of a fixed-pitch wood or metal propeller. The diameter of a skull-cap spinner is the same as that of the propeller hub. The spinner serves as a cover over the propeller retaining bolts or nuts and provides a degree of streamlining.

skunk works. A section of an aircraft factory set aside for research and development of new aircraft. No one is allowed to visit the skunk works except those who are actually involved in the project being developed there.

Skydrol hydraulic fluid. The registered trade name of a synthetic hydraulic fluid used in most modern high-performance aircraft. Skydrol hydraulic fluid has a phosphate-ester base, is nonflammable, and is usable over a wide range of temperatures. Skydrol hydraulic fluid meets Military Specifications MIL-H-8446.

skyspotter (weather observation). A pilot who has received specialized training in observing and reporting inflight weather phenomena.

sky wave (radio transmission). The portion of an electromagnetic signal that radiates upward from the antenna until it strikes the ionosphere, then bounces back to the earth.

slag (welding product). The hard, brittle, glasslike material that covers a weld bead that has been made with a coated welding rod. The flux coating on the rod melts in the heat of the arc and flows out ahead of the bead. The melted flux covers the metal where the weld is being made and keeps oxides from forming in the weld. When the weld is made, the liquid flux hardens into slag that must be chipped off to allow the bead to be inspected.

slam acceleration (gas turbine engine operation). Improper operation of the power control lever of a gas turbine engine in which the control is moved forward too quickly to allow the engine to accelerate as it should. There is danger of a rich flameout if the fuel is metered into the engine before the compressor is able to pull enough air into the engine to furnish the correct fuel-air mixture ratio.

slant-line distance (aircraft navigation). The actual distance between an aircraft and a ground radio facility. A distance measuring equipment (DME) indicator shows the slant-line distance between the aircraft and the ground station. Slant-line distance is the hypotenuse of a right triangle, with the altitude of the aircraft as one side, and the horizontal distance between the ground station and a point directly below the aircraft as the other side.

slant range (radar measurement). The actual distance between a ground-based radar antenna and an airborne target.

slant visibility (meteorology). The distance an airborne observer can see and distinguish objects on the ground.

slash (radar indication). A radar beacon reply displayed on a radar scope as an elongated target.

slat (aircraft control). A secondary control on an airplane that allows the airplane to fly at a high angle of attack without stalling. A slat is a section of the leading edge of the wing mounted on curved tracks. These tracks move into and out of the wing on rollers.

In flight at low angles of attack, the air pressure on the wing holds the slat in, and it forms the leading edge of the wing. At a high angle of attack, aerodynamic forces pull the slat forward on its tracks, and it forms a duct that forces the air down onto the top of the wing to keep it from stalling.

slaved compass. A system whereby the heading gyro is "slaved to" or continuously corrected to bring its direction readings into agreement with a remotely located magnetic direction-sensing device (usually a flux valve or flux gate compass).

slaved gyro (aircraft flight instrument). A gyro-stabilized direction indicator whose directional signals are produced by a flux valve. *See* flux valve.

sleet. *See* ice pellets.

slide caliper. A device often used to measure the length of an object. It provides greater accuracy than a ruler.

slide rule (mathematics). A mechanical calculating device consisting of two side-by-side logarithmically graduated scales. The graduations are spaced according to the logarithm of the number, rather than the number itself. Two numbers are multiplied by adding the lengths of the logarithmic scales representing the numbers.

Slide rules, which are available in both straight and circular forms, are used to make fast calculations involving multiplication and division and the use of logarithms and trigonometric functions. Mechanical slide rules have been almost totally replaced by electronic calculators that can work all of the problems a slide rule can work, as well as many other types, much faster and with a far greater degree of accuracy.

slide switch. A type of electrical switch in which connections are made by sliding a conductor over fixed contacts.

slide valve. A valve that opens or closes a port by sliding back and forth over it. Slide valves are used in reciprocating steam engines to open and close the passage into the cylinder to allow steam to enter and leave.

slide-wire potentiometer. A form of variable resistor in which the amount of resistance used in a circuit is determined by the position of a contact along a length of resistance wire. The amount of resistance is directly proportional to the length of wire in the circuit.

slinger ring (propeller anti-icing system component). A hollow metal ring mounted around the hub of a propeller so that it turns with it. A mixture of alcohol and ethylene glycol is pumped into the slinger ring, and centrifugal force throws the fluid out through short discharge tubes along the leading edges of the propeller blades. The fluid prevents ice from forming on the blades.

sling psychrometer. An instrument used to measure the relative humidity of the air. A sling psychrometer consists of two mercury thermometers mounted on a frame with a handle that allows it to be slung around, so air moves across the thermometers. The bulb of one thermometer is covered with a cloth wick saturated with water. As the air blows over it, the water evaporates and lowers the temperature.

A chart showing the dry-bulb temperature and the difference between the wet-bulb and dry-bulb temperatures is used to find the relative humidity, in percentage, for these conditions.

slip (aircraft flight maneuver). A maneuver in which the aircraft moves through the air sideways, rather than straight ahead. Slipping produces a large amount of drag so the airplane can descend at a steep angle without gaining excessive speed. An airplane is slipped by crossing its controls, using right rudder and left aileron. A forward slip is one in which the aircraft turns its side into the wind, but continues in forward flight. A slide slip is one in which the aircraft continues to point straight ahead, but slips to the side.

slip (induction motor specification). The difference between the synchronous speed of an induction motor (the speed of the rotating magnetic field in the stator) and the actual speed the rotor is turning. An induction motor tries to turn at its synchronous speed, but friction and the mechanical load connected to the rotor prevent it turning at this speed.

The amount the rotor lags behind the rotating field is called slip. It is slip that gives the motor its torque. The greater the slip, the greater the pull between the magnetic fields in the rotor and stator. Slip is measured in percentage of the synchronous speed.

slip clutch (aircraft starter component). A heavy spring-loaded mechanism built into an aircraft reciprocating-engine starter that allows the starter drive to slip enough to take up the initial shock when the starter is engaged. The slip clutch minimizes the shock that could damage the engine or the starter when the starter engages.

slip joint (reciprocating engine exhaust system component). A type of connection used in the exhaust system of a reciprocating engine that provides for the expansion of the system components as they get hot. The exhaust system is assembled and connected together with ball joints, bellows, and slip joints that allow the system to move and not crack. Slip joints fit together loosely when the system is cold, but tighten when the components reach their operating temperature.

slippage mark (tires and tubes). A small mark painted between a wheel and a tube-type tire. The mark is half on the tire and half on the wheel. If the mark on the tire is not lined up with the mark on the wheel, it shows that the tire has slipped on the wheel. When a tire slips, the valve in the tube is likely to be damaged, and the tire should be removed from the wheel and the tube examined.

slip rings (electrical machine). Smooth, continuous rings of brass or copper mounted on the rotor shaft of an electrical generator or alternator. Current used to produce the magnetic field in the rotor of a DC alternator flows into the rotor coil through slip rings. Slip rings also carry current into the deicer heating coils on an airplane propeller blade.

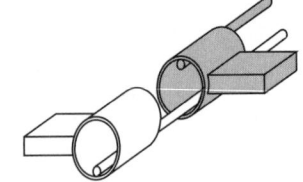

slip rings

slip-roll former (sheet metal tool). A type of sheet-metal shop tool used to form large-radius curves in sheets of metal. Slip-roll formers have three hardened steel rollers mounted in a framework. One roller, the drive roller, is turned with a hand crank to pull the metal through the former. The clamp roller is adjustable up or down to clamp the sheet metal tightly against the drive roller.

The radius roller is adjustable so it can be pressed against the metal to bend it as the metal is pulled by the clamp roller and drive roller. This determines the radius of the bend.

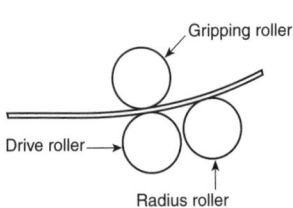

slip-roll former

slip stick (mathematics). A commonly used term for a slide rule. This name comes from the fact that most slide rules have a slide that slips in and out of grooves in the body of the rule.

slipstream (aircraft operation). The strong flow of air moved rearward by an airplane propeller.

slipstream area. For the purpose of rib stitch spacing, the slipstream area is considered to be the diameter of the propeller plus one wing rib on each side.

sloshing compound (fuel tank sealant). A rubbery sealant used to line the inside of built-up metal fuel tanks. The sloshing compound is poured into the tank until the tank is about half full. The filler cap is installed and the tank rotated until the compound covers all of the internal surface. Then the compound is drained from the tank. The compound that sticks to the walls of the tank cures to form a tight seal over all of the seams in the tank.

slot (aerodynamic component). A fixed, nozzle-like opening near the leading edge of an airplane wing, ahead of the aileron. A slot acts as a duct to force air down on the upper surface of the wing when the airplane is flying at a high angle of attack. Forcing the air down on the top of the wing allows the airplane to fly at a higher angle of attack before it stalls. Since the slot is located ahead of the aileron, the aileron remains effective even at very high angles of attack.

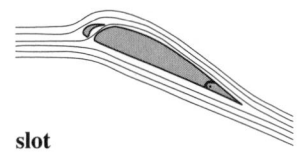

slot

slotted flap (aircraft secondary control). A type of trailing-edge flap that forms a slot between its leading edge and the inside of the flap well in the wing. This slot directs fast-moving air over the lowered flap and prevents it separating from the flap upper surface. The air flowing over the top of the flap increases the lift produced by the wing when the flap is lowered.

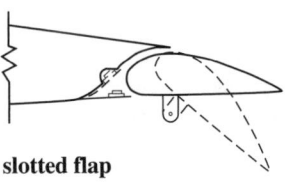

slotted flap

slotted-head screw. A screw having a single, straight slot cut across its head for the blade of a screwdriver to fit.

slotted nut. A regular hexagon nut with slots cut across its top. A cotter pin is installed through a hole in the shank of the bolt and through the slots in the nut to safety the nut to the bolt. Slotted nuts differ from castle nuts in that the sides of slotted nuts are straight, rather than domed.

slow-blow fuse. A special type of fuse that allows a large flow of current for a short period of time, but opens the circuit if current in excess of its rating flows for a longer period. Slow-blow fuses are used in electric motor circuits and circuits with incandescent lamps. Both of these circuits have a large inrush of current when the switch is first closed, but when the motor begins to turn, or when the lamp filaments heat up, the current drops to a much lower value.

slow taxi (float plane operation). To taxi a float plane at low power or low RPM.

sludge. A heavy contaminant that forms in an aircraft engine lubricating oil because of oxidation and chemical decomposition of the oil.

sludge plugs (aircraft reciprocating engine component). Spool-shaped, sheet-metal plugs installed inside hollow crankshaft throws. Sludge carried in the lubricating oil passing through the crankshaft is thrown by centrifugal force to the outside of the chamber formed by the sludge plugs, where it is trapped and held until the engine is disassembled at overhaul.

slug (electrical relay component). A heavy ring of copper or other metal placed over a relay coil. The slug acts as a short-circuited winding, and the magnetic field produced by current induced in the slug slows the operation of the relay.

slug (tuned circuit component). A small cylinder of either powdered iron or copper, placed in the center of a radio-frequency (RF) coil to vary its inductance. When an iron slug is put in the center of the coil, its inductance increases; but when a copper slug is put in, its inductance decreases. Changing the inductance of the coil changes the resonant frequency of the circuit in which the coil is installed.

S

slug (unit of mass). The unit of mass equal to that which experiences an acceleration of one foot per second per second when a force of one pound acts on it. It is equal to 32.174 pounds, or 14.5939 kilograms, of mass. A slug is also called a G-pound.

small aircraft. *14 CFR Part 1:* "Aircraft of 12,500 pounds or less, maximum certificated take-off weight."

small-scale integration (SSI). An integrated circuit chip that contains up to nine gates or gate-equivalent circuits.

smaze (atmospheric condition). A combination of smoke and haze similar to smog (smoke and fog), except it does not contain as much moisture. Smaze is generally found in heavily industrialized areas.

smile (sheet metal damage). A small curved dent in the sheet metal around a rivet head. The smile is caused by the rivet set being held at an angle to the rivet head, rather than straight in line with the head.

smog (atmospheric condition). A mixture of smoke and fog. Smog is a serious obstruction to visibility and is basically natural fog contaminated with industrial pollution.

smoke (meteorology). Restriction to visibility caused by small particles of carbonaceous material suspended in the air. Smoke is a residue from combustion.

smoke detector. A device that warns the flight crew of the presence of smoke in cargo and/or baggage compartments. Some smoke detectors are of the visual type, others are photoelectric or ionization devices.

smoothing filter (electronic component). An electronic filter, usually made of capacitors and inductors. A smoothing filter, also called a ripple filter, is installed between a rectifier and an electrical load to remove the ripple from the DC produced by the rectifier.

snake drill (sheet-metal-working tool). A long, flexible extension with a round shank on one end and a drill chuck on the other. The snake drill is fastened in the chuck of a drill motor, and a twist drill is installed in its chuck. This combination allows holes to be drilled in locations that are inaccessible to other types of drills.

snap-action switch (electrical switch). A type of electrical switch whose contacts are mounted on a spring and held pressed together by the operating handle. As soon as the handle is moved to the OPEN position, the spring snaps the contacts apart. Snap-action switches are used in circuits carrying inductive loads to separate the contacts quickly before the inductance causes an arc to form across the contacts.

snap ring. A small, spring-steel ring that can be fitted into a groove in a shaft or in a groove cut into the walls of a hole. The spring action of the ring holds it tightly in the groove.

snap roll (airplane maneuver). An abrupt maneuver of an airplane in which the airplane does a single turn of a spin while flying in a horizontal direction.

snips (metal-working hand tool). Hand-operated shears used for cutting sheet metal. The most generally used snips are called tin snips, because they are commonly used to cut commercial sheet metal which is often (though incorrectly) called "tin."

snow (type of precipitation). A type of precipitation that forms in the air when water vapor changes directly into crystals of ice. Snow forms when the air temperature is below 0°C.

snow flurry (meteorology). A popular term for snow shower, particularly of very light and brief nature.

snow grains (meteorology). Precipitation of very small, white, opaque grains of ice, similar in structure to snow crystals. The grains are fairly flat or elongated with diameters generally less than 0.04 inch (1 mm).

snow pellets (meteorology). Precipitation consisting of white, opaque ice particles that are approximately round or sometimes conical. The particles have a snowlike structure and are about 0.08 to 0.2 inch in diameter. Snow pellets differ from snow grains in that they are crisp and easily crushed, and they rebound from a hard surface and often break up.

snubber (fluid power system component). A component in a hydraulic or pneumatic actuator that slows the motion of the actuator piston. The snubber absorbs the shock when the actuator piston reaches the end of its travel.

snubber (instrument component). A restrictor fitting installed between an oil pressure gage and the pressure pump. A snubber prevents the indicator pointer from fluctuating.

soak (metal heat treatment). The procedure in which metal being heat-treated is held in an oven at an elevated temperature until it is heated uniformly throughout.

soap. A material used for cleaning or as an emulsifier. Soap is made by the chemical action between the salt of a metal, such as sodium or potassium, and a fatty oil. Soap assists water in penetrating a film of grease or dirt on a surface so it can be washed away.

SOAP (Spectrometric Oil Analysis Program). An oil analysis program in which a sample of oil is burned in an electric arc and an examination is made of the wavelength composition of the resulting light. Each chemical element in the oil, when burned, produces light containing a unique band of frequencies. A computer analyzes the amount of each band of frequencies and prints out the number of parts of the element per million parts of the entire sample. SOAP can predict engine problems by warning the engine operator of an uncharacteristic increase in the amount of any of the elements in the oil.

soap bubble test. A type of test used to check for leaks in almost any kind of system in which a gas is held under pressure. A soap solution is brushed over all areas of a pressurized system where a leak could occur, and if there is a leak, the escaping gas will form bubbles in the soap film.

soapstone. A soft, grayish-white stone composed of talc and chlorite, a mineral similar to mica. Soapstone has a slick, or soapy, feel that gives it its name.

soaring (aircraft flight). A type of flight in which the aircraft, usually a glider or sailplane, flies without the use of engine power. The aircraft is normally pulled into the air with a powered airplane and, when released, it glides down. The pilot circles in a column of rising air, and as long as the air is rising faster than the aircraft is descending, the aircraft goes up in altitude. As soon as an altitude is reached where the air is no longer rising, the pilot leaves that column and searches out another, to continue the flight.

socket-head bolt. A bolt with a socket, usually hexagon-shaped, formed in its head. A hexagon wrench that fits into the socket is used to turn a socket-head bolt.

socket wrench. A type of wrench used to turn a nut or bolt. The socket is a small cylinder of high-strength chrome-vanadium steel. One end of the cylinder has either a 6-point or 12-point opening that fits the nut or bolt head. The other end has a square hole that fits the handle used to drive the socket. These drive holes are usually $\frac{1}{4}$-inch, $\frac{3}{8}$-inch, $\frac{1}{2}$-inch, or $\frac{3}{4}$-inch square, depending on the size nut the socket is designed to turn.

Ratchet handles, breakover handles, and speed handles can be used to drive the socket. Extensions of various lengths, and universal joints may be used between the socket and the drive handle to allow the socket to fit squarely on the nut and be turned by the handle.

sodium. A soft, light, malleable, ductile, silvery-white, metallic chemical element that has a waxy feel. Sodium's symbol is Na, its atomic number is 11, and its atomic weight is 22.9898. Sodium is in the alkaline metal group and is extremely active, combining readily with other chemical elements. Pure sodium metal combines instantly with oxygen when it is exposed to air, and it causes water to decompose with a violent reaction. Because of this, sodium metal must be kept covered with kerosine.

sodium bicarbonate. A white, powdery salt of sodium. When mixed with water, sodium bicarbonate forms a weak alkaline solution. Sodium bicarbonate is useful for neutralizing spilled battery acid and as a fire extinguishing agent. When sodium bicarbonate is heated, it releases carbon dioxide that smothers the fire. Other names for sodium bicarbonate are baking soda and saleratus.

sodium-filled exhaust valve (reciprocating engine component). A hollow exhaust valve that is partially filled with metallic sodium. The sodium is a soft solid at room temperature, but at the operating temperature of the valve, it melts and becomes a liquid that wets the inside surfaces of the hollow valve stem and head. As the valve opens and closes, the sodium sloshes back and forth, picking up heat from the head and carrying it into the stem, where it is transferred through the valve guide into the cylinder head and is subsequently dissipated into the air.

sodium-vapor lamp. A type of lamp used for outdoor lighting, especially along highways. Metallic sodium is vaporized inside a glass tube that contains a low-pressure gas. A voltage is placed across electrodes inside the glass tube, and the gas between the electrodes becomes ionized and glows enough to produce an orange light.

soft-faced hammer. A hammer whose head has one or more soft faces made of plastic, rubber, rawhide, or a soft metal such as lead or aluminum. Soft-faced hammers are used to pound on surfaces that could be damaged by hard hammers.

soft-field landing. A technique for landing on fields that are rough or have soft surfaces, such as snow, sand, mud, or tall grass. The objective is to touch down as smoothly as possible, and at the slowest possible landing speed. The pilot must control the airplane in a manner that the wings support the weight of the airplane as long as practical, to minimize drag and stresses imposed on the landing gear by the rough or soft surface.

soft magnetic material. Ferromagnetic material that is easy to magnetize and demagnetize. Only a small coercive (demagnetizing) force is needed to remove any magnetism from the material. Low-carbon steel is a soft magnetic material.

soft solder. An alloy of tin and lead that melts at a temperature of less than 800°F (427°C). This temperature is much lower than the melting temperature of the metal on which the solder is used. Soft solder is normally available in the form of a hollow wire filled with a resin flux. Soft solder is melted with a hot soldering copper, called a soldering iron, and the liquid solder wets the surface on which it is melted. When the soldering iron is removed, the solder solidifies and forms a bond between the pieces of metal that have been wetted.

Soft solder does not form a physically strong bond, but is used on sheet metal, over a locked seam to make the joint liquid-proof, or on wires after they have been twisted together to make a connection having a low electrical resistance.

soft vacuum tube. A vacuum tube that is faulty because air has leaked into the tube envelope.

software (computer operation). The package of instructions or programs used to control a computer. Software consists of written instructions that can be easily changed by a computer programmer. The electronic components, switches, and wiring used in computer operation are called hardware.

soft X-rays. Low-powered X-rays that have comparatively long wavelengths. Soft X-rays do not penetrate a material nearly as deeply as the high-powered, hard X-rays.

soil cement. A material used as a base for roads and airport runways. Soil cement is made by mixing portland cement with soil and water and then compacting the mixture.

solar cell. A silicon semiconductor device that converts light energy directly into electrical energy. These devices are called solar cells because they are designed to convert energy from the sun directly into electricity.

solar cell

solar radiation. Electromagnetic radiation emitted by the sun.

solder. *See* soft solder and silver solder.

soldered splice (electrical wiring connection). A type of splice used for electrical wires in which the ends of the wires to be joined are twisted together to give them mechanical strength. The joint is then covered with soft solder to decrease its electrical resistance. Soldered splices are not generally recommended for use in aircraft electrical systems.

soldering. A method of thermally joining metal parts with a molten nonferrous alloy that melts at a temperature below 800°F (427°C). The molten alloy is pulled up between close-fitting parts by capillary action. When the alloy cools and hardens, it forms a strong, leak-proof connection.

soldering iron. A handheld tool used to melt solder. Modern soldering irons are electrically heated and use a tinned copper tip (a copper tip covered with solder) to melt the solder.

soldering pistol. A special type of handheld tool used to melt solder. The heating element is a transformer whose secondary winding is a single turn that extends out of the transformer in the form of two connections for the ends of a copper tip. When the solder is ready to be melted, a trigger switch in the primary winding is pulled. When primary current flows, a low voltage but high current is induced into the single-turn secondary. This current flows through the copper tip and heats it enough to melt the solder. As soon as the soldered joint is made, the trigger is released, and the tip cools off.

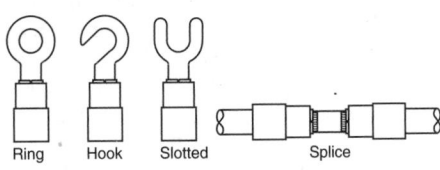

Ring   Hook   Slotted   Splice

solderless connector (electrical wires). A crimped-on connector used to fasten a terminal to an electrical wire.

solderless connector

solenoid. An electromagnet with a movable iron core that can be pulled into the coil. When current flows in the coil, the resulting magnetic field pulls the core into its center. When no current is flowing in the coil, a spring moves the core out of the coil. Solenoids can be used to operate valves, switches, and mechanical locks, as well as many other types of devices.

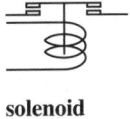

solenoid

solid. A material whose internal structure holds it tightly in its original shape and size. A solid differs from a liquid, whose structure causes it to hold only its size, not its shape, and a gas, that holds neither its size nor its shape.

solid conductor (electrical conductor). An electrical conductor made of a single piece of material, usually wire. Solid conductors are used where vibration is no problem, but stranded conductors are used where vibration is present.

solid fuel (rocket fuel). Rocket fuel made of a mixture of solid materials that, when ignited, combine fast enough to produce a great amount of heat. Solid fuel, which contains all the oxygen needed for the reaction, is molded into a shape that causes it to burn at the correct rate.

solidity (helicopter rotor system). The ratio of the total blade area to the disk area. The disk area is the area of the circle swept by the rotor as it rotates.

solidity ratio (helicopter design). The ratio of the total rotor blade area, which is the combined area of all the main rotor blades, to the total rotor disc area. This ratio provides a means to measure the potential for a rotor system to provide thrust.

solid solution (metal heat treatment). A uniform combination of the alloying elements in a base metal. The alloying elements enter into the solid solution when the metal is heated in a furnace and held at a high temperature long enough for the metal to reach a uniform temperature throughout. When the metal is uniformly hot, it is removed from the furnace and immediately quenched to lock the alloying elements into the solid solution.

solid-state device. An electronic component that controls the flow of electrons without the use of any heated filaments, vacuum spaces, or moving parts. Semiconductor devices such as diodes, transistors, and silicon-controlled rectifiers are examples of solid-state devices.

solo flight (aircraft flight). Flight of an aircraft when there is only one person in the aircraft.

soluble. The condition of a substance that can be dissolved in, or can form a solution with, another substance. Salt is soluble in water, it will dissolve in water to form a solution of salt and water. Oil is soluble in gasoline. Oil and gasoline form a solution when they are mixed.

solution. A homogeneous mixture (a mixture that is the same all the way through) of one or more materials dissolved in another. A solution is a physical mixture, because the parts that make up the solution do not have to be combined in any exact ratio, as they do in a compound. Either a little bit, or a large amount of salt can be dissolved in a container of water, to produce a solution of salt water.

solution heat treatment (metal heat treatment). A type of heat treatment in which the metal is heated in a furnace until its temperature is uniform throughout. It is then removed from the furnace and quenched in cold water. When the metal is hot, the alloying elements enter into a solid solution with the base metal to become part of its basic structure. When the metal is quenched, the alloying elements remain a part of the base-metal structure.

If the metal is not immediately quenched after it is removed from the furnace, some of the alloying elements will precipitate, or settle out, of the solid solution with the base metal, and the grain structure will enlarge. The metal will not be as strong as it would have been if it were properly quenched, and intergranular corrosion is likely to form along the enlarged grain boundaries.

solvent. A liquid able to dissolve certain types of solids. Water is a good solvent for some kinds of chemical materials, such as certain types of salts. Alcohol is a solvent for many materials that cannot be dissolved in water. Some of the stronger acids, such as hydrofluoric acid, are used as solvents for materials that cannot be dissolved in any other solvent.

somatogravic illusion (physiology). The feeling of being in a nose-up or nose-down attitude, caused by a rapid acceleration or deceleration while in flight situations that lack visual reference.

sonar. An electronic detection system used for locating objects in water. Pulses of acoustic energy (energy whose frequency is within the range that can be heard by the human ear) is transmitted through the water. This energy travels until it strikes an object, and part of it is reflected back to the sonar receiver where it is amplified and displayed on a scope or dial.

Sonar is used by the U.S. Navy to detect the presence of submarines and by commercial fishermen to locate schools of fish. Passive sonar does not transmit pulses of energy, but listens for sounds made by the propellers of ships and submarines.

sonic boom. A loud, explosive noise heard on the ground when an airplane passes overhead at a speed faster than the speed of sound. Sound-pressure waves build up as the airplane passes through the air, but because the airplane is flying faster than these waves can move out ahead of it, the sound pressure builds up and forms a shock wave.

The shock wave radiates out from the airplane in the form of a cone. When this cone passes over the ground, the pressure difference between the pressure inside the wave and the pressure of the surrounding air causes the loud explosion-like sound.

sonic cleaning. A method of cleaning delicate mechanical parts. The parts are placed in a sonic cleaning machine and covered with a cleaning fluid. High-intensity sound waves are produced in the cleaning fluid, and the vibrations caused by these waves shake loose any contaminants on the parts being cleaned.

sonic frequencies. Frequencies of mechanical vibrations that can be heard by the human ear. Sonic frequencies are normally considered to be those between 20 hertz and 20,000 hertz (20 kHz).

sonic soldering. A method of soldering metals, such as aluminum, that are normally difficult to solder because of the speed with which surface oxides build up. The surface to be soldered is covered with a flux to prevent oxygen reaching it, and the tip of the soldering iron used to heat the surface is vibrated at a sonic rate. The vibrations loosen the surface oxides, and they float to the top of the flux. Since no new oxides can form under the molten flux, the solder can reach the hot, clean metal and adhere to it.

sonic speed. The speed of sound.

sonic venturi. A venturi in a line between a turbine engine compressor or turbocharger and the pressurization system of an aircraft. When the air flowing through the venturi reaches the speed of sound, a shock wave forms across the throat of the venturi and restricts the flow. A sonic venturi is also called a flow limiter.

soot. A black residue left when a hydrocarbon material is burned in an atmosphere in which there is not enough oxygen for complete combustion. Soot is composed mostly of carbon.

sounding (meteorology). An upper-air observation; a radiosonde observation.

sound suppressor. The airframe component that replaces the turbine engine tail pipe. It decreases the distance sounds made by the exhaust gases can propagate by converting low-frequency vibrations into high-frequency vibrations.

sound waves. Longitudinal pressure waves within an elastic medium, such as air, water, or a solid material, that has been disturbed. Sound waves cannot travel through a vacuum.

source. In communication, the sender, speaker, transmitter, or instructor who composes and transmits a message made up of symbols which are meaningful to listeners and readers.

source region (meteorology). An extensive area of the earth's surface characterized by relatively uniform surface conditions. Large masses of air remain long enough over these surfaces to take on characteristic temperature and moisture properties from the surface.

southern domestic airspace (SDA). All airspace within the Canadian Domestic Airspace that lies south of a line, that, specifically defined by regulation, begins at the Alaska/Canada border on the Arctic Ocean and, more or less, extends southward through Yellowknife to Churchill and thence northeast to Frobisher and the Atlantic Ocean.

south geographic pole. The location of the southern spin axes of the earth. The south geographic pole is located at 90° south latitude.

south magnetic pole. The location near, but not at, the south geographic pole, at which the magnetic lines of flux of the earth's magnetic field enter. These lines of flux are considered to leave from the north magnetic pole and enter at the south magnetic pole.

south pole of a magnet. The pole of a magnet at which lines of magnetic flux are considered to enter after leaving the magnet at its north pole.

space charge (electron tube). The negative charge in an electron tube between the cathode and the plate. This space charge is caused by the cloud of electrons that collect around the cathode of the tube when the cathode emits more electrons than the plate can accept.

spacers. Components used to fill a space between two objects. Washers are commonly used as spacers around a bolt to take up the space between the nut and the surface being clamped by the fastener.

space shuttle. A manned vehicle launched by a rocket, usually a two-stage rocket, and carried to an altitude at which it can orbit the earth. At the completion of its assigned mission, the space shuttle re-enters the earth's atmosphere and glides to a landing.

S

space wave (radio transmission). The portion of an electromagnetic signal that is capable of traveling through the ionosphere.

spade drill. A special drill used for cutting holes in graphite structural materials. The flat surfaces of the drill end allow ample room for the drill dust to leave the hole so it will not abrade the sides of the hole and increase its diameter.

spade drill

spaghetti (electrical insulation). The commonly used name for a type of insulating tubing slipped over the end of an electrical wire. The tubing is put on at the point the wire connects to a terminal, where it is soldered to a component, or where the wire is spliced. Modern spaghetti is often made of some form of polyvinyl chloride tubing, and it can be either transparent or color coded. The name spaghetti comes from the hollow tube of pasta the tubing resembles.

spalling. A type of damage in which chips are broken from the surface of a case-hardened material such as a bearing race. Spalling takes place when a bearing race is put under a load great enough to distort the softer inner part of the metal and cause the hard, brittle surface to crack. Once a crack forms in the surface, chips break out.

span loading (aerodynamic measurement). An aerodynamic measurement found by dividing the span of an airfoil by the total weight the airfoil supports.

spanner. The name generally used by the British for a wrench. In American usage, a spanner is a special type of wrench with a hook-shaped arm and a hole, pin, or projection in its hooked end. A spanner is used to turn ring-shaped nuts.

spanner nut. A special type of round nut with holes, notches, or projections around its periphery. Spanner nuts are turned with a hook spanner or pin spanner.

span of an airfoil. The length of an airfoil measured between its tips.

spanwise. The distance from tip to tip of an airfoil, wing or stabilizer.

spar (airplane wing component). The main spanwise, load-carrying structural member in an airplane wing.

spark. An electrical discharge between two electrodes or points within a circuit having a difference of electrical potential. A spark normally has a very short duration and produces intense heat, light, and electromagnetic radiation that cover a wide band of frequencies. A spark is used inside the cylinder of an internal combustion engine to ignite the fuel-air mixture. A discharge of lightning is an extremely large spark.

spark coil (reciprocating engine ignition system component). A step-up transformer used to produce a high voltage. This high voltage causes a spark to jump across the electrodes of a spark plug inside the cylinder of a reciprocating engine. The primary winding of the spark coil consists of comparatively few turns of heavy copper wire, wound over a soft iron core. When primary current flows through this winding and through the breaker points, a magnetic field is formed that extends out beyond the secondary winding.

The secondary winding consists of many hundreds of turns of very fine copper wire wound on the outside of the primary winding. One end of the secondary winding connects to the primary, and the other end goes to the rotor of the distributor, a high-voltage selector switch that directs the high voltage to the proper spark plug.

When the breaker points open, primary current stops flowing, and its magnetic field instantly collapses. As it collapses, the lines of flux cut across the turns of wire in the secondary winding and induce a high voltage in it. This high voltage produces the spark in the spark plug.

spark-ignition engine (reciprocating engine). A form of reciprocating engine in which the fuel-air mixture inside the cylinder is ignited by an electric spark. The spark is timed to occur when the piston is in the correct position on the compression stroke.

spark plug (reciprocating engine ignition system component). A device in the ignition system of a reciprocating engine that produces the spark which ignites the fuel-air mixture inside the cylinder. A spark plug has a steel shell and an insulated center electrode. Accurately spaced gaps are formed between the ground electrodes on the shell and the insulated center electrode.

The high-voltage lead from the ignition distributor is connected to the insulated terminal of the spark plug and, at the correct time, a pulse of high-voltage electrical energy is sent to the spark plug. As this electrical energy passes to ground, it produces an intense spark between the two electrodes.

spark plug bushing (aircraft reciprocating engine component). A threaded bronze or steel bushing screwed and shrunk into an opening in the cast aluminum cylinder head of an aircraft engine. The spark plugs screw into the bushings which protect the soft aluminum from damage when the spark plugs are changed.

spark plug resistor. A resistor installed in a shielded spark plug between the ignition lead terminal and the center electrode. The capacitance in the shielded ignition lead stores enough energy to keep the spark flowing across the gap long enough to erode the electrodes. The resistor decreases the duration of the spark and thus minimizes electron erosion.

spark suppressor. A device placed across a set of electrical contacts to suppress the spark that forms when the contacts open. Spark suppressors normally consist of a capacitor and resistor and sometimes a diode across the contacts.

spark test (metal identification method). A quick test to identify types of ferrous metal. A sample of the metal is pressed against a grinding wheel, and the pattern of sparks thrown off indicates of the type of metal. When wrought iron which contains no carbon is held against the wheel, the sparks stream out in a straight line. The lines of sparks grow wider and brighter as they stream out behind the wheel.

Mild steel, with its low carbon content, has a spark pattern similar to that of wrought iron, except some of the sparks have tiny forks on them. The spark pattern for tool steel with its high-carbon content is similar to that for mild steel, except there are more forks in the stream, and the forked sparks form close to the wheel. Cast iron produces a large number of sparks close to the wheel, but they die out quickly. The spark pattern for cast iron is very short.

spar varnish. A hard, durable finish for wood that is to be kept outdoors where it is exposed to the weather. Spar varnish is made of a resin mixed with drying oils and thinners, and it is brushed on the surface to be protected. When the drying oils cure, they leave a hard, protective resin film on the wood. Spar varnish is much more durable than spirit varnish.

S

spatial disorientation (physiology). The state of confusion due to misleading information being sent to the brain from various sensory organs, resulting in a lack of awareness of the aircraft position in relation to a specific reference point.

spatula. A tool that looks much like a knife, but has no cutting edge. The thin, flexible, metal blade of a spatula is used to mix, spread, or move soft materials, such as resins.

speaker voice coil. A small coil that rides inside an air gap in a permanent magnet or electromagnet inside a radio speaker. The voice coil is physically attached to the speaker cone, and alternating current from the output of an audio amplifier flows through it. Current flowing in the voice coil produces a magnetic field that either aids or opposes the magnetic field in which the coil is mounted. This interaction between the magnetic fields moves the coil in and out, and as it moves, it vibrates the speaker cone and produces sound waves in the air.

"speak slower" (air traffic control). Used in verbal communications as a request to reduce speech rate.

special activity airspace (SAA). Any airspace with defined dimensions within the National Airspace System wherein limitations may be imposed upon aircraft operations. This airspace may be restricted areas, prohibited areas, military operations areas, air ATC assigned airspace, and any other designated airspace areas.

special emergency (air traffic control). A condition of air piracy or other hostile act by a person or persons aboard an aircraft which threatens the safety of the aircraft or its passengers.

special flight permit. A flight permit issued to an aircraft that does not meet airworthiness requirements but is capable of safe flight. A special flight permit can be issued to move an aircraft for the purposes of maintenance or repair, buyer delivery, manufacturer flight tests, evacuation from danger, or customer demonstration. Also referred to as a ferry permit.

special instrument approach procedure. A procedure approved by the FAA for individual operators, but not published in 14 CFR Part 97 for public use.

special light-sport aircraft. An aircraft issued a special airworthiness certificate in accordance with 14 CFR §21.190 in the light-sport category. These aircraft meet the ASTM industry-developed consensus standards.

special use airspace. Airspace in which flight activities are subject to restrictions that can create limitations on the mixed use of airspace wherein activities must be confined because of their nature and/or wherein limitations may be imposed upon aircraft operations that are not a part of those activities. Refers to prohibited, restricted, warning, controlled firing, military operations, and alert areas.

Special Use Airspace Management System (SAMS). A joint FAA and military program designed to improve civilian access to special use airspace by providing information on whether the airspace is active or scheduled to be active. The information is available to authorized users via an Internet website.

special VFR. *14 CFR Part 1:* "Meteorological conditions that are less than those required for basic VFR flight in controlled airspace and in which some aircraft are permitted flight under visual flight rules."

special VFR operations. *14 CFR Part 1:* "Aircraft operating in accordance with clearances within controlled airspace in meteorological conditions less than the basic VFR weather minima. Such operations must be requested by the pilot and approved by ATC."

specific fuel consumption. A measure of the amount of fuel burned in a heat engine to produce a given amount of power. Specific fuel consumption of a reciprocating engine is expressed in pounds of fuel burned per hour for each horsepower produced.

specific gravity. The ratio of the density of a material to the density of pure water. If the specific gravity of a material is less than 1.0, it will float in water, but if it is greater than 1.0, it will sink.

specific heat. The ratio of the amount of heat energy needed to raise the temperature of a specific mass of material one degree Celsius, to the amount of heat energy needed to raise the temperature of the same mass of pure water one °C. Water has a specific heat of 1.0, and copper has a specific heat of 0.093. Therefore, it takes 10.75 ($\frac{1}{0.093}$) times as much heat to raise the temperature of one gram of water one °C as it does to raise the temperature of one gram of copper one °C.

specific humidity (meteorology). The ratio, by weight, of the water vapor in a sample of air to the combined weight of the water vapor and the dry air.

specific thrust (turbine engine parameter). A measure of performance for turbojet and turbofan engines. It is the ratio of pounds of net thrust developed to the pounds of mass airflow per second.

specific weight (aircraft engine measurement). The ratio of the weight of an aircraft engine to the brake horsepower it produces.

specific weight of air. 0.07651 pounds per cubic foot.

spectrometric oil analysis. *See* SOAP (Spectrometric Oil Analysis Program).

spectrophotometer. A device for measuring light intensity that can measure intensity as a function of the color, or more specifically, the wavelength of light.

speech scrambler (communications device). A security device used with a radio transmitter to make voice transmissions unintelligible to anyone not having the correct descrambling equipment and the correct code for the day. The scrambler circuit modifies the voice signals being transmitted so they no longer resemble the original sound. When the signals are received by the intended receiver, they are passed through a descrambler that changes them back into their original form.

speed. The rate of motion. Speed, which is the distance an object travels in a given length of time, is expressed in such terms as miles per hour, kilometers per hour, knots (nautical miles per hour), feet per second, or meters per second. Speed, unlike velocity, does not take into consideration the direction of travel.

speed adjustment (air traffic control). An ATC procedure used to request pilots to adjust aircraft speed to a specific value for the purpose of providing desired spacing. Pilots are expected to maintain a speed of plus or minus 10 knots or 0.02 Mach number of the specified speed.

speed brakes (aircraft control). A type of secondary control on an airplane, a control which does not rotate the aircraft about any of its three axes. Speed brakes produce drag without affecting lift, or causing the aircraft to pitch. The drag they produce allows a highly streamlined airplane to descend at a steep angle without picking up excessive speed.

speeder spring (propeller governor component). A compression spring in a propeller governor that balances the centrifugal force acting on the flyweights to route oil to or from the propeller to maintain the desired engine RPM. The compression of the spring is controlled by the pilot through the propeller pitch control.

speed instability. A condition in the region of reverse command in which a disturbance that causes the airspeed to decrease causes total drag to increase, which in turn causes the airspeed to decrease further.

speed of light. The speed at which light travels in a vacuum. The speed of light is 299,792.5 kilometers per second, or 186,282 miles per second.

speed of sound. The speed at which the mechanical vibrations of sound travel in an elastic medium. Sound travels in air, under standard atmospheric conditions, at a rate of 760 miles per hour, 340 meters per second, 1,108 feet per second, or 658 knots. The speed of sound is affected by the density of the medium through which it travels. In the air this is determined by the air temperature.

speed-rated engine (gas turbine engine specification). A gas turbine engine whose rated thrust is produced at a specified RPM.

speed segments (air traffic control). Portions of the arrival route between the transition point and the vertex along the optimum flight path for which speeds and altitudes are specified. There is one set of arrival speed segments adapted from each transition point to each vertex, and each set may contain up to six segments.

speed sense. The ability to instantly sense and react to any reasonable variation of airspeed.

speed-sensitive switch (turbine engine control component). A component in a turbine engine fuel control that selects the desired reference speed for start-limiting operation during initial engine starting. The electronic control remains in the start-limiting condition until the speed switch opens. At this point the electronic control switches to normal limiting temperature operation.

S

speed to fly. Optimum speed through a (sinking or rising) air mass to achieve either the furthest glide or fastest average cross-country speed depending on the objectives during a flight.

sphere. A solid with a curved surface, like a ball. All points on the surface of the sphere are the same distance from a point within the sphere called its center.

spider (propeller component). The high-strength steel component in an airplane propeller that attaches to the propeller shaft of the engine and supports the propeller blades. The spider and the roots of the blades are enclosed in the high-strength propeller hub.

spike (electrical disturbance). A transient condition in an electrical circuit in which a pulse of electrical energy with a high voltage and short duration appears in the circuit. Spikes are produced when an inductive load in the circuit is interrupted, and by induction from an outside source, such as a flash of lightning. Special spike-protection circuits are installed in critical electronic equipment to prevent damage from spikes.

spike knot (wood defect). A knot that runs through the depth of a beam, perpendicular to the annual rings. Spike knots appear most frequently in quartersawed wood.

spin (aircraft maneuver). A maneuver of an airplane in which one wing is stalled while the other wing continues to produce lift. An airplane is put into a spin by getting it very nearly into a stall and then quickly rotating it about its vertical axis by pushing on one of the rudder pedals.

As the airplane rotates about its vertical axis, one wing moves backward and stalls. The other wing moves forward and picks up a bit of extra lift. The nose drops, and the airplane descends slowly, with the wing producing lift pulling it around in a spiral path. To recover from a spin, the nose is forced down so air flows over the stalled wing. With both wings producing lift, the airplane recovers from the spin.

spinner (aircraft propeller component). A streamlined housing over the hub of the propeller. A spinner smoothes the airflow as it enters the cooling openings in the engine cowling. It also gives the airplane a streamlined shape.

spin training (flight training). Training on stall awareness, spin entry, spins, and spin recovery procedures.

spiral (aircraft maneuver). A maneuver in which an airplane descends in a steeply banked, turning flight path. A spiral is sometimes confused with a spin, but the two maneuvers are totally different. In a spin, one wing is stalled and the other is producing lift, while in a spiral, both wings produce lift. The airspeed does not increase as an airplane spins, but in a spiral, the speed can increase to a dangerous level if the spiral is allowed to continue.

spiraling slipstream. The slipstream of a propeller-driven airplane spirals around the airplane. This slipstream strikes the side of the vertical fin, causing the aircraft to yaw slightly. Fin offset is sometimes used by aircraft designers to counteract this tendency.

spiral instability. A condition that exists when the static directional stability of the airplane is very strong compared to the effect of its dihedral in maintaining lateral equilibrium.

spirit level. An instrument used to determine whether or not something is level, or perpendicular to a line that points directly toward the center of the earth. A spirit level is a curved glass tube partially filled with liquid. Enough liquid is left out of the tube so there is a bubble in it. The tube is mounted in a long, straight metal or wood bar in such a way that when the bar is level, the bubble in the liquid is in the center of the tube. Spirit levels are also called bubble levels.

spirit varnish. A finishing material for wood made of a resin dissolved in a volatile solvent such as alcohol. The varnish is brushed or sprayed on a surface, and it forms a hard, resin film when the solvent evaporates from it.

splayed patch (plywood patch). A type of patch made in an aircraft plywood structure in which the edges of the patch are tapered for approximately five times the thickness of the plywood. A splayed patch is not recommended for use on plywood less than ¹/₁₀-inch thick.

splice connector (electric wiring). A solderless, crimped-on connector used to join two wire ends. The splice connector is made in the form of an insulated metal tube. The insulation is stripped from the ends of the wires to be spliced, and the bare wire is slipped into the tube. The tube is then crimped onto the wire. A solderless splice connector forms a joint that is physically as strong as the wire, and it has an extremely low electrical resistance. *See* illustration for solderless connectors.

splice knot (aircraft covering material). A special knot used to join two pieces of waxed rib-stitching cord. A splice knot is superior to a square knot because it will not slip.

splined propeller shaft (reciprocating engine component). A propeller shaft with splines along its periphery that fit into mating splines in the steel propeller hub. A splined propeller shaft is indexed to the hub by a master spline which allows the propeller to be installed with only one orientation to the engine crankshaft.

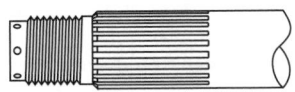

splined propeller shaft

splines. A method of locking a shaft into a wheel or disk. A number of equally spaced parallel slots are cut lengthwise into the surface of a shaft. Matching slots are cut in the inside surface of the hole into which the shaft fits, and the splines prevent the shaft rotating in the hole.

split (wood defect). A longitudinal crack in a piece of wood caused by externally induced stress.

split bus. A type of electrical bus that allows all of the voltage-sensitive avionic equipment to be isolated from the rest of the aircraft electrical system when the engine is being started or when the ground-power unit is connected.

split duty. In flight operations, this is a flight duty period that has a scheduled break in duty that is less than the required rest period.

split-field motor. A reversible DC electric motor that has two separate field windings; one for clockwise rotation and the other for counterclock-wise rotation.

split flaps (aircraft controls). A type of wing flaps in which a part of the under side of the wing or the trailing edge of the wing splits and folds down to increase the curvature (camber) of the bottom of the wing. The increased camber increases the drag and also the lift produced by the wing under low-speed flight conditions.

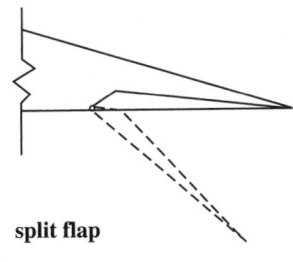

split flap

split lock washer. A heavy spring-steel washer split at an angle across its face and twisted. When a nut is tightened down over a split lock washer, the twist is flattened out, and the spring action of the washer pushes against the nut and holds its threads tight against the threads of the bolt. This pressure between the threads prevents vibration from loosening the nut.

split needles (helicopter instrument indication). The indication on a helicopter tachometer that shows the rotor clutch is not fully engaged. A helicopter tachometer has two needles; one shows the speed of the engine and the other, the speed of the main rotor. When the clutch is fully engaged and the rotor is coupled to the engine, the needles are "married"—one is directly on top of the other. When the engine is started and the rotor is coming up to speed, the engine RPM needle is ahead of the rotor RPM needle. When the engine is throttled back, and the rotor freewheels, the rotor needle is ahead of the engine needle. In either case, the needles are said to be split.

split-phase induction motor. A type of alternating current motor that has a main and an auxiliary winding connected in parallel. The phase of the current flowing in the auxiliary, or start, winding is shifted from that flowing in the main winding, either by a capacitor or by a large difference in the resistance in the two windings. The phase difference between the current flowing in the two field windings produces a rotating magnetic field which starts the rotor spinning. When the rotor is spinning at a specified speed, a centrifugal switch opens the auxiliary-winding circuit, and the motor operates with only the main winding.

split-rocker switch. An electrical switch whose operating control is a rocker, split so one-half of the switch can be opened without affecting the other half. Split-rocker switches are used as aircraft master switches. The battery can be turned on without turning on the alternator, but the alternator

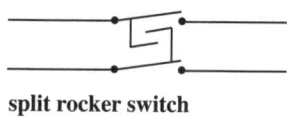

split rocker switch

cannot be turned on without also turning on the battery. The alternator can be turned off without turning off the battery, but the battery cannot be turned off without also turning off the alternator.

split spool compressor (turbine engine component). An axial flow compressor that has two independent spools driven by two separate stages of turbines. The speed of the aft, or high-pressure stage (N_2), is controlled by a governor and the fuel control, while the speed of the forward, or low-pressure stage (N_1), is not governed and it seeks its own best speed.

spoiler (aircraft control). A small deflector that can be raised into the air flowing over an airfoil. When a spoiler is raised into the airstream, it disturbs the smooth flow of air and destroys part of the lift the airfoil is producing. Spoilers are used on high-performance sailplanes to decrease the lift so they will not float during landing.

spokeshave (wood-cutting tool). A short drawknife with handles on each end. The spokeshave cuts as the blade is drawn toward you. A spokeshave is used for rounding the edges of strips of wood. The name comes from its use in shaping the wooden spokes used in the wheels of horse-drawn wagons.

spongy brakes (hydraulic brake condition). The feel of the brake pedal when the hydraulic brake fluid contains air. In normal operation, the brake system is filled with noncompressible brake fluid, and the pedal has a firm feel. But if there is any air in the fluid, the air compresses when the pedal is depressed and gives the pedal a spongy feel.

sponson (aircraft structure). A surface much like a short stub wing that extends out on the side of a flying boat hull near the waterline. Sponsons keep the flying boat level when it is not moving through the water, and they also give it stability and provide some aerodynamic lift.

spontaneous combustion. Self-ignition of a material caused by heat produced in the material as it combines with oxygen from the air. If oily rags are left in a bundle, the heat produced when oxygen in the air reacts with the oil cannot be carried away. The rags get hot enough to burst into flames. They are ignited by spontaneous combustion.

spool (turbine engine component). An axial-flow compressor. Some engines have two or three independent spools, each of which is driven by its own stages of turbines.

sport pilot certificate. An FAA-issued pilot certificate allowing the holder to operate a light-sport aircraft in the category, class, make, and model for which they are endorsed to do so.

spot check. A method of manufacturing inspection in which only a certain percentage of the products are checked. The products to be checked are selected from the production line in a random fashion, so those checked are typical of the entire production run.

spot-facing. A smooth, flat, circular area around a bolt hole that provides a good seat for the bolt head or for a washer under the bolt head.

spotlight. A lighting device that produces a brilliant, concentrated beam of light. Spotlights are used for searching an area at night, because they concentrate the light energy in a small area that allows the beam to extend out for a great distance.

spot welding. A form of electrical resistance welding used for thin sheets of metal. The metal parts are assembled and clamped between the electrodes of the spot welding machine. A timed pulse of current flows between the electrodes and melts a spot of the metal. Pressure on the electrodes forces the molten metal from the two sheets together to form a single spot which joins the sheets. Fuel tanks can be welded with a continuous, leakproof seam by allowing the spots to overlap each other.

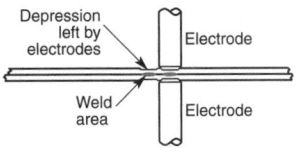

spot welding

spout. A pipe or similar device used to carry a liquid from a container in a stream that is easy to control.

sprag clutch. A form of freewheeling clutch used in the rotor-drive system of a helicopter. The sprag clutch allows the engine to drive the rotor, but, when the engine power is reduced, the clutch allows the rotor to freewheel, and prevents it trying to drive the engine.

spray gun (cleaning tool). A type of maintenance tool used for cleaning parts. Compressed air is blown through the spray gun, and as it passes through a venturi, it produces a low pressure. This low pressure picks up a cleaning solution, such as varsol or naphtha, and sprays it out in the form of tiny drops onto the surface being cleaned. The combined solvent action of the cleaning solution and the force of the high-pressure air removes dirt, grease, or other contaminants from the surface.

spray gun (paint spray gun). A device that breaks a liquid finishing material, such as paint or lacquer, into tiny drops and blows them onto the surface being painted. Two basic types of paint spray guns are: suction-feed and pressure-feed guns. A suction-feed gun uses suction produced by venturi action inside the gun to pick up the finishing material from a cup attached to the gun. The material sprayed by a pressure-feed gun is forced into the gun by air pressure on the fluid stored in a pressure cup or pressure pot.

spray rails. Metal flanges attached to the forward inboard portions of the chines on the floats of a seaplane, intended to reduce the amount of water spray thrown into the propeller.

spray strip (water craft). Small strips of metal mounted on the side of a flying boat hull or seaplane floats. Spray strips throw a spray of water out away from the aircraft and reduce the amount of spray thrown into the propeller.

spreader bar (aircraft floats). Horizontal structural members between the two floats mounted on an aircraft.

springback (aircraft control system). A method used to ensure that the control arm of a device being controlled actually reaches its full-travel stop. There are stops on both ends of an aircraft throttle control. The stop on the carburetor must be contacted first, then the throttle control is moved farther until its stop in the cockpit is reached. This additional movement stretches the control mechanism, and when the throttle control is released, it springs back a slight amount. Technicians often refer to this type of control adjustment as "rigging in the proper cushion." Springback ensures that the stop on the carburetor is contacted before the stop in the cockpit.

springback (sheet metal forming). Springback, in sheet metal forming, is the tendency of the metal to spring back and form an angle less than the angle bent in a brake or a forming block. When a 90° angle is to be bent, the metal must be bent through an angle of about 93° or 94° (depending upon the temper of the metal) so it will spring back to exactly 90°.

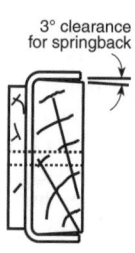

3° clearance for springback

springback

spring-loaded. Components are spring-loaded when one part is held tightly against another by the force of a spring. Relative movement is allowed but the spring returns the parts to their original position.

spring steel. High-carbon steel, a steel containing more than 0.5% carbon, that has been hardened and tempered to give it the maximum amount of elasticity, or the ability to return to its original shape after it has been deflected. Spring steel is hardened and then tempered to remove part of the brittleness by reheating until it turns a uniform dark blue.

spring tab (aircraft controls). A small auxiliary tab, set into the trailing edge of a primary control surface on a high-speed airplane. The control surface is attached to the control horn through a torsion rod. Under normal flight loads, the spring tab remains fixed to the control surface and serves no purpose. But, when the air loads are high and a large amount of force is needed to move

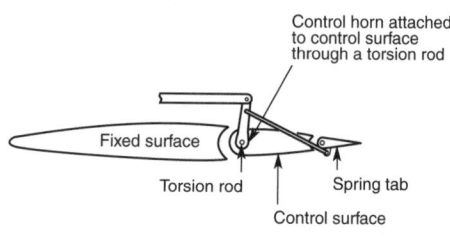

Control horn attached to control surface through a torsion rod

Fixed surface

Torsion rod   Spring tab

Control surface

spring tab

the control surface, the torsion rod twists, and the control rod moves the spring tab in a direction opposite to that of the surface on which it is mounted. It then acts as a servo tab and aids the pilot in moving the control surface. *See* servo tab.

springwood. The lighter, softer part of the grain of wood. The heavier and darker part of the wood grain is the summerwood. The cross section of a tree trunk contains a series of concentric rings, called annual rings. Each ring is made up of a light and a dark area. The light area is the part of the tree that grew at a fast rate in the spring of the year and is called the springwood. The dark area is the part of the tree that grew more slowly during the summer of the year and is called summerwood.

sprue (casting). A hole in a mold through which liquid plastic or molten metal is poured to fill the mold. When the molded material becomes solid, the mold is opened, and the metal which was in the sprue (this metal is also called a sprue) is broken from the casting and discarded.

spur and pinion reduction gear system. A type of reduction gear system that allows one shaft to turn at a speed slower than that of another shaft. A pinion is a small-diameter spur gear, whose teeth mesh with those on the larger-diameter gear. The pinion turns faster than the larger gear, and it turns in the direction opposite to that of the larger gear.

spur gear. A gear wheel with teeth radiating outward around its periphery. The term spur gear comes from the fact that this type of gear looks much like the rowel, or toothed wheel, that was a part of the spur worn by many of the early-day cowboys.

spur gear pump. A form of constant-displacement fluid pump that uses two meshing spur gears mounted in a close-fitting housing. Fluid is taken into the housing where it fills the space between the teeth of the gears and is carried around the housing as the gears rotate.

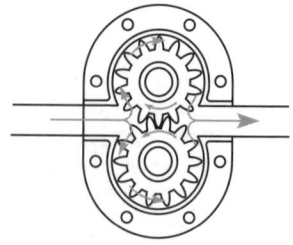

spur-gear pump

spur gear pump. *Continued*
On the discharge side of the pump, the teeth of the two gears mesh, and the fluid is forced out of the pump.

squall (meteorology). A sudden increase in wind speed by at least 15 knots to a peak of 20 knots or more, and lasting for at least one minute. The essential difference between a gust, lasting less than one minute, and a squall is the duration of the peak speed.

squall line (meteorology). Any nonfrontal line or narrow band of active thunderstorms with or without squalls.

square (geometric figure). A closed, plane (flat), four-sided figure. Each angle in a square is a right angle (90°), all sides have the same length, and the opposite sides of a square are parallel.

square drive (mechanical coupling). A mechanical coupling in which the driving element is square and it fits into a square hole in the driven element. Square drives are used between a socket wrench and the handle that turns it.

square engine (reciprocating engine). A reciprocating engine whose bore and stroke have the same dimensions. The bore of the engine is the diameter of the cylinders, and the stroke is the distance the piston moves from the top of its travel to the bottom.

square mil. A unit of area possessed by a square having sides of one mil, or one thousandth of an inch (0.001 inch).

square of a number (mathematics). The product of a number multiplied by itself.

square root (mathematics). A number which, when multiplied by itself, will give a particular number.

square wave (electrical waveform). The waveform produced by pulsating direct current in which the voltage alternates between zero and its maximum value. It changes almost instantaneously from zero to its maximum value, remains at this value for a given period of time, and then returns instantly to zero. The length of time the voltage remains at maximum is the same as the time it remains at zero.

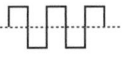

square-wave AC

 Alternating current can also have a square wave if the voltage changes almost instantaneously from its maximum positive value to its maximum negative value. The voltage at both the maximum positive and the maximum negative values remains constant until it shifts to the opposite value. The voltage remains positive for the same length of time it remains negative.

square-wave generator (electronic device). An electronic device that produces alternating current with a square waveform. The frequency and the amplitude of the square-wave AC can be changed to any value desired.

squaring shear (sheet metal shop tool). A large shear used to make straight cuts across a sheet of metal. Squaring shears used for light-gage steel and thin aluminum alloy sheets are operated by a foot pedal, and shears used to cut heavy plate steel are operated by energy stored in a large flywheel by a small electric motor.

squat switch (aircraft safety switch). A switch mounted on the shock strut of an aircraft landing gear. The squat switch is in a circuit whose actuation depends upon the configuration of the landing gear. For example, the squat switch prevents the landing gear retraction handle being moved any time weight is on the landing gear. A squat switch can also be installed in the cabin pressurization system to prevent the cabin being pressurized if the airplane is on the ground and weight is on the landing gear.

"Squawk" (air traffic control). A term used by ATC to request a pilot to activate specific modes, codes, or functions on the aircraft transponder. For example, "squawk three/ alpha, two one zero five, low."

"Squawk ident" (air traffic control). A phrase used by ATC to request a pilot to activate the ident feature on the aircraft transponder. Activation of the ident feature allows the ground controller to immediately identify the aircraft that is squawking.

squealer tip (compressor blade tip). *See* profile tip.

squeegee. A rubber scraper blade mounted on a handle in such a way that the blade forms a T with the handle. Squeegees are used to move a liquid over a surface. Some of the common uses for squeegees are removing water from a window after the window has been washed, spreading paint through the open fibers in a silk screen, and removing water from a photographic print after it has been washed.

squeeze bottle. A bottle made of a soft plastic material. The contents of the bottle can be forced out through a small opening in the cap by squeezing the sides of the bottle.

squeeze riveter. A power riveting tool used to install solid aluminum alloy rivets in a sheet metal structure. The squeeze riveter can be made in the form of a C-clamp or an alligator clamp. One jaw of either type clamp is a fixed part of the riveter frame, and the other jaw is moved against the fixed jaw by the piston in an air cylinder.

The fixed jaw is fitted with a rivet set that fits the manufactured head of the rivet, and the movable jaw is flat. Shims are placed under the rivet set so the jaws come close enough together to form a shop head of the correct thickness. Squeeze riveting is fast, and rivets are more uniform than those driven by a rivet hammer and bucking bar.

squelch circuit (radio receiver circuit). A circuit in a radio receiver that keeps the volume down when no signal is being received. As soon as a signal is received, the squelch circuit allows it to come through loud enough to be comfortably heard. Squelch circuits are used in communications radios that receive long periods of silence between transmissions.

squib (fire extinguishing system component). A small explosive charge that drives a cutter through the seal in a high-rate discharge (HRD) bottle of fire extinguishing agent. The container of fire extinguishing agent is sealed with a thin metal diaphragm. When the operator presses the AGENT RELEASE switch in the cockpit, the squib is ignited. As the squib burns, it produces enough gas pressure to drive a cutter through the metal diaphragm and release the agent into the fire extinguishing system.

squirrel-cage induction motor. A type of AC motor whose rotor has current induced into it from stationary field coils. The rotor is made of a stack of soft iron laminations, mounted on a steel rotor shaft. Heavy copper end plates are fastened to the shaft at each end of the stack of laminations. Copper bars fit into slots in the laminations and are welded to each of the end plates.

Changing magnetic fields, caused by AC flowing in the stator windings, induce a large amount of current into the low-resistance bars and the end plates. This current produces a strong magnetic field that reacts with the field in the stator, and the squirrel-cage rotor spins inside the stator. The speed of the rotor is determined by the frequency of the alternating current flowing in the stator windings.

squitter (ATC transponder signal). (1) A signal transmitted by an ATC transponder without it being interrogated. The squitter does not interrogate other aircraft. (2) The term refers to a system designed to transmit and receive signals from a transponder, without active interrogation of the transponder. It also refers to a signal transmitted by the system. TCAS II requires a Mode S transponder, which is interrogated by other TCAS II equipment and replies to that equipment. A squitter system would be able to transmit and receive any information from the transponders, but it would not actively interrogate other aircraft as a TCAS II would.

SRM. *See* single-pilot resource management.

SRM (Structural Repair Manual). A maintenance manual issued by a manufacturer and approved by the FAA that describes, in detail, specific repairs that are approved for a particular aircraft structure.

SSR. *See* secondary surveillance radar.

SSV. *See* standard service volume.

stabilator (aircraft primary flight control). A single-piece horizontal tail surface on an airplane which serves the purposes of both the horizontal stabilizer and the elevators. A stabilator must have some method of decreasing its sensitivity, and this is done with an antiservo tab on its trailing edge. The antiservo tab automatically moves in the same direction as the stabilator, and the aerodynamic force it produces opposes the movement of the stabilator.

stability (aircraft flight condition). The characteristic of an aircraft that causes it to return to its original attitude after it has been disturbed from this condition.

stability (meteorology). A state of the atmosphere in which the vertical distribution of temperature is such that a parcel of air will resist displacement from its initial level.

stability characteristics, maximum speed for (V_{FC}/M_{FC}). An aircraft's designed stability characteristic V-speed limitation, which represents a speed value midway between the maximum operating limit speed (V_{MO}/M_{MO}) and the demonstrated flight diving speed (V_{DF}/M_{DF}), where the non-subscript "M" refers to a Mach number limitation. M_{FC} need not exceed the Mach number at which an effective speed warning occurs.

stabilized approach. A landing approach in which the pilot establishes and maintains a constant angle glidepath towards a predetermined point on the landing runway. It is based on the pilot's judgment of certain visual cues, and depends on the maintenance of a constant final descent airspeed and configuration.

stabilizer (airplane control surface). The fixed horizontal tail surface on an airplane. The stabilizer is set on the airplane so it provides the correct amount of stabilizing downward aerodynamic force when the aircraft is flying at its normal cruise speed. The elevators are hinged to the trailing edge of the stabilizer.

stabilons (airplane control surface). Small wing-like horizontal surfaces mounted on the aft fuselage of some airplanes to improve longitudinal stability. Stabilons are installed on airplanes that have an exceptionally wide center of gravity range.

stable isotope. An isotope of an element that does not undergo radioactive disintegration. An unstable isotope, or radioisotope, emits radioactive energy as it decays.

stage length. The distance between landing points in airline operation.

stage of a compressor (turbine engines). One disk of rotor blades and the following set of stator vanes in an axial-flow compressor.

stagger (airplane rigging). The relationship between the longitudinal location of the two wings of a biplane. If the upper wing is further forward than the lower wing, the airplane has positive stagger; but if the lower wing is ahead of the upper wing, the airplane has negative stagger.

staggered timing (reciprocating engine ignition). A method of timing the dual ignition of a reciprocating engine. When the timing is staggered, the spark plug nearest the exhaust valve fires before the spark plug nearest the intake valve. In some engines, the exhaust gases are not completely scavenged, and they dilute the fuel-air charge in the cylinder. This diluted charge near the exhaust valve burns more slowly than the undiluted charge near the intake valve, and it is therefore ignited earlier.

stagger wires (airplane rigging component). High-strength steel wires that connect diagonally fore and aft across the cabane struts of an biplane. Adjustment of the length of the stagger wires determines the fore-and-aft relationship of the upper wing to the lower wing.

staging/queuing (air traffic control). The placement, integration, and segregation of departure aircraft in designated movement areas of an airport by departure fix, EDCT, and/or restriction.

stagnation point (fluid dynamics). A location on a body in a stream of moving fluid at which the fluid has stopped—it has no velocity. The stagnation point on an airfoil is at the leading edge where the air splits, with some air passing over the top of the airfoil and the rest passing below it.

stain (finishing material). A form of nonprotective finish used on wood to color the wood without hiding the grain. After a piece of wood is stained, it is usually covered with varnish to protect it.

stainless steel. An alloy of iron, chromium, and nickel that is resistant to rust and corrosion. Stainless steel is more correctly called corrosion-resistant steel. Neither the 200 series nor the 300 series of stainless steel can be hardened by heat treatment, and the steel in both of these series is nonmagnetic. The 400 series of stainless steel which can be hardened by heat treatment and is magnetic is used for knife blades and razor blades.

staking. A method of securing a part in a recess in a metal surface. For example, a disk can be fastened in a counterbored hole by staking the edges of the hole. The disk is put into the hole, and a pointed staking tool is held near the edge of the hole and hit with a hammer. The staking tool forces metal from the edge of the hole over the disk to prevent its from coming out of the hole.

stall (aerodynamic condition). An aerodynamic condition in which the angle of attack, the angle at which the relative wind strikes the airfoil, becomes so steep the air can no longer flow smoothly over the airfoil. When an airfoil stalls, it stops producing lift.

stalled-rotor torque (electric motor characteristic). The amount of torque produced by the rotor of an electric motor when it is fully energized with the correct voltage, but the rotor is held so it cannot turn.

stall strip (airplane wing component). A small triangular metal strip installed along the leading edge of an airplane wing near the root. Many airplane wings begin to stall near the tip, in the area ahead of the ailerons. When this portion of the wing stalls, the pilot no longer has good control of the aircraft. To allow adequate control throughout the stall, the small stall strips force the roots of the wing to stall before the tips. When the wing roots stall, the nose of the aircraft drops, and the aircraft recovers from the stall with complete control throughout.

stall warning system (aircraft flight instrument). A system that warns the pilot when the angle of attack of the wing reaches a point that will likely produce a stall. Stall warning systems measure the angle of attack. Some systems use a small air-operated vane on the leading edge of the wing to detect the high angle of attack. Others use an angle of attack probe on the fuselage. A few of the smaller airplanes have a reed-type horn in the wing that changes its sound as the angle of attack changes.

Some stall warning systems turn on a light or sound a warning horn when the angle of attack gets too near the angle that could cause a stall. Some of the more elaborate systems, called stick shakers, vibrate the control column, and stick pushers actually push the control column forward when a stall is approached.

stand-alone approach. An instrument approach that relies solely on the use of RNAV equipment. If flown with GPS/WAAS-enabled certified equipment in accordance with TSO-C145A or TSO-146A, installed in accordance with the provisions of AC 20-130A or 138A, no conventional navigation equipment alternate approach (VOR/ILS) requirements are necessary, as when flying with TSO-C129 certified equipment.

standard atmosphere. *14 CFR Part 1:* "The atmosphere defined in the U.S. Standard Atmosphere, 1962 (Geopotential altitude tables)."

standard airport traffic pattern. The left-hand turn traffic flow that is prescribed for aircraft landing at, taxiing on, or taking off from an airport.

standard atmospheric conditions. Conditions of the atmosphere that have been agreed upon by scientists and engineers who work with the atmosphere to allow them to correct all measurements to the same conditions.

standard barometric pressure. The weight of gases in the atmosphere sufficient to hold up a column of mercury 760 millimeters high (29.92 inches) at sea level (14.69 psi). This pressure decreases with altitude.

Temperature	15° Celsius
	59° Fahrenheit
Pressure at sea level	29.92 inches of mercury
	1013.2 millibars
	14.69 pounds per square inch
Acceleration due to gravity	32.174 feet per second, per second,
	9.809 meters per second, per second
Specific weight of air...............	0.07651 pounds per cubic foot
	1.225 kilograms per cubic meter
Density...................................	0.002378 slug per cubic foot
	0.1225 kuk per cubic meter
Speed of sound	761.6 miles per hour
	1,225.35 kilometers per hour
	661.7 knots
	34,046.16 centimeters per second

standard atmospheric conditions

standard briefing (weather briefing). The most complete weather briefing and should be requested when a preliminary briefing has not been obtained or when the proposed flight is a cross-country.

standard cell (electrical voltage standard). A cadmium-mercury cell made in a specially shaped glass container in which the two electrodes are covered with an electrolyte of cadmium sulfate. The voltage produced by a standard cell is 1.018636 volts at 20°C. A standard cell is also called a Weston standard cell or a Weston normal cell.

standard day conditions. Conditions that have been decided upon by the ICAO (International Civil Aeronautics Organization) for relating all aircraft and engine performance to a given reference. *See* standard atmospheric conditions.

standard empty weight (GAMA). (1) Weight of a standard airplane including usable fuel, full operating fluids, and full oil. (2) This weight consists of the airframe, engines, and all items of operating equipment that have fixed locations and are permanently installed in the airplane; including fixed ballast, hydraulic fluid, unusable fuel, and full engine oil.

standard-frequency signal (radio-frequency signal standard). A highly accurate radio-frequency signal broadcast from the National Bureau of Standards radio station, station WWV. The standard-frequency signal is broadcast on frequencies of 2.5, 5.0, 10.0, 15.0, 20.0, and 25.0 megahertz.

standard holding pattern (air traffic control). A holding pattern in which all turns are made to the right.

standard instrument departure (SID). Also known as a departure procedure (DP), a preplanned IFR ATC departure procedure printed for pilot/controller use to provide obstacle clearance and a transition from the terminal area to the appropriate enroute structure. SIDs are primarily developed and designed to increase capacity of terminal airspace, effectively control the flow of traffic with minimal communication to reduce pilot/controller workload, and reduce environmental impact through noise abatement procedures. ATC clearance must always be received prior to flying a SID.

standardized taxi routes. Coded taxi routes that follow typical taxiway traffic patterns to move aircraft between gates and runways. ATC issues clearances using these coded routes to reduce radio communication and eliminate taxi instruction misinterpretation.

S

standard-rate turn (aircraft flight maneuver). A turn in which an aircraft changes its direction at a rate of 3° per second (360° in two minutes) for low- or medium-speed aircraft. For high-speed aircraft, the standard-rate turn is $1^1/_2$° per second (360° in four minutes).

standard sea-level pressure. At sea level, 1013.2 millibars, 29.92 inches of mercury, 760 millimeters of mercury, or 14.69 pounds per square inch.

standard sea-level temperature. 59°F or 15°C.

standard service volume (SSV). Defines the limits of the volume of airspace which the VOR serves.

standard terminal arrival. *See* STAR.

standard weights (aircraft operations). Values used when specific weights are not available:

Gasoline ....6.0   pounds/U.S. gallon
Turbine engine fuel..........................6.7   pounds/U.S. gallon
Lubricating oil ....7.5   pounds/U.S. gallon
Water..8.35   pounds/U.S. gallon
Aircraft load
  General aviation
    Crew & passengers 170   pounds
  Air carrier
    Passenger (summer) 160   pounds
    Passenger (winter)...................165   pounds
    Male cabin attendant 150   pounds
    Female cabin attendant...........130   pounds
    Other crewmembers................170   pounds
    Checked baggage ....23.5   pounds
    Carry-on baggage 5   pounds

standing cloud (standing lenticular altocumulus). *See* lenticular cloud.

standing wave (meteorology). A wave in the atmosphere that remains stationary in a moving fluid. The standing waves most commonly encountered in flight are mountain waves, or lee waves.

standing waves (electrical transmission line). Stationary voltage waves existing on an antenna or transmission line that are caused by two waves, identical in amplitude and frequency, but traveling in opposite directions along the conductor.

"Stand by" (air traffic control). A phrase used by ATC meaning that the controller or pilot must pause for a few seconds, usually to attend to other duties of a higher priority. It also means to wait, as in "stand by for clearance." The phrase "stand by" is neither an approval nor denial.

standpipe. A pipe protruding upward from the bottom of a tank, or reservoir, that allows part of the tank to be used as a reserve, or standby, source of fluid. The oil supply tanks for some aircraft engines have a standpipe in them. The main engine-driven oil pump is supplied from the standpipe, and emergency oil to feather the propeller is taken from the bottom of the tank. If an oil leak causes a loss of all of the oil the engine pump can move, there is still enough oil left in the tank to feather the propeller.

staple (fastener). A U-shaped wire loop with sharp points on both ends. Staples are used to fasten wires to a wooden post or wall, and to fasten sheets of paper together.

staple (textile material). The average length of the fibers of a textile material. Cotton, for example, is classified as either long staple or short staple, depending upon the length of the cotton fibers.

stapler. A tool for driving staples through a piece of wood or a stack of paper.

starboard side. The right side of an aircraft or ship as viewed looking forward.

STAR (standard terminal arrival). A preplanned instrument flight rule (IFR) air traffic control arrival procedure published for pilot use in graphic and/or textual form. STARs provide transition from the en route structure to an outer fix or an instrument approach fix/arrival waypoint in the terminal area.

STAR charts (Standard Terminal Arrival charts). Aeronautical charts designed to expedite air traffic control route procedures and to facilitate transition between en route and instrument approach procedures.

start end of runway (SER). The beginning of the takeoff runway available, or where the part of the runway that is available for takeoff begins.

starter (engine component). A device used with either a gas turbine engine or a reciprocating engine that can be coupled to the engine to turn it over fast enough for it to start and run normally.

starter-generator. A combination electrical component installed on some small gas turbine engines. The starter-generator acts as a motor to start the engine, and after it is running, electrical relays change the circuitry inside the unit so it functions as a generator.

starter solenoid (electrical component). An intermittent-duty solenoid that directs the high current needed to operate an aircraft-engine starter.

starting torque (electric motor characteristic). The amount of torque produced by an electric motor when the rotor first begins to turn. Series-wound motors have a high starting torque, and shunt-wound motors have a low starting torque.

STAR transition. A published segment used to connect one or more en route airway, jet route, or RNAV route to the basic STAR procedure. It is one of several routes that bring traffic from different directions into one STAR. AeroNav publishes STARs for airports with procedures authorized by the FAA, included at the front of each Terminal Procedures Publication regional booklet.

start winding (induction motor winding). An auxiliary winding in parallel with the run winding in the stator of a single-phase induction motor. The phase of the current in the start winding is different from that in the run winding. When current is flowing through both windings, a rotating magnetic field is produced which causes the rotor to turn. As soon as the rotor reaches a predetermined speed, a centrifugal switch opens the start winding, and the motor operates on the run windings alone.

starved joint (composites). An adhesive joint which has been deprived of the proper film thickness of adhesive due to insufficient adhesive spreading or by the application of excessive pressure during the lamination process.

state aircraft. Aircraft used in military, customs and police service, in the exclusive service of any government or its political subdivision including the government of any state, territory, or possession of the United States or the District of Columbia. However, this does not include any government-owned aircraft engaged in carrying persons or property for commercial purposes.

state of charge (battery condition). The condition of a storage battery with regard to the amount of charge in it. The state of charge of a lead-acid battery can be determined by measuring the specific gravity of the electrolyte, but the state of charge of a nickel-cadmium battery can be determined only by completely discharging it and measuring the amount of charge put back into it.

state vector. A set of geographical data, used in navigation (such as GPS or inertial navigation), describing exactly where an object is located in space, and how it is moving; using the state vector, the object's current and future position can be determined. Usually it will contain seven pieces of data: the three position coordinates (latitude, longitude, and altitude), three velocity values, and the time at which these were valid.

static. Still, not moving.

static air pressure. The pressure of the ambient air surrounding the aircraft. Static pressure does not take into consideration any air movement.

static air temperature. The temperature of the air when there is no movement.

static balance (aircraft control surface). A condition of balance of an aircraft control surface in which the surface balances about its hinge line. Lead weights are often installed in parts of the surface ahead of the hinge line to balance the surface. Controls are statically balanced to prevent control-surface flutter.

static charge (electrical charge). The electrical charge on a body caused by an accumulation of electrons on one part of the body and a deficiency of electrons on another part. The part having the excess of electrons has a negative charge, and the part with the deficiency of electrons has a positive charge.

static discharger. A device attached to an aircraft control surface to discharge static electricity into the air. Static electricity builds up as air flows across the surface. If it were not discharged, it could build up high enough to cause a spark to jump between the surface and the main structure. Sparks of this type cause radio interference.

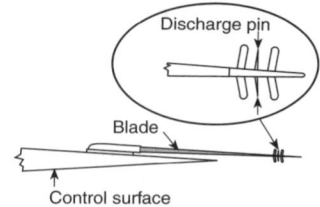

static discharger

Some static dischargers use carbon-impregnated cotton wicks to pick up the static electricity and discharge it off the ends of the cotton fibers. Other dischargers have needle-sharp points from which the static electricity is discharged.

static electricity. Electrical pressure produced by an excess of electrons (a negative charge) or a deficiency of electrons (a positive charge). Static charges accumulate on an insulated surface because of friction, and remain in a still, or static, condition until a conductive path is provided to an oppositely charged surface, or to ground. When a path is provided, electrons flow and neutralize the charge.

static friction. The force that is required to move one body relative to another when they are at rest. It is also known as starting friction.

static instability (aerodynamics). The characteristic of an aircraft, that once disturbed from straight and level flight will tend to move further from its original condition.

static interference (electrical interference). Interference in the communication systems of an aircraft that are caused by static electricity produced by air flowing across an unbonded control surface, or by sparking of an electric motor.

static load. The load imposed on an aircraft structure by the weight of the aircraft and its contents.

static longitudinal stability. The aerodynamic pitching moments required to return the aircraft to the equilibrium angle of attack.

static port (aircraft instruments). A small hole, or port, in the skin of an aircraft at a location where the airflow is not disturbed. The airspeed indicator, altimeter, and vertical speed indicator get their reference static air pressure from this port. Some aircraft pick up their static pressure from a combined pitot-static tube.

static pressure, Ps (fluid pressure). The pressure of a fluid that is still, or not moving, measured perpendicular to the surface exposed to the fluid. Static pressure and dynamic pressure, which is caused by the movement of the air, make up the total pressure of a mass of air. Static air pressure relates to the density of the air, and density is affected by both the altitude (pressure) and the air temperature.

static pressure pickup (aircraft instrument system). The location on the surface of an aircraft where the static air pressure used in the altimeter, airspeed indicator, and the vertical speed indicator is picked up. Static pressure is often taken from flush static ports on the sides of the fuselage or on the sides of the vertical tail surface. In other installations, static pressure is picked up from ports in the side of a combination pitot-static tube. Static pressure pickups must be located in an area where there is no movement of air in a direction that could blow into the static holes.

static radial engine. A type of reciprocating engine in which the cylinders are arranged radially around a small crankcase. Static radial engines are different from rotary radial engines in that their cylinders do not rotate with the propeller. Static radial engines were at one time the most popular configuration of engine used in airplanes, because of their low weight-to-power ratio. But they have so much frontal area that they produce too much drag for modern high-speed aircraft. Radial engines can have three, five, seven, or nine cylinders in one row. Two or four rows of cylinders can be stacked together to make an engine with 14, 18, 28, or 36 cylinders.

static restrictions (air traffic control). Those restrictions that are usually not subject to change, fixed, in place, and/or published.

static RPM (aircraft reciprocating engine operation). The number of revolutions per minute an aircraft engine can produce when the aircraft is not moving. The static RPM is lower than the RPM the engine develops in flight because of the increased power made possible by forward movement ramming air into the carburetor inlet.

static stability (aerodynamics). The characteristic of an aircraft that causes it to try to return to straight and level flight after it has been disturbed from this condition.

static stop (helicopter rotor). A device used to limit the blade or rotor flap at low rpm or when the rotor is stopped.

static system (flight instrument system). The system that provides static air pressure to the airspeed indicator, altimeter, and vertical speed indicator from the static ports.

static test (structural test). A type of test given to such mechanisms as airplane structures. Hydraulic cylinders or sandbags apply forces to simulate loads that could possibly be encountered in flight, and the amount the structure deflects is measured. Some static testing is carried to destruction—the structure is loaded until something breaks. Testing to destruction identifies the weakest point in the structure.

static thrust (gas turbine engines). The amount of thrust produced by a gas turbine engine when the engine is not moving through the air.

static wick. A device used to bleed an accumulated static electrical charge off an aircraft control surface and discharge it into the air. The wick is made of graphite-impregnated cotton fibers, enclosed in a plastic tube. One end of the wick is electrically connected to the trailing edge of a control surface, and the other end of the fibers are spread out of the end of the tube so the hundreds of fiber ends stick out into the air. As the airplane flies through the air, static electricity builds up on the control surfaces, travels through the static wicks, and discharges into the air from the tips of the cotton fibers.

station. A location on an aircraft identified by a number designating its distance in inches from the datum.

stationary front (meteorology). A front that is moving at a speed of less than 5 knots.

stationary reservations. Altitude reservations that encompass activities in a fixed area which may include activities, such as special tests of weapons systems or equipment, certain U.S. Navy carrier, fleet, and anti-submarine operations, rocket, missile and drone operations, and certain aerial refueling or similar operations.

station declination (VOR orientation). The angular difference between true north and the zero radial of a VOR at the time the VOR was last site checked.

station pressure (meteorology). The actual barometric (atmospheric) pressure measured at the observing station.

S

stator (electrical machine component). The part of an electric motor or generator that produces the stationary, or nonmoving, electromagnetic field. In a direct-current alternator, such as is used on most light airplanes, the stator windings are the coils of heavy copper wire in which the output current is produced.

stator (gas turbine engine component). The stationary portion of an axial-flow compressor in a gas turbine engine. A stage of stator vanes is located between each stage of rotor blades. Stator vanes slow the airflow and increase its pressure.

statute mile. A unit of linear measurement in the English system. One statute mile is equal to 5,280 feet, or 1.609 kilometers.

stay (structural member). A structural member in a truss that is loaded in tension only. Stays are usually made of steel wire, and their length is adjusted by turnbuckles.

STC (Supplemental Type Certificate). An approval issued by the FAA for a modification to a type-certificated airframe, engine, or component. More than one STC can be issued for the same basic alteration, but each holder must prove to the FAA that his alteration meets all of the requirements of the original type certificate.

steady-state condition (electrical circuit condition). The condition of an electrical circuit that exists when all of the circuit values are constant. When some circuits are first energized, voltage or current transients cause conditions that are not normal. The steady-state conditions can be measured only after all of these transient conditions have stabilized.

steady-state flight. A condition when an aircraft is in straight-and-level, unaccelerated flight, and all forces are in balance.

steam. Water that has been changed into its vapor state by heating it. Steam is invisible, but the cloud of tiny droplets of water that rises above boiling water is often called steam.

steam cooling. A method of liquid cooling a reciprocating engine in which the coolant, normally water, is allowed to absorb enough heat that it boils, or changes into steam. The steam gives up this heat when it condenses back into a liquid.

steam fog (meteorology). Fog formed when cold air moves over relatively warm water or wet ground.

steatite. A ceramic insulating material used in making insulators for high-voltage, high-frequency radio transmitters. Steatite is mainly a silicate of magnesium.

steel. An alloy of iron that usually contains between 0.1% and 1.5% carbon with other elements. Iron is melted in a furnace, and air or oxygen is blown through it to combine with and get rid of the excess carbon. After sufficient carbon has been removed, the correct amounts of such alloying elements as manganese, molybdenum, chromium, nickel, vanadium, and tungsten are added. The steel is poured from the furnace into ingots, which are rolled or forged into the desired shape or form.

steel wool. A mat of fine threads of steel. Steel wool is used as an abrasive to remove rust or to clean a surface.

steep spiral (flight maneuver). A constant gliding turn, during which a constant radius around a point on the ground is maintained similar to the maneuver, turns around a point.

steep turns (flight maneuver). In instrument flight, anything greater than standard rate; in visual flight, anything greater than a 45° bank.

steering bars. Bars located just aft of the nosewheel and mounted on each side of the aircraft that move forward and back when the pilot applies foot pressure. Pushing either one of the steering bars causes the steering lines to pull down on the corresponding surface of the wing's trailing edge, which banks the PPC into a turn.

stellite. A nonferrous alloy of cobalt, chromium, and tungsten. Stellite is hard, wear- and corrosion-resistant, and does not soften until its temperature is extremely high. Stellite is welded to the face of many reciprocating engine exhaust valves that operate at very high temperatures.

stem. The part of a multiple-choice test item consisting of the question, statement, or problem.

step (seaplane hull design). A break in the bottom of the hull of a flying boat or seaplane float. When a seaplane is taking off, it is rocked back and forth in the water as its speed increases until the float rides high enough for air to pass between the water and the step. Getting a seaplane up on the step decreases the friction of the water against the float.

step descent (balloon operation). A method of allowing a balloon to lower toward the ground by reducing the altitude, leveling-off, and repeating the step, to lower the balloon in increments rather than one continuous motion.

stepdown fix (air traffic control). (1) Permits additional descent within a segment of an IAP by identifying a point at which an obstacle has been safely overflown. (2) A fix permitting additional descent within a segment of an instrument approach procedure by identifying a point at which a controlling obstacle has been safely overflown.

step-down transformer (electrical transformer). A type of electrical transformer with more turns in the primary winding than in the secondary. The secondary voltage of a step-down transformer is lower than the primary voltage, but the secondary current is greater than the primary current.

step leader (meteorology). A path of ionized air which extends downward from a thundercloud during the initial stages of atmospheric breakdown during a lightning strike.

stepped solvents (finishing material component). Solvents in a finishing material that have different rates of evaporation. A finishing material thinned with stepped solvents dries evenly and slowly, as the solvents evaporate out over a long period of time.

stepping motor. A precision electric motor whose output shaft position is changed in steps by pulses from the control device. Stepping motors can make high-torque changes in small angular increments to their output shaft.

stepping relay. A type of relay-operated multipole electrical switch. A relay moves the wiper, or selector, of the switch one step at a time, as pulses of electrical energy are sent into the relay coil. Stepping relays are used in rotary-dial telephone systems.

step position (seaplane operation). The attitude of the seaplane when the entire weight of the aircraft is supported by hydrodynamic and aerodynamic lift, as it is during high-speed taxi or just prior to takeoff. This position produces the least amount of water drag. Also called the planing position, or being on the step.

step stud, stepped stud. A type of stud used to replace a stud that has stripped the threads in a cast housing. A stud is a type of threaded fastener used to fasten a component to a casting; for example, to fasten the cylinders of an aircraft engine to the crankcase. One end of the stud has coarse threads that screw into the soft metal of the casting. The other end has fine threads to accept a nut.

stepped stud

If the threads in the soft casting are stripped, the threads can be drilled out and tapped for a larger stud, and a stepped stud can be used. The coarse threads on the stepped stud are usually one bolt size larger than the fine threads.

step taxi (float plane operation). To taxi a float plane at full power or high RPM.

step turn (float plane operation). A maneuver used to put a float plane in a planing configuration prior to entering an active sea lane for takeoff.

step-up coil (electrical component). A transformer that has more turns in its secondary winding than in its primary winding. The secondary voltage will be greater than the primary voltage by the same ratio as that between the turns in the windings. The secondary current will be less than the primary current by the inverse of this ratio.

step-up transformer (electrical transformer). A type of electrical transformer with more turns in the secondary winding than in the primary. The secondary voltage of a step-up transformer is higher than the primary voltage, but the secondary current is less than the primary current.

stereo route. A routinely used route of flight established by users and ARTCCs identified by a coded name; e.g., ALPHA 2. These routes minimize flight plan handling and communications.

sterile cockpit (flight operation). FAA regulations specifically prohibiting crew member to perform non-essential duties or activities while the aircraft is involved in taxi, takeoff, landing, and all other flight operations conducted below 10,000 feet MSL, except cruise flight.

stick puller. A device that applies aft pressure on the control column when the airplane is approaching the maximum operating speed.

stick pusher. A device that applies an abrupt and large forward force on the control column when the airplane is nearing an angle of attack at which a stall could occur.

stick shaker. An artificial stall warning device that vibrates the control column.

stiffener (sheet metal structural component). A piece of formed sheet metal or extrusion riveted to a larger piece of thin sheet metal to give it rigidity and stiffness. Some types of aircraft sheet metal structure have large areas of thin sheet metal that vibrate and cause noise and weaken the metal. To prevent this metal from vibrating, a stiffener in the shape of a hat section, a channel, or an angle is riveted across the sheet. This stiffens it enough to stop the vibration.

stimulants (physiology). Drugs that excite the central nervous system to produce an increase in alertness and activity.

Stoddard solvent. A petroleum product, similar to naphtha, used as a solvent and a cleaning fluid.

stoichiometric mixture (heat engine fuel-air mixture). The ratio of the mixture of fuel and air that, when burned in a heat engine, leaves no uncombined oxygen nor free carbon. A stoichiometric mixture of gasoline and air contains one pound of gasoline and 15 pounds of air.

STOL (Short TakeOff and Landing). STOL performance of an aircraft is the ability of the aircraft to take off and clear a 50-foot obstruction in a distance of 1,500 feet from the beginning the takeoff run. It must also be able to stop within 1,500 feet after crossing over a 50-foot obstacle on landing.

"Stop altitude squawk" (air traffic control). A phrase used by ATC to inform a pilot to turn off the automatic altitude reporting feature of his transponder. This phrase is used when the verbally reported altitude varies 300 feet or more from the automatic altitude report.

stop and go landing (flight operation). A procedure in which an aircraft lands, makes a complete stop on the runway and then commences a takeoff from that point.

stop countersink (sheet metal tool). A cutting tool used to cut the chamfered holes into which flush rivet heads fit. The cutter, which is driven by a shaft mounted in a handheld drill motor, fits through a bushing in the body of the stop unit and extends out beyond a fiber collar on the end of the body. The body is made in two parts threaded together to allow the length of the body to be adjusted. The body length determines the amount the cutter protrudes, and this, in turn, controls the depth of the hole made by the cutter. A fiber collar prevents the stop scratching the soft metal being countersunk.

stop drilling (method of crack arresting). A method of stopping the growth of a crack in a piece of metal by drilling a small hole at the end of the crack. A crack in a piece of metal subject to vibration will continue to grow because of the stresses concentrated at its end in an extremely small area. Very little force acting on this tiny area will tear the metal. If a small hole is drilled at the end of the crack, the forces, instead of being concentrated at the end of the crack, spread out around the circumference of the hole, and much more force is needed to tear the metal.

stop nut. *See* elastic stop nut.

stopover flight plan (air traffic control). A flight plan format which permits in a single submission, the filing of a sequence of flight plans through interim full-stop destinations to a final destination.

"stop squawk (mode or code)" (air traffic control). Used by ATC to tell the pilot to turn specified functions of the aircraft transponder off.

stop stream (air traffic control). A term used by ATC to request a pilot to suspend electronic attack activity.

stopway. *14 CFR Part 1:* "An area beyond the takeoff runway, no less wide than the runway and centered upon the extended centerline of the runway, able to support the airplane during an aborted takeoff, without causing structural damage to the airplane, and designated by the airport authorities for use in decelerating the airplane during an aborted takeoff."

storage battery. A battery composed of several secondary electrical cells. A discharged storage battery can be recharged by placing it across a source of direct current until the chemical composition of the plates and the electrolyte change to their charged condition.

storm-detection radar (radar meteorology). A weather radar designed to detect hydrometeors of precipitation size. Storm-detection radar is used primarily to detect storms containing large drops of water or hailstones, as opposed to clouds and light precipitation of small drop size.

Stormscope (weather detection indicator). The registered trade name of an instrument that detects severe weather conditions by measuring the amount and intensity of static electrical discharges within the storm.

STOVL (Short TakeOff and Vertical Landing). STOVL performance of an aircraft is the ability of the aircraft to take off and clear a 50-foot obstruction in a distance of 1,500 feet from the beginning of the takeoff run. The aircraft can land vertically, with no forward speed.

straightedge. A bar, or a piece of metal, wood, or plastic, used to check another piece of material or surface for straightness, or used to draw straight lines. A straightedge is similar to a ruler, except a straightedge does not have graduations marked on it.

straight-in IFR approach (air traffic control). An instrument approach in which the final approach is begun without first executing a procedure turn. A straight-in approach is not necessarily completed with a straight-in landing, nor is it made to straight-in landing minimums.

straight-in landing. A landing made on a runway aligned within 30 degrees of the final approach course following completion of an instrument approach.

straight-in landing minimums. *See* landing minimums.

straight-in VFR approach (air traffic control). An entry into an airport traffic pattern by intercepting the extended runway center line without executing any other portion of the traffic pattern.

structural. A type of handheld hammer used for forming sheet metal. One end of the head is round and has a flat face. The other end is wedge-shaped, with the apex (peak) of the wedge parallel to the handle. A cross-peen hammer is much like a straight-peen hammer except the wedge on its head is perpendicular to the handle.

straight-polarity arc welding. DC electric arc welding in which the electrode is negative with respect to the work.

straight-run gasoline (petroleum product). Gasoline refined from crude oil without the addition of any of the additives used in some of the other methods of refining.

straight-through combustor (turbine engine component). A combustor in a gas turbine engine through which the air from the compressor to the turbine flows in an essentially straight line.

strain. A deformation, or physical change, in a material caused by a stress. According to Hooke's law, the strain in a material, the amount it stretches or compresses, is directly proportional to the stress, until the elastic limit of the material is reached. Spring scales and certain types of torque wrenches work on the principle that strain is proportional to stress.

strain gage. A device attached to the surface of a piece of equipment to measure the amount of strain acting on the surface. A strain gage is a piece of extremely fine wire bonded (glued) to the surface, with the length of the wire parallel to direction of the strain to be measured. When the surface is stressed, it is also strained (deformed), and it either stretches or compresses. Since the strain gage is bonded to the surface, it also stretches or compresses. The resistance of the strain gage is measured with a precision bridge-type instrument, and the resistance change caused by the wire stretching or compressing is measured. Strain gages are calibrated so the change in resistance indicates the amount of strain acting on the surface.

strain hardening (metallurgy). A method of hardening metals that cannot be hardened by heat treatment. Copper, some aluminum alloys, and low-carbon steel cannot be hardened by heat treatment, but they can be hammered, rolled, pulled, or bent to change their grain structure enough that they become hard.

strake (helicopter aerodynamics). A flat metal strip attached lengthwise to the left-hand side of the tail boom of a helicopter, slightly above the center of the boom. Downwash air from the main rotor passes over the tail boom in a near vertical direction. As it flows over the boom, according to the Coanda effect, it speeds up and its pressure decreases. The air flowing over the left side of the boom strikes the strake and is made turbulent and slower than the air on the right side. The pressure differential across the tail boom moves it to the right to correct for torque. *See* Coanda effect.

strake (high-speed aerodynamics). A slender forward extension of the inboard area of the wing of a high-speed aircraft. Strakes increase lift during high angle-of-attack maneuvers by allowing the flow to separate along its leading edge and form strong leading-edge vortices. The swirling motion in these vortices create a low pressure area on the upper surface of the strake and produce a lift force which increases as the angle of attack increases.

stranded wire (electrical conductor). An electrical conductor made up of a number of small wires. These wires are either twisted together or braided and are usually enclosed in an insulating material. A stranded wire is often called a cable.

strapdown system. An inertial navigation system, INS, in which the accelerometers and gyros are permanently "strapped down" or aligned with the three axes of the aircraft.

stratiform clouds (meteorology). Clouds that form in stable air and appear to be in layers. Stratus clouds, stratocumulus, and nimbostratus clouds are all stratiform clouds.

stratocumulus (meteorology). Low clouds that are predominantly stratiform in nature. Stratocumulus clouds are gray with some dark parts and often with white patches.

stratopause (meteorology). The dividing line between the stratosphere and mesosphere at an altitude of approximately 160,000 feet.

stratosphere. The upper part of earth's atmosphere. The stratosphere extends upward from the tropopause, which is about seven miles (11 kilometers) above the surface of the earth, to an altitude of about 22 miles (35 kilometers). The temperature of the air in the stratosphere remains constant at −56.5°C (−69.7°F), and since there is no water vapor in the stratosphere, there are no clouds, nor any of the weather conditions that exist at the lower altitudes.

stratus (meteorology). A low, gray cloud layer or sheet with a fairly uniform base. Stratus clouds sometimes appear in ragged patches. They seldom produce precipitation but may produce drizzle or snow grains.

stratus fractus (meteorology). *See* fractus.

streamlined body. A body whose shape is such that fluid moving over it flows in smooth lines with no turbulence. A fish is an excellent example of a streamlined body. The fish can move through the water with a minimum of opposition. Fluid flowing around a flat plate or circular object has a turbulent area behind it. This turbulence causes drag. There is a minimum area of turbulence in the flow of fluid behind a streamlined body.

streamline flow. The flow of a fluid in which there is no turbulence. All particles of the fluid move in continuous smooth lines.

strength. The ability of a material to resist distortion or deformation caused by an external force acting on it. Strength is the ability of a material to resist stresses that try to break it.

stress. A force within an object that tries to prevent any outside force changing its shape.

stress corrosion. A form of intergranular corrosion that forms in metals that are subject to a continuous tensile stress. The tensile stress separates the metal along the internal grain boundaries, and the corrosion acts at the apex of the cracks that form.

stress crack (transparent plastics). External or internal cracks in a plastic caused by tensile stresses which are frequently accelerated by the environment to which the plastic is exposed.

stressed-skin structure. A type of aircraft structure that has a minimum of internal structure and carries all, or most, of the stresses in its outside skin. An egg shell is a perfect example of a natural stressed-skin. All of the stresses acting on an egg are carried in its shell.

stress management (psychology). The personal analysis of the kinds of stress experienced while flying, the application of appropriate stress assessment tools, and other coping mechanisms.

stress relieve (steel heat treatment). A type of heat treatment of steel. When steel parts are forged, machined, or welded, stresses are often locked in them that cause the parts to warp or break. These stresses can be relieved by heating the part until it is red-hot and then allowing it to cool slowly in still air to room temperature. This type of stress relieving is called normalizing.

stress riser. A location on a structure where the cross-sectional area of the part changes drastically. Stresses concentrated at such locations are likely to cause failure. A scratch, gouge, or tool mark in the surface of a highly stressed part can change the area enough to concentrate the stresses, and it becomes a stress riser.

stringer (aircraft structure). A part of an aircraft fuselage structure used to give the fuselage its shape and, in some types of structure, to provide a small portion of the fuselage strength. Formers give the fuselage its cross-sectional shape, and stringers, which are channels or angles of sheet metal or metal extrusions, fill in the shape between the formers. Stringers in a semimonocoque fuselage are covered with sheet metal, and in a truss-type fuselage, with fabric.

S

strobe. A high-intensity white flashing light. Strobe lights are located on aircraft wingtips to increase aircraft visibility in low-light conditions.

stroboscope. A special light that flashes with a brilliant, short-duration flash. A variable-frequency oscillator controls the stroboscope so it flashes at any required interval. Stroboscopes are used to study the motion of rotating or vibrating bodies. The stroboscope is shone on the object, and the frequency of the flashes is adjusted until the object appears to stand still or move in slow motion.

stroboscopic tachometer. A device used to measure rotational speed by the use of a stroboscopic light. A brilliant light which flashes at a controlled rate is shone on the rotating object. When the light is adjusted to flash at the same rate the object is rotating, the object appears to stand still. The flash rate of the light is calibrated in terms of revolutions per minute (RPM).

stroke (reciprocating engine parameter). The linear distance the piston moves inside the cylinder from the top to the bottom.

strontium. A soft, silvery, easily oxidized, metallic chemical element. Strontium's symbol is Sr, its atomic number is 38, and its atomic weight is 87.62. Finely divided strontium ignites spontaneously in air. Strontium is used in the manufacture of pyrotechnic devices.

structural adhesive (composites). A bonding agent strong enough to transfer the required loads between components that are bonded together while exposed to service environments.

structural bond (composites). A bond that joins basic load-bearing parts of an assembly. The load may be either static or dynamic.

structural damage, major. Any damage to an aircraft that requires major repair to restore it to an airworthy condition.

structural failure. The loss of the load-carrying capacity of a component or member within the structure, or of the structure itself. Structural failure is initiated when the material is stressed beyond its ultimate load, thus causing fracture or permanent deformation.

structural icing. The accumulation of ice on the exterior of an aircraft.

strut (aircraft component). A general term used for a structural brace. *See* wing strut, jury strut, compression strut.

stub antenna (radio antenna). A short, wide UHF blade antenna used for DME and ATC transponders.

stud (fastening device). A threaded fastener used to attach components to an engine crankcase or other type of casting. A stud used to fasten a cylinder to a cast aluminum alloy crankcase has threads on both ends. The threads that screw into the soft aluminum crankcase are coarse, and the threads on which a nut is screwed to clamp the cylinder base to the crankcase are fine.

student pilot certificate. An FAA-issued certificate that permits student pilots to exercise solo pilot privileges with limitations. A student's medical certificate becomes their student pilot certificate once it is endorsed by their flight instructor.

stuffing box. A box through which a sliding or rotating shaft passes. The stuffing box contains packing material that can be compressed around the shaft to prevent liquid or gas leaking past the moving shaft.

S-turns across a road (flight training maneuver). A practice wind correction maneuver in which the airplane's ground track describes semicircles of equal radii on each side of a selected straight line on the ground.

Styrofoam. The registered trade name for an expanded (full of bubbles), rigid polystyrene plastic material.

subassembly. An assembly of components that is part of a larger device. A wing is a subassembly of an airplane.

subatomic particles. Particles smaller than an atom. Electrons, protons, and neutrons are subatomic particles.

subfreezing temperature. Temperature lower than that needed to cause water to freeze.

subject matter knowledge codes (SMKC). A list of codes prepared by the FAA to establish specific references for all knowledge standards. The listings contain reference materials to be used when preparing for all airman knowledge tests.

sublimation. The procedure in which a solid material changes directly into a vapor or a vapor changes into a solid without becoming a liquid in the process.

submerged-arc welding. A form of electric arc welding in which a bare rod is used as the electrode. The rod is covered with granulated flux that melts in the arc and flows out ahead of the weld to prevent the formation of oxides in the bead.

subpage. An additional page of information about a particular topic that can be displayed on an FMS/RNAV. Many pages require the use of several subpages to show all information pertaining to any one topic.

subrefraction (radar technology). Less than normal bending of a radar beam, resulting from abnormal vertical gradients of temperature and/or water vapor.

subscript. A number or letter written to the right of, and partially below, an abbreviation or a number. In gas turbine engine operation, the symbol P_{Am} identifies ambient pressure. "P" stands for pressure, and the subscript "$_{Am}$" tells that this pressure is ambient pressure. The chemical formula for water is H_2O. The subscript "$_2$" indicates that two atoms of hydrogen unite with one atom of oxygen to form one molecule of water.

subsidence (meteorology). A descending motion of the air in the atmosphere over a rather broad area.

subsonic flight (aircraft flight). Flight of an aircraft in which all the air passing over the aircraft structure is moving at a speed slower than the speed of sound.

subsonic speed. Speed below the speed of sound.

substandard. The quality of an object that is less than can be considered normal or acceptable.

substantial damage (to an aircraft). Damage or failure that adversely affects the structural strength, performance, or flight characteristics of the aircraft, and would normally require major repair or replacement of the affected component. (*See* 49 CFR §830.2 for more details.)

substitute. To use one material or object to take the place of something else. Plans and specifications often call for a certain type of material to be used. But if this particular material is not available, another material may be used in its place. The material used in place of the one specified is a substitute material.

substitute route (air traffic control). A route assigned to pilots when any part of an airway or route is unusable because of NAVAID status. These routes consist of substitute routes shown on U.S. government charts, routes defined by ATC as specific NAVAID radials or courses, and routes defined by ATC as direct to or between NAVAIDs.

substrate. The wafer of semiconductor material on which the components of integrated circuits are diffused and deposited.

subsystem. A small system inside a larger system. Each subsystem has a job it must perform for the main system to operate properly.

subtraction (mathematics). The mathematical process in which the value of one number is taken from the value of another.

subtrahend (mathematics). The number in a subtraction problem that is to be subtracted.

subtropical jet stream (meteorology). Relatively fast uniform winds concentrated within the upper atmosphere in a narrow band. The subtropical jet stream exists in the subtropics at an altitude of approximately 13 kilometers and flows from west to east with a speed somewhat slower than the polar jet stream.

S

suction. A term commonly used for a negative pressure, or a pressure below atmospheric pressure. The terms suction and vacuum are both used to mean a negative pressure.

suction gage. The instrument that monitors the negative pressure produced by a vacuum pump. The suction gage is often marked to indicate the normal operating range for the pneumatic flight instruments.

suction relief valve (pneumatic system component). A component that holds a constant and steady suction, a pressure lower than that of the atmosphere, on a system. Some gyroscopic instruments used in an aircraft are operated by air pulled into the instrument case by a suction produced by an engine-driven vacuum pump.

A suction relief valve in the line between the pump and the instrument case has a spring-loaded poppet that remains closed until the pressure becomes low enough to allow outside air pressure to force the poppet off its seat, then outside air is taken into the pump through the valve, rather than through the instrument case. This air entering the system holds the pressure inside the instrument case at the value for which the suction relief valve is set.

suction vortex (meteorology). A small but very intense vortex within a tornado circulation.

sudden stoppage (engine operating condition). A condition likely to cause internal damage to an aircraft engine. An engine is said to have a sudden stoppage if it comes to a complete stop within one revolution of the crankshaft.

sulfating (battery condition). A condition in a lead-acid storage battery in which both the positive and negative plates are covered with a hard deposit of lead sulfate. When a lead-acid battery discharges, the active material on both its plates changes into lead sulfate, which can be removed by recharging the battery. But if the battery is allowed to stand in a discharged state for a long period of time, the sulfate hardens and is difficult, if not impossible, to remove by normal recharging.

sulfur. A pale yellow, nonmetallic chemical element. Sulfur's symbol is S, its atomic number is 16, and its atomic weight is 32.064. Sulfur, also spelled sulphur, is extremely important in the manufacture of commercial and industrial compounds and is found in its free state in underground beds along the Gulf coast of Texas and Louisiana.

sum (mathematics). The answer to an addition problem when two or more numbers are added together. In the problem $2 + 4 = 6$, the number 6 is the sum.

summation principle (meteorology). The principle which states that the sky cover assigned to a layer is equal to the summation of the cover of the lowest layer, plus the additional coverage at all successively higher layers, up to and including the layer in question. No layer can be assigned a sky cover less than a lower layer, and no sky cover can be greater than 1.0 (10/10).

summerwood. The less porous, usually harder portion of an annual ring that forms in a tree during the latter part of the growing season, the summer of the year.

sump (aircraft engine component). A low point in an aircraft engine in which lubricating oil collects and is stored or transferred to an external oil tank. A removable sump attached to the bottom of the crankcase of a reciprocating engine is often called an oil pan.

sump (fuel tank component). A low point in an aircraft fuel tank in which water and other contaminants collect and are held until they can be drained out.

sump jar (aircraft battery installation component). A small jar located in the vent line of an aircraft battery box. The sump jar used in a lead-acid battery installation contains a sponge saturated with a solution of bicarbonate of soda and water. Acid fumes from the battery pass through the sump jar where they are neutralized to prevent their causing corrosion in the aircraft structure. The sump jar in a nickel-cadmium battery installation contains a boric acid solution to neutralize the alkaline fumes from this battery.

sunset and sunrise. The mean solar times of sunset and sunrise as published in the Nautical Almanac, converted to local standard time for the locality concerned. Within Alaska, the end of evening civil twilight and the beginning of morning civil twilight, as defined for each locality.

superadiabatic lapse rate (meteorology). A lapse rate greater than the dry-adiabatic lapse rate, greater than 3°F per thousand feet.

supercell thunderstorm (meteorology). A large, powerful type of thunderstorm that forms in very unstable environments with vertical and horizontal wind shear. These are almost always associated with severe weather, strong surface winds, large hail, and/ or tornadoes.

supercharged engine. A reciprocating engine that uses an air compressor to increase the pressure of the air before it enters the engine cylinders.

supercharger (reciprocating engine component). An air pump used to increase the pressure of the air taken into the cylinders of a reciprocating engine. The amount of power a reciprocating engine can develop is determined by the mass, or weight, of the fuel-air mixture taken into the cylinders. By compressing the air before it enters the cylinders, a greater mass of air can be used, and more power can be developed by the engine. Superchargers can be gear-driven from the engine, or they can be driven by a turbine spun by exhaust gases. Superchargers driven by exhaust gases are called turbochargers or turbosuperchargers.

superconductivity. A condition of certain chemical elements (niobium, tantalum, vanadium, tin, and others) when they are held at a temperature near absolute zero. At this low temperature, these metals lose almost all their electrical resistance and become strongly diamagnetic. They try to orient themselves across a magnetic field, rather than aligning with the field.

supercooled water. Water in its liquid form at a temperature well below its natural freezing temperature. When supercooled water is disturbed, it immediately freezes.

supercritical airfoil (aerodynamics). An airfoil section that allows an airplane to cruise efficiently at a speed very near Mach one (the speed of sound). The center portion of the airfoil is nearly flat, and there is a distinct downward curve, or cusp, near the trailing edge. The lower side of the forward part of the airfoil is more curved than the upper side.

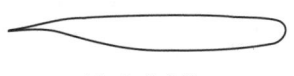

supercritical airfoil

superheat (refrigeration system). Heat energy added to a refrigerant after it changes from its liquid state into a vapor. The thermal expansion valve in a refrigeration system meters just enough liquid refrigerant into the evaporator for all of it to be changed from droplets of liquid into a vapor by the time it reaches the end of the evaporator coils. If all of the refrigerant vaporizes before it reaches the end of the coils, any additional heat raises its temperature. This additional heat is called superheat.

superheated water. Water that has been heated to a temperature above that at which it normally changes its state from liquid into steam. Water may be superheated by holding it under pressure. More heat energy must be added to it before its molecules move fast enough to leave the surface of the liquid and become steam.

superheterodyne radio receiver circuit. The type of circuit used in most modern radio receivers. A radio-frequency signal is received, amplified, and mixed with a signal produced inside the radio by a local oscillator. The frequency of the oscillator signal is always a fixed amount different from the radio-frequency signals being received.

Continued

superheterodyne radio receiver circuit. *Continued*

When the two signals are mixed, two more signals are produced. The frequency of one is the sum of the other two, and the frequency of the other is the difference between them. The signal whose frequency is the difference is called an intermediate frequency, an IF. The IF is amplified and changed into an audio-frequency voltage that duplicates the AF used to modulate the radio-frequency signal in the transmitter.

superhigh frequency (radio frequencies). Electromagnetic radiation whose frequency is between 3.0 and 30.0 gigahertz. At this frequency, the wavelengths are between 100 and 10 millimeters.

superpressure balloon. A type of hot air balloon that has no openings to the atmosphere—the mouth is sealed with a special skirt—and is kept pumped full of air at a higher pressure than the atmosphere by an onboard fan. Used on moored balloons to allow operations in relatively strong wind. In gas ballooning, a sealed envelope in which the internal envelope pressure exceeds that of a nonsealed envelope.

superrefraction (radar technology). More than normal bending of a radar beam resulting from abnormal vertical gradients of temperature and/or water vapor.

supersaturated solution. A solution in which a solid is dissolved in a liquid until the liquid will hold no more. A supersaturated solution of salt and water has some salt crystals in the liquid. The amount of crystals depends upon the temperature of the solution. As the temperature decreases, more crystals precipitate out of the solution.

supersede. To replace, or take the place of, something. When a manufacturer issues a revision to an instruction manual, the revised manual supersedes the original one. If there is a difference in the instructions in the two manuals, the instructions in the latest (the superseding) manual, are to be followed.

supersonic aerodynamics. The branch of aerodynamics that deals with flight at a speed greater than the speed of sound.

supersonic flight. Flight at an airspeed in which all air flowing over the aircraft is moving at a speed greater than the speed of sound.

supersonic speed. Speed above the speed of sound.

supersonic transport. A civil aircraft designed to transport passengers at speeds greater than the speed of sound.

super stream class (air traffic control). Super stream class is used to refer to group of aircraft that share similar scheduling characteristics. Super stream class categories are typically based on engine type (jet or prop), destination airport, and meter fix.

superstructure. The framework of formers and stringers attached to the main truss of a truss-type aircraft fuselage. The superstructure gives the fuselage its shape, but it is not a main strength-carrying part of the fuselage.

supplemental operation. Any common carriage operation for compensation or hire conducted with (1) an airplane with more than 30 passenger seats, excluding crewmember seats; (2) an airplane with a payload capacity of more than 7,500 pounds; (3) a propeller-powered airplane with more than 9 and less than 31 passenger seats, excluding crewmember seats, that is also used in domestic or flag operations and that is so listed in the operations as required for those operations; or (4) a turbojet powered airplane with 1 or more but less than 31 passenger seats, excluding crewmember seats, that is also used in domestic or flag operations and that is so listed in the operations specifications as required for those operations.

In addition, a supplemental operation must be (1) an operation for which the departure time, departure location, and arrival location are specifically negotiated with the customer or the customer's representative; (2) an all-cargo operation; or (3) a passenger-carrying public charter operation conducted under 14 CFR Part 380.

supplemental pilot (unmanned aircraft). A pilot assigned unmanned aircraft (UA) flight duties to augment the pilot in command. It is common in this situation to have both an internal and an external UA pilot, and the supplemental pilot can assume either of these positions. The supplemental pilot may also assume duties of the PIC provided he or she meets the qualifications.

supplemental type certificate (STC). An approval issued by the FAA for a modification to a type certificated airframe, engine, or component. More than one STC can be issued for the same basic alteration, but each holder must prove to the FAA that the alteration meets all the requirements of the original type certificate.

supplemental weather service location. Airport facilities staffed with contract personnel who take weather observations and provide current local weather to pilots via telephone or radio. All other services are provided by the parent flight service station (FSS).

supplementary angles. Any two angles whose sum is 180°. An angle of 30° and one of 150° are supplementary angles; their sum is 180°.

supplement of an angle. One hundred and eighty degrees minus the angle. Thirty degrees is the supplement of 150°.

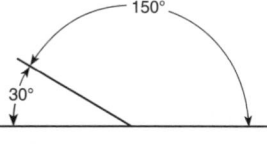

supplementary angles

supply-type test item. A question in which the student supplies answers as opposed to selecting from choices provided. Essay or fill-in-the-blank questions are examples of supply-type test items.

suppressor grid (electron tube component). The grid in a pentode vacuum tube used to suppress secondary emission from the plate of the tube.

SUPPs. Refers to ICAO Document 7030 "Regional Supplementary Procedures." SUPPs contain procedures for each ICAO region which are unique to that region and are not covered in the worldwide provisions identified in the ICAO Air Navigation Plan.

surface analysis chart (weather reporting). A chart report depicting an analysis of the current surface weather, which shows the areas of high and low pressure, fronts, temperatures, dewpoints, wind directions and speeds, local weather, and visual obstructions.

surface area. The airspace contained by the lateral boundary of the Class B, C, D, or E airspace designated for an airport, beginning at the surface and extending upward.

surface corrosion. Corrosion that forms on the surface of a piece of metal covered with some form of electrolyte. Surface corrosion shows up as pits filled with a powdery salt.

surface friction (meteorology). Resistance to movement of air flowing along the surface of the earth or other surface such as an airplane wing.

surface incident. An event during which authorized or unauthorized/unapproved movement occurs in the movement area or an occurrence in the movement area associated with the operation of an aircraft that affects or could affect the safety of flight.

surface inversion (meteorology). A temperature inversion with its base at the surface. Surface inversions are often caused by the air near the surface being cooled by terrestrial radiation, especially at night.

surface movement guidance control system (SMGCS). Facilitates the safe movement of aircraft and vehicles at airports where scheduled air carriers are conducting authorized operations.

surface roughness (cylinder wall condition). The condition of the surface of a reciprocating engine cylinder wall that has been honed to make it hold lubricating oil. Surface roughness is measured in microinches rms (min rms).

S

surface tape (aircraft fabric material). Strips of aircraft fabric that are doped over all seams and all places where the fabric is stitched to the aircraft structure and over wing leading edges where abrasive wear occurs. The edges of surface tape are pinked, or notched, to keep them from raveling before the dope is applied.

surface tension. The cohesive force that causes molecules of a liquid to hold themselves together. Surface tension tries to keep the area of the surface of the liquid as small as possible. It is surface tension that causes a soap bubble to be shaped like a sphere, since a sphere has the smallest surface area possible for its volume.

surface visibility (meteorology). Visibility observed from eye-level above the ground.

surfactant (fuel system contaminant). A surface active agent, or partially soluble contaminant which is a by-product of fuel processing or of fuel additives. Surfactants adhere to other contaminants and cause them to drop out of the fuel and settle to the bottom of the fuel tank as sludge.

surge. A condition of unstable airflow through the compressor of a gas turbine engine in which the compressor blades have an excessive angle of attack. Surge normally affects an entire stage of compression.

surpic. A term of description of surface vessels in the area of a Search and Rescue incident including their predicted positions and their characteristics.

surveillance approach (air traffic control). An instrument approach in which the air traffic controller issues instruction, for pilot compliance, based on the aircraft position relative to the final approach course (azimuth) and the distance (range) from the end of the runway as displayed on the controller's radar scope. The controller will provide recommended altitudes on final approach if requested by the pilot.

SUSP. *See* suspend mode.

suspend mode (SUSP). The name used in some FMS/RNAV units to describe the nonsequencing mode when it has been automatically set by the computer or the pilot.

suspension lines (balloons). Lines descending from the mouth of a balloon envelope from which the basket and heater are suspended.

swaged fitting (fluid line fitting). A nonreusable fitting installed on a flexible hose by forcing the material of the fitting into the hose. Swaged fittings are also installed on rigid fluid lines used in high-pressure hydraulic and pneumatic systems.

swaged terminal (control cable terminal). A terminal pressed onto a steel control cable. A swaged terminal is made in the form of a cylinder into which the steel cable is slipped. This steel cylinder is then swaged (hammered into) the cable with special swaging dies. The swaging dies compress the cylinder, and as the inside of the hole becomes smaller than the outside of the cable, the metal of the terminal is pressed around the wires of the cable. A properly swaged terminal develops the full strength of the steel cable.

SWAP (severe weather avoidance plan) (air traffic control). An approved plan to minimize the effect of severe weather on traffic flows in impacted terminal and/or ARTCC areas. SWAP is normally implemented to provide the least disruption to the air traffic control system when flight through portions of airspace is difficult or impossible due to severe weather.

swash plate. The component in a helicopter control system that consists basically of two bearing races with ball bearings between them. The lower, or nonrotating, race is tilted by the cyclic control, and the upper, or rotating, race has arms which connect to the control horns on the rotor blades. Movement of the cyclic pitch control is transmitted to the rotating blades through the swash plate. Movement of the collective pitch control raises or lowers the entire swash plate assembly to change the pitch of all of the blades at the same time.

sweat soldering. A method of soldering two pieces of sheet metal together. Both surfaces that form the seam are tinned (covered with a thin coating of solder), and the joint is assembled. The entire assembly is put into an oven and heated enough to melt the solder in the joint and produce a tight, uniform seal.

swell (sea condition). Waves that continue after the generating wind has ceased or changed direction. Swells also are generated by ships and boats in the form of wakes, and sometimes by underwater disturbances such as volcanoes or earthquakes. These waves have a uniform and orderly appearance characterized by smooth, rounded, regularly spaced wave crests. Once set in motion, swells tend to maintain their original direction for as long as they continue in deep water, regardless of wind direction, and may be moving into or across the local wind.

swell velocity (sea condition). The velocity with which the swell advances with relation to a fixed reference point, measured in knots. There is little movement of water in the horizontal direction. Each water particle transmits energy to its neighbor, resulting primarily in a vertical motion, similar to the motion observed when shaking out a carpet.

sweptback wing (airplane wing). An airplane wing in which the leading edge angles backward from the fuselage. The leading edge of the wing at the tip is farther back than the leading edge at the root.

swinging choke (electrical component). A special type of iron-core inductor used in a filter circuit for an electrical power supply. A swinging choke is built in such a way that its effective inductive reactance varies with the amount of current flowing through its winding.

swinging the compass. *See* compass compensation.

switch (electrical circuit component). A component used to open or close an electrical circuit or to select paths through the circuit.

switching diode (electronic component). A type of semiconductor diode whose resistance varies with the voltage across it. A switching diode acts as an open switch when the voltage across it is low, but when the voltage rises to a certain value, its resistance decreases, and the diode conducts, acting as a closed switch.

syllabus. A summary or outline of a course of study that is a step-by-step, building block progression of learning with provisions for regular review and evaluations at prescribed stages of learning.

symbols (in teaching/learning process). In communication, simple oral and visual codes such as words, gestures, and facial expressions which are formed into sentences, paragraphs, lectures, or chapters to compose and transmit a message that means something to the receiver of the information.

symbols/symbolization (in teaching/learning process). *See* word/symbol confusion.

symmetrical airfoil. An airfoil that has the same shape on both sides of its center line. A symmetrical airfoil has a very small change in the location of its center of pressure as its angle of attack changes. For this reason, symmetrical airfoils are often used for helicopter rotors.

symmetrical airfoil

symmetrical laminate (composites). A composite laminate in which the ply orientation is symmetrical about the laminate midplane.

symmetry check (rigging check). A dimensional check of an airframe to determine that the wings and tail are symmetrical about the longitudinal axis.

synchro (remote indicating device). A device used to transmit indications of angular movement or position from one location to another. *See* Autosyn system.

synchronous motor (electric motor). An alternating current motor similar to an induction motor, except the rotor is either a permanent magnet or an electromagnet excited by an external source of direct current. The rotor of a synchronous motor turns at a speed directly related to the frequency of the alternating current used to excite its stator.

synchronous speed (induction motor). The speed of an induction motor at which the rotor follows the rotating field in the stator. The synchronous speed, in revolutions per minute, is found by dividing the frequency of the AC, in hertz, by the number of poles in the stator. Then multiplying this answer by 120. A four-pole induction motor, operating on 60-hertz AC, has a synchronous speed of 1,800 RPM.

synchrophasing (propeller operation). A method of synchronizing the propellers of a multiengine aircraft. The engines all turn at the same RPM, and the propellers rotate in such a way that a master blade on each propeller keeps the same relative position in its rotation as the master blade on each of the other propellers.

synchroscope (aircraft instrument). A powerplant instrument used on multiengine aircraft to detect and display the difference in rotational speed of the various engines. One popular type of synchroscope has a small propeller on the face of the instrument. The propeller rotates at a speed and in a direction determined by the difference in RPM of the master engine and the other engine. When the propeller on the instrument face is not rotating, the two engines are turning at exactly the same speed.

synchro system (remote indicating system). A type of remote indicating system that uses synchro motors in the transmitter and the indicator. These synchro motors have a three-phase stator and a single-phase rotor. The stators and rotors of the transmitter and indicator are connected in parallel, and alternating current is used to excite the rotors.

The AC exciting the rotor induces a voltage in the three phases of the transmitter stator, and since the two stators are connected in parallel, the magnetic fields in the indicator are the same as those in the transmitter. The magnetic fields in the indicator stator pull its rotor around so it assumes the same position as the rotor in the transmitter. An Autosyn system is a form of synchro system. *See* Autosyn system.

synoptic chart (meteorology). A chart, such as a weather map, which shows the distribution of meteorological conditions over an area at a given time.

synthetic oil. A type of engine lubricating oil made by chemical synthesis (changing) of a mineral-, animal-, or vegetable-oil base. Synthetic oils have appropriate additives that give them such characteristics as low volatility, low pour point, high viscosity index, good lubricating qualities, low coke and lacquer formation, and low foaming.

Synthetic oils are superior to natural mineral oils because they resist oxidation better, and they are able to be used over a wider range of operating temperatures. Synthetic oils are used in almost all gas turbine engines and are used to some extent in reciprocating engines.

synthetic vision system (SVS). A visual display of terrain, obstructions, runways, and other surface features that creates a virtual view of what the pilot would see out the window. This tool could be used to supplement normal vision in low visibility conditions, as well as to increase situational awareness in IMC.

system pressure regulator (hydraulic power system component). A type of hydraulic system-pressure control valve. When the system pressure is low, as it is when some unit is being actuated, the output of the constant-delivery pump is directed into the system. When the actuation is completed and the pressure builds up to a specified kick-out pressure, the pressure regulator shifts. A check valve seals the system off and the pressure is maintained by the accumulator. The pump is unloaded and its output is directed back into the reservoir with very little opposition. The pump output pressure drops, but the volume of flow remains the same. When the system pressure drops to the specified kick-in pressure, the regulator again shifts and directs fluid into the system.

Spool-type and balanced-pressure-type system pressure regulators are completely automatic in their operation and require no attention on the part of the flight crew. A system pressure regulator is also called an unloading valve.

system strategic navigation. Military activity accomplished by navigating along a pre-planned route using internal aircraft systems to maintain a desired track. This activity normally requires a lateral route width of 10 NM and altitude range of 1,000 feet to 6,000 feet AGL with some route segments that permit terrain following.

system-wide information management (SWIM). An advanced technology program designed to enable and promote greater sharing of Air Traffic Management (ATM) system information, such as airport operational status, weather information, flight data, status of special use airspace, and National Airspace System (NAS) restrictions. SWIM supports current and future NAS programs by providing flexible and secure information management architecture for sharing NAS information.

S

Tango

TA. *See* traffic advisory.

TAA. *See* terminal arrival area.

tab (auxiliary flight control). A small, movable control hinged to the trailing edge of one of an airplane's primary flight control surfaces. Tabs can be used to help the pilot move the primary control surface, or they can be used to produce an aerodynamic load on the primary surface that trims the aircraft for a hands-off flight condition. *See* antiservo tab, balance tab, servo tab, spring tab, trim tab.

TACAN (electronic navigation system). An electronic navigation system, operating in the ultrahigh frequency (UHF) range. The name TACAN is an acronym for TACtical Air Navigation. TACAN is used by military aircraft to give the pilot both the distance and direction from the transmitting stations on the ground. Civilian aircraft have equipment that use the TACAN ground facilities to show the distance to the navigational fix. The equipment used in civilian aircraft is called DME (Distance Measuring Equipment).

TACAN-only aircraft. An aircraft, normally military, possessing TACAN with DME but no VOR navigational system capability. Clearances must specify TACAN or VORTAC fixes and approaches.

tachometer. An instrument used to measure the rotational speed of an object. Tachometers are usually calibrated in revolutions per minute, RPM, or percentage of the maximum rated RPM.

tachometer cable. The flexible drive used to connect the rotating magnet inside a tachometer indicator to the tachometer drive gear inside an engine. A tachometer cable is made of a core of steel wire, around which are wound two concentric coils of steel wire, wound in opposite directions.

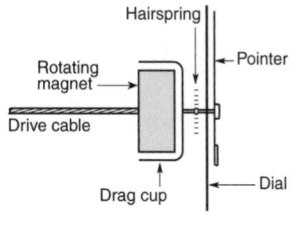

tachometer

tachometer generator. A small alternating current generator, mounted on and driven from the tachometer drive pad on an engine. The frequency of the AC produced by the tachometer generator is proportional to the speed of the engine.

tack coat (aircraft finishing system operation). A coat of finishing material sprayed on a surface and allowed to dry until the solvents evaporate. As soon as the solvents evaporate from the tack coat, a wet, full-bodied coat of the material is sprayed over it.

tackle. An arrangement of ropes and pulleys used to gain a mechanical advantage. Tackle is most frequently spoken of as block and tackle.

tack rag (finishing system component). A clean, lintless rag, slightly damp with thinner. A tack rag is used to wipe a surface to prepare it to receive a coat of finishing material.

tack weld. A method of holding a structure together before it is permanently welded. The parts of the structure are cut and fitted together, and each joint is welded with a small spot. When all of the joints fit and line up as they should, the final welding is done.

tacky (composite condition). The condition of some uncured resins or finishing materials that leave the material sticky to the touch.

tacky (finishing system condition). The condition of a finishing system in which the material is slightly sticky to the touch.

tactical air navigation. An ultra-high frequency electronic rho-theta air navigation aid which provides suitably equipped aircraft a continuous indication of bearing and distance to the TACAN station.

tag wire. Small-diameter, soft steel wire used to tie identification tags to objects.

TAI (Thermal Anti-Ice). *See* thermal anti-icing system.

tail boom (aircraft structure). A spar, or small-diameter structure that connects the tail section of an aircraft to a pod-type fuselage.

tail cone (gas turbine engine component). The cone-shaped section of the exhaust system of a gas turbine engine used to produce the correct change in area of the duct through which the exhaust gases leave the engine.

tailets. Small vertical surfaces mounted on the underside of the horizontal stabilizer of some airplanes to increase directional stability.

tail-heavy (aircraft balance condition). The condition of balance of an aircraft in which the center of gravity is behind its allowable aft limit.

tail load (aerodynamics). The downward aerodynamic force produced by the horizontal tail surfaces of an airplane. Tail load normally acts downward to give the airplane longitudinal stability. The lift produced by the wing of the airplane must overcome the downward-acting tail load, as well as the downward-acting force caused by the weight of the airplane.

tail pipe (engine exhaust system component). The part of the exhaust system of either a reciprocating engine or a gas turbine engine through which the exhaust gases leave the engine. If a muffler is installed in the exhaust system of a reciprocating engine, the tail pipe usually connects to the muffler and carries the exhaust gases away from the airplane.

tail rotor (helicopter component). The small, auxiliary rotor installed on the tail of a single-rotor helicopter. The tail rotor turns in a vertical plane to produce thrust that counteracts the torque produced by the main rotor. The pitch of the tail rotor blades is controlled from the cockpit by the control pedals.

tail skid (airplane landing gear component). A small skid mounted on the bottom of the aft end of the fuselage of an airplane equipped with a tricycle landing gear. The tail skid absorbs the shock and prevents damage to the structure if the airplane should be rotated too abruptly on takeoff. In the early days of aviation when airplanes had no brakes and operated from grass fields, tail skids were used rather than tail wheels to support the tail of the airplane when it was on the ground.

tail warning radar. A radar system installed in military aircraft to warn the pilot of an aircraft approaching from behind.

tail wheel (airplane landing gear component). A small, swiveling or steerable wheel mounted at the aft end of the fuselage of an airplane equipped with a conventional landing gear. The tail wheel supports the rear end of the airplane when it is on the ground.

tailwheel aircraft. *See* conventional landing gear.

tailwheel checkout (pilot endorsement). Flight instruction in a tailwheel aircraft that is required in order to receive an endorsement from a certified flight instructor, which acknowledges a pilot is competent to fly a tailwheel aircraft (*see* conventional landing gear).

tail wind (aircraft navigation). Wind blowing in the same direction the aircraft is moving. When an aircraft is flying with a tail wind, its speed over the ground is equal to its speed through the air, plus the speed the air is moving over the ground.

tailwind component. The component of wind that is blowing in the same direction an aircraft is flying.

takeoff (aircraft flight). The portion of an aircraft flight in which the aircraft leaves the ground.

takeoff briefing. A briefing prior to takeoff that a pilot performs with crewmembers to ensure a safe flight.

takeoff clearance. ATC authorization for an aircraft to depart a runway. It is predicated on known traffic and known physical airport conditions.

takeoff decision speed (V₁). *14 CFR §23.51:* "The takeoff decision speed, V_1, is the calibrated airspeed on the ground at which, as a result of engine failure or other reasons, the pilot is assumed to have made a decision to continue or discontinue the takeoff."

takeoff distance. The distance required to complete an all-engines-operative takeoff to the 35-foot height. It must be at least 15 percent less than the distance required for a one-engine-inoperative takeoff. The takeoff distance is not normally a limiting factor as it is usually less than the one-engine inoperative takeoff distance.

takeoff distance available (ICAO). The length of the takeoff run available plus the length of the clearway, if provided.

takeoff power (aircraft engine specification). The amount of power an aircraft engine is allowed to produce for a limited period of time. The use of takeoff power is normally limited to no more than one minute.

14 CFR Part 1: "(1) With respect to reciprocating engines, means the brake horsepower that is developed under standard sea level conditions, and under the maximum conditions of crankshaft rotational speed and engine manifold pressure approved for the normal takeoff, and limited in continuous use to the period of time shown in the approved engine specification; and (2) With respect to turbine engines, means the brake horsepower that is developed under static conditions at a specific altitude and atmospheric temperature, and under the maximum conditions of rotor shaft rotational speed and gas temperature approved for the normal takeoff, and limited in continuous use to the period of time shown in the approved engine specification."

takeoff run available (ICAO). The length of runway declared available and suitable for the ground run of an airplane takeoff.

takeoff safety speed. *14 CFR Part 1:* "A referenced airspeed obtained after lift-off at which the required one-engine-inoperative climb performance can be achieved."

takeoff thrust. *14 CFR Part 1:* "With respect to turbine engines, means the jet thrust that is developed under static conditions at a specific altitude and atmospheric temperature under the maximum conditions of rotorshaft rotational speed and gas temperature approved for the normal takeoff, and limited in continuous use to the period of time shown in the approved engine specification."

takeoff warning system. An aural warning system that provides an audio signal when the thrust levers are advanced for takeoff if the stabilizer, flaps, or speed brakes are in an unsafe condition for takeoff.

takeoff weight (weight and balance). The weight of an aircraft just before brake release. It is the ramp weight less the weight of the fuel burned during start and taxi.

tandem. One object ahead of another. Tandem seating in an airplane has one seat ahead of the other. The wheels of a bicycle are tandem wheels.

tandem bearings (ball bearing configuration). Two sets of ball bearings mounted on a shaft in such a way that both bearings support the thrust load.

tandem wing configuration. *14 CFR Part 1:* "A configuration having two wings of similar span, mounted in tandem."

tang. A tapered shank sticking out from the blade of a knife or a file. The handle of the knife or file is mounted on the tang.

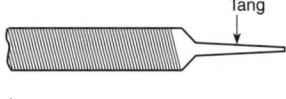

Tang

tang

tangent (geometric tangent). A line that touches a curve at one point only and does not cross the curve.

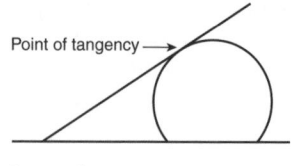

Point of tangency →

tangent

tangent of an angle (trigonometric function). The tangent of an angle in a right triangle is the ratio of the length of the side of the triangle opposite the angle, to the length of the side adjacent to (next to) the angle.

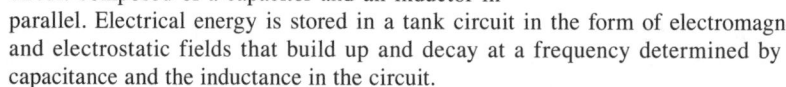

$$\text{Tan } \emptyset \;=\; \frac{\text{opposite}}{\text{adjacent}}$$

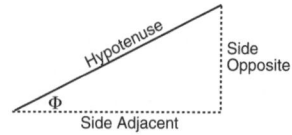

tangent

tangent point (TP). The point on the VOR/DME RNAV route centerline from which a line perpendicular to the route centerline would pass through the reference facility.

tank circuit (electronic circuit). A resonant electronic circuit composed of a capacitor and an inductor in parallel. Electrical energy is stored in a tank circuit in the form of electromagnetic and electrostatic fields that build up and decay at a frequency determined by the capacitance and the inductance in the circuit.

tantalum. A hard, gray, or steel-blue metallic chemical element. Tantalum's symbol is Ta, its atomic number is 73, and its atomic weight is 180.948. Tantalum is used in the manufacture of light bulb filaments, and tantalum oxide is used in electrolytic capacitors.

tantalum carbide. A compound of tantalum and carbon in a hard, crystalline form, used for making cutting tools and dies.

tantalum-foil capacitor. A type of electrolytic capacitor that uses tantalum foil for the plates. An oxide film formed on the anode, the positive plate, serves as the dielectric. Absorbent paper saturated with an electrolyte keeps the plates separated. The large capacity of a tantalum-foil capacitor is caused by the thinness of the oxide-film dielectric.

tap (thread-cutting tool). A metal-cutting tool used to cut threads on the inside of a hole. A taper tap is used to start the threads in the hole; then a plug tap is used to cut threads to almost the full depth of the hole. If it is necessary that the threads extend to the very bottom of the hole, a bottoming tap is used. The threads cut by a bottoming tap are the same from one end to the other.

tap drill. A twist drill of the correct size to drill a hole to be tapped. There is a correct tap drill for each size tap.

tape display. A vertical display format used to portray data such as airspeed and altitude on many primary flight displays. Tape displays are also used to show vertical speeds and many other values such as power settings and powerplant speeds.

tape measure. A long, narrow strip of cloth, paper, or steel with graduations of inches or millimeters marked along its edge.

taper (dimensional change). A gradual change in the width or thickness of an object along its length.

taper (resistance change). The relationship between the change in the resistance of a potentiometer or rheostat and the amount of rotation of its shaft. The resistance of a linear-taper potentiometer or rheostat changes in direct proportion to the number of degrees the shaft is rotated.

tapered pin. A type of hardware used to fasten concentric tubes together or to fasten a sleeve around a solid shaft. A tapered pin is pressed into a tapered hole drilled through the components to be joined. Some tapered pins are secured in place by passing safety wire through a hole in the large end of the pin and then wrapping it around the shaft or tubes. Other tapered pins are secured with a nut screwed onto threads cut onto the small end of the pin.

tapered propeller shaft (reciprocating engine component). A propeller shaft with a tapered end that fits into a tapered hole inside the propeller hub. A tapered propeller shaft is prevented from turning in the hub by a hardened steel key that fits in matching grooves in the shaft and the hub.

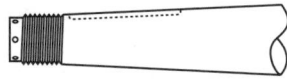

tapered propeller shaft

tapered punch. A handheld punch that is tapered from its full shank size to a smaller diameter at its end. Tapered punches are used to start bolts, pins, or rivets from their holes.

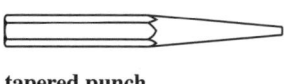

tapered punch

tapered roller bearings. A form of antifriction bearing that uses hardened steel rollers between hardened and polished, cone-shaped steel races. Tapered roller bearings take thrust loads as well as radial loads.

tapered-shank drill. A form of twist drill normally used in a large drill press or a lathe. The shank of the drill is tapered and is held in the spindle by friction. The drill is removed by forcing it out with a tapered wedge driven through an opening in the spindle.

taper reamer (metal-cutting tool). A tool for reaming a drilled hole for a tapered pin or for a taper pipe thread.

taper tap (thread-cutting tool). A type of thread-cutting tap used to start the threads in a hole. The first six or seven threads on the end of the tap are ground in the form of a taper so the tap can easily enter the hole.

tap extractor. A tool used to remove a broken tap from a hole. Taps are made of very hard and brittle steel and they can be broken off in the hole being tapped. The tap extractor has a series of fingers that can be stuck down into the hole through the flutes in the tap. When the tap extractor is turned with a wrench, the fingers turn the tap and screw it out of the hole.

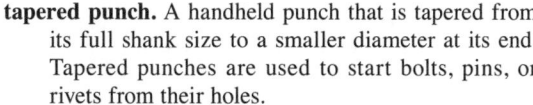

tapped resistor

tapped resistor (electrical component). A type of wire-wound resistor with connections made to the resistance wire at points between its ends. The connection to the resistance wire is permanent in some tapped resistors, but other resistors have a section of the wire left bare. A clamp can be moved to a point where it contacts the wire at the correct point to furnish the desired resistance. The clamp is then tightened.

tappet (reciprocating engine component). The component in the valve train of a reciprocating engine that rides on the lobes of the cam shaft or cam ring and pushes against the pushrod. A tappet is called a cam follower. In many reciprocating engines, the tappet incorporates a hydraulic valve lifter that automatically adjusts for the changes in the length of the valve train mechanism caused by temperature changes.

T

tare weight (aircraft weight and balance). The weight of all the chocks and other items used to secure an aircraft on the scales for weighing. The tare weight must be subtracted from the scale reading to find the weight of the aircraft.

target (radar display). The indication shown on an analog display resulting from a primary radar return or a radar beacon reply.

target (radar technology). Any of the many objects detected by radar.

target blade (helicopter rotor blade). The blade of a helicopter rotor identified as the reference blade when the rotor is being electronically checked for balance.

target resolution (air traffic control). A process to ensure that correlated radar targets do not touch.

target thrust reverser (turbine engine thrust reverser). A form of mechanical-blockage thrust reverser that uses two or more rectangular reverser panels to direct exhaust gases forward to slow the aircraft.

target symbol (radar display). A computer-generated indication shown on a radar display resulting from a primary radar return or a radar beacon reply.

tarmac. The British name for a hard-surfaced area on an airport where aircraft are tied down and serviced. The term tarmac comes from tarmacadam, a mixture of tar and crushed stone, often used as the surfacing material.

tarmac delay. The holding of an aircraft on the ground either before departure or after landing with no opportunity for its passengers to deplane.

tarmac delay aircraft. An aircraft whose pilot-in-command has requested to taxi to the ramp, gate, or alternate deplaning area to comply with the three-hour tarmac rule.

tarmac delay request. A request by the pilot-in-command to taxi to the ramp, gate, or alternate deplaning location to comply with the three-hour tarmac rule.

tarnish. A dull surface which forms on some types of metal when oxygen in the air changes some of the metal into its oxides. Polished aluminum, for example, tarnishes, or turns dull, when aluminum oxide forms on its surface.

tarpaulin. A large piece of heavy, waterproof canvas, fitted along its edges with eyelets. Ropes can be tied through the eyelets to hold the tarpaulin tight over whatever device it is protecting.

TAS. True airspeed. *See* true airspeed.

task. A knowledge area, flight procedure, or maneuver within an area of operation in a practical test standard (PTS).

tautening dope (aircraft finishing material). A finishing material brushed or sprayed on the fabric used to cover the framework of an aircraft. Aircraft dope has a film base of cotton fibers dissolved in certain acids and mixed with solvents and thinners. Plasticizers are mixed into the dope to give it resilience and keep it from being brittle.

When the dope is put on the fabric, it encapsulates, or surrounds, the fibers of the cloth, and as it dries, it shrinks and pulls the fibers close together. This shrinks, or tautens, the fabric on the framework. Some inorganic fabrics used to cover aircraft are shrunk with heat, and a special nontautening dope must be used with them. Nontautening dope does not shrink as much as tautening dope as it dries.

TAWS. *See* terrain awareness warning system.

taxi (aircraft operation). To move an aircraft along the ground or water under its own power, at a slow speed. An aircraft is taxied from an airport terminal to the runway, where it takes off.

taxi light (aircraft external light). A light, similar to the landing light, installed on an aircraft in such a way that it illuminates the runway or taxiway when the aircraft is on the ground in its normal attitude for taxiing.

taxi patterns (airport traffic control). Patterns established to illustrate the desired flow of ground traffic for the different runways or airport areas available for use.

taxiway (part of an airport). A paved strip that parallels the runways. Aircraft move along the taxiways from the terminal to the end of the runway so they will not interfere with aircraft using the runway for takeoff and landing.

taxiway centerline lights (airport lighting). Lights used to facilitate ground traffic under low visibility conditions, these lights are flush to the ground and emit a steady green color. Taxiway centerline lead-off/-on lights extend out from the taxiway centerline onto the runway to provide visual guidance to aircraft exiting/entering the runway and are alternately green and yellow.

taxiway edge lights (airport lighting). Blue-colored omnidirectional lights that outline the edges of a taxiway.

taxi weight (weight and balance). The total weight of a loaded aircraft. It includes all fuel, and is greater than the takeoff weight by the weight of fuel that will be burned during the taxi and runup operations.

taxonomy of educational objectives. A systematic classification scheme for sorting learning outcomes into three broad categories (cognitive, affective, and psychomotor) and ranking the desired outcomes in a developmental hierarchy from least complex to most complex.

TBO (time between overhauls). A time period specified by the manufacturer of an aircraft engine as the maximum length of time the engine should be run between overhauls without normal wear causing parts of the engine to be worn beyond safe limits. TBO depends upon the engine being operated properly and maintained in accordance with the engine manufacturer's recommendations.

The overhaul of an engine when it reaches its TBO hours is not mandatory except for certain commercial operators that have this requirement written into their operations manual.

TCA (terminal control area). Controlled airspace extending upward from the surface or higher to specified altitudes within which all aircraft are subject to operating rules and pilot and equipment requirements specified in 14 CFR Part 91.

TCAS (traffic alert and collision avoidance system). An electronic warning system installed in an aircraft that detects nearby aircraft and warns the pilot, showing the range, altitude, and course of the impending threat. The TCAS informs the pilot of the appropriate maneuver to use to avoid a collision.

TCAS I. *14 CFR Part 1:* "A TCAS that utilizes interrogations of, and replies from, airborne radar beacon transponders and provides traffic advisories to the pilot."

TCAS II. *14 CFR Part 1:* "A TCAS that utilizes interrogations of, and replies from airborne radar beacon transponders and provides traffic advisories and resolution advisories in the vertical plane."

TCAS III. *14 CFR Part 1:* "A TCAS that utilizes interrogation of, and replies from airborne radar beacon transponders and provides traffic advisories and resolution advisories in the vertical and horizontal planes to the pilot."

TCDS (Type Certificate Data Sheet). *See* Type Certificate Data Sheet.

TCH. *See* threshold crossing height.

TCLT (tentative calculated landing time) (air traffic control). A projected time calculated for the adapted vertex for each arrival aircraft based upon runway configuration, airport acceptance rate, airport arrival delay period, and other metered arrival aircraft. TCLT is either the vertex time of arrival (VTA) of the aircraft or the tentative or actual calculated landing time (TCLT/ACLT) of the previous aircraft plus the arrival aircraft interval (AAI), whichever is later. TCLT will be updated in response to the aircraft's progress and its current relationship to other arrivals.

TCO. *See* training course outline.

TCP (trichresyl phosphate). A colorless, combustible compound, $(CH_3C_6H_4O)_3PO$, that is used as a plasticizer in aircraft dope and an additive in gasoline and lubricating oil. TCP aids in scavenging lead deposits left in the cylinders when leaded fuel is burned.

TDC (top dead center). The position of a piston in the cylinder of a reciprocating engine when the piston is at the top of its stroke and the piston pin, crank pin, and the center of the crankshaft are all in line.

TDZE. *See* touchdown zone elevation.

teaching. Instructing, training, or imparting knowledge or skill; the profession of someone who teaches.

teaching lecture. An oral presentation that is directed toward desired learning outcomes. Some student participation is allowed.

tear-down area (overhaul shop). The area in an overhaul shop set aside for disassembling the equipment being overhauled. Tear-down areas are usually located near the point the equipment is received into the shop. There are facilities in the tear-down area to remove most of the grease and dirt from the equipment before it is taken into the main part of the shop.

TEB (triethyl borane). A fuel additive that ignites on contact with oxygen. It is used as a catalyst to ignite the low-flammable JP-7 used in the Lockheed SR-71 fuel during engine start and afterburner lights.

TEC. *See* tower enroute control.

technetium. A synthetically produced, silvery-gray, metallic chemical element. Technetium's symbol is Tc, and its atomic number is 43. Technetium is used in the manufacture of corrosion-resistant steel.

technically advanced aircraft (TAA). A general aviation aircraft that contains a global positioning system (GPS) navigator with a moving map display, plus any additional systems. Traditional systems such as autopilots are included when combined with GPS navigators. This includes aircraft used in both VFR and IFR operations, with systems certified to either VFR or IFR standards.

Technical Standard Order. *See* TSO.

technician. A specialist in one of the technical fields. In research and development, technicians often assist engineers. The engineer's knowledge of the theory behind the project is usually greater than that of the technician, but the technician usually has a more practical approach and is able to build the things the engineer designs.

technique. The manner in which procedures are executed.

tee fitting. A connector, made in the shape of the letter T, for joining either rigid or flexible fluid lines.

teetering hinge (helicopter rotor). A hinge that permits the blades of a semi-rigid rotor system to flap as a unit.

Teflon. The registered trade name for a fluorocarbon resin. Because of its good resistance to chemical action and its strength at elevated temperatures, Teflon is used for fluid lines and backup rings in fluid power components.

TEL (tetraethyl lead). An additive used in aviation gasoline to improve its antidetonation characteristics. Tetraethyl lead, $Pb(C_2H_5)_4$, is a heavy, oily, poisonous liquid mixed with the gasoline at the refinery. Tetraethyl lead increases the critical pressure and temperature of the fuel.

telegraphing (composites). The distortion of the repair plies caused by imperfections in the inner layers showing up in the layers above it.

telemetering. A method used to transmit quantitative information from a vehicle in flight to a station on the ground where this information can be used. Airplanes, missiles, rockets, and other types of complex devices are equipped with many different types of instruments that measure movement, pressure, temperature, acceleration, and strain.

The output from these instruments is coded and transmitted to flight test stations on the ground. Here it is decoded and given to the engineers in a form they can use to determine what is happening to the vehicle in flight.

telephone information briefing service (TIBS). A continuous telephone recording of area and/or route meteorological briefings, airspace procedures, and special aviation-oriented announcements.

telescope (type of movement). To slide one section of an object into another section or into a slightly larger sleeve. The name comes from the sections of a telescope that slide into each other to make the instrument smaller to store when it is not in use.

telescoping gage (measuring tool). A precision measuring tool used to measure the inside diameter of a hole. A telescoping gage consists of a hardened steel pin that slides, or telescopes, into a hardened steel sleeve. The pin is spring-loaded outward, and a T-handle, extending out from the center of the pin and sleeve, can be twisted to lock the pin in the sleeve.

A telescoping gage with the correct range of measurement is put in the hole whose inside diameter is to be measured, and the lock is released. The spring pushes the pin and the sleeve against the sides of the hole. The gage is held level across the hole, and the lock is tightened. The gage is then removed from the hole, and its length is measured with a micrometer caliper.

telling-and-doing technique. A technique of flight instruction that consists of the instructor first telling the student about a new procedure and then demonstrating it. This is followed by the student telling and the instructor doing. Third, the student explains the new procedure while doing it. Last, the instructor evaluates while the student performs the procedure.

tellurium. A brittle, silvery-white, metallic chemical element. Tellurium's symbol is Te, its atomic number is 52, and its atomic weight is 127.60. Tellurium is used in the production of corrosion-resistant steel.

TEMAC. Trailing edge of the mean aerodynamic chord. *See* mean aerodynamic chord.

temper (metal condition). The condition of a metal with regard to its strength and hardness.

temperature. A measure of the intensity of heat, or the hotness or coldness of a body or material. Temperature is measured on one of four scales: Celsius, Fahrenheit, Kelvin, and Rankine. The three reference points used to measure temperature are:

1. Absolute zero, the point at which all molecular activity stops: All molecular activity stops at 0°K, 0°R, –273°C, and –460°F.
2. The point at which pure water changes from a liquid into a solid (freezes): Water freezes at 0°C, 32°F, 273°K, and 492°R.
3. The point at which pure water changes from a liquid into a gas (boils): Water boils at 100°C, 212°F, 373°K, and 672°R.

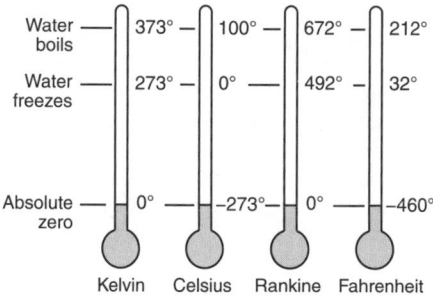

temperature scales

temperature bulb (electrical thermometer component). A temperature-sensing device used with a ratiometer-type thermometer. A length of small-diameter nickel wire is wound around an insulator and enclosed in a thin stainless steel tube. This bulb is surrounded by the medium whose temperature is to be measured so the nickel wire can reach the same temperature as the medium. The resistance of the wire changes with its temperature, and a sensitive resistance-measuring instrument measures the resistance of the wire and displays this resistance in terms of degrees of temperature.

temperature coefficient of resistance (electrical resistance). The change in electrical resistance for each degree Celsius of temperature change.

temperature gauge. The thermometer system, required in all type-certificated hot air balloons, that gives a constant reading of the inside air temperature at the top of the envelope. May be direct-reading or remote—using a thermocouple or thermistor connected to a gauge in the basket, or reading signals sent by a transmitter.

temperature gradient (thermodynamics). The rate of temperature change with distance in a given direction from a specified reference point.

temperature inversion (meteorology). A layer of air in which temperature increases with altitude.

temperature-dew point spread (meteorology). The difference between the temperature of the air and the dew point of the same air. It is an indicator of the probability of fog formation, the smaller the spread the more likely the formation of fog. *See* dew point.

temperature recorder (structural damage monitor). Temperature-sensitive paint that changes its appearance, usually from dull to shiny when a specified temperature has been reached by the surface on which it is applied. This provides a permanent record of the maximum temperature reached.

tempered glass. Glass that has been heat-treated to increase its strength. Tempered glass is used in birdproof, heated windshields for high-speed aircraft.

tempering steel (heat treatment). A process in the heat treatment of steel in which some of its hardness and brittleness are removed. The steel is first hardened by heating it to the correct temperature and then quenching it in oil, water, or brine. This makes the steel hard, but also brittle. The hard steel is then reheated, but to a lower temperature, and held at this temperature for a specified period of time. It is then allowed to cool to room temperature in still air. This reheating and cooling is called tempering.

template (layout tool). An outline pattern made of sheet metal, plastic, or heavy paper that can be traced on the material of which a part is to be made. Much time is saved by using a template rather than having to lay out the outline of the part from the engineering drawing each time a part is to be made.

template (registration numbers)

temporary flight restriction (TFR). Restrictions to flight imposed in order to: (1) Protect persons and property in the air or on the surface from an existing or imminent flight associated hazard; (2) Provide a safe environment for the operation of disaster relief aircraft; (3) Prevent an unsafe congestion of sightseeing aircraft above an incident; (4) Protect the President, Vice President, or other public figures; and, (5) Provide a safe environment for space agency operations. Pilots are expected to check appropriate NOTAMs during flight planning when conducting flight in an area where a TFR is in effect.

tensile strength. The strength of a material that opposes the stresses which try to stretch or lengthen it.

tensile stress. A stress that tries to pull an object apart.

tensiometer. A precision instrument used to measure the tension on a steel control cable installed in an aircraft. The tensiometer holds the cable at two points, and an anvil presses on the cable between these points and deflects it a specific amount. The amount of force needed to deflect the cable is measured, and this value is used on a chart to determine the tension on this particular type and diameter of cable.

tension. Maintaining an excessively strong grip on the control column, usually resulting in an overcontrolled situation.

tension adjusters (aircraft control system components). Devices used in the control system of some large aircraft to maintain a constant tension on the control cables as the aircraft dimensions change because of changes in temperature. The dimensions of the large mass of aluminum of which an airplane is made change a great deal from the time the plane leaves a hot ramp until it reaches the subzero temperatures of high altitude. If tension adjusters were not used, the control cables would become too loose when the metal contracts and the airplane becomes smaller.

tentative calculated landing time. *See* TCLT.

tera. The metric prefix that means a million million, or 1 x 10^{12}.

terbium. A soft, silvery-gray, rare-earth, metallic chemical element. Terbium's symbol is Tb, its atomic number is 65, and its atomic weight is 158.924. Terbium is used in the manufacture of semiconductor devices and in laser technology.

terminal (computer system). The device in a computer system that allows the human operator to interface with the computer. A computer terminal normally contains a video display similar to a television screen and a keyboard much like the keyboard of a typewriter.

terminal (electrical wiring component). A device that is crimped or soldered onto the end of an electrical wire to allow the wire to be attached to a component or terminal strip. Electrical wire terminals may be in the form of a ring, a spade, or a flag, and they may be insulated or uninsulated. *See* illustration for solderless connections.

terminal aerodrome forecast (TAF). A report established for the 5 statute mile radius around an airport which uses the same descriptors and abbreviations as the METAR report.

terminal area (airspace). A general term used to describe airspace in which approach control service or airport traffic control service is provided.

terminal area facility. A facility providing air traffic control service for arriving and departing IFR, VFR, Special VFR, and sometimes enroute aircraft.

terminal arrival area (TAA). The published or assigned track by which aircraft are transitioned from the RNAV en route structure to the terminal area. A terminal arrival area consists of a designated volume of airspace (often called a "T" structure) designed to allow aircraft to enter a protected area with guaranteed obstacle clearance and signal reception where the initial approach course is intercepted. The TAA normally provides a NoPT ("no procedure turn") for aircraft using the approach. The TAA is not found on all RNAV approaches; when the TAA is published, it replaces the minimum safe altitude (MSA) for that approach procedure..

terminal automation system (TAS) (air traffic control). The terminal automation system receives radar data and aircraft flight plan information that is then presented to air traffic controllers on monitors at over 162 radar control facilities and hundreds of FAA and contract control towers. The system consists of processors and displays that present air traffic controllers with the total airspace picture. Controllers use automation to provide ATC service to pilots in the airspace immediately around major airports. These ATC services include the separation and sequencing of air traffic, conflict and terrain avoidance alerts, weather advisories, and radar vectoring for departing and arriving traffic. Some currently-used TAS tracking systems include ARTS IIE, ARTS IIIA, ARTS IIIE, STARS, and MEARTS. *See also* digital terminal automation system (DTAS).

terminal control area. Blocks of airspace surrounding the busiest airports throughout the United States; e.g., Atlanta, Chicago, New York, Los Angeles, and San Francisco. These are typically Class B airports. Terminal Control Area charts should be used when operating in these areas.

terminal data link system (TDLS). A system that provides digital automatic terminal information service (D-ATIS) on a specified radio frequency and also, for subscribers, in a text message via data link to the cockpit or to a gate printer. TDLS also provides pre-departure clearances (PDC) at selected airports to subscribers, through a service provider, in text to the cockpit or to a gate printer. In addition, TDLS emulates the flight data input/output (FDIO) information within the control tower.

T

terminal Doppler weather radar (TDWR). At many U.S. airports this type of radar is used to look at the airspace around and over the airport for detection of microbursts, gust fronts, wind shifts and precipitation intensities. TDWR products advise the controller of wind shear and microburst events impacting all runways and the areas $\frac{1}{2}$ mile on either side of the extended centerline of the runways out to 3 miles on final approach and 2 miles out on departure.

terminal forecast (FT). A forecast that predicts the weather conditions for an area within 5 nautical miles of a runway complex.

terminal mode. In flying an activated GPS or GPS (RNAV) approach procedure, this is the FMS/RNAV sensitivity mode in which the aircraft operates when within 30 NM of an airport. In the terminal mode of the FMS/GPS RNAV unit, the required navigation performance sensitivity of the course deviation indicator becomes 1 NM. Also called approach arm mode.

terminal radar approach control (TRACON). A facility that provides radar and nonradar services at major airports. The primary responsibility of each TRACON is to ensure safe separation of aircraft transitioning from departure to cruise flight or from cruise to a landing approach.

terminal radar service area. *See* TRSA.

terminal strip (electrical system component). A strip of insulating plastic material that contains a number of threaded studs to which electrical wires can be attached. Ring-type terminals on the wires are slipped over the studs and secured with a lock washer and nut. Some terminal strips have barriers between adjacent studs to keep the wires from shorting between the studs.

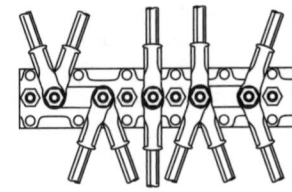

terminal strip

terminal velocity. The maximum speed a freely falling object can reach when falling through the air. At the terminal velocity, the wind resistance trying to slow down the object exactly balances the force of acceleration trying to speed up the object.

terminal velocity descent (balloon operation). A term used by balloonists for the speed obtained when the balloon is allowed to fall until it apparently stop accelerating, at which point the envelope acts as a parachute and its vertical speed is no longer affected by its lifting gas, but only by its shape (which is caused by design), load, and other factors.

terminal VFR radar service. A national program instituted to extend the terminal radar services provided instrument flight rules (IFR) aircraft to visual flight rules (VFR) aircraft. The program is divided into four types service referred to as basic radar service, terminal radar service area (TRSA) service, Class B service and Class C service (*see* AIM). The type of service provided at a particular location is listed in the A/FD.

terminal VOR (electronic navigation facility). A low-powered VOR that is normally located on an airport.

terminating decimal. A decimal fraction which can be expressed as a definite number. The fraction $\frac{2}{5}$ produces a terminating decimal, 0.4. A fraction that cannot be expressed as a definite number is called a repeating decimal. The fraction $\frac{1}{3}$ is a repeating decimal, and it is equivalent to 0.333333333.... .

terneplate. Thin sheets of steel protected from rust with a thin coating of lead. The lead coating allows terneplate to accept solder so the seams in a tank made from terneplate can be made leakproof.

TERPS, or United States Standard for Terminal Instrument Procedures (FAA Order 8260.3). Document published and updated by the FAA that contains the criteria for creation, review, approval, and publication of the procedures for instrument approach and departure of aircraft to and from U.S. civil and military airports. This order prescribes standardized methods for use in designing instrument flight procedures. *See also* TPP, U.S. Terminal Procedures Publications.

terrain and obstacle database. An electronic database storing details of the significant terrain features and obstacles that could potentially pose a threat to aircraft flight. Some obstructions, especially manmade, may not be in the database, even if it is current. Pilots should not plan a flight by depending on the database to keep the aircraft clear of obstacles and obstructions to navigation

terrain awareness warning system (TAWS). An onboard system that can alert the pilot to a number of potential hazards presented by proximate terrain such as excessive rate of descent, excessive closure rate to terrain, and altitude loss after takeoff.

terrain display. A pictorial display that shows surrounding terrain and obstacles that present a potential threat to the aircraft, given present altitude. The display draws terrain information from a terrain and obstacle database.

terrain following (flight operation). The flight of a military aircraft maintaining a constant AGL altitude above the terrain or the highest obstruction. The altitude of the aircraft will constantly change with the varying terrain and/or obstruction.

terrain inhibit switch. A switch that allows the pilot to suppress all visual and auditory warnings given by a terrain system. This switch is often used to silence nuisance alerts when in deliberate operation in the vicinity of terrain.

terrestrial radiation (meteorology). The total infrared radiation emitted by the earth and its atmosphere.

terrain system. Any cockpit system that provides the pilot with a pictorial view of surrounding terrain, and in some cases, visual and/or auditory alerts when the aircraft is operating in close proximity to terrain.

test. A set of questions, problems, or exercises for determining whether a person has a particular knowledge or skill.

test club (type of propeller). A wide-blade, short-diameter propeller used on a reciprocating engine when it is run in a test stand. A test club applies a specific load to the engine and forces the maximum amount of air through the cylinder cooling fins.

test item. A question, problem, or exercise that measures a single objective and requires a single response.

test stand (engine maintenance facility). A facility used for testing and running in engines. It includes an engine mount and a booth with controls and monitoring instruments.

tethering (balloon operation). Operation of a manned balloon secured to the ground by a series of lines.

tetraethyl lead (TEL). A heavy, oily, poisonous liquid, $Pb(C_2H_5)_4$, that is mixed into aviation gasoline to improve its antiknock quality by increasing its critical pressure and temperature.

tetrahedron (wind direction indicator). A large, lightweight framework made in the shape of a tetrahedron, a triangular-shaped solid. The framework is covered with thin metal, wood, or fabric and is painted a bright color. It is mounted on a pivot so it is free to swing with the wind, and is installed near the center of an airport beside the runway, where it is easily visible from the air. The tetrahedron always points into the wind and shows pilots approaching the airport the correct direction to make their landing approach.

tetrode (electron tube). An electron tube with four active electrodes. A tetrode has a cathode, a control grid, a screen grid, and an anode, or plate.

TFR. *See* temporary flight restriction.

thallium. A soft, bluish-white, malleable, highly toxic, metallic chemical element. Thallium's symbol is Tl, its atomic number is 81, and its atomic weight is 204.37. Thallium is used in the manufacture of photocells and infrared detection devices and in poison for rodents.

"that is correct" (air traffic control). A phrase used in ATC–pilot communications to indicate that the other party's understanding of a communicated message is correct.

theater (in flight operations use). A geographical area in which the distance between the flightcrew member's flight duty period departure point and arrival point differs by no more than 60° longitude.

theodolite. An optical instrument used for surveying and weather observation. A theodolite contains a telescope fitted with cross hairs, and mounted on a platform. The platform is fitted with two bubble levels and an accurate magnetic compass. The platform is leveled and pointed toward true north by applying the correction for declination, or variation, to compensate for the difference between magnetic north and true north.

An azimuth scale (a scale that measures the horizontal direction the telescope moves) measures the bearing from the theodolite to any object visible through the telescope. A vertical scale measures the angle the telescope is inclined upward from its level position.

In weather observation, the theodolite is used to track the movement of a weather balloon to find the direction and velocity of the wind at various altitudes. A theodolite is also used with a ceiling light to measure the height of the base of clouds at night.

therapeutic mask adapter (oxygen system component). A type of adapter used in a constant-flow oxygen system to increase the flow of oxygen to a mask being used by a passenger known to have a heart or respiratory problem.

thermal (meteorology). A column of rising air. Buildings and automobile traffic heat the air above cities and this heated air rises in a column, called a thermal. Sailplanes gain altitude by circling in a thermal and being carried upward by it. Thermals are easily found, because clouds normally form at their top. Air containing water vapor is carried upward until it reaches a level at which the vapor condenses and becomes visible droplets of liquid water. These droplets form the cloud.

thermal anti-icing system (TAI). An aircraft anti-icing system that uses hot air to prevent ice forming on the leading edges of the wings and tail surfaces. Hot air from the turbine-engine compressor or from a shroud around the exhaust system of a reciprocating engine flows through ducts in the leading edges of the wings and tail surfaces to heat them so ice cannot form on them.

thermal barrier (high-speed aerodynamics). A term used to describe one of the limits to the speed at which an aircraft can fly. The thermal barrier is the speed limit caused by heat produced by friction of the air passing over the aircraft surfaces. At this speed, the heat is severe enough to damage the aircraft structure.

thermal circuit breaker. A type of circuit breaker that opens an electrical circuit when excessive current flows through it. Movable contacts are mounted on a bimetallic strip which is bent in such a way that they are forced tightly against fixed contacts in the circuit breaker housing. When more current than the circuit breaker is designed to carry flows through the bimetallic strip, the strip heats up and warps. When it warps, it snaps the contacts apart and opens the circuit.

thermal circulation (meteorology). Atmospheric circulation caused by the heating and cooling of air.

thermal coefficient of resistance. The ratio of the change in resistance of a material to a change in its temperature. The coefficient is positive if the resistance of the material increases as its temperature goes up. The coefficient is negative if the resistance becomes less as the material gets hotter. The thermal coefficient of resistance is usually expressed in such units as ohms per degrees Celsius ($\Omega/°C$).

thermal conduction. A method of heat transfer in which heat energy is transferred from one body into another when the bodies are in direct contact.

thermal conductor. A material that transfers heat energy by conduction with very little loss. Most metals are good thermal conductors, and such materials as paper, wood, and water are poor thermal conductors, or are thermal insulators.

thermal cutout (electric motor component). A special circuit breaker mounted inside an electric motor. The thermal cutout opens the power lead to the motor if the motor overheats for any cause. These causes could be: too great a load, too low an operating speed, or lack of cooling airflow. As soon as the motor cools down, the thermal cutout automatically resets itself, and the motor runs again. Thermal cutouts are also called automatic-reset circuit breakers.

thermal decomposition (chemistry). A chemical reaction in which a single compound breaks up into two or more simpler compounds, or elements, when heated.

thermal dimpling. *See* hot dimpling.

thermal efficiency (heat engine specification). The ratio of the amount of useful work produced by a heat engine to the amount of work that could be done by the heat energy in the fuel used.

thermal expansion. The change in the physical size of a material caused by the material absorbing heat. Thermal expansion causes a material to expand both in its length and in its volume.

thermal expansion coefficient. A dimensionless number that relates to the change in the physical dimensions of a material as the temperature of the material changes. The thermal expansion coefficient of aluminum is approximately twice that of steel.

thermal fatigue (metallurgy). Fatigue of a metal caused by repeated heating and cooling.

thermal index (TI) (soaring). For any given level is the temperature of the air parcel having risen at the dry adiabatic lapse rate (DALR) subtracted from the ambient temperature. Experience has shown that a TI should be –2 for thermals to form and be sufficiently strong for soaring flight.

thermal insulator. A material that does not conduct heat. It is used to prevent the transfer of heat from one point to another.

thermalling (glider operations). Locating and utilizing thermals for soaring flight in order to gain altitude (also referred to as "thermal soaring"). The thermal, which is a rising mass of buoyant air in a vertical, convective current, contains "plumes" or "bubbles" that provide lift for soaring flight. The pilot first attempts to find thermals by being aware of lift indicators, and then uses the thermal's plume or bubbles to gain altitude by first entering a thermal, then centering it, and finally leaving it. (*See also* centering.)

thermally actuated switch (electrical component). A switch whose contacts are actuated by changing temperature. The contacts are normally mounted on a bimetallic strip that warps when its temperature changes. When the strip warps, the contacts either snap closed or snap open, depending on whether the switch is actuated by a descending or a rising temperature.

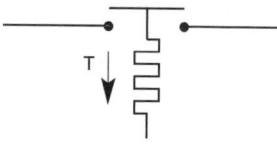

thermally actuated switch

thermal relief valve (hydraulic system component). A pressure relief valve in a hydraulic system that relieves the pressure which builds up when heat expands the fluid. Thermal relief valves are installed in sections of the system in which fluid can be trapped, usually in the lines between the selector valves and the actuators. When fluid in these lines absorbs heat and expands, the thermal relief valve momentarily unseats and releases enough fluid back into the system return manifold to relieve the high pressure and prevent damage to the system.

thermal runaway (nickel-cadmium battery malfunction). A condition that can occur in a nickel-cadmium battery in which the battery overheats because of excess current. A nickel-cadmium battery has a very low internal resistance, but if an excessive amount of current flows from it, even its low resistance will cause it to overheat. The center cells get hotter than the outer cells, which transfer some of their heat to the outside air, and when the center cells overheat, their voltage and resistance both drop.

When the generator puts current back into the battery, the center cells take the most current and get even hotter. As they get hotter, their voltage and resistance continue to drop, and they take more current. This current increase continues until the battery is destroyed.

thermal shock (engine operating condition). The rapid change in engine operating temperature that occurs when engine power is suddenly reduced at the same time the airspeed, thus the cooling, is increased. Thermal shock occurs when an aircraft is required to rapidly descend to a lower altitude.

thermal stress cracking (transparent plastics). Crazing and cracking of some thermoplastic resins caused by exposure to elevated temperatures. *See* crazing.

thermal turbulence (soaring). Thermals, or rising columns of air, in the boundary layer generated by uneven surface heating.

thermal wave (meteorology). Waves, often but not always marked by cloud streets, that are excited by convection disturbing an overlying stable layer. Also called convection waves.

thermionic current. The flow of electrons in a vacuum tube from a heated cathode to a positively charged anode, or plate. When the cathode is heated, electrons gain so much energy that their orbits increase in size enough for them to be influenced by the positive voltage on the plate. They leave the cathode and flow to the plate.

thermistor. A semiconductor device whose electrical resistance varies with its temperature. The resistance of a thermistor material decreases as its temperature increases. Thermistor materials are used in fire detection systems. When the thermistor is cold, its resistance is high, but when it is heated in a fire, its resistance drops enough to operate the fire warning system.

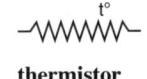

thermistor

thermistor material. A material with a negative temperature coefficient that causes its resistance to decrease as its temperature increases.

thermoammeter. An ammeter used to measure the radio-frequency (RF) alternating current flowing in a circuit. The RF current flows through a short piece of resistance wire and heats it. The amount the wire is heated is proportional to the square of the current flowing through it.

A thermocouple is welded to the center of the resistance wire, and a DC ammeter measures the current produced by the thermocouple. This current is proportional to the temperature of the resistance wire. The dial of the thermocouple instrument is calibrated in amps of RF alternating current.

thermocouple. A device used to generate a small electrical current. A thermocouple is made up of two dissimilar metal wires, such as iron and constantan, copper and constantan, or chromel and alumel. The ends of these wires are joined to form a loop. Electrical current flows through the wires when there is a temperature difference between the junctions, the points at which the wires join. The amount of current flowing in the loop is determined by three things:

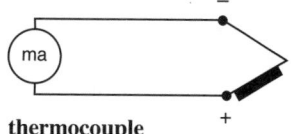

thermocouple

1. The types of metals used for the wires
2. The temperature difference between the two junctions
3. The resistance of the thermocouple wires

Iron and constantan or copper and constantan thermocouples are used to measure the cylinder head temperature of reciprocating engines, and chromel and alumel thermocouples are used to measure the exhaust gas temperature in both reciprocating and gas turbine engines.

thermocouple fire detection system. A fire detection system that works on the principle of the rate-of-temperature-rise. Thermocouples are connected in series and installed in various locations in the area to be protected. One thermocouple is surrounded by insulation that prevents its temperature changing rapidly.

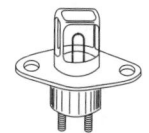

fire-detection thermocouple

In the event of a fire, the temperature of all the thermocouples except the protected one will rise immediately and a fire warning will be initiated. In the case of a general overheat condition, the temperature of all the thermocouples will rise uniformly and since there is no temperature difference between the thermocouples, there will be no fire warning.

thermocouple house thermal (meteorology). A thermal that forms frequently in the same or similar location.

thermodynamic diagram. In general, this type of chart can represent the thermodynamic states of a material, typically a fluid; in meteorology it is used to show an analysis of the state of the atmosphere with the results derived from radiosonde measurements (usually obtained by weather balloon). It presents plotted isopleths (showing the equal or connecting points of the isobars and isotherms) of values of pressure, temperature, and water vapor content, as well as dry and saturated adiabats. Various forms of this chart exist for many different purposes in science and engineering, the most commonly used in meteorology in the U.S. being the "skew-T/log-P" chart. *See* adiabat; skew-T chart.

thermodynamic horsepower. The power that would be produced by a turboprop engine under standard-day sea-level conditions if the engine were run at a maximum turbine inlet temperature.

T

thermodynamics. The branch of physics that deals with mechanical actions caused or controlled by heat.

thermoelectricity. The flow of electrons caused by heat in a metal or in a junction of two metals. The current flowing in a thermocouple circuit is a form of thermoelectricity.

thermograph (meteorology). A continuously recording thermometer.

thermometer. An instrument used to measure temperature. Some thermometers measure the change in the volume of a liquid caused by its expansion or contraction with changes in its temperature. Others measure the change in pressure of a confined gas as its temperature changes. Electrical thermometers measure the current produced in a thermocouple as the temperature difference between the thermocouple junctions changes, and resistance thermometers measure temperature by measuring the current forced by a constant voltage through a resistance that changes with the temperature.

thermonuclear action. The release of energy that takes place when the nucleus of one element is changed into the nucleus of another element by the action of heat.

thermopile. An assembly of thermocouples connected together. These thermocouples can be connected in series to get a higher voltage or in parallel to get a larger amount of current. Thermopiles are used to measure temperature or to change electromagnetic radiant energy into electrical power.

thermoplastic material. A type of plastic material that becomes soft when it is heated, and hardens when it is cooled. Thermoplastic materials can be softened and hardened many times without the strength or quality of the material being affected. Transparent acrylic plastic resin is an example of a thermoplastic material.

thermosetting material. A type of plastic material that, when once hardened by heat, cannot be softened by being heated again. Phenolic resin is an example of a thermosetting material.

thermosphere. The highest layer of the atmosphere that begins above the mesosphere and gradually fades away into space.

thermostat. A temperature-sensitive electrical switch. A thermostat is used with a combustion heater to control the temperature of the air inside the cabin of an aircraft. The thermostat contains an electrical switch that closes when the temperature drops to a preset value. Current flowing through the closed switch opens the heater fuel valve, allowing the heater to begin heating the air. When the cabin air temperature rises to the upper value for which the thermostat is set, the switch opens, and the fuel valve shuts off the flow of fuel to the heater.

thermostatic bypass valve (reciprocating engine lubricating system component). A temperature-sensing valve in an oil cooler that opens when the oil is cold and allows it to flow around the core of the cooler, between the core and the cooler jacket. When the oil is hot, the bypass valve closes and forces the oil to flow through the core of the cooler.

thermostatic expansion valve (air conditioning system component). The component in a vapor-cycle cooling system that meters the refrigerant into the evaporator. The amount of refrigerant metered by the thermostatic expansion valve, or TXV, is determined by the temperature and pressure of the refrigerant as it leaves the evaporator coils. The TXV changes the refrigerant from a high-pressure liquid into a spray of low-pressure liquid.

thermoswitch. An electrical switch that closes a circuit when it is exposed to a specified high temperature.

thickness gage. A precision measuring tool made of a series of narrow strips of steel. Each strip is ground to an accurate thickness with the thickness marked on each gage. Thickness gages are used to measure the clearance, or the distance between parts, by finding the thickest gage that can be slipped between them.

thinner (finishing system component). A solvent mixed with a finishing material, such as lacquer, dope, or enamel, to reduce its viscosity so it can be sprayed.

third-class lever. A lever in which the force is applied between the fulcrum and the weight. The force needed to move the weight is greater than the weight, but the distance moved by the weight is greater than that moved by the force.

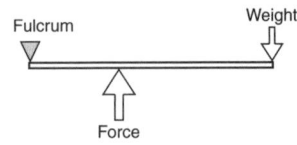

third-class lever

thixotropic (composites). The property of certain gels which liquify when subjected to vibrating forces such as ultrasonic waves or even simple shaking. They resolidify when allowed to stand.

thixotropic agent (plastic resin component). A material, such as microballoons, added to a resin to give it body and increase its workability. *See* microballoons.

thorium. A heavy, silvery-white, malleable, metallic chemical element. Thorium's symbol is Th, its atomic number is 90, and its atomic weight is 232. Thorium is slightly radioactive and is used as an alloy with tungsten to make filaments for incandescent electric lights. It is also a potential source of nuclear energy.

thread (machine fastener component). Helical grooves cut onto the surface of a bolt or screw. Mating threads are cut into the inside of a nut. The threads inside the nut match the threads on the outside of the bolt, and the nut is turned down over the threads of the bolt to produce a clamping action that holds parts of a machine together. A threaded bolt is a form of inclined plane.

thread (textiles). Long filaments made by twisting together short lengths of natural fibers, such as cotton or linen, to form a continuous strand. Threads of synthetic materials are made of a single continuous filament. These are called monofilament threads.

thread chaser (maintenance hand tool). A cutting tool that is used to remove damaged areas in threaded fasteners. There is a cutter for each thread pitch.

thread pitch (threaded fastener specification). The linear distance from the apex (peak) of one thread to the similar position on the next thread on a threaded fastener.

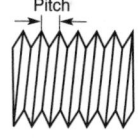

thread pitch

three-axis automatic pilot. An automatic flight control system for an aircraft that controls the movement of the aircraft about all three of its axes.

three-dimensional cam. A drum-shaped cam in a hydromechanical fuel control whose outer surface is precision ground in such a way that followers riding over it as it moves up and down and rotates move mechanical linkages to control the fuel according to a preprogrammed schedule.

three-dimensional object. An object that has length, width, and depth. A cube, for example, is a three-dimensional object. A flat, or plane, surface on the other hand, has only length and width and is two-dimensional.

three-hour tarmac rule. Refers to the Department of Transportation (DOT) "enhancing airline passenger protections" requirement which says, if tarmac delays are anticipated to reach 3 hours, the pilot-in-command (or aircraft operator if the flight crew cannot be reached) can request for an aircraft to return to the ramp, gate, or alternate deplaning area.

three-phase alternating current. The form of alternating current produced by a generator with three sets of windings. The three windings are arranged in such a way that the current and voltage in each winding is 120 electrical degrees out of phase with the current and voltage in either of the other two windings.

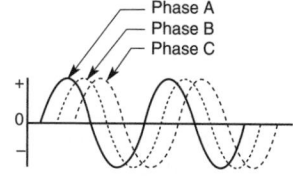

three-phase AC

The three windings can be connected in either a delta or a Y-arrangement. In a delta connection, the three windings are connected in series. The voltage across any one of the three windings is the same as that across the other windings. The total current is 1.73 times the current through any of the individual windings.

In a Y-connected three-phase circuit, one end of each of the windings is connected to a common neutral point. The voltage across any two windings is 1.73 times the voltage between any single winding and the neutral point. The current through any two windings is the same as the current through any single winding.

three-point landing (aircraft operation). A full-stall landing of an airplane equipped with a tail wheel. In a three-point landing, the main wheels and the tail wheel touch the ground at the same time. A three-point landing with a tail wheel airplane is desirable, but landing an airplane with a nose wheel so the main wheels and the nose wheel touch the ground at the same time is not normally considered a good operating procedure.

three-pole, single-throw switch. An electrical switch that has three sets of contacts, controlled by a single operating handle. A three-pole, single-throw switch can select two conditions, such as on and off, in three separate circuits.

three-pole single-throw switch

three-state buffer. A digital logic device used as a switch in an integrated circuit chip. When there is a logic low on the control line, the device acts as a closed switch with the in and out lines connected, a low on the in line produces a low on the out line, and a high on the in line produces a high on the out line. When there is a high on the control line, the device acts as an open switch, placing a high impedance between the in and the out lines.

three-state buffer

three-view drawing. An orthographic drawing showing three views of a part. There are six possible views, but the three most commonly used for aircraft drawings are the front, right-side, and top views.

three-way light switch. A type of switch that allows an electrical light to be turned on or off at either of two locations. Three-way light switches are used at the top and the bottom of stairs and at either end of a long hall.

threshold (runway location). The beginning of that portion of the runway that is usable for landing.

threshold crossing height (TCH). (1) The height of the glide slope above the runway threshold. (2) The theoretical height above the runway threshold at which the aircraft's glideslope antenna would be if the aircraft maintains the trajectory established by the mean ILS glideslope or MLS glidepath.

threshold lights (runway lights). Fixed green lights arranged symmetrically left and right of the runway centerline, identifying the runway threshold.

threshold of pain (intensity of sound). The intensity at which sound begins to cause pain. A sound intensity of 150 decibels which is often produced near an operating jet engine is normally considered to be the threshold of pain.

throatless shears (sheet metal tool). A floor- or bench-mounted metalworking tool used to cut across large sheets of thin metal. Short cutting blades, operated by a lever, cut across the sheet in much the same way scissors cut across a sheet of paper.

throat microphone. A type of microphone used by a person operating in an extremely noisy area such as the cockpit of an airplane. The throat microphone is strapped around the person's neck so the sensitive pickup rests over the larynx (the part of the throat containing the vocal cords). When the person wearing the microphone talks, vibrations of the larynx vibrate the microphone and produce an electrical signal that can be changed into sound.

throttle (aircraft engine control). The control in an aircraft that regulates the power or thrust the pilot wants the engine to develop.

throttle body (fuel metering system component). The component in a reciprocating engine fuel metering system through which all of the air that flows into the engine must pass. A throttle valve controls the amount of air flowing into the engine, and the main metering system meters the proper amount of fuel for this air.

throttle ice (carburetor ice). A type of ice that forms on the throttle valve of an aircraft carburetor when the throttle is partially closed. The temperature drop caused by the pressure drop across the partially closed throttle valve, and by the evaporation of the fuel, forces moisture to condense out of the air and freeze on the throttle-valve plate.

through bolts (reciprocating engine component). Long threaded rods that extend across the crankcase of an aircraft reciprocating engine to hold the crankcase halves together. The through bolts pass through the cylinder base flanges of one cylinder on each side of the crankcase, and nuts on the through bolts hold the cylinders to the crankcase, as well as holding the halves of the crankcase together.

throw (reciprocating engine crankshaft). The offset in the crankshaft of a reciprocating engine to which the connecting rods are attached. Radial engines have only one throw for each row of cylinders. In-line and horizontally opposed engines normally have one throw for every cylinder, and V-engines have one throw for each pair of cylinders.

throwaway part. A part of a mechanism designed and built in such a way that it is not economically repairable. When the part fails, it is more economical to throw it away and put in a new one than it would be to repair it.

throw-over control (airplane controls). A type of airplane control wheel that may be moved from in front of the left seat to a position in front of the right seat. This is done so the airplane can be flown from either seat. To throw the wheel over, a pin in the control column is released, and the upper part of the column on which the wheel is mounted pivots so it can be moved from one side to the other.

thrust (aerodynamic force). The forward aerodynamic force produced by a propeller, fan, or turbojet engine as it forces a mass of air to the rear, behind the airplane. A propeller produces its thrust by accelerating a large mass of air by a relatively small amount. A turbojet engine produces its thrust by accelerating a smaller mass of air by a much larger amount. The mass and acceleration of the air moved by a fan is between those of the propeller and the jet.

thrust augmentation (turbine engine operation). The short-term increase in thrust output of a turbojet or turbofan engine by water injection or afterburning. *See* water injection (gas turbine engines) and afterburner (gas turbine engine component).

thrust bearing. A form of bearing used in a mechanism to absorb rotating loads parallel to the axis of the shaft on which the bearing is mounted. Aircraft engines have thrust bearings to transmit thrust loads from the propeller into the crankcase.

thruster (space vehicle component). A small rocket engine whose thrust is used to change the attitude of a space vehicle.

thrust horsepower (reciprocating or turboprop engine). The actual amount of horsepower an engine-propeller combination transforms into thrust.

thrust horsepower (turbojet or turbofan engine). The horsepower equivalent of the thrust produced by a turbojet or turbofan engine. Since power requires movement, thrust horsepower must take into consideration the speed of the aircraft in which the engine is mounted.

Thrust horsepower may be found by multiplying the net thrust, measured in pounds, by the speed of the aircraft measured in miles per hour or feet per second. This value is then divided by a constant.

$$\text{Thrust Horsepower} = \frac{\text{Thrust (pounds)} \cdot \text{Airplane Speed (mph)}}{375}$$

or

$$\text{Thrust Horsepower} = \frac{\text{Thrust (pounds)} \cdot \text{Airplane Speed (fps)}}{550}$$

thrust line (airplane reference line). An imaginary line, parallel to the propeller shaft of an engine installed in an airplane.

thrust loading. The gross weight of an aircraft, in pounds, divided by the thrust, in pounds, produced by the engines.

thrust loads (bearing loads). Axial loads in a bearing installed in an aircraft engine. These loads are caused by the thrust produced by the engine.

thrust reverser (gas turbine engine component). A device in the tail pipe of a gas turbine engine installed in an airplane that deflects some of the exhaust gases forward to produce a rearward thrust. This reverse thrust slows the aircraft and decreases its landing roll.

thulium. A bright, silvery, rare-earth chemical element. Thulium's symbol is Tm, its atomic number is 69, and its atomic weight is 168.934. Thulium is used as a source of X-rays.

thumbscrew. A type of machine screw with a flat head in line with the length of the screw. A thumbscrew can be turned by hand by gripping the flat head between the thumb and first finger. Thumbscrews are used to lock one part to another when the parts must be locked and released without the use of tools.

thunder (meteorology). The loud rumbling sound caused by lightning. When lightning (a large spark) jumps from one cloud to another or from a cloud to ground, a great amount of heat is produced. This heat causes the air to expand violently, and this expansion causes shock waves that travel outward at the speed of sound. These shock waves cause the noise we know as thunder.

thundercloud (meteorology). The commonly used name for a cumulonimbus cloud. Violent up and down air currents inside the cloud produce static electricity that discharges in the form of lightning. Lightning causes the thunder heard inside thunderclouds.

thunderstorm (meteorology). A local storm invariably produced by a cumulonimbus cloud and always accompanied by lightning and thunder.

thunderstorm, multi-cell (meteorology). A group or cluster of individual thunderstorm cells, with varying stages of development. These storms are often self propagating and may last for several hours.

thunderstorm, severe. Winds of 50 knots or more, hail $\frac{3}{4}$-inch or more in diameter, and/or tornadoes.

thyratron (electronic component). A hot-cathode, gas-filled electron tube in which one or more control electrodes start a flow of electrons between the cathode and anode. A pulse of high voltage on the control grid ionizes the gas inside the tube and allows electrons to flow. The grid loses its control as soon as the electrons begin to flow, and the only way to stop the flow is to reduce the anode voltage to a value that no longer attracts the electrons.

thyrector (electronic component). A special type of semiconductor device used to protect a piece of electronic equipment from being damaged by spikes of voltage. A thyrector contains two zener diodes, connected together back to back. When the circuit voltage is below that for which the diodes are rated, no current flows through them.

thyrector

But if a spike of voltage occurs in the circuit, one of the diodes breaks down and conducts the spike to ground. Since the zener diodes are connected back to back, the thyrector protects against spikes of voltage of either polarity.

thyristor (electronic component). A semiconductor device used as an electrically controlled switch. Two of the most widely used thyristors are silicon controlled rectifiers (SCRs) and triacs. An SCR is a semiconductor device that does not normally allow electrons to flow

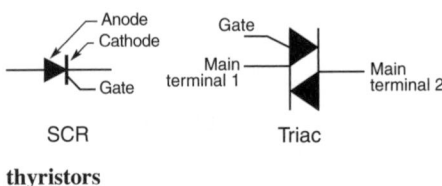

thyristors

through it in either direction. However, if a pulse of voltage of the correct polarity is applied to a third electrode, the gate, the SCR conducts in its forward direction.

The SCR continues to conduct until the voltage across it drops to zero. Once electrons stop flowing through it, the SCR remains shut off until another pulse of voltage is applied to its gate. The triac begins to conduct when a pulse of voltage of either polarity is applied to its gate. Once conducting, it can be turned off only by reducing the voltage across it to a value low enough to stop the current flowing through it.

tickler coil (electronic component). A small coil in series with the collector of a transistor in an oscillator circuit. The tickler coil is part of a feedback circuit. Current flowing through the tickler coil induces a voltage in an inductor in the base circuit.

tiedown area. The parking area on an airport that provides anchors or cables for securing an aircraft by tying it down to prevent it being blown around by the wind.

tie rod (structural member). A high-strength steel rod used to tie parts of a structure together. Tie rods carry only tensile loads.

tight-drive fit. An interference fit between mechanical parts in which the parts can be assembled only by driving them together with a sharp blow from a 12- to 14-ounce hammer.

TIG (tungsten inert gas) welding. A form of electric arc welding in which the electrode is a nonconsumable tungsten wire. TIG welding is now called GTA (gas tungsten arc) welding.

time and opportunity. A perception factor in which learning something is dependent on the student having the time to sense and relate current experiences in context with previous events.

time and speed table (instrument approach chart). A table depicted on an instrument approach procedure chart that identifies the distance from the FAF to the MAP, and provides the time required to transit that distance based on various ground speeds.

time constant (capacitive circuit value). The amount of time, measured in seconds, needed for the voltage across a capacitor to rise to 63.2% of the voltage applied to the circuit. Time constant is determined by the amount of both resistance and capacitance in the circuit.

time constant (inductive circuit value). The amount of time, measured in seconds, needed for the current flowing through an inductive circuit to reach 63.2% of its final value. Time constant is determined by the amount of both resistance and inductance in the circuit.

time constant of an electric motor. The amount of time, measured in seconds, needed for an electric motor to accelerate from standstill to its final no-load speed. Time constant is measured when the motor is connected to a power source having the correct voltage, phase, and frequency.

time-delay relay (electrical circuit component). A slow-acting electrical relay in which there is a measurable delay between the time current is applied to the relay coil and the time the relay contacts close. A time-delay relay is called a slow-closing or a slow-opening relay.

timed turn (instrument flight procedure). A turn in which the clock and the turn coordinator are used to change heading a definite number of degrees in a given time.

time group (air traffic control). Four digits representing the hours and minutes of Coordinated Universal Time (UTC), based on the 24-hour clock system. In this system, the day begins at 0000 and ends at 2359, and is the time along the prime meridian. The FAA uses UTC for all operations and identifies it as Zulu time, or Z time. For example, 0205Z indicates the reference time of 2:05 a.m.

The word "local" or the time zone equivalent is used when local time is given during radio and telephone communications. When written, a time zone designator is used to indicate local time. For example, 0205M is 2:05 a.m. mountain standard time.

time in service. *14 CFR Part 1:* "With respect to maintenance time records, means the time from the moment an aircraft leaves the surface of the earth until it touches it at the next point of landing."

time-limited part (aircraft maintenance term). An item installed on an aircraft that must be replaced when it has been in service for a specified number of hours.

Time-Rite indicator (engine maintenance tool). A patented maintenance tool used to locate the position of the piston in the cylinder of a reciprocating engine. The body of the Time-Rite indicator screws into a spark plug hole and, as the piston moves up in the cylinder, it contacts the indicator arm. A pointer and a scale on the indicator show the number of degrees of crankshaft rotation before top center at which the piston is located.

timing disk (engine maintenance tool). A metal disk with a 360° graduated scale marked on its face and a weighted pointer mounted on a bearing in its center. When the disk is clamped onto the end of the propeller shaft of an aircraft reciprocating engine, the pointer points directly upward. The disk rotates with the propeller but the pointer continues to point straight upward and indicates on the scale the number of degrees the shaft has rotated. The timing disk is used with a top-dead-center indicator to position the crankshaft of the engine for valve and ignition timing.

timing light. An indicator light used when timing magnetos to indicate when the breaker points open. Some timing lights also incorporate an oscillator or buzzer that changes its pitch when the points open.

tin. A lustrous, silvery-white, ductile, malleable, metallic chemical element. Tin's symbol is Sn, its atomic number is 50, and its atomic weight is 118.69. Tin is used as a plating material for steel (tinplate) and as one of the two major alloys in solder. Soft solder contains between 40% and 60% tin; the rest is lead.

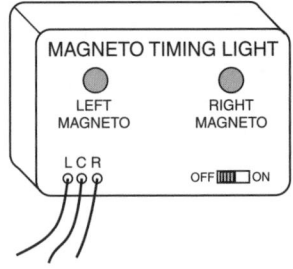

timing light

tinned wire (electrical wire). Copper wire covered with a thin coating of tin or solder, an alloy of tin and lead. The tin coating keeps copper from corroding and makes it easy to solder the wires.

tinner's rivet. A flat-headed solid rivet used in commercial sheet metal work. A tinner's rivet is driven by holding its flat head on an anvil and peening the end of the shank with a peening hammer.

tinplate. Thin sheets of steel coated on one or both sides with a thin layer of tin.

tinsel cord. A type of extra-flexible electric cord used for the leads in headphones. Tinsel cord is made of strips of tinsel, or metal foil, wound around a strong, flexible center cord. The tinsel and the center cord are enclosed in a braided cloth sheath.

tin snips. A commonly used name for hand-held metal-cutting shears. Most tin snips have short blades and relatively long handles to give enough leverage for a person to cut fairly heavy sheet metal.

tip cap (helicopter rotor component). A removable cap mounted on the tip of some helicopter rotor blades. These tip caps often hold the weights used for spanwise blade balance.

tip fin. *See* winglet.

tip floats (seaplane component). Small floats near the wingtips of flying boats or floatplanes having a single main float. The tip floats help stabilize the airplane on the water and prevent the wingtips from contacting the water.

tip-path plane (rotorcraft term). The path followed by the tip of the rotor blade as it rotates.

tip speed (helicopter rotor blade). The rotative speed of a rotor blade, measured at its tip.

tire (landing gear component). A ring, usually made of rubber or rubber compound, that fits around a wheel and serves as a cushion at the point the wheel touches the surface over which it rolls. Most tires are made so that they form a chamber which is filled with compressed air. The compressed air acts as a shock absorber.

tire bead. Bundles of high-strength steel wire used as a foundation for an aircraft tire. The cords of the tire wrap around the bead wires to tie the body of the tire to the bead. Rubber is molded around the bead wires to form an airtight seal with the bead seat area of the wheel.

TIT (turbine inlet temperature) (gas turbine engine parameter). The temperature of the gases from the combustion section of a gas turbine engine as they enter the turbine inlet guide vanes or the first stage of the turbine. TIT is the highest temperature inside a gas turbine engine and is one of the limiting factors of the amount of power the engine can produce. TIT is difficult to measure, but exhaust gas temperature, or EGT, which is the temperature of the gas as it leaves the turbine, relates to TIT and is normally the parameter measured.

titanium. A strong, brittle, lustrous, silvery-gray, metallic chemical element. Titanium's symbol is Ti, its atomic number is 22, and its atomic weight is 47.90. Titanium is malleable when it is hot, but is hard and brittle when it is cold. Titanium is used in its pure state or as an alloy with other metals to increase their strength at high temperatures. Titanium is also used in the manufacture of some ceramic components.

titanium white (paint pigment). A brilliant white paint pigment that contains no lead. Titanium white contains titanium dioxide, which is often mixed with barium sulfate and zinc oxide.

Title 14 of the Code of Federal Regulations (14 CFR). The federal aviation regulations governing the operation of aircraft, airways, and airmen.

title block (aircraft drawing). An information block placed in the lower right-hand corner of an aircraft drawing. This block includes the part number, the part name, and the names of the engineer, draftsman, and checker.

TMC (thrust management computer). A component in the flight management system of a jet transport aircraft that senses the engine parameters and power requests and controls the thrust produced by the engines.

toe-in (airplane wheel alignment). The wheels of an airplane are toed in if lines drawn through the center of the two wheels, perpendicular to the axles, cross ahead of the wheels. As the airplane moves forward, toe-in causes the wheels to try to move closer together.

toe-out (airplane wheel alignment). The wheels of an airplane are toed out if lines drawn through the center of the two wheels, perpendicular to the axles, cross behind the wheels. As the airplane moves forward, toe-out causes the wheels to try to move farther apart.

To-From indicator (electronic navigation system component). An indicator used in aerial navigation with the VOR, very-high-frequency omnirange navigation system. The To-From indicator shows the pilot whether the aircraft is flying toward or away from the station if it is flying at the heading shown on the omni bearing selector (OBS). When an aircraft passes over a VOR antenna, the To-From indicator changes from To to From.

toggle (*noun*). A T-shaped handle fitted onto the end of a cable that is used to move some mechanical device.

toggle (*verb*). To alternate between two or more circuit configurations, normally by the operation of a single switch.

toggle flip-flop. A digital building block that changes the logic state of its output each time a clock pulse is received.

T

toggle switch. An electrical switch with a control handle in the form of a bat, or lever, sticking out of the front of the switch. It is customary when installing a toggle switch to move the toggle up to turn the switch ON, and down to turn the switch OFF.

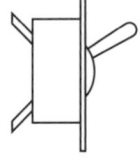

toggle switch

tolerance (dimensions). The difference between the extreme allowable dimensions of a part.

toluene. A liquid hydrocarbon material much like benzene, but less flammable. Toluene is used as a solvent and as an antiknock additive for gasoline used in reciprocating engines.

toluol. A commercial grade of toluene. *See* toluene.

ton. A unit of weight in the English system that is equal to 2,000 pounds.

tonne (metric ton). A unit of mass in the metric system equal to 1,000 kilograms or 2,204.62 pounds of mass.

ton of refrigeration. A measure of the cooling effect of an air conditioning system. One ton of refrigeration is the amount of cooling produced when one ton of ice melts in a 24-hour period.

tooling resins (composites). Plastic resins, chiefly epoxy and silicone, which are used as tooling aids.

tool steel. Any steel that is capable of being hardened sufficiently to be used for making metal-cutting tools.

top dead center (reciprocating engine piston position). *See* TDC.

top of climb (TOC). An identifiable waypoint representing the point at which cruise altitude is first reached. TOC is calculated based on current aircraft altitude, climb speed, and cruise altitude. There can only be one TOC waypoint at a time.

top-of-descent point. The point that the RNAV computer calculates to be the ideal location at which to begin a descent to the planned crossing restriction, given the descent speed and rate that has been entered by the pilot.

topographical database. A volume of information stored in an advanced cockpit system that details the topographical features of the earth's surface. Used by several systems to assess aircraft position and altitude with respect to surrounding terrain.

topographic map. A map depicting area information on a smaller scale than an aviation sectional chart, and of much more value to the balloon pilot. Most topographic charts show areas of vegetation, roads, built-up areas, and the general topography (or terrain) of a given area.

top overhaul (reciprocating engine maintenance). The overhaul of the cylinders, valves, and pistons of a reciprocating engine. A top overhaul does not include opening the crankcase or removing the connecting rods from the crankshaft.

torching (reciprocating engine malfunction). Flames that appear at the end of an exhaust stack of a reciprocating engine that is operating with an excessively rich fuel-air mixture.

tornado (meteorology). A violently rotating column of air hanging down as a funnel-shaped cloud below a cumulonimbus cloud. Tornadoes are the most destructive of all small-scale atmospheric phenomena.

toroidal coil (electrical component). An electrical inductor wound around a ring-shaped core made of a highly permeable material. The ring-shaped core concentrates the magnetic flux and allows a minimum amount of flux to be lost in an external field.

torque. A force that produces or tries to produce rotation. It is measured in such terms as inch-pounds, foot-pounds, or meter-kilograms. One inch-pound of torque is the amount of torque that is produced by a force of one pound acting at a distance of one inch from the axis of rotation.

torque limited (turboprop or turboshaft engine limitation). A limit placed on a turboprop or turboshaft engine that restricts the amount of power the engine is allowed to deliver to the propeller or to the rotor-drive system. This limit is imposed because of the strength of the drive-train mechanism or the strength of the aircraft structure.

torque links (aircraft shock absorber component). A hinged link between the cylinder and piston of an aircraft shock absorber. Torque links prevent the piston from turning inside the cylinder, but they allow it to move up and down to absorb the landing and taxi shocks. Torque links are also called scissors and nutcrackers.

torque meter. An instrument used with some of the larger reciprocating engines and turboprop engines to measure the amount of torque the engine is producing.

torque tube (aircraft control system component). A tube in an aircraft control system that transmits a torsional force from the operating control to the control surface. Torque tubes are often used to actuate ailerons and flaps.

torque wrench (precision measuring tool). A precision hand tool used to measure the amount of torque being applied to a threaded fastener by the wrench. Torque is normally measured by measuring the amount

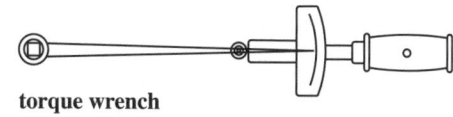

torque wrench

a beam in the wrench bends when the torque is being applied. *See* deflecting-beam torque wrench.

torr (unit of pressure). A unit used to measure a low pressure or vacuum. One torr is equal to one millimeter of mercury, or $\frac{1}{760}$ of the standard atmospheric pressure.

torsional force. A twisting force. A torsional force is made up of a tensile force and a compressive force acting at right angles to each other and at 45° to the axis of the object. Torsional forces are the main forces acting on propeller shafts and helicopter rotor shafts.

torsion rod. A device in a spring tab to which the control horn is attached. For normal operation, the torsion rod acts as a fixed attachment point, but when the control surface loads are high, the torsion rod twists and allows the control horn to deflect the spring tab.

total air temperature (TAT). The temperature a column of moving air will have if it is stopped.

total drag (aerodynamics). The sum of all of the parasite and induced drag of an aircraft.

total estimated elapsed time (ICAO). For IFR flights, the estimated time required from takeoff to arrive over that designated point, defined by reference to navigation aids, from which it is intended that an instrument approach procedure will be commenced, or, if no navigation aid is associated with the destination aerodrome, to arrive over the destination aerodrome. For VFR flights, the estimated time required from takeoff to arrive over the destination aerodrome.

totalizer (fuel quantity indicator). An instrument that indicates the total amount of fuel remaining in all the fuel tanks in an aircraft.

total pressure (Pt). The pressure a moving mass of fluid would have if it were stopped. Total pressure is the sum of static pressure and the pressure due to ram effect.

total temperature (Tt). The temperature of a fluid that is stopped from its motion. Total temperature is the sum of the static temperature of the fluid and the temperature caused by ram effect as the fluid is stopped.

touch and go (aircraft operation). A type of flight practice in which the pilot makes a series of landings and takeoffs. The landing is made, but the aircraft is not allowed to come to a complete stop before power is applied and the takeoff is made.

T

touchdown (flight operation). (1) The point at which an aircraft first makes contact with the landing surface. (2) In a precision radar approach, it is the point at which the glide path intercepts the landing surface.

touchdown and lift-off area (TLOF). The TLOF is a load-bearing, usually paved area at a heliport where the helicopter is permitted to land. The TLOF can be located at ground or rooftop level, or on an elevated structure. The TLOF is normally centered in the final approach and takeoff area (FATO).

touchdown point. The point or intended point at which an aircraft first makes contact with the landing surface.

touchdown RVR. The runway visibility readout values obtained from sensors serving the runway touchdown zone.

touchdown zone (air traffic control). The first 3,000 feet of a runway beginning at the threshold. This area is used for determining the touchdown zone elevation in the development of straight-in landing minimums for instrument approaches.

touchdown zone (ICAO). The portion of a runway, beyond the threshold, where it is intended that landing aircraft first contact the runway.

touchdown zone elevation (TDZE). (1) The highest elevation in the first 3,000 feet of the landing surface, TDZE is indicated on the instrument approach procedure chart when straight-in landing minimums are authorized. (2) The highest elevation in the first 3,000 feet of the landing surface. TDZE is indicated on the instrument approach procedure chart when straight-in landing minimums are authorized.

touchdown zone lights (TDZL) (airport lighting). Two rows of transverse light bars disposed symmetrically about the runway centerline in the runway touchdown zone.

toughness (material characteristic). The characteristic of a material that allows it to be deformed by twisting, pulling, hammering, or bending without its breaking.

towering cumulus (meteorology). A rapidly growing cumulus cloud in which its height is greater than its width.

tower visibility (meteorology). Prevailing visibility as determined from an airport control tower.

towing eye (aircraft structural component). A ring, usually installed on some strong part of the landing gear of an aircraft, to which a tow bar or cable can be attached to move the aircraft on the ground.

Townend ring (aircraft component). A type of ring cowling used over a single-row radial engine. The Townend ring, often called a speed ring, directs the air smoothly over the cylinder heads to increase the cooling and decrease the drag.

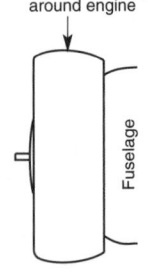

Airfoil-shaped ring around engine

Fuselage

Townend ring

tower (air traffic control facility). A terminal facility that uses air/ground communications, visual signaling, and other devices to provide ATC services to aircraft operating in the vicinity of the airport or on the movement area. Tower controllers authorize aircraft to land or takeoff at the airport or to transit the Class D airspace regardless of flight plan or weather conditions. A tower may also provide approach control services.

tower enroute control (TEC). An ATC program to provide a service to aircraft proceeding to and from metropolitan areas. It links designated Approach Control Areas by a network of identified routes made up of the existing airway structure of the National Airspace System.

towhook (glider operation component). A mechanism allowing the attachment and release of a towrope on the glider or towplane. On gliders, it is located near the nose or directly ahead of the main wheel.

TPP, or United States Terminal Procedures Publication. Booklets published by the FAA Aeronautical Navigation Products division (AeroNav) containing charts of instrument approach and departure procedures for IFR flight to and from U.S. civil and military airports. It is a 26-volume set of printed books containing instrument approach procedures (IAP), departure procedures (DP), standard terminal arrival charts (STAR), and airport diagrams, as well as takeoff, radar, and alternate minima textual procedures, all of which are also available in digital format online.

TPX-42 (air traffic control equipment). A numeric beacon decoder equipment/system, designed to be added to terminal radar systems for beacon decoding. TPX-42 provides rapid target identification, reinforcement of the primary radar target, and altitude information from Mode C.

T/R (transformer/rectifier). A component in a large aircraft electrical system used to reduce the AC voltage and change it into DC for charging the battery and operating DC equipment in the aircraft.

TRACAB (terminal radar approach control in tower cab). A type of air traffic facility that consists of a radar approach control facility located in the tower cab of the primary airport, as opposed to a separate room.

trace (meteorology). An unmeasurable quantity of precipitation, less than 0.01 inches.

traceable pressure standard (weather reporting). The facility station pressure instrument, with certification/calibration traceable to the National Institute of Standards and Technology. Traceable pressure standards may be mercurial barometers, commissioned ASOS or dual transducer AWOS, or portable pressure standards or DASI.

tracer (composites). A fiber, tow, or yarn added to a prepreg material to indicate fiber alignment and, in the case of woven materials, for distinguishing warp fibers from fill fibers.

track (ICAO). The projection on the earth's surface of the path of an aircraft, the direction of which path at any point is usually expressed in degrees from north (true, magnetic, or grid).

track (helicopter rotor blade condition). The path followed by the blade tips of a helicopter rotor as they rotate.

track (propeller). The path followed by a blade segment of a propeller in one rotation.

tracking (flight operation). Flying a heading that will maintain the desired track to or from the station regardless of crosswind conditions.

tracking flag (helicopter maintenance tool). A white cotton flag mounted in line with a wooden pole and attached at both ends. Colored transfer marks are made on the blade tips, and the tracking flag is carefully moved against the tips of the blades as the helicopter is held near a hover. The colored chalk transfers to the tracking flag to show the relative vertical position of the blade tips as they rotate.

tracking reflectors (helicopter maintenance tool). Small colored reflectors installed on the tip of a helicopter rotor to aid in checking the track of the blades. A spotlight is shone on the tip of the rotor, and as it reflects off the reflectors, it shows up as bars of colored light. The bars caused by both reflectors must be superimposed for the rotor blades to be in track.

tracking stick (helicopter maintenance tool). A stick with a rubber wick attached to its end. The wick is coated with Prussian blue dye and is raised up until it touches the rotor blade while the rotor system is turning at the prescribed speed. When the helicopter is shut down, the blades are examined, and the blade riding the lowest in its track will have a blue mark on it.

track of interest (TOI). Displayed data representing an airborne object that threatens or has the potential to threaten North America or national security. Indicators of threat may include, but are not limited to: noncompliance with air traffic control instructions or aviation regulations; extended loss of communications; unusual transmissions or unusual flight behavior; unauthorized intrusion into controlled airspace or an ADIZ; noncompliance with issued flight restrictions/security procedures; or unlawful interference with airborne flight crews, up to and including hijack. In certain circumstances, an object may become a TOI based on specific and credible intelligence pertaining to that particular aircraft/object, its passengers, or its cargo.

track of interest resolution. The resolution of a track of interest (TOI), usually occurring when the aircraft/object is no longer airborne; the aircraft complies with air traffic control instructions, aviation regulations, and/or issued flight restrictions and security procedures; radio contact is re-established and authorized control of the aircraft is verified; the aircraft is intercepted and intent is verified to be nonthreatening/nonhostile; TOI was identified based on specific and credible intelligence that was later determined to be invalid or unreliable; or displayed data is identified and characterized as invalid.

tractor engine. An engine installed on an aircraft in such a way that the propeller faces the front of the aircraft. Thrust produced by the propeller mounted on a tractor engine pulls the aircraft through the air.

tractor propeller (airplane propeller). A propeller mounted on an airplane in such a way that its thrust pulls the airplane through the air. Most modern airplanes use tractor propellers.

trade winds (meteorology). Winds that always blow in the same general direction. In the northern hemisphere, the trade winds blow toward the equator from the northeast. In the southern hemisphere, they blow toward the equator from the southeast. Trade winds are caused by the rotation of the earth and by the friction between the surface of the earth and the air.

traditional assessment. Written testing, such as multiple choice, matching, true/false, or fill-in-the-blank.

traffic. A term used by ATC to refer to one or more aircraft. Also, used by a controller to transfer radar identification of an aircraft to another controller for the purpose of coordinating separation action. Traffic is normally issued in response to a handoff or point out, in anticipation of a handoff or point out, or in conjunction with a request for control of an aircraft.

traffic advisories. Advisories issued to alert pilots to other known or observed air traffic which may be in such proximity to the position or intended route of flight of their aircraft to warrant their attention, based on visual observation, observation of radar identified and nonidentified aircraft targets on an ATC radar display, or verbal reports from pilots or other facilities.

traffic alert and collision avoidance system. Also called traffic collision avoidance system (TCAS), the generic term for the active traffic alerting and collision avoidance systems. An airborne collision avoidance system based on radar beacon signals which operates independent of ground-based equipment. TCAS-I generates traffic advisories only. TCAS-II generates traffic advisories, and resolution (collision avoidance) advisories in the vertical plane.

traffic data system. An advanced avionics system designed to aid the pilot in visually acquiring and maintaining awareness of nearby aircraft that pose potential collision threats.

traffic display. A pictorial display showing any aircraft operating in the vicinity that have been detected by a traffic data system.

traffic flow management system (TFMS). TFMS is a system that the FAA uses in performing traffic flow management, a collaborative effort to manage aircraft operating within the national airspace system (NAS). It consists of an automated data processing system that supports the FAA traffic management functions within ARTCCs and ATC. Traffic management personnel and ATC analyze the demand on the NAS and implement initiatives that are relayed to enroute and terminal controllers. Those controllers, along with other system users, relay information to traffic management personnel for use in their decision-making process.

traffic information service (TIS). An air traffic control service provided by the FAA that transmits traffic information to the cockpit via data link. It is similar to the VFR radio traffic advisories normally received over voice radio, but is available in the cockpit via an automatic display that informs the pilot of nearby traffic and potential conflict situations. The display assists the pilot in the visual acquisition of traffic; TIS is intended to improve the safety and efficiency of the "see and avoid" awareness that pilots must exercise in flight. TIS also employs an enhanced capability of the terminal Mode S radar system, which contains surveillance data as well as the data link required to uplink the information to suitably-equipped aircraft (called the "TIS client"). TIS surveillance data is derived from the same radar used by ATC, and is uplinked to the client aircraft on each radar scan, normally every 5 seconds. *See also* traffic information service – broadcast (TIS-B).

traffic information service-broadcast (TIS-B). (1) An air traffic surveillance system that combines all available traffic information on a single display. (2) Supplement to ATS-B, and provides an integration of data input from other sources that don't have the GPS/Mode S data link. This is particularly valuable where ground radar returns can be added and also for airport surface movement control where the surface radar information can be integrated.

"traffic in sight" (air traffic control). A phrase in ATC–pilot communications, used by pilots to inform a controller that previously issued traffic is in sight.

traffic management advisor (TMA). A computerized tool that assists Traffic Management Coordinators to efficiently schedule arrival traffic to a metered airport, by calculating meter fix times and delays, then sending that information to the sector controllers. TMA has the ability to sequence and schedule aircraft to the outer fix, meter fix, final approach fix, and runway threshold in a way that maximizes airport and TRACON capacity without compromising safety.

traffic management program alert. A term used in a Notice to Airmen (NOTAM) issued in conjunction with a special traffic management program to alert pilots to the existence of the program and to refer them to either the Notices to Airmen publication or a special traffic management program advisory message for program details. The contraction TMPA is used in NOTAM text.

traffic management unit. The entity in ARTCCs and designated terminals directly involved in the active management of facility traffic. Usually under the direct supervision of an assistant manager for traffic management.

"traffic no factor" (air traffic control). A phrase used in ATC–pilot communications, indicating that the traffic described in a previously issued traffic advisory is not a factor.

"traffic no longer observed" (air traffic control). A phrase used in ATC–pilot communications to indicate that the traffic described in a previously issued traffic advisory is no longer depicted on radar, but may still be a factor.

traffic pattern. The traffic flow that is prescribed for aircraft landing at, taxiing on, or taking off from an airport. The components of a typical traffic pattern are: upwind leg, crosswind leg, downwind leg, base leg, and final approach.

T

traffic pattern (airport operation). A published route prescribed for aircraft to fly when approaching or leaving an airport. The possibility of in-flight collision is minimized by all aircraft in the vicinity of the airport using a specified traffic pattern.

14 CFR Part 1: "The traffic flow that is prescribed for aircraft landing at, taxiing on, or taking off from, an airport."

traffic proximity alert system (TPAS). A traffic avoidance system that tells the pilot how far the nearest aircraft is. It includes a highly sensitive microwave receiver and pre-programmed sound alerts that warn the pilot of close traffic.

traffic situation display (TSD). TSD is a computer system that receives radar track data from all 20 CONUS ARTCCs, organizes this data into a mosaic display, and presents it on a computer screen. The display allows the traffic management coordinator multiple methods of selection and highlighting of individual aircraft or groups of aircraft. The user has the option of superimposing these aircraft positions over any number of background displays. These background options include ARTCC boundaries, any stratum of en route sector boundaries, fixes, airways, military and other special use airspace, airports, and geopolitical boundaries. By using the TSD, a coordinator can monitor any number of traffic situations or the entire systemwide traffic flows.

trailing edge (aircraft structure). The back edge of an airfoil, such as a wing, a helicopter rotor, or a propeller blade. It is the edge that passes through the air last.

trailing edge (electrical pulse). The part of an electrical pulse that occurs last. In a pulse whose voltage is higher than the reference voltage, the trailing edge is the part of the pulse where the voltage goes from the high value back to the reference value.

trailing edge flap (airplane secondary control). Flaps mounted on the trailing edge of an airplane wing. Trailing edge flaps are extended in flight to increase the camber of the airfoil section. This increases both the lift and the drag produced by the airfoil.

trailing finger (magneto distributor component). A second finger installed on the rotor of some aircraft magneto distributors. High voltage from an induction vibrator flows to the spark plugs through the trailing finger to produce a hot and late spark in the cylinder when the engine is being started.

training course outline (TCO). A document within a curriculum that describes the content of a particular course by statement of objectives, descriptions of teaching aids, definition of evaluation criteria, and indication of desired outcome.

training media. Any physical means that communicates an instructional message to students.

training syllabus. A step-by-step, building-block progression of learning with provisions for regular review and evaluations at prescribed stages of learning. The syllabus defines the unit of training, states by objective what the student is expected to accomplish during the unit of training, shows an organized plan for instruction, and dictates the evaluation process for either the unit or stage of learning.

trajectory (air traffic control). A URET representation of the path an aircraft is predicted to fly based upon a current plan or trial plan. *See also* user request evaluation tool (URET), current plan, trial plan.

trajectory modeling (air traffic control). The automated process of calculating a trajectory.

tram (*verb*). The procedure used to square up the Pratt truss used in an airplane wing. Trammel points are set on the trammel bar so they measure the distance between the center of the front spar, at the inboard compression strut, and the center of the rear spar at the next compression strut outboard. The drag and antidrag wires are adjusted until the distance between the center of the rear spar at the inboard compression strut and the center of the front spar at the next outboard compression strut is exactly the same as that between the first points measured.

trammel bar. A wood or metal bar on which trammel points are mounted to compare distances.

trammel points (aircraft maintenance tool). A set of sharp-pointed pins that protrude from the side of a long wood or metal bar (a trammel bar). A trammel bar is used to tram, or square up, the Pratt truss used in an airplane wing. *See* tram.

transceiver (communications equipment). A piece of radio communications equipment in which all of the circuits for the receiver and the transmitter are contained in the same housing.

transconductance (electronic measurement). The ratio of the change in plate current to the change in grid voltage in an electron tube when the plate voltage is held constant.

transcribed weather broadcast (TWEB). A continuous recording of meteorological and aeronautical information that is broadcast on L/MF and VOR facilities for pilots. TWEB is provided only in Alaska.

transducer. A device that changes energy from one form into another. A microphone is an example of a transducer. It changes variations in air pressure into variations in electrical voltage. A radio speaker is another type of transducer. A speaker changes variations in electrical voltage into variations in air pressure, or sound.

transfer of control (air traffic control). The action by which the responsibility for the separation of an aircraft is transferred from one controller to another.

transfer of learning. The ability to apply knowledge or procedures learned in one context to new contexts.

transfer punch (sheet metal tool). A special type of punch used to mark the center of a rivet hole when the punch is stuck through an existing rivet hole. The diameter of the shank of the punch near the tip is the same as that of the rivet hole, and the end of the punch is flat; but there is a short, sharp point

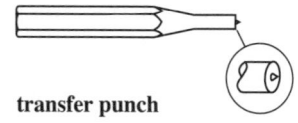

transfer punch

protruding from its center. This point makes a small impression in the metal that is used to start a drill at the location the rivet hole is to be drilled.

transferring controller. A controller/facility transferring control of an aircraft to another controller/facility.

transferring unit/controller (ICAO). Air traffic control unit/air traffic controller in the process of transferring the responsibility for providing air traffic control service to an aircraft to the next air traffic control unit/air traffic controller along the route of flight.

transformer (electrical component). An electrical component used to change the voltage and current in an alternating current circuit. The core of a transformer is made of a stack of soft iron laminations, and the windings, which consist of several coils of insulated wire, are wound around the core. The winding connected to the power source is called the primary winding, and the windings connected to the electrical loads are called secondary windings.

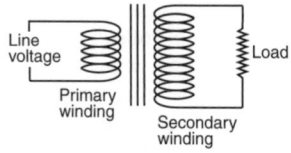

transformer

The voltage difference between that across the primary winding and that across any one of the secondary windings is directly proportional to the ratio of the number of turns in the secondary winding to the number of turns in the primary winding. The higher the ratio, the higher the secondary voltage.

The current difference between that in the primary winding and that in the secondary winding is inversely proportional to the ratio of the number of turns in the secondary winding to the number of turns in the primary winding. The higher the ratio, the lower the secondary current.

transformer/rectifier. *See* T/R.

transistor (electronic component). An active semiconductor device with three electrodes: an emitter, a collector, and a base. A large flow of electrons between the emitter and the collector is controlled by a much smaller flow of electrons between the emitter and the base. Transistors are physically small, require almost no power for their operation, are extremely rugged, and are low in cost. *See* NPN transistor and PNP transistor.

transistor voltage regulator (aircraft electrical system component). A type of voltage regulator used in an aircraft electrical system to control the output voltage of an alternator. A zener diode senses the alternator output voltage, and power transistors control the amount of current flowing through the alternator field coil.

A transistor voltage regulator is not the same as a transistorized voltage regulator. In a transistorized voltage regulator, the alternator or generator output voltage is sensed by an electromagnetic relay. Only a small amount of current flows through the relay contacts, just the base current of an output transistor that controls the larger alternator field current.

transition. The general term that describes the change from one phase of flight or flight condition to another; e.g., transition from en route flight to the approach or transition from instrument flight to visual flight. Also, a published procedure (DP Transition) used to connect the basic DP to one of several en route airways/jet routes, or a published procedure (STAR Transition) used to connect one of several en route airways/jet routes to the basic STAR.

transitional airspace (air traffic control). That portion of controlled airspace in which aircraft change from one phase of flight or one flight condition to another.

transition liner. The portion of the combustor that directs the gases into the turbine plenum.

transition training. An instructional program designed to familiarize and qualify a pilot to fly types of aircraft not previously flown, such as tailwheel aircraft, high-performance aircraft, and aircraft capable of flying at high altitudes.

translational lift (helicopter operation). The additional lift produced by a helicopter rotor as the helicopter changes from hovering to forward flight. The lift produced by a helicopter rotor decreases as the helicopter rises vertically out of ground effect. But if the helicopter moves forward at an airspeed of somewhere around 15 to 20 miles per hour, the rotor system becomes more efficient in forcing the air downward, and the lift increases. This increased lift caused by the forward motion of the helicopter is called translational lift.

transition altitude (QNH). The altitude in the vicinity of an airport at or below which the vertical position of an aircraft is controlled by reference to altitudes (MSL).

transition area (air traffic control). Controlled airspace extending upward from 700 feet or more above the surface of the earth, when designated in conjunction with an airport for which an approved instrument approach procedure has been prescribed—or from 1,200 feet or more above the surface of the earth when designated in conjunction with airway route structures or segments. Unless otherwise limited, transition areas terminate at the base of the overlying controlled airspace.

Transition areas are designated to contain IFR operations in controlled airspace during portions of the terminal operation, and while transitioning between the terminal and en route environment.

transition height (QFE). Transition height is the height in the vicinity of an airport at or below which the vertical position of an aircraft is expressed in height above the airport reference datum.

transition layer. Transition layer is the airspace between the transition altitude and the transition level. Aircraft descending through the transition layer will set altimeters to local station pressure, while departing aircraft climbing through the transition layer will be using standard altimeter setting (QNE) of 29.92 inches of Mercury, 1013.2 millibars, or 1013.2 hectopascals.

transition level (QNE). The lowest flight level available for use above the transition altitude.

transition point. A point at an adapted number of miles from the vertex at which an arrival aircraft would normally commence descent from its en route altitude. This is the first fix adapted on the arrival speed segments.

transition waypoint. The waypoint that defines the beginning of a runway or en route transition on an RNAV SID or STAR.

translating tendency (helicopter operation). The tendency of the single-rotor helicopter to move laterally during hovering flight. Also called tail-rotor drift.

translucent. The condition of a material that diffuses the rays of light passing through it. This diffused light prevents objects being seen clearly when viewed through the material.

transmissometer (meteorology). An instrument system which shows the transmissibility of light through the atmosphere. Transmissibility may be translated either automatically or manually into visibility and/or runway visual range (RVR).

transmission line (electrical conductor). A conductor used to transfer electrical energy from its source to the load using it.

transmit (communications operation). To send information or data from one location to another. When a message is transmitted by radio, the information is changed into electromagnetic waves radiated out into space from the transmitting antenna. Radiated waves of electromagnetic energy are received by another antenna and changed back into the form of the original data.

transmitter (communications equipment). An electronic device that produces a radio-frequency carrier wave that can be modulated with information or data. The RF carrier produces electromagnetic energy that is radiated from an antenna.

transmitting in the blind (radio operation). A transmission from one station to other stations in circumstances where two-way communication cannot be established, but where it is believed that the called stations may be able to receive the transmission.

transom (seaplane float component). The square stern of a seaplane float.

transonic flight. Flight in which an airplane transitions from subsonic speed to a speed at or beyond the speed of sound. Transonic flight is considered to be between about 600 and 900 miles per hour, a speed of between Mach 0.8 and Mach 1.2. At this speed, some air passing over the aircraft is subsonic and other air is supersonic. Abrupt changes in the flight characteristics of an airplane take place in transonic flight.

transparent. The condition of a material that allows rays of light to pass through it without being diffused, or scattered. Clear glass is transparent, allowing objects seen through it to be recognized.

transpiration cooling (rocket motor cooling). Cooling provided by liquid or gaseous coolant through a porous chamber wall at a rate sufficient to maintain the hot-gas chamber wall at the desired temperature.

transponder (radar beacon transponder). The airborne radar beacon receiver/transmitter portion of the air traffic control radar beacon system (ATCRBS). The transponder automatically receives radio signals from interrogators on the ground, and it selectively replies from a specific reply pulse or pulse group only to those interrogations being received on the mode to which it is set to respond. *See* radar beacon transponder.

transponder code. One of 4,096 four-digit discrete codes ATC will assign to distinguish between aircraft.

"transponder observed" (air traffic control). Phraseology used to inform a VFR pilot that the aircraft's assigned beacon code and position have been observed and that its position has been correlated for transit through the designated area.

transport category aircraft. Aircraft certified under 14 CFR Part 25.

transverse pitch (rivet spacing). The distance between the center of rivets in two adjacent rows. Transverse pitch is also called rivet gage. *See* illustration for gage (rivet).

transverse-flow effect (helicopter aerodynamics). A condition in helicopter forward flight when the air flowing through the rear of the disc is more perpendicular than that flowing through the front. This flow causes a decreased angle of attack and the tendency of the rear of the disc to descend. Precession causes the effect to be felt 90° in the direction of rotation and the helicopter has a tendency to roll to the right.

transverse wave. A type of mechanical wave in which the material being vibrated moves in a direction perpendicular to the direction the wave is moving. Transverse waves are formed when a rock is thrown into a pond of water. The surface of the water moves up and down as the wave moves across the pond.

trapezoid. A plane, closed, four-sided figure. Only two of the sides of a trapezoid are parallel to each other.

trapped fuel. Fuel that is undrainable from the fuel tanks.

trend. Immediate indication of the direction of aircraft movement, as shown on instruments.

trapezoid

trend monitoring (turbine engine maintenance). A system for monitoring the performance of a turbine engine by routine comparison of performance parameters with a base line of the same parameters established when the engine was new or newly overhauled. EGT, RPM, fuel flow, and oil consumption are monitored on every flight, and the difference between the current indication and the base line is plotted. Any deviation from a normal increase or decrease warns the technician of an impending problem.

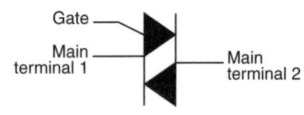

triac (electronic component). A form of thyristor, similar to a silicon controlled rectifier, except it controls current flow in either direction. A triac acts as two SCRs connected in parallel, with the anode of one connected to the cathode of the other. A triac does not conduct until a pulse of voltage is applied to its gate. But once it begins to conduct, it can be turned off only by reducing the voltage across it to a value low enough to stop the current flowing through it. *See* thyristor.

triac

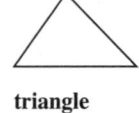

triangle

trial plan. The ATC computer's proposed amendment to the flight plan, a result of the automatic analysis of potential conflicts along the predicted trajectory of the selected aircraft, displayed at the controller's terminal. *See also* current plan.

triangle. A closed, plane, three-sided figure. The sum of the three angles in a triangle is always 180°.

triangulation (navigation). A method of determining the location of an aircraft by radio bearings. Lines are drawn from two or more VOR stations along the radials on which the aircraft is located. The location on the chart where these lines cross is the location of the aircraft.

triboelectricity. Electrostatic charges built up because of friction between different materials.

triboelectric series. A list of materials which can be rubbed together to produce electrostatic charges. When any two materials in this series are rubbed together, the material higher in the list loses electrons and becomes positive with respect to the material lower in the list.

Positive
glass
mica
nylon
fur
silk
paper
cotton
wood
acrylic
polystyrene
rubber
sulfur
Saran Wrap
Negative

triboelectric series

trickle charge (batteries). A continuous, low-current charge used to keep storage batteries fully charged at all times. A trickle charge puts just enough current into the battery to restore the electrical energy lost through the internal resistance of the battery.

trickle charger (battery charger). A small transformer-rectifier connected across a storage battery to charge it at a slow rate. Trickle chargers are limited to a small amount of current by an internal circuit breaker that opens the primary circuit if the battery requires too much current.

tricresyl phosphate (TCP). A chemical compound, $(CH_3C_6H_4O)_3PO$, used in aviation gasoline to assist in scavenging the lead deposits left from the tetraethyl lead that is used in the fuel as an antiknock agent. TCP is also used as a plasticizer in aircraft dope.

tricycle landing gear

tricycle landing gear (aircraft landing gear). A type of aircraft landing gear that uses two main wheels located behind the center of gravity and a nose wheel well ahead of the center of gravity. The ease of ground handling of aircraft with tricycle landing gear has made this the most widely used landing gear configuration.

trigger pulse. A pulse of electrical energy used to initiate an operation in certain types of electronic equipment.

trigonometry (mathematics). The branch of mathematics that deals with the relationships between the angles and the lengths of the sides of a triangle.

trijet (airplane type). A jet-propelled aircraft that has three engines. The Boeing 727, the McDonnell-Douglas MD-11, and Lockheed L-1011 are all trijet airplanes.

trim. To adjust the aerodynamic forces on the control surfaces so that the aircraft maintains the set attitude without any control input.

trim devices (aircraft secondary flight control). Any device designed to reduce or eliminate pressure on the control stick or wheel. When properly trimmed, an aircraft should fly hands off at the desired airspeed with no control pressure from the pilot. Trim mechanisms may be either external tabs on the control surface or a simple spring-tension on the cockpit control.

trimetrogon. A method of aerial mapping in which three photographs are taken at the same time of the area being mapped. One photograph is taken vertically downward and the other two are oblique photographs, taken at two different angles. The three photographs are studied with special instruments that show the contours of the terrain. Maps are made from these photographs.

trimmed flight. A flight condition in which the aerodynamic forces acting on the control surfaces are balanced, and the aircraft is able to fly straight and level with no control input.

trimming (gas turbine engine operation). The procedure of adjusting the fuel control of a gas turbine engine so the engine produces the correct maximum RPM and idling RPM, and functions properly under acceleration and deceleration. Trimming is done to adjust the engine performance to agree with the performance specifications published by the engine manufacturer.

trim tab (aircraft controls). A small movable control mounted on a primary control surface. The trim tab is adjustable in flight to change the aerodynamic load on the control surface. The aerodynamic load produced by the trim tab deflects the control surface enough for it to trim the aircraft for hands-off flight at any normal speed.

trinomial (mathematical term). An algebraic expression that has three terms. $A^2 + 2AB + B^2$ is a trinomial.

triode electron tube. An electron tube with three active electrodes: the cathode, the control grid, and the anode, or plate. Triode electron tubes are used as amplifiers. A small change in voltage between the cathode and the control grid controls a large flow of electrons between the cathode and the anode. Triode electron tubes have, to a large extent, been replaced by the much smaller and more efficient bipolar transistors.

trip-free circuit breaker (electrical component). A circuit breaker that opens a circuit any time an excessive amount of current flows, regardless of the position of the circuit breaker's operating handle. A trip-free circuit breaker cannot be closed into an active electrical fault.

triphibian (aircraft type). An aircraft with a landing gear that allows it to operate from dry ground, snow or ice, or water.

triplane (type of airplane). An airplane with three main supporting wings. Triplanes were used during World War I because they were strong and lightweight, and their short wing span made them highly maneuverable. The additional expense and the drag produced by the third wing caused them to lose in popularity to the biplane and later to the monoplane.

triple-slotted flap (airplane secondary control). A type of trailing-edge wing flap used on some of the larger, high-performance airplanes. Triple-slotted flaps extend from the trailing edge of a wing in three sections. The trailing edge of one section forms a duct with the leading edge of the section behind it to force air down over the top of the flap. Triple-slotted flaps prevent the airflow from separating from the surface of the flap when they are fully extended.

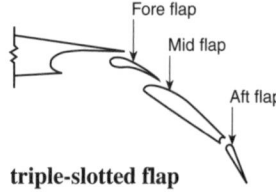

triple-slotted flap

triple-spool engine (gas turbine engine). A type of turbofan engine in which the fan is the first stage of compression, or N_1. The normal low-pressure compressor is N_2, and the high-pressure compressor is N_3. Each stage of compressor is driven by its own turbine, and the N_3 compressor is the only one whose speed is governed by the fuel control. The N_1 and N_2 compressors rotate at their own best speed.

triple thread. A multiple screw thread in which three threads are cut parallel to each other. The starting point of each thread is 120° from the starting point of the others. The lead, or the distance the screw moves forward in one revolution, is three times the pitch (the distance between the threads adjacent to each other).

tritium. An isotope of hydrogen with an atomic weight of three. The nucleus of an isotope of tritium has two neutrons as well as the proton. A normal atom of hydrogen has only one proton and no neutrons in its nucleus.

trivalent element. A chemical element with three electrons in its valence, or outer, shell. Boron, aluminum, gallium, and indium are trivalent elements.

tropical air (meteorology). An air mass with characteristics developed over the low latitudes. Maritime tropical (mT) air, the principal type, is produced over the tropical and subtropical seas and is very warm and humid. Continental tropical (cT) air is produced over subtropical arid regions and is hot and very dry.

tropical cyclone (meteorology). A general term for a cyclone that originates over tropical oceans. By international agreement, tropical cyclones have been classified according to their intensity:
- Tropical depression—winds up to 34 knots
- Tropical storm—winds of 35 to 64 knots
- Hurricane or typhoon—winds of 65 knots or higher.

tropopause. The division between the troposphere, the lower level of the earth's atmosphere, and the stratosphere, the layer of the atmosphere above the troposphere.

troposphere. The lower level of the earth's atmosphere. The troposphere extends upward from the surface of the earth to an altitude of about 36,000 feet (11,000 meters). The temperature drops steadily in the troposphere, and it is in the troposphere that all of the clouds and weather conditions exist.

troubleshooting. A procedure used in aircraft maintenance in which the operation of a malfunctioning system is analyzed to find the reason for the malfunction and to find a method for returning the system to its condition of normal operation.

trough (meteorology). An elongated area of relatively low atmospheric pressure. Troughs are usually associated with and most clearly identified as an area of maximum cyclonic curvature of the wind flow. A trough is the opposite of a ridge.

trough line (meteorology). A line along which pressures are lower than in the surroundings and where the cyclonic curvature of the isobars is a maximum.

TRSA (terminal radar service area) (air traffic control). Airspace surrounding designated airports in which ATC provides radar vectoring, sequencing, and separation on a full-time basis for all IFR and participating VFR aircraft. Service provided in a TRSA is called Stage III service. The *Aeronautical Information Manual* contains an explanation of TRSA, and TRSAs are depicted on VFR aeronautical charts. Pilot participation is urged, but not mandatory.

true airspeed (TAS). The airspeed shown on the airspeed indicator after it has been corrected for nonstandard temperature and pressure. *14 CFR Part 1:* "The airspeed of an aircraft relative to undisturbed air. True airspeed is equal to equivalent airspeed multiplied by $(p0/p)^{1/2}$."

true airspeed indicator (aircraft instrument). A special airspeed indicator that modifies the differential pressure measured by its diaphragm to take into consideration free-air temperature and barometric pressure. The indication of the instrument is in units of true airspeed, rather than indicated airspeed.

true air temperature. Indicated air temperature (IAT) corrected for the heat of compression caused by high-speed flight.

true altitude. The exact height of an aircraft above mean sea level.

true bearing (navigation). The direction between an aircraft and another object measured in degrees clockwise from true north.

true course (navigation). The navigational course for an aircraft measured from the geographic north pole.

true/false test item. A test item consisting of a statement followed by an opportunity for the student to indicate whether the statement is true or false.

true heading (TH) (navigation). The direction, measured in degrees clockwise from true north, which the nose of an aircraft should point to make good the desired course.

true north. True direction on the earth's surface measured from the geographic north pole.

true power (electrical power). The power, measured in watts, actually available in an alternating current circuit. True power is found by multiplying the circuit voltage by the current in phase with this voltage. It may also be found by multiplying the circuit voltage by the total current and then multiplying this by the power factor of the circuit.

true wind direction. The direction, with respect to true north, from which the wind is blowing.

truncated cone. A cone with its point cut off in such a way that its top is parallel with its base.

truss. A fuselage design made up of supporting structural members that resist deformation by applied loads. The truss-type fuselage is constructed of steel or aluminum tubing, with strength and rigidity achieved by welding the tubing together into a series of triangular shapes, called trusses.

T

TR unit. A transformer-rectifier unit. A TR unit reduces the voltage of alternating current and changes it into direct current.

trunnion. Projections from the cylinder of a retractable landing gear strut about which the strut pivots to retract.

truss-type structure. A type of structure made up of longitudinal beams and cross braces. Compression loads between the main beams are carried by rigid cross braces called compression struts. Tension loads are carried by stays, or wires, that go from one main beam to the other and cross between the compression struts.

T-seal. A form of two-way seal used in fluid power components. The cross section of the main seal element is in the shape of the letter T with the edge of the stem providing the sealing surface. The stem is backed up on both sides with Teflon backup rings.

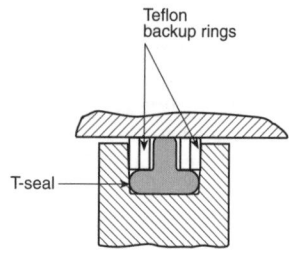

T-seal

TSFC (thrust specific fuel consumption). A measure of the fuel efficiency of a turbojet or turbofan engine. TSFC is the number of pounds of fuel burned per hour for each pound of thrust produced.

TSO (Technical Standard Order). An approval issued by the FAA for the manufacture of a component for installation on a certificated aircraft.

T-tail (aircraft configuration). The configuration of an aircraft empennage in which the horizontal stabilizer has little or no dihedral or anhedral and is mounted at or near the top of the vertical stabilizer, in the form of the letter T.

tubing cutter (mechanic's hand tool). A small hand tool used to make a square cut across the end of a piece of soft metal or plastic tubing. The cutter consists of a set of rollers and a sharp-edged wheel that can be screwed down so it rolls over the surface of the tubing. The tubing is placed on the rollers, and the wheel is screwed down against the surface. The cutter is rotated around the tubing and the wheel is moved in so it cuts deeper into the tubing. This action is continued until the tubing is cut completely through.

tumble limit (gyroscopic flight instrument limitation). The number of degrees of pitch or roll an aircraft is allowed before a gyroscope in a gyroscopic flight instrument contacts the stops in its gimbal system and tumbles.

tuned circuit (electronic circuit). A resonant electronic circuit containing both inductance and capacitance. Either the inductance or the capacitance can be adjusted to change the frequency to which the circuit is resonant.

tungsten. A hard, grayish-white, brittle, corrosion-resistant, metallic chemical element. Tungsten's symbol is W, its atomic number is 74, and its atomic weight is 183.85. Tungsten, which melts at 3,400°C, is used for incandescent lamp filaments and as an alloying element to give steel toughness and strength at high temperature.

tungsten steel. A very hard, heat-resistant steel containing tungsten and other alloys. It is used for making metal-cutting and forming tools.

tunnel diode (electronic component). A semiconductor diode doped with a larger amount of impurity than is used in an ordinary diode. A tunnel diode has a negative resistance region. Forward current increases with an increase in forward voltage until peak current is reached. At this point, forward current decreases with an increase in forward voltage until a valley is reached. This region of decreasing forward current, with an increase in forward voltage, is called the negative resistance region. Tunnel diodes are used as high-speed switching diodes.

turbine (axial). A wheel fitted with vanes, or buckets, radiating out from its circumference. Kinetic energy in a fluid flowing through the vanes is converted into mechanical power by the impulse or reaction of the fluid with the vanes.

turbine blades. The portion of the turbine assembly that absorbs the energy of the expanding gases and converts it into rotational velocity.

turbine discharge pressure (Pt). The total pressure at the discharge of the low-pressure turbine in a dual-turbine axial-flow engine.

turbine disk (turbine engine component). The solid, central portion of a turbine wheel. The turbine blades are attached to its periphery and the shaft is attached to its center.

turbine engine (gas turbine engine). A form of internal combustion engine that consists principally of a turbine-driven air compressor and a combustion chamber. Fuel is sprayed into the compressed air and ignited inside the combustion chamber. Heat from the burning fuel expands the air which is forced through the turbine to spin it and drive the compressor. *See* turbofan engine, turbojet engine, turboprop engine and turboshaft engine.

turbine inlet guide vanes (turbine engine component). The special series of stator vanes immediately ahead of the turbine. The function of the inlet guide vanes is to divert the air to the proper direction to enter the first-stage turbine, and to provide a series of convergent ducts which increase the velocity of the air.

turbine inlet temperature. *See* TIT.

turbine nozzle. Another name for turbine inlet guide vanes.

turbine outlet temperature (TOT). The temperature of the gases as they exit the turbine section.

turbine plenum. The portion of the combustor in which the gases are collected to be evenly distributed to the turbine blades.

turbine rotors. The portion of the turbine assembly that mounts to the shaft and holds the turbine blades in place.

turbine section. The section of the engine that converts high-pressure, high-temperature gas into rotational energy.

turbine stage (turbine engine component). A turbine stage consists of a row of stationary vanes or nozzles, followed by a row of rotating blades. When additional power is needed, more than one stage of turbines is used.

turbine wheel (turbine engine component). A dynamically balanced unit consisting of turbine blades attached to the periphery of a rotating disk. Hot gases from the combustion chamber flow through a series of nozzle vanes to direct them into the turbine blades at the optimum angle. Torque from the turbine wheel drives the compressor.

turbocharger (reciprocating engine component). An exhaust-gas-driven air compressor used to increase the power of a reciprocating engine. A turbocharger uses a small radial-inflow turbine in the exhaust system of the engine to drive a centrifugal-type air compressor mounted on the turbine shaft. Exhaust gases spin the turbine, and the compressor compresses air. This compressed air flows into the cylinders of the engine through the induction system.

A turbocharger uses power from the engine because it increases the exhaust back pressure. But the compressed air it forces into the cylinders produces a greater power increase than the loss of power caused by the turbine. Turbocharger is a shortened name for exhaust-driven turbosupercharger.

turbocompound engine (reciprocating engine type). A type of reciprocating engine that recovers some of the energy normally lost through the exhaust by using a power-recovery turbine (PRT) in the exhaust. Some of the energy remaining in the exhaust gas leaving the cylinders is used to spin a turbine connected through a fluid coupling to the crankshaft. A portion of this energy is returned to the crankshaft.

turbofan engine. A type of gas turbine engine that has a set of lengthened blades on the low-pressure compressor or low-pressure turbine. Air moved by these special blades bypasses the core engine and produces between 30% and 75% of the total thrust produced by the engine.

T

turbojet aircraft. An aircraft having a jet engine in which the energy of the jet operates a turbine which in turn operates the air compressor. *See also* turbojet engine.

turbojet engine. A form of heat engine that produces thrust by accelerating a relatively small mass of air through a large change in velocity. A compressor in the front of the engine compresses the inlet air, and fuel is sprayed into this air and burned. The heat from the burning fuel expands the air and forces it out the back of the engine in the form of a high-velocity jet of hot air. The air leaving the engine flows through a turbine which extracts energy to drive the compressor.

turboprop aircraft. An aircraft having a jet engine in which the energy of the jet operates a turbine which drives the propeller. *See also* turboprop engine.

turboprop engine. A form of gas turbine engine that uses one or more stages of turbines to drive a set of reduction gears, which in turn drives a propeller. Most of the heat energy in the exhaust gases is converted into torque, rather than into a stream of high-velocity exhaust gases, as is done in a turbojet engine.

turboshaft engine. A form of gas turbine engine that uses one or more stages of turbines to drive a transmission, which in turn drives the rotors of a helicopter. A turboshaft engine extracts a maximum amount of the heat energy from the exhaust gas to drive the turbine connected to the transmission.

turbosupercharger. The original name for a turbocharger.

turbulence. A condition of fluid flow in which the flow is not smooth. The velocity of the flow changes rapidly, and the flow direction often reverses itself.

turbulence in and near thunderstorms (TNT). Turbulence associated with thunderstorms that occurs above, below and around them.

turbulence, mechanical (meteorology). Air turbulence caused by eddies produced as air flows over and around such obstructions as buildings, trees, and rough terrain.

turbulent wake (aerodynamics). The wake of a body passing through the air caused by the separation of airflow from the surface of the structure.

turn and bank indicator. The former name for a turn and slip indicator. *See* turn and slip indicator.

turn and slip indicator (flight instrument). A rate gyro flight instrument that gives the pilot an indication of the rate of rotation of the aircraft about its vertical axis. The turn and slip indicator shows the trim condition of the aircraft and serves as an emergency source of bank information in case the attitude gyro fails.

The turn indicator uses a rate gyro attached through a fork and pin mechanism to a vertical pointer. This rate gyro is installed so it measures the rate of rotation about the vertical axis of the aircraft. The vertical pointer shows when a standard rate turn ($3°$ per second for some aircraft, and $1^1/_2°$ per second for others) is being made. The slip indicator is a curved glass tube partially filled with a liquid in which a black glass ball rolls.

When the angle of bank is correct for the rate of turn, centrifugal force and gravity are balanced, and the ball stays in the center of the tube. When the rate of turn is too high for the angle of bank, the centrifugal force is greater than the force of gravity and the ball rolls to the outside of the turn. When the rate of turn is too low for the angle of bank being used, the force of gravity is greater than the centrifugal force, and the ball rolls to the inside of the turn. Turn and slip indicators were once called needle and ball indicators and more recently, turn and bank indicators. *See* illustration for rate gyro.

turn anticipation (navigation). The capability of RNAV systems to determine the point along a course, prior to a turn WP, where a turn should be initiated to provide a smooth path to intercept the succeeding course, and to enunciate the information to the pilot.

turnbuckle. An adjusting device used in a run of aircraft control cable to adjust its tension. A turnbuckle consists of a brass barrel and two threaded cable terminals made of steel. One terminal and one end of the barrel have left-hand threads, and the other terminal and the other end of the barrel have right-hand threads. The cable terminals are both started into the barrel, and as the barrel is turned, the terminals both screw into it. Screwing the terminals into the barrel increases the cable tension by shortening the cable.

turn coordinator (aircraft flight instrument). A rate gyro instrument that shows at a glance when a standard-rate turn is being made. The dial has a symbol which represents the rear of an airplane with marks that align with its wing tip when a standard-rate turn of 3° per second is being made. A black ball in a curved glass tube below the airplane symbol shows when the angle of bank is correct for the rate of turn being made.

The rate gyro is mounted in a canted gimbal (a tilted mounting frame) that allows the gyro to precess, or roll over, when the aircraft rotates about either its vertical or longitudinal axes. The gyro sensing rotation about both axes makes the instrument more sensitive and gives a more accurate indication of the condition of a turn than that shown by a turn and slip indicator.

turning error (magnetic compass error). *See* northerly turning error.

turning vent (balloon component). A vent on the side of a hot air balloon envelope which, when opened, allows escaping air to exit in a manner causing the balloon to rotate on its axis.

turn radius (aircraft performance). The horizontal distance required for an aircraft to complete a turn.

turns around a point (flight training maneuver). A training maneuver that requires the airplane to be flown in two or more complete circles of uniform radii or distance from a prominent ground reference point using a maximum bank of approximately 45° while maintaining a constant altitude.

turn WP (turning point). A waypoint which identifies a change from one course to another.

turpentine. A liquid obtained by distilling the gum from pine trees. Turpentine is used as a solvent and thinner for paints and varnishes.

turret lathe. A type of metal-turning lathe in which the cutting tools are mounted in a turret. For example, a drill, a boring tool, and a chamfering tool can be mounted in the turret. The drill is moved into the work to drill the hole. The drill is then backed out, the turret is rotated to put the boring tool in place, and the hole is counterbored. The boring tool is then backed out and the chamfering tool is rotated into place. The chamfering tool is moved into the work to chamfer the edges of the counterbored hole.

TWEB. *See* transcribed weather broadcast.

twelve-point socket (mechanic's hand tool). A socket wrench with a double hex, or a 12-point, opening broached into its open end. A 12-point socket is easier to position on a nut or bolt head than a six-point socket.

twenty-minute rating (battery capacity rating). The ampere hour rating of an aircraft battery when the current drawn from it will drop its voltage to a predetermined cut-off voltage in twenty minutes.

twilight. The intervals of incomplete darkness following sunset and just preceding sunrise. The time at which evening twilight ends and morning twilight begins is determined by arbitrary convention. *See* civil twilight, nautical twilight, astronomical twilight.

twin-row radial engine (reciprocating engine type). A type of radial engine with two rows of cylinders and a single crankshaft. The cylinders of a radial engine project out from a small crankcase that holds the crankshaft. The piston in one cylinder attaches to a master rod whose large end goes around the crankshaft throw, and the pistons in all of the other cylinders attach to the master rod with link rods.

A twin-row radial engine has a two-throw crankshaft and two rows of cylinders and two master rods. The cylinders in the rear row are staggered between those in the front row for improved cooling. The most popular twin-row radial engines have 14 or 18 cylinders.

T

twist drill. A metal-cutting tool turned in a drill press or a hand-held drill motor. A twist drill has a straight shank and spiraled flutes. A cutting edge is ground on the end of the spiraled flutes. The diameter of twist drills is measured in four different ways: Fractions of an inch, millimeters, letters, and numbers.

twisted pair (electrical cable). A type of electrical cable made up of two insulated wires twisted together and enclosed in an outer insulation. The magnetic fields caused by current flowing in the two conductors of a twisted pair cancel each other and minimize the magnetic field radiating from the conductors.

twister (meteorology). A colloquial term for tornado.

twist grip (helicopter power control). The throttle control on the collective pitch control lever. Twisting the grip controls the amount of fuel supplied to a reciprocating engine, or the amount of power produced by a turboshaft engine.

twist stripe (flexible fluid lines). A colored stripe running along the length of a flexible hose. If this stripe spirals around the hose, it indicates that the hose was twisted when it was installed. Twist stripes are also called lay lines.

two-axis automatic pilot. An automatic pilot that uses a canted rate gyro, similar to that used in a turn coordinator, to sense rotation of the aircraft about its longitudinal and vertical axes. Output from the rate gyro controls a pair of servos in the aileron system that keeps the wings level and the airplane stable in roll and yaw. Two-axis automatic pilots are sometimes called wing levelers.

two-part adhesive. An adhesive packaged in two containers and mixed just before it is used. A two-part adhesive consists of resin and an accelerator to speed up the curing action of the resin.

two-spool engine. *See* dual-spool gas-turbine engine.

two-stroke-cycle engine (reciprocating engine). A simple form of reciprocating engine that completes its operating cycle in two strokes of its piston—one down and one up. When the piston moves up, fuel is pulled into the crankcase at the same time the fuel-air mixture inside the cylinder is being compressed. When the piston is near the top of its stroke, a spark plug ignites the compressed fuel-air mixture, and the expanding gases force the piston down. Near the bottom of its stroke, the piston uncovers an exhaust port, and the burned gases leave the cylinder. When the piston moves farther down, it uncovers an intake port, and fuel and air are forced from the crankcase into the cylinder.

Two-stroke-cycle engines are inefficient in their use of fuel, but their simplicity makes them popular for powering ultralight aircraft where light weight and low cost are paramount.

two-terminal spot-type fire detection system. A fire detection system that uses individual thermoswitches installed around the inside of the area to be protected. These thermoswitches are wired in parallel between two separate circuits. A short or an open can exist in either circuit without disabling the system or causing a fire warning.

two-way communications. Communications in which two stations transmit and receive information. Ordinary telephone communications is an example of two-way communications.

two-way radio communications failure. *See* lost communications.

TYP (drafting term). The word TYP on a mechanical drawing indicates that the part of the drawing referred to is typical for more than one part. If a fastener requires six holes of the same dimensions, it is common practice to show the dimension for one hole and mark it as "TYP FOR 6."

type. *14 CFR Part 1:*

"(1) As used with respect to the certification, ratings, privileges, and limitations of airmen, means a specific make and model of aircraft, including modifications thereto that do not change its handling or flight characteristics. Examples include: DC-7, 1049, and F-27; and

(2) As used with respect to the certification of aircraft, means those aircraft which are similar in design. Examples include: DC-7 and DC-7C; 1049G and 1049H; and F-27 and F-27F.

(3) As used with respect to the certification of aircraft engines means those engines which are similar in design. For example JT8D and JT8D-7 are engines of the same type, and JT9D-3A and JT9D-7 are engines of the same type."

Type Certificate Data Sheet (TCDS). The official specifications of an aircraft, engine, or propeller issued by the Federal Aviation Administration. TCDS lists pertinent specifications for the device, and it is the responsibility of the technician and/or inspector to ensure, on each inspection, that the device meets these specifications. TCDS replaces Aircraft Specifications which were issued to aircraft and components certificated under the CARs (Civil Air Regulations), the forerunner of the FARs, or 14 CFRs.

type certification. Official recognition that the design and operating limitations of an aircraft, engine, or propeller meet the airworthiness standards prescribed by the Code of Federal Regulations for that particular category or type of aircraft, engine, or propeller.

type rating (pilot rating). A rating to a pilot's certificate that states he or she is able to fly a particular type of sophisticated or large aircraft, such as a Cessna Citation X business jet.

typhoon (meteorology). A tropical cyclone in the eastern hemisphere with winds in excess of 65 knots.

Ty-Rap. Patented nylon straps used to tie bundles of wire together. The Ty-Rap is wrapped around the wire bundle, and its toothed strap is passed through a loop having matching teeth. A special tool pulls the strap tight around the bundle, and as it is pulled, the teeth on the strap and the loop mesh and lock the loop in place. Once a Ty-Rap is pulled tight, it must be cut to remove it.

T

UA. *See* unmanned aircraft.

U-bolt. A U-shaped rod threaded on both ends. U-bolts are used to fasten round rods or pipes to a flat surface.

UDF engine (Unducted Fan). The trade name registered by General Electric for type of ultrahigh-bypass turbofan engine that drives one or more propellers which have between 8 and 12 blades. These blades, which are not enclosed in a duct or shroud, are very thin, have wide chords, and are highly swept back with a scimitar shape. An Unducted Fan engine can power airplanes flying at speeds of near Mach 0.8.

UHB engine (ultrahigh-bypass). A gas turbine engine in which a fan, either ducted or unducted, has a bypass ratio greater than 30:1.

UHF (ultrahigh frequencies) (radio frequencies). Frequencies of electromagnetic radiation between 300 and 3,000 megahertz. The wavelengths for ultrahigh frequencies range between 100 and 10 centimeters. The UHF band is between the VHF (very-high-frequency) and the SHF (super-high-frequency) bands.

ultimate load (aircraft structural specification). The amount of load that can be applied to an aircraft structure before it fails. The limit load is the maximum load a structure is designed to carry, and the factor of safety is the percentage of limit load the structure can actually carry before its ultimate load is reached. A structure designed to carry a load of 1,000 pounds with a safety factor of 1.5 has an ultimate load of 1,500 pounds.

ultimate tensile strength. The tensile stress required to cause a material to break or to continue to deform under a decreasing load.

ultrahigh frequencies. *See* UHF.

ultralight vehicle. An aeronautical vehicle operated under 14 CFR Part 103 for sport or recreational purposes which does not require FAA registration, an airworthiness certificate, nor pilot certification. Ultralights are primarily single-occupant vehicles, although some two-place vehicles are authorized for training purposes. Operation of an ultralight vehicle in certain airspace requires authorization from ATC.

ultrasonic cleaning. A method of cleaning mechanical components by vibrating them at an ultrasonic frequency while soaking them in a cleaning solution.

ultrasonic frequencies. Frequencies of vibration higher than the human ear can hear. Ultrasonic frequencies are normally considered to begin at 20,000 hertz.

ultrasonic inspection. A type of nondestructive inspection in which a piece of material is examined for hidden flaws. Pulses of mechanical vibration at an ultrasonic frequency are passed through the part being tested. This vibration produces an electrical signal which is displayed on the screen of a cathode-ray oscilloscope. The display produced by the vibrations passing through the material being tested is compared with the display produced by a vibration of the same frequency passing through a similar material known to have no faults. Any difference in the displays is an indication of an internal fault.

ultrasonics. The branch of science and technology that deals with mechanical vibrations having a frequency higher than the human ear can normally hear. Ultrasonic energy has a frequency greater than 20,000 hertz.

ultrasonic soldering. A method of soldering aluminum with soft solder. Aluminum is difficult to solder because, when it is heated, oxides form on its surface and prevent the solder wetting the metal. The tip of a special soldering iron is vibrated at an ultrasonic frequency as it heats the metal and melts the flux in the solder. This vibration breaks the oxide film away from the surface of the metal, and it floats on top of the flux. The flux covers the hot metal and prevents new oxides forming. Soft solder will stick to aluminum when there are no oxides on it.

ultrasonic vibrations. Vibrations at a frequency higher than the human ear can normally hear. Ultrasonic vibrations are higher than 20,000 hertz (cycles per second).

ultraviolet-blocking dope. Dope that contains tiny aluminum flakes or some other pigment that blocks the passage of ultraviolet rays from the sun. This coat of dope protects the organic fabrics and the clear dope from deterioration by these rays.

ultraviolet lamp. A form of vapor lamp that produces electromagnetic radiation whose wavelength is slightly shorter than that of visible light. Ultraviolet light is often called "black light."

ultraviolet radiation. Radiation of electromagnetic energy whose wavelengths are between about 100 and 4,000 angstroms. *See* angstrom. The wavelengths of ultraviolet rays are just shorter than those of rays visible to the human eye.

umbilical cord (rocket component). A cable used to carry power from a launch pad to a rocket or spacecraft being readied for flight. The umbilical cord is disconnected before the vehicle leaves the pad. An umbilical cord is also used to tether and to supply oxygen to an astronaut when operating outside a spacecraft in space.

"unable" (air traffic control). A phrase used in ATC–pilot communications to indicate inability to comply with a specific instruction, request, or clearance.

unacceptable risk (risk assessment, aeronautical decision making). A result of risk assessment, when a pilot determines that a certain level of risk or hazard is not manageable and is unacceptable for a certain flight. As the first task of system safety, all possible hazards or risks are identified within practical limitations; then those risks are assessed as to their manageability in flight, or whether they can be reduced through some other prior action. In the case of unacceptable risk, the pilot has determined this level of risk cannot be tolerated and needs to be eliminated or controlled. *See also* acceptable risk, residual risk.

unbalanced cell (nickel-cadmium battery condition). A cell in a nickel-cadmium battery that has become discharged to a lower level than the other cells in the battery. An unbalanced cell will take more charging current than the other cells, and this can lead to overheating and thermal runaway of the battery. Unbalanced cells can be corrected by deep-cycling the battery.

unbalanced transmission line (radio transmission line). A form of two-conductor cable used to carry an electromagnetic signal from a transmitter to its antenna. An unbalanced line does not have the same voltage between each of the two conductors and ground. A coaxial cable is a form of unbalanced transmission line.

uncaging (gyro instrument). Unlocking the gimbals of a gyroscopic instrument, leaving the gyro free to tumble and making it susceptible to damage by abrupt flight maneuvers or rough handling.

uncontrolled airport. An airport that does not have an operating control tower. Two-way radio communications are not required at uncontrolled airports, although it is good operating practice for pilots to transmit their intentions on the specified frequency.

uncontrolled airspace. Class G airspace that has not been designated as Class A, B, C, D, or E. It is airspace in which air traffic control has no authority or responsibility to control air traffic; however, pilots should remember there are VFR minimums which apply to this airspace.

uncontrolled lift (aerodynamics). Lift that occurs without specific action by the pilot. Often referred to as false lift.

uncontrolled spin (aircraft flight maneuver). A spin in an airplane in which the controls are ineffective in recovering to straight and level flight. *See* spin.

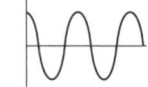

undamped oscillation. Oscillation that continues with an unchanging amplitude once it has started.

undercarriage (aircraft structure). The landing gear of an aircraft.

undercast (meteorology). A cloud layer of ten-tenths (1.0) coverage, as viewed from an observation point above the layer.

undamped oscillation

undercompounded generator (electrical generator). A condition in an electrical generator which has both a series and a shunt field in which the effect of the shunt field is greater than that of the series field. The output voltage tends to drop as the electrical load increases.

undercurrent relay (electrical protection device). An electrical circuit protection device that opens a control circuit when the current drops to a specified low value.

underground fuel hydrant (airport fueling facility). The terminal of an underground fuel system installed at many large airports. The fuel truck which has the required pumps, filters, and metering instruments but no storage tank is connected to the fuel hydrant, and its hoses are connected to the fueling panel of the aircraft.

underpowered (aircraft condition). An aircraft is underpowered when there is not enough power delivered to its propeller or rotor to give it the required performance.

undershoot (aircraft landing). A condition in an aircraft landing in which the aircraft touches the ground before it reaches the end of the runway or the landing strip. A pilot can correct an undershot approach by applying engine power as soon as it is evident the aircraft will not reach the spot of intended touchdown.

underslung rotor (helicopter rotor). A helicopter rotor with its center of gravity below the point at which the rotor is attached to the mast.

underspeed condition (propeller governor condition). A propeller governor is in its underspeed condition when the engine is operating at a speed lower than the governor calls for. The speeder spring holds the pilot valve down and the flyweights in. With the pilot valve down, the governor directs oil in the proper direction to decrease the pitch of the propeller blades. When the blade pitch decreases, the RPM increases, the governor flyweights spin out to an on-speed condition, and oil is trapped in the propeller to hold the pitch.

understanding. A basic level of learning at which a student comprehends or grasps the nature or meaning of something.

under the hood (instrument flight training). A term that indicates that the pilot is using a hood to restrict visibility outside the cockpit while simulating instrument flight. An appropriately rated pilot is required in the other control seat while this operation is being conducted.

undervoltage relay (electrical circuit protection device). A type of electrical circuit protection device that opens the alternator field circuit when the output circuit voltage drops below a specified low value.

underwing fueling (aircraft fuel system). The method of fueling an aircraft in which fuel is pumped into the aircraft tanks through a single-point fueling port located below the wing. Underwing fueling differs from overwing fueling, in which the fuel is pumped directly into the tanks through openings in the tops of the tanks.

U

Underwriters' Laboratories. Independent laboratories recognized in the electrical industry as setting safety standards for electrical equipment and components. Before a piece of electrical equipment is granted the right to carry the UL symbol, it must pass the tests prescribed by the laboratories for that type of equipment.

undrainable oil (aircraft specification). Oil that cannot be drained from an engine lubricating system when the aircraft is in the normal ground attitude and the drain valve is left open. The weight of the undrainable oil is included in the empty weight of the aircraft.

unfeather (propeller operation). To change the blade pitch of a propeller from the feathered high pitch, which prevents air loads windmilling it, to a lower pitch. When a propeller is unfeathered in flight, aerodynamic forces produced by air flowing over the blades cause the propeller to turn the engine.

unfeathering accumulator. A tank that holds oil under pressure, which can be used to unfeather a propeller.

unfrozen (air traffic control). This refers to the state of the scheduled time of arrival (STA) tags for aircraft that are still being rescheduled by traffic management advisor (TMA) calculations. The aircraft will remain unfrozen until the corresponding estimated time of arrival (ETA) tag passes the preset freeze horizon for that aircraft's super stream class. At that point, the automatic rescheduling will stop and the STA becomes "frozen." *See also* super stream class.

UNICOM (radio communications). A privately owned radio station located on an airport. Pilots of aircraft operating from the airport can talk with the operator of the UNICOM station to order service or to have the operator ready to service their aircraft when they land. UNICOM can be used to give advisory information about the airport, but it cannot be used to control traffic around the airport.

unidirectional current (electrical current). Another name for direct current. Unidirectional current flows in one direction only. It does not reverse its direction as alternating current does. It is always either positive or negative, with respect to a reference value.

unidirectional fabric. Fabric in which all of the threads run in the same direction. These threads are often bound with a few fibers which cross them at right angles, just enough to hold the yarns together and prevent their bunching.

uniform acceleration. The speeding up of an object in which the velocity increases at a uniform rate. It changes the same amount each second it moves.

uniform surface corrosion. A mild form of corrosion in which the surface of a piece of metal is covered by the salts of corrosion, but there are no localized pits on the surface.

unijunction transistor (UJT). A three-terminal semiconductor device. A pulse of energy on one terminal controls the flow of electrons between its other two terminals. When a pulse of electrical energy of the correct polarity is applied between the emitter and one of the bases, a negative resistance is produced between the two bases, and electrons flow through the UJT between the two bases.

unimproved airport. An airport with runways made of grass, dirt, or gravel, instead of concrete or asphalt.

union (threaded pipe fitting). A three-piece threaded pipe fitting used to join two pipes or to connect a pipe to a component. A union allows the pipes to be connected without either of the pipes having to be turned.

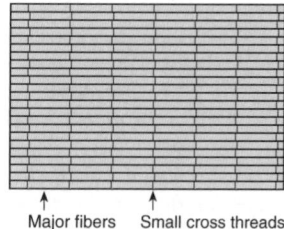

Major fibers   Small cross threads

unidirectional fabric

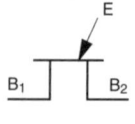

unijunction transistor

United States. *14 CFR Part 1:* "In a geographical sense means: (1) the States, the district of Columbia, Puerto Rico, and the possessions, including the territorial waters, and (2) the airspace of those areas."

United States air carrier. *14 CFR Part 1:* "A citizen of the United States who undertakes directly by lease, or other arrangement, to engage in air transportation."

unit magnetic pole. A magnetic pole that will repel a like pole of equal strength, at a distance of one centimeter, in a vacuum, with a force of one dyne.

universal chuck (machine tool component). A type of clamp used to hold material being turned on a lathe. The three jaws of a universal chuck are moved in and out at the same time by turning a chuck key. A universal chuck holds the work centered as the jaws are clamped tightly on the work.

universal communications (UNICOM). An air-ground communication facility operated by a private agency to provide advisory service at uncontrolled airports.

universal joint. A type of shaft coupling that allows one shaft to drive the other, even if the two shafts are not in perfect alignment. A universal joint has a double hinge, with the axes of the two hinges at right angles to each other.

universal motor. A form of series-wound electric motor that operates equally well on alternating current or direct current. A universal motor has a commutator on its armature, and armature current is fed into the commutator through brushes.

universal propeller protractor. A precision protractor that can be read to one tenth of a degree. Universal propeller protractors are used to check and set the pitch of propeller blades and to measure the amount of movement of aircraft control surfaces.

universal time. Solar time at the prime meridian. Solar time is the time based on the rotation of the earth about the sun, and the prime meridian is the meridian of longitude that passes through the Royal Observatory at Greenwich, England. Universal time is known also as Greenwich mean time (GMT) and Zulu time.

unleaded gasoline (reciprocating engine fuel). A fuel for reciprocating engines that does not contain any tetraethyl lead (TEL). *See* TEL.

unlimited ceiling (meteorology). A clear sky or a sky cover that does not meet the criteria for a ceiling.

unloaded rotor (helicopter rotor condition). The state of a rotor when rotor force has been removed, or when the rotor is operating under a low or negative G condition.

unloading valve (hydraulic system component). A pressure control valve used in an aircraft hydraulic system to unload the engine-driven pump when the system pressure reaches a predetermined value. The unloading valve traps the pressure in the pressure manifold, where it is held by the accumulator, and routes the output of the pump back to the reservoir. When the pressure in the manifold drops to a lower predetermined value, the unloading valve directs the pump output back into the pressure manifold. An unloading valve is also called a system pressure regulator. *See* system pressure regulator.

unmanned aircraft (UA). A device used or intended to be used for flight in the air with no onboard pilot. UA include all classes of airplanes, helicopters, airships, and translational lift aircraft that have no onboard pilot, but only those aircraft controllable in three axes and, therefore, exclude traditional balloons. The United States Air Force (USAF) refers to UA as remotely piloted aircraft (RPA).

An unmanned aircraft system (UAS), associated with a UA, is operated by a pilot-in-command who is responsible for remote piloting duties such as collision avoidance, avoidance of other traffic, clouds, obstructions, and terrain, etc. This person is assisted by a trained observer (or, a "visual observer") who has duties associated with collision

Continued

unmanned aircraft (UA). *Continued*
avoidance and watching the activity of the UA, either from the ground via a visual line-of-sight or in the air by means of a chase aircraft. Additionally, a UAS may use a supplemental pilot, who can be available to augment and/or assume duties of the PIC, provided he or she meets the qualifications. UAS occasionally use both an internal and an external UA pilot, and a supplemental pilot can take either position.

unmanned aircraft system (UAS). A system consisting of an unmanned aircraft (UA), a data link, a ground control station, and any necessary ground support equipment. UAS come in a variety of shapes and sizes and serve diverse purposes. They may have a wingspan as large as a Boeing 737 or be smaller than a radio-controlled model aircraft. A designated pilot-in-command is always in control of a UAS. *See also* unmanned aircraft.

unmetered fuel (pressure carburetor fuel). Fuel in a pressure carburetor after its pressure has been regulated, but before it has been metered by flowing through the metering jet.

unpublished route. A route for which no minimum altitude is published or charted for pilot use. It may include a direct route between NAVAIDs, a radial, a radar vector, or a final approach course beyond the segments of an instrument approach procedure.

unreliable (GPS/WAAS). An advisory to pilots indicating the expected level of service of the GPS and/or WAAS may not be available. Pilots must then determine the adequacy of the signal for desired use.

unscheduled maintenance. Maintenance performed on an aircraft as a result of a problem discovered in the course of normal operation. Scheduled maintenance is maintenance performed according to a predetermined plan or schedule.

unstabilized approach. The final approach of an aircraft that has not achieved a stable rate of descent or controlled flight track by a predetermined altitude, usually 500 feet AGL.

unstable air (meteorology). A mass of air whose temperature lapse rate, the change in temperature as the altitude changes, is greater than that of the air surrounding it. When unstable air is forced upward by flowing up the side of a mountain, for example, it will continue to move upward, increasing its speed as it goes up. This causes updrafts in the air. Cumulus clouds form at the top of a column of rising unstable air.

unusable fuel (aircraft specification). Fuel in an aircraft fuel system that will not flow to the fuel metering system when the aircraft is in its normal flight attitude. This fuel is also called residual fuel. The weight of unusable fuel is included in the empty weight of the aircraft. The amount of unusable fuel and its arm are specified in the aircraft type certificate data sheets.

unusual attitude (flight attitude). An airplane attitude not normally required for instrument flight. Unusual attitudes may result from a number of conditions, such as turbulence, disorientation, instrument failure, confusion, preoccupation with cockpit duties, carelessness in cross-checking, errors in instrument interpretation, or lack of proficiency in aircraft control.

updraft (meteorology). A localized upward current of air.

updraft carburetor (reciprocating engine component). A type of carburetor that mounts below the intake manifold of a reciprocating engine. All of the air flowing into the engine flows upward through the venturi.

upholstery. The fabric, padding, and other components used to make a soft covering for a seat. Upholstery makes the seat comfortable to sit in and attractive to look at.

upper deck pressure (fuel metering system pressure). The pressure that exists between the turbocharger compressor and the throttle plate of a fuel injection system installed on a reciprocating engine. Upper deck pressure, also called turbocharger discharge pressure, differs from manifold pressure by the pressure drop across the throttle valve.

upper front (meteorology). A front aloft that does not extend to the earth's surface.

upset head (rivet head). The head of a rivet formed when the rivet is installed. The upset head is also called the shop head, to distinguish it from the manufactured head on the rivet before it is driven.

upslope fog (meteorology). Fog formed when air flows upward over rising terrain and is cooled adiabatically to a temperature at or below its initial dew point.

upslope wind (meteorology). Stable air moving up sloping terrain.

upswell (sea condition). Motion opposite the direction the swell is moving. If the swell is moving from north to south, a seaplane going from south to north is moving upswell.

upwind. The direction from which the wind is blowing.

upwind leg (airport traffic pattern). A flight path parallel to the landing runway in the direction of landing.

uranium. A heavy, silvery-white, metallic chemical element in the actinide group. Uranium's symbol is U, and its atomic number is 92. An isotope of uranium, U-235, is used as one of the basic atomic fuels. When U-235 is bombarded with neutrons, it changes into smaller atoms, and in making this change, it releases neutrons and produces an enormous amount of heat.

urgency. A condition of being concerned about safety and of requiring timely but not immediate assistance; a potential distress condition.

usability. The functionality of tests.

usable fuel (GAMA). Fuel available for flight planning.

useful lift (load). The potential weight of the pilot, passengers, equipment, and fuel. It is the basic empty weight of the aircraft subtracted from the maximum allowable gross weight.

useful load (aircraft operation). The difference between the maximum allowable weight of the aircraft and its empty weight. The useful load of an aircraft includes the weight of the fuel and oil, the crew, the passengers, all of their baggage, and any cargo carried.

user-defined waypoints (navigation). Waypoint location and other data which may be input by the user; this is the only GPS database that may be altered (edited) by the user.

user request evaluation tool (URET). The user request evaluation tool is an automated tool provided at each radar associate position in selected ATC en route facilities. This tool utilizes flight and radar data to determine present and future trajectories for all active and proposal aircraft and provides enhanced, automated flight data management.

U.S. gallon. A measure of quantity equal to 231 cubic inches, or 0.133 cubic foot.

U.S. Terminal Procedures Publication (TPP). Booklets published in regional format by the NACO that include DPs, STARs, IAPs, and other information pertinent to IFR flight.

utility category aircraft. A classification of aircraft approved for limited acrobatics, which may include spins, lazy eights, chandelles, and steep turns in which the bank angle exceeds sixty degrees. Typical limit load factors for utility category aircraft are +4.4g and −1.76g.

utility finish (type of aircraft finish). The finish of an aircraft that gives the necessary tautness and fill to the fabric and the necessary protection to the metal, but does not have the glossy appearance of a show-type finish.

U-tube manometer. A pressure measuring instrument made of a glass tube bent into the shape of the letter U. A liquid such as water or mercury is poured into the tube until it is filled to a given level. Either a positive or a negative pressure applied to one end of the tube will cause the liquid to rise in one side of the tube and drop in the other side. The difference in the level of the liquid in the two sides of the tube is proportional to the difference in the pressure at the two ends of the tube.

vacuum. A space in which nothing exists, a completely empty space. For practical purposes, a vacuum is considered to be a negative pressure, or a pressure less than that of the surrounding atmosphere.

vacuum bottle. A double-wall container used to store liquified gases such as liquid oxygen or liquid nitrogen. A vacuum bottle is made of thin stainless steel sheet, formed into a double-walled container. All air is pumped out of the space between the two walls, leaving a vacuum. The walls are too thin to transfer much heat into the bottle by conduction, and almost no heat passes across the vacuum. A vacuum bottle is a form of Dewar flask. *See* Dewar flask.

vacuum capacitor (electrical component). A capacitor that uses two concentric tubes as the plates, or conductors, and a vacuum between the tubes as the dielectric. A vacuum capacitor has a higher breakdown voltage than a similar capacitor that uses air as its dielectric.

vacuum distillation. A method of distilling a liquid by boiling it in a vacuum. The material being distilled is placed in a container, and as much air as possible is pumped from it. Because of the low pressure, the liquid boils at a lower temperature which prevents the material being damaged by heat.

vacuum forming. A method of forming parts from thermoplastic resin by using the weight of the atmosphere to apply pressure to the softened material. A sheet of thermoplastic material is placed above a female die and heated to soften it. When it is at the proper temperature, a low pressure, or vacuum, is produced inside the die, and atmospheric pressure forces the softened material into the die.

vacuum metallizing. A method of depositing an extremely thin film of metal on a surface. A metallic vapor is formed by evaporating the metal in a high vacuum, or extremely low absolute pressure. This vapor is attracted to the surface to be metallized where it forms a microscopically thin coating.

vacuum pump. An air pump used to remove air from a container. There are two types of vacuum pumps: those that produce a very low absolute pressure (a high vacuum) with almost no flow of air, and those that produce less vacuum (a higher absolute pressure) but move a much larger volume of air.

vacuum tube (electronic component). An electron control valve that has most of the air removed from the glass or metal envelope in which the electrodes are mounted. After as much air is removed from the envelope as is practical, a "getter" is ignited inside the tube to combine with any oxygen left inside the envelope. *See* getter.

vacuum-tube voltmeter. *See* VTVM.

VAD winds. Velocity azimuth display (VAD) winds are derived from the output of the 160 or more WRS-88 radar sites located throughout the United States. The WRS-88 is configured to produce radar returns off of dust and other particulate matter in the air, which can be used to indicate wind direction and speed at different altitudes. VAD winds are generally reported in 1,000-foot increments.

V

valence electrons. Electrons that spin around the nucleus of an atom in its outer shell. It is the number of valence electrons in an atom that determines its chemical and electrical characteristics, and it is these electrons that can be moved from one atom to another to produce electron, or current, flow.

All chemical elements have between one and eight valence electrons. Elements with between one and three valence electrons are good electrical conductors. Elements with five to eight valence electrons are electrical insulators, and elements with four valence electrons are called semiconductors.

valence shell. The outer shell of electrons spinning around the nucleus of an atom.

validity. The extent to which a test measures what it is supposed to measure.

valley breeze (meteorology). An anabatic wind formed during the day by the heating of a valley floor. As the ground becomes warmer than the surrounding atmosphere, the lower levels of air heat and rise, flowing up the mountainsides.

valve (electronic device). The British name for a vacuum tube.

valve (mechanical component). A device that regulates or controls the flow of a fluid, either a liquid or a gas. Fluid power systems use both flow control and pressure control valves. Aircraft pressurization systems control the cabin pressure with outflow valves, and the fuel-air charge enters the cylinder of a reciprocating engine through the intake valve, and the burned gases leave through the exhaust valve.

valve clearance (reciprocating engine specification). The clearance between the end of the valve stem and the rocker arm when the valve is seated and the cam follower is off the cam lobe.

valve core (aircraft wheel component). A spring-loaded air valve screwed into a metal tube installed in an aircraft wheel. When the tire mounted on the wheel is being inflated, the stem of the valve core is depressed by the air chuck, and air flows into the tire. When the air chuck is removed, the stem seats in the valve core, and the air is trapped in the tire. To deflate the tire, the valve stem is depressed, allowing air to flow out through the core.

valve duration (reciprocating engine specification). The amount of time, usually measured in degrees of crankshaft rotation, an intake or exhaust valve remains off its seat.

valve face (reciprocating engine component). The portion of a poppet valve that forms a seal with the valve seat in an aircraft engine cylinder head. The valve face is ground so it is perfectly smooth and concentric with the valve stem.

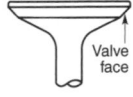

Valve face

valve face

valve float (reciprocating engine operation). The condition of engine operation in which an intake or exhaust valve does not seat when the rocker arm is off the valve stem. It is possible for the engine to operate at a speed at which valves are being opened at the natural, or resonant, frequency of the valve springs. If this happens, the valve springs lose their effectiveness and will not close the valves, and the valves will float. To prevent floating, most aircraft engine valves are closed with more than one spring. These springs are wound with a different pitch and of different size wire, giving them different resonant frequencies.

valve grinding (reciprocating engine overhaul procedure). The step in the overhaul of a reciprocating engine in which the valve faces are ground to remove all pits and the worn surface. The ground surface is smooth and perfectly concentric with the valve stem.

valve guide (reciprocating engine component). Bronze or cast-iron sleeves installed in the cylinder head of an aircraft reciprocating engine. The stems of the intake and the exhaust valves ride up and down in the valve guides which hold them in the exact center of the valve seats.

valve lag (reciprocating engine specification). The number of degrees of crankshaft rotation after the piston passes the top or the bottom center of its stroke at which the intake or exhaust valves open or close. For example, if the exhaust valve closes 15° of crankshaft rotation after the piston passes over top center and starts down on its intake stroke, the exhaust valve lag is 15°.

valve lapping (reciprocating engine overhaul procedure). The procedure in which the intake and exhaust valves are given a final processing so they form an airtight seal with the valve seat. A small amount of a very fine abrasive paste, valve-grinding compound, is spread on the valve face, and the valve is placed in the valve guide. The valve is rotated by hand to lap the valve face and seat together to remove any material that would prevent an airtight seal.

valve lead (reciprocating engine specification). The number of degrees of crankshaft rotation before the piston reaches the top or bottom center of its stroke, at which the intake or exhaust valves open or close. For example, if the intake valve opens when the crankshaft is 15° before the piston reaches the top of the exhaust stroke, the intake valve lead is 15°.

valve lift (reciprocating engine specification). The linear distance a poppet valve in a reciprocating engine moves off its seat when it is opened by the cam.

valve overlap (reciprocating engine operation). The portion of the operating cycle of a four-stroke-cycle reciprocating engine in which both the intake and the exhaust valves are off their seats at the same time. Valve overlap occurs at the end of the exhaust stroke and the beginning of the intake stroke. Valve overlap increases the efficiency of engine operation. The low pressure caused by the exhaust gases leaving the cylinder helps the fresh fuel-air charge start moving into the cylinder.

valve ports (reciprocating engine components). The openings in the cylinder heads of a reciprocating engine through which the fuel-air mixture flows into the cylinder and the burned gases leave.

valve seats (reciprocating engine components). Rings of hardened steel or bronze shrunk into the soft cast-aluminum cylinder head of an aircraft reciprocating engine. The wear caused by the continual hammering of the valves as they close is absorbed by the valve seat, rather than allowing the hammering to ruin the cylinder head. Valve seats are ground with a special seat grinder so that they are perfectly concentric with the valve guide. Worn valve seats can be removed from the cylinder head and replaced with new seats.

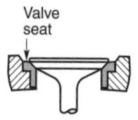

Valve
seat

valve seat

valve springs (reciprocating engine components). Helically wound steel-wire springs used to close the poppet valves in the cylinders of an aircraft reciprocating engine. Almost all aircraft engines use more than one spring to close each of the valves.

valve spring tester (reciprocating engine overhaul equipment). A tester used to determine the amount of force needed to compress a valve spring to a specified height. Weak valve springs do not close the valves tightly enough, and they must be discarded when the engine is overhauled.

valve stem (reciprocating engine component). The portion of a poppet valve that rides in the valve guide in the cylinder head of a reciprocating engine. The rocker arm presses on the end of the valve stem to open the valve.

valve stretch gage (reciprocating engine overhaul tool). A special gage that measures the radius between the valve head and the valve stem. If this radius is greater than that of the gage, the valve has been stretched and it must be discarded.

valve timing (reciprocating engine specification). The relationship between crankshaft rotation and the opening and closing of the intake and exhaust valves in the cylinders of a reciprocating engine. When the valves are properly timed, the intake valve opens a specified number of degrees of crankshaft rotation before the piston reaches the top of the exhaust stroke. The intake valve closes a specified number of degrees after the piston starts moving upward on the compression stroke. The exhaust valve opens a specified number of degrees before the piston reaches the bottom of the power stroke, and the exhaust valve closes at the correct position of the crankshaft after the piston has started down on its intake stroke.

valve-timing clearance (reciprocating engine specification). A specified clearance between the end of the valve stem and the rocker arm of an air-cooled aircraft engine equipped with solid valve lifters. The valves in one cylinder, usually cylinder number one, are adjusted to the valve-timing clearance, and the valve operating cam mechanism is adjusted so the valves in this cylinder open and close when the crankshaft is in the correct position. After the cam mechanism is adjusted, the valves are reset to the correct cold clearance. Valve-timing clearance is also called the hot, or operating, valve clearance of the engine.

valve train (reciprocating engine components). The engine components that are involved in timing and operating the intake and exhaust valves in the cylinder of a reciprocating engine. The train includes the camshaft, valve lifter, push rod, rocker arm, valves, valve springs, and retainers.

vanadium. A silvery-white, ductile, metallic chemical element. Vanadium's symbol is V, its atomic number is 23, and its atomic weight is 50.942. Vanadium is used as an alloying element for steel to increase its hardness and toughness. Vanadium steel alloyed with chromium is used to make mechanics' hand tools.

vane-type pump (fluid pump). A constant-displacement fluid pump that uses sliding vanes to move fluid through the pump. An eccentrically mounted shaft is turned inside a circular housing that has an intake port on one side and an outlet port on the other. Flat vanes are free to slide back and forth through slots in the shaft as it turns.

As the shaft turns, the volume of the chamber connected to the intake port increases and pulls fluid into the pump. This fluid is carried around the inside of the pump until it reaches a point connected to the outlet port. At this point, the vanes sliding through the shaft decrease the volume of the chamber, and fluid is forced out of the pump. Vane-type pumps move a comparatively large volume of fluid, but produce a relatively low pressure and are used as fuel pumps and low-pressure air pumps.

vanishing point (mechanical drawing). The point in a linear perspective drawing at which the lines forming parallel sides of an object meet. Drawings made in linear perspective cause the object to appear to have depth.

vapor. The gaseous state of a material. Water is normally a liquid, but when it evaporates, it turns into invisible water vapor. Certain metals can be turned into a vapor in the intense heat of an electric arc and the low pressure of a vacuum.

vapor-cycle air cooling system. A sealed mechanical refrigeration system used to lower the temperature of the air in an aircraft cabin. A liquid refrigerant, such as R-12 or R-134a, is sprayed into the evaporator coils, and as it evaporates, it absorbs heat from the cabin air blown across the evaporator.

The refrigerant, now in its vapor form, flows from the evaporator into a mechanical compressor where it is compressed, increasing both its temperature and pressure. The hot, high-pressure vapor flows from the compressor through the coils of a radiator-like condenser. Air from outside the aircraft blowing across the condenser coils absorbs heat from the refrigerant vapor, causing it to change back into a liquid. The liquid refrigerant now repeats its cycle through the evaporator and picks up more heat.

vapor degreasing. A method of removing grease and oil from a metal part by spraying it with hot vapors of a solvent such as trichlorethylene.

vaporization. The act of changing of a liquid into a vapor.

vapor lock (reciprocating engine malfunction). A condition of fuel starvation that can occur in a reciprocating engine fuel system. If the fuel in the line between the tank and the carburetor is heated enough to cause it to vaporize, a bubble of fuel vapor will form in the line. If the vapor pressure of this bubble is high enough, it will block the fuel and prevent it from flowing to the engine. This is a vapor lock.

vapor pressure. The pressure of the vapor above a liquid needed to prevent the liquid evaporating, or changing into a vapor. When an aircraft ascends to an altitude at which the air pressure is lower than the vapor pressure of the fuel, vapor leaves the fuel. The fuel "boils." Vapor pressure is measured in pounds per square inch at a specified temperature.

vapor separator (fuel metering system component). The component in a pressure carburetor or fuel injection system that picks up vapors as they are released from the fuel and return them with some fuel to one of the main fuel tanks.

vapor trail. A long trail of visible moisture left by an airplane as it flies at high altitude through very cold air. Vapor trails are caused by the condensation of water vapor in the exhaust gases leaving the engines. Vapor trails look like long, thin clouds, and they are often called con-trails (condensation trails).

vapour. The British spelling of vapor.

VAPC (variable absolute pressure controller). A type of turbocharger controller that uses a cam actuated by the engine throttle to maintain a constant upper-deck pressure for each position of the throttle valve. A VAPC differs from an absolute pressure controller (APC) which maintains a constant upper-deck pressure only for full-throttle operation. The bellows in the VAPC controls the position of the valve, but the throttle controls the position of the valve seat.

variable-angle stator vanes (gas turbine engine component). Compressor stator vanes whose angle is controlled by fuel pressure from the fuel control unit. By varying the stator-vane angle, the air directed into the first stages of the compressor meets the rotor blades at an angle that minimizes the possibility of compressor stall.

variable capacitor (electrical component). A capacitor whose capacity can be changed. The capacity of a variable capacitor can be changed by varying the area of the plates, the distance between the plates, or the dielectric between the plates.

variable capacitor

variable-displacement fluid pump. A type of fluid pump whose output can be changed to suit the demands placed on it. A centrifugal pump moves an amount of fluid determined by the opposition at its discharge port. The less opposition there is, the greater the amount of fluid the pump moves. Variable-displacement piston pumps control their output by either changing the physical distance the pistons move by using a variable wobble plate, or by changing the length of time the intake ports of the cylinders are open.

variable-geometry aircraft. An aircraft whose wings can be moved in flight, to change the amount of sweepback. When flying at a high speed, the wings are sharply swept back; but for takeoff or landing, the wings are moved into a position where there is much less sweepback.

variable-geometry air inlet duct (turbojet airplane component). The type of air inlet duct used on a supersonic airplane. The shape and area of the inlet duct can be varied in flight to provide the correct air velocity and pressure at the inlet of the engine as the airspeed of the airplane changes.

V

variable inductor (electrical component). A coil whose
inductance can be changed. The inductance of a coil
is determined by the number of turns of wire and by
the type of material used as the core. Changing either
of these varies the inductance.

variable inductor

variable-pitch propeller. A propeller whose pitch can be
changed in flight. A two-position propeller is one that can be set to a low pitch angle
for takeoff, and then in flight, the pitch angle can be increased for a more economical
cruise. A constant-speed propeller is a variable-pitch propeller whose pitch is controlled by a governor to keep the RPM of the engine constant as the air loads on the
propeller change.

variable resistor (electrical component). A resistor whose resistance can be changed by
varying the length of the resistance element in the circuit. The most commonly used
variable resistors are rheostats and potentiometers. Rheostats have two terminals,
one at the end of the resistance element and one at the wiper, or movable contact.
Potentiometers have three terminals, one at either end of the resistance element and
one at the wiper.

variable restrictor (fluid flow control device). An adjustable device in a fluid power
system. A variable restrictor is usually some form of variable orifice that controls the
amount of fluid allowed to flow in a given time when it is acted on
by a specific pressure.

Variac. The registered trade name for a toroidal-wound autotransformer.
A portion of the winding is connected to the power line, and it serves
as the primary of the transformer. A carbon brush riding on a bare
portion of the winding is moved by the control knob. The position of
this brush determines the number of turns of wire used as the secondary winding. A Variac can vary the secondary voltage from zero to
approximately 117% of the primary voltage.

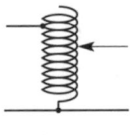

Variac

variation (magnetic compass error). The compass error caused by the difference in the
physical locations of the magnetic north pole, the location to which the magnetic
compass points, and the geographic north pole, the reference from which navigational
charts are drawn. Variation is shown on a chart by isogonic lines, along which the
variation is a constant number of degrees. For land navigation, variation is called
declination.

variometer (sailplane instrument). An extremely sensitive rate-of-climb or descent indicator that measures static pressure between the static ports and an external reference.
Variometers can be mechanical or electrical and can be compensated to eliminate
unrealistic indications of lift and sink due to rapid speed changes.

varistor (electronic component). A special type of semiconductor device whose resistance
varies as the voltage across it changes. A varistor is sometimes called a voltage-
dependent resistor (VDR).

varmeter (electrical measuring instrument). An electrical instrument used to measure the
reactive power in an alternating current circuit. Reactive power is the power caused by
the portion of the current not in phase with the voltage. Reactive power is measured in
volt-amps reactive (VARs) or kilovolt-amps reactive (KVARs).

varnish (finishing material). A material used to produce an attractive and protective coating on wood or metal. Varnish is made of a resin dissolved in a solvent, and thinned
until it is the proper viscosity to spray or brush. The varnish is spread evenly over the
surface to be coated, and when the solvents evaporate, a tough film is left. Enamel is
made by mixing a finely ground colored pigment into a varnish base.

varnish (reciprocating engine damage). A hard, glass-like deposit that forms on the cylinder walls of a reciprocating engine when the lubricating oil bakes onto the surface. Varnish often forms on the cylinder walls of an engine that is not operated properly when it is first run after it has been overhauled. Varnish on the cylinder walls prevents the piston rings seating as they should.

varsol (cleaning fluid). A petroleum product similar to naphtha. Varsol is used in aircraft maintenance shops as a degreaser.

VASI. *See* visual approach slope indicator.

V-bars. The flight director displays on the attitude indicator that provide control guidance to the pilot.

V-belt. An endless belt used to drive a pump or generator from a source of power. The cross section of a V-belt has the shape of a trapezoid, and it fits into V-shaped pulleys, with the top of the V-belt even with the top of the pulleys.

V-blocks (wood). Blocks of wood with a V-shaped cut in one of their edges. Two V-blocks are used to hold a round object when clamping it in a vise.

V-blocks (metal). A fixture that allows a shaft to be centered and rotated to measure any out-of-round condition.

VDP. *See* visual descent point.

vector (aircraft navigation). Aircraft approaching a busy terminal area are directed from the ground by a process known as vectoring. The air traffic controller on the ground has radar contact with the aircraft, and by giving the pilot a vector, or a heading to fly, the aircraft can be positioned to avoid other traffic, to fly around bad weather, or be directed to a position from which a landing can be made.

vector (mathematics). A quantity which has both direction and magnitude.

vectored-thrust engine. A turbojet or turbofan engine whose exhaust nozzle is mounted on a swivel in such a way that it may be rotated in flight to produce forward, vertically upward, or rearward thrust.

vectoring. Navigational guidance by assigning headings.

vectors to final (advanced avionics). A function of FMS/RNAV units allowing the pilot to perform a vectored approach procedure without being required to switch manually to the nonsequencing mode and set the active waypoint and course.

vector sum (mathematics). A single vector with the same magnitude and direction as a number of vectors would have if they acted on a single point, one at a time. The vector representing the vector sum is called the resultant vector, or just the resultant.

veering (meteorology). Shifting of the wind in a clockwise direction with respect to either space or time. Veering, which is the opposite of backing, is commonly used by meteorologists to refer to an anticyclonic shift, clockwise in the northern hemisphere, and counterclockwise in the southern hemisphere.

velocity. A vector quantity expressing both the speed an object is moving and the direction in which it is moving. "One hundred miles per hour" is a measure of speed, because it tells only the rate at which an object is moving. But "one hundred miles per hour, northward" is a measure of velocity. It tells both the rate and the direction the vehicle is moving.

velocity turbine. A turbine designed in such a way that it is driven by forces produced by the velocity, rather than the pressure, of the gases flowing through the vanes. Velocity turbines are used on turbocompound engines as the power recovery turbines (PRTs).

vendor. A person or business that sells goods or services.

veneer (wood product). A thin sheet of wood "peeled" from a log with a knife held against the log as it is rotated in the cutter. Veneer is used for making plywood. Several sheets of veneer are glued together, with the grain of each sheet placed at 45° or 90° to the grain of the sheets next to it.

V-engine (reciprocating engine). A form of reciprocating engine in which the cylinders are arranged in two banks, separated by an angle of between 45° and 90°. Pistons in two cylinders, one in each bank, are connected to each of the crankshaft throws.

vent. An orifice, or hole, in a container that maintains the air pressure inside the container the same as the pressure on the outside.

ventilate. To allow fresh air to circulate through a room or compartment. A compartment is ventilated to remove fumes and make it more comfortable for the occupants.

vent line (balloon operations). The line that activates the cooling vent, or deflation port. *See* red line (where it is defined as a part of balloon operations).

ventral fin (aircraft structural component). A fixed vertical surface on an airplane that extends below the aft end of the fuselage. Ventral fins are used to increase the directional stability of an airplane.

venturi. A specially shaped restriction in a tube designed to speed up the flow of fluid passing through it. According to Bernoulli's principle, any time a fluid is speeded up without losing or gaining any energy from the outside, the pressure of the fluid decreases. Venturis are used in carburetors and in many types of fluid control devices to produce a pressure drop proportional to the speed of the fluid passing through them. *See* Bernoulli's principle.

venturi effect. *See* venturi, Bernoulli's principle.

venturi tube (gyroscopic instrument component). A specially shaped tube mounted on the side of the fuselage, within the slipstream, of an airplane that does not have a vacuum pump. Air flowing through the venturi produces a negative pressure that is directed into the case of a gyroscopic instrument to pull air into the instrument to drive the gyro. Four-inch tubes are used for gyro horizons and directional gyros, and two-inch tubes are used for turn and bank indicators. Venturi tubes are seldom seen on modern airplanes.

verdigris. A green or a greenish-blue deposit that forms on the surface of copper when it is acted on by certain acids or other contaminants.

"verify" (air traffic control). A term used in ATC–pilot communications to request confirmation of information (e.g., "verify assigned altitude").

"verify specific direction of takeoff (or direction of turns after takeoff)" (air traffic control). Used by ATC to ascertain an aircraft's direction of takeoff and/or direction of turn after takeoff. It is normally used for IFR departures from an airport without a control tower. When direct communication with the pilot is not possible, the request and information may be relayed through a flight service station (FSS), dispatcher, or by other means.

vernier. A device used to allow very fine adjustments or very small measurements to be made. A vernier coupling, for example, has two sets of splines, or teeth. One set has 35 teeth and the other set has 36 teeth. When the coupling is moved ahead one tooth on the 35-tooth side, it moves ahead 10.285 degrees ($360 \div 35 = 10.285$). When it is moved back one tooth on the 36-tooth side, it moves back 10 degrees ($360 \div 36 = 10$). By moving the coupling ahead one tooth on the 35-tooth side and back one tooth on the 36-tooth side, the shafts joined by the coupling have been moved by an amount of only 0.285 degree.

vernier caliper. A precision measuring instrument used to make inside or outside measurements with an accuracy in the range of $^1\!/_{1000}$ inch, or $^1\!/_{50}$ millimeter. The movable jaw of the vernier caliper moves a vernier scale next to the main scale. The distance between the end marks on the vernier scale is divided into one more space than the same distance on the main scale.

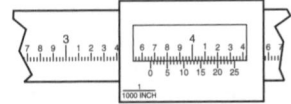

vernier caliper

To read the vernier caliper, read the inches, tenths, and hundredths of an inch from the main scale opposite the zero on the vernier scale. Only one line on the vernier scale lines up with a line on the main scale. Find this line, and it shows the number of thousandths of an inch to be added to the number read from the main scale. In the illustration, the zero on the vernier scale is past the 3.650 mark. The 20 line on the vernier scale lines up with a line on the main scale; so, add 3.650 + .020 = 3.670 inch.

vernier coupling. A timing coupling used with base-mounted magnetos. The vernier coupling allows the timing to be adjusted in increments of considerably less than one degree.

vernier micrometer caliper. A precision measuring device calibrated in units of one ten-thousandth of an inch. A vernier scale consisting of 11 lines (10 spaces), is marked on the barrel of the caliper. Only one of these marks lines up with a mark on the caliper thimble. To find the distance the caliper spindle has moved out from its zero position, add the number of ten-thousandths of an inch shown on the vernier scale to the number of thousandths of an inch read on the sleeve and the thimble.

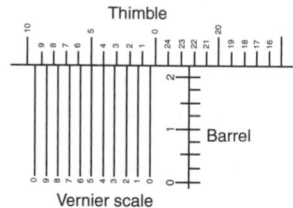

vernier micrometer caliper

In the illustration, the thimble has moved out more than 0.222 inch, as shown by the lines on the barrel scale and the thimble. The 4 line on the vernier scale lines up with a line on the thimble so the final reading is 0.2224.

vernier micrometer caliper (metric). A precision measuring device calibrated in units of one-thousandth of a millimeter. A vernier scale consisting of 6 lines (5 spaces), is marked on the barrel of the caliper. Only one of these marks lines up with a mark on the caliper thimble. To find the distance the caliper spindle has moved out from its zero position, add the number of thousandths of a millimeter shown on the vernier scale to the number of millimeters read on the sleeve and the thimble.

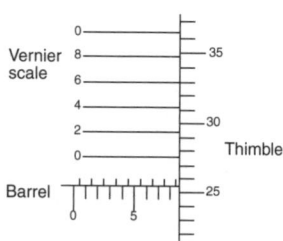

vernier micrometer caliper (metric)

In the illustration, the thimble has moved out more than 8.50 millimeters, as shown by the lines on the barrel scale, and more than 0.25 millimeters as shown on the thimble. The 6 line on the vernier scale lines up with a line on the thimble so the final reading is 8.756 millimeters.

vertex (air traffic control). The last fix for an arriving aircraft. Normally, it is the outer marker of the runway in use. However, it may be the actual threshold or other suitable common point on the approach path for the particular runway configuration.

vertex (part of a cone). The point of a cone, or the part of the cone the greatest distance from the base.

vertex time of arrival. See VTA.

vertical axis of an aircraft. An imaginary line passing vertically through the center of gravity of an aircraft. The vertical axis is called the z-axis, or the yaw axis.

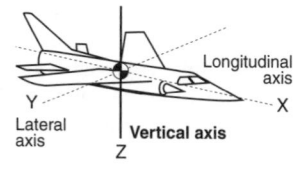

vertical axis

vertical card compass (direction indicator). A magnetic compass that consists of an azimuth on a vertical card, resembling a heading indicator with a fixed miniature airplane which acts as the lubber line. The design uses eddy current damping to minimize oscillation and lead and lag during turns.

vertical component of lift (aerodynamics). A component of flight that works along with the horizontal component, this is the lift that acts vertically and in opposition to weight (gravity). *See also* horizontal component of lift (HCL).

vertical fin (aircraft component). The fixed vertical surface in the empennage of an airplane. The vertical fin acts as a weather vane to give the airplane directional stability.

vertical navigation (VNAV). A function of area navigation (RNAV) equipment that calculates, displays, and provides vertical guidance to a profile or path.

vertical navigation planning. Included within certain STARs is information provided to help reduce the amount of low-altitude flying time for high-performance aircraft, such as jets and turboprops. An expected altitude is given for a key fix along the route. By knowing an intermediate altitude in advance when flying a high-performance aircraft, pilots can plan the power or thrust settings and aircraft configurations that result in the most efficient descent in terms of time, fuel requirements, and engine wear.

vertical separation. Separation established by assignment of different altitudes or flight levels.

vertical-speed indicator (aircraft instrument). An instrument that gives the pilot an indication of the rate at which an aircraft is rising or descending. A vertical-speed indicator is a pressure instrument with a calibrated restriction between the case and a pressure bellows. When the aircraft changes altitude, the pressure inside the case changes immediately. But because of the calibrated restriction, the pressure change inside the bellows lags behind the pressure change in the case.

The difference between the pressure inside and outside of the bellows causes the bellows to expand or collapse, and this change in its dimensions causes a pointer to move over its dial showing the pilot the rate of climb or descent. Vertical-speed indicators are often called rate-of-climb indicators.

vertical speed mode. An FD/autopilot mode that allows constant-rate climbs and descents by selecting a vertical speed on the flight director or autopilot control panel.

vertical stability (aircraft stability). *See* directional stability.

vertical stabilizer. *See* vertical fin.

vertical takeoff and landing aircraft (VTOL). Aircraft capable of vertical climbs and/or descents and of using very short runways or small areas for takeoff and landings. These aircraft include, but are not limited to, helicopters.

vertical tape instrument. A tall rectangular instrument that displays the quantity of the parameter being measured by a movable strip of colored tape. The presentation resembles a vertical bar graph.

vertical vibration (helicopter operation). Up-and-down vibration of a helicopter caused by an out-of-track main rotor.

vertical visibility (meteorology). The distance one can see upward into a surface-based obscuration. It is also the maximum height from which a pilot in flight can recognize the ground through a surface-based obscuration.

vertical wind shear (meteorology). The condition produced by a change in wind velocity (speed and/or direction) with height.

vertigo. A type of spatial disorientation caused by the physical senses sending conflicting signals to the brain. Vertigo is specially hazardous when flying under conditions of poor visibility. The eyes send a signal to the brain telling it the airplane is in one condition, while the deep muscles, "the seat of the pants," tell the brain the airplane is in another condition. The inner ear tells still another story, and the result is confusion—vertigo. Vertigo may cause pilot incapacitation, but may be minimized by confidence in the indication of the flight instruments.

very high frequency. *See* VHF.

very-high-frequency omnirange. *See* VOR.

very low frequency. *See* VLF.

Very signal. A type of emergency light signal used by ships and aircraft. A special pistol, a Very pistol, fires a cartridge that looks much like a shotgun cartridge. The cartridge sends up a ball of white or colored fire that can be seen for several miles during the day or night.

vestibule. The central cavity of the bony labyrinth of the ear, or the parts of the membranous labyrinth that it contains.

VFO (variable-frequency oscillator). An oscillator inside a communications radio receiver that produces radio-frequency alternating current. The frequency produced by the VFO can be changed until it is almost the same as the radio frequency of the carrier being received. When the output of the VFO is mixed with a continuous wave (CW) carrier, an audible signal is produced. VFOs are used to make Morse code signals audible when they are transmitted by continuous wave (CW) transmission. When a VFO is used in this way, it is called a beat-frequency oscillator, a BFO.

VFR (visual flight rules). Flight rules adopted by the Federal Aviation Administration to govern aircraft flight when the pilot has visual reference to the ground at all times. VFR operations specify the amount of ceiling (the distance between the surface of the earth and the base of the clouds) and the visibility (the horizontal distance the pilot can see) that the pilot must have in order to operate according to these rules. When the weather conditions are not such that the pilot can operate according to VFR, he or she must use another set of rules, instrument flight rules (IFR).

VFR aircraft. An aircraft conducting flight in accordance with visual flight rules.

VFR conditions. Weather conditions equal to or better than the minimum for flight under visual flight rules. The term may be used as an ATC clearance/instruction only when (1) an IFR aircraft requests a climb/descent in VFR conditions; (2) the clearance will result in noise abatement benefits where part of the IFR departure route does not conform to an FAA approved noise abatement route or altitude; (3) a pilot has requested a practice instrument approach and is not on an IFR flight plan.

VFR cruising altitude. Specific guidelines for altitudes while flying VFR. When flying above 3,000 feet above the surface on a heading between 0° and 179°, a pilot must fly any odd thousand foot MSL altitude +500 feet (3,500, 5,500, 7,500, etc.). While on a heading of 180° to 360°, a pilot must fly even thousands +500 feet (4,500, 6,500, 85,00, etc.).

VFR military training routes. Routes used by the Department of Defense and associated Reserve and Air Guard units for the purpose of conducting low-altitude navigation and tactical training under VFR below 10,000 feet MSL at airspeeds in excess of 250 knots IAS.

"VFR not recommended." An advisory provided by a flight service station to a pilot during a preflight or inflight weather briefing that flight under visual flight rules is not recommended. To be given when the current and/or forecast weather conditions are at or below VFR minimums. It does not abrogate the pilot's authority to make his/her own decision.

VFR over-the-top. *14 CFR Part 1:* "The operation of an aircraft over-the-top under VFR when it is not being operated on an IFR flight plan."

VFR-On-Top (flight conditions). A flight condition in which a pilot flies an aircraft according to visual flight rules (VFR) above a solid layer of clouds. While flying in the clear above the clouds, the pilot can operate under visual flight rules, but in order to reach VFR-On-Top conditions, the aircraft must pass through the clouds. When flying through the clouds, the aircraft must be operated according to instrument flight rules (IFR).

VFR terminal area chart. An aeronautical chart, drawn to a scale of 1:250,000 (one inch is equal to four statute miles). This chart depicts terminal control area (TCA) airspace which provides for the control or segregation of all aircraft within the TCA. The topographic and aeronautical information depicted on terminal area charts includes visual and radio aids to navigation, airports, controlled airspace, restricted areas, obstructions, and related data.

V-G diagram (operating flight strength limitation). A chart that is usually included in an aircraft flight handbook that relates airspeed to load factor for a specific weight, configuration, and altitude. It shows the positive and negative load factor allowable for a given airspeed. It also shows the limit and ultimate positive and negative load factors and the airspeed limit.

VHF (very-high frequency) (radio frequencies). The range of radio frequencies between 30 megahertz (30,000,000 cycles per second) and 300 megahertz (300,000,000 cycles per second) that are used for aviation communications and navigation. VHF radio waves operate much like light waves, in that they travel in straight lines and are usable only for a line-of-sight distance. VHF radio waves do not follow the curvature of the earth.

VI (viscosity index). A measure of the change in the viscosity of a fluid with a change in its temperature. The higher the viscosity index, the less the viscosity changes with the temperature.

vibrating-reed frequency meter. A type of panel-mounted instrument used to show the frequency of the alternating current being supplied to certain electrical equipment. Metal reeds of different lengths are vibrated by an electromagnet powered by the AC whose frequency is being measured. The reed whose resonant frequency is the same as the frequency of the AC will vibrate with a much greater amplitude than the other reeds. The ends of all of the reeds are visible on the face of the instrument, and each reed is identified by the frequency at which it is resonant. The number beside the reed seen as a wide blur is the frequency of the AC.

vibration. A periodically reversing motion in which a body moves from one side to the other of its at-rest position. Every physical body has a natural resonant frequency at which it vibrates with the greatest amplitude for a given amount of excitation.

vibration isolator. A device installed between a component and a structure to prevent any vibrations present in the structure from being transmitted into the component. Instruments and electronic components are mounted in aircraft with vibration isolators to keep the shocks and vibrations from damaging them. Vibration isolators are often called shock mounts.

vibration loop (fluid lines). A loop formed in a rigid fluid line to prevent vibration from concentrating stresses that could cause the line to break.

vibrator (electrical component). An electromagnetic relay used to change steady direct current into pulsating DC. Current flowing through a relay coil produces an electromagnetic pull that opens a set of contacts that are normally held closed by a spring. The coil and contacts are connected in series so the current flowing in the coil stops as soon as the contacts open. When the contacts open, the coil loses its electromagnetic pull, and the spring closes the contacts, restoring the current to the coil. The frequency of the pulsating DC is determined by the magnetic characteristics of the relay.

vibrator-type voltage regulator (DC generator control). A voltage control used with some of the simpler direct current generators. The voltage sensor is an electromagnetic relay whose coil is connected across the generator output. The relay contacts are in the generator field circuit. As soon as the generator output voltage reaches the value for which the voltage regulator is set, the electromagnetic field in the relay pulls the contacts open. Field current is reduced and the generator output voltage drops. As soon as the voltage is low enough, the relay contacts close and field current again flows. The contacts vibrate open and closed several hundred times a minute to hold the generator voltage within the desired range.

vibratory torque control (reciprocating engine component). A patented coupling between the propeller shaft and the crankshaft of the Continental Tiara series aircraft engines. A short quill shaft absorbs torsional vibrations under certain operating conditions, and a centrifugal lock bypasses the quill shaft under conditions in which a solid shaft will produce less vibration. *See* quill shaft.

Victor airway. (1) Low altitude airspace corridor between 700 feet above ground level to 18,000 feet. (2) Based on a centerline that extends from one VOR or VORTAC navigation aid or intersection, to another navigation aid (or through several navigation aids or intersections); used to establish a known route for en route procedures between terminal areas.

video amplifier (electronic component). An electronic amplifier capable of amplifying alternating current over a wide band of frequencies. Video amplifiers normally amplify AC over a frequency band of from about 15 hertz to five megahertz (5,000,000 hertz).

video map. An electronically displayed map on the radar display that may depict data such as airports, heliports, runway center line extensions, hospital emergency landing areas, NAVAIDs and fixes, reporting points, airway/route center lines, boundaries, hand-off points, special use tracks, obstructions, prominent geographical features, map alignment indicators, range accuracy marks, and minimum vectoring altitudes.

view limiting device (instrument flight training device). A device used primarily during instrument training to limit the view of the pilot to the instrument panel, blocking the ability to see any outside visual references.

VIFF (vectoring in forward flight). The ability of the pilot of an aircraft equipped with a vectored-thrust engine to change the direction of the exhaust gas flow while the aircraft is in forward flight. VIFF allows the pilot to accomplish flight maneuvers that are impossible with a conventional engine installation.

VI (viscosity index) improver. An additive used to produce a multiviscosity lubricating oil. The polymer additive expands as temperature increases and contracts as the temperature decreases. VI improvers cause the viscosity to increase as the oil becomes hot and decrease when it becomes cold.

VIP levels (meteorology). National Weather Service categorization of radar weather echo intensity for precipitation into six levels which are sometimes expressed during communications as "VIP LEVEL" 1 through 6 (derived from the component of the radar that produces the information—video integrator and processor). The levels in relation to the precipitation intensity within a thunderstorm are: Level 1–Weak; Level 2–Moderate; Level 3–Strong; Level 4–Very strong; Level 5–Intense; Level 6–Extreme.

virga (meteorology). Water or ice particles falling from a cloud, usually in wisps or streaks, and evaporating before reaching the ground.

virtual reality (VR). A form of computer-based technology that creates a sensory experience allowing a participant to believe and barely distinguish a virtual experience from a real one. VR uses graphics with animation systems, sounds, and images to reproduce electronic versions of real-life experience.

viscosity. The resistance of a fluid to flow. The viscosity of a liquid is a measure of its internal friction, or its "stiffness."

viscosity index. *See* VI.

viscosity index improver. *See* VI improver.

viscosimeter. An instrument used to measure the viscosity of a fluid. A cup-type viscosimeter is a specially shaped cup with an accurately sized hole in its bottom. The cup is filled with the fluid whose viscosity is to be measured, and the hole is opened so fluid can flow from it. The number of seconds is measured between the beginning of the flow and the time the first break in the flow occurs. This time relates to the viscosity of the fluid.

viscous damping. A method of damping vibration or oscillation by converting some of the vibrational energy into heat. Viscous damping is done by allowing the vibrating object to force a fluid, either a liquid or gas, through a small orifice. The amount of damping is determined by the viscosity of the fluid and the size of the orifice. An aircraft nose wheel shimmy damper operates on the principle of viscous damping. *See* shimmy damper.

vise. A bench-mounted clamp used to hold material while it is being worked on. One jaw of the vise is fixed, and the other is mounted on a screw that allows it to be moved away from or close to the fixed jaw.

Vise-grip pliers. A patented type of pliers in which the jaws can be locked together by the over-center compound action of a toggle. A screw in one handle of the pliers allows the basic size of the jaw opening to be adjusted, and when the handles are squeezed together, the jaws lock tightly on the object between them. Vise-grip pliers are made with many different types and shapes of jaws for many different uses.

visibility. The ability, as determined by atmospheric conditions and expressed in units of distance, to see and identify prominent unlighted objects by day, and prominent lighted objects by night. Visibility is reported in statute miles, hundreds of feet, or meters.

visibility (ICAO). The ability, as determined by atmospheric conditions and expressed in units of distance, to see and identify prominent unlighted objects by day and prominent lighted objects by night.

visible light. The very small range of electromagnetic radiation that produces sensations the human eye and brain can accept. Vibrations making up visible light have wavelengths of between approximately 4,000 and 7,700 angstroms. One angstrom is equivalent to one billionth of a centimeter. The different wavelengths of electromagnetic energy give light its color. Visible light with the shortest wavelength has the color of violet, and that with the longest wavelength has the color of red.

visual approach (air traffic control). An approach conducted on an instrument flight rules (IFR) flight plan which authorizes the pilot to proceed visually and clear of clouds to the airport. The pilot must, at all times, have either the airport or the preceding aircraft in sight. This approach must be authorized and under the control of the appropriate air traffic control facility, and the reported weather at the airport must be: ceiling at or above 1,000 feet and visibility of three miles or greater.

visual approach (ICAO). An approach by an IFR flight when either part or all of an instrument approach procedure is not completed and the approach is executed in visual reference to terrain.

visual approach slope indicator (VASI). The most common visual glidepath system in use. The VASI provides obstruction clearance within 10° of the extended runway centerline, and to 4 nautical miles (NM) from the runway threshold.

visual climb over airport (VCOA). A departure option for an IFR aircraft, operating in visual meteorological conditions equal to or greater than the specified visibility and ceiling, to visually conduct climbing turns over the airport to the published "climb-to" altitude from which to proceed with the instrument portion of the departure. VCOA procedures are developed to avoid obstacles greater than 3 statute miles from the departure end of the runway as an alternative to complying with climb gradients greater than 200 feet per nautical mile. These procedures are published in the "Take-Off Minimums and (Obstacle) Departure Procedures" section of the Terminal Procedures Publications. *See* AIM.

visual descent point (VDP). (1) A defined point on the final approach course of a nonprecision straight-in approach procedure from which normal descent from the MDA to the runway touchdown point may be commenced, provided the runway environment is clearly visible to the pilot. (2) A defined point on the final approach course of a nonprecision straight-in approach procedure from which normal descent from the MDA to the runway touchdown point may be commenced, provided the approach threshold of that runway, or approach lights, or other markings identifiable with the approach end of that runway are clearly visible to the pilot.

visual flight. A flight made by referencing the horizon and other outside landmarks.

visual flight rules (VFR). Rules that govern the procedures for conducting flight under visual conditions. The term "VFR" is also used in the United States to indicate weather conditions that are equal to or greater than minimum VFR requirements. In addition, it is used by pilots and controllers to indicate type of flight plan.

visual holding (flight procedure). The holding of aircraft at selected, prominent geographical fixes which can be easily recognized from the air.

visual line of sight (unmanned aircraft). A method of control and collision avoidance that refers to the pilot or observer directly viewing the unmanned aircraft with human eyesight. Corrective lenses (spectacles or contact lenses) may be used by the pilot or visual observer. Aids to vision, such as binoculars, field glasses, or telephoto television, may be employed as long as their field of view (FOV) does not adversely affect the surveillance task.

visual meteorological conditions (VMC). (1) Meteorological conditions expressed in terms of visibility, distance from cloud, and ceiling meeting or exceeding the minimums specified for VFR. (2) Meteorological conditions expressed in terms of visibility, distance from cloud, and ceiling equal to or better than specified minima.

visual segment, on a published instrument approach procedure. A segment on an instrument approach procedure (IAP) chart annotated as "Fly Visual to Airport" or "Fly Visual." A dashed arrow will indicate the visual flight path on the profile and plan view with an associated note on the approximate heading and distance. The visual segment should be flown as a dead reckoning course while maintaining visual conditions.

visual separation (air traffic control). A means employed by ATC to separate aircraft in terminal areas and en route airspace in the NAS. There are two ways to effect this separation: (1) The tower controller sees the aircraft involved and issues instructions, as necessary, to ensure that the aircraft avoid each other; (2) A pilot sees the other aircraft involved and upon instructions from the controller provides his/her own separation by maneuvering his/her aircraft as necessary to avoid it. This may involve following another aircraft or keeping it in sight until it is no longer a factor.

vitrify. To turn a material into a glasslike substance by heating it enough so that it melts.

vixen file. A metal-cutting hand file that has curved teeth across its faces. Vixen files are used to remove large amounts of soft metal.

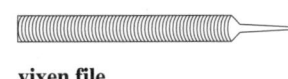

vixen file

VLF (very-low frequency) (radio frequencies). The range of radio frequencies between three kilohertz (3,000 cycles per second) and 30 kilohertz (30,000 cycles per second). VLF radio waves are used for operations that require the signal to travel great distances.

VMC. *See* visual meteorological conditions.

V$_{MC}$ demonstration (flight training). An engine inoperative/loss of directional control demonstration that is a required task on the practical test for a multi-engine class rating.

V$_{NE}$ (never-exceed speed). The maximum speed an aircraft is allowed to attain in any conditions of flight. V$_{NE}$ is marked on the airspeed indicator with a red radial line.

voice switching and control system. The VSCS is a computer controlled switching system that provides air traffic controllers with all voice circuits (air to ground and ground to ground) necessary for air traffic control.

volatile content (composites). The percent of volatile components that are driven off as a vapor from a plastic or an impregnated reinforcement during cure.

volatile liquid. A liquid that evaporates easily, or readily turns into a vapor. Alcohol and gasoline are both volatile liquids.

volatile memory (computer memory). Memory in a computer in which all data is lost when power to the computer is turned off. Dynamic RAMs (random access memories) store data in the form of charges on capacitors. Memory stored in this manner is volatile.

volatility. The characteristic of a liquid that relates to its ability to vaporize, or change into a gas.

volcanic ash. The term for very fine rock and mineral particles less than 2 mm in diameter that are ejected from a volcanic eruptions. The volcanic ash clouds contain an abrasive dust that poses a serious safety threat to flight operations.

VOLMET broadcast (ICAO). Meteorological information for aircraft in flight.

volt (electrical unit). The basic unit of electrical pressure. One volt is the amount of electrical pressure needed to force one ampere of current through a resistance of one ohm. One volt is also the amount of electrical pressure drop that occurs when a current of one ampere produces one watt of power.

voltage amplifier (electronic circuit). An electronic circuit capable of increasing voltage. Voltage amplifiers normally supply an extremely small amount of current.

voltage divider (electrical circuit). An electrical circuit in which a tapped resistor or a series of resistors is installed across a voltage source to provide various output voltages. The sum of the voltage drops across each of the resistances in a voltage divider is the same as the voltage across the entire resistance.

voltage doubler (electrical circuit). An electrical circuit in which alternating current is rectified, and its output is increased to a value of twice its original peak value.

voltage drop. The drop in voltage or electrical pressure caused by current flowing through a resistance. A voltage drop is called an IR (current times resistance) drop.

voltage dropping resistor. A current-limiting resistor in series with an electrical or electronic component that drops the voltage across that component.

voltage quadrupler (electrical circuit). An electrical circuit in which alternating current is rectified, and its output is increased to a value four times its original peak value.

voltage regulation. The maintenance of a constant voltage across an electrical component or electronic circuit as the applied voltage or the load current varies.

voltage regulator (generator or alternator control). A device which holds the output voltage of a generator or alternator constant as its speed changes in normal operation and its load current changes within its rated value.

voltage regulator tube (electron tube). A special gas-filled electron tube. The tube, in series with a resistor, is placed across the output of a DC power supply. The gas in the tube ionizes when a specific voltage is placed across it, and when the gas ionizes, electrons flow through it with very little opposition. The voltage drop across the regulator tube remains constant as the load current changes.

voltage spike (electrical disturbance). A sudden, short-duration surge of high voltage along a power line or in a piece of electrical equipment. Voltage spikes are induced into the system by lightning or by some inductive equipment being turned off. These high-voltage spikes can damage many types of semiconductor devices. Surge protectors are used to bypass voltage spikes to ground, so they cannot cause damage.

voltaic cell. *See* primary cell (electrochemical cell).

voltammeter (electrical measuring instrument). An instrument that can measure both volts and amperes. A switch is built into the instrument to change its function.

volt-amp. The basic unit of apparent power in an AC circuit. A volt-amp is the product of the circuit voltage and all of the current, regardless of its phase. A volt-amp differs from a watt in that a watt is a measure of true power and is the product of the circuit voltage and only that current in phase with it.

voltmeter. An electrical measuring instrument used to measure electrical pressure. Most of the commonly used voltmeters are actually current measuring instruments in series with a high resistance which limits the amount of current that can flow through the meter. The deflection of the meter pointer is proportional to the voltage across the meter and resistance combination.

voltmeter multiplier. A precision resistor in series with a voltmeter mechanism used to extend the range of the basic meter or to allow a single meter to measure several ranges of voltage.

voltmeter sensitivity (electrical measuring instrument specification). The amount of current needed to move the pointer of a voltmeter across its full scale. Voltmeter sensitivity, which is expressed in terms of ohms per volt, is found by dividing the total resistance of the meter by its full-scale voltage.

volt-ohm-milliammeter. *See* VOM.

volume (physical measurement). The amount of space in a container. Volume is measured in cubic units, and it is found by multiplying the area of the base of the container by its height. All measurements must be in the same units.

volume control (electrical circuit). A circuit or control in an audio amplifier that can vary the output volume.

volumetric efficiency (reciprocating engine specification). The ratio of the volume of the charge of fuel and air inside the cylinder of a reciprocating engine to the total physical volume of the cylinder. The fuel-air charge inside the cylinder is reduced to a standard pressure and temperature to measure the volumetric efficiency. The volumetric efficiency of a normally aspirated engine is always less than 100%, but a supercharged engine can have a volumetric efficiency greater than 100%.

VOM (electrical measuring instrument). A combination voltmeter, milliammeter, and ohmmeter, all using a single indicating instrument. One current-measuring instrument and a number of switches, resistors, and rectifiers are used to measure a wide range of voltages, both AC and DC, current, normally in milliamperes and microamperes, and resistance in ohms. A VOM may have either an analog or digital display.

von Ohain, Dr. Hans Pabst. The designer and developer of the first turbojet engine to actually power an airplane. Von Ohain's HeS3b engine was built in Germany by the Heinkel Company, and it flew in a Heinkel HE-178 airplane on August 27, 1939.

VOR (very-high-frequency omnirange navigation equipment). A type of electronic navigation equipment in which the instrument in the cockpit identifies the radial, or line from the VOR station measured in degrees clockwise from magnetic north, along which the aircraft is located. VOR is a phase-comparison system in which two signals transmitted simultaneously from a ground station are in phase only when they are received at a location directly magnetic north of the station. At a location magnetic east of the station, they are 90° out of phase. At magnetic south, they are 180° out of phase, and west of the station, they are 270° out of phase.

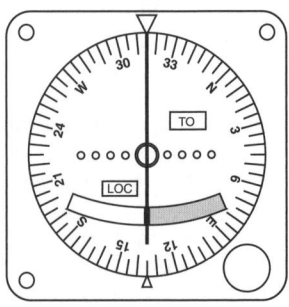

VOR/LOC indicator

The pilot selects on the omni bearing selector (OBS) the radial on which he wants to fly, and the needle of the course deviation indicator (CDI) centers when the aircraft is on the radial. If the aircraft moves off the radial, the needle moves away from center to show the pilot which direction to turn to return the aircraft to the radial. The indictor for the VOR is often also used as the localizer indicator.

VOR test facility (VOT). A ground facility that emits a test signal to check VOR receiver accuracy. Some VOTs are available to the user while airborne, and others are limited to ground use only. Also referred to as "VOR test signal."

VORTAC (electronic navigation system). An electronic navigation system used by both military and civilian aircraft. The name VORTAC is the combination of the names of two types of navigation equipment: VOR, very-high-frequency omnirange navigation equipment, and TACAN, a military pulse-type tactical navigation system. VOR and TACAN equipment are colocated at a VORTAC station, and signals from both systems are transmitted simultaneously.

Military aircraft use the TACAN system for determining their direction and distance from the VORTAC station. Civilian aircraft determine their direction from the station by the VOR and their distance from the station by the distance-measuring portion of TACAN. This distance is shown in the aircraft by the distance measuring equipment (DME).

vortex. A whirling motion in a fluid. The Coriolis force caused by the rotation of the earth causes water to flow out of a drain in a vortex. Air that spills over the wing tips of an airplane spins in the form of vortices. A tornado is an extremely strong vortex of air.

vortex dissipator (turbine powered aircraft component). A high-velocity stream of compressor bleed air blown from a nozzle into an area where vortices are likely to form. Vortex dissipators destroy the vortices that would otherwise suck debris from the ground into engines mounted in pods below the wings.

vortex generators (aerodynamics). Small rectangular, low aspect ratio airfoils mounted on the upper surface of the wings of some high-speed airplanes. Vortex generators are mounted in pairs, and the air spilling over their upper ends forms swirls, or vortices. These vortices pull high-energy air down to the surface of the wing. Vortex generators prevent the air separating from the surface of the wing.

vortex ring state (helicopter flight condition). A transient condition of downward flight (descending through air after just previously being accelerated downward by the rotor) during which an appreciable portion of the main rotor system is being forced to operate at angles of attack above maximum. Blade stall starts near the hub and progresses outward as the rate of descent increases.

vorticity (meteorology). Turning of the atmosphere. Vorticity may be embedded in the total airflow and not readily identified by a flow pattern. *See* absolute vorticity, negative vorticity, positive vorticity, and relative vorticity.

VOT (VOR test signal). A ground facility which emits a test signal to check VOR receiver accuracy. Some VOTs are available to the user while airborne, and others are limited to ground use only.

V-speeds. A series of designators used by the FAA and listed in 14 CFR 1 to describe certain flight conditions.

V_A — design maneuvering speed.

V_B — design speed for maximum gust intensity.

V_C — design cruising speed.

V_D — design diving speed.

V_{DF}/M_{DF} — demonstrated flight diving speed.

V_{EF} — The speed at which the critical engine is assumed to fail during takeoff.

V_F — design flap speed.

V_{FC}/M_{FC} — maximum speed for stability characteristics.

V_{FE} — maximum flap extended speed.

V_{FO} — Maximum flap operating speed (extended or retracted).

V_{FTO} — Final takeoff speed.

V_H — maximum speed in level flight with maximum continuous power.

V_{LE} — maximum landing gear extended speed.

V_{LO} — maximum landing gear operating speed.

V_{LOF} — lift-off speed.

V_{MC} — minimum control speed with the critical engine inoperative.

V_{MD} — Minimum drag speed. Minimum drag speed.

V_{MO}/M_{MO} — maximum operating limit speed.

V_{MU} — minimum unstick speed.

V_{NE} — never-exceed speed.

V_{NO} — maximum structural cruising speed.

V_P — Minimum dynamic hydroplaning speed—the minimum speed required to start dynamic hydroplaning.

V_R — rotation speed.

V_{REF} — Reference landing speed.

V_S — the stalling speed or the minimum steady flight speed at which the airplane is controllable.

V_{S0} — the stalling speed or the minimum steady flight speed in the landing configuration.

V_{S1} — the stalling speed or the minimum steady flight speed obtained in a specific configuration.

V_{SR} — Reference stall speed.

V_{SR0} — Reference stall speed in the landing configuration.

V_{SR1} — Reference stall speed in a specific configuration.

V_{SSE} — Safe, intentional one-engine inoperative speed. The minimum speed to intentionally render the critical engine inoperative.

V_{SW} — Speed at which onset of natural or artificial stall warning occurs.

V_{TOSS} — takeoff safety speed for Category A rotorcraft.

V_X — speed for best angle of climb.

V_{XSE} — Best angle of climb speed with one engine inoperative.

V_Y — speed for best rate of climb.

Continued

V-speeds. *Continued*

V_{YSE} — Best rate-of-climb speed with one engine inoperative. This airspeed provides the most altitude gain in a given period of time in a light, twin-engine airplane following an engine failure.

V_1 — Critical engine failure speed or takeoff decision speed. Engine failure below this speed will result in an aborted takeoff; above this speed the takeoff run should be continued.

V_2 — takeoff safety speed.

V_{2min} — minimum takeoff safety speed.

VSI. *See* vertical speed indicator.

VSWR (voltage standing-wave ratio). A measure of reflected energy in an electrical transmission line such as a waveguide or a coaxial cable. VSWR is the ratio of a voltage maximum to an adjacent voltage minimum.

VTA (vertex time of arrival) (air traffic control). A calculated time of aircraft arrival over the adapted vertex for the runway configuration in use. Vertex arrival time is calculated via the optimum flight path using adapted speed segments.

V-tail (aircraft configuration). An aircraft empennage design which utilizes two slanted tail surfaces to perform the same functions as the surfaces of a conventional elevator and rudder configuration. The fixed surfaces act as both horizontal and vertical stabilizers. The movable control surfaces, which are usually called ruddervators, perform the dual functions of elevator and rudder.

VTOL (vertical takeoff and landing). Aircraft operation in which the aircraft rises and descends vertically without requiring forward motion. A helicopter is capable of VTOL operation.

VTVM (vacuum-tube voltmeter) (electrical measuring instrument). A voltmeter that has a high input impedance so that it does not load the circuit whose voltage is being measured. The voltage to be measured is impressed on the grid of a vacuum tube amplifier, and the resulting plate current is measured. Vacuum-tube voltmeters (VTVM) are being replaced with solid-state field-effect transistor (FET) voltmeters.

vulcanize. A method of treating crude rubber with heat to give it such useful properties as elasticity, strength, and chemical and dimensional stability.

WAAS. *See* wide area augmentation system.

wafer (semiconductor production). A thin slice of silicon or germanium used as the substrate on which the components of an integrated circuit chip are formed. A wafer is also called a slice.

wafer-type selector switch (electrical component). A multicontact switch with the contacts arranged around the outside of a circular wafer. A shaft through the center of the wafer is rotated by a knob to connect a center contact, or wiper, to any one of the contacts around the wafer. Several wafers can be stacked together with their center contacts rotated by the same shaft.

waffle piston (reciprocating engine component). A reciprocating engine piston with fins cast or forged on the bottom of the head, inside the piston. The fins cross to form a pattern that looks much like the surface of a waffle. The fins strengthen the piston head and provide extra surface area to increase the amount of heat the oil can carry away from the piston.

wake. The high-velocity stream of turbulent air behind an operating aircraft engine.

wake turbulence (aircraft operation). The disturbed air left behind an airplane. At one time, it was thought that the rough air behind and below an airplane in flight was caused by the propeller slipstream. But this turbulence is actually caused by air spilling over the wing tips and forming tornado-like vortices. Wake turbulence also includes thrust stream turbulence, jet blast, jet wash, propeller wash, and rotor wash, both on the ground and in the air.

walk-around bottle (oxygen bottle). A small steel cylinder containing aviators breathing oxygen. The walk-around bottle is fastened to the flight suit and attached to the oxygen mask to supply the aviator with oxygen as he or she walks around the aircraft. When the aviator is at his or her regular duty station, the walk-around bottle is disconnected, and the oxygen mask is plugged into the built-in oxygen system.

wall cloud (meteorology). The well-defined bank of vertically developed clouds having a wall-like appearance and which form the outer boundary of the eye of a well-developed tropical cyclone.

Wankel engine. A form of rotary, internal combustion engine. Instead of using cylinders and moving pistons, the Wankel engine uses a rounded, triangular-shaped rotor, with sliding seals that form the combustion space inside an oblong circular chamber. Expanding gases from the burning fuel-air mixture press against the rotor and rotate it and the drive shaft geared to it.

warm. A term used to identify a relative condition of temperature; it is opposed to cool. A warm wind is a movement of air whose temperature is slightly higher than the temperature of the person upon whom it is blowing.

warm front (meteorology). The surface between two air masses in which a mass of warm air is flowing over a mass of colder air. Warm fronts usually bring low ceilings, fog, and light but steady rain.

warm front occlusion (meteorology). An occlusion that occurs when the air ahead of the warm front is colder than the air of the cold front. *See* occluded front (meteorology).

warm sector (meteorology). The area covered by warm air at the surface and bounded by the warm front and cold front of a wave cyclone.

W

warm-up time. The time needed for certain types of components or systems to reach their normal operating temperature. Aircraft reciprocating engines must be operated for a specified warm-up time before they are safe for takeoff.

warning area (aircraft navigation). An area containing hazards to any aircraft not participating in the activities being conducted in the area. Warning areas may contain intensive military training, gunnery exercises, or special weapons testing.

warning horn. An aural warning device that is used in conjunction with warning lights to alert the flight crew of a dangerous condition. A continuous warning horn alerts the pilot that the landing gear is not down and locked when either of the throttles is retarded for landing. An intermittent warning horn sounds when the thrust levers are advanced for takeoff if certain conditions exist that could make takeoff dangerous.

warning lights. Indicator lights installed in the cockpit of an aircraft to warn the flight crew of some unsafe condition. Overheat conditions, low fuel supply, low oil pressure, unlocked doors, or landing gear in an unsafe position are all indicated by warning lights.

warp. The threads in a piece of fabric that run the length of the fabric.

WARP. *See* weather and radar processing.

warpage. (1) Distortion caused by a nonuniform change of internal stresses. (2) In composites, it is the result of distortion caused by shrinkage differences in a reinforced molded part.

warp clock. An alignment indicator included in a structural repair manual to show the orientation of the plies of a composite material. The ply direction is shown in relation to a reference direction.

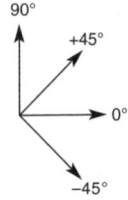

warp clock

warp threads (fabric). Threads that run the length of a piece of fabric. Threads that run across the fabric are called woof, or fill, threads.

warp tracers. Threads of a different color from the warp threads that are woven into a material to identify the direction of the warp threads.

Warren truss. A type of structural truss in which the main lengthwise members are separated by rigid diagonal members that carry both tensile and compressive loads. Most welded-steel truss fuselages are Warren truss structures.

washer (type of hardware). A flat metal disk with a hole in its center used to provide a smooth surface for a nut or the bolt head to seat against. Washers are also used to shim, or fill a space, between a nut and a surface to take up space if the grip length of the bolt is too long for the material being clamped.

wash-in (airplane rigging). A condition in airplane rigging in which a wing is twisted so its angle of incidence is greater at the tip than at the root. Washing-in a wing increases the lift to correct for a wing-heavy condition.

wash-out (airplane rigging). A condition in airplane rigging in which a wing is twisted so its angle of incidence is less at the tip than at the root. Wash-out decreases the lift the wing produces. If an airplane is left-wing-heavy, the left wing can be washed in and the right wing washed out.

wash-out (helicopter rotor design). A design that decreases the blade angle from root to tip by twisting it, which maintains the associated angle of attack or, in many cases, reduces it. Wash-out controls the coefficient of lift from root to tip to ensure even, or controlled, lift production throughout the length of the blade.

wash primer (aircraft finishing system component). A type of primer used to prepare an aluminum or magnesium surface to receive a topcoat of finishing material. Wash primer contains an etchant, a material that chemically roughens the metal, to prepare the surface to accept the topcoat material.

waste gate (turbosupercharger component). A controllable butterfly valve in the exhaust pipe of a reciprocating engine equipped with an exhaust-driven turbocharger. When the waste gate is open, the exhaust gases leave the engine through the exhaust pipe. But when it is closed, the gases must pass through the turbine that drives the turbo-charger compressor. By controlling the amount the waste gate is open, the speed of the turbocharger can be controlled, and this speed determines the manifold pressure in the engine.

water ballast (glider operation). A system of adding water to the wings or tail of a glider to increase weight and optimize CG.

water break test (aircraft finishing). A test to determine that a metal surface is entirely free of contamination and is ready to be painted. The area being tested is covered with a thin film of distilled water. If any of the water beads up rather than flowing out smoothly it indicates that the area has not been sufficiently cleaned and the cleaning process must be repeated.

water equivalent (meteorology). The depth of water that would result from the melting of snow or ice.

water injection (gas turbine engines). Pure water or a mixture of water and alcohol is sprayed into the compressor inlet or the diffuser inlet. When the water evaporates, it absorbs heat from the air and drops its temperature making the air more dense. Increasing the density of the air flowing through the engine increases the mass airflow, and this increases the thrust the engine produces.

water injection (reciprocating engines). A system in which a water and alcohol mixture is injected into the induction system of a reciprocating engine when it is developing full power. When the water injection system (or antidetonation [ADI] system, as it is more properly called) is used, the fuel-air mixture being produced by the carburetor is automatically leaned, or deriched, to allow the engine to develop its maximum power.

The liquid water-alcohol mixture is injected with the fuel and air into the cylinders where it turns into vapor. As it evaporates, it absorbs the heat that would otherwise cause detonation.

waterline (reference line). A horizontal reference line used in lofting (laying out the contour of an airplane fuselage). Waterline zero (WL 0) is used as the reference, and measurements above this line are positive water lines. Measurements below WL 0 are negative waterlines. An object located on WL 104 is 104 inches above WL 0.

water/methanol injection. *See* W/M injection.

water rudders (seaplane float component). Retractable control surfaces on the rear end of each float that can be extended downward into the water to provide more directional control when taxiing. They are attached by cables and springs to the air rudder and operated by the rudder pedals in the cockpit.

waterspout (meteorology). *See* tornado.

water vapor. Water in its vapor state. Water vapor is an invisible gas that is lighter than air and is an important constituent of the lower level of the atmosphere.

watt. The basic unit of mechanical power in the metric system and also as a measure of electrical power. One watt is the amount of power needed to do one joule (0.7376 foot-pound) of work in one second and is also the equivalent of $^1/_{746}$ horsepower. In terms of electrical power, one watt is the amount of electrical power needed to force one ampere of current to flow under a pressure of one volt.

wattage rating (electrical component rating). The maximum power an electrical component can dissipate without becoming overheated or otherwise damaged.

watt-hour. The basic unit of electrical work. One watt-hour is the amount of work done when one watt of power is used for one hour. One watt-hour is equal to 3,600 joules of work.

wattmeter. An indicating instrument that measures electrical power.

watt-second. The amount of work done when one watt of power is used for one second. One watt-second is equal to one joule.

wave cyclone (meteorology). A cyclone which forms and moves along a front. The circulation about the cyclone center tends to produce a wavelike deformation of the front.

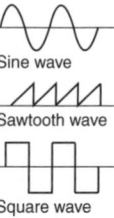

Sine wave

Sawtooth wave

Square wave

waveforms

waveform. The visual or graphic shape of an electromagnetic wave as is seen on a cathode-ray oscilloscope. Some of the more common waveforms are sine waves, square waves, sawtooth waves, and random or complex waves.

waveform analyzer. An electronic instrument that measures the frequency and amplitude of the various components of a complex electromagnetic wave.

wave guide. A hollow transmission line through which high-frequency electromagnetic waves are directed.

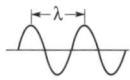

wavelength

wavelength (λ). The distance between a peak or a trough of an electromagnetic wave and the corresponding peak or trough in the next cycle of the wave. Wavelength is inversely related to the frequency of the wave.

wave soldering. A method of soldering components to a printed circuit (PC) board. All the components are assembled on the PC board, and the side of the board on which the copper strips are formed is treated with flux. A tank of molten solder is vibrated so waves form on the surface of the solder, and the board is passed over the solder so the tip of the waves touch the fluxed copper strips. All the component leads protruding through the board are soldered to the copper strips.

wave window (glider operation). Special areas arranged by Letter of Agreement with the controlling ATC wherein gliders may be allowed to fly under VFR in Class A Airspace at certain times and to certain specified altitudes.

waypoint (aerial navigation). The location on a navigational chart to which a VORTAC station has been electronically moved by an Area Navigation (RNAV) system. A waypoint is located by keying in the radial from the VORTAC station on which the waypoint is to be located, and the distance in nautical miles from the station along the selected radial.

By using waypoints, rather than flying directly to the physical station, a flight can be made in a straight line, and radio navigation can be used directly to a destination having no radio facility. A waypoint may be defined relative to a VORTAC station or in terms of latitude/longitude coordinates.

waypoint alerting. The function performed by the FMS/RNAV to alert the pilot at some time or distance prior to, or when reaching, the active waypoint.

waypoint sequencing. The action performed by the FMS/RNAV unit when an aircraft effectively has reached the active waypoint, and the unit automatically switches to the next waypoint in the programmed route. (*See also* turn anticipation.)

WCA. *See* wind correction angle.

wear pads (aircraft brake component). Steel pads riveted to the surface of the stationary disks of a multiple-disk brake. These pads wear away by the abrasive action of the sintered material on the rotating disks as the brake is used. It is more economical to replace the wear pads than to replace an entire disk.

weather. The state of the atmosphere, mainly with respect to its effects on life and human activities. Weather differs from climate in that it refers to instantaneous conditions or short-term changes.

weather advisory. An expression of hazardous weather conditions not predicted in the area forecast, as they affect the operation of air traffic and as prepared by the National Weather Service.

weather and radar processor (WARP). A device that provides real-time, accurate, predictive, and strategic weather information presented in an integrated manner in the National Airspace System (NAS).

weather briefing. The gathering by a pilot of all the available weather information vital to the nature of the flight. Weather briefings are most often obtained from a flight service station (FSS) specialist.

weather depiction chart. A chart which details surface conditions as derived from METAR and other surface observations.

weather radar. Radar specifically designed for observing weather. *See* cloud detection radar and storm-detection radar.

weathervaning (aerodynamics). The tendency of an aircraft to turn until it points into the wind.

weber. The basic unit of magnetic flux. One weber is the amount of magnetic flux in one turn of wire needed to produce one volt of electrical pressure, when the current flowing through the wire is reduced evenly at the rate of one ampere per second.

web of a beam. The part of a structural beam between the caps. A beam is designed in such a way that a bending load is carried as a tensile load in one of the caps and a compressive load in the other. The web between the two caps is subjected to a shear load much lower than the tensile or the compressive load. The web of a structural beam is usually thinner than either of the caps.

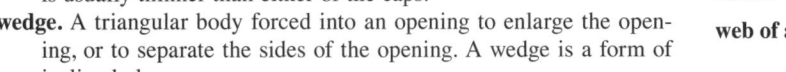

web of a beam

wedge. A triangular body forced into an opening to enlarge the opening, or to separate the sides of the opening. A wedge is a form of inclined plane.

weft direction (fabric). The yarns running perpendicular to the warp in a woven fabric; also called "woof." *See* warp threads.

weft threads. *See* fill threads.

weighing points (aircraft weight and balance). Locations on an aircraft, designated by the manufacturer, for the placement of the scales or load capsules when the aircraft is being weighed.

weigh-off (balloon operation). Determining neutral buoyancy of a gas balloon or airship by taking weight off at launch.

weight. A measure of the force of gravity acting upon a body. Weight and mass are often used interchangeably, but they are not the same thing. Mass is the amount of material in a body and does not consider the effect of gravity acting on it. Weight does take into consideration the effect of gravity acting on the mass.

weight and balance record (aircraft record). The record kept in an aircraft that gives the pilot or flight engineer an accurate account of the total weight of the aircraft and the location of its center of gravity. If the aircraft weight is too great, or if the center of gravity falls outside the allowable limits, the aircraft is not safe to fly.

weight-shift control aircraft (WSC). A powered aircraft with a framed pivoting wing and a fuselage controllable only in pitch and roll by the pilot's ability to change the aircraft's center of gravity with respect to the wing. Flight control of the aircraft depends on the wing's ability to flexibly deform rather than on the use of control surfaces.

W

weld bead. The ridge of metal left along the seam where two pieces of metal are joined by welding. The ridge, caused by the metal from the welding rod, increases the strength of the joint.

welded patch (steel tubular structural repair). A repair of dents or holes in steel tubing by welding a patch of the same material, one gage thicker, over the damaged area.

welding. A method of joining pieces of metal by fusion. The pieces to be joined are placed next to each other, and the surfaces between the two pieces are melted and allowed to flow together. The heat used to melt the edges is produced by a gas flame, an electric arc, or an extremely hot stream of plasma (ionized particles that act as a gas). Most welds are reinforced by adding filler metal to the puddle of molten metal to build up the area where the pieces are joined.

welding flux. A material that melts and flows over the surface of metal being welded. Flux produces an airtight seal which prevents oxygen reaching the surface of the hot metal and forming an oxide film. Oxides on the metal contaminate the weld.

Western Union splice (wire splice). A type of wire splice used to join two pieces of solid copper wire. The insulation is removed from the ends of the two pieces of wire, and the wires are scraped clean of all oxide coating. The wires are crossed and each end is wrapped around other wire; then the joint is coated with molten solder and insulated with tape.

wet-bulb temperature. Temperature measured with a thermometer enclosed in a cloth wick, saturated with water. Evaporation of the water lowers the temperature measured by this thermometer. Relative humidity of the air is found by comparing the wet-bulb temperature with the dry-bulb temperature, which is not affected by evaporation.

wet cell (electrical cell). A primary electrical cell having a liquid electrolyte.

wet lay-up (composites). A method of making a reinforced composite component by applying the resin system as a liquid when the reinforcement is put into place.

wet lease. Any leasing arrangement in which a person agrees to provide an entire aircraft and at least one crewmember. A wet lease does not include a code-sharing arrangement.

wet-out (composites). The condition of an impregnated roving or yarn in which substantially all voids between the sized strands and filaments are filled with resin.

wet-sump engine (lubrication system classification). An aircraft engine that carries its supply of lubricating oil in a sump, or compartment, which is part of the engine itself. After serving its lubricating functions, the oil drains back into the sump by gravity.

A dry-sump engine uses an external oil tank, and the oil, after flowing through the engine, is moved by scavenger pumps to the external tank where it is stored until it is pumped through the engine again.

wet-type vacuum pump. An engine-driven air pump which uses steel vanes lubricated with engine oil drawn into the pump through holes in the base. The oil passes through the pump, where it seals and lubricates, and is then exhausted with the air. Wet-type pumps must have oil separators in their discharge line to trap the oil and return it to the engine crankcase.

wet wing (aircraft structure). A type of aircraft construction in which part of the wing structure is sealed and used as a fuel tank. Wet wings are more properly called integral fuel tanks.

Wheatstone bridge (electrical circuit). A four-arm electrical bridge circuit used to measure resistance. An unknown resistance is placed in one arm of the bridge and is compared with a variable, or known, resistance in an opposite arm. When the variable resistor is adjusted until no current flows through the indicator, the bridge is balanced and the unknown resistance is exactly the same as that of the variable resistor.

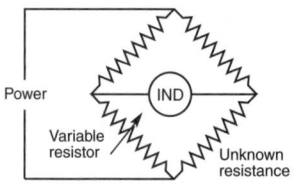

Wheatstone bridge

wheel well (aircraft structural component). A part of an aircraft structure that houses the landing gear when it is retracted. Wheel wells may be part of the wing, engine nacelle, or fuselage.

"When able" (air traffic control). A phrase used in conjunction with ATC instructions that gives the pilot latitude to delay compliance until a condition or event has been reconciled. Unlike "pilot discretion," when an instruction is prefaced with "when able," the pilot is expected to seek the first opportunity to comply. Once a maneuver has been initiated, the pilot is expected to continue until the specifications of the instructions have been met. "When able," should not be used when expeditious compliance is required.

whetstone. An abrasive stone used to wear away, or sharpen, the edges of cutting tools.

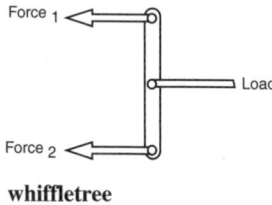

whiffletree

whiffletree. A pivoted beam used in an aircraft control system to allow more than one force to act on a common point. For example, two pulling forces may be applied to the ends of a whiffletree, and the device being pulled is connected to the point between the pulling forces.

whip antenna (radio antenna). A flexible, vertical antenna often used with high-frequency (HF) and very-high-frequency (VHF) radio equipment. The length of a whip antenna is one-quarter the wavelength of the frequency to which the antenna is resonant. A whip antenna is nondirectional; it transmits or receives its signals equally well in all directions.

whirlwind (meteorology). A small, rotating column of air which may be visible as a dust devil. *See* dust devil.

white dew (meteorology). Dew that has frozen as the result of a fall in temperature to below freezing after the original formation of the dew.

whiteout (meteorology). A condition where within the pilot visibility range there are no contrasting ground features resulting in a loss of depth perception. Buildings, people, and dark colored objects appear to float in the air, and the horizon disappears.

Whittle, Sir Frank. The British Royal Air Force Flying Officer who in 1929 filed a patent application for a turbojet engine. Whittle's engine first flew in a Gloster E.28 on May 15, 1941. The first jet flight in America was made on October 2, 1942, in a Bell XP-59A that was powered by two Whittle-type General Electric I-A engines.

whole numbers. A number that is not a fraction. For example, the numbers: 0, 1, 2, 3, 4, 5, and so on.

wicking (soldering problem). A problem that occurs when solder flows up around the individual wires in a stranded electrical conductor until it reaches the insulation. When stranded wire is soldered, there should be a short piece of the bare wire between the end of the solder and the beginning of the insulation. This bare section allows the wire to flex smoothly so it will not break when it is vibrated.

wide area augmentation system (WAAS). A differential global positioning system (DGPS) that improves the accuracy of the system by determining position error from the GPS satellites, then transmitting the error, or corrective factors, to the airborne GPS receiver.

wilco (radio communications). A term meaning "I have received your message, understand it, and will comply with it."

willy-willy (meteorology). A tropical cyclone of hurricane strength near Australia; also, in Australia, a dust devil.

W

winch. A machine used for pulling or moving heavy loads. A cable is wound around a drum turned by a geared hand crank or some type of motor. The load is attached to the cable and is moved by it.

wind (meteorology). Air in motion relative to the surface of the earth. The term wind generally denotes horizontal movement of the air.

winds and temperature aloft forecast (FD). A twice-daily forecast that provides wind and temperature forecasts for specific locations in the contiguous United States.

wind chill factor (meteorology). A measure of the cooling effect of the wind. Wind chill factor is based on both the temperature of the air and the velocity of the wind.

wind correction angle (navigation). WCA is the angle between the desired track and the heading of the aircraft necessary to keep the aircraft flying over the desired track.

wind direction indicator (airport fixture). A device which visually indicates the wind direction for the purpose of determining the direction in which landings and take-offs should be made.

wind drift (navigation). The sideways motion of an aircraft over the ground caused by a crosswind.

wind grid display. A display that presents the latest forecasted wind data overlaid on a map of the ARTCC area. Wind data is automatically entered and updated periodically by transmissions from the National Weather Service. Winds at specific altitudes, along with temperatures and air pressure can be viewed.

windmilling (aircraft engine operation). An aircraft engine is said to be windmilling when it is turned by aerodynamic action of air flowing over the propeller or through the compressor in a gas turbine engine. If an engine fails in flight, air flowing over the propeller or through the compressor produces enough force to keep the engine turning.

When a propeller windmills, it produces so much drag it can cause difficulty in controlling the airplane. For this reason, the propellers of most multiengine airplanes are made so that they can be feathered by turning the blades parallel to the direction of flight. When a propeller is feathered, it does not windmill.

windmilling propeller. The continued rotation of a propeller after the engine is shut down in flight. Aerodynamic forces act on the propeller to keep it turning, or windmilling, with no power from the engine.

window demister. A method of keeping moisture from condensing on the windows of an aircraft operating in the cold air at high altitudes. Warm compressor bleed air is blown between the layers of transparent material of which the windows are made.

wind shear (meteorology). A strong horizontal or vertical wind shift that acts at right angles to the direction the wind is blowing. Wind shear, normally associated with the passage of a front, can be dangerous if an aircraft flies through one when slowed for landing or immediately after takeoff.

wind shear escape. An unplanned abortive maneuver initiated by the pilot-in-command (PIC) when an inadvertent wind shear encounter is experienced or an onboard system issues a warning. Wind shear escapes are characterized by maximum thrust climbs in the low altitude terminal environment until wind shear conditions are no longer detected.

windshield. A transparent glass or plastic covering used to protect the occupants of an aircraft from the wind and rain while allowing forward vision. A windshield is also called a windscreen.

wind sock (wind direction indicator). A long, tapered, cloth tube open at both ends. Its large end is supported and held open by a steel ring mounted in a bearing so it is free to turn. Wind socks are mounted on tall poles so they can catch the wind and stream out in the direction the wind is blowing. Wind socks are normally made of vividly colored cloth and are used on airports and heliports to show the pilot of an arriving aircraft the direction from which the wind is blowing.

wind speed. Rate of air movement in distance per unit time.

wind triangle (navigation). A navigational aid in which a triangle is drawn to scale, one side represents the course and ground speed, one side the wind direction and velocity, and the third side the heading and airspeed. Any value can be found when the other five are known.

wind tunnel testing. A method of determining the aerodynamic characteristics of an aircraft design. An accurate scale model of the aircraft is made and mounted in the wind tunnel on a series of balances, or scales. Wind of an accurately controlled speed is blown across the model, and the balances measure the amount of lift and drag produced by the model at different wind speeds and angles of attack.

windward. Upwind, or the upwind side of an object.

wing (aircraft component). The part of a heavier-than-air aircraft that produces aerodynamic lift to support the aircraft in the air against the force of gravity. The wing of an airplane, a fixed-wing aircraft, is attached rigidly to the aircraft structure, but the wing of a helicopter, a rotor-wing aircraft, is mounted on a mast and is rotated by the engine.

wing area (aircraft wing dimensions). The total surface area of an airplane wing. Wing area is usually measured in square feet, and it is found by multiplying the span of the wing by its chord.

wing chord (aircraft wing dimension). The width of a wing, or the distance from the leading edge to the trailing edge.

wing fences. Vertical vanes that extend chordwise across the upper surface of an airplane wing to prevent spanwise airflow.

wing fillet (aircraft structural component). A streamlined fairing installed between the root of an airplane wing and the fuselage. Wing fillets smooth the airflow where the wing joins the fuselage and reduce the drag caused by this junction.

wing flaps (airplane secondary controls). An auxiliary control on an airplane that can be lowered to increase both the lift and drag the wing produces. Wing flaps are partially lowered for takeoff to allow the airplane to leave the ground at a slow speed. They are fully lowered for landing to allow the airplane to make a steep approach without building up excessive speed. *See* plain flap, split flap, slotted flap, Fowler flap, triple-slotted flap.

wing floats (or, tip floats). *See* wing-tip floats. *See also* sponsons.

wing heavy (flight condition). An out-of-trim condition in which an airplane flies, hands off, with one wing low. A wing-heavy condition is normally corrected by changing the rigging of the wing or by the deflection of one of the trim tabs.

winglet (aerodynamic surface). A vertical or angled extension at the wingtip of many transport and corporate airplanes. Winglets improve the efficiency of an aircraft by decreasing wingtip vortices which cause lift-induced drag. Winglets increase the effective aspect ratio of a wing without adding to the span.

winglet (tip fin). *14 CFR Part 1:* "An out-of-plane surface extending from a lifting surface. The surface may or may not have control surfaces."

wing loading (aircraft performance measure). The amount of load each square foot of airplane wing area must support. Wing loading is found by dividing the maximum weight of the aircraft, in pounds, by the total area of the wing, in square feet.

wing nut. An internally threaded fastener with two wings protruding from its sides. The wings allow the nut to be turned onto a bolt using only the fingers. No provision is made for turning a wing nut with a wrench.

wing panel (airplane structural component). A removable section of an airplane wing. Most airplane wings are made in panels, with a left and a right panel attached to a center section. The center section is often a part of the fuselage.

wing rib (aircraft component). The structural member in an aircraft wing that gives the wing its aerodynamically correct cross-sectional shape. Wing ribs are mounted across the wing spars and are covered with thin sheets of metal, plywood, or cloth fabric.

wing span (aircraft wing dimension). The length of an aircraft wing, or the distance from one wing tip to the other.

WINGS Program. A program that encourages general aviation pilots to continue training and provides an opportunity to practice selected maneuvers in a minimum of instruction time. Participation in the WINGS program relieves a pilot from compliance with flight review requirements, provided all WINGS requirements are met. Previously governed by Advisory Circular 61-91, the WINGS program is available as on online education program at www.faasafety.gov, effective mid-2007.

wing strut (airplane component). The external rigid braces that extend from the bottom of the fuselage, for a high wing airplane, to the wing spars at a point about midway of the span of the wing panel. The strut carries the flight loads in tension and the landing loads in compression. Thin struts are normally fitted with jury struts to prevent vibration and buckling. *See* jury strut.

wing-tip floats (seaplane component). A buoyant body of streamline shape attached to the wing tips of a flying-boat or single-float seaplane to prevent the wing tips from contacting the water.

wing-tip vortices (aircraft operation). Tornado-like disturbances produced at the wing tips any time an airplane wing is producing lift. When a wing produces lift, the air pressure on top of the wing is much lower than the pressure below the wing, and the high-pressure air below the wing spills over to the top at the tip, producing a tight spiral, or vortex, of wind. Wing-tip vortices settle below the airplane, and those produced by heavy airplanes can cause lighter aircraft flying into them to be thrown out of control.

wing twist. A design feature in which a wing panel has a built-in wash-out twist. This twist decreases the angle of incidence near the wing tip and maintains aileron effectiveness by delaying the stall to a higher angle of attack. *See* wash out.

wink Zyglo. *See* blink Zyglo.

wiper (electrical component). The movable contact in a potentiometer, rheostat, or wafer-type switch. The wiper is controlled by rotating the shaft that extends through the center of the device, and as the wiper is rotated, it makes contact with a part of the resistance element or with one of the fixed contacts of the switch.

wire braid. A woven, flexible metal covering placed over electrical wiring that carries alternating current. Energy radiated from the wire is intercepted by the braid and carried to ground, rather than allowing it to cause radio interference.

wire bundle (aircraft electrical system component). A group of electrical wires routed through a compartment of the aircraft. The wires are grouped together and secured with nylon straps or lacing cord into a compact bundle, and the bundle is secured to the aircraft structure with cushioned clamps.

wire cloth. A screen made by weaving wire into a sheet.

wire edge (sheet metal defect). A sharp burr that forms on the edge of a sheet of metal when it is cut with a dull shear.

wireless. The British term that means the same as "radio," used in the United States.

wire stripper (electrical maintenance tool). A tool used to remove insulation from an electrical wire without nicking or otherwise damaging the strands.

wire-wound resistor (electrical component). An electrical resistor made by winding a strip or ribbon of high-resistance metal or high-resistance wire around an insulating core. Connections are made to both ends of the resistance element, which is then covered with a baked-on ceramic material.

wiring diagram. A diagram that shows the electrical wiring and circuitry, coded for identification, of all the electrical appliances and devices used on aircraft.

W/M injection (turbine engine thrust augmentation). A system in which a mixture of water and methanol (methyl alcohol) is injected into the compressor inlet and/or the combustion chamber of a turbine engine. The W/M injection increases the thrust by increasing the mass of the air flowing through the engine. It also cools the gases flowing through the turbine so more fuel can be burned before reaching the limiting turbine inlet temperature. W/M injection is not used on modern turbine engines.

wobble pump (fluid pump). A type of hand-operated pump used to move a fluid such as gasoline or oil. The handle of a wobble pump is attached to a flat plate inside a housing that is equipped with four flapper-type check valves. Moving the handle back and forth (wobbling it) pulls fluid into one side of the pump and forces it out the other side.

Wood's metal. The registered trade name for an alloy of bismuth, lead, tin, and cadmium. Wood's metal melts at 158°F.

woodruff key. A hardened steel key made in the shape of a half circle. The rounded side of the key fits into a semicircular keyway cut into a shaft. The flat end fits into a slot cut into a wheel or disk mounted on the shaft. The key prevents the wheel or disk from turning on the shaft.

woof threads. *See* fill threads.

"words twice" (radio communications). As a request: "Communication is difficult. Please say every phrase twice." As information: "Since communications are difficult, every phrase in this message will be spoken twice."

word/symbol confusion (in teaching/learning process). In explaining concepts or conversing with students, a miscommunication that can occur when the distinction between a word and its connotation (or what it symbolizes) is not made clear by the instructor. Effective communication is easier when speakers and writers are aware of the distinctions of meaning in words they use. Instructors should be careful that their words bring to mind the correct symbols for their students when trying to communicate aviation concepts. *See also* symbols.

work. The physical measurement of the amount of force required to produce a given amount of movement. Work is the product of the force applied to an object, multiplied by the distance the force causes the object to move. Work is measured in such terms as pound-inches, pound-feet, or joules.

work hardening (metal condition). A method of hardening and strengthening metal that cannot be hardened by heat treatment. When the metal is hammered, rolled, bent, or stretched, it becomes work hardened.

working drawings. The classification of drawings that includes detail drawings, assembly drawings, and installation drawings.

working life (composites). The period of time during which a liquid resin or adhesive, after mixing with catalyst, solvent, or other compounding ingredients, remains usable.

working or short-term memory (in learning process). The portion of the brain that receives information from the sensory register and can store information in memory for only a short period of time. If an individual determines that the information is important enough to remember, it must be coded for transmittal to long-term memory.

working voltage (capacitor rating). The maximum amount of DC voltage that can safely be applied across the plates of a capacitor.

world aeronautical charts (WAC) (1:1,000,000). Provide a standard series of aeronautical charts covering land areas of the world at a size and scale convenient for navigation by moderate speed aircraft. Topographic information includes cities and towns, principal roads, railroads, distinctive landmarks, drainage, and relief. Aeronautical information includes visual and radio aids to navigation, airports, airways, restricted areas, obstructions and other pertinent data.

worm gear. A helical gear mounted on a shaft and meshed with a spur gear whose teeth are cut at an angle to its face. A worm gear is an irreversible type of mechanism. Rotating the shaft on which the worm gear is mounted rotates the spur gear, but the worm gear locks the spur gear so its shaft cannot be rotated.

WOXOF (meteorology). A meteorological term meaning visibility zero due to fog.

wrench. A hand tool used to turn threaded fasteners such as bolts and nuts. A wrench has a slot or a hexagonal-shaped hole that fits over the head of the fastener and a handle to which a force is applied to turn the fastener.

wrinkle (composites). A surface imperfection in laminated plastics that has the appearance of a crease or fold in one or more outer laminations. It also occurs in vacuum bag molding when the bag is improperly placed, causing a crease.

wrinkle finish. A rough paint finish that is often applied to aircraft instrument panels. The surface of wrinkle-finish paint dries quickly, and the material below the surface shrinks as it dries. The shrinkage pulls the surface into a series of small wrinkles. A wrinkle finish does not show fingerprints or small scratches as much as a smooth finish.

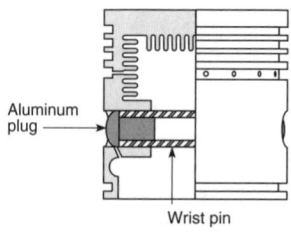

Wrist pin

wrist pin

wrist pin (reciprocating engine component). The hardened and polished steel pin that attaches a piston to the small end of a connecting rod. Wrist pins are called piston pins, and in the United Kingdom, gudgeon pins.

wrist pin boss (reciprocating engine). The enlarged area inside a piston that supports the wrist pin. The additional metal provides a greater bearing area for the pin and strengthens the piston so it can transfer the force acting on the piston to the connecting rod. *See* piston (reciprocating engine component).

wrought iron. A commercial grade of iron used for the manufacture of low-strength items. Wrought iron is malleable (it can be shaped by hammering), tough, and relatively soft.

wye connection (electrical connection). A name that is often used for a Y- or star-connected electrical circuit. *See* Y-connection.

X-ray

X-axis. The longitudinal, or roll axis of an aircraft. The vertical axis is the Z-axis, and the lateral axis is the Y-axis. *See* longitudinal axis.

X-band radar. Radar whose energy is transmitted in a frequency band of between 5.2 and 10.9 gigahertz, and whose wavelength is between about 5.77 and 2.75 centimeters.

xenon. An inert, colorless, odorless, gaseous chemical element. Xenon's symbol is Xe, its atomic number is 54, and its atomic weight is 131.30. Xenon is extracted from liquified air, and it is used to fill stroboscopic lamps because it gives off a brilliant flash of light when it is ionized and current flows through it.

X-ray inspection. A form of nondestructive inspection in which a piece of photographic film is exposed by X-rays passing through a section of the aircraft structure. The density of the structure determines the amount of energy passed to the film. Because of the different densities of the structure, an image of the structure is formed on the film. X-ray inspection is used to examine the inside of a structure for corrosion or damage that deforms the structure.

X-rays. Rays of electromagnetic energy having a wavelength of approximately one angstrom. X-rays are produced by accelerating electrons to a high velocity and then stopping them instantly by collision with a solid object. X-rays are able to penetrate many types of solid objects and are used to produce a photographic record of the inside of an aircraft structure.

xylene. A flammable, oily, aromatic, hydrocarbon fluid. Xylene is mixed with other hydrocarbon fluids and used as a solvent and as an additive to improve the combustion characteristics of reciprocating engine fuels.

X

yagi antenna (radio antenna). A highly directional antenna used for high-frequency (HF) radio communications. A yagi antenna has a single dipole connected to the transmission line (this is the driven dipole) and several unconnected dipoles parallel to the driven dipole. These unconnected dipoles act as reflectors and directors for the radio-frequency energy transmitted from the antenna.

yard (unit of measure). A unit of length in the English system of measurement. One yard is equal to 36 inches, three feet, or 0.9144 meter.

yardstick. A wooden measuring stick with the length of three feet, or one yard. A yardstick is marked at every inch along its length.

yaw (aircraft flight condition). A flight condition of an aircraft in which the aircraft rotates about its vertical axis. Yawing is not the same as turning, because an aircraft can be yawed and continue in straight flight with the wind striking it from the side. When an airplane is turned, it follows a curved flight path, with the wind always flowing parallel to its longitudinal axis.

yaw damper (airplane control). A part of an aircraft automatic flight control system used to keep the aircraft from unwanted yawing. Yaw dampers are generally needed for swept-wing airplanes because of the tendency of this type of airplane to Dutch roll. *See* Dutch roll.

yaw string (yaw indicator). A piece of string or yarn approximately 18 to 36 inches in length, taped to the base of the windshield, or to the nose near the windshield, along the airplane centerline. In two-engine coordinated flight, the relative wind will cause the string to align itself with the longitudinal axis of the airplane, and it will position itself straight up the center of the windshield. This is zero sideslip. Experimentation with slips and skids will vividly display the location of the relative wind.

Y-axis. The lateral, or pitch, axis of an aircraft. The vertical, or yaw, axis is the Z-axis, and the longitudinal, or roll, axis is the X-axis. *See* lateral axis.

Y-connected circuit (electrical circuit). A three-phase alternating current circuit in which one end of each of the three windings of a three-phase generator or transformer is connected to form a common point. In a Y-connected circuit, two windings are in series with each other, and the current flowing in each of the two windings is 120 electrical degrees out of phase with the current flowing in the other windings.

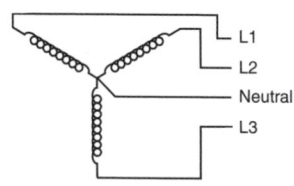

Y-connected circuit

The voltage across the ends of the two windings is 1.73 times the voltage across either of the windings and the common point. A Y-connected circuit is sometimes called a wye-connected circuit or a star-connected circuit.

years in service. The calendar time elapsed since an aircraft was issued its first U.S. or first foreign airworthiness certificate.

Y

yellow arc (aircraft instrument marking). A type of range marking for aircraft instruments that identifies a caution area. A yellow arc on the dial of an airspeed indicator identifies a range of airspeeds that can be safely flown in calm air, but the aircraft must not be flown at these speeds in rough air. There must be no abrupt maneuvers made while flying in this speed range.

yield point (material strength). A measure of the amount of stress needed to permanently deform a material. When a piece of material is stressed to a value within its elastic limit, it will deform, but will return to its original size and shape when the stress is removed. When the material is stressed to its yield point, it will not return to its original size and shape when the stress is removed; it will be permanently deformed.

yield strength. The amount of stress needed to permanently deform a material.

yoke (airplane control). The control column in an airplane on which the control wheel is mounted. Back-and-forth movement of the yoke moves the elevators, and rotation of the control wheel moves the ailerons.

Young's modulus. The ratio of the amount of tensile stress applied to a material to the amount of resulting strain parallel to the stress.

ytterbium. A soft, bright, silvery, rare-earth, metallic chemical element. Ytterbium's symbol is Yb, its atomic number is 70, and its atomic weight is 173.04. Ytterbium is used as an X-ray source and in the study of superconductivity.

yttrium. A silvery, rare-earth, metallic chemical element. Yttrium's symbol is Y, its atomic number is 39, and its atomic weight is 88.905. Yttrium is used in nuclear technology and as an alloy for other metals.

Y-valve (lubrication system component). The oil drain valve for a dry-sump reciprocating engine. One branch of the Y goes to the oil tank, the other to the inlet of the oil pressure pump. The lower branch contains a valve from which the oil is drained.

Zahn cup (viscosity measuring instrument). A specially designed viscosimeter, or cup for measuring the viscosity of a liquid. The Zahn cup is filled with the liquid whose viscosity is to be measured. A specially calibrated hole in the bottom of the cup is opened, and the time needed for the liquid to flow from the cup is measured. The number of seconds between the start of the flow and the time at which the first break in the flow occurs relates to the viscosity of the liquid.

Z-axis. The vertical, or yaw, axis of an aircraft. The X-axis is the longitudinal, or roll axis, and the Y-axis is the lateral, or pitch axis. *See* vertical axis.

zener diode (electronic component). A special type of semiconductor device that allows electrons to flow through it in one direction, but normally opposes flow in the opposite direction. If the voltage across the zener diode, in the direction that does not allow flow, is increased

zener diode

to a specific value, the zener diode will break down, and electrons will flow through it. The voltage at which a zener diode breaks down is called the zener voltage. Zener diodes are also called avalanche diodes.

zenith. The point in the orbit of a satellite or any body rotating around another body, at which the orbiting body is the greatest distance from the object around which it is rotating. The zenith of an orbit is opposite the nadir of the orbit.

zephyr (meteorology). A mild breeze, usually one blowing from the west.

Zeppelin. A large, rigid, lighter-than-air flying machine. The Zeppelin gets its name from Count Ferdinand von Zeppelin who pioneered the design and manufacture of these large, cigar-shaped airships. Zeppelins were used in World War I, and to a limited extent in commercial air travel, until the time the huge German airship *Hindenburg* burned in 1939.

Zerk fitting (grease fitting). The registered trade name for a type of fitting used to put grease into a bearing. A hole is drilled through the structure to the location where grease is needed, and a Zerk fitting is installed in this hole.

The Zerk fitting has a ball-shaped top that is gripped by the nozzle of the grease gun when pressure is applied. Grease is pumped through the fitting into the bearing until it flows out between the surfaces of the bearing. When the grease gun is removed from the Zerk fitting, a check valve inside the fitting prevents grease leaking out, and prevents dirt getting into the bearing through the fitting.

zero (mathematical quantity). A numerical quantity that has no value. Zero is used as a reference point on a number line from which values on both sides of zero are measured.

zero (temperature). A reference used in the measurement of temperature. In the measurement of absolute temperatures using both degrees Kelvin and degrees Rankine, zero is the point at which all molecular movement stops. In the measure of temperature using the Celsius scale (the centigrade scale), zero is the temperature of melting ice. In the measure of temperature using the Fahrenheit scale, zero is the temperature of a mixture of ice and salt water.

zero adjustment (electrical measuring instrument). The adjustment of the pointer of an electrical measuring instrument so that the needle rests over the zero mark on the dial when no current is flowing through the moving coil of the meter.

Z

zero beat (frequency adjustment). A method of determining the exact frequency of an alternating current. Vibrations caused by a variable-frequency alternating current are mixed with vibrations caused by the alternating current whose frequency is to be found. When the two vibrations mix, a third vibration is formed whose frequency is the difference between the frequencies of the first two vibrations. The variable frequency is changed until the third vibration disappears. At this point, the two frequencies are exactly the same. The beat has been reduced to zero.

zero bleed (composites). A laminate fabrication procedure that does not allow loss of resin during cure. Also describes prepreg made with the amount of resin desired in the final part, such that no resin has to be removed during cure.

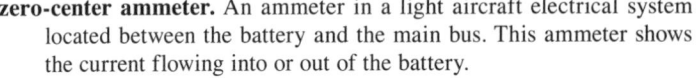

zero-center ammeter. An ammeter in a light aircraft electrical system located between the battery and the main bus. This ammeter shows the current flowing into or out of the battery.

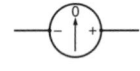

zero-center ammeter

zero fuel weight (aircraft weight). The weight of an aircraft with all of the useful load except the fuel on board.

zero gravity. A condition in which the effect of gravity is cancelled or nullified by the force of inertia. Zero gravity is felt in a high-performance aircraft when it is flying in a parabolic, or curved, flight path, and in a satellite when it is orbiting the earth.

zero-lash valve lifter (reciprocating engine component). A type of valve lifter in a reciprocating engine that uses a hydraulic device to keep all clearance out of the valve train. Each time an intake or exhaust valve is opened, a specific amount of oil leaks from the hydraulic valve lifter, and while the valve is closed, engine oil pressure refills the lifter so it keeps all of the operating clearance out of the valve mechanism.

zero-lift line (aerodynamics). An imaginary line through an airfoil along which air can flow over both sides of the surface of the airfoil and not produce any lift. The zero-lift line is the chord line of a symmetrical airfoil, but it is at a negative angle of attack for an asymmetrical airfoil.

zero sideslip (flight condition). A maneuver in a twin-engine airplane with one engine inoperative that involves a small amount of bank and slightly uncoordinated flight to align the fuselage with the direction of travel and minimize drag.

zero stage (turbine engine). A stage of compressor blades installed ahead of the front of an axial compressor.

zero thrust. An engine configuration with a low power setting that simulates a propeller feathered condition.

zinc. A bluish-white, lustrous, metallic chemical element. Zinc's symbol is Z, its atomic number is 30, and its atomic weight is 65.37. Zinc is used as an alloying agent for other metals and as a corrosion-resistant coating for steel.

zinc chromate primer. An alkyd resin primer used to prepare a metal surface to take a topcoat of paint. Moisture in contact with a coating of zinc chromate primer causes the primer to release chromate ions that inhibit the formation of corrosion on the metal protected by the primer.

zirconium. A lustrous, grayish-white, metallic chemical element. Zirconium's symbol is Zr, its atomic number is 40, and its atomic weight is 91.22. Zirconium is used as an ingredient in ceramics and refractory materials.

Z-marker (aerial navigation). A type of directional radio beacon used to mark a specific location along an airway or along an instrument approach course. A Z-marker transmits a vertical signal on a 75-megahertz carrier modulated with a series of 3,000 hertz dots. The series of dots can be heard over the radio speaker, and the Z-marker also causes the white light on the marker beacon panel to light up in a series of short flashes, the dots.

zonal wind (meteorology). A west wind or the westerly component of a wind. Zonal wind is conventionally used to describe large-scale flow that is neither cyclonic nor anticyclonic.

zone of confusion. Volume of space above a VOR station where a lack of adequate navigation signal directly above the station causes the needle to deviate.

zone numbers (aircraft drawing). Numbers placed along the edges of large aircraft drawings to identify the location of a part on the drawing. Numerals are used along the length of the drawing, and letters are used along the width.

Zulu time. A name for Greenwich mean time, or universal time. *See* universal time.

Zyglo inspection (nondestructive inspection). The registered trade name for a type of nondestructive inspection used to find flaws that extend to the surface of a metallic or nonmetallic material. The part to be inspected is cleaned and soaked in a bath of hot penetrating liquid that contains a fluorescent dye. After the part has soaked for the correct length of time, it is removed from the bath, and all of the penetrant is washed from its surface. The part is then covered with a dry powder that pulls the penetrant from any surface defect. The part is then examined under an ultraviolet light, and any penetrant that has been pulled from a defect shows up as a green mark.

Z

Appendix 1
Acronyms and Abbreviations

A

A&P	Airframe and Powerplant
AAC	Aircraft Administration Communications
AAE	American Association of Airport Executives
AAI	Arrival Aircraft Interval
AAM	Air-to-Air Missile
AAR	Airport Acceptance Rate
AAS	Airport Advisory Service
AAUP	Attention All Users Page
AB	Afterburner
ABC	After Bottom Center
ABS	Absolute
AC	Advisory Circular
A/C	Air Conditioning
AC	Air Corps (an obsolete abbreviation)
AC	Alternating Current
ACARS	ARINC Communication Addressing and Reporting System
ACAS	Airborne Collision and Avoidance System
ACC	Active Clearance Control
ACC	Area Control Center
ACCEL	Acceleration
ACDO	Air Carrier District Office
ACESS	Advanced Cabin Entertainment and Service System
ACLS	Automatic Carrier Landing System
ACLT	Actual Calculated Landing Time
ACM	Air Cycle Machine
ACMI	Air Combat Maneuvering Instrumentation
ACMS	Aircraft Condition Monitoring System
ACT	Active Control Technology
ACU	Acceleration Control Unit
ACU	Antenna Coupling Unit
AD	Airworthiness Directive
A/D	Analog-to-Digital
ADAHRS	Air Data Attitude and Heading Reference System
A/D Conv	Analog-to-Digital Converter
ADC	Air Data Computer
ADDS	Aviation Digital Data Service
ADEU	Automatic Data Entry Unit
ADF	Automatic Direction Finder
ADI	Antidetonation Injection
ADI	Attitude Director Indicator
ADIZ	Air Defense Identification Zone
ADLY	Arrival Delay

ADM .... Aeronautical Decision Making
ADMA .... Aviation Distributors and Manufacturers Association
ADP .... Advanced Ducted Propfan
ADS .... Automatic Dependent Surveillance
ADS–B .... Automatic Dependent Surveillance–Broadcast
ADV .... Air Defense Version
AEA .... Aircraft Electronics Association, Inc.
AEG .... Aircraft Evaluation Group
AEM .... Audio Entertainment Multiplexer
AER .... Approach End of Runway
AEW .... Airborne Early Warning
AF .... Audio Frequency
AFA .... Air Force Association
AFA .... Association of Flight Attendants
AFC .... Automatic Frequency Control
AFCS .... Automatic Flight Control System
A/FD .... Airport/Facility Directory
AFDS .... Autopilot Flight Director System
AFIS .... Automatic Flight Information Service
AFM .... Airplane Flight Manual
AFMS .... Airplane Flight Manual Supplements
AFS .... Aircraft Flight Safety
AFS .... Autoflight System
AFSS .... Automated Flight Service Station
AFTI .... Advanced Fighter Technology Integration
AFVG .... Anglo-French Variable Geometry
A/G .... Air/Ground
AGB .... Accessory Gear Box
AGC .... Automatic Gain Control
AGI .... Advanced Ground Instructor
AGL .... Above Ground Level
AGM .... Air-to-Ground Missile
AGS .... Automatic Gain Stabilization
AHRS .... Attitude and Heading Reference System
AI .... Attitude Indicator
AIA .... Aerospace Industries Association of America, Inc.
AIAA .... American Institute of Aeronautics and Astronautics, Inc.
AID .... Airport Information Desk
AIDS .... Airborne Integrated Data System
AIL .... Aileron
AILS .... Automatic Instrument Landing System
AIM .... Aeronautical Information Manual
AIM .... Avalanche-Induced Migration
AIMS .... Advanced Integrated Manufacturing System
AIP .... Aeronautical Information Publication (ICAO)
AIR .... Aircraft Certification Service
AIRMET .... Airman's Meteorological Information
AIS .... Airborne Instrumentation System
AISI .... American Iron and Steel Institute
AIT .... Automated Information Transfer

AJW-3 ....Aviation System Services (part of FAA's Technical
Operations Services)
A/L ....Autoland
ALAR ....Approach and Landing Accident Reduction
ALARM ....Air-Launched AntiRadiation Missile
ALD ....Available Landing Distance
ALERFA ....Alert Phase (ICAO)
Al-Gate MOS ....Aluminum-Gate Metal Oxide Silicon semiconductor
ALNOT ....Alert Notice
ALOFT ....Airborne Light/Optical Fiber Technology
ALPA ....Air Line Pilot's Association, Intl.
ALRS ....Arithmetic and Logic Register Stack
ALS ....Approach Lighting System
ALSF-I ....Approach Light System with sequenced Flashing lights
in ILS Cat I configuration
ALSF-II ....Approach Light System with sequenced Flashing lights
in ILS Cat II configuration
ALT ....Altitude
ALT ACQ ....Altitude Acquire
ALT HOLD ....Altitude Hold
ALTRV ....Altitude Reservation
ALU ....Arithmetic and Logic Unit
AM ....Amplitude Modulated
AMAD ....Airframe Mounted Accessory Drives
AMASS ....Airport Movement Area Safety System
AME ....Aviation Medical Examiner
AMED ....Advanced Mechanical Engine Demonstrator
AMEL ....Airplane Multi-Engine Land
AMES ....Airplane Multi-Engine Sea
AMETS ....Airplane Maintenance Engineering Time Standard
AMOS ....Automatic Meteorological Observing Station
AMP ....Amplifier
amp ....ampere
AMS ....Aeronautical Materials Specifications
AMSL ....Absolute Mean Sea Level
AMT ....Aviation Maintenance Technician
AMVER ....Automated Mutual-Assistance Vessel Rescue System
AN ....Air Force-Navy or Army-Navy
ANA ....All Nippon Airways
ANCA ....Airport Noise and Capacity Act
ANP ....Actual Navigation Performance
ANR ....Advanced Navigation Route
ANSI ....American National Standards Institute
ANT ....Antenna
AOA ....Airport Operating Area
AOA ....Angle of Attack
AOC..................................Aircraft Operational Communications
AOCC ....Airline Operations Control Center
AOG ....Aircraft on the Ground
AOPA ....Aircraft Owners and Pilots Association
AOSS ....After Over Station Sensor

AP	Autopilot
APB	Automated Problem Detection Boundary
APC	Absolute Pressure Controller
APCU	Auxiliary Power Control Unit
APD	Automated Problem Detection
APDIA	Automated Problem Detection Inhibited Area
APFDS	Autopilot and Flight Director System
API	American Petroleum Institute
APMS	Automatic Performance and Management System
APS	Altitude Preselect
APSB	Altitude Preselect Bracket
APT WP	Airport Waypoint
APU	Auxiliary Power Unit
APV	Approach with Vertical Guidance
AQR	Airline Quality Report
ARAC	Army Radar Approach Control
ARAC	Aviation Rulemaking Advisory Committee
ARC	Aftermarket Risk Contract
ARFF	Aircraft Rescue and Fire Fighting
ARINC	Aeronautical Radio Incorporated
A-RNAV	Advanced Area Navigation
ARO	Airport Reservation Office
ARPT	Airport
ARSA	Aeronautical Repair Stations Association
ARSA	Airport Radar Service Area
ARSR	Air Route Surveillance Radar
ARTC	Air Route Traffic Control
ARTCC	Air Route Traffic Control Center
ARTS	Automated Radar Terminal Systems
AS	Aeronautical Standard
AS, A/S	Airspeed
ASA	American Standards Association
ASA	Autoland Status Annunciator
ASARS	Advanced Synthetic Aperture Radar System
ASC	Aero Sports Connection
ASCB	Avionics Standard Communications Bus
ASCII	American Standard Code for Information Interchange
ASCR	Asymmetrical Silicon Controlled Rectifier
ASD	Aircraft Situation Display
ASDA	Accelerate-Stop Distance Available
ASDAR	Aircraft to Satellite Data Relay
ASDE	Airport Surface Detection Equipment
ASDE–3	Airport Surface Detection Equipment–3
ASDE–X	Airport Surface Detection Equipment–X
ASEL	Airplane Single-Engine Land
ASES	Airplane Single-Engine Sea
ASF	Air Safety Foundation
ASI	Airspeed Indicator
ASI	Aviation Safety Inspector
ASL	Above Sea Level
ASLAR	Aircraft Surge Launch and Recovery

ASM	Air-to-Surface Missile
ASM	Available Seat Mile
A-SMGCS	Advanced Surface Movement Guidance and Control System
ASOS	Automated Surface Observing System
ASP	Arrival Sequencing Program
ASPS	Airborne Self Protection System
ASR	Airport Surveillance Radar
ASRAAM	Advanced Short Range Air-to-Air Missile
ASRS	Aviation Safety Reporting System
ASTM	American Society for Testing and Materials
ASTOVL	Advanced STOVL
ASU	Altitude Sensing Unit
ASW	Anti-Submarine Warfare
ASYM	Asymmetrical
AT	Auto Throttle
ATA	Actual Time of Arrival
ATA	Air Transport Association of America
ATA	Aviation Training Association
ATC	After Top Center
ATC	Air Traffic Control
ATC	Approved Type Certificate
ATCAA	ATC Assigned Airspace
ATCRBS	Air Traffic Control Radar Beacon System
ATCS	Air Traffic Control Specialist
ATCSCC	Air Traffic Control System Command Center
ATCT	Airport Traffic Control Tower
ATCT	Airport Traffic Control Transponder
ATC-TFM	Air Traffic Control Traffic Flow Management
ATD	Actual Time of Departure
ATD	Along Track Distance
ATE	Actual Time Enroute
ATE	Automatic Test Equipment
ATEC	Aviation Technician Education Council
ATF	Aerodynamic Twisting Force
ATFM	Air Traffic Flow Management
ATIRCM	Advanced Threat Infrared Countermeasures
ATIS	Automatic Terminal Information Service
ATLAS	Abbreviated Test Language for Avionics Systems
ATM	Aerodynamic Twisting Moment
ATO	Air Traffic Organization
ATOL	Automatic Test-Oriented Language
ATP	Advanced Turboprop
ATP	Airline Transport Pilot
ATR	Avions de Transport Regional
ATS	Air Traffic Service
ATS	Automated Throttle System
ATSC	Air Traffic Security Coordinator
AT/SC	Auto Throttle/Speed Control
ATT	Attitude
ATU	Antenna Tuning Unit
AUG	Augmentation

AUTO ....Automatic
AUTOB ....Automatic Weather Reporting System
AUW ....All-Up Weight
AUX ....Auxiliary
AVC ....Automatic Volume Control
AVGAS ....AViation GASoline
AVM ....Airborne Vibration Monitor
AVN ....Office of Aviation System Standards
AVT ....Advanced Vectored Thrust
AWA ....Aviation/Space Writers Association
AWACS ....Airborne Warning and Control System
AWC ....Aviation Weather Center
AWG ....American Wire Gage
AWIPS ....Advanced Weather Interactive Processing System
AWOS ....Automated Weather Observing System
AWR ....Airborne Weather Radar
AWSS ....Automated Weather Sensor System
AWTT ....Aviation Weather Technology Transfer
AWW ....Severe Weather Forecast Alert

B

BA ....British Airways
BA ....Bank Angle
BAA ....Bilateral Airworthiness Agreement
BAe ....British Aerospace
BARO ....Barometric
Baro-VNAV ....Barometric Vertical Navigation
BASA ....Bilateral Aviation Safety Agreement
BATT ....Battery
B/B ....Back Beam
BB ....Bar Bias
BBC ....Before Bottom Center
BBD ....Bucket Brigade Device
BC, B/C ....Back Course
BCD ....Binary Coded Decimal
BCSL ....Base-Current Switch Logic
B/D ....Bottom of Descent
BeAMOS ....Beam-Addressed Metal Oxide Silicon semiconductor
BFET ....Bipolar Field Effect Transistor
BFL ....Buffered Field Effect Transistor Logic
BFO ....Beat Frequency Oscillator
BFR ....Biennial Flight Review
BGI ....Basic Ground Instructor
BHP ....Brake Horsepower
BIGFET ....Bipolar Insulated Gate Field Effect Transistor
BIMOS ....Bipolar Metal Oxide Silicon semiconductor
BIT ....Binary Digit
BITE ....Built-In Test Equipment
BLC ....Boundary Layer Control

BM ....Back Marker
BMEP ....Brake Mean Effective Pressure
BML ....Bipolar Memory, Linear
BNR ....Binary Numerical Reference
BOP ....Bipolar Operational Power
BORAM ....Block Oriented Random Access Memory
BOW ....Basic Operating Weight
BPCU ....Bus Power Control Unit
BPR ....Bypass Ratio
BR ....BMW–Rolls-Royce
BRG ....Bearing
BRITE ....Bright Radar Indicator Tower Equipment
B-RNAV ....European Basic RNAV
BSFC ....Brake Specific Fuel Consumption
BSR ....Bit Shift Register
BTB ....Bus Tie Breaker
BTC ....Before Top Center
Btu ....British Thermal Unit
BU ....Buffer Unit

C

CAA ....Civil Aeronautics Administration
CAA ....Civil Aviation Authority (UK)
CAASD ....Center for Advanced Aviation Systems Development
CAB ....Cabin
CAB ....Civil Aeronautics Board
CAD ....Computer-Aided Design
CAD/CAM ....Computer Aided Design and Manufacturing
CADD ....Computer-Aided Design Drafting
CAE ....Computer-Aided Engineering
CALCM ....Conventional Air-Launched Cruise Missile
CAMI ....Civil Aerospace Medical Institute
CAMP ....Continuous Airworthiness Maintenance Program
CANC ....Cancel
CAP ....Capture
CAP ....Civil Air Patrol
CAP ....Combat Air Patrol
CAR ....Civil Airworthiness Regulation
CARF ....Central Altitude Reservation Function
CAS ....Calibrated Airspeed
CAS ....Close Air Support
CAS ....Collision Avoidance System
CASOM ....Conventional Armed Stand-Off Missile
CAT ....Category
CAT ....Clear Air Turbulence
CAT II ....Category II
CAVU ....Ceiling and Visibility Unlimited
CAWS ....Central Aural Warning System
CB ....Circuit Breaker

CBI	Computer-Based Instruction
CBT	Computer-Based Training
CCA	Central Control Actuator
CCCI, C3I	Command, Control, Communications, Intelligence
CCD	Charge Coupled Device
CCIP	Continuously Computed Impact Point
CCL	Convective Condensation Level
CCS	Cabin Configuration System
CCV	Control Configured Vehicle
CCW	Counterclockwise
CD	Clearance Delivery
CD	Convergent-Divergent
CDA	Controlled Diffusion Airfoil
CDI	Course Deviation Indicator
CDL	Configuration Deviation List
CDM	Collaborative Decision Making
CDT	Central Daylight Time
CDT	Clearance Delivery Time
CDT	Controlled Departure Time
CDTI	Cockpit Display of Traffic Information
CDU	Control/Display Unit
CEMF	Counter Electromotive Force
CENRAP	Center Radar ARTS Presentation/Processing
CEP	Central East Pacific
CFA	Controlled Firing Area
CFCF	Central Flow Control Function
CFIT	Controlled Flight Into Terrain
CFM	Cubic Feet per Minute
CFR	Code of the Federal Regulations
CFRP	Carbon Fiber Reinforced Plastic
CG	Center of Gravity
CGD	Combined Graphic Display
CH	Channel
CH	Compass Heading
CHGR	Charger
CHT	Cylinder Head Temperature
CIC	Cabin Interphone Controller
CIS	Commonwealth of Independent States
CIT	Compressor Inlet Temperature
CK	Check
CKT	Circuit
C/L	Center Line
CLC	Course Line Computer
CLK	Clock
CLOS	Command to Line of Sight
CLR	Clear
CLS	Cabin Lighting System
CLT	Calculated Landing Time
CMCS	Central Maintenance Computer System
CMD	Command

CMNPS ....Canadian Minimum Navigation Performance Specification Airspace
CMP ....Configuration, maintenance, and procedures document
CMPTR ....Computer
CMR ....Central Management Unit
CMWS ....Common Missile Warning System
CNF ....Computer Navigation Fix
CNS ....Communication, Navigation, and Surveillance
COA ....Certificate of Waiver or Authorization
COAX ....Coaxial
COMED ....Combined Map and Electronic Display
COMM ....Communication
COMP ....Compressor
COND ....Condition
CONFIG ....Configuration
CONN ....Connection
COP ....Changeover Point
CORR ....Correction
COS/MOS ....Complementary Oxide Silicon/Metal Oxide Silicon
COTS ....Commercial Off The Shelf
CP ....Center of Pressure
CP ....Control Panel
CPB ....Chemically Powered Bomber
CPDLC ....Controller Pilot Data Link Communications
CPL ....Current Flight Plan (ICAO)
CPU ....Central Processor Unit
CRAF ....Civil Reserve Air Fleet
CRC ....Cyclic Redundancy Check
CRCT ....Collaborative Routing Coordination Tool
CRM ....Cockpit (or Crew) Resource Management
CROM ....Control and Read-Only Memory
CRP ....Compulsory Reporting Point
CRS ....Certified Repair Station
CRS ....Computer Reservation System
CRS ....Course
CRT ....Cathode-Ray Tube
CS ....Course Select
CSD ....Constant Speed Drive
CSEU ....Control Systems Electronic Unit
CSL ....Current-Sinking Logic
CST ....Central Standard Time
CT ....Control Tower
CT ....Control Transformer
CTA ....Control Area (ICAO)
CTA ....Controlled Time of Arrival
CTAF ....Common Traffic Advisory Frequency
CTD ....Charge Transfer Device
CTL ....Complementary Transistor Logic
CTM ....Centrifugal Twisting Moment
CTOL ....Conventional Takeoff and Landing
CVFP ....Charted Visual Flight Procedure

CVR ....Cockpit Voice Recorder
CW ....Caution and Warning
CW ....Clockwise
CWA ....Center Weather Advisories
CWS ....Control Wheel Steering
CWSU ....Center Weather Service Unit

D

DA ....Decision Altitude/Decision Height
DA ....Density Altitude
D/A ....Digital-to-Analog
DA ....Drift Angle
DAC ....Digital-to-Analog Converter
DACS ....Digital Aeronautical Chart Supplement
DAD ....Data Acquisition Display
DADC ....Digital Air Data Computer
DAIR ....Direct Altitude and Identity Readout
DAIS ....Digital Avionics Information System
DALR ....Dry Adiabatic Lapse Rate
DAR ....Data-Access Register
DAR ....Designated Airworthiness Representative
DARPA ....Defense Advanced Research Projects Agency
DAS ....Delay Assignment
D-ATIS ....Digital Automatic Terminal Information Service
DB ....Diffusion Bonding
DBRITE ....Digital Bright Radar Indicator Tower Equipment
DBS ....Doppler Beam Sharpening
DC ....Direct Current
DCC ....Discrete Component Circuit
DCDR ....Decoder
DCFL ....Direct-Coupled Field Effect Transistor Logic
DCL ....Direct-Coupled Logic
DCTL ....Direct-Coupled Transistor Logic
DDA ....Derived Decision Altitude
DDB ....Digital Data Bus
DDI ....Dual Distance Indicator
DDS ....Digital Display System
DEM ....Digital Elevation Model
DEMOD ....Demodulator
DER ....Departure End of Runway
DER ....Designated Engineering Representative
DF ....Direction Finder
DFDAU ....Digital Flight Data Acquisition Unit
DFDR ....Digital Flight Data Recorder
DG ....Directional Gyro
D/G ....Driver/Gate
DGPS ....Differential Global Positioning System
DH ....Decision Height
DI ....Digital Interface

DIC ....Digital Integrated Circuit
DIFCS ....Digital Integrated Flight Control System
DIL ....Dual In-line
DIP ....Dual In-line Package
DISTR ....Distributor
DLC ....Direct Lift Control
DMA ....Direct Memory Access
DMAP ....Digital Modular Avionics Program
DMC ....Direct Memory Channel
DME ....Designated Mechanic Examiner
DME ....Designated Medical Examiner
DME ....Distance Measuring Equipment compatible with TACAN
DMLS ....Doppler Microwave Landing System
DMM ....Digital Multimeter
DMOS ....Double-diffused Metal Oxide Silicon semiconductor
DOD ....Department of Defense
DOD ....Domestic Object Damage
DOT ....Department of Transportation
DP ....Departure Procedures
DP ....Differential Protection
DRC ....Dual Remote Compensator
DPE ....Designated Pilot Examiner
DR ....Dead Reckoning
DRVSM ....Domestic Reduced Vertical Separation Minimums
DS ....Directionally Solidified
DSB ....Double-Sided Board
DSC ....Digital-to-Synchro Converter
DSM ....Dynamic Scattering Mode
DSP ....Departure Sequencing Program
DSR ....Display System Replacement
DT ....Delay Time
DTG ....Distance To Go
DTL ....Diode-Transistor Logic
DU ....Display Unit
DUAT ....Direct User Access Terminal (weather briefing)
DUF ....Diffusion Under Epitaxial Film
DVA ....Diverse Vector Area
DVFR ....Defense Visual Flight Rules
DVRSN ....Diversion
DVM ....Digital Voltmeter
DWN ....Down

E

EAA ....Experimental Aircraft Association, Inc.
EAC ....Expect Approach Clearance
EADF ....Electronic Automatic Direction Finder
EADI ....Electronic Attitude Director Indicator
EAROM ....Electrically Alterable Read Only Memory
EARTS ....En Route Automated Radar Tracking System

EAS ....En Route Automation System
EAS ....Equivalent Airspeed
EAT ....Expected Approach Time
EBCDIC ....Extended Binary Coded Decimal Interchange Code
EBW ....Electron Beam Welding
EC ....EICAS Computer
ECAM ....Electronic Centralized Aircraft Monitor
ECCM ....Electronic Counter Countermeasure
ECL ....Emitter-Coupled Logic
ECM ....Electro-Chemical Machining
ECM ....Electronic Countermeasures
ECS ....Environmental Control System
ECTL ....Emitter-Coupled Transistor Logic
E/D ....End of Descent
EDCT ....Expected Departure Clearance Time
EDM ....Electro-Discharge Machining
EDPS ....Electronic Data Processing System
EDSP ....EICAS Display Select Panel
EDT ....Eastern Daylight Time
EDU ....EICAS Display Unit
EEC ....Electronic Engine Control
EELV ....Evolved Expendable Launch Vehicle
EE-PROM ....Electrically Erasable Programmable Read Only Memory
EFAS ....En Route Flight Advisory Service
EFB ....Electronic Flight Bag
EFC ....Expect Further Clearance
EFCU ....Electronic Flight Control Unit
EFD ....Electronic Flight Display
EFI ....Electronic Flight Instruments
EFIS ....Electronic Flight Instrument System
EFISCP ....Electronic Flight Instrument System Control Panel
EFISCU ....Electronic Flight Instrument System Comparator Unit
EFISSG ....Electronic Flight Instrument System Signal Generator
EFL ....Emitter-Follower Logic
EFM ....Enhanced Fighter Maneuverability
EFOGM ....Enhanced Fiber Optic Guided Missile
EFV ....Enhanced Flight Visibility
EFVS ....Enhanced Flight Vision System
EGNOS ....European Geostationary Navigation Overlay System
EGPWS ....Enhanced Ground Proximity Warning Systems
EGT ....Exhaust Gas Temperature
EHF ....Extremely High Frequency
EHP ....Equivalent Horsepower
EHSI ....Electronic Horizontal Situation Indicator
EHSID ....Electronic Horizontal Situation Indicator Display
EHSV ....Electro-Hydraulic Servo Valve
EIA ....Electronic Industries Association
EICAS ....Engine Indicating and Crew Alerting System
EIU ....EFIS/EICAS Interface Units
ELCU ....Electrical Load Control Unit
ELT ....Emergency Locator Transmitter

EMALS ....Electromagnetic Aircraft Launch Systems
EMAS ....Engineered Materials Arresting System
EMFI ....Electromechanical Flight Instruments
EMI ....Electromagnetic Interference
EMP ....Electromagnetic Pulse
EMS ....Emergency Medical Service
EMSAW ....En Route Minimum Safe Altitude Warning
EO ....Electro-Optical
EOPs ....Engine Out Procedures
EOVM ....Emergency Obstruction Video Map
EOW ....Empty Operating Weight
EP ....External Power
EPE ....Estimated Position Error
EPNdB ....Equivalent Perceived Noise Decibels
EPR ....Engine Pressure Ratio
EPROM ....Erasable Programmable Read Only Memory
EPS ....Engineered Performance Standards
EPU ....Emergency Power Unit
ER-OPS ....Extended Range Operations
ERU ....Explosion Release Unit
ESA ....European Space Agency
ESD ....Electrostatic Discharge
ESHP ....Equivalent Shaft Horsepower
ESOP ....Employee Stock Ownership Plan
ESP ....En Route Spacing Program
EST ....Eastern Standard Time
ETA ....Estimated Time of Arrival
ETD ....Estimated Time of Departure
ETE ....Estimated Time En route
ETMS ....Enhanced Traffic Management System
ETOPS ....Extended Operations
EV ....Enhanced Vision
EVA ....Extravehicular Activity
EVO ....Equivalent Visual Operations
EVS ....Electro-Optical Viewing System
EW ....Electronic Warfare
EWINS ....Enhanced Weather Information System
EWIS ....Electrical Wiring Interconnection System
EX LOC ....Extended Localizer

F

FA ....Area weather forecast
FA ....Final Approach
FAA ....Federal Aviation Administration
FAC ....Final Approach Course
FAC ....Flight Augmentation Computer
FAD ....Fuel Advisory Departure
FADEC ....Full-Authority Digital Engine Control
FAE ....Fuel-Air Explosive

FAF	Final Approach Fix
FAMOS	Floating-gate Avalanche-injection Metal Oxide Silicon semiconductor
FAO	Finish All Over
FAP	Final Approach Point
FAR	Federal Aviation Regulations
FATO	Final Approach and Takeoff Area
FAWP	Final Approach Waypoint
FAWS	Flight Advisory Weather Service
FB	Fly-By
FBL	Fly by Light
FBO	Fixed Base Operator
FBW	Fly by Wire
FBWP	Fly-By WayPoint
FCC	Federal Communications Commission
FCC	Flight Control Computer
FCES	Flight Control Electronic System
FCEU	Flight Control Electronic Unit
FCLT	Freeze Calculated Landing Time
FCU	Flight Control Unit
FD	Flight Director
FD	Winds and temperature aloft forecast
FDC	Flight Data Center
FDC NOTAM	Flight Data Center Notice to Airmen
FDE	Fault Detection and Exclusion
FDE	Flight Deck Effect
FDEP	Flight Data Entry Panel
FDI	Flight Director Indicator
FDIO	Flight Data Input/Output
FDP	Flight Data Processing
FDP	Flight Duty Period
FDR	Flight Data Recorder
FDS	Flight Display Screen
FE	Flight Engineer
FED	Field Effect Device
FET	Field Effect Transistor
FF	Feeder Fault
FFP2	Free Flight Phase 2
FFS	Full flight simulator
FGS	Flight Guidance System
FHP	Friction Horsepower
FIFO	First-In First-Out
FIM	Fault Isolation Monitoring
FIM	Flight Information Manual
FIR	Flight Information Region
FIRC	Flight Instructor Refresher Clinic
FIS	Flight Instrument System
FIS-B	Flight Information Service – Broadcast
FISDL	Flight Information Services Data Link
FITS	FAA/Industry Training Standards
FL	Flight Level

FL CHG ....Flight Level Change
FLIP ....FLight Information Publication
FLIR ....Forward-Looking Infra-Red System
FM ....Fan Marker
FM ....Frequency Modulation
FMA ....Flight Mode Annunciator
FMC ....Flight Management Computer
FMCDU ....Flight Management Computer Display Unit
FMCS ....Flight Management Computer System
FMCU ....Flight Management Computer Unit
FMS ....Flight Management System
FO ....Fly-Over
FOD ....Foreign Object Damage
FODTS ....Fiber-Optic Data Transmission System
FOI ....Fundamentals of Instruction
FOM ....Flight Operations Manual
FOWP ....Fly-Over WayPoint
FPA ....Flight Path Angle
FPC ....Fuel Performance Computer
FPLA ....Field-Program Logic Array
FPM ....Feet per Minute
FPM ....Flap Position Module
FPNM ....Feet per Nautical Mile
FPR ....Fan Pressure Ratio
F-PROM ....Field-Programmable Read Only Memory
FPS ....Feet Per Second
FPV ....Flight Path Vector
FRC ....Full Route Clearance
FREQ ....Frequency
FRMS ....Fatigue Risk Management System
FSB ....Flight Standardization Board
FSDO ....Flight Standards District Office
FSEU ....Flap/Slot Electronic Unit
FSL ....NOAA Forecast Systems Laboratory
FSPD ....Freeze Speed Parameter
FSS ....Flight Service Station
FSTD ....Flight simulation training device
FT ....Terminal weather forecast
FTD ....Flight Training Device
FTR ....Force Trim Release
FVC ....Frequency-to-Voltage Converter
FWC ....Flight Warning Computer
FWD ....Forward

G

G ....Gravity
GA ....General Aviation
GA ....Go Around
GaAsFET ....Gallium-Arsenic Field Effect Transistor

GADO ....General Aviation District Office
GAMA ....General Aviation Manufacturers Association
GAO ....General Accounting Office
GAPA ....Ground-to-Air Pilotless Aircraft
GBAS ....Ground-Based Augmentation System
GC ....Ground Control
GCA ....Ground Controlled Approach
GCB ....Generator Circuit Breaker
GCO ....Ground Communication Outlet
GCR ....Generator Control Relay
GCU ....Generator Control Unit
GD ....General Dynamics
GDP ....Ground Delay Programs
GDPE ....Ground Delay Program Enhancements
GEN ....Generator
GEO ....Geostationary Satellite
GFET ....Gate Field Effect Transistor
GFRP ....Glass Fiber Reinforced Plastic
GHz ....Gigahertz
GLONASS ....GLobal Orbiting Navigation Satellite System
GLS ....GNSS Landing System
GMT ....Greenwich Mean Time
GND ....Ground
GND PWR ....Ground Power
GND RET ....Ground Return
GND SVC ....Ground Service
GNE ....Gross Navigation Error
GNSS ....Global Navigation Satellite System
GOES ....Geostationary Operational Environmental Satellite
GPH ....Gallons Per Hour
GPO ....Government Printing Office
GPS ....Global Positioning System
GPSS ....Global Positioning System Steering
GPSW ....Gear Position Switch
GPU ....Ground Power Unit
GPWS ....Ground Proximity Warning System
GRD ....Ground
GS ....Glide Slope
GS ....Ground Speed
GSE ....Ground Support Equipment
GSR ....Ground Service Relay
GSTR ....Ground Service Transfer Relay
GTOSCR ....Gate and Turn-Off Silicon Controlled Rectifier
GUS ....Ground Uplink Station
GW ....Gross Weight
GWS ....Graphical Weather Service

H

HAA	Height Above Airport
HAL	Height Above Landing
HAR	High Altitude Redesign
HARM	High-speed Anti-Radiation Missile
HARS	Heading and Attitude Reference System
HARV	Hybrid Augmented Reusable Vehicle
HAT	Height Above Touchdown
HAZMAT	Hazardous Materials
HCL	Horizontal Component of Lift
HCMOS	High-density Complementary Metal Oxide Silicon semiconductor
HDD	Head-Down Display
HEMS	Helicopter Emergency Medical Services
HF	High Frequency
HFA	High-Frequency Radio Antenna
HFDL	High Frequency Data Link
HGS	Head-up Guidance System
HIALS	High-Intensity Approach Light System
HIC	Hybrid Integrated Circuit
HIIC	High-Isolation Integrated Circuit
HiMAT	Highly Maneuverable Aircraft Technology
HIRL	High Intensity Runway Light System
HITS	Highway In The Sky
HIWAS	Hazardous In-flight Weather Advisory Service
HI Z	High Impedance
HLTTL	High-Level Transistor-Transistor Logic
HMOS	High-Performance Metal Oxide Silicon semiconductor
HNIL	High Noise Immunity Logic
HOBOS	Homing Bomb System
HOCSR	Host/Oceanic Computer System Replacement
HOTAS	Hands-on-Throttle-and-Stick
HP	High Performance
HP	High Pressure
hp	Horsepower
HS	Heading Select
HSCT	High-Speed Civil Transport
HSI	Horizontal Situation Indicator
HT	High Tension
HTFD	Hybrid Thick Film Device
HTL	High-Threshold Logic
HTP	High-Test Peroxide
HUD	Head-Up Display
HVOR	High VOR
HVPS	High-Voltage Power Supply
Hz	Hertz

I

IA	Indicated Airspeed
IA	Indicated Altitude
IA	Inspection Authorization
IA	Intercept Angle
IAC	Instrument Approach Chart
IAE	International Aero Engines
IAF	Initial Approach Fix
IAI	Israel Aircraft Industries
IAM	International Association of Machinists and Aerospace Workers
IAP	Instrument Approach Procedure
IAPS	Integrated Avionics Processor System
IAS	Indicated Airspeed
IATA	International Air Transportation Association
IAWP	Initial Approach Waypoint
IBM	International Business Machines
IC	Integrated Circuit
ICA	Initial Climb Area
ICAO	International Civil Aviation Organization
ICU	Instrument Comparator Unit
IDECM	Integrated Defensive Electronic Countermeasures
IDG	Integrated Drive Generator
IDS	Integrated Display System
IDS	Interdiction Strike
IEEE	Institute of Electrical and Electronics Engineers
IEPR	Integrated Engine Pressure Ratio
IF	Intermediate Fix
IF	Intermediate Frequency
IFF	Identification—Friend or Foe
IF/IAWP	intermediate fix/initial approach waypoint
IFIM	International Flight Information Manual
IFR	Instrument Flight Rules
IFSD	In-flight shutdown
IFSS	International Flight Service Station
IFWP	Intermediate Fix Waypoint
IGFET	Insulated Gate Field Effect Transistor
IGI	Instrument Ground Instructor
IGN	Ignition
IGV	Inlet Guide Vanes
IHP	Indicated Horsepower
IHS	Integrated Heat Sink
IIL, I^2L	Integrated Injection Logic
IIMC	Inadvertent Instrument Meteorological Conditions
IIR	Imaging Infra-Red
IIS	Integrated Instrument System
ILP	Integral Lead Package
ILS	Instrument Landing System
ILS OC	Instrument Landing System On Course
ILS/PRM	Instrument Landing System/Precision Runway Monitor

IM ....ILS Inner Marker
IMC ....Instrument Meteorological Conditions
IMO ....International Meteorological Organization
IMPATT ....Impact Avalanche Transit Time
IMU ....Inertial Measuring Unit
InFO ....Information For Operators
In. Hg. ....Inches of Mercury
INREQ ....Information Request
INS ....Inertial Navigation System
INST ....Instrument
INT ....Intersection
INTFC ....Interface
INTPH ....Interphone
INTR ....Interrogation
INV ....Inverter
INWP ....Intermediate Waypoint
I/O ....Input/Output
IOAT ....Indicated Outside Air Temperature
IOC ....Initial Operational Capability
IOC ....Input/Output Concentrator
IP ....Intermediate Pressure
IPN ....Iso Propyl Nitrate
IPV ....Instrument Procedure with Vertical guidance
IR ....IFR Military Training Routes
IRAN ....Inspect and Repair As Necessary
IRBM ....Intermediate Range Ballistic Missile
IRCM ....Infra-Red Counter Measures
IRMP ....Internal Reference Mode Panel
IRS ....Inertial Reference System
IRST ....Infra-Red Search/Track
IRU ....Inertial Reference Unit
IRVR ....Instrument Runway Visual Range
ISA ....Instrument Society of America
ISA ....International Standard Atmosphere
ISAR ....Inverse Synthetic Aperture Radar
ISIS ....Integrated Sight and Interception System
ISO ....International Standards Organization
ISS ....Inertial Sensing System
ISS ....Instrument Source Select
ITALD ....Improved Tactical Air-Launched Decoy
IVS ....Instantaneous Vertical Speed
IVSI ....Instantaneous Vertical Speed Indicator
IVV ....Instantaneous Vertical Velocity
IWP ....Intermediate Waypoint

J

JAL ....Japan Air Lines
JAR ....Joint Airworthiness Requirements
JAST ....Joint Advanced Strike Technology

JATO ....Jet Assisted Takeoff
JDAM ....Joint Direct Attack Munition
JFET ....Junction Field Effect Transistor
JMCIS ....Joint Maritime Command Information System
JPATS ....Joint Primary Aircraft Training System
JPL ....Jet Propulsion Laboratory
JPT ....Jet Pipe Temperature
JROC ....Joint Requirements Oversight Committee
JSOW ....Joint Stand-Off Weapon
JTIDS ....Joint Tactical Information Distribution System

K

KCAS ....Knots Calibrated Airspeed
kHz ....Kilohertz
KIAS ....Knots Indicated Airspeed
KMH ....Kilometers per Hour
KTAS ....Knots True Airspeed
KV ....Kilovolts
KVA ....Kilovolt-Amps
KVAR ....Kilovolt-Amps Reactive

L

LAA ....Local Airport Advisory
LAAS ....Local Area Augmentation System
LAAS ....Low Altitude Alert System
LAHSO ....Landing and Hold Short Operation
LANTIRN ....Low-Altitude Navigation Targeting Infra-Red for Night
LAPADS ....Light-weight Acoustic Processing and Display System
LAPC ....Laptop Auxiliary Performance Computer
LAPUT ....Light-Activated Programmable Unijunction Transistor
LARAM ....Light-Addressed Random Access Memory
LASCAR ....Light-Activated Silicon Controlled Rectifier
LAU ....Linear Accelerometer Unit
LAWRS ....Limited Aviation Weather Reporting Station
LBS ....Lateral Beam Sensor
LCD ....Liquid Crystal Display
L/D ....Lift/Drag ratio
LD ....Load
LDA ....Landing Distance Available
LDA ....Localizer-type Directional Aid
LED ....Light Emitting Diode
LEMAC ....Leading Edge of the Mean Aerodynamic Chord
LERX ....Leading Edge Root Extensions
LEX ....Leading Edge Extensions
L/F ....Load Factor
LF ....Low Frequency
LFC ....Level of Free Convection

LFR ....Low-Frequency Radio Range
LGB ....Laser-guided Glide Bombs
LIC ....Linear Integrated Circuit
LIFO ....Last In First Out
LINS ....Laser Inertial Navigation System
LIRL ....Low-Intensity Runway edge Lights
LL ....Logic Level
LLTV ....Low-Light Television
LLWAS ....Low Level Windshear Alert System
L/MF ....Low or medium frequency
LMM ....Compass Locator at the Middle Marker
LMT ....Local Mean Time
LNAV ....Lateral Navigation
LO ....Locator Outer marker
LOA ....Letter Of Authorization
LOFT ....Line Oriented Flight Training
LOX ....Liquid Oxygen
LO Z ....Low Impedance
LOC ....ILS Localizer
LOCMOS ....Local Oxidation Complementary Metal Oxide Silicon
                                    semiconductor
LOE ....Line Operating Experience
LOM ....Locator Outer Marker (Compass Locator at the Outer Marker)
LOP ....Line of Position
LORAN ....Long Range Navigation
LP ....Localizer Performance
LP ....Low Pressure
LPV ....Lateral Precision Performance with Vertical guidance
LR ....Lapse Rate
LRCO ....Limited Remote Communications Outlet
LRCS ....Long-Range Communication System
LRMTS ....Laser Ranger and Marked Target Seeker
LRNAV ....Long-Range Navigation
LRNS ....Long-Range Navigation System
LRRA ....Low-Range Radar Altimeter
LRU ....Line Replaceable Unit
LS ....Loud Speaker
LSA ....Light-Sport Aircraft
LSI ....Large-Scale Integration
LSIA ....Large-Scale Integration Array
LSSAS ....Longitudinal Static Stability Augmentation System
LSU ....Logic Switching Unit
LT ....Light
LTA ....Lighter-Than-Air
LTD ....Along Track Distance
LTP ....Landing Threshold Point
LUAW ....Line Up And Wait
LVDT ....Linear Voltage Differential Transducer
LVL CHG ....Level Change
LVPS ....Low-Voltage Power Supply
LZ ....Landing Zone

M

M ....Mach number
MAA ....Maximum Authorized IFR Altitude
MAC ....Mean Aerodynamic Chord
MAD ....Magnetic Anomaly Detector
MAD ....Mutually Assured Destruction
MADGE ....Microwave Aircraft Digital Guidance Equipment
MAHWP ....Missed Approach Holding Waypoint
MALS ....Medium Intensity Approach Light System
MALSF ....Medium intensity Approach Lighting System with sequenced
                                              Flashing lights
MALSR ....Medium Intensity Approach Light System with Runway align-
                                              ment indicator lights
MALU ....Mode Annunciation Logic Unit
MAMS ....Military Airspace Management System
MANPADS ....Man Portable Air Defense Systems
MAP ....Manifold Absolute Pressure
MAP ....Missed Approach Point
MAP ....Mode Annunciator Panel
MAP ....Monitor Alert Parameter
MAR ....Memory Address Register
MARSA ....Military Authority Assumes Responsibility for Separation
                                              of Aircraft
MASPS ....Minimum Aviation System Performance Specification
MAW ....Mission Adaptive Wing
MAWP ....Missed Approach Waypoint
MAWS ....Missile Approach Warning System
MB ....Magnetic Bearing
MB ....Marker Beacon
MBA ....Marker Beacon Antenna
MCA ....Minimum Controllable Airspeed
MCA ....Minimum Crossing Altitude
MCA ....Multichip Array
MCDP ....Maintenance Control and Display Panel
MCP ....Mode Control Panel
MCTMA ....Multi-Center Traffic Management Advisor
MCU ....Modular Concept Unit
MCW ....Modulated Continuous Wave
MD ....McDonnell Douglas
MDA ....Minimum Descent Altitude
MDH ....Minimum Descent Height
MEA ....Minimum En route IFR Altitude
MEADS ....Medium Extended Air Defense Systems
MEAL ....Micro-Extended Assembly Language
MEARTS ....Micro-Enroute Automated Radar Tracking System
MEC ....Main Equipment Center
MEGA ....Million
MEK ....Methyl Ethyl Ketone
MEL ....Minimum Equipment List
MEL ....Multi-Engine Land

MEP ....Mean Effective Pressure
MEPU ....Monofuel Emergency Power Unit
METAR ....Aviation Routine Weather Report
METO ....Maximum Except Take-Off (power)
MF ....Medium Frequency
MFD ....Multi-Function Display
MFT ....Meter Fix Time/Slot Time
MGW ....Maximum Gross Weight
MH ....Magnetic Heading
MHA ....Minimum Holding Altitude
MHz ....Megahertz
MIA ....Minimum IFR Altitude
MIALS ....Medium Intensity Approach Light System
MIC ....Microphone
MIC ....Monolithic Integrated Circuit
MICROM ....Micro Instruction Control Read Only Memory
MIDO ....Manufacturing Inspection District Office
MIL ....Military
Milli ....One Thousandth
MIP ....Maintenance Information Printer
MIR ....Memory Information Register
MIRL ....Medium Intensity Runway Edge Lights
MIS ....Meteorological Impact Statement
MIT ....Miles-In-Trail
MKR BCN ....Marker Beacon
MLDI ....Meter List Display Interval
MLS ....Microwave Landing System
MLW ....Maximum Landing Weight
MM ....ILS Middle Marker
MMEL ....Master Minimum Equipment List
MMWR ....Millimeter Wave Radar
MN ....Magnetic North
MNPS ....Minimum Navigation Performance Specifications
MOA ....Military Operations Area
MOCA ....Minimum Obstruction Clearance Altitude
MOD ....Modulate
MOPS ....Minimum Operational Performance Standards
MORA ....Minimum Off Route Altitude
MOSFET ....Metal Oxide Silicon Field Effect Transistor
MOSIC ....Metal Oxide Silicon Integrated Circuit
MOST ....Metal Oxide Silicon Transistor
MP ....Manifold Pressure
mP ....maritime Polar air
MPH ....Miles Per Hour
MPU ....Microprocessor Unit
MRA ....Minimum Reception Altitude
MRCA ....Multi-Role Combat Aircraft
MRM ....Maintenance Resource Management
MRV ....Maximum Reverse Voltage
MS ....Military Standard
MSA ....Minimum Safe Altitude

MSA	Minimum Sector Altitude
MSAW	Minimum Safe Altitude Warning
MSEC	Millisecond
MSG	Message
MSI	Medium Scale Integration
MSL	Mean Sea Level
MST	Monolithic System Technology
MST	Mountain Standard Time
MSU	Mode Selector Unit
mT	maritime Tropical air
MTA	Minimum Turning Altitude
MTBF	Mean Time Between Failures
MTCA	Minimum Terrain Clearance Altitude
MTFE	Mid-Thrust Family Engine
MTI	Moving Target Indicator
MTL	Merger Transistor Logic
MTOW	Maximum Takeoff Weight
MTP	Maintenance Test Panel
MTR	Military Training Route
μ	Micro
μ SEC	Microsecond
MTSAT	Multifunctional Transport Satellite
MU	Friction value representing runway surface conditions (designation)
MUX	Multiplexer
MV	Millivolt
MVA	Minimum Vectoring Altitude
MVFR	Marginal VFR
MWA	Mountain Wave Activity
MWS	Master Warning System
MZFW	Maximum Zero Fuel Weight

N

N_1	RPM of low-pressure compressor, or fan
N_2	RPM of high-pressure, or intermediate-pressure compressor
N_3	RPM of high-pressure compressor on a triple-spool engine
NA	Not Authorized
NAA	National Aeronautical Association
NACA	National Advisory Committee for Aeronautics
NACG	National Aeronautical Charting Group
NAFI	National Association of Flight Instructors
NAS	National Aircraft Standards
NAS	National Airspace System
NASA	National Aeronautics and Space Administration
NASP	National Aerospace Plane
NASSI	National Airspace System Status Information
NAT	North Atlantic
NATA	National Air Transportation Association, Inc.
NATO	North Atlantic Treaty Organization

NAT/OPS ....North Atlantic Operation
NAV ....Navigation
NAVAID ....Navigational Aid
NAV/COM ....Navigation and Communication Radio
NAVWASS ....Navigation and Weapon-Aiming Sub System
NAWAU ....National Aviation Weather Advisory Unit
NBAA ....National Business Aircraft Association, Inc.
NBC ....Nuclear-Biological-Chemical
NBCAP ....National Beacon Code Allocation Plan
NC ....No Connection
NC ....Normally Closed
NC ....Numerical Control
NCAR ....National Center for Atmospheric Research
NCD ....No Computed Data
NCU ....Navigation Computer Unit
ND ....Navigation Display
NDAA ....Non-Development Airlift Aircraft
NDB(ADF) ....Non-directional Beacon (Automatic Direction Finder)
NDRO ....Non-Destructive Readout
NDT ....Non-Destructive Testing
NEG ....Negative
NESDIS ....National Environmental Satellite Data and Information Service
NEXRAD ....Next generation weather Radar
NextGen ....Next Generation Air Transportation System
N$_f$ ....RPM of free turbine
NFDC ....National Flight Data Center
NFDD ....National Flight Data Digest
N-FET ....N-type conduction Field Effect Transistor
NFH ....NATO Frigate Helicopter
NFPO ....National Flight Procedures Office
NGV ....Nozzle Guide Vanes
NHC ....National Hurricane Center
NIMA ....National Imagery and Mapping Agency
NM ....Nautical Mile
NMAC ....Near Mid-Air Collision
NMC ....National Meteorological Center
N-MOS ....N-Channel Metal Oxide Silicon Semiconductor
NMPH ....Nautical Miles Per Hour
NNEW ....NextGen Network-Enabled Weather
NOAA ....National Oceanic and Atmospheric Administration
NO A/G ....No Air to Ground Communication
NOC ....NAV On Course
NOPAC ....North Pacific
NoPT ....No Procedure Turn Required
NORDO ....No Radio
NOS ....National Ocean Service
NOTAM ....Notice To Airmen
NOTAM D ....Distant NOTAM
NOTAR ....No Tail Rotor
NOZ ....Normal Operating Zone
NPA ....Nonprecision Approach

NPB ....Nuclear-Powered Bomber
NPRM ....Notice of Proposed Rulemaking
NPT ....National (tapered) Pipe Thread
NRO ....National Reconnaissance Office
NRP ....National Route Program
NRR ....Non-Restrictive Routing
NRS ....National Reference System
NSA ....National Security Area
NSEC ....Nanosecond
NSF ....National Science Foundation
NSSFC ....National Severe Storms Forecast Center
NSSN ....National Standards Systems Network
NTAP ....Notice to Airmen Publication
NTS ....Negative Torque Sensor
NTSB ....National Transportation Safety Board
NTSS ....Negative Torque Sensing System
NTZ ....No Transgression Zone
NVM ....Nonvolatile Memory
NVS ....NAS Voice Switch
NWS ....National Weather Service

O

OALT ....Operational Acceptable Level of Traffic
OAT ....Outside Air Temperature
OBS ....Omni Bearing Selector
OC, O/C ....On Course
OCA ....Obstacle Clearance Altitude
OCS ....Obstacle Clearance Surface
OCU ....Operational Conversion Unit
ODA ....Organization Designation Authorization
ODALS ....Omnidirectional Approach Lighting Systems
ODAPS ....Oceanic Display and Planning System
ODP ....Obstacle Departure Procedure
OEI ....One Engine Inoperative
OEM ....Original Equipment Manufacturer
OEP ....Operational Evolution Plan
OF ....Over Frequency
OFT ....Outer Fix Time
OFZ ....Obstacle Free Zone
OIS ....Obstacle Identification Surface
OIS ....Operational Information System
OM ....ILS Outer Marker
OMC ....Onboard Maintenance Computer
ONC ....Operational Navigation Charts
ONER ....Oceanic Navigational Error Report
ONS ....Omega Navigation System
OP AMP ....Operational Amplifier
OpsSpecs ....Operations Specifications
OROCA ....Off-Route Obstruction Clearance Altitude

OSS .... Over Station Sensor
OSV .... Operational Service Volume
OTR .... Oceanic Transition Route
OTS .... Organized Track System
OTS .... Out of Service
OV .... Overvoltage
OVAS .... Ocular Vergence and Accommodation Sensor

P

PA .... Passenger Address
PA .... Precision Approach
PA .... Pressure Altitude
PACOTS .... Pacific Organized Track System
PAFAM .... Performance and Failure Assessment Monitor
PAM .... Pulse Amplitude Modulation
PAm .... Ambient Pressure
PAMA .... Professional Aviation Maintenance Association
PAPI .... Precision Approach Path Indicator
PAR .... Precision Approach Radar
PAR .... Preferential Arrival Route
PARA/SER .... Parallel-to-Serial
PAS .... Performance Advisory System
P ATT .... Pitch Attitude
PATWAS .... Pilots Automatic Telephone Weather Answering Service
PAX .... Passengers
P$_B$ .... Burner Pressure
PBB .... Pitch Bar Bias
PBCT .... Proposed Boundary Crossing Time
PBE .... Protective Breathing Equipment
PBN .... Performance Based Navigation
PC .... Personal Computer
PC .... Proficiency Check
PCA .... Positive Control Area
PCA .... Power Control Actuator
PCB .... Plenum Chamber Burning
PCB .... Printed Circuit Board
PCCD .... Profiled Charge-Coupled Device
PCG .... Positive Course Guidance
PCL .... Pilot Controlled Lighting
PCM .... Pulse-Code Modulation
PCPL .... Pitch Couple
PCU .... Power Control Unit
PCWS .... Pitch Control Wheel Steering
PDAR .... Preferential Departure and Arrival Route
PDC .... Pre-Departure Clearance
PDCS .... Performance Data Computer System
PDO .... Phosphorus-Doped Oxide
PDR .... Preferential Departure Route
PDT .... Pacific Daylight Time

PDU	Pilot's Display Unit
PECO	Pitch Erection Cutoff
PED	Portable Electronic Device
PELS	Precision Emitter Location System
PF	Pilot Flying
pFAST	Passive Final Approach Spacing Tool
PFD	Primary Flight Display
P-FET	P-type conduction Field Effect Transistor
PGM	Precision Guided Munition
P Hold	Pitch Hold
Phot-SCR	Photosensitive Silicon Controlled Rectifier
PI	Principal Inspector
PIBAL	Pilot Balloon Observation
PIC	Pilot In Command
PIDP	Programmable Indicator Data Processor
PinS	Point-in-Space
PIO	Pilot Induced Oscillation
PIREP	Pilot Report
PIU	Peripheral Interface Unit
PJFET	P-type Junction-conduction Field Effect Transistor
PKI	Public/Private Key Infrastructure/Technology
PLA	Power Lever Angle
PLA	Programmable Logic Array
PLL	Phase-Locked Loop
PM	Phase Modulated
PM	Pilot Monitoring
PMA	Parts Manufacturer Approval
PMAT	Portable Maintenance Access Terminal
PMB	Plastic Media Blasting
PMOS	P-type Metal Oxide Silicon semiconductor
PMS	Performance Management System
PNCS	Performance Navigation Computer System
PND	Primary Navigation Display
PNF	Pilot Not Flying
POFZ	Precision Obstacle Free Zone
POH	Pilot's Operating Handbook
POI	Principle Operations Inspector
POS	Positive
POT	Potentiometer
PPC	Powered parachute
PPI	Plan Position Indicator
PPM	Parts Per Million
PPM	Pulse Position Module
PR	Pressure Ratio
PRA	Precision Radar Approach
PRAM	Programmable Analog Module
PRF	Pulse Repetition Frequency
PRL	Parallel
PRM	Precision Runway Monitor
P-RNAV	European Precision RNAV
PROM	Programmable Read Only Memory

PROX	Proximity
PRR	Pulse Repetition Rate
PRT	Power Recovery Turbine
P-S	Parallel-to-Serial
PS	Power Supply
PSAS	Pitch Stability Augmentation System
PSEU	Proximity Switch Electronic Unit
psi	Pounds per square inch
psia	Pounds per square inch, absolute
psid	Pounds per square inch, differential
psig	Pounds per square inch, gage
PSL	Polycrystalline Silicon Layer
PSM	Power Supply Module
PSO	Phase Shift Oscillator
PST	Pacific Standard Time
PSU	Passenger Service Unit
PSU	Power Supply Unit
P SYNC	Pitch Synchronization
PT	Procedure Turn
P$_T$	Total Pressure
PTD	Propagation Time Delay
PTH	Plated-Through Hole
PTM	Pulse Time Modulation
PTP	Point-To-Point
PTR	Part-Throttle Reheat
PTRS	Performance Tracking and Reporting System
PTS	Practical Test Standards
PTT	Push To Talk
PVASI	Pulsating Visual Approach Slope Indicator
PVD	Plan View Display
PW	Pratt & Whitney
PWI	Proximity Warning Indicator
PWR	Power
PWR SPLY	Power Supply

Q

QAR	Quick Access Recorder
QEC	Quick Engine Change
QECA	Quick Engine Change Assembly
QFE	Transition Height
QNE	Transition Level
QNH	Transition Altitude

R

RA	Radio Altimeter
RA	Radio Altitude
RA	Resolution Advisory

RAA ....Regional Airline Association
RAD ....Radio
RADAR ....Radio Detection And Ranging
RADS ....Retardant Aerial Delivery System
RAF ....Royal Air Force
RAIL ....Runway Alignment Indicator Lights
RAIM ....Receiver Autonomous Integrity Monitoring
RAIND ....Radio Altimeter Indicator
RAIS ....Remote Airport Information Service
RAL ....Research Applications Laboratory (part of NCAR)
RALU ....Register and Arithmetic Logic Unit
RAM ....Random Access Memory
RAOB ....Radarsonde Observation
RAPCON ....Radar Approach Control
RAREP ....Radar Weather Report
RAS ....Random Access Store
RAT ....Ram Air Turbine
RATO ....Rocket Assisted Takeoff
RATR ....Radio Altimeter Transmitter/Receiver
RB ....Relative Bearing
RBA ....Radio Bearing Annunciator
RBB ....Roll Bar Bias
RBI ....Relative Bearing Indicator
RBN ....Radio Beacon
RCC ....Rescue Coordination Center
RCCB ....Remote Control Circuit Breaker
RCLM ....Runway Center Line Markings
RCLS ....Runway Center Line Light System
RCO ....Remote Communications Outlet
RCPL ....Roll Coupled
RCR ....Runway Condition Reading
RCTL ....Resistance-Coupled Transistor Logic
RCVR ....Receiver
RCVR/XMTR ....Receiver/Transmitter
RCWS ....Roll Control Wheel Steering
RDF ....Radio Direction Finder
RDMI ....Radio Direction Magnetic Indicator
RDOF ....Radio Failure
RDP ....Radar Data Processing
REIL ....Runway End Identifier/Identification Lights
REV/C ....Reverse Course
RF CYCLE ....Refresh Cycle
RF ....Radio Frequency
RFFS ....Rescue and firefighting services
RFI ....Radio Frequency Interference
R/HOLD ....Roll Hold
RJ ....Regional Jet
RLC ....Radial-Lead Capacitor
RLS ....Remote Light Sensor
RLV ....Reusable Launch Vehicle
RMI ....Radio Magnetic Indicator

RNAV .... Area Navigation
RNP .... Required Navigation Performance
ROB .... Radar Observation
ROC .... Required Obstacle Clearance
ROM .... Read Only Memory
RPA .... Remotely Powered Aircraft
RPAT .... RNP Parallel Approach Runway Transitions
RPM .... Revenue Passenger Mile
RPM .... Revolutions Per Minute
RPS .... Revolutions Per Second
RR .... Radio Range, low- or medium-frequency
RR .... Road Reconnaissance
RSAS .... Roll Stability Augmentation System
RSP .... Runway Safety Program
RSS .... Relaxed Static Stability
RSU .... Remote Switching Unit
R/T or RT .... Receiver/Transmitter
RTCA .... Radio Technical Commission for Aeronautics
RTL .... Resistor-Transistor Logic
RTM .... Rolls-Royce-Turbomeca
RTR .... Remote Transmitter/Receiver
RTU .... Radio Tuning Unit
RVDT .... Rotary Voltage Differential Transmitter
RVR .... Runway Visual Range
RVSM .... Reduced Vertical Separation Minimums
RVV .... Runway Visibility Values
R/W .... Read/Write
RW .... Relative Wind
RWR .... Radar Warning Receiver
RWY .... Runway
RWY WP .... Runway Waypoint

S

SA .... Selective Availability
SA .... Situational Awareness
SA .... Surface Aviation Weather Report
SAAAR .... Special Aircraft and Aircrew Authorization Required
SAE .... Society of Automotive Engineers
SAFO .... Safety Alerts For Operators
SAI .... Standby Attitude Indicator
SALR .... Saturated Adiabatic Lapse Rate
SALS .... Short Approach Lighting System
SALSF .... Short Approach Lighting System with sequenced
Flashing lights
SAM .... Stabilizer Aileron Module
SAM .... Surface-to-Air Missile
SAMS .... Special Use Airspace Management System
SAR .... Search and Rescue
SAR .... Synthetic Aperture Radar

SARB	Search and Rescue Beacon
SARH	Semi-Active Radar Homing
SARPs	Standards and Recommended Practices
SAS	Stability Augmentation System
SAS	Synthetic Aperture Sonar
SATCOM	Satellite Communications
SATNAV	SATellite NAVigation
SAWRS	Supplemental Aviation Weather Reporting Station
SB	Service Bulletin
SBAS	Satellite-Based Augmentation Systems
SBS	Silicon Bilateral Switch
SBT	Scenario-Based Training
SC	Single Crystal
SCAT	Speed Command of Attitude and Thrust
SCDX	Solid-State Control Differential Transmitter
SCM	Spoiler/Speed Brake Control Module
SCR	Silicon Controlled Rectifier
SD	Radar Weather Report
SDC	Synchro-to-Digital Converter
SDF	Simplified Directional Facility
SDR	Service Difficulty Reports
SECNOT	Security Notice
SELCAL	Selective Calling
SEM	Scanning Electron Microscope
SER	Start End of Runway
SFA	Single Frequency Approach
SFAR	Special Federal Aviation Regulation
SFC	Specific Fuel Consumption
SFCC	Slat/Flap Control Computer
SFO	Simulated Flameout
SFSS	Satellite Field Service Station
SG	Specific Gravity
SG	Symbol Generator
SGU	Symbol Generator Unit
SHF	Super-High Frequency
SHORAN	Short Range Navigation
SIAP	Standard Instrument Approach Procedure
SIC	Silicon Integrated Circuit
SID	Standard Instrument Departure
Si-gate MOS	Silicon-gate Metal Oxide Silicon semiconductor
SIGMET	Significant Meteorological Advisory
SIL	Single In-Line
SIP	Single In-Line Package
SLAMMR	Side-Looking Advanced Multimode Maritime Radar
SLAR	Sideways Looking Airborne Radar
SLS	Satellite Landing System
S-LSA	Special Light-Sport Aircraft
SM	Statute Mile
SMA	Surface Movement Advisor
SMGCS	Surface Movement Guidance Control System

SMI	Static Memory Interface
SMS	Surface Management System
S/MTD	STOL and Maneuvering Technology Demonstrator
SNR	Signal-to-Noise Ratio
S/N RATIO	Signal-to-Noise Ratio
SOIA	Simultaneous Offset Instrument Approaches
SOL	Solenoid
SOM	Start of Message
SOP	Standard Operating Procedure
SOS	Silicon-on-Sapphire
SOT	Start of Transmission
SPAN	Stored Program Alphanumeric
SPECI	Non-routine (special) aviation weather report
SPF	Super Plastic Forming
SPKR	Speaker
SPR	Software Problem Report
SQL	Squelch
SR	Status Register
SRA	Surveillance Radar Approach
SRB	Solid Rocket Booster
SRD	Shift Register Decoder
SRM	Single-Pilot Resource Management
SRP	Selected Reference Point
SRT	Shift Register Transistor
SS	Slow Slew
SSALF	Simplified Short Approach Light system with sequenced Flashing lights
SSALS	Simplified Short Approach Light System
SSALSR	Simplified Short Approach Light System with runway alignment indicator lights
SSB	Single Sideband
SSB	Supersonic Bomber
SSCT	Solid-State Control Transformer
SSD	Static Sensitive Device
SSEC	Static Source Error Correction
SSR	Secondary Surveillance Radar
SSR	Solid State Relay
SST	Supersonic Transport
SSTO	Single-Stage To Orbit
SSV	Standard Service Volume
ST	Synchro Transmitter
STA	Scheduled Time of Arrival
STAC	Supersonic Transport Aircraft Committee
STAR	Standard Terminal Arrival Route
STARS	Standard Terminal Automation Replacement System
STBY	Standby
STC	Sensitivity Time Control
STC	Supplemental Type Certificate
STCM	Stabilizer Trim Control Module
STEM	Shaped-Tube Electrolytic Machining

STMP .... Special Traffic Management Program
STOL .... Short Takeoff and Landing
STOVL .... Short Takeoff, Vertical Landing
STS .... Status
STTL .... Schottky Transistor-Transistor Logic
SUA .... Special Use Airspace
SUA/ISE .... Special Use Airspace/Inflight Service Enhancement
SUP .... Suspect/Unapproved Part
SURPIC .... Surface Picture
SVFR .... Special Visual Flight Rules
SVS .... Synthetic Vision System
SW .... Switch
SWAP .... Severe Weather Avoidance Plan
SWIM .... System Wide Information Management
SYM GEN .... Symbol Generator

T

TA .... Traffic Advisory
TAA .... Technically Advanced Aircraft
TAA .... Terminal Arrival Area
TAAS .... Terminal Advanced Automation System
TAC .... TACAN
TAC .... Terminal Area Chart
TACAN .... UHF Tactical Air Navigation
TACEVAL .... Tactical Evaluation
TADS .... Target Acquisition and Designation System
TAF .... Terminal Aviation Forecast
TANS .... Tactical Air Navigation System
TAOARC .... Terminal Area Operations Aviation Rulemaking Committee
TAP .... Technically Advanced Pilot
TAS .... Terminal Automation System
TAS .... True Airspeed
TAT .... Total Air Temperature
TAV .... Trans-Atmospheric Vehicle
TAWS .... Terrain Awareness Warning System
TB .... Track Bar
TBDP .... Tie Bus Differential Protection
TBO .... Time Between Overhauls
T/C .... Top of Climb
TC .... Type Certificate
TCA .... Terminal Control Area
TCAS .... Traffic Alert and Collision Avoidance System
TCC .... Thrust Control Computer
TCDS .... Type Certificate Data Sheet
TCH .... Threshold Crossing Height
TCLT .... Tentative Calculated Landing Time
TCO .... Training Course Outline
TCS .... Touch Control Steering
T/D .... Top of Descent

TDC ....Top Dead Center
TDLS ....Terminal Data Link System
TDM ....Time-Division Multiplex
TDRS ....Tracking and Data Relay Satellite
TDZ ....Touchdown Zone
TDZ/CL ....Touchdown Zone and runway Centerline Lighting
TDZE ....Touchdown Zone Elevation
TDZL ....Touchdown Zone Lights
TEB ....Tri-Ethyl-Borane
TEC ....Tower Enroute Control
TEMAC ....Trailing Edge of Mean Aerodynamic Chord
TERCOM ....Terrain-Commanded
TEREC ....Tactical Electronic Reconnaissance
TERPS ....United States Standard for Terminal Instrument Procedures
TET ....Turbine Entry Temperature
TF ....Track to Fix
TFHC ....Thin-Film Hybrid Circuit
TFM ....Traffic Flow Management
TFMS ....Traffic Flow Management System
TFR ....Temporary Flight Restriction
TFR ....Terrain-Following Radar
TFR ....Transfer
TFT ....Thin-Film Transistor
TFX ....Tactical Fighter Experimental
TGT ....Turbine Gas Temperature
THB ....Through-Hole Board
THP ....Thrust Horsepower
TI ....Texas Instruments
TIAS ....True Indicated Airspeed
TIBS ....Telephone Information Briefing Service
TIG ....Tungsten Inert Gas
TIS ....Traffic Information Service
TIS–B ....Traffic Information Service–Broadcast
TIT ....Turbine Inlet Temperature
TKE ....Track Angle Error
TLOF ....Touchdown and Lift-Off Area
TM ....Traffic Management
TMA ....Traffic Management Advisor
TMC ....Thrust Management Computer
TMS ....Thrust Management System
TMSP ....Thrust Mode Select Panel
TMU ....Traffic Management Unit
TNT ....Turbulence in and Near Thunderstorms
TO ....Technical Order
TOC ....Top Of Climb
TOD ....Top Of Descent
TODA ....Takeoff Distance Available (ICAO)
TOGA ....Takeoff/Go Around
TOI ....Track of Interest
TOPPS ....Turbine Overhaul Power Plant Support
TORA ....Takeoff Run Available (ICAO)

TOT ....Turbine Outlet Temperature
TOW ....Tube-launched, Optically-tracked, Wire-guided
TPA ....Traffic Pattern Altitude
TPP .................................U.S. Terminal Procedures Publication
T-R ....Transformer-Rectifier
TRACAB ....Terminal Radar Approach Control in Tower Cab
TRACON ....Terminal Radar Approach Control
TRL ....Transistor-Resistor Logic
TRP ....Thrust Rating Panel
TRSA ....Terminal Radar Service Area
TRU ....Transformer-Rectifier Unit
TSE ....Total navigation System Error
TSO ....Technical Standard Order
TSOA ....Technical Standing Order Authorization
TSSAM ....Tri-Service Standoff Attack Missile
TSTO ....Two Stage-to-Orbit
TSU ....Telescopic Sighting Unit
T_T ....Total Temperature
TTG ....Time To Go
TTH ....Tactical Transport Helicopter
TTL ....Transistor-Transistor Logic
TTL ....Tuned To Localizer
TTS ....Time To Station
TVCS ....Thrust Vectoring Control System
TVOR ....VHF Terminal VOR
TWA ....Trans World Airlines
TWEB ....Transcribed Weather Broadcast
TWR ....Turbulence-detecting Weather Radar
TWS ....Track While Scan
TWT ....Traveling Wave Tube
TWU ....Tactical Weapons Unit
TXPDR ....Transponder

U

UA ....Pilot Report (PIREP)
UA ....Unmanned Aircraft
UART ....Universal Asynchronous Receiver-Transmitter
UAS ....Unmanned Aircraft Systems
UAV ....Unmanned Aerial Vehicle
UBR ....Utility Bus Relay
UDF ....UnDucted Fan
UF ....Under Frequency
UFET ....Unipolar Field Effect Transistor
UHF ....Ultra High Frequency
UJT ....Unijunction Transistor
UK ....United Kingdom
UN ....United Nations
UNICOM ....Universal Communications
URET ....User Request Evaluation Tool

USAF ....United States Air Force
USDA ....United States Department of Agriculture
USUA ....United States Ultralight Association
UTC ....Coordinated Universal Time
UUA ....Urgent pilot report (message identifier)
UV ....Under Voltage

V

V ....Voltage
V_1 ....Takeoff decision speed
V_2 ....Takeoff safety speed
$V_{2\,min}$ ....Minimum takeoff safety speed
V_A ....Design maneuvering speed
VA ....Volt-Amps
VAC ....Volts, Alternating Current
VAD ....Velocity Azimuth Display
VAFTAD ....Volcanic Ash Forecast Transport And Dispersion
VAPI ....Visual Approach Path Indicator
VAR ....Volt-Amps Reactive
VAS ....Visual Augmentation System
VASI ....Visual Approach Slope Indicator
V_B ....Design speed for maximum gust intensity
VBS ....Vertical Beam Sensor
V_C ....Design cruise speed
VC ....Variable Cycle
VCO ....Voltage-Controlled Oscillator
VCOA ....Visual Climb Over Airport
V_D ....Design diving speed
VDA ....Vertical Descent Angle
VDC ....Volts, Direct Current
V_{DF}/M_{DF} ....Demonstrated flight diving speed
VDP ....Visual Descent Point
VDR ....Voltage Dependent Resistor
VDU ....Visual Display Unit
V_F ....Design flap speed
VFC ....Voltage-to-Frequency Converter
V_{FC}/M_{FC} ....Maximum speed for stability characteristics
V_{FE} ....Maximum flap-extended speed
VFR ....Visual Flight Rules
V_{FTO} ....Final takeoff speed
VG ....Variable Geometry
VGSI ....Visual Glide Slope Indicator
VGU ....Vertical Gyro Unit
V_H ....Maximum level-flight speed with continuous power
VHF ....Very High Frequency
VHIC ....Very High Speed Integrated Circuit
VIFF ....Vectoring in Forward Flight
VIGV ....Variable Inlet Guide Vanes
VLCT ....Very Large Commercial transport

V_{LE} .... Maximum landing gear extended speed
VLJ .... Very Light Jet
VLF .... Very Low Frequency
V_{LO} .... Maximum landing gear operating speed
V_{LOF} .... Lift-off speed
V_{MC} .... Minimum control speed with critical engine inoperative
VMC .... Visual Meteorological Conditions
V_{MINI} .... Minimum speed–IFR
V_{MO}/M_{MO} .... Maximum operating limit speed
VMOS .... Vertical Metal Oxide Silicon semiconductor
V_{MU} .... Minimum unstick speed
VNAP .... Vertical Noise Abatement Procedures
VNAV .... Vertical Navigation
V_{NE} .... Never-exceed speed
V_{NEI} .... Never exceed speed–IFR
V_{NO} .... Maximum structural cruising speed
VOM .... Volt-Ohm-Milliammeter
VOR .... Very high frequency Omnidirectional Range
VOR APPR .... VOR Approach
VOR/DME .... Collocated VOR and DME NAVAIDs
VOR OC .... VOR On Course
VORTAC .... Colocated VOR and TACAN
VOT .... VOR Test signal, or Test facility
VPA .... Vertical Path Angle
V_R .... Rotation speed
VR .... (VFR) military training Route
VR .... Visual Reference
VR .... Volts Regulated
VRA .... Vertical Resolution Advisory
V_{REF} .... Reference landing speed
VRMS .... Volts, Root Mean Square
V_S .... Stalling speed, or the minimum steady flight speed at which the airplane is controllable
VS .... Vertical Speed
V_{S0} .... Stalling speed in the landing configuration
V_{S1} .... Stalling speed for a specified flight configuration
VSCS .... Voice Switching and Control System
VSCU .... Vertical Signal Conditioner Unit
VSI .... Vertical Speed Indicator
V_{SR} .... Reference stall speed
V_{SR0} .... Reference stall speed in the landing configuration
V_{SR1} .... Reference stall speed in a specific configuration
VSTOL .... Vertical or Short Takeoff and Landing
VSV .... Variable Stator Vanes
V_{SW} .... Speed at which onset of natural or artificial stall warning occurs
VSWR .... Voltage Standing Wave Ratio
V_T .... Terminal Velocity
VTA .... Vertex Time of Arrival
VTAS .... Visual Target Acquisition System

VTF .... Vector To Final
VTL .... Variable Threshold Logic
VTOL .... Vertical Take Off and Landing
V$_{TOSS}$ .... Takeoff safety speed for Category A rotorcraft
VVI .... Vertical Velocity Indicator
V$_X$ .... Speed for best angle of climb
V$_{XSE}$ .... Best angle of climb speed with one engine inoperative
V$_Y$ .... Speed for best rate of climb

W

W .... Watts
WA .... AIRMET
WAAS .... Wide-Area Augmentation System
WAC .... World Aeronautical Charts
WAM .... Wide Area Multilateration
WARN .... Warning
WARP .... Weather and Radar Processing
WCA .... Wind Correction Angle
WCMD .... Wind Corrected Munitions Dispenser
WCP .... Weather Radar Control Panel
WD .... Wind Direction angle
WEA .... Weather
WFO .... Weather Forecast Office
WILCO .... Will Comply
WMO .... World Meteorological Organization
WMS .... Wide-area Master Station
WMSC .... national Weather Message Switching Center
WO, W/O .... Washout
W/P .... Waypoint
WP .... WayPoint
WPT .... Waypoint
WRS .... Wide-area ground Reference Station
WS .... SIGMET
WS .... Wind Speed
WSFO .... Weather Service Forecast Office
WSO .... Weather Service Office
WST .... Convective SIGMET
W/V .... Wind Vector
WW .... Severe Weather Watch
W$_X$ .... Weather
WXR .... Weather Radar Transceiver

X

XCVR .... Transceiver
XDCR .... Transducer
XFMR .... Transformer
XMIT .... Transmit

XMOS ....High Speed Metal Oxide Silicon semiconductor
XMTR ....Transmitter
XPDR ....Transponder
XTK ....Cross-Track
XTK DEV ....Cross Track Deviation
X/W ....Crosswind

Y

YD ....Yaw Damper
YDM ....Yaw Damper Module

Z

Z ....Zulu Time (Greenwich Mean Time)
ZFW ....Zero Fuel Weight

Appendix 2
Periodic Table of Chemical Elements

Periodic Table of Elements

Atomic weights in ( ) are mass numbers of the most stable isotope of that element.

Legend (example):
- **4** Atomic number
- **Be** Symbol
- 9.0122 Atomic weight

Heavy Metals: VIB, VIIB
Transition Elements
Group VIII
Light Metals: IA, IIA
Nonmetals: IVA, VA, VIA, VIIA

Period	IA	IIA	IIIB	IVB	VB	VIB	VIIB	VIII	VIII	VIII	IB	IIB	IIIA	IVA	VA	VIA	VIIA	Inert Gases
1	1 **H** 1.00794																	2 **He** 4.0026
2	3 **Li** 6.941	4 **Be** 9.0122											5 **B** 10.811	6 **C** 12.0107	7 **N** 14.0067	8 **O** 15.9994	9 **F** 18.9984	10 **Ne** 20.1797
3	11 **Na** 22.9898	12 **Mg** 24.305											13 **Al** 26.9815	14 **Si** 28.086	15 **P** 30.9737	16 **S** 32.065	17 **Cl** 35.453	18 **Ar** 39.948
4	19 **K** 39.0983	20 **Ca** 40.078	21 **Sc** 44.956	22 **Ti** 47.867	23 **V** 50.9415	24 **Cr** 51.996	25 **Mn** 54.938	26 **Fe** 55.845	27 **Co** 58.9332	28 **Ni** 58.6934	29 **Cu** 63.546	30 **Zn** 65.38	31 **Ga** 69.723	32 **Ge** 72.64	33 **As** 74.9216	34 **Se** 78.96	35 **Br** 79.904	36 **Kr** 83.798
5	37 **Rb** 85.4678	38 **Sr** 87.62	39 **Y** 88.9058	40 **Zr** 91.224	41 **Nb** 92.906	42 **Mo** 95.96	43 **Tc** (98)	44 **Ru** 101.07	45 **Rh** 102.905	46 **Pd** 106.42	47 **Ag** 107.868	48 **Cd** 112.411	49 **In** 114.818	50 **Sn** 118.710	51 **Sb** 121.76	52 **Te** 127.60	53 **I** 126.9045	54 **Xe** 131.293
6	55 **Cs** 132.905	56 **Ba** 137.327	57* **La** 138.905	72 **Hf** 178.49	73 **Ta** 180.948	74 **W** 183.84	75 **Re** 186.2	76 **Os** 190.23	77 **Ir** 192.217	78 **Pt** 195.084	79 **Au** 196.967	80 **Hg** 200.59	81 **Tl** 204.383	82 **Pb** 207.2	83 **Bi** 208.980	84 **Po** (209)	85 **At** (210)	86 **Rn** (222)
7	87 **Fr** (223)	88 **Ra** (226)	89** **Ac** (227)	104 **Rf** (265)	105 **Db** (268)	106 **Sg** (271)	107 **Bh** (272)	108 **Hs** (277)	109 **Mt** (276)	110 **Ds** (281)	111 **Rg** (280)	112 **Cn** (285)	113 **Uut** (284)	114 **Uuq** (289)	115 **Uup** (288)	116 **Uuh** (293)	117 **Uus** (294)	118 **Uuo** (294)

Rare Earth Elements

* Lathanide Series													
58 **Ce** 140.116	59 **Pr** 140.907	60 **Nd** 144.242	61 **Pm** (145)	62 **Sm** 150.36	63 **Eu** 151.964	64 **Gd** 157.25	65 **Tb** 158.925	66 **Dy** 162.50	67 **Ho** 164.930	68 **Er** 167.259	69 **Tm** 168.934	70 **Yb** 173.054	71 **Lu** 174.967

** Actinide Series													
90 **Th** 232.038	91 **Pa** 231.0359	92 **U** 238.03	93 **Np** (237)	94 **Pu** (244)	95 **Am** (243)	96 **Cm** (247)	97 **Bk** (247)	98 **Cf** (251)	99 **Es** (252)	100 **Fm** (257)	101 **Md** (258)	102 **No** (259)	103 **Lr** (262)

Appendix 3
Trigonometric Functions

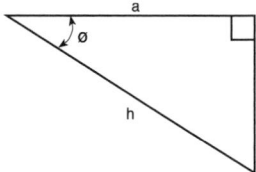

sin ø $= \dfrac{\text{opposite}}{\text{hypotenuse}} = \dfrac{\text{o}}{\text{h}}$

tan ø $= \dfrac{\text{opposite}}{\text{adjacent}} = \dfrac{\text{o}}{\text{a}}$

cos ø $= \dfrac{\text{adjacent}}{\text{hypotenuse}} = \dfrac{\text{a}}{\text{h}}$

ø = angle to be found

a = side adjacent to the angle ø

o = side opposite to the angle ø

h = hypotenuse, the side opposite
    the right angle

Trigonometric Functions

Degree	Sine	Cosine	Tangent		
0	.0000	1.0000	.0000	∞	90
1	.0175	.9999	.0175	57.290	89
2	.0349	.9994	.0349	28.640	88
3	.0523	.9986	.0524	19.080	87
4	.0698	.9976	.0699	14.300	86
5	.0872	.9962	.0875	11.430	85
6	.1045	.9945	.1051	9.514	84
7	.1219	.9926	.1228	8.144	83
8	.1392	.9903	.1405	7.115	82
9	.1564	.9877	.1584	6.314	81
10	.1737	.9848	.1763	5.671	80
11	.1908	.9816	.1944	5.145	79
12	.2079	.9782	.2126	4.705	78
13	.2250	.9744	.2309	4.331	77
14	.2419	.9703	.2493	4.011	76
15	.2588	.9659	.2680	3.732	75
16	.2756	.9613	.2868	3.487	74
17	.2924	.9563	.3057	3.271	73
18	.3090	.9511	.3249	3.078	72
19	.3256	.9455	.3443	2.904	71
20	.3420	.9397	.3640	2.747	70
21	.3584	.9336	.3839	2.605	69
22	.3746	.9272	.4040	2.475	68
23	.3907	.9205	.4245	2.356	67
24	.4067	.9136	.4452	2.246	66
25	.4226	.9063	.4663	2.145	65
26	.4384	.8988	.4877	2.050	64
27	.4540	.8910	.5095	1.963	63
28	.4695	.8830	.5317	1.881	62
29	.4848	.8746	.5543	1.804	61
30	.5000	.8660	.5774	1.732	60
31	.5150	.8572	.6009	1.664	59
32	.5299	.8481	.6249	1.600	58
33	.5446	.8387	.6494	1.540	57
34	.5592	.8290	.6745	1.483	56
35	.5736	.8192	.7002	1.428	55
36	.5878	.8090	.7265	1.376	54
37	.6018	.7986	.7536	1.327	53
38	.6157	.7880	.7813	1.280	52
39	.6293	.7772	.8098	1.235	51
40	.6428	.7660	.8391	1.192	50
41	.6561	.7547	.8693	1.150	49
42	.6691	.7431	.9004	1.111	48
43	.6820	.7314	.9325	1.072	47
44	.6947	.7193	.9657	1.036	46
45	.7071	.7071	1.0000	1.000	45
	Cosine	Sine		Tangent	Degree

Appendix 4
International Phonetic Alphabet and Morse Code

Letter	Word	Morse Code
A	Alfa	· —
B	Bravo	— · · ·
C	Charlie	— · — ·
D	Delta	— · ·
E	Echo	·
F	Foxtrot	· · — ·
G	Golf	— — ·
H	Hotel	· · · ·
I	India	· ·
J	Juliett	· — — —
K	Kilo	— · —
L	Lima	· — · ·
M	Mike	— —
N	November	— ·
O	Oscar	— — —
P	Papa	· — — ·
Q	Quebec	— — · —
R	Romeo	· — ·
S	Sierra	· · ·
T	Tango	—
U	Uniform	· · —
V	Victor	· · · —
W	Whiskey	· — —
X	X-ray	— · · —
Y	Yankee	— · — —
Z	Zulu	— — · ·
1		· — — — —
2		· · — — —
3		· · · — —
4		· · · · —
5		· · · · ·
6		— · · · ·
7		— — · · ·
8		— — — · ·
9		— — — — ·
0		— — — — —